Corpus Linguistics

HSK 29.1

Handbücher zur Sprach- und Kommunikationswissenschaft

Handbooks of Linguistics
and Communication Science

Manuels de linguistique et
des sciences de communication

Mitbegründet von Gerold Ungeheuer (†)
Mitherausgegeben 1985–2001 von Hugo Steger

Herausgegeben von / Edited by / Edités par
Herbert Ernst Wiegand

Band 29.1

Walter de Gruyter · Berlin · New York

Corpus Linguistics

An International Handbook

Edited by

Anke Lüdeling and Merja Kytö

Volume 1

Walter de Gruyter · Berlin · New York

♾ Printed on acid-free paper which falls within the guidelines
of the ANSI to ensure permanence and durability.

Library of Congress Cataloging-in-Publication Data

Corpus linguistics : an international handbook / edited by Anke Lüdeling and Merja Kytö
p. cm. – (Handbooks of linguistics and communication science ; 29.1 – 29.2)
Includes bibliographical references and indexes.
ISBN 978-3-11-018043-5 (hardcover : alk. paper) –
ISBN 978-3-11-020733-0 (hardcover : alk. paper) – 1. Corpora (Linguistics) 2. computational linguistics.
I. Lüdeling, Anke, 1968 – II. Kytö, Merja.
p126.C68C663 2008
410–dc22
2008042529

ISBN 978-3-11-018043-5
ISSN 1861-5090

Bibliografische Information der Deutschen Nationalbibliothek

Die Deutsche Nationalbibliothek verzeichnet diese Publikation in der Deutschen Nationalbibliografie; detaillierte bibliografische Daten sind im Internet über http://dnb.d-nb.de abrufbar.

Printed in Germany
Typesetting: META Systems GmbH, Wustermark
Coverdesign: Martin Zech, Bremen

Introduction

1. Why a handbook on corpus linguistics?

Corpus linguistics today is often understood as being a relatively new approach in linguistics that has to do with the empirical study of "real life" language use with the help of computers and electronic corpora. In the first instance, a "corpus" is simply any collection of written or spoken texts. However, when the term is employed with reference to modern linguistics, it tends to bear a number of connotations, among them machine-readable form, sampling and representativeness, finite size, and the idea that a corpus constitutes a standard reference for the language variety it represents. While linguistics divides up into many research areas depending on complexes of research questions, corpus linguistics in essence behaves diametrically: it offers a set of methods that can be used in the investigation of a large number of different research questions.

For a number of reasons, we think that the time is right for a handbook on this approach: we now have access to large corpora and rather sophisticated tools to retrieve data from them. Over the past few decades, corpus linguists have gained a great deal of experience in dealing with both theoretical and practical problems in their research. In other words, we are now much wiser about the ways in which legitimate claims can be made about language use on the basis of corpora. There is also a new focus on empirical data in theoretical linguistics, with growing interest in the techniques and procedures practised within the corpus linguistic approach.

Our handbook is intended to sketch the history of corpus linguistics, and describe various methods of collecting, annotating and searching corpora as well as processing corpus data. It also reports on a number of case studies that illustrate the wide range of linguistic research questions discussed within the framework.

In this Introduction, we will survey the main areas covered in the 61 articles included in the handbook. In the next section, we first give a brief overview of the "roots" of corpus linguistics and then discuss the role played by corpus linguistics in a number of central fields of linguistics. Our aim is to highlight the various ways in which techniques deriving from these fields have contributed to modern corpus linguistics, and vice versa, the ways in which corpus linguistics has been able to contribute to the advances made in these fields. In section 3, we look at the kinds of data that corpora can give us and the kinds of research questions these data can be used for. In section 4, we look into the issues relevant to corpus design, and in section 5, we turn to the links between corpus linguistics and computational linguistics. Finally, in section 6, we introduce the structure of the handbook and the way in which the articles have been grouped under the main section headings.

2. Origins and history of corpus linguistics

As a methodology, the rise of modern corpus linguistics is closely related to the history of linguistics as an empirical science. Many techniques that are in use in corpus linguistics are much older than computers: many of them are rooted in the tradition of the late eighteenth and nineteenth century when linguistics was for the first time claimed to be a "real", or empirical, science.

2.1. Historical linguistics: Language change and reconstruction

One of the main contributors to modern corpus linguistics is the area of comparative and historical linguistics, the reason being, of course, that historical linguists have always made use of texts or text collections as their material. Many techniques developed in the nineteenth century for reconstructing older languages or recognizing relationships between languages are still in use today. In the Indo-European tradition, the study of language change and the reconstruction effort were dependent on early texts or corpora (cf. Sprachdenkmäler, or "language monuments"). Jacob Grimm and later the Neogrammarians supported their claims about the history and grammars of languages by citing textual data. The Neogrammarians declared that it was the study of present-day language use evidenced in dialects (and not only the study of early texts) that was of utmost importance.

Many ideas and techniques deriving from nineteenth-century scholars were adopted and further developed in modern corpus linguistics. There is currently a great interest in the compilation of historical corpora; historical corpora were also among the first electronically available corpora (e. g. Roberto Busa's pioneering work on the writings of St Thomas Aquinas and Louis Milić's Augustan Prose Sample).

The advent of electronically available texts made it possible to collect vast amounts of data relatively rapidly. This in turn enabled scholars to profit from statistical methods in linguistic analysis and to design and develop new sophisticated tools and models for their research purposes. Today, mathematically complex models of language change can be computed by using data drawn from electronic corpora. Both long-term developments and recent change have been found to be of interest.

2.2. Grammar writing, lexicography and language teaching

Nineteenth-century grammarians illustrated the statements they made by examples taken from the writings of recognized authors, e. g. Hermann Paul in his *Prinzipien der Sprachgeschichte* (Halle: Max Niemeyer, 1st ed. 1880) used German "classics" to exemplify virtually every claim, be it in phonology, in morphology or in syntax. Today, grammar writers may also adopt a corpus-driven approach, but the corpora they now use include not only classics but all kinds of texts. To remedy the so far very much written-biased view, there is also a growing interest in the grammar of spoken language. In grammatical descriptions of a language, corpora can be exploited to arrive at frequency information on usage characteristic of different varieties, registers and so forth.

In lexicography, to take some early examples, the *Oxford English Dictionary*, and many dictionaries of dead languages give citations from texts containing the word under scrutiny in a context. In modern corpus linguistics, this method is materialized in the form of KWIC concordances. Even though computers make it easier to find and classify examples and retrieve multi-word entries (modern lexicographic tools use sophisticated statistics to extract collocations and interesting patterns for each word), the underlying ideas of exploiting corpus texts are still very similar to those used by early lexicographers and philologists who had no access to computer technology.

Traditional school grammars and textbooks tend to contain constructed or edited examples of language use. In the long run, these can provide only limited support for students who are sooner or later faced with authentic language data in their assignments. In this respect, corpora as sources of empirical data play an important role in language pedagogy. They can also be used to assess the validity of the more traditional teaching materials based on constructed examples of language use. In language teaching, corpora provide a source for activating students and engaging them in independent study of authentic usage. An important recent application is computer-assisted language learning (CALL), where corpus-based software is used to support the interactive learning activities students carry out with the help of the computer.

2.3. Sociolinguistics: Language varieties

Another root of modern corpus linguistics is the research on language varieties. It all began with the compilation of dialect maps and collections of dialect expressions in the last third of the nineteenth century. The methods were similar to the methods used in historical linguistics at that time, with one big difference: dialect corpora were systematically compiled according to given criteria. This might perhaps be seen as a precursor of the still ongoing discussion of what to include in a corpus (although, of course, today the issues involved can be very different).

Currently electronic corpora are often used in the research on language varieties (e. g. dialects, sociolects, registers), and mathematical methods (e. g. multifactorial analyses) crucially rely on computationally available data.

2.4. Psycholinguistics and language acquisition

Research in psycholinguistics has traditionally meant experiments carried out in the laboratory environment. However, in the study of many important phenomena, for instance the familiarity of words to a language user in word recognition experiments, corpora have been profitably used for basic frequency data. Similarly, a speaker's overall output can be compared with speech error data drawn from corpora. The analysis of language pathologies also has a great deal to gain from the study of corpus data: with reference to data from corpora, it is possible to build hypotheses on the factors underlying the possible abnormalities detected in a speaker's output.

In the late 1800s and early 1900s, corpora of child language were composed on the basis of parental diaries containing records of children's language. Interest in corpus collection continued even after the diary studies period. Up until the 1960s, large samples of data were collected and analysed in order to arrive at norms of development in child language acquisition. From the 1960s onwards, longitudinal studies have replaced large sample studies; in longitudinal studies data is collected from individual children over time.

In a similar fashion, second or foreign language acquisition can now be studied quantitatively and qualitatively much more easily than ever before by examining learner corpora.

2.5. Structuralism

The Indo-European descriptivist tradition continued in a way in American Structuralism (the focus being of course on the synchronic rather than on the diachronic perspective). The goal was to acquire data from many different languages and to develop systematic ways of describing them. In their work American Structuralists contributed to corpus linguistics in at least two ways. First, they raised the issue of data collection. Second, they developed ways of transcribing oral production in languages that had not been recorded in written form earlier on.

2.6. The philosophical tradition

Language philosophy and rationalist theories (Friedrich Frege, Rudolf Carnap, later Noam Chomsky) are not concerned with the empirical study of language. Instead, statements on language use are based on constructed examples and conscious introspective reflections. The aim is to make claims about the ways in which human beings process language and to arrive at a cognitively plausible model of language. The criticism raised by Chomsky against the empirical corpus linguistics approach is justified in many respects. Among other things, it must be recognized that a corpus is inherently a collection of performance data, mostly limited and constrained by external circumstances. How could such data be the appropriate guide for a linguist aiming at modelling linguistic competence? Yet related criticism can be raised against rationalist methodology. How can any serious model of human behaviour be based on artificial examples?

The debate carried out on such fundamental issues as the aims of linguistic analysis and description, and the nature of the data and the analytical tools used has helped corpus linguists to define and justify their position. Today generative linguists are becoming more and more interested in empirical questions and the use of corpus data. Nor can corpus linguists ignore the need to reflect on the issues relevant to language theory and modelling when working on their data (cf. Charles J. Fillmore's visionary contribution on "'Corpus Linguistics' or 'Computer-aided Armchair Linguistics'" to *Directions in Corpus Linguistics* edited by Jan Svartvik (Berlin and New York: Mouton de Gruyter, 1992, pp. 35–60)).

3. What can corpus data contribute?

What can corpus data contribute, or in other words, what kinds of data can be used for answering which linguistic research questions? Corpus data cannot replace introspection or provide grammaticality judgments. Nor can corpus data replace experimental data or fieldwork. The present section deals with corpus data in theoretical linguistics; we come back to the use of corpus data in computational linguistics, in section 5 below.

Corpora can in principle give us three different kinds of data: (1) empirical support, (2) frequency information, and (3) meta-information.

(1) Many linguists use a corpus as an "example bank", that is, they try to find empirical support for whatever hypothesis, principle or rule they are working on. Examples can, of course, also be made up or simply found by chance, but the corpus linguistics approach provides a search tool which usually enables a good recall of relevant examples in a given corpus. It is often the case that one just "doesn't come to think of" a relevant example. Many long-standing "truths" have been refuted by corpus data (one example is the often repeated claim that particles in German particle verbs do not topicalize; there are many perfectly grammatical examples of particle topicalization in any corpus). Corpus evidence can be found for verifying hypotheses on each linguistic level from speech sounds to entire conversations or texts. Within the framework, it is possible to replicate the analysis and thus reproduce the results, something which is not possible (and not even intended to be possible) in introspection.

(2) While (1) is a qualitative method of corpus exploitation, corpora provide frequency information for words, phrases or constructions that can be used for quantitative studies. Quantitative studies (which are, of course, often based on a qualitative analysis) are used in many areas of theoretical linguistics as well as in computational linguistics. They show similarities and differences between different groups of speakers or different kinds of texts, provide frequency data for psycholinguistic studies, and so forth. This area is especially interesting because of the different mathematical models that can be used in the analysis.

(3) In addition to the linguistic context, a corpus may provide extra-linguistic information (or meta-data) on such factors as the age or gender of the speaker/writer, text genre, temporal and spatial information about the origin of the text, etc. This extra-linguistic information allows comparisons between different kinds of text or different groups of speakers.

To profit from information that can be retrieved from corpora, the end user needs to know how a given corpus was collected, how it is annotated, how it can be searched, and which statistical techniques can be used. It is necessary to understand the potential (and problems) of corpus data. Corpus linguistics provides a methodology that can be rigidly defined (in the same sense that methodology is defined and standardized in psychology or sociology, and in contrast to introspection or consulting language users about e. g. grammaticality judgments).

4. Corpus design

Many agree that the decisive factor in corpus design is the purpose a corpus is intended to be used for. This purpose largely decides whether a corpus will contain written or spoken language, or both, and what registers and varieties will be represented in it.

Multi-purpose corpora typically contain texts representative of various genres whilst specialized corpora can be limited to highlight only one genre, or a family of genres. In balanced corpora the various components are represented in a stratified way, which enables the scholar to map occurrences of the linguistic phenomena investigated against the extra-linguistic variables involved. In unbalanced corpora, other guidelines than representativity have been followed. Understandably enough, it is not always possible to collect data in similar (or even sufficient) quantities for each text category represented in the corpus; this is often the case with historical corpora.

Though a corpus is traditionally understood as a closed set of textual material, some so-called monitor corpora have also been developed, with the aim of storing a continuously growing (non-finite) body of texts in the memory of the computer. These monitor corpora are useful in lexicographical work. Electronic large-scale dictionaries can also be used for data retrieval in ways similar to corpora (e. g. the *Oxford English Dictionary*).

In multilingual corpora two or several languages are brought together to enable research on translation and contrastive studies, language engineering applications, language teaching, etc. Parallel corpora, on the other hand, bring together the same text in its original language and in translation(s) (cf. the "polyglot" bibles in the Middle Ages). Not only translations but also texts from one and the same topic area written independently in two or several languages can be included in a parallel corpus. A relatively recent introduction to the variety of corpora is learner corpora, where samples of learner production appear and enable systematic study of L2 properties.

5. Corpus linguistics and computational linguistics

Ever since computers were introduced in linguistic analysis, computational linguistics and corpus linguistics have been linked in three ways. In computational linguistics and corpus linguistics, techniques have been developed for structuring, annotating and searching large amounts of text. Techniques have also been designed for qualitative and quantitative study of corpus data. In computational linguistics, corpus data are exploited to develop Natural Language Processing (NLP) applications.

5.1. Preprocessing of corpora

Many corpora that are used by linguists are preprocessed in one or another way: for instance, corpora can be tokenized, split into sentences, and annotated with part-of-speech information. In many cases, information about the (inflectional) morphology of a token has also been added, together with the lemma form. Higher-level annotation such as information on syntactic structure (tree banks), or semantics (anaphoric relations, dependency structures) is also available for certain corpora.

Several competing techniques (e. g. rule-based, statistical, constraint-based, hybrid) have been developed to automate these preprocessing steps, enabling the annotation of large amounts of data within a reasonable amount of time and research effort. Two points are important. Firstly, each preprocessing step forces the corpus compiler to make linguistic decisions that will influence further preprocessing steps and the evaluation of the corpus. The end user must be aware of these decisions in order to find what he or she is looking for. For instance, the tokenizer has to decide whether to treat *New York* or *Weil der Stadt* (the name of a German town) as one token or several; it will also need to deal with open word classes such as English compound nouns. Similarly, a lemmatizer has to decide what to do with for example German particle verbs. Secondly, the end user must be aware of the quality of the work done over the preprocessing stage and of the error rates involved, as any coding errors, especially systematic errors, may influence the results.

Once end users are aware of the preprocessing principles, corpus texts can be exploited for solving linguistic research questions and for developing NLP products. In our view it is important for our readers to learn about such issues as the techniques that can be used to preprocess a corpus, the (linguistic) decisions that have been made by corpus compilers, and the errors that can be encountered when exploiting corpora. This is why a number of articles on preprocessing have been included in the handbook.

5.2. Qualitative and quantitative study of corpus data

Developing techniques for the preprocessing of text is not the only computational linguistic contribution to corpus linguistics. In addition, many methods and standards for the qualitative and quantitative study of text have been developed within the two frameworks. Let us mention only two issues in this context, the work done on grammar development and on morphological productivity.

5.3. Corpus data in NLP applications

Many NLP applications rely on the availability of large amounts of textual data. Today, many applications use statistical algorithms that are trained on electronic corpora.

Machine translation is a case in point: with the arrival of fast computers and large amounts of text in the 1970s, it was possible to start using computational techniques for translation purposes. Today, an increasing use is made of parallel corpora and various alignment techniques. While many problems are still waiting for solutions, promising advances have been made within e. g. statistical translation and example-based machine translation.

6. Structure of the handbook

The handbook consists of 61 articles organized in five sections.

Section I: Origins and history of corpus linguistics – corpus linguistics vis-à-vis other disciplines

In section I, articles 1–3 relate the origins of corpus linguistics to the disciplines in linguistics in the nineteenth and twentieth century. Articles 4–8 show how corpus linguistics and corpus study are positioned with respect to certain central branches of linguistics.

Section II: Corpus compilation and corpus types

Section II explains how corpora are collected, discusses the different corpus types, and introduces some existing corpora. In article 9, different strategies for collecting text and designing a corpus are dealt with. Articles 10–19 describe different types of corpora and data collections.

Section III: Existing corpora

In section III, article 20 provides brief introductions to over a hundred influential corpora (different corpus types, different languages), whilst article 21 introduces some examples of corpora of less studied languages and discusses the special problems related to the collection of these corpora.

Section IV: Preprocessing corpora

In section IV, the different preprocessing steps for corpus data are introduced in articles 22–32. Here our focus is not on the detailed description of algorithms (which are dealt with in the HSK volume on *Computational Linguistics*) but rather on the decisions that have to be made, on the potential and limitations of the procedure at different stages, and on possible sources of errors. Articles 33–34 introduce search strategies for linear and non-linear material, and article 35 addresses three important aspects of linguistically annotated corpora, i. e. their quality assurance, reusability and sustainability.

Section V: Use and exploitation of corpora

Section V is devoted to the use that can be or has been made of corpora. Article 36 lays the groundwork for articles 37–38: here the different statistical distributions found in corpora are described (normal distribution, LNRE distribution etc.). Articles 39–60 then show how corpus data can be exploited statistically or made other use of. Finally, article 61 surveys the major research designs used in statistical corpus-based analysis.

Anke Lüdeling (Berlin, Germany) and Merja Kytö (Uppsala, Sweden)

Acknowledgments

This project has been an exciting exploration into the world of words and computers! We wish to express our warmest thanks to all those who contributed to the completion of this handbook.

We are indebted to the reviewers of the handbook articles, who generously gave their time to help our authors improve their texts in so many ways. Among the reviewers were our authors, who all reviewed one or more articles, and the following external reviewers: Jan Aarts, Gisle Andersen, Jörg Asmussen, Angelika Becker, Bettina Berendt, Silvia Bernardini, Lars Borin, Peter Bosch, Christian Chiarcos, Massimiliano Ciaramita, Bengt Dahlqvist, Katrin Dohlus, Adrienne Dwyer, Jürg Fleischer, Felix Golcher, Angela Grimm, Peter Grund, Jörg Hakenberg, Patrick Hanks, Andrew Hardie, Sebastian Hoffmann, Graham Katz, Graeme Kennedy, Göran Kjellmer, Peter Kolb, Olga Krasavina, Brigitte Krenn, Emil Kroymann, Jonas Kuhn, Andreas Lücking, Claudia Maienborn, Anna Mauranen, Paola Merlo, Britta Mondorf, Joybrato Mukherjee, Frank Müller, Victoria Oketch, Ralf Plate, Ines Rehbein, Randi Reppen, Beatrice Santorini, Michael Schiehlen, Thomas Schmidt, Bettina Schrader, Hinrich Schütze, Serge Sharoff, Anna-Brita Stenström, Martin Volk, and Benjamin Weiß. Heartfelt thanks to you all.

We were also fortunate to have Professor Tony McEnery (Lancaster University) join us for the initial stages of the editorial project. We take the opportunity of acknowledging the inspiration and insights with which he contributed to our work.

Further, we would have been lost without our assistants at Institut für deutsche Sprache und Linguistik at Humboldt-Universität zu Berlin. Sabine Krämer processed the first batch of articles, and Amir Zeldes drilled through the rest. It was very much thanks to the unfailing stamina and exemplary organisational skills of Amir that we were able to deal with the stream of contributions flooding in at the various stages of the editorial process.

Finally, we wish to express our gratitude to the Series Editor, Professor Herbert Ernst Wiegand, and Dr Anke Beck at Mouton de Gruyter for trusting us with this book. We are also indebted to Ms Barbara Karlson and Ms Monika Wendland at the publisher's, who always had answers to our questions.

The Editors

Contents

Volume 1

Volume 2

V. Use and exploitation of corpora

I. Origin and history of corpus linguistics – corpus linguistics vis-à-vis other disciplines

1. Pre-electronic corpora

1. Introduction

Although definitions of what constitutes a linguistic corpus will vary, many would agree that a corpus is "a collection of texts or parts of texts upon which some general linguistic analysis can be conducted" (Meyer 2002, xi). There are two types of corpora that meet this definition: pre-electronic and electronic corpora. Pre-electronic corpora were created prior to the computer era, consisted of a text or texts that served as the basis of a particular project, and had to be analyzed through often time-consuming and tedious manual analysis (see e. g. Hofmann 2004). For instance, in the 18th century, Alexander Cruden created a concordance of the King James Version of the Bible, an extremely work-intensive effort that had to be done with pen and paper. Electronic corpora are the mainstay of the modern era and are a consequence of the computer revolution, beginning with the first computer corpora in the 1960s, such as the Brown Corpus (Kučera/Francis 1967) and continuing to the present time.

This article focuses on four types of linguistic projects in which pre-electronic corpora played an important role:

– Biblical Concordances
– Grammars
– Dictionaries
– The Survey of English Usage (SEU) Corpus

Although the discussion is based primarily on English-language corpora, the principles of corpus compilation and analysis described in this article apply to pre-electronic corpora of other languages as well, which will only be referred to briefly in the course of the discussion.

2. Biblical concordances

Kennedy (1998, 13) comments that biblical concordances represent "the first significant pieces of corpus-based research with linguistic associations …". These concordances were written in many languages, among them Latin, Greek, Hebrew, and English and included Cardinal Hugo's Concordance, a Latin concordance of the Bible written in the 13th century; a Hebrew Concordance written by Isaac Nathan ben Kalonymus (also known as Rabbi Mordecai Nathan) in the 15th century; and two English Concordances: John Marbeck's in the 15th century and, as mentioned above, Alexander Cruden's in the 18th century (Keay 2005, 33–34).

Of these concordances, Cruden's stands out as the most ambitious and comprehensive. At approximately 2,370,000 words in length, it is longer than the Bible itself (Keay 2005, 29) and took a surprisingly short period of time to write. As Fraser (1996) notes, while "it had taken the assistance of 500 monks for [Cardinal] Hugo to complete his concordance of the Vulgate", Cruden took only two years to complete his concordance, working 18 hours on it every day. As Cruden describes in the introduction to the first edition in 1737, the concordance consists of three parts. Parts I and II contained an index of common and proper nouns, respectively, in the Old and New Testaments; Part III contained an index of words from books in the Bible that are, in Cruden's words, "Apocryphal"; i. e., not universally accepted as legitimate parts of the Bible.

Cruden's Concordance is lengthier than the Bible because he included entries not just for individual words but for certain collocations as well. In addition, Cruden does not lemmatize any of the entries, instead including separate entries for each form of a word. For instance, he has separate entries for *anoint*, *anointed*, and *anointing* as well as *his anointed*, *Lord's anointed*, and *mine anointed*. For each entry, he lists where in the Bible the entry can be found along with several words preceding and following the entry. Figure 1.1 contains a sample entry for *his anointed*.

His ANNOINTED.
1 *Sam.* 2:10 exalt horn of *his a.*
    12:3 against the L. and *his a.*
    5 the L. and *his a.* is witness
2 *Sam.* 22:51 showeth mercy to
    his a. Ps. 18:50
Ps. 2:2 and against *his a.*
    20:6 the Lord saveth *his a.*
    28:8 saving strength of *his a.*
Is. 45:1 saith L. to *his a.* to C.

Fig. 1.1: Concordance entry for *his anointed* in Cruden's concordance

To create the concordance, Cruden had to manually alphabetize each entry by pen on various slips of paper – an enormous amount of work. As Keay (2005, 32) notes, the letter *C* had "1019 headerwords … of which 153 start with 'Ca'". The concordance was assembled not out of Cruden's interest in language but as a way of helping people gain easy access to the Bible.

The development of biblical concordances was followed in subsequent years by the creation of concordances of more literary texts. For instance, Heenan (2002, 9) describes the creation of a concordance of Chaucer's works, a project that began in 1871 and that consisted of a team of volunteers who were assigned sections of texts and required "to note variant spellings for each word, the definition of each word, its inflectional form, and the rhyming relationships for the final word in every line". Because the project required manual analysis, it did not appear in print until 1927 (see Tatlock 1927 and Tatlock/Kennedy 1963).

3. Early grammars

This section deals with the use of corpora in the compilation of grammars. Again, I will discuss the issues involved by describing English grammars but many of the issues discussed pertain to other European languages as well (see e. g. Jakob Grimm's or the Neogrammarians' grammars for German). In fact, some of the earliest known grammars of the classical languages may be considered corpus based: as early as the 4th century BC, Pāṇini's grammar described the language of the Vedas (alongside Classical Sanskrit), which was no longer spoken in his time and preserved only in the Vedic corpus; and Aristonicus of Alexandria, a 1st century Greek scholar, composed his work *Ungrammatical Words* to deal with irregular grammatical constructions in the corpus of Homer.

Early English grammars too have their roots in the classical tradition, a tradition that was heavily prescriptive and normative and that placed great value on the 'proper' education of students in Greek and Latin language and literature. This influence is particularly evident in many 18th century grammars of English, such as Robert Lowth's 1762 *A Short Introduction to English Grammar*. Lowth had a specific purpose in writing his grammar:

> ... the principal design of a Grammar of any Language is to teach us to express ourselves with propriety in that Language, and to be able to judge of every phrase and form of construction, whether it be right or not. The plain way of doing this, is to lay down rules, and to illustrate them by examples. But besides shewing what is right, the matter may be further explained by pointing out what is wrong. (Lowth 1762, x)

What is particularly noteworthy in this quote is that Lowth did not illustrate common solecisms in English using examples that he himself made up. Instead, he based his analyses and subsequent criticisms on examples taken from famous writers of English. For instance, in discussing subject-verb agreement with second person pronouns, Lowth (1762, 48–49) notes that "*Thou*, in the Polite, and even in the Familiar Style, is disused, and the Plural *You* is employed instead of it: we say *You have*, not *Thou hast*." He regards *You was*, an older form still in use at the time, as "an enormous Solecism; and yet Authors of the first rank have inadvertently fallen into it". He goes on to cite examples from various writers committing this so-called error of usage:

> Knowing that *you was* my old master's friend. (Addison, *Spectator*, #517)
> Would to God *you was* within her reach. (Lord Bolingbroke to Swift, Letter 46)
> I am just now as well, as when *you was* here. (Pope to Swift, P.S. to Letter 56)

While Lowth uses corpus data to provide counter-examples to his very subjective views of English usage and grammar, subsequent linguists and grammarians used such data as the basis of their linguistic descriptions. This trend is particularly evident in the descriptively-oriented grammars of English written in the late 19th and early to mid 20th centuries by individuals such as George Curme, Otto Jespersen, Hendrik Poutsma, Henry Sweet, and Charles Fries. Not all grammarians of this period based their discussions on examples taken from a corpus. For instance, Henry Sweet's (1891–1898) *A New English Grammar* is based entirely on invented examples to illustrate the grammatical categories under discussion. However, one of the more famous grammars of this era, Otto Jespersen's (1909–49) seven volume *A Modern English Grammar on Historical Principles*, is based exclusively on examples taken from an extensive collection of written English that Jespersen consulted for examples. Jespersen was one among many linguists of this period, including the neogrammarian Hermann Paul (cf. Paul 1880), who felt that linguistic description should be based on real rather than made-up examples. As Jespersen comments:

> With regard to my quotations, which I have collected during many years of both systematic and desultory reading, I think that they will be found in many ways more satisfactory than even the best made-up examples, for instance those in Sweet's chapters on syntax. Whenever it was feasible, I selected sentences that gave a striking, and at the same time natural, expression to some characteristic thought; but it is evident that at times I was obliged to quote sentences that presented no special interest apart from their grammatical peculiarities.
> (ibid., vi)

Jespersen's corpus is extensive and consists of hundreds of books, essays, and poems written by well and lesser known authors (ibid., vol. VII, 1–40). Some of the better known authors include Huxley, Austen, Churchill, Darwin, Fielding, Hemingway, Kipling, Locke, Mencken, Shelley, Priestley, Walpole, Wells, and Virginia Wolfe. As this list of names indicates, the writing represented in Jespersen's corpus covers a range of different written genres: fiction, poetry, science, and politics.

Reading Jespersen's description of grammatical categories, one can see that the examples he includes both shape and illustrate the points he makes. Unlike Lowth, Jespersen does not bring to his discussion rigidly held preconceptions of how English should be spoken and written. Instead, he uses the data in his corpus as a means of describing what the language is really like. In this sense, Jespersen is an important early influence on how descriptions of English grammar should be conducted.

A typical entry will be preceded by general commentary by Jespersen, with perhaps a few invented sentences included for purposes of illustration, followed by often lengthy lists of examples from his corpus to provide a fuller illustration of the grammatical point being discussed. For instance, in a discussion of using a plural third person pronoun such as *they* or *their* to refer back to a singular indefinite pronoun such as *anybody* or *none*, Jespersen (ibid., vol. II, 137) notes that number disagreements of this nature have arisen because of "the lack of a common-number (and common-sex) form in the third-personal pronoun … ." He then includes a quote from an earlier work of his, *Progress in Language* (published in 1894), in which he argues that using generic *he* in a tag question such as *Nobody prevents you, does he?* "is too definite, and *does he or she?* too clumsy". He adds that using a plural pronoun in such a construction is in some cases "not wholly illogical; for *everybody* is much the same thing as *all men*", though he notes that for all instances of such usages, "this explanation will not hold good" (ibid., 138). He then very exhaustively illustrates just how widespread this usage exists, giving extensive lists of examples for each of the indefinite pronouns, a sampling of which is given below:

God send *euery one their* harts desire (Shakespeare, *Much Ado About Nothing* III 4.60, 1623)
Each had *their* favourite (Jane Austen, *Mansfield Park*, 1814)
If *anyone* desires to know … *they* need only impartially reflect
(Percy Bysshe Shelley, *Essays and Letters*, 1912)

Now, *nobody* does anything well that *they* cannot help doing
(John Ruskin, *The Crown of Wild Olive*, 1866)

Jespersen even documents instances of plural pronouns with singular noun phrases as antecedents, noting that these noun phrases often have 'generic meaning' (ibid., vol. II, 495):

Unless *a person* takes a deal of exercise, *they* may soon eat more than does them good
(Herbert Spencer, *Autobiography*, 1904)
As for *a doctor* – that would be sinful waste, and besides, what use were *they* except to tell you what you knew? (John Galsworthy, *Caravan*, 1925)

Of course, Jespersen is not the first English grammarian to document uses of *they* with singular antecedents. Curzan (2003, 70–73) notes that such usages can be found as far back as Old English, particularly if the antecedent is a noun phrase consisting of nouns conjoined by *or* (e. g. Modern English *If a man or a woman want to get married, they must get a marriage license*). Most contemporaries of Jespersen, she continues (ibid., 73–79), treated the construction from a prescriptive point of view, in many cases insisting that generic *he* be preferred over *they*. And while Curzan (2003, 76) correctly observes that there is 'a hint at prescriptivism' in Jespersen's discussion when he comments that using a plural pronoun with a singular antecedent 'will not hold good' in all instances, Jespersen's treatment of such constructions nevertheless foreshadows the methodology now common in most corpus analyses: what occurs in one's corpus shapes the grammatical description that results.

This methodology reaches full fruition in the grammatical descriptions found in Charles Carpenter Fries' (1952) *The Structure of English*. While Fries' predecessors based their discussion exclusively on written texts, Fries is the first to use spoken texts as the source of data for his grammar, and to use frequency information taken from this corpus to discover common and uncommon patterns of usage. Fries (1952, 4) takes this approach because he is interested in studying "the 'language of the people' … [not] the language of 'great literature'". To study English grammar in this manner, Fries assembled a 250,000-word corpus based on transcriptions of conversations held between speakers of American English residing in the North Central part of the United States (ibid., viii, 3–4).

Although Fries' grammar has pedagogical aims, he rejects the prescriptive tradition that preceded him, arguing that grammatical discussions of English sentences should be based on the application of "some of the principles underlying the modern scientific study of language" (ibid., 2). In this sense, Fries' grammar is one of the first written for "educated lay readers" (ibid., 7) to embody the traditions of descriptive linguistics. Because Fries is an adherent of American structuralism, his orientation is heavily behaviorist: "… all the signals of structure are formal matters that can be described in physical terms" (ibid., 8).

This orientation is very evident in the "discovery procedures" that Fries employs as he analyzes his corpus and step-by-step reaches a grammatical description based heavily on what he finds in the data. For instance, in chapters II and III, Fries outlines a procedure for determining exactly what kinds of structures qualify as sentences, a procedure grounded in Fries' claim that "more than two hundred different definitions of the sentence confront the worker who undertakes to deal with the structure of English utterances" (ibid., 9). To move beyond descriptions of the sentence that are heavily notional (e. g. a sentence is a 'complete thought'), Fries (1952, 23f.) first divides his corpus into 'utterance units', a level of structure corresponding to the modern notion of 'speaker turn'. A single speaker turn is classified by Fries as a 'single free utterance'. Fries then begins examining the single free utterances (hereafter SFUs) in his corpus, making further subdivisions and uncovering the structures that make up SFUs and ultimately constitute exactly what a sentence is.

In one section, Fries (1952, 42–47) engages in what is now known as conversation analysis by classifying the structure of SFUs in adjacency pairs when the second member of a pair contains some kind of 'oral' response. For instance, the second part can repeat the first part. This repetition can occur at the start of a conversation, where one party might say 'Hello' and the other party reply with 'Hello', or at the end of a conversation, where 'See you later' will be echoed by 'See you later'. Fries also found that such adjacency pairs could contain only partial repetition in the second turn: 'Good morning Happy New Year' is followed by 'Happy New Year'. As Fries continues this kind of inductive analysis, he uses his corpus to uncover further structures found within SFUs. Fries (1952, 57) is quite clear about how his approach differs from previous grammatical treatments of the sentence, noting that it:

> ... starts from a description of the formal devices that are present and the patterns that make them significant *and arrives at the structural meanings as a result of the analysis.*
> (emphasis in original)

The rigidly empirical and behavioristic orientation of Fries' methodology was rejected shortly after the publication of *The Structure of English* by the advent of the Chomskyan revolution in linguistics and the downfall of behaviorist psychology. Nevertheless, even though modern-day corpus linguists do not necessarily follow the types of discovery procedures that Fries advocates, their objections to intuition-based descriptions of language are firmly grounded in Fries' belief that linguistic analysis should be based on naturally occurring data.

4. Early dictionaries

Corpora have a long tradition in lexicography, primarily because they provide a source for illustrative quotations that serve the dual function of helping lexicographers determine the meaning of a word from the context in which it occurs and then illustrating the meaning of the word in the actual dictionary entry itself.

Although Samuel Johnson has been mythologized as the first lexicographer to use illustrative quotations in his 1775 *Dictionary of the English Language*, this practice, as Landau (2001, 64) notes, can be traced back to 16th century Latin and Greek dictionaries as well as a 1598 Italian–English dictionary written by John Florio (see article 4 and especially Hausmann et al. 1990 for a thorough discussion of early lexicography). But while Johnson may not have originated the use of illustrative quotations, he was one of the first lexicographers to use them as extensively as he did: the first edition of his dictionary contained nearly 150,000 illustrative quotations (Francis 1992, 20).

In the early stages of creating his dictionary, Johnson set out ambitious goals for the selection of texts from which he would obtain illustrative quotations. He originally planned to use texts published up until the restoration, since he felt that texts from this period were "the pure sources of genuine diction", while those from later periods would contain too many borrowings, a reflection of the fact that the English language had begun "gradually departing from its original *Teutonick* character, and deviating towards a *Gallick* structure and phraseology, ..." (Johnson 1755, Preface to *Dictionary of the English Language* 1st ed.). Johnson also planned not to use texts from living authors, and to include quotations that did more than simply illustrate the meanings of words. In his 1747 *The Plan of a Dictionary of the English Language*, he states that he wants to select examples that "besides their immediate use, may give pleasure or instruction, by conveying some elegance of language, or some precept of prudence or piety" (Johnson 1747).

However, as is common in large-scale endeavors such as Johnson's, one's plans often do not match the logistical demands of the task being undertaken. Johnson, as Reddick (1990, 33) observes, selected many quotations from authors, such as Pope and Swift, whose works were published after the restoration; he used quotes from "some living authors, including (though usually attributed anonymously) passages from his own works." In addition, because he had to include words of a more technical nature, he was forced to include quotations from individuals not regarded, in Johnson's words "as masters of elegance or models of stile" (Johnson, 'Preface', *Dictionary of the English Language* 1st ed.). The ultimate result is that Johnson's quotations spanned a range of genres, from poetry to history to horticulture (Reddick 1990, 33).

Although the actual corpus of texts that Johnson used is unknown, it is generally acknowledged that Johnson employed a method of selection now known as "haphazard, convenience, or accidental sampling" (Kalton 1983, 90); that is, Johnson used whatever texts he had easy access to, including those he either owned or were obtained from individuals he knew (Reddick 1990, 35). As Johnson went through his corpus, he would mark words and quotations for possible inclusion in his corpus, and then have a small group of amanuenses copy the quotations onto slips. These slips, then, served as a basis for the words and quotations that subsequently found their way into the dictionary. Below is a sample entry in the dictionary:

ARGUE [1] *v.n.* [arguo, Lat.]

1. To reason; to offer reasons.
   I know your majesty has always lov'd her So dear in heart, not to deny her what A woman of less place might ask by law; Scholars allow'd freely to argue for her. *Shakesp. Hen. VIII.*
   Publick arguing oft serves not only to exasperate the minds, but to whet the wits of hereticks. *Decay of Piety.* An idea of motion, not passing on, would perplex any one, who should argue from such an idea. *Locke.*

2. To persuade by argument.
   It is a sort of poetical logick which I would make use of, to argue you into a protection of this play. *Congr. Ded. to Old Bat.*

3. To dispute; with the particles with or against before the opponent, and against before the thing opposed.
   Why do christians, of several persuasions, so fiercely argue against the salvability of each other. *Decay of Piety.*
   He that by often arguing against his own sense, imposes falsehoods on others, is not far from believing himself. *Locke.*
   I do not see how they can argue with any one, without setting down strict boundaries. *Locke.*

Johnson, as Reddick (1990, 36–37) notes, was not very systematic about where in a text he selected quotations: he "appears, frequently, to have simply plunged into his books wherever he chanced to find himself, marking useful passages as he encountered them …".

While lexicographers following Johnson collected texts more systematically (Francis 1992, 20), Johnson's methodology influenced many future dictionaries, particularly the *Oxford English Dictionary*, the largest dictionary ever published. The *OED* was an extremely ambitious project. As articulated in the 1859 statement 'Proposal for the Publication of a New English Dictionary by the Philological Society', the dictionary was to include every word in the English language from 1250 to 1858. Words to be included in the dictionary would be based on vocabulary found in printed matter written during these years. These goals resulted in "the only English dictionary ever created wholly on the basis of citations" (Landau 2001, 191). The heavily empirical nature of the OED placed a great burden on its creators to find individuals willing to read books and create citation slips. To find volunteers, both the 1859 'Proposal' and a later (1879) document, 'An Appeal to the English-speaking and English-reading public to read books and make extracts for the Philological Society's New English Dictionary', written after James A. H. Murray became editor, actively solicited readers.

Because the *OED* was intended to be a historical dictionary, it was decided that it should include vocabulary taken from texts written during three time periods: 1250–1526, 1526–1674, and 1674–1858. These three time-frames were chosen because they delineate periods "into which our language may, for philological purposes, be most conveniently divided, …." (from *Proposal for the Publication of A New English Dictionary by the Philological Society*, Philological Society 1859, 5). The year 1526, for instance, marked the publication of the first printed edition of the New Testament in English, 1674 the death of Milton. While these are certainly important historical events, they hardly correspond to the major periods in the development of English, especially since the OED is based exclusively on written texts, ignoring speech completely. Moreover, as Landau (2001, 207) notes, "the core of citation files tend to be those of the educated and upper classes," hardly making them representative of the language as a whole. But since there was really no feasible way (or desire, for that matter) to collect spoken data during this period, it was unavoidable that the data be biased in favor of written English.

The first edition of the *OED*, published in 1928, was based on words taken from four million citation slips supplied by approximately 2,000 readers (Francis 1992, 21). These individuals, as Gilliver (2000, 232) notes, either provided specific examples of words, or collected them from sources they were asked to read. Gilliver (2000) provides brief descriptions of the contributions that some of these individuals made. For instance, one of the early editors of the *OED*, Frederick James Furnivall, supplied 30,000 quotations taken from newspapers and magazines (ibid., 238). Harwig Richard Helwich, a Viennese philologist, supplied 50,000 quotations, many from a medieval poem entitled *Cursor Mundi*, "the most frequently cited work in the dictionary" (ibid., 239). The physician Charles Gray contributed 29,000 quotations, many providing examples of function words taken from texts written in the 18th century (ibid., 238).

Specific instructions were given to readers telling them how they should collect words for inclusion on citation slips (from the Historical Introduction of the original OED, reprinted in Murray 1971, vi):

> Make a quotation for *every* word that strikes you as rare, obsolete, old-fashioned, new, peculiar, or used in a peculiar way.
> Take special note of passages which show or imply that a word is either new and tentative, or needing explanation as obsolete or archaic, and which thus help to fix the date of its introduction or disuse.
> Make as *many* quotations *as you can* for ordinary words, especially when they are used significantly, and tend by the context to explain or suggest their own meaning. (quoted from 'An Appeal to the English-speaking and English-reading public ....')

After a word was selected, it needed to be included on a citation slip, which had a specific format, illustrated in Figure 1.2 below.

> Britisher
>
> 1883 Freeman Impressions U.S. iv. 29
>
> I always told my American friends that I had rather be called a Britisher than an Englishman, if by calling me an Englishman they meant to imply that they were not Englishmen themselves.

Fig. 1.2: Citation Slip from the *OED* ('An Appeal to the English-speaking and English-reading public ....')

The headword appeared in the upper left-hand corner of the slip, and was followed below by complete bibliographical information of the source from which the word was taken. The quotation itself was placed at the bottom of the slip. The slips were then sent to Oxford, where they were placed in one of the 1,029 pigeon-holes in a *Scriptorium* constructed by the main editor of the *OED*, James A. H. Murray. Murray and his assistants used the citation slips as the basis for entries and illustrative quotations in the *OED*.

While Johnson's dictionary and the *OED* were certainly two of the more significant dictionary projects undertaken in the 18th-20th centuries, they were not the only dictionaries of their era based upon pre-electronic corpora. In the United States, the second edition of *Webster's New International Dictionary* was published in 1934 and was based on 1,665,000 citations systematically collected from books and periodicals not by "volunteers ... [but by] full-time professional lexicographers working together to make sure that all significant sources were searched" (Francis 1992, 22).

Other more specialized dictionaries based on pre-electronic corpora also appeared. Between 1898 and 1905, Joseph Wright published a six-volume dialect dictionary of British English. This dictionary was based on a corpus of 3,000 dialect glossaries and books from which examples were taken. A group of volunteers worked on the project and had produced, as of the publication of the first volume, 1.5 million citation slips (Wright 1898–1905, vol. 1, v). Francis (1992, 23–27) describes other dialect projects, such as the Linguistic Atlas of New England (LANE, see Kurath et al. 1939), that produced works providing descriptions of vocabulary, pronunciations, and grammar particular to various geographical regions. However, linguistic atlas projects such as LANE collected data from interviews and questionnaires rather than pre-electronic corpora. Therefore, unless one wants to consider a collection of questionnaires a corpus (as Francis does), these projects were not really based on pre-electronic corpora, since corpora are generally defined as extended stretches of discourse: either complete texts or text excerpts (see Meyer 2002, xi–xii).

Landau (2001, 273–275) describes a number of pre-electronic corpora designed in the early 20th century for "lexical study". Two corpora he mentions stand out as especially noteworthy, since they are based on corpora compiled specifically for lexical analysis, not a series of books or periodicals analyzed by groups of readers. An 18-million-word corpus was used as the basis of Edward L. Thorndike and Irving Lorge's *The Teacher's Word Book of 30,000 Words*. A five-million-word corpus served as the basis of Ernest Horn's *A Basic Writing Vocabulary: 10,000 Words Most Commonly Used in Writing*. A five-million-word corpus was the basis of Michael West's *A General Service List of English Words*, which contained 2,000 words classified according to their overall frequency and the frequency of the individual meanings that they expressed. These dictionaries had more of a "pedagogical purpose", with Thorndike and Lorge's work being "enormously influential for the teaching of English in many parts of the world over the next 30 years" (Kennedy 1998, 16, cf. also 93–97).

5. The Survey of English Usage (SEU) corpus

The most significant and influential pre-electronic corpus was the Survey of English Usage (SEU) Corpus, a corpus whose compilation began in 1959 at the Survey of English Usage (University College London) under the direction of Randolph Quirk. Quirk developed the SEU Corpus because he saw the need for grammatical descriptions to go beyond those found in the grammars of Poutsma, Kruisinga, and Jespersen. "For all their excellence, ..." Quirk (1974, 167) states, "the big grammars fell short ... for two main reasons." They were based on writing, not speech, Quirk notes, and "their generally eclectic use of [written] source materials too often leaves unclear the distinction between normal and relatively abnormal structures and the conditions for selecting the latter." To remedy these deficiencies, Quirk assembled a corpus containing the text categories listed in Figure 1.3.

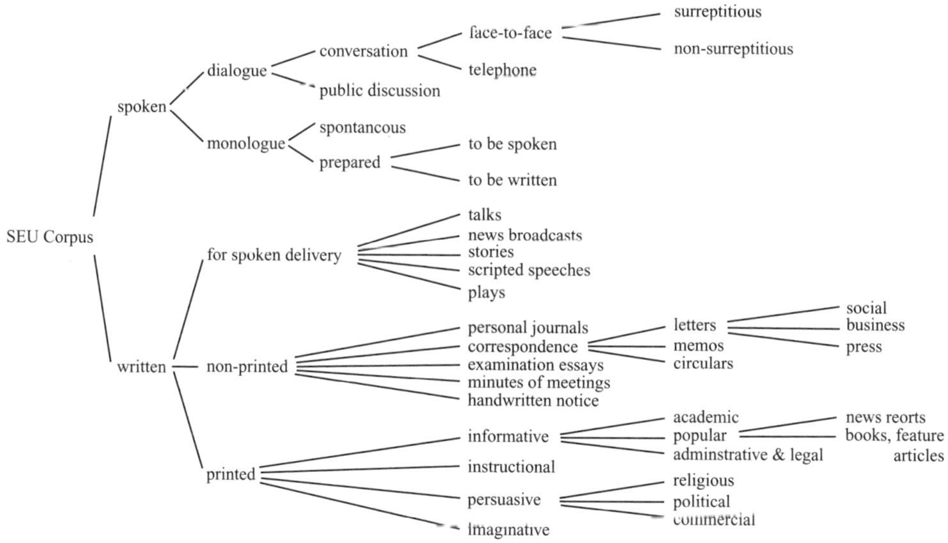

Fig. 1.3: The SEU Corpus (Greenbaum/Svartvik 1990, 13)

The categories in Figure 1.3 were motivated by a series of methodological assumptions concerning not just the content of the corpus but the individuals contributing spoken and written texts to it:

Modes and genres: To enable comprehensive studies of English grammar, a corpus needs to contain not just spoken as well as written texts but a range of different types of each. The many different genres in the SEU Corpus are a consequence of the Firthian influence on linguistics in England at this time (cf. Firth 1957): the notion that language use will vary depending upon the context in which it is used. Therefore, to obtain a complete description of English, it is necessary to study, for instance, spontaneous dialogues (conversations) taking place face-to-face or over the telephone; spontaneous monologues; scripted news broadcasts; personal journals; and so forth. Because the ethics of recording speech were different in the 1950s than in the present time, many conversations in the SEU Corpus were recorded surreptitiously, a practice that is no longer followed.

Speakers and writers: While the SEU Corpus contained a range of different written and spoken genres, the writers and speakers contributing to the corpus were restricted to "educated professional men and women" (Quirk 1974, 167). For the written part of the corpus, this is an inevitable sampling limitation, since only a small percentage of speakers of English, for instance, write news reports. For the spoken component, this is a more significant limitation, one resulting in a corpus that provides only a very narrow sample of the potential speakers of English. Later corpora, such as the British National Corpus, addressed this limitation by planning more carefully the collection of spoken data to insure that a broader range of speakers of British English was represented (Crowdy 1993).

Social relationships: In conversations, because how people speak is determined by the power relationships that exist between them, the SEU Corpus contains samples of speech between equals and disparates. The corpus also contains conversations involving mixed genders as well as only males or only females.

Size: The SEU Corpus is approximately one million words in length and is divided into 5000 word samples. As Quirk (1974, 170) notes, a corpus this size "will not present a complete picture of English usage or anything like it". For this reason, Quirk comments that it is necessary for corpus data to be supplemented with elicitation tests (see Greenbaum/Quirk 1970): tests given to native speakers for purposes of evaluating or eliciting data not found in a corpus. Because the SEU Corpus was intended to be a relatively short corpus, individual samples consist mainly of text excerpts. Sampling texts in this manner ensured that many different examples of a given text-type could be included as well as a range of different speakers and writers.

Transcription: The spoken texts were transcribed not only orthographically but prosodically as well. That is, in addition to containing a transcription of the actual words that speakers spoke, the texts were annotated with markup indicating many prosodic features of speech (e. g. tone unit boundaries, pitch changes, tonic syllables; cf. Svartvik/Quirk 1980 for a more detailed description of the system of transcription that was developed). In linguistics during this period, prosody was considered a very important organizing feature of speech. Thus, the detailed prosodic transcription of the corpus was considered crucial for any grammatical description of English.

Grammatical Analysis: Although linguists studying corpora can do their own grammatical analyses, tailored to their specific needs, the SEU Corpus was grammatically analyzed for "65 grammatical features, over 400 specified words or phrases, and about 100 prosodic paralinguistic features" (Greenbaum/Svartvik 1990, 13–14). Each feature is included on a typed slip containing an example of the particular feature being illustrated, some surrounding text, and information on where in the corpus the feature could be found (e. g. genre, line number, etc.). For instance, Meyer (1987) is a discussion of appositives in English (e. g. constructions such as *my friend, Peter*) based on citation slips for appositives in the SEU Corpus.

To conduct analyses of the SEU Corpus, researchers had to travel to the Survey of English Usage to consult the slips, housed in filing cabinets, relevant to their particular analyses. Electronic corpora have made such long distance travel no longer necessary: in fact, users can now consult the computerized version of the spoken texts found in the SEU Corpus, in the London-Lund Corpus (see Greenbaum/Svartvik 1990 and also article 3 for details). Nevertheless, the importance of the SEU Corpus cannot be underestimated: it was the first corpus created expressly for use by those other than its creators. In addition, the principles of corpus creation that guided its creation are still very relevant and actively applied by those building modern corpora.

6. Conclusions

Although the tedious manual analyses associated with pre-electronic corpora are now considered arcane and unnecessary, these corpora have nevertheless had important influences on the development of corpus linguistics as a field of inquiry. While the many software programs now available for producing concordances have greatly expedited the creation of a concordance, such programs would never have existed had people such as Alexander Cruden not conceptualized the notion of a concordance. Early modern grammarians such as Otto Jespersen demonstrated how one can use a corpus to conduct grammatical analyses and extract relevant examples for purposes of illustration – a methodology still evident in modern corpus-based grammars such as Biber et al.'s (1999) *The Longman Grammar of Spoken and Written English.* Corpora are now commonly used as the basis for creating dictionaries. And the design principles of the SEU Corpus still guide how modern corpora are created. In short, pre-electronic corpus linguistics has a rich history that has over the years contributed to the development of the discipline.

7. Literature

(All URLS were accessed on Dec 9, 2005.)

Biber, Douglas/Johansson, Stig/Leech, Geoffrey/Conrad, Susan/Finegan, Edward (1999), *The Longman Grammar of Spoken and Written English.* Harlow: Pearson Education.

Crowdy, Steve (1993), Spoken Corpus Design. In: *Literary and Linguistic Computing* 8, 259–265.

Curzan, Anne (2003), *Gender Shifts in the History of English.* Cambridge: Cambridge University Press.

Firth, John R. (1957), *Papers in Linguistics 1934–1951.* London: Oxford University Press.

Francis, W. Nelson (1992), Language Corpora B.C. In: Svartvik, Jan (ed.), *Directions in Corpus Linguistics.* Berlin: Mouton de Gruyter, 17–32.

Fraser, Michael (1996), Tools and Techniques for Computer-assisted Biblical Studies. Paper delivered to the New Testament Research Seminar, Faculty of Theology, University of Oxford, June 1996. Available at: http://users.ox.ac.uk/~mikef/pubs/NT_Seminar_Oxford_Fraser_1996.html.

Fries, Charles Carpenter (1952), *The Structure of English.* New York: Harcourt Brace.

Gilliver, Peter (2000), Appendix II: *OED* Personalia. In: Mugglestone, Lynda (ed.), *Lexicography and the OED: Pioneers in the Untrodden Forest.* Oxford: Oxford University Press, 232–252.

Greenbaum, Sidney/Svartvik, Jan (1990), The London-Lund Corpus of Spoken English. In: Svartvik, Jan (ed.), *The London-Lund Corpus of Spoken English: Description and Research.* Lund: Lund University Press, 11–59.

Greenbaum, Sidney/Quirk, Randolph (1970), *Elicitation Experiments in English.* London: Longman.

Grimm, Jakob (1819–1837), *Deutsche Grammatik* (parts 1–4). Göttingen: Dieterich.

Hausmann, Franz Josef/Reichmann, Oskar/Wiegand, Herbert Ernst/Zgusta, Ladislav (eds.) (1990), *Wörterbücher. Ein Internationales Handbuch zur Lexikographie.* (Handbücher zur Sprach- und Kommunikationswissenschaft 3.) Berlin/New York: Walter de Gruyter.

Heenan, Charles H. (2002), Manual and Technology-based Approaches to Using Classification for the Facilitation of Access to Unstructured Text. Available at: http://eil.stanford.edu/publications/charles_heenan/ClassificationPaper_S.pdf.

Hofmann, Walter (2004), Probleme der Korpusbildung in der Sprachgeschichtsschreibung und Dokumentation vorhandener Korpora. In: Besch, Werner/Betten, Anne/Reichmann, Oskar/Sonderegger, Stefan (eds.), *Sprachgeschichte. Ein Handbuch zur Geschichte der deutschen Sprache und ihrer Erforschung.* (Handbücher zur Sprach- und Kommunikationswissenschaft 2.) Berlin/New York: Mouton de Gruyter, 875–889.

Jespersen, Otto (1909–1949), *A Modern English Grammar on Historical Principles.* London: George Allen and Unwin LTD.

Johnson, Samuel (1747), The Plan of an English Dictionary. Available at: http://andromeda.rutgers.edu/~jlynch/Texts/plan.html.

Johnson, Samuel (1755), Preface. Available at: http://andromeda.rutgers.edu/~jlynch/Texts/preface.html.

Kalton, Graham (1983), *Introduction to Survey Sampling*. Beverly Hills, CA: Sage.
Keay, Julia (2005), *Alexander the Corrector: The Tormented Genius whose Cruden's Concordence Unwrote the Bible*. Woodstock and New York: The Overlook Press.
Kennedy, Graeme (1998), An Introduction to Corpus Linguistics. London: Longman.
Kučera, Henry/Francis, W. Nelson (1967), *Computational Analysis of Present-day American English*. Providence, RI: Brown University Press.
Kurath, Hans/Hansen, Marcus L./Bloch, Bernard/Bloch, Julia (1939), *Handbook of the Linguistic Geography of New England*. Providence: Brown University Press.
Landau, Sidney I. (2001), *Dictionaries: The Art and Craft of Lexicography*, 2nd ed. Cambridge: Cambridge University Press.
Lowth, Robert (1762), *A Short Introduction to English Grammar*. Reprinted in: Alston, R. C. (ed.) (1967), *English Linguistics 1500–1800* 18. Menston: Scolar Press.
Meyer, Charles (1987), Apposition in English. In: *The Journal of English Linguistics* 20(1), 101–121.
Meyer, Charles (2002), *English Corpus Linguistics: An Introduction*. Cambridge: Cambridge University Press.
Murray, J. A. H. (ed.) (1971), *The Compact Edition of the Oxford English Dictionary*. London: Oxford University Press.
Paul, Hermann (1880), *Prinzipien der Sprachgeschichte*. Halle: Max Niemeyer.
Philological Society (1859), *Proposal for the Publication of A New English Dictionary by the Philological Society*. Facsimile available at: http://oed.hertford.ox.ac.uk/main/content/view/141/308/.
Quirk, Randolph (1974), *The Linguist and the English Language*. London: Edward Arnold.
Reddick, Allen (1990), *The Making of Johnson's Dictionary, 1746–1773*. Cambridge: Cambridge University Press.
Svartvik, Jan/Quirk, Randolph (1980), *A Corpus of English Conversation*. Lund, Sweden: Gleerup.
Sweet, Henry (1891–1898), *A New English Grammar*. Oxford: Oxford University Press.
Tatlock, John S. (1927), *A Concordance to the Complete Works of Geoffrey Chaucer*. Washington: Carnegie Institute Press.
Tatlock, John S./Kennedy, Arthur (1963), *A Concordance to the Complete Works of Geoffrey Chaucer*. Gloucester, MA: P. Smith.
West, Michael (1953), *A General Service List of English Words*. London: Longman.
Wright, Joseph (1898–1905), *The English Dialect Dictionary*. Oxford: Clarendon Press.

Charles F. Meyer, Boston (USA)

2. Early generative linguistics and empirical methodology

1. Introduction

Early generative linguistics is here defined as the period from Noam Chomsky's first publication in 1953 to the end of the 1960s. During the formative years in the 1950s few others than Chomsky himself were active in developing transformational-generative theory. Therefore an analysis of the relation between early generative linguistics and corpus linguistics is largely a study of the development of Chomsky's methodological practices, especially of how he has used corpus observation methods, native speaker intuitions, and the linguist's own intuitions. Six main chronological phases are discernible: (i) Chomsky's earliest publications 1953–1955 where the seeds of generative grammar already are to be seen, (ii) his 1955 dissertation which contains the basic outline of generative syntax but was not published until 1975, (iii) the important publications from 1956 leading to *Syntactic Structures* 1957 and almost immediate widespread international attention, (iv) work by Chomsky and others now joining him in the period 1958–1964, making the theory more mature and introducing the first comprehensive grammar fragments, ultimately leading to (v) *Aspects of the Theory of Syntax* (1965), the full-blown version of what came to be called the Standard Theory, and finally, (vi) the late 1960s when the generative community was split and generative semantics appeared. Our focus in this overview is on syntax which has always been the central concern of generative linguistics.

When Chomsky entered the trade the immediate linguistic scene he saw was that of North American structuralism. Key conceptions of language and linguistics were reliance on corpora as the starting point of linguistic analysis, emphasis on description rather than on theory formulation, inductivistic discovery procedures, classification of elements, separation of levels in the grammar, insistence on biuniqueness of phonemic transcriptions, physicalistic concept formation, and non-mentalism manifested especially as an aversion for semantics. When this approach was taken to its extremes, a grammar of a particular language was considered to be an inventory of elements (phonemes, morphemes, constructions, etc.), and linguistics was basically conceived as a classificatory type of scholarship.

In judging the data-acquisition methods of any (ordinary working or theoretical) grammarian, transformational-generative ones included, it is important to keep in mind that the following three types of phenomena are ontologically distinct: (i) language data in the form of sentences (utterances), (ii) the mentally represented competence of the native speaker-hearer, i. e. his/her grammatical intuitions (tacit knowledge of the language), and (iii) the spatio-temporal performance processes underlying his/her speaking and understanding. Language data (i) are accessible by observation, i. e. corpus work done for example by authors of comprehensive reference grammars, and elicitation, typically conducted by a field linguist working with an informant, both backed up by introspection in order to ensure that the language specimens so obtained are indeed grammatical. Competence (ii) is accessible by introspection, elicitation, experimental testing, and indirectly by observation of language data. Performance processes (iii) are accessible by observation of language data and by experimental testing, both surely guided by introspective consultation of competence.

2. The early Chomsky (1953–1955)

In his earliest papers, Chomsky adheres (at least on paper) to the empiricist and inductivistic ideas of Zellig S. Harris, with an emphasis on formalization. Thus, Chomsky (1953, 242–244) inquires "into the formality of linguistic method and the adequacy of whatever parts of them can be made purely formal". He wants to "reconstruct the set of procedures" by which the linguist establishes the statements of his/her grammar "from the behavior of language users", which in practice is taken to be "a fixed sample of linguistic material upon which the primitives of the system are experimentally defined".

There has been much confusion as to what the ultimate object of generative description is. As we just saw, this confusion is in evidence on the first page of Chomsky's first publication where he equates the behavior of language users with samples of linguistic material, i. e. corpus data. Taken at face value, the profile of the earliest Chomsky thus somewhat surprisingly is that of a dedicated corpus linguist. But in practice he does not commit himself to the primacy of natural data. The basic corpus of Chomsky (1953) is the constructed "six-sentence text" (1) which is taken to be part of a "reasonably limited sample":

(1) ab, cb, de, fe, axd, cyf

In a footnote Chomsky rejects the idea that the "whole language" would be available as data but he makes some brief general remarks on the feasibility of applying distributional methods to "this situation". The argumentation here builds upon Harris (1951) to whom several references are made.

The second important aim of Chomsky (1953) is to develop an adequate notion of syntactic category to deal with the problem of syntactic homonymy. The explicit treatment of this is one of the cornerstones of generative grammar which consequently was in a germinal stage as early as 1953: "a syntactic analysis will result in a system of rules stating the permitted sequences of the syntactic categories of the analyzed sample of the language, and thus generating the possible or grammatical sentences of the language" (ibid., 243). As far as I know, this is the first mention of generative grammar in the linguistic literature.

Chomsky (1954) is a critical review of a textbook on Modern Hebrew by Eliezer Rieger. Having noted that Rieger confuses prescriptive rules and real usage while being aware that the task of the grammarian is to describe the structure of the language at a given period, Chomsky (1954, 180) then comments on a list of 225 errors collected by Rieger: "The technique by which these 'errors' were collected suggests a method that the linguist might be tempted to use in constructing a linguistic corpus. […] But now, in place of the previous suggestion [to construct] a truly descriptive grammar, it is recommended that this list of 'errors' be used as a guide for a correctional teaching program." This is one of the few places in Chomsky's writings where he comments on the corpus-based work of ordinary working grammarians.

Chomsky (1955) is a critical comment on proposals by Yehoshua Bar-Hillel that linguists should pay more attention to recent advances in logical syntax and semantics. Chomsky sees no linguistic benefits in the purely formal approaches offered by logicians. There are several references to the notion "ordinary linguistic behavior" as central in linguistic description but the notion is not spelt out in detail and therefore one cannot know what Chomsky has in mind, e. g. corpus data (sentences, utterances) or behavior proper as manifest in the processes of speaking and understanding.

3. *The Logical Structure of Linguistic Theory* (LSLT, 1955–56)

In the genesis of transformational-generative grammar, Chomsky's (1975 [1955–1956]) 570-page book *The Logical Structure of Linguistic Theory* (LSLT) occupies a peculiar position. On the one hand, it is the foundational work underlying the whole theory, on the other it was not published until 1975. Chronologically its central parts predate Chomsky's important papers from 1956 as well as *Syntactic Structures* (1957a). In some respects, LSLT still dwells within the tradition of North American structuralism, especially as regards the discussion of discovery methods and substitution procedures in Chapter V. From the viewpoint of corpus linguistics the following programmatic statement in a footnote is highly interesting:

(2) "All of our discussion is based on the assumption that the data have been collected – that the grammar is based on an adequate corpus. We have not discussed the very important question of *how* a corpus is put together and how the linguist obtains the information about linguistic behavior. See Lounsbury, "Field methods and techniques in linguistics" [Lounsbury 1953]; Harris and Voegelin, "Eliciting" [Harris/Voegelin 1953]."
(Chomsky 1975 [1955–1956], 227; emphasis in the original)

At this stage of transformational-generative theory Chomsky indeed seems to have regarded the availability of adequate representative corpora as self-evident points of departure for linguistic description, along with the presumed information about "linguistic behavior". As evidenced by the references to Lounsbury (1953) and Harris/Voegelin (1953), Chomsky basically had in mind the structuralist field methodology of corpus collection based on informant elicitation. Of course this methodology was mainly designed for research on 'exotic' languages not previously known to the field linguist and therefore much of it is not directly relevant to grammatical work on well-known languages with long written traditions and established traditions of basic grammatical description.

It is a striking fact that Chomsky mentions this supposition only in a footnote on page 227, after having made tens of references in passing to the importance of corpora. Some examples: "given a corpus of linguistic material", various proposed grammars can be compared and the best of them selected (p. 61); "given a corpus", a set of compatible descriptive levels may be constructed (p. 68); in grammatical description, "we have [...] only a finite corpus of utterances out of an infinite set of grammatical utterances" (p. 78); "[we] have suggested that a grammar is justified by showing that it follows from application to the corpus of a properly formulated general theory" (p. 86); "[the] grammar must generate a set of grammatical sentences on the basis of a limited corpus" (p. 94); "given a corpus of utterances for which we know in advance that there is some grammar" (p. 166); "given a corpus of sentences", the linguist must determine which of these utterances are phonemically distinct (p. 129); "the set of grammatical sentences cannot be identified with the linguist's corpus of observed sentences" (p. 129); "we must project the class of observed sentences to the […] infinite class of grammatical sentences" (p. 129); "suppose that […] *look at the cross-eyed man* does occur in the corpus" (p. 133); "We are given a corpus *K* which we take to be a set of strings of words." (p. 134); "We define the *distribution* of a word as the set of contexts in the corpus in which it occurs." (p. 137); "Let us suppose […] that all the sentences of the corpus are of the same length." (p. 140); "in actual linguistic material, the selectional restrictions on distribution are extremely heavy" (p. 141); "Given a corpus of sentences, we define the set G to be the set of sentences conforming to the rules established for describing this corpus […]." (p. 147); "The method of §35 cannot furnish a complete answer to the problem of projecting the corpus to a set of grammatical utterances […]." (p. 153); "Having developed the level **P** abstractly, we can now attempt to determine its effectiveness by applying it to the description of actual language material." (p. 223); "Given a set of first-order grammatical categories, and a linguistic corpus, we have a set of sentences generated." (p. 227); "Applying the methods of Chapter V to a linguistic corpus, we […]." (p. 518).

Thus, there is no doubt that in LSLT Chomsky took the structuralist corpus gathering methodology for granted as a self-evident integral component in the toolbox of emergent generative linguistics. But it is also a fact that here, as in later works, he never himself applies this methodology, nor does he pose the question whether the transformational-generative approach to linguistics actually would need an explicit new corpus methodology. Rather, without any principled discussion in LSLT, Chomsky introduces the method of using (more or less) ungrammatical (or otherwise strange) made-up examples, coined by himself on the basis of his native grammatical intuitions, to be used as evidence in his grammatical argumentation. Here is an assortment of examples of this type in LSLT (in 1955–56, the conventions of starring or question-marking ungrammatical or weird examples were not yet in use; the earliest use of stars for indicating ungrammaticality I am aware of is R. B. Lees (1957, 402) who, when discussing compound formation in English, gives examples such as *a book for cooking* vs. **a cooking book*):

(3) Colorless green ideas sleep furiously.
Furiously sleep ideas green colorless.
Sincerity admires John.
Golf admires John.
The admires John.
Of had lunch with Tom.
Look at the cross-eyed from.
The sincerity scratched by John was […]
The table manifested by John was […]
Himself was seen in the mirror by John.
Misery loves company.
old my book
victory's toothache
Victory has a toothache.
a talkative harvest
an abundant man
the considered a fool person
It seems John's.
It seems barking.

He seems forgiven.
John was tired and applauded.
At the clown, everyone laughed.
The office was worked at by John.

Despite the many programmatic references to the importance of corpora, they are not used in LSLT, not even in the form of sporadic authentic examples. But neither does one find an explicitly formulated break with structuralist corpus methodology. Notice, in passing, that Newmeyer (1986, 66) claims that Chomsky's earliest books and papers are filled with polemics against the empiricist conceptions of science held by the structural linguists. I fail to find anything of this in Chomsky's writings prior to 1956.

On the other hand, LSLT also contains many references to the concept of linguistic intuition. In the beginning of the summary chapter, Chomsky (ibid., 61–62) declares that his theory "will shed some light on such facts as the following" which include (i) the capability of the speaker to produce an indefinite number of new utterances which are immediately acceptable to other members of the speech community, and (ii) the capability to have "intuitions about linguistic form", in particular to identify phoneme membership of sounds, to perceive morphological affinities (such as *see* : *sight*), to identify related sentences (such as declaratives and the corresponding questions), to identify sentence schemata (such as various instances of transitive clauses), and to perceive constructional ambiguities (e. g. *They don't know how good meat tastes.*).

A grammar of the language L attempts to deal with such problems in terms of the formal properties of utterances. A theory which defines grammaticality, generates only grammatical sentences when "applied to a finite sample of linguistic behavior", and demonstrates that they are in harmony with native speaker intuitions, corresponds to the intuitive sense of grammaticality of the native speaker and is a "rational account of this behavior, i. e., a theory of the speaker's linguistic intuition" (ibid., 95). Taken at face value, these declarations provide the missing link between corpus data and intuition as input or raw material for the generative description, but we are still left with the fact that corpora are not used in actual practice.

4. The 1956 papers and *Syntactic Structures* (1957)

Syntactic Structures (Chomsky 1957a) was not originally planned to be a monograph on the international linguistic scene, being on the one hand a condensed version of undergraduate lectures that Chomsky had given at MIT, on the other a summary of ideas that he had published in 1956.

The length of Chomsky's (1956a) article "On the Limits of Finite-state Description" is only a page and a half but its repercussions have been enormous, especially as they were communicated to the research community in practically the same form in Chomsky (1956b) and, above all, in *Syntactic Structures*. Chomsky advanced the claim that the syntax of natural languages, as exemplified by English, is not describable by grammars with finite-state power, whereas context-free grammars according to him do have the requisite formal properties. For evidence Chomsky called upon mirror-image languages with sentences like aa, bb, abba, baab, aabbaa, …, and asserted that English sentences have this property. The arguments runs as follows: Let S_1, S_2, S_3, ... be declarative sentences of English. Then the following are all English sentences:

(4) (i) If S_1, then S_2.
(ii) Either S_3, or S_4.
(iii) The man who said that S_5, is arriving today.

These sentences have dependencies between "if" and "then", "either" and "or", and "man" and "is". But any of S_1, S_3, and S_5 in (4i), (4ii), and (4iii) may be chosen as any of (4i), (4ii), and (4iii) themselves. "Proceeding to construct sentences in this way, we arrive at sentences with dependency sets of more than any fixed number of terms [...]. English is therefore not a finite-state language" (ibid., 65). This is the hypothesis of unrestricted center-embedding. Suffice it here to note that the examples (i), (ii), and (iii) are artificial. No independent empirical data were offered in support of the hypothesis. This is the first (but not last) argument in the history of generative grammar resting on intuitively constructed data the grammaticality of which is debatable. This argument is then repeated as such in Chomsky (1956b, 115–116) and, above all, in *Syntactic Structures* (1957a, 20–23) where generations of linguists have made their first acquaintance with it. (In Karlsson (2007) I demonstrated that there is indeed a precise restriction on multiple center-embedding and that restriction is three.)

Chomsky (1956b, 113) states that a primary concern for the linguist is to discover simple and revealing grammars for natural languages and, through analysis of such grammars, to arrive at a general theory of linguistic structure. Grammars are said to be "based on a finite number of observed sentences (the linguist's corpus)" and they "'project' this set to an infinite set of grammatical sentences by establishing general 'laws' (grammatical rules) framed in terms of such hypothetical constructs as the particular phonemes, words, phrases, and so on". If a "large corpus of English" does not contain either of (1) *John ate a sandwhich* or (2) *Sandwhich a ate John*, "we ask whether the grammar that is determined for this corpus will project the corpus to include (1) and exclude (2)".

Syntactic Structures reiterates the same ideas: "given a corpus of sentences", linguistic theory should provide a method for selecting a grammar (p. 11); a language is "a (finite or infinite) set of sentences" (p. 13); one way to test the adequacy of a grammar is to determine whether the sentences it generates "are actually grammatical, i. e., acceptable to the native speaker", which is a "behavioral criterion for grammaticalness" (p. 13); a grammar is "related to the corpus of sentences" it describes (p. 14); "the set of grammatical sentences cannot be identified with any particular corpus of utterances obtained by the linguist in his field work" (p. 15), etc. Corpora figure prominently – in principle – also in the chapter titled "On the goals of linguistic theory" where Chomsky discusses the relations of grammars and corpora to discovery procedures, decision procedures, and evaluation procedures. When dealing with the explanatory power of linguistic theory, he remarks in passing that a grammar designed by the linguist generates "all and only the sentences of a language, which we have assumed were somehow given in advance" (p. 85). This remark runs counter to the many statements e. g. in LSLT boosting the importance of corpora but also confirms the observation already made that no systematic (or even sporadic) attention is paid to corpora.

5. From *Syntactic Structures* towards *Aspects*

Chomsky (1957b) is a review of Roman Jakobson and Morris Halle's book *Fundamentals of Language* and concerned above all with the relationship of phonetic substance to phonological representations. Chomsky develops his fairly critical evaluation as a combination of inductive and deductive elements. The former is represented by "a set of utterances" and "a given corpus" subjected to segmentation and phonological classification, the latter by loosening the structuralist biuniqueness requirement in favor of abstract phonological representations worked on by phonological rules. In addition to corpora Chomsky (1957b) also invokes "the linguistic behavior of an individual" as something to be accounted for by the grammar and the theory it is based on.

Chomsky (1957c) is a review of Charles F. Hockett's book *A Manual of Phonology*. Here some surprising claims about the status of intuition are made:

(5) "One cannot quarrel with Hockett's assertion that intuitive mastery of a language is, in fact, a great aid to a linguist, just as familiarity with his data is an aid to any other scientist. And it is probably true that very little can be said about how one acquires such familiarity, how one 'empathizes' and acquires a 'feel' for a language. But it is important to emphasize that the whole purpose of methodological investigations is to show how, in principle, and in crucial cases, intuition can be avoided. We can [... recognize ...] that study of the intuitive process of discovery (constructing hypotheses, gaining familiarity with the data, and so forth) is really outside the domain of linguistic method proper, and that linguistic theory itself must scrupulously avoid all intuition-based concepts. In other words, when we turn to the question of justification, which is, after all, at the heart of theoretical and methodological study, such notions as 'empathy' can play no role. Such operational devices as the paired utterance test, which Hockett mentions incidentally as an aid to field work, form, in fact, the empirical cornerstone of phonological theory. Compared with the problem of developing objective methods of this sort, discussion of intuitive procedures is of minor importance. [...] I can see no justification for the position that objectivity in linguistics is in principle something different from objectivity in physical science, and that the basic methods in linguistics are empathy and intuition. [...] It may be that grammatical research can best be described as the attempt to reconstruct precisely and explicitly the 'linguistic intuition' of the native speaker. But it does not follow from this that grammatical theory itself must be based on intuition. In fact only a completely objective theory in which empathy, prejudices, unanalyzed notions of 'phonetic realism', and so on, play no part will have any real value as an explanation of 'linguistic intuition'." (Chomsky 1957c, 228; 233–234)

My reading of this passage is that Chomsky confuses intuitions$_1$, which constitute the tacit knowledge making native mastery of the language possible, with the totally different intuitions$_2$ which a competent scholar relies on when she designs scientific hypotheses, theories, tests, etc. It is perplexing to see that Chomsky here is so explicit in condemning the use of intuitions$_1$ in linguistics. After all, it is only because of his native-speaker intuitions$_1$ of English that Chomsky himself is capable of producing and judging e. g. the sentences (3) which do not emanate either from natural corpora or 'linguistic behavior' of naive native speakers. Of course, through the ages it has been part and parcel of the methodology of grammar-writing to allow grammarians to invent example sentences, especially 'clear cases' (or 'bona fide sentences': Lees 1960, 211) such as *John sleeps*, the ultimate source of which is precisely the intuitions$_1$ of the grammarian herself. Surely, regardless of theoretical and methodological convictions, everybody agrees that it would be an idle ceremony to require the grammarian to carefully document the sources of such self-evidently grammatical sentences.

The bottom line is that intuitions$_1$ constitute the irreducible kernel of language ability which must be taken as axioms (also cf. Itkonen 1978). Contrary to what Chomsky declares in (5), it is not possible to give an explication of intuitions$_1$ that does not invoke those same intuitions$_1$. Without intuitions$_1$ (or something derived from them, e. g. elicited informant judgements) as primitive notions we simply do not know which one (if any, or perhaps both, or none) of *Colorless green ideas sleep furiously* and *Furiously sleep ideas green colorless* is syntactically well-formed. This confusion has led to an inconsistent ontological and methodological self-conception of many generative grammarians. On the one hand, the use of intuitions$_1$ is condemned, leading to claims that generative grammars and generative theory would be based on corpora or 'linguistic behavior'. On the other, the real practice of generative grammarians relies precisely on intuitions$_1$, usually coupled to an outright disregard of natural corpora. – Lees (1957, 376; 379), in his review of *Syntactic Structures*, does give an adequate characterization of the importance of intuitions, and grammar writing as an explication of those intuitions, as does Chomsky in several of his later writings.

Chomsky (1957d, 284) defines a grammar of a language as "a theory of the set of sentences constituting the language", i. e. with an explicit ontological commitment to language as sentences. Note that here there is no emphasis on intuitions as the real object of study. Chomsky (1958a, b; 1959a, b) are landmarks in the theory of formal languages but contain nothing of corpus-linguistic relevance.

Chomsky (1959c, 576) is the famous review of B. F. Skinner's book *Verbal Behavior*. There is a surprising statement concerning the object of study: "The behavior of the speaker, listener, and learner constitutes, of course, the actual data for any study of language". Chomsky then concedes that a generative grammar for a language only indirectly characterizes these abilities, but even so, given the context where the claim is made, it must be considered a category mistake. The basic data of grammatical theory and description are (real) sentences (utterances) and intuitions about them. The behavior of the speaker, listener, and learner is studied in empirical psycholinguistics, first-language acquisition research, etc.

The first detailed application of generative grammar to a sizeable morphosyntactic problem was R. B. Lees' (1960, xvii) *The Grammar of English Nominalizations*. Lees defines the task of generative grammar to be to propose and validate maximally simple rules to account for the grammatical structure of an "ever expanding corpus of English sentence types". At the same time, his study is intended to explicate grammatical details "in accordance with our intuitive mastery of the mechanisms we use to construct new English sentences". In the preface to the third printing of the book, Lees (1963, xxvix) notes that there has been widespread confusion in the literature concerning the question: "exactly what does a [generative] grammar purport to describe" (emphasis in the original)? As we have seen, the early Chomsky has not been consistent on this issue when invoking corpora, intuitions, and behavior. Lees' answer is simply that "a grammar describes how the correctly put utterances of a language are put together". In a secondary and indirect manner, a grammar, once made, also is a description of the tacit intuitive knowledge possessed by native speakers. Lees emphatically stresses that grammars are not descriptions of the gross linguistic behavior of speakers. In my opinion, these statements are perfectly correct, and the only possible conclusion to draw from them is that corpus observation supplemented with consultation of correctness notions (intuitions) are the indispensable basic methods of grammatical theorizing and description. This is not the conclusion which Lees draws because next he belittles the requirement "that a serious linguistic study should concern itself with 'real' sentences" and rather defines his object of study by downgrading it to "the principles in accordance with which I in fact construct the real, well-formed sentences of my dialect of English", thereby taking dangerous steps in the direction of solipsistic grammar writing. Note, in passing, that when Lees needs authentic material, he draws upon the copious data-oriented grammars of Curme and Jespersen.

In his review of Lees (1960), Matthews (1961, 205–207) takes issue with Lees' confession that intuitions are indispensable in grammatical analysis. Matthews warns against any use of intuition because that would be impossible to distinguish from a straight appeal to meaning. Matthews also gives a detailed description (of which there are not many in the generative literature) of the basic techniques of transformational analysis. The first step is to "take a text, say (i) the dog was bitten by the cat". But surely this very step presupposes that Matthews consults his intuitions$_1$ to ensure that the text (obviously constructed by himself) is grammatical in the first place, and not e. g. *the the by bitten was dog cat.*

Chomsky (1961a, 121; 127–128) still talks pro forma about corpora: "we ask how a linguistic theory [...] can be constructed so that given a corpus, grammars chosen by the evaluation procedure [...] meet the given empirical conditions of adequacy", but in practice he uses his intuitions$_1$ to coin examples as needed, e. g. *many more than half of the rather obviously much too easily solved problems* and *Why has John been such an easy fellow to please?*

Chomsky (1961b, 221–223; 233–239) offers several important corpus-related remarks and also treats degrees of grammaticality. He makes a distinction between data and facts. The linguist's data consist of observations about the form and use of utterances. The facts of linguistic structure that he hopes to discover go "well beyond" these observations. A grammar of a particular language is a hypothesis about the principles of sentence formation in that language. The truth and falsity of the hypothesis is judged i. a. by considering how well the grammar succeeds in organizing the data and how successfully it accommodates new data. A linguist who confines herself only to data (in the sense defined) has severely limited the scope of her research. A grammatical description that gives only "a compact one-to-one representation of the stock of utterances in the corpus" (here Chomsky cites Harris [1951, 376]) is defective. Chomsky remarks that on the level of syntax the intuitive character of grammatical descriptions is most obvious and that, ultimately, the collection of data is concerned with finding a basis for intuitive judgements. He offers the following list of types of data that generative grammarians utilize:

(6) a. phonetic transcriptions;
 b. judgements of conformity of utterance tokens;
 c. judgements of wellformedness;
 d. ambiguity that can be traced to structural origins;
 e. judgements of sameness or difference of sentence type;
 f. judgements concerning the propriety of particular classifications and segmentations;

However, Chomsky also emphasizes that such data are used specifically for determining the validity of particular proposed grammars and linguistic theory, not for construction of or choice among grammars. This remark in conjunction with the list (6a–f), where only (6a) represents intersubjective data strongly downplays the role of corpus data in the form of real language material. Data such as (6a–f) can also be complemented with results from experimental or behavioral tests. These two approaches are not alternatives but they also do not presuppose one another.

In Chomsky (1961b, 234) the concept "grammatical regularity" is used, as far as I can see, for the first time in his writings, even if it is not made clear if something else is intended than what is normally referred to by grammatical rules. When discussing the nature of deviant sentences, Chomsky cites two authentic examples, Dylan Thomas' *a grief ago* and Thorstein Veblen's *perform leisure*. I have not come across more than a handful of authentic examples in Chomsky's writings from the 1950s and 1960s, certainly much fewer than there are programmatic references in the earlier writings to the use of corpora as input to grammatical analysis. Chomsky notes that *a the ago* and *perform compel* are more deviant than *a grief ago* and *perform leisure*. There is a brief reference to corpora: "It is also easy to drop the restriction [...] that the corpus be finite" (ibid., 388).

Chomsky (1964a [1962]), a paper originally presented at a conference in 1958, states that a grammar should characterize all the utterances of the language. In this paper Chomsky does not in any way mention or invoke the intuitions of the native speaker nor those of the linguist. When discussing iterative applications of transformations, he picks up the method (introduced in *Syntactic Structures*, cf. (4)) of making up overly complex examples and claiming full grammaticality for them, here e. g. *My being prompted to try to visualize myself forcing him to come by this event* (ibid., 239–245).

In contradistinction to Chomsky (1964a [1962]), Chomsky (1962, 533), a paper read in 1960, emphasizes that a formalized grammar is a theory of the linguistic intuition of the native speaker. Operational tests for grammaticality and a description (theory) of English structure must converge on the linguistic intuition of the native speaker. The general theory can be evaluated by determining how well its structural descriptions accord with the intuitions of the native speaker. "[...] there is an enormous variety of perfectly clear cases that provide a very strong, though indirect, empirical condition of adequacy for this general theory. Failure to meet this general condition means that the theory must be revised." Chomsky (1964b, 928) even claims that the theory of generative grammar can suggest an explanation for the speaker's linguistic intuition.

Lees/Klima (1963, 18; 21) are concerned with generative rules for English pronominalization. The difficulties with strongly intuition-based methodology are dawning upon the authors. They have misgivings about their data as witnessed by statements like "the rules we formulate [...] characterize sentences in our own dialect only" and "there will be readers who judge differently certain examples we quote". A humbly submissive attitude is reflected in the statement that it "is also best, no doubt," to reject such sentences as (*)*John is shaved by himself*, where the parentheses around the star inform that the authors are genuinely uncertain about how to interpret the (obviously made-up) sentence.

Chomsky (1963, 326) contains (to my knowledge) his first mention of the notion competence. In this article the use of ungrammatical sentences plays an important role in the argumentation, e. g. **John saw the play and so did Bill the book*; **That one is wider than this one is wide* (ibid., 378). Miller and Chomsky (1963, 471) claim full grammaticality for sentences and phrases such as *That the fact that he left is unfortunate is obvious* and *the cover that the book that John has has* even though it is mentioned that they are preferably transformed into *It is obvious that it was unfortunate that he left* and *John's book's cover*.

Around 1963 the generative reliance on the linguist's intuitions in making up example sentences clearly overstepped the confines of what is methodologically defensible (i. e., to make up clear cases such as *Sue sleeps* on the basis of the linguist's intuition). Thus, Chomsky/Miller (1963, 286–287) say that the English sentence:

(7) The rat the cat the dog chased killed ate the malt.

"is surely confusing and improbable but it is perfectly grammatical and has a clear and unambiguous meaning", and then they continue: "To illustrate more fully the complexities that must in principle be accounted for by a real grammar of a natural language, consider [8]. [...] Of course, we can safely predict that [8] will never be produced except as an example, just as we can, with equal security, predict that such perfectly well-formed sentences as *birds eat*, *black crows are black*, *black crows are white*, *Tuesday follows Monday*, etc., will never occur in normal adult discourse. Like other sentences that are too obviously true, too obviously false, too complex, too inelegant, or that fail in innumerable other ways to be of any use in ordinary human affairs, they are not used. Nevertheless, [8] is a perfectly well-formed sentence with a clear and unambiguous meaning, and a grammar of English must be able to account for it if the grammar is to have any psychological relevance."

(8) Anyone who feels that if so-many more students whom we haven't actually admitted are sitting in on the course than ones we have that the room had to be changed, then probably auditors will have to be excluded, is likely to agree that the curriculum needs revision.

But intersubjective agreement on the status of artefacts like (7), (8) is of course hard to achieve. The grammaticality/acceptability status of such sentences is indeterminate as it lacks backing in real usage.

Chomsky (1964c) is a revised and expanded version of a paper (Chomsky 1964b) read at the Ninth International Congress of Linguists in 1962. A new corpus-related concept is introduced, "primary linguistic data", which refers to authentic samples of speech confronting language-acquiring infants (ibid., 61–64). The important distinctions between three levels of success for grammatical descriptions are made: observational, descriptive, and explanatory adequacy. An observationally adequate level of success is achieved if the grammar presents the observed primary data correctly. The level of descriptive adequacy is reached when the grammar gives a correct account of the intuition of the native speaker. The explanatory level is achieved when the associated linguistic theory succeeds in providing a principled basis for deciding which one of several competing alternative grammars, each satisfying the criterion of descriptive adequacy, should be picked as the optimal one. Chomsky (1964c, 79–81) contains an interesting, and one of the few explicit, discussions in the history of generative grammar of the topic "objectivity of linguistic data". Chomsky emphasizes that introspective judgements are not sacrosanct nor beyond conceivable doubt, but that they can be neglected only at the cost of destroying the discipline. (Notice the contrast with the views expressed in (5).) Consistency among speakers of different backgrounds is relevant information, as is consistency for a particular speaker on different occasions. A key statement is this one: "The possibility of constructing a systematic and general theory to account for these observations is also a factor to be considered in evaluating the probable correctness of particular observations". Operational tests that consistently supported introspective judgements in clear cases would also be considered relevant in determining the correctness of particular observations.

The generative upgrading of the methodological status of linguistic intuition can largely be traced to these very paragraphs. In the next few years to come the theoretical and methodological discussion would mostly concern the levels of descriptive and explanatory adequacy and literally no attention was paid in generative works to the level of observational adequacy which would have been the domain of authentic examples and real language use.

When Chomsky presented these ideas at the Ninth International Congress of Linguists in 1962, they provoked a lively discussion documented in Lunt (ed., 1964). Halliday (1964, 988; 990) remarked that he, as a native speaker of English, found many of Chomsky's claims about English "counter-intuitive", e. g. the rule S → NP VP, and derivations involving deletion. Halliday also pointed out that the full possibilities of observation-oriented taxonomic description had not yet been utilized. Chomsky's (1964d, 990) reply did not address these remarks directly but emphasized the importance of constructing a substantive theory of language with sufficient clarity so that its "empirical adequacy" can be tested, and the choice between competing theories made on "empirical grounds". Pike (1964, 991) made the important remark that introspective judgements are less useful in dealing with preliterate cultures and their languages than the "study of objectively *observable* reactions of native speakers" (emphasis in the original). In his reply Chomsky (1964e, 994) did not address this particular issue. At the same conference, Schachter (1964) read a paper on kernel and non-kernel sentences. In the discussion, E. Hahn (1964, 697) exclaimed: "I am shocked at the suggestion that we are to trust intuition! *Is this science?*" (emphasis in the original).

Paavo Siro (1964, 165) was the first Finnish linguist to become interested in generative grammar. He too attended the 1962 congress. Siro was concerned with designing a unified description of the Finnish system of local case forms, a problem which then-current generative grammar with its obvious Anglocentrism was not particularly well suited to tackle. At the end of his paper Siro makes the interesting remark that his model for the description of simplex sentences can be extended in several directions, but that the "choice of solutions must depend on empirical analysis of large linguistic materials". Such requests are not easy to find in the generative literature, neither in the early nor in the later one. In practice, Siro did not pursue this corpus-linguistic line of research.

Katz/Postal (1964, ix; 75; 123; 144; 148) distinguish sharply between language and speech. A language is a system of abstract objects analogous in significant respects to such a cultural object as a symphony. Speech is the actual verbal behavior that manifests the linguistic competence of someone who has learned the appropriate system of abstract objects. The methodology of using ungrammatical made-up examples sentences is in widespread use, e. g. in the discussion concerning the generative derivation of the imperative construction: **go home, did you*; **go home, must he*; **kill herself*. Controversial grammaticality judgements are easy to spot, e. g. *this washing of the car of John's*. Postal

(1964, v) claims that generative grammar is a "methodological framework" which represents a proposal about the way linguistic research should proceed and the aims it should take. He then states that this framework is "empirically neutral" and excludes no possible claim about the nature of language. Postal talks about the importance of matching the theory with "empirical linguistic data" and "observed data" but nowhere does he spell out or use such data, apart from using examples made up by himself. The same goes for Fodor/Katz (1964b, vii–ix) who repeatedly stress the empiricalness of linguistics and the importance of empirical evidence but fail to use anything but intuitive judgements and to mention what else the empirical evidence could consist of.

Klima's paper (1964, 264–265) on English negation became widely cited. It was one of the earliest in-depth studies of a complex syntactic-semantic problem. As usual the data are intuition-based. Klima is one of the first to note the occasional indeterminacy of intuitive data, and to resolve it by postulating two different idiolects, i. e. by going one step further than Lees/Klima (1963) who, as already noted, restricted their claims to certain (intuitively surmised) dialects of English. Thus, Klima claims that in the less differentiated Idiolect A all negative pre-verbs allow a *neither*-tag, as in the sentence:

(9) Writers will seldom accept suggestions, and neither will publishers.

whereas in a second, more highly differentiated idiolect, Idiolect B, *neither*-tags are allowed to occur only with *not* and *never*, not with e. g. *seldom*. Thus, (9) would be grammatical in Idiolect A but ungrammatical in Idiolect B. Some of Klima's grammaticality judgements are controversial, e. g. the proclaimed ungrammaticality of **Did John drink any bourbon*? or **a not clear formulation* (a search of the Internet supplies several authentic examples of the latter type, e. g. *a not clear enough definition*). These measures of restricting debatable intuition-based generative grammaticality judgements and the theoretical claims resting upon them to dialects and even idiolects were a methodological decline.

6. *Aspects of the Theory of Syntax* (1965)

Aspects doubtless is the most significant contribution to linguistics made by Chomsky (and by generative grammar as a whole). Here the full-blown notion of competence is elaborated in an explicitly mentalistic framework. However, still prevailing are the somewhat contradictory views of the subject matter and the input data of linguistic theory and grammar writing. Chomsky (1965, 4; 8; 15; 20) thus states that the problem for the linguist is to determine "from the data of performance" the underlying system of rules which is a "mental reality underlying actual behavior". Similarly, a generative grammar "assigns structural descriptions to sentences" while it also deals with "mental processes that are far beyond [...] consciousness". Observation of data and introspection are both recognized as legitimate knowledge sources but the importance of observational data is now explicitly downgraded: "observed use of language [...] may provide evidence as to the nature of this mental reality, but surely cannot constitute the actual subject matter of linguistics, if this is to be a serious discipline". It is a "necessity to give [...] priority to introspective evidence and to the linguistic intuition of the native speaker". Furthermore, "sharpening of the data by more objective tests is a matter of small importance for the problems at hand". In view of this, it is no surprise that corpus-oriented methods play no role in *Aspects* (where the word "corpus" is mentioned in passing only once or twice). All examples are made up by Chomsky himself, many of them are of type (3).

A booklet closely related to *Aspects* is *Topics in the Theory of Generative Grammar* (Chomsky 1966, 21–35). This is largely a response to several criticisms of generative theory that had been voiced during the first half of the 1960s. There is an eloquent and irrefutable defense of the importance of intuitions as the indispensable starting-point of grammatical description. There are also a few mentions in passing of "empirically given data", and even of corpora of which three (somewhat hypothetical) examples are programmatically mentioned, the set of sentences in the New York Public Library, in the Congressional Record, and in a person's total experience of his native language.

Taken as a whole, the corpus-related pronouncements in Chomsky (1965, 1966) confirm what had become established practice already in the 1950s, a shift in methodology to full reliance on introspection. Corpora and other empirical considerations might be mentioned but they are never elaborated nor put to use. When real-language data are needed, generative grammarians occasionally turn to the classics of descriptive grammar such as (for English) Curme, Jespersen, and Poutsma. Thus, Rosenbaum (1967, 114) notes that "traditional grammarians were very diligent. They present much data that are quite relevant to the construction of a [generative] grammar for the complement system".

7. The late 1960s

In the late 1960s the practice increased of using strange made-up examples the grammaticality and/or acceptability of which is unclear. (10) presents instances of sentences claimed to be fully grammatical but which are debatable, (11) of sentences claimed to be ungrammatical that rather should be considered grammatical because such structures do in fact occur in current usage (as manifested on the Internet):

(10) It is believed by me that John has convinced Bill. (Rosenbaum 1967, 58)
What is believed by me is that John has convinced Bill. (ibid.)
There is believed by everybody to be three chairs in the room. (ibid., 64)
For there to be three chairs in the room was preferred by everybody. (ibid.)
I believe that John is honest is true. (ibid., 66)
That the plane flew at all was marveled at by them. (ibid., 83)
The giving of the lecture by the man who arrived yesterday assisted us. (Fraser 1970, 91)
The rumor that the report which the advisory committee submitted was suppressed is true is preposterous. (Langendoen 1970, 99)
It proves that it's true that Tom's thinking that it would be a good idea for him to show that he likes it here that he's told everyone that he's staying. (ibid., 101)

(11) *What an idiot I thought Tom was. (Postal 1968, 75; cf. Internet: What an idiot I thought the main character to be.)
*the best of some sheep (Postal 1970a, 60; cf. Internet: the best of some situations)

*it which I ate (ibid., 74; cf. Internet: He brings the same root to it, which is Black American music.)
*John will leave until tomorrow. (Lakoff 1970, 148; cf. Internet: I will leave until tomorrow.)
*John's certainty (likelihood) to win the prize (Chomsky 1970, 189; cf. Internet: Kilbane's certainty to start on the left)
*Physicists like himself don't often make mistakes (Ross 1970, 229; cf. Internet: Fields feels like himself.)
*Harry reminds me of himself. (Postal 1970b; cf. Internet: Joe reminds me of himself.)

Related to these methodological problems is the subjective practice of marking deviant sentences not only with simple stars for ungrammaticality, but also with question-marks and even combinations of question-marks and stars. Thus, Ross (1968, 106–107) uses four markings of deviance in his widely cited PhD dissertation "Constraints on Variables in Syntax", without explaining their precise meaning and mutual differences: *, ?, ??, ?*.

8. Conclusion

At the end of section 1 I defined a number of data-acquisition methods appropriate for the study of (i) language data such as sentences and utterances, (ii) speaker-internal intuitive language competence, and (iii) the behavioral real-time processes of speaking and understanding. The methods are:

(12) observation ('corpus work'),
elicitation ('field work'),
introspective consultation (of native competence),
introspective construction of fully grammatical sentences ('clear cases'),
introspective construction of ungrammatical sentences,
introspective construction of questionable sentences,
experimentation ('psycholinguistic testing'),

where observation and introspective consultation (checking whether the observed material accords with intuitions) normally go together, and introspective construction of ungrammatical and questionable sentences are closely related.

Now let us consider how data are acquired by typical practitioners of various types of the grammar trade. An author of simple school grammars relies mainly on introspective construction of fully grammatical sentences, i. e. the grammarian herself constructs clear cases like *John runs*, *The bottle is on the table*, etc. Occasionally she might use observation, i. e. she spots a relevant example in real texts or discourse and decides to use it, having first introspectively consulted her competence to check that the example is fully grammatical. Authors of comprehensive scholarly oriented reference grammars such as Curme (1931) and Huddleston/Pullum (2002) use observation and introspective consultation (i. e. do critically minded corpus work) to a much larger extent than authors of elementary school grammars but they surely also introspectively construct fully grammatical sentences. Field linguists mainly use elicitation techniques. Often a field linguist does not have native-like competence in the language under study and therefore he is not entitled to use introspective consultation (except for generating hypotheses to be tested with the informant). Psycholinguists typically perform experiments, grammarians (of any type) typically do not.

As we have seen, corpus methodology was rejected by the early Chomsky in practice long before he rejected it in principle (which happened in the early 1960s). From 1955 onwards, Chomsky was relying on intuitions while he continued to say how important empirical data was. This contradictory methodological stance was further complicated when no clear distinction was made between data in the sense of sentences (utterances) vs. (the undefined category of) "linguistic behavior". Generative grammarians introspectively constructed fully grammatical and acceptable sentences, clear cases, much like all grammarians have been doing through the ages. The distinct generative methodological innovations as for data-acquisition were introspectively constructed ungrammatical and questionable sentences. The former proved fruitful in sharpening grammatical argumentation, cf. (3). But the method of introspective construction of questionable sentences often had detrimental consequences, especially when full grammaticality was claimed for very strange made-up sentences (e. g. (8)) which then served as data for strong theoretical claims.

9. Literature

Chomsky, Noam (1953), Systems of Syntactic Analysis. In: *Journal of Symbolic Logic* 18(3), 242–256.

Chomsky, Noam (1954), Review of Eliezer Rieger, *Modern Hebrew*. In: *Language* 30(1), 180–181.

Chomsky, Noam (1955), Logical Syntax and Semantics. Their Linguistic Relevance. In: *Language* 31, 36–45.

Chomsky, Noam (1956a), On the Limits of Finite-state Description. In: *MIT Research Laboratory of Electronics, Quarterly Progress Report* 41, 64–65.

Chomsky, Noam (1956b), Three Models for the Description of Language. In: *IRE Transactions on Information Theory, vol. IT-2, Proceedings of the Symposium on Information Theory*, 113–124.

Chomsky, Noam (1957a), *Syntactic Structures*. The Hague: Mouton.

Chomsky, Noam (1957b), Review of Roman Jakobson & Morris Halle, *Fundamentals of Language*. In: *International Journal of American Linguistics* XXIII, 234–242.

Chomsky, Noam (1957c), Review of Charles F. Hockett, *A Manual of Phonology*. In: *International Journal of American Linguistics* XXIII, 223–234.

Chomsky, Noam (1957d), Logical Structures in Language. In: *American Documentation* 8, 284–291.

Chomsky, Noam (1958a), Finite State Languages. In: *Information and Control* 1, 91–112.

Chomsky, Noam (1958b), Some Properties of Finite-state Grammars. In: *MIT Research Laboratory of Electronics, Quarterly Progress Report* 49, 107–111.

Chomsky, Noam (1959a), On Certain Formal Properties of Grammars. In: *Information and Control* 2, 137–167.

Chomsky, Noam (1959b), A Note on Phrase Structure Grammars. In: *Information and Control* 2, 393–395.

Chomsky, Noam (1959c), A Review of B. F. Skinner, *Verbal Behavior*. In: *Language* 35, 26–58. [Reprinted in Fodor/Katz 1964a, 547–578.]

Chomsky, Noam (1961a), On the Notion "Rule of Grammar". In: Jakobson, Roman (ed.) *Proceedings of Symposia in Applied Mathematics, 12: Structure of Language and its Mathematical Aspects*, 6–24. [Reprinted in Fodor/Katz 1964a, 119–136.]

Chomsky, Noam (1961b), Some Methodological Remarks on Generative Grammar. In: *Word* 17, 219–239. [Partially reprinted under the title "Degrees of Grammaticalness" in Fodor/Katz 1964a, 384–389.]
Chomsky, Noam (1962), Explanatory Models in Linguistics. In: Nagel, E./Suppes, P./Tarski, A. (eds.), *Logic, Methodology and Philosophy of Science: Proceedings of the 1960 International Congress*. Stanford: Stanford University Press, 528–550.
Chomsky, Noam (1963), Formal Properties of Grammars. In: Luce/Bush/Galanter 1963, 325–418.
Chomsky, Noam (1964a [1962]), A Transformational Approach to Syntax. In: Fodor/Katz 1964a, 211–245. [Originally published in: Hill, A. A. (ed.), *Proceedings of the Third Texas Conference on Problems of Linguistic Analysis of English on May 9–12, 1958*. Austin, Texas: The University of Texas Press, 124–158.]
Chomsky, Noam (1964b), The Logical Basis of Linguistic Theory. In: Lunt 1964, 914–978.
Chomsky, Noam (1964c), Current Issues in Linguistic Theory. In: Fodor/Katz 1964a, 50–118.
Chomsky, Noam (1964d), Comment to M. A. K. Halliday. In: Lunt 1964, 990.
Chomsky, Noam (1964e), Comment to Kenneth Pike. In: Lunt 1964, 992–994.
Chomsky, Noam (1965), *Aspects of the Theory of Syntax*. Cambridge, MA: MIT Press.
Chomsky, Noam (1966), *Topics in the Theory of Generative Grammar*. The Hague: Mouton & Co.
Chomsky, Noam (1970), Remarks on Nominalization. In: Jacobs/Rosenbaum 1970, 184–221.
Chomsky, Noam (1975 [1955–1956]), *The Logical Structure of Linguistic Theory*. New York: Plenum Press.
Chomsky, Noam (1986), *Knowledge of Language. Its Nature, Origin, and Use*. New York etc.: Praeger.
Chomsky, Noam/Miller, George A. (1963), Introduction to the Formal Analysis of Natural Languages. In: Luce/Bush/Galanter 1963, 269–321.
Curme, George O. (1931), *A Grammar of the English Language: Syntax*. Boston etc.: D. C. Heath and Company.
Fodor, Jerry A./Katz, Jerrold J. (eds.) (1964a), *The Structure of Language. Readings in the Philosophy of Language*. Englewood Cliffs, New Jersey: Prentice Hall, Inc.
Fodor, Jerry A./Katz, Jerrold J. (1964b), Preface. In: Fodor/Katz 1964a, vii–ix.
Fraser, Bruce (1970), Some Remarks on the Action Nominalizations in English. In: Jacobs/Rosenbaum 1970, 83–98.
Hahn, E. (1964), Comment to Paul Schachter. In: Lunt 1964, 697.
Halliday, M. A. K. (1964), Comment to Noam Chomsky. In: Lunt 1964, 986–990.
Harris, Zellig S. (1951), *Methods in Structural Linguistics*. Chicago: The University of Chicago Press.
Harris, Zellig S./Voegelin, Charles W. (1953), Eliciting. In: *Southwestern Journal of Anthropology* 9, 59–75.
Huddleston, Rodney/Pullum, Geoffrey K. (2002), *The Cambridge Grammar of the English Language*. Cambridge: Cambridge University Press.
Itkonen, Esa (1978), *Grammatical Theory and Metascience: A Critical Investigation into the Methodological and Philosophical Foundations of 'Autonomous' Linguistics*. Amsterdam: Benjamins.
Jacobs, Roderick A./Rosenbaum, Peter S. (eds.) (1970), *Readings in English Transformational Grammar*. Waltham, Mass.: Ginn and Company.
Karlsson, Fred (2007), Constraints on multiple center-embedding of clauses. In: *Journal of Linguistics* 43, 365–392.
Katz, Jerrold J./Postal, Paul M. (1964), *An Integrated Theory of Linguistic Descriptions*. Cambridge: MIT Press.
Klima, Edward (1964), Negation in English. In: Fodor/Katz 1964a, 246–323.
Lakoff, George (1970), Pronominalization, Negation, and the Analysis of Adverbs. In: Jacobs/Rosenbaum 1970, 145–165.
Langendoen, D. Terrence (1970), The Accessibility of Deep Structures. In: Jacobs/Rosenbaum 1970, 99–104.

Lees, Robert B. (1957), Review of Noam Chomsky, *Syntactic Structures*. In: *Language* 33(3), 375–408.
Lees, Robert B. (1960), *The Grammar of English Nominalizations*. Bloomington, IN: Indiana University Press.
Lees, Robert B. (1963), *The Grammar of English Nominalizations*. Third printing. Bloomington: Indiana University / The Hague: Mouton.
Lees, Robert B./Klima, Edward S. (1963), Rules for English Pronominalization. In: *Language* 39(1), 17–28.
Lounsbury, Floyd G. (1953), Field Methods and Techniques in Linguistics. In: Kroeber, A. L. (ed.), *Anthropology Today*. Chicago: University of Chicago Press.
Luce, R. Duncan/Bush, Robert R./Galanter, Eugene (eds.) 1963, *Handbook of Mathematical Psychology. II.* New York: John Wiley and Sons.
Lunt, Horace G. (ed.) (1964), *Proceedings of the Ninth International Congress of Linguists, Cambridge, Mass., August 27–31, 1962.* The Hague: Mouton & Co.
Matthews, Peter H. (1961), Review Article: Transformational Grammar. In: *Archivum Linguisticum* 13(2), 196–209.
Miller, George A./Chomsky, Noam (1963), Finitary Models of Language Users. In: Luce/Bush/Galanter 1963, 419–491.
Newmeyer, Frederick J. (1986), *The Politics of Linguistics*. Chicago: The University of Chicago Press.
Pike, Kenneth (1964), Comment to Noam Chomsky. In: Lunt 1964, 990–992.
Postal, Paul M. (1964), *Constituent Structure. A Study of Contemporary Models of Constituent Structure*. The Hague: Mouton & Co.
Postal, Paul M. (1968), Cross-over Phenomena. A Study in the Grammar of Coreference. In: Plath, W. J. (ed.), *Specification and Utilization of a Transformational Grammar*. Scientific Report No. 3, 1–239. Yorktown Heights, New York: IBM Corporation.
Postal, Paul M. (1970a), On So-called Pronouns in English. In: Jacobs/Rosenbaum 1970, 56–82.
Postal, Paul M. (1970b), On the Surface Verb 'remind'. In: *Linguistic Inquiry* 1, 37–120.
Rosenbaum, Peter (1967), *The Grammar of English Predicate Complement Constructions*. (Research Monograph No. 47.) Cambridge, Mass.: MIT Press.
Ross, John Robert (1968), Constraints on Variables in Syntax. MIT PhD Dissertation, reproduced by the Indiana University Linguistics Club.
Ross, John Robert (1970), On Declarative Sentences. In: Jacobs/Rosenbaum 1970, 222–272.
Schachter, Paul (1964), Kernel and Non-kernel Sentences. In: Lunt 1964, 692–696.
Siro, Paavo (1964), On the Fundamentals of Sentence Structure. In: Lunt 1964, 161–165.

Fred Karlsson, Helsinki (Finland)

3. Some aspects of the development of corpus linguistics in the 1970s and 1980s

1. The breakthrough

Although the roots of corpus linguistics can be traced further back (cf. the introduction to this volume and article 1), the real breakthrough came with the access to machine-readable texts which could be stored, transported, and analysed electronically. Tasks which were previously beyond human capacity, or required an enormous amount of work, such as the compilation of frequency lists and concordances, could now be done easily. In the 1970s and 1980s we find an explosion in the quantity and variety of texts prepared for analysis by computer. The texts were used by a fast increasing number of researchers and for a wide range of purposes. The development was partly connected with technological advances. In this period computers became more powerful and at the same time cheaper and more user-friendly, making the linguist less dependent upon computational expertise. An additional reason for the upsurge of corpus linguistics in this period was the increasing interest of language researchers in language use as opposed to language systems *in abstracto*. It was widely recognised that computer corpora provide an unprecedented way of studying language in use. There was, however, a tension between armchair linguists and corpus linguists, well captured by the caricature in a paper by Fillmore (1992, 35), and the negative view of corpora found in early generative linguistics (cf. article 2 and section 4.1. below) persisted in many circles. It would take some time before it was realised that corpus linguistics can provide theoretically interesting insights, and that there is no necessary conflict between empirical and theoretical work.

Those who want to study the development are recommended to consult collections of papers such as those edited by Bergenholtz/Schaeder (1979), Johansson (1982), and Johansson/Stenström (1991). Note also Geoffrey Leech's (1991) account of the state of the art in corpus linguistics and Ian Lancashire's survey of literary and linguistic computing 1968–1988 (Lancashire 1990) and of corpus linguistics in *The Humanities Computing Yearbook 1989–90* (Lancashire 1991, 159–170). I will draw attention to some of the most significant developments, focusing in particular on the quantity and variety of texts, the annotation of texts, and the uses of corpora. But first there is a need to examine the term 'corpus linguistics', which was introduced in this period.

2. The term 'corpus linguistics'

It took some time of computer corpus use before the term 'corpus linguistics' was introduced. It is found in the title of a collection of papers from the 'Conference on the Use of Computer Corpora in English Language Research', an early ICAME (see section 4.2.) conference held in Nijmegen in 1983: *Corpus Linguistics: Recent Developments in the Use of Computer Corpora in English Language Research* (Aarts/Meijs 1984), a *locus classicus* in corpus linguistics. Jan Aarts informs me that he had used the Dutch equivalent of corpus linguistics, *corpustaalkunde*, a few years earlier, in 1980, as the name of a research programme submitted to the Dutch research council:

> "The programme put the collaboration between the Nijmegen Department of Computer Science and the TOSCA group [see 6.2. below] on a formal footing. The reason for choosing 'corpustaalkunde' as the name of the research programme [...]: it brought two disparate disciplines under a common denominator and the term caught people's attention, because it suggested 'This is NEW!' Throughout the 80s and the 90s I continued using the name 'corpustaalkunde' for the research programmes I had to write, but I've never felt the need to argue that corpus linguistics is a discipline in its own right, as some people do; for me it's always been a means to an end." (Jan Aarts, private communication)

The term 'corpus linguistics' was useful in underlining that this was a new enterprise, in the narrow sense of 'computer corpus linguistics'. But most people agreed that it was not a new linguistic discipline, but rather a tool that could be applied in virtually any branch of linguistics.

3. The rise of computer studies of language

Computer corpus linguistics goes back beyond the period I will be mainly concerned with. McEnery/Wilson (2001, 20–22) draw attention to Roberto Busa's studies of the works of St Thomas Aquinas and Alphonse Juilland's 'mechanolinguistics', which involved the statistical study of words in machine-readable corpora for several languages. The work of these scholars started well before 1970. The 1960s saw the compilation of the classic Brown Corpus, which has been immensely influential in the development of corpus linguistics (see section 4.1.), and the launching of the important journal *Computers and the Humanities*. But it is in the period after 1970 that the compilation and use of computer corpora gained momentum.

A striking feature of the development of the computer analysis of texts is its international aspect, prompted by the need to establish cooperation in the use of the new technology. New organisations were formed, such as the Association for Literary and Linguistic Computing (1973) and the Association for Computing in the Humanities (1978). Centres focusing on linguistic and literary computing were established in a number of countries (see the survey of centres in Lancashire 1991, 548–563). In Italy Antonio Zampolli continued in the footsteps of Roberto Busa, making the University of Pisa a major centre for the computational study of language. A research centre for the *Thesaurus Linguae Graecae* was founded in 1972 at the University of California, Irvine. Centres for computer analysis of German were early established at Bonn, Mannheim, and

Saarbrücken. The Arts Computing centre at Waterloo, Canada, laid the foundation for the work done by its Computer Science Department with Oxford University Press on the *Oxford English Dictionary* (see section 5.4.). In France Bernard Quemada took the initiative to the Institut National de la Langue Française of the Centre National de la Recherche Scientifique (CNRS). In Sweden, as early as 1965, Sture Allén set up the research group *Språkdata* at Gothenburg University, now the home of the Swedish Language Bank. The Norwegian Computing Centre for the Humanities at Bergen was founded in the early 1970s and became an important centre for the distribution of English machine-readable texts (see section 4.2.). The Oxford Text Archive, a repository for machine-readable texts and a channel for their dissemination rather than a research centre, was established in 1976.

The list could be made much longer, but in this brief survey it is not possible to do justice to all the pioneering work done. As English corpus work has been particularly influential, I will focus on English corpus linguistics. The central role of English is commented on by many who touch on the history of corpus linguistics, as in the article on corpora in *The Encyclopedia of Language and Linguistics* (Sebba/Fligelstone 1994, 772): "Even given its status as an international language, the predominance of English-language corpora over all others is striking". There is no doubt a connection with the fact that English is the major world language of science and business and that it is widely known and studied all over the world. Another contributory factor is probably that some early English corpora, notably the Brown Corpus (see section 4.1.), were placed at the disposal of the international community of scholars. This sharing of resources is an important and rather novel aspect of the development of corpus linguistics.

4. First-generation corpora

In his introduction to corpus linguistics Graeme Kennedy (1998) singles out the Brown Corpus, the LOB Corpus, and the London-Lund Corpus as 'first-generation corpora'. Although they are not the only early computer corpora compiled for language research, they are the ones which have been especially influential in the development of English corpus linguistics, and they have no doubt also stimulated corpus studies more generally.

4.1. The significance of the Brown Corpus

Considering the seminal role assigned to the Brown Corpus in most comments on the history of corpus linguistics, it seems appropriate to go into some detail. One of the compilers, W. Nelson Francis, gives a vivid account in his paper on 'Problems of assembling and computerizing large corpora' (Francis 1979). He writes that, when he, with Henry Kučera, was planning the Brown Corpus, they convened a conference of 'corpus-wise scholars' at Brown University, including Randolph Quirk, who had initiated the important pre-computational Survey of English Usage project (cf. article 1), and he continues:

> "This group decided the size of the corpus (1,000,000 words), the number of texts (500, of 2,000 words each), the universe (material in English, by American writers, first printed in

the United States in the calendar year 1961), the subdivisions (15 genres, 9 of 'informative prose' and 6 of 'imaginative prose') and by a fascinating process of individual vote and average consensus, how many samples from each genre (ranging from 6 in science fiction to 80 in learned and scientific)." (Francis 1979, 117)

Table 3.1 summarises the composition of the Brown Corpus and its British counterpart, the LOB Corpus, which we will come back to in section 4.2.

Tab. 3.1: The composition of the Brown Corpus and the LOB Corpus

Text categories		Number of texts in each category	
		Brown	LOB
A	Press: reportage	44	44
B	Press: editorial	27	27
C	Press: reviews	17	17
D	Religion	17	17
E	Skills, trades, and hobbies	36	38
F	Popular lore	48	44
G	Belles lettres, biography, essays	75	77
H	Miscellaneous (government documents, foundation reports, industry reports, college catalogue, industry house organ)	30	30
J	Learned and scientific writings	80	80
K	General fiction	29	29
L	Mystery and detective fiction	24	24
M	Science fiction	6	6
N	Adventure and western fiction	29	29
P	Romance and love story	29	29
R	Humour	9	9
	Total	500	500

In retrospect, it is easy to criticise the composition of the Brown Corpus. Why a total of one million words? Why pick samples of 2,000 words? Why exactly from these text categories? What are the grounds behind the weighting of the text categories? The fact remains, however, that the corpus was large considering the technical resources at the time and that the samples represent a wide range of styles and varieties of texts, including both informative (A–J) and imaginative (K–R) prose. The selection of texts was based on a combination of considered judgement (the choice of text categories and their weighting) and random sampling. The sampling and coding of the texts are explained in the manual for the corpus (Francis/Kučera 1979), which also provides detailed information on the source texts.

As the only method of input of text available at the time was via a punched-card reader, the texts were card-punched with 70 characters per line plus a location marker specifying the text and line number, corresponding to the single line of 80 spaces contained on a single IBM punched card. Figure 3.1 illustrates the original card-image form of the corpus, as it was prepared in 1963–1964 (quoted from Francis/Kučera 1979, 9, where it is pointed out that "owing to corrections, some lines are not filled out"; this accounts for the coding in the second line).

TELEVISION IMPULSES, SOUND WAVES, ULTRA-VIOLET RAYS, ETC**., THAT MAY	1020E1F03
OC*	1025E1F03
CUPY THE VERY SAME SPACE, EACH SOLITARY UPON ITS OWN FREQUENCY, IS INF	1030E1F03
INITE. *SO WE MAY CONCEIVE THE COEXISTENCE OF THE INFINITE NUMBER OF U	1040E1F03
NIVERSAL, APPARENTLY MOMENTARY STATES OF MATTER, SUCCESSIVE ONE AFTER	1050E1F03
ANOTHER IN CONSCIOUSNESS, BUT PERMANENT EACH ON ITS OWN BASIC PHASE O	1060E1F03
F THE PROGRESSIVE FREQUENCIES. *THIS THEORY MAKES IT POSSIBLE FOR ANY	1070E1F03
EVENT THROUGHOUT ETERNITY TO BE CONTINUOUSLY AVAILABLE AT ANY MOMENT T	1080E1F03
O CONSCIOUSNESS.	1090E1F03

Fig. 3.1: A sample from the original card-image form of the Brown Corpus

The text of Figure 3.1 is to be read as transliterating:

> "television impulses, sound waves, ultra-violet rays, etc., that may occupy the very same space, each solitary upon its own frequency, is infinite. So we may conceive the coexistence of the infinite number of universal, apparently momentary states of matter, successive one after another in consciousness, but permanent each on its own basic phase of the progressive frequencies. This theory makes it possible for any event throughout eternity to be continuously available at any moment to consciousness".

The corpus on 100,000 cards was transferred to magnetic tape for use with mainframe computers. Due to the limited character set, the original form of the corpus was in capitals only, and many textual features had to be coded in a cumbersome way. This is not the place to go into details of coding. Suffice it to say that we are very far from what a computer corpus looks like in our days. In the 1970s Knut Hofland at the Norwegian Computing Centre for the Humanities prepared new forms of the Brown Corpus with upper- and lower-case letters and a minimum of special codes, and the corpus later became available for microcomputers by means of diskette and CD-ROM. The new versions are probably the ones that have been most widely used.

The building of the Brown Corpus is remarkable considering the unsupportive environment among leading linguists at the time. This story told by W. Nelson Francis has often been quoted (Francis 1979, 110):

> "In 1962, when I was in the early stages of collecting the Brown Standard Corpus of Ameri can English, I met Professor Robert Lees at a linguistic conference. In response to his query about my current interests, I said that I had a grant from the U.S. Office of Education to compile a million-word corpus of present-day American English for computer use. He looked at me in amazement and asked, 'Why in the world are you doing that?' I said something about finding out the true facts about English grammar. I have never forgotten his reply: 'That is a complete waste of your time and the government's money. You are a native speaker

> of English; in ten minutes you can produce more illustrations of any point in English grammar than you will find in many millions of words of random text.'"

The Brown Corpus has been significant in a number of ways. It established a pattern for the use of electronic corpora in linguistics, at a time when corpora were negatively regarded by many linguists in the United States and elsewhere. It was significant in the care which was taken to systematically sample texts for the corpus and provide detailed documentation in the accompanying manual (Francis/Kučera 1964, 1979). But the world-wide importance of the Brown Corpus stems from the generosity and foresight shown by the compilers in making the corpus available to researchers all over the world.

4.2. The LOB Corpus and the development of ICAME

In the early 1970s Geoffrey Leech at the University of Lancaster took the initiative to compile a British counterpart of the Brown Corpus (see Leech/Leonard 1974). After a great deal of work had been done at Lancaster, the project was taken over and finished in Norway, through cooperation between the University of Oslo and the Norwegian Computing Centre for the Humanities at Bergen. This is how the corpus got its name: the *L*ancaster-*O*slo/*B*ergen Corpus. The LOB Corpus matches its American counterpart as closely as possible; see the detailed documentation on sources, sampling, and coding in the accompanying manual (Johansson/Leech/Goodluck 1978). Compiling the LOB Corpus was no easy task, in spite of the technical advances that had been made in the decade since the Brown Corpus was first produced. One difficult problem, which had threatened to stop the whole project, was the copyright issue. This led indirectly to the beginning of the *I*nternational *C*omputer *A*rchive of *M*odern *E*nglish (ICAME).

In February 1977, a small group of people, including Jostein Hauge, director of the Norwegian Computing Centre for the Humanities, W. Nelson Francis, Geoffrey Leech, Jan Svartvik, and myself, met in Oslo to discuss the copyright issue as well as corpus work in general. The outcome of the meeting was a document announcing the beginning of ICAME. I quote a passage from the text (see the *ICAME Journal* 20, 101 f.):

> "The undersigned, meeting in Oslo in February 1977, have informally established the nucleus of an International Computer Archive of Modern English (ICAME). The primary purposes of the organization will be:
>
> (1) collecting and distributing information on English language material available for computer processing;
> (2) collecting and distributing information on linguistic research completed or in progress on the material;
> (3) compiling an archive of corpuses to be located at the University of Bergen, from where copies could be obtained at cost.
>
> One of the main aims in establishing the organization is to make possible and encourage the coordination of research effort and avoid duplication of research."

The document announcing the establishment of ICAME was circulated to scholars active in the field, and it was used to support applications for permission to include texts in the LOB Corpus.

Texts and concordances were distributed at cost through ICAME to research institutions all over the world, first on magnetic tapes and microfiche sets, later in the form of diskettes and CD-ROMs. At the outset, the material was limited to the Brown Corpus, the LOB Corpus, and the London-Lund Corpus (see section 4.3.), but new corpora were added in the course of the 1980s. ICAME became not just an archive and a distribution centre, but an informal organisation for a growing number of linguists with an interest in the use of English corpora for language research. A newsletter, *ICAME News*, was distributed from 1978; in 1987 this became the *ICAME Journal*. Yearly conferences were organised, the first one in Bergen in 1979. By the end of the period we are concerned with in this chapter, the tenth ICAME conference was arranged, again at the University of Bergen (selected papers were published in Johansson/Stenström 1991).

4.3. The Survey of Spoken English and the London-Lund Corpus

The Survey of Spoken English (SSE) was initiated by Jan Svartvik, Lund University, in 1975. Building on the Survey of English Usage at University College London (cf. article 1), its primary aim was to computerise the spoken corpus material collected and transcribed in London and make it available in machine-readable form. This included editing and checking the corpus, which at the time consisted of 87 texts, each of 5,000 words. The very detailed prosodic and paralinguistic transcription was reduced:

> "[...] the basic prosodic distinctions (tone units, nuclei, boosters, onsets, and stresses) have been retained in the SSE version. Other features, including tempo (allegro, clipped, drawl, etc.), loudness (piano, forte, etc.), modifications in voice quality (pitch range, rhythmicality, and tension), voice qualifiers (whisper, creak, etc.), and voice qualifications (laugh, sob, etc.) have been omitted.
>
> The reasons for reducing the number of features were partly practical and technical, partly linguistic. While we do not want to minimise the importance of paralinguistic features, it is clear that they are less central than the basic distinctions (such as tone units, types of tone, place of nucleus) for most grammatical studies of spoken English."
>
> (Svartvik/Quirk 1980, 14)

The resulting corpus, known as the London-Lund Corpus, was made available in machine-readable form through ICAME, and part of the material (34 texts, representing surreptitiously recorded conversation) was also published in printed form (Svartvik/Quirk 1980). The book, which was very carefully produced to achieve easy readability, was a useful complement at a time when computer corpora were not yet widely used and the handling of complex spoken transcriptions by computer was difficult.

The 13 texts which were missing at the outset were added later, after being processed at the Survey of English Usage "in conformity with the system used in the original London-Lund Corpus" (Greenbaum/Svartvik 1990, 14). The complete London-Lund Corpus thus consists of 100 texts, in agreement with the original plan for the spoken part of the Survey of English Usage. Although some of the information was sacrificed in the machine-readable version and the speakers represented can hardly be said to form a cross-section of the population, there is no doubt that the London-Lund Corpus has profoundly influenced the study of speech (see 7). This reflects the original thinking and foresight of Randolph Quirk, the initiator of the Survey of English Usage, and the equally important contribution of Jan Svartvik, who prepared the material for computer processing and made it available for research to the community of scholars across the world. The London-Lund Corpus was long the most important source for the computational study of spoken English. Due to the difficulties of handling spoken material (to do with recording, transcription, prosodic coding, etc.), spoken corpora have been scarce, and the imbalance in the availability of spoken and written material in machine-readable form is likely to remain for the foreseeable future.

5. Quantity and variety of texts

In the course of the 1970s and 1980s the quantity of machine-readable texts grew immensely, partly because more and more researchers became interested in corpus studies, and partly because of the greatly increased capacity of computers to store and organise large amounts of data. At the same time the building of corpora became less arduous. Whereas the first-generation corpora dealt with above were punched or keyboarded, as time went on it became easier for corpus compilers to draw on machine-readable texts which emerged in increasing numbers as by-products from computer typesetting. And where such texts were not available, printed texts could be scanned using increasingly effective optical scanning equipment, such as the Kurzweil Data Entry Machine (KDEM). The quantity of texts grew not just in the sense that more and more corpora were compiled; the texts contained in the corpora grew beyond the fairly small sample sizes of the first-generation corpora, and the total size of many corpora grew well beyond the million words of the Brown Corpus. By the end of the 1970s Bergenholtz/Schaeder (1979, 325–329) listed 3 English and 14 German corpora, varying between 200,000 and 5 million words. In their survey of English machine-readable corpora, completed in 1989 and printed a couple of years later, Taylor/Leech/Fligelstone (1991, 319–354) provided documentation on 36 corpora, including the Birmingham Corpus with c. 20 million words (and the total Birmingham Collection of Texts was said to contain over 40 million words). The survey also showed how corpora had become more diversified, including corpora of special text types, of different varieties of English, of child language, of historical texts, multilingual corpora, corpora with grammatical annotation, etc. The increasing variety reflects the widening range of purposes the corpora were intended for. As the range of research questions grew, so did the size and variety of corpora.

A thorny issue which remained unresolved is the representativeness of corpora. Francis (1979, 110) defined a corpus as "a collection of texts assumed to be representative of a given language, dialect, or other subset of a language, to be used for linguistic analysis". Other corpus compilers made no strict claims of representativeness. Cf. the wording in the LOB Corpus manual:

> "[...] the present corpus is not representative in a strict statistical sense. It is, however, an illusion to think that a million-word corpus selected randomly from the texts printed during a certain year can be an ideal corpus. What is relevant is not only *what* texts are printed but *how* they are circulated, *by whom* they are read, etc. [...] The true 'representativeness' of the present corpus arises from the deliberate attempt to include relevant categories and subcategories of texts rather than from blind statistical choice. Random sampling simply ensures

> that, within the stated guidelines, the selection of individual texts is free of the conscious or unconscious influence of personal taste or preference."
>
> (Johansson/Leech/Goodluck 1978, 14)

Corpus compilation is to a great extent a question of judgement, taking into account the purposes the corpora are compiled for (for a discussion of issues in corpus design, see article 9).

5.1. Beyond sample corpora

In his 'Reflections on computer corpora in English language research', John Sinclair points out some inadequacies of the Brown Corpus (and similar sample corpora, here used in the sense of corpora of short text extracts of equal length):

> "[...] the limitation on continuous text is 2,000 words, and so any study of largish text patterns is likely to be inappropriate. Its vocabulary is controlled only indirectly via the genre classification, so any study of the patterning of infrequent words is doomed [...]"
>
> (Sinclair 1982, 2)

The problem is not just the short text samples, but also the limited size of the early text corpora. The inadequacy of a million-word corpus for the study of individual words can be illustrated by examining the frequency of words in the LOB Corpus (based on the figures for word-tag combinations in the tagged LOB Corpus; cf. Johansson/Hofland [1989, 21]):

Total number of word types:	56,000
Word-types occurring once:	26,000
Word-types occurring 2–10 times:	22,000
Word-types occurring 11–100 times:	7,000
Word-types occurring 101–1000 times:	900
Word-types occurring 1001+ times:	100

Close to half of the words are *hapax legomena*, i.e. occur once only (this is also true of much larger corpora; cf. article 37). About 85 per cent of the words are instanced just a few times.

John Sinclair pointed out that the progress of hardware and software development offered opportunities for compiling far bigger corpora. Referring to computer type setting and the possibilities for optical scanning, he suggested that "these developments mean that everything which has ever been printed, or will ever be, is within the reach of the determined researcher" (1982, 3). These were the premises for the Birmingham Collection of Texts, which formed the basis for the innovative COBUILD project in lexical computing and the *Collins COBUILD English Language Dictionary* (see the account of the project in Sinclair 1987). As mentioned by Antoinette Renouf in her survey of corpus development in connection with the COBUILD project (Renouf 1987), work on corpora had been going on at the University of Birmingham for over twenty years, but these corpora were comparatively small and were not widely used. The new collection went beyond earlier efforts in a number of respects: extended texts were collected rather than short samples; a wide variety of texts was included, both written texts and transcriptions of speech; the total size was c. 20 million words, including a Main Corpus of 7.3 million words and a Reserve Corpus of 13 million words. The significance of this corpus for lexical studies will be dealt with in 7 below.

5.2. Monitor corpora

In his visionary paper John Sinclair went even further to suggest a new type of corpus, called a *monitor corpus*, where "the whole state of a language can be passed before one's eyes" (Sinclair 1982, 4). No limit was to be set on text length:

> "Sampling can be done to order on gigantic, slowly changing stores of text, and detailed evidence of language evolution can be held efficiently." (Sinclair 1982, 4)

These thoughts were picked up by Antoinette Renouf in her comments on the future of corpus development at the University of Birmingham:

> "We already have considerable experience of text processing and the creation of finite corpora, and our sights are now set on the development of a 'monitor' corpus. This will be a dynamic rather than a static phenomenon, consisting of very large amounts of electronically-held text which will pass through the computer. A certain proportion of the data will be stored at any one time, but the bulk will necessarily be discarded after processing. The object will be to 'monitor' such data, from various points of view, in order to record facts about the changing nature of language." (Renouf 1987, 21)

Here we are very far from the first-generation corpora, and indeed even from the standard conception of a corpus as a finite collection of texts. The potential was not to become clear until much later.

5.3. The continued relevance of sample corpora

The emergence of larger corpora did not mean the end of small sample corpora. As John Sinclair himself pointed out, there was no easy way of compiling large machine-readable corpora of speech or handwritten material. Moreover, sample corpora were well suited for particular research questions, e. g. on language variation. Projects were undertaken to compile counterparts of the Brown and LOB corpora: the Kolhapur Corpus for Indian English (Shastri 1985), the Macquarie Corpus for Australian English (Peters 1987), the Wellington Corpus of New Zealand English (Bauer 1993). Towards the end of the 1980s Sidney Greenbaum took the initiative to compile a new 'family' of comparable corpora for English as used in different parts of the world: the International Corpus of English (Greenbaum 1988, 1991). Like the Brown Corpus and its counterparts, these were to contain one million words representing a wide variety of texts, but unlike the former they were to contain transcriptions of speech as well as printed texts. Another important undertaking in the 1980s was the launching of the Helsinki Corpus, consisting of a diachronic part and a corpus of recordings of contemporary English dialects (to be compiled under the direction of Matti Rissanen and Ossi Ihalainen, respectively). By 1990 the diachronic part of the Helsinki Corpus was completed (see Kytö 1991), but this was just the first stage in the exploration by computer of language variation and change (see articles 4 and 14).

5.4. Machine-readable dictionaries

Besides the preparation of collections of running text, much work was done to convert printed dictionaries into machine-readable databases or build new dictionaries on the basis of large text collections and database and text-analysis tools (see Lancashire 1991, 145–156). One of the greatest achievements in the 1980s was the conversion of the *Oxford English Dictionary* plus supplements into an electronic database with multiple search capabilities, a project undertaken in collaboration between the University of Waterloo in Canada and Oxford University Press.

6. Quality of texts

Before texts can be analysed by computer, they must be encoded in machine-readable form. In addition to representing textual features, it is important for many purposes to annotate texts with additional information, such as lemma or word class (part of speech). In some early projects the annotation was added manually. The general tendency, however, was to devise methods for automatic tagging. Some examples will serve to illustrate the development. Again we will start with the Brown Corpus.

6.1. Part-of-speech tagging

In the course of the 1970s the Brown Corpus was tagged for word class using an automatic tagging program, TAGGIT, written by Greene/Rubin (1971). The operation worked in the following manner:

> "[...] the words of a text are examined against a tagged list of approximately 3,000 entries; words not located in the Word List are tagged by matching their endings against a list of approximately 450 word endings; and, since by this matching procedure many words will have been given more than one tag, automatic context examination, consisting of the application of an ordered set of Context Frame Rules, is then used to resolve many of the ambiguities; those which remain must be eliminated manually." (Greene/Rubin 1971, 2)

As a result of these procedures, each word was assigned one (and only one) out of 86 tags. The tags were mainly indicators of major form classes (noun, verb, adjective, and adverb, including certain subgroups), function words (determiners, prepositions, conjunctions, etc.), and inflectional morphemes. In addition, certain individual words (*not*, existential *there*, etc.) were given special tags. There were also tags for punctuation marks "to aid in disambiguation and syntactic analysis" (Greene/Rubin 1971, 17).

Figure 3.2 illustrates how the tagging procedures worked for one sentence from a test run of the program. As many as nine words were given more than one tag on the basis

PPSS	1	→	VBD	USED	WORD 2
PPSS	1	→	¬VBN	USED	WORD 7
AT	1	→	¬VB	USED	WORD 11
PP$	1	→	¬VB	USED	WORD 13
	1PPS	→	CS	USED	WORD 19
	1PPS	→	¬QL	USED	WORD 19
BEDZ	1JJ	→	QL	USED	WORD 22

1	*I	PPSS			
2	DEFENDED	~~VBN~~	VBD		
3	MYSELF	PPL			
4	,	,			
5	AS	RB	CI		
6	*I	PPSS			
7	IMAGINED	~~VBN~~	VBD		
8	,	,			
9	AGAINST	IN			
10	THE	AT			
11	FEAR	NN	~~VB~~		
12	MY	PP$			
13	FATHER	NN	~~VB~~		
14	MADE	VBN	VBD		
15	ME	PPO			
16	FEEL	NN	VBD		
17	BY	RI			
18	REMEMBERING	VBG			
19	THAT	CS	~~QL~~	~~DT~~	~~WPS~~
20	HE	PPS			
21	WAS	BEDZ			
22	VERY	QL	~~AP~~		
23	OLD-FASHIONED	JJ			
24	.				

Fig. 3.2: Sample output, somewhat simplified, from Greene/Rubin (1971, 52)

of dictionary look-up (use of the tagged word list and the suffix list). Six of these words were disambiguated by the use of the context rules given above the sentence; the ambiguous word is designated by '1'. Words 2 and 7 were tagged VBD (verb, past tense) rather than VBN (verb, past participle) due to the preceding PPSS (other nominative personal pronouns). The VB tag (verb, base form) was eliminated for words 11 and 13 because of the preceding AT (article) and PP$ (possessive personal pronoun), respectively. Word 19, *that*, was identified as CS (subordinating conjunction) as it is followed by PPS (3rd singular nominative personal pronoun), and word 22, *very*, was identified as QL (qualifier) as it follows BEDZ (past tense singular of *be*) and precedes JJ (adjective). In three cases (words 5, 14, and 16) the context rules could not resolve the ambiguity, which means that these words would have to be dealt with manually.

In his account of the Brown Corpus tagging project Francis (1980, 202) reports that about 23% of the words were left with multiple tags after the automatic tagging stage. There followed a "long and tedious" process of manual disambiguation, "open to human failings of inconsistency, misreading, and all kinds of error stemming from fatigue and boredom" (Francis 1980, 202). After several years of checking, the tagged Brown Corpus was completed in 1979.

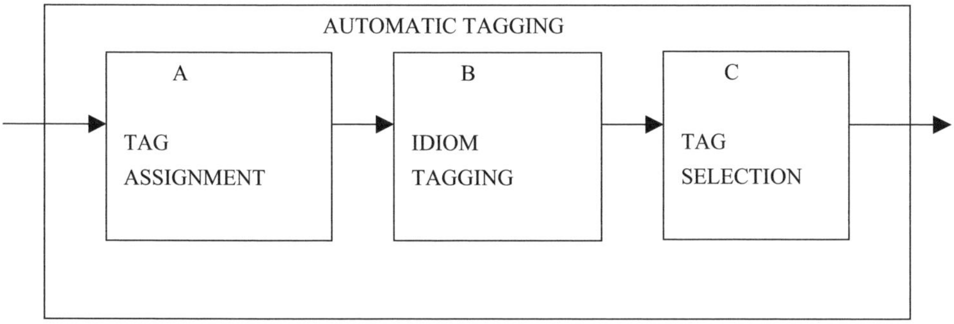

Fig. 3.3: The automatic tagging of the LOB Corpus

The tagging of the Brown Corpus gave the impetus to a similar project for the LOB Corpus. The tagged Brown Corpus and a copy of the TAGGIT program were generously made available for the new project. The aim was to build on previous experiences and, if possible, improve on the performance of TAGGIT. Largely the same set of tags was used, but the number was increased from 86 to 134, to achieve greater delicacy, while preserving comparability with the Brown Corpus. The main stages of the LOB automatic tagging are specified in Figure 3.3; these stages were complemented by manual computer-aided pre-editing and post-editing (for more detail, see Garside/Leech/Sampson 1987).

Stage A was comparable with the initial procedures of the tagging of the Brown Corpus, except that the word list was extended to over 7,000 words and the suffix list to c. 660 word endings. Stage B was added to handle idiosyncratic sequences which would otherwise cause difficulty for automatic tagging, such as *in order that*, *as to*, and *each other* (tagged as a single conjunction, a single preposition, and a single pronoun, respectively). The most innovative part is the tag-selection program. The Brown context rules selected or eliminated tags on the current word by taking into account the tags on the words within a span of two to the left and two to the right of the current word. The rules worked only if one or more of these words were unambiguously tagged. Rather than being rule-based, the LOB tag-selection program was based on statistics of tag combinations, originally derived from the tagged Brown Corpus and adjusted to take account of changes in the tag set. The program computed transitional probabilities between one tag and the next for all combinations of possible tags, and chose the most likely path through a set of ambiguous tags (see Marshall 1987 and Atwell 1987). An example of the output of the program is given in Figure 3.4.

In the output shown in Figure 3.4, the tags supplied by the tag-assignment program are accompanied by a probability expressed as a percentage. For example, the entry for the word *involved* ([VBD]/90 VBN/10 JJ@/0) indicates that the tag VBD (verb, past tense) has an estimated probability of 90%; that the tag VBN (verb, past participle) has an estimated probability of 10%; and that the tag JJ (adjective) has an estimated probability of 0%. The symbol @ after JJ means that the tag-assignment program had already marked the JJ tag as rare for this word. The square brackets enclosing the VBD tag indicate that this has been selected as preferred by the tag-selection program. The program went through a series of improvements and has later become known as *CLAWS* (Constituent-Likelihood Automatic Word-Tagging System); see Garside/Leech/Sampson (1987). The improvements, together with the introduction of the idiom tagging program,

this	DT		
task	NN		
involved	[VBD]/90	VBN/10	JJ@/0
a	AT		
very	[QL]/99	JJB@/1	
great	[JJ]/98	RB/2	
deal	[NN]/99	VB/1	
of	IN		
detailed	[JJ]/98	VBN/2	VBD/0
work	[NN]/100	VB/0	
for	[IN]/97	CS/3	
the	ATI		
committee	NN		

Fig. 3.4: Sample output from the LOB tagging program

resulted in an overall success rate of between 96.0 % and 97.0 %. After a lengthy period of post-editing, the tagged LOB Corpus was finished and made available in 1986; see the manual by Johansson/Atwell/Garside/Leech (1986).

Other programs for word-class tagging were developed in the 1980s using rule-based or statistical approaches, or a combination of the two; see e. g. Eeg-Olofsson (1990). One of most successful is the rule-based Constraint Grammar approach, first presented in Karlsson (1990). Unlike the Brown and LOB tagging programs, this includes both morphological and syntactic annotation. For more information on word-class tagging, see article 24.

6.2. Syntactic annotation

If word-class tagging can be handled quite successfully by automatic tagging programs, the challenges are far greater when such techniques are applied to syntax. In an early project directed by Alvar Ellegård, part of the Brown Corpus was subjected to a very detailed system of grammatical analysis. The texts were analysed manually on three levels, with the aim of providing "an as nearly complete as possible parsing" (Ellegård 1978, 1): (1) clause structure of sentences, (2) constituent structure of clauses, and (3) word class of individual words. Another project which included manual syntactic annotation was the Dutch Computer Corpus Pilot Project (Aarts/van den Heuvel 1980). The corpus was a rather small one, numbering 126,000 words. The annotation included the coding of word class and of syntactic boundaries both at the phrase and the clause level.

As the manual marking of syntax is laborious and error-prone, and inconsistencies are inevitable, it is not surprising that researchers turned to methods of automatizing the process, as in the Constraint Grammar approach mentioned in 6.1. At the University of Lancaster, Garside/Leech (1987) attempted to apply constituent-likelihood grammar to the analysis of syntax, and other approaches, involving human-machine interaction, were developed to build up *treebanks*, i. e. syntactically analysed corpora; see Leech/ Garside (1991). At the University of Nijmegen, Jan Aarts and his team developed the LDB (Linguistic Database), where analytic trees with labelled nodes could be stored, and the TOSCA system (Tools for Syntactic Corpus Analysis), an interactive system for the analysis of corpora; see Aarts/van den Heuvel (1985), Aarts/Oostdijk (1988), and van Halteren/van den Heuvel (1990). But whereas methods of word-class tagging were well established by the end of the 1980s, automatic syntactic analysis was still in its infancy.

6.3. Text encoding guidelines

When the Brown Corpus was card-punched, many features had to be coded (cf. section 4.1.). The London-Lund Corpus had a complex system of prosodic coding, although a number of details had to be sacrificed (cf. section 4.3.). An elaborate coding system was devised for the LOB Corpus, including codes for: typographical shifts, abbreviations, foreign words, editorial comments, etc; see Johansson/Leech/Goodluck (1978). The main guiding principle was to produce a faithful representation of the original text with as little loss of information as possible, at the same time making sure that the coded text was maximally efficient for computational analysis. As more and more texts were prepared in machine-readable form and coding systems turned out to be incompatible and vary widely and were also often inadequately documented, the need was felt to develop general encoding guidelines. This is the background for the Text Encoding Initiative (TEI). A workshop at Vassar College in November 1987 (see Burnard 1988) marked the beginning of a period of intensive work involving a large number of scholars from a variety of fields. The first version of the TEI guidelines (TEI P1) was made public in the summer of 1990 (Sperberg-McQueen/Burnard 1990). Detailed mechanisms were proposed for the encoding of documentation on texts (bibliographic information, information on editorial principles, etc.) and for a wide range of textual features (characters, textual units, editorial changes, etc.), catering for many different types of texts (prose, verse, spoken texts, dictionaries, etc.). The coding was formulated with reference to a consistent syntax, using the Standard Generalized Markup Language (SGML). Although this was only the first step in a continuing effort, it set a new standard for text encoding.

7. Uses of corpora

The rapid growth of corpora is matched by a phenomenal increase in the use of corpora for language research. In his bibliography of publications relating to English computer corpora, covering the period up to 1990, Bengt Altenberg (1991) lists over 600 items. The distribution of publications across time testifies to the astounding growth of corpus linguistics:

–1965	10
1966–1970	20
1971–1975	30
1976–1980	80
1981–1985	160
1986–1990	320

Although the bibliography focuses on five major corpora (the Birmingham Collection of English Text, the Brown Corpus, the LOB Corpus, the London-Lund Corpus, and the Survey of English Usage) and is thus incomplete, the increase is striking. Another notable tendency is the great variety of uses of corpora, which in many cases probably extend far beyond what was imagined by the corpus compilers. We find publications on corpus compilation and software development as well as quantitative and qualitative studies of a wide range of phenomena in lexis, grammar, semantics, discourse, language variation, language change, etc. Important applications include lexicography, language teaching, and natural language processing. Rather than attempting to cover all of these areas, I will single out some which were especially important.

Corpus linguistics is often associated with purely quantitative studies, and these were relatively common in the early stages of computer corpus linguistics, for the simple reason that calculations which were previously very costly and time-consuming could be easily be done when texts were available in machine-readable form. Kučera/Francis (1967) presented information on word frequencies in the Brown Corpus, on word length, and sentence length. On the basis of the tagged Brown Corpus, Francis/Kučera (1982) provided lemmatized frequency lists, information on sentence length and complexity, on word class and contextuality (i. e. the rate of variation across genres), etc. Quantitative information on the LOB Corpus was presented in Hofland/Johansson (1982), which included a comparison of word frequencies in different text categories and in British and American English; and Johansson/Hofland (1989) gave information based on the tagged LOB Corpus (tag and word frequencies, tag and word combinations). There were numerous other works of this kind, for English and other languages. Suffice it to say that quantitative aspects were to remain an important element of corpus linguistics, whether the focus was on lexis, grammar, discourse, or language variation.

An area of great importance, and indeed one which is fundamental for the understanding of language in general, is the study of spoken texts. The launching of the London-Lund Corpus led to a spate of studies on lexis, grammar, prosody, and, especially, discourse structure and function, e. g. Aijmer (1986) on the use of *actually*, Stenström (1986) on *really*, Erman (1987) on *you know*, *you see*, and *I mean*, Svartvik (1980) on *well*, Stenström (1984) on questions and responses in English conversation, Granger (1983) on the passive, and Altenberg (1987) on prosodic patterns in spoken English; see further Svartvik (1990). Spoken and written English were contrasted in a number of studies based on the London-Lund Corpus and the LOB Corpus, e. g. Altenberg (1984) on causal linking, Hermerén (1986) on modality, Collins (1987) on cleft constructions, and Tottie (1988) on negation. Here also belong Douglas Biber's innovative and influential studies of varieties across speech and writing (e. g. Biber 1986, 1988).

A landmark in English linguistics is the comprehensive grammar by Quirk et al. (1985), which could draw directly on corpus evidence as well as on corpus-based grammatical studies, such as Hermerén (1978) and Coates (1983) on modality, Svartvik (1966) and Granger (1983) on the passive, Olofsson (1981) on relative clauses, Breivik (1983) on existential *there*, and Taglicht (1984) on focus and scope in English. Another landmark is the *Collins COBUILD Dictionary* (1987) produced by John Sinclair and his team. The dictionary was innovative in a number of respects: it was based on a large corpus (cf. 5.1.), definitions were written in a new way, examples were naturally occurring ones drawn from the corpus, etc. The COBUILD project set a new standard for dictionary-making, where systematic use of corpora became an essential element. One of the most important aspects of John Sinclair's work is the corpus-based study of collocations, which began in the late 1960s (Sinclair/Jones/Daley 1970) and was more fully developed later by Sinclair and his followers. Important corpus-based work on collocations, using a different approach, was done by Göran Kjellmer (1982, 1984, etc.). Originally advanced in the age before computer corpora and developed in particular by J. R. Firth (see especially Firth 1957), collocations could only be fully explored with access to large collections of texts in machine-readable form, with far-reaching consequences not just for lexicography but also for linguistic theory in general. For more information on corpora and collocations, see article 58.

Towards the end of the period we are concerned with, there was an increasing interest in the use of corpora for computer-based linguistic technologies, though the main developments were to come later. According to Church (2003, 2), following the rationalism which was dominant in the 1970s, empiricism was revived in the 1990s, with data collection efforts such as the Linguistic Data Consortium (LDC, founded in 1992).

8. Corpus linguistics comes of age

Although this survey has focused on developments in English corpus linguistics, it should nevertheless provide a picture of the main trends more generally. At the beginning of the 1970s, corpora were few and small, corpus use was limited and cumbersome, and the users were restricted to a dedicated few outside the mainstream of linguistics at the time. Computer corpus studies rarely went beyond indexes, concordances, and quantitative lexical studies. Twenty years later a fast increasing number of users had easy access to vast amounts of machine-readable text (different types of written and spoken material, modern and historical texts, general and specialized corpora, machine-readable dictionaries), new analysis tools had been developed (concordancers, taggers, text analysis software), and the uses had expanded to encompass a wide range of linguistically sophisticated studies in syntax, lexis, discourse, language variation and change, etc. At this time Jan Svartvik was ready to organise the first Nobel Symposium of Corpus Linguistics, which took place in Stockholm, 4–8 August, 1991. Appropriately the preface to the proceedings had the title 'Corpus linguistics comes of age' (Svartvik 1992, 7). The ground was prepared for the 1990s when corpus linguistics became mainstream (cf. Svartvik 1996).

9. Literature

[Many of the early publications on corpus linguistics were published in journals, conference proceedings, etc. of limited circulation and may not be available in the average university library. The reader is recommended to consult general books like Kennedy (1998) and McEnery/Wilson (2001).]

Aarts, Jan/van den Heuvel, Theo (1980), The Dutch Computer Corpus Pilot Project. In: *ICAME News* 4, 1–8.

Aarts, Jan/van den Heuvel, Theo (1985), Computational Tools for the Syntactic Analysis of Corpora. In: *Linguistics* 23, 303–335.

Aarts, Jan/Meijs, Willem (eds.) (1984), *Corpus Linguistics. Recent Developments in the Use of Computer Corpora in English Language Research*. Amsterdam: Rodopi.
Aarts, Jan/Oostdijk, Nelleke (1988), Corpus-related Research at Nijmegen University. In: Kytö/Ihalainen/Rissanen 1988, 1–14.
Aijmer, Karin (1986), Why is *actually* So Frequent in Spoken English? In: Tottie/Bäcklund 1986, 119–129.
Aijmer, Karin/Altenberg, Bengt (eds.) (1991), *English Corpus Linguistics. Studies in Honour of Jan Svartvik*. London: Longman.
Altenberg, Bengt (1984), Causal Linking in Spoken and Written English. In: *Studia Linguistica* 38, 20–69.
Altenberg, Bengt (1987), *Prosodic Patterns in Spoken English. Studies in the Correlation. Between Prosody and Grammar for Text-to-Speech Conversion.* (Lund Studies in English 76.) Lund: Lund University Press.
Altenberg, Bengt (1991), A Bibliography of Publications Relating to English Computer Corpora. In: Johansson/Stenström 1991, 355–396.
Atwell, Eric (1987), Constituent-likelihood Grammar. In: *ICAME News* 7, 34–67. Reprinted in: Garside/Leech/Sampson 1987, 57–65.
Bauer, Laurie (1993), *Manual of Information to Accompany the Wellington Corpus of Written New Zealand English*. Wellington: Department of Linguistics, Victoria University of Wellington.
Bergenholtz, Henning/Schaeder, Burkhard (eds.) (1979), *Empirische Textwissenschaft: Aufbau und Auswertung von Text-Corpora*. Königstein: Scriptor Verlag.
Biber, Douglas (1986), Spoken and Written Textual Dimensions in English: Resolving the Contradictory Findings. In: *Language* 62, 384–414.
Biber, Douglas (1988), *Variation Across Speech and Writing*. Cambridge: Cambridge University Press.
Breivik, Leiv Egil (1983), *Existential* There: *A Synchronic and Diachronic Study*. (Studia Anglistica Norvegica 2.) Bergen: Department of English.
Burnard, Lou (1988), Report of Workshop on Text Encoding Guidelines. In: *Literary and Linguistic Computing* 3(2), 131–133.
Church, Kenneth W. (2003), Speech and Language Processing: Where Have We Been and Where Are We Going? (EUROSPEECH 2003.) 8th European Conference on Speech Communication and Technology. Geneva, September 1–4, 2003.
Coates, Jennifer (1983), *The Semantics of the Modal Auxiliaries*. London: Croom Helm.
Collins COBUILD English Language Dictionary (1987), London: Collins.
Collins, Peter (1987), Cleft and Pseudo-cleft Constructions in English Spoken and Written Discourse. In: *ICAME Journal* 11, 5–17.
Eeg-Olofsson, Mats (1990), An Automatic Word-class Tagger and a Phrase Parser. In: Svartvik 1990, 107–136.
Ellegård, Alvar (1978), *The Syntactic Structure of English Texts: A Computer-based Study of Four Kinds of Text in the Brown University Corpus*. (Gothenburg Studies in English 43.) Gothenburg: Acta Universitatis Gothoburgensis.
Erman, Britt (1987), *Pragmatic Expressions in English. A Study of* you know, you see *and* I mean *in Face-to-face Conversation*. (Stockholm Studies in English 69.) Stockholm: Almqvist & Wiksell.
Fillmore, Charles J. (1992), 'Corpus Linguistics' or 'Computer-aided Armchair Linguistics'. In: Svartvik 1992, 35–60.
Firth, J. R. (1957), *Papers in Linguistics*. London: Oxford University Press.
Francis, W. Nelson (1979, 1982), Problems of Assembling and Computerizing Large Corpora. In: Bergenholtz/Schaeder 1979, 110–123. Reprinted in: Johansson 1982, 7–24.
Francis, W. Nelson (1980), A Tagged Corpus: Problems and Prospects. In: Greenbaum/Leech/Svartvik 1980, 192–209.
Francis, W. Nelson/Kučera, Henry (1964, 1979), *Manual of Information to Accompany a Standard Sample of Present-day Edited American English, for Use with Digital Computers*. Original ed. 1964, revised and augmented 1979. Providence, R.I.: Brown University.

Francis, W. Nelson/Kučera, Henry (1982), *Frequency Analysis of English Usage: Lexicon and Grammar.* Boston: Houghton Mifflin.
Garside, Roger/Leech, Fanny (1987), The UCREL Probabilistic Parsing System. In: Garside/Leech/Sampson 1987, 66–81.
Garside, Roger/Leech, Geoffrey (1982), Grammatical Tagging of the LOB Corpus: General Survey. In: Johansson 1982, 110–117.
Garside, Roger/Leech, Geoffrey/Sampson, Geoffrey (eds.) (1987), *The Computational Analysis of English. A Corpus-based Approach.* London: Longman.
Granger, Sylviane (1983), *The* be + *Past Participle Construction in Spoken English, with Special Emphasis on the Passive.* Amsterdam: North Holland.
Greenbaum, Sidney (1988), A Proposal for an International Corpus of English. In: *World Englishes* 7, 315.
Greenbaum, Sidney (1991), The Development of the International Corpus of English. In: Aijmer/Altenberg 1991, 83–91.
Greenbaum, Sidney/Leech, Geoffrey/Svartvik, Jan (eds.) (1980), *Studies in English Linguistics for Randolph Quirk.* London: Longman.
Greenbaum, Sidney/Svartvik, Jan (1990), The London-Lund Corpus of Spoken English. In: Svartvik 1990, 11–59.
Greene, Barbara B./Rubin, Gerald M. (1971), *Automated Grammatical Tagging of English.* Providence, R.I.: Department of Linguistics, Brown University.
de Haan, Pieter (1989), *Postmodifying Clauses in the English Noun Phrase. A Corpus-based Study.* Amsterdam: Rodopi.
van Halteren, Hans/van den Heuvel, Theo (1990), *Linguistic Exploitation of Syntactic Databases.* Amsterdam: Rodopi.
Hermerén, Lars (1978), *On Modality in English: A Study of the Semantics of the Modals.* (Lund Studies in English 53.) Lund: CWK Gleerup.
Hermerén, Lars (1986), Modalities in Spoken and Written English. An Inventory of Forms. In: Tottie/Bäcklund 1986, 57–91.
Hofland, Knut/Johansson, Stig (1982), *Word Frequencies in British and American English.* Bergen: Norwegian Computing Centre for the Humanities/London: Longman.
ICAME News. 1978–1986. Newsletter of the International Computer Archive of Modern English. Bergen: Norwegian Computing Centre for the Humanities.
ICAME Journal. 1987–. Journal of the International Computer Archive of Modern English. Bergen: Norwegian Computing Centre for the Humanities.
Johansson, Stig (ed.) (1982), *Computer Corpora in English Language Research.* Bergen: Norwegian Computing Centre for the Humanities.
Johansson, Stig/Atwell, Eric/Garside, Roger/Leech, Geoffrey (1986), *The Tagged LOB Corpus. Users' Manual.* Bergen: Norwegian Computing Centre for the Humanities.
Johansson, Stig/Hofland, Knut (1989), *Frequency Analysis of English Vocabulary and Grammar.* Vol. 1–2. Oxford: Clarendon Press.
Johansson, Stig/Leech, Geoffrey/Goodluck, Helen (1978), *Manual of Information to Accompany the Lancaster-Oslo/Bergen Corpus of British English, for Use with Digital Computers.* Oslo: Department of English, University of Oslo.
Johansson, Stig/Stenström, Anna-Brita (eds.) (1991), *English Computer Corpora. Selected Papers and Research Guide.* Berlin/New York: Mouton de Gruyter.
Karlsson, Fred (1990), Constraint Grammar as a Framework for Parsing Running Text. In: *Proceedings of the 13th International Conference on Computational Linguistics (COLING-90).* Helsinki, 168–173.
Kennedy, Graeme (1998), *Introduction to Corpus Linguistics.* London: Longman.
Kjellmer, Göran (1982), Some Problems Relating to the Study of Collocations in the Brown Corpus. In: Johansson 1982, 25–33.

Kjellmer, Göran (1984), Some Thoughts on Collocational Distinctiveness. In: Aarts/Meijs 1984, 163–171.

Kučera, Henry/Francis, W. Nelson (1967), *Computational Analysis of Present-day American English.* Providence, RI: Brown University Press.

Kytö, Merja (1991), *Manual to the Diachronic Part of the Helsinki Corpus of English Texts: Coding Conventions and Lists of Source Texts.* Department of English, University of Helsinki.

Kytö, Merja/Ihalainen, Ossi/Rissanen, Matti (eds.) (1988), *Corpus Linguistics Hard and Soft.* Amsterdam: Rodopi.

Lancashire, Ian (1990), Back to the Future: Literary and Linguistic Computing 1968–1988. In: Choueka, Yaakov (ed.), *Proceedings of the Fifteenth International Conference on Literary and Linguistic Computing 1988*. Paris-Geneva: Champion-Slatkine, 36–47.

Lancashire, Ian (1991), *The Humanities Computing Yearbook 1989–90. A Comprehensive Guide to Software and Other Resources.* Oxford: Clarendon Press.

Leech, Geoffrey (1991), The State of the Art in Corpus Linguistics. In: Aijmer/Altenberg 1991, 8–29.

Leech, Geoffrey/Candlin, Christopher (eds.) (1986), *Computers in English Language Teaching and Research.* London: Longman.

Leech, Geoffrey/Garside, Roger (1991), Running a Grammar Factory: The Production of Syntactically Analysed Corpora or 'Treebanks'. In: Johansson/Stenström 1991, 15–32.

Leech, Geoffrey/Leonard, Rosemary (1974), A Computer Corpus of British English. In: *Hamburger Phonetische Beiträge* 13, 41–57.

Mair, Christian (1990), *Infinitival Complement Clauses in English. A Study of Syntax in Discourse.* Cambridge: Cambridge University Press.

Mair, Christian (1991), Quantitative or Qualitative Corpus Analysis? Infinitival Complement Clauses in the Survey of English Usage Corpus. In: Johansson/Stenström 1991, 67–80.

Marshall, Ian (1987), Tag Selection Using Probabilistic Methods. In: Garside/Leech/Sampson 1987, 42–56.

McEnery, Tony/Wilson, Andrew (2001), *Corpus Linguistics.* 2nd ed. Edinburgh: Edinburgh University Press.

Olofsson, Arne (1981), *Relative Junctions in Written American English.* (Gothenburg Studies in English 50.) Gothenburg: Acta Universitatis Gothoburgensis.

Peters, Pam (1987), Towards a Corpus of Australian English. In: *ICAME Journal* 11, 27–38.

Quirk, Randolph/Greenbaum, Sidney/Leech, Geoffrey/Svartvik, Jan (1985), *A Comprehensive Grammar of the English Language.* London: Longman.

Renouf, Antoinette (1987), Corpus development. In: Sinclair 1987, 1–40.

Sebba, Mark/Fligelstone, Steven (1994), Corpora. In: Asher, R. E./Simpson, J. M. Y. (eds.), *The Encyclopedia of Language and Linguistics.* Vol. 2. Oxford: Pergamon Press, 769–773.

Shastri, S. V. (1985), Research in Progress. Towards a Description of Indian English: A Standard Corpus in Machine-readable Form. In: *English World-Wide* 6, 275–278.

Sinclair, John M. (1982), Reflections on Computer Corpora in English Language Research. In: Johansson 1982, 1–6.

Sinclair, John M. (ed.) (1987), *Looking Up. An Account of the COBUILD Project in Lexical Computing.* London: Collins ELT.

Sinclair, John M./Jones, Susan/Daley, Robert (1970, 1972), *English Lexical Studies. Final Report to OSTI on Project C/LP/08 for January 1967–September 1969.* Department of English, Birmingham University.

Sperberg-McQueen, C. M./Burnard, Lou (eds.) (1990), *Guidelines for the Encoding and Interchange of Machine-readable Texts. TEI P1. Draft Version 1.0.* Chicago and Oxford: Association for Computers and the Humanities/Association for Computational Linguistics/Association for Literary and Linguistic Computing.

Stenström, Anna-Brita (1984), *Questions and Responses in English Conversation.* (Lund Studies in English 68.) Lund: CWK Gleerup.

Stenström, Anna-Brita (1986), What Does *really* Really Do? Strategies in Speech and Writing. In: Tottie/Bäcklund 1986, 149–163.
Svartvik, Jan (1966), *On Voice in the English Verb*. The Hague: Mouton.
Svartvik, Jan (1980), *Well* in Conversation. In: Greenbaum/Leech/Svartvik 1980, 167–177.
Svartvik, Jan (ed.) (1990), *The London-Lund Corpus of Spoken English: Description and Research*. (Lund Studies in English 82.) Lund: Lund University Press.
Svartvik, Jan (ed.) (1992), *Directions in Corpus Linguistics. Proceedings of Nobel Symposium 82, Stockholm, 4–8 August 1991*. Berlin/New York: Mouton de Gruyter.
Svartvik, Jan (1996), Corpora Are Becoming Mainstream. In: Thomas/Short 1996, 3–13.
Svartvik, Jan/Quirk, Randolph (eds.) (1980), *A Corpus of English Conversation*. (Lund Studies in English 56.) Lund: CWK Gleerup.
Taglicht, Josef (1984), *Message and Emphasis*. London: Longman.
Taylor, Lita/Leech, Geoffrey/Fligelstone, Steven (1991), A Survey of English Machine-readable Corpora. In: Johansson/Stenström 1991, 319–354.
Thomas, Jenny/Short, Mick (eds.) (1996), *Using Corpora for Language Research: Studies in the Honour of Geoffrey Leech*. London & New York: Longman.
Tottie, Gunnel (1988), *No*-negation and *Not*-negation in Spoken and Written English. In: Kytö/Ihalainen/Rissanen 1988, 245–265.
Tottie, Gunnel/Bäcklund, Ingegerd (eds.) (1986), *English in Speech and Writing: A Symposium*. (Studia Anglistica Upsaliensia 60.) Stockholm: Almqvist & Wiksell.

Stig Johansson, Oslo (Norway)

4. Corpus linguistics and historical linguistics

1. Corpora: A window to the past of the language

The introduction of corpora has had a revolutionary effect on language studies in the last few decades. This is particularly true of historical linguistics, which has to rely on written sources only; introspection and native-speaker competence cannot be relied on in the study of the language of previous centuries and millennia. We could even suggest that in the present world the creation of corpora has been a matter of life or death for the future of evidence-based historical linguistics, at least in the study of extensively spoken living languages. In our era of electronic speed and efficiency, young scholars and postgraduate students might be less willing to spend months or even years just collecting material from manuscripts or printed editions, copying examples onto small slips of paper and arranging them in piles on their desks (cf. article 1). Corpora have radically shortened the time needed for collecting evidence from early written sources and made these sources more easily available for research. They have also encouraged scholars and students to aim at more extensive coverage of text material and more thoroughgoing analysis of examples. Quantitative analysis, in particular, has been very much enhanced by corpus methodology.

Corpora have provided remarkable support for most branches of the historical study of language. So far, not surprisingly, the majority of corpus-based studies have dealt with questions of morphosyntax and semantics. In recent years, thanks to the compilation of new corpora with more accurate and multifaceted annotation, they have also shown their value in studies of discourse and pragmatics (cf. article 51). Easy access to a large number of variant forms with chronological and dialectal significance has also contributed to philological text analysis and editing, and to linguistic reconstruction and phylogeny. Corpora have also radically improved the replicability of research results and the ability to check the correctness and accuracy of the linguistic evidence presented in historical language studies that are necessarily based on written material.

In this survey I will first describe the variationist approach to the study of the history of language, with special reference to internal processes of change and to the extralinguistic factors affecting the choice of variant. I will then discuss the usefulness of corpora in analysing variation and change and give an example of this kind of analysis. I will refer to the problems of analysing the spoken language of the past and mention some restrictions of corpus-based analysis.

As the compilation of historical corpora and corpus-based analysis of the language of the past have so far been most intensive in the field of the English language, the following discussion will primarily focus on English. The variationist approach and the methodological questions discussed can, however, be applied to research on other languages as well. We should also keep in mind that important diachronic corpus projects on German, Spanish, French, Czech, Welsh, the Scandinavian languages, Finnish, and various other languages are either completed or in progress. Useful bibliographical information can be found, for example, in article 52.

2. Variationist approach to the study of language

The increasing use and obvious advantages of computerised corpora have led to the adoption of the term "corpus linguistics" with reference to linguistic study based on corpora. While this is a useful term for indicating a particular focus on evidence-based linguistic research, which typically combines qualitative and quantitative analysis and pays particular attention to software developments, it should be kept in mind that the use of corpora is a methodological approach rather than an independent branch of linguistics. The aims and goals of corpus-based research are the same as those of all empirical linguistic research: to understand and explain language as a means of communication between people. Using corpora for collecting and analysing material simply helps us approach and appreciate the richness and variability of language and to understand how linguistic change is related to this variability, caused by both internal processes of change and language-external factors, socio-cultural, regional or genre-based.

If we wish to define a new branch of linguistics supported by computerised corpora, attention should be called to the variationist approach to the analysis and understanding of language. A useful starting-point for describing this approach can be found in M. A. K. Halliday's discussions of language in a social perspective, based on Malinowski's and Firth's views on the social functioning of language (Halliday 1973, 22–47; 48–70). According to Halliday, the basic function of language is "how to mean". The sum total of the meanings of a language forms its meaning potential, which is realised as lexico-grammatical potential, i. e., all the linguistic expressions available to convey the meanings of the language (Halliday 1973, 51–54). It is significant that the same meaning can be expressed in more ways than one, by roughly synonymous expressions (the word "roughly" is, however, important in this context). The groupings of nearly synonymous variant expressions may be called variant fields.

The variationist approach aims at analysing language by describing the structure of the variant fields and comparing the characteristics of the variants within a field, with special reference to the language-internal and external factors affecting the use of the variant. The fields may consist of phonological, morphological, syntactic or lexical, or even discoursal or pragmatic variants. Examples of simple structural variant fields are, for instance, the causative links (English *for*, *because*, *as*, *since*; German *denn*, *weil*; French *car*, *parce que*; Swedish *ty*, *för*, *eftersom*, *därför att*; Finnish *sillä*, *koska*, *kun*, *sen tähden että*). The expressions of various feelings (love, hate, fear, etc.) or colours (shades of blue, red, green, etc.) are typical representatives of semantic variant fields. This approach is of course equally valid in the study of present-day language as in the study of the language of the past. The study of variation at the older stages of language has, however, an additional dimension, as change in language can most naturally be described through changes in the shape and size of the variant fields. When the language changes, some variants may disappear and others may emerge. In English and Swedish, this happened, for instance, to most oblique case forms, which were replaced by prepositions governing the base form. English has also lost the morphological markers of grammatical gender, while German and the Scandinavian and Romance languages still retain these markers, at least to some extent.

More typically, however, some variant forms become more common, unmarked or prototypical, while others may become rarer and restricted to certain contexts, genres, or registers. A good example of this is the preposition or subordinating conjunction *notwithstanding*, which was originally much more common than the synonymous expressions *despite* or *in spite of*, but is now mainly restricted to legal contexts, particularly when it is used as a subordinator (see 3.2.). In Swedish, the use of the preterite subjunctive form of the verb (*finge, ginge*) is now stylistically highly marked (if not obsolete), and in German the dative singular ending of the nouns is disappearing, to mention only a few examples.

Diachronic research into variation can focus on changes in real time or apparent time (cf. this volume, article 52; Labov 2001, 75–78; Nevalainen/Raumolin-Brunberg 2003, 12; 53–100). In real time study, the same variant field is surveyed in two or more subsequent periods, while in apparent time study the occurrence of the variants in the language of different age groups, or of the same individual at different ages, is placed under scrutiny.

The concepts of variation and change through variation are not new. As early as the nineteenth century, scholars called attention to "different ways of saying the same thing" and to the factors explaining the loss and emergence of forms. The systematic study of variation as a means of describing and explaining the development of language was, however, given new vigour and significance by a highly influential essay by Weinreich/Labov/Herzog (1968) and by the studies of Michael Samuels (1972), Suzanne Romaine (1982) and many other scholars in the last few decades. In a nutshell, this approach includes the characterisation of language as "orderly heterogeneity" (Weinreich/Labov/Herzog 1968) and by the statement "[i]t is speakers and not languages that innovate" (Milroy 1992, 169; cf. Nevalainen/Raumolin-Brunberg 2003, 1–2).

The variationist approach has obvious links with cognitive semantics and prototype semantics, which concentrate on the various ways in which meanings and their expressions emerge in human cognition, how some of these meanings are more central and some more peripheral than others, and how these relations may change over time. Comparisons between various languages are particularly interesting. The concept of variation is also important and useful in the study of historical pragmatics, which traces pragmatic meanings and the changes in their realisations over time (see, e. g., Jacobs/Jucker 1995, 13–14; 19).

2.1. Extralinguistic factors affecting the choice of the variant

Although apparent-time synchronic research might be regarded as subordinate to real-time diachronic research, it leads us to the most important aspect of the study of variation. This is the attempt to define and understand the extralinguistic factors and language-internal trends that affect the choices of variants within a field. The most important extralinguistic factors can be grouped in the following way (for a discussion of the internal processes of change, see 2.2.):

(1) Sociolinguistic, including the speaker's or writer's social status and education and the relationship between discourse participants.

(2) Textual, including genre, topic or purpose of text, discourse situation and medium.

(3) Regional, including contact.

It is obvious that the speaker's or writer's social and educational background affects his/her choice of variant expressions. In the same way, differences in the social characteristics, including gender, age, rank, etc., of the speaker/writer and the addressee must be taken into consideration. Family relations form a special kind of social hierarchy. The sociolinguistic aspect is of particular relevance to historical studies of language, as social differentiation, including genre, education and the urban/rural dichotomy, was generally speaking much more marked in previous centuries than it is today; we need only think of the European societies of the Middle Ages or even the early Modern period to confirm this (cf. Nevalainen/Raumolin-Brunberg 2003).

Simple and illustrative examples of the influence of sociolinguistic factors on choice of expression can be found, for example, in the field of address forms, beginning with the use of the singular or plural form of the second person pronoun, English *you/thou*, German *Sie/du*, Swedish *ni/du*, French *vous/tu,* Finnish *te/sinä*, etc. In English, the singular form practically disappeared in the course of the early Modern English period (see, e. g., Nevala 2004; Walker 2005), while in Swedish the use of the polite plural has been rapidly losing ground in the last few decades. A similar trend can be noted in many other European languages.

Quite naturally, too, the type and purpose of text and the discourse situation are highly relevant in the choice of variant expressions. There are vast differences in register or level of formality of expression between, for instance, scientific writing and private letters, and parliamentary debates differ from coffee-table conversations. At a more general level, spoken language is in many ways different from writing. The study of these differences is vital in understanding the long-term development of a language. The development of new genres of writing – officialese, scientific texts, etc. – leads to the adoption of new words and constructions. The standard variety of language is often associated with prestigious genres of writing (cf. Milroy 1992, 129–131; Rissanen 2000), while the natural development of a language can in many cases be best understood as "changes from below" effected by the spoken medium (for "changes from above" and "changes from below", see, e. g., Labov 1994, 78).

The emergence and establishment of new prepositions and subordinating conjunctions, many of them borrowed from French or Latin, illustrates the importance of corpus-based variationist study focusing on genre distribution. It is easy to see that such connectives as *except*, *provided (that)* and *notwithstanding* were in common use in legal and documentary texts as early as the fifteenth century, and that this use in prestigious genres may have contributed to their establishment in the emerging standard (see Rissanen 2002a, 2002b, 2003a).

Geographical separation and distance explain the existence, emergence and further development of different varieties of the same language. If the distance between the varieties is not remarkable, the term "dialect" is generally used, particularly when the varieties are spoken within the same political area. If the separation is more remarkable and connected with the political situation (national independence or autonomy), the term "geographical variety" is preferred, as for instance in the case of American, Canadian, Australian or Indian English, Austrian or Swiss German, or the trans-Atlantic varieties of Spanish or Portuguese. The overseas varieties in particular often show both archaic and innovative features. The former are due to the fact that, particularly in the earlier period, emigrant populations often conservatively maintained the written conventions and literary models of the variety of the mother country; on the other hand, new environment, contacts, and the structure and administration of new society called forth new forms and expressions in language. Contact between speakers using different varieties of the language may cause considerable change and accelerate this process. It is only natural that the role of contact increases in emigrant environments.

As can be seen from this brief summary of the character of extralinguistic factors causing variation and change, these factors are overlapping and research focused on one of them must necessarily also pay attention to others, as well as to the internal processes of change discussed in the next section. Changes in society are related to the development of new genres of writing and to the emergence of standard varieties. Contact and dialectal variation create tensions between the standard language and dialects, including prestigious and stigmatised forms, and these tensions, again, have a close relationship to social aspects of language use.

2.2. Internal processes of change

In our discussion of change in language we also have to consider internal processes of change (cf. Samuels 1972, 6–8 and *passim*). To illustrate the difference between the extralinguistic factors described above and language-internal trends of change, an analogy with the growth and development of human beings can be presented. To describe the development of an individual, we should of course focus on such external factors as parents and other relatives, playmates and schoolmates, education and studies, hometown or village, jobs, colleagues, etc. All these correspond to the extralinguistic factors affecting linguistic change. But the person also inevitably changes and develops in ways that have little or nothing to do with environment: learning to walk, the growth of teeth, puberty with its physical and mental developments, the changes during the person's fifties, old age with its loss of hair and teeth, etc. are all developments that can be compared with the internal processes of linguistic change over a shorter or longer period of time. These internal processes are mainly related to basic patterns of change in meaning, such as metaphor or metonymy, grammaticalisation, and the tendency to seek out new and more emphatic expressions to replace old and partially bleached ones. Furthermore, *inertia*, or the tendency to express oneself with minimum effort (Samuels 1972, *passim*), causes phonological, morphological and even syntactic changes, well-known examples including such colloquial expressions as *ain't* instead of *am not* or *is not,* or the French negative in *n'a, n'est*, etc.

In the last few decades, grammaticalisation has become one of the most researched language-internal types of change. According to a simple definition, it involves the change in which "lexical items and constructions come in certain linguistic contexts to serve grammatical functions and, once grammaticalised, continue to develop new grammatical functions" (Hopper/Traugott 2003, xv). The French negative particle *pas*, which originally meant 'step', is a good example of grammaticalisation, as is the Swedish ending *-en*, *-et* indicating definiteness, originally an independent pronoun placed after the noun and meaning roughly 'that', or the German conjunction *weil*, which was originally a noun indicating a space of time (cf. English *while*). Many prepositions and subordinating conjunctions, such as English *because* or *according to/as* or Swedish *trots att*, go back to phrases with more profound semantic contents.

3. Variationist study and corpora

It is obvious that diachronic variationist study has benefited and will benefit enormously from the easy access to vast amounts of textual evidence provided by corpora and databases. Corpora not only offer examples of the use of variants in various contexts, but also make it possible to observe the relative frequencies of the variants. In the past, descriptions of change in language were often based on information derived from dictionaries and historical grammars and described by the simple formula A > B. This kind of formula does not, however, tell the whole truth about the real-time or apparent-time change of linguistic features within a language community. A more accurate picture of change, supported by corpora, would look like the formula presented in Figure 4.1.

In this formula, A, B, and C are variant forms within a variant field changing in time (from Period 1 to Period 2). The field may of course be phonological, morphological, syntactic, semantic, discoursal or pragmatic. The student should concentrate on defining the factors that result in the diminishing popularity of A and the establishment of B as the unmarked variant in Period 2, on the reasons for the emergence of C, and on the

Fig. 4.1: Change through variation

source from which that variant form is derived. These changes can be explained either by language-internal processes, such as grammaticalisation or levelling and loss of inflectional endings, or by extralinguistic factors, whether sociolinguistic, text and genre-based, or related to contact.

For this kind of variationist analysis both general multipurpose corpora and more focused specialized corpora are indispensable (cf. articles 14, 51, 52). As mentioned above (section 1), historical corpora giving information on a number of languages are available, and ambitious corpus projects are in progress. At the moment, however, the variety of English historical corpora is larger than that of the other languages, and for this reason some of these corpora are introduced in the following discussion, in order to illustrate the dimensions of corpus-based research into the history of language (see, in particular, article 14).

A good starting-point for a long-term diachronic study of the changing shape of any variant field is offered by the *Helsinki Corpus of English Texts* (HC), either the basic version or the grammatically tagged and parsed versions, the *Brooklyn-Geneva-Amsterdam-Helsinki Corpus of Old English*, the *Penn-Helsinki Parsed Corpus of Middle English* and the *Penn-Helsinki Parsed Corpus of Early Modern English*. The *Helsinki Corpus* and its annotated versions cover the period from the earliest Old English to the beginning of the eighteenth century. (The *Penn Parsed Corpus of Modern British English*, including texts from the eighteenth to the twentieth century, is in preparation.) *A Representative Corpus of Historical English Registers* (ARCHER), not yet publicly available, spans the period from the mid-seventeenth century to the 1990s.

Because of their relatively small size of less than two million words, and because they cover a long period of time, both HC and ARCHER may give insufficient evidence of the occurrence of less frequent linguistic features. Even in such cases, they are useful as "diagnostic corpora", giving an overall view of the major lines of development. In many cases, it is easy to supplement the qualitative and quantitative evidence using specialized corpora, particularly as regards the influence of the extralinguistic factors described above. For sociolinguistic factors, i. e. the writer's gender, age, social and educational background, etc., the *Corpus of Early English Correspondence* (CEEC) is most useful. In its present form it covers the time from the fifteenth to the end of the seventeenth century; a continuation including eighteenth-century texts is in preparation (*Corpus of Early English Correspondence Extension*, CEECE). Of the other corpora useful for the study of genre variation, *Middle English Medical Texts* (MEMT) has recently been published, and its Modern English continuation, *Early Modern English Medical Texts* (EMEMT), is in preparation. Evidence for newspaper language can be derived from the *Zürich English Newspaper Corpus*, including English newspaper text from 1671 to 1791. Seventeenth- and eighteenth-century argumentative texts (pamphlets, etc.) can be found in the *Lampeter Corpus*.

Early stages of regional varieties are represented by the *Helsinki Corpus of Older Scots* (1450–1700) and the *Corpus of Irish English*, which includes texts from the fourteenth to the twentieth century. A *Corpus of Early American English* is in preparation. Material giving information on writing which approaches spoken English can be found in the *Corpus of English Dialogues (1560–1760)*, and also in CEEC and in the Early Modern English part of the HC.

New technological developments have also made it possible to combine major dictionary projects with corpus methodology. The *Dictionary of Old English Corpus* is an excellent example of this; the computer tape of practically all Old English texts was generously offered for scholarly use as early as the 1980s, and the corpus, with a sophisticated search program, can now be accessed through the internet. The *Middle English Compendium*, a product of the recently completed *Middle English Dictionary* project, consists of *The Corpus of Middle English Prose and Verse* and all the quotation material of the *Dictionary.* This is a fine resource for all scholars of the history of English whose work is related to Middle English in one way or another. The user has, however, to keep in mind that a search based on the quotations database can give the same passage many times if it is quoted under more than one head-word. The enormous number of quotations in the electronic *Oxford English Dictionary* provides valuable evidence, particularly for the study of diachronic lexicology (cf. article 14).

3.1. The problem of spoken language

The above discussion does not mean, however, that corpora can solve all the problems of finding linguistic evidence for variationist diachronic studies. Written texts from past centuries give us, even at best, an inaccurate and skewed picture of spoken language. Yet it is precisely spoken language that plays a decisive role in variation and change. The hazy picture we have of the speech of the past can, however, be sharpened if we have access to large quantities of different types of writing through structured and textually coded corpora. Speech leaves an imprint on writing. Records of spoken utterances, dialogue in drama and fiction, private letters, and other texts representing colloquial style are of great value, although they never reproduce speech in authentic form. In particular, dialogic face-to-face interaction is regarded as relevant in actuating change (Milroy 1992; Traugott/Dasher 2002; Kytö/Walker 2003); in this respect the *Corpus of English Dialogues 1560–1760* provides particularly interesting material.

A careful and extensive comparative analysis of written texts which stand at different distances from speech may help us in our attempt to reconstruct spoken language. These distances must, of course, be defined by extralinguistic criteria, such as the genre, topic and purpose of the text, the discourse situation, the relationship existing between the writer and real or hypothetical readers, and the writer's educational level and mastery of registers, (cf. the factors discussed above). In this way we may approach changes from below as well as changes from above, developments at the level of orality as well as at the level of literacy.

In our textual comparisons we can apply a simple formula, according to which forms, words or phrases that are frequent in texts close to the spoken expression are more likely to be typical of speech than those that are frequent in texts far removed from speech (Figure 4.2):

	Text	Variant	
		M	N
Literacy	A	60 %	40 %
↕	B	10 %	90 %
Orality			

Fig. 4.2: Reconstructing expressions typical of the spoken language of the past

If we are studying a variant field consisting of two variants, M and N, in two texts, A and B, of which B (e. g. a private letter, drama dialogue, court room examination dialogue) is closer to spoken language than A, and B shows a much higher proportional frequency of the variant N than A, we can assume that the variant N is more typical of the spoken language of the period in question than M. This hypothesis is, however, valid only if we have control of the other factors, referred to above, that can affect the choices between variant forms besides the text's relationship to spoken language. Furthermore, the quantification of the occurrences of the variants must be based on at least some degree of statistical reliability. Both these conditions can most easily be fulfilled with the support of large, structured corpora, in which the changes in the type of text and level of orality are coded. Reliable grammatical annotation facilitates the analysis of course.

3.2. An example: *despite* and *notwithstanding*

The usefulness of corpora in tracing historical developments has been amply demonstrated by studies of grammaticalisation. Recent in-depth studies of various lexico-grammatical phenomena include the rivalry of simple and progressive passive constructions, the development of intensifiers (e. g. *fairly* and *pretty*), connectives (e. g. *beside(s)*) and low-frequency complex prepositions (e. g. *in view of, in consideration of, on account of*); see Lindquist/Mair (2004a). The use of corpora not only allows rigorous and systematic collection of primary data, but also requires methodological refinements as regards grammaticalisation theory, by making it necessary to take into consideration such differences in developments as the rates at which grammaticalisation proceeds in different textual genres (Lindquist/Mair 2004b; Nevalainen 2004).

The development of the roughly synonymous English adverbial connectives (prepositions and conjunctions) *despite*, *in spite of*, and *notwithstanding* are briefly outlined below as an example of the evidence given by historical corpora on grammaticalisation. These connectives appeared in the Middle English period, in the late fourteenth and fifteenth centuries. The first two go back to the phrase *in despite of*; this phrase may have been supported by the French phrase *en dépit de*. In most Middle English instances, the original meaning of the word *despit*, 'a feeling or attitude of contempt' (*Middle English Dictionary*, s. v. *despit* n. 1.), can still be traced. *Notwithstanding* consists of native elements, although it was probably formed after the model of the French and Latin *non obstant(e)*.

Evidence given by historical corpora shows the gradual grammaticalisation of these connectives, including the loss of the prepositions surrounding *despite*, the elision of the prefix *de-* in *in spite of*, and the decreasing popularity of the pre-verbal subject of 'withstand' in *notwithstanding* (as in *this notwithstanding*, which still shows the original idea of "this does not withstand", while in the order *notwithstanding this*, *this* is more clearly governed by the grammaticalised connective).

In Table 4.1, based on the fifteenth century quotation material in the *Middle English Dictionary*, the higher frequency of *notwithstanding* in comparison to the *(de)spite* forms is obvious (see examples 1–3). The figures also show the slow development of the form *spite*.

Tab. 4.1: *(In) despite of*, *in spite of* and *notwithstanding* in the *Middle English Dictionary* quotations corpus (c. 1150–1500). Absolute figures.

	(in) despite of	*(in) spite of*	*notwithstanding*
–1400	5	–	5
1400–1500	24	2	76

(1) And **notwithstanding al our feling**, wo or wele, God will we vnderstond and feithyn [= 'believe'] that we arn more verily in hevyin (c. 1450 Julian of Norwich).

(2) Edward the First .. Wan Scotland .. And al Walis **despite of** al ther myht (c. 1475 John Lydgate; a later manuscript, c. 1500, reads ***spite of** her myght*).

(3) And þow xalt [= 'shalt'] faryn wel, dowtyr, **in spyte of** alle thyn enmys; (c. 1438 Margery Kempe).

Table 4.2 reveals the interesting fact that *notwithstanding* was particularly favoured in officialese, in legal and documentary texts, and that its introduction into English can thus be regarded as a change from above. Comparative statistics of this kind underline the importance of different genres or text types in tracing the paths of grammaticalisation.

Tab. 4.2: *Notwithstanding* in the MED database and the *Helsinki Corpus* M3 and M4 (1350–1500): Occurrences in legal and documentary texts (absolute figures; occurrences per 10,000 words in the HC in brackets)

MED	
Documents	26
Other	55
HC	
Laws and documents	11 (2.3)
Other	9 (0.2)

It is not possible to calculate the proportional frequencies of the MED quotations material in Tables 4.1 and 4.2, but it is obvious that the proportion of documentary texts of all the material in the database is much lower than the proportion of the occurrences of *notwithstanding*, as shown by Table 4.2.

In Early Modern English, in the sixteenth and seventeenth centuries, the frequency of *notwithstanding* remains stable, and it is overwhelmingly more popular than the *(de)-spite* forms. This is clearly seen in the figures based on the Early Modern English part of the *Helsinki Corpus* in Table 4.3.

Tab. 4.3: *(De)spite* and *notwithstanding* in the Early Modern English part of the *Helsinki Corpus* (figures in brackets per 10,000 words)

	(in) despite (of)	*in spite of*	*notwithstanding*
E1 (1500–1570)	1	1	34 (1.8)
E2 (1570–1640)	1	1	35 (1.8)
E3 (1640–1710)	–	2	29 (1.7)

Even the *Corpus of Early English Correspondence Sampler*, which includes texts that are fairly close to informal spoken expression, shows a clear preference for *notwithstanding* and low figures of occurrence for the *(de)spite* forms (Table 4.4). The figures for the occurrence per 10,000 words of *notwithstanding* are, however, lower than in the *Helsinki Corpus*.

Tab. 4.4: *(De)spite* and *notwithstanding* in the *Corpus of Early English Correspondence Sampler* (figures in brackets per 10,000 words)

	(in) despite (of)	*in spite of*	*notwithstanding*
1500–1599	1	4	75 (0.8)
1600–1681	2	4	117 (0.9)

It is of interest that the *Corpus of English Dialogues* figures imply a clear decrease in the frequency of *notwithstanding* in the late seventeenth and in the eighteenth century (Table 4.5). The figures per 10,000 words are lower than in the *Helsinki Corpus* or the *CEEC*.

Tab. 4.5: *(De)spite* and *notwithstanding* in the *Corpus of English Dialogues* (figures in brackets per 10,000 words)

	(in) despite (of)	*in spite of*	*notwithstanding*
1560–1599	1	1	5 (0.2)
1600–1639	1	–	14 (0.7)
1640–1679	2	2	14 (0.5)
1680–1719	–	3	2 (0.1)
1720–1760	–	2	2 (0.1)

Tab. 4.6: *(De)spite* and *notwithstanding* in ARCHER (absolute figures)

	(in) despite (of)	*in spite of*	*notwithstanding*
1650–1700	–	3	22
1700–1750	–	3	18
1750–1800	1	10	36
1800–1850	2	12	14
1850–1900	6	22	13
1900–1950	8	7	4
1950–1990	40	37	2

Although the figures are low, Table 4.5 implies that in the course of the Modern English period *notwithstanding* gradually loses its predominant position to the *(de)spite* forms. Indeed, the figures from ARCHER in Table 4.6 indicate that in the second half of the eighteenth century *in spite of* begins to gain ground; in the early nineteenth century both types are equally common, and from the second half of the nineteenth century on, *notwithstanding* becomes a minority form. The twentieth-century figures for its occurrence are conspicuously low and indicate heavy contextual and genre restrictions, a phenomenon easily verified by a study of Present-day English corpora.

Table 4.6 also shows that *despite* catches up with *in spite of* in frequency only in the twentieth century. The development in which the *(de)spite* forms gradually become more popular than *notwithstanding* may have begun at the spoken level of the language and thus be a change from below, although the Middle English introduction of the borrowed *(de)spite*, just as that of *notwithstanding*, was no doubt a change from above. The length of the four-syllable *notwithstanding*, and its associations with formal language, probably affected and may still affect its diminishing popularity.

It should be emphasized that the corpus-based survey presented above is much simplified, and only calls attention to some factors which may have influenced the grammaticalisation and development of negative concessive connectives. For a more detailed discussion, see Rissanen (2002a), which is also the source of the tables.

3.3. Caveats

Corpus-based research is as important to postgraduate and even advanced undergraduate students as to senior scholars. The time spent on collecting evidence for doctoral dissertations can be radically shortened, and more time spent on the analysis of the material, reading earlier studies, and gaining a profound understanding of the essential character of language and its development. Even seminar papers and master's theses, which are often prepared within severely restricted time limits, may produce more significant results and give more satisfaction for the student if they are based on the rich linguistic evidence offered by corpora. The verifiability and falsifiability of research results is improved decisively. Ideally, a course in corpus methodology, introducing both present-day and historical corpora, should be included in all English and linguistics syllabi at the advanced undergraduate or early postgraduate level, depending of course on the structure of the syllabus and the technological infrastructure available.

It is obvious, however, that corpus-based research also has its restrictions and caveats (cf. article 51; Rissanen 1989, 2003b) and that ill-advised and incompetent use of corpora can adversely affect the results. An awareness of these restrictions is particularly important if and when, as suggested above, young students and scholars are encouraged to use corpora in their first efforts in the field of linguistic research.

The first and perhaps most important restriction to be kept in mind is that corpora only represent a part of linguistic reality. Even the largest corpus does not include all the possible variant expressions of the language (cf. article 9). This is a truism about which we need not be too worried. It is more important to remember that the choice of variant is the sum total of the discourse situation, the purpose of the message, the medium, the relationship between the speaker and the hearer or the writer and the reader, the speaker's ethnic, educational, cultural and social background, etc. Much of this background information can and should be coded in the corpus, but even this coding gives an inaccurate picture of the reality of language; it is not language itself.

This problem in corpus-based studies has sometimes been called "the God's truth fallacy". A large general corpus gives so convincing and easily analysable linguistic evidence that there is a risk that the corpus will be identified with language itself. This risk should be especially remembered in historical studies of language: the language historian is not constantly warned against the restrictions of corpus evidence by his or her own competence regarding the language form studied and is not exposed to limitless evidence of the language in everyday life. Furthermore, multi-purpose corpora are carefully structured to give as multifaceted and "lifelike" a picture of the language as possible. A less experienced scholar or student is easily tempted to argue that "this is true of the linguistic feature or phenomenon A in period X because my corpus says so." A more cautious and appropriate way of argumentation would be, "my corpus suggests that, at least in most circumstances, this may be true of the linguistic feature or phenomenon A in period X."

Connected with this problem is "the mystery of vanishing evidence". In corpus-based studies of less frequent linguistic details, the figures of occurrence given by corpora are too low for any reliable conclusions. The problem is intensified if the figures of occurrence are divided not only chronologically, but according to genre, sociolinguistic parameters, etc. The methods of estimating and calculating the reliability and generalising power of various quantifications based on corpus evidence are discussed in articles 36 to 40.

Another important fact to be kept in mind in historical corpus-based studies is what I have described as "the philologist's dilemma" (Rissanen 1989). The student is only able to draw meaningful and correct conclusions from corpus evidence if he or she has a good command of the language form studied and a fair knowledge of the main characteristics of the literary, social and cultural background from which the texts forming the corpus arise. Otherwise, fatal misinterpretations of textual evidence may take place. Even this simple fact is often forgotten because of the attractiveness of and easy access to corpus evidence. Thus, while the inclusion of corpus courses in language syllabi is to be recommended, competence in corpus use should never replace a profound knowledge of the early forms of the language if the student specializes in historical linguistics.

There are also more practical problems in the use of corpora as a source of evidence in historical linguistics. At the early stages of most languages, the spelling is not established, and the same word can be spelt in dozens of different ways. This naturally makes finding all the occurrences of a word or form difficult. Some corpora are lemmatized, i. e., searching by the normalised spelling will yield all the spelling variants. In the case of most corpora, however, the only way of trying to ensure the inclusion of all variant spellings of a word is by a careful check of the alphabetical word index of the corpus. Regrettably often, however, the medieval scribes' use of irregular and unexpected spelling variants beats the scholar's ingenuity.

Furthermore, most historical corpora only include the transcript of one or perhaps two manuscripts of the text, although the number of extant manuscripts may be much higher. Also, the corpus text is often based on a printed edition rather than on the original manuscript. The user of the corpus should be prepared to go back to the original printed edition of an early text with its footnoted information on variant manuscript readings, if this is important in view of the topic of study. Even study of the original manuscript(s) may prove necessary in some cases (see Kytö/Walker 2003).

Finally, we should keep in mind the slogan often repeated by corpus scholars (cf. article 51): "Research begins where counting ends". Corpus-based evidence is easily quantifiable. Particularly in the early years of historical corpus studies, it was often thought that satisfactory research consisted of collecting all the examples of the linguistic feature under scrutiny, counting the variants and presenting the figures. It is important to note, however, that real research only begins here; it should include a careful analysis of the evidence, with due attention paid to the linguistic processes of change and the extralinguistic factors causing variation, followed by conclusions and generalisations with reference to theoretical implications.

4. To conclude

The emphasis on the corpus-based study of variation and change as a starting point for historical linguistics presented in this article should not be understood as a rejection of more theoretical approaches to linguistics. Although the variationist approach emphasises the communicative aspects of language and the close connection existing between language and its users, it aims at generalisations, testing existing theories and offering a basis for new theory-building. The concept of change through variation has a solid theoretical basis which supports, for instance, cognitive semantics, prototype semantics and historical pragmatics.

The computer-aided variationist approach to the study of the history of English has also improved our ways and means of understanding and explaining the basic character of the present-day language. This approach is a good reminder that even the present-day varieties of language are not static, but constantly changing, as a logical – or less logical – result of variability. The gap which existed between historical and present-day language studies only a couple of decades ago is rapidly disappearing.

One important advantage of the variationist approach is that, even though its primary domain so far has been basic research, the emphasis it lays on the communicative aspects of language makes the step to applied study a short one. The concept of language as an ever-changing series of variant fields, not only those of the present day but also of earlier periods, gives perspective to dictionary making and even to the study of translation. Furthermore, the focus on contact between the speakers of various languages, and between the speakers of different varieties of one and the same language, has a close connection with the study of language learning and teaching.

5. Literature

Firth, J. R. (1957 [1935]), The Technique of Semantics. In: *Transactions of the Philological Society,* 36–72. Reprinted in Firth, J. R., *Papers in Linguistics 1934–1951*. London: Oxford University Press.

Firth, J. R. (1968), Linguistic Analysis as a Study of Meaning. In: Palmer, F. R. (ed.), *Selected Papers of J. R. Firth 1952–59*. London: Longman, 12–26.

Halliday, M. A. K. (1973), *Explorations in the Functions of Language*. London: Edward Arnold.

Hopper, Paul/Traugott, Elizabeth Closs (2003 [1993]), *Grammaticalization*. Cambridge: Cambridge University Press.

Jacobs, Andreas/Jucker, Andreas H. (1995), The Historical Perspective in Pragmatics. In: Jucker, Andreas H. (ed.), *Historical Pragmatics: Pragmatic Developments in the History of English*. Amsterdam/Philadelphia: John Benjamins, 3–33.

Kytö, Merja/Walker, Terry (2003), The Linguistic Study of Early Modern English Speech-related Texts. How "Bad" Can "Bad" Data Be? In: *Journal of English Linguistics* 31(3), 221–248.

Labov, William (1994), *Principles of Linguistic Change. Vol. 1: Internal Factors*. Oxford, UK/Cambridge, MA: Blackwell.

Labov, William (2001), *Principles of Linguistics Change. Vol. 2: Social Factors*. Oxford, UK/Cambridge, MA: Blackwell.

Lindquist, Hans/Mair, Christian (eds.) (2004a), *Corpus Approaches to Grammaticalization in English*. (Studies in Corpus Linguistics 13.) Amsterdam/Philadelphia: John Benjamins.

Lindquist, Hans/Mair, Christian (2004b), Introduction. In: Lindquist/Mair 2004a, ix–xiv.

Malinowski, Bronislaw (1923), The Problem of Meaning in Primitive Languages. Supplement I to Ogden, C. K./Richards, I. A., *The Meaning of Meaning*. London: Routledge/Kegan Paul.

Middle English Dictionary (1956–2001), edited by Hans Kurath et al. Ann Arbor, Michigan: The University of Michigan Press.

Milroy, James (1992), *Linguistic Variation and Change*. Oxford/Cambridge, Mass.: Blackwell.

Nevala, Minna (2004), *Address in Early English Correspondence. Its Forms and Socio-pragmatic Functions*. (Mémoires de la Société Néophilologique de Helsinki 64.) Helsinki: Société Néophilologique.

Nevalainen, Terttu/Raumolin-Brunberg, Helena (2003), *Historical Sociolinguistics: Language Change in Tudor and Stuart England*. (Longman Linguistics Library.) London: Pearson Education.

Nevalainen, Terttu (2004), Three Perspectives on Grammaticalization: Lexico-grammar, Corpora and Historical Sociolinguistics. In: Lindquist/Mair 2004a, 1–31.

Rissanen, Matti (1989), Three Problems Connected with the Use of Diachronic Corpora. In: *ICAME Journal* 13, 16–19.

Rissanen, Matti (2000), Standardisation and the Language of Early Statutes. In: Wright, Laura (ed.), *The Development of Standard English: Theories, Descriptions, Conflicts*. Cambridge. Cambridge University Press, 117–130.

Rissanen, Matti (2002a), *Despite* or *Notwithstanding*? On the Development of Concessive Prepositions in English. In: Fischer, Andreas/Tottie, Gunnel/Lehmann, Hans Martin (eds.), *Text Types and Corpora: Studies in Honour of Udo Fries*. Tübingen: Gunter Narr Verlag, 191–203.

Rissanen, Matti (2002b), "Without except(ing) unless ...": On the Grammaticalisation of Expressions Indicating Exception in English. In: Lenz, Katja/Möhlig, Ruth (eds.), *Of Dyuersite &*

Chaunge of Langage: Essays Presented to Manfred Görlach on the Occasion of his 65th Birthday. Heidelberg: C. Winter Universitätsverlag, 77–87.
Rissanen, Matti (2003a), On the Development and Grammaticalisation of Borrowed Conditional Subordinators in Middle English. In: *Studies in Medieval English Language and Literature* 18, 1–19.
Rissanen, Matti (2003b), Computerised Corpora and the Development of *beside(s)*. In: Amano, M. (ed.), *Creation and Practical Use of Language Texts.* Nagoya: Nagoya University, 87–97.
Romaine, Suzanne (1982), *Sociohistorical Linguistics: Its Status and Methodology.* Cambridge: Cambridge University Press.
Samuels, Michael L. (1972), *Linguistic Evolution, with Special Reference to English.* Cambridge: Cambridge University Press.
Traugott, Elizabeth Closs/Dasher, Richard B. (2002), *Regularity in Semantic Change.* Cambridge: Cambridge University Press.
Walker, Terry (2005), *Second Person Singular Pronouns in Early Modern English Dialogues 1560–1760.* PhD diss., Uppsala University.
Weinreich, Uriel/Labov, William/Herzog, Marvin Y. (1968), Empirical Foundations for a Theory of Language Change. In: Lehmann, W. P./Malkiel, Yakov (eds.), *Directions for Historical Linguistics: A Symposium.* Austin, Texas: University of Texas Press, 95–195.

Matti Rissanen, Helsinki (Finland)

5. Theory-driven and corpus-driven computational linguistics, and the use of corpora

1. Introduction

Computational linguistics and corpus linguistics are closely-related disciplines: they both exploit electronic corpora, extract various kinds of linguistic information from them, and make use of the same methods to acquire this information. Moreover, both were heavily affected by "paradigm shifts" from the prevailing empiricism of the 1950s to rationalism, and then back again with a revival of empirical methods in the 1990s.

Computational linguistics deals with the *formal modelling* of natural language. The formal models can be used to draw conclusions about the structure and functioning of the human language system. They also form the basis of implemented systems for the analysis and generation of spoken or written language in a variety of applications. The methods applied in building these models are of different kinds since, as a result of the above-mentioned paradigm changes, work in computational linguistics has taken two different paths. Both branches of computational linguistics aim to build models of natural language, but each exploits different techniques: the rationalist's branch focuses on *theory-driven, symbolic, nonstatistical* methods, whilst the empiricist's branch focuses on *corpus-driven* and *statistical* techniques. As we will see later, however, the distinction between the branches is these days less clear, and the two fields seem to be coming together again as people successfully combine concepts and methods from each field.

Obviously, the corpus-driven branch of computational linguistics has a natural affinity to corpus linguistics, and a shared interest in corpus exploitation. As a consequence, many research topics can be attributed equally well to either computational linguistics or corpus linguistics; examples include part-of-speech tagging (see article 24), treebanking (article 13), semantic tagging (article 26) and coreference resolution (article 27), to name just a few. At opposite extremes of computational and corpus linguistics, the ultimate goals of corpus exploitation do, however, diverge: certain domains of corpus-driven computational linguistics aim to build "optimal" models "no matter how", and the particular corpus features that find their way into such models are not seen as interesting *per se*; in contrast, corpus linguistics could be said to target exactly these features, the "ingredients" of the models.

The theory-driven branch of computational linguistics does not overlap very much with corpus linguistics (except for their common interest in linguistic issues in general), although corpora do play a (minor) role in theory-driven computational linguistics, as we will show. Thus, we could more accurately rephrase the introductory sentence as follows: "*Corpus-driven* computational linguistics and corpus linguistics are closely-related disciplines."

Another side branch of research goes back to the early days of computational linguistics and is closely tied to artificial intelligence. Traditionally, this field focuses on modelling human behavior, including human actions like communicating and reasoning. A lot of research has gone into the formal description of world knowledge and inference drawing. These topics are nowadays seeing a revival, in the form of ontologies to encode concepts and the relations between them, and instances of the concepts. Current research on dialogue, such as human-machine communication, also draws heavily on this branch of computational linguistics. We will come back to the issue of world knowledge in the concluding section.

This article gives a survey of the research interests and concerns that are found in the theory-driven and corpus-driven branches of computational linguistics, and addresses their relation to corpora and corpus linguistics. Section 2 deals with theory-driven computational linguistics and section 3 with the corpus-driven branch. In section 4, I sketch the history of computational linguistics and trace the development of automatic part-of-speech taggers; this nicely illustrates the role that corpora have played and still play in computational linguistics. Section 5 concludes the article. Needless to say, this paper cannot do justice to all the work that has been done in computational linguistics. I hope, however, that the topics I address convey some of the main ideas and interests that drive research in this area.

2. Theory-driven computational linguistics

As a child of the paradigm shift towards rationalism, this branch of computational linguistics relies on the intellect and on deductive methods in building formal language models. That is, research is driven by *theoretical* concerns rather than empirical ones. The research issues addressed here often take up topics from theoretical linguistics. For instance, various syntactic formalisms have been the object of research in computational linguistics, such as Dependency Grammar (Tesnière 1959), HPSG (Head-Driven Phrase Structure Grammar, Pollard/Sag 1994), LFG (Lexical Functional Grammar, Bresnan 1982) or the Minimalist Program (Chomsky 1993).

Why is computational linguistics interested in linguistic theories? We see two main concerns of such research: firstly, the search for a complete, rigid and sound *formalization* of theoretical frameworks; secondly, concern for *implementation* of linguistic theories. I address both issues in the following sections.

2.1. The formalization of theoretical frameworks

As already stated, computational linguistics aims at a complete and sound formalization of theoretical frameworks. For instance, for the above-mentioned syntactic formalisms, computational linguists have defined formalisms that are mathematically well-understood: Kaplan/Bresnan (1982) for LFG, Kasper/Rounds (1986), King (1989, 1994) and Carpenter (1992) for HPSG, and Stabler (1997) with the "Minimalist Grammar" for the Minimalist Program. (Dependency-based systems come in a variety of realizations, and are in general formalized to a lesser degree than other theories.)

Other frameworks have started out as well-defined, purely-mathematical formalisms which were first studied for their mathematical properties, and have only later been exploited as the representational formats of linguistic theories. Such formalisms include TAG (Tree-Adjoining Grammar, Joshi/Levy/Takahashi 1975, Joshi 1985), CG (Categorial Grammar, Ajdukiewicz 1935, Bar-Hillel 1953), and especially its extension CCG (Combinatory Categorial Grammar, Ades/Steedman 1982, Steedman 1996); the linguistic relevance of these formalisms has been addressed, e. g., by Kroch/Joshi (1985) for TAG, and by Steedman (1985) for CCG.

What do these formalized theories offer? Armed with such a theory, computational linguists can explore the formal properties of the framework, such as its *structural complexity*. A commonly-used way of characterizing the complexity of a framework is by the form of its rules: for instance, a simple grammar rule like $N \rightarrow dog$ replaces (expands) a noun by the word *dog*, regardless of the noun's context. A more complex rule would be $N \rightarrow dog \mid DET\_$, which restricts the replacement to those contexts in which the noun is preceded by a determiner. Grammars are classified according to the most complex rule type that they contain: a grammar with rules like the second example above would be a member of the class of "context-sensitive" grammars. (The term "grammar" is often used to refer to syntactic rule systems. We call a grammar any linguistic rule system, including phonological, morphological, semantic, and pragmatic rule systems.)

This way of characterizing grammars has been introduced by Chomsky (1956, 1959). For each class of grammars, there is a corresponding class of languages that are generated by these grammars, and a corresponding abstract model, the "automaton", which represents an alternative way of defining the same class of languages. The first two columns of Table 5.1 display the four complexity classes as defined by Chomsky, with the most complex class at the top. Each class properly contains the simpler classes below it. This means, e. g., that for any context-free language (or "Type-2" language) we can define a context-sensitive grammar ("Type-1" grammar) to generate that language, but not vice versa. The resulting hierarchy of grammars and languages is known as the *Chomsky Hierarchy*. In the following paragraphs, I show how each of the above-mentioned linguistic frameworks relates to the Chomsky Hierarchy, and then address issues of computational complexity (see last column of Table 5.1).

Tab. 5.1: Structural complexity (Chomsky Hierarchy) and computational complexity.

Structural Complexity		*Computational Complexity*
Grammar/Language Class	*Automaton*	
Type 0	Turing machine	undecidable
Type 1, context-sensitive	linear-bounded automaton	NP-complete
Type 2, context-free	pushdown automaton	$O(n^3)$
Type 3, regular	finite-state automaton	$O(n)$

Unification-based formalisms, such as HPSG and LFG, are in general equivalent to a Turing machine (which generates Type-0 languages). The formalisms of TAG and CCG are less complex, but they can still express the famous cross-serial (= non context-free) dependencies observed in Dutch, Swiss-German, or Bambara (see, e. g., Savitch et al. 1987). TAG and CCG are appealing formalisms because they are only slightly more powerful than context-free grammars; that is, they do not use the full power of context-sensitive grammars and are therefore easier to compute than context-sensitive grammars in general. The complexity class of TAG and CCG is not part of the original Chomsky Hierarchy but lies between Types 1 and 2. Joshi (1985), who defined this class, coined the term "mildly context-sensitive".

The class of languages generated by finite-state automata or regular expressions (Type-3 languages) has received much attention since the early days of research on formal languages (Kleene 1956; Chomsky/Miller 1958; Rabin/Scott 1959). In the following years, finite-state techniques became especially important in the domain of phonology and morphology: with SPE (*The Sound Pattern of English*), Chomsky/Halle (1968) introduced a formalism to express phonological processes, such as Place Assimilation (such as, "'n' in front of 'p' becomes 'm'"). The formalism defined an ordered set of rewriting rules which operated on phonological features such as [+/−nasal] and superficially resembled the rules of context-sensitive grammars: $\alpha \rightarrow \beta \,/\, \gamma \,\_\, \delta$ ("replace α by β in context $\gamma \ldots \delta$"). It turned out though, that the formalism, as used by the phonologists, was in fact equivalent in power to finite-state automata (Johnson 1972; Kaplan/Kay 1981, 1994). Kaplan and Kay showed this by means of a special type of finite-state automata, the so-called finite-state transducers. Their alphabet consists of complex symbols like 'n : m' (or feature bundles representing the phonemes), which can be interpreted as the "deep" (= lexical) and "surface" representations of phonological elements: phonemic 'n' becomes orthographic 'm'. In the formalism of Kaplan and Kay, the rewriting rules are applied in a sequential order. Another way of formalizing the mapping from lexical to surface form was the formalism of "two-level morphology", proposed by Koskenniemi (1983). In this formalism, declarative rules express parallel constraints between the lexical and the surface form. This formalism is again equivalent in power to finite-state automata. As the name suggests, the formalism has been used to formalize morphological phenomena (which in part overlap with phonological phenomena, but also include morphotactics).

Obviously, structural complexity is an important factor for the implementation of a linguistic theory, and implementation is the second concern of theory-driven computational linguistics. Theories that allow for more complex structures require more powerful programs to handle these structures than simpler theories do. For instance, a program that interprets context-sensitive rules (such as $N \rightarrow dog\ /\ DET\ \_$) needs some mechanism to look at the context of the node that is to be expanded, whereas programs for context-free rules can do without such a function.

Complexity is also seen as an issue for theoretical linguistics and psycholinguistics, since it might be related to questions of learnability and processability of language. A sample research question is: what bearing does a certain linguistic constraint have on the system's overall complexity? To answer such questions, computational linguists investigate the effects of adding, removing, or altering constraints, for instance, by (slightly) re-defining one of the "island conditions" or "move-alpha" in Minimalist Grammar. Does this result in a system that is more or less or equally complex as the original system? (One might think, naively, that adding a constraint such as the "shortest move condition" would result in a more restrictive grammar, because it does not allow for many of the things that another system does allow; however, research has shown that intuitions can be misleading.)

Another interesting research topic is the *computational complexity* (or parsing complexity) of a framework: given an input string of length n (e. g., n words or characters), how long does it take (at least) to compute an analysis, and how much storage space does the computation need? As one might expect, computational complexity parallels structural complexity: the simpler a grammar/language, the less time or storage space the computation needs.

For instance, from a computational point of view, finite-state automata (or regular/Type-3 grammars) are highly attractive, since there are efficient algorithms to process Type-3 languages which are linear in time. Thus, given an input of length n, these algorithms roughly need at most n steps to decide whether the input is accepted by a given finite-state automaton, i. e., to decide whether the input belongs to the language defined by that automaton. Using "big-O notation", we say that these algorithms run in $O(n)$ time (see last column of Table 5.1). As a result, finite-state techniques have been and are used for a variety of tasks in computational linguistics, including speech, phonological and morphological processing, as well as syntactic analysis. Since, as is well-known, natural language syntax requires more powerful models than Type-3 grammars, the finite-state approaches *approximate* more powerful grammars, e. g., by a depth cut-off in rule application (and thus disallowing deeply-embedded structures).

For context-free grammars in general, there are also a number of relatively efficient algorithms, such as the Earley algorithm (Earley 1970) and the Cocke-Younger-Kasami (CYK) algorithm (Kasami 1965, Younger 1967), both of which run in $O(n^3)$ time; that is, the algorithm roughly needs at most n^3 steps for processing an input string of length n.

Turning now to the class of Type-0 (Turing-equivalent) languages, Table 5.1 states that these are *undecidable*. This means that, even if provided with huge amounts of storage space and time, there is no general algorithm that would deliver an analysis for any arbitrary input (it could well deliver analyses (or rejections) for the vast majority of possible input data but not necessarily for all of them). The property of *decidability* pertains to questions such as: given a grammar and a sentence, is there a procedure that tells us whether the sentence is accepted/generated by the grammar, in other words, whether the sentence is grammatical or not? The answer is that there is no such procedure for Type-0 languages in general.

As noted above, unification-based formalisms, such as HPSG and LFG, are in general equivalent to a Turing machine. This means that these formalisms would also be undecidable, in general. Since this is a highly problematic property, additional constraints have been proposed and added to the formalisms, to constrain their power and make them decidable. For instance, adding the "off-line parsability constraint" to the LFG formalism makes it decidable, in particular, "NP-complete" (Johnson 1988). As a result processing an LFG grammar on a *nondeterministic* Turing machine takes *polynomial* time ("NP" stands for "nondeterministic, polynomial"): $O(n^k)$, where k stands for some constant (which can be much larger than 3, as in the $O(n^3)$ time complexity of context-free algorithms). Computers themselves correspond to deterministic Turing machines however, so typical algorithms have to simulate non-determinacy and in this way actually take *exponential* time for LFG parsing ($O(k^n)$ – here the input length n provides the exponens of the function rather than the basis; as a consequence, lengthening the input string has a drastic effect on computation time). Nonetheless, since natural languages are mostly equivalent to context-free languages, intelligent algorithms exploit this property and thus arrive at parsing in polynomial time, for most cases.

Abstract algorithms, such as the Earley algorithm, are used in mathematical proofs of complexity. The next step is to turn them into parsing algorithms, which determine mechanical ways of applying the grammar rules and constraints and using the lexicon entries so that, given an input string, the algorithm can finally come up with either an analysis (or multiple analyses) of the input string, or else with the answer that the input string is ungrammatical and no analysis can be assigned to it. This leads us to the second concern of theory-driven computational linguistics: implementing the formalized theories and parsing algorithms.

2.2. Implementation of the theoretical frameworks

Implementations of linguistic theories can be viewed as "proofs of concept": they prove that the formalizations are indeed sound and rigid, and exhibit the predicted complexity properties. An implementation consists of two parts: (i) a language-specific grammar (e. g. an LFG grammar for English) and (ii) a parser, which analyzes input strings according to that grammar (and the underlying formalism). It is the parser that knows how to "read" the grammar rules and to construct the trees or feature structures that constitute the analyses of the input strings.

The parsers are often embedded in "grammar development platforms", workbenches (software packages) which support the grammar writer in writing and debugging the grammar rules, e. g., by checking the rule format ("do all grammar rules end with a full stop?") or by displaying the output analyses in accessible formats. Important platforms for syntactic formalisms are: XLE (Xerox Linguistic Environment, from the NLTT group at PARC) for LFG implementations, LKB (Lexical Knowledge Builder, Copestake 2002) for HPSG grammars, but also used for implementing CCG grammars, and XTAG (Paroubek/Schabes/Joshi 1992) for TAG grammars.

For the implementation of phonological and morphological analyzers, widely-used tools are KIMMO (Karttunen 1983) and its free version, PC-KIMMO, from the Summer Institute of Linguistics (Antworth 1990), which embody the two-level rules of Koskenniemi (1983). The Xerox research groups have developed a collection of finite-state tools, which, among other things, implement rewriting rules (see, e. g. Beesley/Karttunen 2003). Computational linguists have also worked on formalizing and implementing semantics. CCG traditionally uses the lambda-calculus, building semantic structures in parallel with categorial structures (Steedman 2000). In the LFG world, the formalism of Glue Semantics has been both developed and implemented (Dalrymple 1999); in the HPSG world, MRS (Minimal Recursion Semantics, Copestake et al. 2005) has been applied.

An implementation does not only serve as proof of the sound formalization of a theoretical framework. It can also serve linguists by verifying their formalization of specific linguistic phenomena within this framework. Development platforms can support the linguist user in the formulation and verification of linguistic hypotheses: by implementing a grammar of, e. g., phonological or syntactic rules and lexicon entries, the user can verify the outcome of the rules and entries and experiment with variants. As early as 1968, Bobrow and Fraser implemented such a system, the "Phonological Rule Tester", which allowed the linguist user to define rewriting rules as presented in SPE, and to test the effect of the rules on data specified in form of bundles of phonemic features.

The earliest implementations consisted of grammar fragments or "toy grammars", which could handle a small set of selected phenomena, with a restricted vocabulary. With the advent of more powerful computers, both in speed and storage, and of the availability of large electronic corpora (see article 3), people started to work on broader coverage. Adding rules and lexicon entries to a grammar can have quite dramatic effects however, because of unexpected and, usually, unwanted interferences. Such interferences can lead to rules cancelling each other out, or else they give rise to additional, superfluous analyses. Interferences can provide important hints to the linguist and grammar writer, by pointing out that some grammar rules are not correctly constrained. The problem, though, is that there is no procedure to automatically diagnose all the interference problems of a new rule. A useful approximation of such a procedure is the use of *test suites* (see article 13), which are representative collections of grammatical and ungrammatical sentences (or words, in the case of phonological or morphological implementations). After any grammar modification, the grammar is run on the test suite, and the outcome is compared to previous test runs.

2.3. Theory-driven computational linguistics and corpora

I conclude this section by briefly summarizing the main points of interest of theory-driven computational linguistics and then address the role of corpora and the relation to corpus linguistics. As the name suggests, computational linguistics deals with "computing linguistics": linguistic phenomena and theories are investigated with regard to formal correctness, and structural and computational complexity. A second aspect is the development and verification of language-specific grammars, in the form of implementations.

What role do corpora play in this field? Firstly, as in research in (corpus-based) linguistics, corpora serve in computational linguistics as a "source of inspiration"; they are used to obtain an overview of the data occurring in natural language and to determine the scope of the phenomenon that one wants to examine. Secondly, corpus data drive the usual cyclic process of theory construction: we start by selecting an initial set of examples that we consider relevant for our phenomenon; next, we come up with a first working model (in the form of a set of linguistic rules or an actual implementation), which accounts for our initial set of examples; we then add more data and test how well the first model fits the new data; if necessary, we adjust the model, such that it accounts for both the initial and new data; then we add further data again, and so on. Test suites with test items (sentences or words) for all relevant phenomena can be used to ensure that the addition of rules for new phenomena does not corrupt the analysis of phenomena already covered by the model.

In the early days of (toy) implementations, *evaluation* did not play a prominent role. However, with more and more systems being implemented, both assessment of the systems' quality (performance) and comparability to other systems has become an issue. The performance of a system can be evaluated with respect to a standardized gold standard, e. g., in the form of test suites or corpora with annotations, such as "treebanks" (see article 13). Performance is usually measured in terms of the grammar's coverage of the gold standard. Other measures include the time needed to parse the test corpus, or the average number of analyses. As we will see in the next section, thorough evaluation, according to standardized measures, has become an important topic in computational linguistics.

In the scenarios described above, both the analysis and the use of corpus data is mainly *qualitative*. That is, the data is inspected manually and analyses are constructed manually, by *interpreting* the facts and hand-crafting rules that fit the facts. Data selection and analysis are driven by theoretical assumptions rather than the data itself. In this respect, theory-driven computational linguistics is closely related to (introspective) theoretical linguistics – and is unlike corpus linguistics.

An alternative strategy is to automatically derive and "learn" models from corpora, based on quantitative analyses of corpora. This method is more consistent with the empiricist paradigm, which relies on inductive methods to build models bottom-up from empirical data. The empiricist's branch of computational linguistics is addressed in the next section.

3. Corpus-driven computational linguistics

Up to the late 1980s, most grammars (i. e., phonological, morphological, syntactic, and semantic analyzers) consisted of knowledge-based expert systems, with carefully handcrafted rules, as described in section 2. At some point, though, manual grammar development seemed to have reached its limit and no further progress seemed possible. However, the grammars had not yet arrived at a stage that would permit development of useful applications (something that was urgently requested by funding agencies). In general, common deficiencies of hand-crafted systems were:

(i) Hand-crafted systems do not easily *scale up*, i. e., they are not easily extensible to large-scale texts. As described in the previous sections, early implementations consisted of toy grammars, which covered a small set of phenomena, with a restricted vocabulary. When such systems are augmented, e. g., to cover real texts rather than artificial examples, interferences occur that are not easy to eliminate. The grammars of natural languages are complex systems of rules, that are often interdependent and, thus, difficult to manage and maintain.
(ii) Hand-crafted systems are not *robust*. Real texts (or speech) usually contain many words that are unknown to the system, such as many proper nouns, foreign words, hapax legomena and spelling errors (or mispronunciations). Similarly, real texts contain a lot of "unusual" constructions, such as soccer results ("1 : 0") in sports news, verbless headers in newspaper articles, syntactically-awkward and semantically-opaque idiomatic expressions, and, of course, truly-ungrammatical sentences. For each of these "exceptions", some "workaround" has to be defined that can provide some output analysis for them. More generally speaking, "the system needs to be prepared for cases where the input data does not correspond to the expectations encoded in the grammar" (Stede 1992, 383). In the case of spelling errors and ungrammatical sentences, it is obvious that workarounds such as additional rules or constraint relaxation risk spoiling the actual grammar itself and causing it to yield incorrect (or undesirable) analyses for correct sentences.
(iii) Hand-crafted systems cannot easily deal with *ambiguity*. Natural languages are full of ambiguities; famous examples are PP attachment alternatives ("The man saw the woman with the telescope") or the sentence "I saw her duck under the table", with (at least) three different readings. In fact, people are usually very good at picking out the reading which is correct in the current context, and indeed are rarely conscious of ambiguities and (all) potential readings. For example, Abney (1996) shows that the apparently impossible "word salad" sequence "The a are of I" actually has a perfectly grammatical (and sensible) NP reading, wich can be paraphrased as "The are called 'a', located in some place labeled 'I'" ('are' in the sense of 1/100 hectare). Ambiguity is a real challenge for automatic language processing, because *disambiguation* often needs to rely on contextual information and world knowledge. Moreover, there is a natural tradeoff between coverage/robustness and ambiguity: the more phenomena a grammar accounts for, the more analyses it provides for each input string. This means that having arrived at a certain degree of coverage, research then has to focus on strategies of disambiguation.
(iv) Hand-crafted systems are not easily *portable* to another language. Development of a grammar for, e. g., Japanese, is of course easier for a grammar writer if he or she has already created a grammar for English, because of his or her experience, and the rules of "best practice" that he or she has developed in the first implementation. It is, however, not often feasible to reuse (parts of) a grammar for another language, especially if the two languages are typologically very different, such as English and Japanese.

For the initial purposes of theory-driven computational linguistics, these deficiencies were not so crucial. For *applied* computational linguistics, which focuses on the development of real applications, the shortcomings posed serious problems. Thus researchers in applied computational linguistics sought alternative methods of creating systems, to overcome the deficiencies listed above. They found what they were looking for among the speech-processing community, who were working on automatic speech recognition (ASR) (and speech synthesis, TTS, text-to-speech systems). Speech recognition is often regarded as a topic of physical, acoustic engineering rather than linguistic research, and researchers had successfully applied statistical methods to it on a large scale in the late 1970s. With the success of the ASR systems, people tried, and successfully applied, the same methods in other tasks, starting with part-of-speech tagging, and then moving on to syntax parsing, etc. The large majority of today's applications in computational linguistics make use of quantitative, statistical information drawn from corpora.

Interestingly though, statistical techniques are not really new to the field of computational linguistics, which in fact started out as an application-oriented enterprise, using mainly empirical, statistical methods. The earliest statistical applications are machine translation (e. g., Kaplan 1950, Oswald 1952), speech recognition (Davis/Biddulph/Balashek 1952), optical character recognition (OCR, Bledsoe/Browning 1959), authorship attribution (Mosteller/Wallace 1964), or essay grading (Page 1967). It was only after the influential ALPAC report in 1966 (ALPAC 1966), and in the wake of Chomsky's work (e. g., Chomsky 1956, 1957, see article 2), that the focus of research switched to rationalism-based, non-statistical research (with the exception of speech recognition), and gave rise to the branch of research that we called "theory-driven computational linguistics" (this switch is addressed in more detail in section 4). However, the severe shortcomings of the theory-driven (toy) implementations led researchers to look for alternative methods, and to re-discover corpus-driven techniques. But it was not until the 1980s that people started to apply statistical methods (on a large scale) to tasks such as part-of-speech tagging, parsing, semantic analysis, lexicography, and collocation or terminology extraction. Indeed it was even longer before statistical methods were once again reintroduced into research on machine translation.

The reasons mentioned so far for re-discovering statistical methods are rather pragmatic, technically-motivated reasons. Following Chomsky, one could say that corpus-driven approaches are misguided, since they model language *use*, i. e., performance rather than competence, in Chomsky's terms. However, many people today claim that competence grammar takes an (overly) narrow view of natural language, by restricting language to its algebraic properties, and that statistical approaches can provide insights about other linguistically-relevant properties and phenomena of natural language, such as language change, language acquisition, and gradience phenomena (see, e. g., Klavans/Resnik 1996; Bod/Hay/Jannedy 2003; Manning/Schütze 1999, ch. 1). Thus there may be theory-driven reasons to re-focus on corpus-driven methods. In the next section, I present prominent concepts and methods used in statistical approaches and then discuss how statistical methods overcome the above-mentioned deficiencies.

3.1. Concepts and methods of statistical modelling of language

In section 2, formal models of language in the form of formal grammars and automata as defined by the Chomsky Hierarchy were introduced. These models take words or sentences as input and produce linguistic analyses as output, e. g. part-of-speech tags or syntactic trees, or else the input can be rejected as ungrammatical. *Statistical* (or *probabilistic*) formal models also take words or sentences as input and produce linguistic analyses for them. In addition, they assign *probabilities* to all input-output pairs. For instance, a statistical part-of-speech tagger might assign probability 0.7 to the input-output pair *book-NN* ("book" as singular noun) and 0.3 to the pair *book-VB* ("book" as verb base form). Ungrammatical and absurd analyses like *book-CD* (cardinal number) would receive very low or zero probability.

The models used in corpus-driven computational linguistics are probabilistic variants of the formal grammars and automata defined by the Chomsky Hierarchy. For instance, a *probabilistic context-free grammar* (PCFG) can be seen as an ordinary context-free (Type-2) grammar whose analyses are augmented by probabilities. Applying an implementation of a PCFG, e. g. for English, to an input sentence typically results in a huge number of different syntactic analyses (thousands or even millions), each supplied with a probability. The probabilities impose a natural order on the different analyses: the most probable analyses are the most plausible ones, and indeed most likely the correct ones. In sum then, the probabilistic models arrange the individual analyses of some input along a scale of probabilities, marking them as more or less plausible, relative to each other.

Due to their favorable computational properties, Type-3 models are again highly popular, just as in theory-driven computational linguistics. The most prominent probabilistic Type-3 models are *n-gram models* (which are described in more detail below) and *Hidden Markov Models*. Most work on statistical syntactic parsers deals with PCFGs (Type-2 models), while comparatively less research has been devoted to probabilistic variants of Type-1 grammars.

Comparing statistical with non-statistical models, we could say that non-statistical models are simplified versions of statistical models in that they assign just two "probability values": "1" to all grammatical inputs (= "accept"), and "0" to all ungrammatical ones (= "reject"). It is the task of the grammar writer to write the grammar rules in such a way that all and only the correct input words or sentences are accepted. In contrast, rules of statistical models are usually written in a very general way (similarly to underspecified rules in "universal grammar"), and may – at least in theory – even include absurd assignments such as *book-CD*, or rules that are ungrammatical in the language under consideration, such as $PP \rightarrow NP\ P$ in an English grammar. The probabilities that are assigned to these rules would be very low or equal to zero, and all analyses that these rules participate in would "inherit" some part of the low probability and thus be marked as rather implausible.

Where do the probabilities for the rules come from? The models themselves only define the factors (*parameters*) that are assigned the probabilities. For PCFGs, these factors are context-free grammar rules. For simpler models, the factors can be word forms, part-of-speech (PoS) tags, sequences of PoS tags, pairs of word forms and PoS tags, etc. For instance, a model could define that the probability of a PoS assignment such as *book-NN* depends on the individual probabilities of the word and PoS tag in isolation ("How probable is it that the word 'book' occurs in some text, compared to all other words? How probable is the tag 'NN', compared to all other PoS tags?"). The question is then where the individual probabilities come from and how their probabilities are combined to produce the overall probability of *book-NN*.

The answer to the first question is that the probabilities can be derived from *corpus statistics*. The basic idea in statistical modelling of linguistic phenomena is to "take a body of English text (called a *corpus*) and learn the language by noting statistical regularities in that corpus" (Charniak 1993, 24). Put in technical terms then, most statistical modelling relies on the assumption that the *frequencies* of so-called events (the occurrences of a certain word, part-of-speech tag or syntactic configuration), as observed in a corpus, can be used to compute (or estimate) the *probabilities* of these linguistic events, and thereby to detect regularities and generalizations in the language.

For instance, an existing, non-statistical grammar can be augmented with probabilities by running the original grammar on a corpus and keeping a record of how often the individual rules are applied in the analyses (as in Black/Lafferty/Roukos 1992). Another way is to use annotated corpus data (e. g., treebanks) both to induce grammar rules by reading off rules from the corpus, and to assign probabilities to them (e. g., Charniak 1996, Bod 1998). Finally, plain text data, without annotations, can also be used to induce statistical grammars, such as syntactic parsers (van Zaanen 2000).

The process of calculating probabilities on the basis of a model and corpus data is called *parameter estimation* (or *training*): the fillers of the parameters are assigned probabilities, resulting in an instance of the formal model. A model instance can in turn be used to predict future occurrences of linguistic events, and thereby be applied to analyse previously-unseen language data. How the individual probabilities result from corpus frequencies and combine to an overall probability is a matter of probability theory. Statistical models are based on the (simplifying) assumption that their parameters are statistically independent. The individual probabilities of "competing candidates" therefore sum up to 1. In a PCFG, for instance, the probabilities of all rules with the same left-hand side (e. g., $NP \rightarrow N$, $NP \rightarrow DET\ N$, $NP \rightarrow ...$) sum up to 1. The probability of a PCFG analysis of a complete sentence is then computed as the product of the probabilities of the rules that participate in the analysis.

How the parameters are actually assigned their probabilities depends on the algorithm that is applied. For Type-3 models, a commonly-used estimator algorithm is the "forward-backward algorithm" (also called "Baum-Welch algorithm", Baum 1972); for PCFGs, the "inside-outside algorithm" is used (Baker 1979). Both types of algorithms are specific instances of a general algorithm called "Expectation Maximization" (EM, Dempster/Laird/Rubin 1977).

Having built a model instance, we need algorithms to apply the model to new input data, similar to the algorithms that interpret and apply the grammars within theory-driven computational linguistics; this task is often called *decoding*. The Earley and CYK algorithms for context-free grammars, which we mentioned in section 2.1., can be modified and applied to PCFGs. For Type-3 and Type-2 models, the most prominent decoding algorithm is the Viterbi algorithm (Viterbi 1967). As with theory-based computational linguistics, computational complexity of the frameworks is an important issue: the training and decoding algorithms mentioned above are of polynomial computational complexity.

We now address selected concepts and methods of statistical modelling in more detail.

3.1.1. Noisy channel

The task of decoding is neatly illustrated by the metaphor of the *noisy channel*. As already mentioned, many statistical approaches were inspired by work in the area of speech recognition. The aim of speech recognition is to map speech signals to words, and to this end, the acoustic signal must be analyzed. Very often the system cannot uniquely determine a particular word, e. g., words such as "big" or "pig" are hard to distinguish on an acoustic basis only.

In his theory of communication ("Information Theory"), Shannon (1948) develops the metaphor of the noisy channel to describe problems such as these, which arise in the process of communication. According to the noisy-channel model, communication proceeds through a "channel" which adds "noise" to the signal: *original signal → noisy channel → perturbed signal*. For instance, a source word like "pig" might be "disturbed" by the channel and come out as or be misheard as "big". Or else a source word might be disturbed in that one of its letters is deleted, resulting in a spelling error. The aim of information theory, and cryptography in general, is to reconstruct (decode) the original source signal from the perturbed signal at the end of the channel. How can this be done automatically? For this, we combine three types of information: (i) the perturbed signal (which we have at hand); (ii) some measure of "similarity" between the perturbed signal and all source signal candidates (we prefer signal pairs that are rather similar to each other than dissimilar); (iii) the prior (unconditioned) probability of the source candidates, specifying how probable it is that the speaker actually uttered that source signal (we prefer source signals that are usual, frequent signals, over infrequent ones).

For calculating similarity (ii) and prior probability (iii), we can use statistics derived from corpora: (iii) can be estimated on the base of a large (balanced) corpus, by counting word occurrences (or occurrences of parameters other than wordforms, as specified by the model at hand). We thus might learn that "big" is a highly probable word, and "pig" is less probable. For (ii), we need a list of word pairs that are commonly mixed up (or misspelt) and the numbers for how often that happens. This information can be calculated on the basis of a corpus that is annotated with the relevant information. In this way, we might learn that "pig" is often misheard as "big". Based on this information, we can calculate the optimal candidate for the source signal, which realizes the best combination of being similar to the perturbed signal and of being a probable word itself (although what counts as "similar" depends on the specific task).

3.1.2. Bayes' rule

The three components (i)–(iii) of the noisy-channel model stand in a certain relation to each other, and this relation is made explicit by an equation, called *Bayes' rule* (or *Bayes' law*). The equation captures the fact that we can swap the dependencies between source and perturbed signal: we are interested in determining the most probable source signal (what we are trying to reconstruct) given a perturbed signal: $argmax_{source \in X}\ P(source|perturbed)$, where X is a set of alternative sources for the given "perturbed". According to Bayes' rule, this can be computed as $argmax_{source \in X}\ P(perturbed|source) * P(source)$, in which the arguments of the probability function P are switched. In fact we effectively applied this rule already in our informal reasoning of how to reconstruct the source signal: the first factor of the product expresses our vague notion of similarity (ii), the second factor captures the prior probability of the source signal (iii).

Bayes' rule is not restricted to linguistic applications but can be found in every-day reasoning. For instance, a doctor usually applies Bayes' rule in the diagnosis of a disease (example from Charniak 1993, 23). The doctor's task is to determine, given a certain symptom, the most probable disease (*P(disease|symptom)*). Often, the doctor does not know the values for all possible diseases (a symptom can co-occur with a number of different diseases). However, he or she knows quite well which symptoms are usually associated with a disease (*P(symptom|disease)*). Put differently, the doctor's knowledge is indexed by diseases, whereas the task at hand requires an index of symptoms. In addition, however, the doctor knows how often a disease occurs (*P(disease)*), i. e., which diseases are worthy of consideration. With this knowledge, he or she can derive the most probable disease given the symptom (*P(disease|symptom)*).

3.1.3. N-gram models (= Markov Models) and Hidden Markov Models

Up to now, we have applied the noisy-channel model to decode isolated words, and this approach seems sensible for simple tasks like spelling correction. For speech recognition and other tasks, however, it may make a big difference whether we look at isolated words or words in context: the prior probability of "big" might well be higher than that of "pig"; however, in a context such as "The nice _ likes John", we know for sure that it is more probable that "pig" will occur than "big", and corpus data should somehow provide evidence for that. In fact, we have to deal with entire sentences (or even complete texts) rather than just words. We thus need to know the prior probability of source candidates that consist of entire sentences, and we need likewise to measure similarity between pairs of sentences. Obviously, however, we do not have corpora that contain all possible source sentences (because language is infinite), so that we could directly read off the information. Instead, we have to approximate the information by looking at spans of words rather than entire sentences. The spans usually consist of two words (bigrams) or three words (trigrams). For instance, the sentence "The nice pig likes John" contains the trigrams "The nice pig", "nice pig likes", and "pig likes John".

A list of *n-grams* (for some natural number *n*) together with their probabilities derived from a corpus (by counting their occurrences) constitutes an instance of a Markov model and is called a *language model*. Using a bigram or trigram language model, a speech analysis system can now compute that it is much more probable that "pig" will occur than "big" in the context "Another nice _ likes Mary" (even if this particular sentence was not part of the training corpus).

The noisy-channel model and n-gram models can be applied in a large variety of tasks. One of the earliest considerations of automatic machine translation refers to the noisy-channel model and cryptography: "When I look at an article in Russian, I say 'This is really written in English, but it has been coded in some strange symbols. I will now proceed to decode.'" (Weaver 1949; also see section 4.1. below). According to this view, an extreme form of "perturbation" has occurred when an English source text is affected in such a way that it comes out as a Russian text. The same statistical methods above can be used in reconstructing the source, i. e., in translating Russian "back" to English.

The model can also be used for linguistic analyses, such as part-of-speech tagging. Here, the "perturbed" signal is words in a text, and we use the model to reconstruct the corresponding parts-of-speech of the words as the assumed source signal. For this kind of task, *Hidden Markov Models* (HMM) are used, an extension of n-gram (Markov) models. In a HMM, multiple paths can lead to the same output, so that the functioning of the automaton can be observed only indirectly, from where the term "hidden". For example, the task of a PoS tagger is to deliver the correct PoS tags of some input words. The "visible" information is then the sequence of input words, and the "hidden" information is the corresponding sequence of PoS tags (which we are interested in). HMMs combine the probabilities of the visible information with those of the hidden information, so that we can reconstruct the PoS tag sequence from the word sequence.

The shared assumption of n-gram-based approaches is that linguistic phenomena of different kinds depend, to a large extent, on "some" local context information only. For instance, one might assume that for modelling word-related phenomena such as parts-of-speech, only the current word and its immediate neighbours, or only up to two words to the left, are "relevant"; for modelling constituent-related phenomena, only up to two constituents to the left are relevant, etc. (this is called a "Markov assumption", here of the second order, because probabilities depend on two items preceding the current word/constituent: its two neighbours). These assumptions seem justified in the light of the cognitive, iconic Proximity Principle: "Entities that are closer together functionally, conceptually, or cognitively will be placed closer together at the code level, i. e., temporally or spatially" (Givón 1990, 970). Certainly, it is true that there are many linguistic phenomena that involve "long-distance dependencies", such as circumfixes in morphology and agreement or *wh*-movement in syntax – however, the idea is that a "sufficient" amount of data can be modeled successfully by looking at local context only. For instance, Marshall (1983) observes that in general a local context of two words provides enough information to yield "satisfactory results" in the automatic assignment of part-of-speech tags (see section 4.2.4. below).

3.1.4. Supervised and unsupervised learning

I already mentioned that a probabilistic CFG can be trained on the basis of annotated or raw corpus data (for further discussion, see articles 39 and 40). If, due to annotations, the parameters of the probabilistic model are directly observable in the training corpus, we are dealing with "supervised" learning; if the parameters are not observable, it is called "unsupervised" learning.

In the scenarios described above, we measured "similarity" between the observed signal and source signal candidates. To do this, we need corpora that are annotated with the relevant information. A program that should learn to correct spelling mistakes needs a training corpus of real text whose spelling errors are annotated with the corrected version; a PoS tagger, which should learn to automatically assign parts-of-speech to words, needs a training corpus whose words are annotated with PoS tags; and so on. Training on annotated corpora is called "supervised learning", and the task that the program has to learn is called a "classification task": the system classifies each input according to a predefined set of classes (categories).

In unsupervised learning, the system is confronted with unannotated data only. It then tries to group (to cluster) the data in such a way that the clusters are distinguished from each other by characteristic combinations of certain features. What are these features? Suppose, for instance, we want to learn PoS tagging by unsupervised learning. That is, we feed the system with unannotated text and expect it to somehow come up with clusters that (more or less) correspond to linguistic PoS categories. The basic idea is that the system can learn these classes simply by comparing distribution in texts (thus implementing Firth's much-cited slogan "You shall know a word by the company it keeps!", Firth 1957), since we know that parts-of-speech reflect/encode distributional similarity. For instance, all words of the category "noun" show similar distribution and occur in similar contexts: contexts like "the ... is" or "a ... has" are characteristic of nouns. In this scenario, the features that the learning algorithm uses would be the word's neighboring words. The system then starts by assigning random probabilities (instead of probabilities derived from annotated corpora), then iteratively adjusts these values to maximize the overall probability of the entire text. It could thus learn, e. g., that "in" and "on" are members of the same cluster since they share many leftward and rightward neighbors. Of course, the system will not be able to guess the labels of the clusters (like "preposition" or "noun"), nor even the number of clusters that it is supposed to identify.

To sum up, supervised and unsupervised learning are two different approaches to machine learning: a system is fed (trained) with example data and derives generalizations from the data; after the training phase, the system can be applied to new, hitherto unseen data and classify (or cluster) this data according to the generalizations. To date unsupervised systems cannot in general learn highly fine-grained tagsets, and do not yet achieve the performance levels of systems that have been trained on annotated data.

3.1.5. Sparse data

The features that a system makes use of during training are obviously crucial to the success of the enterprise: there is probably no corpus so large that simple features like neighboring words would provide enough evidence for learning algorithms. In fact, there are no corpora so large that all possible kinds of phenomena would really occur in them, or that their frequencies would be high enough for learning algorithms. This is called the *sparse-data problem*. To overcome this problem, more abstract features have to be used, which generalize over relevant properties of the underlying words. For instance, in the clustering task above, the training features might consist of affixes of *n* characters length rather than full word forms. The learning algorithm would then cluster and generalize over strings like "-able" or "-ally". Another kind of generalization can be provided by annotations. No generalization, however, can compensate for the sparse-data problem completely.

Automatic selection of suitable training features is an important topic: the system itself aims at finding the optimal subset of features from among a predefined set; the predefined set often consists of linguistically-motivated features but also includes superficial features like word length or position (in the text).

Another method to cope with the sparse data problem is a technique called *smoothing*: smoothing decreases the probabilities of all seen data, then redistributes the saved amount (probability mass) among the unseen data, by assigning them very small probabilities of equal size.

3.1.6. Corpus annotation

As we have seen, annotated corpora are a vital prerequisite of supervised learning, and, in view of the sparse data problem, of unsupervised learning as well: corpora provide suitable abstraction layers over the training data. Annotated corpora are similarly important for theoretical linguists, and resources of this kind are being successfully exploited by both camps (see article 13). Annotations encode diverse kinds of information, such as part-of-speech (article 24), lemma (article 25), word sense (article 26), syntax trees (article 13), etc. Applied computational linguistics is also interested in broader regions of text, like paragraphs or entire texts. Annotations can thus also encode, e. g., the logical document structure, by marking regions as "header" or "footnote", or the content structure of texts, by labeling regions as "introduction" or "conclusion". A further example is alignment of comparable regions from different (possibly multilingual) sources.

Such corpora are usually first annotated manually, and subsequently exploited for training. Further annotation can then be performed (semi-)automatically, by applying the system that has been trained on the first data. An example bootstrapping approach of this kind is the PoS tagger CLAWS, which is presented in section 4.

Due to the interest in annotated corpora, a lot of work in computational linguistics has been devoted to the development of corpus tools, such as tools to assist the annotator in the annotation, or search tools that support the use of linguistically-motivated search operators like "linear precedence" or "structural dominance", the basic relations of theoretical syntax. In this area, computational and corpus linguistics completely overlap in their interest in tools and methods.

3.1.7. Evaluation

As with linguistic theories, trained systems can be evaluated by testing their performance on new, unseen data, i. e., by evaluating whether the predictions of the theory or system fit the unseen data. Of course, computational linguistics aims at automatic evaluation, since systems nowadays deal with large amounts of data and are supposed to handle unrestricted texts. There are different methods of evaluation. Firstly, a supervised-learning system can be trained and evaluated on the same type of data. In this case, only part of the data (e. g., 90 %) is used for training (and system development), and the remaining data is used as test (= evaluation) data. It is crucial that neither the system nor the system's developer make any use of the test data other than for the very final evaluation, otherwise, the evaluation cannot be used as an indication of how well the system performs on genuinely new data. For testing, the trained system is run on the test data with the annotations stripped off. The output of the system is then compared with the original annotation, and the system's performance is computed in terms of measures such as *precision* and *recall*. Precision measures how accurate the system's predictions are; for instance, if a certain system assigns 10 NP chunks, and 8 of them are correct, then the system's precision equals $8/10 = 0.8$. If the system should actually have marked 20 NP chunks but it found only 8 of them, then its recall equals $8/20 = 0.4$. The measures thus encode both the fact that if this system marks an NP, it is usually correct, and the fact that it misses many of the NPs. A measure combining precision and recall is the *F-score*, the harmonic mean of both; in our example: $2 * (0.8 * 0.4)/(0.8 + 0.4) = 0.533$.

If the performance of several systems is to be compared, a gold standard corpus is usually used as the test corpus (see section 2.3.), such as the Penn Treebank (Marcus/Santorini/Marcinkiewicz 1993). A disadvantage of this type of evaluation is that the outputs of the systems are often not easily mapped onto the gold standard, for example due to theory-dependent discrepancies, with the result that the performance of a system might actually be better than the evaluation outcome suggests. With unsupervised-learning systems especially, the discrepancies between a linguistically-motivated gold standard and the clusters of a system can be enormous.

For certain tasks like Information Retrieval, Machine Translation (see article 56) or Automatic Text Summarization (article 60), no gold standard is immediately available for evaluation, and with these tasks, it is hard to define "the best solution". Depending on the user and the situation, a range of different document selections might count as optimal for a specific Information Retrieval task. Similarly, there are always many alternative ways of translating or summarizing a text, and a gold standard would have to account for all these alternatives. In these cases then, manual inspection of the system output is often deemed necessary, and (subjective) measures like "quality" or "informativeness" are used.

The evaluation methods addressed so far are instances of *intrinsic* evaluation, because the performance of the system is measured by evaluating the system itself. Another method is *extrinsic* evaluation, in which the system is embedded in another application and the overall performance is measured. For instance, in order to evaluate a summarization system, one first asks people to assess the relevance of particular documents to a certain topic, or to answer document-related questions. It can then be measured whether these people perform similarly when confronted with automatically-generated summaries of the documents instead of the full text; if so, the summarization system does a good job.

Evaluation nowadays plays an important role in applied computational linguistics, and researchers who develop new methods or tools are expected to provide the results of standardized evaluations alongside presentation of the system. A series of conferences focusing on evaluation issues has been initiated in the U.S., starting with MUC (Message Understanding Conference, since 1987; see also article 27) and TREC (Text REtrieval Conference, since 1992). These conferences in fact consist of competitions: each year, the conference organizers define a set of specific tasks, such as "for each open class word in the text, determine its sense according to the WordNet (Fellbaum 1998) synsets". They also provide researchers with relevant training data, well in advance of the conference, so that the system developers can tune and adapt their systems to the task and data. During the conference, the organizers present comparative evaluations of the systems that have been "submitted" to the conference.

To conclude this section, let us quickly review the deficiencies of handcrafted systems identified at the beginning of this section and compare them to the outcomes of statistical methods.

(i) Scalability: usually, statistical methods scale up well; if the training data is too small and does not include (enough) instances of certain phenomena, then the training corpus has to be enlarged, but the overall training method can be kept unchanged. (ii) Robustness: input data that does not meet the expectations of the system can be handled by smoothing, which assigns very low probabilities to unseen (and hence unexpected) data. However, scalability as well as robustness of a system are often sensitive to the types and domains of text that the system is confronted with: if the system has been trained on a certain text type and domain, its performance usually suffers if it is fed with texts of other types and domains. (iii) Ambiguity: ambiguities such as "The man saw the woman with the telescope" actually require some sort of semantic, contextual or even world knowledge to resolve. However, useful approximations of such knowledge are provided by statistical methods that take lexical, collocational information into account: certainly the lemma "telescope" co-occurs with the lemma "see" more often than with "man"; similar preferences can be derived from (large) treebanks. (iv) Portability: usually the techniques applied in statistical approaches are language-independent, so portability is not an issue, in principle; the features that are used in training must be carefully selected however; e. g., it makes no sense to use affix-like features in an isolating language like Chinese.

3.2. Statistical computational linguistics and corpora

The previous sections have shown clearly that texts and annotated corpora play a predominant role in application-oriented and statistical computational linguistics. They are a *sine qua non* condition both in training and in evaluating statistical systems. Linguistic information in the form of annotation is usually part of the training data (other kinds of resources, such as WordNet (Fellbaum 1998), often provide additional information). Corpus annotation and corpus tools are thus a concern of both corpus and computational linguistics and annotation-related research, and methods can often be attributed to both disciplines. Similarly, just as in corpus-based linguistic research, techniques in computational linguistics that make use of corpus frequencies are faced with the fact that corpora are finite samples and, to generalize from such samples, statistical inference is needed (see article 36), and methods like n-gram approximations and smoothing have to be applied.

As already mentioned, at opposite extremes of computational and corpus linguistics, the ultimate goals of corpus exploitation do, however, diverge in that the features that turn out to be useful for language models are not seen as interesting *per se* by certain domains of corpus-driven computational linguistics. Indeed, many researchers think it would be most desirable to let the algorithms specify (define) the features fully automatically – and some of these researchers only care about the performance of the system rather than the features used by the system. Unfortunately for them, corpus data is too restricted to provide enough evidence for all sorts of conceivable features that an algorithm might come up with (and, probably, computer capacities also set limits to such an enterprise). Therefore, a set of features has to be predefined that the algorithms can choose from. These sets often contain both linguistic and non-linguistic features and, very often, simple non-linguistic features such as the average word or sentence length, the standard deviation of word/sentence length, the number of periods, question marks, commas, parentheses, etc., are successfully exploited by learning algorithms. These features are certainly reflections of interesting linguistic phenomena, e. g., the number of commas can give hints about the syntactic complexity of the sentences. However, the connection between the features and the linguistic properties is rather loose, so that corpus linguists would not be so interested in such features. They usually select the features that they are interested in very carefully.

In contrast to theory-driven computational linguistics, corpora are mainly used quantitatively. The knowledge encoded in annotations thus becomes part of any language model derived on the basis of the data. However, the development of statistical models can also involve qualitative analysis: for example, during the development phase, researchers will quite carefully inspect the data (and its annotation) in order to identify an optimal set of discriminative features for use in training. Similarly, evaluations are usually accompanied by more or less detailed *error analyses*, to facilitate better understanding of the weaknesses and shortcomings of the system; for this, researchers will scrutinize that part of the test data that most often causes the system to fail.

We now proceed to section 4, which presents a short historical overview of the origins and early development of computational linguistics, focussing on early machine translation and the evolution of part-of-speech tagging. This area neatly illustrates the application of hand-crafted rules in the first generations of PoS taggers, which were later supplemented and finally replaced by corpus-driven techniques.

4. Computational linguistics: A brief history

4.1. The emergence of computational linguistics: First steps in machine translation

The origins of computational linguistics can be traced back (cf., e. g., Hutchins 1997, 1999) to the American mathematician Warren Weaver, director of the Natural Sciences Division of the Rockefeller Foundation, who during World War II became acquainted with the development of electronic calculating machines and the application of statistical techniques in cryptography. In July 1949, he wrote his famous memorandum, "Translation", suggesting that automatic translation might be feasible (Weaver 1949 [1955], see section 3.1.3.). At that time, early experiments in machine translation had already been conducted on the basis of word-by-word translation of scientific abstracts. The results of these translations were of course far from satisfactory – as will be obvious to anyone with basic linguistic knowledge.

In his memorandum, Weaver made four proposals as to how to overcome the problems of word-by-word translation, two of which we address here because they refer to information that can be extracted from raw texts. (The other proposals relate to the "logical character" of language and the existence of language universals.) Weaver's first proposal concerned the disambiguation of word meaning:

> "If one examines the words in a book, one at a time through an opaque mask with a hole in it one word wide, then it is obviously impossible to determine, one at a time, the meaning of words. "Fast" may mean "rapid"; or it may mean "motionless"; and there is no way of telling which. But, if one lengthens the slit in the opaque mask, until one can see not only the central word in question but also say N words on either side, then, if N is large enough one can unambiguously decide the meaning." (Weaver 1949 [1955], 20–21)

The second proposal concerned the application of cryptographic methods (Shannon 1948), based on "frequencies of letters, letter combinations, intervals between letters and letter combinations, letter patterns, etc. ..." (Weaver 1949 [1955], 16).

In both proposals, information is gained from texts and contexts: in the first proposal, a word can be disambiguated by examining its *current* context. The second proposal suggests that such tasks might also be achieved by examining the *usual* context of a word, i. e., the contexts in which the word commonly (most frequently) occurs. The n-gram example in section 3.1.3., disambiguating "big/pig", implements these proposals.

4.2. The emergence of symbolic methods in computational linguistics

Returning to the evolution of machine translation, the next major event after the Weaver memorandum was the publication of the ALPAC report in 1966. At this time, most US funding for computational linguistics had gone into projects on machine translation. In 1964, a committee of experts were asked to judge whether this funding was justified, and in their final report (ALPAC 1966) they came to the devastating conclusion that none of the applications developed so far were satisfactory, and that employing human translators would not only yield better results but would also be cheaper. The report suggested abandoning the funding of scientific research on machine translation, but, instead, encouraged the support of fundamental research in computational linguistics in general. In particular, the ALPAC report recommended the following:

> "(1) basic developmental research in computer methods for handling languages, as tools to help the linguistic scientist discover and state his generalizations, and as tools to help check proposed generalizations against data; and (2) developmental research in methods to allow linguistic scientists to use computers to state in detail the complex kinds of theories (for example, grammars and theories of meaning) they produce; so that the theories can be checked in detail." (ALPAC 1966, vi)

Clearly, the main role of computational linguistics was seen as assisting linguists in the formalization and assessment of linguistic theories, very much as described in section 2. The ALPAC report had a tremendous impact on the course of computational linguistics research in the following years, causing a major change in the focus of research: a shift from mainly statistical methods to rationalist approaches, using symbolic, linguistic features, rather than numerical values, such as probabilities. More emphasis was put on the analysis of the nature of the underlying categories that constitute natural language, and on their interaction, introducing different levels of categories and structures, such as simple part-of-speech (PoS) tags or complex syntactic structures.

In our presentation here, we focus on PoS tagging (see also article 24). We will see that the very first automatic PoS taggers implemented versions of Weaver's first proposal, in the form of context rules. These rules were created manually, but later taggers derived them from annotated corpora, thus implementing Weaver's second proposal (applying his proposal to annotations rather than words). We will further see that people then started to use annotated corpora to evaluate the performance of their system.

4.2.1. The TDAP parser

Probably the first automatic PoS tagger was implemented by Zellig S. Harris in 1958/59 (cf. Jurafsky/Martin 2000, 317). The tagger was designed as a preprocessing component of the TDAP parser ("Transformation and Discourse Analysis Project", Harris 1962;

reimplemented as "Uniparse" by Joshi/Hopely 1998). In this architecture, the tagger first assigns to each word a set of tag candidates, which are looked up in a lexicon. Next, a series of rules are run, eliminating tags that are incompatible with the local context, thus implementing Weaver's first proposal. For instance, the tag "V" (verb) is deleted from the set of candicates if the word is followed by the preposition "of", although a set of designated verbs, such as "think, consist", are exempted from this rule. All in all, the system comprised 14 hand-written rules for PoS disambiguation, which were run in cycles until no further disambiguation was possible.

On top of these PoS-disambiguation rules, another series of cascaded rules was applied to the previously-identified PoS tags, to parse the sentence. Thus, the tagger functioned as a preprocessor for the parser, by introducing a first layer of abstract linguistic categories (parts-of-speech) to encode syntax-relevant information in the text. The parser could recognize basic, non-recursive syntactic constituents, such as base NPs and PPs. The parser rule for NPs, for instance, which was applied from right to left, recognized tag sequences of the form "N A* (T)", using a longest-match strategy. That is, it first allocated the head noun (N), next, arbitrarily many adjectives (A*) preceding that head noun, and, finally, an optional determiner (T). An example TDAP parse is shown in (1) (taken from Bangalore 1997, 21); [ ] indicate NPs, { } verb sequences, and ( ) adjuncts.

(1) [Those papers] {may have been published} (in [a hurry]).

The TDAP parser could not handle unknown words. One of the reasons was certainly the limited computational capacities available at that time, both in terms of storage size and processing speed. At that time implementations could only be fed small amounts of data, so there was no need to process large amounts of free text, featuring unknown words.

4.2.2. The CGC tagger

The next step in the evolution of PoS tagging was made by Klein/Simmons (1963), who developed a tagger in the context of a natural language question-answering system. The tagger, called "CGC" (computational grammar coder), assigned PoS tags based on suffixes rather than words. The algorithm first looked up each word in dictionaries of approximately 400 function words (articles, prepositions, pronouns, ...) and 1,500 irregular forms (nouns, verbs, adjectives). For the remaining words, tag candidates were assigned according to the suffix of each word. For instance, the test "Suffix Test 1" handled English inflection: it marked, e. g., words ending in "-ies", such as "nationalities", as NOUN/VERB (plural noun or 3rd person singular verb). The algorithm would then replace the presumed suffix "-ies" by "y" ("nationality") and perform another test, "Suffix Test 2", on the new form. "Suffix Test 2" included information about derivational suffixes, so that the newly-created word ending in "-ity" would be recognized as NOUN. After running a series of such tests, the individual results were intersected; in our example, "Suffix Test 1" (NOUN/VERB) and "Suffix Test 2" (NOUN) would be resolved to NOUN as the final tag. For remaining ambiguities, or words that had not yet been assigned some tag, the "Context Frame Test" could delete, or add, tag candidates, based on a hand-crafted list of about 500 permissible tag sequences. As with the above disambiguation rules, the Context Frame Test implements Weaver's first proposal.

Besides the fact that the CGC tagger needed small lexica only, it had the enormous advantage of being robust: regardless of the input, the tagger always came up with some analysis. Since it was the first system that was actually able to deal with unrestricted text, it now made sense to evaluate the CGC tagger, by tagging previously-unknown text. Klein/Simmons (1963, 344) report that they tagged "several pages" of a children's encyclopedia, and the tagger "correctly and unambiguously tagged slightly over 90 per cent of the words". This is a surprisingly good result; however, it is not fully clear from their paper whether or not they had used the evaluation data in the development of the system. If so, this would mean that their system was optimized for this data and could not be expected to yield similarly good results for unseen texts. Moreover, since all of the knowledge resources of the system (dictionaries, suffix tests, context frame test) were hand-crafted, it is not obvious whether the system would scale up, i. e., be extensible to large-scale texts.

4.2.3. TAGGIT

Continuing the work of Klein/Simmons, TAGGIT (Greene/Rubin 1971) was the first tagger that was actually applied to large-scale texts, namely the Brown Corpus (Kučera/Francis 1967; see article 20). Like the CGC tagger, TAGGIT used a dictionary, with about 3,000 entries, then applied a suffix list of about 450 strings, followed by a filtering through 3,300 context frame rules (which play the role of the Context Frame Test of the CCG tagger). In comparison to the CGC tagger, TAGGIT used a more fine-grained tagset (82 tags, as opposed to 30 CGC tags), and the suffix list was derived from lexicostatistics of the Brown Corpus. Crucially, and in contrast to the previous approaches, the TAGGIT context rules were acquired semi-automatically: the tagger (without context frame rules) was run on a subset of 900 sentences from the Brown Corpus, and for all ambiguous cases the correct tag was determined manually; a program was then run to produce and order all of the context frame rules that would have been needed for the disambiguation. According to Francis/Kučera (1982), TAGGIT correctly tagged approximately 77 % of the Brown Corpus. In the 1970s, TAGGIT was used to annotate the entire Brown Corpus; any words that did not receive a unique tag from TAGGIT were manually disambiguated. The Brown Corpus is therefore not only the first large-scale *electronic* corpus, and the first *annotated* corpus, but also the first corpus which was ever annotated by an *automatic* tagger.

4.2.4. ... and back to statistics: CLAWS

The Brown Corpus, which consists of texts of American English, was soon complemented by a corresponding corpus of British English, the LOB corpus (Leech/Garside/Atwell 1983). Similarly to the Brown Corpus, the LOB corpus was intended to be enriched by PoS tags. For this task, Leech and colleagues benefited from the annotated Brown Corpus and the TAGGIT program itself. TAGGIT had an accuracy of 77 %; this means that, assuming an average sentence length of 19 words, every sentence would contain, on average, 4 ambiguous tags, which had to be manually post-edited. This heavy load of human intervention was obviously a serious problem for further large-scale annotation. To improve the performance of TAGGIT, the LOB group developed a program that applied statistical methods, known as the "tagging suite", later called "CLAWS" ("Constituent-Likelihood Automatic Word-Tagging System", Marshall 1983, Leech/Garside/Atwell 1983). CLAWS inherited much from TAGGIT: it comprised a lexicon of 7,000 entries, derived from the tagged Brown Corpus, plus a list of 700 suffixes, and rules for certain words. The important innovative aspect of CLAWS was the implementation of the context frame rules, by means of a statistical program called the Tag Selection Program (Marshall 1983). The program used PoS-bigram frequencies computed from the Brown Corpus. Given a sequence of ambiguous tags, which had been assigned in previous steps, the program first enumerated all possible disambiguated tag sequences. Next, it computed the probability of the entire sequence as the normalized product of all of the individual bigram frequencies occurring in the sequence. Finally, the tag sequence that maximized the probability was chosen.

To give an example: suppose lexicon lookup and suffix rules resulted in the following ambiguous tag sequence (example from Marshall 1983):

(2)	Henry	NP
	likes	NNS VBZ
	stews	NNS VBZ
	.	.

This sequence compiles into four disambiguated tag sequences:

(3) a. NP NNS NNS .
b. NP NNS VBZ .
c. NP VBZ NNS .
d. NP VBZ VBZ .

The frequency for each tag bigram ("NP NNS", "NNS NNS", "NNS VBZ", etc.) is computed from the Brown Corpus; e. g., freq(NP NNS) = 17, freq(NNS NNS) = 5, freq(NNS .) = 135, etc. The probability of the complete sequence "NP NNS NNS ." (3a) is then computed as the product of the individual bigrams, i. e., 17 * 5 * 135 = 11,475, divided by the sum of the values for all possible sequences (38,564), resulting in the probability P("NP NNS NNS .") = 0.3.

Marshall observed that, in general, bigram frequencies yielded satisfactory results. In certain cases, however, bigrams could not encode enough information: for instance, in sequences of the form "verb adverb verb" (as in "has recently visited"), the second verb was often incorrectly analyzed as past tense ("VBD") instead of the correct past participle ("VBN"). To extend the context window, selected tag triples (or trigrams) were added to the program to avoid such errors. For certain cases, it proved useful to exploit the probability of a word-tag assignment, derived from the Brown corpus, as an alternative method of calculating the most probable tag. CLAWS has been used to tag the entire LOB Corpus and achieved an overall success rate of between 96% and 97% (which is very close to the performance of today's taggers).

The development we have traced, by looking at part-of-speech tagging algorithms, clearly shows how theory-driven methods were applied to make explicit the information contained in a corpus, through analysis of linguistic expressions in terms of more abstract linguistic categories and structures. This information was exploited again, to train statistical methods, but on the basis of yet more abstract linguistic structures than the original surface-oriented methods. At the same time, the annotated corpus was also used to evaluate the performance of the automatic systems.

5. Conclusion

In summary then, the history of computational linguistics started out with a strong focus on statistics, which were computed on raw, unanalyzed texts, then moved on to research on theoretical frameworks and theory-driven, more linguistically-informed methods (by introducing linguistic categories like PoS tags), and, finally, came back again to the use of statistics on annotated texts. Needless to say not all research in computational linguistics fits exactly into this picture.

As we have seen, computational linguistics started out as an application-focused task, namely automatic translation, and from there evolved into a broad research area, comprising different research methodologies (corpus- and theory-driven), fundamental and application-oriented research, and involving different linguistic disciplines. Interestingly, the methods that were judged to be useless in the beginning were later successfully revived, but combined with more substantial, linguistically-informed, formal models of language. Today, statistical approaches are prevalent in many areas of computational linguistics; e. g., the majority of approaches presented at the most important conferences of computational linguistics – most prominently, the conferences of the Association for Computational Linguistics (ACL, EACL, NAACL), or COLING, the International Conference on Computational Linguistics – are oriented towards statistical language modelling. Why are statistical methods nowadays so successful, in contrast to earlier attempts in machine translation, and in contrast to purely-symbolic approaches? Here are some possible reasons: firstly statistics can these days draw information from annotated texts, which means that the input provides relevant information in a focused, condensed way. Secondly, the amount of data available for training has increased immensely. Thirdly, and in contrast to symbolic approaches, statistical methods are robust and can easily deal with defective input. Martin Kay, one of the pioneers of computational linguistics, adds another reason (e. g., Kay 2004): what was missing from the early approaches, and is indeed still missing today, is world knowledge. For successful language understanding, we need knowledge about objects in the world, about their relations to other objects, about the knowledge of the speaker and hearer about these objects, about their mutual beliefs, etc. Such knowledge is in part encoded in resources like WordNet; however, these resources are rather small and confine themselves to relations that are linguistic in nature, such as lexical relations of synonymy or hypernymy. They do not encode world knowledge, such as "in restaurants, meals are served by waiters". The representation of world knowledge is the domain of Artificial Intelligence. However, the modelling of world knowledge and commonsense reasoning is a difficult and complex task, and as of today there are no large-scale implementations that would allow for practical applications in computational linguistics. Statistical methods can derive world knowledge from corpora to a certain extent. For instance, words like "restaurants, meals, waiters" will often co-occur in narrow contexts, if enough data is available that contains these words, and thus statistics can be used as a "poor man's" substitute for underlying world knowledge. Similarly, ambiguities such as "The man saw the woman with the telescope" can be resolved by collocational information derived from corpora: certainly the lemma "telescope" co-occurs with the lemma "see" more often than with "woman".

These days then, we see an increasing tendency to rely on a mixture of both linguistic knowledge – whether explicitly encoded in the form of rules (e. g., tagger or grammar rules) or implicitly encoded in the form of annotated corpora – and statistical methods.

6. Literature

Abney, Steven (1996), Statistical Methods and Linguistics. In: Klavans/Resnik 1996, 1–26.

Ades, Anthony/Steedman, Mark (1982), On the Order of Words. In: *Linguistics and Philosophy* 4, 517–558.

Ajdukiewicz, Kazimierz (1935), Die syntaktische Konnexität. In: *Studia Philosophica* 1, 1–27.

ALPAC (1966), *Language and Machines: Computers in Translation and Linguistics.* A Report of the Automatic Language Processing Advisory Committee (ALPAC), Division of Behavioral Sciences, National Research Council. Publication 1416. Washington, DC: National Academy of Sciences.

Antworth, Evan L. (1990), PC-KIMMO: A Two-level Processor for Morphological Analysis. (Occasional Publications in Academic Computing 16.) Dallas, TX: Summer Institute of Linguistics.

Baker, James K. (1979), Trainable Grammars for Speech Recognition. In: Wolf, Jared J./Klatt, Dennis H. (eds.), *Speech Communication Papers Presented at the 97th Meeting of the Acoustical Society of America.* MIT, Cambridge, MA, 547–550.

Bangalore, Srinivas (1997), *Complexity of Lexical Descriptions and its Relevance to Partial Parsing.* PhD thesis, University of Pennsylvania, IRCS Report 97–10.

Bar-Hillel, Yehoshua (1953), A Quasi-arithmetical Notation for Syntactic Description. In: *Language* 29, 47–58.

Baum, Leonard E. (1972), An Inequality and Associated Maximization Technique in Statistical Estimation for Probabilistic Functions of Markov Processes. In: *Inequalities* 3, 1–8.

Beesley, Kenneth R./Karttunen, Lauri (2003), *Finite State Morphology.* Stanford, CA: CSLI Publications.

Black, Ezra/Lafferty, John D./Roukos, Salim (1992), Development and Evaluation of a Broad-coverage Probabilistic Grammar of English-language Computer Manuals. In: *Proceedings of the 30th Annual Meeting of the Association for Computational Linguistics.* Newark, DE, 185–192.

Bledsoe, Woodrow W./Browning, Iben (1959), Pattern Recognition and Reading by Machine. In: *Proceedings of the Eastern Joint Computer Conference.* Boston, MA, 225–232.

Bobrow, Daniel G./Fraser, J. Bruce (1968), A Phonological Rule Tester. In: *Communications of the Association for Computing Machinery (ACM)* 11, 766–772.

Bod, Rens (1998), *Beyond Grammar: An Experience-based Theory of Language.* Stanford, CA: CSLI Publications.

Bod, Rens/Hay, Jennifer/Jannedy, Stefanie (eds.) (2003), *Probabilistic Linguistics.* Cambridge, MA: MIT Press.

Bresnan, Joan, (ed.) (1982), *The Mental Representation of Grammatical Relations.* Cambridge, MA: MIT Press.

Carpenter, Bob (1992), *The Logic of Typed Feature Structures.* (Cambridge Tracts in Theoretical Computer Science 32.) Cambridge: Cambridge University Press.

Charniak, Eugene (1993), *Statistical Language Learning.* Cambridge, MA: MIT Press.

Charniak, Eugene (1996), *Tree-bank Grammars*. Technical Report CS-96–02, Department of Computer Science, Brown University.

Chomsky, Noam (1956), Three Models for the Description of Language. In: *IRE Transactions on Information Theory* 2, 113–124.

Chomsky, Noam (1957), *Syntactic Structures*. The Hague: Mouton.

Chomsky, Noam (1959), On Certain Formal Properties of Grammars. In: *Information and Control* 2(2), 137–167.

Chomsky, Noam (1993), A Minimalist Program for Linguistic Theory. In: Hale, Kenneth/Keyser, Samuel Jay (eds.), *The View from Building 20*. Cambridge, MA: MIT Press, 1–52.

Chomsky, Noam/Halle, Morris (1968), *The Sound Pattern of English*. New York: Harper and Row.

Chomsky, Noam/Miller, George A. (1958), Finite State Languages. In: *Information and Control* 1(2), 91–112.

Copestake, Ann (2002), *Implementing Typed Feature Structure Grammars*. Stanford, CA: CSLI Publications.

Copestake, Ann/Flickinger, Dan/Sag, Ivan/Pollard, Carl (2005), Minimal Recursion Semantics: An Introduction. In: *Journal of Research on Language and Computation* 3(2–3), 281–332.

Dalrymple, Mary (ed.) (1999), *Semantics and Syntax in Lexical Functional Grammar: The Resource Logic Approach*. Cambridge, MA: MIT Press.

Davis, K. H./Biddulph R./Balashek, S. (1952), Automatic Recognition of Spoken Digits. In: *Journal of the Acoustical Society of America* 24(6), 637–642.

Dempster, Arthur/Laird, Nan/Rubin, Donald (1977), Maximum Likelihood from Incomplete Data via the EM Algorithm. In: *Journal of the Royal Statistical Society*, Series B, 39(1), 1–38.

Earley, Jay (1970), An Efficient Context-free Parsing Algorithm. In: *Communications of the Association for Computing Machinery* 13(2), 94–102.

Fellbaum, Christiane (ed.) (1998), *WordNet: An Electronic Lexical Database*. Cambridge, MA: MIT Press.

Firth, John Rupert (1957), A Synopsis of Linguistic Theory, 1930–1955. In: *Studies in Linguistic Analysis*. Special volume of the Philological Society. Oxford: Basil Blackwell, 1–32.

Francis, W. Nelson/Kučera, Henry (1982), *Frequency Analysis of English Usage: Lexicon and Grammar*. Boston: Houghton Mifflin.

Givón, Talmy (1990), *Syntax: A Functional-typological Introduction*. Volume II. Amsterdam/Philadelphia: Benjamins.

Greene, Barbara B./Rubin, Gerald M. (1971), *Automatic Grammatical Tagging of English*. Technical report, Department of Linguistics, Brown University, Providence, Rhode Island.

Harris, Zellig S. (1962), *String Analysis of Sentence Structure*. The Hague: Mouton.

Hutchins, John (1997), First Steps in Mechanical Translation. In: Teller, Virginia/Sundheim, Beth (eds.), *Proceedings of MT Summit VI: Past, Present, Future*. San Diego, CA, 14–23.

Hutchins, John (1999), Warren Weaver Memorandum: 50th Anniversary of Machine Translation. In: *MT News International* 8(1) (= issue 22), 5–6.

Johnson, C. Douglas (1972), *Formal Aspects of Phonological Description*. The Hague: Mouton.

Johnson, Mark (1988), *Attribute-value Logic and the Theory of Grammar*. (CSLI Lecture Notes No. 16.) Stanford, CA: CSLI.

Joshi, Aravind K. (1985), Tree Adjoining Grammars: How Much Context-sensitivity is Required to Provide Reasonable Structural Descriptions? In: Dowty, David R./Karttunen, Lauri/Zwicky, Arnold (eds.), *Natural Language Parsing*. Cambridge: Cambridge University Press, 206–250.

Joshi, Aravind K./Hopely, Philip D. (1998), A Parser from Antiquity. In: Kornai, András (ed.), *Extended Finite State Models of Language*. Cambridge: Cambridge University Press, 6–15.

Joshi, Aravind K./Levy, Leon S./Takahashi, Masako (1975), Tree Adjunct Grammars. In: *Journal of the Computer and System Sciences* 10(1), 136–163.

Jurafsky, Daniel S./Martin, James H. (2000), *Speech and Language Processing: An Introduction to Natural Language Processing, Computational Linguistics, and Speech Recognition*. Upper Saddle River, NJ: Prentice Hall.

Kaplan, Abraham (1950), *An Experimental Study of Ambiguity and Context*. Santa Monica: The RAND Corporation. Reprinted in: *Mechanical Translation* 2, 39–46 (1955).

Kaplan, Ronald M./Bresnan, Joan (1982), Lexical-functional Grammar: A Formal System for Grammatical Representation. In: Bresnan 1982, 173–281.

Kaplan, Ronald M./Kay, Martin (1981), Phonological Rules and Finite-state Transducers. Paper presented to the Winter Meeting of the Linguistic Society of America, New York.

Kaplan, Ronald M./Kay, Martin (1994), Regular Models of Phonological Rule Systems. In: *Computational Linguistics* 20(3), 331–378.

Karttunen, Lauri (1983), KIMMO: A General Morphological Processor. In: *Texas Linguistic Forum* 22, 163–186.

Kasami, Tadao (1965), *An Efficient Recognition and Syntax-analysis Algorithm for Context-free Languages*. Scientific report AFCRL-65-758, Air Force Cambridge Research Lab, Bedford, MA.

Kasper, Robert T./Rounds, William C. (1986), A Logical Semantics for Feature Structures. In: *Proceedings of the 24th Annual Meeting of the Association for Computational Linguistics*. Morristown, NJ: ACL, 257–266.

Kay, Martin (2004), Introduction. In: Mitkov, Ruslan (ed.), *The Oxford Handbook of Computational Linguistics*. Oxford: Oxford University Press, xvii-xx.

King, Paul John (1989), A Logical Formalism for Head-driven Phrase Structure Grammar. Ph.D thesis, University of Manchester.

King, Paul John (1994), *An Expanded Logical Formalism for Head-driven Phrase Structure Grammar*. (Arbeitspapiere des SFB 340.) Tübingen: University of Tübingen.

Klavans, Judith L./Resnik, Philip (eds.) (1996), *The Balancing Act: Combining Symbolic and Statistical Approaches to Language*. Cambridge, MA: MIT Press.

Kleene, Stephen Cole (1956), Representations of Events in Nerve Sets and Finite Automata. In: Shannon, Claude E./McCarthy, John (eds.), *Automata Studies*. Princeton, NJ: Princeton University Press, 3–41.

Klein, Sheldon/Simmons, Robert F. (1963), A Computational Approach to Grammatical Coding of English Words. In: *Journal of the ACM* 10(3), 334–347.

Koskenniemi, Kimmo (1983), *Two-level Morphology: A General Computational Model for Word-form Recognition and Production*. (Publication No. 11.) Helsinki: University of Helsinki, Department of General Linguistics.

Kroch, Anthony S./Joshi, Aravind K. (1985), *The Linguistic Relevance of Tree Adjoining Grammar*. Technical Report, MS-CIS-85-16, University of Pennsylvania.

Kučera, Henry/Francis, W. Nelson (1967), *Computational Analysis of Present-day American English*. Providence, RI: Brown University Press.

Leech, Geoffrey/Garside, Roger/Atwell, Eric (1983), *The Automatic Grammatical Tagging of the LOB Corpus*. In: *Newsletter of the International Computer Archive of Modern English (ICAME)* 7, 13–33.

Manning, Christopher D./Schütze, Hinrich (1999), *Foundations of Statistical Natural Language Processing*. Cambridge, MA: MIT Press.

Marcus, Mitchell P./Santorini, Beatrice/Marcinkiewicz, Mary Ann (1993), Building a Large Annotated Corpus of English: The Penn Treebank. In: *Computational Linguistics* 19, 313–330.

Marshall, Ian (1983), Choice of Grammatical Word class without Global Syntactic Analysis: Tagging Words in the LOB Corpus. In: *Computers and the Humanities* 17, 139–150.

Mosteller, Frederick/Wallace, David L. (1964), *Inference and Disputed Authorship: The Federalist*. Reading, MA: Addison-Wesley.

Oswald, Victor A. (1952), Microsemantics. Paper presented at the MIT Conference on Mechanical Translation. Cambridge, MA.

Page, Ellis B. (1967), Statistical and Linguistic Strategies in the Computer Grading of Essays. In: *Proceedings of COLING (Conférence internationale sur le traitement automatique des langues)*. Grenoble, France, 1–13.

Paroubek, Patrick/Schabes, Yves/Joshi, Aravind K. (1992), XTAG – a Graphical Workbench for Developing Tree-adjoining Grammars. In: *Proceedings of the 3rd Conference on Applied Natural Language Processing (ANLP)*. Trento, Italy, 223–230.

Pollard, Carl/Sag, Ivan A. (1994), *Head-driven Phrase Structure Grammar*. Stanford, CA: CSLI, and Chicago: University of Chicago Press.

Rabin, Michael O./Scott Dana (1959), Finite Automata and their Decision Problems. In: *IBM Journal of Research and Development* 3(2), 114–125.

Savitch, Walter J./Bach, Emmon/Marsh, William/Safran-Naveh, Gila (eds.) (1987), *The Formal Complexity of Natural Language*. (Studies in Linguistics and Philosophy 33.) Dordrecht: Reidel.

Shannon, Claude E. (1948), A Mathematical Theory of Communication. In: *Bell System Technical Journal* 27, 379–423 and 623–656.

Stabler, Edward (1997), Derivational Minimalism. In: Retore, Christian (ed.), *Logical Aspects of Computational Linguistics, LACL'96*. Berlin: Springer, 68–95.

Stede, Manfred (1992), The Search for Robustness in Natural Language Understanding. In: *Artificial Intelligence Review* 6, 383–414.

Steedman, Mark (1985), Dependency and Coordination in the Grammar of Dutch and English. In: *Language* 61, 523–568.

Steedman, Mark (1996), *Surface Structure and Interpretation*. (Linguistic Inquiry Monograph No. 30.) Cambridge, MA: MIT Press.

Steedman, Mark (2000), *The Syntactic Process*. Cambridge, MA: MIT Press.

Tesnière, Lucien (1959), *Eléments de syntaxe structurale*. Paris: Éditions Klincksieck.

Viterbi, Andrew J. (1967), Error Bounds for Convolutional Codes and an Asymptotically Optimum Decoding Algorithm. In: *IEEE Transactions on Information Theory* 13(2), 260–269.

Weaver, Warren (1949 [1955]), *Translation*. Reprinted in: Locke, William Nash/Booth, Andrew Donald (eds.), *Machine Translation of Languages: Fourteen Essays*. New York: Wiley, 15–23.

Younger, Daniel H. (1967), Recognition and Parsing of Context-free Languages in Time n^3. In: *Information and Control* 10(2), 189–208.

van Zaanen, Menno (2000), ABL: Alignment-based Learning. In: *Proceedings of the 18th Conference on Computational Linguistics*, Volume 2. Saarbrücken, Germany, 961–967.

Stefanie Dipper, Bochum (Germany)

6. Corpus linguistics and sociolinguistics

1. Introduction

Sociolinguistics and corpus linguistics share a natural affinity. There is a sense in which one could say that sociolinguistics is corpus linguistics, at least with respect to one prominent branch of sociolinguistics devoted to the study of spoken and written language in context. One goal of this kind of sociolinguistics is to compile a corpus of data suitable for quantitative analysis of linguistic and social variables, such as social class, gender, region, ethnicity, style, and age. Although sociolinguistics began before the use of electronic corpora and computers became widespread, today new technologies assist and enhance methods linguists and philologists have used for a very long time. Like many of the great grammarians, lexicographers, and dialectologists, the earliest sociolinguists worked from manually compiled and analyzed corpora (cf. article 1). Most of these consist of tape recordings and transcriptions (often not in electronic form) that are not in the public domain.

Despite the fact that most contemporary sociolinguists use computers to analyze the data they collect, and store it in electronic databases, most still design and compile their own corpora based on the particular variables under investigation and annotated for their own specific purposes (cf. articles 9 and 53) rather than rely on commercially available electronic corpora. There are a variety of reasons for this. Perhaps the main one is the emphasis within corpus linguistics on standard written forms of language. Texts found within most corpora do not contain the kind of material of greatest interest to most sociolinguists, namely, casual everyday speech, often from non-standard language varieties. Large corpora of spontaneously occurring spoken data are still expensive and time-consuming to compile due to problems of transcription and input (cf. articles 11 and 47).

This article provides examples of how one can use existing corpora to investigate some common social variables based primarily on English because it is the language for which the largest collections of data exist, much of it acquired for academic, industrial or commercial research (cf. article 20). However, resources for corpus-based sociolinguistic research on other large European languages such as German, French, Spanish, and smaller ones such as Dutch are steadily increasing. The Institute for German language in Mannheim houses 38 spoken corpora in its Archive for spoken German (Archiv für Gesprochenes Deutsch or AGD) (http://www.ids-mannheim.de/ksgd/agd/). The Meertens Institute in Amsterdam has a unit devoted to variationist studies (http://www.meertens.knaw.nl/meertensnet/wdb.php?url=/variatielinguistiek/), and the Institute for Dutch lexicology has a number of electronic corpora (http://www.inl.nl). The Spanish Royal Academy of Language makes available on-line its *Diccionario de la Lengua Española* (Dictionary of the Spanish Language) and the *Banco de datos del español* (Spanish language database) (http://www.rae.es). Pusch (2002) provides an overview of Romance language corpora (cf. article 21 for other languages). An increasing number of parallel corpora also present opportunities for sociolinguistic research (cf. article 16). The Europarl Corpus of proceedings from the European Parliament features 11 languages (French, Italian, Spanish, Portuguese, English, Dutch, German, Danish, Swedish, Greek and Finnish). The Nordic Teenage Language Project (UNO), a network of researchers investigating the language of teenagers, have compiled or made use of corpora in various Nordic languages (http://www.uib.no/uno/) Hasund's (2002) comparison of the discourse markers *like* and *liksom* among English and Norwegian teenagers relied on a Norwegian and English corpus of teenage language (see also Hasund/Stenström 2005).

The principal social dimensions sociolinguists have been concerned with are social class, age, ethnicity, sex, and style. Of these, social class has been one of the most researched. Most sociolinguists take as their starting point the notion that social stratification will be an important dimension in accounting for linguistic variation in all speech communities. Most studies have employed what can be referred to as quantitative variationist methodology (sometimes also called the quantitative paradigm or variation theory) to reveal and analyze sociolinguistic patterns, i. e. correlations between variable features of the kind usually examined in sociolinguistic studies of urban speech communities, such as post-vocalic /r/ in New York City (Labov 1966), initial /h/ in Norwich (Trudgill 1974), etc., and external social factors (e. g. social class, age, ethnicity, sex, network, and style). A major finding of urban sociolinguistic work is that differences among social dialects are quantitative and not qualitative. The usual sorts of queries/searches routinely performed on corpora produce various kinds of data that can be analyzed using sociolinguistic methods (Milroy/Gordon 2003). The occurrence of words, word forms, constructions, etc. can all be correlated with the usual social variables investigated by sociolinguists whenever corpora provide reliable information on the social categories of users. A number of studies of discourse phenomena ranging from intonation, pragmatic particles and discourse markers to conversational routines have been carried out using corpora (see Aijmer 2002; Aijmer/Stenström 2004; cf. article 49).

2. Corpora of particular interest to sociolinguists

The following list gives no more than a brief hint at some of the currently available corpora that might be of interest to sociolinguists, some of which will be used to illustrate the discussion of variables in this article (cf. articles 10, 11 and 20 for fuller lists).

2.1. The British National Corpus (BNC)

100 million words of written (90 %) and spoken (10 %) British English from the 1990s (http://www.natcorp.ox.ac.uk/). The corpus is annotated with metadata pertaining to demographic variables such as age, gender and social class, and textual features such as register, publication medium and domain. The spoken part includes informal, unscripted conversation by speakers of different ages, regions, and social classes, as well as spoken language from formal meetings, radio shows, phone-ins, and other situations (see Aston/Burnard 1998, chapter 6 for examples of how to use the corpora for analyzing social variables). The spoken texts in the corpus include both men and women from three geographic regions: south, midland, north. The speakers are further classified according to age (0–14; 15–24; 25–34; 35–44; 45–59; 60+) and social class. The BNC categorizes social class membership into four groups based on occupation, a commonly used indicator of socio-economic status. From highest to lowest ranked, these are: AB (top or middle management, administrative or professional), C1 (junior management, supervisory or clerical), C2 (skilled manual), DE (semi-skilled and unskilled manual). Unfortunately, this demographic information is not given for all speakers in all texts but is unevenly distributed across the corpus. This limits the use that can be made of the corpus and the conclusions that can be drawn about social variables. Only about 20 % of the material in the spoken component is coded for the speaker's social class and education. The only speakers for whom the social class coding can be trusted are the recruited

respondents who were asked to record conversations. Similarly, one must be careful when using the corpus to look at regional variation because the corpus codes the region where the recording was made, not the variety used by the speakers.

2.2. Brown Corpus of American English (Brown)

1 million words of written American English from 1961. This corpus provided a model for a set of parallel corpora (LOB, Frown and FLOB), all of which contain a million words and are constructed in parallel fashion so that they contain 500 word samples from 15 genres of written text. Brown and LOB (Lancaster-Oslo/Bergen Corpus of British English) represent American and British English in 1961 (http://khnt.hit.uib.no/icame/manuals/lob/index.htm), while Frown (Freiburg Brown Corpus of American English) and FLOB (Freiburg LOB Corpus of British English) were compiled at the University of Freiburg as matching databases representing the state of the two varieties in 1992 and 1991 respectively. These and other widely used corpora are distributed by the International Computer Archive of Medieval and Modern English (ICAME). Further information and on-line versions of the manuals are available at http://nora.hd.uib.no/icame.html.

2.3. Australian Corpus of English (ACE)

1 million words of written Australian English compiled in 1986 as a parallel corpus to Brown.

2.4. Wellington Corpus of Written and Spoken New Zealand English (WCNZE)

1 million words of spoken and written New Zealand English compiled in 1986–1990 as a parallel corpus to LOB.

2.5. London-Lund Corpus of Spoken English (LLC)

1 million words comprising 200 samples of 5000 words of spoken and written English collected from 1959 to 1988. The spoken texts contain both dialogue and monologue. The written texts include not only printed and manuscript material but also examples of English read aloud, as in broadcast news and scripted speeches.

2.6. International Corpus of English (ICE)

In 1990 the International Corpus of English began to assemble parallel one million word corpora of spoken and written material from 20 major varieties of English spoken around the world. Each corpus follows a standard design and grammatical annotation, thus permitting the examination of regional variation (http://www.ucl.ac.uk/english-usage/ice/).

2.7. American National Corpus (ANC)

In progress, 100 million words of spoken and written American English parallel to BNC (http://americannationalcorpus.org/).

2.8. Corpus of Spoken, Professional American-English (CSPA)

Short conversational interchanges recorded between 1994 and 1998 from ca. 400 speakers centered on professional activities broadly tied to academics and politics, including academic politics (http://www.athel.com/cpsa.html).

2.9. Corpus of London Teenage Language (COLT)

500,000 words of spontaneous conversations between 13 to 17 year old boys and girls from socially different school districts in London (http://torvald.aksis.uib.no/colt/). In 1994–95 the conversations were transcribed orthographically, and tagged for word-classes by a team at Lancaster University. In this form, COLT became part of BNC.

3. Investigating sociolinguistic variables using corpora

Variationist methodology came into prominence in the late 1960s primarily to fill perceived gaps in traditional studies of variability which for the most part were concerned with regional variation. Dialectologists in the 19th and early 20th centuries concentrated their efforts on documenting the rural dialects which they believed would soon disappear. A primary concern was to map the geographical distribution across regions of forms that were most often different words for the same thing, e. g. *dragon fly* v. *darning needle*; some phonological and grammatical features were also included. The results often took many years to appear in print and were generally displayed in linguistic atlases of maps showing the geographical boundaries between users of different forms (cf. articles 1 and 53). More recently, some of these projects have made some of their material available in electronic form for downloading and/or on-line searches. The website for the Linguistic Atlas Projects contains an overview of these projects and the materials collected in various regions of the United States (http://hyde.park.uga.edu/). In addition to regional variation, it is possible to use some of the data to analyze other kinds of variation of interest to sociolinguists. The informants for the various surveys were classified according to social criteria (degree of formal education, occupation, age, sex).

By contrast, sociolinguists turned their attention to the language of cities, where an increasing proportion of the world's population lives in modern times. Aided by the mass-production of recording equipment, sociolinguists collected spoken data that were transcribed and analyzed, paying attention to easily quantifiable linguistic features, e. g. post-vocalic /r/ in words such as *cart*, etc. Most of the variables studied in detail have tended to be phonological, and to a lesser extent grammatical, although in principle any instance of variation amenable to quantitative study can be analyzed in similar fashion. Counting variants of different kinds in tape-recorded interviews and comparing their incidence across different groups of speakers revealed that when variation in the speech of and between individuals was viewed against the background of the community as a whole, it was not random, but rather conditioned by social factors such as social class, age, sex and style in predictable ways. Thus, while idiolects (or the speech of individuals) considered in isolation might seem randomly variable, the speech community as a whole behaved regularly. Using these methods, one could predict, for example, that a person of a particular social class, age, sex, etc. would pronounce post-vocalic /r/ a certain percent of the time in certain situations. Some variables are unique to particular communities, while others are shared across the English-speaking world. The replication of a number of sociolinguistic patterns across many communities permits some generalizations about the relationship between linguistic variables and society (Romaine 2000).

3.1. Region

The so-called 'first generation' corpora (Brown, LOB etc.) along with ICE and BNC are ideal for comparing features across different varieties of English. They provide a rich source of information on lexical, spelling and grammatical differences among the major regional varieties of English. Table 6.1 compares the use of *film* vs. *movie* and *journey* vs. *trip* in Brown, Frown, LOB and FLOB. Results are given in terms of number of hits as well as in the form of a ratio calculated by dividing the number of hits for *movie/trip* by the number of hits for *film/journey* respectively. A ratio of more than 1.00 indicates that *film/trip* are more common than *movie/journey,* and a ratio of less than 1, that *film/journey* are more common.

The corpus results do not bear out the common assumption that *movie* is preferred over *film* in American English, either in 1961 (Brown) or 1991 (Frown). Although the rate of occurrence of *movie* increases in relation to that of *film* in Frown, *film* is still the

Tab. 6.1: Comparison of *film/movie* and *journey/trip* in four corpora

	N of hits			N of hits		
Corpus	*film*	*movie*	Ratio	*journey*	*trip*	Ratio
Brown	126	67	.53	30	109	3.63
Frown	178	119	.67	3.4	85	2.5
LOB	243	7	.03	69	45	.65
FLOB	119	41	.34	66	74	1.12

preferred term in both British and American English. Comparing LOB and FLOB, however, shows that *movie* is increasing at the expense of *film*. In the case of *journey/trip*, however, American usage favors *trip* in both Brown and Frown, while British English favors journey in LOB, but not FLOB, where *trip* is more common than *journey*. Data from BNC, however, suggest that *trip* is slightly favored over *journey* only in spoken but not written English. There are 236 hits for *journey* and 256 for *trip* in the spoken component. The word *film* is preferred over *movie* in both the spoken and written components.

The comparisons can be extended by considering ACE and WCNZE. In some instances Australian usage aligns itself with the norms of American English, preferring, for example, *movie* over *film* and *trip* over *journey*, but in other cases, with that of British English, favoring, for example, *holiday* over *vacation*. The use of *movie* is less common in New Zealand than Australia, while the preference for *trip* over *journey* is in line with the Australian tendency towards the American variant *trip*, as is the greater use of *holiday* over *vacation*. Australian English is also like American English in disfavoring the use of the suffix *-st* on *while* and *among*. With respect to spelling, there are also divergent tendencies, with <or> on the increase in Australian English, e. g. *color*. By mid-1985 six of Australia's major urban newspapers used the American <or> spellings, but when it comes to words with <re> instead of <er>, e. g. *theatre*, both Australia and New Zealand favor the British variant. Although most Australians have learned at school to take an anti-American stance in language, especially in spelling, it is not necessarily the case that Australian English is becoming unilaterally more Americanized (Peters 1998).

Similarly, in Britain departures from British spelling norms in favor of American ones have not been welcomed in all quarters and have attracted attention. When in 2000 it was suggested that Britain should adopt internationally standardized spellings of scientific terms, such as *fetus* and *sulfate* (instead of *foetus* and *sulphate*), there were complaints. Looking at BNC, it is evident that the American spelling *fetus*, has already made considerable inroads into written British English. Just over one third (36 %) of the 353 examples follow the American spelling, and 64 % use the traditional British spelling *foetus*. The trend for *sulphate/sulfate*, however, runs in favor of the British spelling *sulphate*; only 3 % of the 410 occurrences of the word use the American spelling *sulfate*. In the case of other words such as *globalization/globalisation*, the American spelling predominates in 63 % of the 64 occurrences, and the British variant, *globalisation* is in the minority with 37 %.

Indeed, the very occurrence of this term can be used as an index of the spread of a new term and the process of globalization in world English. It is a truism that the history of words offers a window into the history of a language. A closer examination of the history of the word *globalization* and its spread is itself instructive of the forces that many now seek to understand. Corpora can be used to show how linguistic changes having their origin in social and cultural developments can be manifested in vocabulary. Neither Brown nor Frown contains any occurrences of the word; nor does LOB. FLOB contains only one example, but the BNC has 64.

These findings are interesting in the light of Giddens's (2000, 25) comment that the term *globalization* came seemingly from nowhere and now it is everywhere. Although the word *global* is over 400 years old, the terms *globalization* and *globalize* began to be used in the 1960s, and spread thereafter, especially in 1980s onwards. This is reflected in the corpus findings. It is also sometimes said that globalization is moving the world inexorably toward greater homogeneity in the direction of American language and culture, and that the normative basis for World English has shifted from British to American English. In this view the global village has become a homogenized McWorld, where everyone speaks English, drinks Coke, and eats at McDonalds. Although this is clearly an exaggerated view of the extent of (American) English influence, there is little evidence of a wholesale shift towards American norms. Global English is still best described as a 'pluricentric' language, i. e. one whose norms are focused in different local centers, capitals, centers of economy, publishing, education and political power.

3.2. Social class

In the mid 1950s Ross (1980) suggested that certain lexical and phonological differences in English could be classified as U (upper class) or non-U (lower class), e. g. *serviette* (non-U) vs. *table-napkin* (U), to take what was then one of the best known of all linguistic class-indicators of England. Other notable pairs he mentioned were *have one's bath* (U) vs. *take a bath* (non-U), *writing paper* vs. *note paper* (non-U), *pudding* (U) vs. *sweet* (non-U), or what would be called *dessert* in the US. Such claims can be tested against corpora such as BNC that include information about the social status of speakers. Compare the results in Table 6.2 for *settee/couch/sofa* and *lounge/living room/sitting room*. For each term, the number is bold-faced for the social group showing the highest usage.

Tab. 6.2: Social distribution of selected lexical items in BNC: hits/million words for *settee/sofa/couch* and *lounge/living room/sitting room*

Social class	*settee*	*sofa*	*couch*	*lounge*	living room	sitting room
AB	12.32	2.7	0	11.09	12.32	**13.55**
C1	18.02	2.57	5.5	32.18	9.01	9.01
C2	13.98	**8.39**	**8.39**	**48.93**	13.98	5.59
DE	**31.21**	4.46	0	8.92	**22.9**	8.92

p is less than or equal to 0.01; distribution is significant for *settee/sofa/couch*.
p is less than or equal to 0.001; distribution is significant for *lounge/living room/sitting room*.

Looking first at variation in terms for the item of furniture, all four social groups use both *settee* and *sofa*; the term *couch* does not occur for the highest and lowest social group. The lowest social group strongly favors the term *settee*; the highest social group uses that term least. The term *sofa* occurs most frequently among class C2 followed by DE, but is less often used by two highest classes AB and C1. As for the room where this item of furniture is found, all social groups use all three terms. The middle and lower middle classes (C1 and C2), however, are the greatest users of the term *lounge*. The highest group leads in the use of the term *sitting room*, and the lowest in the use of the term *living room*. Thus, the upper class displays a tendency to sit in the sitting room, while the working class is more likely to sit on a settee in the living room, and the middle class to sit either on a sofa or couch in the lounge.

3.3. Gender

In a pioneering work on the relationship between language and gender, Lakoff (1975) suggested that women made use of a larger color vocabulary than men. In particular, she noted that women were more likely to use non-basic color terms such as *mauve*, *beige*, etc. as well as more secondary color terms such as *sky blue*, *pale green*, *hot pink*, etc. She also said that women used a different set of evaluative adjectives she called 'empty adjectives' more frequently than men, including words such as *lovely*, *divine*, *adorable*, *sweet*, *cute*, etc. Her claims can readily be tested with corpora such as BNC that include information on the sex of the speaker/author. Table 6.3 shows the distribution of the color terms *mauve*, *beige*, *pink*, *maroon* and the use of the descriptive adjective *pale* followed by a color term, along with three evaluative adjectives (*lovely*, *nice* and *cute*). The results for color words are not statistically significant, probably because the number of occurrences is small; *mauve*, for instance occurred only 13 times, and *beige* only 9. Yet the general trends are still in line with Lakoff's suggestions. Women used *mauve* 11 times and men only 2. For *beige*, there were 18 occurrences split equally between men and women. The results for the use of the three adjectives are significant. Indeed, *lovely* and *nice* are among the 25 most frequently used words by women in the spoken BNC (Rayson/Leech/Hodges 1997). The word *adorable*, however, occurred only three times in the spoken corpus and all users were male.

Tab. 6.3: Frequency per million words of selected color terms and evaluative adjectives in spoken component of British National Corpus

	Female	Male
mauve	3.37	.41
beige	2.75	1.83
pink	59.68	25.61
maroon	3.37	.61
pale + color term	4.28	2.44
lovely	437.04	135.15
nice	998.33	445.87
cute	10.1	2.85

p is less than or equal to 0.01; distribution is significant for evaluative adjectives.

Lakoff, along with a number of researchers, suggested that women used more standard forms and that they avoided 'bad' and 'taboo' expressions. The swear words *fuck* and *fucking* are among the most 25 most frequent words used by men in the spoken component of the BNC (Rayson/Leech/Hodges 1997). Stenström (1991) found that in LLC women used proportionally more weaker expletives such as *heavens* than men, as indicated in Table 6.4.

Because situation is an important variable, it is crucial to compare only data collected in comparable communicative contexts, e. g. mixed sex groups vs. single sex groups, etc.

Tab. 6.4: Some swear words used by men and women in the London-Lund Corpus (adapted from Stenström 1991)

	Female	Male
heavens	7.35	4.67
damn	36.73	29.02
blimey	22.04	10.57
fuck	32.75	68.28

p is less than or equal to 0.001; distribution is significant.

(cf. articles 9 and 49). Talk between men in a pub, women in a kitchen, between a male interviewer and female interviewee, or among men watching a football match on TV represent instances of situations that may affect amount and type of data obtained.

3.4. Style

Style is a notoriously difficult term to define, but at its simplest, variation between genres, text types, etc. can be thought of as kinds of stylistic differences. One of the first observations made by early corpus linguists working with the first generation of computerized corpora was that syntactic constructions such as the passive were unevenly distributed across text types. Svartvik (1966, 155) found that their rate of occurrence in the Survey of English Usage comprising the written component of LLC ranged from a low of 3.2/1,000 words in advertisements to a high of 23.1/1,000 words in scientific texts. In the corpus as a whole they occurred at a rate of 11.3/1,000 words, as shown in Table 6.5.

Tab. 6.5: Passives per 1,000 words in the Survey of English Usage (adapted from Svartvik 1966, 155, Table 7.4)

Genre	Hits/1,000 words
Science	23.1
News	15.8
Arts	12.7
Speech	9.2
Sports	9.0
Novels	8.2
Plays	5.3
Advertising	3.2
Whole Corpus	11.3

Many studies have investigated differences between speech and writing, examining features such as negation, contraction, etc. Verb contraction is more frequent in speech than in writing, as can be seen in Table 6.6 comparing the frequency of contraction of *be* and *have* in written and spoken components of the BNC. The ratio is calculated by dividing the number of contracted forms by the number of uncontracted forms. A ratio of more than 1.00 indicates that the contracted form is more common than the uncontracted form. In the spoken texts all the ratios are higher than those for writing; three (*'m*, *'s*, *'s*) exceed 1.00. Even in the written texts the contracted first person singular form *I'm* for *I am* is more common than the uncontracted form.

Tab. 6.6: Ratio of contracted and uncontracted forms in the written and spoken components of the BNC (adapted from Leech/Rayson/Wilson 2001, 130)

	Speech			Writing		
	contracted	uncontracted	ratio	contracted	uncontracted	Ratio
'm:am	2512	252	9.97	443	250	1.77
're:are	4255	4663	.91	439	4712	.09
's:is	15818	10164	1.56	1729	1729	.17
'd:had	575	2835	.20	284	4639	.06
's:has	1844	1598	1.15	119	2708	.04
've:have	4637	7488	.62	440	4416	.10

Other more sophisticated analyses of vocabulary are possible, but as these go beyond simple word/phrase searches, they require more effort (see articles 38 and 50). One such study examined the density of Latinate diction as a stylistic index in the collected speeches, letters and internal monologues of the characters in Jane Austen's novels. The study required assembling an electronic corpus of Austen's work (relying on the Oxford Electronic Text Library Edition of *The Complete Works of Jane Austen*). Such corpora of the texts of individual authors can nowadays be easily assembled form a variety of text banks, databases and archives. The study also required a way of identifying and counting words of Latinate origin, e. g. *artist*, *deception*, etc. This was done by means of a program called JALATIN devised by the researchers, which revealed that overall just over 36% of the words used by Austen were of Latinate origin. There was, however, considerable variation among and within the novels.

Compare these two extracts from Austen's *Mansfield Park* (1814) contrasting the manor at Mansfield belonging to Fanny Price's uncle with her parents' house in Portsmouth.

- The elegance, propriety, regularity, harmony,- and perhaps, above all, the peace and tranquillity of Mansfield, were brought to her remembrance every hour of the day, by the prevalence of everything opposite to them here.
- Every body was noisy, every noise was loud. Whatever was wanted, was halloo'd for, and the servants halloo'd out their excuses from the kitchen. The doors were in constant banging, the stairs were never at rest, nothing was done without a clatter.

When Fanny Price is exiled to Portsmouth to live with her parents in a squalid noisy house, she pines there for her uncle's elegant manor. The Latinate words convey the stately atmosphere of the house, while the Germanic words suggest the chaos and squalor prevailing in her parents' home.

The study actually followed a long tradition of similar stylistic investigations done by earlier scholars who did not have the advantage of modern methods relying on computers and corpora of electronic texts, but who nevertheless examined the proportion of Germanic vs. Romance vocabulary used by influential authors such as Chaucer, who introduced many French words in his works. English has a long tradition of extending its lexical resources through borrowing words from other languages, particularly Latin and French. Historians of English have discussed the impact of these borrowings on English, both in terms of their tendency to cluster in certain semantic domains, e. g. science and technology, as well as in terms of the addition of new roots and their derivational system (cf. *happiness* and *felicity*). As soon as French and Latin words were borrowed, native prefixes and suffixes were added to them, and when a sufficient number of foreign words were borrowed for their word formation patterns to be transparent and isolable, they could be used productively with both native and newly borrowed foreign words. Pairs such *dine/eat*, *commence/begin,* etc. illustrate social and stylistic stratification. The native Germanic members of these doublets are in everyday use, while the borrowings represent a higher, more refined stylistic level. Such choices can then be used by speakers/writers as stylistic resources. Authors such as Chaucer experimented with competing forms such as *frailness* vs. *frailty, stableness/stability/mutability,* etc.

Austen's novel *Pride and Prejudice* (1813) features a range of characters, who differ in the extent to which they use Latinate vocabulary. Table 6.7 shows the percentage of Latinate vocabulary used by the narrator and three women in the Bennett family. Mary, for instance, is bookish and pretentious and, not surprisingly, has the highest index of Latinate words, or for that matter of any character in any Austen novel. Lydia and Kitty Bennett, on the other hand, do not speak like well-educated characters and are at the opposite end of the stylistic and social spectrum. A low index of Latinate vocabulary is an index of low educational level, or low birth or both.

Tab. 6.7: Percentage of Latinate words used by characters in Austen's *Pride and Prejudice* (adapted from DeForest/Johnson 2000, 25)

Character	% of Latinate words
Mary Bennett	33.8
Lydia Bennett	6.3
Kitty Bennett	4.3
Narrator	25.4
All females	19.3

3.5. Age

The age distribution of a variable may be an important clue to on-going change in a community (see article 52). Some patterns of 'age grading' (i. e. variation correlated to age) may reflect a passing fad (e. g. teenage slang), or be repeated anew in each generation (e. g. swearing by young males) and not lead to long-term change in the community as a whole (see Stenström/Andersen/Hasund 2002). In other cases, however, age grading or change in apparent time may lead to change in real time (Bauer 2002). Once new variants spread, they often follow predictable paths through social and linguistic structures, as new members adopt an innovation.

As a simple example of age-grading, take the distribution of the word *wireless* 'radio' in the spoken component of the BNC shown in Table 6.8. It is used only by those over 25, and even then only infrequently (N = 14) at a rate of 2.37 times per million words. It is most frequent in the oldest age group comprising those over 60. The more frequent term for all age groups is *radio*, especially in the younger age groups. The slang term *tranny* for 'transistor radio' is nearly obsolete, occurring only 11 times in the whole corpus of 100 million words. The BNC is not recent enough to show many instances of the new meaning of *wireless* that has arisen to refer to a variety of new wireless mobile communication devices such as wireless internet service, etc. To document such new uses it would be profitable to use the Web itself as a corpus, but that method would not be able to uncover the age and social distribution of the users (see article 18).

Tab. 6.8: Occurrence of *radio* and *wireless* by age group in spoken component of the BNC

Age	Number of hits		Hits/million words	
	radio	*wireless*	*radio*	*wireless*
60+	57	7	50.47	6.2
45–59	87	2	53.55	1.23
35–44	94	2	88.09	1.87
25–34	58	3	52.19	2.7
15–24	23	0	38.97	0
0–14	34	0	88.72	0

p is less than or equal to 0.05; distribution is significant.

Table 6.9 shows a similar age-graded distribution for *movie.* As suggested in section 3.1., *movie* may be increasing at the expense of *film.* The most frequent users are under 25, and the word is especially common among the youngest age group of those 14 and under. To confirm this trend, one would need to monitor usage over the coming years.

Another word that shows an age graded distribution is *bollocks.* Indeed, it is one of the ten most frequently used 'dirty' words in COLT, with differences between boys (58 instances) and girls (32 instances) (Stenström/Andersen/Hasund 2002, 32). Rayson/Leech/Hodges (1997) also found that *fucking/fuck* were among the words more frequently used by those under 35 in the spoken component of BNC.

One can also use parallel corpora collected at different points in time such as Brown/Frown and LOB/FLOB to investigate change in real time (cf. article 52). Holmes (1999) compared these four corpora with the written component of the Wellington Corpus of New Zealand English to investigate Lakoff's (1975) claim that the term *lady* (which she considered a patronizing, trivializing, non-sexual, polite euphemism for *woman*), was in the process of replacing *woman.* Holmes found that references to adult females had more

Tab. 6.9: Distribution of *movie* by age in spoken component of the BNC

Age group	Hits/million words
0–14	33.92
15–24	8.47
25–34	4.5
35–44	4.69
45–59	3.08
60+	3.54

Tab. 6.10: Distribution of *bollocks* by age in the spoken component of the BNC

Age group	Hits/million words
0–14	60.02
15–24	91.48
25–34	13.5
35–44	3.75
45–59	1.85
60+	3.54

than doubled overall, but this increase was not due to a rise in the use of the term *lady/ ladies*, whose number of occurrences had barely altered over the 30 years between the appearance of Brown/LOB and Frown/FLOB.

4. Correlations among variables and the social embedding of variation and change

Some of the same linguistic features figure in patterns of both regional and social dialect differentiation at the same time as they also display correlations with other social factors. Generally speaking, the use of non-standard forms increases, the less formal the style and the lower one's social status. All groups recognize the overt greater prestige of standard speech and shift towards it in more formal styles. Another sociolinguistic pattern is that women, regardless of other social characteristics such as class, age, etc., tend to use more standard forms than men.

Berglund (1999) found evidence of such classic sociolinguistic patterns in her study of variation in the BNC between the phonologically condensed form *gonna* and the full form *going to*. That is, the form *gonna* was more frequent in the spoken component, in informal contexts, among the youngest two age groups, and men. Table 6.11 shows the

Tab. 6.11: Percent of *gonna* in the BNC for men and women in formal and informal style (adapted from Berglund 1999)

Style	Men	Women
Informal	81	70
Formal	45	26

interaction between style and gender; *gonna* is most frequently used in male informal speech and least in female formal speech.

Similar patterns can be found for other variables in BNC. McEnery/Xiao (2004) examined the occurrence of one common swear word (and its morphological variants) within and across all the spoken and written registers in BNC. They found the use of the word *fuck* to be more frequent in speech than writing, among men than women, among young people and teenagers more than among those over 35, and among the two lower social classes. In addition, their findings for the spoken component suggest that swearing may be increasing among women compared to Stenström's (1991) finding for LLC (see Table 6.4).

5. Limitations of corpora for sociolinguistic research

Although the availability of public corpora greatly increases the range of variables that can be studied in English and other languages, corpora also severely limit the phenomena that can be investigated to those that are most easily retrievable (cf. article 33). There are two reasons why many large public corpora are not well suited to the kinds of analysis undertaken by sociolinguists. Firstly, most corpora are composed primarily of written material in standard English and other standardized language varieties and are best suited to the study of lexical and grammatical variation. Sociolinguists, however, have been concerned primarily with non-standard spoken varieties. Secondly, there is often little or no information on many of the social variables such as class, ethnicity, gender, age, etc. that sociolinguists are most interested in. Nevertheless, the increasing availability of corpora of spoken language, often enhanced with sound files, has opened up possibilities for sociolinguistic analysis (cf. article 11). Despite this, even where phonetically transcribed corpora exist, automatic search and retrieval of the kind of variables of interest to sociolinguists can be extremely difficult; each token of a variable may have innumerable variants and sound files may not always be available (cf. articles 11 and 53).

Studies that would once have taken many years to complete can now be conducted more rapidly and have opened up linguistic phenomena to empirical investigation on a scale previously unimaginable. This article has illustrated how corpora can be used to test hypotheses and to examine the occurrence of many variables in relation to the parameters encoded.

6. Literature

Aijmer, K. (2002), *English Discourse Particles. Evidence from a Corpus.* Amsterdam: John Benjamins.

Aijmer, K./Stenström, A.-B. (eds.) (2004), *Discourse Patterns in Spoken and Written Corpora*. Amsterdam: John Benjamins.
Aston, G./Burnard, L. (1998), *The BNC Handbook – Exploring the British National Corpus with SARA*. Edinburgh: Edinburgh University Press.
Bauer, L. (2002), Inferring variation and change from public corpora. In: Chambers, J. K./Trudgill, P./Schilling-Estes, N. (eds.), *Handbook of Linguistic Variation and Change*. Oxford: Blackwell, 97–113.
Berglund, Y. (1999), *Gonna* and *Going to* in the Spoken Component of the British National Corpus. In: Mair, C./Hundt, M. (eds.), *Corpus Linguistics and Linguistic Theory*. Amsterdam: Rodopi, 35–51.
DeForest, M. M./Johnson, E. (2000), Computing Latinate Word Usage in Jane Austen's novels. In: *Computers and Texts* 18/19, 24–25.
Giddens, A. (2000), *Runaway World*. London: Routledge.
Hasund, I. K. (2002), 'Congratulations, like!' – 'Gratulerer, liksom!' Pragmatic Particles in English and Norwegian. In: Breivik, L. E./ Hasselgren, A. (eds.), *From the COLT's mouth ... and others'. Language and Corpora Studies in Honour of Anna-Brita Stenström*. Amsterdam: Rodopi, 125–139.
Hasund, I. K./Stenström, A.-B. (2005), Conflict Talk: A Comparison of the Verbal Disputes between Adolescent Females in Two Corpora. In: Sampson, G./McCarthy D. (eds.), *Corpus Linguistics: Readings in a Widening Discipline*. London: Continuum, 326–334.
Holmes, J. (1999), *Ladies* and *Gentlemen*: Corpus Analysis and Linguistic Sexism. In: Mair, C./ Hundt, M. (eds.), *Corpus linguistics and Linguistic Theory*. Amsterdam: Rodopi, 141–155.
Labov, W. (1966), *The Social Stratification of English in New York City*. Washington, DC: Center for Applied Linguistics.
Lakoff, R. (1975), *Language and Woman's Place*. New York: Harper.
Leech, G./Rayson, P./Wilson, A. (2001), *Word Frequencies in Written and Spoken English: Based on the British National Corpus*. London: Longman.
McEnery, T./Xiao, Zh. (2004), Swearing in Modern British English: The Case of *Fuck* in the BNC. *Language and Literature* 13(3), 235–268.
Milroy, L./Gordon, M. (2003), *Sociolinguistics: Method and Interpretation*. Oxford: Blackwell.
Peters, P. (1998), Australian English. In: Bell, P./Bell, R. (eds.), *Americanisation and Australia*. Sydney: University of New South Wales Press, 32–44.
Pusch, C. D. (2002), A Survey of Spoken Language Corpora in Romance. In: Pusch, C. D./Raible, W. (eds.), *Romanistische Korpuslinguistik – Korpora und gesprochene Sprache. Romance Corpus Linguistics – Corpora and Spoken Language*. Tübingen: Gunter Narr Verlag, 245–264.
Rayson, P./Leech, G./Hodges, M. (1997), Social Differentiation in the Use of English Vocabulary: Some Analyses of the Conversational Component of the British National Corpus. In: *International Journal of Corpus Linguistics* 2(1), 133–152.
Romaine, S. (2000), *Language in Society. An Introduction to Sociolinguistics*. Oxford: Oxford University Press.
Ross, A. S. C. (1980), U and non-U. In: Mitford, N. (ed.), *Noblesse oblige*. London: Futura, 11–38.
Stenström, A.-B. (1991), Expletives in the London-Lund Corpus. In: Aijmer, K./Altenberg, B. (eds.), *English Corpus Linguistics in Honour of Jan Svartvik*. London: Longman, 230–253.
Stenström, A.-B./Andersen, G./Hasund, I. K. (2002), *Trends in Teenage Talk. Corpus Compilation, Analysis and Findings*. Amsterdam: John Benjamins.
Svartvik, J. (1966), *On Voice in the English Verb*. The Hague: Mouton.
Trudgill, P. (1974), *The Social Differentiation of English in Norwich*. Cambridge: Cambridge University Press.

Suzanne Romaine, Oxford (UK)

7. Corpora and language teaching

1. Introduction

1.1. Corpus linguistics and language teaching

Over the past two decades, corpora (i. e. large systematic collections of written and/or spoken language stored on a computer and used in linguistic analysis) and corpus evidence have not only been used in linguistic research but also in the teaching and learning of languages – probably a use that "the compilers [of corpora] may not have foreseen" (Johansson 2007). There is now a wide range of fully corpus-based reference works (such as dictionaries and grammars) available to learners and teachers, and a number of dedicated researchers and teachers have made concrete suggestions on how concordances and corpus-derived exercises could be used in the language teaching classroom, thus significantly "[e]nriching the learning environment" (Aston 1997, 51). Indicative of the popularity of pedagogical corpora use and the need for research in this area is the considerable number of books and edited collections – some of which are the result of the successful "Teaching and Language Corpora" (TaLC) conference series – that have recently been published on the topic of this article or which bear a close relationship to it (cf. Ädel 2006; Aston 2001; Aston/Bernardini/Stewart 2004; Bernardini 2000a; Botley et al. 1996; Braun/Kohn/Mukherjee 2006; Burnard/McEnery 2000; Connor/Upton 2004; Gavioli 2006; Ghadessy/Henry/Roseberry 2001; Granger/Hung/Petch-Tyson 2002; Hidalgo/Quereda/Santana 2007; Hunston 2002; Kettemann/Marko 2002; Mukherjee 2002; Nesselhauf 2005; Partington 1998; Römer 2005a; Schlüter 2002; Scott/Tribble 2006; Sinclair 2004a; Wichmann et al. 1997).

In this article I wish to examine the relationship between corpus linguistics (CL) and language teaching (LT) and provide an overview of the most important pedagogical applications of corpora. As Figure 7.1 aims to illustrate, this relationship is a dynamic one in which the two fields greatly influence each other. While LT profits from the resources, methods, and insights provided by CL, it also provides important impulses that are taken up in corpus linguistic research. The requirements of LT hence have an pact on research projects in CL and on the development of suitable resources and tools. The present article will investigate what influence CL has had on LT so far, and in what ways corpora have been used to improve pedagogical practice. It will also discuss further possible effects of CL on LT and of LT on CL, and highlight some future tasks for researchers and practitioners in the field.

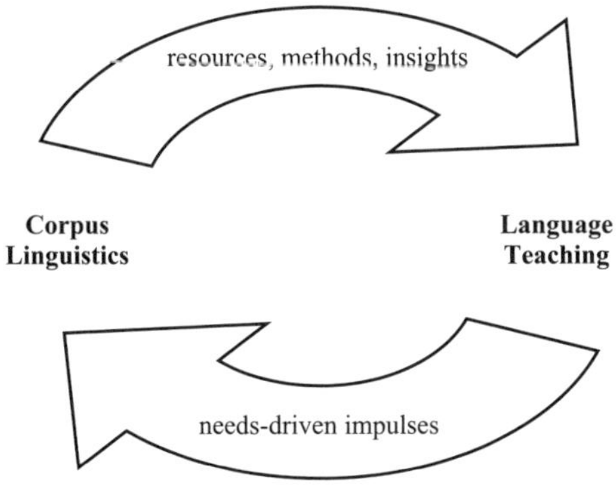

Fig. 7.1: The relationship between corpus linguistics (CL) and language teaching (LT)

1.2. Types of pedagogical corpus applications

When we talk about the application of corpora in language teaching, this includes both the use of corpus *tools,* i. e. the actual text collections and software packages for corpus access, and of corpus *methods,* i. e. the analytic techniques that are used when we work with corpus data. In classifying pedagogical corpus applications, i. e. the use of corpus tools and methods in a language teaching and language learning context, a useful distinction (going back to Leech 1997) can be made between direct and indirect applications. This means that, 'indirectly', corpora can help with decisions about what to teach and when to teach it, but that they can also be accessed 'directly' by learners and teachers in the LT classroom, and so "assist in the teaching process" (Fligelstone 1993, 98), thus affecting how something is taught and learnt. In addition to direct and indirect uses of

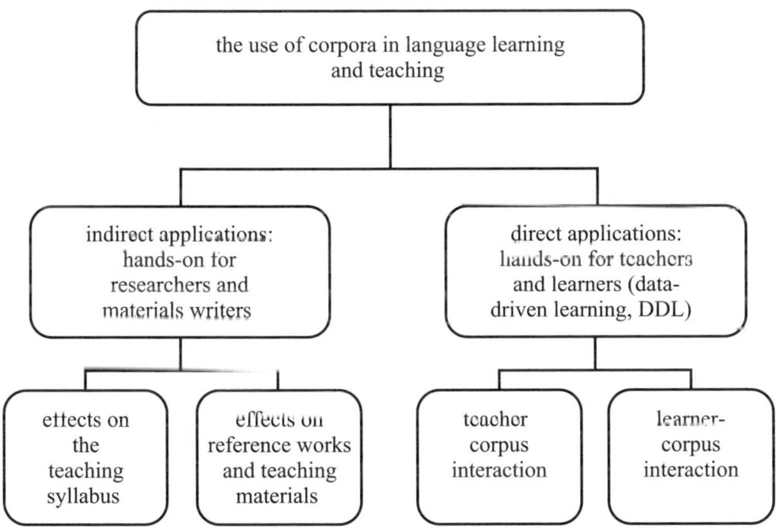

Fig. 7.2: Applications of corpora in language teaching

corpora in LT, Leech (1997, 5–6) talks about a third, in his opinion less-central component which he labels "further teaching-oriented corpus developments" (e. g. LSP corpora and learner corpora). These developments will, however, not be treated as marginal aspects here, but integrated in the discussion of direct and indirect pedagogical corpus applications. Sections 2 and 3 of this article will feature the most important lines of research and developments in both areas as presented in Figure 7.2. As the figure shows, we can identify different types of direct and indirect applications, depending on who or what is affected by the use of corpus methods and tools. In our discussions below, we will consider these distinctions and refer throughout to the pedagogical uses of general corpora, such as the BNC (British National Corpus, see articles 9, 10, 20), as well as specialised corpora, such as MICASE (the Michigan Corpus of Academic Spoken English, see articles 9, 47).

2. Indirect applications of corpora in language teaching

As Barlow (1996, 32) notes, "[t]he results of a corpus-based investigation can serve as a firm basis for both linguistic description and, on the applied side, as input for language learning." This implies that corpora and the evidence derived from them can greatly affect course design and the content of teaching materials (see also Hunston 2002, 137). Existing pedagogical descriptions are evaluated in the light of "new evidence" (Sinclair 2004c, 271), and new decisions are made about the *selection* of language phenomena, the *progression* in the course, and the *presentation* of the selected items and structures (cf. Mindt 1981, 179; Römer 2005a, 287–291). This kind of indirect pedagogical corpus use benefits from research based on or driven by general and specialised corpora.

2.1. Indirect applications of general corpora

2.1.1. Corpora and the teaching syllabus

Large general corpora have proven to be an invaluable resource in the design of language teaching syllabi which emphasise communicative competence (cf. Hymes 1972, 1992) and which give prominence to those items that learners are most likely to encounter in real-life communicative situations. In the context of computer corpus-informed English language teaching syllabi, the first and probably most groundbreaking development was the design of the *Collins COBUILD English Course* (CCEC; Willis/Willis 1989), an offshoot of the pioneering COBUILD project in pedagogically oriented lexicography (cf. Sinclair 1987; articles 3 and 8). The contents of this new, corpus-driven "lexical syllabus" are "the commonest words and phrases in English and their meanings" (Willis 1990, 124). With its focus on lexis and lexical patterns, the CCEC responds to some of the most central findings of corpus research, namely that language is highly patterned in that it consists to an immense degree of repeated word-combinations, and that lexis and grammar are inseparably linked (cf. Hoey 2000; Hunston 2002; Hunston/Francis 2000; Partington 1998; Römer 2005a, 2005b; Sinclair 1991; Stubbs 1996; Tognini Bonelli 2001). Also worth mentioning is a much earlier attempt to improve further the teaching of

English vocabulary that was made long before the advent of computers and electronic corpora. In 1934, Michael West organised a conference "to discuss the part played by corpus-based word lists in the teaching of English as a foreign language" (Kennedy 1992, 327). About 20 years later, West's (1953) *General Service List of English Words* (GSL) was published and has since then exerted great influence on curriculum design (cf. Kennedy 1992, 328; Willis 1990, 47). As the title indicates, West's GSL suggests a syllabus that is based on words rather than on grammatical structures. It is also based on *frequently occurring* rather than on rare words. Of course, frequency of occurrence is not the only criterion that should influence decisions about the inclusion of items in the teaching syllabus (there are other relevant criteria, such as "range, availability, coverage and learnability (Mackey 1965, 188)" (Kennedy 1992, 340); cf. also Nation 1990, 21), but it is certainly an immensely important one (see also Aston 2000, 8; Leech 1997, 16). It can be safely assumed that learners will find it easier to develop both their receptive and productive skills when they are confronted with the most common lexical items of a language and the patterns and meanings with which they typically occur than when the language teaching input they get gives high priority to infrequent words and structures which the learners will only rarely encounter in real-life situations.

Another strand in applied corpus research that aims to inform the teaching syllabus and also stresses the importance of frequency of occurrence, examines language items in actual language use and compares the distributions and patterns found in general reference corpora (of speech and/or writing) with the presentations of the same items in teaching materials (coursebooks, grammars, usage handbooks). The starting point for these kinds of studies is usually language features that are known to cause perpetual problems to learners, for example, for German, discourse particles (Jones 1997), modal verbs (Jones 2000), the passive voice (Jones 2000) prepositions (Jones 1997), or, for English, future time expressions (Mindt 1987, 1997), *if*-clauses (Römer 2004b), irregular verbs (Grabowski/Mindt 1995), linking adverbials (Conrad 2004), modal verbs (Mindt 1995; Römer 2004a), the present perfect (Lorenz 2002; Schlüter 2002), progressive verb forms (Römer 2005a, 2006) and reflexives (Barlow 1996). For all these phenomena, researchers have found considerable mismatches between naturally-occurring German or English and the type of German or English that is put forward as a model in the examined teaching materials. They have, as a consequence, called for corpus-inspired adjustments in the language teaching syllabus (particularly as far as selection and progression are concerned) and for revised pedagogical descriptions which present a more adequate picture of the language as it is actually used. A case in point here is the misrepresentation of the functions and contextual patterns of English progressive forms in EFL teaching materials used in German schools. Progressives that refer to repeated actions or events, for example, are considerably more frequent in 'real' English than in textbook English where the common function "repeatedness" is rather neglected and the focus is on single continuous events (cf. Römer 2005a, 261–263).

2.2.2. Corpora and reference works and teaching materials

The results of the abovementioned corpus-coursebook comparisons do not only inform the language teaching curriculum but also help with decisions about the presentation of items and structures in reference works and teaching materials. Research on general corpora has exerted a huge influence on reference publishing and has led to a new generation of dictionaries and grammar books. Nowadays, "people who have never heard of a corpus are using the products of corpus research." (McEnery/Xiao/Tono 2006, 97) In the context of ELT (English Language Teaching), the publications in the Collins COBUILD series constitute a major achievement. Based on real English and compiled with the needs of the language learner in mind, the COBUILD dictionaries, grammars, usage guides, and concordance samplers (cf. Capel 1993; Carpenter 1993; Goodale 1995; Sinclair et al. 1990; Sinclair et al. 1992; Sinclair et al. 2001) offer teachers and learners more reliable information about the English language than any of the more traditional reference grammars or older non-corpus-based dictionaries. Two major advantages of the COBUILD and other corpus-based reference works for learners, e. g. those published in the past few years by Longman, Macmillan, OUP and CUP (cf. e. g. Abbs/Freebairn 2005; Biber/Leech/Conrad 2002; Hornby 2005; Peters 2004; Rundell et al. 2002) are that they incorporate corpus-derived findings on frequency distribution and register variation, and that they contain genuine instead of invented examples. Particularly worth mentioning here is the student version of the entirely corpus-based *Longman Grammar of Spoken and Written English* (Biber et al. 2002). The importance of presenting learners with authentic language examples has been stressed in a number of publications (cf. de Beaugrande 2001; Firth 1957; Fox 1987; Kennedy 1992; Römer 2004b, 2005a; Sinclair 1991, 1997). Kennedy (1992, 366), for instance, cautions that "invented examples can present a distorted version of typicality or an over-tidy picture of the system", and Sinclair (1991, 5) calls it an "absurd notion that invented examples can actually represent the language better than real ones". Thanks to the 'corpus revolution', the language learner can today choose from a range of reference works that are thoroughly corpus-based and that offer improved representations of the language she or he wants to study. While coursebooks and other materials used in the LT classroom have long been lagging behind this development and been rather unaffected by advances in CL (at least as far as the EFL (English as a Foreign Language) market is concerned), the first attempts are now being made to produce textbooks which draw on corpus research and are fully based on real-life data, i. e. on language that has in fact occurred (cf. Barlow/Burdine 2006; Carter/Hughes/McCarthy 2000; McCarthy/McCarten/Sandiford 2005).

Another branch of general corpora research that has exerted some influence on the design of reference works and, to a lesser extent, teaching materials is the area of phraseology and collocation studies. Scholars like Biber et al. (1999), Hunston/Francis (2000), Kjellmer (1984), Lewis (1993, 1997, 2000), Meunier/Gouverneur (2007), Nattinger (1980), Pawley/Syder (1983), and Sinclair/Renouf (1988) have emphasised the importance of recurring word combinations and prefabricated strings in a pedagogical context because of their great potential in fostering fluency, accuracy and idiomaticity. Although corpus-based collocation dictionaries (e. g. Hill/Lewis 1997; Lea 2002) are available, and although information on phraseology (i. e. about the combinations that individual words favour) is implicitly included in learners dictionaries in the word definitions and the selected corpus examples – and sometimes even explicitly described, e. g. in the grammar column in the COBUILD dictionaries and in the *COBUILD Grammar Patterns* reference books (cf. Francis/Hunston/Manning 1996, 1998) – such information and exercises on typical collocations are as yet largely missing from LT coursebooks (or they are inadequate; cf. Meunier/Gouverneur 2007). Like Hunston/Francis (2000, 272), I see a necessity in and "look forward to [more] information about patterns being incorporated in language teaching materials."

2.2. Indirect applications of specialised corpora

Like general corpora, corpora of specialised texts (e. g. from one particular field of expertise, such as economics, or a narrowly defined group of speakers/writers, such as learners with a particular L1 and a certain level of proficiency) and research findings based on them can also be used to improve pedagogical practice and affect LT syllabi or the design of teaching materials. I would like to distinguish three different types of specialised corpora: LSP (language for special purposes) corpora, learner corpora, and parallel or translation corpora.

"LSP is the language that is used to discuss specialized fields of knowledge", and it is the purpose of this language "to facilitate communication between people who wish to discuss a specialized subject" (Bowker/Pearson 2002, 25, 27). Corpora that capture a particular LSP, e. g. a corpus of Italian business letters or a corpus of English chemistry textbooks, can have a positive impact on the design of syllabi and materials of LSP courses. As Gavioli (2006, 23) states with reference to courses of English for special purposes (ESP), "working out basic items to be dealt with is a key teaching problem." ESP corpora can help solve this problem. To give just two examples, Flowerdew (1993) demonstrates how frequency and concordance data from a corpus of English biology lectures and readings can be used in the creation of a course syllabus and teaching materials for students of science, and that such corpus-derived materials enable LSP teachers to teach those words and expressions (and those uses of them) that the learners will need later on in order to handle texts in their subject area. Focussing on academic English in general, Coxhead (2002) uses corpus evidence to compile an Academic Word List (AWL) which contains those vocabulary items that are most relevant and useful to the learners. Coxhead's AWL has become an important tool in learning and teaching EAP (English for Academic Purposes). Other related studies deal with the pedagogical implications of corpora of English tourism industry texts (Lam 2007), meat technology English (Pereira de Oliveira 2003), or English letters of application (Henry/Roseberry 2001). Henry/Roseberry (2001, 121), for example, suggest that to compile genre-specific compendia or glossaries which they term "Language Pattern Dictionaries" based on their specialised corpus (see also Bowker/Pearson 2002, 137) would bring the learner more "success in job hunting" (Henry/Roseberry 2001, 117).

Studies on learner corpora, i. e. systematic computerised collections of the language produced by language learners (article 15), are also highly relevant for syllabus design (cf Aston 2000, 11; Granger 2002, 22) since they provide insights on "the needs of specific learner populations" (Meunier 2002, 125) and help to test teachers' intuitions about whether a particular phenomenon is difficult or not (Granger 2002, 22). It has been shown how the findings of such studies (e. g. those based on the International Corpus of Learner English, "ICLE", or on the German error-annotated learner corpus "Falko", cf. Aijmer 2002; Altenberg/Granger 2001; Granger 1999; Leriko-Szymanska 2007; Lorenz 1999; Lüdeling et al. 2005; Nesselhauf 2004, 2005) can "enrich usage notes" in learners' dictionaries (Granger 2002, 24), or how they "can provide useful insights into which collocational, pragmatic or discourse features should be addressed in materials design" (Flowerdew 2001, 376–377). Researchers like Granger (e. g. 2002, 2004) have also given the suggestion of linking up learner corpora work with contrastive analyses and using findings from corpora of the learner's mother tongue to interpret the results of learner corpus studies. Contrastive work (i. e. research based on parallel or translation corpora; article 16) is clearly invaluable for the selection of "elements the learner is likely to mistreat because they are different [...] from those in his [or her] native language" (Kjellmer 1992, 375). Parallel corpora are, in Teubert's (2004, 188) words, "the repositories of source language units of meaning and their target language equivalents." A corpus-enhanced knowledge of these equivalents (approached from different source language perspectives) is undoubtedly of use for language material developers and compilers of reference works (e. g. bilingual dictionaries), as is a knowledge about language items which cause translation problems for learners (cf. Schmied 1998 and article 54).

3. Direct applications of corpora in language teaching

While the indirect approach centres on the impact of corpus evidence on syllabus design or teaching materials, and is concerned with corpus access by researchers and – though to a lesser extent – materials designers, the direct approach is more teacher- and learner-focused. Instead of having to rely on the researcher as mediator and provider of corpus-based materials, language learners and teachers get their hands on corpora and concordancers themselves and find out about language patterning and the behaviour of words and phrases in an "autonomous" way (cf. Bernardini 2002, 165). Tim Johns, who, strongly supported by Tony Dudley-Evans and Philip King, pioneered direct corpus applications in grammar and vocabulary classes in the English for International Students Unit at the University of Birmingham in the 1980s (John Sinclair, personal communication), made the suggestion to "confront the learner as directly as possible with the data, and to make the learner a linguistic researcher" (Johns 2002, 108). Johns (1997, 101) also referred to the learner as a "language detective" and formulated the motto "Every student a Sherlock Holmes!" This method, in which there is either an interaction between the learner and the corpus or, in a more controlled way, between the teacher and the corpus (cf. Figure 7.2) is now widely known under the label "data-driven learning" or DDL (cf. Johns 1986, 1994). DDL activities with language learners can be based on (usually larger) general reference corpora or on (smaller) specialised corpora.

3.1. Direct applications of general corpora

Following Johns' example, a number of researchers have discussed ways in which general corpora and concordances derived from them can be used by language learners. Bernardini (2002, 165), for instance, describes the positive effects of "corpus-aided discovery learning" with the BNC, and describes corpora as "rich sources of autonomous learning activities of a serendipitous kind" (ibid.; cf. also Bernardini 2000b, 2004). She sees the learner in the role of a *"traveller* instead of a *researcher*" (Bernardini 2000a, 131; italics in original), and is less "interested in the starting or end point of a learning experience" than in what the learner experiences in between, on her or his journey (Bernardini 2000a, 142). Kettemann (1995, 30) too stresses the exploratory aspect of DDL and considers concordancing in the ELT classroom "motivating and highly experiential" for the learner.

The DDL method of using learner-centred activities with the teacher as a facilitator of these activities has, however, not only been discussed with reference to English language teaching and English language corpora, but has also been applied in teaching other languages. Whistle (1999), for example, reports on introducing DDL activities to the teaching of French in order to supplement other CALL (computer-assisted language learning) tasks. Dodd (1997) and Jones (1997) show how corpora of written and spoken German can be exploited "to give students a richer language-learning experience in the foreign language environment" (Dodd 1997, 131), and Kennedy/Miceli (2001, 2002) suggest corpus consultation for learners of Italian. To give an example of a possible DDL task, learners could be asked to compile concordances of a pair of near-synonyms (such as 'speak' and 'talk' in English or 'connaître' and 'savoir' in French; cf. Chambers 2005, 117) and work out the differences in the collocational and phraseological behaviour of these words (see concordance samples in Figure 7.3). Further examples of DDL activities with English, German, Italian, and Spanish corpora are described in Aston (1997, 2001); Brodine (2001); Coffey (2007); Davies (2000, 2004); Dodd (1997); Fligelstone (1993); Gavioli (2001); Hadley (1997, 2001); Johns (1991, 2002); Stevens (1991); Sripicharn (2004); Tribble (1997); Zorzi (2001); and especially in Tribble/Jones (1997).

```
1    ery? Can I think.  .. Well I 'd like to speak about the gallery I like to speak for m
2    d morning.   Hello! Yeah,  I 'd like to speak about the the squeeze on the benefits.
3    ught people might be less willing to to speak at the meeting if they knew it was bein
4    d   pointing. And er when you get up to speak at the conference,  you have to give yo
5    re 's not quite as bad as when I had to speak for Amnesty on Radio Essex last year an
6    ke to speak about the gallery I like to speak for myself and er just the visual arts
7    't got a word  . you 're not allowed to speak for the rest of the week. he 's hiding
8    Well football fans? well David I ca n't speak on behalf of Hibs,  all I can say Mm. i
9    a member of the public I 'm not here to speak on behalf of the theatre at all. I migh
10   rhaps people could as actually come and speak to me afterwards,  if they, if they thi
11   e will if you 'd like to come along and speak to him individually afterwards he will
12   hat, then.  When do you start again? I speak to Stella now Do you speak, do you star
13   e appropriate way of doing it.  Shall I speak to Paula about that then?  Yeah. Paula,
14   er Okay.   I 'll speak to Simon.  I 'll speak to Simon erm about borrowing his P C at
15   ot to go     home and do? Are you sure? Speak to me Yes Okay,  right, one person from
16   rt is to go back one step,  not just to speak to people who are experiencing hurt, bu
17   ikey.  Speak up loud, you 've got ta be speak up loud and clear.  No. Uniform. Unifor
18    I think that they may be frightened to speak up and that they 're scared that if the
19    of talking about.  Excuse me could you speak up just a little bit?  Yes yes er Thank
20    first floor.   Oh I 'm sorry!  Can you speak up then?  Oh sorry!  Have I Mm mm. Have

1    ney. All of that being said and Mr will talk a bit more about the figures when he com
2     have an M P here on the phone line and talk about this er proposed pay rise. They ca
3    ? Mm.   . Erm I just want to go back and talk about a few things we just touched on ea
4    are?   Erm Without drawing it,  try and talk about a square.  What would happen? Erm
5     Mm.   Like we had you know,  who could talk about experiences you know,  in a, in a
6    ey include Gerry Addams and we we could talk about the other side,  we could talk abo
7    ot  , you know, I 'm not er gon na even talk about the disaster at airport things, yo
8    Mm.   And basically,  again can we just talk about what we 're trying to achieve? My
9     on, and Mr   I know in a minute we 'll talk about the number of people who attend co
10    Becky. No, Becky. Becky  .  And we 'll talk about this in committee and let you   kn
11   ople or all about that I do n't want to talk about that I want to talk I want to talk
12    get them around the table and begin to talk about those sort of things.  Show a bit
13    bit, we just have done.  We started to talk about the solar system.  How far have we
14   them   anyway. Right.  What else did we talk about and we need to know, we have n't g
15   ber   of possible pieces there,  Did we talk about this?  We did.  Ah, right, yes. So
16   .   They look tired and worn out.  They talk quietly amongst themselves sometimes fin
17   s boss, the professor to come along and talk to us,  and let,  some of their time is
18   than then, because as a kid they do n't talk to you about them things do they like, y
19    going to talk to somebody who will not talk to you,  who will not s possibly even sm
20   how nice the man was when he started to talk to Jason oh I 'll go and help you how fr
```

Fig. 7.3: Concordance samples of 'speak' and 'talk', based on the spoken part of the British National Corpus

Advantages of corpora work with learners have been formulated by scholars like Sinclair (1997, 38), who notes that, for the learner, "[c]orpora will clarify, give priorities, reduce exceptions and liberate the creative spirit." Likewise, many researchers and teachers in the TaLC (Teaching and Language Corpora) tradition are convinced that DDL can empower learners to find out things for themselves, and that corpora have a great pedagogic potential. The effectiveness of DDL has actually been proven in studies on the teaching and learning of vocabulary by Cobb (1997), Cresswell (2007) and Stevens (1991). Concordancing has not only been shown to be a useful way "to mimic the effects of natural contextual learning" (Cobb 1997, 314), researchers have recently also highlighted its use and usefulness for error correction in foreign or second language writing (cf. Bernardini 2004; Chambers 2005; Gaskell/Cobb 2004; Gray 2005). These studies demonstrate that corpora nicely complement existing reference works and that they may provide information which a dictionary or grammar book may not provide.

The immediate accessibility of authoritative information about the language is also a major advantage for language *teachers* who decide to interact with a corpus. As a recent survey on teachers' needs has shown (cf. Römer forthcoming), teachers often require native-speaker advice on language points. Computer corpora that have been described as "tireless native-speaker informant[s], with rather greater potential knowledge of the language than the average native speaker" (Barnbrook 1996, 140), can offer help in such situations. In the sense of a modified type of DDL, teachers could also access corpora to create DDL exercises for learners, tailored to their learners' proficiency level and their particular learning needs. Such exercises would enable teachers to "present the structures [they wish to introduce] and their lexis at the same time" (Francis/Sinclair 1994, 200). Emphasising the great potential of corpus analysis in a pedagogical context, Hunston/Francis (2000, 272) suggest that teachers, especially those in training, "should be encouraged to identify patterns as a grammar point for learners to notice". Concordancing can certainly help teachers create a data-rich learning environment and "enrich their own knowledge of the language" (Barlow 1996, 30), as well as that of their pupils.

3.2. Direct applications of specialised corpora

Data-driven learning activities are not restricted to large general corpora but can also be based on the types of small and specialised corpora that have been discussed in section 2.2. of this article: LSP corpora, learner corpora and parallel corpora. Classroom concordancing in Johns' or Bernardini's sense is regarded as a useful tool in teaching LSP by a number of researchers and teachers in this field (for an overview, see Gavioli 2006, ch. 4). Mparutsa/Love/Morrison (1991) comment, for example, on the problems ESP students may have with general words (such as 'price') that are used in special ways and in particular (fixed) expressions in certain genres (cf. Brodine 2001, 157; cf. also Thurstun/Candlin 1998). In "[w]orking with corpora," Gavioli (2006, 131) states, "ESP students become familiar with a productive idea of idiomatic language features, [and] they learn to use and adapt language patterns to their own needs". In a similar vein, Bondi (2001, 159) discusses DDL in LSP contexts as a language awareness-raising strategy. Providing examples of useful worksheets, she points out that "[s]tudents of economics, for example, could become much better readers by developing an awareness of the forms and functions of different meta-argumentative expressions [e. g. 'considers' or 'examined'] and by learning to understand the different role they play in the different genres". Small and specialised corpora can also function as the source for DDL materials in general language teaching (cf. Tribble 1997), e.g. in the teaching of conversational skills. This particular use is exemplified by Pérez Basanta and Rodríguez Martín (2007) who extract typical features of spoken English from a corpus of film transcripts (a collection of subtitles from movie DVDs) to be used in DDL tasks in EFL conversation classes.

What has been said above about the awareness-raising potential of DDL activities with LSP corpora is also true for DDL with learner corpora (article 15). Taking up Granger/Tribble's (1998) suggestion to combine data from native and learner corpora in the LT classroom, Meunier (2002, 130–134) presents examples and describes the advantages of DDL exercises with parallel native and learner concordances (cf. also Papp 2007). However, such exercises should, according to Meunier (2002, 134), "only be used, here and there, to complement native data and to illustrate [...] universally problematic areas" (e.g. verb or noun complementation). Seidlhofer (2000, 207) also comments on "using learner corpora for learning", though with a shift in focus from learner errors to dealing with questions learners have about what they and their classmates have written. This focus on familiar texts (i.e. on texts the learners themselves have produced) ensures motivation and, in Seidlhofer's (2000, 222) terms, "the consideration of two equally crucial points of reference for learners: where they are, i.e. situated in their L2 learning contexts, and where they eventually (may) want to get to, i.e. close to the native-speaker language using capacity captured by L1 corpora." Pedagogical applications of such "local learner corpora" (Seidlhofer 2002, 213) have also been discussed by Mukherjee/Rohrbach (2006; cf. also Turnbull/Burston 1998). In their paper on error analysis in a local learner corpus, the authors claim that their learners do "not only profit from the correction of their own mistakes but also from the analysis of their fellow-students' errors and their corrections" (Mukherjee/Rohrbach 2006, 225). Local learner corpora like the ones described by Seidlhofer and by Mukherjee/Rohrbach could easily be compiled by a larger number of teachers and lecturers by simply collecting their students' writings in electronic format, and subsequently serve as an exciting source of data to inspire the creation of DDL materials.

The third type of specialised corpus described in section 2.2., the parallel or translation corpus (i.e. a corpus that consists of original texts and their translations), also lends itself to the kind of DDL exploitation that we have envisaged for LSP and learner corpora. In coming to terms with the meaning(s) of an item in a foreign language, it can be extremely helpful for learners to create a parallel concordance and look at the translation equivalents of this item in their native language, or, the other way round, look for perhaps partly unknown translation equivalents of a selected native language item in the target language. Another promising use of parallel corpora in LT lies in highlighting collocational and phraseological differences between a word in the target language and its dictionary translation in the source language. Gavioli (1997), for example, reports that classroom work based on concordances of English 'crucial' and Italian 'cruciale/cruciali' has led her Italian students to illuminating findings about the different behaviour of these words. Johns (2002, 114) discusses the potential of parallel corpora for the creation of "reciprocal language materials", i.e. "materials which could be used both to teach language A to speakers of language B, and language B to speakers of language A." He provides examples of exercises derived from English-French parallel concordances. Similar exercises, but resulting from English-Chinese parallel concordancing, have been designed by Wang (2001; cf. also Ghadessy/Gao 2001). Parallel or comparable corpora (i. e. text collections in different languages but of similar text types) have also been described as "aids in translation activities" (Zanettin 2001, 193) and as useful tools in the training of professional translators and interpreters (cf. e. g. Bernardini 2002; Bowker/Pearson 2002, ch. 11). Johansson (2007) gives examples of using the English-Norwegian Parallel Corpus (article 16) with a group of Norwegian students in solving the students' learning problems and in dealing with problems of translation. Concordancing activities in the education of translators are described by Gavioli/Zanettin (1997) and by Bernardini (1997). According to Gavioli/Zanettin (1997, 6), comparable corpora provide "a repertoire of naturally occurring contexts in the target language onto which hypothesised translations can be mapped." They hence "problematize the choices of the translator" (ibid.) or trainee translator, and help him or her find the most adequate and acceptable translation.

4. Tasks for the future

Despite the progress that has unquestionably been made in the field of pedagogical corpus applications, there is still scope for development. A number of tasks can be formulated to foster both the indirect and the direct use of corpora in language learning and teaching. Referring back to what has been mentioned in section 1.2., the next two sections will examine what further effects CL could have on LT and vice versa.

4.1. Fostering the indirect use of corpora in language teaching

We have seen that corpora and corpus evidence have already had an immense impact on teaching syllabi, teaching materials, and especially reference works like dictionaries or grammars (see the discussions in sections 2.1. and 2.2.). I would, however, argue that general and specialised corpora could be even better exploited to positively affect pedagogical practice. I am thinking here of further research activities that are inspired or driven by the needs of learners and language teaching practitioners. No matter how promising the advances made in the field of TaLC are, we still have a long way to go in providing more adequate descriptions of different types of language (different text types, registers and varieties), based on larger collections of data. I expect, for instance, that the place that LSP has in the language teaching domain will become increasingly significant in the future, and that more and better teaching materials tailored to the communication needs of students of economics or participants of business English courses, to mention only two groups of learners, will be required. These teaching and learning resources should ideally be based on expert performances (as opposed to apprentice performances; cf. Tribble 1997) in the selected field and, if possible, on large amounts of genuine language material. This implies the need to compile more and larger corpora of different types of written and especially spoken data. A task for the corpus researcher will then be to derive from these corpora those items and meanings that are most relevant for the learner group in question (cf. the publications in the *CorpusLab* series that are tailored to different groups of learners; e. g. Barlow/Burdine 2006). If we wish to tailor materials to learners' needs and focus on language points that tend to be particularly troublesome, we also ought to create more learner corpora of different kinds and find out more about the characteristics of learner language, so that, in the future, a larger number of dictionaries, grammars, and textbooks will not only be corpus- but also learner corpus-informed.

Further important insights to boost indirect corpus applications in LT could come from contrastive linguistic research on the basis of parallel or comparable corpora – another field of research in which significant developments are to be expected in the next few years (cf. articles 16 and 54). A number of comparative analyses of selected lexical-grammatical features in corpora and coursebooks have been carried out, mainly based on English language corpora and EFL teaching materials (cf. section 2.1.). More investigations of this type, in particular for different languages but also for different varieties of English, could help to isolate further mismatches between 'real' language and 'school' language, which could then lead to further improvements of teaching materials (cf. also Johansson/Stavestrand 1987, 147).

4.2. Fostering the direct use of corpora in language teaching

Although a lot is still left to be done as far as the indirect use of corpora in LT is concerned, there is probably even more scope for development with respect to direct applications. The gap between corpus linguistics and the teaching reality described by Mukherjee (2004), is still far too wide, and the extent to which corpora and concordances have actually been used in LT classrooms is, unfortunately, as yet fairly limited. Now that we know how beneficial corpus work can be to the learner, I think that it is the applied corpus linguist's task to, as Chambers (2005) and Mukherjee (2004) call it, "popularise" corpus consultation and the work with corpus data in schools. In order to achieve this, some obstacles have of course to be overcome and a DDL-friendly environment has to be created. First of all, schools have to be equipped with corpus computers and appropriate software packages. For this purpose, new concordance programs that are appealing and easy to use may have to be written so that teachers and learners are not put off from working with corpora right away because the software is too complex or not user-friendly enough. John Sinclair (personal communication) has recently initiated a project which will provide broadband and corpus access for every classroom in Scotland by 2007 with the aim to support written literacy of the 12+-year-olds. We are thus coming closer to Fligelstone's (1993, 100) hoped for scenario in which learners can access corpora whenever they want and simply "go to any of the labs, hit the icon which says 'corpus' and follow the instructions on the screen" – but we are not quite there yet. Projects like Sinclair's Scotland project ought to be encouraged in different countries. An alternative to providing direct corpus access in the classroom would be to introduce learners and teachers to the resources that are accessible online and show them the potential of the Web as a huge resource of language data (article 18). Boulton/Wilhelm (2006) in this context talk about freely available corpus tools that learners have a right to use and that ought to be put in the hands of the learner.

A second and very important step towards creating a DDL-friendly environment will be to guide teachers and learners and give them a basic training in accessing corpora and in working with and evaluating concordances. Such a training is crucial because, as

Sinclair (2004b, 2) puts it, "a corpus is not a simple object, and it is just as easy to derive nonsensical conclusions from the evidence as insightful ones" (cf. also Gavioli 1997, 83). Guidance for teachers in how to read concordances and advice on what types of DDL exercises they could create can be found in Sinclair (2003) and Tribble/Jones (1997). Once they are familiar with the basics of corpus work and have learnt to deal with their new role as facilitators of autonomous learning activities, a follow-up task for teachers will be to "create conditions to make it [i. e. corpus work] relevant for" their learners (Gavioli 2006, 133) and to encourage DDL activities of an inductive and exploratory kind. It would probably also be helpful for learners and teachers of different languages if more DDL materials with ready-made exercises and photocopiable work-sheets on selected language points were available, but both groups might profit a lot more from getting their hands on corpora themselves.

5. Concluding remarks

This article has focussed on the relationship between corpus linguistics and language teaching. I hope to have shown that corpus resources and methods have a great potential to improve pedagogical practice and that corpora can be used in a number of ways, indirectly to inform teaching materials and reference works, or directly as language learning tools and repositories for the design of data-intensive teaching activities. I have also tried to make clear that a lot still remains to be done in research and practice before corpus linguistics will eventually 'arrive' in the classroom. Communication between corpus researchers and practitioners has to be improved considerably so that teachers and learners get the support they need and deserve.

As for the development of the CL-LT relationship and going back to what is shown in Figure 7.1 above, I would predict that the requirements of language learners and teachers will keep affecting corpus research and the creation of suitable tools and resources. In the future, more and more developments in corpus linguistics will probably be oriented towards language teaching and learning. Among other things I envisage a stronger emphasis on learner corpora, spoken language corpora, and specialised corpora – corpora that are tailored to the target learner group and its needs. As suitably formulated by Aston (2000, 16), "language pedagogy is increasingly designing its own corpora to its own criteria". We do not know exactly how these criteria will develop in the next few decades. One thing that we can be sure of, however, is that the field of corpus linguistics and language teaching has an exciting future that both researchers and teachers can, and should, look forward to.

6. Literature

Abbs, Brian/Freebairn, Ingrid (eds.) (2005), *Longman Dictionary of Contemporary English.* Munich: Langenscheidt-Longman.

Ädel, Annelie (2006), *Metadiscourse in L1 an L2 English.* Amsterdam: John Benjamins.

Aijmer, Karin (2002), Modality in Advanced Swedish Learners' Written Interlanguage. In: Granger/Hung/Petch-Tyson 2002, 55–76.

Altenberg, Bengt/Granger, Sylviane (2001), The Grammatical and Lexical Patterning of MAKE in Native and Non-native Student Writing. In: *Applied Linguistics* 22(2), 173–195.

Aston, Guy (1997), Enriching the Learning Environment: Corpora in ELT. In: Wichmann et al. 1997, 51–64.

Aston, Guy (2000), Corpora and Language Teaching. In: Burnard/McEnery 2000, 7–17.

Aston, Guy (ed.) (2001), *Learning with Corpora.* Bologna: CLUEB and Houston, TX: Athelstan.

Aston, Guy/Bernardini, Silvia/Stewart, Dominic (eds.) (2004), *Corpora and Language Learners.* Amsterdam: John Benjamins.

Barlow, Michael/Burdine, Stephanie (2006), *American Phrasal Verbs.* (CorpusLAB Series.) Houston, TX: Athelstan. http://www.corpuslab.com (accessed 12 September 2006).

Barlow, Michael (1996), Corpora for Theory and Practice. In: *International Journal of Corpus Linguistics* 1(1), 1–37.

Barnbrook, Geoff (1996), *Language and Computers. A Practical Introduction to the Computer Analysis of Language.* Edinburgh: Edinburgh University Press.

Beaugrande, Robert de (2001), *Twenty Challenges to Corpus Research. And how to Answer them.* http://beaugrande.bizland.com/Twenty%20questions%20about%20corpus%20research.htm (accessed 22 August 2006).

Bernardini, Silvia (1997), A 'Trainee' Translator's Perspective on Corpora. Paper presented at: *Corpus Use and Learning to Translate (CULT),* Bertinoro, 14–15 November 1997. http:// www.sslmit.unibo.it/cultpaps/trainee.htm (accessed through http://web.archive.org, 22 August 2006).

Bernardini, Silvia (2000a), *Competence, Capacity, Corpora. A Study in Corpus-aided Language Learning.* Bologna: CLUEB.

Bernardini, Silvia (2000b), Systematising Serendipity: Proposals for Concordancing Large Corpora with Language Learners. In: Burnard/McEnery 2000, 225–234.

Bernardini, Silvia (2002), Exploring New Directions for Discovery Learning. In: Kettemann/Marko 2002, 165–182.

Bernardini, Silvia (2004), Corpora in the Classroom: An Overview and Some Reflections on Future Developments. In: Sinclair 2004a, 15–36.

Biber, Douglas/Johansson, Stig/Leech, Geoffrey/Conrad, Susan/Finegan, Edward (1999), *Longman Grammar of Spoken and Written English.* Harlow: Pearson Education.

Biber, Douglas/Leech, Geoffrey/Conrad, Susan (2002), *Longman Student Grammar of Spoken and Written English.* London: Longman.

Bondi, Marina (2001), Small Corpora and Language Variation: Reflexivity across Genres. In: Ghadessy/Henry/Roseberry 2001, 135–174.

Botley, Simon/Glass, Julia/McEnery, Tony/Wilson, Andrew (eds.) (1996), *Proceedings of Teaching and Language Corpora 1996.* Lancaster: University Centre for Computer Corpus Research on Language.

Boulton, Alex/Wilhelm, Stephan (2006), Habeant Corpus – they Should Have the Body: Tools Learners Have the Right to Use. Paper presented at: *27e Congrès du GERAS "Cours et Corpus".* Université de Bretagne Sud, Lorient, France, 23–25 March 2006.

Bowker, Lynne/Pearson, Jennifer (2002), *Working with Specialized Language. A Practical Guide to Using Corpora.* London: Routledge.

Braun, Sabine/Kohn, Kurt/Mukherjee, Joybrato (eds.) (2006), *Corpus Technology and Language Pedagogy.* Frankfurt: Peter Lang.

Brodine, Ruey (2001), Integrating Corpus Work into a Academic Reading Course. In: Aston 2001, 138–176.

Burnard, Lou/McEnery, Tony (eds.) (2000), *Rethinking Language Pedagogy from a Corpus Perspective.* Frankfurt: Peter Lang.

Capel, Annette (1993), *Collins COBUILD Concordance Samplers 1: Prepositions.* London: HarperCollins.

Carpenter, Edwin (1993), *Collins COBUILD English Guides 4: Confusable Words.* London: HarperCollins.

Carter, Ronald/Hughes, Rebecca/McCarthy, Michael (2000), *Exploring Grammar in Context. Grammar Reference and Practice.* Cambridge: Cambridge University Press.
Chambers, Angela (2005), Integrating Corpus Consultation in Language Studies. In: *Language Learning and Technology* 9(2), 111–125.
Chambers, Angela (2005), Popularising Corpus Consultation by Language Learners and Teachers. In: Hidalgo/Quereda/Santana 2007, 3–16.
Cobb, Tom (1997), Is there Any Measurable Learning from Hands-on Concordancing? In: *System* 25(3), 301–315.
Coffey, Stephen (2007), Investigating Restricted Semantic Sets in a Large General Corpus: Learning Activities for Students of English as a Foreign Language. In: Hidalgo/Quereda/Santana 2007, 161–174.
Connor, Ulla/Upton, Thomas A. (eds.) (2004), *Applied Corpus Linguistics. A Multi-dimensional Perspective.* Amsterdam: Rodopi.
Conrad, Susan (2004), Corpus Linguistics, Language Variation, and Language Teaching. In: Sinclair 2004a, 67–85.
Coxhead, Averil (2002), The Academic Word List: A Corpus-based Word List for Academic Purposes. In: Kettemann/Marko 2002, 73–89.
Cresswell, Andy (2007), Getting to 'Know' Connectors? Evaluating Data-driven Learning in a Writing Skills Course. In: Hidalgo/Quereda/Santana 2007, 267–288.
Davies, Mark (2000), Using Multi-million Word Corpora of Historical and Dialectal Spanish Texts to Teach Advanced Courses in Spanish Linguistics. In: Burnard/McEnery 2000, 173–185.
Davies, Mark (2004), Student Use of Large, Annotated Corpora to Analyze Syntactic Variation. In: Aston et al. 2004, 259–269.
Dodd, Bill (1997), Exploiting a Corpus of Written German for Advanced Language Learning. In: Wichmann et al. 1997, 131–145.
Firth, John R. (1957), *Papers in Linguistics 1934–1951.* London: Oxford University Press.
Fligelstone, Steve (1993), Some Reflections on the Question of Teaching, from a Corpus Linguistics Perspective. In: *ICAME Journal* 17, 97–109.
Flowerdew, John (1993), Concordancing as a Tool in Course Design. In: *System* 21(2), 231–244 (reprinted in Ghadessy/Henry/Roseberry 2001, 71–92).
Flowerdew, Lynne (2001), The Exploitation of Small Learner Corpora in EAP Materials Design. In: Ghadessy/Henry/Roseberry 2001, 363–380.
Fox, Gwyneth (1987), The Case for Examples. In: Sinclair 1987, 137–149.
Francis, Gill/Sinclair, John McH. (1994), 'I Bet he Drinks Carling Black Label': A Riposte to Owen on Corpus Grammar. In: *Applied Linguistics* 15(2), 190–202.
Francis, Gill/Hunston, Susan/Manning, Elizabeth (1996), *Collins COBUILD Grammar Patterns 1: Verbs.* London: HarperCollins.
Francis, Gill/Hunston, Susan/Manning, Elizabeth (1998), *Collins COBUILD Grammar Patterns 2: Nouns and Adjectives.* London: HarperCollins.
Gaskell, Delian/Cobb, Tom (2004), Can Learners Use Concordance Feedback for Writing Errors? In: *System* 32, 301–319.
Gavioli, Laura/Zanettin, Federico (1997), Comparable Corpora and Translation: A Pedagogic Perspective. Paper presented at: *Corpus Use and Learning to Translate (CULT).* Bertinoro, 14–15 November 1997. http://www.sslmit.unibo.it/cultpaps/laura-fede.htm (accessed through http://web.archive.org, 22 August 2006).
Gavioli, Laura (1997), Exploring Texts through the Concordancer: Guiding the Learner. In: Wichmann et al. 1997, 83–99.
Gavioli, Laura (2001), The Learner as Researcher: Introducing Corpus Concordancing in the Classroom. In: Aston 2001, 108–137.
Gavioli, Laura (2006), *Exploring Corpora for ESP Learning.* Amsterdam: John Benjamins.
Ghadessy, Mohsen/Gao, Yanjie (2001), Small Corpora and Translation: Comparing Thematic Organization in Two Languages. In: Ghadessy/Henry/Roseberry 2001, 335–359.

Ghadessy, Mohsen/Henry, Alex/Roseberry, Robert L. (eds.) (2001), *Small Corpus Studies and ELT. Theory and Practice.* Amsterdam: John Benjamins.
Goodale, Malcolm (1995), *Collins COBUILD Concordance Samplers 4: Tenses.* London: HarperCollins.
Grabowski, Eva/Mindt, Dieter (1995), A Corpus-based Learning List of Irregular Verbs in English. In: *ICAME Journal* 19, 5–22.
Granger, Sylviane (1999), Uses of Tenses by Advanced EFL Learners: Evidence from an Error-tagged Computer Corpus. In: Hasselgård/Oksefjell 1999, 191–202.
Granger, Sylviane (2002), A Bird's-eye View of Learner Corpus Research. In: Granger/Hung/Petch-Tyson 2002, 3–33.
Granger, Sylviane (2004), Computer Learner Corpus Research: Current Status and Future Prospects. In: Connor/Upton 2004, 123–145.
Granger, Sylviane/Hung, Joseph/Petch-Tyson, Stephanie (eds.) (2002), *Computer Learner Corpora, Second Language Acquisition and Foreign Language Teaching.* Amsterdam: John Benjamins.
Granger, Sylviane/Tribble, Chris (1988), Learner Corpus Data in the Foreign Language Classroom: Form-focused Instruction and Data-driven Learning. In: Granger, Sylviane (ed.), *Learner English on Computer.* London: Longman, 199–209.
Gray, Bethany E. (2005), *Error-specific Concordancing for Intermediate ESL/EFL Writers.* http://dana.ucc.na4.edu/~bde6/coursework/Projects/PedagogicalTip/homepage.html (accessed 28 January 2008).
Hadley, Gregory (1997), *Sensing the Winds of Change: An Introduction to Data-driven Learning.* http://www.nuis.ac.jp/~hadley/publication/windofchange/windsofchange.htm (accessed 22 August 2006).
Hadley, Gregory (2001), *Concordancing in Japanese TEFL: Unlocking the Power of Data-driven Learning.* http://www.nuis.ac.jp/~hadley/publication/jlearner/jlearner.htm (accessed 22 August 2006).
Henry, Alex/Roseberry, Robert L. (2001), Using a Small Corpus to Obtain Data for Teaching a Genre. In: Ghadessy/Henry/Roseberry 2001, 93–133.
Hidalgo, Encarnacion/Quereda, Luis/Santana, Juan (eds.) (2007), *Corpora in the Foreign Language Classroom.* Amsterdam: Rodopi.
Hill, Jimmie/Lewis, Michael (1997), *LTP Dictionary of Selected Collocations.* Hove: Language Teaching Publications.
Hoey, Michael (2000), The Hidden Lexical Clues of Textual Organisation: A Preliminary Investigation into an Unusual Text from a Corpus Perspective. In: Burnard/McEnery 2000, 31–41.
Hornby, Albert S. (ed.) (2005), *Oxford Advanced Learner's Dictionary.* Oxford: Oxford University Press.
Hunston, Susan/Francis, Gill (2000), *Pattern Grammar. A Corpus-driven Approach to the Lexical Grammar of English.* Amsterdam: John Benjamins.
Hunston, Susan (2002), *Corpora in Applied Linguistics.* Cambridge: Cambridge University Press.
Hymes, Dell (1972), On Communicative Competence. In: Pride, John B./Holmes, Janet (eds.), *Sociolinguistics.* Harmondsworth: Penguin, 269–293.
Hymes, Dell (1992), The Concept of Communicative Competence Revisited. In: Pütz, Martin (ed.), *Thirty Years of Linguistic Evolution. Studies in Honour of Rene Dirven on the Occasion of his Sixtieth Birthday.* Amsterdam: John Benjamins, 31–57.
Johansson, Stig (2007), Using Corpora: From Learning to Research. In: Hidalgo/Quereda/Santana 2007, 17–30.
Johansson, Stig/Stavestrand, Helga (1987), Problems in Learning – and Teaching – the Progressive Form. In: Lindblad, Ishrat/Ljung, Magnus (eds.), *Proceedings from the Third Nordic Conference for English Studies, Hässelby, Sept 25–27, 1986, vol. 1.* Stockholm: Almquist & Wiksell, 139–148.
Johns, Tim (1986), Microconcord: A Language-learner's Research Tool. In: *System* 14(2), 151–162.

Johns, Tim (1991), Should you Be Persuaded – Two Samples of Data-driven Learning Materials. In: Johns, Tim/King, Philip (eds.), *Classroom Concordancing* (*ELR Journal* 4), 1–16.

Johns, Tim (1994), From Printout to Handout: Grammar and Vocabulary Teaching in the Context of Data-driven Learning. In: Odlin, Terence (ed.), *Perspectives on Pedagogical Grammar.* Cambridge: Cambridge University Press, 27–45.

Johns, Tim (1997), Contexts: The Background, Development and Trialling of a Concordance-based CALL Program. In: Wichmann et al. 1997, 100–115.

Johns, Tim (2002), Data-driven Learning: The Perpetual Challenge. In: Kettemann/Marko 2002, 107–117.

Jones, Randall L. (1997), Creating and Using a Corpus of Spoken German. In: Wichmann et al. 1997, 146–156.

Jones, Randall L. (2000), Textbook German and Authentic Spoken German: A Corpus-based Comparison. In: Lewandowska-Tomaszczyk, Barbara/Melia, Patrick James (eds.), *PALC'99: Practical Applications in Language Corpora.* Frankfurt: Peter Lang, 501–516.

Kennedy, Claire/Miceli, Tiziana (2001), An Evaluation of Intermediate Students' Approaches to Corpus Investigation. In: *Language Learning and Technology* 5(3), 77–90. http://llt.msu.edu/vol5num3/kennedy/ (accessed 22 August 2006).

Kennedy, Claire/Miceli, Tiziana (2002), The CWIC Project: Developing and Using a Corpus for Intermediate Italian Students. In: Kettemann/Marko 2002, 183–192.

Kennedy, Graeme (1992), Preferred Ways of Putting Things with Implications for Language Teaching. In: Svartvik 1992, 335–373.

Kettemann, Bernhard/Marko, Georg (eds.) (2002), *Teaching and Learning by Doing Corpus Analysis. Proceedings of the Fourth International Conference on Teaching and Language Corpora, Graz 19–24 July, 2000.* Amsterdam: Rodopi.

Kettemann, Bernhard (1995), On the Use of Concordancing in ELT. In: *Arbeiten aus Anglistik und Amerikanistik* 20, 29–41.

Kjellmer, Göran (1984), Some Thoughts on Collocational Distinctiveness. In: Aarts, Jan/Meijs, Willem (eds.), *Corpus Linguistics. Recent Developments in the Use of Computer Corpora in English Language Research.* Amsterdam: Rodopi, 163–171.

Kjellmer, Göran (1992), Comments. In: Svartvik 1992, 374–378.

Lam, Peter Y. W. (2007), A Corpus-driven Lexico-grammatical Analysis of English Tourism Industry Texts and the Study of its Pedagogic Implications in English for Specific Purposes. In: Hidalgo/Quereda/Santana 2007, 71–90.

Lea, Diana (ed.) (2002), *Oxford Collocations Dictionary for Students of English.* Oxford: Oxford University Press.

Leech, Geoffrey (1997), Teaching and Language Corpora: A Convergence. In: Wichmann et al. 1997, 1–23.

Leńko-Szymańska, Agnieszka (2007), Past Progressive or Simple Past? The Acquisition of Progressive Aspect by Polish Advanced Learners of English. In: Hidalgo/Quereda/Santana 2007, 253–266.

Lewis, Michael (1993), *The Lexical Approach.* Hove: Language Teaching Publications.

Lewis, Michael (1997), *Implementing the Lexical Approach.* Hove: Language Teaching Publications.

Lewis, Michael (2000), *Teaching Collocation. Further Developments in the Lexical Approach.* Hove: Language Teaching Publications.

Lorenz, Gunter (1999), *Adjective Intensification – Learners versus Native Speakers. A Corpus Study of Argumentative Writing.* Amsterdam: Rodopi.

Lorenz, Gunter (2002), Language Corpora Rock the Base: On Standard English Grammar, Perfective Aspect and Seemingly Adverse Corpus Evidence. In: Kettemann/Marko 2002, 131–145.

Lüdeling, Anke/Walter, Maik/Kroymann, Emil/Adolphs, Peter (2005), Multi-level Error Annotation in Learner Corpora. In: Hunston, Susan/Danielsson, Pernilla (eds.), *Proceedings from the Corpus Linguistics Conference Series (Corpus Linguistics 2005, Birmingham, 14–15 July 2005).* http://www.corpus.bham.ac.uk/PCLC (accessed 22 August 2006).

Mackey, William Francis (1965) *Language teaching analysis*. London. Longman.
McCarthy, Michael/Jeanne McCarten/Sandiford, Helen (2005), *Touchstone Student's Book 1.* Cambridge: Cambridge University Press.
McEnery, Tony/Xiao, Richard/Tono, Yukio (2006), *Corpus-based Language Studies. An Advanced Resource Book.* London: Routledge.
Meunier, Fanny/Gouverneur, Celine (2007), The Treatment of Phraseology in ELT Textbooks. In: Hidalgo/Quereda/Santana 2007, 119–140.
Meunier, Fanny (2002), The Pedagogical Value of Native and Learner Corpora in EFL Grammar Teaching. In: Granger/Hung/Petch-Tyson 2002, 119–141.
Mindt, Dieter (1981), Angewandte Linguistik und Grammatik für den Englischunterricht. In: Kunsmann, Peter/Kuhn, Otto (eds.), *Weltsprache Englisch in Forschung und Lehre. Festschrift für Kurt Wächtler.* Berlin: Schmidt, 175–186.
Mindt, Dieter (1987), *Sprache – Grammatik – Unterrichtsgrammatik. Futurischer Zeitbezug im Englischen I.* Frankfurt: Diesterweg.
Mindt, Dieter (1995), *An Empirical Grammar of the English Verb: Modal Verbs.* Berlin: Cornelsen.
Mindt, Dieter (1997), Corpora and the Teaching of English in Germany. In: Wichmann et al. 1997, 40–50.
Mparutsa, Cynthia/Love, Alison/Morrison, Andrew (1991), Bringing Concord to the ESP Classroom. In: Johns, Tim/King, Philip (eds.), *Classroom Concordancing* (*ELR Journal* 4), 115–134.
Mukherjee, Joybrato (2002), *Korpuslinguistik und Englischunterricht. Eine Einführung.* Frankfurt: Peter Lang.
Mukherjee, Joybrato (2004), Bridging the Gap between Applied Corpus Linguistics and the Reality of English Language Teaching in Germany. In: Connor/Upton 2004, 239–250.
Mukherjee, Joybrato/Rohrbach, Jan-Marc (2006), Rethinking Applied Corpus Linguistics from a Language-pedagogical Perspective: New Departures in Learner Corpus Research. In: Kettemann, Bernhard/Marko, Georg (eds.), *Planing, Gluing and Painting Corpora. Inside the Applied Corpus Linguist's Workshop.* Frankfurt: Peter Lang, 205–232.
Nation, Paul (1990), *Teaching and Learning Vocabulary.* Boston: Heinle & Heinle.
Nattinger, James R. (1980), A Lexical Phrase Grammar for ESL. In: *TESOL Quarterly* 14(3), 337–344.
Nesselhauf, Nadja (2004), How Learner Corpus Analysis Can Contribute to Language Teaching: A Study of Support Verb Constructions. In: Aston/Bernardini/Stewart 2004, 109–124.
Nesselhauf, Nadja (2005), *Collocations in a Learner Corpus.* Amsterdam: John Benjamins.
Papp, Szilvia (2007), Inductive Learning and Self-correction with the Use of Learner and Reference Corpora. In: Hidalgo/Quereda/Santana 2007, 207–220.
Partington, Alan (1998), *Patterns and Meanings. Using Corpora for English Language Research and Teaching.* Amsterdam: John Benjamins.
Pawley, Andrew/Syder, Frances H. (1983), Two Puzzles for Linguistic Theory: Native-like Selection and Native-like Fluency. In: Richards, Jack C./Schmidt, Richard W. (eds.), *Language and Communication.* London: Longman, 191–226.
Pereira de Oliveira, Maria José (2003), Corpus Linguistics in the Teaching of ESP and Literary Studies. In: *ESP World* 6(2). http://www.esp-world.info/articles_6/Corpus.htm (accessed 22 August 2006).
Pérez Basanta, Carmen/Martín, María Elena Rodríguez (2007), The Application of Data-driven Learning to a Small-scale Corpus: Using Film Transcripts for Teaching Conversational Skills. In: Hidalgo/Quereda/Santana 2007.
Peters, Pam (2004), *The Cambridge Guide to English Usage.* Cambridge: Cambridge University Press.
Römer, Ute (2004a), A Corpus-driven Approach to Modal Auxiliaries and their Didactics. In: Sinclair 2004a, 185–199.
Römer, Ute (2004b), Comparing Real and Ideal Language Learner Input: The Use of an EFL Textbook Corpus in Corpus Linguistics and Language Teaching. In: Aston/Bernardini/Stewart 2004, 151–168.

Römer, Ute (2005a), *Progressives, Patterns, Pedagogy. A Corpus-driven Approach to English Progressive Forms, Functions, Contexts and Didactics.* Amsterdam: John Benjamins.
Römer, Ute (2005b), Shifting Foci in Language Description and Instruction. In: *Arbeiten aus Anglistik und Amerikanistik* 30(1–2), 145–160.
Römer, Ute (2006), Looking at *Looking:* Functions and Contexts of Progressives in Spoken English and 'School' English. In: Renouf, Antoinette/Kehoe, Andrew (eds.), *The Changing Face of Corpus Linguistics.* Amsterdam: Rodopi, 231–242.
Römer, Ute (forthcoming), Corpus Research and Practice: What Help Do Teachers Need and what Can we Offer? In: Aijmer, Karin (ed.), *Teaching and Corpora* (provisional title). Amsterdam: John Benjamins.
Rundell, Michael (ed.) (2002), *Macmillan English Dictionary for Advanced Learners.* Oxford: Macmillan.
Schlüter, Norbert (2002), *Present Perfect. Eine korpuslinguistische Analyse des englischen Perfekts mit Vermittlungsvorschlägen für den Sprachunterricht.* Tübingen: Narr.
Schmied, Josef (1998), Differences and Similarities of Close Cognates: English *with* and German *mit.* In: Johansson, Stig/Oksefjell, Signe (eds.), *Corpora and Cross-linguistic Research. Theory, Method and Case Studies.* Amsterdam: Rodopi, 255–274.
Scott, Mike/Tribble, Christopher (2006), *Textual Patterns. Key Words and Corpus Analysis in Language Education.* Amsterdam: John Benjamins.
Seidlhofer, Barbara (2000), Operationalizing Intertextuality: Using Learner Corpora for Learning. In: Burnard/McEnery 2000, 207–223.
Seidlhofer, Barbara (2002), Pedagogy and Local Learner Corpora: Working with Learning-driven Data. In: Granger/Hung/Petch-Tyson 2002, 213–234.
Sinclair, John McH. (ed.) (1987), *Looking Up. An Account of the COBUILD Project in Lexical Computing.* London: HarperCollins.
Sinclair, John McH. (1991), *Corpus Concordance Collocation.* Oxford: Oxford University Press.
Sinclair, John McH. (1997), Corpus Evidence in Language Description. In: Wichmann et al. 1997, 27–39.
Sinclair, John McH. (2003), *Reading Concordances.* London: Longman.
Sinclair, John McH. (ed.) (2004a), *How to Use Corpora in Language Teaching.* Amsterdam: John Benjamins.
Sinclair, John McH. (2004b), Introduction. In: Sinclair 2004a, 1–10.
Sinclair, John McH. (2004c), New Evidence, New Priorities, New Attitudes. In: Sinclair 2004a, 271–299.
Sinclair, John McH./Renouf, Antoinette (1988), A Lexical Syllabus for Language Learning. In: Carter, Ronald/McCarthy, Michael (eds.), *Vocabulary in Language Teaching.* London: Longman, 140–158.
Sinclair, John McH. et al. (eds.) (1990), *Collins COBUILD English Grammar.* London: HarperCollins.
Sinclair, John McH. et al. (eds.) (1992), *Collins COBUILD English Usage.* London: HarperCollins.
Sinclair, John McH. et al. (eds.) (2001), *Collins COBUILD English Dictionary for Advanced Learners.* London: HarperCollins.
Sripicharn, Passapong (2004), Examining Native Speakers' and Learners' Investigation of the Same Concordance Data and its Implications for Classroom Concordancing with EFL Learners. In: Aston/Bernardini/Stewart 2004, 233–245.
Stevens, Vance (1991), Concordance-based Vocabulary Exercises: A Viable Alternative to Gap-fillers. In: Johns, Tim/King, Philip (eds.), *Classroom Concordancing* (*ELR Journal* 4), 47–63.
Stubbs, Michael (1996), *Text and Corpus Analysis: Computer-assisted studies of language and culture.* Oxford: Blackwell.
Svartvik, J. (ed.) (1992), *Directions in Corpus Linguistics: Proceedings of Nobel Symposium 82 Stockholm, 4–8 August 1991.* Berlin/New York: Mouton de Gruyter.

Teubert, Wolfgang (2004), Units of Meaning, Parallel Corpora, and their Implications for Language Teaching. In: Connor/Upton 2004, 171–189.
Thurstun, Jennifer/Candlin, Christopher (1998), Concordancing and the Teaching of the Vocabulary of Academic English. In: *English for Specific Purposes* 17, 267–280.
Tognini Bonelli, Elena (2001), *Corpus Linguistics at Work.* Amsterdam: John Benjamins.
Tribble, Chris (1997), Improvising Corpora for ELT: Quick-and-dirty Ways of Developing Corpora for Language Teaching. In: Lewandowska-Tomaszczyk, Barbara/Melia, Patrick J. (eds.), *Practical Applications in Language Corpora. The Proceedings of PALC '97.* Lodz: Lodz University Press. http://www.ctribble.co.uk/text/Palc.htm (accessed 22 August 2006).
Tribble, Chris/Jones, Glyn (1997), *Concordances in the Classroom. A Resource Book for Teachers.* Houston, TX: Athelstan.
Turnbull, Jill/Burston, Jack (1998), Towards Independent Concordance Work for Students: Lessons from a Case Study. In: *On-CALL* 12(2). http://www.cltr.uq.edu.au/oncall/turnbull122.html (accessed through http://web.archive.org, 22 August 2006).
Wang, Lixun (2001), Exploring Parallel Concordancing in English and Chinese. In: *Language Learning and Technology* 5(3), 174–184.
West, Michael (1953), *A General Service List of English Words.* London: Longman.
Whistle, Jeremy (1999), Concordancing with Students Using an 'off-the-Web' Corpus. In: *ReCALL* 11(2), 74–80. Available at: http://www.eurocall-languages.org/recall/pdf/rvol11no2.pdf.
Wichmann, Anne/Fligelstone, Steven/McEnery, Tony/Knowles, Gerry (eds.) (1997), *Teaching and Language Corpora.* London: Longman.
Willis, Dave/Willis, Jane (1989), *Collins COBUILD English Course.* London: HarperCollins.
Willis, Dave (1990), *The Lexical Syllabus. A New Approach to Language Teaching.* London: HarperCollins.
Zanettin, Federico (2001), Swimming in Words: Corpora, Translation, and Language Learning. In: Aston 2001, 177–197.
Zorzi, Daniela (2001), The Pedagogic Use of Spoken Corpora. In: Aston 2001, 85–107.

Ute Römer, Hannover (Germany)

8. Corpus linguistics and lexicography

1. Introduction

1.1. Objectives and structure of this article

The production of dictionaries is one of the "clients" of corpus linguistics, insofar as many dictionaries of recent date have been created in some way "on the basis" of corpora. This reliance on corpus data concerns the selection of raw material from which the lexicographer gets evidence (including both qualitative and quantitative criteria, see section 2), the selection of types of linguistic data to be extracted in order to feed into dictionaries (section 3), as well as corpus-linguistic tools for the actual manipulation of corpus data in lexicographic work (section 4).

These three aspects seem to suggest an exclusively supportive role of corpora and corpus linguistics for lexicography. However, in recent years, new products which combine dictionary and corpus data have been conceived, and Natural Language Processing (NLP) has been characterized by a number of two-way interactions between the two fields: from the simple fact that lexical data are used for corpus annotation, to tools and procedures which abstract lexical descriptions from annotated corpora (see section 5). This article ends with a short historical overview (section 6) which will allow us to draw lines of development, with respect to the kinds of relationships between corpus linguistics and lexicography discussed previously.

The interaction between corpus linguistics and lexicography has been summarized in manuals of both disciplines. Examples from lexicography include van Sterkenburg (2003, 18–25, 167–193, 228–239), Gouws/Prinsloo (2005, 21–37), and Bergenholtz/Tarp (1995, 90–95). The most detailed account of lexicography at large is found in Hausmann et al. (1989–1990). Examples from corpus linguistics: McEnery/Xiao/Tono (2006, 80–85), McEnery/Wilson (1996, 90–93) and, with selected practical examples, Biber/Conrad/Reppen (1998, 21–54).

1.2. Notions of lexicography

Much lexicographic activity is aimed at the production of dictionaries. There are several metalexicographic theories and traditions which discuss the foundation and objectives of lexicography (for a detailed overview, see Wiegand 1998). In this article, we take work by Wiegand (2001) and in particular Bergenholtz/Tarp (2002) and Tarp (2006) as a metalexicographic starting point. Bergenholtz/Tarp see dictionaries as utility products which provide people with data about linguistic objects (e. g. words, morphemes, word groups). The creation of human use dictionaries is based or should be based on an analysis of the users, their needs and their prior knowledge. Bergenholtz/Tarp (2002) and Tarp (2006) distinguish two main types of user needs, communication-oriented needs and knowledge-oriented needs.

Communication-oriented needs may concern one language or two (covered by monolingual as opposed to bilingual dictionaries), be it the mother tongue of the user or (one of) his/her foreign language(s); and in each case, the dictionary may be intended to support the user with respect to language reception (understanding and reading) or to language production (speaking and writing). This gives four basic types of needs (receptive needs with respect to the mother tongue, receptive needs with respect to the foreign language, production needs with respect to mother tongue and foreign language, respectively), as well as (at least) two types of translation needs (from the mother tongue to the foreign language, and vice versa).

Knowledge-oriented needs concern information (i. e. a possibility to learn something) about general cultural and encyclopedic facts, about a certain field of specialization (e. g. organic chemistry, computer science, American law on food and drugs), or about a language (e. g. facts about the etymology of words).

Following Bergenholtz/Tarp's theory of dictionary functions (in Danish *Funktionsteori*), one may see dictionaries as "knowledge tools"; this implies that not only the needs of users, but also the knowledge already present in the users play an important role for dictionary design. Lexicographers should thus keep track of the linguistic knowledge of the users, and of their non-linguistic knowledge. The former concerns their mastery of their mother tongue and/or of a foreign language, both with respect to general language and to the specialized language of a given domain. The types of non-linguistic knowledge mentioned by Bergenholtz/Tarp (2002) include general cultural and encyclopedic knowledge, and knowledge of a given domain (like organic chemistry etc.). Obviously, linguistic and non-linguistic knowledge interact in many ways, and the distinction between dictionaries for general language and dictionaries for specialized language is not necessarily congruent with the dividing line between the two types of knowledge. A good dictionary of the specialized language of organic chemistry, for example, will have to describe the specialized language use of words and word groups in written and spoken communication of the organic chemistry domain, including, for example, their valency, their preferred adjuncts, or their frequent collocations.

Both, user needs and the users' (assumed) background knowledge influence dictionary design. To give an (oversimplified) example: monolingual learner's dictionaries assume a certain type of users (e. g. school pupils) with a certain amount of background knowledge about their mother tongue (e. g. the 5,000 most frequent words of daily conversation), about cultural and encyclopedic facts (rather not much, which is why many such dictionaries contain, among other things, pictures of objects labelled with words), and with a predominant need to get support for the production of texts in their mother tongue (thus, the dictionaries contain many collocations, examples illustrating the syntactic valency properties of words, etc.).

User needs, the users' background knowledge, and the dictionary design in turn influence the use of corpora for the creation of a given dictionary. This affects the choice of corpus material (which (kinds of) texts are used as a corpus for writing a dictionary?) and the kinds of data extracted from the corpus and presented in the dictionary (which head words, which kinds of properties of these words?). We will come back to this interdependency throughout the remainder of this article.

The abovementioned aspects obviously concern primarily the creation of dictionaries for human users. There are other lexicographic activities as well, and moreover, the notion of 'lexicography' is broader than just that of 'dictionary making'. As mentioned, Natural Language Processing (NLP) is also in need of dictionaries, and the model of Bergenholtz/Tarp is only partly applicable to this situation. The needs of language processing systems (symbolic, statistical, hybrid), the kinds of representations used by the targeted system (both, with respect to contents and formalization) and the intended coverage play a role in the design of NLP dictionaries, and all this also has implications for corpus use (see section 5).

As noted, the broad sense of the term "lexicography" includes more than dictionary making, even though the theory and practice of the design and production of dictionaries are at the heart of lexicographic science. Dictionary making can be analyzed from the user angle (see above, cf. Bergenholtz/Tarp 2002), from the point of view of the dictionary product (e. g. in terms of its textual components and structures, cf. Wiegand 1990) or in terms of the workflow and processes which lead to dictionaries (see, section 4 and, for example, part II of van Sterkenburg 2003, with contributions to the topic of "Linguistic corpora (databases) and the compilation of dictionaries"). Other subfields include research into dictionary use (relevant for the analysis of user needs and of the functionality of lexicographic devices), dictionary assessment and criticism and the history of lexicography (for an overview of all fields, see Hausmann 1985, 368–372).

2. Corpora as a source for lexicography: Corpus composition

2.1. General observations

In section 1.2., we mentioned that the users of a dictionary, their needs and their prior knowledge (should) have an influence on the corpora used as a basis for the creation of the dictionary. This problem presents itself in different forms, depending on the types of targeted dictionaries. Within monolingual dictionaries, a main distinction concerns dictionaries for general vs. specialized language (sometimes abbreviated as LGP vs. LSP dictionaries, *l*anguage for *g*eneral/*s*pecific *p*urposes); and obviously, the creation of bilingual dictionaries has its own implications on corpus use.

A few corpus linguistic fundamentals are however common to all corpus lexicographic work. These include corpus data selection and corpus representativity. Most corpora contain written material from (professional) authors, such as books, magazines, newspapers, etc. It has often been argued that this should be counterbalanced by spoken text, ideally from free conversational production. 10 % of the text of the British National Corpus (BNC) is transcribed spoken material. Higher percentages are rare, at least in large corpora, due to transcription costs. Questions of corpus authenticity, balance and sampling methodology (see article 9 of this handbook) and of the (im-)possibility of creating representative corpora are particularly important for lexicography: lexicographers should carefully decide which language sample(s) they want to be working on (cf. e. g. the discussion in Tognini Bonelli 2001, 55–64).

Consequently, emphasis has been put on the development of text classification criteria (cf. Biber/Conrad/Reppen 1998, 133–171, 203–229) both internal (linguistic) and in particular external (non-linguistic), on the use of annotation systems (metadata tagsets and guidelines for their annotation) and on possibilities for lexicographers to keep track of and to cite the source of a given corpus instance in detail. An early, quite influential paper discussing these questions in a general way is Atkins/Clear/Ostler (1992). The paper is not exclusively targeted at lexicographers (although the authors are lexicographers), but it introduces, among other things, sets of criteria for corpus classification and annotation.

2.2. Corpora for monolingual general language dictionaries

General language has often been described as evenly covering, at least in a shallow way, a broad range of fields of knowledge, i. e. as not focusing on one field; many words and word groups from general language seem to be shared by a broad range of text types from many fields. This kind of "unmarked" language is supposed to be covered in general language dictionaries, mostly for a public of non-specialists. Lexicographers are thus interested in equally "unmarked" corpora.

General language dictionaries vary considerably in size, depending on the public; their vocabulary may go from 5,000 to well over 100,000 items, and the books may be published in one or several volumes (cf. Pruvost 2006, 83–92, 137, 150–153). Single volume dictionaries include monolingual defining dictionaries intended for a broad public (such as *Duden Universalwörterbuch* (DUW), *Zingarelli, Le Petit Robert* (PR) etc.; references to all the dictionaries mentioned in this articles are given in the literature section), as well as general language dictionaries for specific types of users, in particular learners' dictionaries. Examples of the latter include the *Oxford Advanced Learner's Dictionary* (OALD), the *Dictionnaire du français contemporain* (DFC) etc. A particularly interesting learners' dictionary in this respect is the *Nuwe Woordeboek sonder grense* (Gouws/Stark/Gouws 2004), an Afrikaans learners' dictionary for school children, which is based not only on a general corpus, but also on a corpus of texts from school manuals (see also De Schryver/Prinsloo 2003). The *English G Wörterbuch* is similar: it is targeted at German high school learners of English.

Multivolume dictionaries are supposed to provide a detailed description of the lexical inventory of a language at a given point in time or over a certain time span, which implies both broad (and the broadest possible) coverage and a considerable degree of descriptive detail. Examples of such dictionaries are the *Oxford English Dictionary,* the *Trésor de la langue française* (cf. Imbs/Quémada 1971–1994) or *Den Danske Ordbog.* Similar undertakings in terms of electronic dictionaries on the internet are planned and under way, for example for German: *elexiko* (see Klosa/Schnörch/Storjohann 2006) and the plans for *Digitales Wörterbuch der deutschen Sprache* (DWDS, cf. Geyken 2003, http://www.dwds.de). There are also CD-ROM versions of several multivolume dictionaries, for example of *Grand Robert* and of *Trésor de la langue française* for French.

Obviously, the intended size of the dictionary has a major impact on the size and composition of the corpora used as sources of data. Work on the six-volume *Den Danske Ordbog* was based on an initial corpus of about 40 million words, later enlarged with another 28 million (Korpus 2000, cf.: http://korpus.dsl.dk, Norling-Christensen/Asmussen 1998). The ongoing electronic dictionary projects for German intend to rely on much larger corpora: *elexiko* is based, as of mid-2006, on 1,400 million words, and the corpus of DWDS is about 1,000 million words. The assumption is that larger corpora allow for broader coverage, more detail and more reliable frequency data for larger numbers of lexical items. As lexicographers would not consider items with a frequency of less than 5 (because such figures could equally well be a result of chance, see Evert 2005, 119–133 and article 37 of this handbook), the total amount of items covered increases with the size of the corpus.

2.3. Large corpora used for lexicography

The abovementioned reasoning about the relationship between corpus size and the coverage of a dictionary has led to the creation of large national text corpora. The British National Corpus, BNC (cf. BNC, Clear 1993), was the first one to be created, and it was initiated by a lexicographic consortium and used by several dictionary publishers.

The same holds for the attempts to create an American National Corpus, ANC, (cf. Ide/Suderman 2004), for the corpora used for *Den Danske Ordbog,* for the Corpus de la Real Academia Española (CREA, Corpus de Referencia del Español Actual) and for the ever expanding Bank of English, which was created to support the production of the *COBUILD* dictionary.

BNC has 100 million words and is composed according to a detailed and fully reproducible set of (annotated) text typological and text structural criteria (cf. Clear 1993). It served as a model for the ANC and to some extent for the Czech National Corpus, CNC (cf. Cermák 1997). Part of the corpus of the Berlin-Brandenburgische Akademie der Wissenschaften, the Kernkorpus, intended to serve the creation of DWDS, is carefully sampled in terms of time slices (ca. 100 million words evenly covering the period between 1900 and 2000), as is the Danish Korpus 2000, which covers the Danish language of the turn of the millennium.

More generally, lexicographers agree that a corpus of at least ca. 60 to 100 million words is needed to get enough data for a dictionary of ca. 50,000 to 60,000 head words, if these are to be described in some detail.

2.4. Corpora for dictionaries of the language of specialized domains

The creation of dictionaries for specialized domains has its own corpus methodology (cf. Bergenholtz/Tarp 1995, 32–37, 90–96; Bergenholtz/Pedersen 1994); it aims at describing the way in which experts speak about a given domain. The more restricted the domain, the smaller the vocabulary to be covered; many dictionaries of specialized language contain only a few hundred or a few thousand entries. Bergenholtz/Tarp (1995, 95) report that a corpus of less than one million words, chosen from specialized literature, manuals, handbooks, general descriptions of the domain, etc. was sufficient as a material basis for a specialized dictionary of DNA technology (cf. Kaufmann/Bergenholtz 1992). On the other hand, a dictionary covering a broad domain of knowledge (say biotechnology or biology at large) would require a larger corpus.

A major issue in corpus design for specialized lexicography is the selection of appropriate texts to go into the corpus. The more specialized the domain, the easier it becomes to decide whether a given text belongs to the targeted domain or not: the field of "biology" is not only vast, but also has overlaps with physics, chemistry etc. The biochemical subfield of DNA technology is easier to delimit, especially on the basis of a systematic description of the main (classes of) facts of the domain (a sort of domain ontology, cf. e. g. Kaufmann/Bergenholtz 1992, 26–61). Once these central facts are noted, a corpus can be collected which contains texts about these facts.

An additional important problem of corpus design for specialized lexicography is the typology of users of the texts included in the corpus. Specialized communication between experts differs from that between experts and semi-experts or experts and laymen, and the corpus texts should parallel the intended user group(s) of the dictionary.

Within the research field of terminology and terminography, the use of corpus data is advocated by those who wish to provide not only lists of terms and their equivalents, but also data about the use of these terms in texts. This includes collocations, term variants, and morphosyntactic properties of terms. In France and Canada, proponents of "*terminologie textuelle*" (e. g. Condamines/Rebeyrolle 2001, cf. also Pearson 1998, 41–66, 121–167) place corpus data at the centre of their research, to identify the above mentioned properties and to analyze the function of terms within texts for specialized communication. In contrast, for mainly taxonomical concept-oriented terminographic work, corpora play a less important role.

2.5. Corpora for bilingual dictionaries

Most bilingual dictionaries are conceived as general language dictionaries with a rather comprehensive lemma list.

There is debate about the use and usefulness of parallel corpora (cf. article 16 of this handbook) for bilingual lexicography. A carefully aligned corpus (aligned at least at sentence level, and ideally also at the level of phrases, chunks and/or words) would obviously support lexicographers quite well in providing syntagmatic data about the use of words in both languages. This approach is only starting to be explored, for example by Citron/Widmann (2006); on the basis of a correctly sentence aligned English/French literary corpus of 2 million words per language, the authors check frequent words "backwards", i. e. they extract source language words that have given rise to a certain translation, in order to improve equivalent proposals in their dictionary. A major obstacle for a broader use of this approach is that only few parallel corpora are available, and many of them are specialized in terms of text types (e. g. parliament debates) and/or domains (e. g. technical documentation). Thus, for the moment, this method is only applicable for high frequency words.

From a theoretical point of view, there may be a problem with the use of parallel corpora: a parallel corpus reflects the translation work of one or more individual translators. The translations provided are bound to the context: at sentence level, at text level, and even with respect to the wider interpretational context. Such translations may be specific, sometimes more specific than needed in a general bilingual dictionary. Citron/Widmann (2006, 255) counterbalance this by checking source language items which have been translated with the word they want to verify, "catching writers unaware", i. e. by searching backwards, from L_2 to L_1.

Comparable corpora, if large enough and constructed according to the criteria mentioned above in section 2.1., could indeed serve the needs of lexicographers writing bilingual dictionaries, as they would provide texts about the same topics, in both languages, and each (typically) written by a native speaker. Again, data collection cost is still a hindrance to the realization of large projects of this kind. The methodology applied in the creation of bilingual specialized dictionaries (see above, section 2.3.) can however be seen as an instance of this approach.

Lexicographers involved in the production of bilingual dictionaries have developed their own procedures to cope with the lack of appropriate corpus data. An example is the use of a bilingual framework, i. e. a pair of monolingual descriptions of lexical items in the dictionary's languages, based on a corpus, with subsequent translation. An early example of a bilingual dictionary developed in this way is *The Oxford-Hachette French Dictionary* (Corréard/Grundy 1994, cf. its introduction).

2.6. Data from the internet as a source for lexicography

Researchers in linguistics and lexicography have recently started to get interested in the use of World Wide Web data as corpora (cf. Scholze-Stubenrecht 2001, Kilgarriff/ Grefenstette 2003 and the articles in the special issue of *Computational Linguistics* introduced by this article; cf. also article 18 of this handbook). There are also some experimental lexicographic products available which are partly based on Web data (cf. the Wortschatz project at Leipzig University, Biemann et al. 2004).

For large scale lexicographic work, problems of at least two kinds need to be addressed before web data can be exploited in dictionary making. The first is the quality of text data on the internet. There is a need for a minimum of metadata (author, person responsible for the text, date of production of the text, "nativeness" of the author, site and institution to be cited, etc.), to allow the lexicographer to interpret the source in terms of reliability. Secondly, any quantitative statements derived from a snapshot of the Web are problematic; one reason for this is the fact that the actual size of the Web corpus can only be known if a snapshot is downloaded (but not if a search engine is used). A second reason is that there are many repetitions, redundancies, citations of other people's texts etc. on the internet. Thus the basic problems of text selection for lexicography remain the same, also for the Web (see section 2.1. and article 18 of this handbook). Finally, many texts published on the Web require a non-trivial amount of text handling work before they can be exploited for lexicography.

3. Corpora as a source for lexicography: Using corpus data as evidence

Most descriptive work in corpus-based lexicography is semi-automatic, in the sense that tools serve to extract candidate data from the corpus, and the lexicographer's task is to interpret these data. Intuitively, one thinks of the lexicographer as interpreting, sorting and grouping concordance lines. However, there are more ways of using corpus data; this section will present them, starting from the two main structure types present in dictionaries, macrostructure and microstructure, or, entry words and linguistic facts about entry words.

A more general note is however needed at this point, about the relationship between text data found in a corpus and lexicographic data in a dictionary ("Angaben" in Wiegand's terms, cf. Wiegand 1990). The latter are meant to allow a user to infer information about properties of words, word groups etc. The former are typically used by lexicographers to infer such properties themselves, and to serve as examples of those properties which the lexicographers find important enough to be presented to a given user group. As in all language description work which uses corpus data, there are different methodological approaches to the identification, classification and sorting of corpus data for the creation of lexicographic data.

In line with the "corpus-driven" position (cf. e. g. Tognini Bonelli 2001, 177–179, Sinclair 2004), one may wish to avoid as much as possible the a priori projection of linguistic categorizations onto a corpus, relying essentially on the observation of distributional facts identified in the corpus; this view tends to exclude or minimize corpus preprocessing as it is discussed below, in section 4.1., relying only or mainly on statistically derived distributional data presented to the lexicographer, and assuming that combinatorial, semantic and to some extent syntactic properties of words and word combinations can be intellectually inferred from the observed distributional data (cf. Perkuhn et al. 2005, 67 f. for an example).

Alternatively, one may accept computational linguistic preprocessing of corpora (and potential errors it may introduce) and use descriptive linguistic hypotheses as a basis for automatic search and retrieval, trying to automatically pre-classify some of the corpus data given to lexicographers as an input to the construction of lexicographic data (examples include work by Kilgarriff/Tugwell 2001 and Heid et al. 2004, see section 4.3.). This second view rather corresponds to the "corpus-based" paradigm of corpus linguistics.

3.1. Corpus evidence for treatment units of a dictionary: General problems

According to everybody's intuitive notion, dictionaries contain entries labelled by "words". However, single words are by no means the only linguistic objects that can be such "headwords", i. e. have lemma status in dictionaries. Bound morphemes (e. g. derivational affixes like *-able, -(t)ion, -ment* etc.) as well as multiword items (e. g. multiword prepositions, adverbs and conjunctions, like French *sans que, parce que* etc.; idioms; multiword names, and so on) can also have lemma status. And many linguistic objects described by lexicographers within dictionary entries are not listed as lemmas (have no full article), but are sublemmas, i. e. mentioned in the horizontal text structure of an entry. Thus, to avoid confusion and to clarify that we denote a large variety of linguistic objects described in different ways, we speak of *treatment units,* i. e. linguistic objects that receive a lexicographic description in a dictionary (cf. Gouws/Prinsloo 2005, 13, 18, 85–91).

When lexicographers use corpus evidence, there may be a mismatch between the targeted treatment units and the linguistic objects which can be extracted from the corpus. Among the reasons for this are, as in any lexical data extraction from corpora, problems of homonymy and polysemy. Homonymy (e. g., $risk_N$ vs. $risk_V$) can to a large extent be handled by the use of word class tagged and lemmatized corpora, and by means of restricted search. Polysemy, on the other hand, requires thorough manual intervention on the side of the lexicographer. At most he or she may be able to sort or group certain types of contexts in a way that tells different readings apart semi-automatically; Hanks/Pustejovsky (2005) have designed a procedure which they call *Corpus Pattern Analysis*: it leads to verb readings annotated syntactically and with semantic types and semantic roles. Proponents of a corpus-driven approach would rely, for both homonymy and polysemy, on clustering of distributional data. Finally, there is also an integrative approach, where the lexicographer looks at senses of morphologically related items in one go (cf. Fillmore/Atkins 1994 on *risk,* especially 371).

Overall, problems of polysemy are hard both from a theoretical viewpoint (what are the criteria for a reading distinction) and from a practical one (what are the boundaries of readings, should one "split" the observed corpus data into several readings or "lump" them together?). Consequently, hardly any two unrelated dictionaries will show a large overlap in their reading distinctions (cf. Fillmore/Atkins 1994, 350–363, in particular 356 f.).

Another general problem of the lexicographic use of corpus data is the size of the relevant context. Many properties of words and word combinations can be explained by means of sentence-length contexts, but in some cases more context may be needed. In addition, the context may contain numerous lexicographically relevant facts which may need to be recorded alongside a given phenomenon. Examples are negative polarity items (which require a negation in their context), or collocations which show up more likely in the passive than in the active, or the syntactic construction of a verb like *[to] calculate* which takes a *that*-clause primarily when not appearing in the present tense. These "lexicographically relevant" context parameters again tend to manifest themselves in the sentence or in the wider context. Details of the notion of "lexicographic relevance" are discussed in Atkins/Fillmore/Johnson (2003) from a frame semantic point of view, and more generally in Atkins/Grundy (2006). Lexicographers have to carefully design their corpus and the pertaining data extraction, in order to get access to as much context as needed for a particular type of description.

3.2. Corpus use for lemma selection

A frequently used argument among lexicographers to motivate the use of corpus data is that an up-to-date corpus will provide an up-to-date lemma candidate list; the presence of neologisms (new words) and of "fashion words" (see Prinsloo/Gouws 2006 for a corpus-based account of these phenomena) is a selling point for commercial dictionaries.

Thus, obviously, lists of treatment unit candidates with frequency indications are extracted from corpus data. Frequency counts may contain figures for text types, registers, domains, regions or time periods. As speakers have little intuition about word frequency, such counts are lexicographically relevant and have been used, among other things, as a basis for a broad indication of frequency (e. g. in the form of five frequency bands), in dictionaries such as the *Collins COBUILD English Dictionary* or the *Macmillan English Dictionary for Advanced Learners (MEDAL)*.

Word frequency has been the starting point for determining the size of the lemma inventory (the nomenclature) of dictionaries. On the assumption that learners should first learn frequent words, frequency lists have been used to determine the 3,000, 5,000 etc. most frequent words as a basis for learners' dictionaries. Work in this direction goes back to early frequency dictionaries for didactic purposes, such as Michael West's *Definition Vocabulary* (1935), Vander Beke's *French Word Book* (1935), Ogden's *Basic English* (1930) etc. A detailed account of frequency-based work on (French) basic vocabularies can be found in Berré (to appear).

Word frequency in corpora has also been used, among other criteria, to determine inclusion and removal candidates in the updating of existing dictionaries: frequent words from the corpus not yet covered by the dictionary would be considered for inclusion, and certain words from the dictionary found rarely (or not at all) in a corpus of several hundred million words would be earmarked for removal (cf. Heid et al. 2004, Geyken 2004).

However, lemma and word form frequency counts are evidently not sensitive to polysemy, and thus the above mentioned polysemy-related problems also persist for these frequency counts.

3.3. Corpus-based control of a dictionary's nomenclature

An issue in the design of a dictionary's macrostructure is not only the size of its overall list of treatment units (its nomenclature), but also the proportions of each letter of the alphabet (and, possibly, of the word classes). When it comes to deciding about the inclusion into the dictionary, the number of words starting with "a", "b" etc. must be determined. Prinsloo/De Schryver (2002) thus propose a "ruler", derived from a large, ideally lemmatized corpus: it indicates the proportion of corpus words per initial letter, and allows the lexicographer to adjust the size of the respective alphabetical sections of the dictionary accordingly.

The ruler can be applied also to ongoing dictionary projects, as De Schryver did in the case of the *Woordeboek van die Afrikaanse Taal* (WAT, cf. De Schryver 2005), a multivolume dictionary which has been worked on for many years, and which saw changes in editorial policy at several points in time. De Schryver checked the page allocation in the existing dictionary, compared it with ruler data extracted from a large Afrikaans news corpus and noticed, among other things, that the letter "K" was overtreated (many more entries than the corpus-based ruler would predict), whereas other letters were undertreated (not enough entries). Even though the method has problems, e. g. to account adequately for productive and non-productive prefixation and compounding (which items to count in the corpus, which ones to include in the dictionary?), it is a valuable tool for the design of nomenclatures. An extension of the notion of ruler with respect to proportions of word classes could be equally useful.

3.4. Corpus evidence for microstructural data

The text of a dictionary article is called its microstructure: this is the sequence of indications ("Angaben") given about a treatment unit, to allow the user to deduce information about its linguistic properties. Typically, dictionaries for different user groups have different microstructural programs, i. e. they contain different kinds of indications.

For the purpose of the present article, we may broadly subclassify microstructural lexicographic data into the following types:

- indications of readings of the treatment units: meaning explanations, paraphrases, definitions, and the subdivision of the article according to the readings of a polysemous treatment unit,
- indications of (syntagmatic) properties of the treatment units, pertaining to different levels of linguistic description: these include for example morphological indications (e. g. about plural formation of nouns), distributional syntactic indications (e. g. about the position of an adjective with respect to a noun), valency indications, indications of collocations, indications of selectional restrictions;
- indications of (paradigmatic) relations between treatment units: these include most prominently synonymy and antonymy, but also morphological relations (word family relationships) etc.;
- indications of equivalence in bilingual dictionaries;
- indications of frequency, preferences or diasystematic markedness: these are in a way second order properties, as they may denote properties of one of the four kinds of

facts discussed above: a reading may (predominantly) exist in a geographic area or in the language of a group (and thus receive a diasystematic mark as being regional or youth speak, etc.); similarly a collocation may have morphosyntactic preferences, or a synonymy or equivalence relation may hold in a particular sublanguage only.

The situation with respect to the use of corpus linguistic work to provide evidence for these lexicographic data types is rather uneven; this has to do with the possibilities of data extraction from corpora.

Despite the large amount of work on word sense disambiguation and on the automatic identification of synonyms in NLP (cf. article 26 of this handbook), these approaches are only starting to have an impact on or a direct use in lexicography (see e. g. Perkuhn et al. 2005). Mostly the distinction of readings of polysemous words and the identification of synonyms is carried out manually by lexicographers. As mentioned above (cf. section 3.1.), the study of the word *risk* by Fillmore/Atkins (1994) has highlighted the well-known fact that different dictionaries do not necessarily agree in their reading distinctions.

Most use has been made of corpus data for the identification of evidence for syntagmatic properties of words: syntactic data from corpora (e. g. subcategorization patterns) are found in the *COBUILD* dictionary, but also in many others. Collocations extracted from the BNC have found their way, among others, into the *Macmillan Dictionary MEDAL.*

Frequency and preference data can typically only be gained from corpora. As mentioned in section 3.2., word frequency and lemma frequency are much used in lexicography. As it is much more demanding (in terms of corpus linguistic tools, e. g. parsing) to determine the frequency of syntactic constructions, let alone of readings of polysemous words, there is much less practical use made of attempts of this kind. An example is Schulte im Walde (2002), a study on the identification and frequency ranking of German verb subcategorization frames and their lexicographic evaluation. With the advent of more performant and more precise tools for corpus-based data extraction, more lexicographic applications of this sort will become possible.

The determination of diasystematically marked uses of words or word groups is possible when the corpora used for data extraction carry the necessary metadata, e. g. a mark of register, style, regional use or an indication of the time when the texts were produced.

3.5. Corpus evidence for lexicographic examples

Many dictionaries contain textual examples, and one of their most prominent functions is to illustrate the (syntagmatic) use of the respective treatment units (for an overview of the functions of examples, as well as of related problems, from the French perspective, see Heinz 2005). *COBUILD* was one of the first monovolume definition dictionaries to use (edited) corpus sentences from the Bank of English as examples (see the introduction to the dictionary, p. IX). In scholarly lexicography, as well as in large multivolume dictionaries, it is customary to cite full-length sentences or edited sentences from literary works or from other corpus data, along with a philologically detailed indication of the source. In learners' dictionaries, often only syntagms or made-up example sentences are used.

The choice of examples, the degree to which the lexicographer edits or condenses them and the philological detail with which they are cited, depend on the primary user group for which a dictionary is conceived. But even made-up examples are typically inspired by the corpus data a lexicographer has at hand when compiling his entry.

4. Corpus linguistic tools for lexicography

Above, at the beginning of section 3, we mentioned the corpus-driven vs. the corpus-based methodology of corpus exploitation and their respective application in lexicography. The corpus-driven approach relies essentially on statistical tools, such as clustering and association measures for the determination of significant word cooccurrences (for theoretical details on such tools, see Evert 2005 and article 58; a repository of association measures can be found at http://www.collocations.de/AM).

Obviously, concordancing (see section 4.2. and article 33 of this handbook) is mostly independent from the distinction between corpus-driven and corpus-based, whereas preprocessing (section 4.1.) belongs completely, and work described in section 4.3. mainly, to the corpus-based paradigm.

4.1. Preprocessing of corpora

Obviously, lexicographic data description is highly dependent on high quality corpus data. If computational linguistic corpus technology is used, this includes tokenizing, part of speech tagging, lemmatization and possibly chunking or parsing (see section IV of this handbook for details on these techniques). There is however no specifically lexicographic need with respect to preprocessing, and lexicographers can work perfectly with standard corpus tools.

Data quality (precision of analyses and recall across a large corpus) is very important. Another aspect of data quality is the availability of metadata; to be able to cite corpus data, lexicographers insist on a coherent annotation of the corpus texts in terms of authors/responsibles, publication dates, places, etc.

4.2. Concordancing as a lexicographic tool

Concordancers, i. e. generators of KWIC-Indices (key-word in context), are the most widespread corpus tool type in lexicography. Dictionary publishing houses either have their own custom-made tools (cf. e. g. Walter/Harley 2002), or they make use of one or several of the well-known tools which come with the large national corpora; examples of the latter are BNC and the Sara/Xaira tool, the query tools of the Bank of English, the COSMAS tool for the corpora of the Institut für deutsche Sprache (cf. URL: http://www.ids-mannheim.de/cosmas2/), or *Frantext,* to name but a few. Other publishers use commercial products or open source tools, such as the IMS open Corpus Workbench (http://cwb.sourceforge.net, cf. Hoffmann/Evert 2006).

Typically, for work on semasiological dictionaries, word and word group-based search functions, sorting functions, frequency counts etc. are needed. Tools must be aware of metadata and able to account for metadata in frequency listings. For interactive lexicographic work, the full potential of regular expression search is rarely needed; rather, lexicographers prefer to have libraries of ready-made search functions which provide certain types of evidence, e. g. for typical word combinations, for distributional facts etc. Wishlists for corpus search functions are included in Atkins (1992–1993) and, more than ten years later, in De Schryver (2003).

4.3. Lexicography-specific corpus tools

Above, in section 4.1., we mentioned that no specific tools for corpus preprocessing are needed for lexicography. In a functional sense, this also holds for corpus exploration tools; what lexicography can use are mainly tools for data extraction from corpora: collocation extraction, valency extraction, etc.

What is indeed specific to lexicography is the way in which such tools are integrated into lexicographic workflows. Most lexicographic work proceeds in a word-wise semasiological way. Often many lexicographers work in parallel, some of them on specific sets of treatment units. Corpus exploration is then meant to support them with corpus instances, ideally grouped according to certain types of phenomena (see section 3.4.). Two types of issues need to be addressed in particular, namely on the one hand the scarcity of corpus evidence (for specific linguistic phenomena) and, on the other hand, the abundance of (repetitive, redundant) corpus evidence. Tasks for lexicographic tools are thus:

– to find evidence for typical syntagmatic properties of words or word combinations: collocations, typical subjects or objects to illustrate selection properties, sets of contexts illustrating particularly frequent uses etc.
– to condense similar corpus instances into a sort of "type": for high frequency words, several hundreds or thousands of similar contexts may be retrieved by the corpus query tool. Ideally, a generalization into one "context type", plus corpus frequency and possibly some statistical significance data should be provided.

Specialized corpus lexicographic tools have been created over the last few years to provide a combination of the two abovementioned functions. The WASPS workbench (Kilgarriff/Tugwell 2001) and its commercial successor *Sketch Engine* (Kilgarriff et al. 2004) are the most well-known tools of this kind. WASPS tackles the abundancy problem and provides, for nouns, verbs and adjectives in English, a collection of syntagmatic query results from the corpus, generalized by types of syntagmatic contexts (e. g. English verbs plus object nouns, extracted from a sequence of a verb and a subsequent noun phrase); context types include, for example, combinations of verbs and subjects, verbs and objects, the occurrence of an item in a coordination, and typical verb+adverb combinations. For each type, the most significant word combinations are provided, along with a significance measure and BNC frequency. Lexicographers can inspect BNC corpus evidence for each word combination type, and they can label it with a reading tag. Once a sufficient number of cooccurrence types is labelled for the readings of the keyword, this material can be used for a machine learning-based search for similar cases in the BNC.

Sketch Engine is a generic version of the tool, not bound to BNC; it can be used for other languages, provided extraction patterns for relevant combination types are written.

Extraction patterns are typically regular expressions over word forms, lemmas, parts of speech, etc., depending on the annotations available in the corpus used. *Sketch Engine* was used in the creation of the Macmillan English dictionary, *MEDAL*.

A similar type of tools was developed for German, and tested in the updating of monolingual and bilingual dictionaries for German (Heid et al. 2004, Docherty/Heid 1998). The difference to *Sketch Engine* is that existing lexicographic data (from the electronic version of a printed dictionary) are compared with the corpus data, so as to propose candidates for inclusion in an updated version of the dictionary, as well as candidates to be potentially removed from the dictionary (see the discussion about the use of frequency data for that purpose, in section 3.2. above). The German tools cover lemmas, collocations, syntactic valency, and distributional properties of words.

5. Two-way interaction between lexicography and corpus linguistics

In sections 2 to 4, mainly support functions of corpus linguistics for lexicography have been discussed. This section is devoted to examples of a two-way interaction between the two fields, mainly from NLP and from new, mixed products which integrate lexicon and corpus.

5.1. Corpus analysis and lexicography in NLP

90% of NLP work is targeted at the analysis of natural language text. To this end, grammars and lexicons are designed and implemented. Corpus annotation (as done in part-of-speech tagging) serves the same purpose. Some large-scale natural language analysis projects aim at covering the full analysis pipeline, from corpus tokenizing and tagging over flat syntactic analysis to a deep syntactic and semantic analysis. Examples include the broad coverage grammar projects *LinGO* and *Pargram*.

NLP dictionaries are typically conceived to be exactly compatible with the grammars used for analysis. But in principle, the same holds (or could hold) for lexicons and tagsets. If corpus tagging is seen as a first step towards syntactic analysis, it makes sense to base distinctions in pos-tagsets on the same grammatical categorizations as those in formal grammars and lexicons. Obviously, corpus tagging typically remains at a level of coarse-grained categorization, whereas grammars and lexicons provide more fine-grained distinctions. But it makes sense to ensure a basic compatibility between both, with lexical specifications providing a more fine-grained subclassification of the broader classes introduced at the level of tagging. The EAGLES proposals for part of speech tagsets have to some extent be conceived with this basic idea in mind (cf Leech 1997, 24–29).

The same idea of a basic parallelism in the underlying descriptive classification between corpus tagging and lexical description is found in work on standards for corpora and lexicons. In the framework of the International Organization for Standardization, ISO (ISO TC37 / SC4), work towards a morphological annotation framework (MAF, cf. Clément/de la Clergerie 2005) and towards a syntactic annotation framework is ongoing.

Similar ideas of convergence, exchange and interoperability of NLP resources and tools underlie formal linguistic ontologies and proposals for resource combination (Bertagna et al. to appear). Resources have long been developed independently, and sharing, compatibility and interoperability are needed.

5.2. Combined resources: Corpus and lexicon

The strict separation between corpora and lexicons which is often taken for granted is not a necessity, but rather the result of developments of the last 20 years. And in fact, instead of a dictionary, many people use a corpus or right away a web search engine to test their lexical hypotheses, e. g. about orthography or collocations, by simply comparing them against the number of hits found in texts. Thus they use corpora or the Web as a source of lexical information.

A similar position is argued for by Tarp (2006, 143–147), on the basis of Bergenholtz (1998): they suggest that a combination of static lexical knowledge (as it is found in a lexical database or in a dictionary) and of dynamic possibilities to query a large collection of texts (as is the case with corpus query and/or web search engines) may best serve the needs of users. Tarp calls such a lexical information system a "leximat" (lexical automaton): data from a dictionary database and from a web search, as well as possibly from searches in specifically designed text corpora would flow together to provide a synthetic synopsis for the user. In particular, the texts and the web search results would "take over", where the dictionary has not enough data to offer.

A simple implemented version of a related concept has been realized by Køhler Simonsen (2006), for the field of zoology, under the assumption that most zoological terms are monosemous and that appropriate data to illustrate meaning and use of such terms can be found by means of word or lemma-based search in (web) texts.

Learner lexicography goes a step into the same direction: for French collocations, Verlinde's *Base Lexicale du Français* (*BLF*, Verlinde et al. 2006) provides a detailed lexical description, represented in a manually corrected data collection (a database) prepared on the basis of large corpora. If the advanced learner is interested in exploring the collocational potential of a given word beyond the contents of the database, collocation extraction tools are run on the underlying corpus and their raw output is displayed to the learner as collocation candidates. In a similar fashion, there are plans to extend the Italian/German learners' dictionary *ELDIT* in such a way as to give access to example sentences from a corpus (Knapp/Gamper/Brusilowsky 2004).

The common access portal to corpus data and to dictionary entries from the *Wörterbuch der deutschen Gegenwartssprache* made available by the DWDS project (see above, section 2.2.) is an attempt to combine lexicon and corpus not only at the level of learners' dictionaries, but also of broad-coverage general-language dictionaries. The Danish Korpus 90/Korpus 2000 of DSL, Det Danske Sprog- og Litteraturselskab (cf. Andersen/Asmussen/Asmussen 2002, URL: http://www.dsl.dk), provides end user access to a corpus of contemporary Danish, along with an integrated dictionary lookup for orthography, morphology and multiwords related to the searched item. In a similar spirit to DWDS, the Danish web site Ordnet.dk (http://www.ordnet.dk, cf. Trap-Jensen 2006, 349) is intended to provide integrated access to a redesigned version of *Den Danske*

Ordbog (cf. Lorentzen 2004), to the older 28-volume *Ordbog over det danske Sprog* (cf. Asmussen 2003) and to various corpus resources. As of early 2007, only *Ordbog over det danske Sprog* and Korpus 2000 are accessible.

With these developments, the road towards broader information for the user seems to be open. However, for the moment, this breadth is compromised by a certain lack of depth: the collocation candidates in BLF which are extracted from the corpus are given without lexicographic classification or analysis. And Køhler Simonsen's approach is (rightly) restricted to specific corpus texts (in this case texts from the Copenhagen Zoo) and to monosemous terms, in order to avoid the polysemy problems discussed in section 3.1., above. For such integrated lexical information systems to become more powerful, more (and also, as far as possible, semantically informed) corpus linguistic processing seems to be necessary, for example a semi-automatic classification of corpus instances with respect to the query task.

Experimental research in NLP is aimed at deriving lexical resources from annotated corpora directly, so as to be able to recompile an up-to-date dictionary each time new annotations are added to the corpus. Spohr et al. (2007) describe a system which is based on the German SALSA corpus, a corpus annotated manually at the levels of syntax (TIGER treebank) and semantics (Frame Semantics, cf. Baker/Fillmore/Cronin 2003). On the basis of a formal model of valency descriptions and semantic frames according to Frame Semantics, it is possible to derive lexical data by means of a query to the annotated corpus. The system also allows the user to search in ways which a traditional dictionary would not support, e. g. by combining query constraints concerning the corpus annotations with constraints concerning the Frame Semantics model.

We expect more integrated resources to come up over the next years, as they broaden the possibilities for end users to get information about lexical items. The issue of tailoring the data provided to the actual user needs, and the question of how to provide reliable corpus analyses when going beyond the contents of a dictionary seem to be the major challenges in this context.

6. Historical note

The history of corpus linguistics is described elsewhere in this volume (see articles 1−3). But the interaction between corpus linguistics and lexicography also has a historical dimension, albeit covering only a relatively short time span.

Obviously, the use of concordances of the Holy Bible and of ancient authors in the middle ages, as well as the use of translations in two languages as a sort of "parallel corpus" and the annotation of Latin texts with interlinear translations, all of which was intended as material for language learning, can be seen in a way as the pre-history of corpus lexicography. A well-known related example is the earliest written text of medieval Castilian, the *Glosas Emilianenses* of the end of the 11th century found in San Millán de la Cogolla (Rioja).

At the end of the 19th century, Käding's work on a German frequency dictionary (Käding 1897), based on an 11 million-word corpus manually analysed by over 80 collaborators, is the first truly corpus-based lexicographic enterprise. More frequency dictionaries and basic word lists follow in the 1920s and 1930s (cf. Berré to appear), up to

Charles Muller's and A. Juilland's work on lexical statistics (cf. Juilland/Chang-Rodriguez 1964) inspired by Zipf (1949) and his laws on statistical correlations between frequency and ranking. Thus, most of the early corpus lexicographic work was in fact devoted to frequency dictionaries.

On the other hand, the early computational corpora with around one million words, such as the Brown Corpus, the Lancaster-Oslo/Bergen Corpus (*LOB*) etc., though being used for grammar writing (cf. the *Survey of English Usage*, in the 1960s, which provided material some of which was later used in Quirk et al.'s famous *Comprehensive Grammar of the English Language*, Quirk et al. 1985), did not massively impact lexicography, mostly because of their (restricted) size.

The first dictionaries created, at least partly, on the basis of (then purely internal) electronic text corpora were the *Trésor de la langue française* (Imbs/Quémada 1971–1994), the *Oxford English Dictionary* and, obviously, *COBUILD*. With *COBUILD*, corpus lexicography became established and very quickly gained ground. An English monovolume monolingual dictionary could not be produced today in another way than on a corpus basis.

A good overview of the developments of the 1990s in the field of corpus linguistics and lexicography can be gained from the *Complex* conferences, organized by the Hungarian Academy of Sciences, in 1990, 1992, 1994, 1996, 1999, 2003 and 2005 (cf. Kiefer/Kiss/Pajzs 2005). The conferences were called "conference(s) on computational lexicography and text research" and provided a specialized platform for the interaction between computational lexicography and corpus linguistics. This interaction has long gained ground in a broad range of international conferences, and much of the research published, among others, in the lexicon and corpus tracks of the biennial *Linguistic Resources and Evaluation Conference*, is also of this nature.

7. Literature

All URLs in this article were checked in February 2007.

7.1. Corpora

ANC: American National Corpus, URL (22. 02. 2007), http://www.americannationalcorpus.org/.

BNC: British National Corpus, URL (22. 02. 2007), http://www.natcorp.ox.ac.uk/.

BoE: Bank of English, URL (22. 02. 2007), http://www.cobuild.collins.co.uk/.

CNC: Czech National Corpus, URL (22. 02. 2007), http://ucnk.ff.cuni.cz/.

Corpus of *Digitales Wörterbuch der deutschen Sprache (DWDS-Kernkorpus)*, URL (22. 02. 2007), http://www.dwds.de/textbasis/kerncorpus.

CREA, Corpus of the Real Academia Española: URL (22. 02. 2007), http://corpus.rae.es/creanet.html.

Korpus 90, Korpus 2000, URL (22. 02. 2007), http://korpus.dsl.dk/korpus2000/.

SALSA, Saarbrücken Lexical Semantics Annotation Project: URL (22. 02. 2007), http://www.coli.uni-saarland.de/projects/salsa/

7.2. Dictionaries

Abel, A./Knapp, J. (2002), *ELDIT, Elektronisches Lernerwörterbuch Deutsch/Italienisch*. URL (22. 02. 2007), http://dev.eurac.edu:8081/MakeEldit1/Eldit.html.

Collins COBUILD English Dictionary (1995). 1st edition 1987. London: Harper Collins.

Corréard, M. H./Grundy, V. (dir.) (2004 [1994]), *The Oxford-Hachette French Dictionary French–English/English–French*. Oxford: Oxford University Press and Paris: Hachette.

Den Danske Ordbog (2003–2005). København: Det Danske Sprog- og Litteraturselskab/Gyldendal.

Dubois, J. (dir.) (1980) *Dictionnaire du français contemporain* [= DFC]. 1st edition 1968. Paris: Larousse.

Dubois, J./Dubois-Charlier, F. (dir.) (1978–1979), *Dictionnaire du français langue étrangère* [= DFLE]. Paris: Larousse, Niveau 1: 1978, Niveau 2: 1979.

DUW: *Duden Deutsches Universalwörterbuch*, (2007). 6th edition. Mannheim: Dudenverlag.

DWDS, *Digitales Wörterbuch der deutschen Sprache*. URL (22. 02. 2007), http://www.dwds.de.

Elexiko. URL (22. 02. 2007), http://www.elexiko.de.

English G 2000 Wörterbuch. Das Wörterbuch zum Lehrwerk. Englisch–Deutsch; Deutsch–Englisch (2002). 1st edition. Berlin: Cornelsen and Berlin/München: Langenscheidt.

Gouws, R./Stark, M./Gouws, L. (2004), *Nuwe Woordeboek sonder grense*. Kaapstad: Maskew Miller Longman.

Hornby, A. S./Cowie, A. P. (eds.) (2005), *Oxford Advanced Learner's Dictionary of Current English* [= OALD, OALDCE]. 7th edition, 4th edition 1989. Oxford: Oxford University Press.

Imbs, P./Quémada B. (dir.) (1971–1994), *Trésor de la langue française. Dictionnaire de la langue du XIXe et du XXe siècle (1789–1960)* [= TLF]. Paris: Editions du CNRS/Gallimard.

Juilland, A./Chang-Rodriquez, E. (1964), *Frequency Dictionary of Spanish Words*. Den Haag: Mouton.

Käding, F. W. (1897), *Häufigkeitswörterbuch der deutschen Sprache*. Berlin: Privately published.

Kaufmann, U./Bergenholtz, H. (1992), *Genteknologisk ordbog*; *Dansk–engelsk/engelsk–dansk molekylærbiologi og DNA-teknologie*. København: G. E. C. Gads Forlag.

The Oxford English Dictionary (1989) [= OED]. 2nd edition. URL: http://www.oed.com.

Rey, A./Rey-Debove, J. (coords.), *Le Petit Robert. Dictionnaire alphabétique et analogique de la langue française* [= PR]. Paris: Le Robert.

Rundell, M. (ed.) (2002), *Macmillan English Dictionary for Advanced Learners* [= MEDAL]. Oxford: Macmillan.

Trésor de la langue française informatisé (2004) [= TLFi]. Cédérom du texte integral et son livre d'accompagnement. Paris: CNRS Editions.

Verlinde S./Binon, J./Selva, T., *Base lexicale du français* [= BLF]. URL (22. 02. 2007), http://www.kuleuven.be/ilt/blf/.

Woordeboek van die Afrikaanse Taal (1951–) [= WAT]. Stellenbosch: Bureau van die WAT.

Wortschatz, Deutscher Wortschatz. URL (22. 02. 2007), http://wortschatz.uni-leipzig.de/.

Zingarelli, N. (2002), *Vocabolario della lingua italiana*. Bologna: Zanichelli.

7.3. Other references

Andersen, M. S./Asmussen, H./Asmussen, J. (2002), The Project of Korpus 2000 Going Public. In: Braasch, A./Povlsen, C. (eds.), *Proceedings of the Xth EURALEX International Congress*. København: Center for Sprogteknologi, 291–299.

Asmussen, J. (2003), Zur geplanten Retrodigitalisierung des Ordbog over det danske Sprog. Konzeption, Vorgehensweise, Perspektiven. In: Burch, T./Fournier, J./Gärtner, K./Rapp, A. (eds.), *Standards und Methoden der Volltextdigitalisierung. Beiträge des Internationalen Kolloquiums der*

Universität Trier, 8./9. Oktober 2001, Abhandlungen der Akademie der Wissenschaften und der Literatur Mainz. Mainz: Akademie der Wissenschaften und der Literatur. Stuttgart: Franz Steiner Verlag, 161–175.

Atkins, B. T. S. (1992–1993), Tools for Computer-aided Corpus Lexicography: The Hector Project. In: *Acta Linguistica Hungarica* 41(1–4), 5–71.

Atkins, B. T. S./Clear, J./Ostler, N. (1992), Corpus Design Criteria. In: *Journal of Literary and Linguistic Computing* 7(1), 1–16.

Atkins, B. T. S./Fillmore, Ch. J./Johnson, C. R. (2003), Lexicographic Relevance: Selecting Information from Corpus Evidence. In: *International Journal of Lexicography* 16(3), 251–280.

Atkins, B. T. S./Grundy, V. (2006), Lexicographic Profiling: An Aid to Consistency in Dictionary Entry Design. In: Corino, E./Marello, C./Onesti, C. (eds.), *Proceedings – XIIth Euralex International Congress*, Torino, Italy. Alessandria: Edizioni dell'Orso, 1097–1107.

Baker, C./Fillmore, C. J./Cronin, B. (2003), The Structure of the Framenet Database. In: *International Journal of Lexicography* 16, 281–296.

Bergenholtz, H. (1998), Das Schlaue Buch: Vermittlung von Informationen für textbezogene und textunabhängige Fragestellungen. In: Zettersten, A./Mogensen, J. E./Hjørnager Pedersen, V. (eds.), *Symposium on Lexicography VIII. Proceedings of the Eighth International Symposium on Lexicography May, 2–5, 1996, at the University of Copenhagen*. Tübingen: Niemeyer, 93–110.

Bergenholtz, H./Pedersen, J. (1994), Zusammensetzung von Textkorpora für die Fachlexikographie. In: Schaeder, B./Bergenholtz, H. (eds.), *Fachlexikographie. Fachwissen und seine Repräsentation in Wörterbüchern*. Tübingen: Narr, 161–176.

Bergenholtz, H./Tarp, S. (1995), *Manual of Specialised Lexicography. The Preparation of Specialised Dictionaries*. Amsterdam/Philadelphia: John Benjamins.

Bergenholtz, H./Tarp, S. (2002), Die moderne lexikographische Funktionslehre. Diskussionsbeitrag zu neuen und alten Paradigmen, die Wörterbücher als Gebrauchsgegenstände verstehen. In: *Lexicographica* 18, 253–263.

Berré, M. (to appear), Enseignement des langues et vocabularies de base: Quelques observations sur le Basis-woordenschat de Verlée (1954) et le *Dictionnaire fondamental de la langue française* de Gougenheim (1958). To appear in: Heinz, M. (ed.), *Le dictionnaire maître de langue – lexicographie et didactique*. Tübingen: Niemeyer (2008).

Bertagna, F./Calzolari, N./Monachini, M./Soria, C./Hsieh, S./Huang, C./Marchetti, A./Tesconi, M. (to appear), Exploring Interoperability of Language Resources: The Case of Cross-lingual Semi-automatic Enrichment of Wordnets. In: *Natural Language Engineering.*

Biber, D./Conrad, S./Reppen, R. (1998), *Corpus Linguistics. Investigating Language Structure and Use*. Cambridge: Cambridge University Press.

Biemann, C./Bordag, S./Heyer, G./Quasthoff U./Wolff, C. (2004), Language-independent Methods for Compiling Monolingual Lexical Data. In: *Lecture Notes in Computer Science* 2945. Berlin/Heidelberg: Springer-Verlag, 217–228.

Cermák, F. (1997), Czech National Corpus: A Case in Many Contexts. In: *International Journal of Corpus Linguistics* 2(2), 181–197.

Citron, S./Widmann, T. (2006), A Bilingual Corpus for Lexicographers. In: Corino, E./Marello, C./Onesti, C. (eds.), *Proceedings – XIIth Euralex International Congress*, Torino, Italy. Alessandria: Edizioni dell'Orso, 251–255.

Clear, J. H. (1993), The British National Corpus. In: Landow, G. P./Delany, P. (eds.), *The Digital Word: Text-based Computing in the Humanities*. Cambridge, MA: MIT Press, 163–187.

Clément, L.,/de la Clergerie, É. (2005), MAF: A Morphosyntactic Annotation Framework. In: *Proceedings of the 2nd Language and Technology Conference (LT'05)*. Poznań, Poland, 90–94.

Condamines, A./Rebeyrolle, J. (2001), Searching for and Identifying Conceptual Relationships Via a Corpus-based Approach to a Terminological Knowledge Base (CTKB). Methods and Results. In: Bourigault, D./Jacquemin, C./L'Homme, M-C. (eds.), *Recent Advances in Computational Terminology*. Amsterdam/Philadelphia: John Benjamins, 127–148.

Copestake, A./Lambeau, F./Villavicencio, A./Bond, F./Baldwin, T./Sag, I. A./Flickinger, D. (2002), Multiword Expressions: Linguistic Precision and Reusability. In: *Proceedings of the Linguistic Resources and Evaluation Conference 2002*. Las Palmas de Gran Canaria, Spain, 1941–1947.

Docherty, V./Heid, U. (1998), Computational Meta-lexicography in Practice – Corpus-based Support for the Revision of a Commercial Dictionary. In: Fontenelle, T./Hiligsmann, P./Michiels, A./Moulin, A./Theissen, S. (eds.), *Actes EURALEX '98*. Liège: Universite de Liège, 333–346.

EAGLES (1996), *Recommendations for the Morphosyntactic Annotation of Corpora*. URL (22. 02. 2007), http://www.ilc.cnr.it/EAGLES96/annotate/annotate.html.

Evert, S. (2005), *The Statistics of Word Cooccurrences – Word Pairs and Collocations*. Stuttgart: University of Stuttgart, IMS. Also URL, http://www.collocations.de/phd.html.

Fillmore, Ch. J./Atkins, B. T. S. (1994), Starting Where the Dictionaries Stop: The Challenge of Corpus Lexicography. In: Atkins, B. T. S./Zampolli, A. (eds.), *Computational Approaches to the Lexicon*. Oxford: Oxford University Press, 349–393.

Geyken, A. (2003), Digitales Wörterbuch der deutschen Sprache des 20. Jahrhunderts. In: Städtler, T. (ed.), *Wissenschaftliche Lexikographie im deutschsprachigen Raum*. Heidelberg: Winter, 439–446.

Geyken, A. (2004), Korpora als Korrektiv für einsprachige Wörterbücher: Philologie auf neuen Wegen. In: *LiLi. Zeitschrift für Literaturwissenschaft und Linguistik* 34(136), 72–100.

Gouws, R. H./Prinsloo, D. J. (2005), *Principles and Practice of South African Lexicography*. Stellenbosch: SUN PReSS.

Hanks, P./Pustejovsky, J. (2005), A Pattern Dictionary for Natural Language Processing. In: *Revue Française de Linguistique Appliquée* 10(2), 63–82.

Hausmann, F. J. (1985), Lexikographie. In: Schwarze, Ch./Wunderlich, D. (eds.), *Handbuch der Lexikologie*. Königstein: Athenäum, 367–411.

Hausmann, F. J./Reichmann, O./Wiegand, H. E./Zgusta, L. (eds.) (1989–1990), *Wörterbücher, Dictionaries, Dictionnaires. An International Encyclopedia of Lexicography*. Berlin: de Gruyter, 3 vols.

Heid, U./Säuberlich, B./Debus-Gregor, E./Scholze-Stubenrecht, W. (2004), Tools for Upgrading Printed Dictionaries by Means of Corpus-based Lexical Acquisition. In: *Proceedings of the Fourth Language Resources and Evaluation Conference*. Lisboa: ELRA, 419–423.

Heinz, M. (ed.) (2005), *L'exemple lexicographique dans les dictionnaires français contemporains: Actes des "Premieres Journees allemandes des dictionnaires" (Klingenberg am Main, 25–27 juin 2004)*. Tübingen: Niemeyer.

Hoffmann, S./Evert, S. (2006), BNCweb (CQP-Edition): The Marriage of Two Corpus Tools. In: Braun, S./Kohn, K./Mukherjee J. (eds.), *Corpus Technology and Language Pedagogy: New Resources, New Tools, New Methods*. (English Corpus Linguistics 3.) Frankfurt am Main: Peter Lang, 177–195.

Ide, N./Suderman, K. (2004), The American National Corpus First Release. In: *Proceedings of the Fourth Language Resources and Evaluation Conference*. Lisboa: ELRA, 1681–1684.

Kiefer, F./Kiss, G./Pajzs, J. (eds.) (2005), *Papers in Computational Lexicography – COMPLEX 2005*. Budapest: Hungarian Academy of Sciences, Linguistics Institute.

Kilgarriff, A./Grefenstette, G. (2003), Introduction to the Special Issue on the Web as Corpus. In: *Computational Linguistics* 29(3), 333 – 347.

Kilgarriff, A./Rychly, P./Smrz, P./Tugwell, D. (2004), The Sketch Engine. In: Williams, G./Vessier, S. (eds.), *Proceedings of the XIth EURALEX International Congress*. Lorient: Université de Bretagne Sud, 105–116.

Kilgarriff, A./Tugwell, D. (2001), WASPBENCH: A Lexicographic Tool Supporting WSD. In: *Proceedings of the ACL-SIGLEX SENSEVAL Workshop*. Toulouse, France, 151–154.

Klosa, A./Schnörch, U./Storjohann, P. (2006), ELEXIKO – A Lexical and Lexicological, Corpus-based Hypertext Information System at the Institut für deutsche Sprache, Mannheim. In: Corino, E./Marello, C./Onesti, C. (eds.), *Proceedings – XIIth Euralex International Congress*, Torino, Italy. Alessandria: Edizioni dell'Orso, 425–430.

Knapp, J./Gamper, J./Brusilowsky, P. (2004), Multiple Use of Content in a Web-based Language Learning System. In: *Proceedings of ICALT 2004*. Joensuu, Finland, 750–752.

Køhler Simonsen, H. (2006), Zoolex: The Wildest Corporate Reference Work in Town? In: Corino, E./Marello, C./Onesti, C. (eds.), *Proceedings – XIIth Euralex International Congress*, Torino, Italy. Alessandria: Edizioni dell'Orso, 787–794.

Leech, G. (1997), Grammatical Tagging. In: Garside, R./Leech, G./McEnery, T. (eds.) (1997), *Corpus Annotation. Linguistic Information from Computer Text Corpora*. London/New York: Longman, 19–33.

LinGO Project. URL (22.02.2007), http://lingo.stanford.edu/.

Lorentzen, H. (2004), The Danish Dictionary at Large: Presentation, Problems and Perspectives. In: Williams, G./Vessier, S. (eds.), *Proceedings of the XIth EURALEX International Congress*. Lorient: Université de Bretagne Sud, 285–294.

McEnery, T./Wilson, A. (1996), *Corpus Linguistics*. Edinburgh: Edinburgh University Press.

McEnery, T./Xiao, R./Tono, Y. (2006), *Corpus-based Language Studies. An Advanced Resource Book*. Abingdon: Routledge.

Norling-Christensen, O./Asmussen, J. (1998), The Corpus of the Danish Dictionary. In: *Lexikos* 8, Afrilex Series 8, 223–242.

Ogden, C. K. (1930), *Basic English*. London: Kegan Paul.

Pargram Project. URL (22.02.2007), http://www2.parc.com/istl/groups/nltt/pargram/.

Pearson, J. (1998), *Terms in Context*. Amsterdam/Philadelphia: John Benjamins.

Perkuhn, R./Belica, C./al-Wadi, D./Lauer, M./Steyer, K./Weiß, C. (2005), Korpustechnologie am Institut für Deutsche Sprache. In: Schwitalla, J./Wegstein, W. (eds.), *Korpuslinguistik deutsch: Synchron – diachron – kontrastiv*. Tübingen: Niemeyer, 57–70.

Prinsloo, D. J./Gouws, R. H. (2006), Fashion Words in Afrikaans Dictionaries: A Long Walk to Lexicographic Freedom or Just a Lexical Fly-by-night? In: Corino, E./Marello, C./Onesti, C. (eds.), *Proceedings – XIIth Euralex International Congress*, Torino, Italy. Alessandria: Edizioni dell'Orso, 301–312.

Prinsloo, D. J./De Schryver, G. M. (2002), Designing a Measurement Instrument for the Relative Length of Alphabetical Stretches in Dictionaries, with Special Reference to Afrikaans and English. In: Braasch, A./Povlsen, C. (eds.), *Proceedings of the Xth EURALEX International Congress*. København: Center for Sprogteknologi, 483–494.

Pruvost, J. (2006), *Les dictionnaires français outils d'une langue et d'une culture*. Paris: Ophrys.

Quirk, R./Greenbaum, S./Leech, G./Svartvik, J. (1985), *A Comprehensive Grammar of the English Language*. London and New York: Longman.

Scholze-Stubenrecht, W. (2001), Das Internet und die korpusgestützte praktische Lexikographie. In: Korhonen, J. (ed.), *Von der mono- zur bilingualen Lexikografie für das Deutsche*. Frankfurt: Peter Lang, 43–64.

De Schryver, G. M. (2003), Lexicographers' Dreams in the Electronic-dictionary Age. In: *International Journal of Lexicography* 16(2), 143–199.

De Schryver, G. M. (2005), Concurrent Over- and Undertreatment in Dictionaries – the *Woordeboek van die Afrikaanse Taal* as a Case in Point. In: *International Journal of Lexicography* 18(1), 47–75.

De Schryver, G. M./Prinsloo, D. (2003), Compiling a Lemma-sign List for a Specific Target User Group: The Junior Dictionary as a Case in Point. In: *Dictionaries. Journal of the Dictionary Society of North America* 24, 28–58.

Schulte im Walde, S. (2002), Evaluating Verb Subcategorization Frames Learned by a German Statistical Grammar against Manual Definitions in the *Duden* Dictionary. In: Braasch, A./Povlsen, C. (eds.), *Proceedings of the Xth EURALEX International Congress*. København: Center for Sprogteknologi, 187–198.

Sinclair, J. (2004), *Trust the Text: Language, Corpus and Discourse*. London: Routledge.

Spohr, D./Burchardt, A./Padó, S./Frank, A./Heid, U. (2007), Inducing a Computational Lexicon from a Corpus with Syntactic and Semantic Annotation. In: Geertzen, J./Thijsse, E./Bunt, H./

Schiffrin, A. (eds.), *Proceedings of the Seventh International Workshop on Computational Semantics (IWCS-7)*. Tilburg, The Netherlands, 210–222.

van Sterkenburg, P. (ed.) (2003), *A Practical Guide to Lexicography*. (Terminology and Lexicography Research and Practice 6.) Amsterdam/Philadelphia: John Benjamins.

Tarp, S. (2006), *Leksikografien i grænselandet mellem viden og ikke-viden. Generel leksikografisk teori med særlig henblik på lørnerleksikografi*. Århus: HHÅ Center for Leksikografi, to appear in English in 2008 (Tübingen: Niemeyer).

Tognini Bonelli, E. (2001), *Corpus Linguistics at Work*. Amsterdam/Philadelphia: John Benjamins.

Trap-Jensen, L. (2006), Making Dictionaries for Paper or Screen. In: Corino, E./Marello, C./Onesti, C. (eds.), *Proceedings – XIIth Euralex International Congress*, Torino, Italy. Alessandria: Edizioni dell'Orso, 349–355.

Vander Beke, G. E. (1935), *French Word Book*. (Publications of the American and Canadian Committees on Modern Languages 15.) New York: Macmillan.

Verlinde, S./Selva, T./Binon, J. (2006), The Base Lexicale du Francais (BLF): A Multifunctional Online Database for Learners of French. In: Corino, E./Marello, C./Onesti, C. (eds.), *Proceedings – XII Euralex International Congress*, Torino, Italy. Alessandria: Edizioni dell'Orso, 471–482.

Walter, E./Harley, A. (2002), The Role of Corpus and Collocation Tools in Practical Lexicography. In: Braasch, A./Povlsen, C. (eds.), *Proceedings of the Xth EURALEX International Congress*. København: Center for Sprogteknologi, 851–857.

West, M. P. (1935), *Definition Vocabulary*. (Bulletin No. 4.) Toronto: University of Toronto, Dept. for Educational Research.

Wiegand, H. E. (1990), Printed Dictionaries and their Parts as Text. An Overview of More Recent Research as an Introduction. In: *Lexicographica* 6, 1–126.

Wiegand, H. E. (1998), *Wörterbuchforschung. Untersuchungen zur Wörterbuchbenutzung, zur Theorie, Geschichte, Kritik und Automatisierung der Lexikographie*. Berlin/New York: de Gruyter.

Wiegand, H. E. (2001), Was eigentlich sind Wörterbuchfunktionen? Kritische Anmerkungen zur neueren und neuesten Wörterbuchforschung. In: *Lexicographica* 17, 217–248.

Zipf, G. K. (1949), *Human Behaviour and the Principle of Least Effort*. Cambridge, MA: Addison-Wesley.

Ulrich Heid, Stuttgart (Germany)

II. Corpus compilation and corpus types

9. Collection strategies and design decisions

1. Introduction

Corpora range in type from general, reference corpora designed to investigate a given language as a whole, to specialised corpora designed to answer more specific research questions (cf. article 3). They can be carefully planned and have a long 'shelf-life', or they can be 'disposable' (Bernardini/Baroni 2004), quickly constructed for a specific purpose and as rapidly discarded. This article deals with some of the issues involved in planning and compiling a corpus. As will be seen in this article, this is an area prone to paradox, where even the apparently simplest decisions can have extensive ramifications.

Any corpus, unless it is unusually specific in content, may be perceived as a collection of sub-corpora, each one of which is relatively homogenous. The sub-corpora are determined by a template of variables that creates a number of cells, each of which constitutes a sub-corpus. For example, a researcher may wish to investigate the written language of Economics and of Social Science, and may wish to include academic articles, university textbooks and popular articles in the corpus. These design criteria may be expressed as a grid, cf. Table 9.1.

Tab. 9.1: A grid of corpus design criteria

	Economics	Social Sciences
Academic articles	1	2
University textbooks	3	4
Popular articles	5	6
Student essays	7	8

The corpus compiler collects texts to fit into each of the eight cells and may wish to specify, for example, the relative size of each sub-corpus in terms of texts, or of tokens.

If the corpus is being built for a specific purpose, as in this example, the variables will be determined by the parameters of the study – in this case the distinction between two academic disciplines and the genres that constitute them. If not, the criteria may be drawn from theories of language variation. Aston and Burnard (1998, 23; 29–33), for example, refer to systemic linguistic concepts of *field, tenor* and *mode* variables; these are (just) recognisable in the design criteria of the British National Corpus (BNC) which include Domain (i. e. the subject-matter of written texts), Interaction type (for the spoken texts), and Medium (e. g. book, periodical, written-to-be-spoken). On the other hand, lists of variables are more often recognisable as 'common-sense' distinctions rather than as the outcomes of any one given theory. For example Nelson/Wallis/Aarts (2002, 307–308) describe the British component of the International Corpus of English (ICE-GB) as being subdivided into:

Spoken vs. Written	
(In spoken)	Dialogue vs. Monologue
(In dialogue)	Private vs. Public
(In private)	Face-to-face conversation vs. Telephone

and so on. Other variables often used in sociolinguistics, such as age, sex, region and social class are also used as design criteria.

The purpose of identifying and filling each cell in the template may be to allow comparison between them. Biber (1988, 3), for example, concentrates on this aspect. Alternatively, it may simply be to ensure that the widest possible range of texts is included. Our hypothetical researcher into Economics and Social Sciences, for example, may wish to compare student essays in each discipline, or to compare academic articles with popular articles, in both disciplines. Equally possibly, however, he or she may wish to compile a lexicon for students of these subjects, and may include a number of different genres only in order to ensure that no crucial items of vocabulary are missed.

Many corpora are, of course, much more complex than the example above, and the hypothetical grid may quickly become multi-dimensional. (Our hypothetical researcher may choose to distinguish between texts published in Britain and in the US, for example, and/or between textbooks aimed at different kinds of students.) Much of the debate over corpus design focuses on how the parameters of the grid are to be determined, and what the relationship between the cells should be. This article will consider such questions, and is organised as follows: section 2 makes the point that a corpus cannot be judged except in the context of its purpose; sections 3, 4 and 5 identify some practical constraints on corpus design, and on the construction of written and spoken corpora; sections 6, 7 and 8 discuss some theoretical issues in corpus design.

2. Corpus use and corpus design

If a corpus is compiled in order to carry out research only on its own content, identifying what that content should be is straightforward. For example, Barr (2003) carries out a stylometrics study comparing texts from the New Testament, using a corpus comprising those texts. In many cases, however, it is clearly impossible to put all the texts that are the object of research into a corpus. Even a fairly restricted topic of study – lectures delivered in American universities during the year 2004, for example – involves too many texts for a corpus of all the relevant texts to be compiled. Instead a sub-set of the possible candidate texts is selected, and in that selection lies corpus design.

It is a truism that there is no such thing as a 'good' or a 'bad' corpus, because how a corpus is designed depends on what kind of corpus it is and how it is going to be used.

Articles 10 to 17 give detailed information about types of corpora. Here, I shall simply give some examples to show how the design of a corpus depends on its purpose.

A corpus intended to facilitate research into a single register, such as university lectures, will contain texts from the range represented by that register. It is likely that researchers will wish to compare lectures in different disciplines and/or introductory lectures with more advanced ones. The corpus designer may decide to select as many disciplines as resources will allow, and to include lectures from all stages of the students' career in each discipline. Even if some disciplines are more 'lecture based' than others, so that in the university as a whole more Law lectures, say, are given each year than Geography ones, the corpus designer may choose to include roughly equal numbers of each to make comparison easier. In other words, strict sampling techniques may give way to the need for comparability (cf. sections 6 and 7).

In an example such as this one, the texts are selected on external criteria. For example, a text may be included because it is a transcript of a lecture given in the Law department to first year students, not because it covers a particular topic or because it contains instances of a particular word or phrase. The design of most corpora is based on such external criteria, that is, using situational determinants rather than linguistic characteristics, as the parameters of composition (Biber 1988, 68). However, where the purpose of the research project is to discover how a particular cultural keyword (Stubbs 1996, 157–195) is used, or how a word has changed its meaning or function over a period of time (Teubert 2004, 138–155), a corpus consisting of texts selected precisely because they contain that item might be justified. This is particularly true if the item concerned is relatively infrequent, or if data from a specific time period is required. In these cases even a very large general corpus may be inadequate to represent the item in its required contexts. For example, to test the hypothesis that the affective meaning of the words *unilateral, unilateralism, unilaterally* is different in British and American English, and that it has changed since 2001, requires a corpus of texts containing those words, from the two countries, covering a number of specific years, and of a sufficient size to allow comparison to take place. (This example is based on Rottweiler 2006.) The texts therefore have to be selected using both internal criteria (they contain at least one of the target words at least once) and external criteria (there are an approximately equal number originating in Britain or America, and in each of the years 1999–2003).

The contents of a corpus designed for research purposes, whether general or specialised, need to be carefully considered. On the other hand, a language teacher may wish to compile a small corpus for his or her students to use in checking how particular words and phrases in the target language are typically used. The students may not need a corpus that is a balanced representation of the language as a whole, but a ready reference that can be cross-checked against books and the teacher's intuition where necessary. A corpus of newspaper texts on CD-ROM, or texts downloaded from the Internet, will be a sufficient source of information about how the most frequent words and phrases in the language are used. Design of the corpus will depend more on what is freely available in an easily-converted format than on other criteria.

3. Practical constraints on corpus design

All corpora are a compromise between what is desirable, that is, what the corpus designer has planned, and what is possible. There are many practical constraints on corpus building, of which the most important are: software limitations, copyright and ethical issues, and text availability. Each of these will be dealt with briefly.

Useful corpus size may be limited by the search software that is to be used. Readily available software packages, such as WordSmith Tools (Scott 2004), work on raw text, and can deal with a corpus of tens of millions of tokens in size. Larger corpora often work with software that demands that the tokens are converted into digits (each type being represented by a unique sequence of digits). This enables the search software to work more quickly. Even so, complex operations on corpora of many hundreds of millions of words can take some time to complete.

Storing electronic versions of published texts is illegal in most countries unless copyright permission has been given. Such permission is often difficult to obtain, and even when given may restrict the availability of the corpus (Meyer 2002, 62). The design of many corpora is determined to a large extent by the availability or otherwise of copyright permissions. Corpora consisting of unpublished material, such as student essays or transcripts of conversations, do not run into copyright problems as such, but ethical considerations must be taken into account. Informed consent for the material to be used must be obtained, and this has to include permission for the corpus to be made publicly available, if this is what is intended. Ensuring anonymity for participants in spoken interactions is possible (for example, names can be changed or deleted in transcripts: Meyer 2002, 75), but not if the transcripts are linked to sound files.

The third practical issue to be taken into account is the availability of texts, and their availability in a usable form. Historical corpora, in particular, are constrained by the limitations on what texts from earlier times are currently available. It is often pointed out, for example, that obtaining spoken texts from an era before the invention of tape recorders is impossible, and corpus designers hoping to include such material must depend on transcripts of situations such as court proceedings, or on fictional representations of speech (Biber and Finegan 2001, 69; Meyer 2002, 37). In either case, the accuracy of the data as a representation of actual speech is always questionable. Written texts are easier to obtain, but in some cases they may be available only in paper form rather than electronically. Unless very large resources are available for scanning and keying in (cf. section 4), a corpus designer may choose to avoid texts that are not available electronically. Thus, once again, ideal corpus design may take second place to availability (see article 14).

Practical constraints operate also in cases where a corpus is designed to be non-finite and where it will be added to over time in order to track changes in a language (i. e. a 'monitor corpus' as described by Sinclair 1991, 24–26 and Teubert 2003, 12). It is unlikely that the resources necessary for compiling a carefully balanced and varied corpus will be available in perpetuity, and monitor corpora may need to make use of texts that are available cheaply and easily, relying on internet and/or journalistic texts.

4. Collecting written texts

There are three methods of acquiring written texts in a form that can be used to create a corpus. In increasing level of technological sophistication, and ease, they are: keying-in, scanning, and obtaining texts electronically.

Keying texts in by hand is obviously very time-consuming and is generally avoided unless the texts concerned are unavailable in any other way, as may be the case, for example, with older manuscripts, or handwritten letters, or learner essays. During the keying-in process, decisions may have to be taken, for example, whether to normalise unconventional spelling.

Scanning was the usual method of building corpora in the 1980s (Renouf 1987, 5) and is still used where print quality is sufficient, and where a text cannot be obtained in electronic form. With the larger corpora that are expected today, however, obtaining text in electronic form, either from a publisher or from the internet, is the optimum way of building a corpus of written texts.

It is no exaggeration that the availability of the internet, with its instant access to millions of downloadable texts, has transformed corpus building (see article 18). In most cases, corpus builders find the internet a more convenient source of texts than material in paper form. Bernardini/Baroni (2004), for example, describe software designed to trawl the internet and compile a 'quick and dirty' corpus of texts on topics chosen by the compiler. Such a corpus is not designed as a permanent research tool, but as a useful temporary aid for a language learner seeking to extend their familiarity with lexis in a given domain. These 'disposable' corpora are a far cry from the carefully designed and painstakingly constructed corpora of the twentieth century. Meyer (2002, 63) also approves of the relative ease of building a corpus using internet texts, but warns that such texts may not be identical to those that appear in print, so that an 'internet corpus' is an artefact of a particular kind, representing language on the internet, not written language in general.

Teubert (2001, 45–46) takes a more robust attitude. Describing a corpus of texts produced by British Euro-sceptics (those who oppose Britain's membership of the European Union) and posted on web-sites, he argues that such texts, because of their ready availability to the average web-user, are more influential upon public discourse than those that could be found in newspapers or in more esoteric publications such as Hansard (the record of proceedings in the British parliament). Compiling a corpus exclusively of such texts, therefore, is not simply a matter of convenience, but of policy.

5. Collecting spoken texts

The larger corpora become, therefore, the more corpus builders tend to rely on material that is easily available in written form. This is at odds with the procedures necessary for collecting spoken data. There are several well-known spoken corpora (see articles 11 and 30 for a description of many of them). Many are relatively specialised, focusing on the interactions of particular sections of a community. More ambitious in design is the spoken component of the British National Corpus, which attempts to include speakers of all ages, socio-economic groups, and regions in Britain, and to represent a wide range of interaction types (Leech/Rayson/Wilson 2001, 2–4). The compilers of the British spoken sub-corpus of the Bank of English took a more serendipitous approach to build as large a sub-corpus as possible (20 million words): it contains a wide variety of social situations, such as casual conversation among friends, seminars, meetings, service encounters, unscripted local radio broadcasts, and interviews conducted by researchers in

History and Sociology, but there is no attempt to control for a balance of gender, age, region or class.

Three questions face the compiler of a corpus of spoken language. One is the selection of speakers and social contexts; another is the management of data collection; the third is the choice of transcription system. Some aspects of the selection of speakers and contexts might be determined by the aim of the corpus. For example, the age range of speakers in the COLT corpus is limited by the requirement to obtain teenage language. The Santa Barbara corpus includes only casual conversation. Many learner corpora, designed to investigate the interlanguage of learners, take oral language tests, which are usually tape-recorded as a matter of course, as their component texts. These have the advantage of adding a measure of uniformity to the texts, as the learners are performing similar tasks. On the other hand, what is investigated is the language of learners under test conditions rather than the totality of their production.

Those projects, such as the BNC, that attempt to represent the spoken language of a nation, require ingenuity to overcome the inevitable difficulties. The compilers of the BNC used market-research interviewers to identify a cross-section of speakers who would be willing to record themselves over a period of time. They were therefore drawing on the expertise and recognised procedures of a profession accustomed to sampling populations. As Aston and Burnard (1998, 31) make clear, however, such sampling was successful in obtaining interactions in some social situations only, and further collection, not sampled demographically, had to be done in order to obtain examples of lectures, legal proceedings, radio broadcasts and so on. The result is a corpus of two halves, one balanced in terms of speaker age, sex and so on only, the other balanced in terms of interaction type only.

The questions of data collection and transcription are similar to those faced by any researcher into spoken interaction, but exacerbated by the need to have a relatively large number of texts. Meyer (2002, 56–61) describes some of these: the need to obtain informed consent from all speakers, the choice of recording equipment, and the problems caused by the speakers' awareness that they are being recorded. He notes that some corpus compilers have adopted techniques such as giving target speakers recording equipment and asking them to turn on the recorder whenever they wish. This avoids the difficulty of requiring very large numbers of researchers to obtain the necessary amount of data. A corpus also puts constraints upon transcription systems. Because of the need to search the corpus by entering a search word orthographically, normalised spelling is usually used, rather than the spelling representing sound used by conversation analysts. Timing features such as overlaps need to be represented through symbol rather than by the layout of the text, as the corpus will be stored purely linearly. Other than that, the amount of information encoded in the transcript depends largely on the size of the corpus. Meyer (2002, 71) notes two extremes: the Corpus of Spoken Professional English ⟨http://www.athel.com/corpdes.html⟩ which consists of ready-made transcripts produced by professional transcribers who were nonetheless not transcribing for the purposes of linguistic analysis, and the Santa Barbara Corpus, which is a faithful transcription, of the standard expected for conversation analysis, including hesitations, false starts and also information about intonation. The time and level of expertise needed to undertake such a detailed transcription means that the corpus is of necessity relatively small.

As Meyer (2002, 72) points out, a written representation of speech can be only partially informative, however accurate the transcription, and this is why many corpora of spoken interaction are now linked to sound files. However, corpus linguistics has yet to embrace fully the issues involved in transferring its principles to interactions in other media. The mainstays of corpus research, such as concordance lines and word lists, assume a written medium. Other media, such as film, will need different methods of presenting data. Baldry/Thibault (2005), for example, report a multi-media corpus that is actually a collection of video-clips, heavily annotated so that they can be searched for specific instances of given semiotic categories. The need to devise methodologies for exploring multi-media corpora is particularly acute when sign languages are being studied, as these do not have an accepted written form and can currently be studied only through video-recordings of signed texts.

6. The corpus and the object of investigation

There are three issues which are typically taken into account when designing a corpus. These are sometimes referred to as representativeness, balance, and size. They will now be discussed in turn, in each case taking an example of a publicly-available corpus.

Representativeness is the relationship between the corpus and the body of language it is being used to represent. A corpus is usually intended to be a microcosm of a larger phenomenon, except where the corpus is the whole, as in the Barr (2003) example mentioned above. As such, although some statements can be made with absolute confidence about the corpus itself, the value of the corpus lies in being able to make somewhat more tentative statements about the body of language as a whole. Thus a corpus that is unrepresentative is very limited in usefulness.

For example, the ICLE corpus and the LOCNESS corpus (Granger 1998, 9–10; 13) both consist of expository essays written by university students in English. In the case of the ICLE corpus, the writers are learners of English, whereas the LOCNESS writers are native speakers of English. Aijmer (2002, 61) reports that the Swedish component of the ICLE corpus contains many more instances of modals such as *will, would, have to, should* and *might* than the LOCNESS corpus does. This is a fact about these two corpora only. Most researchers, including Aijmer, however, would wish to go further and claim that, on the whole, Swedish learners of English use more of those modals in expository writing than native English speakers do. In making such a claim, they are assuming that the Swedish component of the ICLE corpus, and the LOCNESS corpus, are both representative of the written English of native speakers of Swedish and of English respectively. It is worth considering what would make such a claim invalid. If all the essays in the Swedish corpus were written by one or two learners, for example, it would increase the chances that the evidence relates only to the idiolect of a few learners rather than to Swedish learners as a whole. Alternatively, if all the essays in one corpus (but not the other) were on the same topic and if that topic necessitated a high use of *will, would* and so on, then the judgement that the corpus accurately represented modal use by the two groups would again be thrown into doubt. If, however, each corpus can be shown to include a range of topics and a range of writers, confidence that it is representative is increased. Two further points need to be made here. Firstly, if a range of topics and writers is to be included in the corpus, it must be of a sufficient size to allow this. Thus, representativeness and size are connected. Secondly, the figures for modal use (or use of any other feature) are averaged across the corpus/corpora. They do not take into account possible differences between learners in the same cohort. Thus, whereas we might say with confidence that Swedish learners as a group tend to use a lot of modals such as *will, would* and so on, we cannot say that every individual learner will do so. The corpus is representative of the group, not of the individual.

Finally, of course, it is not possible to extrapolate with certainty from the ICLE corpus, which contains examples of written expository English, to learners' use of a language feature in other written registers, such as narrative, or in speech, or to more advanced learners. It may be reasonable to hypothesise that Swedish learners will use the relevant modals more than native English speakers whether they are writing or speaking, and whatever kind of writing and speaking they are doing, but this remains a hypothesis until tested. On the other hand, teachers of English in Sweden may well decide that they have enough evidence to start devising ways of encouraging their learners to adopt alternative strategies to using modals, that is, that the ICLE corpus is for practical purposes representative of Swedish use of English in general.

Similar issues can be raised about any specialised corpus, but the question of representativeness really becomes controversial when applied to a general corpus, that is, one that aims to represent (a variety of) a language as a whole. There is widespread agreement that such a corpus should include texts from as many different categories of writing and speech as resources will allow. The categories are likely to include: topic areas (books and magazines on various subjects, both fiction and non-fiction, for instance); modes of publication (books, newspapers, leaflets, for example, as well as unpublished materials such as letters and diaries); social situation (casual conversation, service encounters, interviews, lessons, for example); and interactivity (monologue, dialogue and multi-party conversation). Corpora of spoken language often use standard social categories such as age, sex, socio-economic class and region to identify the different groups of people whose speech they wish to include (Leech/Rayson/Wilson 2001, 2–4). A second criterion of representativeness is that the quantity of text from a given category in the corpus would reflect its significance in the society that the corpus is to represent. For example, if twice as many books are published each year on 'social sciences' as on 'world affairs', the corpus might include twice as much text from the former as from the latter. If 15% of a population are over 60 years of age, the same proportion of the spoken component of the corpus should comprise speakers of that age.

There are, of course, considerable problems with this ideal of representativeness. One is that it is not possible to identify a complete list of 'categories' that would exhaustively account for all the texts produced in a given language. No list of domains, or genres, or social groupings can ever be complete, and indeed most general corpora explicitly exclude very specialised kinds of discourse. The ICE corpus, for example, does not include written legal discourse (Meyer 2002, 36). Those categories that are identifiable may in fact be far from homogeneous. One example is the category of 'academic discourse', which forms one of the registers used in Biber et al. (1999), but which is a composite of several different genres and many subject areas, all of which can be demonstrated to have different linguistic characteristics. Thus the 'coverage' apparently afforded by the presence of various categories may be illusory. The question of proportions is even more vexed. Gellerstam (1992, 154), for example, points out that the composition of a corpus will be very different depending on whether it is based on the amount of each kind of language that is produced or on the amount of each kind of language that most people come into contact with. He gives the example of parliamentary proceedings, which are produced in large quantities but read by few people. In other words, there is no true measure of the 'significance' of a type of discourse to a community. Even where the ideal proportions seem to be obvious, there may be several complicating factors. Meyer (2002, 48–49), for example, reports that achieving representation of gender in a spoken corpus is a complex matter, because it is not sufficient to have equal numbers of men and women speakers, representing the broadly equal numbers in the society. As it is known that men and women tend to speak differently depending on whether they are speaking to men or women, and in what situation, a truly representative corpus needs to have equal proportions of male speakers talking to male and female addressees, in single sex and mixed groups, and the same for female speakers. What appears at first to be a simple binary distinction in fact involves at least half a dozen situational configurations, and those configurations change with each speaker change in a conversation.

There are three possible responses to the problems posed by the notion of representativeness in a general corpus. One is to avoid the notion of representation altogether, and to treat the corpus as a collection of different registers, each of which occurs frequently in the target community, but without claiming comprehensive coverage. Biber's work on register variation, for example, selects registers without claiming that together they make up a representation of English. A second is to acknowledge the problems but to do the best that is possible in the circumstances and to be transparent about how the corpus has been designed and what is in it. This allows the degree of representativeness to be assessed by the corpus user. For example, Leech/Rayson/Wilson (2001, 3) record the percentage of speech produced by speakers of different age groups in their corpus of British English conversation; the user can then decide whether this accurately reflects the distribution of ages in Britain. A third alternative is to seek to include texts from as many different sources as possible in the corpus but to treat the resulting corpus as a collection of sub-corpora rather than as a single entity. This is feasible only when each sub-corpus is of a reasonable size. The principle might be illustrated by considering the written and spoken components respectively of the British National Corpus. The spoken component comprises only 10% of the whole, which is clearly not representative either of production or of reception, but which is explained by the heavy resources required to collect spoken data in electronic form. However, 10% of 100 million words is a corpus of a respectable size that allows research to be carried out into spoken British English. The process of normalisation is used to allow valid comparisons between the written and the spoken components (Leech/Rayson/Wilson 2001). The problem of a lack of representativeness disappears. The principle of allowing size to compensate for other issues might be applied to a difficulty raised by Gellerstam (1992, 154), ironically a difficulty caused by representativeness. Gellerstam notes that 75% of all written output in Swedish in any given year comprises newspaper texts. A corpus of written Swedish that consisted of this proportion of newspaper text, and so was representative in that sense, would include only small amounts of other kinds of Swedish. A user of the corpus would be in danger of seeing nothing but the newspaper texts. This would be true, unless the corpus as a whole was large enough so that even 25% of the total could comprise hundreds of millions of words, and unless it was possible to access the various components of the corpus independently. In that case, non-journalistic Swedish could be investigated and compared with the newspaper texts when required.

7. The corpus as artefact

The second issue often discussed in terms of corpus design is balance. Balance refers to the internal composition of the corpus, that is to the proportions of the various sub-corpora that make it up. A corpus that consists of much more of one kind of text than another may be said to be unbalanced. It is immediately obvious, as illustrated by Gellerstam's discussion of Swedish corpora, that balance (equality between sub-corpora) may be at odds with representativeness (each sub-corpus in proportion to its significance). An issue that illustrates this is the decision that the corpus-builder has to take between 'number of texts' and 'number of tokens'. A hypothetical researcher may wish to study newspaper editorials. Obviously, a balanced corpus would consist of the same amount of text from each of the newspapers concerned. However, if some newspapers typically print more, or longer, editorials than others, the problem of 'sameness' arises. The corpus builder could select the same number of editorials from each newspaper, in which case the sub-corpora would contain unequal numbers of words because some texts are longer than others. On the other hand, balancing the sub-corpora in terms of tokens would lead to inequality in terms of number of texts, and would in addition be unrepresentative of the balance of text actually produced by the newspapers concerned.

An example of a corpus designed to be balanced is the Michigan corpus of Spoken Academic English, or MICASE. Its contents are subdivided by speech event type (lecture, discussion group, seminar, meetings, office hours, service encounters etc.), by academic subject (physical sciences, social sciences, humanities etc.), by 'participant level' (undergraduate student, postgraduate student, junior or senior faculty etc.), and by primary discourse mode (monologue, discussion etc.). The corpus is also divisible by the attributes of the speakers: their age, sex, first language, and so on. An argument for the balance of the corpus is that each set of subdivisions is roughly equal. For example: 46% of the speech is produced by men, 54% by women; 49% is produced by faculty, 44% by students; and approximately a quarter of the content of the corpus comes from each of the four main academic subject areas (the actual figures are between 19% and 26%). However, only 12% of the speech is from non-native speakers of English, and only 8% belongs to the discourse mode classified as 'panel' (where a group of speakers each produces a short monologue in turn). These figures presumably reflect the relatively low proportion of non-native speakers of English on the Michigan campus and the relative infrequency of panel-type discourse. Furthermore, only 14% of the speech in the 'monologic' mode is produced by students, with the rest being produced by faculty. Although overall male/female proportions are roughly equal, the numbers are not equal in all the subject areas. The biggest discrepancy is in Social Sciences and Education, where 63% of the speech is produced by female speakers. Again, this is no doubt an inevitable consequence of the contexts of recording: few lectures are given by students and there are sex imbalances in some academic disciplines. Although the corpus designers planned MICASE as a balanced, rather than a representative, corpus, lack of balance in the context has affected the corpus to some extent.

Although the need for balance in a corpus may appear obvious, it is worth considering precisely what benefits a balanced corpus offers. To take an example: a researcher looking at a particular language feature in monologic discourse in MICASE does not need to worry that the prevalence or absence of the feature is due to the peculiarities of male or female speech rather than to the nature of monologue, because the monologic discourse component of the corpus is split exactly 50:50 between men and women. If it is found that the feature occurs more frequently in monologues by women than in monologues by men, on the other hand, this can confidently be ascribed to a difference in gendered speech rather than to a difference in the proportions of men and women in that component of the corpus. It should be noted, however, that a similar effect can be obtained by normalising the frequency of an item, so that differences between the sizes of sub-corpora are overcome. When Poos/Simpson (2002) normalise the frequency of hedges such as *kind of* and *sort of* in MICASE monologues, they find that the frequency per thousand words is practically the same for men and women. They express greater confidence in this finding for those disciplines where the quantity of male and female speech in monologues is approximately the same than in those where it is markedly different. In the Physical Sciences, for example, although the per thousand word frequency is almost the same for men and women, there are only two female speakers, and the number of words produced by them is less than half that produced by the male speakers (Poos/Simpson 2002, 8). It is possible, then, that one or two of the female speakers have used an abnormal number of hedges, so skewing the results. In other words, the authors argue that a lack of balance may lead to a lack of representativeness, in that women producing monologues in the Physical Sciences are under-represented in this corpus.

This suggests that the real benefit of a balanced corpus is that each of its various components is large enough to make comparisons feasible. In MICASE there are sufficient quantities of male and female speech, of speech by students and faculty, of monologic and interactive speech, and of speech in the various subject areas, to warrant comparisons between these categories, even though the total word count of the corpus (about 1.5 million words) is not huge. Another point to be made is that balance, like representativeness, implies explicitness in corpus description. Poos/Simpson (2002, 7) point out that an imbalance in a corpus does not matter so long as it is known and hypotheses can be adjusted accordingly. They note, for instance, that in MICASE there is more interactive speech, proportional to monologue, in Biology than in Social Sciences. If a language feature were found to be more prevalent in Biology than in Social Sciences, then, a possible explanation would be that this feature was frequent in interactive speech generally. This would have to be explored before an association between the feature and discipline was proposed.

The explicitness of description, however, can only be partial. In fact, arguments that a particular corpus is representative, or balanced, are inevitably circular, in that the categories we are invited to observe are artefacts of the design procedure. The categories that have formed the basis of the corpus design are, indeed, representative or balanced, but other categories may be less representative or balanced and less observable. Meyer's discussion of gender balance is an example of this. If the only categories considered are 'male' versus 'female', then a corpus may be designed to capture an equal amount of speech from men and women, and the results may show that this has been achieved. Other categories, such as 'addressee', that have not been built into the corpus design, may be in the end very unbalanced. The women may have chosen to make recordings only when speaking to other women, for example, or the men may have avoided recording all-male chat.

8. Large and small corpora

In looking at the issue of corpus size, we are once again faced with a paradox. On the one hand, it might said of any corpus that the larger it is, the better, the only upper constraint being computational capacity and speed of software (Sinclair 1991, 18; Meyer 2002, 33). As has been indicated above, some of the difficulties posed by seeking to make a corpus balanced and representative can be lessened by having a corpus large enough for each of its constituent components to be of a substantial size (cf. Aston/Burnard 1998, 21). The only advantage of a small corpus is that the occurrence of very frequent words is low enough to make observation of all instances feasible, whereas in a large corpus some kind of sampling has to take place (Carter/McCarthy 1995, 143). The counter-argument is that such sampling can incorporate the observation of large-scale patterning rather than simply taking a small sub-set of the whole. For example, collocation lists can be used to summarise the information from a large number of concordance lines so that a smaller number of lines incorporating more specific phraseologies can then be examined in detail. This is true even of very frequent grammatical items, if these are considered to be the locus of phraseology rather than simply a grammatical category. For example, Groom (2007) investigates the behaviour of very frequent items, such as prepositions, in corpora of academic writing distinguished by discipline. He notes certain phraseologies that are typical of one discipline rather than another, such as the sequence 'It is in … that' which is an identifying phraseology of Literary Criticism and which functions as an introduction to an interpretative observation (e. g. *it is in the exchanges between these characters that Shakespeare can again emphasise the political ambiguity of language*). This sequence was identified in the course of an investigation of the very frequent word *in*. Sequences such as this one are potentially so long, however, that even Groom's Literary Criticism corpus of 4 million words, with its many thousands of instances of *in*, cannot always show more than a handful of each.

It would appear, then, that any corpus should simply be as large as possible, and that to achieve this the corpus should continue being added to over the lifetime of its use. In most situations, however, this is impractical. The need to plan the resources involved in a research project, including the time and money involved, make it necessary to specify in advance the size of the corpus to be compiled. If a corpus is extensively annotated, and especially if some of this annotation has to be done or edited manually, increasing the size of the corpus greatly increases the amount of effort involved. Adding to the corpus once the resources allocated to its compilation have been used up is impossible. Even if such problems do not exist, if a corpus is converted to digits for storage, enlarging the corpus means re-converting the whole entity. As a result, additions cannot be made with great frequency.

Connected to the issue of corpus size is that of sample size. A corpus of a million words or so cannot afford to include whole books which might be up to 100,000 words in length, and as a result text sampling is often used. The British component of the International Corpus of English, for example, consists of 'texts' of 2,000 words each (Nelson/Wallis/Aarts 2002, 4). Each 'text' consists either of part of a longer entity, such as a novel, or of a collection of smaller entities, such as business letters. Such uniformity ensures maximum control over the content of the corpus, which is advantageous in a situation where corpora (in English, from around the world) are to be compared. Sinclair (1991, 19), however, argues that sampling can lead to differences between parts of a text being overlooked. The 'whole text' policy that he advocates, however, does necessitate the collection of a much larger corpus if one or two large publications are not to affect the output disproportionately.

In the long run, then, the issue of corpus size becomes a set of interconnecting issues that concern the aims and methods of investigation as well as the question of size. Where resources are limited, or where close control is needed to ensure comparability between corpora, or where a very accurate transcription or extensive annotation is required, the corpus will tend to be relatively small, and, if it is a general corpus, will probably consist of samples of texts rather than whole texts. If size and whole texts are seen as priorities, annotation is likely to be minimal and comparability, even between sections of the corpus, is unlikely to be exact. Conversely, a small corpus is most useful if it is annotated, and in turn an annotated corpus is most useful for investigating the relative frequency and other aspects of instances of the categories for which it has been annotated. For example, Semino and Short's study of speech, thought and writing representation in newspapers, novels and biographies is based on a corpus of just under 260,000 words that is, nonetheless, minutely annotated (Semino/Short 2004, 19). A large corpus is most useful for studying less frequent items or, crucially, the macro-patterning of language that is not amenable to intuition and is ignored by grammatical tradition, and that can only be seen when many instances of relatively long sequences of items are brought together.

9. Conclusion

Corpus design and compilation seems like a simple matter. The researcher decides what the various components of the corpus are to consist of and what the size relationship between the components will be. He or she then identifies places where the desired texts can be found, and so builds the corpus. In practice, the situation is likely to be much more complex. Practical issues such as copyright restrictions, or availability in electronic form, may determine which texts are used and as a consequence which variables can be taken into account. In considering the relative size of components, the researcher may need to choose between balance and representativeness. What would constitute 'representation' may not be identifiable anyway.

In addition, although in theory a corpus is a neutral resource that can be used in research from any number of standpoints (Leech 1997, 7), in practice the design of the corpus may strongly constrain the kind of research that is carried out (Sinclair 1992). Most obviously, a corpus that is limited in time-period precludes discourse studies that depend on a diachronic dimension to intertextuality (Teubert 2003, 12). A corpus that is small and balanced prioritises the investigation of variation using grammatical categories (Biber et al. 1999, 15–24). A very large corpus facilitates the study of phraseology and macro-patterning (Sinclair 2004, 24–48).

Far from being neutral, then, issues of corpus design and building take us to the heart of theories of corpus linguistics. Questions of what goes into a corpus are largely answered by the specific research project the corpus is designed for, but are also connected to more philosophical issues around what, potentially, corpora can show us about language.

10. Literature

Aijmer, K. (2002), Modality in Advanced Swedish Learners' Written Interlanguage. In: Granger, S./Hung, J./Petch-Tyson, S. (eds.), *Computer Learner Corpora, Second Language Acquisition and Foreign Language Teaching*. Amsterdam: Benjamins, 55–76.

Aston, G./Burnard, L. (1998), *The BNC Handbook: Exploring the British National Corpus with SARA*. Edinburgh: Edinburgh University Press.

Baldry, A./Thibault, P. (2005), Multimodal Corpus Linguistics. In: Thompson, G./Hunston, S. (eds.), *System and Corpus: Exploring Connections*. London: Equinox, 164–183.

Barr, G. K. (2003), Two Styles in the New Testament Epistles. In: *Literary and Linguistic Computing* 18, 235–248.

Bernardini, S./Baroni, M. (2004), Web-mining Disposable Corpora in the Translation Classroom. Paper read at the 6th TALC Conference, Granada, 2004.

Biber, D. (1988), *Variation Across Speech and Writing*. Cambridge: Cambridge University Press.

Biber, D./Finegan, E. (2001), Diachronic Relations among Speech-based and written registers in English. In: Conrad, S./Biber, D. (eds.), Variation in English: Multidimensional Studies. Harlow etc.: Longman, 66–83.

Biber, D./Finegan, E./Atkinson, D. (1994), ARCHER and its Challenges: Compiling and Exploring a Representative Corpus of Historical English Registers. In: Fries, U./Tottie, G./Schneider, P. (eds.), *Creating and Using English Language Corpora: Papers from the Fourteenth International Conference on English Language Research on Computerized Corpora, Zürich 1993*. Amsterdam: Rodopi, 1–14.

Biber, D./Johansson, S./Leech, G./Conrad, S./Finegan, E. (1999), *Longman Grammar of Spoken and Written English*. Harlow: Pearson Education.

Carter, R./McCarthy, M. (1995), Grammar and the Spoken Language. In: *Applied Linguistics* 16(2), 141–158.

Du Bois, J./Chafe, W./Meyer, C./Thompson, S. (2000), *Santa Barbara Corpus of Spoken American English, Part 1*. Philadelphia: Linguistic Data Consortium.

Du Bois, J./Chafe, W./Meyer, C./Thompson, S. (2003), *Santa Barbara Corpus of Spoken American English, Part 2*. Philadelphia: Linguistic Data Consortium.

Gellerstam, M. (1992), Modern Swedish Text Corpora. In: Svartvik, J. (ed.), *Directions in Corpus Linguistics*. Berlin/New York: Mouton de Gruyter, 149–163.

Granger, S. (1998), The Computer Learner Corpus: A Versatile New Source of Data for SLA Research. In: Granger, S. (ed.), *Learner English on Computer*. London: Longman, 3–18.

Groom, N. (2007), Phraseology and Epistemology in Humanities Writing: A Corpus-driven Study. PhD thesis, University of Birmingham.

Francis, N./Kučera, H. (1982), *Frequency Analysis of English Usage: Lexicon and Grammar*. Boston: Houghton Mifflin.

Leech, G. (1997), Introducing Corpus Annotation. In: Garside, R./Leech, G./McEnery, A. (eds.), *Corpus Annotation: Linguistic Information from Computer Text Corpora*. London: Longman, 1–18.

Leech, G./Rayson, P./Wilson, A. (2001), *Word Frequencies in Written and Spoken English: Based on the British National Corpus*. London: Longman.

Meyer, C. (2002), *English Corpus Linguistics: An Introduction*. Cambridge: Cambridge University Press.

Nelson, G./Wallis, S./Aarts, B. (2002), *Exploring Natural Language: Working with the British Component of the International Corpus of English*. Amsterdam: John Benjamins.

Poos, D./Simpson, R. (2002), Cross-disciplinary Comparisons of Hedging: Some Findings from the Michigan Corpus of Academic Spoken English. In: Reppen, R./Fitzmaurice, S./Biber, D. (eds.), *Using Corpora to Explore Linguistic Variation*. Amsterdam: Benjamins, 3–23.

Renouf, A. (1987), Corpus Development. In: Sinclair, J. (ed.), *Looking Up: An Account of the COBUILD Project in Lexical Computing*. London: HarperCollins, 1–40.

Rottweiler, G. (2006), Evaluative Meanings, Social Values, and One Lexical Set: A Corpus Analysis of *Unilateral, Unilaterally, Unilateralism*, and *Unilateralist/s*. MPhil thesis, University of Birmingham.
Scott, M. (2004), *WordSmith Tools*, version 4.0. Oxford: Oxford University Press.
Semino, E./Short, M. (2004), *Corpus Stylistics: Speech, Writing and Thought Presentation in a Corpus of English Writing*. London: Routledge.
Sinclair, J. (1991), *Corpus, Concordance Collocation*. Oxford: Oxford University Press.
Sinclair, J. (1992), The Automatic Analysis of Corpora. In: Svartvik, J. (ed.), *Directions in Corpus Linguistics*. Berlin/New York: Mouton de Gruyter, 379–397.
Sinclair, J. (2004), *Trust the Text: Language, Corpus and Discourse*. London: Routledge.
Stubbs, M. (1996), *Text and Corpus Analysis:* Computer-Assisted Studies of Language and Culture. Oxford: Blackwell.
Teubert W. (2001), A Province of a Federal Superstate, Ruled by an Unelected Bureaucracy: Keywords of the Euro-sceptic Discourse in Britain. In: Musolff, A./Good, C./Points, P./Wittlinger, R. (eds.), *Attitudes Towards Europe*. Aldershot: Ashgate, 45–86.
Teubert W. (2003), Writing, hermeneutics, and corpus linguistics. In: *Logos and Language* 4, 1–17.
Teubert, W. (2004), When did we Start Feeling Guilty? In: Weigand, E. (ed.), *Emotion in Dialogic Interaction*. Amsterdam: Benjamins, 121–162.

Susan Hunston, Birmingham (UK)

10. Text corpora

1. Introduction

Among corpora, one often distinguishes between text corpora (consisting of written material – both published and unpublished), spoken corpora (cf. article 11) and multimodal corpora (cf. article 12). More specialized types of corpora are treebanks (cf. article 13), historical, learner, or parallel corpora (cf. articles 14, 15 and 16, respectively). On closer inspection, the distinction between text and speech corpora is not as straightforward as it appears to be. The article will therefore begin with a discussion of the notions 'text' and 'speech'. Section 1.1.1. will consider how far text corpora can be defined as collections of written texts and what it means for a text to be 'written'. Corpora further have to be distinguished from mere text databases or text archives (section 1.1.2.). An outline of topics treated in the remaining sections of this article will be given in section 1.2.

1.1. Definition of 'text' corpus

Biber et al. (1998, 4) define a corpus as "a large and principled collection of natural texts". This general definition of what a corpus is (or should be) can be taken as a useful starting point for the definition of 'text corpus'. The relevant key words are 'text' and 'principled'.

1.1.1. Spoken vs. written 'texts'

Biber et al. (1998) include both written and spoken registers in their notion of the 'text'. The focus in this article is on prototypically 'written' corpora. For primarily spoken corpora, cf article 11. However, the distinction between text corpora, on the one hand, and speech corpora, on the other hand, is somewhat artificial. It is a problematic distinction for two reasons, one theoretical, the other practical. These will be addressed in turn.

The terms 'written' and 'spoken' are normally taken to refer to the (primary) channel of transmission: texts can be transmitted in the written or spoken medium. But they can also be written to be spoken (for example lectures, political speeches, some kinds of radio broadcasts) or they can be transcribed speech (i. e. medially 'written' recordings of originally 'spoken' language). Therefore, in addition to the medial aspect (i. e. the channel of transmission), a distinction has to be made between conceptually 'literal' and 'oral' texts. Both aspects – the medial and the conceptual – overlap. Closer analysis of medially spoken and written language shows that, conceptually and linguistically, we are dealing with a cline that ranges from prototypically written texts to prototypically spoken texts (cf. Chafe 1982; Koch/Österreicher 1985; Biber 1988; Häcki Buhofer 2000). A personal letter, for instance, is conceptually less 'written' than an academic text book. Published texts, in general, have a tendency to be more 'written' than unpublished material. Some popular newspapers, however, attempt a more oral style. This does not imply that they are approximations of language transmitted in the spoken medium. Fowler (1991, 39) has labelled this style of writing a 'social construct': "Through the use of colloquialisms, incomplete sentences, questions and varied typography suggesting variations of emphasis, the written text mimics a speaking voice, as of a person talking informally […]." The literacy-orality cline also has repercussions for the practical decision-making in corpus compilation. In a corpus of Korean, for instance, comics and 'conversations' in novels were included in the spoken section (see Kang/Kim/Huh 2003). The literacy-orality cline is also a major issue for a corpus of computer-mediated communication (cf. article 17). For an obvious reason, namely the relatively recent availability of technical facilities to preserve spoken language in the spoken medium, historical corpora tend to be corpora of written texts. The written-spoken or literal-oral cline, however, also applies to these corpora as some text-types (for example personal letters, depositions from criminal investigations, dramatical or fictional dialogue) are conceptually closer to the spoken end of the text-speech cline (cf. article 14).

In the following, the term 'text corpus' is used to refer mainly to the channel of transmission – i. e. medially 'written' texts – regardless of their degree of (conceptual) orality or literacy.

Secondly, the distinction between text and speech corpora is also somewhat artificial for a very practical reason. A lot of existing corpora aim at being representative or at least balanced (cf article 9) collections of language in use, and therefore have sampled both written and spoken texts. These 'mixed' corpora (for example the Survey of English Usage (SEU), the International Corpus of English (ICE) or the British National Corpus (BNC)) will be treated in section 3.

1.1.2. Text corpus vs. text database

If a corpus is defined as a principled or structured (Kennedy 1998, 3) collection of texts, it has to be distinguished from a more arbitrary collection of material or 'text database'. This opens up questions such as (a) how well-defined the sampling frame for genres or text-types has to be to make a text database into a 'corpus', or (b) how 'open' a corpus is allowed to be. According to McEnery/Wilson (1996, 24), for instance, a prototypical corpus in the corpus linguistic sense is a "finite-sized body of machine-readable text". In addition, corpora rather than text-databases are usually annotated collections of text, i. e. they are often provided with a header, some structural annotation and sometimes also positional annotation. These points are treated in more depth elsewhere (cf. article 9 on issues of corpus design, article 3 on sample vs. monitor corpora, and article 22 on annotation schemata). The borderline between a well-defined corpus and a random collection of texts is unlikely to be a clear-cut one, however.

1.2. Outline

Corpora in the narrow sense are described in sections 2 and 3. Emphasis will be on publicly available or accessible, computerized corpora of modern languages (for a discussion of pre-electronic corpora, cf. Kennedy 1998, 13−19; for historical text corpora, cf. article 14). The corpus on which the *Longman Grammar of Spoken and Written English* (Biber et al. 1999) is based, for instance, would fit with the mixed corpora described in section 3 but has not been made publicly available. Sections 2 and 3 do not attempt to give an exhaustive overview of all available written or mixed corpora. At the beginning of the 21st century, this task is no longer achievable with several projects underway for various languages, as Kennedy (1998, 13) points out (for an overview of well-known and/or influential corpora, see article 20). Sections 2 and 3 are slightly biased towards corpora of English since English-based corpus linguistics has played a pioneering role in the field (cf. article 3), but the comments also apply to corpora of other languages (for corpora of other languages, cf. articles 20 and 21).

Apart from the text corpora in the narrow, corpus-linguistic sense defined above, various other collections of written texts are available in the form of newspaper archives, fiction databases, or digitally stored dictionaries. Section 4 discusses whether these might be considered as single-register corpora (as opposed to the general reference corpora). The final section illustrates how prototypical corpora can be combined with text databases in corpus-based research.

2. Standard written corpora

Among the written corpora, we find what could be termed 'general language' corpora and principled collections of more specialised written texts (for example learner corpora, cf. article 15, or corpora of computer mediated communication, cf. article 17). The focus in this section is on 'standard' general reference corpora and their sampling frame.

2.1. First-generation corpora

For the English language, a ground-breaking development was the compilation at Brown University of a one-million word corpus intended as a representative sample of written American English published in 1961 (see article 3). The 500 samples of approximately 2,000 words each are spread over a range of non-fictional and fictional text categories (see Table 10.1). In the late 1970s, a matching corpus of British English was compiled at the universities of Lancaster, Oslo and Bergen, commonly abbreviated as the LOB corpus.

A word of caution is in order with respect to different text categories. The text categories sampled in the Brown corpus have often been referred to as 'text types' or 'genres'. In the narrower, text linguistic sense, the use of this terminology is hardly justified. The categories are only a fairly rough-and-ready classification of texts. Research by Biber (1988) has shown, for instance, that sometimes more variation within traditional text categories (such as 'newspapers') exists than between different text categories. For scientific writing, for instance, not only the difference between natural and social sciences

Tab. 10.1: Sampling frame for the Brown corpus of written AmE (1961)

Text category	Category label	Number of samples	Approximate number of words
Press: reportage	A	44	88,000
Press: editorials	B	27	54,000
Press: reviews	C	17	34,000
Religion	D	17	34,000
Skills and hobbies	E	36	72,000
Popular lore	F	48	96,000
Belles letters, biography, etc.	G	75	150,000
Miscellaneous	H	30	60,000
Learned	J	80	160,000
General fiction	K	29	58,000
Mystery and detective fiction	L	24	48,000
Science fiction	M	6	12,000
Adventure and western fiction	N	29	58,000
Romance and love story	P	29	58,000
Humor	R	9	18,000
Total		500	1,000,000

might be relevant. Within both categories, articles from scientific journals and theses are likely to be quite different from introductory text books which sometimes try to sound 'chatty and user-friendly' and may feature elements that are intended to simulate direct interaction between the author and the reader, such as question-answer sequences or imperatives. In other words, the definition of text categories is a fairly subjective, notional one in corpus compilation and not a linguistic one that is based on a multi-feature/multi-dimensional model of the type employed by Biber. Furthermore, the assignment of individual text samples to a category of the corpus may also be a problematic issue (some examples will be discussed in connection with the BNC in section 3). Text category labels thus often have to be taken with a grain of salt in corpus linguistic research.

It is important to bear in mind that, whereas the Brown corpus as a whole was intended to be representative of written American English at the time, this was not the case for the sub-sections of the corpus. As far as more coarse-grained categorisations are concerned, it should further be noted that the non-fictional part of the corpus is much larger (approximately 75%) than the fictional part (roughly 25%). Hofland/Johansson (1989, 27) use four different macro-categories, namely Press (18%), General Prose – the most heterogeneous category (41%), Learned (16%) and Fiction (25%). These are useful distinctions for cross-corpus comparison that will be used below.

What the list of text categories in Table 10.1 does not reveal is the fact that, as part of category H ('Miscellaneous'), transcripts of parliamentary or other public speeches were included. These texts are not usually faithful transcriptions of the oral delivery but have been adapted to publication in the written medium, for instance by leaving out false starts, repetitions, etc. (cf. Slembrouck 1992 and Mollin forthcoming). For examples of these conceptually more 'oral' texts in standard reference corpora of written English, see Figures 10.1 and 10.2. Typical of the more oral style is the relatively frequent use of first and second pronouns. Text type-specific oral features are formulaic address forms (*Mr Speaker* or *the right hon. Gentleman*). The combination of two optional adverbials in sentence initial position in H15, 3–4 also reflects that the text is a transcript of spoken language.

H03	0010	You have heard him tell these young people that during his almost
H03	0020	50 years of service in the Congress he has seen the Kaisers and
H03	0030	the Hitlers and the Mussolinis, the Tojos and Stalins and Khrushchevs,
H03	0040	come and go and that we are passing on to them the freest Nation
H03	0050	that mankind has ever known. Then I have seen the pride of country
H03	0060	well in the eyes of these young people. So, I say, Mr& Speaker,
H03	0070	God bless you and keep you for many years not only for this body
H03	0080	but for the United States of America and the free world. You remember
H03	0090	the words of President Kennedy a week or so ago, when someone
H03	0100	asked him when he was in Canada, and Dean Rusk was in Europe, and
H03	0110	Vice President JOHNSON was in Asia, "Who is running the
H03	0120	store"? and he said "The same fellow who has been running it, SAM
H03	0130	RAYBURN".

Fig. 10.1: Example of a transcript of a parliamentary speech (from the 87th Congress; Brown corpus)

```
H15   1  **[279 TEXT H15**]
H15   2     |^*0I do not know what the right \0hon. Gentleman means by *"large
H15   3  part of the country.**" ^For all I know, over a geographical area what
H15   4  he says may be true. ^For example, let us consider the area in which
H15   5  the \0hon. Member for Exeter plays such a large part. ^If the
H15   6  Government knock down one cottage in the middle of Dartmoor, they may
H15   7  be removing all the slums over a wide area. ^But if the Minister
H15   8  means, by *"large part**", areas where people are living in great
H15   9  concentrations of population, then the answer is that the areas that
H15  10  are not keeping up with the slum clearance programme represent the
H15  11  majority of unfit houses in the country.
```

Fig. 10.2: Example of a transcript of a parliamentary speech (March 20, 1961; LOB corpus)

Written representations of spoken language are, to a certain extent, also included in newspaper writing as quotations of direct speech or in fiction as passages of dialogue (according to the manual of the Brown corpus, fictional texts that contained more than 50% dialogue were therefore excluded from the sampling process). Like the transcripts of speeches, however, these more 'oral' passages are heavily adapted to publication in the written medium. The Brown and LOB corpus are samples of published material, i. e. they are biased towards the standard variety of the language. (Occasionally, however, instances of non-standard language use may occur in fictional writing or in more popular newspapers). The bias towards the standard variety is not necessarily inherent in written text corpora, however, as will become evident in section 3.

A number of other corpora of English (both as a first and a second language) took the Brown-LOB sampling frame as a model (for the slight deviations from the original sampling frame, notably with respect to such categories as 'Adventure and western fiction', see the various manuals for these corpora). Examples of other first-language corpora would be the Wellington Corpus of Written New Zealand English (compiled from material published in the years 1986–1990) or the Macquarie University Corpus of Australian English (sampling texts that were published in 1986). The Kolhapur Corpus of Indian English contains samples of English used as a second language that were published in 1978. In the early 1990s, replicas of the original Brown and LOB corpus were compiled from texts published in 1992 and 1991, respectively (named Frown and FLOB since they were compiled at the University of Freiburg). In Lancaster, a comparable British corpus was compiled from material published in the late 1920s/early 1930s; a matching corpus for American English is currently being compiled at the Universitiy of Zürich. In addition to research on regional (national) varieties of English, this family of comparable 'standard' one-million-word corpora allows linguists to study short-term diachronic change in the twentieth century in two major varieties, British and American English (cf article 52). The sampling frame of the Brown corpus has also been applied in the collection of a non-English corpus, namely the Lancaster Corpus of Mandarin Chinese (cf. article 20).

Most of these corpora are available as lexical corpora. Some of them have also been annotated with part-of-speech tagging (for example Brown, LOB, Frown and FLOB) or have been syntactically parsed (for example parts of the LOB corpus have been made available as the 'Lancaster Parsed Corpus' (LPC)).

2.2. Second-generation corpora

Recently, a standard reference corpus for modern written Italian has been made available, namely the Corpus di Italiano Scritto (CORIS). This is one of the 100-million-word corpora which, due to their size, are often referred to as 'second-generation' corpora. Compiled at the University of Bologna, it includes written texts from six major text categories, namely press (38 million words), fiction (25 million words), academic prose (12 million words), legal and administrative prose (10 million words), a category of 'miscellaneous' texts, for example religious books, travelogue, skills and hobbies (10 million words), and a category labelled 'ephemera' in which letters (both private and public), leaflets and instructions are sampled (5 million words). With the exception of the 'ephemera' category, the sampling frame for the text categories thus resembles the one used for the Brown-type corpora. As in the first-generation corpora, the proportion of non-fictional to fictional texts is about 75% to 25%. A closer look at the non-fictional texts, however, shows that CORIS contains a larger proportion of press texts than the first generation corpora (see Table 10.2).

Tab. 10.2: Comparison of sampling frames (Brown-type corpora vs. CORIS)

Macrocategory	Brown-type corpora	CORIS
Press	18%	38%
General Prose	41%	25%
Learned	16%	12%
Fiction	25%	25%

Another difference between Brown and CORIS is that, with advances in computer technology, the appropriate size for the Italian corpus was taken to be one hundred million words rather than the one million words of the first generation corpora of the Brown-type. Unlike the standard one-million-word corpora of English, CORIS contains whole texts rather than text samples of a defined size. This option is only open to large corpora, however, since the one-million word corpora of the first generation could not possibly sample whole scientific articles, for instance, let alone complete monographs. In the newspaper section, however, even the two-thousand word samples of the one-million word corpora obviously had to sample whole texts, as a single newspaper article hardly ever yields the required number of words.

CORIS is a synchronic corpus in the wider sense of the word, as the texts were produced mostly in the 1980s and 1990s. The dichotomy of sample vs. monitor corpora does not apply to this text corpus, either: it is available both as a sample corpus (for example on CD-ROM) and as a monitor corpus that will continually be updated bi-annually, so as to remain a sample of modern Italian over the years. Finally, to enable linguists to carry out comparative research across various languages, a dynamic version of CORIS is available that allows for the creation of sub-corpora of practically any size and composition (see Rossini Favretti et al. 2003).

With an increasing array of general language corpora that will obviously not be perfect fits for cross-corpus comparisons, a flexible corpus structure that allows users to adapt the size and composition of the corpora will be a convenient solution. (Note, however, that comparison across corpora or between corpora and text databases does not necessarily depend on perfectly matching sets of samples, as will be shown in section 5). In a way, dynamic corpora challenge the notion of a corpus as a well-defined, principled collection of texts because they are more open. In their totality, they may be standard reference corpora in the more narrow sense defined above; at the same time, however, the principles of corpus compilation or rather corpus definition can be adapted to the specific research requirements of individual projects.

3. Mixed corpora

The Brown corpus was not the first one-million-word corpus intended as a representative collection of texts. The Survey of English usage corpus (SEU), compiled at University College, London, is also a one-million-word corpus. Unlike the 'standard' corpora of English described in the previous section, however, it comprises both written and spoken 'texts' – i. e. it is a 'mixed' corpus. Furthermore, it was originally compiled on slips of paper (which have, in the meantime, been digitalized). It also differs from the standard written corpora of English in that it is not a synchronic corpus: the texts sampled in the SEU corpus were produced between the years 1955 and 1985. Another difference between the Brown-type corpora and the SEU corpus is the number and size of the individual samples: the latter contains fewer and larger individual text extracts. 100 samples of approximately 5,000 words each make up the written component of the SEU corpus. The sampling frame for this mixed corpus is also wider than that for the Brown-type corpora in that it includes both published and unpublished texts (see Figure 10.3). The fact, that speech and text corpora form a cline rather than two neat distinct categories, is also reflected in the SEU corpus: the written part of the corpus includes written-to-be-spoken texts like news broadcasts or talks, whereas the spoken component has samples of prepared monologue like sermons, lectures or addresses by lawyers in a court room. They also include samples of monologue that are intended to be written down, i. e. dictated letters. The main difference between the written texts for spoken delivery and the prepared monologue is that monologues are not simply read faithfully from a script and are thus slightly more spontaneous than scripted speeches. In other words, they are more 'oral'.

The sampling frame for another set of mixed corpora, namely the different regional components of the International Corpus of English (ICE), resembles that of the SEU corpus in so far as it consists of spoken and written texts. In the ICE corpora, however, the balance between spoken and written texts has been changed: the spoken component is larger than the written component, with approximately 600,000 and 400,000 words, respectively. Furthermore, texts written for oral delivery are included among the spoken texts (as part of the category of scripted monologue) in the ICE corpora, and not among the written texts, as in the SEU. Like the SEU corpus, the written component of the ICE corpora contains both printed and non-printed texts (see Figure 10.4). (Note that *non-printed* is used in the sense of 'unpublished' in the SEU and ICE framework, as non-printed texts also include business letters which are no longer handwritten).

A comparison of Figures 10.3 and 10.4 shows that the SEU has a much wider variety of non-printed texts, but these are not necessarily of the informal type. Memos and minutes of meetings, for instance, tend to be more formal than certain kinds of 'chatty' editorials. With only 50 samples of non-printed texts against 150 samples of printed texts, the emphasis in the written component of the ICE corpora is definitely on published material. The inclusion of unpublished material, however, opens up the (theoreti-

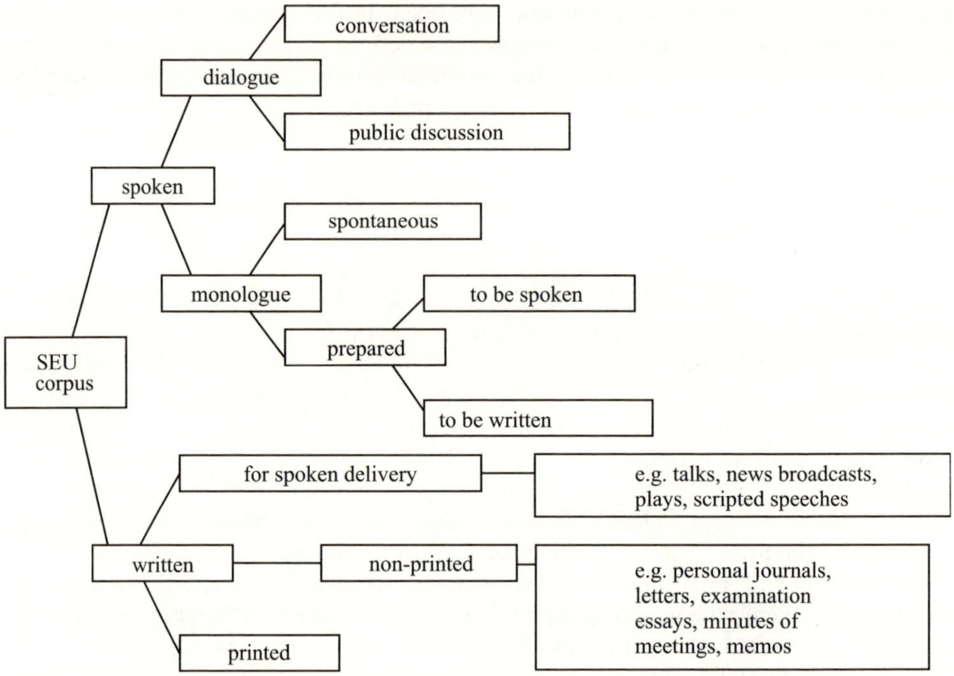

Fig. 10.3: Structure of the SEU corpus

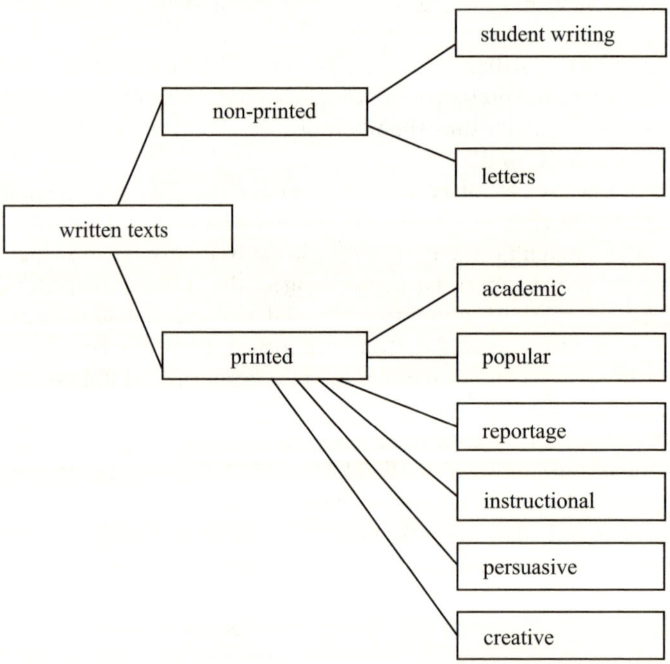

Fig. 10.4: Sampling frame for the written component of the ICE corpora

cal) possibility that non-standard features are included in the corpus to a greater extent than in corpora which sample only published texts. Social letters are probably the most likely text category for non-standard language use. This is particularly an issue for the second-language ICE corpora, as the extract from ICE-East-Africa in (1) illustrates.

(1)

W1B-SK02
<I> <name/> dear,
[...]
Sorry I had promised to write first and I failed. All the same I thank God <slang/>coz of a dear friend of Mine somewhere who said 'better late than never'. <ea/>Ama? Anyway I <slang/>juz wanted to fetch some news for you.
[...]
<ea/>Hakika I <-/recieved> yours <ea/>na <ea/>kusema <ea/>ukweli I was so glad though I felt <-/guity> for failing to fulfill the promise. which? All the same take it <slang/>coooo-oolly.
[...]
<slang/>Tiz my deep desire, hope and sincere prayer that it may never happen on the planet earth. It would better happen to <ea/>akina Jupiter and <-/mars> and never here.
[...]
<name/> greets you so much, says she never made it for the interviews <slang/>coz of money problems.
There is <-/alot> to say as you can <-/guezz> but time factor and <-/commitements> here and there are forcing me to call it off.
Share my love with <name/> and your other friends.
Bye!
Call her
</I>

In this corpus, non-standard features are marked-up as <slang/>. On closer analysis, all of the non-standard features in this letter are actually non-standard spellings which may also, occasionally, be used as sensational spellings in news writing.

The BNC is another corpus that 'mixes' both spoken and written texts. Like the SEU and the CORIS, the BNC can be considered a 'synchronic' corpus only in the wider sense of the word, since the texts that were sampled for the BNC date from between 1960 and 1993 (with the majority from the period between 1975 and 1993). It resembles the SEU in that texts that were written for oral delivery are included in the written rather than the spoken part of the corpus. The major part of the texts in the written component of the corpus consists of published material, with unpublished texts only comprising about 4 million words (i. e. less than 10% of the written material). In the ICE corpora, on the other hand, non-printed material amounts to 25% of the written component.

It is not possible to compare the composition of the written components of the three mixed corpora with respect to the macro-categories established by Hofland/Johansson (1989) that were introduced in the previous section. Comparison of the BNC with the Brown-type corpora is only sometimes possible – one category used in the BNC comprises leisure writing which is probably similar to the 'skills and hobbies' section in the Brown-type corpora. For other standard text categories, however, there are no equivalents in the BNC sampling frame. There is no separate category of journalistic prose, for example. Instead, the BNC classification has two categories in which newspaper articles may be included, i.e. world affairs (reportage) and belief & thought (editorials and reviews).

Tab. 10.3: Non-fictional vs. fictional writing in the written part of three mixed corpora

	SEU	ICE	BNC
Non-fiction	92%	90%	75%
Fiction	8%	10%	25%

The text categories on which the sampling for the informative prose in the BNC was based shows once more that text categories or labels are more of the rough-and-ready type than based on careful text linguistic principles: for scientific writing, for instance, three sub-categories (natural, applied and social science) are distinguished. Even more problematic than the rather vague category labels is the fact that sometimes, individual texts are not assigned to the category where one would expect them to occur. An extract from *Gardener's World*, for instance, is included in the domain 'natural and pure science' of the BNC, as is an excerpt from Stephen Hawking's *A Brief History of Time*. The 'applied science' domain features extracts from the same author's *Black Holes and Baby Universes* along with samples from *Nursing Times*, lectures on electromagnetic theory, and texts from do-it-yourself guides (which might be more appropriately classified as part of the 'leisure' domain).

Unlike the other 100-million-word corpus described in section 3 (CORIS), the BNC contains mostly text samples rather than complete texts. For a discussion of whether this might increase the representativeness of the sample, cf. articles 3 and 9.

4. Text databases

Collections of computerized texts are not only available in the form of carefully designed reference corpora. Typesetting of texts for publication is nowadays no longer done mechanically but electronically. As a result, the body of electronically stored text that can easily be made available is constantly growing. At the same time, 'conventionally' produced, older publications are converted into electronically readable texts. The question is whether some of the resulting text databases can be considered as single-register 'corpora' or not.

Kennedy (1998, 4) defines a text database or archive as "a text repository, often huge and opportunistically collected, and normally not structured". (For an overview of text archives, see Kennedy 1998, 57–60.) In the following, three different types of archive will be considered, namely newspaper collections, fiction databases and electronic dictionaries. The use of another huge electronic source of textual data as a corpus – namely the internet – is discussed in articles 9 and 18. A very large but mixed archive – the electronic texts available at the Institut für deutsche Sprache (IdS) – will serve as a case study for the discussion of what the difference between text archives and dynamic corpora might be.

4.1. Newspaper collections

Before large corpora like the BNC became available, newspapers on CD-ROM were used by various linguists as a source of data for corpus-based analyses that require huge amounts of data. The question is whether one year's worth of *The Guardian* or *The Times* can be considered a single-register corpus or not. As pointed out in sections 2.1. and 3, texts from newspapers are not homogeneous and have either been divided into various sub-sections (for example in the Brown-type corpora) or included in different notional text categories of a corpus (for example in the BNC). In addition, a whole year of any one particular newspaper is not a sample but the whole population of possible texts from that newspaper and particular year. In that way, *The Guardian* from 2005, for instance, is fully representative of the language used in *The Guardian* in 2005, but it is obviously not representative of BrE journalistic prose of that year. In other words, there is a clear and obvious bias in these kinds of 'corpora'. Findings based on a single newspaper may have been influenced by the particular house-style of the paper (see section 5 for an example). One possible strategy of dealing with this problem would be to consider information from the house-internal style-guides of a newspaper. Very often, however, this kind of information is not made available by the publishers. Another possible bias that has to be considered in the use of newspaper editions on CD-ROM concerns the social stratification of different newspapers – language use in British up-market, mid-market and tabloid newspapers is quite different and, as a result, evidence from a single newspaper is not representative of the range of newspaper writing produced in BrE. Whenever comparisons across different national varieties of a language are attempted it is therefore essential to compare newspapers of the same stylistic background. Another problem in the study of national varieties of a language, for instance, is the fact that newspapers include both locally produced texts and material from press agencies or guest writers. In a carefully constructed corpus, texts with an obvious international bias or 'foreign' material can be excluded from the sampling process. In the use of newspaper collections on CD-ROM, the linguist has little if any control over the inclusion of material from international press agencies. These issues have to be considered in the careful analysis of individual examples and the cautious interpretation of the overall findings from such obviously biased sources of information.

A more practical problem in the use of newspapers on CD-ROM concerns the size of these databases. For standard reference corpora, the size of the sample – i.e. the number of running words – is known for the corpus as a whole and for individual samples in the corpus (see, for example, Table 10.1). For text databases like newspaper collections, this is not the case. There is usually no information on the number of words or sentences included in the database as they are not specifically produced for the purpose of linguistic investigation.

The solution to this problem is to either define the linguistic variable or to sample the evidence in a way that allows comparison with findings from other sources. The frequency of a variant can be measured against the frequency of another variant of the same variable, for instance; alternatively, evidence can be sampled until a previously defined number of hits (for example 100 instances) have been reached (see section 5 for examples).

Single-register corpora (in the more narrow, corpus-linguistic sense of the word) can be compiled from the online versions of newspapers. For an example of such an approach to principled corpus building, see Mazaud (2004).

4.2. Fiction databases

Fictional texts – including some contemporary authors – are available from several electronic text archives, such as the Oxford Text Archive (OTA), Project Gutenberg or the electronic text center at the university of Virginia, US. Sometimes, individual texts can be searched on-line (for example the searches at OTA for individual texts even produce keyword-in-context concordances). For literary scholars, this approach might be useful. For a linguistic investigation that aims at collecting evidence from a large number of different texts, such a piecemeal procedure hardly seems practical. At the Project Gutenberg and the electronic text center, full text searches are possible across a larger selection of texts, and the available search tools even allow for a definition of the range of works or contexts (like fictional vs. non-fictional or, in the case of the electronic text center, a search in speeches from drama texts). The usefulness of fiction text archives for the description of current usage is rather limited, however. Because recent fictional publications tend to be subject to copyright, text archives like OTA or the Project Gutenberg are a more valuable source of texts for historical studies. Commercially available full-text databases of fictional texts are published by Chadwyck-Healey, but like the texts available from the public domain, they tend to be more valuable for historical research (cf article 14 and Hoffmann (2005) for an example of a custom-built 'corpus' sampled from Project Gutenberg material). Full-text databases of fictional writing can also be used as a basis for principled corpus compilation, resulting in specialised rather than general reference corpora. It is thus the research question that defines the usefulness of such specialised 'corpora' which are likely to have a certain idiolectal bias if various works by the same author are included. One possible application might be the construction of a corpus that allows linguists or literary critics to study the usage of a particular group of authors as a 'community of practice'.

4.3. Electronic dictionaries

Machine-readable dictionaries can be a source of data if they are corpus-based themselves and make use of attested examples from corpora to illustrate word meanings or grammatical patterns. The major difference between a text corpus in the traditional sense and a dictionary as an archive is the fact that text corpora are samples of whole texts or larger excerpts from texts, whereas the examples in an electronic dictionary are a sample of unconnected sentences. One of the problems in the use of dictionaries as corpora is connected with the sampling unit of the sentence. Unlike text corpora, hits in key-word-in-context concordances from electronic dictionaries provide only very limited context information. As a result, phenomena that run across sentence boundaries (anaphoric use of pronouns and connected issues of pronominal concord, for instance) cannot be studied in a meaningful way in a dictionary database. Another problem is the fact that the source of the examples might have been a well-defined corpus or a collection of texts with a bias towards a certain text type, period or variety of English (on the use of the *Oxford English Dictionary* as a corpus, cf. article 14 or Hoffmann 2004).

4.4. Archive or dynamic corpus?

Standard, well-defined general language corpora of German are not available. Instead, archives have so far been the main source of data for German corpus linguists. One example would be the text corpora available at the IdS, Mannheim. The material in this archive is extremely varied. It includes, for instance, not only written and spoken 'texts', several years of various newspapers (representing all national varieties of German), complete literary texts, but also machine-readable lexicographic databases (for example the Korpus Kartei der Gesellschaft für deutsche Sprache). Furthermore, some of the sub-corpora were compiled for specific research projects, like the grammar corpus (gr1) which comprises 8 fictional texts, some from the 1970s, some from 1990, or the topical Wendekorpus (wk) which contains texts produced between 1989 and 1990 and, in addition to East and West German newspapers, sampled political leaflets and fliers as well as speeches. Moreover, the text corpora at the IdS include material of modern German as well as historical texts. Finally, the archive of the IdS is continually growing, much like the monitor corpora used for lexicographic research (for example the Bank of English or the Kerncorpus used for *Das Digitale Wörterbuch der deutschen Sprache des 20. Jahrhunderts*). In other words, this huge archive does not constitute 'a' corpus in itself, but it can be used to define virtual corpora for specific research projects. Regional variation in standard national varieties of German could, for instance, be studied on the basis of the newspaper material from the 1990s. Such an approach would have to consider the possible skewing effects from a single-register corpus.

The advantage that this archive has over other archives or text-databases is the fact that all texts can be accessed through the same concordancing software (COSMAS) which has been specifically designed for the needs of linguistic research. One of the disadvantages of the more dynamic approach of corpus building lies in the fact that the overall collection of corpora or text-databases at the IdS is not intended as a representative sample of German (unlike, for instance, the CORIS, which is a general reference corpus for Italian that can be used for dynamic corpus building). The written material of the IdS is biased towards certain text types (newspaper language and fiction, for instance), whereas the categories general prose or academic writing are underrepresented. It is also not possible to select individual text types (for example transcripts of parliamentary speeches) included in some of the sub-corpora. In other words, it is virtually impossible for an outside user to construct a balanced general-language reference corpus from the material available at the IdS that would be comparable to the first generation corpora of the Brown-type. It is therefore not surprising that one of the recent projects of the IdS has been to compile a reference corpus for German (Deutsches Referenzkorpus or DEREKO) which (because of copyright restrictions) has not been made publicly available (see http://www.sfs.nphil.uni-tuebingen.de/dereko/).

5. Application

The focus in this section will not be on the many different quantitative and qualitative analyses of existing text corpora in the narrow sense. (The reader is referred, to the ICAME bibliography (http://korpus.hit.uib.no/icame/bib/) that documents the rich research tradition in this area of corpus linguistics and the articles in section V of this handbook.) Instead, a methodological problem will be addressed, i. e. that of combining text corpora with other, less principled sources of data.

Standard general reference corpora of English described in section 2 have many advantages, but one problem frequently encountered in the study of infrequent constructions is that they simply do not yield conclusive evidence. In these cases, the trends indicated in the data from more principled, closed collections of text can be tested against evidence from text databases or archives. This section will illustrate how prototypical text corpora can be combined with less principled collections of text in corpus-based research. One type of text database will be used, namely newspapers on CD-ROM. In the discussion of the results one important question to be addressed is whether single-register corpora allow us to draw conclusions about the larger language population. In other words, how likely is it that results obtained from a single newspaper only are likely to reflect more general tendencies found, for instance, in written English?

5.1. Complementation of *different*

In English, the comparative adjective can be followed by three prepositions, *from, to* and *than*. Historically, *different to* is the oldest variant, *different from* and *different than* are more recent. Nevertheless, prescriptivists have always favoured *different from* as the 'logical' choice, since *from* is also the preposition that collocates with the verb. *Different than* is said to be the variant preferred in American English (AmE), where it can even be used to introduce a noun phrase rather than a clause (e. g. *My parents are very different than yours.*) The variant with *to* is said to be used in colloquial British English (BrE). The comparative adjective *different* occurs rather frequently in the Brown-type corpora, but only a small number of these occurrences give evidence of the co-occurrence patterns with prepositions.

Tab. 10.4: Prepositions after *different* (based on Hundt 2001)

	Brown (1961)	Frown (1992)	LOB (1961)	FLOB (1980s)	WCNZE (1980s)
total number of occurrences	281	388	367	449	367
different from	39	44	34	52	47
different to	0	0	7	9	8
different than	6	5	1	0	2

The figures in Table 10.4 provide preliminary confirmation of the intuitions about regional differences in the use of prepositions after *different*: *from* is the preferred option in all varieties, *than* is more frequently found in AmE, whereas *to* is attested in BrE and New Zealand English (NZE). Additional data from newspaper databases were collected to verify these trends. For BrE and AmE, 100 instances of the variable were collected from the *Guardian* (1991) and *Miami Herald* (1992) on CD-ROM, respectively. For NZE, all instances of *different* followed by a preposition were collected from the database of

Tab. 10.5: Prepositions after *different* in three newspaper databases (from Hundt 1998)

	Miami Herald	*Guardian*	*Dominion/ Evening Post*
from	65	89	109 (67 %)
to	0	8	48 (30 %)
than	35	3	5 (3 %)
Total	100	100	162 (100 %)

the *Dominion/Evening Post*, two Wellington-based newspapers, in February 1995. The results are summarized in Table 10.5.

Even though the additional data were sampled from text databases rather than corpora in the narrow sense, they confirm that *different from* is the preferred variant in all three varieties. *Different than* is avoided in both BrE and NZE; if it is used, it usually precedes a clause, a context in which *different from* is considered a clumsy alternative. In a few cases (quotations of direct speech) *different than* is used before a simple noun phrase in BrE and NZE. In AmE, however, *different than* is a well-established variant which is not only used before a clause but also fairly often before a simple noun phrase (19 occurrences). *Different to* is not attested in the American newspaper. Evidence from spoken corpora (see Mair, 2007) indicates that *different to* is also used (infrequently) in AmE. In the British newspaper material, it is an occasional variant, whereas the New Zealand data indicate a greater acceptability of this variant in NZE.

5.2. Collective nouns

In English, collective nouns like *crew, government* or *team* can be used with either singular or plural concord. Mixed concord is also possible, for example if a collective noun is followed by a singular verb and a plural pronoun, as in *The committee has not yet decided how they should react to the proposal.* As in the previous case, individual collective nouns as such occur fairly frequently in standard one-million-word corpora, but the syntactic variable (singular vs. plural concord) is infrequent. In the vast majority of cases, concord is not a relevant category. There are various reasons for this. Nouns often occur in the modifier position of a noun phrase (e. g. *government officials* or *family estate*) or they may be the head of a noun phrase that does not function as the subject of the clause and therefore the verb does not have to agree with the collective noun. Finally, collective nouns with subject function are sometimes followed by a verb phrase that is neutral with respect to number marking, i. e. it is a past tense, modal or non-finite verb phrase. For the nouns *government* and *family*, for instance, a search in the Brown corpus produces a total of 435 and 343 occurrences, respectively, but fewer than 100 instances illustrate the variable concord pattern: for *government*, the dominant pattern is singular concord at 52 : 1 instances; for *family*, plural concord is more frequent at 3 : 26 occurrences, all of them of the pronominal type. Nouns like *committee* and *team* have a lower overall frequency, but they may not necessarily yield proportionately fewer instances of the syntactic variable: *committee* occurs only 170 times in the Brown corpus, but 26 concordance entries show variable concord (again predominately of the singular type at 24:2); out of the 88 instances of the noun *team*, 13 are examples of the syntactic variable (with only one instance illustrating plural concord). At best, these figures indicate trends in the data, i.e. that nouns like *government* heavily tend towards singular concord and that a noun like *family* is slightly more likely to allow for plural concord, particularly of the pronominal type. Other nouns – like *police* and *couple* – have a propensity for plural concord: for *police*, all 29 instances of the syntactic variable in the Brown corpus are examples of plural concord; for *couple*, plural concord in the Brown corpus outnumbers singular concord at 8: 6. For less frequent nouns like *clergy*, standard text corpora are too small to even indicate trends (of the twelve occurrences of the noun, two were examples of the syntactic variable, exclusively of the verbal plural type). But even for relatively frequent nouns, a more fine-grained analysis that takes into account syntactic, semantic and lexical factors which may influence the choice of singular or plural (verbal and pronominal) concord requires a much larger amount of data. Hundt (1998, 80–89) and Levin (2001) are studies that – for the analysis of concord patterns in written texts – make use exclusively of newspapers on CD-ROM. Hundt analyses the *Miami Herald* (1992) for AmE and the *Guardian* (1991) for BrE; Levin uses the *New York Times* (1995) for AmE and the *Independent* (1995) for BrE.

Tables 10.6 and 10.7 show that the results from different newspapers for verbal concord are very similar, more so for AmE than for BrE. This indicates that newspapers on CD-ROM are fairly reliable sources of information and can be used as single-register corpora – provided they are newspapers of the same type. At least for up-market newspapers, the results from newspapers on CD-ROM produce evidence of a slight regional difference between AmE and BrE: singular verbal concord is more firmly established in the American than in the British variety.

Tab. 10.6: Singular vs. plural concord (percentages) with collective nouns in AmE

	Verbal concord		Pronominal concord	
	Hundt (1998)	Levin (2001)	Hundt (1998)	Levin (2001)
government	100:0	100:0	95:5	90:10
committee	100:0	100:0	91:9	90:10
team	98:2	99:1	65:35	67:33
family	97:3	96:4	18:82	27:73

Tab. 10.7: Singular vs. plural concord (percentages) with collective nouns in BrE

	Verbal concord		Pronominal concord	
	Hundt (1998)	Levin (2001)	Hundt (1998)	Levin (2001)
government	100:0	95:5	96:4	86:14
committee	97:3	91:9	92:8	72:28
team	62:38	63:37	23:77	19:81
family	72:28	63:37	26:74	11:89

The results for pronominal concord are slightly more divergent (especially for BrE). This has to do with the fact that pronominal concord – due to the larger distance between the antecedent and the pronoun – allows for more variation. Even in AmE newspapers, which show exclusive or almost exclusive singular concord with *government*, *committee*, *team* and *family*, pronominal concord has a higher probability of yielding plural marking. In both AmE and BrE, *team* and *family* yield higher percentages of plural pronominal concord marking than *government* and *committee*. These results are in accordance with the general trends obtained from large, balanced (but publicly unavailable) corpora, as published in Biber et al. (1999, 188).

That house-styles may have an impact on the results can be illustrated with data on concord patterns with the noun *government*. Siemund (1995, 368f.) compares the results from a manually compiled corpus based on editorials of *The Times*, only (Bauer 1994) with data from the press section of the LOB corpus. Usage patterns found in Bauer's *Times* corpus turn out to be conservative (i. e. in the use of plural concord with the British government) when compared with the more balanced LOB sample (see Table 10.8).

Tab. 10.8: Concord with *government* in *The Times* corpus and LOBpress (Siemund 1995, 369)

	British government		Non-British government	
	Singular	Plural	Singular	Plural
The Times (1960)	0	23	8	0
LOBpress (1961)	61	3	27	2

Note, however, that Bauer's corpus was restricted not only to one particular paper but also to a specific section of that paper (editorials). If a wider range of sections from a newspaper is analyzed, the effect of house-styles might be less pronounced. Sports reportage, for instance, tends to be less conservative than business reports (on the effect of register internal variation, see for instance Mazaud 2004). Furthermore, skewing effects might be exaggerated if only one particular lexical item is studied.

6. Summary

The focus in the discussion of text corpora has been on two major clines: one ranging from written or conceptually literal texts to spoken or conceptually oral texts, the other ranging from carefully compiled, finite-size reference corpora on the one hand to text archives on the other hand. The two most important methodological caveats for the corpus linguist that emerge from this article are that firstly, whether a collection of texts can be defined as a corpus probably often depends on the research question that is being pursued, and that secondly, evidence from corpora in the more narrow sense can be combined with less rigidly defined sources of data if the findings are interpreted with the necessary discretion.

7. Literature

Bauer, Laurie (1994), *Watching English Change. An Introduction to the Study of Linguistic Change in Standard Englishes in the Twentieth Century*. London: Longman.

Biber, Douglas (1988), *Variation across Speech and Writing*. Cambridge: Cambridge University Press.

Biber, Douglas/Conrad, Susan/Reppen, Randi (1998), *Corpus Linguistics. Investigating Language Structure and Use*. Cambridge: Cambridge University Press.

Biber, Douglas/Johansson, Stig/Leech, Geoffrey/Conrad, Susan/Finegan, Edward (1999), *Longman Grammar of Spoken and Written English*. Harlow: Pearson Education.

Brinker, Klaus/Antos, Gerd/Heinemann, Wolfgang/Sager, Sven F. (eds.) (2000), *Text- und Gesprächslinguistik*. (HSK Vol. 16.1.) Berlin: de Gruyter.

Chafe, Wallace (1982), Integration and Involvement in Speaking, Writing, and Oral Literature. In: Tannen 1982, 35–53.

Fowler, Roger (1991), *Language in the News: Discourse and Ideology in the Press*. London/New York: Routledge.

Häcki Buhofer, Annelie (2000), Mediale Voraussetzungen: Bedingungen von Schriftlichkeit allgemein. In: Brinker et al. 2000, 251–61.

Hoffmann, Sebastian (2004), Using the OED Quotations Database as a Corpus – A Linguistic Appraisal. In: *ICAME Journal* 28, 17–30.

Hoffmann, Sebastian (2005), *Grammaticalization and English Complex Prepositions: A Corpus-based Study*. London: Routledge.

Hofland, Knut/Johansson, Stig (1989), *Frequency Analysis of English Vocabulary and Grammar: Based on the LOB corpus*. Oxford: Clarendon.

Hundt, Marianne (1998), *New Zealand English Grammar. Fact or Fiction?* Amsterdam/Philadelphia: John Benjamins.

Hundt, Marianne (2001), Grammatical Variation in National Varieties of English – The Corpus-based Approach. In: *Revue Belge de Philologie et d'Histoire* 79, 737–756.

Hundt, Marianne/Nesselhauf, Nadja/Biewer, Carolin (eds.) (2007), *The Web as Corpus*. Amsterdam: Rodopi.

Kang, Beom-mo/Kim, Hung-gyu/Huh, Myung-hoe (2003), Variation Across Korean Text Registers. In: Wilson/Rayson/McEnery 2003, 51–57.

Kennedy, Graeme (1998), *An Introduction to Corpus Linguistics*. London: Longman.

Koch, Peter/Österreicher, Wulf (1985), Sprache der Nähe – Sprache der Distanz: Mündlichkeit und Schriftlichkeit im Spannungsfeld von Sprachtheorie und Sprachgeschichte. In: *Romanistisches Jahrbuch* 36, 15–43.

Levin, Magnus (2001), *Agreement with Collective Nouns in English*. (Lund Studies in English 103.) Lund: Lund University Press.

Mair, Christian (2007), Ongoing Change and Variation in English: Integrating the Analysis of Closed Corpora and Web-based Monitoring. In: Hundt, Marianne/Nesselhauf, Nadja/Biewer, Carolin, 233–247.

Mazaud, Carolin (2004), Complex Premodifiers in Present-day English: A Corpus-based Study. PhD dissertation, University of Heidelberg.

McEnery, Tony/Wilson, Andrew (1996), *Corpus Linguistics*. Edinburgh: Edinburgh University Press.

Mollin, Sandra (forthcoming), The Hansard Hazard. Gauging the Accuracy of British Parliamentary Transcripts. To appear in *Corpora* 2: 2.

Rossini Favretti, Rema/Tamburini, Fabio/De Santis, Cristiana (2003), A Corpus of Written Italian: A Defined and A Dynamic Model. In: Wilson/Rayson/McEnery 2003, 27–38.

Siemund, Rainer (1995), 'For Who the Bell Tolls' – Or Why Corpus Linguistics Should Carry the Bell in the Study of Language Change in Present-day English. In: *Arbeiten aus Anglistik und Amerikanistik* 20(2), 351–377.

Slembrouck, Stef (1992), The Parliamentary Hansard 'Verbatim' Report: The Written Construction of Spoken Discourse. In: *Language and Literature* 1(2), 101–119.
Tannen, Deborah (ed.) (1982), *Spoken and Written Language: Exploring Orality and Literacy.* Norwood, NJ: Ablex Publishing.
Wilson, Andrew/Rayson, Paul/McEnery, Tony (eds.) (2003), *A Rainbow of Corpora: Corpus Linguistics and the Languages of the World.* Munich: Lincom.

Marianne Hundt, Zurich (Switzerland)

11. Speech corpora and spoken corpora

1. Spoken language and speech corpora

The heading of this article may appear to imply that 'speech' and 'spoken language' are in some ways different phenomena. This is of course not the case. There are indeed many different dimensions to spoken language. Dimensions such as varieties of style, register, accent and dialect, for example, are justifiably the focus of much research. However, the distinction being made here is not a linguistic one: it is a distinction that relates more closely to the practicalities of research aims and methods than to the phenomenon that is being investigated. It relates in particular to the broad division between those researchers who focus on technological applications of speech research and those whose focus is the study of human language and communication for its own sake. As with all categorisation, these boundaries are less clear-cut than the binary distinction suggests, but the fact remains that not all corpora can serve the needs of different users. This article focuses on the use of spoken corpora to investigate the sounds of spoken texts. In particular, it is concerned with the use of corpora for prosodic analysis as opposed to lexical, syntactic or pragmatic analysis.

1.1. Speech databases

Speech databases or corpora are typically compiled for specific purposes, generally with a view to developing consumer applications. The compilers and users tend to be speech technologists rather than linguists. Applications include automatic speech recognition (ASR), speech synthesis and, more recently, automatic dialogue systems that involve both of the latter. This clearly has an influence on the kind of data required. Automatic speech recognition systems are most successful when the language content is highly constrained, the environment free from extraneous noise, and when the system has been trained on an individual speaker. There are many situations, however, in which these conditions cannot be met. Most recognition systems have to operate in the real world outside the sound-proofed laboratory, and the real world is often noisy. They also have to deal with real people, whose speaking habits display wide variation. On the other hand, most ASR systems are designed for a particular situation (e. g. service encounters) where the range of language used is naturally constrained. Corpora intended for research towards specific ASR applications are therefore typically compilations of speech from the same narrow domain, whether relating to train enquiries, baggage handling or air traffic control. It is also essential to collect unscripted speech, however difficult to handle, since systems trained on fluent, scripted speech will by definition have trouble processing natural unscripted speech, however constrained, with its repetitions, discontinuities and disfluencies.

Speech synthesis operates on different principles; so far, there appears to be no desire on the part of commercial developers to generate speech that contains the disfluencies and prosodic mannerisms typical of human speech (House/Youd 1991). Research into speech synthesis therefore requires a different model on which to build. Corpora designed for work in speech synthesis typically contain scripted or prepared data, recorded in a controlled environment without extraneous noise. Some may be naturally-occurring, such as collections of broadcast texts, but others may consist of material elicited expressly for the corpus. In many applications, the synthesiser generates the equivalent of monologue, but in some mixed environments, e. g. human-machine dialogue systems, the synthesised speech has to take interactional features into consideration, including indication of speech act (querying, confirming) and turn-taking signals.

From all of the above it will be clear that speech corpora are compiled for applications concerning the sounds of speech, both segmental and prosodic. The availability of sound files is therefore of prime importance and the research for which they are used is frequently focused on the speech signal itself. This contrasts starkly with many spoken language corpora, both in the way they are compiled, the availability of the sound files, and the kind of research for which they are intended.

1.2. Spoken language corpora

Spoken language corpora are generally compiled to serve the interests of linguists whose main aim is not a particular commercial application but to understand the nature of human language and communication. The focus is for the most part on spontaneous, or at least unscripted, speech, in other words the kind of speech that is created by the speaker in real time and that represents both process and product simultaneously. In contrast to scripted speech, which of course reflects the structures of the written text, spontaneous speech is not only differently structured (see Biber et al. 1999) but normally contains disfluencies that provide evidence of the speaker's cognitive processing and are also assumed to benefit the hearer.

There are, of course, many different motivations among linguists for studying spoken data, including interest in lexical, syntactic and stylistic variation, and also, more recently, an interest in cognitive processes (cf. Schönefeld 1999, cited in Mukherjee 2004). This has an influence on corpus design. Since such corpora are intended to be useful to a wide variety of linguistic interests, attempts are usually made to include representative samples of different speech genres – e. g. scripted vs. unscripted, prepared vs. unprepared (cf. Wichmann 2000) – so that linguistic phenomena may also be related to extra-linguistic variables. The primary data of such corpora, the sound recordings themselves, are not always widely available, often for ethical reasons, and the orthographic transcription of the original recordings is often treated as data in its own right and analysed in the same way as one would analyse a corpus of writing, dealing, for example, with orthographic representations of filled pauses as lexical items. In this way, it is possible to study the lexical and grammatical features of spoken language, but not the sound patterns. What corpus data is able to reveal about a language, or language in general, depends on one's view of language. Performance data is of no interest to generative linguists, and only of limited interest to some functional linguists, whose notion of 'context' tends to be far wider than that provided by a single corpus. Adherents of a usage-based model approach to grammar (e. g. Bybee 2001), by contrast, believe that a language system emerges from the interaction between human cognitive capacity and language use, the basic premise being that frequency of use affects the cognitive representation of forms in the brain. Reliable frequency information such as corpora can provide is therefore valuable not only at a purely descriptive level, but is also a potential source of information about the nature of language itself.

It is often harder to use such corpora as a basis for speech research. The quality of the sound files varies considerably, and is closely linked to specific genres. Files of broadcast speech are generally of high quality, but recordings of informal conversations are often noisy, for the obvious reason that such informal conversations rarely take place in soundproofed recording studios. They are more likely to occur in homes or public places with inevitable background noise. There are therefore certain trading relations in the study of speech – clean recordings that lend themselves to instrumental analysis can be made in dedicated environments but cannot be representative of how people speak in their natural habitat. Natural habitats, on the other hand, tend to be noisy and the resulting sound files are therefore often not suitable for instrumental analysis, but on the other hand the speech that has been recorded is probably much more representative of the category 'informal conversation'.

1.3. Techniques for collecting/eliciting data

Where there is a need for highly constrained but unscripted speech, particular elicitation methods have to be devised. Many of these are drawn from the games used in the teaching of foreign languages, emerging from the need to encourage learners to talk but within the constraints of their vocabulary and grammatical knowledge. They are usually dialogue exercises that present partners with problems to solve. The participants may be given two similar but not identical pictures, with the task of establishing the differences without being able to see the partner's version. It may involve drawing a route on a map, as in the Map Task Corpus (Anderson et al. 1991) (cf. 2.1.1.), or it may consist of recreating a design or arrangement of figures described by the partner. Swerts/Collier

(1992), for example, elicit spontaneous speech by using an arrangement of geometrical shapes (e. g. *the blue square is above the red triangle and to the left of the green circle*) which one participant describes so that the other can re-create the same pattern. In these exercises the speech is spontaneous, i. e. unscripted, but very limited both in terms of vocabulary and discourse structure. In terms of speech acts, for example, they may simply consist of a list of instructions and responses. The limitations of Map Task data in terms of speech act identification has been observed by Shobbrook/House (2003), who noted that even such basic acts as questions and statements were difficult to distinguish. Nonetheless, they provide a situation in which many variables can be controlled, including choice of speakers (their age, gender, native language, language variety, etc.) and lexis.

A different approach to eliciting data within specific constraints, in this case the domain of 'meetings', is exemplified by the ICSI (International Computer Science Institute) Meetings Corpus, a collection of 75 meetings of a research team (Berkeley, California) of approximately 1 hour each. The participants also read digit strings, providing a supplement to the natural conversational data. Although the meetings were in English, a number of the speakers were not native speakers of the language. In fact, the degrees of fluency were reported to vary considerably from 'nearly native' to 'challenging-to-transcribe'. Here then we have an example of a corpus in which the nature of the interaction is controlled, but the speaker variables, including language variety, are not.

As with any non-surreptitious data, collections of naturally-occurring speech are, of course, subject to the observer's paradox. This arose with the collection of the speech of London teenagers (COLT corpus, see section 2.2.2.), who explicitly assumed that the researchers were particularly interested in obscenities, and obligingly provided them.

2. Content and design of corpora

Given the wide range of interests represented in corpus collection, it is obvious that the structure and compilation methods will also vary. Differences include the genres that are represented, the degree of constraint on the content or structure of the data, and whether the speech occurs naturally or is elicited for the purpose of data collection. In the following section I will discuss some of these dimensions, which inevitably intersect at a number of points.

2.1. Genre

2.1.1. Dialogue

Both speech scientists and linguists have an interest in dialogue, albeit for different reasons. What constitutes a 'dialogue', however, can be interpreted in many different ways. The canonical form of dialogue for many linguists is spontaneous, unscripted conversation. This is the kind of conversation whose main function is phatic – oiling the social wheels – and the aim of the participants is generally to sustain the conversation: silences are uncomfortable, and efforts are made to introduce new topics when old ones have run their course. The function of a service encounter, on the other hand, is to achieve a practical outcome, and the aim of the participants is to bring the encounter successfully to an end rather than to sustain it. In other kinds of dialogue, such as broadcast interviews, the participant roles are asymmetrical, most of the talk being expected from the interviewee. Such dialogues contain much longer turns, and could be better characterised as prompted monologues. In this situation the talk is also intended to benefit not only the participants but also a wider audience, and the presence of multiple addressees has an inevitable effect on what is said and how it is said.

The Air Traffic Control Corpus consists of approximately 70 hours of voice communication between controllers and pilots in the vicinity of three American airports. The dialogue in this corpus is strictly functional, but unlike service dialogues, the 'successful' outcome, the safe landing and taking off of aeroplanes, is a matter of life and death. The data is entirely naturally-occurring; in other words it was not produced for the sake of compiling a corpus but would have occurred, and indeed been recorded, whether or not it was to be used for corpus research. It is however very highly constrained data, with a limited vocabulary and regulated alternation of speaker turns, leaving no opportunity for speech overlap. It is also unusual in that such tightly constrained dialogue also occurs against the background of extreme noise. In fact this corpus was designed specifically for research into speech recognition in conditions such as those found in this context: a range of speakers, noisy channels, a relatively small vocabulary and constrained language.

The TRAINS corpus (http://www.cs.rochester.edu/research/cisd/projects/trains/), another corpus of dialogue, is also highly constrained and task-oriented. On the other hand it is not naturally-occurring but elicited through role-play, and recorded in a soundproofed environment in order to eliminate noise. Compiled in Rochester 1993, it contains 98 dialogues with 34 speakers. The dialogues were collected with human-machine dialogue in mind, and the participant roles were 'user' and 'system' respectively. In each conversation one participant, the 'user', was given a task to complete and the other played the role of the system 'by acting as planning consultant'. The tasks included transporting oranges to orange juice factories, and making and transporting orange juice. The speakers performed under time constraints and were not allowed to see each other. This is the kind of task-oriented dialogue that is of particular interest to those working on human-machine interaction. It is useful to exclude the overlaps that occur in normal conversation, since these are difficult to deal with in ASR, and can be avoided in human-machine systems by controlling the turn taking. The lack of face-to-face contact excludes the possibility that gestures are used instead of speech in the interaction, so that all meaning has to be communicated in speech. This situation was naturally inherent in the case of air traffic control interaction, but has been artificially introduced in the compilation of the TRAINS corpus.

A similar approach to eliciting unscripted but constrained dialogue was adopted by the compilers of the Map Task Corpus. The team recorded 128 dialogues with 64 speakers. Half of the participants were allowed to see each other, the other not. Each participant was given a map, but only one of the maps had a route drawn on it. One person had to describe the route in order for the other to replicate it on his or her map. The maps were not identical, although the speakers did not know this at the outset, and this of course generated phases of negotiation and questioning in the dialogue. Nonetheless, these dialogues are asymmetrical and provide only limited material for the study of dialogue. Much of the dialogue is one-sided – a series of instructions punctuated by backchannel responses. However, it provides a wealth of phonetic material around a controlled set of items (the landmarks on the map, such as *tree, house, windmill,* etc.) which are repeated many times.

A corpus of speech that is naturally occurring but nonetheless constrained by topic and participants, is the American English Meetings Corpus, described in 1.3. above. Even the canonical dialogue – casual, informal conversation – can be constrained in a number of ways. Two large corpora of American English, the CALLHOME corpus and the Switchboard corpus, consist of telephone conversations between family members and strangers respectively. The Switchboard corpus contains 3 million words of telephone conversations between people who were paid to participate, and who had no control over their choice of interlocutor. The telephone situation provides for relatively controlled recording quality.

Conversation does not, of course, always only involve two interlocutors and can therefore not necessarily be classed as dialogue, as for example with the multi-party conversations included in the ICE-GB (cf. 2.2.1.). Many of those take place in homes, often when participants are eating a meal, and the sound of plates and cutlery provides a background to the talk. This means that the sound files cannot be systematically investigated instrumentally, since a computer cannot distinguish between human speech and the sound of cutlery. On the other hand, this kind of conversation comes closest to what we think of as 'normal' unconstrained conversation.

2.1.2. Monologue

Like 'dialogue' the notion of monologue covers a wide variety of speech types that include reading aloud, unscripted but prepared speeches and story-telling. Speech corpora may contain monologue for a variety of reasons, depending on the intended use. The Spoken English Corpus (SEC) (Knowles et al. 1996), for example, was designed to provide a model for the prosody component of speech synthesis. This is a small corpus of approximately 50,000 words of British English speech, and was compiled in collaboration between Lancaster University and IBM UK. The focus is on high quality, noise-free recordings, much of it radio broadcast or recorded in a studio environment. The corpus consists largely of prepared or scripted monologue: prepared monologue is closest in structure to written language, and it provides a good model for automatic speech synthesis (text-to-speech), since most applications are designed to convert written text into speech. For those concerned with the segmental aspects of generating synthetic speech, a far more highly controlled set of data is necessary. Some corpora consist, therefore, of read aloud digits, phrases and sentences out of context, designed carefully for their phonetic content (e. g. TIMIT – http://www.ldc.upenn.edu/Catalog/readme_files/timit.readme.html; SCRIBE – http://www.phon.ucl.ac.uk/resource/scribe/). These compilations are generally referred to as speech databases rather than corpora, and provide a basis for micro-level applications (diphone, phoneme by rule) in speech synthesis.

2.2. Variation in language (geographical, individual, contextual)

Corpora are sometimes compiled to represent a particular variety of speech: this can be a relatively permanent accent typical of a particular geographical region or a particular social class. Less permanent variation can be related to age: the majority of corpora contain the speech of educated adults, but some attempts have been made to record younger speakers. There are also more transient effects on the voice, such as health, emotion and stress.

2.2.1. Other Englishes, other languages

Regional variation

A corpus that was collected in order to compare regional varieties of British English is the IViE corpus (Intonation Variation in English) (Grabe et al. 2001). This used the elicitation method devised by the Map Task Corpus, together with others such as reading aloud and free conversation, but using young participants from different regions of Britain. The purpose of the corpus was explicitly to examine the speech patterns, specifically the intonation, of different varieties of British English, including that of ethnic minorities. The accents represented are London Caribbean, Cambridge, Leeds, Bradford Punjabi, Newcastle, Belfast and Dublin; they thus include a variety close to the standard (Cambridge), the most marked regional accents from the North of England, together with those of speakers of Afro-Caribbean and of Asian origin. By some standards this is a small corpus (36 hours of speech) but still too large for a complete prosodic analysis to be practicable, since this requires skill and is extremely time-consuming. (See section 4.)

Other Englishes

A particularly ambitious project designed to represent different varieties of English is the ICE project. This is the International Corpus of English that has as its aim the collection of comparable corpora of speech and writing from different World Englishes: British, Singapore, New Zealand, Australia, East Africa. The most advanced so far is the collection of British English (mainly southern standard), the ICE-GB (Nelson/Wallis/Aarts 2002). The corpus contains 1 million words of English: the spoken component consists of 600,000 words and the written component 400,000 words. The whole corpus (the written texts and the orthographic transcriptions of the speech section) has been parsed and tagged, and the transcribed speech contains some prosodic information in the form of pause marking. The spoken section contains dialogue and monologue, in both the public and private domain. Dialogues include conversations, phone calls, broadcast discussions and interviews, parliamentary debates, and legal cross-examinations; monologues include unscripted commentaries, speeches and legal presentations, and scripted broadcast news and talks.

Other languages

As pointed out by McCarthy/O'Keeffe (article 47), speech corpora have been dominated in the past by collections of English, but there are now many projects, ongoing and completed, to collect speech data in other languages. The Spoken Dutch Corpus (Oostdijk et al. 2002) and the French corpora pooled in the ELICOP project (Brosens 1998) are examples of spoken corpus development of other European languages. The standardised markup of French corpora that the ELICOP project aims to achieve includes both prosodic (e. g. pauses and syllable lengthening) and segmental (liaison, elision, gemination) encoding. An example of spoken corpus development of a non-European language is the Corpus of Spoken Hebrew (Izre'el/Hary/Rahav 2001). This employs, at least in its preliminary stage, the transcription conventions that were developed by Du Bois et al. (1993) and used in the Corpus of Spoken American English (CSAE – see also section 4.1.). Since standard Hebrew orthography is from right to left, annotation software has to be designed accordingly.

Finally, spoken corpora, and the development of tools for managing spoken resources, play a significant part in the efforts to document and study endangered languages as in the DoBeS project (Dokumentation bedrohter Sprachen) which is documenting endangered languages in Africa, North and Middle America, South America, Eurasia, SE Asia and Austronesia (see article 21). Such projects are a driving force behind the development of modern state-of-the-art technology, including archival formats and recording and analysis formats, to ensure long-term preservation and accessibility.

Diachronic change

Given the fact that interest in spoken corpora seems a relatively recent development of corpus linguistics as a whole, it is remarkable that we already have access to a diachronic spoken corpus, by means of which it will be possible to trace changes in speech over a period of 25 to 30 years. The Diachronic Corpus of Present-day Spoken English (DCPSE) is a project recently completed at the Survey of English Usage, at University College London (see http://www.ucl.ac.uk/english-usage/diachronic). The corpus contains directly comparable material, 800,000 words in all, from the London-Lund Corpus (LLC) (Svartvik 1990), collected in the 1970s–1980s, and the British component of the International Corpus of English (ICE-GB) collected in the late 1990s. Both sets of texts have been parsed and tagged, and are linked to the relevant sound recordings. This will serve linguists who are particularly interested in recent change.

2.2.2. Age-related variation

By far the majority of spoken corpora contain the speech of educated adults. One interesting attempt to redress this balance is represented by the COLT corpus, the Corpus of London Teenager Language (a subset of the British National Corpus). Unlike the IViE corpus, which used young adults in order to control for regional accent, the COLT corpus was designed for the study of teenager speech *per se*. Young people's language is particularly innovative, and reveals interesting developments in discourse phenomena, such as the emergence of discourse markers via a process of grammaticalisation. Stenström et al. (2002), for example, suggest that *cos* (because) is developing a new sentence-independent function and becoming grammaticalised, or perhaps, more properly, pragmaticalised. Similar observations on markers such as *like, yeah, what* and *innit* have been made by Andersen (2000, 2001), also based on data from the COLT corpus.

2.2.3. Speaker states: Physiological and emotional variation

Speech is known to vary according to transient features affecting the individual speaker, such as stress (induced by time pressure, importance of task, or fear), sleep deprivation, illness and inebriation. A speaker with a severe cold, or who is out of breath or drunk, will sound different from a healthy speaker. A very simple example of how this is relevant for speech technology is the fact that a voice recognizer, such as may be used instead of a key to give access to a room or building, may have to be robust enough to recognize the identity of the speaker regardless of their current state of health. Acoustic effects of physical context must therefore be to some extent filtered out by the voice recognizer, and research is geared to finding out features of the voice that are not relevant and should be ignored by the system. Less trivial is the need to study the effect of speech in stressful conditions associated with the many military applications of ASR. Verbal instructions issued by the pilot of an aircraft in combat are likely to be different in quality from those issued to an electronic door key, and ASR systems need to be trained accordingly. One such study used the techniques of the Map Task to investigate speech produced under stress. Collected by Canada's Defense and Civil Institute of Environmental Medicine (DCIEM), the corpus contains 216 unscripted dialogues. The speakers were adults in the course of a major sleep deprivation study. The pressure of combat is not only related to sleep deprivation, of course, and can cause the voice to betray a range of emotions generated by such a situation.

There is currently considerable interest in the study of emotional speech, but this has proved challenging to speech researchers. The challenge lies not only in the problem of defining and categorising emotions, but also in the fact that adults are mostly socially constrained not to display strong emotions except in private. It is therefore difficult to find emotionally laden speech to record in ethically acceptable ways. Even attempts at eliciting emotional speech by, for example, asking people to recount sad or happy events, is generally unsuccessful because of the lack of intimacy in such situations. A corpus of emotional speech collected at Queen's University Belfast (Douglas-Cowie et al. 2003) used broadcast television entertainment programmes in which guests voluntarily faced provocative and emotional situations that elicited strong reactions. To some extent these situations are clearly artificially heightened for the benefit of the audience, and the emotional displays cannot necessarily be seen as 'natural'. However, the fact that the material is in the public domain avoids the ethical issues that might otherwise arise. Unlike the structure of many corpora, this corpus contains only selected extracts of the most emotional-sounding speech, so that it is more akin to application-driven speech databases than to spoken corpora. An earlier corpus of emotional speech was collected as part of the Emotion in Speech project (EISP) in Reading (Greasely et al. 1995). This too relied primarily on broadcast speech for data, including documentary programmes, talk shows and sports commentary. In both cases the problems of data collection were matched by the problems of annotation and transcription (see section 3.3.).

3. Status of sound files

3.1. What is the primary data?

Most corpora are annotated at least to the level of an orthographic transcription. The problems involved in creating this transcription itself are considerable, depending on the nature of the speech. Scripted text is relatively straightforward, although, as Oostdijk/Boves point out (article 30), readers frequently depart from their scripts, and the original script, if available, is not reliable as a representation of the spoken version. Spontaneous speech is more difficult to transcribe. Even with ideal recording conditions, there will be natural speech disfluencies to deal with, such as false starts, hesitations and repetitions. There are, of course, many vocalisations that cannot be captured orthographically, but are useful in the interpretation of the data, such as laughter, coughing, sharp intakes of breath, as well as the common phenomenon of filled pauses (*uhm uh*).

Many users of spoken language corpora are content to treat the orthographic transcription of speech as their primary data, and because they are interested in lexical, grammatical and discourse phenomena, such corpora tend to be much more richly annotated than speech databases. The ICE-GB, for example, is tagged and parsed and can be searched on the basis of both the orthographic transcription and the annotation categories. However, phoneticians and speech engineers see this differently: "it is assumed, with modern technological progress, that all users of a spoken language corpus will have ready access to the sound recording, which can therefore be regarded as the basic record of any spoken language data" and hence "orthographic transcription loses its observational primacy" (Gibbon et al. 2000, 1). In the following I will therefore examine the ways in which this 'primary data' can be made available as part of a spoken corpus.

3.2. Accessibility, linking of sound and transcription

Even orthographic transcriptions, particularly of dialogue, rely heavily on suprasegmental and extra-linguistic information. For example, the choice between representing a stretch of speech as a single long utterance or two shorter separate utterances is guided by prosodic information. Prosodic information is often necessary where decisions have to be made about what constitutes a turn at speaking. There are also cases where the prosody does not necessarily affect the orthography, but very much affects the meaning (e. g. *sorry* can mean *please repeat* or *I apologise*). (See section 5.)

For those whose interest lies primarily in the sounds of speech rather than the words, the accessibility of sound files is crucial but has often been impractical, not least because of issues of anonymity. The alternative is to provide users with a detailed written prosodic annotation that captured as much as possible of the prosodic information. An early spoken corpus that paid great attention to prosody, the London-Lund Corpus (Svartvik 1990), provided a very detailed auditory prosodic analysis of the text, one that is heavily used by discourse researchers even today (e. g. Aijmer 1996) but did not make the sound files readily available. (The sound is now available as part of DCPSE, and will also be made available separately.) Many researchers who use the corpus are happy to rely on the skills of the original annotators, but others would like to be able to consult the original files, not only to check the annotation against their own perceptions but also to investigate prosodic features that are not captured by the system used. The annotation does not make the sound files redundant, as Oostdijk/Boves point out in article 30. Indeed this corpus was annotated prosodically at a time when the systematic study of prosody was in its infancy.

The rapid increase in availability of cheap speech analysis software, a useful consumer spin-off from developments in speech technology and signal processing, means that inspection of the phonetic characteristics of the raw data is no longer the prerogative of those working in expensive laboratories, but can now be done by almost anyone with a computer at home. This has radically changed what can be done in prosody research. It presupposes, however, that the speech files are available to the researcher. The Spoken English Corpus, one of the few other publicly available corpora that are prosodically annotated, does have accompanying sound files. The annotation is embedded in the orthographic transcription, and can thus be searched together with the text, and the annotation can be checked against the original speech. However, even though the raw data is available, it is not time-aligned with the transcription and annotation. A later incarnation of this corpus, the Aix-Marsec corpus, has endeavoured to remedy this. Researchers at the speech and language laboratory in Aix-en-Provence (Laboratoire langue et parole, Universite de Provence Aix-Marseille 1), have taken the existing machine readable version (Auran et al. 2004) and aligned the orthographic transcription with the speech signal, in addition to an automatically generated phonemic transcription, and a pitch analysis. The disadvantage of this version is that it can only be searched using specially written scripts, thus making it inaccessible to many corpus-linguists who are more familiar with concordancing software. The corpus is also relatively small by today's standards and is limited in speaking styles to scripted or highly prepared speech.

The much larger British National Corpus contains 10 million words of naturally-occurring speech, including teenager speech (also available separately as the COLT corpus). However, with the exception of the COLT component, for which the sound files are available, the corpus was published without sound files, and subsequent efforts to make these available have floundered on two counts. The first is the promise made to participants that their identities would not be revealed, and the second is the fact that their permission was sought only for publication of the transcriptions and not the recordings themselves. The anonymisation carried out now makes it difficult to return to the original respondents to ask for the additional permission. These issues are described in greater details by Burnard (2002). The fact that the publication of sound files was not envisaged from the start is an illustration of the continued divide between corpus linguists who regard the orthographic transcription of speech as their primary data, and those who are interested in the prosody of naturally-occurring speech.

A development that showed a little more foresight in this respect is the ICE project – the International Corpus of English (see section 2.2.1.). The British English version (ICE-GB) has been created in such a way that sections of the sound files are aligned with sections of the transcription. This has the advantage of allowing repeated playback of small sections of the recorded data to permit auditory prosodic analysis of whatever subset of the data is of interest. The time-consuming nature of prosodic annotation, and the high degree of training required, means that such annotation is left largely to individual researchers, who may then invest the time available in annotating only those aspects of the corpus that are of interest. The visual inspection of the speech signal is of course also possible, but the recordings were designed to provide maximum naturalness of situation and are thus in many cases too noisy for useful instrumental analysis.

Some speech software allows the speech signal to be annotated directly, using a number of tiers for different levels or kinds of annotation. An example of this is 'Praat' (Dutch for 'talk'), a program created by Paul Boersma and David Weeninck of the Institute of Phonetic Sciences of the University of Amsterdam (Boersma/Weeninck 2005). A corpus that has used such software is the IViE corpus, a corpus designed to investigate intonation variation in British English. Figure 11.1 shows a screen shot of a speech pressure wave, IViE prosodic annotations, and a fundamental frequency trace.

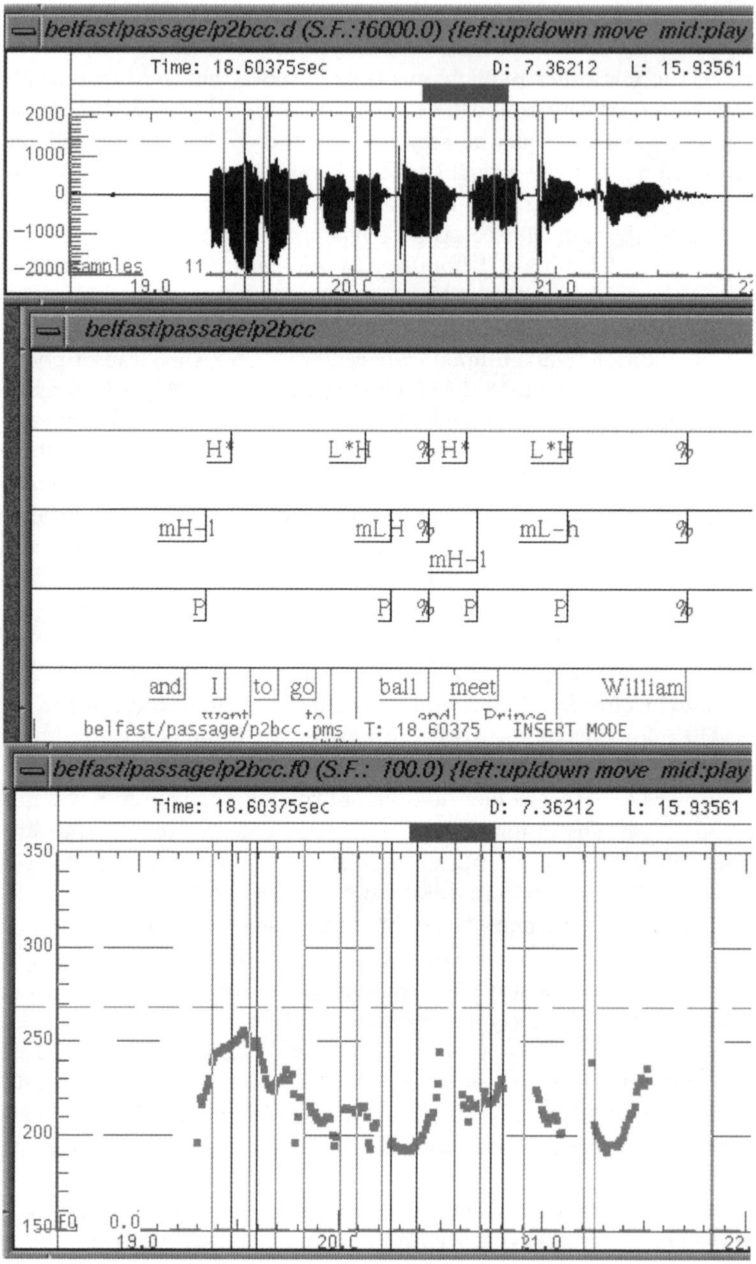

Fig. 11.1: This shows a screen shot of a sound wave in the upper section and in the central frame a sample of IViE annotations in several transcription tiers, including orthographic and prosody. The lowest frame shows the fundamental frequency trace (the pitch contour or 'melody'). The information in all frames is time aligned (marked with vertical lines) so that exact alignment can be found, for example, of pitch peaks with the segmental structure of a stressed syllable. This pitch trace illustrates the typical rising contour at the end of a phrase in Northern Irish English (on 'ball' and 'William').

Only a subset of the corpus has been annotated in this way, with the intention of providing a model for users should they wish to analyse more of the data. A total of five hours of data has been labelled with phonetic and phonological annotations, a considerable amount given the time-consuming nature of such transcription, and given that there is very little publicly available intonation data that has been labelled in this way.

4. Prosodic transcription of corpora

Phonetic / phonological annotation of corpora can include reference to both segmental (phonemic, broad and narrow phonetic) and prosodic information. The techniques and approaches to segmental annotation are dealt with in detail in article 30. In what follows I will therefore focus on attempts to extract suprasegmental (prosodic) information from spoken language corpus data. I will briefly consider methods for the automatic extraction of prosodic features, and then describe more fully the issues surrounding manual prosodic annotation, including a description of existing prosodically transcribed corpora.

4.1. Automatic annotation

If a corpus user wants more than an orthographic representation of the speech it contains, there are various ways of doing it. Manual annotation is clearly the most time-consuming approach, and requires skilled annotators. In some cases we find whole 'factories' of students being employed to carry out the analysis manually. However, the availability of engineers appears to be greater than that of trained manual annotators, and automatically calculated values have the advantage of seeming objective, in contrast to the subjectivity, and hence unreliability of manual annotation. Some researchers therefore limit their study to features that can be identified automatically.

The principal components of prosody are pitch (intonation), timing (including pauses, segment duration and syllable duration), loudness, and voice quality. All of these features can be extracted to some extent automatically from the speech signal: for a given stretch of speech, for example, it is possible to calculate automatically the speech and articulation rate, the overall pitch range, the high points and the low points, and also average range and pitch movements. What cannot be done automatically is to ascertain which of these features are linguistically important and which are not, unless they can be analysed in relation to linguistically meaningful units (phonemes, intonation units, utterances, discourse acts).

An example of a corpus-based study using mainly automatically extracted features is Koiso et al. (1998), who used the Japanese Map Task corpus to analyse turn-taking. Their data was separated automatically into 'Inter Pause Units' (IPUs), i.e. stretches of speech bounded by pauses of more than 100ms, a decision based on the assumption that 'turn exchanges occur most frequently at or during pauses' (Koiso et al. 1998, 298–299). This is an approach that is based perhaps more on what is practical than on a sophisticated view of turntaking phenomena, but typical of work carried out with speech technology applications in mind. Even this study, however, relied on some hand labelling (identifying the final mora and final phoneme in each IPU). The complexity of the automatic extraction procedures, together with the need to examine each unit of utterance individually for hand labelling, meant that in fact although the data was taken from the Map Task Corpus, only 40 minutes of speech, a very small subset, was used.

4.2. Manual annotation

Corpus compilers have in general decided to leave prosodic annotation largely to the consumer. Given the lack of agreement over which system to use this is a wise decision. Early attempts to represent the pitch component of prosody (intonation) used a variety of visualisations, ranging from a quasi musical notation on a stave to crazy type (Bolinger 1989) and the tadpole transcription (Cruttenden 1996; see Williams 1996 for an overview). None of these representations, however, make much attempt to reduce the perceived overall contour to the representation of broader phonological categories, but are mainly attempts at visualising the 'tune' and in some cases indicating the more prominent syllables.

There are broadly two systems of intonation currently in use for English: the British system and the American Autosegmental system. The first treats pitch movement as the smallest unit of analysis, while in the Autosegmental model, pitch movements are further decomposed into high and low pitch targets. The autosegmental equivalent of a falling 'nuclear tone' in the British system is the interpolation between a high and a low pitch target. (See Wichmann 2000 for further comparison.) An adaptation of the autosegmental model, ToBI (Tones and Break Indices) is by far the most frequently used model in current intonational phonology as it is particularly well-suited to computational uses. A binary system of H and L tones is more compatible with computer modelling than holistic patterns of pitch movement. It is also being used in adapted form to analyse languages other than English, thus providing an international standard for comparison. However, the two corpora of British English that have detailed prosodic annotations, the LLC and the SEC, and the Corpus of Spoken American English (CSAE), each use a form of the iconic British system.

The LLC annotation is the richest in terms of the number of features captured, which include both paralinguistic and categorical linguistic elements. It is based closely on the system developed by Crystal (1969) and includes the marking of tone unit boundaries, degrees of stress, pauses, degree of pitch range, and pitch movement on nuclear tones. The disadvantage of this system is that it takes some time to internalise and makes interpretation difficult if the researcher is not extremely practised at reading it.

The Spoken English Corpus is also transcribed using the same theoretical framework (nuclear tones, tone groups, etc.) but using a much pared down set of iconic symbols that are much easier to read but inevitably capture fewer features than the full Crystal system (Knowles et al. 1996). As in all models, the boundaries are annotated between tone groups (or 'intonation phrases' or 'intonation groups' or 'tone units'). The SEC uses two levels: major and minor, the former equating approximately to a sentence break and the latter to lesser breaks, usually containing (since this is mostly formal scripted speech) around 4–6 syllables. (Note that since the SEC contains largely scripted speech the term 'sentence' here is still appropriate. For unscripted speech it would be preferable to refer to 'utterances'.) Pauses are only annotated if they occur inside a tone group, and can be classed as hesitations or rhetorical pauses. Grammatical pauses are not indicated. The only paralinguistic indication of pitch range is by means of the up-arrow ↑ and down-arrow ↓ ('higher than expected' and 'lower than expected'), and relative pitch height is indicated by the use of high and low versions of the symbols for pitch movement (e. g. high fall and low fall). Only accented syllables are annotated (with indication of pitch movement); the pitch of unstressed syllables is assumed to be largely predictable. No indication of any other paralinguistic features (tempo, loudness, voice quality) is included in the annotation.

The purpose of this corpus was to serve developments in the automatic synthesis of natural-sounding intonation, which is why the annotation was kept to a minimum. Work in speech technology, whether for speech synthesis or recognition is, however, now completely geared to the autosegmental system. The iconic system of annotation is now largely used for teaching purposes – it lends itself well to teaching about intonation (Wichmann et al. 1997) to non-specialist students of English.

There is a particular issue with the labelling of paralinguistic or attitudinal information. Crystal's original transcriptions contained considerable paralinguistic information, including overall pitch height (*high, low*), pitch range (*wide, narrow*), tempo (*allegro, lento, allegrissimo*), loudness (*forte, fortissimo, piano, pianissimo, crescendo, diminuendo*). These impressionistic labels contain information that modern annotation software would accommodate on a paralinguistic tier, and could be kept apart from the more linguistic analysis. Such an annotation was used for the Reading Emotion Corpus (see Figure 11.2). This corpus, as others, was compiled on the assumption that there is a systematic link to be found between psychological analysis and speech characteristics. This link has so far proved elusive, not least because listeners have great difficulty in identifying specific emotions from the voice alone, and it seems that the cues to emotional expression are more closely bound to context than has previously been thought (Stibbard 2000, 2001).

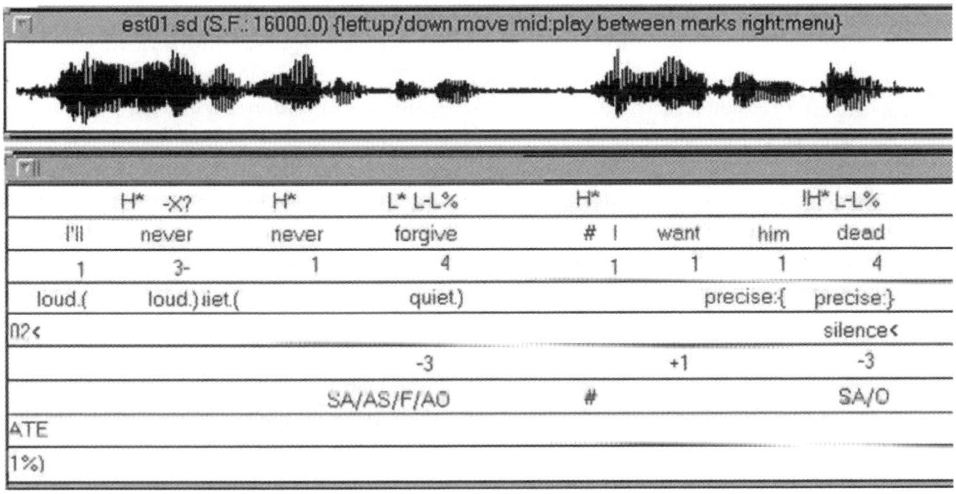

Fig. 11.2: This shows a sound wave and annotations on several levels including pitch, orthography, break indices and paralinguistic effects. The data is taken from the Emotion in Speech project, Reading University.

The representation of prosodic information, both linguistic and paralinguistic, utilised in the Santa Barbara Corpus of Spoken American English owes some features to the British system of intonation. The text is laid out to indicate prosodic units (tone groups), and is marked up to show intonation contours, using an iconic system similar to the British system of tones, and a range of other phonetic features. Other conventions are controversial, such as using functional or discourse-related symbols (e. g. 'finality', 'continuation', 'appeal') together with formal indicators such as 'falling terminal'. Nonetheless, this is a valuable and widely used corpus, providing access to original sound files as well as a detailed transcription.

The annotation system of the CSAE is similar to and derived from the system used by Conversation Analysts which was devised by Gail Jefferson. It was motivated by the understandable desire not to pre-select segmental or suprasegmental features for annotation, and thus not to pre-judge the analysis. The Jefferson transcription system uses a non-standard spelling system to capture prosodic features, and also indicates some segmental features such as syllable lengthening or vowel reduction, e. g. [so:::::: when ya comin?]. The argument underlying this system is that we should transcribe everything we hear, because we do not know in advance what will be important. Unfortunately it is naive to imagine that we 'hear everything'. Indeed recent developments in the study of the prosody of conversation (e. g. Couper-Kuhlen/Selting 1996, Couper-Kuhlen/Ford 2004), have investigated the function of phonetic features that would have been impossible for anyone but a trained auditory and acoustic phonetician to observe, such as the alignment between pitch contours and segments, the slope of pitch contours, and changes in voice quality. The insights derived from phonetic analyses in the CA framework are extremely valuable, both for the insights in human communicative behaviour and for their potential applications. It would be a considerable step forward for Conversation Analysis if this attention to phonetic detail was expressed in a shift to more appropriate annotation methods, for example using tiered annotation such as has already been described.

Prosodic analysis can never be theory neutral and thus any prosodic labelling of a corpus presupposes a choice of theoretical framework. The transcriptions of the corpora described above are based entirely on auditory analysis, relying on the trained ear of the experienced phonetician. The use of the ToBI framework, which is currently the dominant model, has coincided with the much wider availability of speech software, enabling the transcriber to inspect the fundamental frequency contours, the waveform and the spectrogram to reinforce or counter auditory impressions. This has led people to believe that the system is thus less reliant on subjective impression and therefore more reliable. The findings of inter-rater reliability studies, however, suggest that this is an optimistic view. Large corpora cannot be labelled for prosody single-handedly and teams of labellers are needed. However, even highly trained labellers have been found to disagree and this detracts from the usefulness of the resulting transcription. Oostdijk/Boves (article 30) suggest that a reduced label set (including break indices / boundary strength, and the identification of prominent syllables) leads to a more reliable transcription. It should be pointed out, incidentally, that labellers should be native-speakers of the language they are analysing. Apparently simple things such as identifying prominent syllables is not so easy when other languages are involved. It is common, for example, for speakers of standard southern British English, to misinterpret pitch prominence in French as a sentence accent, and to perceive final high syllables in Northern Irish English as accented when they are actually part of a post-nuclear melody. In other words, the acoustic cues to sentence accent (or stress) vary across languages, and one's perceptions are in the main guided by one's own language.

A good example of just how labour-intensive the prosodic and linguistic labelling of a speech corpus can be is to be found in a study by Shriberg et al. (1998). This is an investigation into the prosodic cues to 'dialogue acts' including statements, questions, backchannels, and agreements, and uses data from the Switchboard corpus. The published article not only has 10 authors from 8 different institutions, but also acknowledges a team of 8 dialogue labellers and a team of 5 intonation labellers. In addition to the work of these labellers, automatic extraction methods were used to establish utterance duration, pauses, pitch range, pitch movements, energy and speech rates. The automatic identification of prominent syllables and the pitch value before a boundary (pitch accents and boundary tones) was compared to results of hand labelling but reached only an accuracy of 31.7%.

Purely manual analysis of prosody using corpus data is not common outside large research units. Individuals working on prosody and corpora now tend to use conventional search methods (concordancing software) such as is provided for ICE-GB, that allows a search for any lexical item or any grammatical structure included in the annotation. This means that one can extract a set of utterances containing a particular word or phrase, e. g. *please* (see Wichmann 2004, 2005), or all backchannel responses, and then restrict the labour intensive transcription process to that particular subset of the data.

5. Sociolinguistic and pragmatic applications of spoken corpora

Spoken language corpora provide information about spoken grammar and the spoken lexicon, and also about recurring sequences and collocations, discourse particles and short responses, pauses, filled pauses and verbal fillers, etc. (see article 47). Most of this information is derived from the transcription alone, but there are further insights to be gained from the combined information of text and sounds. In this section I will outline some of the research that reflects work at this interface between what people say and how they say it, focusing on efforts to understand human communication rather than on work aimed at recognising or imitating human dialogue in machine systems.

5.1. Prosodic variation

The study of socio-phonetic variation has been restricted mainly to segmental differences and some observation of intonation patterns of a given variety (e. g. regional varieties of British English). The close analysis required for this work has meant that it is mainly based on a small database of utterances, and little work is based on systematically compiled corpora. An exception is the current work on the IViE project (see section 2.2.1.). Work so far has investigated systemic differences, including the intonation of declaratives and modal questions in different varieties of English, and phonotactic differences including the permitted sequencing of nuclear and prenuclear tones, and also phonetic realisational differences of tonal contours (Grabe 2004). While currently restricted to varieties of English, the methodology being developed in these studies is laying the foundation for much wider typological studies of intonation across and within languages.

5.2. Discourse and pragmatics

Some work in this area relies on analysis of annotation categories, either using a pre-annotated corpus (e. g. LLC, SEC) or using the user's own annotations (IViE, ICE-GB). Most work is focused on usage. In a study (Aijmer 1996) of the various ways of expressing thanks, apologies and requests, based on quantitative data from the LLC, discussion of the prosodic patterning of these speech acts (for example the different ways of saying 'sorry'), although only a small part of the study, is derived from the prosodic annotation of the corpus. Hedberg et al. (2006) studied the intonation contours of yes/no questions in the American Callhome corpus, by selecting 104 examples from the corpus and analysing the phonological constituents and their realisation. Another approach to the prosody of speech acts is represented by the study of Shriberg et al. (1998) (see section 4.1.). While Aijmer and Hedberg examined the role of phonological phenomena (nuclear tone choice, accent placement and intonational phrasing), Shriberg et al. base their study on automatic analysis of global prosodic features (e. g. pitch range, amplitude variation).

Interest in discourse prosody is not restricted to speech acts. The role of intonation in the signalling of topic and paragraph structure is well known (Lehiste 1975; Wichmann 2000). Some annotation schemes, such as those used in the LLC and SEC, which include an indication of unusual pitch resets, can shed light on this function. For the most part however this work has involved instrumental phonetic analysis. Extra high initial accented syllables have been found to signal the beginning of a topic or paragraph. By means of close analysis of the alignment of such an initial pitch peak with the associated syllable, it has also been found that initiality is signalled not only by peak height but by peak delay (Wichmann et al. 1999).

5.3. Emotion and attitude

The affective function of prosody is known to be an important dimension of speech research, and much work has been done on the effect of emotion and other speaker states on speech prosody (see section 2.2.3.). The notion of 'attitude', however, is more controversial. It is often conflated with emotion, but Wichmann (2000) argues that it should be kept apart, being treated as a pragmatic inference or implicature arising from speech in a particular context. Attitudinal meanings arise not from any 'attitudinal' tone of voice, but often from a mismatch between a prosodic choice (accent placement, tonal contour) and context. A study of *please*-requests (Wichmann 2005), based on the International Corpus of English (GB), shows how *please* in English can be not only a neutral expression of courtesy but also an attitudinally marked appeal or entreaty; the difference can be accounted for not by a special 'tone of entreaty' but within a pragmatic framework by the exploitation in context of limited 'normal' intonational resources – accent placement and tone choice.

6. Summary

It is evident from the above account that the compilation of speech corpora and spoken corpora is motivated in a variety of ways, and that the design and analysis of the corpora vary in equal measure depending on the application envisaged. Developments in speech analysis are at present driven by the needs of speech technology, and this fact accounts for the preference for automatic methods of analysis. Advances in prosodic phonology, the linguistic study of the structure of prosody, are being made on the basis of laboratory experiments rather than on corpus data. Linguists interested in the relationship between prosody and discourse, while they have access to a number of spoken corpora described above, are ultimately reliant on very small subsets of data given the time-consuming nature of the annotation, or the technical difficulties in accessing pre-annotated data such as Aix-Marsec. One hopes that future spoken corpora will provide linguistically sophisticated syntactic, pragmatic and discourse annotation together with an equally sophisticated prosodic annotation that can then be complemented by automatic analysis of global trends, such as pitch, pause, loudness and voice quality. At present, the technology outstrips the linguistics.

7. Literature

Aijmer, K. (1996), *Conversational Routines in English*. London: Longman.

Andersen, G. (2000), The Role of the Pragmatic Marker *like* in Utterance Interpretation. In: Andersen, G./Fretheim, T. (eds.), *Pragmatic Markers and Propositional Attitude*. Amsterdam: John Benjamins, 17–38.

Andersen, G. (2001), *Pragmatic Markers and Sociolinguistic Variation*. Amsterdam: John Benjamins.

Anderson, A. H./Bader, M./Gurman Bard, E./Boyle, E./Doherty, G./Garrod, S./Isard, S./Kowtko, J./McAllister, J./Miller, J./Sotillo, C./Thompson, H. S./Weinert, R. (1991), The HCRC Map Task Corpus. In: *Language and Speech* 34, 351–366.

Auran, C./Bouzon, C./Hirst, D. (2004), The Aix-MARSEC Project: An Evolutive Database of Spoken British English. In: *Proceedings of Speech Prosody 2004*. Nara, Japan, 561–564.

Biber, D./Johansson, S./Leech, G./Conrad S./Finegan, E. (1999), *Longman Grammar of Spoken and Written English*. Harlow: Pearson Education.

Boersma, P. (2001), Praat, a System for Doing Phonetics by Computer. In: *Glot International* 5(9/10), 341–345.

Boersma, P./Weenink, D. (2005), *Praat: Doing Phonetics by Computer (Version 4.3.04)*. [Computer program.] Retrieved March 8, 2005, from ⟨http://www.praat.org/⟩.

Bolinger, D. (1989), *Intonation and Its Uses*. London: Edward Arnold.

Brosens, V. (1998), Le projet ELICOP, Etude LInguistique de la Communication Parlée. Presented at the AFLS Colloquium (Association for French Language Studies), East Anglia, 4–6 September 1998, (Français oral, français écrit à l'ère des nouvelles technologies (resume in *Cahiers AFLS*, 4.2. Summer 1998, p. 4).

Burnard, L. (2002), The BNC: Where Did We Go Wrong? In: Kettemann, B./Marko, G. (eds.), *Teaching and Learning by Doing Corpus Analysis: Proceedings of the Fourth International Conference on Teaching and Language Corpora*. Amsterdam: Rodopi, 51–72.

Bybee, J. (2001) *Phonology and Language Use*. Cambridge: Cambridge University Press.

Couper-Kuhlen, E./Ford, C. E. (eds.) (2004), *Sound Patterns in Interaction: Cross-linguistic Studies from Conversation*. Amsterdam/Philadelphia: John Benjamins.

Couper-Kuhlen, E./Selting, M. (eds.) (1996), *Prosody in Conversation. Interactional Studies*. Cambridge: Cambridge University Press.

Cruttenden, A. (1986), *Intonation*. Cambridge: Cambridge University Press.

Crystal, D. (1969), *Prosodic Systems and Intonation in English*. Cambridge: Cambridge University Press.

Douglas-Cowie, E./Campbell, N./Cowie, R./Roach, P. (2003), Emotional Speech: Towards a New Generation of Databases. In: *Speech Communication* 40(1–2), 33–60.

Du Bois, J. W./Cumming, S./Schuetze-Coburn, S./Paolino, D. (1993), Outline of Discourse Transcription. In: Edwards, J. A./Lampert, M. D. (eds.), *Talking Data: Transcription and Coding in Discourse Research*. Hillsdale, New Jersey: Lawrence Erlbaum, 45–89.

Gibbon, D./Mertins, I./Moore, R. K. (eds.) (2000), *Handbook of Multimodal and Spoken Dialogue Systems*. Dordrecht: Kluwer.

Grabe, E. (2004), Intonational Variation in Urban Dialects of English Spoken in the British Isles. In: Gilles, P./Peters, J. (eds.), *Regional Variation in Intonation*. Tuebingen: Niemeyer, 9–31.

Grabe, E./Post, B./Nolan, F. (2001), *The IViE Corpus*. University of Cambridge, Department of Linguistics. ⟨http://www.phon.ox.ac.uk/~esther/ivyweb⟩

Greasely, P./Setter, J./Waterman, M./Sherrard, C./Roach, P./Arnfield, S./Horton, D. (1995), Representation of Prosodic and Emotional Features in a Spoken Language Database. In: *Proceedings of the 13th ICPhS Stockholm* 1, 242–245.

Hedberg, N./Sosa, J. M./Fadden, L. (2006), Tonal Constituents and Meanings of Yes-No Question in American English. In: Hoffmann, R./Mixdorff, H. (eds.), *Proceedings of Speech Prosody, 3rd International Conference, Dresden*, on CD-Rom.

House, J./Youd, N. (1991), Stylised Prosody in Telephone Information Services: Implications for Synthesis. In: *Proceedings of the 12th ICPhS*. Aix-en-Provence, Vol. 5, 198–201.

Izre'el, Sh./Hary, B./Rahav, G. (2001), Designing CoSIH: The Corpus of Spoken Israeli Hebrew. In: *International Journal of Corpus Linguistics* 6, 171–197.

Knowles, G./Williams, B./Taylor, L. (eds.) (1996), *A Corpus of Formal British English Speech*. London: Longman.

Koiso, H./Horiuchi, Y./Tutiya, S./Ichikawa, A./Den, Y (1998), An Analysis of Turn Taking and Backchannels on Prosodic and Syntactic Features in Japanese Map Task Dialogs. In: *Language and Speech* 41(3–4), 295–321.

Ladd, D. R. (1996), *Intonational Phonology*. Cambridge: Cambridge University Press.

Lehiste, I. (1975), The phonetic structure of paragraphs. In: Cohen, A./Nooteboom, S. G. (eds.), *Structure and Process in Speech Perception*. N.Y.: Springer Verlag, 195–206.

Mukherjee, J. (2004), The State of the Art in Corpus Linguistics: Three Book-length Perspectives. In: *English Language and Linguistics* 8(1), 103–119.

Nelson, G./Wallis, S./Aarts, B. (2002), *Exploring Natural Language: Working with the British Component of the International Corpus of English*. Amsterdam: John Benjamins.

Ooostdijk, N./Goedertier, W./Van Eynde, F./Boves, L./Martens, J.-P./Moortgat, M./Baayen, R. H. (2002), Experiences from the Spoken Dutch Corpus Project. In: Gonzalez-Rodriguez, M./Paz Suárez Araujo, C. (eds.), *Proceedings from the Third International Conference on Language Resources and Evaluation*. Las Palmas de Gran Canaria, 330–347.

Schönefeld, D. (1999), Corpus Linguistics and Cognitivism. In: *International Journal of Corpus Linguistics* 4, 137–171.

Shobbrook, K./House, J. (2003), High Rising Tones in Southern British English. In: *Proceedings of 15th ICPhS*. Barcelona, 1273–1276.

Shriberg, E./Bates, R./Stolcke, A./Taylor, P./Jurafsky, D./Ries, K./Coccaro, N./Martin, R./Meteer, M./Van Ess-Dykema, C. (1998), Can Prosody Aid the Automatic Identification of Dialog Acts in Conversational Speech? In: *Language and Speech* 41(3–4), 443–492.

Stenström, A.-B. (1998), From Sentence to Discourse: *cos (because)* in Teenage Talk. In: Jucker, A./Ziv, Y (eds.), *Discourse Markers: Descriptions and Theory*. Amsterdam: John Benjamins, 127–146.

Stenström, A.-B./Andersen, G./Hasund, I. K. (2002), *Trends in Teenage Talk*. Amsterdam: John Benjamins.
Stibbard, R. M. (2000), Automated Extraction of ToBI Annotation Data from the Reading/Leeds Emotion in Speech Corpus. In: Cowie, R./Douglas-Cowie, E./Schröder, M. (eds.), *Proceedings of the ISCA Workshop on Speech and Emotion*. Belfast: Textflow, 60–65.
Stibbard, R. M. (2001), Vocal Expression of Emotions in Non-laboratory Speech: An Investigation of the Reading/Leeds Emotion in Speech Project Annotation Data. Unpublished PhD dissertation, University of Reading.
Svartvik, J. (ed.) (1990), *The London-Lund Corpus of Spoken English: Description and Research*. (Lund Studies in English 82.) Lund: Lund University Press.
Swerts, M./Collier, R. (1992), On the Controlled Elicitation of Spontaneous Speech. In: *Speech Communication* 11, 463–468.
Wichmann, A. (2000), *Intonation in Text and Discourse*. London: Longman.
Wichmann, A. (2004), The Intonation of *please*-requests: A Corpus-based Study. In: *Journal of Pragmatics* 36(9), 1521–1549.
Wichmann, A. (2005), *Please* – from Courtesy to Appeal: The Role of Intonation in the Expression of Attitudinal Meaning. *English Language and Linguistics* 9(2), 229–253.
Wichmann, A./Fligelstone, S./McEnery, A./Knowles, G. (eds.) (1997), *Teaching and Language Corpora*. London: Longman.
Wichmann, A./House, J./Rietveld, T. (1999), Discourse Structure and Peak Timing in English: Experimental Evidence. In: *Proceedings of the International Congress of Phonetic Sciences (ICPhS)*. San Francisco, USA, 1765–1768.
Williams, B. (1996), The Formulation of an Intonation Transcription System for British English. In: Knowles, G./Wichmann, A./Alderson, P. (eds.), *Working with Speech*. London: Longman, 38–57.

Anne Wichmann, Preston (UK)

12. Multimodal corpora

The structure of this paper is the following. In section 1, multimodal corpora are defined and described, in section 2, reasons are given why multimodal corpora are created, and in section 3, there is a discussion of some issues to keep in mind when creating and analyzing a multimodal corpus. There is also a discussion of some research directions. In section 4, possible applications are mentioned and section 5, finally, contains some concluding remarks.

1. What are multimodal corpora?

The Latin word "corpus" (body) is used to metaphorically describe a collection of language and communication data, see Lewis/Short (1966). In what follows, I will assume that the corpus is stored on a computer, i. e. a digitized corpus. A digitized corpus is, thus, a kind of database of language related material. Although computer-based corpora were planned in the 1940's (cf. http://en.wikipedia.org/wiki/Roberto_Busa), the first appeared in the 1950's and contained written language excerpts. They were an attempt to replace earlier manually collected and stored sets of written excerpts with a set stored on a computer. During the 1960's corpora of transcriptions of spoken language also appeared. For a history of corpora, see McEnery/Wilson (2001) and the articles in section I of this volume. If we want to find out when the first multimodal corpora appeared, the answer to this question is dependent on how we define a "multimodal corpus". In the widest sense, it may be a collection of analog films, which are registered in a paper file or on a computer. In a slightly more narrow sense, which will be the sense I will discuss here, it would only include material that has been digitized, i. e., the films would have to be digitized rather than just available in an archive. A first attempt at a definition might now be to say that a multimodal digitized corpus is a computer-based collection of language and communication-related material drawing on more than one sensory modality or on more than one production modality (see below). Depending on how narrow we want our sense of "corpus" to be, we might then, for example, revise this definition to say that a multimodal corpus is a digitized collection of language and communication-related material, drawing on more than one modality. In a more narrow sense, we might require that the audiovisual material should be accompanied by transcriptions and annotations or codings based on the material. This definition is more narrow, since there is a specification of the nature of the language and communication related material, i. e. it should contain recordings, transcriptions and annotations. The first definition leaves the nature of the corpus open.

Examples of multimodal corpora might, thus, be a digitized collection of texts illustrated with pictures and/or diagrams or a digitized collection of films with associated transcriptions of the speech in the films.

Another issue, already hinted at, is what is meant by multimodality. The term "modality" can be used in many ways, but the definition we will adopt is that "multimodal information" is information pertaining to more than one "sensory modality" (i. e., sight, hearing, touch, smell or taste) or to more than one "production modality" (i. e., gesture (the term "gesture" will, in this paper, be used in the sense of any body movement), speech (sound), touch, smell or taste). If we assume that there are five or more sensory modalities (e. g. vision, hearing, touch, smell, and taste) only two of these have really been made use of so far in multimodal corpora, namely vision and hearing (which corresponds to the production modalities of gesture and speech in face-to-face communication). The term "multimodal" can, thus, be contrasted with the term "multimedial" which has a slightly different sense, relying on the notion of "medium". This term can also be used in many ways and is sometimes taken in more or less the same sense we have given to "multimodal" above. However, in order to maintain a contrast, we will define a "communication medium" as the physical carrier of multimodal information. Thus, the medium for sight is light waves, the medium for hearing is sound waves, the medium for touch is physical pressure and the medium for smell and taste various types of chemical molecules.

Multimodal corpora are multidimensional, not only from a modality point of view, but also from a semiotic point of view. Often, all the three Peircean information carrying relations are present, i. e. index, icon and symbol (cf. Peirce 1955). Even though still pictures and motion pictures are themselves iconic in nature, both types can iconically represent indexical, symbolic and even iconic information (a picture of a picture). This is also true of sound recordings, where the recorded sound is an iconic representation of the original sound which in itself can contain indexical, symbolic and even iconic information (e. g. a sound recording of an imitated sound).

Besides what is iconically represented in this way by audio or video recordings, the corpus can contain symbolic textual information which can add to, supplement and complement the recordings. Let us distinguish three cases:

(i) Texts describing pictures

Pictures give concrete iconic details, e. g. a particular brown horse on a particular field, while words give more abstract symbolic information. The word "horse" does not tell us what color the horse has, but it is impossible to depict a horse without depicting a particular color. Words can add focus, identification and perspective to a pictorial representation. In fact, most existing multimodal corpora rely on textual identifying information in searching the corpus. This is so, since present technology mostly does not really allow efficient search using the iconic elements themselves. So texts in a multimodal corpus can be used for identification but also to give historical or background information.

(ii) Audio-video recordings with annotations or codings

A special case of texts describing pictures is provided by text (usually called annotations or codings) which gives a kind of descriptive running commentary on what occurs in the recording. This kind of textual information is often used to describe gestures, prosody or other aspects of sound quality. It can also be used to capture features of context or various types of semantic-pragmatic information.

(iii) Audio-video recordings with transcriptions

A second special case (in fact a special case of annotations and codings) is provided by so called transcriptions, i. e. text which gives a more direct representation (usually symbolic) of what is said or done. The most common type of transcriptions (cf. Allwood et al. 2000) are related to audio recordings and represent segmental speech sounds, leaving out gestures, prosody and other aspects of sound quality. There are, however, special types of transcription which include such information. For gestures, see, for example, Birdwhistell (1952) or Laban (1974) and for prosody, see, for example, Svartvik/Quirk (1980) or Brazil (1985). The difference between transcriptions and annotations (or codings) lies in the attempt of transcription to give a direct moment to moment representation of what is said, rather than to give a more indirect and mostly less continuous description of certain properties of what is said or done.

For all these three types of textual information, the question may be raised how they relate to the recorded material. To ease comprehension, the general principle adopted for all three types is that of spatio-temporal contiguity. A text occurs at the same point in time as the event it describes or represents. Sometimes, it is even placed at the same point in space, as for example when a label for an object or the name of a person is placed on or in the immediate vicinity of the iconic object it identifies. Usually, however, only temporal contiguity is maintained. When temporal contiguity concerns the relation between transcribed speech (or gesture) and recorded speech (or gesture), it is often referred to as "synchronized alignment" of recording and transcription. The degree of synchronization can vary from the subtitles conventionally used in translating commercial movies which usually occur on an utterance level, in such a way that the whole transcribed utterance is visible as it is being said, to the more fine-grained synchronized alignment used in studies of phonetics, where each phoneme is aligned with a feature in an indexical representation of the acoustic features of the utterance. What synchronization means is that for every part of the transcription (given a particular granularity), it is possible to hear and view the part of the interaction it is based on and that for every part of the interaction, it is possible to see the transcription of that part.

In general, synchronization of information in different modalities has turned out to be a difficult problem in assembling a multimodal corpus. It concerns not only the relation between text and iconic representation but also between different means of recording in the same or different modalities. For example, how should several cameras recording the same event from different perspectives be synchronized or how should several microphones recording a multiparty conversation be synchronized and how should sound and pictures be synchronized? There are two main ways of handling the problem:

(i) Synchronization can be done by a computer program, already while making the recording. This is the most convenient solution (cf. the AMI project, http://www.amiproject.org, and The CHIL project, http://chil.server.de/servlet/is/101/, or Zhang et al. 2006, for interesting examples of how this can be done).
(ii) Synchronization can also be done after the recordings have been made.

In addition, it is possible to mix these two approaches, so that some synchronization is done during the recording and some more is done using the finished recordings.

The kind of multimodal corpus we will be mostly interested in below can be characterized as a digitized collection of audio- and video-recorded instances of human communication connected with transcriptions of the talk and/or gestures in the recordings. The two modalities are, thus, hearing and vision. There are audio recordings of the speech and there are video recordings of the body movements of the participants in the interaction. In addition, there are the transcriptions, which, as we have mentioned, are a kind of visual symbolic representation of the speech (and more rarely of the gestures that occur in the recordings). The form of connection between the transcriptions and the material in the recordings can vary from just being a pairing of a digitized transcription with a digitized video or audio recording (both recording and transcription exist but they have not yet been synchronized) to being a complete temporal synchronization of recordings and transcription.

2. Why multimodal corpora?

The basic reason for collecting multimodal corpora is that they provide material for more complete studies of "interactive face-to-face sharing and construction of meaning and understanding" which is what language and communication are all about. Such studies are not fully possible in corpora which contain linguistic material of a less comprehensive kind, since much of the sharing and construction of information is done multimodally through a combination of gestures and speech (including prosody), i. e. concern processes which integrate multimodal information (in perception and understanding) and distribute information multimodally in production. These are processes of which we often have a low degree of awareness.

Examples of such, often very automatic types of processes can, for example, be found in the head nods by which one speaker gives feedback to another speaker (while he/she is speaking), or in the head movements which a speaker uses to elicit attention from other interlocutors. For an account of processes of this kind, see Goodwin (1981) and Allwood (2001a, 2002).

Another reason is that speech and gestures, unlike written language, are transient objects: they disappear when they have been produced. Given that our intuitions about the nature of naturalistic speech and gesture are usually very unreliable, there is a need for a less transient type of object to study. A corpus of multimodal communication is this kind of object.

Simplifying the matter slightly, the study of multimodal communication enables us to highlight how we continuously in interaction incrementally combine communicative actions with other instrumental actions in order to share information, e. g. compare a situation where I pour coffee into a cup and hand it over to you saying *coffee* with a rising intonation, with a situation where I lift an empty cup directing it to you (you are sitting next to the coffee pot) and say *coffee* with a falling intonation. The former might be construed as an offer while the latter perhaps might be construed as a slightly impolite demand. In both cases, our interpretation is dependent on an integration of signaled verbal linguistic information with indicated and displayed non-linguistic actions (cf. Allwood 2002).

The general problem of how information from communicative actions is combined with information from instrumental actions which are not primarily communicative, has not been extensively studied so far. However, the more limited problems of describing the function of visual communicative gestures (cf. Poggi 2002; Kendon 2004; Argyle 1988; Allwood 2001a) and describing the integration of words, with prosody and gestures have been somewhat more studied (cf. Allwood 2002).

If we turn to the functions of the different modalities in communication, we may say that vocal verbal elements (what is usually captured in conventional writing systems) are our primary source of factual information. In addition, this vocal verbal information is often supplemented by conventional symbolic gestures and illustrative iconic gestures. Vocal verbal information is also used for communication management, prosody gives us information about information structure and emotions/attitudes, while gestures primarily give us information both about emotions/attitudes and communication management. Sometimes the word "social" is used for aspects of communication that do not relate to factual information. Even though this is not a very good term (since communication is always social and what is social often encompasses factual information and what is non-factual is not always social), it should be clear that the "social" functions of language, to a very high degree, rely on information which is gestural and prosodic, i. e. necessitate a multimodal approach to communication.

In any case, we can see that, given the central role of prosody and gestures for the communication of emotion and attitude, studies of affective behavior and affective display which are to have ecological validity, are highly dependent on creation of reliable naturalistic multimodal corpora.

In the following example we illustrate some of the types of behavior and processes that are involved in multimodal communication.

Example 1. Video-based analysis of vocal verbal and gestural elements in a case of hesitation, i. e. OCM "own communication management"

Speaker: *å där så de e som en e // sportspår där som vi springer*
and there so it is like a eh // sportstrack where we run

A closer look at the relationship between vocal words and gestures in the OCM part of the utterance (the phrase *en e // sportspår)* is provided in Table 12.1.

Tab. 12.1: Multitrack annotation of an example of own communication management

Speech	en	e	//	sportspår
Type	Indef article	OCM word	pause	Noun
Gesture	hand circling, illustrating track	turns away head aze gaze		Head and gaze back

If we start by examining the temporal relation between the vocal-verbal and gestural production, we see that an illustrating gesture occurs before the OCM word *e* and pause, which both precede the word *sportspår (sportstrack*). We interpret this as indicating that the speaker has a problem in choosing and producing the right word and that this is reflected in the use of the OCM word and pause to gain time. We can also see that the gesture occurs as the article preceding the OCM word is produced. The gesture might in this case be an illustrating iconic gesture, which could have occurred even if the speaker had no need for support in finding the word, but it might also have a self-activating word finding function for the speaker. The gesture also serves to keep the floor and to give a clue about the meaning of the coming word to the listeners.

Simultaneously with the OCM word and pause, the speaker turns his head and gaze away from the interlocutors, indicating memory search and giving further support for turnkeeping. When he produces the noun he moves his head back facing the interlocutor, indicating that the memory search is completed.

Thus, the example indicates that normal face-to-face communication contains a wealth of multimodal information, vocal-verbal as well as gestural and that the temporal relation between the modalities is not simple. The example is fairly typical of the complex relation between speech and gesture, the study of which is facilitated by the kind of data that are available in a multimodal corpus.

A multimodal corpus, in this way, gives one an opportunity to capture not only written language (or a written transcription of spoken language) but provides an opportunity to include information of a contextual and cultural kind. This means that multimodal corpora are excellent instruments for a more holistic documentation of cultural and linguistic processes (as is currently going on in relation to the endangered languages of the world, see article 21). It also means that theories of language and communication, by giving access to more relevant data, potentially can provide a better and more correct description, understanding and explanation of the nature of language.

In line with what has been said above, another area that is currently driving the need for multimodal corpora is the construction of so called embodied conversational agents or avatars, i. e. artificial computer-based communicators that have a more or less artificial face and body. Such avatars are today becoming more and more human-like. This means that they are being equipped with the same kind of communicative behavior and communicative functions that humans have. Among other things, this means that they are capable of showing emotions and attitudes. For interesting examples of avatars (or ECAs) of this type see the HUMAINE network (http://emotion-research.net); Cassell et al. (2000); Gratch/Mao/Marcella (2006).

Since the approach relies on simulating multimodal human communication, there is a great need for more exact information of this type. The primary source of this information is corpora of multimodal communication, cf. Martin et al. (2005).

Also in the area of computer mediated communication (CMC) use is made of corpora of multimodal communication. An important goal of CMC is to facilitate human communication in various ways, e. g. in order to bridge gaps of space and time or to provide summarization of meeting contents. (Cf. the AMI project at http://amiproject.org for interesting examples of techniques to create so called "virtual meeting rooms", Nijholt/op den Akker/Heylen (2006), and article 17). If this is to be done efficiently, the suggestions made have to be based on studies of actual human communication. Otherwise, there is an obvious risk that what will be produced will never be used. Again, the key is to have information on actual multimodal human communication available in corpus form.

3. Creating a multimodal corpus

Let us now take a look at some of the considerations that need to be kept in mind, in constructing a multimodal corpus based on recordings of face-to-face communication. We will consider the following issues (some of which are also covered in article 31):

1. What should we record?
2. How should we record?
3. How should we keep track of the recordings?
4. Should we transcribe and, if so, how?
5. How should we keep track of the transcriptions?
6. How should we analyze recordings and transcriptions?
7. What should we analyze?

3.1. What should we record?

What we should record depends on the purpose of our investigation (cf. also article 9). There are many possible criteria for deciding on what data should be recorded and included in the corpus. What sampling criteria for the corpus (e. g. speaker characteristics like age, sex, social class, personality type, level of education, ethnic background, occupation or regional background) should be chosen is dependent on what we are investigating and what is important for this investigation. However, since a corpus is often collected in order to be a resource for more than one purpose, many researchers are interested in getting a balanced sample in the sense of taking into account as many of the sampling criteria as possible. What this could mean is that our corpus should not only contain women but both men and women, not only children but children, adults and persons of old age, etc. In some cases, however, one does not want a balanced sample but rather a specialized sample of only women or only young men of working class background, etc.

Another problem that arises is the choice of persons within each category. For example, could we merely record the persons we happen to run into in each category? This is sometimes done and can provide interesting results. Another possibility is to use some type of random sampling within each category. This requires getting a list of the possible candidates and then using some method of random sampling to pick out the persons who will be recorded. A third possibility is to use some sort of strategic sampling, where the theory to be investigated decides what data to choose.

Instead of basing our corpus on speaker characteristics, we could choose to sample on the basis of social activity or type of organization. We could, for example, try to record activities related to, e. g., research, education or manual work (e. g. fishing, hunting, farming, crafts), industrial work, commerce, religious practice, healthcare, judicial (law) practice, entertainment, mass media, transportation, building, professional food, military or everyday life (including relaxation). Even if the main purpose in gathering data according to social activity would be to record communication in the mentioned activities irrespective of the personal characteristics of the participants, it may still be desirable to keep track of these characteristics. They will, however, usually be of secondary interest and we would normally accept an activity-based corpus that had more women than men or more middle class people than upper class people, etc., since we are primarily interested in the nature of the activity-based interaction rather than in the influence of the participants' personal characteristics on the interaction.

Unfortunately, the answer to the question of what a balanced sample is is even more unclear in relation to social activities, than it is in relation to personal characteristics. The list of activities given in the previous paragraph represents an effort to find such a list but there is no guarantee that something important is not missing. In many cases, the nature of the list is also culture-dependent and is therefore going to change with time and be different in different cultures.

3.2. How should we record?

Once we have decided what to record, we have to decide how to do this. Since this topic will be covered in more detail elsewhere in this book (see articles 30 and 31), I will restrict myself to a few of the relevant issues.

The first issue concerns choice of medium for registering data. Should we, for example, rely on memory, use written notes (the classical anthropological field notes) or use audio and video recordings? Probably, we will end up with a combination of all three of these methods.

When it comes to recording, we are faced with many options and questions that need to be answered regarding choice of equipment. For example regarding

- choice of audio/video recorder (analog/digital, size of recorder, number of channels)
- choice of microphone (directed, wide angle, radio)
- choice of camera
- choice of lens
- choice of lighting
- choice of view, focus, panorama, etc.
- choice of tape/digital memory

It is not always easy to make the right decisions since the relevant technology is changing very quickly. What is impossible today might very well be possible tomorrow.

Let me just stress a few points.

(i) It is very important to establish routines to be followed in making the recordings, e. g. concerning what to do before in preparation, what to do during the recording and what to do afterwards regarding storage and access.

(ii) In making video recordings that have as a purpose to document regularities and interactive mechanisms in normal communication, it is not a good idea to shift focus or to move the camera from one speaker to another. In order to capture the interaction, the camera should have a constant wide-angle view, trying to get a picture of all participants. If the focus keeps shifting from speaker to speaker, the interaction is lost. A compromise, if your resources allow it, is to have a second camera following the current speaker while keeping the first camera constant on the interaction. In editing the recordings, the second camera recording can then be synchronized with the first camera recording and inserted in a corner of the wide-angle view, thus providing both interaction and focus on speaker.

(iii) Another point concerning video recordings and the study of gestures is that we should be aware that many positions, e. g. sitting down around a table, limit both our freedom to gesture and our ability to record and observe what gestures occur. As usual, the purpose of our investigation is important here. If we only want to study facial gestures and hand movements, probably the rest of the body is less important. But if we want a more holistic impression of multimodal communication, perhaps the best choice is to record communicators who are standing up and moving about.

(iv) In general, as recording of multimodal communication is getting more sophisticated, we are presently moving from using one microphone or camera to the use of several microphones and cameras. As already discussed above, this raises the problem of synchronization of recording devices while the recordings are being made. This area is currently under rapid development and many new computer-based algorithms for synchronization of data are currently being tried out, cf. the AMI project (http://www.amiproject.org). It also raises the problem of how the data from several recordings is going to be presented to a human researcher. There is a need for more research on how to best visualize complex multimodal data in such a way that the constraints and capacities of human cognition are respected (cf. Nijholt et al. 2006). This is one of the concerns motivating the suggestion made in point (ii) above.

(v) Finally, there is a never-ending tension between the desire to get high quality sound and video recordings (this is a must for many types of analysis) and the desire to get naturalistic recordings with high ecological validity (cf. Brunswick 1969), outside of the studio, with no interference from the researcher. This tension is a challenge to try to optimize on both of these criteria as much as possible, i. e. to always opt for as high a quality as possible and as much ecological validity as possible.

3.3. How should we keep track of the recordings?

All recordings that are made should be described with as much relevant background information as possible, e. g. date of recording, person who did the recording, type of recorder, length of recording, purpose of recording, what has been recorded, participants and characteristics of the participants (i. e., age, gender, social class; see section 3.1. above, concerning "personal characteristics"). This information is essential for the build-up of a systematic database containing the recordings. It is also very valuable for the person(s) who are going to transcribe the recordings, since they might not always be the same persons as the ones who made the recordings. The information makes it easier to understand what is going on, how many speakers there are, who is speaking, etc.

As recordings and transcriptions accumulate, the background information can be used to structure the actual physical archive or digital memory space allotted to the recordings (according to whether they are in analog or digital form). It can also be used for retrieval purposes, e. g. to find all recordings of auctions or of doctor-patient consultations. If personal characteristics rather than activities are the basis for the recordings, one might want to find all recordings of women who are middle-aged or men who are speakers of a particular dialect. What can be searched for and retrieved later when we want to use the corpus, entirely depends on what information about the recordings and transcriptions has been entered into the data base, when it was created.

If the recordings and transcriptions are not described, marked and registered (in the way suggested above) gradually as they come in, they usually end up in a more or less serious state of chaos, giving considerably more work to yet another person who gets the job of structuring the data and who, because of lack of information, usually is never able to do more than a partial job.

3.4. Should we transcribe and, if so, how?

One of the first issues to decide on after we have made our recordings (or in some other way obtained audio/video material) is the question of whether the recordings should be transcribed or not. Transcription is certainly not the only way in which audio and video data can be studied. As we have seen above, one might, for example, attempt some sort of direct automatic computer-based analysis using speech recognition or attempt to annotate and code the material directly without also having made a transcription. For additional discussion, see article 30. There are many advantages to doing this, in terms of time and money, since transcriptions are both time-consuming and costly.

Another question concerns how the transcriptions should be produced, since transcriptions could, in principle, be produced online by speech recognition algorithms, as the recording is made. However, this is still not really possible, as there are too many mistakes in the output of the recognition algorithms. This means that transcriptions have to be made either in the traditional manual way by listening (observing) and transcribing what is heard or seen or by using automatically recognized speech (or gesture) as a first step and then correcting this step manually on the basis of listening and observation. The further synchronized alignment of transcriptions and recorded material can now take place, either by synchronizing the recording with the transcription (at the desired level of granularity) as the transcription is being made or by creating the synchronization at a later stage by matching transcription with recording. The second option is often a necessity if one wishes to align corpora of spoken language or multimodal communication, which were made before support of on-line synchronization was available. An interesting issue in this latter case is the creation of algorithms that can achieve synchronized alignment with recordings that have varying sound quality and contain overlapping speech.

We may here note that there probably are advantages to an automatic analysis in terms of not introducing biases, the most important of which probably derive from standard written language, involving such things as word spacing, spelling, capitalization and punctuation (none of which actually occur in normal face-to-face communication). An automatic type of analysis might enable us to get closer to the real properties of the acoustical and optical signal and, thus, perhaps also closer to more detail concerning how we perceive speech and gestures.

If we decide to transcribe, the question of what to transcribe needs to be answered. Should we attempt to transcribe the gestures (in the wide sense of all body movements), or should we restrict transcription to communicatively relevant body movements or perhaps even more to some more limited set of gestures, such as head or hand movements? Should we leave out gestures altogether and restrict transcription only to sound, perhaps limited to only some aspects of the speech signal?

If we decide to transcribe gestures (body movements), there are very many schemes available starting, for example, with Birdwhistell's proposals in the 1950's (cf. Birdwhistell 1952). Laban's choreographically inspired proposals for posture and large scale gestures (Laban 1974), the various proposals that exist for deaf sign language (Stokoe 1978; Bellugi 1972; Nelfelt 1998; Prillwitz et al. 1989) or proposals inspired by the work of David McNeill (McNeill 1979), Kita/van Gijn/van der Hulst (1997) and Månsson (2003).

Since a holistic transcription of gestures is so time-consuming as to be almost impossible, most researchers usually decide on a system of annotation and coding that is oriented toward some communicative functions and thus does not cover everything (cf. for example, the gesture annotation schemas in Allwood 2001b, and Allwood et al. 2005).

In a similar way, we have to decide how speech and sound are to be transcribed. Should we adopt a system which is close to standard orthography or should we adopt a system which captures as much fine-grained detail in the speech sounds as possible? The most detailed system of transcription is probably some version of the IPA (International Phonetic Alphabet). Related to the IPA (http://www2.arts.gla.ac.uk/IPA/ipa.html) there are then systems like SAMPA (http://www.phon.ucl.ac.uk/home/sampa/home.htm), which make the IPA ASCII-compatible, systems which extend the IPA and a host of less fine-grained systems than the IPA. Among the less fine-grained systems, one might distinguish, e. g. phonemic systems and orthographic systems as well as several systems which propose a series of modifications to standard orthography, in order to get closer to various noticeable features of spoken interaction. Examples of two systems which employ such modifications of standard orthography are the system employed in Conversation Analysis (CA) (see Jefferson 1984) and the GTS (Göteborg Transcription Standard) (see Nivre et al. 2004).

3.5. How should we keep track of the transcriptions?

Most of what has been said above about keeping track of recordings is also relevant for keeping track of transcriptions. It is advisable either to initiate each transcription with a section giving all the relevant background information about the transcription or to have separate background posts or files for all transcriptions enabling one to retrieve all the transcriptions which have the prerequisite background information attached to them.

3.6. How should we analyze recordings and transcriptions?

The most important factor in determining how we should analyze our recordings and transcriptions is, of course, our theoretical perspective and research objective, i. e., what we think we are investigating and why we are doing it. Since empirical reality potentially has a very large, probably infinite number of properties and relations, any standard of transcription or schema of annotation/coding is dependent on a theoretical perspective and objective, which will select what empirical data are seen as relevant, determining what properties are picked up by the transcription or annotation and what properties are not picked up. This is so even if the adherents of the system of transcription or annotation claim they have no theory. Given the potential richness of empirical data, any transcription or coding must be the result of a selective procedure, even if the grounds of this procedure are not clearly articulated.

However, while fully acknowledging that the theoretical perspective, even if it is not very explicit, in the end is the most important determining factor, there are some general considerations that if taken into account will make a multimodal corpus more fully exploitable.

One such consideration is that the tools you employ for analysis should allow for simultaneous access to the relevant parts of the transcriptions and recordings. As we have already mentioned, a way to achieve this is to try to align the transcriptions and recordings so that there is a direct relationship between what is said or done and what is transcribed, i. e., in reading the transcription on-line you are also able to open one or more other windows on your computer monitor, where you can see the relevant part of the video recording and hear the corresponding part of the audio recording. This means that there is synchronization between transcriptions and audio/video recordings. All three types of files are time-stamped and the time points can be used for temporal alignment.

The synchronization between transcription and audio/video recordings can then further be extended so that all types of analysis that are done using the recordings or using the transcriptions are made accessible together with recordings or transcriptions. For example, we might be able to open windows for acoustic analysis, gesture analysis or functional analysis that are synchronized with the files containing recordings or transcriptions. With tools allowing this type of analysis, we can avail ourselves of the information available in the multimodal corpus to a greater extent. For this reason, during the last few years, several tools for analysis of multimodal corpora have been developed which have some of the characteristica described above concerning synchronization between recordings, transcriptions and types of analysis. Some of these are:

ANVIL – http://www.dfki.de/~kipp/anvil/
MULTITOOL – http://www.ling.gu.se/projekt/tal/multitool
WAVESURFER – http://www.speech.kth.se/wavesurfer
NITE/MATE – http://nite.nis.sdu.dk/ and http://mate.nis.sdu.dk/

All systems have their strong points and their weak points and no system exists yet that has all desirable qualities. Most of the systems run better on PCs than on Mac computers.

A second general consideration concerns whether the analysis should be done manually or automatically. If done automatically, it could, for example, be based on pattern recognition, sequential Markov models or be rule-based. It could also possibly involve machine learning techniques. We should note that there is no absolute distinction between computer-based automatic analysis and computer-based manual analysis. Rather, there are many forms of partially manual and partially automatic analysis. Thus, we may speak of Computer Aided Manual Analysis (CAMA) and Manually Aided Computer Analysis (MACA).

A third relevant issue concerns whether our analysis should aim for representativity or not. Obviously a multimodal corpus can be used as a basis for one or more case studies and since analysis of multimodal data is often very time-consuming and therefore costly, in the past recorded multimodal material has often primarily resulted in case studies. This is completely acceptable and often what is needed in the initial stages of development of a field of inquiry. However, it might also be said that it does not fully exploit the potential which exists in a corpus. This potential is mostly made more full use of by a series of case studies or by a more frequency and statistics-based analysis of patterns in the data than by a single case study.

3.7. What can we analyze?

Finally, we come to the question of what we can analyze in a multimodal corpus. Obviously, this question has no definite answer, since the limits are set by the creativity and insight of the researchers who are doing the analysis. All we can do is point to some examples where multimodal corpora have been used or could be used. The examples will be grouped in three areas, (i) human-human face-to-face communication, (ii) media of communication, and finally in section 4, applications.

(i) Human-human face-to-face communication

In many ways this area is the basic area of investigation for multimodal communication. The following are some of the topics that can be investigated in the area. The list is in no way exhaustive.

(i) The nature of communicative gestures. Work has been done on basic taxonomies of both the content/function of gestures and the particular types of expressive behaviour which is employed; cf. Ekman/Friesen (1969), Hjortsjö (1969) or Peirce (1955) for a more general semiotic classification of gestures.

(ii) The nature of multimodal communication with a particular communicative function like feedback (cf. Allwood/Cerrato 2003), own communication management (Allwood/Nivre/Ahlsén 1990) or symbolic gestures (Poggi 2002) hesitation: word finding.

(iii) The relations between gestures of different types, resulting for example in questions like: to what extent are feedback gestures symbolic and to what extent are they iconic or indexical? Symbolic feedback gestures here usually involve head movements for *yes* and *no* that can vary from one cultural and linguistic area to another. There are two main variants for *yes* (i) nodding (most European influenced cultures) and (ii) sideways movement of the head back and forth (India). Similarly, there are two main variants for *no* (i) shaking (most European influenced cultures) and (ii) backwards head jerk (the Balkan area, Turkey and the Middle East). There is also iconic feedback, as when one communicator repeats or imitates the movements of another in order to indicate (or display) consensual coordination or agreement. Finally, there is indexical feedback which can be given, for example, by facial gestures, indicating or displaying emotions and attitudes.

A more specific inquiry might here concern when and where in relation to the interlocutor's communication, the different kinds of feedback are used, e. g. when do communicators indicate friendliness by a smile and when do they signal it symbolically by a phrase like *I am so happy to see you*? When are both means used to support each other and when is only one means sufficient?

(iv) The issues raised in (iii) fairly directly lead to the more general question of what kind of relations hold between speech and gestures. What information is usually spoken and what information is usually gestured? How do the two types of information influence each other? How is information distributed between these two modes of production and how is it integrated by us in interpreting other people's contributions to communication. As an extension of this, we can also study the relationship between text and picture in illustrated written text. What information is contributed by text and what information by pictures? How do the modes of representation influence each other (see below)?

Another issue here concerns the temporal relation between spoken utterances and gestures with related content. Is there a fixed temporal order, so that the gestures always come before, after or simultaneously with the related words, or is it possibly the case that the order depends on the circumstances of communication in such a way that there is no fixed order? Psychologists like Goldman-Eisler (1968) and Beattie (2003) have claimed that gestures precede speech, while other psychologists, like McNeill (1979), have claimed that they are simultaneous with speech. The issue is not settled and it is likely that more studies of naturalized multimodal corpora will be helpful in deciding.

(v) Multimodal communication in different social activities. How are speech and gestures used for political rhetoric? Compare, for example, a speech in a TV studio versus in front of a large crowd. How are speech and gestures used in relaxed talk or, for example, in conducting auctions?
(vi) Multimodal communication in different national/ethnic cultures. What multimodal differences exist, for example, between two Swedes, two Chinese and two Italians quarrelling or flirting publicly (cf. Allwood 1985)?
(vii) Communication and consciousness/awareness. To what extent do different components of multimodal communication reveal differences in degrees of awareness/consciousness regarding what we are communicating about (cf. Allwood 2002)?
(viii) Communication and emotion. One of the most important functions of gestures in communication is to express emotion. How is this done by different types of people in different activities, in different national/ethnic cultures?
(ix) Communication and power. How is power expressed multimodally? Is it true that more powerful people (cf. Mehrabian 1972) have larger and more powerful gestures and that less powerful people have smaller and more constrained gestures?
(x) The relation between primarily communicative and primarily non-communicative action. Mostly when communication occurs at the service of a practical activity, there is a mixture of action which is not primarily communicative with action that is primarily communicative, e. g. a shop assistant silently hands a customer a product or some change (money) and the customer bows and says thank you, etc.
(xi) Differences between persons belonging to different genders, age groups, social classes, regional groups are not only constructed and/or expressed through spoken language but are constructed and/or expressed just as much through gestures and clothes.
(xii) How is multimodal integration in general (often also called "fusion") achieved in perception and understanding of communication? How do we integrate visual and auditive information in order to arrive at an integrated audio/visual interpretation of what is being communicated?
(xiii) How is multimodal distribution in general (often also called "fission") achieved in communicative production? What information is expressed through words, through prosody or through gestures?

(ii) Multimodality in relation to various media of communication

There are also a large number of issues pertaining to the use of more than one modality in relation to media of communication other than those used in face-to-face communication.

(i) Multimodality in writing (books, magazines, newspapers, advertising). A lot more work can be done here, but see some interesting studies by Kress/Leeuwen (2001) and Halliday (1978).
(ii) Multimodality in films: in principle, many of the topics suggested above for face-to-face communication can also be studied in films with attention to the extra (aesthetic) dimensions added to capture an audience.
(iii) Multimodality in songs and music. Performance and experience of music are multimodal. What we see and what we hear influence each other. This can clearly be seen in opera and rock videos but to some extent in all music.

(iv) Multimodality in visual art and sculpture. Disciplines like art history are already developing corpora and data bases of paintings. Probably some of the analytical tools developed here could also be used in studies of face-to-face communication.

4. Applications of multimodal communication

Multimodal corpora can provide useful resources in the development of many different computer-based applications, supporting or extending our possibilities to communicate.

(i) Better modes of multimodal human-computer communication (or more generally human-machine communication). See the discussion of embodied conversational agents and avatars above.
(ii) Better computer support for multimodal human-human communication. See the discussion above and the contributions discussed in the AMI project (http://amiproject.org).
(iii) Better modes of multimodal communication for persons who are physically challenged (handicapped).
(iv) Better modes of multimodal presentation of information from databases, for example for information extraction or for summarization.
(v) Better multimodal modes of translation and interpretation. For example, when will we get a system that takes as input a person speaking Italian with Italian gestures and gives as output the same person speaking Japanese with Japanese gestures?
(vi) Better modes of multimodal distance language teaching (including gestures).
(vii) Better modes of multimodal distance teaching (and instruction) in general.
(viii) Better multimodal modes of buying and selling (over the internet, object presentation in shops, etc.).
(ix) Computerized multimodal corpora can, of course, also be useful outside of the areas of computer-based applications. In general, they can provide a basis for the study of any kind of communicative behavior in order to fine-tune and improve this behavior. This could, for example, apply to areas like public oratory or presentation techniques, but also to any kind of service or teaching related communication, like doctor-patient communication, lawyer-client communication, teacher-student etc.

The list can be made much longer and the preceding topics are mostly intended as a pointer to some of the many possibilities.

5. Concluding remarks

This paper has discussed what might be meant by a digitized multimodal corpus and presented some of the factors that might be relevant in establishing multimodal corpora. I have also presented some of the possible research objectives where multimodal corpora could play an instrumental role.

In doing this, I hope to have provided support for the growing realization that if human (linguistic) communication is basically multimodal (which it seems to be from a phylogenetic, ontogenetic and interactive dynamic perspective), then it also requires us to study language and communication multimodally. This, in turn, means that the creation, maintenance and use of multimodal corpora will remain a very important part of the research agenda for studies of language and communication in the future.

6. Literature

Allwood, J. (1985), Intercultural Communication. In: Allwood, J. (ed.), *Tvärkulturell kommunikation.* (Papers in Anthropological Linguistics 12.) Göteborg: Department of Linguistics, Göteborg University. Available at: http://www.ling.gu.se/~jens/publications/docs001-050/041E.pdf

Allwood, J. (2001a), Cooperation and Flexibility in Multimodal Communication. In: Bunt, H./ Beun, R.-J. (eds.), *Lecture Notes in Computer Science* 2155. Berlin/Heidelberg: Springer Verlag, 113–124.

Allwood, J. (2001b), Dialog Coding – Function and Grammar: Göteborg Coding Schemas. In: *Gothenburg Papers in Theoretical Linguistics*, GPTL 85. Dept. of Linguistics, University of Göteborg, 1–67.

Allwood, J. (2002), Bodily Communication – Dimensions of Expression and Content. In: Karlsson, I./House, D./Granström, B. (eds.), *Multimodality in Language and Speech Systems.* Dordrecht: Kluwer Academic Publishers, 7–26.

Allwood, J./Björnberg, M./Grönqvist, L./Ahlsén, E./Ottesjö, C. (2000), The Spoken Language Corpus at the Department of Linguistics, Göteborg University. In: *FQS – Forum Qualitative Social Research* 1(3). Available at: http://www.qualitative-research.net/fqs-texte/3-00/3-00allwoodetal-e.htm.

Allwood, J./Cerrato, L. (2003), A Study of Gestural Feedback Expressions. In: *First Nordic Symposium on Multimodal Communication.* Copenhagen, Denmark, 7–22.

Allwood, J./Cerrato, L./Dybkjaer, L./Jokinen, K./Navaretta, C./Paggio, P. (2005), The MUMIN Multimodal Coding Scheme. In: *NorFa Yearbook 2005*, 129–157.

Allwood, J./Nivre, J./Ahlsén, E. (1990), Speech Management: On the Non-written Life of Speech. In: *Gothenburg Papers in Theoretical Linguistics*, 58. University of Göteborg, Dept. of Linguistics. Also in: *Nordic Journal of Linguistics* 13, 3–48.

Argyle, M. (1988), *Bodily Communication.* London: Methuen.

Beattie, G. (2003), *Visible Thought: The New Psychology of Body Language.* Routledge: London.

Bellugi, U. (1972), Studies in Sign Language. In: O'Rourke, T. J. (ed.), *Psycholinguistics and Total Communication: The State of the Art.* Silver Spring: American Annals of the Deaf, 68–84.

Birdwhistell, R. (1952), *Introduction to Kinesics.* Louisville: University of Louisville Press.

Brazil, D. (1985), *The Communicative Value of Intonation in English.* English Language Research, University of Birmingham.

Brunswick, E. (1969), *The Conceptual Framework of Psychology.* Chicago: University of Chicago Press.

Cassell, J./Sullivan, J./Prevost, S./Churchill, E. (eds.) (2000), *Embodied Conversational Agents.* Cambridge, MA: The MIT Press.

Ekman, P./Friesen, W. (1969), The Repertoire of Nonverbal Behavior: Categories, Origins, Usage and Coding. In: *Semiotica* 1, 49–98.

Goldman-Eisler, F. (1968), *Psycholinguistics: Experiments in Spontaneous Speech.* New York: Academic Press.

Goodwin, C. (1981), *Conversational Organization: Interaction between Speakers and Hearers.* New York: Academic Press.

Gratch, J./Mao, W./Marcella, S. (2006), Modeling Social Emotions and Social Attributions. In: Sun, R. (ed.), *Cognitive Modeling and Multi-agent Interaction*. Cambridge: Cambridge University Press, 219–251.

Halliday, M. A. K. (1978), *Language as Social Semiotic*. London: Edward Arnold.

Hjortsjö, C. H. (1969), *Människans ansikte och mimiska språket*. Malmö: Studentlitteratur.

Jefferson, G. (1984), Transcript Notation. In: Atkinson, J. M./Heritage, J. (eds.), *Structures of Social Action: Studies in Conversation Analysis*. Cambridge: Cambridge University Press.

Kendon, A. (2004), *Gesture: Visible Action as Utterance*. Cambridge: Cambridge University Press.

Kita, S./van Gijn, I./van der Hulst, H. (1998), Movement Phases in Signs and Co-speech Gestures, and their Transcription by Human Coders. In: *Proceedings of Gesture and Sign Language in Human-Computer Interaction, Bielefeld, Germany, September 1997*. Berlin, Heidelberg: Springer Verlag, 23–36.

Kress, G./van Leeuwen, T. (2001), *Multimodal Discourse – the Modes and Media of Contemporary Communication*. New York: Oxford University Press.

Laban, R. (1974), *The Mastery of Movement*. London: Macdonald & Evans.

Lewis, C. T./Short, C., (eds.) (1966), *A Latin Dictionary*. Oxford: Clarendon Press.

Månsson, A.-C. (2003), *The Relation between Gestures and Semantic Processes*. Göteborg: Department of Linguistics, Göteborg University, Sweden.

Martin, J.-C./Pelachaud, C./Abrilian, S./Devillers, L./Lamolle, M./Mancini, M. (2005), Levels of Representation in the Annotation of Emotion for the Specification of Expressivity in ECAs. In: *Proceedings of Intelligent Virtual Agents 2005*. Kos, Greece, 405–417.

McEnery, T./Wilson, A. (2001), *Corpus Linguistics: An Introduction*. Edinburgh: Edinburgh University Press.

McNeill, D. (1979), *The Conceptual Basis of Language*. Hillsdale: Lawrence Erlbaum.

Mehrabian, A. (1972), Nonverbal Communication. In: Cole, J. K. (ed.), *Nebraska Symposium on Motivation, 1971*, vol. 19. Lincoln, NE: University of Nebraska Press, 107–161.

Nelfelt, K. (1998), *Simultaneous Sign and Speech: A Multimodal Perspective on the Communication of Hearing-impaired Children*. Göteborg: Department of Linguistics, Göteborg University.

Nijholt, A./op den Akker, R./Heylen, D. (2006), Meetings and Meeting Modeling in Smart Environments, AI and Society. In: *The Journal of Human-centred Systems* 20(2), 202–220.

Nijholt, A./Rienks, R. J./Zwiers, J./Reidsma, D. (2006), Online and Off-line Visualization of Meeting Information and Meeting Support. In: *The Visual Computer* 22(12). Berlin, Heidelberg: Springer, 965–976.

Nivre, J./Allwood, J./Grönqvist, L./Gunnarsson, M./Ahlsén, E./Vappula, H./Hagman, J./Larsson, S./Sofkova, S./Ottesjö, C. (2004), *Göteborg Transcription Standard v6.4*. Department of Linguistics, Göteborg University.

Peirce, C. S. (1955), *Philosophical Writings of Pierce*. Buchler, J. (ed.). New York: Cover.

Poggi, I. (2002), Symbolic Gestures: The Case of the Italian Gestionary. In: *Gesture* 1, 71–98.

Prillwitz, S./Leven, R./Zienert, H./Hanke, T./Henning, I. (1989), *HamNoSys. Version 2.0; Hamburger Notationssystem für Gebärdensprache. Eine Einführung*. (Internationale Arbeiten zur Gebärdensprache und Kommunikation Gehörloser 6.) Hamburg: Signum.

Stokoe, W. C. (1978), Sign Language versus Spoken Language. In: *Sign Language Studies* 18, 69–90.

Svartvik, J./Quirk, R. (1980), *A Corpus of English Conversation*. Lund: Gleerup.

Zhang, Z./Potamianos, G./Liu, M./Huang, T. S. (2006), Robust Multi-view Multi-camera Face Detection Inside Smart Rooms using Spatio-temporal Dynamic Programming. In: *Proceedings of Int. Conf. Face Gesture Recog. (FG)*. Southampton, United Kingdom, 407–412.

Transcription systems

IPA – International Phonetic Alphabet http://www2.arts.gla.ac.uk/IPA/ipa.html

SAMPA – http://www.phon.ucl.ac.uk/home/**sampa**/home.htm

CA – transcription. Cf. e. g. Jefferson 1984 above.
GTS Göteborg Transcriptions Standard – http://www.ling.gu.se/projekt/tal/index.cgi?PAGE=3 (See Nivre et al. 2004 above)

Tools for multimodal analysis

MULTITOOL
http://www.ling.gu.se/projekt/tal/multitool
ANVIL
http://www.dfki.de/~kipp/anvil/
WAVESURFER
http://www.speech.kth.se/wavesurfer
NITE/MATE
http://nite.nis.sdu.dk/
http://mate.nis.sdu.dk/

Network and project homepages

http://www.amiproject.org (AMI)
http://chil.server.de/servlet/is/101 (CHIL)
http://emotion-research.net (HUMAINE)

All URLs were accessed in January, 2007.

Jens Allwood, Göteborg (Sweden)

13. Treebanks

1. Introduction

A *treebank* can be defined as a linguistically annotated corpus that includes some grammatical analysis beyond the part-of-speech level. The term 'treebank' appears to have been coined by Geoffrey Leech (Sampson 2003) and obviously alludes to the fact that the most common way of representing the grammatical analysis is by means of a tree structure. However, in current usage, the term is in no way restricted to corpora containing tree-shaped representations, but applies to all kinds of grammatically analyzed corpora.

It is customary to restrict the application of the term 'treebank' to corpora where the grammatical analysis is the result of manual annotation or post-editing. This is in contrast to the term 'parsed corpus', which is more often used about automatically analyzed corpora, whether the analysis has been manually corrected or not. This is also the usage that will be adopted here, although it is worth pointing out that the two terms are sometimes used interchangeably in the literature (cf. Abeillé 2003b).

Treebanks have been around in some shape or form at least since the 1970's. One of the earliest efforts to produce a syntactically annotated corpus was performed by Ulf Teleman and colleagues at Lund University, resulting in close to 300,000 words of both written and spoken Swedish, manually annotated with both phrase structure and grammatical functions, an impressive achievement at the time but unfortunately documented only in Swedish (cf. Teleman 1974; Nivre 2002). However, it is only in the last ten to fifteen years that treebanks have appeared on a large scale for a wide range of languages, mostly developed using a combination of automatic processing and manual annotation or post-editing. In this article, we will not attempt to give a comprehensive inventory of available treebanks but focus on theoretical and methodological issues, referring to specific treebanks only to exemplify the points made. A fairly representative overview of available treebanks for a number of languages can be found in Abeillé (2003a), together with a discussion of certain methodological issues. In addition, proceedings from the annual workshops on *Treebanks and Linguistic Theories* (TLT) contain many useful references (Hinrichs/Simov 2002; Nivre/Hinrichs 2003; Kübler et al. 2004). Cf. also article 20 for some of the more well-known and influential treebanks.

The rest of this article is structured as follows. We begin, in section 2, by discussing design issues for treebanks, in particular the choice of annotation scheme. We move on, in section 3, to the development of treebanks, discussing the division of labor between manual and automatic analysis, as well as tools to be used in the development process. In section 4, we briefly discuss the usage of treebanks, focusing on linguistic research and natural language processing. We conclude, in section 5, with a brief outlook on the future.

2. Treebank design

Ideally, the design of a treebank should be motivated by its intended usage, whether linguistic research or language technology development (cf. section 4 below), in the same way that any software design should be informed by a requirements analysis (cf. article 9 on design strategies). However, in actual practice, there are a number of other factors that influence the design, such as the availability of data and analysis tools. Moreover, given that the development of a treebank is a very labor-intensive task, there is usually also a desire to design the treebank in such a way that it can serve several purposes simultaneously. Thus, as observed by Abeillé (2003b), the majority of large treebank projects have emerged as the result of a convergence between computational linguistics and corpus linguistics, with only partly overlapping goals. It is still a matter of ongoing debate to what extent it is possible to cater for different needs without compromising the usefulness for each individual use, and different design choices can to some extent be seen to represent different standpoints in this debate. We will return to this problem in relation to annotation schemes in section 2.2. But first we will consider the choice of corpus material.

2.1. Corpus material

The considerations involved in selecting the data to include in a treebank are essentially the same as for any (annotated) corpus (cf. article 9). Therefore, we will limit the discussion here to a few observations concerning current practice.

One basic design choice is whether to include written or spoken language, or both, in the treebank. For linguistic corpora in general, written language is much more widely represented than spoken language, and this tendency is even stronger with respect to treebanks, partly because theories of syntactic representation have focused more on written language data, which makes the grammatical annotation of spoken language an even more challenging task. Nevertheless, there now exist quite a few treebanks involving spoken language data, especially for English, such as the CHRISTINE Corpus (Sampson 2003), the Switchboard section of the Penn Treebank (Taylor et al. 2003), and the better part of the ICE-GB Corpus (Nelson et al. 2002). In addition, we have the Tübingen Treebanks of spoken German, English and Japanese (Hinrichs et al. 2000), and the Spoken Dutch Corpus (CGN) (Wouden et al. 2002). It can be expected that the number of spoken language treebanks will increase considerably in the future.

Another basic consideration that any corpus project has to face is whether to construct a balanced sample of different text genres (whether written or spoken) or to concentrate on a specific text type or domain. Historically speaking, treebanks have often been based on previously established corpora, which means that they inherit the design choices of the original corpus. Thus, the SUSANNE Corpus (Sampson 1995) is based on a subset of the Brown Corpus of American English (Kučera/Francis 1967), which is a typical balanced corpus. By and large, however, the majority of available treebanks for written language are based on contemporary newspaper text, which has the practical advantage of being relatively easily accessible. An important case in point is the Wall Street Journal section of the Penn Treebank (Marcus et al. 1993), which has been very influential as a model for treebanks across a wide range of languages.

Although most treebanks developed so far have been based on more or less contemporary data from a single language, there are also exceptions to this pattern. On the one hand, there are historical treebanks, based on data from earlier periods of a language under development, such as the Penn-Helsinki Parsed Corpus of Middle English (Kroch/Taylor 2000) and the Partially Parsed Corpus of Medieval Portuguese (Rocio et al. 2003). On the other hand, there are parallel treebanks based on texts in one language and their translations in other languages. The Prague Czech-English Dependency Treebank has been developed for the specific purpose of machine translation at Charles University in Prague (Čmejrek et al. 2004), and several other projects are emerging in this area (cf. Cyrus et al. 2003; Volk/Samuelsson 2004).

Finally, we have to consider the issue of corpus size. Despite recent advances in automating the annotation process, linguistic annotation is still a very labor-intensive activity. Consequently, there is an inevitable tradeoff in corpus design between the amount of data that can be included and the amount of annotation that can be applied to the data. Depending on the intended usage, it may be preferable to build a smaller treebank with a more detailed annotation, such as the SUSANNE corpus (Sampson 1995), or a larger treebank with a less detailed annotation, such as the original bracketed version of the Penn Treebank (Marcus et al. 1993). Because the annotation of grammatical structure is even more expensive than annotation at lower levels, treebanks in general tend to be one or two orders of magnitude smaller than corresponding corpora without syntactic annotation. Thus, whereas an ordinary corpus of one million running words is not considered very big today, there are only a few treebanks that reach this size, and most of them are considerably smaller.

2.2. Annotation scheme

When discussing the annotation format for a treebank, there are at least two different levels that need to be distinguished. On the one hand, we have the level of linguistic analysis, with certain assumptions about the nature of syntactic structure, a specific choice of linguistic categories, and guidelines for the annotation of particular linguistic phenomena. This level, which is what is normally referred to as an *annotation scheme*, is the level that concerns us in this section (although the discussion of guidelines will be postponed until section 3.1.). On the other hand, we have the level of formal representation, or *encoding*, which is where we decide whether the annotation should be represented using a special markup language or ordinary text, whether it should be stored in one file or several files, etc. The encoding of syntactic annotation will be discussed briefly in section 3.2., and for the time being we will assume that annotation schemes are independent of encoding schemes, although this is strictly speaking not true. (For a general discussion of annotation schemes and standards, cf article 22.)

Most treebank annotation schemes are organized into a number of layers, where the lower layers contain word-level annotations, such as part-of-speech, often supplemented with morpho-syntactic features, lemmatization or morphological analysis. Figure 13.1 shows a representative example taken from the SUSANNE Corpus (Sampson 1995), where each token is represented by one line, with part-of-speech (including morpho-syntactic features) in the first column, the actual token in the second column, and the lemma in the third column.

In the following, we will not discuss word-level annotation but concentrate on the annotation of syntactic (and to some extent semantic) structure, since this is what distinguishes treebanks from other annotated corpora. Moreover, word-level annotation tends to be rather similar across different treebank annotation schemes.

The choice of annotation scheme for a large-scale treebank is influenced by many different factors. One of the most central considerations is the relation to linguistic theory. Should the annotation scheme be theory-specific or theory-neutral? If the first of these options is chosen, which theoretical framework should be adopted? If we opt for the second, how do we achieve broad consensus, given that truly theory-neutral annotation is impossible? The answers to these questions interact with other factors, in particular the grammatical characteristics of the language that is being analyzed, and the tradition of descriptive grammar that exists for this language. In addition, the relation to annotation schemes used for other languages is relevant, from the point of view of comparative studies or development of parallel treebanks. To this we may add the preferences of different potential user groups, ranging from linguistic researchers and language technology developers to language teachers and students at various levels of education. Finally, when embarking on a large-scale treebank project, researchers usually cannot afford to disregard the resources and tools for automatic and interactive annotation that exist for different candidate annotation schemes.

AT	The	the
JJ	grand	grand
NN1c	jury	jury
VVDv	took	take
AT1	a	a
NN1c	swipe	swipe
II	at	at
AT	the	the
NNL1n	State	state
NN1u	Welfare	welfare
NNJ1c	Department	department
GG	+<apos>s	–
VVGt	handling	handle
IO	of	of
JJ	federal	federal
NN2	funds	fund
YG	–	–
VVNt	granted	grant
IF	for	for
NN1c	child	child
NN1u	welfare	welfare
NN2	services	service
II	in	in
VV0t	foster	foster
NN2	homes	home
YF	+.	–

Fig. 13.1: Word-level in the SUSANNE Corpus

The number of treebanks available for different languages is growing steadily and with them the number of different annotation schemes. Broadly speaking we can distinguish three main kinds of annotation in current practice:

- Constituency annotation
- Functional annotation
- Semantic annotation

In addition, we can distinguish between (more or less) theory-neutral and theory-specific annotation schemes, a dimension that cuts across the three types of annotation. It should also be noted that the annotation found in many if not most of the existing treebanks actually combines two or even all three of these categories. We will treat the categories in the order in which they are listed above, which also roughly corresponds to the historical development of treebank annotation schemes.

The annotation of constituent structure, often referred to as bracketing, is the main kind of annotation found in early large-scale projects such as the Lancaster Parsed Corpus (Garside et al. 1992) and the original Penn Treebank (Marcus et al. 1993). Normally, this kind of annotation consists of part-of-speech tagging for individual word tokens and annotation of major phrase structure categories such as NP, VP, etc. Figure 13.2

```
[N Vous_PPSA5MS N]
[V accedez_VINIP5
   [P a_PREPA
      [N cette_DDEMFS session_NCOFS N]
   P]
   [Pv a_PREP31 partir_PREP32 de_PREP33
      [N la_DARDFS fenetre_NCOFS
         [A Gestionnaire_AJQFS
            [P de_PREPD
               [N taches_NCOFP
               N]
            P]
         A]
      N]
   Pv]
V]
```

Fig. 13.2: Constituency annotation in the IBM Paris Treebank

shows a representative example, taken from the IBM Paris Treebank using a variant of the Lancaster annotation scheme.

Annotation schemes of this kind are usually intended to be theory-neutral and therefore try to use mostly uncontroversial categories that are recognized in all or most syntactic theories that assume some notion of constituent structure. Moreover, the structures produced tend to be rather flat, since intermediate phrase level categories are usually avoided. The drawback of this is that the number of distinct expansions of the same phrase category can become very high. For example, Charniak (1996) was able to extract 10,605 distinct context-free rules from a 300,000 word sample of the Penn Treebank. Of these, only 3943 occurred more than once in the sample.

A variation on the basic constituency analysis is to annotate syntactic chunks (Abney 1991) rather than a complete phrase structure tree. This kind of annotation is found in the French treebanks described in Abeillé et al. (2003) and Vilnat et al. (2003), respectively. As a further variation, the Tübingen Treebanks of German introduces a layer of topological fields on top of the basic constituent structure (Hinrichs et al. 2000).

The status of grammatical functions and their relation to constituent structure has long been a controversial issue in linguistic theory. Thus, whereas the standard view in transformational syntax and related theories since Chomsky (1965) has been that grammatical functions are derivable from constituent structure, proponents of dependency syntax such as Mel'čuk (1988) have argued that functional structure is more fundamental than constituent structure. Other theories, such as Lexical-Functional Grammar, steer a middle course by assuming both notions as primitive. When it comes to treebank annotation, the annotation of functional structure has become increasingly important in recent years. The most radical examples are the annotation schemes based on dependency syntax, exemplified by the Prague Dependency Treebank of Czech (Hajič 1998; Böhmová et al. 2003), where the annotation of dependency structure is added

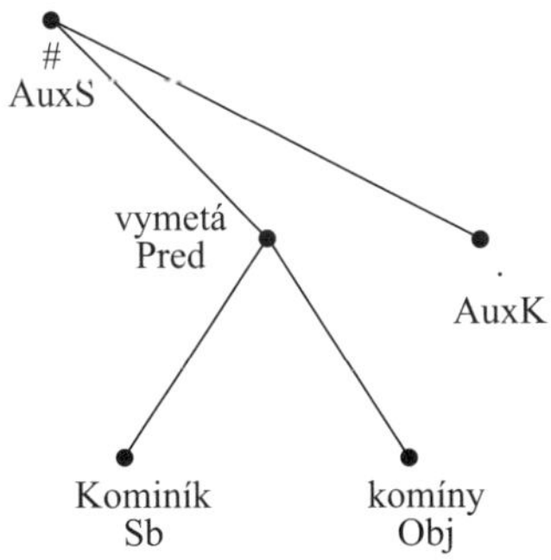

Kominík	vymetá	komíny	.
Chimney-sweep	sweeps	chimney	.

Fig. 13.3: Functional annotation in the Prague Dependency Treebank

directly on top of the morphological annotation without any layer of constituent structure, as illustrated in Figure 13.3.

Other examples of treebanks based primarily on dependency analysis is the METU Treebank of Turkish (Oflazer et al. 2003), the Danish Dependency Treebank (Kromann 2003), the Eus3LB Corpus of Basque (Aduriz et al. 2003), the Turin University Treebank of Italian (Bosco/Lombardo 2004), and the parsed corpus of Japanese described in Kurohashi/Nagao (2003).

The trend towards more functionally oriented annotation schemes is also reflected in the extension of constituency-based schemes with annotation of grammatical functions. Cases in point are SUSANNE (Sampson 1995), which is a development of the Lancaster annotation scheme mentioned above, and Penn Treebank II (Marcus et al. 1994), which adds functional tags to the original phrase structure annotation. A combination of constituent structure and grammatical functions along these lines is currently the dominant paradigm in treebank annotation and exists in many different variations. Adapted versions of the Penn Treebank II scheme are found in the Penn Chinese Treebank (Xue et al. 2004), in the Penn Korean Treebank (Han et al. 2002) and in the Penn Arabic Treebank (Maamouri/Bies 2004), as well as in a treebank of Spanish (Moreno et al. 2003). A similar combination of constituency and grammatical functions is also used in the ICE-GB Corpus of British English (Nelson et al. 2002).

A different way of combining constituency and functional annotation is represented by the TIGER annotation scheme for German (Brants et al. 2002), developed from the earlier NEGRA scheme, which integrates the annotation of constituency and dependency in a graph where node labels represent phrasal categories while edge labels represent syntactic functions, and which allows crossing branches in order to model discontinuous constituents. Another scheme that combines constituent structure with functional annotation while allowing discontinuous constituents is the VISL (Visual Interactive Syntax Learning) scheme, originally developed for pedagogical purposes and applied to 22 languages on a small scale, subsequently used in developing larger treebanks in Portuguese (Afonso et al. 2002) and Danish (Bick 2003). Yet another variation is found in the Italian Syntactic-Semantic Treebank (Montemagni et al. 2003), which employs two independent layers of annotation, one for constituent structure, one for dependency structure.

From functional annotation, it is only a small step to a shallow semantic analysis, such as the annotation of predicate-argument structure found in the Proposition Bank (Kingsbury/Palmer 2003). The Proposition Bank is based on the Penn Treebank and adds a layer of annotation where predicates and their arguments are analyzed in terms of a frame-based lexicon. The Prague Dependency Treebank, in addition to the surface-oriented dependency structure exemplified in Figure 13.3, also provides a layer of tecto-grammatical analysis involving case roles, which can be described as a semantically oriented deep syntactic analysis (cf. Hajičová 1998). The Turin University Treebank also adds annotation of semantic roles to the dependency-based annotation of grammatical functions (Bosco/Lombardo 2004), and the Sinica treebank of Chinese uses a combination of constituent structure and functional annotation involving semantic roles (Chen et al. 2003).

Other examples of semantic annotation are the annotation of word senses in the Italian Syntactic-Semantic Treebank (Montemagni et al. 2003) and in the Hellenic National Treebank of Greek (Stamou et al. 2003). Discourse semantic phenomena are annotated in the RST Discourse Treebank (Carlson et al. 2002), the German TIGER Treebank (Kunz/Hansen-Schirra 2003), and the Penn Discourse Treebank (Miltsakaki et al. 2004). Despite these examples, semantic annotation has so far played a rather marginal role in the development of treebanks, but it can be expected to become much more important in the future.

Regardless of whether the annotation concerns constituent structure, functional structure or semantic structure, there is a growing interest in annotation schemes that adhere to a specific linguistic theory and use representations from that theory to annotate sentences. Thus, Head-Driven Phrase Structure Grammar (HPSG) has been used as the basis for treebanks of English (Oepen et al. 2002) and Bulgarian (Simov et al. 2002), and the Prague Dependency Treebank is based on the theory of Functional Generative Description (Sgall et al. 1986). CCG-bank is a version of the Penn Treebank annotated within the framework of Combinatory Categorial Grammar (Hockenmaier/Steedman 2002), and there has also been work done on automatic f-structure annotation in the theoretical framework of Lexical-Functional Grammar (see, e. g., Cahill et al. 2002).

Whereas theory-neutral annotation caters for a larger group of users, it runs the risk of not being informative enough or containing too many compromises to be useful for special applications. On the other hand, theory-specific treebanks are clearly more useful for people working within the selected theoretical framework but naturally have a more restricted user group. Recently, there have been attempts at combining the best of both worlds and maximize overall utility in the research community through the use of rich annotation schemes with well-defined conversions to more specific schemes (Nivre 2003; Sasaki et al. 2003). In addition to minimizing the effort required to produce a set of theory-specific treebanks based on the same language data, such a scheme has the advantage of allowing systematic comparisons between different frameworks.

The discussion throughout this section has been focused on the annotation of written language data, as exemplified in the majority of available treebanks across the world. The annotation of spoken language data poses special difficulties that call for an extension of existing annotation schemes. One example is the annotation of so-called disfluencies, which is included in the Switchboard section of the Penn Treebank (cf. Taylor et al. 2003). But more generally, it remains an open question to what extent the annotation schemes developed for written language are adequate for the annotation of spoken language, where interactively defined notions such as turns or dialogue acts may be more central than the syntactic notion of sentence inherited from traditional syntactic theory. Nevertheless, the currently available treebanks of spoken language are all annotated using relatively minor adaptations of schemes originally developed for written language.

3. Treebank development

The methods and tools for treebank development have evolved considerably from the very first treebank projects, where all annotation was done manually, to the present-day situation, which is characterized by a more or less elaborate combination of manual work and automatic processing, supported by emerging standards and customized software tools. In section 3.1., we will discuss basic methodological issues in treebank development, including the division of labor between manual work and automatic processing. In section 3.2., we will then give a brief overview of available tools and standards in the area. We will focus on the process of syntactic annotation, since this is what distinguishes treebank development from corpus development in general.

3.1. Methodology

One of the most important considerations in the annotation of a treebank is to ensure consistency, i. e. to ensure that the same (or similar) linguistic phenomena are annotated in the same (or similar) ways throughout the corpus, since this is a critical requirement in many applications of treebanks, be it frequency-based linguistic studies, parser evaluation or induction of grammars (cf. section 4 below). This in turn requires explicit and well-documented annotation guidelines, which can be used in the training of human annotators, but which can also serve as a source of information for future users of the treebank. Besides documenting the general principles of annotation, including the annotation scheme as described in section 2.2., the guidelines need to contain detailed examples of linguistic phenomena and their correct annotation. Among linguistic phenomena that are problematic for any annotation scheme, we can mention coordination structures, discontinuous constituents, and different kinds of multi-word expressions. The need to have a rich inventory of examples means that the annotation guidelines for a large treebank project will usually amount to several hundred pages (cf. Sampson 2003).

Another important methodological issue in treebank development is the division of labor between automatic annotation performed by computational analyzers and human annotation or post-editing. Human annotation was the only feasible solution in early treebank projects, such as Teleman (1974) and Järborg (1986) for Swedish, but has the drawback of being labor-intensive and therefore expensive for large volumes of data. In addition, there is the problem of ensuring consistency across annotators if several people are involved. Fully automatic annotation has the advantage of being both inexpensive and consistent but currently cannot be used without introducing a considerable proportion of errors, which typically increases with the complexity of the annotation scheme.

Hence, fully automatic annotation is the preferred choice only when the amount of data to be annotated makes manual annotation or post-editing prohibitively expensive, as in the 200 million word corpus of the Bank of English (Järvinen 2003). In addition, fully automatic analysis of a larger section of the treebank can be combined with manual post-correction for smaller sections, as in the Danish Arboretum, which contains a "botanical garden" of a few hundred thousand words completely corrected, a "forest" of one million words partially corrected, and a "jungle" of nine million words with automatic analysis only (Bick 2003).

Given the complementary advantages and drawbacks of human and automated annotation, most treebank projects today use a combination of automatic analysis and manual work in order to make the process as efficient as possible while maintaining the highest possible accuracy. The traditional way of combining automated and manual processing is to perform syntactic parsing (complete or partial) followed by human post-editing to correct errors in the parser output. This methodology was used, for example, in the development of the Penn Treebank (Taylor et al. 2003) and the Prague Dependency Treebank (Böhmová et al. 2003). One variation on this theme is to use human disambiguation instead of human post-correction, i. e. to let the human annotator choose the correct analysis from a set of possible analyses produced by a nondeterministic parser. This approach is used in the TreeBanker (Carter 1997) and in the development of the LinGO Redwood Treebanks (Oepen et al. 2002).

Regardless of the exact implementation of this methodology, human post-editing or parse selection runs the risk of biasing the annotation towards the output of the automatic analyzer, since human editors have a tendency of accepting the proposed analysis even in doubtful cases. The desire to reduce this risk was one of the motivating factors behind the methodology for interactive corpus annotation developed by Thorsten Brants and colleagues in the German NEGRA project (Brants et al. 2003), which uses a cascade of data-driven computational analyzers and gives the human annotator the opportunity to correct the output of one analyzer before it is fed as input to the next (Brants/Plaehn 2000). Data-driven analyzers also have an advantage in that they can be used to bootstrap the process, since their performance will steadily improve as the size of the treebank grows.

Another issue to consider is the order in which data are fed to human annotators for post-correction. Wallis (2003) argues that transverse correction, i. e. checking all instances of a particular construction together, can improve the consistency of the annotation, as compared to traditional longitudinal correction (sentence-by-sentence). On the other hand, transverse correction is harder to implement and manage. A related issue is the order in which different layers of a multi-layered annotation scheme should be processed and whether different layers should be annotated together or separately. In many cases, there are dependencies between layers that dictate a particular order, but it may also be possible to annotate layers in parallel (cf. Taylor et al. 2003). Whether the work is done in sequence or in parallel, it is usually considered best to let each annotator work with a single layer at a time.

Finally, it is worth mentioning that consistency in treebank annotation can be improved by letting several people annotate or correct the same sentences and compare their work. However, this procedure is very expensive and can therefore normally be used only for a small subpart of the treebank, often with the specific purpose of investigating inter-annotator agreement. A less expensive method is to use automated analysis to detect potential errors or inconsistencies in the annotation, as proposed by Dickinson/Meurers (2003) and Ule/Simov (2004), among others.

3.2. Tools and standards

Many of the software tools that are used in treebank development are tools that are needed in the development of any annotated corpus, such as tokenizers and part-of-speech taggers (cf. article 24). Tools that are specific to treebank development are primarily tools for syntactic preprocessing (cf. article 28) and specialized annotation tools.

Well-known examples of syntactic parsers used in treebank development are the deterministic Fidditch parser (Hindle 1994), used in the development of the Penn Treebank, and the statistical parser of Collins et al. (1999), used for the Prague Dependency Treebank. It is also common to use partial parsers (or chunkers) for syntactic preprocessing, since partial parsing can be performed with higher accuracy than full parsing.

Breaking down the parsing process into several steps has the advantage that it allows human intervention between each step, as discussed in connection with interactive corpus annotation above. This is one of the motivations behind the Annotate tool (Brants/Plaehn 2000), which is a tool for interactive corpus annotation incorporating a cascade of data-driven analyzers for tagging and chunking. Another annotation tool developed especially for treebank annotation is the graphical editor TrEd, developed in the Prague Dependency Treebank project, but it is also quite common to use more or less sophisticated extensions to existing editors such as Emacs (cf. Taylor et al. 2003; Abeillé et al. 2003).

As a general assessment of the state of the art in treebank development, it seems fair to say that there is a lack of standardized tools and that most projects tend to develop their own tools suited to their own needs. To some extent this can be explained by the fact that different projects use different annotation schemes, motivated by properties of the particular language analyzed and the purpose of the annotation, and that not all tools are compatible with all annotation schemes (or software platforms). However, it probably also reflects the lack of maturity of the field and the absence of a widely accepted standard for the encoding of treebank annotation. While there have been several initiatives to standardize corpus encoding in general (cf. article 22), these recommendations have either not extended to the level of syntactic annotation or have not gained widespread acceptance in the field. Instead, there exist several *de facto* standards set by the most influential treebank projects, in particular the Penn Treebank, but also the Prague Dependency Treebank for dependency representations. Another popular encoding standard is TIGER-XML (König/Lezius 2003), originally developed within the German TIGER project, which can be used as a general interchange format although it imposes certain restrictions on the form of the annotation.

As observed by Ide/Romary (2003), there is a widely recognized need for a general framework that can accommodate different annotation schemes and facilitate the sharing of resources as well as the development of reusable tools. It is part of the objective of the ISO/TC 37/SC 4 Committee on Language Resource Management to develop such a framework, building on the model presented in Ide/Romary (2003), but at the time of writing there is no definite proposal available.

4. Treebank usage

Empirical linguistic research provided most of the early motivation for developing treebanks, and linguistic research continues to be one of the most important usage areas for parsed corpora. We discuss linguistic research in section 4.1. below. In recent years, however, the use of treebanks in natural language processing, including research as well as technical development, has increased dramatically and has become the primary driving force behind the development of new treebanks. This usage is the topic of section 4.2. (cf. also article 35).

The use of treebanks is not limited to linguistic research and natural language processing, although these have so far been the dominant areas. In particular, there is a great potential for pedagogical uses of treebanks, both in language teaching and in the teaching of linguistic theory. A good example is the Visual Interactive Syntax Learning (VISL) project at the University of Southern Denmark, which has developed teaching treebanks for 22 languages with a number of different teaching tools including interactive games such as Syntris, based on the well-known computer game Tetris (see http://visl.edu.dk).

4.1. Linguistic research

Treebanks are in principle a useful resource for any kind of corpus-based linguistic research that is related to syntax. This includes not only syntactic research in a narrow sense but research on any linguistic phenomenon that is dependent on syntactic properties. One of the main advantages of using a treebank, rather than an ordinary corpus, is that it enables more precise queries and thereby reduces the noise in the answer set. To take one concrete example, in a recent corpus-based study of English quantifiers, the use of *all* as a so-called floating quantifier (*they all laughed*) had to be excluded from the study, simply because there was no way of constructing the query precisely enough to extract the relevant examples from the much more numerous examples of other uses of *all* (Estling 2004). Given a properly annotated treebank, this methodological problem should not arise. However, it is important to remember that an efficient use of treebanks in corpus-based research requires adequate tools for searching and browsing treebanks. We refer to article 34 for a discussion of this topic.

Treebank data, like other corpus data, can be used in a variety of ways in linguistic research. Some of them are qualitative, such as finding an authentic example of a certain linguistic construction, or a counter-example to an empirical claim about syntactic structure, but arguably the most important uses of treebank data are found in quantitative studies of different kinds, where treebanks provide an invaluable source of information about frequencies, cooccurences, etc. For a long time, frequency information has by a majority of linguists been considered as complementary to, but not directly relevant for, theoretical accounts of linguistic structure. However, this is a position that is increasingly called into question, and there are now a number of proposals that incorporate frequency, or probability, into the theoretical description of linguistic categories and rules (see, e. g., Bod et al. 2003). Since corpus-based syntactic research and its relation to syntactic theory is treated in depth in other articles, in particular articles 42 and 43, we will not pursue these issues further here.

4.2. Natural language processing

Broadly speaking, we can distinguish two main uses of treebanks in natural language processing. The first is the use of treebank data in the evaluation of natural language processing systems, in particular syntactic parsers. The second is the induction of linguistic resources from treebanks, especially the use of machine learning to develop or optimize linguistic analysers (cf. article 39).

Empirical evaluation of systems and components for natural language processing is currently a very active field. With respect to syntactic parsing there are essentially two types of data that are used for evaluation. On the one hand, we have so-called test suites, i. e. collections of sentences that are compiled in order to cover a particular range of syntactic phenomena without consideration of their frequency of occurrence (cf. Lehmann et al. 1996). On the other hand, we have treebank samples, which are extracted to be representative with respect to the frequency of different phenomena. Both types of data are clearly relevant for the evaluation of syntactic parsers, but it is also clear that the resulting evaluation will focus on different properties. Test suite evaluation measures the coverage of a syntactic parser in terms of the number of constructions that it can handle, without considering the relative frequency of these constructions. Treebank evaluation, on the other hand, measures the average performance that we can expect from the parser when applied to naturally distributed data from the same source as the evaluation corpus.

An important methodological issue in treebank evaluation is the way in which performance of a parser is measured relative to a manually annotated treebank sample (a so-called *gold standard*). An obvious metric to use is the proportion of sentences where the parser output completely matches the gold standard annotation (the *exact match* criterion). However, it can be argued that this is a relatively crude evaluation metric, since an error in the analysis of a single word or constituent will have the same impact on the result as the failure to produce any analysis whatsoever. Consequently, the most widely used evaluation metrics measure various kinds of partial correspondence between the parser output and the gold standard parse.

The most well-known evaluation metrics are the PARSEVAL measures (Black et al. 1991), which are based on the number of matching constituents between the parser output and the gold standard, and which have been widely used in parser evaluation using data from the Penn Treebank. As an alternative to the constituency-based PARSEVAL measures, several researchers have proposed evaluation schemes based on dependency relations and argued that these provide a better way of comparing parsers that use different representations (Lin 1998; Carroll et al. 1998).

A very successful use of treebanks during the last decade has been the induction of probabilistic grammars for parsing, with lexicalised probabilistic models like those of Collins (1999) and Charniak (2000) representing the current state of the art. An even more radical approach is Data-Oriented Parsing (Bod 1998), which eliminates the traditional notion of grammar completely and uses a probabilistic model defined directly on the treebank. But there has also been great progress in broad-coverage parsing using so-called deep grammars, where treebanks are mainly used to induce statistical models for parse selection (see, e. g., Riezler et al. 2002; Toutanova et al. 2002). In fact, one of the most significant results in research on syntactic parsing during the last decade is arguably the conclusion that treebanks are indispensable in order to achieve robust broad-coverage parsing, regardless of which basic parsing methodology is assumed.

Besides using treebanks to induce grammars or optimize syntactic parsers, it is possible to induce other linguistic resources that are relevant for natural language processing. One important example is the extraction of subcategorization frames (cf. Briscoe/Carroll 1997). Cf. also articles 35 and 39.

5. Conclusion

Treebanks have already been established as a very valuable resource both in linguistic research and in natural language processing. In the future, we can expect their usefulness to increase even more, with improved methods for treebank development and usage, with more advanced tools built on universal standards, and with new kinds of annotation being added. Treebanks with semantic-pragmatic annotation have only begun to emerge and will play an important role in the development of natural language understanding. Parallel treebanks, which hardly exist at the moment, will provide an invaluable resource for research on translation as well as the development of better methods for machine translation. Spoken language treebanks, although already in existence, will be developed further to increase our understanding of the structure of spoken discourse and lead to enhanced methods in speech technology.

6. Literature

Abeillé, A. (ed.) (2003a), *Treebanks: Building and Using Parsed Corpora*. Dordrecht: Kluwer.

Abeillé, A. (2003b), Introduction. In: Abeillé 2003a, xiii–xxvi.

Abeillé, A./Clément, L./Toussenel, F. (2003), Building a Treebank for French. In: Abeillé 2003a, 165–187.

Abney, S. (1991), Parsing by Chunks. In: Berwick, R./Abney, S./Tenny, C. (eds.), *Corpus-based Methods in Language and Speech*. Dordrecht: Kluwer, 257–278.

Aduriz, I./Aranzabe, M. J./Arriola, J. M./Atutxa, A./Díaz de Ilarraza, A./Garmendia, A./Oronoz, M. (2003), Construction of a Basque Dependency Treebank. In: Nivre/Hinrichs 2003, 201–204.

Afonso, S./Bick, E./Haber, R./Santos, D. (2002), Floresta Sintá(c)tica, a Treebank for Portuguese. In: *Proceedings of the Third International Conference on Language Resources and Evaluation*. Las Palmas, Spain, 1698–1703.

Bick, E. (2003), Arboretum, a Hybrid Treebank for Danish. In: Nivre/Hinrichs 2003, 9–20.

Black, E./Abney, S./Flickinger, D./Gdaniec, C./Grishman, R./Harrison, P./Hindle, D./Ingria, R./Jelinek, F./Klavans, J./Liberman, M./Marcus, M./Roukos, S./Santorini, B./Strzalkowski, T. (1991), A Procedure for Quantitatively Comparing the Syntactic Coverage of English Grammars. In: *Proceedings of the DARPA Speech and Natural Language Workshop*. Pacific Grove, CA, 306–311.

Bod, R. (1998), *Beyond Grammar*. Stanford, CA: CSLI Publications.

Böhmová, A./Hajič, J./Hajičová, E./Hladká, B. (2003), The Prague Dependency Treebank: A Three-level Annotation Scenario. In: Abeillé 2003a, 103–127.

Bosco, C./Lombardo, V. (2004), Dependency and Relational Structure in Treebank Annotation. In: *Proceedings of the Workshop Recent Advances in Dependency Grammar*. Geneva, Switzerland, 9–16.

Brants, T./Plaehn, O. (2000), Interactive Corpus Annotation. In: *Proceedings of the Second International Conference on Language Resources and Evaluation*. Athens, Greece, 453–459.

Brants, S./Dipper, S./Hansen, S./Lezius, W./Smith, G. (2002), The TIGER Treebank. In: Hinrichs/Simov 2002, 24–42.

Brants, T./Skut, W./Uszkoreit, H. (2003), Syntactic Annotation of a German Newspaper Corpus. In: Abeillé 2003a, 73–87.

Briscoe, E./Carroll, J. (1997), Automatic Extraction of Subcategorization from Corpora. In: *Proceedings of the Fifth Conference on Applied Natural Language Processing*. Washington, DC, 356–363.

Cahill, A./McCarthy, M./Van Genabith, J./Way, A. (2002), Evaluating F-structure Annotation for the Penn-II Treebank. In: Hinrichs/Simov 2002, 43–60.

Carlson, L./Marcu, D./Okurowski, M. E. (2002), *RST Discourse Treebank*. Philadelphia, PA: Linguistic Data Consortium.

Carroll, J./Briscoe, E./Sanfilippo, A. (1998), Parser Evaluation: A Survey and a New Proposal. In: *Proceedings of the First International Conference on Language Resources and Evaluation (LREC)*. Granada, Spain, 447–454.

Carter, D. (1997), The TreeBanker: A Tool for Supervised Training of Parsed Corpora. In: *Proceedings of the ACL Workshop on Computational Environments for Grammar Development and Linguistic Engineering*. Madrid, Spain, 9–15.

Charniak, E. (1996), Tree-bank Grammars. In: *Proceedings of the Thirteenth National Conference on Artificial Intelligence (AAAI '96)*. Portland, OR, 1031–1036.

Charniak, E. (2000), A Maximum-Entropy-Inspired Parser. In: *Proceedings of the First Conference of the North American Chapter of the Association for Computational Linguistics*. Seattle, WA, 132–139.

Chen, K./Luo, C./Chang, M./Chen, F./Chen, C./Huang, C./Gao, Z. (2003), Sinica Treebank. In: Abeillé 2003a, 231–248.

Chomsky, N. (1965), *Aspects of the Theory of Syntax*. Cambridge, MA: MIT Press.

Čmejrek, M./Cuřín, J./Havelka, J./Hajič, J./Kuboň, V. (2004), Prague Czech-English Dependency Treebank: Syntactically Annotated Resources for Machine Translation. In: *Proceedings of the IV International Conference on Language Resources and Evaluation*. Lisbon, Portugal, 1597–1600.

Collins, M. (1999), Head-driven Statistical Models for Natural Language Parsing. PhD Thesis, University of Pennsylvania.

Collins, M./Hajič, J./Brill, E./Ramshaw, L./Tillmann, C. (1999), A Statistical Parser of Czech. In: *Proceedings of the 37th Annual Meeting of the Association for Computational Linguistics*, 505–512.

Cyrus, L./Feddes, H./Schumacher, F. (2003), FuSe – A Multi-layered Parallel Treebank. In: Nivre/Hinrichs 2003, 213–216.

Dickinson, M./Meurers, W. D. (2003), Detecting Inconsistencies in Treebanks. In: Nivre/Hinrichs 2003, 45–56.

Estling, M. (2004), *Syntactic Variation in English Quantified Noun Phrases with* All, Whole, Both *and* Half. Växjo: Växjo University Press.

Garside, R./Leech, G./Varadi, T. (compilers) (1992), Lancaster Parsed Corpus. A Machine-readable Syntactically Analyzed Corpus of 144,000 Words. Available for Distribution through ICAME. Bergen: The Norwegian Computing Centre for the Humanities.

Hajič, J. (1998), Building a Syntactically Annotated Corpus: The Prague Dependency Treebank. In: *Issues of Valency and Meaning*. Prague: Karolinum, 106–132.

Hajičová, E. (1998), Prague Dependency Treebank: From Analytic to Tectogrammatical Annotation. In: *Proceedings of the First Workshop on Text, Speech, Dialogue*. Brno, Czech Republic, 45–50.

Han, C./Han, N./Ko, S. (2002), Development and Evaluation of a Korean Treebank and its Application to NLP. In: *Proceedings of the Third International Conference on Language Resources and Evaluation*. Las Palmas, Spain, 1635–1642.

Hindle, D. (1994), A Parser for Text Corpora. In: Zampolli, A. (ed.), *Computational Approaches to the Lexicon*. New York: Oxford University Press, 103–151.
Hinrichs, E./Simov, K. (eds.) (2002), *Proceedings of the First Workshop on Treebanks and Linguistic Theories*. Sozopol, Bulgaria.
Hinrichs, E. W./Bartels, J./Kawata, Y./Kordoni, V./Telljohann, H. (2000), The Tübingen Treebanks for Spoken German, English and Japanese. In: Wahlster, W. (ed.), *Verbmobil: Foundations of Speech-to-Speech Translation*. Berlin: Springer, 552–576.
Hockenmaier, J./Steedman, M. (2002), Acquiring Compact Lexicalized Grammars from a Cleaner Treebank. In: *Proceedings of the Third International Conference on Language Resources and Evaluation*. Las Palmas, Spain, 1974–1981.
Ide, N./Romary, L. (2003), Encoding Syntactic Annotation. In: Abeillé 2003a, 281–296.
Järborg, J. (1986), *Manual för syntaggning*. Göteborg University: Department of Swedish.
Järvinen, T. (2003), Bank of English and Beyond. In: Abeillé 2003a, 43–59.
Kingsbury, P./Palmer, M. (2003), PropBank: The Next Level of TreeBank. In: Nivre/Hinrichs 2003, 105–116.
König, E./Lezius, W. (2003), *The TIGER Language – A Description Language for Syntax Graphs. Formal Definition*. Technical Report, IMS, University of Stuttgart.
Kroch, A./Taylor, A. (2000), Penn-Helsinki Parsed Corpus of Middle English. URL: 〈http://www.ling. upenn. edu/mideng/.〉
Kromann, M. T. (2003), The Danish Dependency Treebank and the DTAG Treebank Tool. In: Nivre/Hinrichs 2003, 217–220.
Kübler, S./Nivre, J./Hinrichs, E./Wunsch, H. (eds.) (2004), *Proceedings of the Third Workshop on Treebanks and Linguistic Theories*. Tübingen, Germany.
Kučera, H./Francis, W. N. (1967), *Computational Analysis of Present-day American English*. Providence, RI: Brown University Press.
Kunz, K./Hansen-Schirra, S. (2003), Coreference annotation of the TIGER treebank. In: Nivre/Hinrichs 2003, 221–224.
Kurohashi, S./Nagao, M. (2003), Building a Japanese Parsed Corpus. In: Abeillé 2003a, 249–260.
Lehmann, S./Oepen, S./Regnier-Prost, S./Netter, K./Lux, V./Klein, J./Falkedal, K./Fouvry, F./Estival, D./Dauphin, E./Compagnion, H./Baur, J./Balkan, L./Arnold, D. (1996), TSNLP – Test Suites for Natural Language Processing. In: *Proceedings of the 16th International Conference on Computational Linguistics*. Copenhagen, Denmark, 711–716.
Lin, D. (1998), A Dependency-based Method for Evaluating Broad-coverage Parser. In: *Journal of Natural Language Engineering* 4, 97–114.
Maamouri, M./Bies, A. (2004), Developing an Arabic Treebank: Methods, Guidelines, Procedures, and Tools. In: *Proceedings of the Workshop on Computational Approaches to Arabic Script-based Languages*. Geneva, Switzerland, 2–9.
Marcus, M. P./Santorini, B./Marcinkiewics, M. A. (1993), Building a Large Annotated Corpus of English: The Penn Treebank. In: *Computational Linguistics* 19, 313–330.
Marcus, M. P./Kim, G./Marcinkiewics, M. A./MacIntyre, R./Bies, A./Ferguson, M./Katz, K./Schasberger, B. (1994), The Penn Treebank: Annotating Predicate Argument Structure. In: *Proceedings of the Human Language Technology Workshop*. Plainsboro, NJ, 114–119.
Mel'čuk, I. (1988), *Dependency Syntax: Theory and Practice*. New York: State University of New York Press.
Miltsakaki, E./Prasad, R./Joshi, A./Webber, B. (2004), The Penn Discourse Treebank. In: *Proceedings of the IV International Conference on Language Resources and Evaluation*. Lisbon, Portugal, 2237–2240.
Montemagni, S./Barsotti, F./Battista, M./Calzolari, N./Corazzari, O./Lenci, A./Zampolli, A./Fanciulli, F./Massetani, M./Raffaelli, R./Basili, R./Pazienza, M. T./Saracino, D./Zanzotto, F./Nana, N./Pianesi, F./Delmonte, R. (2003), Building the Italian Syntactic-semantic Treebank. In: Abeillé 2003a, 189–210.
Moreno, A./López, S./Sánchez, F./Grishman, R. (2003), Developing a Spanish Treebank. In: Abeillé 2003a, 149–163.

Nelson, G./Wallis, S./Aarts, B. (2002), *Exploring Natural Language: Working with the British Component of the International Corpus of English*. Amsterdam: John Benjamins.
Nivre, J. (2002), What Kinds of Trees Grow in Swedish Soil? A Comparison of Four Annotation Schemes for Swedish. In: Hinrichs/Simov 2002, 123–138.
Nivre, J. (2003), Theory-Supporting Treebanks. In: Nivre/Hinrichs 2003, 117–128.
Nivre, J./Hinrichs, E. (eds.) (2003), *Proceedings of the Second Workshop on Treebanks and Linguistic Theories*. Växjö, Sweden: Växjö University Press.
Oepen, S./Flickinger, D./Toutanova, K./Manning, C. D. (2002), LinGO Redwoods: A Rich and Dynamic Treebank for HPSG. In: Hinrichs/Simov 2002, 139–149.
Oflazer, K./Say, B./Hakkani-Tür, D. Z./Tür, G. (2003), Building a Turkish Treebank. In: Abeillé 2003a, 261–277.
Riezler, S./King, M./Kaplan, R./Crouch, R./Maxwell, J. (2002), Parsing the Wall Street Journal Using a Lexical-functional Grammar and Discriminative Estimation Techniques. In: *Proceedings of the 40th Annual Meeting of the Association for Computational Linguistics*, 271–278.
Rocio, V./Alves, M. A./Lopes, J. G./Xavier, M. F./Vicente, G. (2003), Automated Creation of a Medieval Portuguese Treebank. In: Abeillé 2003a, 211–227.
Sampson, G. (1995), *English for the Computer. The SUSANNE Corpus and Analytic Scheme*. Oxford: Clarendon Press.
Sampson, G. (2003), Thoughts on Two Decades of Drawing Trees. In: Abeillé 2003, 23–41.
Sasaki, F./Witt, A./Metzing, D. (2003), Declarations of Relations, Differences and Transformations between Theory-specific Treebanks: A New Methodology. In: Nivre/Hinrichs 2003, 141–152.
Sgall, P./Hajičová, E./Panevová, J. (1986), *The Meaning of the Sentence in its Semantic and Pragmatic Aspects*. Dordrecht: Reidel.
Simov, K./Osenova, P./Kolkovska, S./Balabanova, E./Doikoff, D./Ivanova, K./Simov, A./Kouylekov, M. (2002), Building a Linguistically Interpreted Corpus of Bulgarian: The BulTreeBank. In: *Proceedings of the Third International Conference on Language Resources and Evaluation*. Las Palmas, Spain, 1729–1736.
Stamou, S./Andrikopoulos, V./Christodoulakis, D. (2003), Towards Developing a Semantically Annotated Treebank Corpus for Greek. In: Nivre/Hinrichs 2003, 225–228.
Taylor, A./Marcus, M./Santorini, B. (2003), The Penn Treebank: An Overview. In: Abeillé 2003a, 5–22.
Teleman, U. (1974), *Manual för grammatisk beskrivning av talad och skriven svenska*. Lund: Studentlitteratur.
Toutanova, K./Manning, C. D./Shieber, S. M./Flickinger, D./Oepen, S. (2002), Parse Disambiguation for a Rich HPSG Grammar. In: Hinrichs/Simov 2002, 253–263.
Ule, T./Simov, K. (2004), Unexpected Productions May Well Be Errors. In: *Proceedings of the Fourth International Conference on Language Resources and Evaluation*. Lisbon, Portugal, 1795–1798.
Vilnat, A./Paroubek, P./Monceaux, L./Robba, I./Gendner, V./Illouz, G./Jardino, M. (2003), EASY or How Difficult Can It Be to Define a Reference Treebank for French. In: Nivre/Hinrichs 2003, 229–232.
Volk, M./Samuelsson, Y. (2004), Bootstrapping Parallel Treebanks. In: *Proceedings of the 5th International Workshop on Linguistically Interpreted Corpora*. Geneva, Switzerland, 63–70.
Wallis, S. (2003), Completing Parsed Corpora: From Correction to Evolution. In: Abeillé 2003a, 61–71.
Wouden, T. van der/Hoekstra, H./Moortgat, M./Renmans, B./Schuurman, I. (2002), Syntactic Analysis in the Spoken Dutch Corpus. In: *Proceedings of the Third International Conference on Language Resources and Evaluation*. Las Palmas, Spain, 768–773.
Xue, N./Xia, F./Chiou, F.-D./Palmer, M. (2004), The Penn Chinese Treebank: Phrase Structure Annotation of a Large Corpus. In: *Natural Language Engineering* 11, 207–238.

Joakim Nivre, Växjö and Uppsala (Sweden)

14. Historical corpora

1. Defining *historical* corpus

With the passage of time, every corpus will eventually turn into one that can be used for historical study, but strictly speaking a 'historical corpus' is one which is intentionally created to represent and investigate past stages of a language and/or to study language change. In all other respects, the defining characteristics of a corpus apply: it is a finite electronic collection of texts or parts of texts by various authors which is based on well-defined and linguistically relevant sampling criteria and aims for some degree of representativeness. A historical corpus concerns periods before the present-day language, which may be taken to end roughly thirty to forty years (one generation) before the present: in other words, any corpus compiled in or around 2000 that goes back beyond ca. 1960/1970 can be called historical. The corpus can extend into the immediate present, as *A Representative Corpus of Historical English Registers* (ARCHER) does, as long as its earliest samples lie sufficiently in the past as defined above.

Historical corpora can be either synchronic or diachronic. In the former case, the corpus represents a specific period seen as a self-contained unit: the *Century of Prose Corpus* (COPC), for example, represents a defined English literary epoch (1680−1780). The diachronic type, for which the *Helsinki Corpus of English Texts* (HC), spanning ten centuries (ca. 750−1710), is a good example, is concerned with linguistic development over (as a rule) longer periods. Subsections of such a diachronic corpus (e. g. Middle English (1150−1500) or the even smaller subsection Middle English 4 (ME4: 1420−1500) of the HC) can also be used as synchronic historical corpora, however. A secondary type of historical corpus is the combination of clone corpora covering discrete periods with an identical setup, e. g. the 1990s and (prospective) 1930s clones of the 1960s LOB and Brown corpora. This latter type will not be treated explicitly in this article.

Like modern corpora, historical corpora can be designed for rather general purposes, enabling a wide range of linguistic investigations, or for a more narrowly focused research agenda, e. g. specific socio-pragmatic concerns. This distinction often correlates with the difference between multi- or single-genre corpora, such as HC vs. *A Corpus of Early English Correspondence* (CEEC). According to standard corpus definitions, electronic versions of the works of one author (e. g. Chaucer: Canterbury Tales Project, Cicero: La Banque de Textes du LASLA) or of one single work (e. g. *Electronic Beowulf*) are strictly speaking not corpora. However, they could be seen as extreme cases of highly focused corpora, which adds the corpus-linguistic perspective to the traditional philological and literary study of such texts. Because of the special restrictions applying to historical (corpus) linguistics, what has been regarded and used as a corpus(-like) base has occasionally been given a wider definition in this field. Accordingly, this article will also discuss collections which might not be corpora under a very strict definition of the term (e. g. ICAMET, Corpus of Early English Medical Writing).

English-language corpora will be used predominantly as examples throughout this article, reflecting the fact that English linguistics has been fairly prolific in this area.

2. The framework: Times and texts

Historical corpora are of necessity written corpora, so that the aspects treated in article 10 apply to them as well. Thus, this article will pay particular attention to some aspects peculiar to or of special importance for historical corpora. The present section will deal with time frames and overall size as well as with the (in)completeness of included texts.

The time frame of a historical corpus is an issue of major importance. Some modern 'snapshot' corpora represent solely one year *(Brown:* 1961) or only a few years (*BNC*: early 1990s), but this type is almost non-existent in the historical sphere, for two reasons: first, such a narrow chronological focus is not fruitful for language-change research (with the exception of combining various clone snapshot corpora), although it may be useful for other precisely defined research questions; secondly, the further back one goes, the harder it is to find sufficient material for a given corpus (partly also due to the dating problems of older texts). Thus, longer periods providing a satisfactory amount of material are necessary and, in fact, historical corpora are usually concerned with time spans of one hundred years or longer. One hundred years, spanning roughly three generations of successive speakers, are taken as the basis in King's model of language change (Polomé 1990, 5) and can be regarded as sufficient for documenting change. Corpora of around this size include the *Zurich English Newspaper Corpus* (ZEN, 1661–1791), the *Lampeter Corpus* (LC, 1640–1740) and the *Corpus of Nineteenth-Century English* (CONCE, 1800–1900). However, shorter periods, such as half a generation to two generations (Labov 1981), may also provide sufficient evidence, in particular as not every change proceeds at the same speed. Furthermore, changes that have been going on for some time in speech can appear rather abruptly, i. e. within a very short period, in the written language (Nevalainen/Raumolin-Brunberg 1996). Nevertheless, few corpora span periods shorter than 100 years, e. g. the *Newdigate Newsletters* (1673–1692) or the *Lancaster Newsbook Corpus* (1653–1654), the latter being concerned with a very specialised question, namely that of text re-use in early news reportage. In contrast, stretches of time exceeding 100 years are covered by the CEEC (1417–1681), the *Corpus of English Dialogues* (CED, 1560–1760), ARCHER (1650–1990), and, in particular, the HC. Non-English corpora seem to specialise in longer periods, e. g. *Frantext* (16th–20th century), *Corpus del Espanol* (1100–1900) or the *Bonner Frühneuhochdeutsches Korpus* (1350 – 1700). Long corpora crucially also have an internal temporal structure, i. e. sub-periods which have a parallel or closely comparable composition: in the case of CONCE, for example, there are three periods of 20–30 years each containing an identical range of registers. The larger the time-frame, the more difficult it may be to keep to the parallel structure, so that the HC has dispensed with a strictly symmetrical structure (Kytö/

Rissanen 1993, 6). The sub-period chunks need to have a certain critical size and to exhibit enough internal variation in order to be as representative of their sub-period as the corpus is of the whole period (cf article 9 for a discussion of representativeness). It may be advantageous to link internal sub-periods to those used in other corpora, as was partly done with the CED with reference to the HC (Culpeper/Kytö 1997, 72), in order to facilitate multi-corpus use and inter-corpus comparisons. The internal composition of subparts is less of an issue in the case of single genre corpora, e. g. the letters in CEEC, but finding enough texts of the same kind or enough writers fulfilling the defined parameters for an equal coverage of the whole corpus period may still present a problem.

Another important matter apart from the time span concerns the precise start and end dates. Selecting these dates is intimately connected with the intended research purpose of the corpus. If it is a fairly broad and unfocused purpose or the corpus is explicitly intended as a multi-purpose one, a possible solution is to link up to linguistic periodisation: thus the *Innsbruck Computer Archive of Middle English Texts* (ICAMET) covers the Middle English period, and the HC Old, Middle, and Early Modern English. Nevertheless, this approach is neither simple nor unproblematic, as periodisation as such is an idealisation and suggested dates are often disputed or pragmatically chosen landmarks. The HC, for example, ends in 1710, but arguments could be found for various dates between 1660 and 1800 for the end of Early Modern English. By staying too close to (established) period frames, a corpus may not actually be promoting new insights, as transitional periods might be neglected. One such important time of transition for English, the 18th century, is certainly still insufficiently covered by the available corpora. In contrast to the period approach, the ZEN, the research aim of which is to document newspapers as a newly emerging register, takes suitable extralinguistic events, namely the beginning of newspaper publication as such (1661) together with the first publication of *The Times* (1791) as a first culmination of press development, as its time frame. The COPC has a literary-stylistic purpose and focuses on what can be defined as 18th-century literature (Milić 1990, 203). The dates may also be determined by the sheer (un)availability of suitable material: extending the CED to earlier periods than 1560 would be problematic for lack of appropriate dialogic material, while obtaining good first-hand access to a wide range of pamphlets was best for the period 1640–1740 in the case of the LC. Sometimes, it may be practicable to simply select one whole century, as the compilers of CONCE have done (1800–1900), in particular if, as here, the period in question is under-researched.

The date of the sampled texts is of great importance with regard to the time frame and the internal sub-periods. However, a precise dating is not always possible, particularly in the case of old manuscripts. The date of composition, copying or publication can also differ to a (considerable) extent. Milić (1990, 205) considered the publication date the relevant one for linguistic usage and sampled accordingly for the COPC, but in most cases it is rather the composition date which is largely responsible for the linguistic characteristics of the text. Where, for example, would one want to place *Beowulf* in the chronology of Old English? While the manuscript was written around the year 1000, proposals for dating the original composition range from the early 8th to the late 10th century. In this case, we cannot even ascertain how much linguistic restructuring might have occurred, as we have only one single manuscript. The HC deals with such cases with the help of three codes for date of original text (O), date of manuscript (M), and contemporarity (K), which yields <O X>, <M 950–1050>, <K NON-CONTEMP>

for *Beowulf*, where X stands for 'unknown'. In the classifier and part of corpus codes (Q & C), it is accordingly marked OX for the original (Old English, sub-period unknown) and O3 for the manuscript (Old English, period 3). Similar problems, though less controversial and often more easily solvable, can also occur in later periods. In the LC, for instance, second or consecutive prints of pamphlets were only included in the corpus if they were substantial re-writes; this procedure was especially important as this corpus has a small-scale decade sub-structure, which can easily be disrupted.

The question of corpus size is partly connected with the time frame, i. e. the larger the frame, the bigger potentially the corpus. This rule of thumb does not always apply: the *Bonner Frühneuhochdeutsches Korpus* spans the period 1350–1700 with a mere 16,000 characters. If the purpose of the corpus is to chart language change, each sub-period of the corpus must contain a sufficient amount of text. The question of what counts as sufficient has no easy answer. The received wisdom (based on modern corpora) is that frequent grammatical phenomena can be researched on the basis of one million words, while infrequent and lexical features need a larger textual basis. However, whereas modern corpora concentrate the one million words in one fairly short temporal span, historical corpora spread them over a whole century (e. g. CONCE, LC) or more (HC, covering about ten centuries with 1.5 million words). The size may thus be adequate, e. g., to analyse the 19th century as a unit, but it may not be big enough to satisfactorily chart less frequent linguistic developments (the three subparts of CONCE, for example, are sized from 298,796 to 346,176 words). In fact, one would need to test the result of language-change research with corpora of different sizes in order to determine the statistically valid size. This has been done by Nurmi (2002) with respect to the development of periphrastic *do* and modal verbs in the full CEEC and the CEEC Sampler; she found that by and large results obtained from the two corpora match fairly well. As a rule, the available historical corpora of English, in particular if used in combination, have proved adequate for most research to date. For languages other than English, the situation may be less favourable; there is, for example, only one historical corpus of Slavic, the *ACT* corpus of Old Church Slavonic covering the period 1230–1450 with ca. 700,000 words.

As a rule, historical corpora are smaller than modern ones: the largest English historical corpora at present are the HC with 1.5 million words, ARCHER with ca. 1.7 and CEEC with 2.7. Some non-English corpora exceed these figures by far, such as the *Mittelhochdeutsche Begriffsdatenbank* with 5.7 million words or the *Corpus del Espanol* with 100 million words covering the period from 1100 to 1900. There are several aspects which have generally restricted the size of historical corpora: (i) the manual process of compilation (to be treated in section 4 below), (ii) the availability of suitable material (historical/cultural factors), (iii) the accessibility of material and (iv) copyright. As to (ii), texts may simply not exist in certain types and/or in sufficient numbers. The Old English textual base, for example, is finite and restricted in its internal variability. On the one hand, one can sample everything for one's collection, in which case it would be an electronic text library/archive rather than a principled and balanced corpus, such as the *Corpus Scriptorum Latinorum* (an index of all Latin texts available online) or the *Old English Corpus* (OEC), which contains every surviving Old English text (in one or more copies). Alternatively, one can construct a criteria-based corpus, which, given the 'skewed' nature of the Old English text base (e. g. translations, dialectally mixed texts, dating problems etc.), would probably not much exceed one million words. While the textual situation becomes better after the Middle Ages with regard to both amount and variation, the historical corpus linguist will always face shortages of some nature before the late 19th century. Culpeper/Kytö (forthc.), for example, have found it difficult to find printed witness depositions and even prose fiction containing a sufficient amount of speech representation for some parts of the CED. As regards point (iii) above, it may be the case that the available texts are not easily accessible, because they exist in manuscript form, or because they are spread among many libraries and can only be examined in situ. While this problem is potentially alleviated by such initiatives as *Early English Books Online* (http://eebo.chadwyck.com/home), the following point (iv) certainly applies to this avenue as well. Aspect (iv) highlights the fact that, as with modern corpora, there may be copyright problems. Libraries and archives may sometimes be much more forthcoming than publishing houses, but payment for copyright will mostly be necessary. A way out may be to work with editions that have fallen out of copyright (e. g. OEC, HC), but this solution has potential drawbacks as such sources may reflect out-dated linguistic evidence (cf 3). Another way to deal with the problem, if perhaps only for a transitional period, is to publish those parts of the corpus for which copyright is available, as has been done with the CEEC Sampler, which contains half a million of the overall 2.7 million words.

The question of the completeness of texts may not seem peculiar to historical corpora, but given the traditional connection of *historical* linguistics and philology it is in fact an important one (cf. article 4). Philology is crucially concerned with texts, not with smaller text chunks such as (modern) corpora usually include. Historical corpora can of course be based on text chunks of ca. 2,000 words (cf. COPC), but with the increasing interest in historical discourse and genre studies historical corpora have also included longer or full texts, even complete publications (e. g. ICAMET, LC, ZEN, CEEC). Quasi-complete texts can also be fairly self-contained parts of larger works, such as chapters of a book as opposed to the whole book, which one might not want to include in a corpus. The chunk approach has the advantage of making for greater overall textual variety in the corpus and of being ideally balanced, but the complete-text approach enables text-linguistic and stylistic studies on a broader level, by paying attention to the potentially unequal spread of linguistic features across textual subparts. The latter approach is nevertheless the trickier one, as it will be necessary to control for (unnecessarily heavy) skewing in working with the corpus. In the case of the text-chunk approach, chunks may be related in some systematic way to the complete text length and also be selected from different parts of the text – one 2,000-word passage might be fairly representative of a 10,000-word text, but certainly less so of a 100,000-word text. The HC, for instance, includes complete short texts and varies the size of extracts from longer texts from 2,500 to 20,000 words (Kytö/Rissanen 1993, 1).

3. Restrictions and peculiarities of historical corpora

This section highlights the ways in which extralinguistic conditions in various historical periods and problems or accidents of textual transmission crucially influence and to a certain extent limit the make-up of historical corpora.

Corpora ideally should be representative and balanced (cf. article 9), completely representing the variability of a population. This is problematic enough for modern corpora, but the problems for historical corpora are multiplied. Precisely defining the total target population, which is crucial for representativeness (Biber 1993, 243), is almost impossible for past periods with any reasonable degree of statistical validity. The texts transmitted to the present represent a random subsample of the whole population, due to largely extra-linguistic accidents. Thus, historical corpora can never even remotely capture the full variety of language.

Among other restrictions and problems, the most obvious is the lack of spoken language evidence before the 20th century. Given the prominence of speech, its clear differences from written language, and its (actuating) role in language change, historical corpus linguists have sought to at least partly remedy this shortcoming by sampling speech-related and/or more informal types of linguistic production. The most easily accessible type concerns written-to-be-spoken productions, i. e. speeches and sermons (included in HC and LC, for example); however, these are usually 'polished' for publication and only very rarely present a verbatim transcription of the actual delivery. Crucially, they are also monologic in character, while the majority of naturally occurring speech is dialogic. Prose drama, while presenting dialogue, has the drawback of being fictional and of a literary nature; linguistically, it may be advantageous to select comedy, often dealing with middle or lower class characters and (thus) containing potentially less formal language, and even works of 'lesser' literary merit (cf. CED). It may be of additional interest in this context to compare authentic and constructed speech, in historical as well as modern contexts, in order to gauge the usefulness of historical fictional material for researching speech (cf. Culpeper/Kytö 2000). Transcriptions of parliamentary debates, of court trials and of witness depositions reflect more authentic, even dialogic, speech, albeit in a formal setting, but scribal interference and smoothing have to be reckoned with. Furthermore, not all trial proceedings are reproduced in direct speech. The compilers of the CED originally made a three-fold division between recorded (based on notes taken during a speech event), re-constructed (recreation of actual dialogue by, ideally, an earwitness) and constructed (imaginary) dialogue (Culpeper/Kytö 1997, 63); while these are important distinctions, the 're-constructed' category proved too time-consuming with respect to locating fitting texts, and so the division was reduced to a two-fold classification. Letters, in particular private ones, and diaries which were not written with a view to publication, while not actually connected to spoken production, are presumably less formal, potentially less carefully drafted and in that respect closer to speech. All these approximations to the spoken medium thus have their drawbacks, but are nevertheless valuable if careful use is made of them.

The written medium, too, is underrepresented by the extant texts. The least problems certainly occur if a corpus focusses largely on literary texts, as has been done for *Frantext* (80% literary texts, 20% technical texts). But forms of non-literary, 'informal', private and (from ca. 1500 onwards) unpublished writing are either in the minority, completely missing for some periods and/or not easily accessible for researchers. Registers and genres are unequally spread across the history of the language, affecting the possible make-up of corpora spanning longer periods (e. g. HC, ARCHER), which ideally need similarly structured subparts, and the ease of comparison of (data from) different corpora. Press and natural science writing (in the modern sense) are two examples of late emerging registers, which are simply not present before the late 17th century or even later. Attempts to extend research in these areas back in time have to deal with texts such as herbals and astrological or practical surgical texts (for science), or newsletters, newsbooks and pamphlets (for press), which are more or less clear historical precursors of the modern texts sharing some features with them and some with other texts/registers. That is, one is concerned with transitional periods in terms of register/genre and also with (partly radically) different world-views and categorizations. The *Corpus of Early English Medical Writing* (1375–1750), for instance, focusses on an early period of an evolving register with the explicit aim of investigating its developing features with regard to content, thought processes, style and text-type (Taavitsainen et al. 2002). Some registers or genres are present throughout history, but with different functions and thus with partly different linguistic realisations (e. g. history writing) – in other words, while the genre remains constant, the linguistic text type undergoes change (e. g. Biber/Finegan 1989). This is detectable with text chunks, but complete texts may even be more enlightening in this respect. Other genres are present in crucially varying proportions throughout history. For instance, religious writing (e. g. sermons) becomes more prominent and more varied, the further back one goes, and its importance in earlier periods stands in stark contrast to its importance today. All these points may have to be taken into account when constructing and using a corpus.

Despite the potential problems listed above, the selection of written texts is broad enough for most periods to construct varied corpora. Accordingly, both those with a broader register/genre/text-type outlook, i. e. multi-purpose corpora (e. g. HC, ICAMET, ARCHER), and those with a narrower focus, i. e. single-purpose corpora (CEEC: letters, CED: speech-related material, LC: pamphlets, ZEN: newspapers), are thus found in the historical sphere (Rissanen 1992). But even single-purpose corpora may exhibit considerable textual variety: in the case of the ZEN one finds such textual classes as 'foreign news', 'proclamation', 'advertisement' or 'letters', while the LC contains sermons, biographical narratives, and instructional material.

A further problem area concerns sociolinguistic considerations, in so far as it is difficult or even completely impossible to fully represent or document the scope of past societies. The majority of the population before the (late) 19th century was illiterate and thus could not produce any linguistic sources (with the exception e. g. of witness depositions and letters taken down by scribes); illiteracy in particular affected the lower and middle segments of society, so that historical corpora to a large extent reflect the language of the social and educational elite – which in earliest times mostly overlaps with the religious elite.

Illiteracy combined with a male-dominated societal structure also means that the language of women is necessarily underrepresented in historical corpora. The language of women is especially of interest, as research on modern changes has shown women to often be leaders of linguistic change. While the uniformitarian principle (Labov 1972) points to the likelihood of women playing a similar role in the past, the CEEC researchers have also found evidence to the contrary (Nevalainen 2000). Further research into the role of women as catalysts or adopters of linguistic change is thus necessary. The 'private' language of women (letters, diaries) is relevant for another reason: because of their receiving little or no exposure to explicit language instruction, female writers may produce forms that are closer to everyday and spoken usage. Phonetic spellings, for example, are especially frequent in women's letters in the *Helsinki Corpus of Scots* (HCOS) (Meurman-Solin 1999, 308). Even when women were literate and wrote texts, it was not always easy for them to find any means of publication: thus, there are only two female writers among the 120 pamphleteers represented in the LC.

Another potential problem is posed by anonymous texts, which are almost the rule in medieval times but are also found in later periods, e. g. with pamphlet literature produced under censorship conditions. Publication under a pseudonym is also not uncommon, and where these cases cannot be clarified beyond doubt they are treated as anonymous works. Whether the anonymity of authors and participants really constitutes a problem depends on the research agenda: for many or even most linguistic questions it does not play a role, whereas it is inevitably a very relevant aspect for sociolinguistic and also for some pragmatic (e. g. politeness) research. In spite of the authorship problems just mentioned, historical sociolinguistics is possible, and, if an appropriate text type is selected, also amenable to the corpus approach. The CEEC is a case in point here, with its collection of late medieval and early modern letters written by 677 known individuals, both men and women (although the latter represent only a fifth of the CEEC (Nurmi 1998)), as well as by people of different social status. This corpus pays attention to such variables as socioeconomic status, gender, age, provenance, relation to the recipient and social/geographical mobility (even if this information is unfortunately not included in the published sampler version of the corpus). It may be necessary to weigh corpus compilation parameters against the quality of sources; in the case of the CEEC wider representativeness could only be achieved by accepting not only autograph letters, but also scribal letters and copies (Nurmi 1998).

Regional variation is another parameter that a historical corpus might be expected to represent, in particular for periods preceding standardisation. The *Bochumer Mittelhochdeutsch Korpus* (1070–1350), for example, covers eleven regional varieties (e. g. Bavarian, Swabian, West Middle German). However, not every linguistic period allows full documentation of this variation. For Old English, most extant texts are of the West Saxon variety; a balanced corpus can thus represent West Saxon only, or, alternatively, reflect all four dialects in equal manner but in doing so ignore most of the data present, resulting in a very small corpus (cf also the necessarily 'unequal' representation of OE in the HC). For later periods (ca. 16th century onwards), it is possible to concentrate on the standard variety as the precursor of the modern language (as done by the HC); strictly speaking, however, no such privileged varieties exist in Old and Middle English. Varieties can be contrasted with the help of different corpora: thus the HC is complemented in its late Middle and Early Modern part by the HCOS (1450–1700), while Hickey has produced a *Corpus of Irish English*. An unequal regional spread of texts (or text types) is found even in later periods: the British printing presses, for example, which are relevant especially for all press publications and (often anonymous) miscellaneous material, were located in a few big cities, and in particular in London for most of the past. Another problem is the unknown or disputed provenance of texts (e. g. in Middle English). In case of too many unlocalizable texts, it will not be possible to use dialectal variation as a corpus parameter. Historical corpora can nevertheless be constructed with the explicit aim of dialectological research, as is the case with the corpora for the *Linguistic Atlas of Early Middle English* and the *Linguistic Atlas of Older Scots* in preparation at the University of Edinburgh.

As the above points illustrate, the available options for constructing historical corpora are crucially dependent on the socio-historical conditions of the past. Nevertheless, a substantial variety of corpora has been produced and successfully exploited, including those with highly focussed research questions, demonstrating that the restrictions posed by the historical conditions are challenges to be overcome, rather than insurmountable obstacles.

4. Processing historical texts

Historical texts come in three guises: (i) manuscripts of a pre-print culture, (ii) manuscripts in a print culture and (iii) (early) printed texts. Additionally, there are early sound documents (20th century), whose transcription follows the same principles as that of modern corpora (cf. article 30); however, this last type will be excluded from the discussion here. It is necessary to distinguish between (i) and (ii) above, because the former are as a rule public and/or official documents, while the latter tend to be more private texts, something which has consequences e. g. for the care taken with the manuscript, the standardisation of letter shapes and of orthography etc., and thus also for the ease of their corpus-linguistic adaptation. With regard to (iii), printed matter from the 19th century onwards is basically modern, whereas prints of the Early Modern era have special characteristics, which need to be taken into account in corpus construction and use. Additionally, historical texts are often also available in editions. Historical corpus compilation is thus faced with the choice between originals and modern editions and, in the former case, with the challenges presented by the form of early texts.

Corpus linguists have often opted for editions (e. g. HC, ARCHER, CEEC; TITUS = *Thesaurus Indogermanischer Text- und Sprachmaterialien, Augustana*). Some corpora, such as *Textes de Français Ancien*, use a mix of editions and manuscripts as their basis. The advantages of the 'edition approach' are obvious: the works are fairly easily available, they can be used at the place of corpus compilation, the editorial work with all its decision-making has already been done, and the texts may be in such a shape that scanning in of the text is possible or that manual keying in can at least proceed fast and efficiently. The potential disadvantages are the following. First, editions of many kinds of texts (e. g. letters, historical documents) are often the work not of linguists but of historians, whose concerns are not necessarily geared towards linguistic interest and accuracy. The CEEC compilers have noticed an editorial predilection for historically important letter-writers and for letters dealing with important events (Nurmi 1999, 54), while linguists would prefer a wider range of writers and a fair spread of topics, walks of life and thus also styles. Secondly, in the case of non-linguist editors, the linguistic decisions made (e. g. spelling normalisation) may not be optimally documented in the edition, and are therefore not documentable at the time of inclusion in a corpus − yet nevertheless become the basis of further linguistic research. And thirdly, editions may be copyrighted and thus crucially restrict the availability of the resultant corpus. One potential solution, that of taking older, non-copyrighted editions, has its own drawbacks: these may be even less satisfactory as regards modern linguistic standards than later ones. A possible way out of the edition dilemma is to indeed use editions but to cross-check the computerised material against the manuscript originals in dubious cases as far as possible. This has been done in the case of the CED and the CEEC, as well as in TITUS. The endeavours of the CEEC compilers have also shown that most of the editions were in fact quite reliable for the purpose of morphological and syntactic studies, but not for the study of orthography. A mixed approach with regard to originals and editions is also possible: for the CEEC, some of the included letters were edited by the compilers in order to close gaps in representativeness. From a purely linguistic point of view, working with originals is of course the preferred option (cf. Walker/Kytö 2003 for a discussion). This is usually complicated and even restricted by the fact that manuscripts and early prints are stored in various, potentially distant archives, museums and libraries, with consequences for both finances and working conditions.

In addition to above considerations, there are characteristics of the texts themselves which present challenges for digitisation. A corpus is not and cannot be an edition, it cannot have a huge critical apparatus – but in effect it is an edited form of an old text and thus has to clearly document the decisions made in the accompanying manual in a form suitable for corpus linguists. Some of the following text characteristics may need to be dealt with in compilation and kept in mind in corpus use. Old texts can simply be in a bad physical state (burnt, torn, holes, faded etc.), which can make parts of them barely or not at all legible; this goes for manuscripts and early printed material alike. Legibility problems can of course occur regardless of physical text quality, for instance with private manuscripts such as letters or diaries. For some periods or text types there may not be the option of excluding such problematic material, because of the sheer lack of other suitable material. Thus, the compiler both has to decide the cut-off point for inclusion (what percentage of the text needs to be unharmed) and in what way to deal with the legibility problem in transcription (cf. section 5). Older texts can contain unfamiliar graphemes, which on the one hand may be hard to correctly decipher for the untrained eye and on the other hand need to be coded in ASCII-compatible type (cf. section 5). Digitisation is not uncommonly done by (student or other) assistants, for whom such matters can be highly problematic, even in the case of fairly modern texts, e. g. from the 17th century, where long <s> and <f> lead to confusion (such errors are to be found in the LC and the ZEN, for example). In the case of private manuscripts, identification can be difficult even for the specialist – linguists are not necessarily paleographers. Texts may further contain additions, corrections and the like by a non-original hand, glosses in medieval texts being a particularly well-known and common example. These can either be included or ignored in the transcription, depending to some extent on the purpose of the corpus. Linguistic glosses are clearly of great interest, while other annotations add a reader perspective and an interactiveness to the texts which is otherwise missing. Even if the annotator is unknown, it may thus be of great interest to include these additions. Historical texts contain instances of code-mixing or code-switching much more commonly than modern ones, i. e. words and whole passages in other languages, in particular but not exclusively in Latin. While words and phrases integrated into the textual flow cannot be left out, a decision has to be made for or against the inclusion of longer and syntactically self-contained foreign-language sections. On the one hand, their presence can distort the word count and consequently the statistics derived from the corpus, unless one finds coding and programming means of avoiding this. On the other hand, they were intended as an integral part of the text in which they occur and from a philological point of view they are essential. If the corpus contains complete texts, they will necessarily be included. If the text chunk approach has been chosen by the compiler, however, textual parts with (too many) foreign elements can be avoided, as was done in the COPC (Milić 1990, 204).

Whatever the problems and decisions, originals certainly have to be dealt with manually, i. e. keyed in and proof-read. The double-keying and consequent comparing process makes the outcome more reliable (e. g. done for the *Mittelhochdeutsche Wörterbücher*). This is a laborious and time-consuming process, which contributes to restricting the size of historical corpora (cf. section 2 above). Ongoing work on improving OCR for older texts might change this in the future.

One important decision to be made before transcription is whether the original spelling or some form of regularized spelling is to be used. The COPC, for example, has opted for a regularisation of orthography and capitalization, based on the American standard as found in the Merriam-Webster dictionaries (Milić 1990, 204). While wordlists and search routines thus become easier to handle and some results are less error-prone, one research avenue is completely blocked off. Given the literary-stylistic aim of the COPC and its compiler, normalisation may be a defensible procedure, while it is more problematic with the multi-purpose and equally regularized ICAMET and *Tycho Brahe Parsed Corpus of Historical Portuguese*. Moreover, much more variation is lost in the latter (Middle English, Portuguese starting 1550) than in the former (18th century). Considering the amount of work going into corpus compilation, it is certainly an asset for a corpus to be useful for as diverse a range of research questions as possible. A way out of the dilemma of faithfulness *vs.* ease of retrievability is to represent both original and regularized spelling in the corpus, either through an annotation system (as in the *Lancaster Newsbook Corpus*, the *Mittelhochdeutsche Begriffsdatenbank* or through a multi-level architecture as in the prospective *DeutschDiachronDigital* (see Lüdeling/Poschenrieder/Faulstich 2005), or through a link to a normalized index.

5. Corpus annotation

Corpus annotation is understood here as the provision of text headers, textual markup for capturing layout and other surface properties, and grammatical annotation in the form of tagging and parsing.

Background information about the texts and their authors is provided as a rule in the text headers and, ideally, in a comprehensive manual accompanying the corpus which also explains the compilation principles in detail. Background information is vital for both compiler(s) and users in order to ensure and judge respectively the representativeness of the corpus. As linguists are not necessarily also historians, the required amount of information to be found and given as well as the detail of explanation will clearly exceed that of comparable modern corpora. The socio-economic rank or class of an author, for instance, cannot simply be given by an established and cross-referenced socio-political label (as in the *BNC*), but has to be (re)constructed on the basis of (potentially conflicting) historical research, and the system used has to be explicitly explained, as has been done for the CEEC and the LC. The compilers need to decide what kinds of information are to be provided, to which level of detail and precision, both for their own purposes and for those of prospective users, who may have very diverse research agendas. Types of information to be given can comprise the following: (i) on the text: title, publication format, register, text type/genre, content (library keyword style), style (formal/informal etc.), medium (written/spoken), language use (prose/verse; dialect; foreign languages etc.), date(s) (if composition and copy diverge), references to established citation systems (e. g. Wing), original/edition used for the corpus; and (ii) on the author: age, gender, social rank/class, parentage, education, profession(s), residence, dialect, type of author-recipient relationship (if interactive). Inevitably, not all of the relevant information is available in every case or for every text (cf. the X value in HC headers). As headers can be used to automatically construct sub-corpora, most of the information can be presented in a generalized as well as an individual form, e. g. period label, age range of author, region of a pre defined grouping, in addition to more precise statements (if available) of text date, age of author, and place of origin of text/author. In some cases, more generalized information can be given even where precise information is lacking, e. g. dialect region of a text/author (place of birth/residence unknown), age bracket extrapolated from the time an author received his M.A. (date of birth unknown, cf. LC). Text headers for historical corpora come either in the COCOA format (cf. HC) or in SGML/XML-TEI-conformant style (cf. LC), both of which can accommodate the same kinds of information. As a brief illustration of the two systems, some of the author information (name, gender, age, status) of text CEEDUC2A of the HC and text RelA1669 of the LC may suffice:

HC: <A BRINSLEY JOHN>
<X MALE>
<Y 40–60>
<H PROF>

LC: <person role="author" sex="m" age="50 : 59">
<persName>Richard Sherlock</persName>
<socecstatus>professions (clergy)</socecstatus>

As stated above, older texts often have a surface appearance that is very different from modern specimens, and if the compiler uses originals the question arises of how many of these characteristics are to be retained by encoding them in the corpus version of the text. With regard to individual characters, there are solutions such as those evolved for the HC, which uses +t, +d for Old and Middle English thorn and eth. Another option can be seen in SGML/XML entity references (as used in the LC), which frame a code for the symbol in question by ‘&’ and ‘;’, e. g. æ for the ligature æ. A further, perhaps better, alternative, namely using the Unicode system, is promoted by the Medieval Unicode Fonts Initiative (MUFI, cf. www.mufi.info/fonts). All these solutions are computer-friendly, but not necessarily user-friendly, as the texts become basically ‘unreadable’ for the human eye and as one has to take these transliterations into account when constructing search routines (e. g. with non-SGML-aware programs). A question to be discussed in this context is when it is actually necessary to encode a certain grapheme or grapheme variant. In general, certain orthographical or similar studies are simply better done with originals than with corpora, but that does not mean that everything can be ignored in corpora. It is certainly desirable to transcribe thorn in some form distinct from digraph <th>-forms in Middle English, but it is not really necessary to distinguish long <s> from <s> in Early Modern English printed texts, as there is regular complementary distribution of the two forms (cf. LC). Similarly, different realisations of the ampersand, common in the Early Modern period, can probably be safely ignored. Some other typographical features are meaningful and need to be transcribed, such as italics for highlighting, but does that also apply to the completely conventional italicization of proper names, as in the LC? And what about varying font sizes, spaces, indentation, various types of ornamentation (including initial capitals), physical manuscript damage and the like? One possible stance is that a written text is also a visual object, and that, given the pronounced human visual orientation, its characteristics ought to be represented. This would of course entail an immense wealth of encoding – and has not been carried through for any corpus, though RET editions encode the original layout fully (word separation, lineation, indentation, paragraphing, pagination). These *Renaissance Electronic Texts* (RET) are based on especially created Encoding Guidelines, which are geared to period-typical textual characteristics. If one really wishes to capture the textual object, it is possible to include facsimiles or selected pictures in the published corpus (cf. the LC's accompanying images). Another option is to concentrate only on those visual features which are of some linguistic relevance. Furthermore, there is the pragmatic compromise, which basically concentrates on linguistically relevant annotation, but also includes other mark-up for items which are highly prominent, easy to encode etc. The LC compilers, for instance, decided that word separation is linguistically relevant and encoded each occurrence, while line breaks in general were not coded, on the assumption that by 1640 printing technique was so advanced that spelling variants were no longer used to fill out or compress lines. On the other hand, two linguistically irrelevant features, large or ornamented initial capitals and page breaks were encoded, simply because this is fairly easy. Changes and/or additions to the original text (cf. section 4) are found in manuscripts, but sometimes also in later texts such as the LC pamphlets. When they are included, it is necessary to ensure that they are kept clearly apart from the main text. The Text Encoding Initiative (TEI) Guidelines (P5) include a chapter (18) on the transcription of primary sources, which, among many other things, offers ways of dealing with additions (18.1.4.). Chapter 19 of the same document, entitled 'Critical apparatus', provides for the encoding of editorial decisions. Both of these are very useful for historical corpus compilation, as are the Renaissance Electronic Texts (RET) Encoding Guidelines mentioned above. The latter also employ SGML and even many TEI elements (cf. article 22).

Another type of annotation is the grammatical one, i. e. tagging (part-of-speech annotation for every lexeme) and parsing (grammatical-functional labelling of phrases and clauses). The amount of grammatically annotated historical material is still relatively scant in comparison to modern corpora. This fact is connected to the problem that the relevant tagging systems and software (cf. article 23) have been developed for the modern language stage. It is by no means a trivial matter to adapt the software with a reasonable degree of accuracy to varieties which (i) diverge from modern usage in various/many respects and (ii) may often be much more variable internally than modern standardised languages. The pragmatic decision was thus taken for the *Penn-Helsinki Parsed Corpus of Middle English* not to employ the category VP in parsing, as the order of the verb and its complements is too variable in Middle English (Taylor 1999). While the accuracy rate for automatic tagging lies at about 96–97% for modern texts, the corresponding figures e. g. for Early Modern English material can vary from mid-90% to as low as 80%, depending on the exact date. It is claimed that the CLAWS-tagged *Nameless Shakespeare* is 99% accurate, but this figure was only reached after several rounds of manual correction. Other corpora, such as the German *Bonner Frühneuhochdeutsch Korpus*, have been tagged completely manually. More manual intervention and proof-reading is therefore necessary with historical texts than with modern ones. Some problems may be solvable fairly easily, such as Early Modern English 'd-spellings (e. g. *call'd*), which can be specified as past tense or participial forms unless preceded by a pronominal form or by the sequence 'space + *cou-, shou-, wou-*'. Other problems are more intractable, however, among them Early Modern English *-s/-'s* endings, which can be plural, genitive (sg./pl.), 3rd person sing. (*he intend's*), or a contraction for *has/is;* the plural-genitive confusion is particularly hard to disambiguate. Similar problems arise with conjunctions, prepositions and determiners, whose usage can diverge considerably from the modern situation.

Historical English corpora which are tagged and/or parsed include at the time of writing the *York-Helsinki Parsed Corpus of Old English Poetry*, the *York-Helsinki Parsed Corpus of Old English Prose*, the *Brooklyn-Geneva-Amsterdam-Helsinki Parsed Corpus of Old English* (a preliminary version of the preceding corpus), the first and second editions of the *Penn-Helsinki Parsed Corpus of Middle English*, and the *Penn-Helsinki Parsed Corpus of Early Modern English*, all of which have required a considerable amount of manual work. Experiments with the ENGCG tagger have further been carried out on parts of the HC (Kytö/Voutilainen 1995), and parsed versions of the Early Modern English part of the HC and the CEEC are under construction.

The last, and still rare, kind of annotation to be mentioned here only briefly is of a semantic kind. The most prominent example of this type is the *Mittelhochdeutsche Begriffsdatenbank*, which annotates words with the semantic concepts they belong to.

6. Dictionaries as corpora?

Insofar as dictionaries do not include recognizable primary texts, they cannot be seen as real corpora. However, two aspects make them potentially relevant here: (i) they themselves can be treated as primary texts, and (ii) they can be seen as databases. Approach (i) is currently found only in the *Early Modern English Dictionary Database* (Lancashire), which represents a web-searchable corpus of 16 bilingual and monolingual works published between 1530 and 1657. In this case, the dictionaries themselves are the object of study, and, given the nature of English pre-Johnsonian lexicography, they can be used exclusively for questions of a lexical, semantic or lexicographical-historical nature. More comprehensive invidual dictionaries which are available in electronic form can also be used for a corpus-linguistic approach, e. g. Samuel Johnson's *Dictionary of the English Language* (1755/1773) on CD-Rom or the German dictionary of Jacob and Wilhelm Grimm (*Der Digitale Grimm*).

For approach (ii), the two dictionaries of prime interest are the *Oxford English Dictionary* (OED) and the *Middle English Dictionary* (MED), as well as, once concluded, the *Dictionary of Old English* (DOE). As the corpora the two latter are based on are accessible on their own – *Corpus of Middle English Prose and Verse* (cf. also Middle English Compendium) and *The Dictionary of Old English Corpus* –, I will concentrate on the OED here. While text corpora contain raw data, dictionaries present a circumscribed selection of data, dependent among other aspects on the specific aims of the dictionary, its lexicographical principles, and the (perceived) institutionalisation of words. The interesting part of the dictionary for corpus linguists is not the entries as such but the illustrative quotations, of which the OED in its second edition contains about 2.4 million. Assuming the average length of a quotation to be ca. 13 words, the OED probably contains something in the range of 33–35 million searchable words and is thus much bigger than any other available historical corpus (Hoffmann 2004). As the quotations serve particular lexicographical functions, they cannot be seen as representative of the corpus of texts behind the dictionary; moreover, this 'corpus' itself need not be representative in any corpus-linguistic sense. There is some noticeable bias in its selection of sources towards great literary writers or even individuals such as Shakespeare, which means that 'everyday' English is under-represented in this dictionary and that there is in general no full or equal representation of various genres and registers, in spite of considerable variation. Furthermore, the OED gives some preference to 'explanatory' quotations which themselves illuminate the sense of the word in question, thus focusing on potentially restricted contexts. The quotations themselves of course offer very limited context and are even shortened in many cases by editorial deletion, something not always explicitly indicated (Hoffmann 2004). While the OED is not geared to any specific historical period, it nevertheless does not provide full diachronic representation, as it excludes the Old English period by its decision to include only words in use after 1150; moreover, the chronological distribution of quotation material is fairly uneven (Hoffmann 2004). A last point to be mentioned here concerns the search and retrieval possibilities offered by the OED, which are quite extensive and varied (e. g. affix searches, combinations with dates/authors etc.). But these were not constructed with the corpus linguist in mind (e. g. results are not presented in KWIC format), of course, and as the quotations cannot be extracted for use with other programs there remain certain obstacles for corpus-linguistic research.

Despite some lexicographical peculiarities and drawbacks, and as long as allowance is made for them, historical dictionaries and the OED in particular can nevertheless be suitable sources in addition to corpus-based studies, for example as complementary sources or as preliminary pilot studies indicating promising research avenues. It is obvious that dictionaries favour certain research questions, such as those from the fields of lexicology, word formation and semantics, while they tend to disfavour others, such as those concerned with syntax, pragmatics, register studies/stylistics etc. Moreover, dictionary studies are suitable for the type-approach (both forms and senses), but not so much for corpus-linguistic token-oriented research, as is obvious in Kettemann et al.'s (2003) comparison of the morpheme *eco-* in the OED and the BNC, for instance. However, Schmid's (1997) study on the semantic development of *idea* succeeds in making good use of (relative) frequencies as well and, additionally, in proving the compatibility of dictionary and corpus results.

7. Final remarks

As the above survey of historical corpora has shown, there is by now quite a wealth of corpus material available. However, there are still also substantial gaps in historical corpus compilation, which are in need of filling. Such gaps may concern particular periods of a language, as for example the 18th and early 20th centuries for English, with the latter period actually being dealt with at the time of writing (the corpora Lancaster 1901, Lancaster 1931 being compiled by Rayson, Leech, Wynne, and Smits (cf. Leech/Smits 2005) and B-Brown by Hundt). Or they may concern whole languages, for example in the case of the largely non-existing historical corpora for the Scandinavian languages (with the exception of a Swedish drama corpus; see Melanda Marttala/Östman 2000; Melanda Marttala/Strömquist 2001). However, there are also new avenues to explore. From a cultural-historical perspective, it would be interesting to link several European languages in a corpus of parallel texts or translations, in particular given the importance of the latter in European history. The planned *Corpus Bibliorum Aetatis Reformationis*, assembling Bible translations of the 16th and 17th centuries in several languages, is a start in this direction.

8. Literature

Biber, Douglas (1993), Representativeness in Corpus Design. In: *Literary and Linguistic Computing* 8(4), 243–257.

Biber, Douglas/Finegan, Edward (1989), Drift and the Evolution of English Style: A History of Three Genres. In: *Language* 65, 487–517.

Biber, Douglas/Finegan, Edward/Atkinson, Dwight (1994), ARCHER and its Challenges: Compiling and Exploring a Representative Corpus of Historical English Registers. In: Fries, Udo/Tottie, Gunnel/Schneider, Peter (eds.), *Creating and Using English Language Corpora*. Amsterdam: Rodopi, 1–13.

Claridge, Claudia (1999/2003), *"Life is ruled and governed by opinion": The Lampeter Corpus of Early Modern English Tracts. Manual of Information*. ⟨http://khnt.hit.uib.no/icame/manuals/index.htm⟩ Accessed Nov. 29, 2005.

Culpeper, Jonathan/Kytö, Merja (1997), Towards a Corpus of Dialogues, 1550–1750. In: Ramisch, Heinrich/Wynne, Kenneth (eds.), *Language in Time and Space*. Stuttgart: Franz Steiner Verlag, 60–73.

Culpeper, Jonathan/Kytö, Merja (2000), Data in Historical Pragmatics: Spoken Interaction (Re)cast as Writing. In: *Journal of Historical Pragmatics* 1(2), 175–199.

Culpeper, Jonathan/Kytö, Merja (forthc.), *Early Modern English Dialogues: Spoken Interaction as Writing*. Cambridge: Cambridge University Press.

Hoffmann, Sebastian (2004), Using the *OED* Quotations Database as a Corpus – a Linguistic Appraisal. In: *ICAME Journal* 28, 17–30.

Johnson, Samuel (1755/1773/1996), *A Dictionary of the English Language*. CD-Rom, ed. by Anne McDermott. Cambridge: Cambridge University Press.

Kettemann, Bernhard/König, Martina/Marko, Georg (2003), The BNC and the OED. Examining the Usefulness of Two Different Types of Data in an Analysis of the Morpheme *eco*. In: Granger, Sylviane/Petch-Tyson, Stephanie (eds.), *Extending the Scope of Corpus-based Research: New Applications, New Challenges*. Amsterdam: Rodopi, 135–148.

Kytö, Merja (1996), *Manual to the Diachronic Part of the Helsinki Corpus of English Texts*. Helsinki: Department of English, University of Helsinki.

Kytö, Merja/Rissanen, Matti (1993), General Introduction. In: Rissanen, Matti/Kytö, Merja/Palander-Collin, Minna (eds.), *Early English in the Computer Age. Explorations through the Helsinki Corpus*. Berlin/New York: Mouton de Gruyter, 1–17.

Kytö, Merja/Rissanen, Matti (1995–2000), English Historical Corpora: Report on Developments in [year]. In: *ICAME Journal* 19, 20, 21, 22, 23, 24.

Kytö, Merja/Voutilainen, Atro (1995), Applying the Constraint Grammar Parser of English to the Helsinki Corpus. In: *ICAME Journal* 19, 23–48.

Kytö, Merja/Rudanko, Juhani/Smitterberg, Erik (2000), Building a Bridge between the Present and the Past: A Corpus of 19th-century English. In: *ICAME Journal* 24, 85–97.

Kytö, Merja/Walker, Terry (2003), The Linguistic Study of Early Modern English Speech-related Texts: How "Bad" Can "Bad" Data be? In: *Journal of English Linguistics* 31(3), 221–248.

Labov, William (1972), Some Principles of Linguistic Methodology. In: *Language in Society* 1, 97–120.

Labov, William (1981), What Can be Learned about Change in Progress from Synchronic Description? In: Sankoff, David/Cedergren, Henrietta (eds.), *Variation Omnibus*. Edmonton, Alberta: Linguistic Research, 177–201.

Lancashire, Ian (1993), The Early Modern English Renaissance Dictionaries Corpus. In: Aarts, Jan/de Haan, Pieter/Oostdijk, Nelleke (eds.), *English Language Corpora: Design, Analysis and Exploitation*. Amsterdam: Rodopi, 11–24.

Lancashire, Ian (1994), *Renaissance Electronic Texts: Encoding Guidelines*. Toronto: University of Toronto, Centre for Computing in the Humanities. ⟨http://www.library.utoronto.ca/utel/ret/guidelines/guidelines0.html⟩ Accessed Nov. 29, 2005.

Leech, Geoffrey/Smits, Nick (2005), Extending the possibilities of corpus-based research on English in the twentieth century: A prequel to LOB and FLOB. In: ICAME Journal 29, 83–98.

Lüdeling, Anke/Poschenrieder, Thorwald/Faulstich, Lukas C. (2005) DeutschDiachronDigital – Ein diachrones Korpus des Deutschen. In: *Jahrbuch für Computerphilologie* 2004, 119–136. Available online at http://computerphilologie.uni-muenchen.de/jg04/luedeling/ddd.html.

Melander Marttala, Ulla/Östman, Carin (2000), *Svensk dramadialog under tre sekler – en projektbeskrivning*. FUMS-rapport nr 200.

Melander Marttala, Ulla/Strömquist, Siv (2001), *Korpusen svensk dramadialog. Användarhandbok*. FUMS-rapport nr 202.

Meurman-Solin, Anneli (1999), Letters as a Source of Data for Reconstructing Early Spoken Scots. In: Taavitsainen, Irma/Melchers, Gunnel/Pahta, Päivi (eds.), *Writing in Nonstandard English*. Amsterdam: Benjamins, 305–322.

Middle English Dictionary & Middle English Compendium. ⟨http://ets.umdl.umich.edu/m/med⟩ Accessed Nov. 29, 2005.

Milić, Louis (1990), The Century of Prose Corpus. In: *Literary and Linguistic Computing* 5(3), 203–208.

Nevalainen, Terttu (2000), Gender Differences in the Evolution of Standard English: Evidence from the Corpus of Early English Correspondence. In: *Journal of English Linguistics* 28(1), 38–59.

Nevalainen, Terttu/Raumolin-Brunberg, Helena (eds.) (1996), *Sociolinguistics and Language History. Studies Based on the Corpus of Early English Correspondence*. Amsterdam: Rodopi.

Nurmi, Arja (ed.) (1998), *Manual for the Corpus of Early English Correspondence Sampler CEECS*. Helsinki: Department of English, University of Helsinki. Available at ⟨http://khnt.hit.uib.no/icame/manuals/ceecs/INDEX. HTM ⟩.

Nurmi, Arja (1999), The Corpus of Early English Correspondence Sampler. In: *ICAME Journal* 23, 53–64.

Nurmi, Arja (2002), Does Size Matter? The Corpus of Early English Correspondence and its Sampler. In: Raumolin-Brunberg, Helena/Nevala, Minna/Nurmi, Arja/Rissanen, Matti (eds.), *Variation Past and Present: VARIENG Studies on English for Terttu Nevalainen*. Helsinki: Société Néophilologique, 173–184.

Polomé, Edgar (ed.) (1990), *Research Guide on Language Change*. Berlin/New York: Mouton de Gruyter.

Rissanen, Matti (1992), The Diachronic Corpus as a Window to the History of English. In: Svartvik, Jan (ed.), *Directions in Corpus Linguistics*. Berlin/New York: Mouton de Gruyter, 185–209.

Rissanen, Matti (2000), The World of English Historical Corpora. From Cædmon to the Computer Age. In: *Journal of English Linguistics* 28, 7–20.

Rissanen, Matti/Kytö, Merja/Palander-Collin, Minna (eds.) (1993), *Early English in the Computer Age*. Berlin/New York: Mouton de Gruyter.

Rissanen, Matti/Kytö, Merja/Wright, Susan (eds.) (1994), *Corpora across the Centuries: Proceedings of the First International Colloquium on English Diachronic Corpora*. Amsterdam: Rodopi.

Santorini, Beatrice (2005), *Annotation Manual for the PPCME2, PPCEME and PCEEC*. Release 1. ⟨http://www.ling.upenn.edu/hist-corpora/⟩ Accessed Nov. 29, 2005.

Schmid, Hans Jörg (1997), The Historical Development and Present-day Use of the Noun Idea as Documented in the OED and Other Corpora. In: *Poetica* 47, 87–128.

Sperberg-McQueen, C. M./Burnard, Lou (eds.) (2001, 2002, 2004), *TEIP4: Guidelines for Electronic Text Encoding and Interchange. XML-compatible edition* & *TEI P5*, TEI homepage: www.tei-c.org/index.xml Accessed Nov. 29, 2005.

Taavitsainen, Irma/Pahta, Päivi/Leskinen, Noora/Ratia, Maura/Suhr, Carla (2002), Analysing Scientific Thought-styles: What Can Linguistic Research Reveal about the History of Science? In: Raumolin-Brunberg, Helena/Nevala, Minna/Nurmi, Arja/Rissanen, Matti (eds.), *Variation Past and Present: VARIENG Studies on English for Terttu Nevalainen*. Helsinki: Société Néophilologique, 251–270.

Taylor, Ann (1999), *PPCME Lite: A Brief Introduction to the Syntactic Annotation System of the PPCME2*. (Now replaced by Santorini 2005.)

Claudia Claridge, Duisburg/Essen (Germany)

15. Learner corpora

1. Introduction

Learner corpus research is a fairly young but highly dynamic branch of corpus linguistics, which began to emerge as a discipline in its own right in the late 1980's/early 1990's. Learner corpora, which can be roughly defined as electronic collections of texts produced by language learners, have been used to fulfil two distinct, though related, functions: they can contribute to Second Language Acquisition theory by providing a better description of interlanguage (i. e. transitional language produced by second or foreign language learners) and a better understanding of the factors that influence it; and they can be used to develop pedagogical tools and methods that more accurately target the needs of language learners.

2. Definition and typology

2.1. Definition

Learner corpora have all the characteristics commonly attributed to corpora (cf. articles 10 and 11), the only difference being that the data come from language learners. Though put like this, the concept of a learner corpus may sound relatively straightforward, it requires clarification both as regards the status of the speakers involved and the type of data they produce.

2.1.1. Language learners

The language learners whose language is covered by learner corpora are to be understood as foreign language learners, i. e. speakers who learn a language which is neither their first language nor an institutionalized additional language in the country where they live. While this definition is unproblematic for a wide range of languages, its application to a global language like English is far from straightforward. In its most common acceptation, the notion of learner corpus only covers varieties of English in Kachru's (1985) expanding circle. This means that we speak of a learner corpus if the data collected come from learners of English in Spain, Sweden or China, where English has no official status and is not used in education or administration, but not if the speakers belong to Kachru's (1985) outer circle, i. e. live in countries such as India, Nigeria or the Philippines, which have developed nativized varieties of English that have achieved the status of official language and/or language of education or administration. However, as the distinction between the expanding circle and the outer circle is becoming increasingly blurred (Lowenberg 2002, 434), it is not always easy to decide whether language data qualify as learner corpus data. The picture is made even more complex by the emerging concept of speakers of English as a Lingua Franca (ELF), i. e. proficient non-native speakers of English who use English as a means of communication with speakers of different first languages (cf Seidlhofer 2004; Mauranen 2003). The learner corpus approach and the ELF approach to non-native language are sometimes presented as opposed, but in fact they should rather be regarded as two sides of the same coin. The main difference between learner corpora and ELF corpora "lies in the researchers' orientation towards the data and the purposes they intend the corpora to serve" (Seidlhofer 2004, 224). If the speakers are non-native speakers who are still in the process of learning the language, the analysts' focus is likely to be (at least partly) on the gap that needs to be filled for the learners to become proficient speakers. If the speakers are non-native speakers who use English in their daily communications, the focus will be more on how they are able to communicate successfully and less on deviations from native speaker norms that do not hinder communication (Seidlhofer 2004). The two approaches should join forces as they are currently faced with the same challenge, that of uncovering the features that characterize non-native discourse and "the bulk of the descriptive work still needs to be done" (ibid, 222).

2.1.2. Learner data

The second difficulty pertains to the type of language data. One of the major distinguishing features of corpus data is authenticity, which Sinclair (1996) describes as follows: "All the material is gathered from the genuine communications of people going about their normal business" unlike data gathered "in experimental conditions or in artificial conditions of various kinds". This raises a problem for learner corpus data as learners, especially foreign language learners, rarely use the target language to go about their normal business. In fact, learner production data display a wide range of degrees of naturalness, with some tasks like reading aloud or fill-in the blanks exercises ranking very low on the naturalness continuum, and others, like informal interviews or free compositions, ranking much higher. Between these two extremes, there are many intermediate categories such as picture descriptions, summaries or translations. While it is important not to adopt an overly dogmatic attitude to this issue, it is essential to bear in mind that the notion of 'continuous text' lies at the heart of corpushood. A series of decontextualized words or sentences produced by learners, while being bona fide learner production data, will never qualify as learner corpus data. In addition, it is best to restrict the term 'learner corpus' to the most open-ended types of tasks, viz. those tasks that allow learners to choose their own wording rather than being requested to produce a particular word or structure. Instead of disqualifying from learner corpus status the more controlled types of text such as compositions guided by pictures, it might be a good idea to follow Nesselhauf's (2004a, 128) suggestion to refer to them as peripheral types of learner corpora. A good example of an emerging type of peripheral learner corpus is the translation learner corpus (Uzar/Walinski 2001).

2.2. Typology

In view of the pace at which learner corpora are being collected worldwide, any attempt at drawing up an inventory of learner corpora will quickly become outdated. Pravec's (2002) inventory is a useful starting-point, however, although it focuses exclusively on English and is restricted to writing. In the following sections, rather than drawing up an inventory, we set out to situate current learner corpora along a series of dimensions with a view to bringing out some of their main characteristics.

2.2.1. Commercial vs. academic

Computer learner corpora fall into two major categories: commercial learner corpora, initiated by major publishing companies, and academic learner corpora, which are compiled in educational settings. While there are more academic than commercial corpora, commercial corpora tend to be much larger and have a wider range of mother tongue backgrounds. For English, there are two major commercial learner corpora – the *Longman Learners' Corpus* and the *Cambridge Learner Corpus*, both of which contain over 10 million words and represent a myriad of mother tongue backgrounds. Academic corpora, on the other hand, come in all shapes and sizes and usually cover learners from only one mother tongue background, the *International Corpus of Learner English* (cf. section 2.2.3.) being a notable exception in this respect.

2.2.2. Big vs. small

As learner corpus data is stored electronically, it is possible to collect a large amount of it fairly quickly. As a result, learner corpora usually contain millions, rather than thousands or hundreds of words. However, while size is clearly a major asset in terms of representativeness of the data and generalizability of the results, small corpora are also of considerable value. As pointed out by Ragan (2001: 211), "the size of the sample is less important than the preparation and tailoring of the language product and its subsequent corpus application to draw attention to an individual or group profile of learner language use". A detailed longitudinal study of one single learner is of great value if the focus is on individual interlanguage development. In addition, size is only really useful if the corpus has been collected on the basis of strict design criteria (cf. section 3).

2.2.3. English vs. non-English

English clearly dominates the learner corpus scene. It can lay claim to some quite large collections, such as the *International Corpus of Learner English (ICLE)*, a 2.5 million-word corpus which covers learners from 11 different mother tongue backgrounds (Granger/Dagneaux/Meunier 2002; Granger 2003a) and the 25 million-word *Hong Kong University of Science and Technology Learner Corpus*, which contains data exclusively from Chinese learners of English (Milton 1998). In addition, it is also the targeted language of a large number of smaller collections, like the *EVA* corpus of speech from Norwegian learners (Hasselgren 1997) or the *APU* Spanish learner corpus (Ife 2004). Despite this prevalence of English corpus data, the number of learner corpus projects on languages other than English is on the increase. Among the languages covered are French (Debrock/Flament-Boistrancourt 1996; Bartning 2000; Myles/Mitchell 2004), Swedish (Hammarberg 1999), Norwegian (Tenfjord/Meurer/Hofland 2004), Dutch (Degand/Perrez 2004), Spanish (Ife 2004) and German (Lüdeling et al. 2005). In addition, mention should be made of Tagnin's (2003) *Multilingual Learner Corpus*, which contains data from learners with a common mother tongue background (Brazilian Portuguese) learning different languages (English, German and Spanish). There is thus no lack of learner corpora although their restricted availability to the academic community is an issue which needs addressing.

2.2.4. Writing vs. speech

Unsurprisingly perhaps, there are many more written than spoken learner corpora. The language covered is predominantly Language for Academic Purposes, which gets the lion's share because of its importance in the foreign language context. This is likely to change, however, as increased use of information and communication technologies (ICT) in foreign language teaching allows for quick and easy compilation of a wide variety of computer-mediated communication between learners. Telecollaborative language courses, for example, which involve language learners from different mother tongue backgrounds, can give rise to large bilingual learner corpora such as *Telekorp*, which results from five years of computer-mediated communication between learners of German in the US and learners of English in Germany (Belz forthcoming). This type of project, which illustrates "the convergence of the learner corpus research with research on a learning task", provides "insights for both SLA and language teaching through technology" (Chapelle 2004, 595). The difficulty of collecting and transcribing speech is multiplied by a factor of 10 in the case of learner data, which explains the relative scarcity of spoken learner corpora. The difficulty is compounded in the case of multimedia learner corpora, which contain learners' texts linked to audio-video recordings (Reder/Harris/Setzler 2003).

2.2.5. Longitudinal vs. cross-sectional

Another dimension along which learner corpora can be classified is the longitudinal vs. cross-sectional dimension. The overwhelming majority of learner corpora covering more than one type of interlanguage data are cross-sectional, i. e. they contain data gathered from different categories of learners at a single point in time. Genuine longitudinal corpora, where data from the same learners are collected over time, are very few and far between. For this reason, researchers interested in interlanguage development tend to collect quasi-longitudinal corpora, i. e. corpora gathered at a single point in time but from learners of different proficiency levels. The growing use of computer-mediated communication in foreign language teaching may well help to make up for the current dearth of good longitudinal data.

2.2.6. Immediate vs. delayed pedagogical use

Recent developments in academic learner corpora have led to a distinction between corpora compiled for delayed pedagogical use and those compiled for immediate pedagogical use. In the first case, learner corpora are not used directly as teaching/learning materials by the learners who have produced the data. They are compiled with a view to providing a better description of one specific interlanguage and/or designing tailor-made pedagogical tools which will benefit similar-type learners, i. e. learners with the same profile as the students who have produced the corpus data (same mother tongue background, same level of proficiency, etc.). In the second case, the learners are at the same time producers and users of the corpus data. The corpus data are collected by teachers as part of their normal classroom activities. As stated by Ragan (2001, 210) this type of corpus is not representative in the usual sense of the word: "[it] only represents itself providing specific information and a basis for generalizations concerning the limited range of the variety of language being produced and studied by a small number of students".

3. Learner corpus design

Nesselhauf (2004b, 40) defines learner corpora as "systematic computerized collections of texts produced by language learners". The adjective 'systematic' highlights the need for strict design criteria in learner corpus compilation. Learner language is influenced by a wide variety of linguistic, situational and psycholinguistic factors, and failure to control for these factors greatly limits the reliability of findings in learner language research. The high degree of control governing learner corpus building sets learner corpus

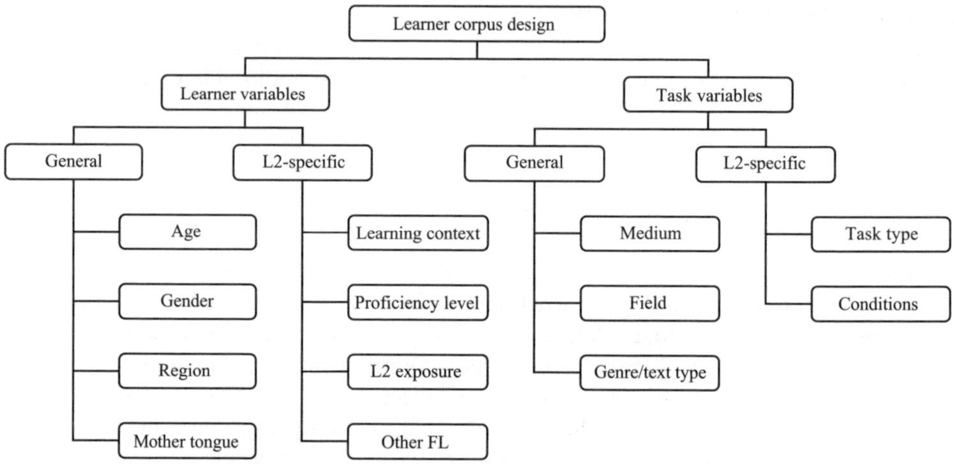

Fig. 15.1: Learner corpus design

data apart from the samples of language use commonly used in cross-sectional SLA studies and for which "there is often no detailed information about the learners themselves and the linguistic environment in which production was elicited" (Gass/Selinker 2001, 33).

Atkins/Clear/Ostler (1992) list 29 variables which corpus builders should consider (see also article 9). While many of these variables are also relevant for learner corpus building, the specific nature of learner language calls for the incorporation of L2-specific variables. Figure 15.1 represents some major variables that need to be controlled when compiling a learner corpus. Following Ellis (1994, 49), a distinction is made between learner variables which characterize the learner and task variables which pertain to the language situation. Each category contains general variables, i. e. variables that apply to any corpus building activity, and L2-specific variables, which are proper to learner corpus compilation. Note that Figure 15.1 is not complete and in fact cannot hope to be as "the factors that can bring about variation in learner output are numerous, perhaps infinite" (ibid).

Of the eight major learner variables represented in Figure 15.1, four are general (learner's age, gender, region and mother tongue background) and four L2-specific (learning context, proficiency level, amount of L2 exposure and knowledge of other foreign languages). Proficiency level is a highly important variable but it is also one that is particularly difficult to establish. The dominant proficiency level covered in current learner corpora falls in the intermediate-advanced range. This somewhat vague description reflects the well-known fact that "one researcher's advanced category may correspond to another's intermediate category" (Gass/Selinker 2001, 37). The fuzziness is compounded by the fact that compilers, following established corpus design practices (see Atkins/Clear/Ostler 1992, 5), have tended to use external criteria to compile their corpus. As regards proficiency, this comes down to favouring the criterion of 'institutional status' (computed in terms of number of years of English, for example) over other criteria such as specific research-designed tests or standardised tests (Thomas 1994). The problem with external assessment of proficiency is that it may cover varying degrees of linguistic proficiency. This has recently been proved with respect to the *ICLE* database. Although all the *ICLE* data come from English majors in their second, third or fourth year at university, a recent study by Granger/Thewissen (2005) shows that the proficiency levels range from B2 to C2 of the Common European Framework of Reference for Languages (http://www.coe.int/t/dg4/linguistic/Source/Framework_EN.pdf). If the learner corpus has been compiled on the basis of external criteria, it is therefore essential to resort to other proficiency measures when analysing the data. Failure to do so might lead researchers to attribute to factors such as the learners' mother tongue background language features that are in fact related to proficiency level.

In addition to the general task variables of medium, field and genre/text type, there is also a wide range of L2-specific task variables, which are roughly categorised as 'task type' and 'conditions' in Figure 15.1. 'Task type' refers to the type of activity learners are engaged in: role-play, informal interview, spontaneous conversation, argumentative essay or letter writing, picture description, etc. The term 'conditions' refers to the many factors that can influence learner production: time limitation, topic, possibility of using reference tools, mother tongue of interlocutor or interviewer, exam status of the activity, etc.

4. Raw vs. annotated learner corpora

Learner corpora also differ in their degree of processing. While most current learner corpora consist of raw data, i. e. they contain the learner texts with no added linguistic annotation, there are several projects based on part-of-speech (POS)-tagged corpora. The number of error-tagged learner corpora is also on the increase.

4.1. Grammatical annotation

While a raw learner corpus is in itself a highly useful resource, it is even more useful if it contains an extra layer of information, which can also be counted, sorted and compared. To this end, researchers can use ready-made annotating tools. However, it is important to bear in mind that all these programs – whether lemmatizers, POS-taggers, or parsers – have been trained on the basis of native speaker corpora and there is no guarantee that they will perform as accurately when confronted with learner data. While the success rate of POS-taggers has been found to be quite good with advanced learner data (Meunier 1998, 21), it has proved to be very sensitive to morpho-syntactic and orthographic errors (Van Rooy/Schäfer 2003) and success rate will therefore tend to decrease as the number of these errors increases. Pilot studies aimed at testing the reliability of linguistic annotation, which are recommended whatever the type of corpus used, are therefore a must with learner corpora. Similarly, while lemmatizers are potentially very useful for lexical analyses of inter language, researchers have to be aware that only the standard realisations of the lemma will be retrieved, i. e. for the lemma LOSE, the standard forms *lose/loses/losing/lost*, but not the (sometimes equally frequent!) non-standard forms *loose/looses/loosing/loosed*. If proved reliable, a POS-tagged learner corpus is a very powerful resource, enabling detailed studies of the use of grammatical categories, such as prepositions, phrasal verbs, modals, passives, etc.

4.2. Error annotation

POS-taggers and lemmatizers have undeniable advantages, not least of which is the fact that they generate an automatic linguistic analysis of the data and therefore considerably reduce the amount of manual work. However, researchers may want to add other types of annotation to the text, for which there are no ready-made programs. Any type of annotation is potentially useful (discourse annotation, syntactic annotation, etc.) and can be inserted into the text files with the help of editing tools. Error annotation is particularly relevant for interlanguage studies and is becoming increasingly popular. Several systems have been developed (Milton/Chowdhury 1994; Dagneaux/Denness/Granger 1998; Granger 2003b; Nicholls 2003; Lüdeling et al. 2005) and exploited in a series of innovative pedagogical applications. The error annotation system for English devised by Cambridge University Press uses “a two-letter coding system in which the first letter represents the general type of error (e. g. wrong form, omission), while the second identifies the word class of the required word” (Nicholls 2003, 573). A similar system devised for French as a Foreign Language is based on a three-tiered annotation system: error domain (form, morphology, grammar, lexis, etc), error category (number, tense, etc.) and word category of the misused item (verb, noun, etc.) (Granger 2003b). Sentences 1 and 2 illustrate the two error coding systems: a missing preposition error annotated using the Cambridge system (1), and an adjective gender agreement error annotated using the Louvain error coding system for French (2) (Granger 2003b).

(1) He said <#MT>|to</#MT> me that
(2) L’héritage du passé est très <G><GEN><ADJ> #fort$ forte </ADJ></GEN></G>

Error annotation usually includes the correction of the error, which means that a researcher has the option to start from a particular correction and find the full range of forms that have given rise to that correction or conversely, to retrieve all the possible corrections of a particular erroneous item. An interesting new development is the multi-level error annotation system which makes it possible to encode competing analyses of learner errors on several independent levels (Lüdeling et al. 2005).

While undoubtedly very useful, error annotation is also beset with difficulties. All three stages of the error coding procedure – error detection, correction and annotation – involve a high degree of subjectivity. To minimise subjectivity and increase inter-coder reliability, it is essential to have a coherent error coding system and a detailed error tagging manual, where all the error categories and error coding principles are defined and illustrated. Last but not least, it is important to design standardized XML-based error annotation systems which make interchange of annotated learner data easier and allow for the development of interoperable applications.

5. Learner corpus analysis

For a field that is still very young, learner corpus research has already generated a very rich and diversified body of research. The online learner corpus bibliography (http://cecl.fltr.ucl.ac.be) contains c. 300 publications and is a good starting point for any researcher wishing to embark on learner corpus analysis, as are the two edited volumes on learner corpus research, Granger (1998) and Granger/Hung/Petch-Tyson (2002). Up to now, the two most frequently-used methods of analyzing learner data are contrastive interlanguage analysis and computer-aided error analysis.

5.1. Contrastive interlanguage analysis

The contrastive interlanguage analysis (CIA) methodology involves comparing learner data with native speaker data (L2 vs. L1) or comparing different types of learner data (L2 vs. L2) (Granger 1996). The bulk of learner corpus studies to date have used this approach to investigate a wide range of topics, some of which – like high frequency vocabulary, modals, connectors and phraseological units – have received particular attention. Most of these CIA studies are based on unannotated learner corpora. A few, however, have used POS-tagged corpora to compare the frequency of grammatical categories or sequences of grammatical categories in native and learner corpora. These studies have all helped to bring to light the words, phrases, grammatical items and syntactic structures that are over- or underused by learners and which therefore contribute to the foreign-soundingness of perhaps otherwise error-free advanced interlanguage. The concordances in Figures 15.2 and 15.3 bring out some typical patterns of use of the verb *argue* in a large academic corpus of English and a comparable corpus of EFL learner writing.

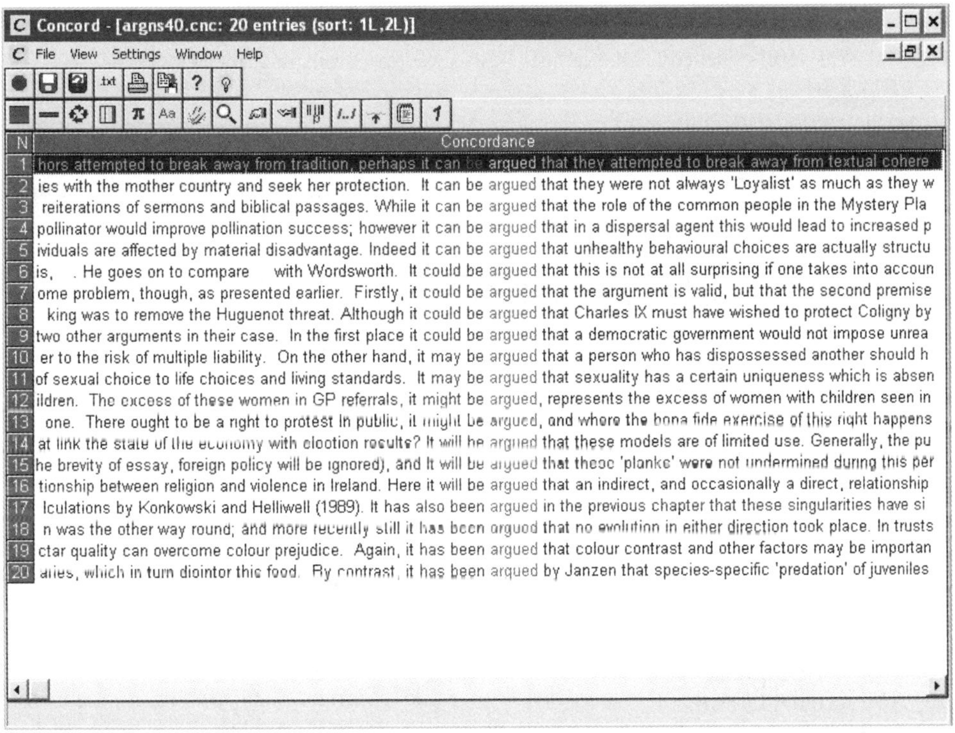

Fig. 15.2: The verb *argue*: concordance lines from a native corpus of academic writing

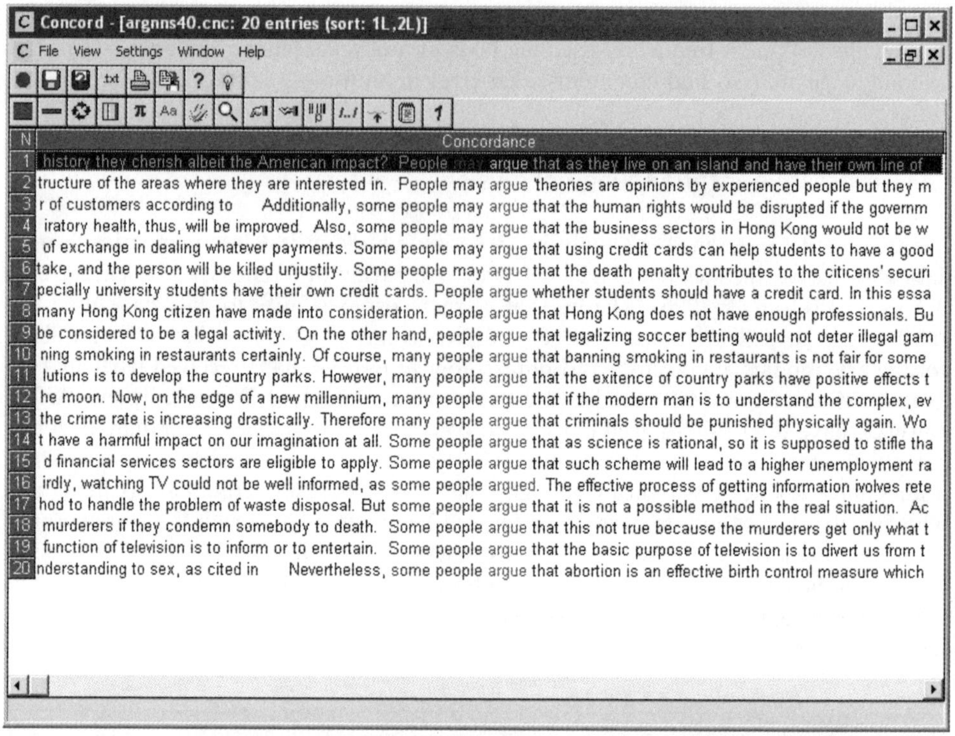

Fig. 15.3: The verb *argue:* concordance lines from a learner corpus of academic writing

5.2. Computer-aided error analysis

Computer-aided error analysis (CEA) involves analyzing learner errors on the basis of learner corpora in which error tags and possible corrections have been inserted with the help of a purpose-built editing tool. It differs from previous error analysis studies in some major respects, not least of which is the fact that errors are not isolated from the texts in which they originated, as was the case in traditional EA, but rather are studied in context alongside cases of correct use and over- and underuse. This approach has led to a much more limited number of publications than CIA, partly due to the difficulty of error annotation and the investment of time it involves, but also to the unpopularity of error analysis within the SLA community and a more general rejection of the notion of error in SLA and FLT. Recent years, however, have seen a revival of interest in error analysis, especially in pedagogical lexicography and language testing (cf. section 7).

6. Learner corpora and second language acquisition research

Learner corpora have a lot to contribute to SLA research. They lead researchers to a better understanding of how second languages are learned and can help them answer questions at the heart of SLA research, such as the as yet unresolved issue of the exact role of transfer in second language acquisition and the notion of avoidance. In spite of this, learner corpus research has failed to arouse great enthusiasm from SLA researchers so far, partly perhaps because they prefer to work with more controlled data, but also perhaps because of the extreme scarcity of longitudinal learner corpora. Another possible reason for the lack of enthusiasm of the SLA community is the use of the CIA approach, which compares interlanguage (IL) to native language and therefore views it not in its own right but rather as an incomplete version of the target language. This practice, which is referred to as the 'comparative fallacy', is presented as follows by Larsen-Freeman/Long (1991, 66): "researchers should not adopt a normative TL perspective, but rather seek to discover how an IL structure which appears to be non-standard is being used meaningfully by a learner". Hunston (2002, 211−212) expresses a similar view when she writes that one of the drawbacks of the CIA approach is that "it assumes that learners have native speaker norms as a target". However, she adds that the learner corpus approach also has two advantages: first, the standard is clearly identified and if felt to be inappropriate can be changed and replaced by another standard; and second, the standard is realistic; it is "what native/expert speakers actually do rather than what reference books say they do". More importantly perhaps, it should be pointed out that learner corpus research need not involve a comparison with native speaker norms (L2 vs. L1). Learner language can simply be studied in its own right or in comparison to other L2 varieties (L2 vs. L2).

The learner corpus studies conducted over the last decade or so have given us a much more accurate picture of advanced EFL interlanguage. This appears clearly from a study by Cobb (2003) who replicated three European learner corpus studies with Canadian data and found a high degree of similarity. The three studies highlighted the following characteristics of advanced interlanguage: overuse of high frequency vocabulary (Ringbom 1998), high frequency of use of a limited number of prefabs (De Cock et al. 1998) and a much higher degree of involvement (Petch-Tyson 1998). Several other studies point to the stylistic deficiency of advanced learner writing, which is often characterised by an overly spoken style or a somewhat puzzling mixture of formal and informal markers. All in all, learner corpus studies show that advanced interlanguage is the result of a highly complex interplay of factors: developmental, teaching-induced and transfer-related, some shared by several learner populations, others more specific. They suggest that "advanced learners are not defective native speakers cleaning up a smattering of random errors, but rather learners working through identifiable acquisition sequences. The sequences are not the *-ing* endings and third person *-s* we are familiar with, but involve more the areas of lexical expansion, genre diversification, and others yet to be identified" (Cobb 2003, 419).

Some recent studies show that the SLA community is beginning to see the interest of using learner corpus data to test SLA hypotheses (Housen 2002; Wible/Huang 2003). Housen (2002, 78) remarks that "computer-aided language learner corpus research provides a much needed quantificational basis" for current SLA hypotheses and makes it possible to "empirically validate previous research findings obtained from smaller transcripts, as well as to test explanatory hypotheses about pace setting factors in second language acquisition" (ibid, 108).

7. Learner corpora and language learning and teaching

Any link between learner corpora and language learning and teaching should be preceded by a major caveat. No rash links should be made between the descriptions of learner language based on CIA and/or CEA analyses and pedagogical applications. It is not because a feature has been found to function differently in learners and native speakers that it must be acted upon in language teaching. As Seidlhofer (2004, 25) puts it, talking of the possible application of ELF findings to teaching: "Language pedagogy should thus refer to, but not defer to, linguistic descriptions" (see also Widdowson 2003). Many factors govern the content and format of teaching, prime among which are teaching objectives. One should not attach the same importance to confusion between the relative pronouns 'that' and 'which' in a communication-oriented course for businessmen and an accuracy-oriented course for trainee translators or future teachers of English. Leech (1998, xix–xx) also warns learner corpus researchers against "the temptation to confuse description and prescription".

This said, learner corpus research opens up exciting pedagogical perspectives in a wide range of areas of language teaching pedagogy: materials design, syllabus design, language testing, and classroom methodology. Of these four fields, only the first can boast a number of concrete achievements.

7.1. Materials design

7.1.1. Reference tools

The latest edition of the *Longman Dictionary of Contemporary English* (2003), the second edition of the *Macmillan English Dictionary for Advanced Learners* (2007) and the new *Cambridge Advanced Learner's Dictionary* (2003), have drawn on large bodies of learner corpus data and added very useful 'common learner error' sections or 'warning notes' to draw learners' attention to common mistakes, such as the plural use of the noun *news* (*I was surprised by *these news*) or the use of the preposition *about* after the verb *discuss* (*we discussed * about the plans for the wedding*). This type of note is especially relevant in an advanced learners' dictionary, as at an advanced proficiency level, many errors have become fossilized and learners tend not to notice them, particularly as many do not hinder communication. The explicit negative feedback provided by warning notes can help learners notice their errors, an essential step towards their eventual eradication. An examination of these notes (De Cock/Granger 2005) shows that most of them target attested learner difficulties, but selection remains a critical issue as even advanced learner corpora contain a high number of errors, and space restrictions dictate that only a very small proportion can be included in paper versions of dictionaries. There is no doubt, however, that subsequent electronic versions of these dictionaries, where space is no longer so much of an issue, will be able to include more learner corpus-derived information and crucially to provide much more L1-specific information, currently sorely lacking, but which is so important to learners who, even at an advanced stage of proficiency, still have considerable difficulty with transfer-related errors.

While learner corpus data have begun to have a marked impact on dictionaries, at least for English, they have yet to find their way into learner grammars. However, it seems both inevitable and highly desirable that learner corpus data will become an essential component of grammar design in years to come. The high number of current error-tagging projects, in both academic and commercial sectors, suggests that progress will be rapid. Fully error-tagged learner corpora make it possible to identify the difficulties of learners at different proficiency levels. This in turn will help materials designers to select the topics for inclusion in EFL grammars and determine the weighting to be given to each of them.

7.1.2. Courseware

The impact of learner corpus studies on courseware has been greater on electronic tools than traditional textbooks. The reason is the high flexibility of the electronic medium, which enables academics to bypass publishers and produce their own tools directly. The pioneer of learner-corpus-informed CALL programs is Milton (1998), who has developed a writing kit called *WordPilot*, which targets Hong Kong learners' difficulties. Other packages include Cowan/Choi/Kim's (2003) *ESL Tutor* program, an error correction courseware tool that contains units targeting persistent grammatical errors produced by Korean ESL students. Another fine achievement is Wible et al.'s (2001) web-based writing environment, which contains a learner interface, where learners write their essays, send them to their teacher over the Internet and revise them when they have been corrected by the teacher, as well as a teacher interface, where teachers correct the essays using their favourite comments (comma splice, article use, etc.) stored in a personal Comment Bank. This environment is extremely attractive both for learners, who get immediate feedback on their writing and have access to lists of errors they are prone to produce, and for teachers, who progressively and painlessly build a large database of learner data which they can use to develop targeted exercises. Finally, Allan's (2002) web-based *TeleNex* project shows that learner corpora can also be put to good use in the field of teacher training. A large learner corpus, the *TELEC Student Corpus*, has been used to inform a teaching grammar hyperlinked to a database of graded teaching materials.

7.1.3. Syllabus design, language testing and classroom methodology

There are other areas of pedagogical application, such as syllabus design, language testing and classroom methodology, where the potential of learner corpus data is relatively unexploited. In both syllabus design and language testing, learner corpora can help practitioners select and rank teaching and/or testing material at a particular proficiency level (Barker 2003). As for classroom methodology, ideas about how to integrate learner corpus data have been put forward by several researchers, among whom Granger/Tribble (1998), Hewings (2000), Seidlhofer (2002), Pérez Paredes/Cantos-Gómez (2004) and Nesselhauf (2004a). However, here as for all uses of corpus data in teaching, there is a need for empirical validation. Tests so far have been few and far between and have mainly involved native speaker corpora (Cobb 1997; Gaskell/Cobb 2004). The use of learner corpus data in the classroom needs to be carefully monitored, but evidence of the value of explicit negative feedback in SLA suggests that learners might stand to gain from language-awareness exercises involving learner corpus data.

8. Conclusion

Learner corpus research sits at the crossroads between three fields: corpus linguistics, second language acquisition and foreign language teaching. While it has found a secure foothold in corpus linguistics, as evidenced by the presence of a learner corpus section in this handbook, it still has only limited influence in the other two fields. Interest is admittedly growing fast in the SLA and FLT communities, but for a major breakthrough to occur serious advances need to be made in the following areas. First, a wider range of learner corpora, in particular longitudinal, spoken and domain-specific, need to be compiled and disseminated. Secondly, more research should be devoted to learner corpus annotation, especially POS-tagging and error annotation. And last but certainly not least, learner corpora need to be carefully analysed and the results interpreted in the light of current SLA theory and incorporated in syllabus and materials design. Then and only then will learner corpus research have come into its own.

9. Literature

Allan, Q. G. (2002), The TELEC Secondary Learner Corpus: A Resource for Teacher Development. In: Granger/Hung/Petch-Tyson 2002, 195–212.

Atkins, B. T. S./Clear, J./Ostler, N. (1992), Corpus Design Criteria. *Literary and Linguistic Computing* 7(1), 1–16.

Barker, F. (2003) Learner Corpora and Testing Applications. Paper presented at the 25th Language Testing Research Colloquium, Reading, 22–25 July 2003.

Bartning, I. (2000), Gender Agreement in L2 French – Pre-advanced vs Advanced Learners. In: *Studia Linguistica* 54(2), 225–237.

Belz, J. A. (forthcoming), Telecollaboration, Contrastive Learner Corpus Analysis, and Data-driven Learning: Implications for Language Program Direction. In: Belz, J. A./Thorne, S. L. (eds.), *Internet-mediated Intercultural Foreign Language Education*. Boston: Heinle & Heinle.

Chapelle, C. (2004), Technology and Second Language Learning: Expanding Methods and Agendas. In: *System: An International Journal of Educational Technology and Applied Linguistics* 32, 593–601.

Cobb, T. (1997), Is There Any Measurable Learning From Hands-on Concordancing? In: *System: An International Journal of Educational Technology and Applied Linguistics* 25(3), 301–315.

Cobb, T. (2003), Analyzing Late Interlanguage with Learner Corpora: Quebec Replications of Three European Studies. In: *The Canadian Modern Language Review/La Revue canadienne des langues vivantes* 59(3), 393–423.

Cowan, R./Choi, H. E./Kim, D. H. (2003), Four Questions for Error Diagnosis and Correction in CALL. In: *CALICO Journal* 20(3), 451–463.

Dagneaux, E./Denness, S./Granger, S. (1998), Computer-aided Error Analysis. In: *System: An International Journal of Educational Technology and Applied Linguistics* 26(2), 163–174.

Debrock, M./Flament-Boistrancourt, D. (1996), Le corpus LANCOM: Bilan et perspectives. In: *ITL – Review of Applied Linguistics* 111–112, 1–36.

De Cock, S./Granger, S. (2005), Computer Learner Corpora and Monolingual Learners Dictionaries: The Perfect Match. In: Teubert, W./Mahlberg, M. (eds.), The Corpus Approach to Lexicography. Special issue of *Lexicographica* (20), 72–86.

De Cock, S./Granger, S./Leech, G./McEnery, T. (1998), An Automated Approach to the Phrasicon of EFL Learners. In: Granger, S. (ed.), *Learner English on Computer*. London/New York: Addison Wesley Longman, 67–79.

Degand, L./Perrez, J. (2004). Causale connectieven in het leerdercorpus Nederlands. In: *N/F* 4, 129–144.

Ellis, R. (1994), *The Study of Second Language Acquisition*. Oxford: Oxford University Press.

Gaskell, D./Cobb, T. (2004), Can Learners Use Concordance Feedback for Writing Errors? In: *System: An International Journal of Educational Technology and Applied Linguistics* 32(3), 301–319.

Gass, S. M./Selinker, L. (2001). *Second Language Acquisition. An Introductory Course*. Mahwah, NJ: Lawrence Erlbaum.

Granger, S. (1996), From CA to CIA and back: An Integrated Approach to Computerized Bilingual and Learner Corpora. In: Aijmer, K., Altenberg, B./Johansson, M. (eds.), *Languages in Contrast*. Lund: Lund University Press, 37–51.

Granger, S. (ed.) (1998), *Learner English on Computer*. London/New York: Longman.

Granger, S. (2003a), The International Corpus of Learner English: A New Resource for Foreign Language Learning and Teaching and Second Language Acquisition Research. In: *TESOL Quarterly* 37, 538–546.

Granger, S. (2003b), Error-tagged Learner Corpora and CALL: A Promising Synergy. In: *CALICO* 20(3), 465–480.

Granger, S./Dagneaux, E./Meunier, F. (eds.) (2002), *The International Corpus of Learner English. Handbook and CD-ROM. Version 1.1*. Louvain-la-Neuve: Presses universitaires de Louvain. Available from (http://www.i6doc.com).

Granger, S./Hung, J./Petch-Tyson, S. (eds.) (2002), *Computer Learner Corpora, Second Language Acquisition and Foreign Language Teaching*. (Language Learning and Language Teaching 6.) Amsterdam/Philadelphia: Benjamins.

Granger, S./Thewissen, J. (2005), Towards a Reconciliation of a 'Can do' and 'Can't do' Approach to Language Assessment. Paper presented at the EALTA (European Association for Language Testing and Assessment) Conference held at Voss, Norway, 2–5 June 2005.

Granger, S./Tribble, C. (1998), Learner corpus Data in the Foreign Language Classroom: Form-focused Instruction and Data-driven Learning. In: Granger, S. (ed.), *Learner English on Computer*. London/New York: Longman, 199–209.

Greenbaum, S. (1996), Introducing ICE. In: Greenbaum, S. (ed.), *Comparing English Worldwide. The International Corpus of English*. Oxford: Clarendon Press, 3–12.

Hammarberg, B. (1999), *Manual of the ASU Corpus, A Longitudinal Text Corpus of Adult Learner Swedish with a Corresponding Part from Native Swedes*. Stockholm: Stockholms universitet, Institutionen för lingvistik.

Hasselgren, A. (1997), The EVA Corpus of Norwegian School English. In: *ICAME Journal* 21, 123–124.

Hewings, M. (2000), Using Computer-based Corpora as a Teaching Resource. Available from (http://artsweb.bham.ac.uk/MHewings/grammar.htm).

Housen, A. (2002), A Corpus-based Study of the L2-acquisition of the English Verb System. In: Granger/Hung/Petch-Tyson 2002, 77–117.

Hunston, S. (2002), *Corpora in Applied Linguistics*. Cambridge: Cambridge University Press.

Ife, A. (2004), The L2 Learner Corpus: Reviewing its Potential for the Early Stages of Learning. In: Baynham, M./Deignan, A./White, G. (eds.), *Applied Linguistics at the Interface*. (British Studies in Applied Linguistics 19.) London: Equinox, 91–103.

Kachru, B. (1985), Standards, Codification and Sociolinguistic Realism. The English Language in the Outer Circle. In: Quirk, R./Widdowson, H. G. (eds.), *English in the World: Teaching and Learning the Language and Literatures*. Cambridge: Cambridge University Press, 11–30.

Larsen-Freeman, D./Long, M. H. (1991), *An Introduction to Second Language Acquisition Research*. London & New York: Longman.

Leech, G. (1998), Learner Corpora: What they are and What Can be Done with them. In: Granger, S. (ed.), *Learner English on Computer*. London/New York: Addison Wesley Longman, xiv–xx.

Lowenberg, P. H. (2002), Assessing English Proficiency in the Expanding Circle. In: *World Englishes* 21, 431–435.

Lüdeling, A./Walter, M./Kroymann, E./Adolphs, P. (2005), Multi-level Error Annotation in Learner Corpora. *The Corpus Linguistics Conference Series 1, 1. Corpus Linguistics 2005*. Available from (http://www.corpus.bham.ac.uk./PCLC).

Mauranen, A. (2003), Academic English as lingua franca – A Corpus Approach. In: *TESOL Quarterly* 37, 513–527.

Meunier, F. (1998), Computer Tools for the Analysis of Learner Corpora. In: Granger, S. (ed.), *Learner English on Computer*. London/New York: Addison Wesley Longman, 19–37.

Milton, J. (1998), Exploiting L1 and Interlanguage Corpora in the Design of an Electronic Language Learning and Production Environment. In: Granger, S. (ed.), *Learner English on Computer*. London/New York: Addison Wesley Longman, 186–198.

Milton, J./Chowdhury, N. (1994), Tagging the Interlanguage of Chinese Learners of English. In: Flowerdew, L./Tong, K. K. (eds.), *Entering Text*. Hong Kong: The Hong Kong University of Science and Technology, 127–143.

Myles, F./Mitchell, R. (2004), Using information technology to support empirical SLA research. In: *Journal of Applied Linguistics* 1(2), 169–196.

Nesselhauf, N. (2004a), Learner Corpora and their Potential in Language Teaching. In: Sinclair, J. (ed.), *How to Use Corpora in Language Teaching*. Amsterdam: Benjamins, 125–152.

Nesselhauf, N. (2004b), *Collocations in a Learner Corpus*. Amsterdam/Philadelphia: Benjamins.

Nicholls, D. (2003), The Cambridge Learner Corpus – Error Coding and Analysis for Lexicography and ELT. In: Archer, D./Rayson, P./Wilson, A./McEnery, T. (eds.), *Proceedings of the Corpus Linguistics 2003 Conference*. UCREL, Lancaster University, 572–581.

Pérez-Paredes, P./Cantos-Gómez, P. (2004), Some Lessons Students Learn: Self-directory and Corpora. In: Aston, G./Bernardini, S./Stewart, D. (eds.), *Corpora and Language Learners*. Amsterdam/Philadelphia: Benjamins, 247–257.

Petch-Tyson, S. (1998), Writer/Reader Visibility in EFL Written Discourse. In: Granger, S. (ed.), *Learner English on Computer*. London/New York: Addison Wesley Longman, 107–118.

Pravec, N. (2002), Survey of Learner Corpora. In: *ICAME Journal* 26, 81–114.

Ragan, P. H. (2001), Classroom Use of a Systemic Functional Small Learner Corpus. In: Ghadessy, A./Henry, A./Roseberry. R. L. (eds.), *Small Corpus Studies and ELT. Theory and Practice*. Amsterdam/Philadelphia: Benjamins, 207–236.

Reder, S./Harris, K./Setzler, K. (2003), The Multimedia Adult ESL Learner Corpus. In: *TESOL Quarterly* 37(3), 546–557.

Ringbom, H. (1998), Vocabulary Frequencies in Advanced Learner English: A Cross-linguistic Approach. In: Granger, S. (ed.), *Learner English on Computer*. London/New York: Addison Wesley Longman, 41–52.

Seidlhofer, B. (2002), Pedagogy and Local Learner Corpora: Working with Learning-driven Data. In: Granger/Hung/Petch-Tyson 2002, 213–234.

Seidlhofer, B. (2004), Research Perspectives on Teaching English as a lingua franca. In: *Annual Review of Applied Linguistics* 24, 209–239.

Sinclair, J. (1996) *EAGLES. Preliminary Recommendations on Corpus Typology*. Available from (http://www.ilc.cnr.it/EAGLES/corpustyp/corpustyp.html).

Tagnin, S. (2003), A Multilingual Learner Corpus in Brazil. In: Archer, D./Rayson, P./Wilson, A./McEnery, T. (eds.), *Proceedings of the Corpus Linguistics 2003 conference*. UCREL, Lancaster University, 940–945.

Tenfjord, K./Meurer, P./Hofland, K. (2004), The ASK corpus – A Language Learner Corpus of Norwegian as a Second Language. Paper presented at the TALC 2004 conference, Granada – Spain, 6–9 July 2004.

Thomas, M. (1994), Assesment of L2 Proficiency in Second Language Acquisition Research. In: *Language Learning* 44(2), 307–336.

Uzar, R./Walinski, J. (2001) Analysing the Fluency of Translators. In: *International Journal ofCorpus Linguistics 6*, 155–166.
Van Rooy, B./Schäfer, L. (2003), Automatic POS Tagging of a Learner Corpus: The Influence of Learner Error on Tagger Accuracy. In Archer, D./Rayson, P./Wilson, A./McEnery, T. (eds.), *Proceedings of the Corpus Linguistics 2003 conference*. UCREL, Lancaster University, 835–844.
Wible, D./Huang, P-Y. (2003), Using Learner Corpora to Examine L2 Acquisition of Tense-aspect Markings. In: Archer, D./Rayson, P./Wilson, A./McEnery, T. (eds.), *Proceedings of the Corpus Linguistics 2003 conference*. UCREL, Lancaster University, 889–898.
Wible, D./Kuo, C-H./Chien, F-Y./Liu, A./Tsao, N-L. (2001), A Web-based EFL Writing Environment: Integrating Information for Learners, Teachers, and Researchers. In: *Computers and Education* 37, 297–315.
Widdowson, H. G. (2003), *Defining Issues in English Language Teaching*. Oxford: Oxford University Press.

Sylviane Granger, Louvain-la-Neuve (Belgium)

16. Parallel and comparable corpora

1. Introduction

Parallel texts, that is, the same text in several languages, have of course been around long before the use made of them in corpus linguistics. A famous example is the Rosetta stone, erected in Egypt in 196 B.C. What makes the Rosetta stone interesting is that the writing on it is in two different languages (Egyptian and Greek) using three different scripts (hieroglyphic, Demotic and Greek). The structure of the hieroglyphic script was a riddle to scholars for several centuries until it was finally deciphered by the Frenchman Jean-Frangois Champollion in the 19th century. Champollion used his knowledge of Greek and Coptic (the later language of Christian era Egypt) and worked out the hieroglyphic inscriptions on the stone on the assumption that they were translations.

Present-day parallel texts have little in common with the original Rosetta stone. Nowadays there are sophisticated techniques for linking sources and translations, and the corpora are available electronically. The growth of parallel corpora and the development of new corpus techniques have gone hand in hand with an increased demand for multilingual competence and translation. There are, for example, 20 official languages in the European Union, and laws and other important documents have to be translated into one or several of the official languages in order to be legally binding in the member states. Moreover, prospective member countries have to translate a corpus of about 12 million words into their native language before they can join the union (Teubert 2002, 190). This situation provides a challenge for Translation Studies and for the practical training of translators and interpreters. Translators not only need a good multilingual competence but they also need to know about corpora and the possibilities these offer, such as providing terminological databases and translation memories (see article 55). Parallel corpora are also important in the field of language engineering. They provide large amounts of aligned bilingual or multilingual data which can be used for machine translation and bilingual and multilingual dictionary projects. Moreover the advent of parallel corpora on the corpus scene has led to a new interest in contrastive linguistics and its applications in second language teaching. Learners can use data from parallel corpora, for instance, to discover more about linguistic phenomena which are different in the two languages in question (see also article 7).

Contrastive corpus studies have a forum in the new journal *Languages in Contrast*, and international conferences (such as CULT – Corpus Use and Learning to Translate), workshops and projects all bring together linguists and practitioners with an interest in the design and use of multilingual corpora.

I will clarify my use of the terms *parallel corpus* and *comparable corpus* and discuss their advantages and disadvantages in section 2. Section 3 is devoted to the applications of multilingual corpora in different areas. In section 4 parallel corpora will be discussed from the point of view of the technology and the design features which make them different from monolingual corpora. A model and method of using parallel corpora are discussed in section 5. Section 6 reviews some parallel corpus projects. Finally, section 7 suggests some challenges for the future.

2. Parallel and comparable corpora

There are two types of multilingual corpora (see Figure 16.1). A fundamental distinction is that between parallel and comparable corpus. Parallel corpora consist of a source text and its translation into one or more languages. They can be further characterised in terms of the direction of the translation. If a corpus consists of e. g. English texts translated into Swedish, it is unidirectional; on the other hand, if this corpus also contains translations into English, it is bidirectional. Very often parallel corpora are aligned, either by sentence or by word (see article 32).

A comparable corpus on the other hand does not contain translations but consists of texts from different languages which are similar or comparable with regard to a number of parameters such as text type, formality, subject-matter, time span, etc.

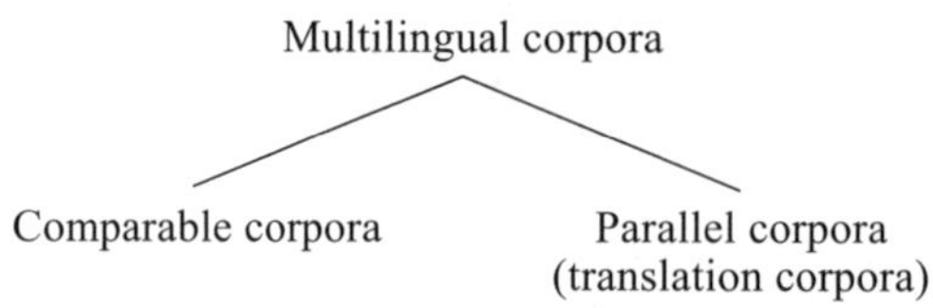

Fig. 16.1: Types of multilingual corpora

Not all researchers use the same terminology and 'translation corpus' is sometimes used instead of parallel corpus to refer to a source and its target (S. Johansson 1998). However the term is confusing since 'translation corpus' is used by translation theorists (especially by Baker, e. g. 1995) to refer to a collection of translation texts (without their sources).

In a multilingual parallel corpus there is a core language which has translations into many different languages (note that most existing parallel corpora are bilingual). Multilingual parallel corpora allow comparisons between more than two languages using many translations of the same original text. Such corpora are obviously more difficult to build since we need to find translations into more than one language. However they open up the possibility of carrying out truly multilingual research and extended language research, thus revitalizing the old paradigm of translation comparison (Viberg 2002, 121).

An early multilingual corpus consisting of non-fiction texts only is the Pedant Corpus (Danielsson/Ridings 1996) which includes Swedish, English, German and French parallel texts. The texts in the corpus are parallel in pairs: in the Pedant Corpus the core language is Swedish and one can search for combinations of Swedish-English, English-Swedish, Swedish-German, German-Swedish, etc. The Oslo Multilingual Corpus is organized as seen in Figure 16.2. The corpus consists of English original texts and their translations into German, Norwegian, Dutch and Portuguese (S. Johansson 1997a; see also http://www.hf.uio.no/german/sprik/english/corpus.shtml).

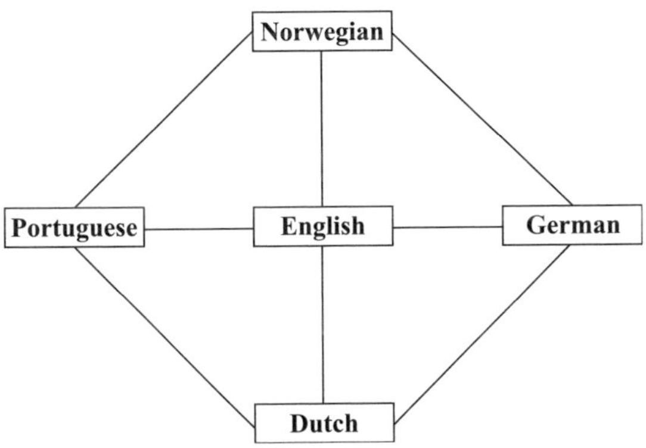

Fig. 16.2: Multilingual comparisons of English with translations into other languages in the Oslo Multilingual Corpus

The corpus can be used both for studying a particular text pair such as English and Portuguese and also for extracting multiple translations of a lexical item or construction in several languages.

Parallel corpora can be combined for cross-linguistic studies. Aijmer/Simon-Vandenbergen (2003) used the English Swedish Parallel Corpus, the Oslo Multilingual Corpus and the Triptic Corpus containing English-Dutch-French texts (see Paulussen 1999) to study translations of *well* into Swedish and Dutch. However in this setup the original texts were not the same.

Both parallel corpora and comparable corpora have their advantages and disadvantages. Comparable corpora may be easier to assemble since one can use already existing corpora. For example, Heyvaert (1998) used the COBUILD Corpus and the Dutch INL

(Instituut voor Nederlandse Lexicologie) Corpus to compare non-agentive deverbal *-er* nominalisations in English and Dutch (such as *bestseller*). Moreover it is sometimes necessary to use comparable corpora rather than parallel corpora, for example if one wants to compare varieties that are seldom or never translated, such as authentic spoken language, radio talk (Engel 1999), corporate brochures (McLaren 1999) or tourist information (Tognini Bonelli/Manca 2004). Comparable corpora have been used especially for contrastive analysis of languages for special purposes e. g. in areas such as contract law and genetic engineering (Lauridsen 1996).

However, comparable corpora are not ideal for contrastive analysis. Since it is difficult to guarantee the comparability of texts in different languages, a comparable corpus gives a less clear picture of the correspondences of a lexical item or construction than does a parallel corpus. For example, modal auxiliaries in one language can correspond more naturally to adverbs in another language (Løken 1997; Aijmer 1999), a fact which could be overlooked in a comparable corpus which does not provide sets or paradigms of translations.

The rationale for using translations is that they are a way of tapping native speakers' intuitions. The translator knows both languages involved and on the basis of this knowledge makes judgements on the meanings of words or constructions in order to produce a translation. Sinclair (1996) describes "translated" corpora as "large repositories of the decisions of professional translators, supplied together with the evidence they had for those decisions" (Sinclair 1996, 174); Noël (2003, 739) refers to parallel corpora as "a collection of informants' judgments about the meaning of the linguistic forms in the source texts, with the added advantage that they are readily available to the linguist, who does not have to worry about setting up an experimental setup".

A parallel corpus is unrivalled when it comes to discovering translation correspondences and displaying them as a set or a paradigm. The results based on the translations can be tested by studying monolingual corpora in the languages compared. Parallel corpora can also be used to establish contrastive lexical-semantic fields. This is done by going back and forth between translations.

A disadvantage of the parallel corpora which have been compiled for contrastive analysis and translation studies is their small size and the restriction to genres which are available in translation. Other objections have to do with the nature of the data. Thus the decisions made by the translators need not be trustworthy because translations are affected by the translation task and reflect the translator's personal style (Lauridsen 1996, 67). What is tested is therefore the behaviour of the translators rather than the translations themselves. This criticism can be met by having many different translators and a large number of translations as the empirical foundation for research.

Moreover, translated texts have special 'interlanguage' properties which are the effect of the translation process such as simplification or explicitation (Baker 1993) or 'translationese' (reflections of the source language in the target language: Gellerstam 1996; S. Johansson 2001). For example, English *probably* is translated into Swedish *förmodligen*, because the English and Swedish adverbs have the same semantic value, but they are not translation equivalents since they do not have the same stylistic value and frequency (Aijmer 2001).

Ebeling (2000, 25–26) summarises the criticism:

"1. translations distort the target language because of influence from the source language

2. translated language is different from original language
3. translators are unreliable and make mistakes
4. translations differ depending upon the individual translator
5. translations are unpredictable, motivated by reference to the text and its circum stances only".

3. Applications of multilingual corpora

In the 1990s, the technology and expertise were available for building multilingual corpora for cross-linguistic studies, and there was a revival of interest in cross-linguistic studies and in translation. Moreover researchers interested in natural language processing were turning more and more to parallel aligned corpora both for direct translation (Statistical Machine Translation, see article 56) and for examples based on translation (see articles 32 and 55). Brown et al. (1990), for example, introduced a statistical translation system based on an aligned French-English parallel corpus which computed language model probabilities (based on the ordering of words in three-word sequences or 'trigrams') and translation probabilities, and suggested a method for searching among source sentences for those providing the best probable translations on the basis of alignment. Another application of large parallel aligned corpora is to provide examples of translations on the basis of knowledge stored in the corpus (example-based machine translation). For example, if we have to translate a sentence in language A into language B, we can examine if we already have that sentence in language A and thus find its translation via alignment (McEnery/Wilson 1996, 157; see also article 56).

The impact of parallel corpora has been dramatic. With globalization, translation has become a centre-stage activity. It is obvious that corpora provide an enormous potential both for translators and students of translation. Parallel corpora are used in translation studies to investigate translator behaviour and how translations are constrained by factors such as translation norms.

Equally important, parallel corpora provide the means for identifying or highlighting similarities and differences between languages. They therefore complement the picture of what is universal in language familiar from the heyday of generative grammar.

Parallel corpora can, for example, be used to test hypotheses based on the monolingual corpora or on intuition. One such hypothesis is that the passive is a less 'strong', or frequent category if the language in question also has a generic pronoun. The translations can show in one or several languages whether the passive is retained or another correspondence is chosen.

The advantages of an aligned parallel corpus can be illustrated by a three-way comparison of expressions of the 'generic person' *one* in English and *man* in German and Norwegian (see example (1), taken from S. Johansson 1997a, 285). Although similar generic pronouns occur in all three languages, it is not self-evident that they are equivalent. The corpus can show both where they are equivalent and where they differ. The analysis of the corpus occurrences shows that, in comparison with German and Norwegian, English reveals a greater semantic variability of the subject and a stronger preference for the passive. Many differences are quantitative. While the second person pronoun may be used in all three languages (example (2), taken from S. Johansson 1997a, 287), it is used most frequently in Norwegian. Johansson finds interesting stylistic and semantic factors to explain this.

(1) a. All of a sudden *one* no longer feels at ease in what has always been one's own world. (ABR)
b. Plötzlich fühlt *man* sich nicht mehr ganz zu Hause in dem, was bisher stets die „eigene" Welt gewesen ist.
c. Plutselig føler *man* seg ikke hjemme i det som bestandig har vert ens „egen" verden.

(2) a. *One* may take one's health for granted.
b. *Man* mag seine Gesundheit als etwas Selbstverständliches nehmen.
c. *Du* kann ta det for gitt at du er frisk.

It is difficult to see how any other method could give such a clear and detailed picture of the relationship between the languages and contribute to the language-specific description of the languages compared.

The use of parallel corpora in translation studies is growing (see article 55). The approach known as Descriptive Translation Studies (DTS) emphasises empirical data and translations as they actually occur (Kenny 2001, 49; Olohan 2004). Several types of parallel corpora are used in translation studies. In these corpora, literary texts may be used; these texts are translated less literally than texts issued by political institutions. An example is the German-English Parallel Corpus of Literary Texts (GEPCOLT) which consists of one million words in each language. Some of the works were chosen because they were supposed to contain examples of lexical creativity (Kenny 2001).

To turn to another approach, Mona Baker is interested in translations rather than originals or the relationship between originals and translations and therefore compiled a corpus consisting of translations only (Baker 1995).

The Translation English Corpus (TEC) at the University of Manchester consists of translations of the same English text into several languages and has been used for the study of general features of translated texts such as explicitation, simplification, and normalisation (Holmes 1988; Laviosa 2002).

Parallel corpora are also used in translation training and teaching. An example is the ACTRES project which is concerned with building an English-Spanish corpus for teaching and research. The aim of the project goes from providing a descriptive framework for analysing translational shifts to the formulation of translational options to be used by translators and in translation training (Zanettin/Bernardini/Stewart 2003). Bowker/Pearson (2002) have drawn attention to how corpora can be used in LSP (language for special purposes) learning and translator training to build language-specific term banks.

The revival in contrastive linguistics has gone hand in hand with an interest in pragmatics and discourse, and the focus has been on language use as well as language systems. In what follows, I mention further contrastive work using the potential of parallel corpora both in more established areas such as lexicography and in pragmatics and discourse. The focus of these studies is on applications in language teaching and dictionaries.

3.1. Parallel corpora and multilingual lexicography

A parallel corpus functions like a bilingual dictionary. We can 'look up' the correspondences of a source item in a different language. However, the parallel corpus provides a richer inventory of meanings, and more context. Dictionaries also try to take into account larger patterns, but because of their limited size they cannot describe all the correspondences of a lexical item and explain how they are used. Not surprisingly, parallel corpora have important applications in lexicography (see Gellerstam et al. 1996 for a description of several large European bilingual projects and Altenberg/Granger 2002 for an overview of the research in bilingual and multilingual lexicography).

With the help of multilingual parallel corpora, linguists can investigate issues which are overlooked in traditional lexicography (Teubert 2001, 2002). For example, the 30-million word French-German Parallel Corpus (GeFre PaC), which records the legal and administrative language of the European Commission, has been used for a project with the aim of showing that parallel corpora are needed to complement traditional bilingual dictionaries (Teubert 2002, 203). This was accomplished by compiling bilingual French-German dictionaries containing those words which have been overlooked or not properly described in the traditional dictionaries. Teubert showed for instance that the French standard equivalent *travail* for German *Arbeit* was rare and that many other nouns were used as equivalents, some of which were not found in dictionaries (Teubert 2002, 206f).

A challenge to bilingual lexicography is to use parallel corpora to describe words with mainly pragmatic meaning. S. Johansson/Løken (1997) studied Norwegian modal particles and showed that they exhibit a much wider range of meanings in the English-Norwegian Parallel Corpus than in bilingual dictionaries. Some of the meanings which were frequent in the corpus were not mentioned at all in the dictionaries.

3.2. Parallel corpora and grammar

Parallel corpora can shed new light on grammatical phenomena which have mainly been studied on the basis of monolingual corpora. Information structure phenomena are of particular interest since we can expect translators to be sensitive both to the linguistic structure and to the structuring of information on the text level. For example, in translating the passive there may be a tension between focusing on the information structure and translating verbatim, which may be resolved differently depending on the language. M. Johansson (2002) has shown that cleft constructions differ in their distribution and function in English and Swedish. Although *it*-clefts occur in both English and Swedish, they appear in Swedish more frequently than in English and are often translated into English as 'unmarked' SOV constructions. One of the factors in this is, as Johansson suggests, that English requires contrastive contexts to licence clefting to a higher extent than Swedish. Another factor might be functional differences between clefts in the two languages. Concurring results are given in Ahlemeyer/Kohlhof (1999).

3.3. Parallel corpora and metaphor

The use of parallel corpora has been extended to more and more areas sometimes only as a complement to other corpus studies. This is particularly true if we investigate infrequent phenomena. Pioneering research has for instance been carried out in the area of metaphor. Established metaphors can be searched for automatically. For example, body metaphors in several languages can be studied in this way, although such studies may need to be complemented by monolingual studies (Mol 2004; Cardey/Greenfield 2002). Metaphorical extensions can also be investigated using parallel corpora. Thus Chun (2002) compared the metaphorical uses of *up/down* in English and the correspondences in Chinese in a cognitive semantic framework. Parallel corpora have also been used to study innovative metaphors and the images they call up in translations into other languages (Wikberg 2004). However, the metaphors could not be searched for automatically in this case: the whole source text had to be read.

4. Design of a parallel corpus

The design of a parallel corpus involves a number of issues that do not have to be taken into account in the design of a monolingual corpus. It is not always easy to get a particular text or text type with a translation (or translations), because many text types are rarely translated. Sometimes the direction of the translation might restrict the sample. For example, while a large number of non-fiction texts have been translated from English into Swedish, there are hardly any translations in the opposite direction. EU documents seem to be a good starting-point for assembling parallel texts, but it is sometimes difficult to decide which of the texts is the original one (Lauridsen 1996). Moreover, copyright has to be obtained for each of the paired texts before they can be included in the corpus.

We cannot discuss language sampling and size of a parallel corpus without considering the purpose of the corpus. The compilation of parallel corpora for language engineering and for machine translation is regulated by other principles than those for parallel corpora assembled for cross-linguistic research or translation studies. For machine translation purposes, corpora must be large and the composition may not be as important. For contrastive studies corpora can be quite small, but have to be much more carefully designed. Ideally the sampling should be based on a large number of text categories.

Preprocessing of the corpus involves 'sentence breaking' and tokenization (cf. article 32): marking up the structure of the text using a mark-up language such as SGML (S. Johansson/Ebeling/Hofland 1996) or XML makes it possible to identify the major units of text such as chapters, paragraphs and sentences (s-units). (See further Sperberg-McQueen/Burnard 1994 and http://www.tei-c.org/ on the guidelines set up by the Text Encoding Initiative; see also article 22).

The usefulness of a parallel corpus can be enhanced by part-of-speech tagging using one of the available tagging programs, using e. g. constraint grammar (Karlsson 1990; also, see article 24). After tagging, one can carry out more sophisticated linguistic analyses. Grammatical tagging of the parallel corpus makes it easier to compare linguistic phenomena in two languges. S. Johansson (1997b) for instance compared different negation types in English and Norwegian on the basis of the part-of-speech tagging in the English-Norwegian Parallel Corpus. Tagging is especially helpful if a construction first needs to be disambiguated. For example, in English the passive uses of the verbal participle have to be distinguished from other uses of the verbal participle before the parallel corpus can be used to investigate the correspondences between passives (Fredriksson 2004).

Alignment is required if we want to make use of the corpus for language engineering, and is also helpful for other purposes. Put simply, alignment implies that sentences (words or paragraphs) are linked to corresponding units in the target text (see article 32). An aligned parallel corpus can for instance be used in addition to other natural language processing tools to build terminology banks, to construct bilingual dictionaries, and for statistical and example-based machine translation (Veronis 2000; for details see also article 32). It is also vital for exploring fine-grained differences between languages which can be explained as due to the language system or to the translator.

A great deal of work on alignment of sentences uses the method of anchor words (Simard/Foster/Isabelle 1992). Johansson/Hofland (1994) use a combination of sentence length, shared 'anchor words' as defined in a bilingual word list, and some additional criteria to establish correspondences between sentences for the English-Norwegian Parallel Corpus. Other methods for sentence alignment are based on statistical calculations of sentence length in the source language and the target language (Church/Gale 1991). Word alignment is more difficult to achieve but is important as an aid to creating bilingual dictionaries and terminology databases automatically (cf. Choueka/Conley/Dagan 2000 and the references to recent publications on word alignment). The results for alignment of multiword units are also promising (Gaussier/Langé/Meunier 1992).

Cognates play an important role in machine translation as anchor words in aligning sentences and words. The term 'cognate' is used in alignment in a slightly different way than in historical linguistics: here cognates are formally similar words. However, the use of 'cognates' is not always straightforward since not all formally similar words are semantic equivalents in two languages (cf. the issue of the so-called 'false friends'). Even in the cases of correspondence, intertranslatability seldom reaches 100% and is confined to specific contexts. In order to use the notion for translation studies, language teaching and machine translation, we need a more refined description of equivalence.

Viberg (1996, 1999), for example, has shown that the intertranslatability between English *go* and its Swedish cognate *gå* is low. The congruent cases represent 35% of all the cases of *gå* and a little more than 33% of all the occurrences of *go*. Most of the congruent cases represent the prototypical meaning 'motion by a human being'. However there is very little overlap between the grammatical constructions involving *go* and *gå*. For instance, there is no use of *gå* that would correspond to the *be+going to future*.

If the texts are word-aligned it is possible to use a search engine such as the Translation Corpus Explorer (Ebeling 1998) to search for corresponding lexical items. If the corpus is sentence-aligned, a search for a particular lexical item (or construction) in L1 yields the sentence containing the item searched for as well as its translation into the other language. In addition to such 'browsers', which also allow complex searches, one can use parallel concordancers such as ParaConc (Barlow 1995) to produce equivalents of the source item.

The above mentioned English-Norwegian Parallel Corpus (ENPC) is an example of a corpus designed for contrastive research and translation studies. It contains both translations and comparable (monolingual) texts. The potential of the English-Norwegian Parallel Corpus is illustrated by the boxes in the diagram in Figure 16.3.

The corpus is bidirectional (there are translations from English into Norwegian and from Norwegian into English). In this way it is possible to test whether the similarities and differences between the languages are genuine or due to translation processes. This possibility is spelled out in M. Johansson's Translation Mirror Principle (TMP) (M. Johansson 2002, 52):

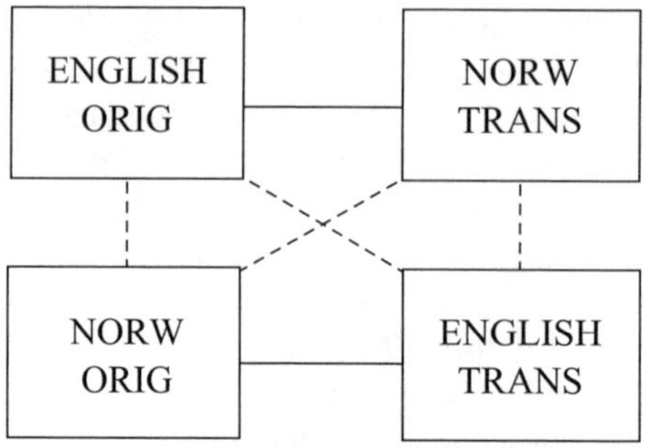

Fig. 16.3: The structure of the English-Norwegian Parallel Corpus

> "Statistical similarities and differences in a comparison of a corpus of original texts from L1 and L2 represent genuine similarities and differences to the extent that they are mirrored, in a significant way, in translations from L1 into L2 and from L2 into L1."

The parallel corpus makes it possible to measure to what degree a certain translation is 'successful' or 'natural'. By comparing correspondences in translations and sources we can compute a measure of mutual correspondence (Altenberg 1999). This value is 100% if there is complete cross-linguistic correspondence between an item in the source language and the target language, and zero if there is no correspondence between the items. The mutual correspondence value is established by comparing the translations in both directions. Items having a mutual correspondence value of 75% represent a stronger degree of intertranslatability than items with a mutual correspondence of only 10%.

5. The parallel corpus – a model and a method

As mentioned above, translations and parallel corpora have contributed to the exploration of similarities and differences between languages (see e. g. the articles in the volume edited by Johansson/Oksefjell 1998, and Hasselgård/Oksefjell 1999). The steps in the analysis and the discussion of 'the parallel corpus method' are inspired by Dyvik (1998, 1999, 2004) and involve notions such as 'semantic mirror', 'translation paradigm' and 'cross-linguistic semantic fields'. According to Dyvik meanings are 'mirrored' in the translations. Semantic equivalence is not straightforward, and the translations need to be analysed in terms of ambiguity, polysemy or vagueness. The verb *think*, for example, has three different translations in Swedish, each representing a separate reading: *tänka* ('cogitation'), *tycka* ('subjective evaluation') and *tro* ('belief') (Aijmer 1998), and a similar distinction is made in Dutch (Simon-Vandenbergen 1998). The question, then, is whether *think* in English should be regarded as ambiguous.

Words or constructions exhibit their meanings in the form of a translation paradigm consisting of all their translations into another language. The translation paradigm provides a 'rich' description of what a lexical element or construction means, and how it functions, by considering the translations into one or more languages.

Tab. 16.1: *of course* and its equivalents in Swedish and Dutch based on Simon-Vandenbergen/Aijmer (2004, 38). ESPC stands for the English-Swedish Parallel Corpus and OMC for the Oslo Multilingual Corpus; the figures refer to the number of occurrences retrieved from the corpora

Swedish translation	ESPC	Dutch translation	OMC
förstås ('of course')	63	natuurlijk 'naturally'	76
naturligtvis ('of course')	57	uiteraard 'of course'	13
givetvis	28		
det är klart (att) ('it is clear that')	17		
Ø	6	Ø	1
visst ('certainly')	5		
fast det är klart ('although it is clear')	4		
ju ('of course', 'to be sure', 'why!')	3		
ja det är klart ('yes, it is clear')	2		
visserligen ('it is true','certainly')	2		
javisst ('oh yes')	1		
men ...ju ('but ... of course' etc.)	1		
naturellement ('naturally')	1		
självfallet ('obviously', 'evidently')	1		
självklart ('obviously', 'evidently')	1		
genast ('at once')	1		
jo det är klart ('yes, it is clear')	1		
TOTAL	192		90

Table 16.1 illustrates a simplified paradigm for *of course* in Swedish and Dutch based on Simon-Vandenbergen/Aijmer (2004, 38).

As shown in Table 16.1, there is only weak equivalence between the languages. Even the most frequent or prototypical translations (Swe. *förstås*, Du. *natuurlijk*) have a correspondence ratio far below 100%.

Parallel corpora can also be used to establish contrastive lexical-semantic fields. This is done by going back and forth between translations. Words which share a number of translations are semantically close. If, on the other hand, words in the two languages do not share any translations, they do not belong to the same semantic field. In this way we can establish systems and subsystems based on the strength of the equivalents. Altenberg (1999), for instance, has studied the area of contrastive conjuncts as a *tertium comparationis* (that which constitutes the common ground) and shown that it can be structured into different subfields on the basis of translations.

Translation paradigms contain (structurally) congruent translations and non-congruent (divergent) translations. The non-congruent translations can be accounted for by differences in the language system or by other linguistic factors such as the context, register, medium or by general factors involved in the translation process as such.

One type of non-congruent translation is represented by 'omission'. Omission or zero-correspondences in the translation may have several motives (Aijmer/Altenberg 2001). The amount of omission in a parallel corpus may be related to the way the alignment is carried out or it can be a result of the translation process itself. Omission may also be of interest for contrastive analysis and translation studies. The cases of omission which are of particular interest for contrastive analysis are those where omission signals that there is a lexical gap. For example, "small" words such as *well* and *oh* often lack direct correspondences in other languages and are therefore omitted in the translation. *Well* was omitted in translations from English into Swedish in 21 % of the examples (Aijmer/Simon-Vandenbergen 2003) and in 39 % of the examples from English into Italian (Bazzanella/Morra 2000; Fischer 2000).

The quantitative nature of the data influences how the analysis on the basis of parallel corpora is carried out. The use of quantitative methods in parallel corpus studies goes beyond counting frequencies. On the basis of the frequencies, statistical significance for the reliability of the correspondences, for instance, can be calculated. There are also more sophisticated statistical methods which can be used to establish word pairs in the corpus. Mutual information rather than simple frequencies, for instance, can be used to show which word pairs in an aligned parallel corpus are statistically most significant (McEnery/Wilson 1996). The more frequently two items occur together, the higher their mutual information score will be. Mutual information can also be used to calculate the strength of association between the elements in collocations (e. g. 'strong tea') and variable phrases (but see article 36).

Parallel corpora provide the data for different theories and approaches and are studied using different methods. In multilingual computational linguistics and machine translation the basis is often Transformational Grammar or another formal syntactic theory. The focus is on the syntactic differences or transfers between the source language and the target language. Roughly speaking, a source language sentence is parsed and the parse tree is then transferred into a syntactic tree in the target language from which a translation can be generated. However, syntactic theory has generally very little to say about the variation between languages and the motives for it except in very simple cases of word order change. Thus a translation may be syntactically correct but semantically or pragmatically inappropriate. Certain correspondences would therefore be difficult to account for. For example, there is a literal correspondence between the modal auxiliary *may/might* in English and *kan* in Swedish. However, the best translation is with the modal adverb *perhaps* in the epistemic meaning (Aijmer 1999; cf. Løken 1997 on Norwegian). For this reason, some projects in machine translation have also built very elaborate formal representations of the semantic structure (for example the Verbmobil project, see Wahlster 2000).

Parallel corpora could also help in researching typological differences between languages. However, they are not yet widely used, since many typologists are looking for universal categories and similarities between languages and are not concerned with differences between languages which become evident when we compare texts in a corpus.

Both contrastive linguistics and translation theory start from the analysis of actual texts. However, the concerns of contrastive linguistics and translation studies are different. For example translation theorists (Olohan 2004) would account for deviations such as zero translations, overuse and underuse in terms of general translation features such as simplification, omission or normalization (Baker 1995). It can be argued that the focus on translation strategies can lead to a neglect of underlying differences between the languages both with regard to language system and language use.

Contrastive analysis is also based on the study of similarities and differences between the languages in texts but explains them in terms of differences between the language systems rather than in terms of the translation situation. There may, however, be several factors explaining why a certain translation is chosen, including translation norms (see also article 54).

6. Parallel corpora – an inventory

Characterising the state of the art in parallel corpus studies is difficult because parallel corpora are constructed for so many different purposes. It is, however, possible to make an inventory of some of the language pairs which are represented. Let me mention a few projects, some of them already touched upon above. In the Scandinavian countries the English-Norwegian Parallel Corpus (S. Johansson 1998) and the English-Swedish Parallel Corpus (Altenberg/Aijmer 2000) are sister projects designed in the same way. Finland is represented in the Scandinavian group through the Finnish-English Contrastive Corpus Studies (FECCS) project at the University of Jyväskylä (Mauranen 1999). The English-Norwegian corpus has been an inspiration for other corpora e. g. the English-Italian Translational Corpus (Zanettin 2000). The Chemnitz English-German Translation Corpus includes a large number of text types, including academic textbooks and EU publications (Schmied 2004). The INTERSECT Corpus contains about 1.5 million words including articles from *Le Monde* and their translations in the *Guardian Weekly*, texts from international organisations, modern fiction and academic textbooks (Salkie 1997). It has been aligned and can be searched with the help of ParaConc. In the COMPARA/DISPARA project the goal is to provide Portuguese parallel text aligned with other languages (Santos 1998).

Probably the best known parallel corpus is the Canadian Hansards Corpus, containing debates from the Canadian Parliament which have been published in the country's official languages, English and French (Germann 2001; Och/Ney 2000). Such texts are available on the World Wide Web and they provide large quantities of literal translations. The corpus, which was collected during the eighties, has been used, for instance, to add and improve on information in machine-readable bilingual dictionaries. There are now several multilingual aligned corpora which include many different languages besides English. The *Europarl* Corpus is a multilingual corpus available in 11 languages, consisting of over 20 million words per language, which is mainly used for statistical machine translation (Köhn 2005). In the OPUS Corpus the translated texts come from the public domain and have been collected from the World Wide Web. It is one of the largest statistical machine translation systems, including 110 language pairs (Tiedemann/Nygaard 2003). Another well-known parallel corpus is the corpus of Plato's *Republic*; the text has been translated into seventeen languages (Erjavec/Lawson/Romary 1998).

The majority of existing parallel corpora deal with European languages which are typologically similar. Parallel corpora are not in principle restricted to languages which are structurally related; however, we need more sophisticated alignment methods to identify the matching linguistic units when the languages are unrelated. An interesting parallel corpus project is, for instance, the English-Chinese Parallel Corpus, which has been used to compare the aspect systems of English and Chinese (McEnery/Xiao 1999, see article 46).

7. Challenges for the future

The future of parallel corpora looks bright. The number of parallel corpora for different purposes is increasing, and they are growing in size. The parallel corpora of the future will be able to use the resources of the Web and include large amounts of translated texts in many languages. The almost unlimited size of the new parallel corpora makes it possible to refine alignment techniques and to improve the success rate for the alignment of words and phrases.

It is likely that the parallel corpora used by researchers in contrastive linguistics and translation studies will remain fairly small because of the problems of finding texts which offer good correspondences. Parallel corpora were first used for lexical and grammatical studies but corpora are also helpful in other areas because they provide authentic data in different languages. Thus we can expect to see more cross-linguistic studies in text linguistics, genre analysis, and in cognitive semantics in the areas of metaphor and metonymy.

Parallel corpora have applications in many different fields. The growing global market will result in an increased need for translators and more resources for translation training. The pedagogical implications of parallel corpora are still in their infancy. Parallel corpora provide a window on similarities and differences between languages and will be useful in second-language teaching for raising the learners' awareness not only of the large systematic differences between languages but also of more fine-grained differences. Parallel corpora are indispensable tools for bilingual lexicography, extraction of term banks and for translation memories. They have led to a revival of contrastive linguistics by giving contrastive studies a firmer empirical footing (see also article 54).

The empirical studies of linguistic phenomena on the basis of parallel corpora show that there is much to discover about translation from actual texts. However, as also discussed in article 55, interaction between scholars using parallel corpora as a source of data in different disciplines is only a recent phenomenon. In the future we would expect much more cross-fertilization between disciplines under the banner of a common interest in translation and parallel corpora.

8. Literature

Ahlemeyer, B./Kohlhof, I. (1999), Bridging the Cleft: An Analysis of the Translation of English *it*-clefts into German. In: *Languages in Contrast* 2(1), 1−25.

Aijmer, K. (1998), Epistemic Predicates in Contrast. In: Johansson/Oksefjell 1998, 277−295.

Aijmer, K. (1999), Epistemic Possibility in an English-Swedish Contrastive Perspective. In: Hasselgård/Oksefjell 1999, 301−323.

Aijmer, K. (2001), *Probably* in Swedish Translations − a Case of Translationese? In: Allen, S./Berg, S./Malmgren, S.-G./Norén, K./Ralph, B. (eds.), *Gäller stam, suffix och ord.* Göteborg: Meijerbergs institut för svensk etymologisk forskning, 1−13.

Aijmer, K./Altenberg, B. (2001), Zero Translations and Cross-linguistic Equivalence: Evidence from the English-Swedish Parallel Corpus. In: Hasselgren, A./Breivik, L. E. (eds.), *From the COLT's Mouth, and Other Places: Studies in Honour of Anna-Brita Stenström.* Amsterdam: Rodopi, 19−41.

Aijmer, K./Altenberg, B. (eds.) (2004), *Advances in Corpus Linguistics. Papers from the 23rd International Conference on English Language Research on Computerized Corpora (ICAME 23), Göteborg 22−26 May 2002.* Amsterdam: Rodopi.

Aijmer, K./Altenberg, B./Johansson, M. (eds.) (1996), *Languages in Contrast: Papers from a Symposium on Text-based Cross-linguistic Studies.* Lund: Lund University Press.

Aijmer, K./Simon-Vandenbergen, A.-M. (2003), The Discourse Particle *well* and its Equivalents in Swedish and Dutch. In: *Linguistics* 41(6), 1123−1161.

Altenberg, B. (1999), Adverbial Connectors in English and Swedish: Semantic and Lexical Correspondences. In: Hasselgård/Oksefjell 1999, 249–268.

Altenberg, B./Aijmer, K. (2000), The English-Swedish Parallel Corpus: A Resource for Contrastive Research and Translation Studies. In: Mair, C./Hundt, M. (eds.), *Corpus Linguistics and Linguistic Theory. Papers from the 20th International Conference on English Language Research on Computerized Corpora (ICAME 20) Freiburg im Breisgau (1999)*. Amsterdam/Philadelphia: Rodopi, 15–33.

Altenberg, B./Granger, S. (eds.) (2002), *Lexis in Contrast: Corpus-based Approaches*. Amsterdam: Benjamins.

Baker, M. (1993), Corpus Linguistics and Translation Studies: Implications and Applications. In: Baker, M./Francis, G./Tognini-Bonelli, E. (eds.), *Text and Technology: In Honour of John Sinclair*. Amsterdam/Philadelphia: John Benjamins, 233–250.

Baker, M. (1995), Corpora in Translation Studies: An Overview and Some Suggestions for Future Research. In: *Target* 7(2), 223–243.

Barlow, M. (1995), ParaConc: A Concordancer for Parallel Texts. In: *Computers and Texts* 10, 14–16.

Bazzanella, C./Morra, L. (2000), Discourse Markers and the Indeterminacy of Translation. In: Korzen, I./Marello, C. (eds.), *Argomenti per una linguistica della traduzione, On Linguistic Aspects of Translation, Notes pour une linguistique de la traduction*. Alessandria: Edizioni dell' Orso, 149–157.

Bowker, L./Pearson, J. (2002), *Working with Specialized Language. A Practical Guide to Using Corpora*. London/New York: Routledge.

Brown P. F./Cocke, J./Della Pietra, V. J./Jelinek, F./Mercer, R. L./Roossin, P. (1990), A Statistical Approach to Machine Translation. In: *Proceedings of the 12th International Conference on Computational Linguistics (COLING'88)*. Budapest, Hungary, 71–76.

Cardey, S./Greenfield, P. (2002), Computerised Set Expression Dictionaries: Analysis and Design. In: Altenberg/Granger 2002, 231–248.

Choueka, Y./Conley, E. S./Dagan, I. (2000), A Comprehensive Bilingual Word System. Application to Disparate Languages: Hebrew and English. In: Veronis, J. (ed.), *Parallel Text Processing. Alignment and Use of Translation Corpora*. Dordrecht/Boston/London: Kluwer Academic Publishers, 69–96.

Chun, L. (2002), A Cognitive Approach to *Up/Down* Metaphors in English and *Shang/Xia* Metaphors in Chinese. In: Altenberg/Granger 2002, 151–174.

Church, K. W./Gale, W. A. (1991), Concordances for Parallel Text. In: *Using Corpora: Proceedings of the Eighth Annual Conference of the UW Centre for the New OED and Text Research* (Oxford, September 29–October 1, 1991), 40–62.

Danielsson, P./Ridings, D. (1996), *Pedant: Parallel Texts in Göteborg*. (Research Reports from the Department of Swedish, GU-ISS-96-2.) Göteborg University: Språkdata.

Dyvik, H. (1998), A Translational Basis for Semantics. In: Johanssson/Oksefjell 1998, 51–86.

Dyvik, H. (1999), On the Complexity of Translation. In: Hasselgård/Oksefjell 1999, 215–230.

Dyvik, H. (2004), Translations as Semantic Mirrors: From Parallel Corpus to Wordnet. In: Aijmer/Altenberg 2004, 311–326.

Ebeling, J. (1998), The Translation Corpus Explorer: A Browser for Parallel Texts. In: Johansson/Oksefjell 1998, 101–112.

Ebeling, J. (2000), *Presentative Constructions in English and Norwegian. A Corpus-based Contrastive Study*. (Acta Humaniora 68.) Oslo: Unipub forlag.

Engel, D. M. (1999), Radio Talk: French and English Perfects on Air. In: *Languages in Contrast* 1(2), 255–277.

Erjavec, T./Lawson, A./Romary, L. (eds.) (1998), *East Meets West: A Compendium of Multilingual Resources*. Mannheim: Institut für Deutsche Sprache/TELRI Association e.V.

Fischer, K. (2000), *From Cognitive Semantics to Lexical Pragmatics. The Functional Polysemy of Discourse Particles*. Berlin/New York: Mouton de Gruyter.

Fredriksson, A.-L. (2004), Exploring Theme Contrastively: The Choice of Model. In: Aijmer/Altenberg2004, 353–370.

Gaussier, E./Langé, J. M./Meunier, F. (1992), Towards Bilingual Terminology. In: *Proceedings of the Joint ALLC/ACH Conference*. Oxford, United Kingdom, 121–124.

Gellerstam, M. (1996), Translations as a Source for Cross-linguistic Studies. In: Aijmer/Altenberg/Johansson 1996, 53–62.

Gellerstam, M./Järborg, J./Malmgren, S.-G./Norén, K./Rogström, L./Röjder Papmehl, C. (eds.) (1996), *Euralex '96 Proceedings I–II. Papers Submitted to the Seventh Euralex International Congress on Lexicography in Göteborg, Sweden*. Göteborg: Department of Swedish, University of Göteborg.

Germann, U. (2001), *Aligned Hansards of the 36th Parliament of Canada*. http://www.isi.edu/natural-language/download/hansard.

Hasselgård, H./Oksefjell, S. (eds.) (1999), *Out of Corpora: Studies in Honour of Stig Johansson*. Amsterdam: Rodopi.

Heyvaert, L. (1998), Non-agentive Deverbal *-er* Nominalization in English and Dutch: A Contrastive Analysis. In: *Languages in Contrast* 1(2), 211–243.

Holmes, J. S. (1988), *Translated! Papers on Literary Translation and Translation Studies*. Amsterdam: Rodopi.

Johansson, M. (2002), Clefts in English and Swedish: A Contrastive Study of IT-clefts and WH-clefts in Original Texts and Translations. PhD Thesis, University of Lund.

Johansson, S. (1997a), Using the English-Norwegian Parallel Corpus – a Corpus for Contrastive Analysis and Translation Studies. In: Lewandowska-Tomasczyk, B./Melia, J. (eds.), *PALC '97. Practical Applications in Language Corpora*. Lodz: University of Lodz, 282–286.

Johansson, S. (1997b), In Search of the Missing *not:* Some Notes on Negation in English and Norwegian. In: Fries, U./Müller, V./Schneider, P. (eds.), *From Ælfric to the New York Times. Studies in English Corpus Linguistics*. Amsterdam/Atlanta, GA: Rodopi, 197–214.

Johansson, S. (1998), On the Role of Corpora in Cross-linguistic Research. In: Johansson/Oksefjell 1998, 3–24.

Johansson, S. (2001), Translationese: Evidence from the English-Norwegian Parallel Corpus. In: Allen, S./Berg, S./Malmgren, S.-G./Norén, K./Ralph, B. (eds.), *Gäller stam, suffix och ord*. Göteborg: Meijerbergs institut för svensk etymologisk forskning, 162–176.

Johansson, S./Ebeling, J./Hofland, K. (1996), Coding and Aligning the English-Norwegian Parallel Corpus. In: Aijmer/Altenberg/Johansson 1996, 87–112.

Johansson, S./Hofland, K. (1994), Towards an English-Norwegian Parallel Corpus. In: Fries, U./Tottie, G./Schneider, P. (eds.), *Creating and Using English Language Corpora*. Amsterdam: Rodopi, 25–37.

Johansson, S./Løken, B. (1997), Some Norwegian Discourse Particles and their English Correspondences. In: Bache, C./Klinge, A. (eds.), *Sound, Structures and Senses. Essays Presented to Niels Davidsen-Nielsen on the Occasion of his Sixtieth Birthday*. Odense: Odense University Press, 149–170.

Johansson, S./Oksefjell, S. (eds.) (1998), *Corpora and Cross-linguistic Research: Theory, Method, and Case Studies*. Amsterdam: Rodopi.

Karlsson, F. (1990), Constraint Grammar as a Framework for Parsing Unrestricted Text. In: Karlgren, H. (ed.), *Proceedings of the 13th International Conference of Computational Linguistics*, Vol. 3. Helsinki, Finland, 168–173.

Kenny, D. (2001), *Lexis and Creativity in Translation. A Corpus-based Study*. Manchester, UK/Northampton, MA: St. Jerome Publishing.

Köhn, P. (2005), Europarl: A Parallel Corpus for Statistical Machine Translation. In: *Proceedings of the Tenth Machine Translation Summit*. Phuket, Thailand, 79–86. Available at: http://www.iccs.inf.ed.ac.uk/~pkoehn/publications/europarl-mtsummit05.pdf.

Lauridsen, K. (1996), Text Corpora and Contrastive Linguistics: Which Type of Corpus for which Type of Analysis? In: Aijmer/Altenberg/Johansson 1996, 63–71.

Laviosa, S. (2002), *Corpus-based Translation Studies. Theory, Findings, Applications*. Amsterdam: Rodopi.
Løken, B. (1997), Expressing Possibility in English and Norwegian. In: *ICAME Journal* 21, 43–59.
Mauranen, A. (1999), What Sort of Theme is There? A Translational Perspective. In: *Languages in Contrast* 1(2), 57–85.
McEnery, A./Wilson, A. (1996), *Corpus Linguistics*. Edinburgh: Edinburgh University Press.
McEnery, A./Xiao, Z. (1999), Domains, Text Types, Aspect Marking and English–Chinese Translation. In: *Languages in Contrast* 2(2), 211–229.
McLaren, Y. (1999), Text Structure and Politeness in French and English Corporate Brochures. In: *Languages in Contrast* 1(2), 231–254.
Mol, S. (2004), *Head* and *Heart:* Metaphors and Metonymies in a Cross-linguistic Perspective. In: Aijmer, K./Hasselgård, H. (eds.), *Translation and Corpora*. (Gothenburg Studies in English 89.) Göteborg: Acta Universitatis Gothoburgensis, 87–111.
Noël, D. (2003), Translations as Evidence for Semantics: An Illustration. In: *Linguistics* 41(4), 757–785.
Och, F. J./Ney, H. (2000), Improved Statistical Alignment Models. In: *Proceedings of the 38th Annual Meeting of the Association for Computational Linguistics*. Hongkong, China, 440–447.
Olohan, M. (2004), *Introducing Corpora in Translation Studies*. London/New York: Routledge.
Paulussen, H. (1999), A Corpus-based Contrastive Analysis of English *on/up*, Dutch *op* and French *sur* within a Cognitive Framework. Unpublished PhD thesis, University of Ghent.
Salkie, R. (1997), INTERSECT: Parallel Corpora and Contrastive Linguistics. In: *Contragram Newsletter* 11 (Oct 17), 6–9; available on the Web: http://bank.rug.ac.be/contragram/newsle11.html#INTERSECT.
Santos, D. (1998), Perception Verbs in English and Portuguese. In: Johansson/Oksefjell 1998, 319–342.
Schmied, J. (2004), Translation Corpora in Contrastive Research, Translation and Language Teaching. In: *TradTerm10 (Revista do centro interdepartamental de traducao e terminologia FFLCH/USP)*. Sao Paulo: Humanitas FFLCH/USP, 83–115.
Simard, M./Foster, G. F./Isabelle, P. (1992), Using Cognates to Align Sentences in Bilingual Corpora. In: *Proceedings of the Fourth International Conference on Theoretical and Methodological Issues in Machine Translation*. Montreal, Canada, 67–81.
Simon-Vandenbergen, A.-M. (1998), I *think* and its Dutch Equivalents in Parliamentary Debates. In: Johansson/Hasselgård 1998, 297–317.
Simon-Vandenbergen, A.-M./Aijmer, K. (2004), The Expectation Marker *of course* in a Cross-linguistic Perspective. In: *Languages in Contrast* 4(1), 13–43.
Sinclair, J. M. (1996), Multilingual Databases: An International Project in Multilingual Lexicography. In: Sinclair, J. M./Palyne, J./Perez Hernandez, C. (eds.), *Corpus to Corpus: A Study of Translation Equivalence International Journal of Lexicography* 9(3), 180–196.
Sperberg-McQueen, C. M./Burnard, L. (1994), *Text Encoding Initiative. Guidelines for Electronic Text Encoding and Interchange*. Chicago/Oxford: TEI Consortium.
Teubert, W. (2001), Corpus Linguistics and Lexicography. In: *International Journal of Corpus Linguistics* 6, 125–153.
Teubert, W. (2002), The Role of Parallel Corpora in Translation and Multilingual Lexicography. In: Altenberg/Granger 2002, 189–214.
Tiedemann, J./Nygaard, L. (2003), OPUS – an Open Source Parallel Corpus. In. *Proceedings of the 13th Nordic Conference on Computational Linguistics*, http://stp.ling.uu.se/~joerg/#publications.
Tognini Bonelli, E./Manca, E. (2004), Welcoming Children, Pets and Guests: Towards Functional Equivalence in the Languages of 'Agriturismo' and 'Farming Holidays'. In: Aijmer/Altenberg 2004, 371–385.
Veronis. J. (ed.) (2000), *Parallel Text Processing. Alignment and Use of Translation Corpora*. Dordrecht/Boston/London: Kluwer Academic Publishers.

Viberg, Å. (1996), Cross-linguistic Lexicology. The Case of English *go* and Swedish *gå*. In: Aijmer/Altenberg/Johansson 1996, 153–182.
Viberg, Å. (1999), The Polysemous Cognates Swedish *gå* and English *go:* Universal and Language-specific Characteristics. In: *Languages in Contrast* 2(1), 87–113.
Viberg, Å. (2002), Polysemy and Disambiguation Cues across Languages: The Case of Swedish *få* and English *get*. In: Altenberg/Granger 2002, 119–150.
Wahlster, W. (ed.) (2000), *Verbmobil: Foundations of Speech-to-Speech Translation*. Berlin: Springer Verlag.
Wikberg, K. (2004), English Metaphors and their Translation: The Importance of Context. In: Aijmer, K./Stenström, A.-B. (eds.), *Discourse Patterns in Spoken and Written Corpora*. Amsterdam/Philadelphia: John Benjamins, 245–265.
Zanettin, F. (2000), Parallel Corpora in Translation Studies: Issues in Corpus Design. In: Olohan, M. (ed.), *Intercultural Faultlines. Research Methods in Translation Studies I: Textual and Cognitive Aspects*. Manchester: St Jerome, 105–118.
Zanettin, F./Bernardini, S./Stewart, D. (eds.) (2003), *Corpora in Translator Education*. Manchester: St. Jerome.

Karin Aijmer, Gothenburg (Sweden)

17. Corpora of computer-mediated communication

1. Introduction

"Computer-Mediated Communication (CMC)" is a research field that explores the social, communicative and linguistic impact of communication technologies, which have continually evolved in connection with the use of computer networks (esp. the Internet). Early work on CMC investigated the use of e-mail, mailing lists, Usenet discussion groups, Multi User Dimensions/Dungeons (MUDs) and Internet Relay Chats (IRC) (e. g. Reid 1991; Maynor 1994; Vilmi 1994; Herring 1996). Since the mid-90ies, when web-based CMC tools made computer-based communication even easier to use and more widespread, the investigation of features and processes particular to CMC has established itself as an independent research field with specialized journals and workshops, e. g. *Journal of Computer-Mediated Communication, Journal of Interactive Media in Education, Journal of Online Behaviour* and *Language@Internet* or the minitrack on persistent conversation at the annual *Hawaii International Conference on System Sciences* (*HICSS*). By browsing John December's portal of CMC resources and research (http://www.december.com/cmc/info/), one may get an impression of the broad range of CMC-related topics, as well as of the rapid change and the continuous evolution of new CMC tools and genres, such as Instant Messaging Services (e.g. *ICQ*; Leung 2001; Grinter/Palen 2002; Leung 2002), weblogs (e.g. Herring et al. 2004) or Wiki-based applications such as "Wikipedia" (e.g. Viegas/Wattenberg/Dave 2004; Pfeil/Zaphiris/Ang 2006).

CMC research is an interdisciplinary field: psychological issues such as motivation, understanding and decision-making in CMC environments are investigated within the context of e-learning and professional collaboration via the Internet. Social science categories such as identity, gender, trust, and confidence are crucial for studies of online communities and social networks. Linguists investigate how language is used in computer-mediated settings and how the technical and pragmatic conditions of the underlying technology affect the strategies of language production and understanding (Herring 2001; Herring 2004). Crystal (2001) uses the term "netspeak" to cover the broad range of peculiarities and specific features of discourse produced on the Internet, the most well-known of which being emoticons, acronyms (*IMHO* = *in my humble opinion*, *AFK* = *away from keyboard*), speedwriting and abbreviations (*4* = *for*, *g* = *grin*) and conventions for simulating prosodic features (e.g. upper case = loud voice). Research on discourse structure in CMC usually distinguishes between two main genres, namely synchronous and asynchronous CMC (cf. Herring 2001, 614). In synchronous CMC, such as chat or Instant Messaging, people exchange messages instantaneously and in real-time; all participants are simultaneously online and react immediately and only with a slight delay to messages from other participants. In asynchronous CMC, such as e-mail, mailing lists or discussion groups, users do not have to be online at the same time to communicate; the addressee of a message may both read and respond to it at a later time.

A central issue in the linguistic CMC-related discussion is the status of computer-mediated discourse relative to the distinction of orality and literacy, especially its status within the dichotomy of writing and speaking. This has to do with the observation that written language produced by means of CMC devices, although represented graphically, often shows features particular to speech and interactive discourse and, thus, differs stylistically from "traditional writing" in similar genres. On the other hand, synchronous text-based CMC, as found in chat environments, differs considerably from face-to-face conversations (Crystal 2001; Storrer 2001a; Zitzen/Stein 2004). Although methods and categories developed in conversation analysis play a central role in describing how people manage to establish and maintain interactional coherence in CMC discourse, obviously central notions – such as "turn", "turn-taking", "speakerhood" and "floor-holding" – have to be adapted and reconsidered, especially with regard to synchronous CMC (Herring 1999; Beißwenger 2003; 2007; Zitzen/Stein 2004).

The focus of our article is on corpora that may serve to support empirical research on linguistic aspects of CMC discourse. In section 2 we present a short overview of different types of existing CMC corpus resources and give examples of how they have been used to study "netspeak" properties and other CMC peculiarities. In section 3 we discuss problems and issues with which designers of CMC corpora are confronted, especially when building resources that are linguistically annotated and enhanced with meta-data.

The main focus of current CMC research is on Internet-based technologies and their genres (including videoconferencing and multimedia applications). However, a clear line between these genres, genres of telecommunication (such as SMS) and other, more "traditional" media (interactive television, Internet broadcasting) cannot be drawn, because computer technology and other communication and entertainment media coalesce in the digital age. In this article we concentrate on corpora of prototypical Internet-based discourse genres such as e-mail, mailing lists, chats and discussion groups, which reveal typical "netspeak" peculiarities and have been collected in the context of CMC research.

The corpora mentioned in our overview are not intended to form a complete list; the selection was motivated by the goal of finding prototypical examples for our typology. The selection given below is accompanied by a list of WWW resources available at http://www.cmc-corpora.de.

2. Overview of CMC corpora

For our overview we found it useful to establish some classification criteria that serve as the basis for a typology of existing CMC corpus resources. (For the interdependence between design strategies and corpus types cf. article 9).

Initially, one may differentiate between *project-related corpora* and *corpora for general use*. The former are compiled as an empirical basis for questions in a particular project; the latter do not directly pertain to a particular project, but were established rather as a data pool for the investigation of diverse potential research questions. Depending on the amount of work spent structuring and annotating the corpus data with respect to potential research questions, one may, furthermore, differentiate between *corpora of raw data* and *annotated corpora*. In *annotated corpora*, the data have been subjected to annotation processes (e. g. an SGML/XML-based annotation of data segments that may be relevant for purposes of analysis) (For issues in corpus pre-processing cf. articles 23–32). In contrast, the data in *corpora of raw data* have been left in the condition in which they were originally acquired from the Internet. Figure 17.1 shows the four main types of CMC corpora, which result from these classification criteria; in the following we will illustrate each type using prototypical examples.

Data edited for purposes of analysis? / The corpus was originally designed to be ...	**No**	**Yes**
... project-related	1 *corpora of raw data*	3 *annotated corpora*
... for general use	2 *corpora of raw data*	4 *annotated corpora*

Fig. 17.1: Types of CMC corpora

2.1. Type 1: Project-related corpora of raw data

Research on Computer-Mediated Communication is presently conducted for the most part with *project-related corpora of raw data*. This is due to the fact that CMC research is a relatively new field and that CMC genres currently are not at all or only marginally represented in large balanced corpora. Thus, at the present time, the assortment of large accessible corpora that were exclusively designed for analyzing CMC phenomena is rather unsatisfactory. Therefore, for empirical studies, corpora often have to be individually acquired from the Internet or obtained from users of CMC facilities. Examples of such type 1 corpora are, for instance, Yates' *CoSy:50*-Corpus, which comprises 50 submissions each, from 152 computer conferences (described in Yates 1996), Todla's *Thai Chat Corpus* (used in Todla 1999 and Panyametheekul/Herring 2003), Janich's corpus with messages from a university mailing list (used in Janich 2002), Berjaoui's corpus with logfiles from Moroccan IRC channels (cf. Berjaoui 2001), the extensive Swiss-German webchat corpus (15,86 million words) recorded by Siebenhaar (cf. e. g. Siebenhaar 2006) or Pankow's contrastive German-Swedish *IRC-Corpus* (used in Pankow 2003). Type 1 corpora usually have a manageable size and are often not compiled with a potential third party user in mind (who possibly pursues other research questions). Accordingly, corpora of this kind are often just rudimentarily documented (i. e. only in the publications in which they are cited). Moreover, they are usually only accessible through the scholars who compiled them for their own purposes.

2.2. Type 2: Corpora of raw data for general use

Contrary to their project-related equivalents, *corpora of raw data for general use* are compiled in order to give scholars a data pool for the empirical study of diverse research questions. Examples are the *Netscan Usenet database* (http://netscan.research.microsoft.com/), the *Korpus deutschsprachiger Newsgroups* (cf. Feldweg/Kibiger/Thielen 1995), the *Enron Email Dataset*, which holds over half a million business-related e-mail messages (http://www-2.cs.cmu.edu/~enron/), the *WWE-2006 weblog dataset* which was temporarily available to the participants of the *3rd Annual Workshop on the Weblogging Ecosystem* (see http://www.blogpulse.com/www2006-workshop/), and the *SpamAssassin Public Corpus* (http://spamassassin.apache.org/publiccorpus/) from the *Apache SpamAssassin Project*, in which approximately 6,000 e-mail messages were compiled as a discretionary data pool for research in automatic e-mail classification.

2.3. Type 3: Project-related annotated corpora

Project-related annotated corpora of CMC data are compiled in order to empirically conduct a particular research project. When building up corpora of this type, the data are subjected to a coding process, which facilitates both the work with the corpus and the access to and analysis of the data. An example of a type 3 corpus is the e-mail corpus of Declerck and Klein (cf. Declerck/Klein 1997), collected in the framework of the *COSMA* project and comprising 160 e-mail messages with appointment arrangements. The data of this corpus have been syntactically and semantically annotated with a research objective in mind – the development and evaluation of the analysis component of a dialogue system for appointment scheduling. Another type 3 example is Paolillo's 24-hour logfile from an IRC channel, in which types of messages and selected linguistic features were coded in order to apply quantitative methods for the analysis of textual

CMC data (cf. Paolillo 1999). In Naumann's corpus (used e. g. in Naumann 2005), logfiles from "virtual classrooms" were linguistically annotated for an analysis of conversational rules in educational chat applications. A large type 3 corpus of personal homepages has been compiled in Rehm's *Hypnotic* project in order to develop procedures for automatic web genre classification. Aside from HTML documents, *Hypnotic* also contains files with news articles, as well as over 1,000 e-mails archived from the WWW (cf. Rehm 2002, 2006). Another large annotated corpus of websites (a "web genre document bank") has been compiled within the *Indogram* project. The particular design and annotation principles are described in Mehler/Gleim (2006).

2.4. Type 4: Annotated corpora for general use

At present, there are few corpora whose data pool has been collected *ab ovo* as a resource for CMC research and edited with regard to various possible research questions. The *Düsseldorf CMC Corpus* (as described in Zitzen 2004, 14–36) contains grammatically annotated data from various synchronous and asynchronous CMC genres (e-mail, mailing lists, newsgroups, guest books, chats) and has a scope of approximately 230,000 tokens. The *Dortmund Chat Corpus* (http://www.chatkorpus.uni-dortmund.de) comprises 511 logfiles with a total of some 1.000.000 tokens from various chat applications (chats in professional contexts such as, for example, teaching, learning, counseling and media contexts, as well as "social chats" within and outside of media contexts) and has been processed for linguistic research purposes on the basis of an XML annotation.

3. Collection and linguistic annotation of CMC corpora

The mere acquisition of data for CMC corpora can be accomplished rather easily. With little effort, linguistic data can be retrieved from public access CMC platforms or from the archives of client programs of e-mail, news and instant messaging services, IRC- or MUD-facilities, which have been made accessible to the researcher. The sheer availability of data that can easily be retrieved does not imply that the design of CMC corpora for linguistic research purposes is trivial. Instead, the design of CMC corpora involves an array of challenges and preliminary decisions that do not arise in a similar way when designing corpora of "traditional" text or speech genres. This is due to, on the one hand, the communicative frameworks of CMC genres and, on the other hand, the embedding of CMC data in Internet-based storage and presentation formats.

3.1. Challenges in data acquisition and documentation

Above all, questions relating to the management and structuring of data are crucial to the acquisition and documentation of content for CMC corpora. Furthermore, with regard to purposes of analysis, the question arises as to which technical, conversational and sociological meta-information should be captured during the collection of the data and which ethical aspects should be considered when designing CMC corpora.

3.1.1. Data sampling

Indeed, textual CMC data are available in large numbers and are simple to archive; however, the data for a CMC corpus should be acquired depending on the purposes that the corpus should serve (for project-related corpora, e. g. with regard to the pursued research questions). Should the data be compiled by the principle of convenience, randomly or according to particular linguistic phenomena? Herring (2004) gives a detailed overview of the advantages and disadvantages of various data compilation techniques for the purpose of Computer-Mediated Discourse Analysis (for issues involved in data collection in general cf. article 9).

3.1.2. Format of the original data

Language data found in individual CMC environments can either be saved in their original form (i. e. including all possibly relevant layout and structure information) or in reduced form (reduced to pure character strings). The decision as to which starting format one would like to use in corpus design should depend on the intended or potential research questions, for the processing of which the corpus should deliver the empirical basis. Especially with regard to CMC genres that use the layout and multimedia properties of WWW-based online publishing, it may be relevant to capture the data not only in the form of pure character strings, but rather as a kind of rich data, which also include layout information such as typeface, font, color, size, manual vs. forced line break, paragraph structure, etc. However, layout properties of written contributions in WWW-based discussion forums, chats and in newer e-mail client programs can adopt pragmatic functions and, thus, are often more than just text decoration within communicative exchanges. Therefore, when choosing a reduced starting format, one should carefully take into consideration that the archived data may have lost some visual properties that were functional in the original context. Furthermore, since the use of graphic elements within CMC environments has become more and more common over the last years, it may be relevant to also represent certain graphic encoding formats in the corpus. In online forums, guest books, weblogs and webchats, graphics can be used as a substitute for emoticons, e. g. by selecting them per mouse click from a selection menu. These graphics – like emoticons – can assume evaluative, expressive or regulative functions (cf. Runkehl/Schlobinski/Siever 1998, 98), sometimes even illustrative or emblematic functions. Capturing data for CMC corpora in ASCII format by simply saving screen content not only implies the loss of potentially relevant layout information but also the loss of graphics. Incidentally, this is not merely applicable to WWW-based CMC applications, but also to e-mail and other non-WWW-based CMC applications, whose client software allows the integration of media objects (graphic, audio, video).

3.1.3. Representation format

Depending on the starting format, it is important to choose an appropriate representation format for the language data contained in the corpus. If the original data were generated with diverse CMC systems (e. g. on the basis of different forum or chat software) and/or represent different CMC genres, then one should choose a representation format that accommodates all of these systems and genres. With regard to long-term data storage and portability, one should choose an interchange format that can be processed and converted regardless of specific applications or special software (e. g. a description format based on an SGML or XML language). Furthermore, a decision must be made as to whether and in which way meta-information that is already contained in the original data should be transferred into the chosen representation format. This applies e. g. to the so-called "header information" in e-mails (cf. Evert/Fitschen 2001, 371). In this context, the establishment of a standardized framework for the representation and exchange of CMC data is a strong desideratum (cf. Bruckman et al. 2000).

3.1.4. Capturing hard-coded references (e. g. hyperlinks)

In the acquisition of data and their representation in the corpus, also non-sequential structures, if applicable, must be taken into consideration: communicative contributions that are captured from WWW-based CMC environments may contain hyperlinks, with which reference is made to external resources. The reconstruction of the content of these resources may be important for the corpus-based analyses of the respective contributions. Furthermore, the structural embedding of a contribution within its context (e. g. of a single posting within the thread structure of a forum) can, in its original presentation format (e. g. the WWW-interface of the respective forum system), also be organized through hyperlinks. On the one hand, there are *system-generated hyperlinks*, which embed the single contribution into the structural and/or thematic organization of the CMC application. On the other hand, there are *hyperlinks that are manually defined* by the users. System-generated hyperlinks would be e. g. those that link single postings in an online forum together into threads and, thus, create a navigation design, which makes all contributions to a thread accessible per mouse click. Likewise, hyperlinks that (a) mark a posting as a reply to a preceding posting by another author and (b) make the latter accessible via mouse click can also be deemed system-generated. An example of a manually set hyperlink would be e. g. a hyperlink that is inserted by the author in the text of his posting in order to refer to a posting in another thread of the forum or to an external website. Another example are associative hyperlinks which lead from one article of a Wiki resource to another. If such referential structures are not represented in the corpus, then coherence relations that refer beyond the single communicative contribution or article cannot be reconstructed. Moreover, when saving CMC data, one should keep in mind that hyperlinks on the user interface are not always simply displayed in the form of a clickable target resource URL, but may also appear in the form of textual link buttons (e. g. "for more information, click here"). In such cases, the URL information can only be obtained from the source code. When saving just the screen data, the respective URL information becomes lost.

3.1.5. Capturing implicit references (e. g. cross-media)

In some cases, CMC facilities in the media context can correspond to and accompany media events outside of the Internet. Examples would be chat events accompanying the matches in a soccer championship or the Tour de France, or moderated chat events with studio guests from a preceding TV show (specifically, talk shows with political or "infotainment" formats). In these types of CMC events, topics that were initiated outside (e. g. in the TV broadcast) may be perpetuated or taken up again within the particular CMC environment. Furthermore, certain issues addressed within the CMC event may only fully be understood by examining the corresponding passages of the parallel TV broadcast. In teaching and learning contexts, CMC facilities are often supplemented through resources that are stored on external platforms – e. g. on an accompanying website or in a "materials" section of the e-learning platform used. Users of the particular CMC environments may not explicitly link to these external resources when they discuss them because they can assume that each user knows where the respective materials are located. It may be important to either incorporate the respective resources (each as a whole) into the corpus or to at least have precise descriptions of them available. While making corpus analyses, this would help resolve linguistic references made to them. The same goes for chat conversations that are conducted using a so-called "shared whiteboard system". A "shared whiteboard" is a kind of virtual chalkboard, on which – parallel to the chat activity – graphics, visual aids and tasks can be provided for the participants, drawings can be created or documents can be collaboratively edited. The content of the whiteboard is not usually documented in the logfile. Therefore, when capturing data from such systems, it may be necessary to decide to which extent the content displayed or produced on the whiteboard (or a description of it) should also be included in the corpus.

3.1.6. Capturing metadata concerning the communication environment

Technical factors that are formative for the structure of communicative events must be taken into consideration when documenting corpus data (e. g. program functions of the respective chat or forum system). Without this information, certain linguistic and interactional characteristics of the data may not be interpreted adequately. The same holds for socio-communicative roles (e. g. the role of a forum or chat moderator) and the communicative authority connected with these roles (e. g. the authority to delete or edit messages written by other users, the authority to revoke a user's right to post further messages), which either apply to an entire CMC platform or are only defined for a singular communicative event on the respective platform (e. g. within the framework of a single expert chat conducted on the e-learning platform used in a "blended learning" seminar). Depending on the technical conditions, both the linguistic form and the conversational structures in one and the same CMC genre can vary considerably, as can be seen in, for example, a comparison between non-moderated chats (e. g. social chats on IRC or the web) and technically moderated chats (e. g. celebrity chat events) (cf. Storrer 2007). The contributions in both of these subtypes of chat discourse differ not only with respect to their average length (5.38 versus 17.22 tokens per message, according to an unpublished spot survey by the authors); they also differ with respect to the frequency of split moves: the partitioning of a communicative move onto several messages does not occur in technically moderated chats (cf. Beißwenger 2003, 219–224). Moreover, and also due to the technical framework, the contributions not only tend to be much longer in the technically moderated chats, but also much more elaborate than contributions in other types of chat applications. The patterns of communicative moves that can be observed in technically moderated chats are also much more rigid than those in non-moderated chats.

3.1.7. Capturing sociological meta-information

Sociological meta-information about the CMC user groups is of great importance for the field of sociolinguistic and socio-psychological CMC research. The analysis of corpus data and the differentiation between group-specific stylistic features and ranges of linguistic variation (cf. Androutsopoulos 2003) will strongly benefit from information about the users of the CMC environments from which the corpus data were recorded. This includes e. g. information about the users' average age, gender and level of education, about the degree of acquaintance among the users and the degree of attachment to the respective platform (as a member of an "online community"). A typological approach to "online communities", which combines the technical and communicative frameworks, as well as pragmatic and sociological meta-information about CMC platforms, can be found in Porter (2004).

3.1.8. Questions concerning research ethics

Ethical questions should be taken into consideration in the creation of CMC corpora in order to protect the personal rights of the users recorded in the corpus data. In order for the research to remain ethically justifiable, it would be ideal to inform people when they or their statements are being recorded for research purposes. Due to reasons of practicability when collecting data from publicly accessible CMC environments, it is unrealistic to obtain a declaration of consent for the recording and subsequent use of users' statements for research purposes, since such environments often have many, and sometimes even frequently alternating, users. Moreover, an *informed consent*, received in advance, would in many cases compromise the authenticity of the communicative behavior of the users. However, obtaining the consent of the participants retrospectively is often just as unrealistic, since the participants are registered under pseudonyms. Although users of publicly accessible IRC, MUD, webchat and forum environments already operate under these self-chosen pseudonyms ("nicknames"), that does not necessarily mean that data recorded in such environments may be used without anonymizing them for research purposes. After all, a third party may happen to meet the respective users when logging onto the environment from which the corpus data had been recorded. Furthermore, in CMC environments in which the users can create "user profiles" with personal information, there is even a possibility that the real person behind the CMC character could be identified through a targeted inspection of the contact information provided by the user (e. g. e-mail address, ICQ or telephone number). Whether a retrospective anonymization of the participant names or a mere omission of details about the particular CMC platform's location is more appropriate from an ethical point of view is a question still being discussed and approached differently by various scholars: "some feel that they have a moral obligation to obtain explicit permission from the authors for *publishing* logs in academic papers (...); others collect logs without asking for permission but the logs are then only processed by statistical software and not read by humans (...); many others simply do not declare explicitly whether permission was obtained for their logs" (Paccagnella 1997). With regard to research ethics, Paccagnella stresses even further, "changing not only real names, but also aliases or pseudonyms (where used) proves the respect of the researchers for the *social reality* of cyberspace." A good overview of the discussion about how to handle CMC data in an ethically justifiable manner – in the frame of which questions concerning authorship and copyright are also addressed – is provided e. g. by Bruckman et al. (2000), Crystal (2001, 191–194) and Döring (2003, 236–242).

3.2. Challenges in data editing and annotation

When annotating CMC data, one should both carefully develop appropriate description categories and document grammars, which grasp the linguistic particularities of CMC genres, and modify existent tools for the linguistic preprocessing of speech data (e. g. morphosyntactic taggers).

3.2.1. Description categories

Categories that were developed for the annotation of structural and functional units in "traditional" discourse genres (text and speech genres) cannot be used for the description of CMC discourse without first being adapted with regard to the particularities of CMC. Thus, there is a need for categories that account for the unclear position of CMC between orality and literacy. Central concepts of discourse analysis must thereby be evaluated and reinterpreted. For instance, in synchronous CMC, simultaneous backchannel feedback is not possible – but this does not inevitably mean that in synchronous CMC there are absolutely no functional *equivalents* to the backchannel behavior in face-to-face conversations. Likewise, one should consider to which extent it is appropriate to describe conversation structures in synchronous CMC by uncritically using categories such as "turn", "turn taking" and "sequentiality" (cf. e. g. Murray 1989; Werry 1996; Garcia/Jacobs 1999; Herring 2001; Beißwenger 2003; 2007).

3.2.2. Interpretative description of conversation structures

When annotating conversation structures in logfiles from synchronous CMC genres, one should keep in mind that the reconstructive assignment of the participant's contributions to thematic threads or patterns of communicative moves (e. g. "question–answer") is always a matter of the researcher's interpretation. Due to the lack of para- and nonverbal data and due to the technical (not pragmatic) sequencing of participant submissions (see section 3.3.), there is a larger margin for interpretation (or speculation) in the modelling of CMC data than in the modelling of data from (oral/face-to-face) conversations. Example (1a) shows a sequence of two messages from a one-to-one chat in the context of psychosocial counseling. The respective logfile was kindly provided by the project "Psychosoziale Hilfe online" (cf. van Eckert 2005).

Due to its move types ("question" and "assertion"), the sequence could be interpreted as the realization of a "question-answer" pattern. But when analyzing this example in its larger context, as provided in (1b), the previously assumed answer ("my mother is going crazy") is actually revealed to be just part of an answer to an earlier question, which was broken up into several messages by the respective user. Due to the lack of means for simultaneous coordination between the participants, it is displayed after the communication partner's next question. This interpretation of example (1b) is substantiated when one considers the message's time of arrival at the server, which is documented by some chat systems in the form of a so-called "timestamp" in the logfile. It is quite unlikely that B could have received, read and answered question A "may I ask how old you are?" within two seconds.

(1) a. A: darf ich fragen, wie alt du bist?
may I ask how old you are?
B: meine mutter is hysterisch
my mother is going crazy

b.

Timestamp	*message*
15:52:42	A: wie sieht denn die krise in der familie bei dir aus? *tell me about the crisis in your family.*
15:53:08	B: meine ma redet nicht mit meinemdad und andersrum *my mom won't speak to my dad and vice versa*
15:53:22	B: mein bruder redet nicht mit ihnen und andrsrum *my brother won't speak to them and vice versa*
15:53:37	B: ich rede wenig mit ihnen und sie gar nicht *i hardly speak to them and they don't speak at all with me*
15:53:50	B: meine eltern wollen sich scheiden *my parents want to divorce*
15:54:01	A: darf ich fragen, wie alt du bist? *may I ask how old you are?*
15:54:03	B: meine mutter is hysterisch *my mother is going crazy*
15:54:06	B: 12 *12*

3.2.3. Linguistic preprocessing and annotation

Tools developed for the automatic annotation of linguistic data (sentencizers, POS taggers, lemmatizers, chunk parsers) cannot be used for processing CMC data without being adapted. This problem is due to some characteristics of language use in CMC that we briefly mentioned in our introduction: speedwriting (e. g. *you* > *U, two/too* > *2, please > plz*; cf. Danet 1997), non-standard spellings (e. g. Engl. *out of > outta, see you > cee ya*; cf. Crystal 2001, 164 – or French *quelqu'un > qqn, c'est > c*; cf. Werry 1996, 55), highly colloquial (slang) or conceptionally oral forms (in German e. g. *ne* (< *nicht wahr?*), *haste* (< *hast du*), *willste* (< *willst du*), in English e. g. *gonna, gotta*), letter repetition as a means of emulating prosody (*uiiiiiii, sooooo, helloooooo*), written dialect (which may be used either non-intentionally or to mimic the style of particular discourse communities, e. g. of Australian speakers of English; cf. Werry 1996, 58) and abbreviations (*btw* for *by the way*, *lol* for *laughing out loud*, *aka* for *also known as*). In order to successfully process CMC data, the search patterns or lexica of the respective tools must be extended to include these typical "netspeak" elements and treat them appropriately.

Furthermore, the frequent omission of upper case may lead to false categorizations when using tools that were developed for parsing "traditional" text genres (cf. Ooi 2001). This is especially important when processing languages in which the distinction between lower case and upper case signifies part-of-speech information, as e. g. in German orthography, where nouns are capitalized. Moreover, the creative or expressive use of punctuation marks and special characters must be taken into account: emoticons emulate typed facial expressions by means of punctuation marks and special characters; verbalizations of gesture or physical action (engl. **smile**, **grin**, **hugs**, **shakes hand**; germ. **knuddel** "hug", **tassekaffeeanbiet** "offercupofcoffee") are often enclosed in asterisks (cf. e. g. Reid 1991; Werry 1996, 60; Runkehl/Schlobinski/Siever 1998, 106, Beißwenger 2000, 105–116). Likewise, typography and layout can provide significant characteristics for identifying typical CMC categories (e. g. angle brackets or bold type and a preceding forced line break to distinguish strings of the type "nickname"). Unusual word order and elliptic constructions in CMC discourse may, in addition, pose problems for frequency-based part-of-speech taggers that have been trained on corpora with written standard language, e. g. newspaper corpora (see article 24).

All in all, tools for corpus search and annotation, developed with standard orthography and "traditional" text genres in mind, need to be adapted to the peculiarities of CMC discourse.

3.3. The status of logfiles of synchronous CMC and their value as source material

The starting point and empirical foundation of CMC research are those data that are exchanged between users of CMC systems for the purpose of communication and that can be saved through one of the users' computers or through the intermediary server. In synchronous text-based CMC, these types of data are usually organized and displayed in the form of scroll-like records (the so-called *logfiles*). The way in which the individual users' messages are arranged in these records can vary; in standard systems (as used in IRC or many social chats on the web), messages are arranged by a "first come, first served" principle, according to the chronological order in which they reach the server. This generates coherence problems such as disrupted adjacency (Herring 1999) or scrambled threads (Storrer 2001a), which are crucial for synchronous CMC discourse and which, therefore, must be taken into consideration for the analysis.

When acquiring logfiles of synchronous CMC for the design of CMC corpora, one must consider whether one is dealing with *server logs* or *client logs*. The former are recorded directly from the server and represent the complete communicative activity of a "channel", "room" or "separée" of the respective CMC platform; the latter can be created by capturing the communicative activity which can be observed on one of the users' computers and which, in many cases, only represents the user's individual view of the communicative event in which he is involved. Most of the synchronous CMC systems operate with the use of the social deictic *you* in the automatically generated system messages, which display the changes in the communicative status of the users (e. g. *You entered the channel Detroit Rock City*). Therefore, when using client logs, it is advisable to document whose view of the communicative event is being represented in the logfile.

Furthermore, one must consider to what extent data which can be acquired from the user's screen or the intermediary server and which can be fixed through saving, are sufficient when the purpose is to investigate how synchronous CMC users organize their exchange. The term "synchronous CMC" means that the users must be logged in synchronously on the particular CMC platform; it does *not* mean that communication in webchat, IRC or Instant Messaging proceeds *simultaneously*. Rather, messages are first produced, then subsequently sent to the server and, lastly, transferred en bloc from there to the addressees' computers. Information about when, for how long and, if applicable, with which disruptions and revisions a message is produced is completely indiscernible for the other participants. A message first becomes visible when it appears on the screen as a text block. Therefore, in synchronous CMC – contrary to face-to-face conversations – a runtime negotiation of turns is not possible. Likewise, which messages have already been read by a user during the production of his/her new message (and which have not) is not documented in the logfile at all. Merely the fact that something is visible on the screen does not necessarily mean that the user in front of the screen has taken notice. The difference to face-to-face conversation becomes clear here as well: while it is virtually impossible not to perceive something that is orally expressed by a communicative partner, it could very well happen that something displayed graphically on a screen is not at all or not directly perceived by its addressee (e. g. because he is composing his own message and, hence, looking at the keyboard or the text submission field and not at the logfile) (cf Beißwenger 2007).

Thus, in many regards, logfiles of synchronous CMC render considerably less information about the conversational process than transcripts of verbal conversations. While the latter are prepared by linguists through an intellectual interpretation of audio or video recordings for the purpose of linguistic analysis, logfiles at best have the status of machine-made "recordings". They neither represent the communicative moves in the sequence in which they were intended by the participants, nor do they document the process of message production – instead, messages in logfiles are represented as text blocks that do not analogously develop over time. Features on the linguistic surface of messages and rhetorical relations between them can thus only be explained through speculation, as long as the analyst is left to rely solely on the data given in logfiles. Therefore, for various purposes of analysis, it is wise to collect additional data aside from just logfile recordings. In order to gather data about the message production processes, Garcia/Jacobs (1999) base their analysis of discourse organization in IRC on video recordings of the users' screens. Ogura/Nishimoto (2004) or Vronay/Smith/Drucker (1999) incorporate typing histories and client-side logging of keytrokes and mouse actions as additional data in their investigation of synchronous text-based CMC. Jones (2001) analyzes series of screenshots from the users' desktops ("screen movies"), in order to investigate how users manage multiple and parallel conversations. A research design for the collection of logfile data in combination with video screen capturing and a video observation of the users is described in Beißwenger (2007).

4. Conclusion and future perspectives

With the increasing amount of reading and writing that people do on the Internet, corpus designers who set out to provide balanced corpora that include all relevant text types of contemporary language, should henceforth include CMC discourse as well. At present, online text corpora of contemporary language, such as the *British National Corpus* (*BNC*, http://www.natcorp.ox.ac.uk/), do not; nor do the German corpora available through the *COSMAS* search tool (http://www.ids-mannheim.de/cosmas2/) or the online corpus of the German language of the 20th century compiled within the framework of the online dictionary project *DWDS* (http://www.dwds.de). In "older" corpus collections, such as the *Brown Corpus* (available through *ICAME*, http://nora.hd.uib.no/whatis.html), the reason for the lack of CMC genres is simply that at the time of the corpus creation CMC was non-existent. In more recently collected language corpora, such as the above-mentioned, the disregard for CMC in corpus building may be due to the unclear status of CMC discourse with regard to the spoken–written dichotomy. Since this dichotomy is crucial for the categorization into speech and text corpora, it is difficult to decide whether CMC discourse should form part of text or speech corpora.

It may have become evident from our review that the compilation and annotation of CMC corpora may be regarded as a challenging task, for which special methods and devices are needed. Standard tools for linguistic annotation of text corpora are only suitable to a limited extent for CMC corpora, since in interactive CMC discourse punctuation marks are often used in a non-standard way or are even completely neglected. Typing errors and typical "netspeak" items (abbreviations, smileys and the like) create obstacles for morphological analyzers or lemmatization tools. Furthermore, the peculiarities of CMC discourse compromise the precision and recall of corpus search tools. The automatic recognition of sentence boundaries alone requires robust techniques that accommodate the informal use of punctuation marks typical to CMC. System-generated markup, e. g. the labeling of quotations in e-mails and forum postings and/or the marking of nicknames and system messages in chats, have to be filtered out and separated from the actual CMC discourse. With regard to the ethical aspects addressed in section 3.1.8., the archiving of CMC discourse should preferably be carried out with the permission of the participants. If this is not possible, then CMC discourse units should at least be anonymized. Moreover, a range of to some extent important tasks must be accomplished before the data can be integrated into a publicly accessible corpus. Typical "netspeak" elements and phenomena of "written speech", such as the English *gotta* (< *got to)* and *dunno* (< *don't know*) or the German *haste* (< *hast du*), *ham* (< *haben*) and *willste* (< *willst du*; cf. section 3.2.3.), must be processed correctly by search tools. In order to deal with typing errors, one can possibly revert to spelling tolerant search techniques as used e. g. in digital dictionaries. All in all, a range of non-trivial tasks must be accomplished before the data can be integrated into a publicly accessible corpus.

Preferably, the construction and the processing of CMC corpora should henceforth be more strongly geared toward methods and standards from corpus linguistics. However, a current desideratum would be appropriate annotation standards that are suited to capturing the specific discourse structures of interactive multiparty CMC genres, such as threads in discussion groups or chat-logfiles. Influential standards for corpus annotation, such as the guidelines of the *Text Encoding Initiative* (*TEI*), do not yet account for CMC genres. Such an extension would be very beneficial, especially for the development of specialized search tools. Up to now, many assumptions about the Internet's impact on language change have been based upon small datasets and a lot of intuition. Preferably, one should be able to compare CMC corpora, in which various CMC genres are contained in a balanced way, with corpora of other genres (e. g. newspaper articles, fiction, as well as oral discussions, interviews and counseling interviews). This would allow for empirically-based statements about language change due to digital media and the Internet and, furthermore, about how and with what effects people communicate in computer networks. It would be easier to investigate how the users linguistically adapt to the functions of CMC devices and how new patterns and genres emerge on the basis of existing patterns of verbal interaction. Our outline in section 3 showed that some challenges still have to be overcome for this purpose. The growing relevance of the Internet for global communication shows that it is worthwhile to dedicate more attention to this area of corpus linguistics.

5. Literature

All URLs were checked on February 02, 2008.

Androutsopoulos, Jannis K. (2003), Online-Gemeinschaften und Sprachvariation. Soziolinguistische Perspektiven auf Sprache im Internet. In: *Zeitschrift für germanistische Linguistik* 31(2), 173–197.

Beißwenger, Michael (2000), *Kommunikation in virtuellen Welten: Sprache, Text und Wirklichkeit.* Stuttgart: ibidem.

Beißwenger, Michael (2003), Sprachhandlungskoordination im Chat. In: *Zeitschrift für germanistische Linguistik* 31(2), 198–231.

Beißwenger, Michael (2007), *Sprachhandlungskoordination in der Chat-Kommunikation.* Berlin/New York: de Gruyter.

Beißwenger, Michael/Storrer, Angelika (eds.) (2005), *Chat-Kommunikation in Beruf Bildung und Medien: Konzepte – Werkzeuge – Anwendungsfelder.* Stuttgart: ibidem.

Berjaoui, Nasser (2001), Aspects of the Moroccan Arabic Orthography with Preliminary Insights from the Moroccan Computer-mediated Communication. In: Beißwenger, Michael (ed.), *Chat-Kommunikation. Sprache, Interaktion, Sozialität & Identität in synchroner computervermittelter Kommunikation. Perspektiven auf ein interdisziplinäres Forschungsfeld.* Stuttgart: ibidem, 431–465.

Bruckman, Amy/Erickson, Thomas/Fisher, Danyel/Lueg, Christopher et al. (2000), *Dealing with Community Data: A Report on the CSCW 2000 Workshop.* (http://www.visi.com/~snowfall/CSCW00CommDataReport.html).

Crystal, David (2001), *Language and the Internet.* Cambridge: Cambridge University Press.

Danet, Brenda (1997), *Language, Play and Performance in Computer-mediated Communication. Final Report submitted to the Israel Science Foundation.* (http://pluto.mscc.huji.ac.il/~msdanet/report95.htm).

Declerck, Thierry/Klein, Judith (1997), *Ein Email-Korpus zur Entwicklung und Evaluierung der Analysekomponente eines Terminvereinbarungssystems.* Paper presented at the 6. Fachtagung der Sektion Computerlinguistik der Deutschen Gesellschaft für Sprachwissenschaft (DGfS/CL 97), In-

tegrative Ansätze in der Computerlinguistik, 08.–10. Oktober, Heidelberg, Germany, 1997. (http://www.dfki.uni-sb.de/Lt/publicatios_show.php?id=179).
Döring, Nicola (2003), *Sozialpsychologie des Internet. Die Bedeutung des Internet für Kommunikationsprozesse, Identitäten, soziale Beziehungen und Gruppen.* 2nd ed. (Neue Medien in der Psychologie 2.) Göttingen etc.: Hogrefe.
Ellis, R. (1994), *The Study of Second Language Acquisition.* Oxford: Oxford University Press.
Evert, Stefan/Fitschen, Arne (2001), Textkorpora. In: Carstensen, Kai-Uwe/Ebert, Christian/Endriss, Cornelia/Jekat, Susanne/Klabunde, Ralf (eds.), *Computerlinguistik und Sprachtechnologie. Eine Einführung.* Heidelberg/Berlin: Spektrum, 369 – 376.
Feldweg, Helmut/Kibiger, Ralf/Thielen, Christine (1995), Zum Sprachgebrauch in deutschen Newsgruppen. In: Schmitz, Ulrich (ed.), *Osnabrücker Beiträge zur Sprachtheorie* 50, 143–154.
Garcia, Angela Cora/Jacobs, Jennifer Baker (1999), The Eyes of the Beholder: Understanding the Turn-taking System in Quasi-synchronous Computer-mediated Communication. In: *Research on Language and Social Interaction* 32(4), 337–367.
Grinter, Rebecca E./Palen, Leysia (2002), Instant Messaging in Teen Life. In: Proceedings of the 2002 ACM Conference on Computer Supported Cooperative Work. November 16–20, 2002, New Orleans/Lousiana, 21–30.
Herring, Susan C. (1999), Interactional Coherence in CMC. In: *Journal of Computer-mediated Communication* 4(4). (http://jcmc.indiana.edu/vol4/issue4/herring.html).
Herring, Susan C. (2001), Computer-mediated discourse. In: Schiffrin, Deborah/Tannen, Deborah/Hamilton, Heidi E. (eds.), *The Handbook of Discourse Analysis.* Oxford: Blackwell, 612–634.
Herring, Susan C. (2004), Computer-mediated Discourse Analysis: An Approach to Researching Online Behavior. In: Barab, S. A./Kling, R./Gray, J. H. (eds.), *Designing for Virtual Communities in the Service of Learning.* New York: Cambridge University Press, 338–376.
Herring, Susan C. (ed.) (1996), *Computer-mediated Communication. Linguistic, Social and Cross-cultural Perspectives.* (Pragmatics & Beyond New Series 39.) Amsterdam/Philadelphia: John Benjamins.
Herring, Susan C./Scheidt, Lois Ann/Bonus, Sabrina/Wright, Elijah (2004), Bridging the Gap: A Genre Analysis of Weblogs. In: *Proceedings of the 37th Hawaii International Conference on System Sciences.* Big Island, HI. (http://csdl2.computer.org/comp/proceedings/hicss/2004/2056/04/205640101b.pdf).
Janich, Nina (2002), Von Lust und Leid. Metakommunikation in der E-Mail am Beispiel einer universitären Mittelbau-Initiative. In: Ziegler, Arne/Dürscheid, Christa (eds.), *Kommunikationsform E-Mail.* (Reihe Textsorten, Bd. 7.) Tübingen: Stauffenburg, 217–243.
Jones, Rodney (2001), *Beyond the Screen. A Participatory Study of Computer Mediated Communication among Hong Kong Youth.* Paper presented at the Annual Meeting of the American Anthropological Association Nov. 28–Dec. 2, 2001. (http://personal.cityu.edu.hk/~enrodney/Research/ICQPaper.doc).
Journal of Computer-mediated Communication (*JCMC*). Online-journal. (http://jcmc.indiana.edu/).
Journal of Interactive Media in Education. Online-journal. (http://www-jime.open.ac.uk).
Journal of Online Behaviour. Online-journal. (http://www.behavior.net/JOB/).
Language@Internet. Online-journal. (http://www.languageatinternet.de).
Leung, Louis (2001), College Student Motives for Chatting on ICQ. In: *New Media & Society* 3(4), 483–500.
Leung, Louis (2002), Loneliness, Self-disclosure, and ICQ ("I Seek You") Use. In: *CyberPsychology & Behavior* 5(3), 241–251.
Maynor, Natalie (1994), The Language of Electronic Mail: Written Speech? In: Little, Greta D./Montgomery, Michael (eds.), *Centennial Usage Studies.* Tuscaloosa: University of Alabama, 48–54.
Mehler, Alexander/Gleim, Rüdiger (2006), The Net for the Graphs – Towards Webgenre Representation for Corpus Linguistic Studies. In: Baroni, Marco/Bernardini, Silvia (eds.), *WaCky! Working Papers on the Web as Corpus.* Bologna: GEDIT, 191–224.

Murray, Denise E. (1989), When the Medium Determines Turns: Turn-taking in Computer Conversation. In: Coleman, Hywel (ed.), *Working with Language. A Multidisciplinary Consideration of Language Use in Work Contexts.* (Contributions to the Sociology of Languages 52.) Berlin/New York: Mouton de Gruyter, 319–337.

Naumann, Karin (2005), Kann man Chatten lernen? Regeln und Trainingsmaßnahmen zur erfolgreichen Chat-Kommunikation in Unterrichtsgesprächen. In: Beißwenger/Storrer 2005, 257–272.

Ogura, Kanayo/Nishimoto, Kazushi (2004), *Is a Face-to-Face Conversation Model Applicable to Chat Conversations?* Paper presented at the Eighth Pacific Rim International Conference on Artificial Intelligence (PRICAI2004). (http://ultimavi.arc.net.my/banana/Workshop/PRICAI 2004/Final/ogura.pdf).

Ooi, Vincent B.Y. (2001), Aspects of Computer-mediated Communication for Research in Corpus Linguistics. In: *Language and Computers* 36(1), 91–104.

Paccagnella, Luciano (1997), Getting the Seats of Your Pants Dirty: Strategies for Ethnographic Research on Virtual Communities. In: *Journal of Computer-mediated Communication* 3(1). (http://jcmc.indiana.edu/vol3/issue1/paccagnella.html).

Pankow, Christiane (2003), Zur Darstellung nonverbalen Verhaltens in deutschen und schwedischen IRC-Chats. Eine Korpusuntersuchung. In: *Linguistik online* 15. (http://www.linguistik-online.de/15_03/pankow.pdf).

Panyametheekul, Siriporn/Herring, Susan (2003), Gender and Turn Allocation in a Thai Chat Room. In: *Journal of Computer-mediated Communication* 9(1). (http://jcmc.indiana.edu/vol9/issue1/panya_herring.html).

Paolillo, John (1999), The Virtual Speech Community: Social Network and Language Variation on IRC. In: *Journal of Computer-mediated Communication* 4(4). (http://jcmc.indiana.edu/vol4/issue4/paolillo.html).

Pfeil, Ulrike/Zaphiris, Panayiotis/Ang, Chee Siang (2006), Cultural Differences in Collaborative Authoring of Wikipedia. In: *Journal of Computer-mediated Communication* 12(1). (http://jcmc.indiana.edu/vol12/issue1/pfeil.html).

Porter, Constance Elise (2004), A Typology of Virtual Communities: A Multi-disciplinary Foundation for Future Research. In: *Journal of Computer-mediated Communication* 10(1). (http://jcmc.indiana.edu/vol10/issue1/porter.html).

Rehm, Georg (2002), Schriftliche Mündlichkeit in der Sprache des World Wide Web. In: Ziegler, Arne/Dürscheid, Christa (eds.), *Kommunikationsform E-Mail.* (Reihe Textsorten 7.) Tübingen: Stauffenburg, 263–308.

Rehm, Georg (2006), *Hypertextsorten: Definition, Struktur, Klassifikation.* Dissertation, Universität Giessen. (http://geb.uni-giessen.de/geb/volltexte/2006/2688/).

Reid, Elizabeth M. (1991), *Electropolis: Communication and Community on Internet Relay Chat.* (http://www.irchelp.org/irchelp/misc/electropolis.html).

Runkehl, Jens/Schlobinski, Peter/Siever, Torsten (1998), *Sprache und Kommunikation im Internet. Überblick und Analysen.* Opladen/Wiesbaden: Westdeutscher Verlag.

Siebenhaar, Beat (2006), Code Choice and Code-switching in Swiss-German Internet Relay Chat Rooms. In: Androutsopoulos, Jannis (ed.), Sociolinguistics and Computer-mediated Communication. Theme Issue, *Journal of Sociolinguistics* 10(4) (September 2006), 481–509.

Storrer, Angelika (2001a), Getippte Gespräche oder dialogische Texte? Zur kommunikationstheoretischen Einordnung der Chat-Kommunikation. In: Lehr, Andrea/Kammerer, Matthias/Konerding, Klaus-Peter/Storrer, Angelika/Thimm, Caja/Wolski, Werner (eds.), *Sprache im Alltag. Beiträge zu neuen Perspektiven in der Linguistik. Herbert Ernst Wiegand zum 65. Geburtstag gewidmet.* Berlin: de Gruyter, 439–465.

Storrer, Angelika (2001b), Sprachliche Besonderheiten getippter Gespräche: Sprecherwechsel und sprachliches Zeigen in der Chat-Kommunikation. In: Beißwenger, Michael (ed.), *Chat-Kommunikation. Sprache, Interaktion, Sozialität & Identität in synchroner computervermittelter Kommunikation. Perspektiven auf ein interdisziplinäres Forschungsfeld.* Stuttgart: ibidem, 3–24.

Storrer, Angelika (2007), Chat-Kommunikation in Beruf und Weiterbildung. In: *Der Deutschunterricht 1/2007*, 49–61.
Todla, Sunisa (1999), Patterns of Communicative Behaviour in Internet Chatrooms. Unpublished master's thesis, Chulalongkorn University.
van Eckert, Edgar (2005), Termingebundene Chats *one-to-one* in der psycho-sozialen Beratung. In: Beißwenger/Storrer 2005, 349–359.
Viegas, Fernanda B./Wattenberg, Martin/Dave, Kushal (2004), *Studying Cooperation and Conflict between Authors with History Flow Visualizations*. Paper presented at the Conference on Human Factors in Computing Systems, Vienna. (http://web.media.mit.edu/~fviegas/papers/history_flow.pdf).
Vilmi, Ruth (1994), *Global Communication through Email: An Ongoing Experiment at Helsinki University of Technology*. Paper presented at EUROCALL 94 Conference, Karlsruhe. (http://www.tkk.fi/Units/LangSpeech/Ruth/Publication/global.html).
Vronay, David/Smith, Marc A./Drucker, Steven (1999), Alternative Interfaces for Chat. In: *Proceedings of the 12th Annual ACM Symposium on User Interface Software and Technology* (CHI Letters 1,1), 19–26.
Werry, Christopher C. (1996), Linguistic and Interactional Features of Internet Relay Chat. In: Herring 1996, 47–63.
Yates, Simeon J. (1996), Oral and Written Linguistic Aspects of Computer Conferencing. In: Herring 1996, 29–46.
Zitzen, Michaela (2004), Topic Shift Markers in Asynchronous and Synchronous Computer-mediated Communication (CMC). Doctoral Thesis, Universität Düsseldorf. (http://diss.ub.uni-duesseldorf.de/ home/etexte/diss/file?dissid=771).
Zitzen, Michaela/Stein, Dieter (2004), Chat and Conversation: A Case of Transmedial Stability? In: *Linguistics* 42(5), 983–1021.

Michael Beißwenger and Angelika Storrer, Dortmund (Germany)

18. Web linguistics

1. Introduction

The term *Web linguistics* was introduced in a recent article by Bergh (2005) to name empirical language research based on textual material collected from the Web. It is a recent branch of modern corpus linguistics which has grown rapidly since the mid-1990s. As an initial snapshot of the discipline, including its textual substrate and working potential, consider the following suite of quotes, gleaned eclectically from a handful of publications in the field:

> *The swiftness of the World Wide Web's ascension from obscure experiment to cultural icon has been truly remarkable.* (O'Neill/Lavoie/Bennett 2003, no page number)

> *The Web has brought the entire spectrum of knowledge and information to our desktop.* (Fletcher 1999, no page number)

> *The Web is immense, free and available by mouse click. It contains hundreds of billions of words of text and can be used for all manner of language research.* (Kilgarriff/Grefenstette 2003, 333)

> *The World Wide Web, whilst intended as an information source, is an obvious resource for the retrieval of linguistic information, being the largest store of texts in existence, freely available, covering a range of domains, and constantly added to and updated.* (Renouf 2003, 39).

> *The corpus of the new millennium is the Web.* (Kilgarriff 2001, 344)

While serving as a general introduction to Web linguistics, each of the above quotes also identifies important aspects of its framework. In particular, this is so in the sense that the first quote describes the general cultural revolution caused by the emergence of the Web; the second highlights the tremendous increase in accessibility to global digital information offered by it; the third recognizes the Web as a unique and powerful alternative for different forms of empirical language research; the fourth establishes its extensive coverage, variability, freshness and open-endedness; and the fifth brings to the fore its status as a language corpus with great momentum for further advance in the field of corpus linguistics. Cumulatively, all five of them also carry a distinct implication of size and potential, i. e. that the iconic Web, unparallelled by any finite corpora, forms an enormous searchable repository of electronic text, a supercorpus (Bergh/Seppänen/Trotta 1998) or corpus colossal (*The Economist* January 20, 2005) which is able to shed new light on many topical research questions.

However, the Web is not just a treasure-trove of possibilities for linguists to explore: with quantity of information surpassing overall quality, there are also problems, in particular related to the composition of the Web and its user-friendliness as a source for linguistic research activities, as indicated by the next suite of quotes, collected as above:

> *The Web is anarchic, and its use is not in the familiar territory of computational linguistics.* (Kilgarriff/Grefenstette 2003, 335)

> *The Web is different from other monitor corpora, such as the Bank of English Corpus, because we do not know its precise size or the kinds of texts that comprise it.* (Meyer et al. 2003, 242)

> *It is a huge ragbag of digital text, whose content and balance are largely unknown. It is, in the jargon, a highly skewed archive, in that some text types are very well represented, and others are hardly present at all.* (Rundell 2000, no page number)

> *It is a muddle of multilinguality; it operates a loose definition of text which includes all manner of extraneous matter; text dating is sporadic and linguistically uninterpretable.* (Renouf 2003, 39–40)

> *Web pages are typically anonymous and Web server location is no certain guide to origin, so it is difficult to establish authorship and provenance and to assess the reliability, representativeness and authoritativeness of text, both for their linguistic form and their content.* (Fletcher, 2004b, 192).

Taken together, these extracts accentuate the heterogeneous and somewhat intractable character of the Web. Its textual material, contrary to sampled corpora, is not controlled, limited or balanced in any way, leading to a situation where variables such as language, text type, age, provenance, authorship, format and originality remain largely unaccounted for. This is tantamount to saying that the Web linguist is likely to face a number of problems, both quantitative and qualitative, when working with this open-ended data source, problems affecting everything from, say, general material extraction for corpus-building projects, via modelling studies of different language varieties or text types, to minute diachronic or sociolinguistic analysis of the usage of individual language items. Thus, reflecting one of the quotes above, it seems that the use of language material from the Web often brings with it a challenge to established empiricist notions such as reliability, representativeness and authoritativeness.

With these initial observations in mind, possibilities as well as problems, it is obvious that the Web constitutes an unprecedented supply of unfiltered, up-to-date electronic text, freely available and maximally broad in topicality, diversity and domain coverage. Combined with appropriate software tools, it provides a virtually inexhaustible resource for further advancement in the field of corpus linguistics, enabling researchers to study the most provocative questions about the nature of language use today. Yet, the Web is dogged by its anarchic character. Its haphazard composition of texts and text fragments tends to have a hampering effect on the systematic exploitation of online data, requiring judicious selection of language material for each individual research initiative. As discussed in several recent papers (e. g. Renouf 2003; Fletcher 2004b; Bergh 2005; Lüdeling et al. 2007), however, there are ways of circumventing many of the structural and methodological problems of the Web, although it may require some extra effort. This can be done, for example, by restricting searches for target items to particular languages, domains or text types, or by employing specialized software for the retrieval of relevant pages and reliable texts. In the words of Kilgarriff (2001, 342):

> *For the Web to be useful for language study, we must address its anarchy.*

It is the purpose of the present article to contribute to that goal by outlining some of the research efforts in Web linguistics in the last decade or so.

2. Structure of the Web

In order to understand the dynamics of online data, let us start by examining briefly some of the basic structural properties of the Web. In particular, this purports a look at its size and growth as well as its language coverage and textual composition.

2.1. Size

When considering the size of the Web, it is important to keep in mind that, from the point of view of accessibility, there are two different aspects to it. On the one hand, there is the visible (surface, open, public, indexable) Web, which offers unlimited access to a variety of common pages, featuring everything from coherent academic prose, news material, advertising copy to simple text fragments. This is also the part which search engines are able to crawl and index. On the other hand, there is the invisible (deep, closed, hidden, shadow) Web, which is likely to be considerably bigger, perhaps five to ten times the size of the public Web (e. g. Hadenius 2004; Fletcher 2007). More dramatic figures were given in October 2005 by Eric Schmidt, Google's CEO, who indicated that his company had only been able to index 170 out of the 5 million terabytes of data available on the Internet (News.com, http://news.com.com/2100-1024_3-5891779.html). This hidden part of the Web consists of a variety of pages which are difficult to access for engine robots, e. g. password-protected sites, pages with no links to them or which simply block indexation, or pages dynamically generated in response to user interaction (i. e. the results of a query to an online database of lawsuits). In view of this imposed division, it is only natural that researchers have been confined to the visible Web in calculations of size, in particular as indexed by general-purpose search engines.

As the Web is continuously changing and growing, even the best assessment can only approximate its size. Such calculations can take different forms: one is to count the number of pages available (in absolute numbers), another is to work with page size estimates (in kilobytes); a third is to use frequency-based extrapolation techniques (in relative numbers of word/phrase occurrences). Notably, while the former two are only general measures of size, the latter features the possibility of providing figures also for specific languages. For example, using a general approach to size, Lawrence/Giles (1999) showed that in 1999 there were about 800 million pages available on the visible Web, each of them containing an average of 7.3 kilobytes of non-markup text. Simple multiplication of these data yields an estimated size of about six billion kilobytes, or, to use a more manageable figure, six terabytes (cf. Meyer et al. 2003; Kilgarriff/Grefenstette 2003). In 2004, based on the indexation of the Web by Google, corresponding figures were worked out by Bergh (2005), indicating a total size of more than eight billion pages and about 50 terabytes of text, respectively. Even more recent estimates of size suggest that the indexable Web is now in the range of more than 10 billion pages (Gulli/Signorini 2005). In comparative terms, then, these studies imply that the indexable Web has become approximately ten times bigger from 1999 to 2004.

From the calculated 50 terabytes of text, furthermore, it is possible to obtain an assessment also of the number of words available on the Web. At an average of 10 bytes per word, a generous estimate for Latin-based languages (Kilgarriff/Grefenstette 2003), these figures suggest a bulk of more than five trillion (5,000 billion) words in one form or another (Bergh 2005). Thus, this awesome figure gives emphatic confirmation of the previous description of the visible Web as a "corpus colossal", i. e. an enormous repository of self-renewing electronic text whose abundance is likely to provoke linguists from various quarters.

2.2. Contents

With a rough idea of the magnitude of the Web, we may turn next to its contents, in terms of languages as well as text types. One of the initial quotes of this paper has already set the scene for this topic, describing the Web as "a muddle of multilinguality" (Renouf 2003). This colourful image expresses the fact that a broad range of languages are represented online, everything from, say, English and Japanese, Malay and Esperanto, to Welsh and Albanian (cf. Kilgarriff/Grefenstette 2003), distributed over a wide variety of different Web servers and content domains, and sometimes mixed even within the same page. Yet, the usage proportions for the various languages differ substantially. Pleasants (2001), for example, reports the top-10 breakdown of the percentage of Web pages in different languages in 2001, see Table 18.1.

Tab. 18.1: Top-10 list of language usage on the Web as reported in Pleasants (2001)

Language	Per cent
English	68.4
Japanese	5.9
German	5.8
Chinese	3.4
French	3.0
Spanish	2.4
Russian	1.9
Italian	1.6
Portuguese	1.4
Korean	1.3

As to the dominant language on the Web, the figures speak for themselves: English leads the pack in splendid isolation, verbalizing more than two thirds of the indexed pages. Following at a distance are major Asian and continental European languages, all of them in the single-digit percentage range. In recent years, however, the dominance of English seems to have diminished somewhat in favour of native languages used by a majority of the world's population (e. g. Grefenstette/Nioche 2000; O'Neill/Lavoie/Bennett 2003), a development which is likely to continue as the Web expands into further non-western areas of the world. Incidentally, this trend is also reflected in the changing distribution of active Web users. Pleasants (2001), for example, notes that, although most Web pages are in English, the majority of users are not native speakers of English (in 2001 52 per cent). An observation to the same effect was communicated in 2004 by Global Reach, an internet marketing communications consultancy, announcing that in 1996 only 20 per cent of the online population were native speakers of non-English languages, whereas in 2004 the corresponding figure was 65 per cent. Another indication of this changing trend, albeit limited to a very specific portion of the Web, is offered by a more recent report by Technorati (http://www.sifry.com/alerts/archives/000433.html) on the status of the so-called blogosphere, i. e. the community of blog users: the survey showed that in September 2005 Japanese was used in 37 per cent of tracked blogs, surpassing for the first time English, which was used in "only" 31 per cent of tracked blogs.

Yet, notwithstanding this dwindling trend, it is clear that the current Web is primarily a corpus of English (e. g. Meyer et al. 2003; Fletcher 2007). On the assumption that the English portion adds up to roughly 60 per cent of the indexable Web, Bergh (2005) estimated it to comprise at least three trillion (3,000 billion) words of English in 2004.

Further, as regards its textual composition, the Web has been depicted impressionistically as "a huge ragbag of digital text" (Rundell 2000). While this may seem true in many instances – in particular where "unpolished ephemera abound alongside rare treasures" (Fletcher 2004a), interfoliated by textual fragments, tables, stock phrases and stretches of impoverished language – there are still some tentative claims made about the proportions of textual content. Lawrence/Giles (1999), for example, report the percentages for the major content areas of the publicly-accessible Web as summarized in Table 18.2.

Tab. 18.2: Percentages for the major content areas on the Web as reported in Lawrence/Giles (1999)

Content area	Per cent
commercial	83.0
scientific and educational	6.0
health	3.8
personal Web pages	2.2
societies	2.0
pornography	1.5
community	1.4
government	1.1
religion	0.9

The problem with these figures, though, is that they seem to derive from a simple classification of domain addresses, notably referring to English-based servers. This implies that .com pages would contain business-related text only, .edu pages scientific and educational text only, and so on. In reality, however, that is not the case. In addition to commercial data, many .com pages feature a great deal of journalistic material, legal text, etc; likewise, many .edu pages supplement their educational and scientific content with discussion of, for example, administration, health and religion. Thus, these observations suggest that the figures of Lawrence/Giles may not be fully accurate, but that the current situation is more in line with the ideas of Fletcher (2004a), proposing that prose texts on the Web consist primarily of legal, journalistic, commercial and academic texts, i. e. such texts which are major ingredients in most finite corpora. Similar observations also argue in favour of a higher proportion of informal, personal text than suggested by Lawrence/Giles, in particular such encouraged in chat rooms, news lists and Web logs (cf. Renouf 2003; Fletcher 2007), i. e. the type of spontaneous language which provides an unfiltered view of authentic language usage (cf. also article 17 for an extensive coverage of corpora of computer-mediated communication). A further refinement in this context is suggested by Sharoff (2006), who reports that texts from arts and the humanities tend to be generally underrepresented on the Web, whereas technical texts tend to be overrepresented.

3. Working with the Web

Having outlined the basic size and composition of the Web, we may turn next to its methodological sphere. With this huge body of easy-to-access data at hand, it is important to consider ways of evaluating and exploiting it efficiently, aspects which are intimately tied to the application of general search strategies as well as the selection of appropriate software tools.

3.1. Search strategies

In Web linguistics there are two main approaches to the exploitation of online data. One is referred to as Web for Corpus (WfC), or Corpora from the Web, and is concerned with corpus compilation of textual data from the Web; the other is known as Web as Corpus (WaC) and involves direct utilization of the Web as a corpus (e. g. de Schryver 2002). It is worth noting, however, that very often the term WaC is used to indicate all aspects of Web linguistics, even those that, according to the definition given above, should go under the label of WfC. In retrieving such online information, there are different strategies available, which Hawkins (1996) has captured in terms of a tripartite metaphorical framework – hunting, grazing and browsing. Linguistically speaking, hunting is equivalent to a procedure where specific language elements are sought for directly, e. g. checking the usage pattern of a particular word or phrase directly on the Internet using one or more search engines; grazing, on the other hand, involves collection of prefabricated data sets maintained by an information provider, e. g. systematically downloading newspaper texts from selected Web sites; and browsing, finally, is defined as the process of coming up with relevant language data by chance, e. g. accumulating examples of concord mistakes by perusing a set of Web logs. While each strategy can serve as a model for both corpus compilation and direct usage of online data for corpus study, there seems to be a correlation in the sense that grazing strategies are typically employed in WfC projects and hunting strategies in WaC projects (e. g. Fletcher 2007).

3.2. Software tools

The properties of WfC and WaC may be developed further by considering what the software market has to offer in this context. These exploratory approaches imply a focus on general-purpose search engines, and by extension recently developed middleware applications for compilation and concordancing purposes.

As generally recognized, the traditional type of search software for information retrieval on the Web is the search engine. Created for the general public and driven by commercial interest, this tool was constructed to search for information (content) rather than particular strings (form), making its services useful to language scholars "by coincidence, not design" (Fletcher 2004a). As such it constitutes a sophisticated piece of state-of-the-art technology which is able to serve a set of different purposes, such as navigational, informational and transactional aims (Broder 2002), and which is capable of catering to the increasing needs of individual users in terms of precision and, to a lesser degree, recall, be it search skills proper, as in first-generation engines, e. g. AltaVista and AlltheWeb, page ranking principles, as in second-generation engines, e. g. Google and Teoma, or query-based needs analyses, as in third-generation engines, e. g. Eurekster and Brainboost (e. g. Hadenius 2004, Fletcher 2007).

For the Web linguist, however, the search engine can be a baffling experience. This is due to the fact that the tool is not adapted for linguistic research, since it incorporates a number of constraints which are not seen in corresponding offline applications. For example, although there is a great deal of variation to be found in this field, the average search engine tends to (i) cover only a slice of the visible Web, (ii) yield only one hit per Web page; (iii) restrict its return to 1,000 hits; (iv) supply no or very little linguistic context; (v) vary its results according to engine load, etc.; (vi) rank results on the basis of linguistically irrelevant factors; (vii) block searches based on specified linguistic categories, e. g. word classes (cf. Kilgarriff/Grefenstette 2003); and (viii) change search terms heuristically to block distinctions between, say, *lawyers fees* and *lawyer fees* (Rosenbach 2007). Adding to the adversity, search engines also seem to be in a constant flux, "opening up, closing down, amalgamating, adding new functionality, and imposing new restrictions" (Renouf/Kehoe/Mezquiriz 2004, 406). Today Google, Yahoo, MSN and Teoma are considered the only large, well-established and independent search engines available, maintaining indices over two billion pages each (Fletcher 2007).

Despite quirks and constraints, search engine-based research is a vital part of Web linguistics. Drawing on built-in refinements for precision and recall, search engines can be used for specifically targeted searches according to language, domain, format, content, date, etc. (e. g. Bergh 2005). Such work is particularly common in the context of hunting/WaC, but there are also corresponding initiatives in grazing/WfC projects. Yet, in those cases where search engines have fallen short of expectations, more linguistically-oriented applications have been developed to handle the situation, in WfC typically corpus compilation software and in WaC Web concordancers. Running on top of existing search engines, such middleware applications represent a gradual transition from process to product by offering online tailored access to the Web. Below we will look briefly into two such applications, KWiCFinder and WebCorp, adding a note also on the Linguist's Search Engine.

Developed and described by Fletcher (2001, 2004a), KWiCFinder is a search agent which is geared towards grazing/WfC research in the sense that it collects Web pages as corpus data. This is done by automatic finding, analyzing and saving of online documents matching a predefined set of search criteria. Initially, the tool helps users formulate a well-formed query and submits it to a search engine. It then retrieves candidate pages and produces a KWiC concordance at the rate of up to 20 online documents per minute. There are several noise reduction measures available: Fletcher (2004b) reports making use of filtering techniques for ruling out duplicates, virtually identical documents (VIDs) and highly repetitive documents, as well as methods for eliminating texts which are fragmentary or too long/short. The performance of the tool is impressive: in the quoted study the author reports having downloaded over 22,000 Web pages in just a few hours time by running 20 independent KWiCFinder searches simultaneously.

WebCorp, on the other hand, is a Web concordancer which can be profitably employed in hunting/WaC projects. Designed by the Research and Development Unit for English Studies at Liverpool (RDUES), this search tool is intended to provide contextualized examples of language usage from the Web, and to present them in a form tailored for linguistic analysis. As such, then, it adds a layer of refinement to standard Web searches by offering a wider range of search possibilities and presentational means than search engines proper. WebCorp works in a set of different stages. When a query is formulated, the tool first interfaces with the search request and converts it to a format acceptable to search engines. It then "piggy-backs" on the selected search engine, which finds the search term through its index and provides a URL for the relevant source text. WebCorp downloads that text temporarily, extracts the search term and the appropriate linguistic context, collates it, and finally presents it to the user in the desired format, prototypically as a KWiC concordance (Renouf 2003; Renouf/Kehoe/Mezquiriz 2004).

A different approach in this context, finally, is adopted by the Linguist's Search Engine (or LSE, available at http://lse.umiacs.umd.edu), which uses corpora of texts downloaded from the Internet Archive. The aim of the LSE is to provide a "linguist-friendly" access to Web data, thus enabling users to perform searches that are not possible with commercial search engines. At the time of writing, the LSE supports two languages, English and Chinese.

4. Linguistic usage of the Web

Having considered the structural and functional properties of the Web, we may now take a look at instances of actual usage, that is at how language scholars have tried to capitalize on its different linguistic possibilities and relative ease of access by means of various search engines and similar applications. This entails that we keep our focus steadily on research activities drawing on the accumulation of machine-readable text, while leaving aside ready-made linguistic applications which are published, but not created, through this channel, notably learner-oriented resources such as electronic dictionaries (e. g. Cambridge Online Dictionaries), electronic grammars (e. g. The Internet Grammar), automatic translation facilities (e. g. Babelfish), and similar applications.

As we have already seen, there are two main types of linguistic usage of the Web, which have been captured in terms of the distinction between WfC and WaC. In particular, WfC concerns the usage of online data as a pure textual resource, providing raw material for different types of corpus building (so-called Do-It-Yourself or DIY corpora), be it in terms of domain-specific corpora or corpora representing language in a more general sense. WaC, on the other hand, forms the basis for investigation of the distribution of language elements and structures, notably frequency-based usage patterns in different languages. One important aspect in this context is the extraction of statistical language models (SLM), i. e. lists of weighted words used to estimate as accurately as possible the distribution of language in different domains. Based on the idea of expressing language phenomena in terms of simple parameters (cf Biber 1988), such models are typically used in speech recognition to predict word combinations in sound streams, in grammatical annotation to produce part-of-speech tagging, in machine translation to identify eligible translation candidates, and in information retrieval to identify words indicative of a particular topic (cf. Kilgarriff/Grefenstette 2003). Below a brief overview will be given of different approaches to research within WfC and WaC, respectively.

4.1. A source for corpus compilation

4.1.1. Monolingual corpora

In WfC projects, documents are typically collected from the Web and stored locally for various types of post-processing. The most common method involves identification and automatic downloading of Web pages by means of a set of iterative search engine queries. Ghani/Jones/Mladenic (2001), for example, showed that by using a variety of term selection methods and query lengths, it is possible to generate queries that perform well at collecting corpora for specific languages. In particular, they demonstrated that opting for terms according to their odds-ratio scores works well for several languages, and that a variety of keywords supplied by the user yield similar performance. This approach has proven particularly effective in the construction of large corpora of minority languages, as demonstrated by the *An Crúbadán* Web crawler (cf. article 21).

A similar study is reported by Baroni/Bernardini (2004), based on their work with the BootCaT toolkit. With a small set of seed terms as input, they managed to bootstrap domain-specific corpora from the Web via a series of automated Google queries. The corpus data and the seeds were then used to extract multi-word terms in two languages (English and Italian) in the domain of psychiatry.

Another study in the same vein is found in Fletcher (2004b), who queried the Alta Vista search engine by means of the 21 most frequent words in the BNC to create a corpus of English online documents. After applying various noise filtering techniques and removing repetitive documents, he concluded that Web pages under 5 KB or over 200 KB seem to exhibit such a low "signal-to-noise" ratio that they can be excluded a priori in WfC downloads. The study also included a comparison of his Web corpus with the BNC, in which he found the rank frequency lists of the two corpora to be quite similar, even though the Web corpus indicated a preference for a more personal style, in which first and second person forms abound along with a greater use of the present tense, as opposed to the more narrative style found in the BNC, where third person and past tense forms are more common.

Ciaramita/Baroni (2006) explored the possibility of determining whether a Web corpus can be used as a general purpose corpus, i. e. if it is comparable to other balanced corpora such as the BNC and the Brown corpus. The assumption behind this study is that the Web forms a basically biased collection, since many pages contain either linguistically uninteresting data (e. g. stock quotes and weather forecasts) or an overrepresentation of certain genres (e. g. computer-related technical articles). In order to evaluate the randomness of the collected documents, they developed a quantitative method for evaluating and comparing corpora by setting the word frequency distribution of a reference corpus against word frequency distributions constructed using queries to a search engine for deliberately biased seeds. The results of the study suggest that seeds used to construct a balanced corpus from the Web should be selected among mid-frequency words rather than high or low-frequency words.

4.1.2. Multilingual corpora

Broadening the perspective to multilingual aspects, Resnik (1999) pioneered the issue of mining parallel corpora from the Web. He demonstrated that language parallels of different text documents exist on the Web, and that, by exploiting AltaVista's advanced search, it was possible to locate them on the basis of their structural similarity. As a result of this work, he proposed an approach to obtaining parallel corpora from the Web, the so-called STRAND system, which was later updated in a follow-up study by Resnik/Smith (2003) to include several additional features: (i) a "spider" component for locating pages that might have translations; (ii) a content-based method for identifying translations complementing the previous structure-based method, the new component requiring only a word-to-word translation lexicon; and (iii) a methodology for mining the Internet Archive, which dramatically improves performance on the task of identifying pairs of translated Web pages.

The automatic construction of parallel corpora is explored also in Kraaij/Nie/Simard (2003) and in Tomás/Casacuberta/Lloret (2005). The former study introduces the PTMiner system, though its main focus is on information retrieval (cf. section 4.2.), whereas the latter presents a software tool capable of mining parallel corpora starting from a manually prepared list of URLs. The main advantage of the proposed system is that it requires only limited resources: it uses its own crawler to find candidate translated pages (i. e. it does not require a search engine) and, since it uses a statistical translation model trained on the fly (unlike other software packages, which employ bilingual lexicons), it just needs a small sample of translated text with which to train the algorithm.

In addition to managing corpora comprising downloaded texts from the Web, it is possible to work with "open-source corpora", i. e. corpora consisting of lists of selected URLs referring to Web pages suitable for downloading. The concept is first suggested in Kilgarriff (2001), who launched the idea of a framework for distributed corpora (Distributed Data Distributed Collection Initiative, or D3CI) in terms of a virtual multicorpus Web site. Though not as yet realized, the main idea of the project is to make corpora available in the form of lists of URLs that users can download and use for their own purposes. The main advantage of providing lists of URLs instead of ready-made corpora is that lists of addresses (unlike the pages they refer to) are not protected by copyright and can therefore be freely redistributed. This approach is found again in Sharoff (forthcoming), who actually created several open-source corpora (i. e. lists of URLs) in various languages (Chinese, English, French, Italian, German, Polish, Russian and Spanish) using automated Google queries (cf. http://corpus.leeds.ac.uk/internet.html). The corpora were then made available in two ways: (i) as collections of texts searchable through an online Web form, and (ii) as lists of URLs, together with the seeds used to obtain them, supplemented by the queries issued to the search engine and a step-by-step guide to replicating the procedure.

Another method for building large-scale corpora is to "spider" the Web, i. e. to make crawls of the Web which are later managed by an ad hoc search engine. One such experiment was carried out by Clarke at al. (2003) to create a large corpus starting from a set of 2,392 seed URLs. The resulting corpus consisted of about one terabyte of HTML data and formed the basis of an automated question answering system.

A similar "crawling" approach is found in Baroni/Kilgarriff (2006) and in Baroni/Ueyama (2006), who created general-purpose annotated corpora of German and Italian. Both studies applied the same methodology, first, a selection of seed URLs was made by querying Google for random combinations of mid-frequency words. From these URLs, Web pages were then retrieved using the Heritrix crawler (cf. http://crawler.archive.org/), which were filtered according to a procedure involving four different stages: (i) "boilerplate" stripping, i. e. removal of parts of pages which were the same across many pages, such as navigational links, menus etc. (at this stage java script and HTML tags were also removed); (ii) function word filtering, i. e. removal of pages with an insufficient proportion of function words; (iii) pornography filtering, i. e. removal of pages containing pornography, since they tend to contain randomly generated text, keyword lists etc.; and (iv) near-duplicate filtering, i. e. removal of documents sharing a fixed number of n-grams. Finally, the remaining language material was annotated using automated part-of-speech tagging and lemmatization.

The large-scale character of the approach is epitomized by its outcome: a corpus of German with 1.71 billion tokens and a corpus of Italian with 1.9 billion tokens, respectively. Despite the clear advantages of having access to such a large amount of data, this approach presents a few drawbacks: for example, there is virtually no control over the contents of the corpus, apart from the Internet domain (.de, .uk, .it, etc.) from which documents are downloaded. Consequently the only metadata available are the sources of documents, information which is often useless given the volatile nature of Web pages, which frequently change or sometimes disappear altogether in a matter of weeks. It is thus clear that current Web corpora cannot be employed to answer linguistic questions that require a certain degree of control over parameters such as, for instance, age, provenance, or degree of education of the speaker. It is equally clear, however, that Web corpora are extremely valuable, in particular in answering research questions that can only be properly addressed by examining large amounts of data.

4.2. A searchable linguistic database

Flipping the coin over to WaC aspects of Web linguistics, we may start by noting that online data has been explored at various linguistic levels. Most of the research concerns lexical or grammatical topics, but there are also interesting reports on the use of Web resources within the applied fields of translation and language learning. These studies often involve a comparison with ordinary corpora of different kinds, not least when such collections of data have had very little or nothing to say on the topic in question.

In the realm of vocabulary studies, corpus linguists have typically crawled the Web for usage patterns of lexical items, expressed as a function of spelling variation, frequency, genre distribution or collocation. The most elementary use of the Web as a vocabulary resource is probably that in the capacity of a spell checking facility. For example, based on the assumption that the most frequent spelling variant of a word is likely to represent its correct spelling, different forms of (preferably language-specific) words can be looked up and compared as regards their relative frequency. Table 18.3 shows the results of such a check by means of Google (November 2004), involving arbitrarily chosen forms of the English words *thorough*, *disappear* and *pronunciation*, often considered orthographically "difficult".

Tab. 18.3: Number of hits by Google for three spelling variants of *thorough, disappear* and *pronunciation*, respectively

Correct form	*thorough*	*disappear*	*pronunciation*
Hits	4,690,000	3,220,000	1,670,000
Incorrect form Hits	*thourough* 16,000	*disapear* 36,500	*pronounciation* 97,800
Incorrect form	*thorogh*	*dissappear*	*prounounciation*
Hits	1,910	35,000	339

Obviously, while all three spelling variants are multiply indexed by the search engine, there is a vast difference in the number of instances found, with the correct form representing no less than 99.6 per cent of the hits for *thorough*, 97.8 per cent for *disappear*, and 94.1 per cent for *pronunciation*. The results of this limited study thus show that while there is a substantial proportion of "noise" (i. e. erroneous forms) on the Web, there is still no question about which the orthographically correct form is when relative frequencies are considered. Concomitantly, the collected data provide interesting information on spelling variation and "level of difficulty" for different lexical items.

As regards the usage of different vocabulary items, there are studies addressing several linguistic perspectives, such as general frequency, synonyms, ontology and language modelling. The typical Web-based study of vocabulary is concerned with some measure of relative frequency. To take a simple example, Brekke (2000) carried out a study of the expansion of two trendy words, *chaos* and *quantum*, comparing their relative frequency and usage patterns in the BNC and on the Web. The main results are shown in Table 18.4.

Tab. 18.4: Number of occurrences of the words *chaos* and *quantum* in the BNC and on the Web, respectively, as reported in Brekke (2000)

Search item	BNC	Web
chaos	1,605	604,622
quantum	820	820,158

Apart from indirectly confirming the vast difference of size between the two collections of text, the data reveal an interesting crossover in the frequency pattern: *chaos* is more frequent in the texts from the early 1990s (the BNC), whereas *quantum* is more frequent in the texts from the late 1990s (the Web). Hence, as these elements have gradually extended their usage outside their original scientific domain, the Web data suggest that *quantum* has been subject to a more rapid increase than *chaos*.

Another study is reported by Meyer et al. (2003), in which the distribution of the words *chairman, chairperson* and *chairwoman* was investigated. Drawing on data from the AltaVista search engine, they set out to measure the relative proportions of these words on the Web, computing also the ratio between page hits and actual string matches. The results are shown in Table 18.5.

Tab. 18.5: Number of page hits and string matches for the words *chairman*, *chairperson* and *chairwoman* as reported in Meyer et al. (2003)

Search item	Page hits	String matches
chairman	3,023,125	6,015,339
chairperson	391,262	904,303
chairwoman	59,786	81,026

The figures confirm two things. On the one hand, they establish what may be called the expected hierarchy of "chair-words": *chairman* dominates the scene with 87 per cent of the recorded page hits, followed by *chairperson* with 11 per cent and *chairwoman* with only three per cent. On the other hand, they show that the number of string matches for these words is quite different from that of page hits, accentuating the importance of keeping these two categories separate. Yet, when relative figures are computed also for the string matches, it turns out that the proportions between the words remain roughly the same (86, 13 and 1 per cent, respectively).

One particularly profitable area is that involving rare or relatively new lexical items. As finite corpora tend to fall short of expectations in this context, not producing a sufficient number of matches, linguists have often turned to the Web, capitalizing on its size and freshness. One such approach is found in Ohlander/Bergh (2004), who investigated the development of the English loan word *Taliban* in the last decade or so. With no instances of this word found in the BNC, the authors used Google to mirror the extensive development of this word in the media of the early 21st century, showing that *Taliban* in fact has become a frequent word in English today, occurring on no less than 360 000 different Web pages. Other similar approaches to vocabulary studies are mentioned in Renouf (2003) and Rundell (2000), discussing problems in connection with the representation of the neologisms *Sophiegate* and *eye candy*, respectively. The former study, highlighting the lag of search engine indexation, showed that *Sophiegate*, of April 1st 2001 vintage, did not occur in Google's periodically updated index in early May the same year. The latter study, focusing on textual imbalances on the Web, indicated that the phrase *eye candy*, normally taken to mean something that is visually appealing but does not have much content, turns out to be associated with software accessories instead, e. g. screensavers or desktop graphics, due to the apparent overrepresentation of such pages on the Web.

Other researchers have focused on the semantic relations between words. Turney (2001), for example, carried out a study on synonymy. Starting out from the hypothesis that a student's ability to recognize synonyms can be used as a test of the mastery of a foreign language, basically in accordance with the ideas underlying the Test Of English as a Foreign Language (TOEFL) and the English as a Second Language test (ESL), he tried to perform the same synonym task with an unsupervised learning algorithm called PMI-IR (Information Retrieval to collect data from the Web, with Pointwise Mutual Information to analyse them). Pages were collected from the Web by issuing various different queries to the AltaVista search engine and then analysing the results using PMI. The algorithm was tested on 80 questions from the TOEFL test and 50 questions from the ESL test, yielding scores of 73.7 and 74 per cent respectively. By comparison, a large sample of applicants to US colleges from non-English-speaking countries obtained an average score of 64.5 per cent, figures which demonstrate the validity of the algorithm.

Baroni/Ueyama (2004) also used mutual information, now coupled with log-likelihood, to extract Japanese terms from a Web corpus constructed on-the-fly using the BootCaT procedure (see above). They reported that the results obtained are comparable to those from a previous study on English and Italian term extraction (Baroni/Bernardini 2004), thus suggesting that the same methodology can be adapted to both Indo-European and non-Indo-European languages.

In the field of ontology studies, finally, Agirre et al. (2000) described a method for enriching the WordNet ontology using data downloaded from the Web. In particular, they exploited information already present in WordNet to build a separate set of search engine queries for each word sense. The documents found by the search engine were retrieved and organized in collections (one per word sense), from which word frequencies were then computed. Words that tend to show a distinct frequency in each collection are dubbed topic signatures for that word sense, which in their turn can be used to create topical links among concepts and improve sense disambiguation.

On the grammatical side of Web-based language research, most studies seem to deal with phrases of different kinds, but occasionally work is also reported on tagging and parsing, and on clausal structures. Given the size of the Web, the focus on phrases is not unexpected, since multi-word searches tend to limit the number of hits to a workable level. One example of this is the study by Meyer et al. (2003), investigating the extent to which the relative pronoun *who* is used in contexts where normally one would expect *whom*. In particular, by combining the target element with a specific transitive verb *(like, know, call, give* and *take*) and a commonly occurring subject (*I*), thus forming a regular monotransitive construction, the authors managed to derive the figures from the Web given in Table 18.6.

Tab. 18.6: Number of page hits for the strings *who I* VP and *whom I* VP with five common transitive verbs, as reported in Meyer et al. (2003)

Search item	Page hits	Per cent
who I VP	11,752	49
whom I VP	12,152	51

As an offset to previous claims that relative *whom* is generally much rarer than *who* (e. g. Biber et al. 1999), the present data show that in certain contexts *whom* is actually preferred to *who*, and that this is the case not only following a preposition but also with a range of transitive verbs.

By the same token, Bergh/Seppänen/Trotta (1998) used the Web to study the distribution of a highly infrequent syntactic pattern in English. Targeting a specific type of finite subjectless clause, previously noted only in historical English, as in the string ...*which is hoped will* ..., the authors managed to show that while such a structure was not represented in any of the ordinary corpora available at the time, the Web provided a good crop of the construction from a range of different English-based Web sites. The results thus argued in favour not only of its existence in present-day English but also of its grammaticality, suggesting yet another fruitful topic for standard reference grammars to deal with in the future.

Another type of study is represented by Volk (2002). Drawing on the vast textual resources of the Web as a means to improve parsing capabilities, the author set himself the task of trying to disambiguate PP attachments on the basis of statistical profiling, e. g. in pairs such as *Peter reads a book about computers* and *Peter reads a book in the subway*. In particular, he used search engines to calculate co-occurrence frequencies for triples such as V + P + N2 and N1 + P + N2, with the subsequent PP attachment decision being based on the highest figure emanating from the formula cooc(X, P, N2) = freq(X, P, N2)/freq(X). For the evaluation of the procedure, 4,383 ambiguous PP constructions were extracted from a German treebank, where 61 per cent of the cases had been previously classified as noun attachments and 39 per cent as verb attachments. On the basis of triple co-occurrence values derived through the AltaVista search engine, the method proved to be applicable on 63 per cent of the test cases, and exhibited a 75 per cent PP disambiguation accuracy.

Furthermore, Web resources have been influential in natural language processing and in the applied fields of translation and language learning. Varantola (2003), for example, reports on the results of a workshop on the use of DIY "disposable" corpora for translation. Participants were asked to build specialized corpora by manually downloading documents from the Web and use them as a linguistic resource in various translation tasks. The results of the study indicate that the two main obstacles encountered by translators were the level of computer literacy required, and the cost of building a corpus for just one specific translation task. Along the same lines, Bernardini (2005) argues that corpora in translation teaching have been widely used also because teachers and learners alike can build their own corpora by downloading texts from the Internet, solving the problem of cost-effectiveness by using the Web to automatically build two disposable corpora of farmhouse descriptions (one in English, the other in Italian). The study shows the usefulness of using ad hoc corpora, not only in finding the most appropriate translation for specific expressions, but also to increase the familiarity of trainee translators with different textual genres.

In the field of machine-translation, Grefenstette (1999) used the AltaVista search engine to find the correct English translation of German and Spanish compounds. Each of the constituents of the compound was first translated into English using an online dictionary, where multiple equivalents of each constituent were given, and where all possible combinations were considered valid. Candidate translations were then sent to the search engine as phrasal queries, and the number of occurrences provided by the engine was noted. In 87 per cent of cases, the query with the highest number of hits turned out to be the correct translation.

Kraaij/Nie/Simard (2003) report on an interesting experiment in cross-language information retrieval. First, using a series of heuristics, they collected parallel corpora from the Web for several language pairs (although all couples contained an English component, i. e. English-Dutch, English-Chinese etc.). The collected corpora were used as training material for statistical translation models, where the effectiveness of the system was tested by translating the same set of queries using the Systran machine translation system and the statistical translation models. The queries were then used to retrieve documents on a certain topic from different corpora. The results showed that the performance of the queries obtained with the Web-based translation models was at least on a par with that obtained from the Systran system, and in some cases it was in fact even better.

In the realm of language learning, finally, Fletcher (2001) offers an extensive overview of how the Web can be used in various pedagogical circumstances. He does so by providing examples of creative usage of search engines in different contexts, suggesting tools and methods for collecting examples to be used in the classroom or independently by students. In particular, it is worth mentioning the Grammar Safari project (http://www.iei.uiuc.edu/student_grammarsafari.html), an online grammar resource for teachers and learners of English. This site provides suggestions on how to create class activities that use the Web as the primary source of examples on various grammatical points. It also details strategies and tutorials for advanced students wishing to investigate particular syntactic structures.

5. Conclusion

This article deals with Web linguistics, a recent branch of corpus linguistics which employs the Web as a source of linguistic data. First, a description is given of the structure of the Web, providing different estimates of its size and composition. As there is no comprehensive "index" of its contents, it proves virtually impossible to determine the exact amount of information available, as well as its distribution into different text types. Then, the two main approaches to Web linguistics are presented, Web for Corpus (WfC) and Web as Corpus (WaC), including the basics of those search strategies and software tools that are typically part of these methodologies. Finally, a survey is provided of the different studies that have been carried out in this field, both as regards usage of the Web as a source for corpus compilation projects and as a searchable linguistic database.

Summarizing the implications of the present discussion, we may note that there seems to be a great potential for Web linguistics in the future, especially within three main areas: (i) as a resource for learning about authentic language structure and use, (ii) as a provider of raw material for both DIY disposable corpora and more "stable" collections, and (iii) as a test bed for the training of various software applications. However, many issues of viability and exploitation of the Web as a linguistic resource must still be resolved. In particular with regard to three aspects: (i) user-friendliness (as the Web was not originally designed for linguistic research), (ii) representativeness (as the Web does not constitute a balanced corpus), and (iii) composition (as very little metainformation exists to categorize its contents according to the traditional parameters of corpus linguistics).

6. Literature

Agirre, E./Ansa, O./Hovy, E./Martínez, D. (2000), Enriching Very Large Ontologies Using the WWW. In: *Proceedings of the Ontology Learning Workshop*. Berlin: ECAI, 73–77.

Banko, M./Brill, E. (2001), Scaling to Very Very Large Corpora for Natural Language Disambiguation. In: *Proceedings of the 39th Annual Meeting of the Association for Computational Linguistics*. Toulouse, France, 26–33.

Baroni, M./Bernardini, S. (2004), BootCaT: Bootstrapping Corpora and Terms from the Web. In: *Proceedings of LREC 2004*. Paris: ELRA, 1313–1316.

Baroni, M./Kilgarriff, A. (2006), Large Linguistically-processed Web Corpora for Multiple Languages. In: *Proceedings of EACL 2006*. Trento, Italy, 87–90.

Baroni, M./Ueyama, M. (2004), Retrieving Japanese Specialized Terms and Corpora from the World Wide Web. In: *Proceedings of KONVENS 2004*. Vienna, Austria, 13–16.

Baroni, M./Ueyama, M. (2006), Building General- and Special-purpose Corpora by Web Crawling. In: *Proceedings of the NIJL Workshop on Language Corpora*. Tokyo, Japan, 31–40.

Bergh, G. (2005), Min(d)ing English Language Data on the Web. What Can Google Tell us? In: *ICAME Journal* 29, 25–46.

Bergh, G./Seppänen, A./Trotta, J. (1998), Language Corpora and the Internet: A Joint Linguistic Resource. In: Renouf, A. (ed.), *Explorations in Corpus Linguistics*. Amsterdam: Rodopi, 41–54.

Bernardini, S. (2005), Tools for Translators: Machine Readable Corpora as Resources for Translators. In: Brown, K. (ed.), *The Encyclopaedia of Language & Linguistics*. 2nd edition. London: Elsevier, 358–375.

Biber, D. (1988), *Variation across Speech and Writing*. Cambridge: Cambridge University Press.

Biber, D./Johansson, S./Leech, G./Conrad, S./Finegan, E. (1999), *Longman Grammar of Spoken and Written English*. Harlow: Pearson Education.

Brekke, M. (2000), From the BNC toward the Cybercorpus: A Quantum Leap into Chaos? In: Kirk, J. M. (ed.), *Corpora Galore. Analyses and Techniques in Describing English*. Amsterdam: Rodopi, 227–247.

Broder, A. (2002), A Taxonomy of Web Search. In: *ACM SIGIR Forum* 36(2), 3–10.
Ciaramita, M./Baroni, M. (2006), Measuring Web-corpus Randomness: A Progress Report. In: Baroni, M./Bernardini, S. (eds.), *WaCky! Working Papers on the Web as Corpus*. Bologna: Gedit, 127–158.
Clarke, C. L. A./Cormack, G. V./Laszlo, M./Lynam, T. R./Terra, E. L. (2003), The Impact of Corpus Size on Question Answering Performance. In: *Proceedings of the 25th Annual International A CM SIGIR Conference on Research and Development in Information Retrieval*. Tampere, Finland, 369–370.
de Schryver, G.-M. (2002). Web for/as Corpus: A Perspective for the African Languages. In: *Nordic Journal of African Studies* 11, 266–282.
Fletcher, W. (1999), Language Studies. Solving Online Research Problems with KWICfinder. Available from: http://www.usna.edu/LangStudy/computation/problem_solving_fletcher.html.
Fletcher, W. (2001), Concordancing the Web with KWICfinder. In: *Third North American Symposium on Corpus Linguistics and Language Teaching*. Boston, MA, 23–25.
Fletcher, W. (2004a), Facilitating the Compilation and Dissemination of Ad-hoc Web Corpora. In: Aston, G./Bernardini, S./Stewart, D. (eds.), *Corpora and Language Learners*. Amsterdam: Benjamins, 273–300.
Fletcher, W. (2004b), Making the Web More Useful as a Source for Linguistic Corpora. In: Connor, U./Upton, T. (eds.), *Applied Corpus Linguistics: A Multidimensional Perspective*. Amsterdam: Rodopi, 191–205.
Fletcher, W. (2007), Concordancing the Web: Promise and Problems, Tools and Techniques. In: Hundt, M./Biewer, C./Nesselhauf, N. (eds.), *Corpus Linguistics and the Web*. Amsterdam: Rodopi, 25–45.
Ghani, R./Jones, R./Mladenic, D. (2001), *Building Minority Language Corpora by Learning to Generate Web Search Queries*. Technical report, Carnegie Mellon University, Center for Automated Learning and Discovery.
Grefenstette, G. (1999), The World Wide Web as a Resource for Example-based Machine Translation Tasks. In: *Proceedings of the Twenty-First International Conference on Translating and the Computer*. London. Available from: http://www.xrce.xerox.com/Publications/Attachments/1999-004/gg_aslib.pdf.
Grefenstette, G./Nioche, J. (2000), Estimation of English and Non-English Language Use on the WWW. In: *Proceedings of the RIAO (Recherche d'Informations Assistée par Ordinateur)*. Paris, France, 237–246.
Gulli, A./Signorini, A. (2005), The Indexable Web is More than 11.5 Billion Pages. Available from: http://www.cs.uiowa.edu/~asignori/pubs/web-size/.
Hadenius, P. (2004), Googles dagar är räknade. In: *Forskning & Framsteg* 7/04, 42–45. Available from http://fof.se/.
Hawkins, D. (1996), Hunting, Grazing, Browsing: A Model for Online Information Retrieval. In: *Online Magazine*. Available from: http://www.infotoday.com/online/JanOL/hawkins.html.
Keller, F./Lapata, M./Ourioupina, O. (2002), Using the Web to Overcome Data Sparseness. In: *Proceedings of the Conference on Empirical Methods in Natural Language Processing*. Philadelphia, PA, 230–237.
Kilgarriff, A. (2001), Web as Corpus. In: *Proceedings of the Corpus Linguistics 2001 Conference*. Lancaster, United Kingdom, 342–344.
Kilgarriff, A./Grefenstette, G. (2003), Introduction to the Special Issue on the Web as Corpus. In: *Computational Linguistics* 29(3), 333–347.
Kraaij, W./Nie, J.-Y./Simard, M. (2003), Embedding Web-based Statistical Translation Models in Cross-language Information Retrieval. In: *Computational Linguistics*, 29(3), 381–419.
Lawrence, S./Giles, L. (1999), Accessibility of Information on the Web. In: *Nature* 400(6740), 107–109.
Lüdeling, A./Evert, S./Baroni, M. (2007), Using Web Data for Linguistic Purposes. In: Hundt, M./Biewer, C./Nesselhauf, N. (eds.), *Corpus Linguistics and the Web*. Amsterdam: Rodopi, 7–24.

Meyer, C./Grabowski, R./Han, H.-Y./Mantzouranis, K./Moses, S. (2003), The World Wide Web as Linguistic Corpus. In: Leistyna, P./Meyer, C. (eds.), *Corpus Analysis: Language Structure and Language Use*. Amsterdam: Rodopi, 241–254.
Ohlander, S./Bergh, G. (2004), Taliban – a Rogue Word in Present-day English Grammar. In: *English Studies* 85, 206–229.
O'Neill, E./Lavoie, B./Bennett, R. (2003), Trends in the Evolution of the Public Web: 1998–2002. Available from: http://www.dlib.org/dlib/april03/lavoie/04lavoie.html.
Pleasants, N. (2001), Languages of the Web. In: *ClickZ Today*, May 11, 2001.
Renouf, A. (2003), WebCorp: Providing a Renewable Data Source for Corpus Linguists. In: Granger, S./Petch-Tyson, S. (eds.), *Extending the Scope of Corpus-based Research: New Applications, New Challenges*. Amsterdam: Rodopi, 39–58.
Renouf, A./Kehoe, A./Mezquiriz, D. (2004), The Accidental Corpus: Some Issues in Extracting Linguistic Information from the Web. In: Aijmer, K./Altenberg, B. (eds.), *Advances in Corpus Linguistics. Papers from the 23rd International Conference on English Language Research on Computerized Corpora (ICAME 23)*. Amsterdam: Rodopi, 403–419.
Resnik, P. (1999), Mining the Web for Bilingual Text. In: *Proceedings of the 37th Meeting of ACL*. College Park, MD, 527–534.
Resnik, P./Smith, N. A. (2003), The Web as a Parallel Corpus. In: *Computational Linguistics* 29(3), 349–380.
Rosenbach, A. (2007), Exploring Constructions on the Web: A Case Study. In: Hundt, M./Biewer, C./Nesselhauf, N. (eds.), *Corpus Linguistics and the Web*. Amsterdam: Rodopi, 167–190.
Rundell, M. (2000), The Biggest Corpus of All. In: *Humanising Language Teaching* 2(3). Available from: http://www.hltmag.co.uk/may00/idea.htm.
Sharoff, S. (2006), Creating General-purpose Corpora Using Automated Search Engine Queries. In: Baroni, M./Bernardini, S. (eds.), *WaCky! Working Papers on the Web as Corpus*. Bologna: Gedit, 63–98.
Sharoff, S. (forthcoming), Open-source Corpora: Using the Net to Fish for Linguistic Data. In: *International Journal of Corpus Linguistics* 11(4), 435–462.
Tomás, J./Casacuberta, F./Lloret, J. (2005), WebMining: An Unsupervised Parallel Corpora Web Retrieval System. In: Danielsson, P./Wagenmakers, M. (eds.), *Proceedings from the Corpus Linguistics Conference* 1(1). Birmingham. Available at: http://www.corpus.bham.ac.uk/PCLC/WebMining.pdf.
Turney, P. (2001), Mining the Web for Synonyms: PMI-IR versus LSA on TOEFL. In: *Proceedings of the Twelfth European Conference on Machine Learning (ECML-2001)*. Freiburg, Germany, 491–502.
Varantola, K. (2003), Translators and Disposable Corpora. In: Zanettin, F./Bernardini, S./Stewart, D. (eds.), *Corpora in Translator Education*. Manchester: St. Jerome, 55–70.
Volk, M. (2002), Using the Web as a Corpus for Linguistic Research. In: *Tähendusepüüdja. Catcher of the Meaning. A Festschrift for Professor Haldur Õim*. University of Tartu: Publications of the Department of General Linguistics 3. Available at: http://www.ifi.unizh.ch/cl/volk/papers/Oim_Festschrift_2002.pdf.

Gunnar Bergh, Härnösand (Sweden) and Eros Zanchetta, Bologna (Italy)

19. Large text networks as an object of corpus linguistic studies

1. Introduction

In simple mathematical terms, a corpus of natural language texts can be defined as a set which abstracts from any order of its elements with respect to each other so that each element is separately processed by some corpus linguistic operation (e. g., of collocation statistics). This view implies the absence of structure formation within the corpus or at least disregards it from the point of view of text representation and subsequent corpus building. Of course, a corpus of natural language texts is more than just a *set* of linguistic units. There is structure formation above the level of single texts which can be made accessible to corpus linguistic studies. According to Stubbs (1996), texts are oriented to routines and conventions; they are shaped by prior texts to which they make intertextual references, possibly (or preferably) included in the same corpus. In this sense, Stubbs (2001) points out:

> "Analysis cannot be restricted to isolated texts. It requires an analysis of intertextual relations, and therefore comparison of individual instances in a given text, typical occurrences in other texts from the same text-type, and norms of usage in the language in general."
> (Stubbs 2001, 120).

With the advent of web-based communication, more and more corpora are accessible which manifest such intertextual relations and thus structure formation in large text networks. Moreover, the WWW does not only manifest a tremendous set of text types (genres and registers) which already existed before the appearance of WWW-based communication, but also a vast number of instances of newly emerging document types, e. g., *corporate sites, Wikis, weblogs or personal academic home pages* (Mehler/Gleim 2006, 2005; Thelwall/Wouters 2005). Theoretically, this makes the web the source of choice for extracting large corpora of certain genres, registers and other linguistic varieties. It also makes the web the reference point of studying the emergence of *hypertext types* as well as the growth, maturity stage and dying of their instances manifested by websites and their constitutive pages. Thus, the web has become increasingly important as a quasi inexhaustible resource of corpus formation (Baroni/Bernardini 2004; Keller/Lapata 2003; Kilgarriff/Grefenstette 2003; Resnik/Smith 2003; Santamaría/Gonzalo/Verdejo 2003).

Of course, the web is not the only resource of large networks of textual units. There exist special areas of textual networking which become accessible to corpus linguistic studies not only because of their web-based interfaces, but also due to digitised or *e*-text releases (Hockey 2000). This includes the area of *scientific communication* (e. g. CiteSeer or CiteBase as examples of digital libraries), *press communication* (e. g. the *New York Times* or the *German Süddeutsche Zeitung*, which link articles to thematically related ones), *technical communication* (e. g. the Apache Software Foundation's technical documentations of open source projects) and *electronic encyclopedias* (e. g. Wikipedia and its releases in a multitude of languages) which can be analysed in terms of corpora of networked units. These are examples of large corpora of interlinked texts which in the majority of cases utilise HTML in order to manifest intertextual relations, such as, for example, citation links (digital libraries), content-based add-ons (online press communication) and links to related lexicon articles (electronic encyclopedias). From a corpus linguistic point of view, several scientific questions come to the fore regarding the formation of such networks:

1. Preprocessing: *How to provide a uniform, generic interface to the analysis of intertextual relations as manifested in web-based communication?*
2. "Co-textualising" corpus linguistic analyses: *How to explore text linkage in large text networks as a source of corpus linguistic studies?*
   This question is related to the position of Fairclough (1992), who argues for an intertextual view of analysing, for example, pre-constructed phrases and fixed collocations. In this sense, digital manifestations of intertextual links provide a source of exploring linguistic structures which are confirmed by intertextually related texts. Cf. also Mehler/Gleim (2006) for the notion of collocation analyses which are sensitive to genre-specific structures.
3. Exploring structure formation in large text networks: *What are the regularities of the distributed formation of large text networks subject to the limitations of the medium in use?*
   As structure formation in large text networks cannot be reduced to the intentionality of single authors, the question of distributed processes of text production and processing – distributed over thousands of collaborating/competing authors – comes to the fore.

This article reviews the state of the art in these areas. As corpus linguistic studies of large text networks are at the very beginning, this will relate especially to the third question. Interestingly, arguments in support of the need of text network analyses come from computer science and, especially, from the field of text and web mining (Mehler/Wolff 2005). This relates to the so-called *link-content conjecture* of Menczer (2004), who states that *the content of a web page is similar to the content of the pages that link to it*. As Menczer approaches content in terms of Information Retrieval (IR) and, thus, in lexical terms, this hypothesis can be reformulated as follows: *A page's lexical organisation is similar to the lexical organisation of the pages that link to it*, where lexical similarity is measured in the framework of the vector space model based on a tf-idf weighting scheme and the cosine measure. The tf idf weighting scheme is a function of the term and document frequency of candidate terms; it is used to filter out non-descriptive terms in the sense of IR, e. g., words which are evenly distributed over all texts of the corpus and, thus, do not contribute to thematically separating them. For more details on this model, cf. Baeza-Yates/Ribeiro-Neto (1999).

Menczer (2004) presents data in support of this conjecture which also points at an exponential decay of the similarity in question from the point of view of a focal page when following hyperlinks from page to page. As will be motivated, this observation is in accordance with so-called small world models of social-semiotic networks (cf., for example, Albert/Jeong/Barabási 1999). Supposing that Menczer's hypothesis is continuingly supported, it implies that additional data in support of the data being observed on a focal page comes from its neighborhood in the web – by analogy with the argument of Stubbs (2001) cited at the beginning of this section. Although this hypothesis has not yet been investigated in the case of more traditional text networks, it is nevertheless plausible to conjecture it in these cases too. This may look as follows: *A text's linguistic organisation is similar to the linguistic organisation of the texts that relate to it by means of intertextual relations.* In order to substantiate this conjecture, the notion of *linguistic similarity* needs to be operationalised as well as the aspect of linguistic organisation under consideration and the type of intertextual relation for which this conjecture actually holds. *Text network analysis* is a step in this direction as it investigates principles of intertextuality which should be taken into account in the course of corpus building in order to meet the requirement of Stubbs (2001) and related requirements.

This article puts emphasis on the state of the art of network analysis (Newman 2000, 2003b) and its utilisation in the area of linguistic systems (cf. Ferrer i Cancho/Riordan/Bollobás 2005). Amongst others, this includes approaches to the notion of the small world of social systems (Watts/Strogatz 1998; Watts 1999). From the point of view of quantitative linguistics, this comprises cluster and pathway analysis (Newman 2003a, 2003b). Moreover, non-linear regression analyses of degree distributions (based on the number of in- and outgoing links) which relate to Zipfian regularities (Rapoport 1982) are reviewed too. The article demonstrates this analytical apparatus by example of some document networks. The aim is to exemplify the state of the art of quantitative network analysis in the area of linguistic networks. From the point of view of corpus linguistics, the significance of this kind of analysis is due to the fact that it gives hints at how to quantify validity constraints of corpora based on intertextual regularities of their constitutive texts.

Text network analysis is at its very beginning, in corpus linguistics as well as in computational and quantitative linguistics. Although the notion of intertextuality has been coming into age (Fix 2000), it nevertheless has been addressed in terms of qualitative, descriptive, but not of exploratory corpus linguistics. Theoretical definitions which allow to demarcate the field of document network analysis are still missing. Accordingly, the subsequent section introduces some preliminary notions for this task.

1.1. A short note on the corpus linguistic relevance of complex network analysis

The analysis of complex text networks is about structure formation in corpora of textual units. For decades, text linguistics has argued that intertextuality is a source of structure formation *above* the level of single texts (de Beaugrande 1980, 1997; Heinemann 1997; Hoey 1995; Holthuis 1993; Jakobs 1999; Raible 1995). This kind of structure formation has two aspects: in terms of the development of text types and in terms of the networking of their textual instances. Following this line of argumentation, Fairclough (1992) points out that intertextual relations allow to explore related texts and, thus, to identify significant cotexts as additional, viable data resources of corpus linguistic studies: if two texts x and y are intertextually related due to their common or related functions or topics, they probably contain common or related linguistic manifestations of these functions or topics, respectively, and, thus, are more likely structured in a similar way (Biber 1995; Brinker 1991). This correlation may hold on the level of lexico-grammatical patterns (Halliday 1966) as well as on the level of textual superstructures (van Dijk/Kintsch 1983). In other words: studying intertextually related texts provides additional data to lexical and grammatical patterns and their variation subject to the change of the underlying genres or registers, respectively (Biber 1995; Ventola 1987). However, in order to benefit from intertextuality as a data resource we need to explore its principles first. That is, we need to make it an object of computational linguistics, not only on the level of pairwise linked texts, but on the level of whole networks based thereon. *This is the task of complex text network analysis.*

On the other hand, knowing the principles of intertextual structure formation (i. e. of the development of complex text networks) provides knowledge about constraints of the "naturalness" or "non-artificiality" of text corpora *by analogy with Zipf's first law* in the case of lexical systems. This can be explained as follows: it is well confirmed in quantitative linguistics that the ranked frequency distribution of lexical text constituents is highly skewed in a way which departs from the normal distribution, but is more reliably modelled by a power-law or some related distribution (Baayen 2001; Rapoport 1982; Wimmer/Altmann 1999a; Zipf 1972). Accordingly, a "text candidate" which heavily departs from this Zipfian distribution indicates it is a mixture of different texts (possibly written by different authors) or to be an artificial product which was produced under "unusual" conditions disturbing the process of text production (Orlov 1982). Analogously, a corpus of texts whose intertextual networking departs from the principles of text networks may indicate artificiality in the sense of being a mixture of topically or functionally highly divergent and, thus, unrelated texts. Using such a corpus as a starting point of inductive reasoning in corpus linguistics (Stubbs 2006) is, thus, problematic. Complex network analysis allows the exploration of such naturalness constraints of corpus formation.

In summary, the intertextual formation of linguistic patterns as well as quality constraints of text corpora are two reference points in support of the relevance of complex network analysis in corpus linguistics. This article surveys the state of the art in this field of research.

1.2. Text and document networks

Structure formation above the level of texts is based on intertextual relations which span *networks* in which nodes denote texts (or textual components thereof) and links manifest coherence relations of these nodes. With the advent of web-based communication, text networking is not only accessible by means of e-texts and their networks, but also by hypertexts which utilise hyperlinks in order to make intertextual relations explicit (Mehler 2005). Starting from the notion of a document which integrates textual content with hypertextual add-ons (Kuhlen 1991), all three kinds of networks are taken into account in this survey: *text*, *e-text* and (hypertext) *document networks*; see Table 19.1. For reasons of terminological simplicity we simply speak of *text* and *document networks*

Tab. 19.1: Levels of structuring of text, *e*-text and hypertext document networks (cf. Storrer 2002; Mehler 2005)

	text area	*e*-text area	hypertext area
atomic level	text component	*e*-text component	text module
intermediate level	text	*e*-text	hypertext document
network level	text network	*e*-text network	hypertext document network

and use both terms interchangeably (while we make it explicit if only one, but not the other term is adequate).

Generally speaking, such networks are characterised as follows:

- *Intertextuality:* Text and document networks are units to which intertextuality can be ascribed as a gradual, quantifiable property by analogy with textuality as a property of single texts.

  Intertextual cohesion or coherence relations interrelate different texts or documents in order to build (not necessarily mutual) constraints on their interpretations. For a formal model of such constraints (with a focus on intratextual ones), cf. Mehler (2007). A survey of this notion is out of reach of the present paper; cf. Mehler (2005) for such a survey. We only stress the fundamental distinction of *referential* and *typological intertextuality* (Heinemann 1997): whereas the former comprises immediate text-to-text relations, which authors manifest more or less explicitly by surface structural markers, it is the shared usage of the same or alike patterns within different texts which mediates their typological, but not necessarily intended relatedness. Since intertextual relations are in many cases *implicit*, they first need to be explored in order to become an object of network analysis. Intertextual relations of web documents may, but do not need to be manifested by hyperlinks. As in the case of cohesion and coherence in general, there are many resources of intertextuality so that ascribing this property to a text or document network is bound by vagueness and under-specification due to a diversity of possibly competing criteria. Even in the case of citation relations, exploring intertextual relations can be a demanding task in terms of computational linguistics and machine learning (Giles/Bollacker/Lawrence 1998). In any case, the starting point of analysing text and document networks is a network of textual units which is spanned by their intertextual relations. Thus, complex text or document network analysis is about structural analyses of networks whose links are spanned by cohesion or coherence relations, which in the majority of cases are meaning- or content-based.
- *Chaining and clustering:* Intertextuality results from producing or processing intertex tual relations. These relations generate chains or clusters of thematically related texts/documents which manifest the same, similar or otherwise associated themes, topics or fields. On the other hand, the chains or clusters may be induced by schematically ordered texts/documents which manifest the same or related text types, patterns or superstructures. Note that whereas chains are partially ordered, clusters are clumps of interrelated units. Finally, as the chains and clusters overlap or intersect, respectively, they constitute networks.
- *Variability:* As intertextual relations are genre-sensitive or genre-specific (e. g. citations in scientific communication vs. content-based links in online press communica-

tion), text and document networks as a whole are genre-sensitive, too. That is, for different genres (e.g. of scientific, technical or press communication) variations in topological and statistical characteristics of the networks of these genres are expected. That is, genres are expected to be distinguishable in terms of the characteristics of their document networks.

- *Distributed cognition:* The production and reception of text and document networks is necessarily *distributed* over possibly hundreds and thousands of agents. They result from cooperative or competitive sign processes in the sense of distributed cognition (Hollan/Hutchins/Kish 2000) and, thus, manifest a kind of superindividual structure formation which cannot be reduced to intentional acts of individual interlocutors, *comparable to the language system, but on the level of its manifestation.* That is, as the lexicon of a language cannot be attributed to single interlocutors, text networks are (because of their size) structured in a way which is not controlled by any (group of) such interlocutors separately. But whereas the lexicon is part of the language system, texts and the networks they induce are manifestation units.

In order to grasp the principles of this kind of networking, a combined approach which integrates at least topological and statistical methods is needed. This can be motivated as follows: according to Bense (1998), the formal branch of text linguistics includes *algebraical, topological* and *statistical* aspects. Whereas algebraic approaches to discourse grammars rely on the notion of *constituency* and *dependency* (Polanyi 1988), it is the notion *of distance* and *neighborhood* which underlies topological models (Brainerd 1977). In contrast to this, the notions of *occurrence, co-occurrence* and *repetition* are the core of statistical approaches (Altmann 1988). A central aim of quantitative linguistics is to investigate those types of repetition which bring about the statistical nature of linguistic structure formation in-between the extreme values of complete randomness and determinism.

Because of their non-linear, non-hierarchical structure formation, text and document networks are only adequately described by means of *graph theory* (Schenker et al. 2005) and *network analysis* (Newman 2003b). Moreover, because of the size of these networks of hundreds and thousands of nodes, there is no alternative to *automatic statistical* analyses. By analogy with stochastic discourse grammars, which combine algebraic with statistical modelling, exploring these kinds of networks demands integrating topological and statistical approaches. Thus, the methods of *statistical network analysis* as elaborated in social science and subsequently sophisticated in physics builds the methodic core of this survey.

1.3. Delineation and terminological notes

This survey is about regularities of large networks of textual units as a special kind of complex networks. A network is called *complex* if it consists of hundreds and thousands or even millions of nodes in a way which affects its self-regulation and -organisation (Milgram 1967; Newman 2003b). The aim of analysing complex networks of texts or documents is to investigate indicators of structure formation which can be utilised for the task of corpus building and maintenance. In his survey of the structure and function of complex networks, Newman (2003b) reports on results of analysing social, informational, technical and biological networks. Amongst others, this comprises co-authorship and company director networks, WWW-based networks and citation networks, the Internet and peer-to-peer networks as well as protein interaction and neural networks. Focusing on social, technical and informational networks, Park (2003) interrelates these areas as follows: as a sort of informational network, hyperlink networks are based on the Internet as a kind of technological network which, in turn, manifests a communication network as a sort of social network in which nodes denote interconnected individuals.

Starting from this general view, we can delineate the object of the present survey as follows: generally speaking, it does not regard social networks in which nodes denote individuals, agents, actors or communities thereof and where links represent social (communication) relations of these agents (Wasserman/Faust 1999; Kautz/Selman/Shah 1997; Otte/Rousseau 2002). Unlike these and related analyses, this review deals with networks whose nodes are linguistic units down from the level of words and up to the level of texts and hypertexts, where the main focus is on the latter. Nevertheless, this review is not restricted to *hyperlink networks* (Park 2003), but takes networking within *old* and *new* media into account thereby stressing the need to explore intertextual relations beyond hyperlinks as a source of networking within text corpora. As pointed out by the three-layer model in Figure 19.1, this does not deny the fact that text and document networks are manifestations of some linguistic system which, in turn, is enclosed by a corresponding social system (e. g. a speech community). Rather, it has to be understood as an indispensable reduction of the variety of network studies to be surveyed within this article. As will be shown in the subsequent section, this includes a wide area of text and document networks ranging from social software-based networks to networks in scientific and press communication.

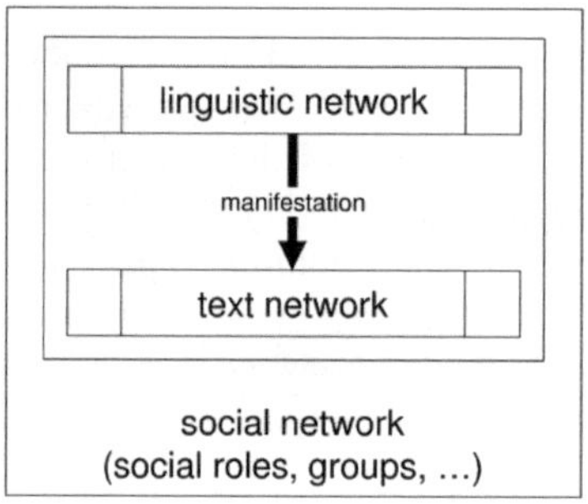

Fig. 19.1: A three-level model of networking

A note on terminology: The terms *node* and *link* will be used when speaking about networks, while *vertex* and *edge* are used when speaking about graphs as formal models thereof. Further, as the apparatus of complex network analysis has predominantly been developed by example of social networks, we will use the term *social-semiotic* network in order to stress the encompassing field of linguistic, text and social networks as interrelated in Figure 19.1.

This article deals with complex networks of textual units. Such networks do not only form a special kind of complex networks but also large corpora. In other words, networks of textual units are a sort of *large linguistic corpora* whose specificity is due to their structuring based on the network inducing intertextual relations of their constitutive units. For the annotation and representation of large linguistic corpora in general, see article 35 in this volume. A more specialised case of a complex network of textual units is given by networks whose nodes denote *web* documents. Analogously, we have a special kind of *web corpus* structured by the hyperlinks of its constitutive elements when dealing with complex networks of web documents. For web corpora as an object of corpus linguistics in general, see article 18 in this volume; see also article 17 on various corpora of computer-mediated communication including web corpora. This article deals more specifically with aspects of networking in corpora of textual units, its graph-theoretical representation and quantitative modelling in various areas of text and document networks.

The article is organised as follows: section 2 introduces graph theoretical notions and outlines some results of the theory of complex networks as needed subsequently. This relates especially to the so-called small-world property which allows to separate the area of random and social-semiotic networks. Section 3 surveys network-oriented studies in corpus, computational and cognitive linguistics as well as in computer science. This includes but is not limited to lexical, sentence and WWW-based networks. Finally, section 4 gives a conclusion and prospects future directions within the present field of research.

2. Structure formation in large networks

The concept of a social-semiotic network in general and that of a small world in particular is formally narrowed down in terms of graph theory. That is, networks to be analysed as candidates of small worlds are, first of all, modelled as *graphs*. The following sections survey this kind of modelling: section 2.1 starts with an overview of some notions of graph theory as used subsequently. The classical model of small worlds as introduced by Watts/Strogatz (1998) which, since then, has been applied in various areas of network formation is described in section 2.2. Section 2.3 overviews the alternative model of Barabási/Albert (1999), who – unlike Watts/Strogatz – take the temporal aspect of network growth into account. In the meantime, several more indices have been introduced in order to quantitatively classify networks. This relates especially to what is called assortative mixing as a characteristic of social instead of technical networks. Section 2.4 gives a short summary of it. Next, section 2.5 describes concepts of structure formation within complex networks above the level of local clusters as considered in the model of Watts/Strogatz. Finally, section 2.6. reconsiders time-dependent constraints of network formation.

2.1. Graph theoretical preliminaries

This subsection briefly surveys fundamental notions of graph theory as they are needed for complex network analysis. Table 19.2 summarises these and other definitions introduced subsequently. For a more thorough introduction to graph theory, cf. Diestel (2005), Melnikov et al. (1998) and Bronstein et al. (1999).

Tab. 19.2: Basic graph theoretical notions used throughout the article

Notation	Description
$C_{WS}(G)$	The cluster value of graph G according to Watts/Strogatz (1998).
$C_{BR}(G)$	The cluster value of graph G according to Bollobás/Riordan (2003).
$d(G)$	The average degree of vertices of graph G.
$d_G(v)$	The degree of vertex v_i of graph G.
$\Delta(G)$	The diameter of graph G.
$E(G)$	The set of edges of graph G.
$\varepsilon(G)$	An alternative coefficient of the average degree of vertices of graph G.
γ	The exponent of a power law fitted to the degree distributions of a given graph.
γ_{in}	The exponent of a power law fitted to the in-degree distributions of a given graph.
γ_{out}	The exponent of a power law fitted to the out-degree distributions of a given graph.
$L(G)$	The average geodesic distance of vertices of graph G.
$r(G)$	The correlation coefficient of the degrees of interlinked vertices of G.
θ	The exponent of a power law fitted to the cluster coefficient $C(k)$ as a function of degree k.
$V(G)$	The set of vertices of graph G.

Let $[X]^k$ be the set of all subsets of k elements of X. A simple undirected graph G is a pair $G = (V, E)$ where V is the set of *vertices* and E the set of *edges* such that $E \subseteq [V]^2$. If $G = (X, Y)$ is a graph, then $V(G) = X$ denotes its *vertex set* and $E(G) = Y$ its *edge set*. The *order* $|G|$ of a graph G is the number of its vertices. An edge $e = \{v, w\} \in E$ is *ending at* v and w which are both *incident* with e and thus *adjacent* or *neighbors*. We also say that two edges are adjacent if they end at least at one common vertex. E (v) is the set of all edges to which v is incident. G is *complete* if all its vertices are pairwise adjacent. A complete graph of order n is denoted by K_n. A *triangle* is a complete graph K_3 of order 3. $N_G(v)$ is the *set of neighbors* of $v \in V(G)$. Usually, the subscript is omitted if the graph referred to is evident. The *degree* $d_G(v_i) = k$ of a vertex v_i is the number $|E(v)|$ of edges ending at v. Evidently, $|E(v)| = |N(v)|$ (note that E is a set and therefore does not contain multiple edges which are introduced in Figure 19.2).

A graph is called *regular* (or *k-regular*) if all its vertices have the same degree (k). The *average degree* of a graph G is $d(G) = \frac{1}{|V|} \sum_{v_i \in V} d_G(v_i)$. In the following sections, we will alternatively refer to the ratio

$$\varepsilon(G) = |E(G)|/|V(G) = \frac{1}{2}\, d(G). \tag{1}$$

A sequence $P = (v_{i_0}, e_{j_1}, v_{i_1}, e_{j_2}, ..., v_{i_{n-1}}, e_{j_n}, v_{i_n})$, $n > 0$, is called a *walk* of *length n* between v_{i_0} and v_{i_n} in G, if for $k = 1, ..., n : e_{j_k} = \{v_{i_{k-1}}, v_{i_k}\} \in E(G)$. v_{i_0} and v_{i_n} are called *end vertices* of P. All other vertices are called *inner* with respect to P. A walk is called a *path* if all its

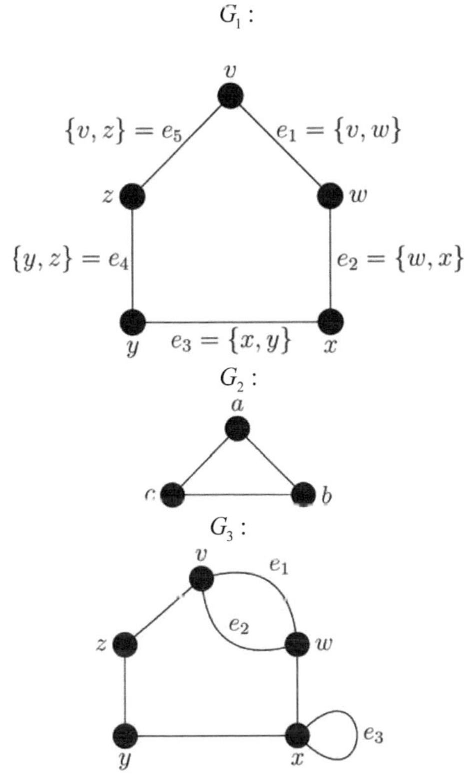

Fig. 19.2: A graphical representation of an undirected graph $G_1 = (V, E)$ with $V = \{v, w, x, y, z\}$ and $E = \{e_1, ..., e_5\}$ G_1 is of order $|G_1| = 5$. Edge $e_3 = \{x, y\}$ is ending at vertex x and y. e_3 is adjacent with e_2 and e_4. Vertex x is adjacent to two edges, that is, $E(x) = \{e_2, e_3\}$. Further, $N_{G_1}(x) = \{w, y\}$ is the set of neighbors of x. The degree of x is $d_{G_1}(x) = |E(x)| = |N_{G_1}(x)| = 2$. G_1 is *not* complete. A triangle, that is, a complete graph of order 3, is exemplified by G_2. Note that G_1 and G_2 are both 2-regular graphs. Thus, $d(G_1) = d(G_2) = 2$ and $\varepsilon(G_1) = \varepsilon(G_2) = 1$. $(v, e_1, w, e_2, x, e_3, y)$ is a simple path with end vertices v and y. The distance $\delta(v, y)$ is 2 since (v, e_5, z, e_4, y) is the shortest path between v, y in G_1. The diameter $\Delta(G)$ of G is 2. Obviously, G_1 and G_2 are connected. G_3 demonstrates a multi- and pseudograph, respectively, with multiple edges e_1 and e_2 as well as a loop e_3

edges are distinct. A path is called *simple* if all its inner vertices are distinct. A path is called *cyclic* if its end vertices are equal. The *distance* $\delta(v, w)$ of two vertices v, w, $v \neq w$, is the length of the shortest path ending at v and w. The *diameter* $\Delta(G) = \max_{v, w \in V(G), v \neq w} \delta(v, w)$ of a graph G is the maximal distance between any pair of vertices in $V(G)$. A non-empty graph G is *connected* if for any pair of vertices $v, w \in V(G)$ there exists a path ending at v and w. A maximal connected subgraph of G is called a *component* of G. A graph G is called *bipartite* if its vertex set $V(G)$ is partitioned into non-empty disjunct subsets A, B such that every edge $\{v, w\} \in E(G)$ is ending at vertices $v \in A$ and $w \in B$. For reasons of clarity, we will call A and B the modes of the bipartite graph G and speak, more specifically, of the *bottom mode* and the *top mode* where the latter is seen to be placed "over" the former (see Figure 19.3).

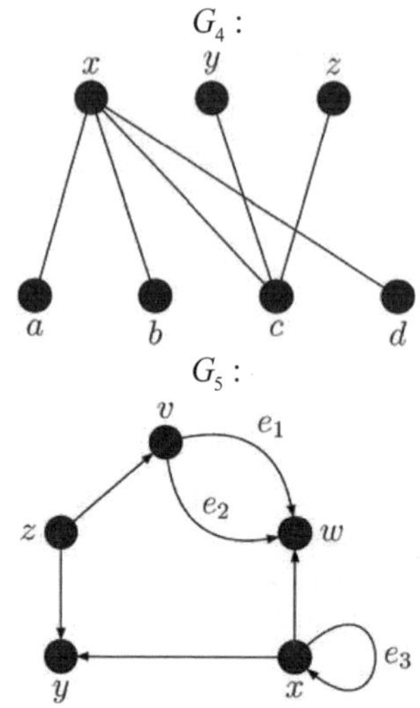

Fig. 19.3: A bipartite graph G_4 whose vertex set $V(G_4)$ is separated by its edge set into the subsets $A = \{a, b, c, d\}$ and $B = \{x, y, z\}$. As a matter of convention we call A the top mode and B the bottom mode of G_4. G_5 exemplifies a directed graph where $\text{in}(e_1) = \text{in}(e_2) = v$ and $\text{out}(e_1) = \text{out}(e_2) = w$. Thus, e_1 and e_2 are not only multiple, but also parallel in G_5. G_5 is an orientation of G_3

So far we neither considered loops, nor multiple, parallel or directed edges which are grasped by the following definitions. These additional definitions are needed in order to map, for example, reflexive links from a web page to itself (i. e. loops) or different links between the same Wikipedia articles (i. e. parallel edges):

1. A *multigraph* is a pair (V, E) whose edge set E is defined as a *collection* of subsets of $[V]^2$ and, thus, may – in contrast to simple graphs – contain several copies of the same elements of $[V]^2$ where equal elements of E are called *multiple edges*.
2. A *pseudograph* is a pair (V, E) where E is defined as a collection of unordered pairs of not necessarily different vertices of V. Thus, pseudographs may – in contrast to multigraphs – also contain loops.
3. A *directed graph* (or digraph) is a pair (V, E) of a vertex set V and an edge set E together with two functions in: $E \rightarrow V$ and out: $E \rightarrow V$ such that for every edge $e \in E$, $\text{in}(e)$ is the *initial vertex* and $\text{out}(e)$ the *end vertex* of e. Edges e_i, e_j, for which $\{\text{in}(e_i), \text{out}(e_i)\} = \{\text{in}(e_j), \text{out}(e_j)\}$, are called *multiple*. Edges e_i, e_j, for which $\text{in}(e_i) = \text{in}(e_j)$ and $\text{out}(e_i = \text{out}(e_j))$, are called *parallel*. Finally, an *orientation* $D = (V, X)$ of an undirected graph $G = (V, E)$ is a directed graph such that for every edge $e \in X$: $\{\text{in}(e), \text{out}(e)\} \in E$. A graph is called *mixed* if it contains two sets E_1, E_2 of undirected and directed edges, respectively.
4. A graph is called *uniquely labelled* if its vertices have pairwise different labels. In order to simplify notation, we assume that indexed vertices $v_i, v_j \in V(G)$, $i, j \in N$, are labelled by their indices. Thus, we sometimes will abbreviate v_i by i.

For additional notions of social network analysis which are used in order to characterise graphs in quantitative terms, cf Otte/Rousseau (2002). This relates, amongst others, to the notion of *components* and *cliques* on the one hand and of *density*, *centrality*, and *cohesion* (Egghe/Rousseau 2003) on the other hand. See also Wasserman/Faust (1999) for a comprehensive overview on graph theoretical concepts in network analysis. For a survey of complex network analysis and its various fields of application see Newman (2000, 2003b). See also Watts (1999, 2003) and Strogatz (2001) for thorough introductions to this field. Further, see Thelwall/Vaughan/Björneborn (2006) for a comprehensive overview of network analysis by example of the WWW. Finally, www.cs.cornell.edu/courses/cs685/2002fa is an excellent collection of links on complex network analysis.

The subsequent sections survey indicators of small world formation in complex networks as they have been introduced in the literature. By default, these indicators are introduced for *simple undirected graphs* – in some cases, their derivation for directed and multi-graphs will be described.

2.2. Short cuts and clusters

As regards the overall structure of complex networks, these and related questions are, for the time being, investigated in terms of so-called *Small Worlds* (SW) (Newman 2003b). Since its invention by Milgram (1967), this notion had awaited formalisation as a measurable property of large, complex networks which allows to distinguish them from random graphs. Milgram started from a social network of persons and their acquaintance (or friendship) links. He asked, so to speak, about the expected value of the shortest chain of such links which connect agents of a starting population from well specified target persons in a given population. More specifically, an agent of the starting population is presented with a description of a target person and asked to advance a letter to him or her by sending it to an acquaintance whom he or she considers more likely than him or herself to know the target. Each of these persons in turn advances the letter by the same procedure until the target person is reached. In social network analysis (Wasserman/Faust 1999) this is a classical question about the cohesion of a network which affects the network's efficiency and vulnerability of information flow. In Milgram's model, the *short-cut* property, that is, the characteristic short average distance between any randomly chosen pair of nodes of a network, is seen as the central small world indicator. But this property alone does not delineate small worlds from random networks which also have the short-cut property, but obviously miss the kind of structure formation known from social networks. A first formalisation of small worlds was introduced by Watts/Strogatz (1998), who characterise them by *two* properties:

- Compared to *random graphs*, small worlds show a considerably higher level of *cluster formation*.
- Compared to *regular graphs*, any randomly chosen pair of vertices in a small world has, on average, a considerably shorter *distance*.

In order to operationalise these statements, Watts/Strogatz introduce two indicators of clustering and density, respectively. First, *clustering* in a simple undirected graph G is measured by the mean of the *cluster value* $C_{v_i}(G)$ of its vertices $v_i \in V(G)$. More precisely, clustering is measured as the mean of the ratio of the number $\mathrm{adj}(v_i)$ of edges ending only at neighbors of v_i to the number of edges in a corresponding complete graph of order $|N_G(v_i)|$ (i.e. a graph in which all neighbors of v_i are adjacent) (note that in a simple undirected graph $adj(v)$ equals the number of triangles incident with v):

$$C_{vi}(G) = \frac{adj(v_i)}{\binom{d_G(v)}{2}} = \frac{adj(v_i)}{d(v_i)\,d(v_i) - 1)/2} \in [0, 1] \tag{2}$$

This allows to define the cluster value $C_{WS}(G)$ of G as (note that $n = |V(G)|$)

$$C_{WS}(G) = \frac{1}{n} \sum_{i=1}^{n} C_{v_i}(G) \in [0, 1] \tag{3}$$

C_{WS} measures the average proportion of the neighbors of vertices that are themselves neighbors. It estimates the probability that two vertices *v*, *w* are themselves adjacent when commonly linked with the same vertex *u*. In terms of friendship networks, for example, in which vertices denote individuals, a high cluster value C_{WS} means that the friend of a friend of a person is probably also a friend of that person.

The notion of clustering relates to the notion of *transitivity* in social networks: a triad of agents *a*, *b*, *c* is said to be transitive if whenever *a* links to *b* (i. e. $a \rightarrow b$) and $b \rightarrow c$, then $a \rightarrow c$ (Wasserman/Faust 1999, 243). See Rapoport (1953) for an early study of transitivity patterns in social networks. As the term *clustering* has a completely different meaning, e. g., in explorative data analysis (Bock 1994), the term *transitivity* is preferred in the network literature (Newman 2003b). Following this manner of speaking, a *network* is said to be *transitive* to the amount of the probability that if any of its vertices *a, b* and *b, c* are linked, then *a* and *c* are linked, too. In this sense, C_{WS} is a candidate measure to estimate this probability.

Of course, the reasoning behind edge formation varies with the network being modelled. In the area of social-semiotic networks, vertices may represent, for example, interlocutors which are seen to be linked whenever they communicate. Alternatively, vertices may represent the linguistic manifestations of this communication in the form of discourse units which are seen to be linked whenever they are related by one or more *intertextual* coherence relations. In this case, a high C_{WS} value means that if a focal discourse unit *a* is simultaneously related to some units *b* and *c*, then there is a high probability that there is an intertextual relation linking *b* and *c*, too.

A drawback of the definition of C_{WS} is that it does not appropriately operate on multigraphs. The reason is that it counts a triple only once even if spanned by multiple edges between the same vertices. Therefore, Bollobás/Riordan (2003) alternatively propose the cluster coefficient $C_{BR}(G)$ as the fraction of the number of triangles within G and the number of pairs of adjacent edges:

$$C_{BR}(G) = \frac{3 \times \text{number of triangles of } G}{\text{number of pairs of adjacent edges of } G} \in [0, 1] \tag{4}$$

High values of $C_{BR}(G)$ and $C_{WS}(G)$ indicate that linkage in G tends to be *transitive* in the sense that if any vertex $u \in V(G)$ is linked with vertices v, $w \in V(G)$, then v and w are probably linked, too. Once more, this notion of clustering is not to be confused with cluster analysis in which clusters of any size are computed which optimise the proportion of cluster internal homogeneity and cluster external heterogeneity in the sense of the underlying similarity measure (Bock 1994). In contrast to this, the reference point of clustering according to CBR and C_{WS} is the local notion of a *triangle* based on *three* vertices. This "restriction" has been the starting point of developing more elaborate models of local structure formation; see, e. g., Milo et al. (2002) and section 2.5.

A central observation of Watts/Strogatz (1998) is that in regular graphs of the sort they examined, clustering is high, whereas in random graphs it is low. This value distribution is reversed by the average distances within regular and random graphs measured as follows:

$$L(G) = \frac{1}{\binom{|V(G)|}{2}} \sum_{\{v,w\} \in [V]^2} \delta(v,w) \tag{5}$$

Note that in the case of large networks (of hundreds and thousands of nodes), $L(G)$ is estimated by means of random samples of up to some thousand vertices of G and their geodesic distances.

Bollobás/Riordan (2003) point out that although by definition $L(G) \leq \Delta(G)$, $L(G)$ is mostly *not much smaller* than $\Delta(G)$. Therefore, $\Delta(G)$ is referred to as an alternative indicator of distance formation in small worlds (Albert/Jeong/Barabási 1999).

In the case of hypertext networks, for example, small values of $L(G)$ indicate that the topic of pages changes fast, i. e., already after a couple of clicks when following the hyperlinks between their modules, supposing that the basic population is thematically diversified as, for example, in the case of Wikipedia. Generally speaking, small average geodesic distances indicate rapid changes of a given variable V (e. g. topic, genre, register etc.) when following links between nodes of a network suggesting that the values of V are diversified within this network.

Starting from $L(G)$ and $C_{WS}(G)$, Watts/Strogatz (1998) narrow down their notion of a small world, henceforth called *WS model* (note that WS abbreviates the initials of the authors of this model). Their basic idea is to start with a regular graph whose edges are stepwise rewired with probability p such that for certain values of p small worlds emerge which simultaneously have high cluster values and short average distances. More specifically, they start from a $2r$-regular graph C_n^r, i. e. the rth power of an n-cycle, of fixed order $n > 2r$ in which vertices are adjacent whose distance within the n-cycle C_n is at most r (Bollobás/Riordan 2003). Next, they derive a random graph $G(p)$ from C_n^r by rewiring a proportion $p \in (0, 1]$ of its edges. The "'surprising' phenomenon" (Bollobás/Riordan 2003, 6) is that even for small values of p, that is, for the introduction of a small amount of randomness, small worlds emerge which share high cluster values with regular graphs and short distances with random graphs, that is:

$$C_X(G_{regular}) \sim C_X(G_{sw}) \gg C_X(G_{random})$$

and

$$L(G_{regular}) \gg L(G_{sw}) \sim L(G_{random})$$

for $X \in \{WS, BR\}$. This is summarised in Table 19.3 in which estimators of L and C_{WS} are given for the corresponding regular and random graphs of equal order (i. e. size) C_{WS} and average degree $d(G)$ (as an index of sparsity or density) (cf Bollobás/Riordan 2003).

Tab. 19.3: Cluster values and average distances in small worlds compared to regular graphs and random graphs. Estimators are given for corresponding random and regular graphs subject to the condition that $n \gg k \gg \log n \gg 1$ (Watts/Strogatz 1998) where $n = V$ and $k = d(G)$. $k \gg \log n$ ensures that the corresponding random graph is connected (Baldi/Frasconi/Smyth 2003)

Graph	Clustering	$C_{WS}(G)$	$C_{BR}(G)$	Distance	$L(G)$
regular	high	$k < \frac{2}{3}n \Rightarrow C = \frac{3(k-2)}{4(k-1)}$	cf. Bollobás/ Riordan (2003)	long	$L = \frac{n}{2k} \gg 1$
SW	high	see Formula 3	see Formula 4	short	see Formula 5
random	low	$C = k/n$	cf. Bollobás/ Riordan (2003)	short	$L \sim \frac{\ln(n)}{\ln(k)}$

In summary, the WS model combines cluster formation with the formation of short distances by means of some short-cuts which provide efficient information flow within the network. In the area of social-semiotic networks, this property has been demonstrated by example of the WWW, collocation networks and thesauri. This is described in detail in section 3.

The notion of a small world as emerging from introducing a small amount of randomness which generates short-cuts within initially regular graphs has been the starting point of a critical review of the WS model (Newman 2000). One reason is that social networks are expected to be structured *far away from* the topology of regular graphs. Another reference point is the focus of the WS model on cluster and distance values and, thus, on node indices. $L(G)$ indicates a *global* network property in the sense that it aggregates values which interrelate all pairs of nodes of a network. In contrast to this, $C_{WS}(G)$ indicates a *local* network property. The reason is that although cluster values are aggregated for the whole network, their reference points are triangles and connected triples of vertices. Thus, both indices, $L(G)$ and $C_{WS}(G)$, focus on single moments of the distributions of the corresponding input values and thus fail to describe these distributions in more detail. The following section describes a model which tackles this shortcoming.

2.3. Scale-free networks

Whereas the WS model describes small worlds from a static perspective, it is the dynamic perspective of network growth from which small worlds are described in the *preferential attachment model* of Barabási/Albert (1999), henceforth called *BA model*. It starts from the observation that the vertex connectivities of some complex networks are distributed according to a scale-free power law *in addition to their common property of short-cuts and local clustering*. More precisely, Barabási/Albert return to the observation – confirmed by many social-semiotic networks, but not, for example, by instances of the random graph model of Erdős/Rényi (cf. Bollobás 1985) – that the number of links per vertex can be reliably predicted by means of a power law. In other words: the probability $P(k)$ that a randomly chosen vertex interacts with k other vertices of the same graph representing a network is approximately:

$$P(k) \sim k^{-\gamma} \tag{6}$$

where γ is often between [1.5,3.5] (Newman 2003b; Milo et al. 2002).

In the present case, in which power laws are fitted to the degree distributions of vertices of an undirected graph, this indicates that connectivity is scale-free and thus relates to the Zipfian nature of many social-semiotic phenomena (Rapoport 1982) as, for example, in the case of the rank-frequency distribution of lexical units. Thus, networks with a power law-like degree distribution are called *scale-free networks* (Barabási/Albert 1999). The exponent of the power law fitted to the degree distribution of a network is an indicator of the kind of its structuring, which, in turn, is related to its *procedural* characteristics: scale-free networks are known for their low vulnerability and fault tolerance (Albert/Jeong/Barabási 1999). Generally speaking, a function $f(x)$ is called scale-free if it remains unchanged under rescaling of the variable x in the sense that $f(ax) = bf(x)$, $a, b \in R$. Solutions to this equation have a power law form (Newman 2005; van Raan 2005). In the case of degree distributions, scale-freeness means that there are no typical nodes which represent all others because of their typical behavior (Barabási/Oltvai 2004; Newman 2005).

Power law-like degree distributions are contrasted by the Poisson distribution of node connectivity in random graphs (Bollobás 1985). The Poisson distribution models the effect that the probability to find highly connected nodes decreases exponentially with k. This property also holds for the WS model, *contrary to empirical observations* which are better fitted by scale-free power laws (Barabási/Albert 1999).

A power law can be fitted to the *rank-degree* distribution (where rank is determined by the decreasing order of node connectivity) or to the *size-degree* distribution (based on the number of vertices of degree one up to the number of vertices of highest degree). Fitting can be restricted to the distribution of vertex *in* or *out* degrees within directed graphs. Note that simple graphs do not distinguish multiple edges and may, therefore, displace the observed distribution. In the present context, successfully fitting a power law indicates that the majority of nodes is poorly connected, while a selected minority of *hubs* is very highly connected (Watts 2003). These hubs are mainly responsible for providing cohesion as they integrate the majority of nodes into the network (Ravasz et al. 2002). Thus, for a fixed number of links, the smaller the value of γ, the shallower the slope of the curve in a log-log plot, the higher the probability of higher connected hubs. In contrast to this, if the number of vertices of a certain degree decays exponentially with increasing degree, highly connected vertices (i. e. hubs) are very unlikely or do not exist. Three general remarks on power law-fittings:

- Firstly, although there is a definite relationship of rank (degree) distributions on the one hand and their cumulative correspondents or size-degree distributions on the other hand, the values of the exponents of power laws fitted separately to these distributions systematically depart from each other. This is explained in detail by Adamic (2000) and Newman (2005).
- Secondly, not only does the algebraic sign of a power law's exponent matter, but also its absolute value as it determines the existence and range of the expected value and variance of the corresponding theoretical distributions under the assumption of additivity; see Newman (2005) for these details. Thus, when comparing two studies we do not only need to know which empirical distribution (rank-degree or size-degree) was fitted, but also by means of which exponent.

- Thirdly, power laws are candidate distributions to be fitted to empirical distributions of, e. g., vertex degrees. Because of theoretical considerations as well as empirical observations or other restrictions, alternative distributions can be checked for their fitting as well; cf. Wimmer/Altmann (1999b) for the whole range of discrete probability distributions, many of which have become relevant in quantitative linguistics.

In order to derive a model which explains the *emergence* of power law-like node connectivities in networks *subject to their growth*, Barabási/Albert (1999) no longer view the number of vertices to be fixed and being rewired with a uniform probability as assumed by the WS model. Instead, they account for the dynamics of networks whose vertex set is continually growing by preferably linking new vertices with already highly connected ones. This preferential attachment produces a so-called *Matthew effect* (Simon 1955) as it predicts that older nodes get rich in links at the expense of younger ones (Watts 2003). In the case of text networks, the BA model says that newly added nodes tend to be added with texts providing a high amount of network coherence. As an example think of a citation network in which new documents tend to cite already frequently cited ones or of Wikipedia in which new articles are predicted to preferably refer to already much discussed ones.

The basic idea of Barabási/Albert (1999) is that scale-invariant degree distributions result from the growth of networks subject to preferential attachment. More specifically, they assume that the probability $P(k_v)$ that a new vertex will be connected to vertex v is a function of the connectivity k_v of v (w runs over all vertices already inserted into the graph):

$$P(k_v) = \frac{k_v}{\sum_w k_w} \tag{7}$$

In several experiments, Barabási/Albert (1999) show that networks which grow according to this model evolve into 'a scale-invariant state' in which node connectivity is distributed according to a power law with an exponent $\gamma = 2.9 \pm 0.1$. It is worth noting that the BA model does not produce networks which obey the WS model; such a combined model was proposed by Steyvers/Tenenbaum (2005) (see section 3).

Although this model overcomes a central aspect of the invariability of the WS model, it is open to many objections as it disregards other aspects of network dynamics. Amongst others, this relates to the fact that networks grow by the number of vertices *and* edges which may also decrease or stagnate if their birth and death rates accord. Another reference point for revising the BA model is its assumption that the choice of nodes to be linked with newly added ones solely depends on the connectivity patterns of the former. Actually, it is unrealistic to assume that a new vertex is linked with an old one simply because of the connectivity rate of the latter. Rather, linkage depends on the opportunities of old and new nodes to get in contact at all which, in turn, depends on the contexts in which members of the network can "meet" each other (Watts 2003). In other words, high connectivity does not automatically mean being met by newly added members of a network. Moreover, Sigman/Cecchi (2002) have exemplified topologically quite different graphs which, nevertheless, share the same degree distribution. In this sense, the BA model is not selective enough. For a comprehensive mathematical review of the BA model and several alternatives to it, see Bollobás/Riordan (2003).

These and related objections have led to a stepwise search for further network characteristics which separate them more precisely from purely random graphs. This includes what is called *assortative mixing* and *community structure*.

2.4. Assortative mixing

Newman (2002, 2003a) proposes a model in which the probability of a link between two nodes depends on the connectivity of both. This model serves to account for social networks in which vertices tend to be linked when they share certain properties, a tendency which is called *assortative mixing*. It reflects what is circumscribed by the expression *birds of a feather flock together*. According to Newman/Park (2003), this principle distinguishes social networks from non-social (e. g. artificial or biological) ones, even if both are uniformly attributed as small worlds according to the WS model. Newman (2002) exemplifies this by assortative mixing of vertex degrees. He confirms that the degrees of interlinked nodes are highly positively correlated in the case of social, while being negatively correlated in the case of technical networks (e. g. the Internet) which show *disassortative mixing*. Newman derives a correlation coefficient $r(G)$ in order to measure mixing in undirected graphs G (for $r(G)$ of *directed* graphs G see Newman 2002, footnote 35):

$$r(G) = \frac{\frac{1}{m}\sum_i j_i k_i - \left[\frac{1}{m}\sum_i \frac{1}{2}(j_i + k_i)\right]^2}{\frac{1}{m}\sum_i \frac{1}{2}(j_i^2 + k_i^2) - \left[\frac{1}{m}\sum_i \frac{1}{2}(j_i + k_i)\right]^2} \in [-1, 1] \tag{8}$$

where i denotes the edge ending at vertices j and k of degree j_i and k_i, respectively, and $m = E$, $G = (V, E)$. Assortative mixing occurs if $r(G) \gg 0$, otherwise, if $r(G) \ll 0$, disassortative is diagnosed.

Although $r(G)$ separates social from other types of networks, it does not explain the emergence of mixing. Like all other coefficients presented so far, it stays on the level of graph indices and, thus, disregards higher order structure formation within complex networks. The starting-point of such an extended view is, as Newman/Park (2003) argue, *community structure*.

2.5. Community building

The probability of the members of a social network interacting depends on the social groups (e. g. family, association etc.) and contexts (e. g. attending the same concert, waiting for the same metro etc.) in which they commonly participate (Watts 2003). Sharing group or context membership raises the probability of interaction. Thus, agents entering a network do not necessarily have a uniform chance of interacting with any of its highly connected members, *in contrast to what is assumed by the BA model*. Analogously, textual manifestations of social interaction are recursively clustered according to the various genres and registers (Martin 1992) they instantiate. Thus, the probability of an intertextual relation between two texts analogously rises with their common membership in the same or related genres or registers. The models presented so far do not account for such constraints on linkage within a network.

Newman/Watts/Strogatz (2002) take this as a starting point for studying *affiliation networks* in order to overcome this deficit. Affiliation networks are exemplified by networks of collaborating scientists where membership in the same group or context is defined by co-authorship. Affiliation networks are modelled as *bipartite graphs* of group and actor vertices where every actor is linked to the group to which he belongs. This bipartite model is transformed into a unipartite graph in which nodes denote agents who are linked if they commonly belong to at least one group. Finally, the unipartite graph is input into a calculation of cluster values and average distances as before. A central conclusion of Newman/Watts/Strogatz is that compared to random graphs (according to the model of Erdős/Rényi), clustering is always higher in such affiliation networks. The reason is that the higher the number of groups and their extent, the more actor triangles exist within the network. This accords with the expectation, that groups raise the probability of transitive closures, that is, an interaction of vertices v, w which are commonly adjacent to a vertex u of the same group. Another implication is that assortative mixing naturally emerges in networks with community structure although it may also be present in networks without it (Newman 2003b). This further implies that networks with community structure supersede measuring assortative mixing.

The affiliation model leads back to a network model to which all standard indicators of small worlds are applied. Thus, it does not go far beyond the insights already inherent to the WS model. A more thorough approach to the formation of significantly *recurrent sub-networks* – which may represent, for example, structures of thematically or functionally homogeneous units – is presented by Milo et al. (2002) and Itzkovitz et al. (2003). They explore subgraphs G' of a graph G representing a network which occur more often in G than expected by chance, that is, than in collections of corresponding random graphs of equal order and the same number of edges (Bollobás 1985) where degree is Poisson distributed and the vertices have the same single-vertex characteristics as in the input graph. A class of such subgraphs is called a *motif*. That is, a motif represents a class of sub-networks whose number is significantly higher within the input network than in its randomised counterpart. One of the observations of Milo et al. (2002) and Itzkovitz et al. (2003) is that exploring the motifs of different networks allows distinguishing biological, technical and informational networks well, as they show different patterns of subgraphs recurrent within them, despite being uniformly attributed as small worlds.

The motif model looks for recurrent network patterns. It is a local model of networking, as motifs represent rather small subgraphs. Further, the motif model does not look for the recursive organisation of such motifs into highly connected modules organised into larger, less cohesive units up to the network as a whole. Such a model has been introduced by Ravasz et al. (2002) and Ravasz/Barabási (2003). They start from the dilemma that while scale-free networks miss any modularity, as their hubs provide the predominant part of network cohesion, modular networks fail to have a scale-free degree distribution, as they consist of inherently highly connected modules interlinked only by a couple of links, so that vertices tend to have a uniform degree. Ravasz et al. present a graph model which has both a modular structure as well as a scale-free degree distribution. This graph model has an inherent hierarchical structure in the sense that it recursively builds around a kernel of a couple of highly clustered vertices more and more peripheral zones which are decreasingly clustered. A central observation of Ravasz et al. (2002) is that such *hierarchical networks* can be distinguished from non-hierarchical, though scale-free networks by the function $C(k)$ of the cluster coefficient C as a function of the degree k. Ravasz et al. (2002) observe that in hierarchical networks $C(k)$ decays – unlike in purely scale-free and simply modular networks – as a power law with the degree k, that is,

$$C(k) \sim k^{-\theta} \tag{9}$$

Thus, this model reduces the measurement of structure formation within complex networks to a node-related coefficient. Such a hierarchical, modular network is exemplified by a text network in which modularity is defined by thematic criteria where the central module represents a general topic and where peripheral modules denote topics derived from the topic of their immediate neighbor, more central modules.

As an indicator of structure formation within linguistic networks, θ has been first computed by Ferrer i Cancho/Solé/Köhler (2004). These and related applications of models of complex networks to linguistic networks are reviewed within the subsequent sections.

2.6. Networks evolving in time

Apart from the BA model, all network characteristics considered so far focus on static graphs as snapshots of complex networks at certain points in time. In contrast to this, the BA model and its derivations (Bollobás/Riordan 2003) start from a given set of vertices to which in every subsequent point in time a fixed number of nodes with a fixed number of links is added. Although the underlying model of preferential attachment already allows deriving degree distributions in correspondence to existing networks, this model nevertheless departs from empirical findings in support of what Leskovec/Kleinberg/Faloutsos (2005) call the *densification* and *shrinking* of evolving networks:

- Firstly, Leskovec/Kleinberg/Faloutsos (2005) observe that complex networks such as, e.g., (scientific or patent) citation networks (cf section 3.4.) tend to become more and more dense over time. This means that the average degree of their vertices is increasing with the aging network. Interestingly, Leskovec/Kleinberg/Faloutsos (2005) successfully adapt a power law to this growth process with a positive exponent $1 < \alpha < 2$

  $$e(t) \sim n(t)^{\alpha} \tag{10}$$

  where $e(t)$ is the number of edges at time t while $n(t)$ denotes the number of vertices at that point in time. Leskovec/Kleinberg/Faloutsos (2005) speak of a *densification* or *growth power law*.

- Secondly, they find that what they call the *effective diameter* decreases over time. The effective diameter of a network is defined by means of the cumulative distribution of distances between connected nodes of a network: if $(d, \#(d))$ is the ordered pair of the number $\#(d)$ of vertices in the graph induced by the focal network which are at most d edges separated from each other, the effective diameter of this network is the number d_{eff} of vertices for which $d_{\mathrm{eff}}/n = 0.9$ (i. e. 90% of the vertices in the graph – $n = |V|$).

As it is possible to generate networks which only have one of these two characteristics, it is worth considering them separately in empirical studies. Moreover, insofar as these characteristics depart from assumptions underlying traditional small world models, they give reason to reconsider and further develop the apparatus of complex network analysis in terms of time-dependent models; cf. Leskovec/Kleinberg/Faloutsos (2005) for two models of such processes. With the accessibility of document networks such as, for example, wiki-based systems (cf. section 3.6.), which make any change of their textual nodes and links transparent, this diachronic turn becomes a realistic endeavor of corpus linguistic analyses of complex document networks.

2.7. Summary

The progression of the models discussed in the last four sections mirrors a gradual revision of assumptions about constraints on vertex connectivity and structure formation in networks. Starting from the WS model which does not reflect constraints on degree distributions, extensions regarding aspects of network growth and community structure were discussed. For the time being, small-world formation is indicated by "sparsity, a single connected component containing the vast majority of nodes, very short average distances among nodes, high local clustering, and a power law degree distribution [...]." (Steyvers/Tenenbaum 2005, 54). For alternative models of structure formation in large networks, see Newman (2003b) and Bornholdt/Schuster (2003). These models were initially developed in order to analyse social, biological and technological networks, but also to analyse linguistic networks. The question is whether there exist principles of linguistic networks which can be explored by complex network analysis, by analogy to the Zipfian nature of many frequency distributions of linguistic units explored in quantitative linguistics. The following section reviews studies which deal, directly or indirectly, with this question.

3. Models of networking of linguistic units

In this section, small-world models are reviewed which focus on linguistic networks, that is, on graphs whose vertices represent, for example, words, sentences or texts. Table 19.4 summarises these approaches with respect to the criteria of networking they apply and the network characteristics they compute. The majority of these approaches analyses WWW-based graphs whose vertices represent *web pages* and whose edges stand for hyperlinks. The remaining set of approaches concentrates on networks spanned by lexical or sentential units and their lexical or syntactical relations. Generally speaking, all these approaches should (but often fail to) answer the following questions:

Tab. 19.4: Studies of complex networks of linguistic units

Graph	Source Network	Vertex	Edge	Orient.	$\|V(G)\|$	$\varepsilon(G)$	$L(G)$	$C_{BR}(G)$	$C_{WS}(G)$	γ	$r(G)$	Reference
association graph	free-association data	word	association	undir.	5,018	22.0	3.04	n.s.	0.186	3.01	n.s.	Steyvers/Tenenbaum (2005)
association graph	free-association data	word	association	dir.	5,018	12.7	4.27	n.s.	0.186	1.79	n.s.	Steyvers/Tenenbaum (2005)
citation graph	ISI citation network	bibliographic record	citation (citing)	dir./bipar.	1,099,017	4.437	n.s	n.s.	n.s.	$\gamma_{out} \approx 3.5$	n.s.	van Raan (2005)
citation graph	ISI citation network	reference	citation (cited)	dir./bipar.	4,876,752	3.14	n.s.	n.s.	n.s.	$\gamma_{in} \approx 3.1$	n.s.	van Raan (2005)
collocation graph	BNC corpus	word	collocation	undir.	460,902	70.13	2.67	n.s.	0.437	1.5 / 2.7	n.s.	Ferrer i Cancho/Solé (2001)
collocation graph	wortschatz.uni-leipzig.de	word	collocation	undir.			3.8	n.s.	0,05		n.s.	Heyer/Quasthoff/ Wittig (2006)
concept graph	WordNet	word	sense relation	undir.	122,005	S. 3	10.56	n.s.	0.0265	3.11	n.s.	Steyvers/Tenenbaum (2005)
co-occurrence graph	BNC corpus	word	co-occurrence	undir.	478,773	74.2	2.63	n.s.	0,687	1.5 / 2.7	n.s.	Ferrer i Cancho/Solé (2001)
newspaper graph	Süddeutsche Zeitung 1997	newspaper article	*quod vide* link	undir.	87,944	24.78	4.245	0.664	0.684	0.1146	0.699	Mehler (2006)
sentence graph	Czech tree bank	word	dependency relation	undir. i. a.	33,336	13.4	3.5	n.s.	0.1	≈2.29	0.06	Ferrer i Cancho/ Solé/Köhler (2004)
sentence graph	German tree bank	word	dependency relation	undir. i. a.	6,789	4.6	3.8	n.s.	0.02	≈2.23	0.18	Ferrer i Cancho/ Solé/Köhler (2004)
sentence graph	Romanian tree bank	word	dependency relation	undir. i. a.	5,563	5.1	3.4	n.s.	0.09	≈2.19	0.2	Ferrer i Cancho/ Solé/KÖhler (2004)

Tab. 19.4: (continued)

Graph	Source Network	Vertex	Edge	Orient.	$\|V(G)\|$	$\varepsilon(G)$	$L(G)$	$C_{BR}(G)$	$C_{WS}(G)$	γ	$r(G)$	Reference
thesaurus graph	Moby's thesaurus	word	sense relation	undir.	30,244	59.9	3.16	n. s.	0.53	S. 3	n. s.	Motter et al. (2002)
thesaurus graph	Roget's Thesaurus	word	sense relation	undir.	29,381	S. 3	5.60	n. s.	0.875	3.19	n. s.	Steyvers/ Tenenbaum (2005)
web graph	search engine crawl	website	hyperlink	undir.	153,127	n. s.	3.1	n. s.	0.1078	n. s.	n. s.	Adamic (1999)
web graph	search engine crawl (SCC)	website	hyperlink	dir.	64,826	n. s.	4.228	n. s.	0.081	n. s.	n. s.	Adamic (1999)
web graph	search engine crawl (SCC)	.edu website	hyperlink	dir.	3,456	n. s.	4.062	n. s.	0.156	n. s.	n. s.	Adamic (1999)
wiki graph	German Wikipedia	wiki entry page	hyperlink	undir.	303,999	19.39	3.247	0.01	0.223	0.4222	−0.1	Mehler (2006)
wiki graph	German Wikipedia	wiki entry page	hyperlink	undir.	406,074	15.88	3.554	0.01	0.186	0.5273	−0.09	Mehler (2006)
wiki graph	German Wikipedia	wiki entry page	hyperlink	undir.	796,454	11.50	4.004	0.007	0.139	0.7405	−0.05	Mehler (2006)
wiki graph	wiki.apache.org/ jakarta	wiki entry page	hyperlink	undir.	916	23.84	4.488	0.162	0.539	0.2949	−0.5	Mehler (2006)
wiki graph	wiki.apache.org/ struts	wiki entry page	hyperlink	undir.	1,358	29.93	4.530	0.162	0.402	0.2023	−0.45	Mehler (2006)
wiki graph	wiki.apache.org/ws	wiki entry page	hyperlink	undir.	1,042	22.91	4.541	0.175	0.485	0.1989	−0.48	Mehler (2006)
wiki graph	11 Wikipedia releases	wiki entry page	hyperlink	dir.	n. s.	n. s.	4.53	cf. ref.	n. s.	$\gamma_{in} \approx 2.15$	≈ -0.1	Zlatic et al. (2006)
wiki graph	11 Wikipedia releases	wiki entry page	hyperlink	undir.	n. s.	n. s.	3.32	cf. ref.	n. s.	$\gamma_{un.} \approx 2.35$	≈ -0.1	Zlatic et al. (2006)

1. *What are the criteria for network formation?* In other words: *what do the vertices represent and subject to which criteria are they linked?*
2. *What is the reason for network analysis?* In other words: *why are the networks being analysed or what is the research interest in analysing these networks?*
3. *Which small-world or complex network indicators are being investigated?*
4. *Which reasons are assumed to evoke the small-world property if observed?*
5. *Is there any account of network growth or of any other aspect of network dynamics?*

The review is ordered by increasing complexity of the signs denoted by the nodes of the networks: it starts with lexical networks in order to approach textual and document networks via so-called sentence networks.

3.1. Co-occurrence graphs and collocation graphs

Collocation analysis is a well established field of corpus linguistics (Sinclair 1991; Stubbs 1996, 2001). It follows the Firthian tradition according to which collocations manifest lexical semantic affinities beyond grammatical restrictions (Halliday 1966). Collocation analysis aims at discovering semantically related words based on (e. g. similarity) functions of their co-occurrences. In computational linguistics, several measures exist for distinguishing collocations from insignificant, though recurrent co-occurrences (Manning/Schütze 1999). Starting from a pairwise computation of lexical affinities by means of such measures, the network perspective is obvious: if two units *a, b* are related in terms of collocation statistics as the units *b, c* are, an indirect relation between *a* and *c* is implied even if not directly confirmed by a collocation of *a* and *c* – by analogy with semantic networks (cf section 3.3.). Following this procedure, a network of units linked by collocation arises whose graph theoretical representation will, thus, be called *collocation network*. Following this line of argumentation, several approaches analyse the *topology of large collocation networks* (Dorogovtsev/Mendes 2001; Ferrer i Cancho/Solé 2001; Heyer/Quasthoff/Wittig 2006). These networks are seen to be partitioned into a kernel lexis and more peripheral sociolects or topic specific terminologies. In such networks, lexical units are not immediately related to every other unit. Rather, there is mediation by means of common words of the kernel vocabulary in the role of hubs (Kleinberg 1999) or long-range nodes which have connections to many local word clusters and, thus, interrelate the different fields of lexis (Tuldava 1998). Moreover, the word clusters are themselves seen to be highly interwoven so that short paths emerge (Bordag/Heyer/Quasthoff 2003). From this perspective, lexis is seen as a complex network which is based in part on collocational regularities (i. e. beyond sense relations) and, thus, can be studied for its SW properties.

A first experiment in this area is described by Ferrer i Cancho/Solé (2001), who analyse the British National Corpus (BNC) from which they extract two graphs:

– Firstly, a so-called *co-occurrence graph* G_1 in which words are linked if they co-occur in at least one sentence within a span of maximally three tokens; see also Widdows/Dorow (2002), who explore the BNC corpus in order to extract a co-occurrence graph whose extraction is constrained by means of PoS relationships.
– Secondly, a *collocation graph* G_2 is extracted in which only those links of G_1 are retained whose end vertices co-occur more frequent than expected by chance.

Generally speaking, a co-occurrence graph is a graph whose edges represent single co-occurrence events of word forms without abstracting over sets of alike events. In contrast to this, a collocation graph is a graph whose edges represent significant co-occurrences where significance is established according to the evaluation of some set of such events by means of some collocation measure.

Ferrer i Cancho/Solé observe the small-world property in the case of both networks, according to the WS model and the BA model (see Table 19.4). But unlike the BA model, they separately fitted a power law to the degree distribution of the so-called kernel vocabulary (including the 5,000 topmost connected vertices) for which they yielded an exponent γ closer to the range of values predicted by the BA model. Dorogovtsev/Mendes (2001) took this empirical finding as a starting point and developed a theoretical model of network growth which reproduces both power laws with a greater exponent of the law fitted to the kernel vocabulary.

By analogy with the model of Ferrer i Cancho/Solé, Bordag/Heyer/Quasthoff (2003) analyse a collocation graph extracted from a German corpus of newspaper articles (cf. wortschatz.uni-leipzig.de). Unlike Ferrer i Cancho/Solé, they apply a log-likelihood-related measure for exploring collocations based on sentence co-occurrences. Their findings confirm the small-world property of the collocation graph being analysed. The numerical results of this study are published in Heyer/Quasthoff/Wittig (2006).

3.2. Sentence graphs

In the last section, co-occurrence graphs were described as a special case of lexical networks in which words, whose co-occurrences are observed in a given input corpus, are linked. These graphs were used as a starting point for deriving collocation graphs by retaining only those edges which manifest collocations (i. e. significant co-occurrences in the sense of some appropriate statistical measure). Another point of departure in dealing with co-occurrence graphs is to consider only those co-occurrences which manifest syntactic dependency relations, e. g. between the verb of a sentence and a noun manifesting its subject. This is the basic building principle of so-called *sentence graphs* (Ferrer i Cancho/Solé/Köhler 2004): a sentence graph is a directed graph in which vertices represent lexical units which are linked if they co-occur at least in one sentence in the role of a modifier (source vertex) and head (target vertex), respectively. In corpus linguistics, sentence graphs have already been analysed by Hoey (1991), who spans networks of sentences which are linked if they share at least two lexically cohesive words.

In the experiments reported by Ferrer i Cancho/Solé/Köhler (2004), directed edges are only considered with respect to power law fitting. As links represent syntactic dependency relations, each input sentence induces a subgraph of the sentence graph, thus justifying its name.

In order to determine the properties of such networks, Ferrer i Cancho/Solé/Köhler (2004) analyse tree banks of Czech, German and Romanian sentences annotated with respect to their dependency structure. They show that sentence graphs have the small-world property according to the WS and the BA model. Additionally, Ferrer i Cancho et al. compute the clustering coefficient $C(k)$ as a function of the degree k. In Ravasz et al. (2002), the distribution of C over k was analysed as an indicator of latent hierarchical structures within networks; see section 2.5. Ferrer i Cancho/Solé/Köhler do not observe this property in the case of sentence graphs. That is, $C(k)$ does not decay according to a scale-free power law, despite being highly skewed. As a further indicator of structure formation, Ferrer i Cancho/Solé/Köhler observe disassortative mixing. Therefore, highly connected words tend to be linked with lowly connected ones – in accordance with what is expected according to the usage of function words, common nouns etc. An extension of the model presented in Ferrer i Cancho/Solé (2001) and Ferrer i Cancho/Solé/Köhler (2004) is elaborated in Ferrer i Cancho/Riordan/Bollobás (2005) which starts from a simplified bipartite "form-meaning" graph in order to derive a network of linguistic units.

3.3. Concept graphs, thesaurus graphs and association graphs

Whereas collocation graphs directly build on observable co-occurrences of lexical units in large text corpora, *lexical reference systems* or *terminological ontologies* (e. g. WordNet), *thesauri* (e. g. Roget's Thesaurus) and related systems build – sometimes additionally – on expert knowledge of lexicographers in order to define *sense relations* (e. g. synonymy, antonymy, homonymy) between words, or *conceptual relations* between concepts (e. g. hypernymy, co-hyponymy, metonymy). As in the case of collocation graphs, but unlike in the case of co-occurrence and sentence graphs, sense relations are meaning-based. The difference between collocation graphs and the type of networks to be surveyed in this section relates to the distinction made by Halliday/Hasan (1976) between unsystematic lexical cohesion based on collocation and systematic lexical cohesion based on sense relations.

An alternative source of exploring meaning-based relations of lexical units which relate to, but are not identical with collocations, are regularities of *association* or, more specifically, *word priming:* in the case of word priming, lexical units are used as primes in order to let test subjects associate sense or form-related words (Kintsch 1988). In the line of this argumentation, association graphs of lexical units are built whose vertices represent primes and responses linked from the former to the latter.

Based on these preliminary considerations, the following graphs can be distinguished:

- *Thesaurus graphs* are graphs in which vertices denote words, whereas edges represent sense relations thereof (cf. Kinouchi et al. 2002).
- In contrast to this, *concept graphs* are graphs in which vertices represent concepts, whereas edges denote conceptual relations thereof.
- Finally, *association graphs* are graphs in which vertices denote words – as in the case of thesaurus graphs – whereas edges represent association or priming relations as observed in cognitive-linguistic experiments.

As these preliminary considerations motivate a network perspective on sense relations and association data, questions with respect to structure formation within such networks and their overall topology likewise arise:

1. In the case of thesaurus graphs based on the expertise of lexicographers and corpus linguists, network properties can be interpreted as indicators of thesaurus quality or consistency. As networks of this kind represent lexical semantic knowledge of a given

language, their analysis also provides an access to the semantic system of that language, that is, to the overall organisation of its lexical subsystem (Sigman/Cecchi 2002).

2. In the case of association networks, a corresponding argumentation applies: according to the hypothesis that association is one of the principles of memory organisation, the question is raised which network topologies support an efficient organisation in terms of time and space complexity. This is the starting point of Motter et al. (2002), who interpret the small-world property of association networks as an indicator of efficient information storage and retrieval (cf. Sigman/Cecchi 2002; Steyvers/Tenenbaum 2005): firstly, the existence of many local clusters is seen as a necessary condition of effective associations. Secondly, the existence of short path lengths is seen to guarantee fast information search (or spreading activation) since any "pieces of information" are on average separated only by a couple of associations − *irrespective of how different they are.*

In addition to collocation graphs, these two research directions − the more language- and the more memory-oriented one − leave the narrow view on word-to-word relations in order to focus whole networks thereof and, thus, lexical subsystems based on corpus-linguistic collocations, cognitive associations or lexicographical sense relations. This section reviews these kinds of approaches. First of all, this includes the study of Motter et al. (2002), who analyse the so-called *Moby thesaurus* in the form of its *e*-text release as part of the Project Gutenberg (cf. ftp://ibiblio.org/pub/docs/books/gutenberg/etext02/mthes10.zip). Motter et al. extract an undirected graph from this thesaurus in which vertices represent *root words* which are linked if the one word occurs in the root word list of the other (cf. also Holanda et al. 2003). As shown in Table 19.4, network analysis indicates that this thesaurus has the small-world property. Regarding scale-freeness, Motter et al. do not directly fit a power law, but observe a crossover from a more exponential behavior of $P(k)$ to a more power law-like behavior for higher values of k (with $\gamma = 3.5$). Albert/Barabási (2002) report on a related experiment of Yook, Jeong and Barabási in which a thesaurus graph (which also shows the small-world property) is extracted from the *Merriam-Webster dictionary* by exploring synonymy relations.

Sigman/Cecchi (2002) extract a concept graph from WordNet (Miller et al. 1990). They extract a graph of *lexicalised concepts* or *word meanings* in which vertices stand for synsets and edges for their meaning relations; 'synset' is a short form of *synonym set* representing a single word meaning (cf. Miller et al. 1990). In such a graph, edges are typed according to the meaning relation they represent. Sigman/Cecchi take *antonymy, hypernymy, meronymy* and *polysemy* relations into account; note that antonymy and polysemy relations are symmetric, whereas hypernymy and meronymy relations have *hyponymy* and *holonomy* as their inverses. Nevertheless, the concept graph extracted by Sigman/Cecchi is an undirected graph whose vertices solely represent *noun* meanings.

Generally speaking, hyponymy relations induce a kernel hierarchical structure of the concept graph extracted from WordNet. This hierarchical skeleton is superimposed by polysemy relations defined between any word meanings whose synsets share at least one (polysemous) word form. Sigman/Cecchi explore these relations as an additional source of edge generation. Their findings indicate that the inclusion of polysemy relations convert the concept network into a small world whose degree distribution follows a power law and in which subgroups of fully connected meanings emerge; for numerical details see Table 19.4. This result fails to appear when antonymy or meronymy relations are added to the hierarchical skeleton instead of the polysemy relations. Sigman/Cecchi conclude that polysemy has the effect of generating the small-world property and view this to be an explanation of its emergence in natural language. In other words: polysemy is seen to convert hyponymy-based concept networks into compact, clustered graphs which allow efficient storage and retrieval of lexical knowledge.

A comprehensive network analysis of lexical-semantic units is performed by Steyvers/Tenenbaum (2005). They analyse networks based on *Roget's Thesaurus*, WordNet and *free-association data* of lexical units:

- *Experiment I:* Steyvers/Tenenbaum start with an *association graph* whose vertices denote cue and response words which are linked whenever at least two participants of the underlying free-association experiment associated the same response to the same input cue. This graph is by definition simple and undirected. Steyvers/Tenenbaum derive a directed graph from this graph by means of its orientation along the association from the cue to the response word. Thus, *two* variants of an association graph are analysed.
- *Experiment II:* As *Roget's Thesaurus* defines a bipartite graph whose *top-mode* vertices represent semantic categories and whose *bottom-mode* vertices stand for words, Steyvers/Tenenbaum derive a unipartite *thesaurus graph* thereof in which words are linked whenever they are commonly classified by at least one category. *Roget's Thesaurus* is also explored by Leicht/Holme/Newman (2006) for the task of complex network analysis.
- *Experiment III:* Essentially, WordNet also has a bipartite structure based on the many-to-many relation of word forms and synsets. Thus, word form-to-word form edges (denoting, for example, antonymy relations) have to be distinguished from word form-to-synset and synset-to-synset edges (representing, for example, hypernymy or meronymy relations). Steyvers/Tenenbaum explore this bipartite structure in order to extract a unipartite graph of vertices denoting word forms (although they separately display $\langle d \rangle$ of the set of synsets). As Steyvers/Tenenbaum extract a graph of lexical, but not of conceptual nodes, it is not a concept graph; nevertheless we will retain this label as the predominant source of linkage are semantic relations as represented by means of links of synsets.

Steyvers/Tenenbaum compute the average degree, average geodesic distances of all vertices (experiment I) or a sample of 10,000 vertices (experiment II and III), diameters, cluster values C_{WS} and power law exponents γ for all four input graphs; see Table 19.4 for the results. All computations were made for the largest strongly connected component which covered at least 96% of the vertices. All networks demonstrate the small-world property, according to the WS model as well as according to the BA model. But Steyvers/Tenenbaum (2005) go beyond the present apparatus of complex network analysis as they develop a model of network growth which departs from the BA model of Barabási/Albert (1999) in that it additionally focuses on cluster formation as observed according to the WS model. In order to do that, they start from a linguistic assumption on the linkage of words newly added to a network at a given point in time. This model hints at promising extensions of the BA model from the point of view of (cognitive) linguistics and, thus, may serve as a starting point for critically extending complex network analysis in the light of linguistic research.

All studies surveyed so far focused on networking of linguistic units *below the text level*. The remaining three sections review studies which analyse text or document networks instead.

3.4. Citation graphs and sitation graphs

The quantitative study of networks of scientific documents linked by bibliographic relations is one of the earliest approaches to document networking (Garfield 1963; de Solla Price 1965). This field of research is separated into *informetrics, bibliometrics, scientometrics* and *webometrics* depending on the provenance of the not necessarily textual units whose linkage is studied (cf. Björneborn 2004):

- *Informetrics* is the most encompassing field of applying quantitative methods to studying processes of information transfer in networks of whatever information units, irrespective of the underlying transfer medium (Ravichandra Rao 1996).
- In contrast to this, *bibliometrics* "is the quantitative study of literatures as they are reflected in bibliographies" (White/McCain 1989, 119). Unlike webometrics, it is mainly based on *printed*, but not on WWW data (Bar-Ilan 2001).
- *Scientometrics* is a kind of bibliometrics with a focus on scientific communication. It aims at evaluating the impact factor of scientists, scientific discoveries or publication media. Further, it explores topological regularities of scientific document networks and maps the topological relatedness of authors, documents and publication media in order to derive recommendations for improving the retrieval of scientific publications (cf. Hummon/Doreian 1989; Larson 1996; Ravichandra Rao 1996).
- With the advent of the WWW, the hyperlink-based classification of web documents became a further research topic not only in *web mining*, but also in *webometrics*. Its basic idea is to apply the methodical apparatus of bibliometrics to web documents and their hyperlinks by analogy with scientific documents and their citation relations, in spite of the many differences due to possibly bidirectional hyperlinks, the lack of peer reviewing and of knowledge about the motives of hyperlinking (for a critical review of this concept, cf. Prime/Bassecoulard/Zitt 2002). According to Björneborn/Ingwersen (2001), webometrics aims at exploring the regularities of the content and structure of web documents and, thus, is connected to web *content* and *structure* mining (Kosala/Blockeel 2000).

The present section focuses on the scientometric study of networks of scientific documents (e. g. conference papers, journal articles, reviews, book chapters, scientific notes etc.) as part of scientific communication. These approaches are split into two groups of which only the second will be reviewed; for an overview of computational linguistic approaches to the first group cf. Leopold (2005):

- Firstly, there exists a group of approaches which explore the vocabularies of texts as a source of intertextual linkage (Leydesdorff 2001).
- Secondly, there is the group of approaches which explore citation and other reference relations as a source of intertextual linkage provided that they are explicitly marked within the input texts.

The latter approaches deal with *referential intertextuality* in the sense of Heinemann (1997), while the former can be said to focus on *typological intertextuality*.

Serving as input to the scientometric way of network analysis are so-called *citation networks*, in which nodes denote scientific publications which are linked from the citing to the cited publication. By example of the OpCit project (opcit.eprints.org) based on the *Los Alamos Eprint Archive* (LANL, cf. xxx.lanl.gov), Harnad/Carr (2000, 629) speak of "citation linked online digital" corpora which can easily be made an object of complex network analysis. Nevertheless, it is worth noting that the majority of these approaches explore bibliographic records (White/McCain 1989) as collected, for example, by the *Institute for Scientific Information* (ISI; cf. Garfield (1994, scientific.thomson.com/free/essays/citationanalysis/scientography or www.isinet.com)) and, thus, metadata descriptions, without exploring the underlying documents directly, unless approaches to referential and typological intertextuality are amalgamated as, for example, by Glenisson/Glänzel/Persson (2005). The ISI integrates the Science Citation, the Social Science Citation and the Arts & Humanities Citation Index. It covers articles, notes, letters, reviews, editorials, corrections, meeting-abstracts and related document types of scientific communication (Sigogneau 2000). Note that, besides proceedings, scientometrics only occasionally analyses citation relations of books, but tends to concentrate on scientific articles and related types of publications (White/McCain 1989). WWW-based resources of citation networks are digital libraries such as, for example, CiteSeer, CiteBase or, as a kind of social software-based digital library, CiteULike.

Citation networks allow distinguishing two fundamental scientometric relations as exemplified in Figure 19.4

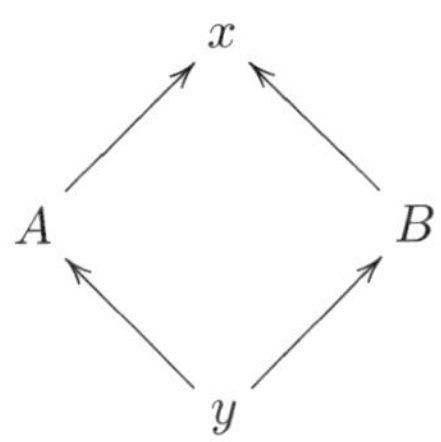

Fig. 19.4: Two fundamental relations within citation networks according to Fang/Rousseau (2001): the *bibliographic coupling* of A and B via x and the *co-citation* of A and B via y

- First of all, two documents A and B are said to be *bibliographically coupled* if there exists at least a third document x commonly cited by A and B (Kessler 1963). In terms of scientometrics: two *citing items* are bibliographically coupled if they have at least one reference (i. e. *cited item*) in common (Glänzel/Czerwon 1996). Coupling relations induce *bibliographic coupling networks* or *BC networks* for short. These networks are induced by analogy with scientific collaboration or co-author networks (van Raan 2005) in which author nodes are linked if they co-authored at least one publication. Within BC networks, link weighting naturally arises from counting and appropriately standardising the number of common references of two publications. BC graphs are inferred from BC networks by means of a bipartite graph model in which the top mode consists of vertices representing so-called *references* cited by *items* represented by vertices of the bottom-mode; see Figure 19.5. This allows interlinking any two *bibliographically coupled* publications whenever the corresponding vertices are linked to the same top-mode vertex. Next, publications sharing the same reference are collected into so-called *BC clusters* – by analogy with collaboration clusters in co-author networks whose affinity is affected by at least one publication whose authorship they share. Further, *BC chains* are paths $(v_{i_0}, e_{j_1}, v_{i_1}, e_{j_2}, ..., v_{i_{n-1}}, e_{j_n}, v_{i_n})$ in which neighboring vertices $v_{i_j}, v_{i_{j+1}}, j \in \{0, ..., n-1\}$, denote bibliographically coupled items; see Figure 19.5.

As references are nothing else but publications, BC networks are – in spite of their analogy to co-author networks – homogeneous in the sense that they consist of nodes of the same sort. Note further that any inference of a BC network necessarily includes two time windows: the window of those publications whose references are studied and the window spanned by the publication dates of these references. Redner (1998), for example, analyses a one-year time window of references cited by publications within the years 1981–1997. In contrast to this, van Raan (2005) analyses a one-year time window of publications and their references within the preceding publication years.

– A second type of relation is co-citation: two documents *A* and *B* are said to be *co-cited* if there exists at least a third document *y* commonly citing *A* and *B* (cf Small 1973); see Figure 19.4. CC graphs are inferred from the same bipartite model as BC graphs, but with the reverse perspective on the top-mode units. Likewise, *CC clusters* and *chains* are defined according to the same analogy; see Figure 19.5.

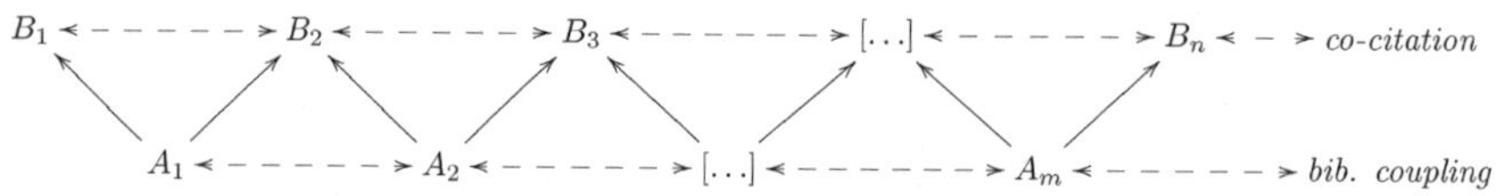

Fig. 19.5: Co-citation and bibliographic coupling chains (cf. Björneborn 2004)

Obviously, citation relations are not symmetric and, thus, induce *directed* edges, while co-citation and bibliographic coupling are symmetric and, therefore, are represented by *undirected* edges. Further, edges representing co-citation or bibliographic coupling relations are straightforwardly weighted by means of functions of the number of their occurrences (Small 1999). Note also that citation patterns vary among scientific communities so that findings in one of them do not necessarily characterise another one adequately. This observation is important when it comes to normalising numerical indicators in order to secure the comparability of different communities (Pinski/Narin 1976).

In citation networks, the *in-degree* distribution is induced by the number of times a publication is cited, whereas the *out-degree* distribution is induced by the number of citations a publication is making. In this context, Redner (1998) distinguishes two types of distributions within citation networks related to the scale-freeness of complex networks:

– firstly, the so-called Zipfian *rank-frequency* distribution of the number of citations ranked in decreasing order where the first rank denotes the most cited publication down to those publications which are only cited once or not at all;
– secondly, the *size-frequency* distribution of the number $N(x)$ of publications with x citations which relates to the Lotka law of scientometrics which is a power law $y_x = c/x^a$ where y_x is the number of items with x occurrences of the focal type (Rousseau/Rousseau 2000).

> In the case of co-citation networks, successfully fitting a power law to a size-frequency distribution indicates that the majority of (pairs of) documents are not co-cited at all, many others are co-cited only once etc. till the region of those hubs are reached which are co-cited very often.

In the case of the rank-frequency distribution, Redner (1998) fits a power law with exponent $y \approx -0.5$ for the part of the distribution from rank 1 (8,904 citations) to rank 12,000 (of about 85 citations). For a large x, this corresponds to fitting a power law $N(x) \propto x^{-\alpha}$ to the corresponding size-frequency distribution with $\alpha \approx 3$. These findings indicate that nearly one half of the papers is un-cited. In the area of webometrics which analyses hyperlinks by analogy with citations as sitations (see below), Prime/Bassecoulard/Zitt (2002) find three regimes of the out-degree distribution of external links within web pages which allow distinguishing, firstly, general portals (first regime) with a high number of external links from, secondly, more specialised portals and, thirdly, from web documents of varying size with few internal and external links. Prime/Bassecoulard/Zitt successfully fit a power law to the distribution of incoming links, that is, to the in-degree distribution of vertices representing web pages.

BC networks are analysed, for example, by van Raan (2005); see Table 19.4. He explores a corpus of 1,099,017 publications (mainly articles, reviews, notes and letters) citing 4,876,752 references. Van Raan considers three degree distributions: firstly, he adapts a power law to the in-degree distribution of references, that is, to the distribution of the number of citing publications per cited reference. Secondly, he considers the number of references per publication in order to adapt an out-degree distribution in the sense of the bipartite graph model presented in Figure 19.5. Thirdly, he studies the number of bibliographically coupled documents per publication. The central observation of van Raan is that within this corpus, power laws are only successfully fitted if all references are taken into account, while scale-freeness disappears when references are separately accounted for by their age. He concludes that references to "younger" publications have other functions (e. g. including topic specific references) than references to older ones (e. g. referring to "classic" works in the corresponding field). This observation points to the significance of time dependent, nonstationary characteristics of document networking. In this sense, Seglen (1992, 629) describes changes in citedness of articles depending on their age where "citedness declines steadily as a function of time since publication", indicating increasing obsolescence where only a few articles are accepted as classic work for a longer time period.

Citation, BC and CC networks are easily made input to multivariate statistics. Based on matrices of co-citation or coupling frequencies, correlation coefficients of documents can be computed as an input to cluster or principle components analysis in order to derive clusters or factors, respectively, which represent sets of topically or otherwise related documents (Larson 1996). Any such cluster can then be described in terms of its size, the mean year of publication of its elements or according to the distribution of these elements over the set of scientific genres. That is, citation, BC and CC networks are input to deriving large sub-networks thereof based on publication medium-, genre-, document type- or topic-related criteria. Hummon/Dorcian (1989) analyse, for example, a citation network which solely consists of publications on DNA theory. Likewise, Schummer (2004) analyses citation networks incorporating articles on nanotechnology only. Further, citation networks may be confined to certain publication media (e. g. journals or proceedings) – leaving out other media of scientific communication (cf Seglen

1992) – or certain pragmatic parameters (e. g. common author, time or location of production etc.) (cf. Sigogneau 2000).

Based on these considerations, the following approaches can be distinguished which focus on structure formation derived from citation relations: Glänzel/Czerwon (1996) present a method for identifying research topics as clusters of bibliographically coupled items. They define *core documents* as items with a higher-than-average number of links. Core documents are analysed with respect to their distribution over journals, scientific subfields and corporate addresses (e. g. of universities). In summary, Glänzel/Czerwon analyse the formation of sub-networks within BC networks and their *macro*-level segmentation according to the criteria just mentioned. Identifying (mainstream) research topics and exploring their life cycle are further parts of this agenda. A further topic is to identify so-called sleeping beauties (van Raan 2004), that is, publications which remain unnoticed for a longer period of time and then, suddenly, get cited to a high degree. A network perspective on the contributions to conference series is provided by Chen/Czerwinski (1998), who apply Latent Semantic Analysis (Landauer/Dumais 1997) in order to automatically link topically related documents. Chen (1999) applies this apparatus to co-citation networks in order to explore predominant research fields as sub-networks. Small (1999) analyses co-citation chains in order to examine cross-disciplinary citations interrelating document networks of different scientific disciplines. He applies cluster analysis to recursively identify sub-networks of high co-citation density which are traversed by means of *pathways* (Björneborn/Ingwersen 2001) of cross-disciplinary citations.

A further research topic is the temporal dynamics of scientific communication. This relates, for example, to studying the life cycle of scientific fields based on their citation relations (Otte/Rousseau 2002). As the set of scientific publications is rapidly growing, citation-based clusters are continually shaped by newly entering or dropping out documents. They may merge or split into new clusters or may even disappear completely (White/McCain 1989).

Distributions of URL-based references to web documents within scientific articles are studied by Brown (2004). He gives a perspective on integrating document networks within more traditional and online media and, thus, leads over to the study of so-called *sitations*. In webometrics, hyperlinks between web documents (e. g. pages or websites) are analysed by analogy with citation relations as sitations (Rousseau 1997; Faba-Pérez/Guerrero-Bote/Moya-Anegón 2003; Björneborn 2004). Rousseau (1997) shows that the distribution of sitations obeys a power law with an exponent of 2.345. He analyses the distribution of the number $N(x)$ of websites with x sitations, that is, with x inlinks. Earlier, Larson (1996) applied co-citation analysis in order to cluster topically related pages. Inlink distributions are, further, analysed by Thelwall/Tang (2003), Tang/Thelwall (2004), and Li et al. (2005a, 2005b), who concentrate on academic websites in order to measure the impact factor of universities and their departments subject to situational parameters and membership in scientific disciplines. Outlink distributions are analysed by Ajiferuke/Wolfram (2004), who concentrate on web pages of top level domains. More recently, Björneborn (2004) has extend webometrics by defining co-linking and co-linked pages by analogy with bibliographic coupling and co-citation, respectively; see Figure 19.5. He explores *co-linkage chains* by analogy with *co-citation chains* (Small 1999) in order to identify pathways of topically related, though *un*-co-linked pages (cf. Garfield 1994). Björneborn gives a comprehensive scientometric perspective on the study of networking in WWW-based scientific communication and, thus, can be seen as leading over to the study of document networking in the WWW as surveyed in the next section.

Tab. 19.5: Reference points of document network analysis by example of the WWW

Level	Unit of Research	Approaches
macro level	network	complex network analysis
meso level	sub-network	exploring web communities, broad topics etc.
micro level	web document	segmentation & categorisation of websites and pages

3.5. Web graphs

A well explored area of network analysis is the World Wide Web (WWW). From the beginning of statistical analyses of small worlds on, it has been made an object of this kind of research (cf. the survey of Newman 2003b). Seen as a network of hypertext documents in the form of websites or pages, the WWW is by now the best studied document network. Because of the many surveys of WWW-oriented studies – cf., for example, Chakrabarti (2002) and Baldi/Frasconi/Smyth (2003) for two excellent books surveying this area – the present section concentrates on a general account of their reference points, which are *macro, meso* and *micro* level units (see Table 19.5) as input to what is called *web content* and *structure mining* (Kosala/Blockeel 2000):

– On the *macro level*, the WWW as a whole is made an object of complex network analysis. The starting point of this kind of research is, more or less explicitly, the seminal paper of Botafogo/Rivlin/Shneiderman (1992) on so-called *hypertext graphs*. Botafogo/Rivlin/Shneiderman generally describe hypertexts in terms of vertices and edges denoting hypertext modules and their hyperlinks, respectively, in order to analyse their structural characteristics in terms of compactness and hierarchical structure formation. In web mining, this graph-theoretical format is utilised in order to represent the WWW or parts of it by means of so-called *web graphs* (Chakrabarti 2002), that is, directed graphs whose vertices denote pages and whose edges denote hyperlinks in-between (Björneborn/Ingwersen 2001); cf. Park (2003), who speaks of *hyperlink network analysis* when it comes to exploring the WWW as a graph. Although the page level is the accentuated reference point of web-based link manifestation and, thus, of networking in the WWW, its networking may also be observed on the level of websites and conglomerates thereof when viewed as vertices; cf. the layered graph model of Mukherjea (2000) and especially the document model of Björneborn (2004) and Björneborn/Ingwersen (2004), who describe a graph model in terms of webometrics, which bridges analyses of the WWW in general and those of document networks in scientific communication. Generally speaking, macro level studies examine the principles of the overall topology of the WWW (Barabási/Albert/Jeong 1999) in terms of clustering and geodesic distances (Adamic 1999), its diameter (Albert/Jeong/Barabási 1999), the degree distribution of pages (Barabási/Albert 1999; Kleinberg et al. 1999; Adamic/Huberman 2001; Barabási et al. 2000) and the web's characteristic motifs (Milo et al. 2002). A seminal paper in this area is Adamic (1999), who analyses the SW property of the web. He refers to websites as the operative units for vertex extraction where a site *A* is seen to be linked with a site *B* if it contains a page linked with a page in *B*. The resulting graph is analysed in three variants: as an undirected, as a directed and as a subgraph containing solely websites of a certain top level domain (e. g. .edu). A purely structural perspective on the overall topology of the WWW is induced by its so-called *bow tie-structure* (Broder et al. 2000), which segments the WWW into four topological regions of roughly equal size (cf Baldi/Frasconi/Smyth 2003): first, the *Strongly Connected Component* (SCC) contains all pages that are reachable from each other by directed paths. In contrast to this, the IN component includes all pages that can reach members of the SCC, but cannot be reached by them in terms of directed paths. Analogously, the OUT component contains all pages that are reachable from the SCC, but are not linked with any member of the SCC. Finally, there are, amongst others, components consisting of pages which are disconnected from the SCC as well as from the IN and OUT component. This model sheds light on the necessity of segmenting sub-networks of the WWW which obviously vary with respect to their structural characteristics. This is done on a meso level of analysis.

- *On the meso level*, the WWW is studied as a heterogeneous network which does not simply consist of pages and their links, but is clustered into large, functionally as well as thematically heterogeneous sub-networks whose segmentation is the focus of inter est on this level. Gibson/Kleinberg/Raghavan (1998) and Flake/Lawrence/Giles (2000), for example, extract so-called *web communities*, that is, networks of websites which have more links to members of the same community than to sites outside of it. Web communities are induced by exploring the link structure of pages. In contrast to this, Chakrabarti et al. (2002) explore so-called *broad topics* manifested by large clusters of thematically homogeneous web pages whose size distribution they study. See also Mukherjea (2000), who likewise distinguishes sub-networks in terms of the matic criteria. A very interesting observation of Chakrabarti et al. (2002) as well as of Pennock et al. (2002) is that generically or topically demarcated sub-networks of the WWW show strikingly different regularities of their degree distributions in comparison to the WWW as a whole. This observation hints at the genre/register sensitivity of network analyses and, thus, on the necessity to further investigate and extract significant sub-networks of the WWW as the proper input of complex net work analysis. Another reference point on the meso level (as a byproduct of inferring web communities and related units) is the classification of vertices of web graphs in terms of so-called *authorities* (i. e. "popular" pages linked by many other pages) and *hubs* (i. e. pages which list links to many authorities) (Kleinberg 1999).
- The genre-sensitivity of large scale network characteristics hints at the fact that, by analogy with texts, hypertexts manifest functionally/thematically demarcated *hypertext types* where instances of the same type tend to be similarly structured, while instances of different types are more likely dissimilarly structured. The general idea is that knowledge about hypertext types and their prototypical instances facilitates hypertext production and reception. This assumption is reflected by the notion of a *web genre* (Dillon/Gushrowski 2000; Firth/Lawrence 2003) which is defined in functional terms as a type of web documents serving a certain recurrent function of web-based communication. Manifestations of web genres and related units are, more or less explicitly, analysed in terms of *compound documents* (Eiron/McCurley 2003), *logi-*

cal domains (Li et al. 2000), *logical documents* (Tajima/Tanaka 1999; Li et al. 2002) or *multipage segments* (Craven et al. 2000). In the majority of cases, instances of web genres are analysed on the level of single pages (Rehm 2002). A smaller group of approaches analyses instances of webgenres in terms of websites as systems of pages whose links are likewise analysed in terms of genre-specific functions (Mehler/Gleim 2006).

This series of approaches of increasing resolution of the units being segmented hints at the necessity to further study the functional/thematic structures of elementary web documents in order to better understand their networking. This is due to the fact that linkage of a page may be due to its membership in a web community, its role in manifesting a broad topic, its function as a hub or authority or as a component of a website manifesting a certain webgenre. Generally speaking, these considerations hint at the need to further integrate linguistic models of document types in order to ground document network analysis not only in terms of (social science and) statistics, but also of linguistics. Future elaborations of this apparatus will need to follow this direction in order to better grasp the genre/register sensitivity of the characteristics of document networks. This includes also networks whose generation is restricted by the kind of web-based software as surveyed in the subsequent section.

3.6. Social software-based networks

With the advent of the so-called *Web 2.0* (O'Reilly 2005; Bächle 2006), a further, hardly foreseen media change is taking place. In some areas of the web, a kind of 'content provider' who generates his or her offer of information in cooperation with other members of the same social network takes the place of the classical WWW user in the role of a passive information recipient. That is, some parts of the web evolve as a medium of distributed cognition (Hollan/Hutchins/Kirsch 2000) by utilising so-called *social software* which covers, amongst others, fora, networked blogs and countless wikis of knowledge or technical communication. The central aim of social software is to support the web-based buildup and self-organisation of social networks in the form of virtual communities of members which – without the need for face-to-face communication – cooperatively/competitively perform some task (e. g. writing a technical documentation, programming open source software, building an electronic encyclopedia etc.) *without involving any kind of central supervision*. In this sense, one may speak of *social software-mediated communication*. In this section, we review approaches to document networks which were cooperatively produced by means of some social software. This includes internet mailing lists (IML), fora, networked weblogs and wiki-based document networks. Other areas of the web 2.0 relevant for document networking but not taken into consideration include *social bookmarking* and *social networking* systems.

3.6.1. Web fora

A (web) (discussion) forum or (electronic bulletin) board is a website which supports asynchronous discussions on certain topics within groups of posters who possibly registered to the forum (Bächle 2006; Fisher 2003). A forum and its sub-fora are usually bound to a certain topic and its sub-topics, respectively (Bächle 2006). It is built around the postings of its posters, where postings on the same subject as part of the same discussion are organised into a thread (see below). In this section, we will review approaches to forum-based document networking by example of Usenet newsgroups.

Usenet newsgroups span a worldwide system of electronic bulletin boards where each newsgroup organises discussions on a certain topic (Bar-Ilan 1997). Usenet is hierarchically organised in a way which is reflected by the newsgroup names (Meinel/Sack 2004; Smith 2003). A newsgroup name is prefixed by the name of the topmost group to which the newsgroup belongs. It is followed by a sequence of period-separated subgroup names indicating – with increasing thematic resolution – the topic of the newsgroup (Bar-Ilan 1997). For the number and diversity of newsgroups, see (Kot/Silverman/Berg 2003; Smith 2003). Each newsgroup may organise several discussions possibly in parallel to each other. Each discussion is organised as a thread which finally consists of single postings, i. e. messages or news items. As a user can reply to a message posted earlier, a post order of hierarchically threaded postings emerges. That is, a thread is a hierarchically ordered series of news items usually about a single topic instantiated by the thread's root or initial message where succeeding messages uniquely refer to a previous one. In its header, a news item identifies its submitter and subject while its body contains the message content. As there is no subscription procedure for newsgroups, one can easily participate in a discussion via e-mail, although newsgroups may be moderated. The moderator may decide, for example, to crosspost a message, that is, to post it in different newsgroups.

Usenet contains science-related newsgroups and, thus, supports scientific communication. The BIOSCI/bionet newsgroup, for example, "is a series of freely accessible electronic communication fora (i. e., electronic bulletin boards or "newsgroups") for use by biological scientists worldwide" (www.bio.net/docs/biosci.FAQ.html – cf also Kot/Silverman/Berg 2003). Its aim is "to promote communication between professionals in the biological sciences" (ibid.). But as Usenet postings are not refereed, they cannot be compared with related forms of collaborative, peer-reviewed publication in scientific communication (Bar-Ilan 1997). Moreover, unlike Wiki-based systems, once statements are posted in a newsgroup, they are, usually, no longer editable, let alone collectively.

Reflecting the thematic focus of Usenet newsgroups, related models of document networking concentrate on the time-related principles of postings on single topics. Bar-Ilan (1997), for example, analyses a corpus of about 16,000 Usenet messages on the *mad cow disease* in a period of one hundred days starting around the beginning of this "food scandal". She studies the growth function of topic-specific messages within certain periods of time in order to analyse time-dependent phenomena such as topic spread and burst. This approach is related to the study of Sengupta/Kumari (1991) of the growth rate of AIDS related publications. Unlike Bar-Ilan, they observe an "epidemic", exponential growth of such publications during the period of 1976 to 1986. In a related context, but with a focus on the WWW, Bar-Ilan/Echermane (2005) analyse web pages linking to contributions on the anthrax scare.

The diversity of newsgroups is studied by Kot/Silverman/Berg (2003) by example of a group of 107 bioscience related newsgroups as can be downloaded from ftp://ftp.bio.net/BIOSCI/ARCHIVE. They show that the number of postings of contributors ranked by decreasing number obeys Zipf's law. Kot/Silverman/Berg develop a model in terms of a stochastic process which accurately predicts the contribution of posters with respect to their number, size and the total number of postings within the simulated newsgroup.

A power law-like characteristic of newsgroup postings is explored by Agrawal et al. (2003), who fit a power law (with exponent $\gamma \approx 0.8$) to the ranked-size distribution of (the number of) postings per author. But unlike the studies just reviewed, Agrawal et al. do not consider document, but agent networks in which nodes denote posters which are linked if one has quoted from an earlier posting written by the other.

3.6.2. Internet mailing lists

An Internet Mailing List (IML) as uniquely identified by its name and address collects the list of e-mail addresses of its members. A member can post a message which is then sent to all other members unless censored by the list moderator. The reason to submit may be to initiate a discussion by posting a question, hypothesis, or an issue for debate (Kuperman 2005). Inter-discussion links occur subject to referential links (e. g. references *to* or quotations *from* preceding discussions) or thematic relatedness and, thus, give rise to networking beyond single discussions. As topic-based links are not explicit, they need to be explored in order to contribute to a networked corpus. The members of a list can actively participate in a discussion or passively follow it in the role of a so-called *lurker*. As submitters reply to messages posted earlier, a hierarchically threaded structure of *e-mail* postings emerges by analogy with web fora. That is, an IML thread is a hierarchically ordered series of messages discussing a single topic with a unique initial message. Alternatively, threads may be simply linearly ordered as in the LINGUIST LIST in which postings are linked as sequels of the same discussion. According to Zelman/Leydesdorff (2000), threaded e-mail messages are the fundamental communication units of IML-based computer-mediated communication (CMC). In scientific communication, they are characterised by their size and thematic homogeneity, as their submitters are known for their expertise (Thelwall/Wouters 2005), clearly affecting the self-organisation of these IMLs, although the extent of this impact has yet to be proven (Zelman/Leydesdorff 2000). IMLs are, usually, moderated to a higher degree than newsgroups, but to a lower degree than conventional scholarly publications. Moderation is based on publication policies. It may concern the format, content and size of postings as well as preventing repeated discussions. Comparably to newsgroups, but unlike in conventional scholarly publications, IML-based postings are less restricted with respect to their number, size, frequency and related restrictions induced by the publishing medium. On the other hand, scholarly IMLs are characterised by having more qualified contributions than unmoderated newsgroups (Hernandez-Borges/Macias/Torres 1998). Thus, moderated IMLs of scientific communication can be settled in-between less moderated newsgroups and scholarly publications which are restricted in terms of their access, number, size, and frequency of publication (Kuperman 2005). For the time being, a standard format for archiving and retrieving IMLs is missing (Zelman/Leydesdorff 2000) as is the case for web fora.

Kuperman (2005) reports on a bibliometric analysis of the productivity of two IMLs. He analyses a corpus of 5,016 e-mails from the LINGUIST LIST (cf linguistlist.org/issues/master.html) and a corpus of 3,023 e-mails from the History of the English Language List (cf. listserv.linguistlist.org/archives/hel-l.html). Kuperman shows that members of the power law family, e. g. Lotka's law, Zipf's law, Zipf-Mandelbrot's law or the Yule, Yule-Simon or the Waring distribution (Simon 1955; Rapoport 1982; Wimmer/Altmann

1999b) poorly fit the ranked-size distribution of postings over authors in *unmoderated* lists. Goodness of fit is better in lists with a higher level of moderation. This result is in support of locating IMLs in-between the area of unmoderated newsgroups and conventional scholarly publications. It was the latter area for which power laws have been successfully fitted in scientometrics. In order to generalise this observation, we may hypothesize that the less restricted the publication process, the less distinctive the incentive to publish, the less "Zipfian" the order of publications (e. g. postings). This finding is supported by Zelman/Leydesdorff (2000), who analyse eleven IMLs of *scientific* communication which include, for example, IMLs on *Self-Organisation* and *Science & Technology Studies*. This corpus includes mailing lists of scientific projects as well as intermediate and field level lists. Zelman/Leydesdorff (2000) aim at describing the dynamics of IMLs by means of statistical indices. Amongst others, this includes counting the number of messages per thread and, subsequently, fitting a function in double-logarithmic scale to the distribution of the frequencies of thread size which allows deriving a corresponding power law with an exponent $-0.42 \leq \gamma \leq -0.47$.

3.6.3. Networked blogs in blogspace

A *weblog* or *blog* for short is a web site which, in the majority of cases, is authored by a single author, i. e. a *blogger*, with the help of a *weblog system* (Glance/Hurst/Tomokiyo 2004). As the word *blog* may denote the action of blogging, its end product (i. e. a blog) or the software that enables blogging (Gill 2005), we will solely refer to the product perspective when using this term. According to Kumar et al. (2003) and Gill (2004), blogs consist of time-aligned, date-stamped, possibly archived entries that are reversely chronologically ordered and additionally contain links to related entries of the same or other blogs in conjunction with so-called blogrolls (as lists of links to recommended blogs).

According to Kumar et al. (2003, 568), blogs are "quirky, highly personal, often consumed by regular repeat visitors and highly interwoven into a network of small but active micro-communities." This network of interrelated blogs is called *BlogSphere, blogosphere* or *blogspace*. Generally speaking, blogs can be characterised with respect to their structure, content and the functions they provide. Nardi et al. (2004) point out the thematic heterogeneity of blogs and stress the wide range of motivations of bloggers to blog, which make network analysis a hard task in this area. Likewise, Schmidt/Schönberger/Stegbauer (2005) state that blogs serve divergent functions including that of a personal diary, journalistic publishing or also of knowledge or organisational communication. Accordingly, (personal) *online diaries* or *journals*, *blogs of pundits* (i. e. self-declared knowledge experts), *news filter blogs* (based on RSS aggregators), *writer* or *artist blogs, marketing blogs*, and *spam blogs* are distinguished as some examples of weblog genres (Gruhl et al. 2004; Glance/Hurst/Tomokiyo 2004; Bächle 2006). Krishnamurthy (2002) presents a two-dimensional model of classifying weblogs according to their *personal* vs. *thematic* and *community* vs. *individual* orientation.

Evidently, network studies focusing on a single one of the dimensions just mentioned face the risk of overgeneralising to the disadvantage of the disregarded dimensions and their impact on networking within the blogspace (Schmidt/Schönberger/Stegbauer 2005). Thus, the sampling of blogs by example of which the network structure of the blogspace is investigated has to be carefully considered. From a structural point of view, the following types of links between blogs can be explored for this task (Glance/Hurst/Tomokiyo 2004): (friendship indicating) links as part of the *blogroll* of a blog, *trackbacks* (linking blogs whose bloggers have linked the focal entry), *permalinks* (as URLs which uniquely identify posts irrespective of whether they have been archived or not) as well as hyperlinks within a blog entry (to other blogs or web pages outside the blogspace). Blogs manifest intra links (interrelating entries of the same blog) as well as extra links which settle them, for example, in the neighborhood of related blogs (participating in the same discussion) (Gruhl et al. 2004). As all these kinds of links are not (necessarily) mutual, graphs derived thereof are necessarily directed. Starting from these structural notions, several reference points of complex network analysis come into play:

- Firstly, so-called *small communities* in the sense of Kumar et al. (2003), that is subnetworks of blogs which link to each other's postings while discussing some topic within a certain period of time.
- Secondly, a large component of interlinked blogs or, alternatively, a *blog site* collecting hundreds and thousands of (links to) blogs (cf. Kumar et al. 2004) may be made an object of network analysis. See Adar et al. (2004) for an enumeration of such sites.
- Thirdly, the system of blog sites as interlinked by means of their component blogs may be made an object of network analysis.
- This leads, fourthly, to the whole blogspace as a candidate input for complex network analysis.

A system for building blog corpora is described by Glance/Hurst/Tomokiyo (2004). It includes a URL harvester, a blog crawler, a time aligner (for mapping blog entries to timestamps) and an indexer for making the collected blogs retrievable. The corpus builder also comprises text mining software for exploring thematic trends and, thus, time-dependent structure formation. As a sample corpus, Glance/Hurst/Tomokiyo crawl about 100,000 weblogs.

Herring et al. (2005) show that blog networks have SW-related characteristics such as, for example, preferential attachment. They investigate the formation of so-called *blog dyads* constituted by their manyfold mutual links and "textual interaction" by means of reciprocal verbal exchange manifesting a sort of "conversation" between the corresponding bloggers. Herring et al. point out that – in contrast to what is propagated by the blogger community – blog linkage is an infrequent phenomenon making such dyads a rather rare event: "the blogosphere appears to be selectively interconnected, with dense clusters in parts, and blogs minimally connected in local neighborhoods, or free-floating individually, constituting the majority." Likewise, Herring et al. (2004) present frequencies of various types of links which in spite of their wide range indicate that linking is a rare phenomenon in blogspace. This is more or less in accordance with successfully fitting power laws to the in-degree distribution of blogs – for related studies of power law fitting, cf. Glance/Hurst/Tomokiyo (2004). See also Tricas/Ruiz/Merelo (2004), who fit a power law with an exponent $\gamma \approx -0.58$, although they report on problems with fitting. The relevance of such analyses is confirmed by studies which show that users tend to focus on highly linked blogs. This hints at preferential attachment, as a minority of authoritative blogs (Herring et al. 2005) is preferably linked from other blogs as well as from outside the blogosphere.

By analogy with web fora and internet mailing lists, networked blogs have also been made an object of investigating time-dependent structure formation. The aim of this research is to investigate the life cycle of thematic spreads and bursts within the blogosphere. This is made possible by the timestamps of blog entries. In this context, the study of Kumar et al. (2003, 2004) is of special interest. Kumar et al. (2003) introduce the notion of a *time graph* in order to describe link generation in the blogspace as a function of time. Time graphs are used to explore the build-up of blog communities and to separate recurrent periods of time within their life cycle. The formation of *small* communities (of about three to twenty members, cf Kumar et al. 2004) is described as a characteristic of the blogspace. That is, blogs are seen to be networked – unlike newsgroups – on the basis of small communities (of blogs whose authors mutually link each other within their blogrolls and respond to newly posted content within the corresponding community). Moreover, unlike "classic" web communities (Gibson/Kleinberg/Raghavan 1998), blog communities show a strikingly temporal characteristic as they evolve subject to temporarily arising debates during which linkages of the blogs involved into community building rapidly grow before they decrease with the debate fading away. Kumar et al. (2004) distinguish three periods of time in the life cycle of blog communities as they, firstly, undergo a sudden burst of activity of rapid-fire discussion in a small period of time before they, secondly, lie, so to speak, dormant for weeks and are, thirdly, replaced by a subsequent burst. A characteristic trait of their study is that unlike many other approaches they analyse a large corpus of about one million interwoven blogs. Extending the analysis of Kumar et al. (2003), they include the spatial and topical dimension in network analysis. Such a spatial restriction, which has already been taken into account in scientometrics, is also considered by Lin/Halavais (2004).

Adar et al. (2004) develop the notion of an information epidemics spreading over the blogosphere. They analyse a corpus of about 40,000 blogs with about 175,000 links in order to classify sitations (see section 3.4.) within blogs dependent on their time characteristics. Likewise, Gruhl et al. (2004) describe the long-term propagation of topics which are referred to in order to segment the blogspace on a macroscopic level. They distinguish spikes and chatters, that is, ongoing and short-term, but highly intensive discussions, respectively.

3.6.4. Wiki-based document networks

A fourth example of social software which became prominent through the online encyclopedia *Wikipedia* (wikipedia.org) is wiki software.

By analogy with weblogs, one has to distinguish *wiki software* (e. g. Media Wiki, cf. www.mediawiki.org/wiki/MediaWiki, or TWiki, cf. www.twiki.org) from the *document networks* (as exemplified in Table 19.6) generated with this software. For a comparative overview of wiki software see www.wikimatrix.org. In the present review we refer to the product perspective when using the term *wiki* and, thus, refer by this term to document networks generated by means of some wiki software. Generally speaking, a wiki is a website which, by means of the corresponding software, allows collaborative writing, editing and revising the collection of pages and links this site consists of. By analogy with social software and its output, the generation of wikis is a self-organised process initiated and continued by a multitude of cooperating/competing authors who may, but in general do not have exclusive access to editing the wiki (Kuhlen 2004). In other words, wikis manifest a sort of distributed, non-linear production and revision of hypertext documents and, thus, a sort of hyper-textually manifested distributed cognition including

Tab. 19.6: Some wikis of knowledge and technical communication

Wiki	URL	Language
a city wiki	ka. stadtwiki .net/Hauptseite	de
a wiki about the Wikimedia Foundation's projects	meta. wikimedia.org/wiki/Main_Page	en
a wiki-based dictionary of French	fr.wiktionary.org/wiki/	fr
Ward Cunningham's wiki (alias WikiWikiWeb)	c2.com/cgi/wiki	en
wiki of the Firefox project	www.firefox-browser.de/wiki/Hauptseite	de
wiki of the MediaWiki software	www.mediawiki. org/wiki/MediaWiki	en
wiki of the Mozilla project	wiki .mozilla. org/Main_Page	en
wiki of the OpenOffice.org	wiki.services.openoffice.org/wiki/Main_Page	en
wiki of the swarm project	www.swarm.org/wiki/Main_Page	en
wiki of the Wikibooks project of free textbooks	en.wikibooks.org/wiki/Wikibooks_portal	en
wiki of the wikis of the Apache.org projects	wiki.apache.org/general/	en
wiki of the W3C RIF Working Group (restricted access)	www.w3.org/2005/rules/wg/wiki/	en

social tagging (Mika 2005) as exemplified by the category system of Wikipedia (tools. wikimedia.de/~daniel/WikiSense/Category Tree. php). Unlike "classic" websites, wikis are continually and cooperatively updated. Unlike weblogs and mailing lists, wiki software-mediated communication is, in principle, symmetric in the sense that every (registered or permitted) user can respond to, continue or edit the contribution of any other wiki author. Thus, the need for a thread-based organisation does not apply, although changes are archived by means of history pages accompanying each article page (see below). For a general discussion of wiki software-mediated communication, the underlying wiki software, some structural, statistical characteristics of wikis and their impact on knowledge communication, see Ebersbach/Glaser/Heigl (2005), Voss (2005), Holloway/Božičevic/Börner (2005) and Kuhlen (2004), respectively.

This section concentrates on wikis built by means of the MediaWiki software. It is used by the Wikimedia Foundation (wikimediafoundation.org/wiki/Home), which hosts the Wikipedia project and its language specific releases which, together, are the largest wikis on the web. The dumps of these releases and those of many other wikis of the Wikimedia Foundation are accessible via download.wikimedia.org, which – in spite of the size of these files – makes wiki network analysis a manageable task. An alternative way of downloading wikis is to explore wiki pages listing, if existing, all entry pages of the corresponding wiki such as, for example, www.firefox-browser.de/wiki/Spezial:Allpages, the Firefox browser wiki. This gives access to all pages of the focal wiki website which need to be further analysed in order to explore their links.

Network extraction in the case of Wiki-based networks faces the situation of the rich type system of node and link types as exemplified by Wikipedia. That is, network extraction cannot be performed by simply extracting all wiki *article* pages, as this may disregard other types of nodes and links (see Table 19.6). Thus, the question which node and link types shall be taken into account has to be carefully considered. A starting point for distinguishing most elementary node types in MediaWiki-based networks is what will be called a wiki document which consists of an article page (describing a certain entry of the wiki), a corresponding *discussion* (or *talk*), history and *edit this* or *view source* page, which together form a flatly structured document.

Due to namespace conventions, some additional types of nodes can be distinguished by example of Wikipedia. Table 19.7 lists all node types as found within its German release or additionally introduced in order to span a hierarchical type system. The central heuristic for extracting instances of node types relates to the URL of the corresponding document module and its namespace prefix. Category, portal and media wiki pages, for example, contain the namespace prefix Kategorie (*category*), Portal (*portal*) and MediaWiki, respectively. The prefix is separated by a colon from the corresponding page name suffix. de.wikipedia.org/wiki/Kategorie:Musik, for example, references the page of the *music* category, whereas de.wikipedia.org/wiki/Portal:Musik identifies the German Wikipedia portal on music. Finally, de.wikipedia.org/wiki/Musik references the standard German Wikipedia article on music. That is, URLs of standard wiki articles do not include a special namespace prefix.

Table 19.7 lists the frequencies of the instances of the node types as found in the input release of Wikipedia. The types are ordered into an inclusion hierarchy in which the child nodes dominated by the same type (e. g. talk) are ranked according to their frequencies in descending order. Further, the frequency of a dominating node is the sum of the frequencies of its child nodes. Analogously, Table 19.7 lists all edge types as found within the input wiki or additionally introduced into the study in order to span a hierarchical type system.

From the point of view of network extraction, *redirect nodes* and *links* which manifest transitive and, thus, mediate links of content-based units are of special interest. An article node v may be linked, for example, with a redirect node r which in turn redirects to an article w. In this case, the document network contains two edges (v, r), (r, w) which have to be resolved to a single edge (v, w) if redirects are to be excluded in accordance with what the MediaWiki system does when processing them. That is, a user, when clicking on the corresponding lexical or phrasal anchor of the link (v, r) does not enter r, but is redirected to the node w. Such redirects may include more than one redirect node r.

A further peculiarity of Wikipedia are portals which introduce a further level of structuring above the level of wiki documents and below the level of the wiki website as a whole. Entry pages of portals are identified by means of the corresponding namespace prefix. Other ways of typing nodes in wiki-based networks, which are not (necessarily) reflected by a namespace prefix, operate on user or entry page statistics. This is exemplified by stubs, that is, Wikipedia entries which are too short to be a useful encyclopedia article.

Complex network and other statistical analyses of wiki-based networks are performed, amongst others, by Voss (2005), Capocci et al. (2006), Zlatic et al. (2006) and – in comparison to other text and document networks – by Mehler (2006).

Tab. 19.7: The system of node and link types and their frequencies by example of the German release of Wikipedia (download in November 14, 2005)

Type	Frequency	Type	Frequency
Pages total	796,454	Links total	17,814,539
Article	303,999	Interlink	12,818,378
Redirect Node	190,193	Category Link	1,415,295
Talk	115,314	Categorises	704,092
Article Talk	78,224	Categorised by Category	704,092
User Talk	30,924	Associates with	7,111
Image Talk	2,379	Topic of Talk	103,253
Wikipedia Talk	1,380	Talk of Topic	88,095
Category Talk	1,272	Hyponym of	26,704
Template Talk	705	Hyperonym of	26,704
Portal Talk	339	Inter Portal Association	1,796
Mediawiki Talk	64	Broken	2,361,902
Help Talk	27	Outside	1,276,818
Image	97,402	Inter Wiki	789,065
User	32,150	External	487,753
Disambiguation	22,768	Intra	1,175,290
Category	21,999	Kernel	1,153,928
Template	6,794	Across	6,331
Wikipedia	3,435	Up	6,121
Mediawiki	1,575	Reflexive	5,433
Portal	791	Down	3,477
Help	34	Redirect	182,151

Voss (2005) suggests that Lotka's law also characterises authorship in Wikipedia with respect to the distribution of the number of edits ranked by the number of authors which are responsible for the respective number of edits. Voss reports a low exponent $\gamma \approx 0.5$. Further, he considers the distribution of the number of authors ranked by the number of distinct articles they are authors of and also finds a highly skewed distribution (i.e. very many authors have contributed to only one article whereas only a small minority of persons authored very many articles, and there is a smooth transition between these two extreme cases.

Capocci et al. (2006) analyse the topology of the English and of the Portuguese release of Wikipedia in terms of the bow-tie model of Broder et al. (2000) (cf. section 3.5.). They observe that most of the entry pages of Wikipedia belong to its SCC, that is, almost any of its pages can be reached from any other of these pages. Capocci et al. fit a power law to the in-degree and to the out-degree distribution of entry pages (which types of pages were actually considered is not mentioned in the paper). In both cases, fitting is successful with an exponent $2 \leq \gamma^{\text{in,out}} \leq 2.2$. Further, Capocci et al. observe a lack of correlation regarding the in-degree of vertices and the average in-degree of its neighboring vertices; this observation is in accordance with computing assortative mixing in the wiki medium (see below). Finally, Capocci et al. consider a model of network growth based on *directed* graphs. They simulate growth in terms of preferential attachment where the probability of acquiring a new edge is separately computed for incoming and outgoing edges subject to the present in-degree and out-degree of vertices, respectively. This model does not only distinguish the direction of newly added edges, but also whether they link already existing vertices or end at newly added ones. A central conclusion of Capocci et al. is that Wikipedia resembles the WWW in terms of the characteristics they measured.

Zlatic et al. (2006) is the most comprehensive Wikipedia-based network study. They analyse the releases of ten languages (including English, German, Japanese, French and Spanish) by taking different node types into account; cf. Table 19.7. But although Zlatic et al. distinguish *article*, *talk*, *help*, *user*, *category*, *redirect* and *template* pages as well as *images* and *multimedia* resources, they report only on calculations with articles, redirects and templates thereby distinguishing broken and non-broken links. A central aim of their study is to distinguish network characteristics common to all releases from those which select singletons of them. Zlatic et al. fit power laws to the in and out-degree distributions of directed graphs extracted from Wikipedia releases as well as to the degree distributions of their undirected counterparts (see Table 19.4). Further, they fit a power law in order to predict the growth of links between entry pages as a function of the number of those pages and observe approximately a linear increase of the number of links and pages. Zlatic et al. compute the rate of assortative mixing within the different releases, compute their cluster values and estimate the average geodesic distance of their entry pages (see Table 19.4). Interestingly, they observe that clustering in Wikipedia generally decreases with the growth of the network. Generally speaking, the growth dependent variation of network characteristics will be a promising future direction of complex network research where Wikipedia provides a tremendous set of information in support of this kind of research. Zlatic et al. also explore motifs of wiki networks by analogy with those found to be characteristic of the WWW. In spite of this and some other characteristics in support of assuming the resemblance of the and Wikipedia, Zlatic et al. find characteristic differences between these networks, for example, in terms of their reciprocity, that is the non-random existence of reciprocal edges between pairs of vertices (Garlaschelli/Loffredo 2004). Further, they observe − unlike in the WWW − a higher stability of the average geodesic distance and ask whether these and related differences are due to the specific growth dynamics of wiki-based networks or due to the structure of the underlying knowledge system approximated by them. These are just two more questions which are still open for future research.

Another perspective on exploring wiki-based networks is opened by Mehler (2006), who comparatively studies document networks in knowledge, technical, press and WWW-based communication. He analyses three variants of the German release of Wikipedia dependent on the different types of nodes and links taken into account. This ranges from a variant based on article pages and their links only to the whole spectrum of entry pages and their different types of links as distinguished in Table 19.7 (except for broken and external links leading to pages outside the input wiki). Further, Mehler (2006) analyses three wiki networks ofApache.org which belong to the topic of technical communication and, thus, considers wikis of different areas of WWW-based communication. He computes the cluster coefficients and average geodesic distances of input networks, fits power laws to the degree distributions of undirected graphs extracted from them and calculates the rate of assortative mixing within these networks (see Table 19.4). As in the case of the studies summarised above, Mehler (2006) observes a latent tendency towards disassortative mixing in wiki networks, and they can definitely be regarded as small worlds according to the WS model. Note that Mehler (2006) reports on very small values of the exponent γ of the BA model (i.e. $\gamma \approx 0.5$) in the case of Wikipedia and even smaller values in the case of the wikis of technical communication. These differences are clarified by hinting at the choice of k_{min} and k_{max} as the degrees *from which* and *up to which* power laws are fitted. In Mehler (2006), the whole degree distributions are fitted while Zlatic et al. use a higher value of k_{min} and a lower value of k_{max} – Capocci et al. (2006) do not report on the choice of k_{min} and k_{max}.

A central outcome of Mehler's study is that the different areas of document networking show striking differences with respect to their network characteristics (except in their average geodesic distances). This result supports the view that the small-world property and related characteristics of complex document networks vary significantly with the underlying genre or area of communication and that these characteristics denote non-categorical, graded network properties.

4. Conclusion and future perspectives

This article surveyed approaches to text and document networks which mostly refer to small-world models. The article reviewed studies in support of the view that these networks share topological characteristics, so that one may speak of principles of the collaborative formation of intertextual structures in corpora of natural language texts. In spite of these commonalities, the article also hinted at the genre-sensitivity of these principles. In this sense, the small-world property, for example, cannot be attributed categorically, but varies with the underlying text and document genre which, thus, is not only mirrored on the level of *text internal characteristics* but also by *principles of intertextual networking*.

These and related findings raise the question of the corpus linguistic importance of complex network analysis. From a corpus linguistic point of view, the small-world property of text networks can be seen as an argument in favor of representative samples as input to computing, for example, cognitively plausible models of lexical association. Although it is known from quantitative linguistics that such samples are hardly possible – cf., for example, Orlov (1982) – the small-world property can at least be utilised as a necessary condition which has to be fulfilled by a corpus in order to be judged as a reliable data base for computing lexical memory models showing the small-world property on their own. Moreover, knowing that a given corpus has the small-world property, one can infer a certain rate of change of a given variable (e.g. topic) when following intertextual relations. That is, the notion of *intertextual neighborhood* relevant to studying a given text, as claimed by Stubbs (2001), can be approached in this framework.

From this perspective, at least three challenging research questions can be identified as an object of future research in this field:

- What do more realistic, linguistically grounded network models look like which do not only account for the genre-sensitivity of intertextuality in more detail, but can be used to simulate the generation of such networks in order to investigate network states which, for the time being, are empirically unobservable (e.g. because of their complexity or the impossibility of parameter variation in the case of real networks)?
- What are the interrelationships of quantitative principles on the level of texts (e.g. vocabulary growth) and those restricting their networking? Is there a unifying, so to

speak Zipfian theory which grasps principles of intra- *and* intertextual structure formation?
- What do text-technological representation formats and their operations, which are expressive enough to manage document networks of the complexity mentioned above and to compute related network characteristics, look like?

5. Acknowledgement

The author thanks Vinko Zlatic (Rudjer Boskovic Institute, Theoretical Physics Division), Ramon Ferrer i Cancho (Universitat de Barcelona), the editors of this handbook as well as the anonymous reviewers of this article for their careful proof-readings and fruitful hints.

6. Literature

Adamic, L. A. (1999), The Small World of Web. In: Abiteboul, S./Vercoustre, A.-M. (eds.), *Research and Advanced Technology for Digital Libraries*. Berlin: Springer, 443–452.

Adamic, L. A. (2000), *Zipf, Power-law, Pareto – a Ranking Tutorial*. Available at: http://www.hpl.hp.com/research/idl/papers/ranking/ranking.html.

Adamic, L. A./Huberman, B. A. (2001), The Web's Hidden Order. In: *Communications of the ACM* 44(9), 55–59.

Adar, E./Zhang, L./Adamic, L. A./Lukose, R. M. (2004), Implicit Structure and the Dynamics of Blogspace. In: *Proceedings of the Workshop on the Weblogging Ecosystem at the 13th International Conference on World Wide Web (WWW'04)*. New York, NY. Available at: http://www.blogpulse.com/papers/www2004adar.pdf.

Agrawal, R./Rajagopalan, S./Srikant, R./Xu, Y. (2003), Mining Newsgroups Using Networks Arising from Social Behavior. In: *Proceedings of the 12th International Conference on World Wide Web (WWW'03)*. New York: ACM Press, 529–535.

Ajiferuke, I./Wolfram, D. (2004), Modelling the Characteristics of Web Page Outlinks. In: *Scientometrics* 59(1), 43–62.

Albert, R./Barabási, A.-L. (2002), Statistical Mechanics of Complex Networks. In: *Reviews of Modern Physics 74*, 47.

Albert, R./Jeong, H./Barabási, A.-L. (1999), Diameter of the World Wide Web. In: *Nature* 401, 130–131.

Altmann, G. (1988), *Wiederholungen in Texten*. Bochum: Brockmeyer.

Baayen, R. H. (2001), *Word Frequency Distributions*. Dordrecht: Kluwer.

Bächle, M. (2006), Social Software. In: *Informatik Spektrum* 29(2), 121–124.

Baeza-Yates, R./Ribeiro-Neto, B. (eds.) (1999), *Modern Information Retrieval*. Harlow: Addison-Wesley.

Baldi, P./Frasconi, P./Smyth, P. (2003), *Modeling the Internet and the Web*. Chichester: Wiley.

Bar-Ilan, J. (1997), The "Mad Cow Disease", Usenet Newsgroups and Bibliometric Laws. In: *Scientometrics* 39(1), 29–55.

Bar-Ilan, J. (2001), Data Collection Methods on the Web for Infometric Purposes – a Review and Analysis. In: *Scientometrics* 50(1), 7–32.

Bar-Ilan, J./Echermane, A. (2005), The Anthrax Scare and the Web: A Content Analysis of Web Pages Linking to Resources on Anthrax. In: *Scientometrics* 63(3), 443–462.

Barabási, A.-L./Albert, R. (1999), Emergence of Scaling in Random Networks. In: *Science* 286, 509–512.

Barabási, A.-L./Albert, R./Jeong, H. (1999), Scale-free Characteristics of Random Networks: The Topology of the World Wide Web. In: *Physica A* 281, 69–77.

Barabási, A.-L./Albert, R./Jeong, H./Bianconi, G. (2000), Power-law Distribution of the World Wide Web. Response to Adamic & Huberman (2000). In: *Science*, 287(12), 2115a.

Barabási, A.-L./Oltvai, Z. N. (2004), Network Biology: Understanding the Cell's Functional Organization. Nature Reviews. In: *Genetics* 5(2), 101 – 113.

Baroni, M./Bernardini, S. (2004), BootCaT: Bootstrapping Corpora and Terms from the Web. In: *Proceedings of LREC 2004.* Lisbon: ELDA, 1313–1316.

Bense, M. (1998), *Ausgewählte Schriften. Band 3. Ästhetik und Texttheorie.* Stuttgart: Metzler.

Biber, D. (1995), *Dimensions of Register Variation: A Cross-linguistic Comparison.* Cambridge: Cambridge University Press.

Björneborn, L. (2004), *Small-world Link Structures across an Academic Web Space: A Library and Information Science Approach.* PhD thesis, Royal School of Library and Information Science, Department of Information Studies, Denmark.

Björneborn, L./Ingwersen, P. (2001), Perspectives of Webometrics. In: *Scientometrics* 50(1), 65–82.

Björneborn, L./Ingwersen, P. (2004), Towards a Basic Framework for Webometrics. In: *Journal of the American Society for Information Science and Technology* 55(14), 1216–1227.

Bock, H. H. (1994), Classification and Clustering: Problems for the Future. In: Diday, E./Lechevallier, Y./Schader, M./Bertrand, P./Burtschy, B. (eds.), *New Approaches in Classification and Data Analysis.* Berlin: Springer, 3–24.

Bollobás, B. (1985), *Random Graphs.* London: Academic Press.

Bollobás, B./Riordan, O. M. (2003), Mathematical Results on Scale-free Random Graphs. In: Bornholdt, S./Schuster, H. G. (eds.), *Handbook of Graphs and Networks. From the Genome to the Internet.* Weinheim: Wiley-VCH, 1–34.

Bordag, S./Heyer, G./Quasthoff, U. (2003), Small Worlds of Concepts and Other Principles of Semantic Search. In: Unger, H./Böhme, T. (eds.), *Innovative Internet Computing Systems Second International Workshop (IICS '03).* Berlin: Springer, 10–19.

Bornholdt, S./Schuster, H. G. (2003), *Handbook of Graphs and Networks. From the Genome to the Internet.* Weinheim: Wiley-VCH.

Botafogo, R. A./Rivlin, E./Shneiderman, B. (1992), Structural Analysis of Hypertexts: Identifying Hierarchies and Useful Metrics. In: *ACM Transactions on Information Systems* 10(2), 142–180.

Brainerd, B. (1977), Graphs, Topology and Text. In: *Poetics* 1(14), 1–14.

Brinker, K. (1991), Aspekte der Textlinguistik. Zur Einführung. In: Brinker, K. (ed.), *Aspekte der Textlinguistik.* Hildesheim: Georg Olms, 7–17.

Broder, A./Kumar, R./Maghoul, F./Raghavan, P./Rajagopalan, S./Stata, R./Tomkins, A./Wiener, J. (2000), Graph Structure in the Web. In: *Computer Networks* 33, 309–320.

Bronstein, I. N./Semendjajew, K. A./Musiol, G./Mühlig, H. (1999), *Taschenbuch der Mathematik.* Frankfurt am Main: Harri Deutsch.

Brown, C. (2004), The Matthew Effect of the *Annual Reviews* Series and the Flow of Scientific Communication through the World Wide Web. In: *Scientometrics* 60(1), 25 – 30.

Capocci, A./Servedio, V. D. P./Colaiori, F./Buriol, L. S./Donato, D./Leonardi, S./Caldarelli, G. (2006), *Preferential Attachment in the Growth of Social Networks: The Case of Wikipedia.* Available at: http://www.citebase.org/cgi-bin/citations?id= oai:arXiv.org:physics/0602026.

Chakrabarti, S. (2002), *Mining the Web: Discovering Knowledge from Hypertext Data.* San Francisco: Morgan Kaufmann.

Chakrabarti, S./Joshi, M./Punera, K./Pennock, D. M. (2002), The Structure of Broad Topics on the Web. In: *Proceedings of the 11th International World Wide Web Conference.* New York: ACM Press, 251–262.

Chen, C. (1999), Visualising Semantic Spaces and Author Co-citation Networks in Digital Libraries. In: *Information Processing and Management* 35, 401–420.

Chen, C./Czerwinski, M. (1998), From Latent Semantics to Spatial Hypertext: An Integrated Approach. In: Grønbæk, K./Mylonas, E./Shipman, F. M. (eds.), *Proceedings of the 9th ACM Conference on Hypertext and Hypermedia*. New York: ACM, 77–86.
Craven, M., DiPasquo, D./Freitag, D., McCallum, A. K./Mitchell, T. M./Nigam, K./Slattery, S. (2000), Learning to Construct Knowledge Bases from the World Wide Web. In: *Artificial Intelligence*, 118(1–2), 69–113.
de Beaugrande, R. A. (1980), *Text, Discourse, and Process. Toward a Multidisciplinary Science of Texts*. (Advances in Discourse Processes 4.) Norwood: Ablex.
de Beaugrande, R. A. (1997), *New Foundations for a Science of Text and Discourse: Cognition, Communication, and the Freedom of Access to Knowledge and Society*. Norwood: Ablex.
de Solla Price, D. J. (1965), Networks of Scientific Papers. In: *Science* 149(3683), 510–515.
Diestel, R. (2005), *Graph Theory*. Heidelberg: Springer.
Dillon, A./Gushrowski, B. A. (2000), Genres and the WEB: Is the Personal Home Page the First Uniquely Digital Genre? In: *Journal of the American Society of Information Science* 51(2), 202–205.
Dorogovtsev, S. N./Mendes, J. F. F. (2001), Language as an Evolving Word Web. In: *Proceedings of the Royal Society of London. Series B, Biological Sciences* 268(1485), 2603–2606.
Ebersbach, A./Glaser, M./Heigl, R. (2005), *WikiTools*. Berlin: Springer.
Egghe, L./Rousseau, R. (2003), A Measure for the Cohesion of Weighted Networks. In: *Journal of the American Society for Information Science and Technology* 54(3), 193–202.
Eiron, N./McCurley, K. S. (2003), Untangling Compound Documents on the Web. In: *Proceedings of the 14th ACM conference on Hypertext and Hypermedia*. Nottingham, UK, 85–94.
Faba-Pérez, C./Guerrero-Bote, V. P./Moya-Anegón, F. D. (2003), "Sitation" Distributions and Bradford's Law in a Closed Web Space. In: *Journal of Documentation* 59(5), 558–580.
Fairclough, N. (1992), *Discourse and Social Change*. Cambridge: Polity Press.
Fang, Y./Rousseau, R. (2001), Lattices in Citation Networks: An Investigation into the Structure of Citation Graphs. In: *Scientometrics* 50(2), 273–287.
Ferrer i Cancho, R./Riordan, O./Bollobás, B. (2005), The Consequences of Zipf s Law for Syntax and Symbolic Reference. In: *Proceedings of the Royal Society* 272, 561–565.
Ferrer i Cancho, R./Solé, R. V. (2001), The Small-world of Human Language. In: *Proceedings of the Royal Society of London. Series B, Biological Sciences* 268(1482), 2261–2265.
Ferrer i Cancho, R./Solé, R. V./Köhler, R. (2004), Patterns in Syntactic Dependency-networks. In: *Physical Review* E(69), 051915.
Firth, D./Lawrence, C. (2003), Genre Analysis in Information Systems Research. In: *Journal of Information Technology Theory and Application* 5(3), 63–87.
Fisher, D. (2003), Studying Social Information Spaces. In: Lueg/Fisher 2003, 3–19.
Fix, U. (2000), Aspekte der Intertextualität. In: Brinker, K./Antos, G./Heinemann, W./Sager, S. F. (eds.), *Text- und Gesprächslinguistik / Linguistics of Text and Conversation – Ein internationales Handbuch zeitgenössischer Forschung*, volume 1. Berlin/New York: De Gruyter, 449–457.
Flake, G./Lawrence, S./Giles, C. L. (2000), Efficient Identification of Web Communities. In: *Sixth ACM SIGKDD International Conference on Knowledge Discovery and Data Mining*. Boston, MA, 150–160.
Garfield, E. (1963), Citation Indexes in Sociological and Historical Research. In: *American Documentation* 14(4), 289–291.
Garfield, E. (1994), Scientography: Mapping the Tracks of Science. In: *Current Contents: Social & Behavioural Sciences* 7(45), 5–10.
Garlaschelli, D./Loffredo, M. I. (2004), Patterns of Link Reciprocity in Directed Networks. In: *Physical Review Letters* 93, 268701.
Gibson, D./Kleinberg, J./Raghavan, P. (1998), Inferring Web Communities from Link Topology. In: *Proceedings of the 9th ACM Conference on Hypertext and Hypermedia: Links, Objects, Time and Space – Structure in Hypermedia Systems*. Pittsburgh, PA, 225–234.

Giles, C. L./Bollacker, K./Lawrence, S. (1998), CiteSeer: An Automatic Citation Indexing System. In: Witten, I./Akscyn, R./Shipman III, F. M. (eds.), *Digital Libraries 98 – The Third ACM Conference on Digital Libraries*. Pittsburgh, PA: ACM Press, 89–98.

Gill, K. E. (2004), How Can we Measure the Influence of the Blogosphere? In: *Proceedings of the Workshop on the Weblogging Ecosystem at the 13th International Conference on World Wide Web (WWW'04)*. New York, NY. Available at: http://faculty.washington.edu/kegill/pub/www2004_blogosphere_gill. pdf.

Gill, K. E. (2005), Blogging, RSS and the Information Landscape: A Look at Online News. In: *Proceedings of the 2nd Annual Workshop on the Weblogging Ecosystem: Aggregation, Analysis and Dynamics at the 14th International Conference on World Wide Web (WWW'05)*. Chiba, Japan. Available at: http://www.blogpulse.com/papers/2005/gill.pdf.

Glance, N./Hurst, M./Tomokiyo, T. (2004), BlogPulse: Automated Trend Discovery for Weblogs. In: *Proceedings of the 2nd Annual Workshop on the Weblogging Ecosystem: Aggregation, Analysis and Dynamics at the 14th International Conference on World Wide Web (WWW'05)*. Chiba, Japan. Available at: http://www.blogpulse.com/papers/www2004glance.pdf.

Glänzel, W./Czerwon, H.-J. (1996), A New Methodological Approach to Bibliographic Coupling and its Application to the National, Regional and Institutional Level. In: *Scientometrics* 37(2), 195 221.

Glenisson, P./Glänzel, W./Persson, O. (2005), Combining Full-text Analysis and Bibliometric Indicators. A Pilot Study. In: *Scientometrics* 63(1), 163–180.

Gruhl, D./Guha, R./Liben-Nowell, D./Tomkins, A. (2004), Information Diffusion through Blogspace. In: *Proceedings of the 13th International Conference on World Wide Web (WWW'04)*. New York: ACM Press, 491–501.

Halliday, M. A. K. (1966), Lexis as a Linguistic Level. In: Bazell, C. E./Catford, J./Halliday, M. A. K./Robins, R. (eds.), *In Memory of J. R. Firth*. London: Longman, 148–162.

Halliday, M. A. K./Hasan, R. (1976), *Cohesion in English*. London: Longman.

Harnad, S./Carr, L. (2000), Integrating, Navigating and Analyzing Eprint Archives through Open Citation Linking (the OpCit Project). In: *Current Science* 79(5), 629–638.

Heinemann, W. (1997), Zur Eingrenzung des Intertextualitätsbegriffs aus textlinguistischer Sicht. In: Klein, J./Fix, U. (eds.), *Textbeziehungen: linguistische und liter aturwissenschaftliche Beiträge zur Intertextualität*. Tübingen: Stauffenburg, 21–37.

Hernandez-Borges, A. A./Macias, P./Torres, A. (1998), Are Medical Mailing Lists Reliable Sources of Professional Advice? In: *Medical Informatics* 23(3), 231–236.

Herring, S. C./Kouper, I./Paolillo, J. C./Scheidt, L. A./Tyworth, M./Welsch, P./Wright, E./Yu, N. (2005), Conversations in the Blogosphere: An Analysis "from the Bottom Up". In: *Proceedings of the 38th Annual Hawaii International Conference on System Sciences (HICSS'05)*. Los Alamitos: IEEE Press. Available at: http://www.blogninja.com/hicss05.blogconv.pdf.

Herring, S. C./Scheidt, L. A./Bonus, S./Wright, E. (2004), Bridging the Gap: A Genre Analysis of Weblogs. In: *Proceedings of the 37th Annual Hawaii International Conference on System Sciences (HICSS'04)*. Big Island, HI. Available at: http://www.ics.uci.edu/~jpd/classes/ics234cw04/herring.pdf.

Heyer, G./Quasthoff, U./Wittig, T. (2006), *Text Mining: Wissensrohstoff Text*. Herdecke: W3L.

Hockey, S. (2000), *Electronic Texts in the Humanities*. Oxford: Oxford University Press.

Hoey, M. (1991), *Patterns of Lexis in Text*. Oxford: Oxford University Press.

Hoey, M. (1995), The Lexical Nature of Intertextuality: A Preliminary Study. In: Wårvik, B./Tanskanen, S.-K./Hiltunen, R. (eds.), *Organization in Discourse. Proceedings from the Turku Conference*. Turku: University of Turku, 73–94.

Holanda, A. de J./Torres Pisa, I./Kinouchi, O./Souto Martinez, A./Seron Ruiz, E. E. (2003), Basic Word Statistics for Information Retrieval: Thesaurus as a Complex Network. In: *Anais XVI Brazilian Symposium on Computer Graphics and Image Processing*. Sao Carlos, Brazil. Available at: http://www.nilc.icmc.usp.br/til2003/oral/holanda15.pdf.

Hollan, J./Hutchins, E./Kirsh, D. (2000), Distributed Cognition: Toward a New Foundation for Human-computer Interaction Research. In: *ACM Transactions on Computer-Human Interaction* 7(2), 174–196.
Holloway, T./Božičević, M./Börner, K. (2005), Analyzing and Visualizing the Semantic Coverage of Wikipedia and its Authors. Available at: http://tw.arxiv.org/abs/cs.IR/0512085.
Holthuis, S. (1993), *Intertextualität. Aspekte einer rezeptionsorientierten Konzeption.* Tübingen: Stauffenburg.
Hummon, N. P./Doreian, P. (1989), Connectivity in a Citation Network: The Development of DNA Theory. In: *Social Networks* 11, 39–63.
Itzkovitz, S./Milo, R./Kashtan, N./Ziv, G./Alon, U. (2003), Subgraphs in Random Networks. In: *Physical Review E* 68, 026127.
Jakobs, E.-M. (1999), *Textvernetzung in den Wissenschaften.* Tübingen: Niemeyer.
Kautz, H./Selman, B./Shah, M. (1997), Referral Web: Combining Social Networks and Collaborative Filtering. In: *Communications of the ACM* 40(3), 63–65.
Keller, F./Lapata, M. (2003), Using the Web to Obtain Frequencies for Unseen Bigrams. In: *Computational Linguistics* 29(3), 459–484.
Kessler, M. M. (1963), Bibliographic Coupling between Scientific Papers. In: *American Documentation* 14, 10–25.
Kilgarriff, A./Grefenstette, G. (2003), Introduction to the Special Issue on the Web as Corpus. In: *Computational Linguistics* 29(3), 333–347.
Kinouchi, O./Martinez, A./Lima, G./Lourenço, G./Risau-Gusman, S. (2002), Deterministic Walks in Random Networks: An Application to Thesaurus Graphs. In: *Physica A* 315, 665–676.
Kintsch, W. (1988), The Role of Knowledge in Discourse Comprehension: A Construction-integration Model. In: *Psychological Review* 95(2), 163–182.
Kleinberg, J. M. (1999), Authoritative Sources in a Hyperlinked Environment. In: *Journal of the ACM* 46(5), 604–632.
Kleinberg, J. M./Kumar, R./Raghavan, P./Rajagopalan, S./Tomkins, A. S. (1999), The Web as a Graph: Measurements, Models, and Methods. In: Asano, T./Imai, H./Lee, D. T./Nakano, S./Tokuyama, T. (eds.), *Computing and Combinatorics: 5th Annual International Conference (COCOON'99), Tokyo, Japan, July 1999.* Berlin/New York: Springer, 1–18.
Kosala, R./Blockeel, H. (2000), Web Mining Research: A Survey. *SIGKDD Explorations: Newsletter of the Special Interest Group (SIG) on Knowledge Discovery & Data Mining* 2(1), 1–15.
Kot, M./Silverman, E./Berg, C. A. (2003), Zipf's Law and the Diversity of Biology Newsgroups. In: *Scientometrics* 56(2), 247–257.
Krishnamurthy, S. (2002), The Multidimensionality of Blog Conversations: The Virtual Enactment of September 11. Paper presented at *Internet Research 3.0.* Maastricht, Holland.
Kuhlen, R. (1991), *Hypertext: Ein nichtlineares Medium zwischen Buch und Wissensbank.* Berlin: Springer.
Kuhlen, R. (2004), Kollaboratives Schreiben. In: Bieber, C./Leggewie, C. (eds.), *Interaktivität – ein transdisziplinärer Schlüsselbegriff.* Frankfurt: Campus-Verlag, 216–239.
Kumar, R./Novak, J./Raghavan, P./Tomkins, A. (2003), On the Bursty Evolution of Blogspace. In: *Proceedings of the 12th International Conference on World Wide Web (WWW'03).* New York: ACM Press, 568–576.
Kumar, R./Novak, J./Raghavan, P./Tomkins, A. (2004), Structure and Evolution of Blogspace. *Communications of the ACM* 47(12), 35–39.
Kuperman, V (2005), Productivity in the Internet Mailing Lists: A Bibliometric Analysis. In: *Journal of the American Society for Information Science and Technology* 57(1), 51–59.
Landauer, T. K./Dumais, S. T. (1997), A Solution to Plato's Problem: The Latent Semantic Analysis Theory of Acquisition, Induction, and Representation of Knowledge. In: *Psychological Review* 104(2), 211–240.
Larson, R. R. (1996), Bibliometrics of the World-wide Web: An Exploratory Analysis of the Intellectual Structure of Cyberspace. In: *Proceedings of the Annual Meeting of the American Society for Information Science.* Baltimore, MD, 71–78.

Leicht, E. A./Holme, P./Newman, M. E. J. (2006), Vertex Similarity in Networks. In: *Physical Review E 73*, 026120.

Leopold, E. (2005), On Semantic Spaces. In: *LDVForum* 20(1), 63–86.

Leskovec, J./Kleinberg, J./Faloutsos, C. (2005), Graphs over Time: Densification Laws, Shrinking Diameters and Possible Explanations. In: *KDD '05: Proceeding of the Eleventh ACM SIGKDD International Conference on Knowledge Discovery in Data Mining*. New York: ACM Press, 177–187.

Leydesdorff, L. (2001), *The Challenge of Scientometrics. The Development, Measurement, and Self-organization of Scientific Communications*. Parkland, FL: Universal Publishers.

Li, W-S./Candan, K. S./Vu, Q./Agrawal, D. (2002), Query Relaxation by Structure and Semantics for Retrieval of Logical Web Documents. In: *IEEE Transactions on Knowledge and Data Engineering* 14(4), 768–791.

Li, W-S./Kolak, O./Vu, Q./Takano, H. (2000), Defining Logical Domains in a Web Site. In: *Proceedings of the 11th ACM on Hypertext and Hypermedia*. San Antonio, TX, 123–132.

Li, X./Thelwall, M./Wilkinson, D./Musgrove, P. (2005a), National and International University Departmental Web Site Interlinking. Part 1: Validation of Departmental Link Analysis. In: *Scientometrics* 64(2), 151–185.

Li, X./Thelwall, M./Wilkinson, D./Musgrove, P. (2005b), National and International University Departmental Web Site Interlinking. Part 2: Link Patterns. In: *Scientometrics* 64(2), 187–208.

Lin, J./Halavais, A. (2004), Mapping the Blogosphere in America. In: *Proceedings of the Workshop on the Weblogging Ecosystem at the 13th International Conference on World Wide Web (WWW '04)*. New York, NY. Available at: http://www.blogpulse.com/papers/www2004linhalavais.pdf.

Lueg, C./Fisher, D. (2003), *From Usenet to Co Webs. Interacting with Social Information Spaces*. London: Springer.

Manning, C. D./Schütze, H. (1999), *Foundations of Statistical Natural Language Processing*. Cambridge, MA: MIT Press.

Martin, J. R. (1992), *English Text. System and Structure*. Philadelphia: John Benjamins.

Mehler, A. (2005), Zur textlinguistischen Fundierung der Text- und Korpuskonversion. In: *Sprache und Datenverarbeitung* 1, 29–53.

Mehler, A. (2006), Text Linkage in the Wiki Medium – a Comparative Study. In: Karlgren, J. (ed.), *Proceedings of the EACL Workshop on New Text – Wikis and Blogs and Other Dynamic Text Sources, April 3–7, 2006*. Trento, Italy, 1–8.

Mehler, A. (2007), Compositionality in Quantitative Semantics. A Theoretical Perspective on Text Mining. In: Mehler, A./Köhler, R. (eds.), *Aspects of Automatic Text Analysis, Studies in Fuzziness and Soft Computing*. Berlin/New York: Springer, 139–167.

Mehler, A./Gleim, R. (2005), Polymorphism in Generic Web Units. A Corpus Linguistic Study. In: *Proceedings of Corpus Linguistics '05, July 14–17, 2005*. (Corpus Linguistics Conference Series 1(1).) Birmingham, UK. Available at: http://www.corpus.bham.ac.uk/PCLC/Alexander_Mehler_and_Ruediger_Gleim_Corpus_Linguistics_2005.pdf.

Mehler, A./Gleim, R. (2006), The Net for the Graphs – towards Webgenre Representation for Corpus Linguistic Studies. In: Baroni, M./Bernardini, S. (eds.), *WaCky! Working Papers on the Web as Corpus*. Bologna: Gedit, 191–224.

Mehler, A./Wolff, C. (eds.) (2005), *Text Mining*. Volume 20(1) of *LDV Forum*.

Meinel, C./Sack, H. (2004), *WWW*. Berlin: Springer.

Melnikov, O./Sarvanov, V./Tyshkevich, R./Yemelichev, V (1998), *Exercises in Graph Theory*. Dordrecht: Kluwer.

Menczer, F. (2004), Lexical and Semantic Clustering by Web Links. In: *Journal of the American Society for Information Science and Technology* 55(14), 1261–1269.

Mika, P. (2005), Ontologies are us: A Unified Model of Social Networks and Semantics. In: *Proceedings of the 4th International Semantic Web Conference (ISWC 2005)*. (LNCS 3729.) Berlin/ Heidelberg: Springer, 1–18.

Milgram, S. (1967), The Small-world Problem. In: *Psychology Today* 2, 60–67.

Miller, G. A./Beckwith, R./Fellbaum, C./Gross, D./Miller, K. J. (1990), Introduction to WordNet: An On-line Lexical Database. In: *International Journal of Lexicography* 3(4), 235−244.
Milo, R./Shen-Orr, S./Itzkovitz, S./Kashtan, N./Alon, D. C. U. (2002), Network Motifs: Simple Building Blocks of Complex Networks. In: *Science* 298(5594), 824−827.
Motter, A. E./de Moura, A. P. S./Lai, Y-C./Dasgupta, P. (2002), Topology of the Conceptual Network of Language. In: *Physical Review E* 65, 065102.
Mukherjea, S. (2000), Organizing Topic-specific Web Information. In: *Proceedings of the 11th ACM Conference on Hypertext and Hypermedia*. San Antonio, TX, 133−141.
Nardi, B. A./Schiano, D. J./Gumbrecht, M./Swartz, L. (2004), Why we Blog. In: *Communications of the ACM* 47(12), 41−46.
Newman, M. E. J. (2000), Models of the Small World. In: *Journal of Statistical Physics* 101, 819−841.
Newman, M. E. J. (2002), Assortative Mixing in Networks. In: *Physical Review Letters* 89(20), 208701.
Newman, M. E. J. (2003a), Mixing Patterns in Networks. In: *Physical Review E* 67, 026126.
Newman, M. E. J. (2003b), The Structure and Function of Complex Networks. In: *SIAM Review* 45, 167−256.
Newman, M. E. J. (2005), Power Laws, Pareto Distributions and Zipf's Law. In: *Contemporary Physics* 46, 323−351.
Newman, M. E. J./Park, J. (2003), Why Social Networks are Different from Other Types of Networks. In: *Physical Review E* 68, 036122.
Newman, M. E. J./Watts, D. J./Strogatz, S. H. (2002), Random Graph Models of Social Networks. In: *Proceedings of the National Academy of Sciences of the United States of America* 99(1), 2566−2572.
O'Reilly, T. (2005), *What is Web 2.0? Design Patterns and Business Models for the Next Generation of Software*. Available at: http://www.oreillynet.com/pub/a/oreilly/tim/news/2005/09/30/what-is-web-20.html.
Orlov, J. K. (1982), Dynamik der Häufigkeitsstrukturen. In: Orlov, J. K./Boroda, M. G./Nadarejšvili, I. S. (eds.), *Sprache, Text, Kunst. Quantitative Analysen*. Bochum: Brockmeyer, 82−117.
Otte, E./Rousseau, R. (2002), Social Network Analysis: A Powerful Strategy, Also for the Information Sciences. In: *Journal of Information Science* 28(6), 441−454.
Park, H. W. (2003), Hyperlink Network Analysis: A New Method for the Study of Social Structure on the Web. In: *Connections* 25(1), 49−61.
Pennock, D. M./Flake, G. W./Lawrence, S./Glover, E. J./Giles, C. L. (2002), Winners don't Take All: Characterizing the Competition for Links on the Web. In: *Proceedings of the National Academy of Sciences* 99(8), 5207−5211.
Pinski, G./Narin, F. (1976), Citation Influence for Journal Aggregates of Scientific Publications: Theory, with Application to the Literature of Physics. In: *Information Processing and Management* 12, 297−312.
Polanyi, L. (1988), A Formal Model of Discourse Structure. In: *Journal of Pragmatics* 12, 601−638.
Prime, C./Bassecoulard, E./Zitt, M. (2002), Co-citations and Co-sitations: A Cautionary View on an Analogy. In: *Scientometrics* 54(2), 291−308.
Raible, W. (1995), Arten des Kommentierens − Arten der Sinnbildung − Arten des Verstehens. Spielarten der generischen Intertextualität. In: Assmann, J./Gladigow, B. (eds.), *Text und Kommentar*. München: Fink, 51−73.
Rapoport, A. (1953), Spread of Information through a Population with Sociostructural Basis: I. Assumption of Transitivity. In: *Bulletin of Mathematical Biophysics* 15, 523−543.
Rapoport, A. (1982), Zipf's Law Re-visited. In: Guiter, H./Arapov, M. V. (eds.), *Studies on Zipf's Law*. Bochum: Brockmeyer, 1−28.
Ravasz, E./Barabási, A.-L. (2003), Hierarchical Organization in Complex Networks. In: *Physical Review E* 67, 026112.

Ravasz, E./Somera, A. L./Mongru, D. A./Oltvai, Z. N./Barabási, A.-L. (2002), Hierarchical Organization of Modularity in Metabolic Networks. In: *Science* 297, 1551–1555.
Ravichandra Rao, I. K. (1996), Methodological and Conceptual Questions of Bibliometric Standards. In: *Scientometrics* 35(2), 265–270.
Redner, S. (1998), How Popular is your Paper? an Empirical Study of the Citation Distribution. In: *European Physical Journal* B(4), 131–134.
Rehm, G. (2002), Towards Automatic Web Genre Identification – a Corpus-based Approach in the Domain of Academia by Example of the Academic's Personal Homepage. In: *Proceedings of the Hawaii International Conference on System Sciences*. Big Island, HI, 101. Available at: http://georg-re.hm/pdf/Rehm-HICSS35.pdf.
Resnik, P./Smith, N. A. (2003), The Web as a Parallel Corpus. In: *Computational Linguistics* 29(3), 349–380.
Rousseau, B./Rousseau, R. (2000), LOTKA: A Program to Fit a Power Law Distribution to Observed Frequency Data. In: *Cybermetrics* 4(1), paper 4. Available at: http://www.cindoc.csic.es/cybermetrics/articles/v4i 1p4.pdf.
Rousseau, R. (1997), Sitations: An Exploratory Study. In: *Cybermetrics* 1(1), paper 1. Available at: http://www.cindoc.csic.es/cybermetrics/articles/v1i1p1.pdf.
Santamaría, C./Gonzalo, J./Verdejo, F. (2003), Automatic Association of Web Directories to Word Senses. In: *Computational Linguistics* 29(3), 485–502.
Schenker, A./Bunke, H./Last, M./Kandel, A. (2005), *Graph-theoretic Techniques for Web Content Mining*. New Jersey/London: World Scientific.
Schmidt, J./Schönberger, K./Stegbauer, C. (2005), Erkundungen von Weblog-Nutzungen. Anmerkungen zum Stand der Forschung. In: *kommunikation@gesellschaft*, 6.
Schummer, J. (2004), Multidisciplinarity, Interdisciplinarity, and Patterns of Research Collaboration in Nanoscience and Nanotechnology. In: *Scientometrics* 59(3), 425–465.
Seglen, P. O. (1992), The Skewness of Science. In: *Journal of the American Society for Information Science (JASIS)* 43(9), 628–638.
Sengupta, I. N./Kumari, L. (1991), Bibliometric Analysis of AIDS Literature. In: *Scientometrics* 20(1), 297–315.
Sigman, M./Cecchi, G. A. (2002), Global Organization of the Wordnet Lexicon. In: *Proceedings of the National Academy of Sciences* 99(3), 1742–1747.
Sigogneau, A. (2000), An Analysis of Document Types Published in Journals Related to Physics: Proceeding Papers Recorded in the Science Citation Index Database. In: *Scientometrics* 47(3), 589–604.
Simon, H. A. (1955), On a Class of Skew Distribution Functions. In: *Biometrika* 42, 425–440.
Sinclair, J. (1991), *Corpus, Concordance, Collocation*. Oxford: Oxford University Press.
Small, H. (1973), Co-citation in the Scientific Literature: A New Measure of the Relationship between Two Documents. In: *Journal of the American Society of Information Science* 24, 265–269.
Small, H. (1999), A Passage through Science: Crossing Disciplinary Boundaries. In: *Library Trends* 48(1), 72–108.
Smith, M. A. (2003), Measures and Maps of Usenet. In: Lueg/Fisher 2003, 47–78.
Steyvers, M./Tenenbaum, J. (2005), The Large-scale Structure of Semantic Networks: Statistical Analyses and a Model of Semantic Growth. In: *Cognitive Science* 29(1), 41–78.
Storrer, A. (2002), Coherence in Text and Hypertext. In: *Document Design* 3(2), 156–168.
Strogatz, S. H. (2001), Exploring Complex Networks. In: *Nature* 410, 268–276.
Stubbs, M. (1996), *Text and Corpus Analysis. Computer-assisted Studies of Language and Culture*. Oxford: Blackwell.
Stubbs, M. (2001), *Words and Phrases. Corpus Studies of Lexical Semantics*. Oxford: Blackwell.
Stubbs, M. (2006), Inferring Meaning: Text, Technology and Questions of Induction. In: Mehler, A./Köhler, R. (eds.), *Aspects of Automatic Text Analysis. Part IV – Corpus Linguistic and Text Technological Modeling*. (Studies in Fuzziness and Soft Computing 209.) Berlin: Springer, 233–253.

Tajima, K./Tanaka, K. (1999), New Techniques for the Discovery of Logical Documents in Web. In: *International Symposium on Database Applications in Non-Traditional Environments*. Washington, DC: IEEE, 125–132.

Tang, R./Thelwall, M. (2004), Patterns of National and International Web Inlinks to US Academic Departments: An Analysis of Disciplinary Variations. In: *Scientometrics* 60(3), 475–485.

Thelwall, M./Tang, R. (2003), Disciplinary and Linguistic Considerations for Academic Web Linking: An Exploratory Hyperlink Mediated Study with Mainland China and Taiwan. In: *Scientometrics* 58(1), 155–181.

Thelwall, M./Vaughan, L./Björneborn, L. (2006), Webometrics. In: *Annual Review of Information Science Technology* 6(8), 81–135.

Thelwall, M./Wouters, P. (2005), What's the Deal with the Web/Blogs/the Next Big Technology: A Key Role for Information Science in E-social Science Research? In: *Proceedings of the 5th International Conference on Conceptions of Library and Information Sciences (CoLIS'05)*. Glasgow, UK, 187–199.

Tricas, F./Ruiz, V./Merelo, J. J. (2004), Do we Live in a Small World? Measuring the Spanish-speaking Blogosphere. In: *Blogtalk 2.0, June 5–6, Wien*. Available at: http://www.blogalia.com/pdf/20030506blogtalk.pdf.

Tuldava, J. (1998), *Probleme und Methoden der quantitativ-systemischen Lexikologie*. Trier: Wissenschaftlicher Verlag.

van Dijk, T. A./Kintsch, W. (1983), *Strategies of Discourse Comprehension*. New York: Academic Press.

van Raan, A. F. J. (2004), Sleeping Beauties in Science. In: *Scientometrics* 59(3), 467–472.

van Raan, A. F. J. (2005), Reference-based Publication Networks with Episodic Memories. In: *Scientometrics* 63(3), 549–566.

Ventola, E. (1987), *The Structure of Social Interaction: A Systemic Approach to the Semiotics of Service Encounters*. London: Pinter.

Voss, J. (2005), Measuring Wikipedia. In: *Proceedings of the 10th International Conference of the International Society for Scientometrics and Informetrics*. Stockholm, Sweden, 221–231.

Wasserman, S./Faust, K. (1999), *Social Network Analysis. Methods and Applications*. Cambridge: Cambridge University Press.

Watts, D. J. (1999), *Small Worlds. The Dynamics of Networks between Order and Randomness*. Princeton: Princeton University Press.

Watts, D. J. (2003), *Six Degrees. The Science of a Connected Age*. New York/London: W. W. Norton & Company.

Watts, D. J./Strogatz, S. H. (1998), Collective Dynamics of 'Small-world' Networks. In: *Nature* 393, 440–442.

White, H. D./McCain, K. W. (1989), Bibliometrics. In: *Annual Review of Information Science Technology (ARIST)* 24, 119–165.

Widdows, D./Dorow, B. (2002), A Graph Model for Unsupervised Lexical Acquisition. In: *19th International Conference on Computational Linguistics, August 24–September 1, 2002*. Taipei, Taiwan, 1–7.

Wimmer, G./Altmann, G. (1999a), Review Article: On Vocabulary Richness. In: *Journal of Quantitative Linguistics* 6(1), 1–9.

Wimmer, G./Altmann, G. (1999b), *Thesaurus of Univariate Discrete Probability Distributions*. Essen: Stamm Verlag.

Zelman, A./Leydesdorff, L. (2000), Threaded Email Messages in Self-organization and Science & Technology Studies Oriented Mailing Lists. In: *Scientometrics* 48(3), 361–380.

Zipf, G. K. (1972), *Human Behavior and the Principle of Least Effort. An Introduction to Human Ecology*. New York: Hafner Publishing Company.

Zlatic, V./Božičević, M./Stefancic, H./Domazet, M. (2006), Wikipedias: Collaborative Web-based Encyclopedias as Complex Networks. Available at: http://www.citebase.org/cgi-bin/citations?id=oai:arXiv.org:physics/0602149.

Alexander Mehler, Bielefeld (Germany)

III. Existing corpora

20. Well-known and influential corpora

1. Introduction

As corpus building is an activity that takes times and costs money, readers may wish to use ready-made corpora to carry out their work. However, as a corpus is always designed for a particular purpose, the usefulness of a ready-made corpus must be judged with regard to the purpose to which a user intends to put it. There are thousands of corpora in the world, but most of them are created for specific research projects and are not publicly available. This article introduces well-known and influential corpora, which are grouped in terms of their primary uses so that readers will find it easier to choose corpus resources suitable for their particular research questions. Note, however, that overlaps are inevitable in our classification. It is used in this article simply to give a better account of the primary uses of the relevant corpora. The higher number of English corpora covered here might reflect the fact that English was the forerunner in corpus research, though as we will see shortly, many other languages are catching up. Information on the web site addresses for the corpora discussed in this article are given in the appendix.

2. National corpora

National corpora are normally general reference corpora which are supposed to represent the national language of a country. They are balanced with regard to genres and domains that typically represent the language under consideration. While an ideal national corpus should cover proportionally both written and spoken language, most existing national corpora and those under construction consist only of written data, as spoken data is much more difficult and expensive to capture than written data. This section introduces a number of major national corpora.

2.1. The British National Corpus

The first and best-known national corpus is perhaps the British National Corpus (BNC), which is designed to represent as wide a range of modern British English as possible so as to "make it possible to say something about language in general" (Burnard 2002, 56). The BNC comprises approximately 100 million words of written texts (90 %) and transcripts of speech (10 %) in modern British English. Written texts were selected using three criteria: "domain", "time" and "medium". Domain refers to the content type (i. e. subject field) of the text; time refers to the period of text production, while medium refers to the type of text publication such as books, periodicals or unpublished manuscripts. Table 20.1 summarizes the distribution of these criteria (see Aston/Burnard 1998, 29–30).

Tab. 20.1: Composition of the written BNC

Domain	%	Date	%	Medium	%
Imaginative	21.91	1960–74	2.26	Book	58.58
Arts	8.08	1975–93	89.23	Periodical	31.08
Belief and thought	3.40	Unclassified	8.49	Misc. published	4.38
Commerce/Finance	7.93			Misc. unpublished	4.00
Leisure	11.13			To-be-spoken	1.52
Natural/pure science	4.18			Unclassified	0.40
Applied science	8.21				
Social science	14.80				
World affairs	18.39				
Unclassified	1.93				

The spoken data in the BNC was collected on the basis of two criteria: "demographic" and "context-governed". The demographic component is composed of informal encounters recorded by 124 volunteer respondents selected by age group, sex, social class and geographical region, while the context-governed component consists of more formal encounters such as meetings, lectures and radio broadcasts recorded in four broad context categories. The two components of spoken data complement each other, as many types of spoken text would not have been covered if demographic sampling techniques alone were used in data collection. Table 20.2 summarizes the composition of the spoken BNC. Note that in the table, the first two columns apply to both demographic and context-governed components while the third column refers to the latter component alone.

In addition to part-of-speech (POS) information (see article 24 for POS tagging), the BNC is annotated with rich metadata (i. e. contextual information) encoded according

Tab. 20.2: Composition of the spoken BNC

Region	%	Interaction type	%	Context-governed	%
South	45.61	Monologue	18.64	Educational/informative	20.56
Midlands	23.33	Dialogue	74.87	Business	21.47
North	25.43	Unclassified	6.48	Institutional	21.86
Unclassified	5.61			Leisure	23.71
				Unclassified	12.38

to the TEI guidelines, using ISO standard 8879 (i. e. SGML, see article 22). Because of its generality, as well as the use of internationally agreed standards for its encoding, the BNC corpus is a useful resource for a very wide variety of research purposes, in fields as distinct as lexicography, artificial intelligence, speech recognition and synthesis, literary studies and, of course, linguistics. There are a number of ways one can access the BNC corpus. It can be accessed online remotely using the BNC Online service (see appendix), the BNCWeb interface (see appendix), or more recently the BNCWeb CQP Edition (see appendix), which integrates the strengths of both BNCWeb and CQP (Corpus Query Processor) (cf Hoffmann/Evert 2006). Another online interface to the BNC (World Edition) is "Variation in English Words and Phrases" (i. e. VIEW, see appendix). Users interested in phrases in English can also access the BNC (World Edition) via "Phrase in English" (PIE, see appendix), a simple yet powerful interface that allows users to study words and phrases up to six words long. Alternatively, if a local copy the corpus is available, the BNC can be explored using corpus exploration tools such as WordSmith (Scott 2004) and Xaira (see below).

The current version of the full release of the BNC is BNC-2, the World Edition. This version has removed a small number of texts (less than 50) which restrict the worldwide distribution of the corpus. The BNC World has also corrected errors relating to mislabeled texts and indeterminate part-of-speech codes in the first version, and has included a classification system of genre labels developed by Lee (2001) at Lancaster. The World Edition, originally marked up in TEI-compliant SGML, has now been replaced with the BNC XML Edition. With a few exceptions, the XML edition contains almost the same texts as in the previous World Edition, but this latest release has corrected many known errors and inconsistencies and included lemma information together with some other improvements. The BNC XML Edition is released on two DVD-ROMs, including the XML-aware corpus indexing and exploration tool Xaira (see appendix) as well as an indexed version of the BNC corpus ready for use. As a prelude to this full release of the XML version, a four-million-word subset of the BNC – BNC Baby – was released in October 2004 together with the XML-aware corpus tool Xaira (see appendix). BNC Baby was originally developed as a manageable subcorpus from the BNC for use in the language classroom, consisting of comparable samples for four kinds of English – unscripted conversation, newspapers, academic prose and written fiction (Burnard 2003).

The BNC model for achieving corpus balance and representativeness has been followed by a number of national corpus projects including, for example, the American National Corpus, the Polish National Corpus and the Russian National Corpus.

2.2. The American National Corpus

The American National Corpus (ANC) project was initiated in 1998 with the aim of building a corpus comparable to the BNC. While the ANC follows the general design of the BNC, there are differences with regard to its sampling period and text categories. The ANC only samples language data produced from 1990 onward whereas the sampling period for the BNC is 1960–1993. This time frame has enabled the ANC to cover text categories which have developed recently and thus were not included in the BNC, e.g. e-mails, web blogs, web pages, and chat room talks, as shown in Table 20.3. In addition to the BNC-like core, the ANC will also include specialized "satellite" corpora (cf. Reppen/Ide 2004, 106–107).

Tab. 20.3: Text categories in the ANC (Second release)

Channel	Text category	%
Written	Books (informative texts for various domains and imaginative texts of various types)	22
	Newspapers, magazines and journals	38
	Electronic (e-mails, web pages etc.)	18
	Miscellaneous (published and unpublished)	5
Spoken	Face-to-face/phone conversations, speech, meetings	17

The ANC corpus is encoded in XML, following the guidelines of the XML version of the Corpus Encoding Standard (XCES, see article 22). The standalone annotation, i.e. with the primary data and annotations kept in separate documents but linked with pointers, has enabled the corpus to be POS tagged using different tagsets (e.g. Biber's (1988) tags, the CLAWS C5/C7 tagsets (Garside/Leech/Sampson 1987) and the Penn tags (see Marcus/Santorini/Marcinkiewicz 1993) to suit the needs of different users.

The second release of the ANC, which has become available since October 2006, contains 22 million words of written and spoken data (18.5 million words for writing and 3.9 million words for speech, but not balanced for genre). In subsequent releases a target size of 100 million words is expected to be reached. The corpus is currently annotated for lemma, part-of-speech, noun chunks, and verb chunks. All data in the second release is POS tagged applying the Penn tagset while many documents are also tagged using Biber's tagset. The ANC corpus is distributed by the Linguistic Data Consortium (LDC, see appendix). In addition, the ANC website offers the Open ANC, which comprises approximately 14 million words (3.2 spoken and 11.4 written) from the second LDC release. The Open ANC is licensed free of charge and can be downloaded from the corpus website.

Another sizeable corpus worth mentioning is the BYU Corpus of American English, which currently contains 360 million words equally sampled from five sources (spoken, fiction, popular magazines, newspapers, and academic journals), with 20 million words for each of the 17 years during the period 1990–2007. The corpus is designed following a dynamic model, meaning that it will grow by 20 million words each year. The BYU corpus website (see appendix) provides a freely accessible interface with the same functionalities as the BNC VIEW interface, allowing users to search by word, phrase, substring, part-of-speech, collocates, etc.

2.3. Reference Corpora of Polish

This section introduces three large reference corpora of Polish, the PELCRA Reference Corpus of Polish, the PWN Corpus of Polish, and the IPI PAN Corpus of Polish. While three corpora are introduced in this section, there is presently no agreed upon national corpus of Polish, though the aim of the PELCRA project (Polish and English Language Corpora for Research and Application) was to build the Polish National Corpus – "with a well planned structure, balanced data etc., replicating the structure of the BNC" (Barbara Lewandowska Tomaszczyk, personal communication), and the PELCRA Reference Corpus was named as such from the outset (see Lewandowska-Tomaszczyk 2003, 106). The controversy over the title of the Polish national corpus has now turned into an interesting cooperative project, with the aim of creating a truly national corpus of Polish, by a consortium including the creators of the three Polish corpora mentioned above (Adam Przepiórkowski, personal communication).

As noted, the PELCRA Reference Corpus of Polish is created at the PELCRA project, which is undertaken jointly by the Universities of Łódź and Lancaster. The project aims to develop a large, fully annotated reference corpus of native Polish, "mirroring the BNC in terms of genres and its coverage of written and spoken language" (Lewandowska-Tomaszczyk 2003, 106). The corpus consists of 100 million words of running text, which covers genres and styles comparable in proportions to those included the BNC. An important difference lies in that the PELCRA corpus contains whole texts whereas the BNC is composed of text samples. The PELCRA corpus is TEI-compliant and is annotated for part-of-speech. Presently, it can be accessed at the corpus website via an online interface that can be used to search not only for simple words and phrases but for frequencies and occurrences of morphologically related words as well, using the so called "Inflections Concordancer". In addition, the interface allows for statistical analysis such as computation of word frequency and collocation.

The PWN corpus is a corpus of native Polish which is used by the Polish scientific publishers PWN primarily in dictionary making. The corpus consists of 60 million words of texts from the 20th and 21st centuries together with three million words from earlier periods. It keeps growing over time. An online version of the corpus, which is available for access for a fee, consists of 40 million words of samples taken from books, press publications, web pages and advertising leaflets and other ephemera, as well as transcripts of spoken data. A demonstration version of this online corpus (totaling 7.5 million words) is also accessible free of charge at the PWN site (see appendix).

The IPI PAN Corpus is presently the largest corpus of Polish, consisting of over 250 million segments (approximately 200 million orthographic words) in its second edition. Developed at the Institute of Computer Science (IPI) of the Polish Academy of Sciences (PAN), this giant corpus is morpho-syntactically annotated. While the corpus as a whole is not balanced, a balanced sample of 30 million segments is also available, which is composed of contemporary prose (10 %), older prose (10 %), non-fiction (10 %), newspapers (50 %), parliamentary proceedings (15 %) and law (5 %). The IPI PAN corpus, as well as its balanced component, is available to the public free of charge. Both can be downloaded together with the accompanying concordancer (i. e. Poliqarp) from the IPI PAN corpus website (see appendix), which also provides the online searching function.

2.4. The Czech National Corpus

The Czech National Corpus (CNC) consists of two sections: synchronous and diachronic. The synchronous section is designed to include written and spoken components. The texts in this section stem from a collection of electronic documents in legacy formats. There are plans for dialectal components of both the synchronous and the diachronic section, which currently are hardly more than blueprints for future work. We will thus only introduce the written and spoken components in the synchronous section.

The written component of the synchronous section, which contains 100 million words, was completed in 2000 and thus named SYN2000. SYN2000 includes both imaginative (15 %) and informative (85 %) texts, each being divided into a number of text categories, as shown in Table 20.4 (see Kučera 2002, 247–248). The technical and specialized texts in the corpus proportionally cover nine domains: lifestyle (5.55 %), technology (4.61 %), social sciences (3.67 %), arts (3.48 %), natural sciences (3.37 %), economics/management (2.27 %), law/security (0.82 %), belief/religion (0.74 %) and administrative texts (0.49 %).

The spoken component of the synchronous section, the so-called Prague Spoken Corpus (PMK), contains 800,000 words of transcription of authentic spoken language sampled in a balanced way according to four sociolinguistic criteria: speaker sex, age, educational level and discourse type, as shown in Table 20.5. The data contained in the Prague

Tab. 20.4: Design of SYN2000

Major category	Genre	%
Imaginative (15 %)	Fiction	11.02
	Poetry	0.81
	Drama	0.21
	Other literary texts	0.36
	Transitional text types	2.6
Informative (85 %)	Journal	60
	Technical/specialized texts	25

Tab. 20.5: Sampling frame of the Prague Spoken Corpus

Criterion	Type	Proportion
Speaker sex	Male	50 %
	Female	50 %
Speaker age	21–35	50 %
	35+	50 %
Education level	Secondary school	50 %
	University	50 %
Discourse type	Formal	50 %
	Informal	50 %

Spoken Corpus consists exclusively of impromptu spoken language (roughly equivalent to the demographically sampled component in the BNC). Texts representing various blends of written and spoken language such as lectures, political speeches and play scripts are included in a special section in the written corpus (cf. Kučera 2002, 248, 253).

Both SYN2000 and the Prague Spoken Corpus are marked up in TEI-compliant SGML and tagged to show part-of-speech categories. SYN2000 is licensed free of charge for non-commercial use. A scaled-down version of SYN2000, PUBLIC, which contains 20 million words with the same genre distribution, is accessible online at the corpus website (see appendix).

2.5. The Hungarian National Corpus

The Hungarian National Corpus (HNC, see Váradi 2002) is a balanced reference corpus of present-day Hungarian. The corpus contains 187.6 million words of texts produced from the mid-1990s onwards, which are divided into five subcorpora, each representing a written text type: press, literature, science, official, and personal (electronic forum discussions). It is particularly interesting to note that in addition to stratification in genres, the HNC is also regionally stratified, covering language variants beyond the border of Hungary such as those from Slovakia, Subcarpathia, Transylvania and Vojvodina. Table 20.6 shows the sizes of these components.

Tab. 20.6: Components of the HNC corpus

	Hungary	Slovakia	Subcarpathia	Transylvania	Vojvodina	Total
Press	71.0	5.7	0.7	5.5	1.5	84.5
Literature	35.5	1.4	0.4	0.8	0.2	38.2
Science	20.5	2.3	0.7	1.6	0.3	25.5
Official	19.9	0.2	0.3	0.6	0.1	20.9
Personal	17.8	0.0	0.4	0.4	0.1	18.6
Total	164.7	9.5	2.5	8.9	2.0	187.6

The HNC is encoded in SGML in compliance with the Corpus Encoding Standard (CES) and annotated with part-of-speech and morphological information. The corpus can be accessed free of charge after registration via a sophisticated online query system at the corpus site (see appendix), which uses CQP functionality to enhance the search engine.

2.6. The Russian National Corpus

The Russian National Corpus (RNC or Natsionalny Korpus Russkogo Yazyka in Russian), which was known as the Russian Reference Corpus (BOKR), is designed as a Russian match for the BNC (see Sharoff 2006, where the corpus design is discussed under its pilot project name BOKR). The corpus contains over 147 million words, of which the BNC-comparable modern language subset amounts to 109 million words, with the rest coming from the 18–19th centuries and the first half of the 20th century. The

Tab. 20.7: Text categories covered in the BNC and RNC corpora

Text category	BNC	RNC
Spoken	10.7%	5%
Life (imaginative texts in the BNC)	16.7%	30%
Natural sciences	3.8%	5%
Applied sciences	7.2%	10%
Social sciences	14.2%	12%
Politics (world affairs in the BNC)	18.9%	15%
Commerce	7.6%	5%
Arts	6.8%	5%
Religion and philosophy (belief and thought in the BNC)	3.1%	3%
Leisure	11.2%	10%

modern language component includes 39.7% of imaginative writing, 56.4% of informative writing and 3.9% of spoken data (see RNC in appendix). Table 20.7 compares text categories covered in the BNC and RNC corpora (cf. Sharoff 2006, 172).

The RNC corpus is encoded in TEI-compliant SGML and annotated for part-of-speech. As Russian is a highly inflective language, the technique used in annotating English corpora with complex POS tags is impractical for Russian, because that would entail thousands of tags which would make corpus exploration ineffective, if not completely impossible. Hence in the Russian National Corpus, each word is annotated with a bundle of lexical and syntactic features such as part-of-speech, aspect, transitivity, voice, gender, number and tense. Separate features from a feature bundle associated with each word can be selected in a window in the query interface. The corpus was completed in 2005 (Serge Sharoff, personal communication) and a pilot version is now accessible online (see Ruscorpora in appendix).

2.7. The CORIS corpus

The CORIS (Corpus di Italiano Scritto) corpus is a general reference corpus of present-day Italian. It contains 100 million words of written Italian sampled from five text categories, which constitute five subcorpora, as shown in Table 20.8.

Unlike most national corpora that are sample corpora, the CORIS corpus follows a dynamic corpus model, which will be updated every two years by means of a built-in monitor corpus (Rossini Favretti/Tamburini/de Santis 2004). The current version of the corpus can be accessed online free of charge via a web-based query system at the corpus website (see appendix).

2.8. The Hellenic National Corpus

The Hellenic National Corpus is a 47-million-word corpus of written Modern Greek sampled from several publication media covering various genres (articles, essays, literary

Tab. 20.8: Components of the CORIS corpus

Category	Subcategory	Words (million)
Press	Newspapers, periodicals, supplement	38
Fiction	Novel, short stories	25
Academic prose	Human sciences, natural sciences, physics, experimental sciences	12
Legal and administrative prose	Legal, bureaucratic, administrative documents	10
Miscellaneous	Books on religion, travel, cookery, hobbies, etc.	10
Ephemeral	Letters, leaflets, instructions	5
	Total size	100

works, reports, biographies etc.) and domains (economy, medicine, leisure, art, human sciences etc.) published from 1976 onwards. Of the five types of medium, newspapers account for 62.83% of the total texts, books 8.23%, magazines 5.19%, Internet texts 0.3%, and miscellaneous (leaflets pamphlets, typed material, reports etc.) 23.49%. In terms of genres, the HNC covers a wide variety including fiction, non-fiction, feature articles, informative writing, official documents, as well as advertising, private material and discussion.

The text classification with regard to medium, genre and domain follows the standards established on the PAROLE project (see section 11.11.). This taxonomy information, together with the bibliographic information, is encoded in TEI-compliant SGML (cf Hatzigeorgiu et al. 2000, 1737). The corpus is constantly being updated and can be accessed online at the corpus site (see appendix), where users can make queries concerning the lexicon, morphology, syntax and usage of Modern Greek (e. g. words, lemmas, part-of-speech categories or combinations of the three).

2.9. The DWDS corpus

The DWDS corpus is a product of the DWDS (Digital Dictionary of the 20th Century German Language) project. The corpus is divided into two parts, a 100-million-word balanced core and a much larger opportunistic subcorpus with a target size of 500 million words. This section introduces the core corpus, which is roughly comparable to the British National Corpus, covering the whole 20th century (1900–2000). Table 20.9 shows the text categories covered in the corpus.

The metadata such as genre information is encoded in XML. Linguistic annotation consists basically of lemmatization, part-of-speech and semantic annotation on the word level, as well as prepositional phrase and noun phrase recognition on the phrase level (Cavar/Geyken/Neumann 2000). The core corpus is available for online search after free-of-charge registration at the DWDS website (see appendix), which provides quite sophisticated tools for searching and presenting search results. These tools are primarily focused on lexicological research.

Tab. 20.9: Design criteria of the DWDS Corpus

Text category	Proportion
Literature	26%
Journalistic prose	27%
Scientific texts	22%
Specialized texts (advert, manuals, etc.)	20%
Spoken (everyday language, televised debates, dialect, etc.)	5%

2.10. The Slovak National Corpus

The Slovak National Corpus (SNK) is a large database of contemporary Slovak texts covering a broad range of genres and language styles. The latest release of the corpus, version 3.0, contains 339 million tokens taken from journalistic text (60.6%), fiction (17.5%), specialized texts (11.6%) and other sources (10.3%) published since 1955. In-addition to the SNK as a whole, there is a cleaned up version of the corpus of approximately 319 million tokens which contains only non-linguistic texts of standard quality (correct diacritics, standard contemporary language from the territory of Slovakia).

The texts in the Slovak National Corpus are morphologically annotated and lemmatized automatically. There is also a small subcorpus (approximately half a million tokens) with hand-crafted morphological annotation and lemmatization, which can be used to train morphological taggers (cf. Gianitsová 2005; Šimková 2005; Garabík 2006). In addition to such linguistic analyses, the texts are encoded with source (bibliographical and style-genre) information.

The SNK corpus is available to the public for research, educational, and other strictly non-commercial purposes. Users can access the corpus using a simple online query system at the SNK website (see appendix). More complex searches require the corpus manager client program (Bonito), which supports regular expressions and can be downloaded at the same website. Online registration is also required in order to login using the client program.

We have so far introduced national corpora for European languages. The next two sections will introduce two national corpora of Asian languages, namely Chinese and Korean; Japanese corpora are discussed in article 21.

2.11. The Modern Chinese Language Corpus

The Modern Chinese Language Corpus (MCLC) is China's national corpus built under the auspices of the National Language Committee of China. The corpus contains 100 million Chinese characters of systematically sampled texts produced during 1919–2002, with the majority of texts produced after 1977. 1919 is generally considered as the beginning of modern Chinese. The corpus covers three large categories (humanities/social sciences, natural sciences, and miscellaneous text categories such as official documents, ceremony speech and ephemera) including more than 40 subcategories. Text categories containing over five million characters include literature, society, economics, newspapers,

Tab. 20.10: Components of the MCLC corpus

Domain	Category
Humanities and social sciences (8 categories)	Politics and laws, history, society, economics, arts, literature, military and physical education, life
Natural sciences (6 categories)	Mathematics and physics, biology and chemistry, astronomy and geography, oceanology and meteorology, agriculture and forestry, medical and health
Miscellaneous (6 categories)	Official documents, regulations, judicial documents, business documents, ceremonial speech, ephemera

miscellaneous, and legal texts, with literary texts accounting for the largest proportion (nearly 30 million characters). Table 20.10 shows the components of the corpus. Most samples in the corpus are approximately 2,000 characters in length, with the exception of samples taken from books, which may contain up to 10,000 characters. The digitalized texts were proofread three times so that errors are less than 0.02 % (see Wang 2001, 283).

All text samples in the MCLC corpus are encoded with detailed bibliographic information (up to 24 items) in the corpus header. A core component of the corpus, which is composed of 50 million Chinese characters, has been tokenized (with an error rate of 0.5 ‰) and POS-tagged (with an error rate of 0.5 %), while a small part of it (one million characters, in 50,000 sentences) has been built into a treebank.

Presently, a scaled down version of the corpus, which contains 20 million characters proportionally sampled from the larger corpus, has been made available to the public free of charge for online access at the MCLC website (see appendix).

2.12. The Korean National Corpus

The Korean National Corpus (KNC) is under construction on the 21st Century Sejong project, which was launched in 1998 as a ten-year development project to build various kinds of language resources including Korean corpora and Korean electronic dictionaries. One of the goals of the project is to construct a balanced national corpus comparable to the BNC (Kang/Kim 2004). The initial target size was 500 million eojuls (similar to tokens but different from English words – an eojul is a morpho-syntactic combination of a word plus particle(s), or a word plus ending(s), or simply a word alone). However since the annotated part of the corpus has been increased, the current goal of the corpus size is 200 million eojuls.

The KNC consists of two components, namely, the primary corpus and the specialized corpus. The primary corpus division deals with the Korean language as used in South Korea, with some parts annotated with various types of linguistic information. The current version of the primary corpus consists of four components – raw corpus (63,899,412 eojuls), grammatically tagged corpus (15,226,186 eojuls), parsed corpus (570,064 eojuls), and semantically tagged corpus (10,132,348 eojuls) – totaling 89,830,015 eojuls. The raw corpus contains data from a range of genres including newspapers (20%), magazines (10%), academic writing (35%), literary works (20%), quasi-spoken data (10%) and others (5%). The special corpus division is largely concerned with language variation and parallel corpus construction. Presently the following specialized corpora are available: a corpus of transcribed colloquial discourse (3,390,533 eojuls), a historical corpus (5,291,215 eojuls), a corpus of international Korean (9,096,159 eojuls), and a Korean-English parallel corpus (5,616,313 eojuls).

Texts in the Korean National Corpus are encoded in SGML, applying the TEI (Text Encoding Initiative) P3 standard. The simplified TEI header shows details such as bibliography, text category, history of computerization, and record of correction. As the Text Encoding Initiative has been updated to TEI P5 based on XML, there is a plan to migrate the KNC corpus to the new standard (see Kim 2006).

The corpus is accessible over the Internet after registration at the corpus site (see KNC in appendix).

2.13. Other National corpora

In addition to those introduced above, there are a number of nation-level corpora which are either already available or are under construction. They include, for example, the FRANTEXT Database for French (see appendix), the Croatian National Corpus (101.3 million tokens, see appendix), Korpus 2000 for Danish (28 million words, see appendix), the National Corpus of Irish (30 million words, see appendix). A number of corpora representing other national languages are also under construction, including, for example, Norwegian (Choukri 2003), Dutch (Wittenburg/Brugman/Broeder 2000), Maltese (Dalli 2001), Basque (Aduriz et al. 2003), Kurdish (Gautier 1998), Nepali (Glover 1998), Tamil (Malten 1998) and Indonesian (Riza 1999).

3. Monitor corpora

While most of the national corpora introduced in section 2 follow a static sample corpus model, there are also corpora which are constantly updated to track rapid language change, such as the development and the life cycle of neologisms. Corpora of this type are referred to as monitor corpora.

The best-known monitor corpus is the Bank of English (BoE), which was initiated in 1991 on the COBUILD (Collins Birmingham University International Language Database) project. The corpus was designed to represent standard English as it was relevant to the needs of learners, teachers and other users, while also being of use to researchers in present-day English language. Written texts (75%) come from newspapers, magazines, fiction and non-fiction books, brochures, reports, and websites while spoken data (25%) consists of transcripts of television and radio broadcasts, meetings, interviews, discussions, and conversations. The majority of the material in the corpus represents British English (70%) while American English and other varieties account for 20% and 10% respectively. Presently the BoE contains 524 million words of written and spoken English. The corpus keeps growing with the constant addition of new material (cf the BoE website at Collins, see appendix).

The BoE corpus is particularly useful for lexical and lexicographic studies, for example, tracking new words, new uses or meanings of old words, and words falling out of use. A 56-million-word sampler of the corpus can be accessed online free of charge at the corpus website. Access to larger corpora is granted by special arrangement.

Another corpus of the monitor type is the Global English Monitor Corpus, which was started in late 2001 as an electronic archive of the world's leading newspapers in English. The corpus aims at monitoring language use and semantic change in English as reflected in newspapers so as to allow for research into whether the English language discourses in Britain, the United States, Australia, Pakistan and South Africa have changed in the same way or differently. As the Global English Monitor Corpus will monitor as accurately as conceivable all relevant changes of attitudes and beliefs, it will prove a useful tool not only for lexicographers, historical linguists and semanticists, but also for those interested in social and political studies all over the world. With its first results having become available at the end of 2003, the corpus is expected to reach billions of words within a few years (cf. the corpus website, see appendix).

4. Corpora of the Brown family

The first modern corpus of English, the Brown University Standard Corpus of Present-day American English (i. e. the Brown corpus, see Kučera/Francis 1967), was built in the early 1960s for written American English. The population from which samples for this pioneering corpus were drawn was written English text published in the United States in 1961, while its sampling frame was a list of the collection of books and periodicals in the Brown University Library and the Providence Athenaeum. The target population was first grouped into 15 text categories, from which 500 samples of approximately 2,000 words were then drawn proportionally from each text category, totaling roughly one million words.

The Brown corpus was constructed with comparative studies in mind, in the hope of setting the standard for the preparation and presentation of further bodies of data in English or in other languages. This expectation has now been realized. Since its completion, the Brown corpus model has been followed in the construction of a number of corpora for synchronic and diachronic studies as well as for cross-linguistic contrast. Table 20.11 shows a brief comparison of these corpora.

As can be seen, these corpora are roughly comparable but have sampled different languages or language varieties. Their sampling periods are either similar for the purposes of synchronic comparison or distanced by about three decades for the purposes of diachronic comparison. For example, the Brown and LOB (the Lancaster/Oslo-Bergen corpus of British English, see Johansson/Leech/Goodluck 1978) can be used to compare American and British English as used in the early 1960s. The updated versions of the two corpora, Frown (see Hundt/Sand/Skandera 1999) and FLOB (see Hundt/Sand/Siemund 1998) can be used to compare the two major varieties of English as used in the early 1990s. Other corpora of a similar sampling period, such as ACE (the Australian Corpus of English, also known as the Macquarie corpus), WWC (the Wellington Corpus of Written New Zealand English) and Kolhapur (the Kolhapur Corpus of Indian English), together with FLOB and Frown, allow for comparison of "world Englishes". For

Tab. 20.11: Corpora of the Brown family

Corpus	Language variety	Period	Samples	Words (million)
Brown	American English	1961	500	One
Frown	American English	1991–1992	500	One
LOB	British English	1961	500	One
Lancaster 1931	British English	1931 +/− 3 years	500	One
FLOB	British English	1991–1992	500	One
Kolhapur	Indian English	1978	500	One
ACE	Australian English	1986	500	One
WWC	New Zealand English	1986–1990	500	One
LCMC	Mandarin Chinese	1991 +/− 3 years	500	One

diachronic studies, the Brown vs. Frown on the one hand, and the Lancaster 1931 (see Leech/Smith 2005), LOB and FLOB corpora on the other hand, provide a reliable basis for tracking recent language change over 30-year periods. The LCMC corpus (the Lancaster Corpus of Mandarin Chinese, see McEnery/Xiao/Mo 2003), when used in combination with the FLOB/Frown corpora, provides a valuable resource for contrastive studies between Chinese and two major varieties of English (see LCMC in appendix).

In comparing these corpora synchronically, caution must be exercised to ensure that the sampling periods are similar. For example, comparing the Brown corpus with FLOB would involve not only language varieties but also language change. Also, as the Brown model may have been modified slightly in some of these corpora, account must be taken of such variation in comparing these corpora across text categories by normalizing the raw frequencies to a common basis. Table 20.12 compares the text categories and number of samples for each category in these corpora.

It can be seen from the table that the two American English corpora (Brown and Frown) have the same numbers of samples for each of the 15 text categories while the British English corpora share the same proportions. The two groups differ in the numbers of samples for categories E, F, and G. The WWC and LCMC corpora follow the model of FLOB. There are important differences between the Kolhapur corpus and others in both sampling periods and the proportions of text categories. The ACE corpus covers 17 text categories instead of 15. All of these differences should be taken into account when comparing these corpora.

With the exceptions of the Lancaster 1931 corpus, which has not been released to the public presently, and LCMC, which is distributed by the European Language Resources Association (ELRA, see appendix), all of the corpora of the Brown family are available from the International Computer Archive of Modern and Medieval English (ICAME, see appendix).

The corpora of the Brown family are balanced corpora representing a static snapshot of a language or language variety in a certain period. While they can be used for synchronic and diachronic studies, more appropriate resources for these kinds of research are synchronic and diachronic corpora, which will be introduced in the following two sections.

Tab. 20.12: Text categories in the corpora of the Brown family

Code	Text category	Brown	Frown	LOB	FLOB	Lancaster 1931	Kolhapur	ACE	WWC	LCMC
A	Press reportage	44	44	44	44	44	44	44	44	44
B	Press editorials	27	27	27	27	27	27	27	27	27
C	Press reviews	17	17	17	17	17	17	17	17	17
D	Religion	17	17	17	17	17	17	17	17	17
E	Skills, trades and hobbies	36	36	38	38	38	38	38	38	38
F	Popular lore	48	48	44	44	44	44	44	44	44
G	Biographies and essays	75	75	77	77	77	70	77	77	77
H	Miscellaneous (reports, official documents)	30	30	30	30	30	37	30	30	30
J	Science (academic prose)	80	80	80	80	80	80	80	80	80
K	General fiction	29	29	29	29	29	59	29	29	29
L	Mystery and detective fiction	24	24	24	24	24	24	15	24	24
M	Science fiction	6	6	6	6	6	2	7	6	6
N	Western and adventure fiction	29	29	29	29	29	15	8	29	29
P	Romantic fiction	29	29	29	29	29	18	15	29	29
R	Humour	9	9	9	9	9	9	15	9	9
S	Historical fiction	–	–	–	–	–	–	22	–	–
W	Women's fiction	–	–	–		–	–	15	–	–

5. Synchronic corpora

While the corpora of the Brown family are generally good for comparing language varieties such as world Englishes, the results from such a comparison must be interpreted with caution if the corpora under examination were built for different periods or the Brown model has been modified. A more reliable basis for comparing language varieties is a synchronic corpus.

5.1. The International Corpus of English

A typical corpus of this type is the International Corpus of English (ICE), which is specifically designed for the synchronic study of world Englishes. The ICE corpus consists of a collection of twenty corpora of one million words each, each composed of written and spoken English produced during 1990–1994 in countries or regions in which English is a first or official language (e. g. Australia, Canada, East Africa, Hong Kong as well as Great Britain and the USA). As the primary aim of ICE is to facilitate comparative studies of English worldwide, each component follows a common corpus design as well as a common scheme for grammatical annotation to ensure direct comparability among the component corpora. All ICE corpora contain 500 texts of approximately 2,000 words each, sampled from a wide range of spoken (60 %) and written (40 %) genres, as shown in Table 20.13 (see Nelson 1996, 29–30).

The ICE corpora are marked up and annotated at various levels. In written texts, features of the original layout are marked, including sentence and paragraph boundaries, headings, deletions, and typographic features, while spoken texts are transcribed orthographically, and are marked for pauses, overlapping strings, discourse phenomena such as false starts and hesitations, and speaker turns. The bibliographic markup, which gives a complete description (e. g. text category, date, and publisher) of each text, is stored in the corpus header of each file. While uniform criteria for data collection and markup style have been applied for all ICE corpora, different levels of linguistic annotation have been undertaken for different components. While the British component (ICE-GB) is POS tagged and parsed (see section 9.6. for further discussion), others are currently available as unannotated lexical corpora, e. g. the components for East Africa, Hong Kong, India, the Philippines, New Zealand, and Singapore. With the exceptions of ICE-GB and ICE-New Zealand, which can be ordered on CD-ROMs, all other currently available ICE corpora are licensed free of charge and can be downloaded at the ICE website (see appendix), but users must sign a license agreement in order to receive the passwords to decompress the corpus files.

5.2. The Longman/Lancaster Corpus

The Longman/Lancaster Corpus consists of about 30 million words of published English. British data takes up 50 % and American data 40 % while the other 10 % represents other varieties such as Australian, African and Irish English. One half of the samples were selected randomly ("microcosmic texts") and the other half selected by a panel of experts

Tab. 20.13: Corpus design of ICE

Spoken (300)	Dialogues (180)	Private (100)	Conversations (90) Phone calls (10)
		Public (80)	Class lessons (20) Broadcast discussions (20) Broadcast interviews (10) Parliamentary debates (10) Cross-examinations (10) Business transactions (10)
	Monologues (120)	Unscripted (70)	Commentaries (20) Unscripted speeches (30) Demonstrations (10) Legal presentations (10)
		Scripted (50)	Broadcast news (20) Broadcast talks (20) Non-broadcast talks (10)
Written (200)	Non-printed (50)	Student writing (20)	Student essays (10) Exam scripts (10)
		Letters (30)	Social letters (15) Business letters (15)
	Printed (150)	Academic (40)	Humanities (10) Social sciences (10) Natural sciences (10) Technology (10)
		Popular (40)	Humanities (10) Social sciences (10) Natural sciences (10) Technology (10)
		Reportage (20)	Press reports (20)
		Instructional (20)	Administrative writing (10) Skills/hobbies (10)
		Persuasive (10)	Editorials (10)
		Creative (20)	Novels (20)

("selective texts") Most texts in the corpus are about 40,000 words long but no whole texts are used.

Both imaginative and informative text categories are included. Imaginative texts come from well-known literary works and works randomly sampled from books in print; informative texts come from natural and social sciences, world affairs, commerce and finance, the arts, leisure, and so on. Imaginative texts are mainly works of fiction in book form while informative texts comprise books, newspapers and journals, unpublished and ephemera. Four external criteria have been used in text selection (see Holmes-Higgin/Abidi/Ahmad 1994): "region" (language varieties), "time" (1900s–1980s), "medium" (books 80 %, periodicals 13.3 % and ephemera 6.7 %), and "level" (literary, middle and popular for imaginative texts, and technical, lay and popular for informative texts). As part of the Longman Corpus Network (see appendix), the Longman/Lancaster Corpus is not available for public access.

5.3. The Longman Written American Corpus

The Longman Written American Corpus contains over 100 million words of running texts taken from newspapers, journals, magazines, best-selling novels, technical and scientific writing, and coffee-table books. The design of the Longman Written American Corpus is based on the general design principles of the Longman/Lancaster Corpus and the written section of the BNC. The corpus is dynamically refined and keeps growing with the constant addition of new materials. Like the other components of the Longman Corpus Network (cf. the corpus website), this corpus does not appear to allow public access.

5.4. The CREA corpus of Spanish

The CREA (Corpus de Referencia del Español Actual) is a corpus of standard varieties of Spanish. The corpus currently contains 150 million words sampled from a wide range of written and spoken text categories produced in all Spanish speaking countries (European Spanish 83 million words and American Spanish 67 million words). The domains covered in the corpus include science and technology, social sciences, religion and thought, politics and economics, arts, leisure and ordinary life, health, and fiction.

The CREA was designed as a monitor corpus which is continually updated so that it always represents the last twenty-five years of the history of Spanish. New data is added proportionally to maintain the corpus balance and to ensure that the various trends in current Spanish are represented.

The CREA corpus is marked up in SGML. Bibliographic and taxonomic information is encoded in the corpus header of each file. For written texts, both structural (paragraph and page number) and intratextual (notes, formulas, tables, quotations, foreign words etc.) marks are encoded. For spoken texts, the markup scheme indicates structural (speech turns) and non-structural (overlapping, tottering, anacoluthon, etc.) marks (cf. Guerra 1998).

The modular structure of the CREA corpus allows for flexible searches using geographical, generic, temporal, and thematic criteria. The corpus is accessible on the Internet (see appendix).

5.5. The LIVAC corpus of Chinese

The LIVAC (Linguistic Variation in Chinese Speech Communities) project started in 1993 with the aim of building a synchronous corpus for studying varieties of Mandarin Chinese. For this purpose, data has been collected regularly and simultaneously, once every four days since July 1995, from representative Mandarin Chinese newspapers and the electronic media of six Chinese speaking communities: Hong Kong, Taiwan, Beijing, Shanghai, Macau and Singapore. The contents of these texts typically include the editorial, and all the articles on the front page, international and local news pages, as well as features and reviews. The corpus is planned to cover a 10-year period between July 1995 and June 2005, capturing salient pre- and post-millennium evolving cultural and social fabrics of the diverse Chinese speech communities (Tsou et al. 2000). The collection of materials from these diverse communities is synchronized with uniform calendar reference points so that all of the components are comparable. The LIVAC corpus contains over 150 million Chinese characters, with 720,000 word types in its lexicon.

All of the corpus texts in LIVAC are segmented automatically and checked by hand. In addition to the corpus, a lexical database is derived from the segmented texts, which includes, apart from ordinary words, those expressing new concepts or undergoing sense shifts, as well as region specific words from the six communities. The database is thus a rich resource for research into linguistics, sociolinguistics, and Chinese language and society.

As LIVAC captures the social, cultural, and linguistic developments of the six Chinese speaking communities within a decade, it allows for a wide range of comparative studies on linguistic variation in Mandarin Chinese. The corpus also provides an important resource for tracking lexical development such as the evolution of new concepts and their expressions in present-day Chinese. While the access to the entire corpus is restricted to registered users only, a sample (covering the period from 1 July 1995 to 30 June 1997) can be searched using the online query system at the LIVAC site (see appendix), which shows KWIC concordances as well as frequency distributions across the six speech communities.

6. Diachronic corpora

Another way to explore language variation is from a diachronic perspective using diachronic corpora. A diachronic (or historical) corpus contains texts from the same language gathered from different time periods. Typically that period is far more extensive than that covered by Brown/Frown and LOB/FLOB or a monitor corpus such as the Bank of English. Diachronic corpora are used to track changes in language evolution. This section introduces a number of corpora of this kind.

6.1. The Helsinki Corpus of English Texts

Perhaps the best-known historical corpus is the diachronic part of the Helsinki Corpus of English Texts (i. e. the Helsinki Corpus), which consists of approximately 1.5 million words of English in the form of 400 text samples, dating from the 8th to the 18th centuries. The corpus is divided into three periods (Old, Middle, and Early Modern English) and eleven subperiods, as shown in Table 20.14 (cf. Kytö 1996).

In addition to the basic selection of texts as indicated in the table, there is a supplementary part in the Corpus, which focuses on regional varieties. This part consists of 834,000 words of Older Scots (in international distribution) and 300,000 words of early

Tab. 20.14: Periods covered in the Helsinki Diachronic Corpus

Period	Subperiod	Words	Percent	Overall
Old English	I. –850	2,190	0.5	413,250
	II. 850–950	92,050	22.3	
	III. 950–1050	251,630	60.9	
	IV. 1050–1150	67,380	16.3	
	Total	413,250	100	26.27%
Middle English	I. 1150–1250	113,010	18.6	608,570
	II. 1250–1350	97,480	16.0	
	III. 1350–1420	184,230	30.3	
	IV. 1420–1500	213,850	35.1	
	Total	608,570	100	38.70%
Early Modern English	I. 1500–1570	190,160	34.5	
	II. 1570–1640	189,800	34.5	
	III. 1640–1710	171,040	31.0	
	Total	551,000	100	35.03%
Total		1,572,820		100%

American English (in compilation). While the primary selectional criteria are the dates of texts, the Helsinki Corpus has sought to reflect socio-historical variation (e. g. author sex, age and social rank) and a wide range of text types (e. g. law, handbooks, science, trials, sermons, diaries, documents, plays, private and official correspondence, etc.) for each specific period. The textual markup scheme includes more than thirty genre labels, which indicate, whenever available, parameter values for the dialect and the level of formality of the text, the relationship between the writer and the receiver as well as the author's age, sex, and social rank (Rissanen 2000).

As the Helsinki Corpus has not only sampled different periods covering one millennium, but also encoded genre and sociolinguistic information, this corpus allows researchers to go beyond simply dating and reporting language change, by combining diachronic, sociolinguistic and genre studies. The Helsinki Corpus can be ordered from ICAME (see appendix) or the Oxford Text Archive (OTA, see appendix).

6.2. The ARCHER corpus

ARCHER, an acronym for "A Representative Corpus of Historical English Registers", contains 1.7 million words of data in the form of 1,037 texts sampled from seven 50-year historical periods covering both Early and Late Modern English (1650–1990). The corpus is designed as a balanced representation of seven written genres (journal-diaries, letters, fiction, news, science, etc.) and three speech-based ones (fictional conversation, drama and sermons-homilies) in British (two thirds of the corpus) and American (one third, data available only for the periods 1750–1799, 1850–1899, 1950–1990) English. Each 50-year subcorpus includes 20,000–30,000 words per register, typically containing ten texts of approximately 2,000–3,000 words each (cf. Biber/Finegan/Atkinson 1994). ARCHER is tagged for grammatical/functional categories. It allows for a wide variety of investigations on recent linguistic change and change in discourse and genre conventions. The corpus is presently being expanded with more American texts to make the American and British data comparable. The expanded version will also enable a systematic comparison of the two varieties of English diachronically. However, because of copyright problems, ARCHER is not publicly available at the moment.

In addition to the Helsinki and ARCHER corpora, which cover many centuries, there are a number of well-known historical corpora focusing on a particular period or a specific domain or genre, which will be introduced in the following sections.

6.3. The Lampeter Corpus of Early Modern English Tracts

The Lampeter Corpus of Early Modern English Tracts is a balanced corpus covering one century between 1640 and 1740, which is divided into ten decades. Each decade consists of data sampled from six domains (religion, politics, economics/trade, science, law and miscellaneous). Two complete texts, ranging from 3,000 to 20,000 words, are included for each domain within each decade, totaling approximately 1.1 million words (Schmied 1994).

The Lampeter corpus is encoded in TEI-compliant SGML. The TEI headers provide the framework for historical, sociolinguistic and stylistic investigations, including information regarding authors (name, age, sex, place of residence, education, social status, political affiliation), printers/publishers, place and date of print, publication format, text characteristics and bibliographical sources. As the corpus includes whole texts rather than smaller samples, the corpus is also useful for study of textual organization in Early Modern English. The Lampeter corpus can be ordered from ICAME or OTA (see appendix).

6.4. The Dictionary of Old English Corpus in Electronic Form

The Dictionary of Old English Corpus in Electronic Form (DOEC, the 2004 release) contains 3,047 texts of Old English, totaling four million words, in addition to two million words of Latin. The texts in the corpus are practically all extant Old English writings. The DOEC corpus includes at least one copy of each surviving text in Old English while in cases where it is significant because of dialect or date, more than one copy is included. These texts cover six text categories: poetry, prose, interlinear glosses, glossaries, runic inscriptions, and inscriptions in the Latin alphabet. In the prose category in particular, a wide range of text types are covered which include, for example, saints' lives, sermons, biblical translations, penitential writings, laws, charters and wills, records (of manumissions, land grants, land sales, land surveys), chronicles, a set of tables for computing the moveable feasts of the Church calendar and for astrological calculations, medical texts, prognostics (the Anglo-Saxon equivalent of the horoscope), charms (such as those for a toothache or for an easy labour), and even cryptograms (cf. the corpus website). The texts in the corpus are encoded in HTML, TEI-compliant SGML, and XML. The DOEC corpus can be ordered on CDs or assessed online by institutional site license at the corpus website (see appendix). The web-based query system allows for searches by single words, word combinations, word proximity and bibliographic sources.

6.5. The EEBO and ECCO databases

Early English Books Online (EEBO) is a joint effort launched in 1999 between the University of Michigan, Oxford University and ProQuest Information and Learning to create a full-text archive of Early English. From the first book published in English through the age of Spenser and Shakespeare, the EEBO collection now contains about 100,000 of over 125,000 titles listed in Pollard & Redgrave's *Short-Title Catalogue (1475–1640)* and Wing's *Short-Title Catalogue (1641–1700)* and their revised editions, as well as the *Thomason Tracts (1640–1661)* collection and the *Early English Books Tract Supplement*, covering a wide range of domains including, for example, English literature, history, philosophy, linguistics, theology, music, fine arts, education, mathematics and science (cf. the corpus website). The remaining titles will be digitized and added to the database in the near future. The database can be accessed online at the EEBO website (see appendix).

Note that Early English Books Online is more of an archive than a corpus. Another similar database is the Eighteenth Century Collections Online (ECCO), which claims to be the most ambitious single digitization project ever undertaken. It includes all significant English-language and foreign-language titles printed in Great Britain during the eighteenth century as well as thousands of important works from the Americas, covering a great variety of materials ranging from books and directories, Bibles, sheet music and sermons to advertisements, and amounting to more than 26 million pages in 150,000 printed volumes. This database is available for a free trial at the ECCO website (see appendix).

6.6. The Corpus of Early English Correspondence

The Corpus of Early English Correspondence (CEEC) is nowadays a cover term for a family of corpora. The full version completed in 1998 consists of 96 collections of 6,039 personal letters written by 778 people (women accounting for 20%) between 1417 and 1681, totaling 2.7 million words. The corpus is accompanied by a sender database, which offers users easy access to various sociolinguistic variables, including writer age, gender, place of birth, education, occupation, social rank, domicile and the relationship with the addressee. CEEC is a balanced corpus which can be neatly divided into two parts, both covering chronologically fairly equal periods: the first from ca. 1417 to 1550 and the second from 1551 to 1680 (cf. Laitinen 2002). Table 20.15 shows the proportions in terms of writers' social ranks and domiciles (see Nevalainen 2000, 40).

As the copyright problem has prevented public access to the full release of the CEEC corpus, a CEEC sampler (CEECS) was published by ICAME, which represents the non-

Tab. 20.15: The CEEC corpus by rank and domicile

Rank	%	Domicile	%
Royalty	2.4	Court	7.8
Nobility	14.7	London	13.9
Gentry	39.3	East Anglia	17.1
Clergy	13.6	North	12.5
Professionals	11.2	Other regions	48.6
Merchants	8.4		
Other nongentry	9.4		

copyrighted materials included in CEEC. The sampler reflects the structure of the full CEEC only in some respects. The time covered is nearly the same (1418–1680), which is divided into two parts. CEECS1 (246,055 words) covers the 15th and 16th centuries while CEECS2 (204,030 words) covers the 17th century. The sampler corpus consists of 23 collections of 1,147 letters with 194 informants, totaling 450,085 words. The CEEC sampler is available from ICAME or the Oxford Text Archive.

A more recent release of the annotated CEEC corpus (PCEEC) is now available from the Oxford Text Archive, which includes the bulk of the original corpus, with 2.2 million words in total (4,979 letters from 657 writers). This new release is part-of-speech tagged and fully parsed.

CEEC is now supplemented by an extension (CEECE, 1681–1800, ca. 2.2 million words) and a supplement (CEECSU 1402–1663, 0.44 million words). These two corpora are currently not available for public use.

6.7. The Zurich English Newspaper Corpus

The Zurich English Newspaper Corpus (ZEN) is a 1.2-million-word collection of newspapers in Early English, covering 120 years (from 1671 to 1791) of British newspaper history. To achieve a representative coverage, a wide variety of newspapers were included. Up to ten issues per newspaper were selected at ten-year intervals throughout the whole period. With the exception of stock market reports, lottery figures, long lists of names and poetry, the whole newspapers were included in the corpus. The news stories are grouped into two major categories: foreign news and home news, with each news category further classified according to its own text genre definition (cf. Fries/Schneider 2000). The corpus is split into four periods in order to track potential language change, as shown in Table 20.16 (see Schneider 2002, 202).

The ZEN corpus is SGML-conformant. It not only allows for linguistic analysis of different types of news stories in the 17th and 18th centuries, it has also made it possible to compare news texts in Early English with modern newspaper language. The ZEN query system (see appendix) allows restricted access to the online database.

Tab. 20.16: The ZEN corpus

Section	Period	Words	Sentences
A	1670–1709	242758	7642
B	1710–1739	347825	12163
C	1740–1769	339362	14112
D	1770–1799	298249	11843
Total		1228194	45760

6.8. The Innsbruck Computer Archive of Machine-Readable English Texts

The Innsbruck Computer Archive of Machine-Readable English Texts (ICAMET) contains ca. 500 Middle English texts totaling 5.7 million words. The database comprises three parts, namely, the Prose Corpus (129 texts written during 1100–1500, accounting for two thirds of the total), the Letter Corpus (254 letters written during 1386–1688, arranged in diachronic order), and the Prose Varia Corpus (mainly translations or normalized versions of Middle English texts). An advantage of ICAMET is that the database consists of complete texts instead of extracts, which allows literary, historical and topical analyses of various kinds, particularly studies of cultural history (Marcus 1999). Nevertheless, the copyright issue has restricted public access to many prose texts in the corpus. A sampler containing half of the prose texts and all letters is available from ICAME.

6.9. The Corpus of English Dialogues

The Corpus of English Dialogues (CED) contains 1.2 million words of Early Modern English dialogue texts produced over a 200-year period between 1560 and 1760. This sampling period is divided into five time spans of 40 years, with each including approximately 200,000 words. While the spoken language of the past is inaccessible directly to modern speakers, it is recorded in speech related texts. The CED corpus has sampled from six such text categories, including trial proceedings, witness depositions, drama, fictional dialogues, didactic works in dialogue form comprising the sub-categories of language teaching texts and other didactic works, and a residual category of miscellaneous texts (cf. Culpeper/Kytö 1997, 2000, and forthcoming).

The focus on dialogue will allow insight into the nature of impromptu speech and interactive two-way communication in the Early Modern English period – aspects which have received little research attention. The CED corpus was released by the Universities of Uppsala and Lancaster in spring 2006. A user's guide accompanying the corpus (Kytö/Walker 2006) is also available.

6.10. A Corpus of Late Eighteenth-Century Prose

A Corpus of Late Eighteenth-Century Prose contains 30,000 words of unpublished letters transcribed from the originals dated from the period 1761–1790. The corpus is distributed in both plain text (extended ASCII) and HTML versions. The text version can be used with a concordancer while the HTML version facilitates viewing the corpus in a browser. The plain text version is marked up in the COCOA format, giving information on writer, date and page breaks, etc. The corpus is intended to complement major diachronic corpora like the Helsinki Corpus, which stop in the early eighteenth century. Another aim of the corpus is "to illustrate non-literary English and English relatively uninfluenced by prescriptivist ideas, in the belief that it might help with research into change in (ordinary, spoken) language in the late Modern English period" (van Bergen/Denison 2004, 228). The corpus is by no means uniform, nor is it balanced. Nevertheless, because of the nature of the material, it is of great use to both linguists and historians. The corpus can be ordered from the Oxford Text Archive, free of charge, for use in education and research.

6.11. A Corpus of Late Modern English Prose

A Corpus of Late Modern English Prose contains 10,000 words of informal private letters written by British writers between 1861 and 1919. All decades in this period are represented, with about 6,000 words for the decade 1880–1889, 13,000 words for 1890–1899 and 20,000 words for the other four decades each. These blocks of texts are sampled from five sources.

Stored in seven extended (8-bit) ASCII text files, the corpus is marked up following the conventions used in the Helsinki Corpus, with information on writer, recipient, relationship, date, genre, and page etc. encoded in COCOA-style brackets (see Denison 1994). The corpus can be ordered at no cost from the Oxford Text Archive.

In addition to the diachronic corpora introduced in the previous sections, there are a number of online databases which are accessible on the Internet, for example, Michigan Early Modern English Materials (MEMEM, see appendix), the Corpus of Middle English Prose and Verse (CME, see appendix), the Middle English Collection (MidEng, see appendix), and the Korpus of Early Modern Playtexts in English (KEMPE, see appendix).

6.12. Corpus del Espahol

Corpus del Espanol contains 100 million words of Spanish texts covering periods from the 1200s to post-1900s which are distributed as follows: 20 million words from the 1200s-1400s, 40 million from the 1500s-1700s, 40 million from the 1800s-1900s, and 20 million from the 1900s. The data from the 1900s is divided equally among literature, oral texts, and newspapers/encyclopedias.

A unique feature of this corpus lies in its use of relational databases, which are used to store texts and various types of annotation. These databases are linked to a very powerful web interface that supports different types of search such as patterns/wildcards, collocations, word forms, lemmas, synonyms, and grammatical categories. The corpus can be accessed online over the Web (see *Corpus del Español* in appendix).

6.13. Corpus do Português

Corpus do Portugues contains more than 45 million words in more than 50,000 Portuguese texts from the 1300s to the 1900s. The structure of the corpus allows for easy comparison of the frequency and distribution of words, phrases, and grammatical constructions across different parameters, e. g. historical period (data for each century forms a subcorpus), dialect (Portugal and Brazil Portuguese), and register (oral, fiction, newspaper, and academic writing).

The corpus is open to the public free of charge via the Web interface (see *Corpus do Português* in appendix), which allows users to search for exact words or phrases, substrings, lemmas, part-of-speech, or any combinations of these. It is also possible to search for collocates within a ten-word window (five to the left and five to the right of the search term).

7. Spoken corpora

While general corpora like national corpora may contain spoken material, there are a number of well-known publicity available spoken English corpora, which will be introduced in this section.

7.1. The London-Lund Corpus

The London-Lund Corpus (LLC), as the first electronic corpus of spontaneous language, is a corpus of spoken British English recorded from 1953–1987. The corpus derived from two projects: the Survey of English Usage (SEU) at University College London and the Survey of Spoken English (SSE) at Lund University. There are two versions of LLC, the original version consisting of 87 transcripts from SSE totaling 435,000 words, and the complete version, which has been augmented by 13 supplementary transcripts from SEU. The full LLC corpus comprises 100 texts, each of 5,000 words, totaling half a million running words. A distinction is made between dialogue (e. g. face-to-face conversations, telephone conversations, and public discussion) and monologue (both spontaneous and prepared) in the organization of the corpus (cf. Greenbaum/Svartvik 1990). This textual information is encoded together with speaker information (e. g. gender, age, occupation). The texts in the corpus are transcribed orthographically, with detailed prosodic annotation. The LLC corpus is available from ICAME.

7.2. SEC, MARSEC and Aix-MARSEC

The Lancaster/IBM Spoken English Corpus (SEC) consists of approximately 53,000 words of spoken British English, mainly taken from radio broadcasts dating between 1984 and 1991. For a corpus of this size, it is impossible to include samples of every style of spoken English. The SEC corpus has been designed to cover speech categories suitable for speech synthesis, as shown in Table 20.17 (see Taylor/Knowles 1988).

Tab. 20.17: The SEC categories

Code	Category	Words	Proportion
A	Commentary	9066	17%
B	News broadcast	5235	10%
C	Lecture aimed at general audience	4471	8%
D	Lecture aimed at restricted audience	7451	14%
E	Religious broadcast including liturgy		
F	Magazine-style reporting	4710	9%
G	Fiction	7299	14%
H	Poetry	1292	2%
J	Dialogue	6826	13%
K	Propaganda	1432	3%
M	Miscellaneous	3352	6%
Total		52637	c. 100%

In the SEC corpus, efforts have been made to achieve a balance between the highly stylized texts (e. g. poetry, religious broadcast, propaganda) and dialogue, and between male and female speakers. Of the 53 speakers in the corpus, 17 are female, representing 30% of the corpus. The higher proportions of male speakers in the news and commentary categories reflect the tendency of the BBC (at the time when the texts in the corpus originated) to use mainly male speakers in these types of programmes.

SEC is available in orthographic, prosodic, grammatically tagged and treebank versions, which should prove most useful to those who research in the speech synthesis or speech recognition fields. The corpus can be ordered from ICAME.

The Machine Readable Spoken English Corpus (MARSEC) is an extension of SEC in which the original acoustic recordings were digitalized, and word-level time-alignment between the transcripts and the acoustic signals was included. Tonetic stress marks were also converted into ASCII symbols to make the corpus machine-readable. The prosodically annotated word-level alignment files are available at the MARSEC website (see appendix).

The Aix-MARSEC database is a further development of MARSEC. The database consists of two major components: the digitalized recordings from MARSEC and the annotations. Annotations have so far been undertaken at nine levels such as phonemes, syllables, words, stress feet, rhythm units, and minor and major turn units. Two supplementary levels, the grammatical annotation by CLAWS and a Property Grammar system developed at Aix-en-Provence, are to be integrated soon (cf. Auran/Bouzon/Hirst 2004). The database, together with tools, is available under GNU GPL licensing at the Aix-MARSEC project site (see appendix).

7.3. The Bergen Corpus of London Teenage Language

The Bergen Corpus of London Teenage Language (COLT) is the first large English corpus focusing on the speech of teenagers. It contains half a million words (about 55 hours of recording) of orthographically transcribed spontaneous teenage talk recorded in 1993 by 31 volunteer recruits from five socially different school boroughs. The speakers in the corpus are classified into six age groups: preadolescence (0−9 years old), early adolescence (10−13), middle adolescence (14−16), late adolescence (17−19), young adults (20−29) and older adults (30+). As the name of corpus suggests, the core of the corpus represents teenagers. The early, middle and late adolescence groups account respectively for 24%, 61% and 9%, totaling 94% of the corpus. The older adult group, mostly parents and teachers, takes up 6%. As regards speaker gender, girls and boys contributed roughly the same amount of text: the male speakers about 51.8% (230,616 words) and the female speakers 48.2% (214,215 words). In terms of social class, only about 50% of the corpus material can be assigned a social group value. The material that has been classified is evenly distributed across the three social groups: high, middle, and low. While a wide range of settings are present in the COLT corpus, settings in connection with school (48%) and home (32%) are the most common. Speaker-specific information (speaker age, gender, social class, etc.) and conversation-specific information (location and setting) is encoded in the header of each corpus text. In the body of the text, paralinguistic features and non-verbal sounds are also marked up (cf Haslerud/Stenström 1995).

The corpus constitutes part of the British National Corpus. In addition, COLT is released in both orthographically transcribed (pure text) and tagged versions (using the CLAWS C7 tagset). A prosodically annotated version (a representative selection amounting to approximately 150,000 words) is also available. The corpus is free for non-commercial purposes and can be accessed online by registered users (COLT, see appendix) or ordered form ICAME.

7.4. The Cambridge and Nottingham Corpus of Discourse in English

The Cambridge and Nottingham Corpus of Discourse in English (CANCODE) is part of the Cambridge International Corpus (CIC, see appendix). The corpus comprises five million words of transcribed spontaneous speech recorded in Britain and Ireland between 1994 and 2001, covering a wide variety of mostly informal settings: casual conversation, people working together, people shopping, people finding out information, discussions and many other types of interaction. As CANCODE is designed as a contextually and interactively differentiated corpus, the data has been carefully collected and sociolinguistically profiled with reference to a range of different speech genres and with an emphasis on everyday communication.

A unique feature of CANCODE is that the corpus has been coded with information pertaining to the relationship between the speakers: whether they are intimates (living together), casual acquaintances, colleagues at work, or strangers. For this purpose, CANCODE is organized along two main axes: context-type and interaction-type. Alongside the axis of context-type are, on the cline from "public" to "private", transactional, professional, socializing and intimate. Alongside the axis of interaction-type are, on the cline from "collaborative" to "non-collaborative", information provision, collaborative idea, and collaborative work. The interactions between the two axes, together with typi-

Tab. 20.18: CANCODE text types

Context-type Information provision	Interaction-type		
	Collaborative idea	Collaborative work	
Transactional	commentary by museum guide	chatting with hairdresser	choosing and buying a television
Professional	oral report at group meeting	planning meeting at place of work	colleagues window-dressing
Socializing	telling jokes to friends	reminiscing with friends	friends working together
Intimate	partner relating the story to a film seen	siblings discussing their childhood	couple decorating a room

cal settings, are shown in Table 20.18 (see Carter/McCarthy 2004, 67). This coding allows users to look more closely at how different levels of familiarity (formality) affect the way in which people speak to each other. The corpus is not currently available to the public.

7.5. The Spoken Corpus of the Survey of English Dialects

A corpus that was built specifically for the study of English dialects is the spoken corpus of the Survey of English Dialects (SED, see Beare/Scott 1999). The Survey of English Dialects was started in 1948 by Harold Orton at the University of Leeds. The initial work comprised a questionnaire-based survey of traditional dialects based on extensive interviews of about 1,000 people from 313 locations all over rural England. During the survey, a number of recordings were made as well as the detailed interviews. The recordings, which were made during 1948–1961, consist of about 60 hours of dialogue of people aged 60 or above talking about their memories, families, work and the folklore of the countryside from a century ago. Elderly people were chosen as subjects because they were most likely to speak the traditional, "uncontaminated" dialect of their area.

The spoken corpus derived from SED consists of transcripts of 314 recordings from 289 (out of the 313) SED localities in England, totaling roughly 800,000 running words. The original recordings were transcribed, with sound files linked to transcripts. The corpus is marked up in TEI-compliant SGML and POS tagged using CLAWS.

While the spoken corpus of SED comprises data invariably produced by elderly people, as the survey was conducted nationwide, covering every county of England, it has, for the first time, made it possible to conduct a detailed study of the regional variation in English dialects on a national level. Also, as the data reflects a society which was different in many ways from today, the corpus is a valuable resource for dialectologists and historical linguistics as well as historians. The CD-ROM of the spoken corpus is published by Routledge, London.

7.6. The Intonational Variation in English Corpus

The Intonational Variation in English (IViE) corpus was constructed for the investigation of cross-varietal and stylistic variation in British English intonation, focusing on nine urban varieties of English spoken in the British Isles, i. e. Belfast, Bradford, Cambridge, Cardiff, Dublin, Liverpool, Leeds, London, and Newcastle. The corpus comprises 36 hours of speech data in five different speaking styles: phonetically controlled sentences (statements, questions without morpho-syntactic markers, WH-questions, inversion questions, coordination structures), a read text (the fairy tale *Cinderella*), a retold version of the same text, a map task ("find your way around a small town") and free conversations (on the assigned topic of smoking). The data was collected in urban secondary schools, and the speakers were 16 years old at the time when the recordings were made. A minimum of six male and six female speakers from each variety were recorded, though more speakers were included for some of the varieties, totaling 116 speakers in all (cf. Grabe/Post/Nolan 2001). The corpus is available free of charge for non-commercial use only. Orthographic and prosodic transcriptions, together with digitalized sound files can be ordered on CDs or downloaded from the corpus website (see appendix).

7.7. The Longman British Spoken Corpus

The Longman British Spoken Corpus contains 10 million words of natural, spontaneous conversations from a representative sample of the population in terms of speaker age, gender, social group and region, and from the language of lectures, business meetings, after dinner speeches and chat shows. The design criteria are discussed in detail in Crowdy (1993). The Longman British Spoken Corpus is the first large scale attempt to collect spoken data in a systematic way. The corpus is part of the spoken section of the British National Corpus (see section 2.1.).

7.8. The Longman Spoken American Corpus

The Longman Spoken American Corpus comprises five million words of spoken data collected from everyday conversations of more than 1,000 Americans of various age groups, levels of education, and ethnicity from over 30 US States. Equal numbers of participants were chosen from each region, and a balance was struck between the numbers of participants from rural and city areas within those regions. Recordings were made of four-hour chunks of the normal daily conversations of each participant over periods of at least four days. The participants were chosen to be representative for gender, age, ethnicity and education, as shown by the latest US demographic census statistics (Table 20.19, see Stern 1997). As part of the Longman Corpus Network (see appendix), the Longman Spoken American Corpus is a property of the Longman publishers for in-house use only.

Tab. 20.19: Demographic distribution of the Longman Spoken American Corpus

Variable	Proportions
Gender	Male: 50 %; Female: 50 %
Age	18–24: 20 %; 25–34: 20 %; 35–44: 20 %; 45–60: 20 %; 60+: 20 %
Ethnicity	White: 75 %; Black: 13 %; Hispanic: 8 %; Asian: 4 %
Education	Degree/Higher degree: 33 %; College: 33 %; High school: 33 %

7.9. The Santa Barbara Corpus of Spoken American English

The Santa Barbara Corpus of Spoken American English (SBCSAE) is based on hundreds of recordings of spontaneous speech from all over the United States, representing a wide variety of people of different regional origins, ages, occupations, and ethnic and social backgrounds. It reflects the many ways that people use language in their lives: conversation, gossip, arguments, on-the-job talk, card games, city council meetings, sales pitches, classroom lectures, political speeches, bedtime stories, sermons, weddings, etc. (cf. Du Bois et al. 2000–2004).

The corpus is particularly useful for research into speech recognition as each speech file is accompanied by a transcript in which phrases are time-stamped to allow them to be linked with the audio recording from which the transcription was produced. Personal names, place names, phone numbers, etc. in the transcripts have been altered to preserve the anonymity of the speakers and their acquaintances, and the audio files have been filtered to make these portions of the recordings unrecognizable. The SBCSAE corpus is distributed by the LDC in five parts, the first four of which have become available. The corpus (including both transcripts and digital audio files) can also be downloaded freely at the TalkBank site (see TalkBank SBCSAE in appendix).

7.10. The Saarbrucken Corpus of Spoken English

The Saarbrücken Corpus of Spoken English (SCoSE) consists of five parts. Parts 1 (Stories) and 3 (Jokes) comprise excerpts transcribed from audio-taped real conversations among family members and friends, fellow students and colleagues at Northern Illinois University and at Saarland University. Part 2 (Indianapolis Interviews) includes transcripts of stories recorded in interviews with senior citizens aged 80 and older in a retirement community in Indianapolis, Indiana in the summer of 2002. Conversations included in Part 4 (Complete Conversations) are transcripts from recordings made by two students in their junior year at a large state university near Chicago as a class assignment to record family and friends in natural settings during their Thanksgiving break at the end of November. The final part (Drawing Experiment) of the corpus consists of transcripts of conversations in which one subject describes a drawing to the other in the same pair who has not seen the picture. All subjects are young students aged 20–25 at various colleges near Chicago. In all of these parts, speech turns are indicated. The hard copy of the corpus (in PDF format), together with a description of transcription conventions, is available at no cost at the corpus site (cf. see SCoSE in appendix). The electronic copy of the corpus, together with digitalized audio files, is downloadable at the TalkBank site (see appendix).

7.11. The Switchboard Corpus

The Switchboard Corpus (SWB) is a corpus of 2,438 spontaneous telephone conversations, averaging 6 minutes in length, recorded for over 542 speakers of both sexes from every major dialect of American English in the early 1990s. The transcripts total three

Tab. 20.20: The Switchboard corpus

Dialect	Speaker age	Speaker sex	Education
South Midland (155) Western (85) North Midland (77) Northern (75) Southern (56) NYC (33) Mixed (26) New England (21)	20–29 (140) 30–39 (179) 40–49 (112) 50–59 (87) 60–69 (13)	Male (292) Female (239)	High school – (14) College – (39) College (309) College + (176) Unknown (4)

million words (over 240 hours of recordings). Information relevant to speakers' sex, year of birth, education level and dialect region is available in the documentation accompanying the corpus. Table 20.20 shows the distribution of major sociolinguistic variables (see Linguistic Data Consortium (1995), the Switchboard User's Manual).

As each transcript in the corpus is time-aligned at the word level, the corpus is useful for sociolinguistic studies as well as for speech recognition. The corpus is distributed by the LDC. A subcorpus annotated with various types of linguistic information (e. g. POS tagging and parsing) is also freely available for download at the TalkBank site (see TalkBank SWB in appendix). It can also be searched over the Web (see SWB online in appendix).

7.12. The Wellington Corpus of Spoken New Zealand English

The Wellington Corpus of Spoken New Zealand English (WSC) comprises one million words of spoken New Zealand English in the form of 551 2,000-word extracts collected between 1988 and 1994 (99 % of the data from 1990–1994, the exception being eight private interviews). A very stringent criterion was adopted to ensure the integrity of the New Zealand samples included in the corpus. Data was collected only from those who had lived in New Zealand since before the age of 10, had spent less than 10 years (or half their lifetime, whichever was greater) abroad, and had not made an overseas trip during the year before data collection. The extracts are classified into 15 text categories covering a wide range of contexts in which each style of speech is found, as shown in Table 20.21 (cf. Holmes/Vine/Johnson 1998).

The formal speech section (12 %) in the WSC corpus includes all monologue categories and "parliamentary debate" in the public dialogue category. The semi-formal section (13 %) includes the three types of interview (both public and private). All of the other text categories make up the informal speech section (75 %), with private conversation alone accounting for 50 % of the corpus. In terms of speaker gender, women contributed 52 % and men 48 % of the final transcribed words, reflecting the New Zealand population balance. With regard to speaker age, data for the age group 20–24 accounts for more than 20 % of the corpus, and the proportions for age groups 45–49 and 40–44 both exceed 10 % while there is little data for those aged over 70. The distribution across different age groups generally mirrors the population structure in New Zealand. The corpus data also reflects the distribution of population across ethnic groups, with data

Tab. 20.21: Composition of the WSC corpus

Category	Text category	Words
Monologue: Public scripted, broadcast	Broadcast news	28,929
	Broadcast monologue	11,205
	Broadcast weather	3,641
Monologue: Public unscripted	Sports commentary	26,010
	Judge's summation	4,489
	Lecture	30,406
	Teacher monologue	12,496
Dialogue: Private	Conversation	500,363
	Telephone conversation	70,156
	Oral history interview	21,972
	Social dialect interview	31,058
Dialogue: Public	Radio talkback	84,321
	Broadcast interview	96,775
	Parliamentary debate	22,446
	Transactions and meetings	102,332
Total		1,046,599

collected for Pakeha accounting for 76%, and for Maori 18%. Every speech sample included in the corpus is described as fully as possible in terms of sociolinguistic variables such as the gender, age, regional origin, social class, level of education and occupation of its contributor.

The unusually high proportion of private material and the rich sociolinguistic variation make the WSC corpus a valuable resource for research into informal spoken registers as well as for sociolinguistic studies. The corpus is available from ICAME.

7.13. The Limerick Corpus of Irish English

The Limerick Corpus of Irish English (L-CIE) comprises one million words in the form of 375 transcripts of naturally occurring conversations recorded in a wide variety of speech contexts throughout Ireland (excluding Northern Ireland). Speakers range from 14 to 78 years of age and there is an equal representation of both male and female speakers. While the corpus consists mainly of casual conversation, it also has over 200,000 words of professional, transactional and pedagogic Irish English which, along with the casual conversation data, were carefully collected with reference to a range of different speech genres. The corpus follows the design of CANCODE by organizing the corpus alongside the axes of context type and interaction type, as shown in Table 20.22 (cf. Farr/Murphy/O'Keeffe 2004).

Tab. 20.22: Design of the L-CIE corpus

	Information provision	Collaborative idea	Collaborative task
Pedagogic	80,253 words e. g. linguistics lecture	60,473 words e. g. English poetry tutorial	10,000 words e. g. one-to-one computer lesson
Professional	145,000 words e. g. real-estate office talk	100,000 words e. g. team meeting	60,000 words e. g. waitresses washing dishes
Socializing	50,000 words e. g. describing a new bar	54,356 words e. g. friends discussing college	30,000 words e. g. friends assembling a bed
Intimate	60,000 word e. g. mother storytelling	266,000 words e. g. partners making holiday plans	60,000 word e. g. family preparing dinner
Transactional	5,000 words e. g. product presentation	10,000 words e. g. chatting in a taxi	1,000 words e. g. eye examination

While it is not designed to be geographically representative – it does not include data from every county in the Republic of Ireland, the L-CIE corpus has developed a careful sociolinguistic classification scheme which facilitates inter-corpus comparisons, especially with regard to linguistic choices and the relationships that hold between the speakers. The corpus website (see appendix) allows online access by registered users.

7.14. The Hong Kong Corpus of Spoken English

The Hong Kong Corpus of Spoken English (HKCSE) comprises 200 hours of orthographically transcribed recordings. The corpus is divided into four subcorpora (conversations, academic discourses, business discourses and public discourses, with about 50 hours of recordings for each), amounting to approximately two million words. The four subcorpora represent the main overarching spoken English discourses in Hong Kong. The compilation work began in the mid-1990s when half a million words of natural

Tab. 20.23: Structure of HKCSE

Subcorpus	Speech type	Size
Academic discourse	Lectures, seminars, student presentations, tutorials and supervisions, workshops for staff	28 hours 30 minutes
Business discourse	Service encounters, meetings, interviews, presentations and announcements, conference calls and videoconferencing, informal office talks, workplace phone calls	29 hours and 14 minutes
Public discourse	Speeches, talks plus interaction, press briefings with/without interaction, TV/radio interviews, discussion forums	25 hours
Conversation	Naturally occurring conversations	27 hours

conversations were recorded between Hong Kong Chinese and non-Cantonese speakers (mostly native speakers of English).

In addition to the orthographic transcription, part of the corpus has been annotated prosodically to enable the examination of the communicative role of intonation. Presently, 1.06 million words have been annotated, covering 53 % of the orthographic version of the corpus. Table 20.23 shows the contents of the HKCSE corpus (cf. Cheng/Greaves/Warren 2005).

Presently the prosodic version of HKCSE is perhaps the largest English corpus which has been annotated with prosodic details. In addition, a computer program (iConc) is specifically developed for the prosodic version of the corpus, which can search for tags for various prosodic features such as tone unit, tones, prominence, termination and key. The prosodic version of the corpus is expected to be released on CD-ROMs.

8. Academic and professional English corpora

As language may vary considerably across genre and domain, specialized corpora provide valuable resources for investigations in the relevant genres and domains. Unsurprisingly, there has recently been much interest in the creation and exploitation of specialized corpora in academic or professional settings. This section introduces a number of well-known English corpora of this kind.

8.1. The MICASE and MICUSP corpora

The Michigan Corpus of Academic Spoken English (MICASE) contains approximately 1.8 million words in the form of 152 transcripts of nearly 200 hours of recordings of 1,571 speakers, focusing on contemporary university speech within the domain of the University of Michigan. Table 20.24 shows the structure of the corpus (cf. English Language Institute (2003), the MICASE Manual).

Tab. 20.24: The MICASE corpus

Criterion	Distribution
Speaker gender	Male (46 %) Female (54 %)
Academic role	Faculty (49 %) Students (44 %) Other (7 %)
Language status	Native speakers (88 %) Non native speakers (12 %)
Academic division	Humanities & Arts (26 %) Social Sciences & Education (25 %) Biological & Health Sciences (19 %) Physical Sciences & Engineering (21 %) Other (9 %)
Primary discourse mode	Monologue (33 %) Panel (8 %) Interactive (42 %) Mixed (17 %)
Speech event type	Advising (3.5 %) Colloquia (8.9 %) Discussion sections (4.4 %) Dissertation defenses (3.4 %) Interviews (0.8 %) Labs (4.4 %) Large lectures (15.2 %) Small lectures (18.9 %) Meetings (4.1 %) Office hours (7.1 %) Seminars (8.9 %) Study groups (7.7 %) Student presentations (8.5 %) Service encounters (1.5 %) Tours (1.3 %) Tutorials (1.6 %)

In the MICASE corpus, speakers are divided into four age groups: 17–23, 24–30, 31–50, and 51+. In terms of academic role, they are classified into a number of categories: junior and senior undergraduates, junior and senior postgraduates, junior and senior faculty and researchers, etc. The language status can be native speaker (North American English), other native speaker (non-American English), near native speaker, and non-native speaker.

The MICASE corpus was originally marked up in TEI-compliant SGML. All of the SGML files have now been converted to the XML format in order to meet the requirements for further corpus development including a web-based search interface and the streaming web delivery of the sound recordings, synchronized with the transcripts. At present, only the orthographically transcribed version of the corpus is available, though future releases will include various kinds of annotations such as part-of-speech, lemmas and discourse-pragmatic categories. The MICASE corpus can be searched online free of charge or ordered at a nominal fee at the corpus website (see appendix).

MICUSP is an acronym for Michigan Corpus of Upper-level Student Papers, an ongoing project which aims to compile a 1.6-million-word collection of 500 to 1,000 word samples of writing by students at different stages of undergraduate and graduate level study in both humanities and science subjects, both native and non-native speakers, from across the University of Michigan (see the MICUSP project site for updates).

8.2. The British Academic Spoken English corpus

The British Academic Spoken English (BASE) corpus, which is designed as a British counterpart to MICASE, was constructed jointly by the Universities of Warwick and Reading. The corpus comprises a collection of recordings and marked up transcripts of 160 lectures and 40 seminars, totaling approximately 196 hours of recordings and 1.6 million words. The lectures and seminars spread evenly across four subject areas, as shown in Table 20.25.

Tab. 20.25: Components of the BASE corpus

Subject area	Lectures	Seminars
Arts and Humanities	42	10
Social Studies and Sciences	40	11
Physical Sciences	40	9
Life and Medical Sciences	39	10
Total	161	40

Unlike MICASE, the BASE corpus only covers two types of speech event, lectures and seminars. Most of the recordings were made on digital video instead of audiotapes. All of these recordings have been transcribed and marked up in TEI-compliant XML. The corpus will not only enable research into spoken academic English at the lexical and structural levels, it will also make it possible, when used in combination with MICASE, to compare academic spoken English in British and US university settings. The British

Academic Spoken English data (transcripts in plain text and XML formats and audio/video files) can be downloaded at the BASE website (see BASE in appendix), but only authorized users can access them.

The British Academic Written English (BAWE) corpus of student writing is a British cousin of MICUSP. This is a selection of about 3,000 student assignments from four disciplinary groupings (Arts and Humanities, Life Sciences, Physical Sciences, and Social Sciences), which are sampled in 28 departments across the three British universities (Oxford Brookes, Reading and Warwick). These samples represent both undergraduate work (typically three years of study) and postgraduate work (typically one year of study) of a high quality (graded II.i (B+) or above). The corpus is marked up in TEI-compliant XML, with metadata such as student gender, year of birth, first language, course of study, year of study, module name and code, etc. recorded in the corpus header. Textual organization in each assignment is also marked up to show title and title page, table of contents, abstract or summary, section headings, figures and diagrams, lists (simple, bulleted and ordered), quotations, bibliography, and appendices. Boundaries for paragraphs and sentences are also marked up. The structure of the BAWE corpus together with the metadata encoded make it possible to compare textual organization across years, text types, disciplines and disciplinary groupings. This corpus is freely available to researchers who agree to the license conditions (see BAWE in appendix).

8.3. The Reading Academic Text corpus

The Reading Academic Text (RAT) corpus is a collection of academic texts written by academic staff and research students at the University of Reading. The initial corpus was composed of twenty research articles written by staff and a small number of PhD theses contributed by successful doctoral candidates in the Faculty of Agriculture, totaling nearly a million words. The theses included in the corpus are all written by native speakers. Since the corpus was created in 1995, the number of theses has increased from 8 to 38. The corpus is still expanding further to represent the discourses of a greater range of disciplines covering both the natural and social sciences as well as a wider range of text types including dissertations, projects, laboratory reports, and samples of textbook readings for Master's courses. In addition to the original files, the texts have been converted to an HTML version which allows the full text to be viewed in a browser, and a plain text version used for linguistic analysis and for the coding of the corpus (see Thompson 2001). The RAT corpus has been used to study text construction practices in academic settings such as the organization of theses in different disciplines as well as the various uses of citations. At present, access to the corpus is restricted to the staff and researchers at the School of Linguistics and Applied Language Studies of Reading University, though it is possible for other users to access the corpus on a Research Attachment arrangement.

8.4. The Academic Corpus

The Academic Corpus is a written corpus of academic English developed at Victoria University of Wellington. The corpus contains approximately 3.5 million words, covering 28 subject areas from four faculty sections (arts, commerce, law, and science), as shown in Table 20.26 (cf. Coxhead 2000, 220).

Tab. 20.26: Subject areas in the Academic Corpus

Faculty	Arts	Commerce	Law	Science	Total
Texts	122	107	72	113	414
Words	883,214	879,547	874,723	875,846	3,513,330
Subject areas	Education History Linguistics Philosophy Politics Psychology Sociology	Accounting Economics Finance Industrial relations Management Marketing Public policy	Constitutional law Criminal law Family law and medicolegal International law Pure commercial law Quasi-commercial law Rights and remedies	Biology Chemistry Computer science Geography Geology Mathematics Physics	

Each of these faculty sections is divided into seven subject areas of ca. 125,000 words, totaling 875,000 words for each section. The corpus comprises 414 academic texts by more than 400 authors which were sampled from journal articles, book chapters, course workbooks, laboratory manuals, course notes and the Internet. With the exception of 41 excerpts from the Brown corpus, 31 excerpts from LOB and 42 excerpts from the Wellington Corpus of Written New Zealand English, full texts (excluding bibliographies) are included. The majority of the texts were written for an international audience, with 64% sourced in New Zealand, 20% in Britain, 13% in the United States, 2% in Canada and 1% in Australia. The texts were selected according to whether they were of suitable length (over 2,000 running words) and were representative of the academic genre in that they were written for an academic audience. Efforts have also been made to balance the corpus with respect to the number of short (2,000–5,000 words), medium-length (5,000–10,000 words) and long (over 10,000 words) texts in the four faculty sections.

The corpus has been used to develop an Academic Word List (AWL) containing 570 word families (see Coxhead 2000), which is available at the AWL site (see appendix).

8.5. The Corpus of Spoken Professional American English

The Corpus of Spoken Professional American English (CSPAE) has been constructed using a selection of transcripts of interactions of various types occurring in professional settings recorded during 1994–1998. The corpus contains two million words of speech involving over 400 speakers. The CSPAE corpus has two main components. The first component is made up of transcripts (0.9 million words) of press conferences from the White House, which contains almost exclusively question and answer sessions in addition to some policy statements by politicians and White House officials. The second component consists of transcripts (1.1 million words) of faculty meetings and committee meetings related to national tests, which involve statements and discussions, as well as questions (cf. Barlow 1998).

The transcripts in the corpus have been marked up in a minimal but consistent way. The markup scheme only indicates speech turns by identifying the last name of the speaker (or VOICE if the name is unknown) with the <SP> element, and puts non-verbal events such as laughter in the brackets. Two versions of the corpus are available, a raw text version and an annotated version tagged by the Lancaster CLAWS tagger. Both versions can be ordered from the corpus website (see CSPAE in appendix).

8.6. The Corpus of Professional English

A much more ambitious project has been initiated by the Professional English Research Consortium (PERC), which aims to create a 100-million-word Corpus of Professional English (CPE). The corpus is expected to include both spoken and written discourse used by working professionals and professionals-in-training, covering a wide range of domains such as science, engineering, technology, law, medicine, finance and other professions. The CPE corpus is designed as a balanced representation of professional English via texts published between 1995 and 2001 by over 1,000 major review and research journals, trade magazines, and textbooks, in American and British English, based on selection criteria such as impact factors provided by the *Journal of Citation Reports*, and other pertinent criteria (cf. Rayson et al. 2005).

The Corpus of Professional English is marked up in XML. Contextual information such as author's name, title, publication year and journal title is stored in the corpus header. Structural information is also encoded to show paragraphs, sections, headings and similar features in written texts. Linguistic annotations such as POS and semantic tagging will be carried out on the corpus using tools developed at Lancaster University.

The CPE corpus can be used for linguistic research as well as for the development of educational resources, such as specialized dictionaries, handbooks, language tests, and other materials that will be useful to working professionals and professionals-in-training. The corpus, when completed, will be made available to consortium members for online access at the PERC website (see PERC in appendix).

9. Parsed corpora

Parsing, also called treebanking, is a form of corpus annotation (see article 13). It is independent of corpus design criteria. Hence, a corpus, whether balanced or specialized, whether written or spoken, can be syntactically parsed. However, as parsing is a much more challenging task which often necessitates human correction, parsed corpora are typically very small in size. Of the corpora we have introduced so far, only ICE-GB is parsed. This section introduces a number of well-known parsed corpora.

9.1. The Lancaster-Leeds Treebank

The Lancaster-Leeds Treebank is perhaps the first syntactically parsed corpus. The corpus is a subset of 45,000 words taken from all text categories in the LOB corpus, which was parsed manually by Geoffrey Sampson using a specially devised surface-level phrase structure grammar compatible with the CLAWS word-tagging scheme (cf. Sampson 1987). The annotation scheme used in the Lancaster-Leeds Treebank, which consisted of 47 labels for daughter nodes (14 phrase and clause classes, 28 word classes and five classes of punctuation marks), represented surface grammar only, without indications of logical form. This hand-crafted treebank provided training data for the automatic probabilistic parser which was used to analyze the Lancaster Parsed Corpus. The corpus was not published but is available from UCREL at Lancaster University (see appendix).

9.2. The Lancaster Parsed Corpus

The Lancaster Parsed Corpus (LPC) is a much larger sample of approximately 144,000 words taken from the LOB corpus that has been parsed. Except for categories M (science fiction, six samples) and R (humor, nine samples), which are included in their entirety, LPC takes the first 10 samples from each of the other 13 text categories in LOB, totaling 145 files which account for 13.29% of the full LOB corpus. Even in these 145 samples, longer sentences have been excluded from the parsed corpus because the parser was unable to process sentences over 20–25 words in length, with the result that the parsed corpus no longer contains LOB text extracts in their entirety. The errors resulting from automatic parsing were corrected by hand to ensure the corpus is reasonably error free (cf Garside/Leech/Váradi 1992).

The Lancaster Parsed Corpus can be regarded as a treebank broadly representative of the syntax of written English across a great variety of styles and text types. It provides a testbed for wide-coverage general-purpose grammars and parsers of English and a valuable resource for quantitative linguistic studies of English syntax. The corpus is available through ICAME.

9.3. The SUSANNE corpus

The SUSANNE (an acronym for "surface and underlying structural analysis of natural English") is a 130,000-word sub-sample taken from the Brown corpus of American English that has been parsed. The parsed corpus comprises 64 text samples, with 16 taken from each of the four text categories: A (press reportage), G (belles-letters, biography and memoir), J (learned writing) and N (adventure and Western fiction).

The parsing was largely undertaken manually in accordance with the SUSANNE analytic scheme developed by Geoffrey Sampson in collaboration with Geoffrey Leech on the basis of samples from written British and American English. The SUSANNE scheme is perhaps the first serious attempt to produce a comprehensive, fully explicit annotation scheme for English grammatical structure.

In SUSANNE, a parse tree is represented as a bracketed string, with the labels of non-terminal nodes inserted between opening and closing brackets. There are three types of information in the parsing scheme: a form tag, a function tag and an index. The hierarchy of form tag ranks (word, phrase, clause and root) defines the shape of a parse tree. The function tags identify surface roles such as surface and logical subject, agent of passive, and time and place adjuncts. An index shows referential identity between nodes (cf. Sampson 1995).

The SUSANNE corpus was first released in 1992 and its latest version, Release 5, was published in 2000. Each successive release has corrected errors found in earlier releases. The latest release, together with the documentation accompanying the corpus, is distributed free of charge at the SUSANNE website (see appendix).

More recently two derivations of the SUSANNE Treebank have been produced. One is SEMiSUSANNE, which covers 33 of the 64 texts from SUSANNE, and supplements the grammatical annotations of the SUSANNE scheme with semantic annotations identifying the WordNet (1.6) senses in which vocabulary items are used. SEMiSUSANNE is freely available at the SUSANNE website. The other recent version of SUSANNE is in XML-based GXL (Graph eXchange Language), which can be downloaded freely at the Indogram (Induction of Document Grammar for Webgenre Representation) project site (see XGL in appendix).

9.4. The CHRISTINE corpus

The CHRISTINE corpus is a spoken counterpart to SUSANNE, developed by Geoffrey Sampson and his team. It is one of the first treebanks of spontaneous speech. The CHRISTINE analytic scheme includes explicit extensions to the SUSANNE annotation which are designed to handle speech phenomena such as pauses, discourse items and speech repairs. The first stage of CHRISTINE (CHRISTINE/I), which was released in 1999, is based on 40 extracts chosen at random from the demographically sampled component in the spoken BNC and other sources, totaling approximately 80,500 words of spoken data representing 147 identified speakers in addition to a great number of unidentifiable speakers. The information about speakers and the metadata originally contained in the BNC corpus header were converted into database files accompanying the corpus (cf Sampson 2000).

The full version of the CHRISTINE corpus includes 66 further texts drawn from the spoken BNC and other sources. The overall proportion of the BNC data accounts for 50 % of the full CHRISTINE corpus, with 40 % from the London-Lund corpus and 10 % from the Reading Emotional Speech Corpus (see Stibbard 2001 for a description). The full release also incorporates a minor change in the distribution of analytic information between the fields to make it more compatible with SUSANNE and easier to read. This version became available in 2000. At present CHRISTINE in plain text and XML can be downloaded at the corpus website (see CHRISTINE and XGL in appendix).

9.5. The LUCY corpus

The LUCY corpus is the third in Sampson's series of treebanks. This corpus represents written English in modern Britain, ranging from published prose to the less skilled writing of young adults, and spontaneous writing by children aged 9–12. To deal with writing of this latter type, the LUCY parsing scheme contains some further extensions to the SUSANNE scheme which can identify cases where an unskilled writer fails to put words together in a meaningful way (cf. Sampson 2005).

There are 239 text files in LUCY, amounting to 165,000 words. The corpus consists of three sections: polished writing (41 text files, 102,000 words), young adult writing (48 text files, 33,000 words), and child writing (150 files, 30,000 words). The polished texts are taken from both informative and imaginative categories in the written section of the

British National Corpus. The young adult writing comprises three groups, namely, A-level general study scripts, access-course coursework, and first-year undergraduate essays. The child writing section is composed of material from the Nuffield corpus, a collection of writing by children aged between 9 and 12 years in 1965.

In addition to providing a valuable source of information on the realities of skilled written usage in modern Britain, LUCY holds the promise to support study of the process through which English-speaking children acquire writing skills. The current version of the corpus is Release 2, which became available in late 2005, and has corrected a number of errors in the initial release of 2003. As the data from the BNC (about half of the corpus) is copyright protected, a copyright free edition and an unreduced edition were prepared. The only difference is that in the copyright free edition, for those files where copyright is an issue, the words of the original texts are replaced by abbreviations. While these abbreviations may be recoverable to human eyes, they are by no means recoverable computationally. This reduced version is available from LUCY website (see appendix). The unreduced edition is only available to those who have purchased a copy of the BNC corpus. The XML version is also available (see XGL in appendix).

9.6. ICE-GB

The British component of the International Corpus of English (ICE-GB) is the first corpus that has been completed in the ICE series. Like all of the ICE components, ICE-GB comprises 300 spoken and 200 written texts from 32 categories, amounting to one million words. As noted in section 5.1., this corpus is not only POS tagged but also fully parsed and hand checked. The corpus contains 83,394 parse trees, including 59,640 in the spoken part of the corpus. Each node in the tree is labelled with up to three types of information: word class/syntactic category, syntactic function and features (e. g. transitivity), the latter being optional (cf Nelson/Wallis/Aarts 2002).

Unlike the SUSANNE, CHRISTINE and LUCY corpora, which come without retrieval software, ICE-GB is distributed together with a utility program, ICECUP, which allows very complex queries of various kinds, e. g. markup queries, exact and inexact grammatical node queries, text fragment queries, Fuzzy Tree Fragment (FTF) queries, and sociolinguistic variable queries.

The second full release of the corpus and ICECUP can be ordered on CD-ROMs from the ICE-GB website (see appendix). The ICE-GB sampler, which includes ICECUP and ten ICE-GB texts, is also available free of charge at the site. The digitized speech recordings of the spoken part of the corpus, aligned with the text, can be ordered as an option (11 CD-ROMs) with Release 2 of ICE-GB, which also includes an updated version of ICECUP (3.1) that can play audio files. This feature allows researchers to hear the original source of what they see on-screen. In addition to the online help included in ICECUP, Nelson/Wallis/Aarts (2002) provides a comprehensive reference guide to both corpus and software.

9.7. The Diachronic Corpus of Present-Day Spoken English

The Diachronic Corpus of Present-Day Spoken English (DCPSE) is composed of 400,000 words from the spoken section of ICE-GB (collected in the early 1990s, see section 9.6.) and 400,000 words from the London-Lund Corpus (late 1960s–early 1980s, see section 7.1.). The corpus DCPSE was parsed using ICE-GB as a gold standard, and the parsing has been corrected by a variety of methods to ensure a high quality. The corpus is particularly useful in research of recent change in grammar of spoken English. This resource is available for order on CD-ROM (see DCPSE in appendix), which comes with ICEUP, the same exploration tool as ICE-GB.

9.8. The Penn Treebank

The Penn Treebank (PTB) is an example of skeleton parsing. Three releases of the treebank have so far been published by the LDC. The original release (Penn Treebank I, 1992) contains over 4.5 million words of American English data. The whole corpus is POS tagged while two thirds of the data is parsed. All of this material has been corrected by hand after automatic processing. Table 20.27 shows the components of Penn Treebank Release I (cf. Marcus/Santorini/Marcinkiewicz 1993).

Tab. 20.27: Penn Treebank Release I

Component	Parsed words	Parsed words
Dow Jones news stories	3,065,776	1,061,166
Brown corpus retagged	1,172,041	1,172,041
Dept. of Energy abstract	231,404	231,404
MUC-3 messages	111,828	111,828
Library of America texts	105,652	105,652
IBM manuals	89,121	89,121
Dept. of Agriculture bulletins	78,555	78,555
ATIS sentences	19,832	19,832
WBUR radio transcripts	11,589	11,589
Total	4,855,798	2,881,188

Penn Treebank Release I applies a parsing scheme which is extended and modified on the basis of the Lancaster parsing scheme. While both annotation schemes employ a phrase structure grammar which covers noun, verb, adjective, adverbial and prepositional phrases, the Lancaster scheme also distinguishes between different clause types such as adverbial clause, comparative clause, nominal clause and relative clause whereas the Penn Treebank scheme differentiates between different types of *wh*-clauses (e. g. noun, adverb and prepositional phrases). The latter also includes a variety of null elements which indicate, for example, the understood subject of infinitive or imperative verbs, and its zero variant in subordinate clauses.

Penn Treebank Release 2, which was published in 1995, features the new Treebank II bracketing style. The new bracketing style is designed to facilitate the extraction of simple predicate/argument structure (see Marcus et al. 1994). Penn Treebank Release 2 contains one million words of 1989 *Wall Street Journal* material and a small sample of ATIS-3 material annotated in Treebank II style in addition to a cleaned copy of the Release 1 material annotated in Treebank I style. Penn Treebank Release 3 (1999) includes tagged and parsed Switchboard transcripts which are also dysfluency-annotated, as well as the parsed texts from the Brown corpus. The Penn Treebank can be ordered on CD-ROM from the LDC. The corpus is also searchable free of charge via the LDC Online (see Penn Treebank in appendix).

9.9. Parsed historical corpora

In addition to the treebanks of present-day English introduced above, this section introduces a number of parsed historical corpora. These corpora are largely based on the diachronic part of the Helsinki Corpus.

The Penn-Helsinki Parsed Corpus of Middle English version 2 (PPCME2) is a corpus of prose text samples of Middle English, annotated for syntactic structure to allow searching not only for words and word sequences but also for syntactic structures. Based on the Middle English section of the Helsinki Corpus (with additions and deletions), PPCME2 comprises 55 text samples amounting to 1.3 million words. The annotation scheme for the corpus follows the basic formatting conventions of the Penn Treebank (Kroch/Taylor 2000). PPCME2 is an improved and extended version of an earlier corpus, PPCME1, which was smaller (510,000 words) and which used a simpler annotation scheme (no POS tagging, no indication of the internal structure of noun phrases, less detailed annotation of several complex sentence and phrase types). Both versions of the corpus are available at the corpus website (see appendix). PPCME1 is free for downloading while PPCME2 can be ordered on CD-ROM at a nominal cost. The corpus search tool, CorpusSearch, is freely available.

The York-Helsinki Parsed Corpus of Old English Poetry is a selection of poetic texts from the Old English Section of the Helsinki Corpus which have been annotated to facilitate searches on lexical items and syntactic structures. The corpus contains 71,490 words of Old English text samples ranging from 4,000 to 17,000 words in length. The Brooklyn-Geneva-Amsterdam-Helsinki Parsed Corpus of Old English is a selection of texts from the Old English Section of the Helsinki Corpus. The corpus contains 106,210 words of Old English text samples, ranging 5,000 to 10,000 words in length, which represent a range of dates of composition, authors and genres. A much larger corpus with much more detailed annotation is the York-Toronto-Helsinki Parsed Corpus of Old English Prose (YCOE), which contains 1.5 million words of Old English prose texts taken from the Toronto Dictionary of Old English Corpus, with special formatting which has made it possible to search conveniently for syntactic structures using a computer search engine. These corpora apply the PPCME2 annotation scheme. They are available at no cost for non-commercial use at the corpus website (see appendix) or via OTA.

10. Developmental and learner corpora

Two types of corpora are particularly relevant to language learning: developmental corpora and learner corpora. A learner corpus is a collection of the writing or speech produced by learners acquiring a second language (L2). The term is used here as opposed to a developmental corpus, which consists of data produced by children acquiring their first language (L1). This section introduces well-known corpora of these two types.

10.1. The Child Language Data Exchange System

The Child Language Data Exchange System (CHILDES) is an international database organized for the study of first and second language acquisition. The database consists of three parts: Codes for the Human Analysis of Transcripts (CHAT), Computerized Language Analysis (CLAN), and a database. The CHILDES database contains transcripts of data collected from children and adults who are learning both first and second languages. The total size of the database is now approximately 300 million characters. The database, which includes a wide variety of language samples from a wide range of ages and situations, consists of five major components: English data, non-English data, narrative data, data from clinical populations, data from bilinguals and second-language acquisition. Some files have associated audio and video recordings. The transcripts from English-speaking children constitute over half of the total CHILDES database, but up to 26 languages are currently covered. All of the data is transcribed in the CHAT format and can be analyzed using the CLAN programs, which support four basic types of linguistic analysis: lexical analysis, morpho-syntactic analysis, discourse analysis, and phonological analysis (cf MacWhinney 1995).

The CHILDES database has been used in a wide range of research of normal and abnormal child language. The database and computer programs are freely available for research at the CHILDES website (see appendix).

10.2. The Louvain Corpus of Native English Essays

The Louvain Corpus of Native English Essays (LOCNESS) is a corpus of argumentative essays on a great variety of topics written by native British and American university students (cf. Granger/Tyson 1996). The LOCNESS corpus comprises three parts, 114 British pupils' A-Level essays (60,209 words), 90 British university students' essays (95,695 words), and 232 American university students' essays (168,400 words), totaling 324,304 words. As the age group of those students is comparable to that of the non-native EFL students in the International Corpus of Learner English (ICLE, see section 10.4.), LOCNESS provides control data in comparing writings of native and non-native learners. The corpus can be ordered from the Centre for English Corpus Linguistics at the University of Louvain (CECL, see appendix).

10.3. The Polytechnic of Wales corpus

The Polytechnic of Wales (POW) corpus contains 65,000 words of informal conversations of about 120 6 to 12-year-old children, which were collected between 1978 and 1984 in South Wales. The children were selected in order to minimize any Welsh or other second language influence and divided into four groups of 30, each within three months of the ages 6, 8, 10, and 12. These groups were subdivided by sex (boys, girls) and socio-economic class (A, B, C, D). The corpus is fully parsed by hand using a Systemic Functional Grammar with rich syntactico-semantic categories, capable of handling raising, dummy subject clauses, ellipsis, and replacement strings (cf. Souter 1993). The corpus contains 11,396 parse trees in 184 files, each file with a reference header which identifies the age, sex and social class of the child, and whether the text is from a play session or an interview. Only the parsed corpus is available in machine readable form via ICAME or OTA. The recorded tapes and 4-volume transcripts with intonation contours are available in hard copy from the British Library.

10.4. The International Corpus of Learner English

The first and best-known learner corpus is the International Corpus of Learner English (i. e. ICLE). The corpus comprises argumentative essays written by advanced learners of English, i. e. university students of English as a foreign language (EFL) in their 3rd or 4th year of study. The primary goal of ICLE is the investigation of the interlanguage of the foreign language learner (cf. Granger 2003).

ICLE version 1.1, published on CD-ROM in 2002, contained over 2.5 million words in the form of 3,640 texts ranging between 500−1,000 words in length written by EFL learners from 11 mother tongue backgrounds, namely, Bulgarian, Czech, Dutch, Finnish, French, German, Italian, Polish, Russian, Spanish, and Swedish. The corpus is still expanding with additional subcorpora (each containing 200,000 words) of ten other L1 backgrounds including Brazilian Portuguese, Chinese, Greek, Japanese, Lithuanian, Norwegian, Portuguese (Portugal), Slovene, South African (Setswana) and Turkish (cf. the ICLE website, see appendix). ICLE published on CD-ROM (version 1.1) is not tagged for part-of-speech or learner errors. The error and POS-tagged versions of the corpus are expected to become available in the near future.

In addition to allowing the comparison of the writing of learners from different backgrounds, the corpus can be used in combination with LOCNESS to compare native and learner English. The ICLE corpus is available for linguistic research but cannot be used for commercial purposes. The ICLE corpus (version 1.1) on CD-ROM accompanied by a handbook can be ordered by following the link at the website of the Centre for English Corpus Linguistics (see CECL in appendix).

10.5. The LINDSEI corpus

The Louvain International Database of Spoken English Interlanguage (LINDSEI) is a spoken counterpart to ICLE. Each subcorpus represents an L1 background and comprises transcripts of fifty 15-minute interviews with 3rd and 4th year university students. The first component of LINDSEI contains transcripts of interviews with 30 female and 20 male French learners of English, totaling ca. 100,000 words. The database has now been expanded with additional components representing other L1 backgrounds including Bulgarian, Chinese, Dutch, German, Greek, Italian, Japanese, Polish, Spanish, and Swedish (see LINDSEI in appendix). As most learner corpora have used written data only, this type of data allows new research into a wide range of features of oral interlanguage by comparing learner data with comparable native speaker data or data produced by learners from different L1 backgrounds.

10.6. The Longman Learners' Corpus

The Longman Learners' Corpus contains ten million words of essays written during 1990–2002 by students of English at a range of levels of proficiency from 20 different L1 backgrounds. The elicitation tasks varied, ranging from in-class essays with or without the use of a dictionary to exam essays or assignments. Each script in the corpus is coded for the student's L1 background, proficiency level, text type (essay, letter, exam script, etc.), target variety (British, American or Australian English), and for the country of residence. This corpus has been designed to provide balanced and representative coverage for each of these categories (cf. Gillard/Gadsby 1998, 160). Taken as a whole it offers a multi-faceted picture of interlanguage, which can be explored in a variety of ways. The Longman Learners' Corpus is not POS tagged, but part of the corpus has been error-tagged manually, although this portion is only for internal use by the Longman publishers. The Longman Learners' Corpus is a commercial corpus, but it is also available for academic use. At present around 10 million words can be supplied. Users can also order a subcorpus for a certain proficiency level or L1 background. For details, see the Longman website (see appendix).

10.7. The Cambridge Learner Corpus

As part of the Cambridge International Corpus (CIC), the Cambridge Learner Corpus (CLC) is a large collection of examples of English writing from learners of English all over the world. The English in the CLC comes from anonymized exam scripts written by students taking Cambridge ESOL English exams worldwide. The corpus currently contains over 22 million words in the form of 85,000 scripts from 180 countries (representing 100 different L1 backgrounds) and it is expanding continually. Each script is coded with information about the student's first language, nationality, level of English, age, etc. Over twelve million words (or about 35,000 scripts) have been coded for errors using the Learner Error Coding system developed by Cambridge University Press. CLC is a commercial corpus. Currently the corpus can only be accessed by authors and writers working for Cambridge University Press and by members of staff at Cambridge ESOL (cf. the CLC site, see appendix).

10.8. Other learner corpora

In addition to the corpora which cover multiple L1 backgrounds as introduced above, there are a number of learner corpora specific to one particular mother tongue.

The HKUST Corpus of Learner English is one such example. The corpus contains 25 million words of essays and exam scripts of upper-secondary and tertiary-level Chinese learners of English in Hong Kong (mainly Cantonese speakers). The average length of these essays is 1,000 words. The corpus is partly tagged for part-of-speech and learner error (see Milton/Chowdhury 1994). The HKUST learner corpus is available to the public for use in research on a collaborative basis.

The Chinese Learner English Corpus (CLEC) contains one million words of writing produced by Chinese learners of English from five proficiency levels: high-school students, junior and senior non-English majors, and junior and senior English majors. The five types of learners are equally represented in the corpus. The CLEC material includes writings for tests, guided writings and free writings. The corpus is not POS tagged, but it is fully annotated with learner errors using an annotation scheme which consists of 61 error types clustered in 11 categories (see Gui/Yang 2002). The CLEC corpus can be searched online at the CLEC website (see appendix).

The JEFLL (Japanese EFL Learner) is a 700,000-word collection of spontaneous compositions (without the help of dictionaries or any careful revision, completed in 20 minutes) written by more than 10,000 Japanese learners of English at beginning and intermediate levels, covering mainly junior and senior high school students in Japan. The essay task used in data collection is carefully controlled so that each subcorpus can be comparable across topics, proficiency, school years, and school types, among others. JEFLL is POS tagged and tagged for learner errors. The corpus is made publicly available for free online access via the Shogakukan Corpus Network (see appendix).

The Standard Speaking Test (SST) corpus, also known as the NICT JLE (Japanese Learner English) Corpus, contains one million words of error-tagged spoken English produced by Japanese learners. Based entirely upon the audio-recordings of an English oral proficiency interview test called the Standard Speaking Test (SST), the corpus comprises 1,200 samples transcribed from 15-minute oral interview tests (around 300 hours of recording in total). This is the largest spoken learner corpus which has been built to date. The subjects are classified into nine SST proficiency levels, thus making it possible to compare speech across different learner proficiency groups. Two types of tagging have been used in the SST corpus: discourse tagging and error tagging. The tags are XML-compliant. More than 30 basic tags are used to mark up discourse phenomena in the learners' utterances, which are clustered into four main categories: tags for representing the structure of the entire transcription file, tags for the interviewee's profile, tags for speaker turns, and tags for representing utterance phenomena such as fillers and repetitions (see Izumi/Uchimoto/Isahara 2004, 34). The error tagging scheme consists of 47 tags. Each tag shows three types of information: part-of-speech, a grammatical/lexical rule, and a corrected form (cf Izumi/Isahara 2004). More details on the SST corpus can be found at the SST corpus website (see appendix).

The Thai English Learner Corpus (TELC) currently contains 1.5 million words of writings by Thai learners of English. One half of the materials were taken from university entrance exams at the Institute for English Language Education (IELE, Assumption University) and the other half came from writings by 4th-year undergraduate students of EFL at Assumption University. The TELC corpus is tagged for part-of-speech and lemma. The corpus is presently not open to the public.

The Uppsala Student English (USE) corpus contains 1.2 million words in the form of 1,489 essays written during 1999–2001 by 440 Swedish university students of English at three different levels, the majority in their first term of full-time studies. These essays were written out of class, against a deadline of 2–3 weeks, with length limitations imposed (usually 700–800 words), and suitable text structure suggested. There are a variety of essay types in the corpus, including evaluation, argumentation, and discussion, etc. The corpus is available for non-commercial research and educational use only. More information about the corpus is available at the USE site (see USE in appendix) and the corpus can be ordered via the Oxford Text Archive (see OTA in appendix).

The Polish Learner English Corpus is designed by the PELCRA project (see section 2.3.) as a half-a-million-word corpus of written learner data produced by Polish learners of English from a range of learner styles at different proficiency levels, from beginning learners to post-advanced learners (cf. Lewandowska-Tomaszczyk 2003, 107). The data was collected between 1998 and 2000 from the exam essays of Polish learners of English at the Institute of English Studies in Łódź and two teacher-training colleges affiliated with the University of Łódź. Each data file contains a "TEI lite" conformant header. The corpus is tagged using CLAWS with the standard C7 tagset. Learner errors are identified by comparing the questionable language portions in the learner corpus with materials from native English corpora (e. g. the BNC and ANC) on the one hand, and the PELCRA corpus of native Polish on the other. Some sample files are available at the PELCRA project site (see appendix).

The JPU (Janus Pannonius University) learner corpus contains 300,000 words of essays and research papers by advanced level Hungarian university students, which were collected from 1992 to 1998. JPU has five subcorpora: Postgraduate, Writing and Research Skills, Language Practice, Electives and Russian Retraining (cf. Horváth 1999). The essays are available at the JPU corpus site (see appendix) while the whole corpus is searchable via the website Lexical Tutor (see appendix).

All of the learner corpora introduced above are for English, given the status of English as an international language. There are, however, a number of existing interlanguage corpora for other languages. For example, the Progression Corpus is a longitudinal corpus of French which was developed to investigate progression in foreign language learning in the early years of secondary schooling, with specific reference to French as a first foreign language. The corpus contains around 200 hours of spoken French produced by a cohort of 60 children who were tracked through two years (six terms) of classroom French, from the second term of year 7 until the first term of year 9 inclusive. The corpus is encoded following the CHAT standards of the CHILDES system (see section 10.1.). The transcripts and audio files of the corpus can be accessed at website of the French Progression Corpus (see appendix). Another learner corpus of spoken French is the Linguistic Development Corpus, which was created to complement the Progression Corpus. This is a cross-sectional corpus which is composed of 240 digitally recorded sound files, as well as their transcripts and tagged files (also in CHAT format). The data contained in this corpus was produced by children of years 9, 10 and 11 of secondary (aged 13–16) education in the UK context. The corpus is accessible at the French Development Corpus website (see appendix).

The Chinese Interlanguage Corpus contains over one million Chinese characters in the form of 1,731 writing samples produced by 740 learners of Mandarin Chinese as a foreign language in nine universities in China. The data was sampled from 5,574 compositions and exercises (totaling over 3.5 million Chinese characters) produced by 1,635 Chinese learners from 96 countries and regions. The corpus is richly encoded with 23 items of metadata information including for example, learner's name, sex, age, nationality, native language, education level, textbooks used, and date of writing. Errors of various types (mainly lexical errors) are also tagged and indexed for easy retrieval. The corpus comes with an integrated system that allows users to perform tasks such as keyword and full text searching, as well as data browsing and processing. The corpus is currently open to on-site use only.

11. Multilingual corpora

We have so far introduced major monolingual corpora of English and a number of other languages. This section introduces multilingual corpora. The term multilingual is used here in a broad sense to include bilingual corpora. Multilingual corpora can be parallel or comparable. Corpora of this kind are particularly useful in translation and con-trastive studies.

11.1. The Canadian Hansard Corpus

The earliest and perhaps best-known parallel corpus is the Canadian Hansard Corpus, which consists of debates from the Canadian Parliament published in the country's official languages, English and French. While its content is limited to legislative discourse, the corpus covers a broad range of topics and styles, e. g. spontaneous discussion, written correspondence, as well as prepared speeches.

There are several versions of the Canadian Hansard parallel corpus. The USC version comprises 1.3 million pairs of aligned text chunks (i. e. sentences or smaller fragments) from the official records (*Hansards*) of the 36th Canadian Parliament (1997–2000) with ca. 2 million words in English and French each. This version is freely downloadable at the USC site (USC Hansard, see appendix). TransSearch (see appendix) offers an online service which allows subscribed users to access all of the Hansard texts from 1986 to February 2003 (approximately 235 million words). The LDC released a collection of Hansard parallel texts in 1995, covering a time span from the mid-1970s through 1988. This version is available on CD-ROM from the LDC. The Canadian Hansard Treebank contains 750,000 words of skeleton-parsed texts from proceedings in the Canadian Parliament, which is available from UCREL of Lancaster University.

11.2. The English-Norwegian Parallel Corpus

The English-Norwegian Parallel Corpus (ENPC) is one of the earliest and best-known parallel corpora. The corpus is bi-directional in that it contains both original and translated texts in the two languages. ENPC consists of 100 original texts between 10,000 to 15,000 words in length in English and Norwegian together with their corresponding translations in the two languages, totaling 2.6 million words. Unlike most parallel corpora which are limited to a particular domain or text type, efforts have been made to balance the ENPC corpus. Both fiction (30 originals plus translations in each language) and non-fiction (20 originals plus translations in each language) texts are sampled. Fiction texts include children's fiction, detective fiction and general fiction. Non-fiction texts cover religion, social sciences, law, natural sciences, medicine, arts, and geography/history (see Johansson/Ebeling/Oksefjell 2002). ENPC is marked up in TEI-compliant SGML. Both English and Norwegian texts in the corpus are POS tagged and lemmatized. The corpus is aligned at the sentence level. The ENPC corpus is available for non-commercial research. Registered users can access the corpus online. See the corpus homepage (ENPC, see appendix) for details on registration.

11.3. The English-Swedish Parallel Corpus

The English-Swedish Parallel Corpus (ESPC) follows ENPC in its design. The corpus consists of 64 English text samples and their translations into Swedish and 72 Swedish text samples and their translations into English, amounting to 2.8 million words. The samples from each language have been drawn from two main text categories, fiction and non-fiction. The fiction categories include children's fiction, crime and mystery fiction, and general fiction, while non-fiction texts cover memoirs and biography, geography, humanities, natural sciences, social sciences, applied sciences, legal documents, and prepared speech. The text types of the originals from both languages are comparable in terms of genre, subject matter, type of audience and register (cf. Altenberg/Aijmer/Svensson 2001). ESPC is aligned at the sentence level and marked up in TEI-compliant SGML. The corpus is for non-commercial research and only registered users can access it. See the ESPC site (see appendix) for contact details.

11.4. The Oslo Multilingual Corpus

The Oslo Multilingual Corpus (OMC) is an extension of ENPC which covers more languages including, in addition to English and Norwegian, also German, French, Swedish, Dutch, Finnish and Portuguese. The corpus is composed of many subcorpora that differ in composition with regard to languages and number of texts included. Apart from ENPC and ESPC, the corpus currently includes a French-Norwegian subcorpus Corpus (FNPC, ca. 0.86 million words), a German-Norwegian subcorpus (GNPC, ca. 1.3 million words), an English-German-English subcorpus (En-Ge-En, 1.5 million words), a German-Norwegian-German subcorpus (Ge-No-Ge, 1.8 million words), a Norwegian-English-German subcorpus (En-Ge-No, 289,230 words of Norwegian original texts, 432,500 words of English original texts, and 287,400 words of German original texts, plus the translations in the other two languages), an English-Dutch subcorpus (En-Du, 0.3 million words), an English-Norwegian-Portuguese subcorpus (En-No-Po, 0.6 million words), a Norwegian-French-German subcorpus (No-Fr-Ge, 1.5 million words), a Norwegian-English-French-German subcorpus (No-En-Fr-Ge, 1.7 million words), and an English-Finnish subcorpus (0.3 million words).

OMC has been constructed following the same principles as ENPC; and like ENPC, the corpus is coded and marked up in TEI-compliant SGML. The OMC corpus is for academic, non-commercial purposes but it can be accessed only by registered users. See the OMC homepage (see appendix) for the current status of the corpus.

11.5. The ET10/63 and ITU/CRATER parallel corpora

ET10/63 is a bilingual parallel corpus of English and French, containing ca. one million words of EC official documents on telecommunications in each language. The corpus is POS tagged and also lemmatized. This bilingual parallel corpus has been extended to include Spanish on the Corpus Resources and Terminology Extraction project. The extension is thus named the CRATER parallel corpus, which contains one million words in each of the three languages. The corpus is sentence aligned and tagged with part-of-speech in all three languages (cf. Garside et al. 1994). An expanded version of the CRATER corpus, CRATER 2, has increased the size of the English and French components of the parallel corpus from one million to 1.5 million words. Both versions of CRATER are available via ELRA. The corpus can also been accessed online or downloaded via FTP at the CRATER site (see appendix).

11.6. The IJS-ELAN Slovene-English Parallel Corpus

The Slovene-English Parallel Corpus (IJS-ELAN) contains one million words from 15 terminology-rich bilingual texts produced in the 1990s. One half of the corpus (in terms of text size) consists of 11 Slovene texts and their English translations while the other half comprises four English texts and their Slovene translations. The corpus is aligned at the sentence level (cf. Erjavec 2002). Two versions of the IJS-ELAN corpus are available, with one version marked up in SGML/TEI P3 and the other encoded in XML/TEI P4 and lemmatized and POS tagged. Both versions are freely available for downloading at the corpus website (see appendix), which also allows free online access.

11.7. JRC-ACQUIS Multilingual Parallel Corpus

The JRC-ACQUIS Multilingual Parallel Corpus is a truly multilingual corpus, covering 22 European languages: Bulgarian, Czech, Danish, German, Greek, English, Spanish, Estonian, Finnish, French, Hungarian, Italian, Lithuanian, Latvian, Maltese, Dutch, Polish, Portuguese, Romanian, Slovak, Slovene, and Swedish. The current version 3.0 contains 463,792 texts of EU legislation between the 1950s and 2006, totaling over one billion words. The current release contains pairwise alignment for 231 language pairs. It has also made some corrections in the Bulgarian subcorpus. The corpus is marked up in XML/TEI P4 and currently aligned at the paragraph level. The corpus is distributed for research purposes and can be downloaded at the corpus website (see ACQUIS in appendix).

11.8. The CLUVI parallel corpus

The CLUVI (Linguistic Corpus of the University of Vigo) parallel corpus is an open textual corpus of specialized registers (taken from fiction, computing, journalism and legal and administrative fields), totaling eight million words of running texts. The corpus currently comprises seven main sections. They are the LEGA parallel corpus of Galician-Spanish legal texts (6.33 million words), the UNESCO parallel corpus of English-Galician-French-Spanish scientific-technical divulgation (3.72 million words), the LOGALIZA corpus of English-Galician software localization (1.98 million words), the TECTRA parallel corpus of English-Galician literary texts (1.47 million words), the FEGA Corpus of French-Galician literary texts (1.27 million words), the CONSUMER corpus of Spanish-Galician-Catalan-Basque consumer information (5.59 million words), and the LEGE-BI corpus of Basque-Spanish legal texts (2.38 million words). The corpus is being expanded with six additional sections: Galician-Spanish economy texts, English-Portuguese literary texts, English-Spanish literary texts, German-Galician literary texts, English-Galician film subtitling, and Portuguese-Spanish postcolonial literature (cf. Gómez Guinovart/Sacau Fontenla 2004). The completed sections of the corpus are freely accessible at the CLUVI website (see appendix), which permits both simple and very complex searches of isolated words or sequences of words.

11.9. European Corpus Initiative Multilingual Corpus I

European Corpus Initiative Multilingual Corpus I (ECI/MCI) was released in 1994 by ELSNET (see section 13). The corpus contains 98 million words of texts from 27 languages, covering most of the major European languages as well as some non-European languages such as Chinese, Japanese and Malay. The corpus has 48 components, 12 of which are parallel corpora composed of 2–9 subcorpora. It also includes a great diversity of text types such as newspapers, novels and stories, technical papers and dictionaries and wordlists, though most components are quite homogeneous in contents (cf. Armstrong-Warwick et al. 1994).

ECI/MCI is marked up in TEI P2 conformant SGML, but the markup has been undertaken in such a way that users can also get easy access to the source text without markup. The corpus is available from ELSNET (see appendix) or the LDC.

11.10. The MULTEXT corpora

Multilingual Tools and Corpora (MULTEXT) is a series of projects whose aims are to develop standards and specifications for the encoding and processing of linguistic corpora, and to develop tools, corpora and linguistic resources embodying these standards. The multilingual corpus used for developing linguistic tools is the JOC (*Official Journal of European Community*) corpus, which comprises 40 files in five languages: English, German, Italian, Spanish and French. Of these, ten files in five languages (English, French, German, Spanish and Italian) are POS tagged and 10 files in four language pairs (English-French, English-German, English-Italian and English-Spanish) are aligned at the sentence level. The corpus is conformant with the Corpus Encoding Standard (CES, see article 22). The availability of the corpus is unknown, but some samples can be downloaded at the MULTEXT website (see appendix).

MULTEXT-East is a project which is intended to extend the scope of MULTEXT by transferring MULTEXT's expertise, methodologies, and tools to Central and Eastern European countries, thus enabling the extension and validation of these methodologies and tools on a new range of languages. The latest release of MULTEXT-East resources, version 3, became available in July 2004. It is marked up in XML/TEI P4.

The MULTEXT-East dataset has four components: morpho-syntactic lexica, a parallel corpus, a spoken corpus, and a comparable corpus. The parallel corpus consists of the English original of George Orwell's *Nineteen Eighty-Four* (100,000 words) together with its translations into the nine project languages: Bulgarian, Czech, Estonian, Hungarian, Lithuanian, Romanian, Russian, Serbian, and Slovene. The translations of *Nineteen Eighty-Four* are POS tagged manually and sentence aligned with the English original, with tagging and alignment validated by hand. The spoken corpus, which covers seven languages (Romanian, Slovene, Estonian, Hungarian, English, Czech, Bulgarian), is composed of the translations (from English) of forty short passages of five thematically connected sentences. For the first four languages in the above list, the texts have also been read, recorded and included in the distribution. The MULTEXT-East multilingual comparable corpus comprises a fiction subset and a news subset of at least 100,000 words each, for each of the six project languages (Bulgarian, Czech, Estonian, Hungarian, Romanian and Slovene). Each language component is comparable in terms of the number and size of texts. The multilingual comparable corpus is marked up in CES format with over 40 different elements (see Erjavec 2004). The comparable spoken corpus (transcripts and audio files) is freely downloadable, while the parallel and comparable corpora, together with other MULTEXT-East language resources, are subject to license and restricted to research use only. Licensed users can browse or download full resources. Registrations can be made on the MULTEXT-East website (see appendix).

11.11. The PAROLE corpora

PAROLE (Preparatory Action for Linguistic Resources Organization for Language Engineering) represents a large-scale harmonized effort to create comparable text corpora and lexica for EU languages. Fourteen languages are involved on the PAROLE project: Belgian French, Catalan, Danish, Dutch, English, French, Finnish, German, Greek, Irish, Italian, Norwegian, Portuguese and Swedish. Corpora containing 20 million words and lexica containing 20,000 entries were constructed for each of these languages using the same design and composition principles during 1996–1998. These corpora all include specific proportions of texts from the categories book (20%), newspaper (65%), periodical (5%) and miscellaneous (10%) within a settled range.

The PAROLE corpora are marked up according to CES-conformant PAROLE DTD (Document Type Declaration). An equal proportion of the texts (up to 250,000 running words) in each PAROLE corpus was POS tagged according to a common PAROLE tagset and morpho-syntactic annotation standards. Part of the tagged data was validated: 50,000 words checked for maximum granularity and 200,000 for part-of-speech. For some PAROLE corpora, only a copyright-free subset is available to the public. The PAROLE corpora that are currently available are distributed by ELRA.

11.12. Multilingual Corpora for Cooperation

Multilingual Corpora for Cooperation (MLCC) is a corpus acquisition project which aims to collect a set of texts representing a substantial improvement in range, quantity and quality of corpus material available. The MLCC multilingual data consists of the Multilingual Parallel Corpus and the comparable Polylingual Document Collection. The parallel corpus comprises translated data in nine European languages: Danish, Dutch, English, French, German, Greek, Italian, Portuguese and Spanish. This corpus has two datasets, with one set taken from the *Official Journal of the European Commission*, C Series: Written Questions 1993, totaling approximately 10.2 million words (1.1 million words per language), and the other set taken from the *Official Journal of the European Commission*, Annex: Debates of the European Parliament 1992–1994, with 5–8 million words for each language. The comparable corpus includes financial newspaper articles from the early 1990s in six European languages: Dutch (8.5 million words), English (30 million words), French (10 million words), German (33 million words), Italian (1.88 million words), and Spanish (10 million words). The MLCC multilingual and parallel corpora are marked up in TEI-compliant SGML (cf. Armstrong et al. 1998). The resources are available via ELRA.

We have so far introduced multilingual corpora of European languages. The following sections are concerned with corpora involving other languages.

11.13. The EMILLE Corpus

The EMILLE Corpus is a product of the Enabling Minority Language Engineering project which develops language resources for South Asian languages. Two versions of the EMILLE Corpus are available: the EMILLE/CIIL Corpus distributed free of charge for non-commercial research, and the EMILLE/Lancaster Corpus for commercial use only.

The EMILLE/CIIL Corpus consists of three components: monolingual, parallel and annotated corpora. There are fourteen monolingual corpora, including both written and (for some languages) spoken data for fourteen South Asian languages: Assamese, Bengali, Gujarati, Hindi, Kannada, Kashmiri, Malayalam, Marathi, Oriya, Punjabi, Sinhala, Tamil, Telegu and Urdu. The EMILLE monolingual corpora contain approximately 92,799,000 words (including 2,627,000 words of transcribed spoken data for Bengali, Gujarati, Hindi, Punjabi and Urdu). The parallel corpus consists of 200,000 words of text in English and its accompanying translations in Hindi, Bengali, Punjabi, Gujarati and Urdu. The annotated component includes the Urdu monolingual and parallel corpora annotated for part-of-speech, together with twenty written Hindi corpus files annotated to show the nature of demonstrative use. The EMILLE/Lancaster Corpus consists of three components: monolingual, parallel and annotated corpora. This version differs from the EMILLE/CIIL Corpus in its monolingual component, which consists of monolingual corpora covering seven South Asian languages (Bengali, Gujarati, Hindi, Punjabi, Sinhala, Tamil, and Urdu), totaling approximately 58,880,000 words (including 2,627,000 words of transcribed spoken data for Bengali, Gujarati, Hindi, Punjabi and Urdu). The parallel and annotated components are the same as in the EMILLE/CIIL Corpus (cf. Baker et al. 2004).

The EMILLE Corpus is marked up using CES-compliant SGML, and encoded using Unicode. More information about the corpus is available on the EMILLE website (see appendix). Both versions of the corpus are distributed via ELRA.

11.14. The BFSU Chinese-English Parallel Corpus

The BFSU (Beijing Foreign Studies University) Chinese-English Parallel Corpus contains 30 million words. Presently it is the largest parallel corpus of English and Chinese. The corpus is composed of four subcorpora, i. e. Balanced Corpus, Translation Corpus, Bilingual Sentences Corpus and Corpus for Specific Purpose. The bidirectional parallel corpus includes both literary (fiction, prose and play scripts) and non-literary texts, which are sampled from 12 text categories covering three major domains: humanities, social sciences and natural sciences. The Chinese-English and English-Chinese texts account for 40% and 60% respectively while literary and non-literary texts account for 55% and 45% respectively. The BFSU parallel corpus is automatically sentence aligned and hand validated. It has been annotated in such a way as to allow concordances of words, phrases, collocations, and sentence patterns (cf. Wang 2004). The corpus is available from the China National Research Centre for Foreign Language Education (see Sinotefl in appendix).

11.15. The Babel Chinese-English parallel corpora

The PKU Babel Chinese-English Parallel Corpus hosted at Peking University contains 20 million Chinese characters and 10 million English words of bilingual texts sampled from a great variety of text categories including government documents, news, academic prose, fiction, play scripts, and speech, among other text categories. It is designed as a balanced corpus covering three styles (literature, practical writing and news), six fields (arts, business/economics, politics, science, sports, and society/culture), two modes (written, spoken), and four periods (ancient, early modern, modern, and contemporary for Chinese texts, and Old English, Middle English, Early Modern English and present-day English for English texts). Presently only contemporary/present-day written texts are included, and about 400,000 sentence pairs have been aligned (cf. Bai/Chang/Zhan 2002). The Babel parallel corpus is marked up in XML. Each document has two parts, the text header and the text body. The header part shows Chinese and English titles, author, translator, style, field, mode and period. The text body is annotated for paragraphs, aligned anchoring points, sentences, and words. The Chinese texts in the corpus are tokenized and POS tagged while the English texts are POS tagged and lemmatized. The completed part of the corpus can be accessed online at the PKU Babel website (see appendix).

The Babel English-Chinese parallel corpus hosted at Lancaster University consists of 327 English articles and their translations in Mandarin Chinese collected from two online bilingual magazines in 2000 and 2001, totaling half a million words. The corpus is tagged for part-of-speech for both English and Chinese and is aligned at the sentence level. It is also marked for paragraph and sentence boundaries. The corpus can be accessed online at the Lancaster Babel website.

11.16. Hong Kong Parallel Text

Hong Kong Parallel Text is a large parallel corpus released by the LDC in 2004. The corpus contains approximately 59 million English words and 49 million Chinese words (or 98 million Chinese characters). It consists of the updates of three parallel corpora published in 2000: Hong Kong Hansards, Hong Kong Laws, and Hong Kong News. The Hong Kong Hansards component contains excerpts from the Official Record of Proceedings of the Legislative Council of the HKSAR from October 1985 to April 2003, totaling 36,140,737 English words and 56,618,181 Chinese characters. The Hong Kong Laws component contains statute laws of Hong Kong in English and Chinese, constitutional instruments, national laws and other relevant instruments published by the Department of Justice of the HKSAR up to the year 2000, amounting to 8,396,243 English words and 14,868,621 Chinese characters. The Hong Kong News component contains press releases from the Information Services Department of the HKSAR between July 1997 and October 2003, amounting to 14,798,671 English words and 26,677,514 Chinese characters. All of the three components in the Hong Kong Parallel Text corpus are aligned at the sentence level. The English and Chinese texts are kept in separate files, with alignment indicated by corresponding sentence numbers. The corpus is available from the LDC.

11.17. The OPUS parallel corpus

OPUS is a publicly available, open-source parallel corpus which consists of translated texts collected from the Web. It covers not only European languages but also Asian languages such as Chinese and Japanese. The corpus is constantly growing with fresh data. The current version has seven components.

The OpenSubtitles corpus comprises 361 bitexts in 30 languages, amounting to 23.4 million tokens in 20,722 files. The subcorpus of European constitution is composed of 210 aligned bitexts in 21 European languages, totaling 987 files and three million tokens. The OpenOffice corpus consists of 2,014 documents in English original (about half a million words) and their partial translations into five languages (French, Spanish, Swedish, German, and Japanese), totaling 10,983 files and 2.6 million tokens. All documents in this subcorpus are tokenized and, except for the Spanish part, tagged with part-of-speech, while the English part is marked with syntactic chunks as well. The subcorpus of KDE system messages consists of 1,830 bitexts in 61 languages, totaling 24,586 files and 20 million tokens. The KDE manual corpus has 226 bitexts in 24 languages with a total of 3.8 million words in 3,736 files. The EUROPARL subcorpus comprises 55 bitexts of European Parliament Proceedings (1996–2003) in 11 languages, amounting to 296 million tokens in 5,214 files. Finally, the PHP manual corpus consists of 231 bitexts in 22 languages, totaling 3.3 million tokens in 71,518 files.

This OPUS parallel corpus is marked up in XML. All components of the corpus, as well as some corpus building tools, can be downloaded at the OPUS site (see appendix), which also provides a multilingual and a bilingual query interface.

12. Non-English monolingual corpora

We have so far been concerned with well-known and influential English corpora and multilingual corpora involving English, in addition to some national corpora. This section introduces a number of major monolingual corpora of other languages.

12.1. The COSMAS corpora

COSMAS (Corpus Search, Management and Analysis System) is a large collection of German text corpora developed at the Mannheim IDS (Institut für deutsche Sprache). With a size of almost two billion words, this is the world's largest, ever-growing collection of German online corpora for linguistic research. The collection covers a wide variety of sources, e. g. classic literary texts, national and regional newspapers, transcribed spoken language, morpho-syntactically annotated texts and several unique corpora.

The copyright free part of the COSMAS collection (over 1.1 billion words) is publicly available free of charge for searching via the COSMAS online toolbox (see appendix), which allows complex queries, collocation analysis, clustering, and virtual corpus composition, etc. The COSMAS corpora are only available for non-commercial use and anonymous COSMAS sessions are limited to 60 minutes.

12.2. The CETEMPúblico Corpus

The CETEMPublico (Corpus de Extractos de Textos Electronicos MCT/Pųblico) corpus includes the text of around 2,600 editions of the Portuguese daily newspaper *Público*, written between 1991 and 1999, amounting to approximately 180 million words. The corpus is marked up in SGML. Having removed some repeated extracts from version 1.0, CETEMPublico version 1.7 consists of over 1.5 million extracts. The first million words (8,043 extracts) have been parsed. This subset represents a balanced selection from the whole period (1991–1999) rather than early years alone. It also covers all of the categories included in the full corpus (cf. Santos/Rocha 2001). CETEMPublico can be used for research and technological development, but direct commercial exploitation is not permitted. There are a number of ways to access the corpus: CD-ROM from the LDC, FTP download, and online access at the corpus website (see appendix).

12.3. The INL corpora

The Institute for Dutch Lexicology (INL) has offered three corpora over the Web. The Five Million Words Corpus 1994 has diversified compositions. It comprises texts of present-day Dutch derived from 17 text sources dating from 1989–1994, including books, magazines, newspapers and TV broadcasts which cover topics such as journalism, politics, environment, linguistics, leisure and business/employment (see Kruyt 1995). The 27 Million Words Dutch Newspaper Corpus 1995 consists of newspaper texts derived from issues published in 1994–1995 by a major national newspaper, NRC (see Kruyt et al. 1996). The 38 Million Words Corpus 1996 has three main components: a component with varied composition (books, magazines, newspaper texts, TV broadcasts, parliamentary reports, 1970–1995, 12.7 million words), a newspaper component (*Meppeler Courant*, 1992–1995, 12.4 million words), and a legal component (Dutch legal texts operative in 1989, with some dating back as early as 1814, 12.9 million words) (see Kruyt/Dutilh 1997). All three corpora are lemmatized and tagged for part-of-speech and users can define subcorpora using the parameters encoded therein. They are available for non-commercial research purposes only. Access to these corpora is free of charge but subject to an individual user agreement, which can be obtained from the INL website (see appendix).

12.4. The CEG corpus

The CEG (Cronfa Electroneg o Gymraeg) corpus contains one million words of written Welsh prose. The corpus is designed as a Welsh parallel to the Brown and LOB corpora, consisting of five hundred 2,000-word samples selected from a representative range of text types to illustrate modern (mainly post 1970) Welsh prose writing. However, the text categories and their proportions in the corpus are different from those in Brown and LOB. The texts in CEG are grouped into two broad categories: factual prose and fiction. There are seven types of fiction such as novels and short stories, while the factual prose is further divided into 22 categories such as various types of press material, administrative documents, academic texts and biography (see Ellis et al. 2001).

The corpus is of value for lexical and syntactic analyses of modern Welsh prose. It is available as both raw and annotated texts. Annotations include lemmatization and POS tagging. Both versions are available at the CEG website (see appendix).

12.5. The Scottish Corpus of Texts and Speech

The Scottish Corpus of Texts and Speech (SCOTS) is an ongoing project which aims to build a large electronic corpus of both written and spoken texts for the languages of Scotland, aiming to cover the period from 1945 to the present day (with most spoken texts recorded since 2000). Currently the corpus (SCOTS Dataset 12) consists of 1,175 documents (4,024,343 words), which include written, spoken and visual materials from a range of genres such as conversation, interviews, correspondence, poetry, fiction and prose. The corpus includes samples from Scots and Scottish English, in addition to a small number of Scottish Gaelic texts. Great efforts have been made on the SCOTS project to render the corpus as balanced as practically possible, by including a wide range of texts of different language varieties, genres and registers, and including speakers and writers from a wide range of geographical locations, backgrounds, age and gender groups as well as occupations, etc. However, SCOTS does not claim to be a truly representative corpus because some genres (e. g. newspaper articles, personal diaries, business correspondence) are not covered owing to practical issues such as permissions, copyright and text availability.

The SCOTS corpus is marked up in SGML. The extensive sociolinguistic metadata includes, for example, resource type, text type, setting, medium, audience, text details, author/speaker details (gender, age, geographic region, education, occupation, religious background, languages used, etc.), and copyright information (see SCOTS in appendix). The current version of the SCOTS corpus is not linguistically annotated, but the transcripts of spoken data are aligned with digital audio/video recordings. The available texts can be searched at the SCOTS project site (see appendix).

12.6. The FIDA Corpus of Slovenian

FIDA is a monolingual reference corpus of the Slovene language which contains just over 100 million words of contemporary Slovene texts. The corpus covers a broad range of Slovene language variants and registers as found in the Slovene press, complemented by some texts from the Internet and speech transcripts. Both literary (poetry, prose and drama, 5.9 %) and non-literary (scientific texts in both natural and social sciences as well as non-scientific writing, 94.1 %) texts are included. In terms of media, newspapers (46.6 %), journals (23.9 %) and books (22.7 %) account for over 93.2 % of the whole corpus.

FIDA can be searched via its web-based interface at the corpus site (see FIDA in appendix), but the access is not free of charge. Only users with a valid account can access the corpus, though a guest account is also available for users to test-run the query system.

12.7. The Nova Beseda corpus of Slovenian

Nova Beseda is another large collection of Slovenian texts which started with web presentation of a three-million-word electronic collection of Slovenian fiction in 1999. In the years that followed the corpus grew in both size and diversity so that it has increased to 240 million words, with most texts taken from publications from the 1990s. All of the texts are marked on the sentence level.

Tab. 20.28: Structure of the Nova Beseda corpus

Part	Contents	Words (million)	Proportion
A	Fiction in Slovenian	12	5 %
B	Non-fiction in Slovenian	2	0.8 %
C	Scientific and technical publications	3	1.3 %
D	Delo Slovenian daily (1998–2007)	169	70.4 %
G	Slovenian National Assembly session transcripts (1996–2007)	31	12.9 %
P	Delo FT, Jana, Mladina, Monitor, National Geographic, Viva magazines	21	8.8 %
S	Republic of Slovenia Legislation	2	0.8 %
	Total	240	

The corpus has seven parts as shown in Table 20.28. As can be seen, newspaper texts account for 70 % of the total number of tokens. The corpus can be searched online freely at the Nova Beseda website (see appendix).

12.8. The Prague Dependency Treebank

The Prague Dependency Treebank (PDT, version 2.0) contains two million words of texts drawn from the Czech National Corpus (see section 2.4.) which have been annotated morphologically and syntactically. Of the texts included in the treebank, general newspaper articles related to politics, sports, culture, hobbies, etc. account for 60 %, economic news and analyses 20 %, and popular science magazines 20 %. PDT version 2.0 is marked up in XML. The annotation scheme consists of three levels. The morphological level assigns a lemma and a morphological tag to each token. The analytical level uses dependency grammar to annotate the structure of the parse tree and the analytical function of every node, which determines the relationship between the dependent node and its governing node one level higher in the tree. The highest level of annotation, the tectogrammatical level, uses the dependency framework to describe the linguistic meaning of a sentence (see Böhmová et al. 2003). The third level annotation has been added in PDT version 2.0. The same texts are annotated on all three levels, but the amount of annotated material decreases with the complexity of the levels, specifically about two million tokens on the morphological level, about 1.5 million tokens at the analytical level, and 0.8 million tokens on the tectogrammatical level (see Hajič 2004). The Prague Dependency Treebank version 2.0 is available on CD-ROM from the LDC. It can also be accessed at the PDT website (see appendix) using an online tool which allows users to search for and view parse trees.

12.9. The Sinica corpora of Chinese

The Academia Sinica Balanced Corpus (ASBC) is the first annotated corpus of modern Chinese. The corpus is a representative sample of Mandarin Chinese as used in Taiwan. The current version (3.1) of the corpus contains five million words of texts sampled from different areas and classified according to five criteria: genre, style, mode, topic, and source. Table 20.29 (cf. Huang/Chen 1995/1998) shows the proportions of texts and categories in terms of these criteria.

The values of these parameters, together with bibliographic information, are encoded at the beginning of each text in the corpus. The whole corpus is tagged for part-of-

Tab. 20.29: Composition of ASBC (version 3.1)

Criterion	Proportions
Genre	Press reportage: 56.25 %, Press review: 10.01 %, Advert: 0.59 %, Letter: 1.29 %, Fiction: 10.12 %, Essay: 8.48 %, Biography and diary: 0.50 %, Poetry: 0.29 %, Quotes: 0.03 %, Manual: 2.03 %, Play script: 0.05 %, Public speech: 8.19 %, Conversation: 1.34 %, Meeting minutes: 0.11 %
Style	Narrative texts: 70.66 %, Argumentative texts: 12.24 %, Expository texts: 14.72 %, Descriptive texts: 2.83 %
Mode	Written: 90.14 %, Written-to-be-read: 1.38 %, Written-to-be-spoken: 0.82 %, Spoken: 7.29 %, Spoken-to-be-read: 0.35 %
Topic	Philosophy: 8.68 %, Natural science: 12.97 %, Social science: 34.99 %, Arts: 9.28 %, General/leisure: 17.89 %, Literature: 16.20 %
Source	Newspaper: 31.28 %, General magazine: 29.18 %, Academic journal: 0.70 %, Textbook: 4.08 %, Reference book: 0.13 %, Thesis: 1.36 %, General book: 8.45 %, Audio/video medium: 22.83 %, Conversation/interview: 1.63 %, Public speech: 0.25 %

speech and a range of linguistic features such as nominalization and reduplication. The Sinica corpus is accessible online at the ASBC website (see appendix) using the query system which also allows users to define subcorpora.

A new version with a target size of 10 million words has been completed and is expected to become available soon (cf. Huang 2006). The texts in the new release have been sampled mainly from 1996 onwards, in a balanced way in terms of five criteria: genre, style, mode, topic, and source. In this version, the proportions for each topic are as follows: philosophy (10 %), science (10 %), society (35 %), art (5 %), life (10 %), and literature (20 %). As in the current version, the new release is tokenized and POS tagged.

The Academia Sinica Tagged Corpus of Early Mandarin Chinese is another Chinese corpus built by the Academia Sinica. This corpus is divided into three subcorpora according to stages of grammatical developments: Old Chinese (from Pre-Qin to Pre-Han, 5,128,068 characters), Middle Chinese (from Late Han to the Six Dynasties, 8,101,662 characters), and Early Mandarin Chinese (from Tang to Qing, 4,406,381 characters). Presently most parts of the subcorpora for Old Chinese and Early Modern Chinese have been tokenised and POS tagged. The corpus is accessible using the online query system at the corpus website (see Early Mandarin in appendix), which permits keyword searching, statistics, and collocation analysis.

12.10. The Sinica Treebank

The Sinica Treebank (version 3.0) contains 361,834 words extracted from the ASBC corpus, covering subject areas such as politics, travel, sports, finance and society. There are 61,087 structural trees in the treebank. Like the Prague Dependency Treebank, the thematic relation between a predicate and an argument is marked in addition to grammatical categories in the Sinica Treebank. Six non-terminal phrasal categories are annotated in the treebank: S (a complete tree headed by a predicate), VP (a verb phrase headed by a predicate), NP (a noun phrase headed by a noun), GP (a phrase headed by locational noun or locational adjunct), PP (a prepositional phrase headed by a preposition), and XP (a conjunctive phrase that is headed by a conjunction). There are three different kinds of grammatical heads: Head, head and DUMMY. Head indicates a grammatical head in a phrasal category; head indicates a semantic head which does not simultaneously function as a syntactic head; and DUMMY indicates the semantic head(s) whose categorical or thematic identity cannot be locally determined. A total of 63 thematic roles are annotated in the treebank including, for example, agent, causer, condition and instrument for verbs, and time and location for nouns (see Huang et al. 2000). The Sinica Treebank can be accessed online (see appendix) using the web-based interface which allows users to search the treebank and view diagrammatical parse trees. A sample of 1,000 syntactic tree structures is available for free download.

12.11. The Penn Chinese Treebank

The current version (version 6.0) of the Penn Chinese Treebank (CTB) consists of 780,000 words (over 1.28 million Chinese characters) that are segmented, part-of-speech tagged and fully bracketed. A total of 2,036 text files are included in this release, covering newswire texts from Xinhua News Agency, articles from Sinorama Magazine, news stories from the website of the Hong Kong Special Administrative Region, and transcripts from various news broadcast programs.

The annotation format of CTB follows that of the Penn English treebank. The formal structural properties are represented with structural labels (such as NP, VP) in brackets while the functional properties are represented with functional labels such as -ADV, -TMP, and -SBJ. Six main grammatical relations are represented in the Chinese treebank, with complementation, adjunction and coordination represented structurally, while predication, modification and apposition are represented non-configurationally (see Xue et al. 2005). There are 28,295 parsed sentences in the treebank. The corpus is available from the LDC.

12.12. The Spoken Chinese Corpus of Situated Discourse

The Spoken Chinese Corpus of Situated Discourse (SCCSD) is an ongoing project under the auspices of the Chinese Academy of Social Science which aims to collect 1,000 hours of recordings of Mandarin Chinese spoken in China. The corpus consists of three subcorpora, one for workshop discourse, one for major dialects in China, and one for speeches. At present, 600 hours of audio and 50 hours of video recordings have been collected. The sampling frame for the societal discourse was established sociologically on the basis of a yellow book while the familial discourse was defined in terms of habitation and occupation, as shown in Table 20.30 (cf. Gu 2002).

Tab. 20.30: Discourse types in SCCSD

Category	Subcategory	Example
Societal	Major activities of organization	government and political discourse, business discourse, educational and academic discourse, legal and mediatory discourse, mass media discourse, discourse of medicine and health, discourse of sports, public service discourse, public welfare discourse, religious and superstitious discourse
	Activities common to organization	administrative discourse, banquet discourse, discourse of celebration and ceremony, discourse of entertainment and leisure, office discourse, political study discourse, telephone discourse
	Special discourse	pathological discourse, criminal discourse, military discourse, miscellaneous
Familial discourse	Family discourse in a metropolis	family of high-ranking officials, family of entrepreneurs, family of businessmen, family of academics, family of white collar, family of blue collar, family of suburb farmers, family of immigrant labor
	Family discourse in a small town	family of academics, family of white collar

The corpus is presently being transcribed and annotated, with segmented audio/video chunks linked to the corresponding transcripts. When the corpus is completed, about 50–100 hours will be mounted at the SCCSD website (see appendix) and made available on the Internet in a multimedia form.

12.13. The PKU Chinese corpora

The PKU-CCL-Corpus has two components, one for Modern Chinese and the other for Ancient Chinese. The Modern Chinese subcorpus has reached a size of 264 million Chinese characters, covering a variety of genres such as newspapers, magazines, literary texts, applied writing, and speeches, while the ancient Chinese subcorpus comprises 84 million Chinese characters of running texts sampled from different historical periods from Old Chinese to Early Modern Chinese. The texts in the corpus are not tokenized or POS tagged, but basic bibliographic information such as title and author is provided. Both Modern and Ancient Chinese components of the corpus can be searched via the online query system at the corpus website (see PKU-CCL-Corpus in appendix).

In addition to the unannotated Chinese corpus introduced above, Peking University has also been developing a Chinese treebank PKU-CTB, with a target size of one million words of Chinese texts with syntactic bracketing. The corpus consists of four parts: (1) Chinese government white papers, (2) newspaper articles, (3) Chinese textbooks of primary/middle/high schools, and (4) test sentences used for machine translation evaluation. At present, a total of 271,460 words in 19,560 sentences have been collected, which are parsed into 207,539 phrases tagged with 22 phrases categories. PKU-CTB differs from the Penn Chinese Treebank in that their parsing schemes contain different numbers and types of phrase labels, and more importantly, different approaches to phrase bracketing have been used. Phrase bracketing in Penn Chinese Treebank is based on generative grammar whereas PKU-CTB is bracketed under the paradigm of traditional structuralism, especially the method of immediate constituent analysis (cf. Zhan et al. 2006). As the corpus is still under construction, its availability is unknown at the time of writing.

13. Well-known distributors of corpus resources

While many corpora introduced in this article are made available at individual project or corpus websites, there are a number of organizations which aim at creating, collecting and distributing corpus resources. The best-known of these include CSLU, ELRA/ELD A, ELSNET, ENABLER, ICAME, the LDC, OTA, and TELRI/TRACTOR.

CSLU (Centre for Spoken Language Understanding) is a research centre at the Oregon Graduate Institute of Science and Technology (OGI) that focuses on spoken language technologies. The centre offers a range of products and services. For non-commercial purposes (educational, research, personal and evaluation), most products are freely available. Some products (generally source codes) are also available for commercial use via a membership agreement. CSLU has created, collected and distributed telephone and cellular speech data in over 20 languages for use in the area of voice processing. A description of the corpora currently available from the centre is available at the CSLU website (see appendix).

ELRA (The European Language Resources Association) is a non-profit organization established in 1995 with the goal of promoting the creation, validation, standardization, and distribution of language resources (LRs) for the Human Language Technology (HLT) community, and evaluating language engineering technologies. Many of these tasks are carried out by ELRA's operational body ELDA (Evaluations and Language Resources Distribution Agency), which is set up to identify, classify, collect, validate and produce language resources. The language resources available from ELRA are classified into four major categories: spoken LRs (telephone/microphone recordings, speech related resources), written LRs (corpora, monolingual and multilingual lexicons), terminological resources (monolingual, bilingual and multilingual), and multimodal/multimedia LRs. See the ELRA catalogue for the available language resources.

ELSNET (European Network in Language and Speech) is a Europe-based forum which aims to advance human language technologies in a broad sense in Europe, by bringing together Europe's key players in research, development, integration or deployment in the field of language and speech technology and neighboring areas. See the ELSNET resources page for the corpora made available or supported by ELSNET.

The ENABLER (European National Activities for Basic Language Resources) Network aims at improving cooperation among the national activities which provide language resources for their respective languages. ENABLER has worked in close collaboration with ELSNET to develop the Language Resources Roadmap and the Language Resources Landscape. Resources offered by ENABLER include written, spoken, and multimodal corpora, as well as lexical resources. See the ENABLER catalogue (see appendix) for a list of available corpora.

ICAME (International Computer Archive of Modern and Medieval English) is an international organization of linguists and information scientists working with English corpora. The aim of the organization is to collect and distribute information on English language material available for computer processing, and on linguistic research completed or in progress on the material, to compile an archive of English text corpora in machine-readable form, and to make material available to research institutions. About 20 corpora amounting to 17 million words are currently available on CDs from ICAME.

The LDC (Linguistic Data Consortium) is an open consortium of universities, companies and government research laboratories which creates, collects and distributes speech and text databases, lexicons, and other resources for research and development purposes. The LDC is the largest distributor of corpus resources, but most LDC resources are specialized corpora which are more geared towards language engineering than linguistic analysis. See the LDC catalogue for a list of available corpora.

OTA (Oxford Text Archive) is one of the oldest and best-known electronic text centres in the world. It works closely with members of the Arts and Humanities academic community to collect, catalogue, and preserve high-quality electronic texts for research and teaching. OTA currently distributes more than 2,500 resources in over 25 different languages covering all areas of literary and linguistic studies, which include a great variety of language corpora in addition to electronic editions of works by individual authors, manuscript transcriptions and reference works. See the OTA catalogue for available resources.

TRACTOR is the TELRI (Trans-European Language Resources Infrastructure) Research Archive of Computational Tools and Resources, which aims at collecting, promoting, and making available monolingual and multilingual language resources and tools for the extraction of language data and linguistic knowledge, with a special focus on Central and Eastern European languages. The TRACTOR archive features monolingual and multilingual corpora as well as lexicons in a wide variety of languages, currently including Bulgarian, Croatian, Czech, Dutch, English, Estonian, French, Finnish, German, Greek, Hungarian, Italian, Latvian, Lithuanian, Polish, Romanian, Russian, Serbian, Slovak, Slovene, Swedish, Turkish, Ukrainian and Uzbek. Resources distributed through TRACTOR (see appendix) are available for non-commercial use only, but TRACTOR aims to promote and foster commercial links between academic and industrial researchers.

14. Conclusion

This article introduced well-known and influential corpora for various research purposes, including national corpora, monitor corpora, corpora of the Brown family, synchronic corpora, diachronic corpora, spoken corpora, academic/professional corpora, parsed corpora, developmental/learner corpora, multilingual corpora, and non-English monolingual corpora. This discussion, however, only covers a very small proportion of the available corpus resources. The classification used in this article was for illustrative purposes only. The distinctions given have been forced by the purpose of this introductory article. It is not unusual to find that any given corpus will be a blend of many of the features introduced here.

With a few exceptions, most of the corpora introduced in this article are publicly available, either free of charge or at an affordable cost. Many of these corpora are searchable or downloadable over the Internet. This article has introduced well-known and influential corpora for English as well as a wide range of European and Asian languages such as French, German, Spanish and Chinese, most of which have been subject to much study. The next article introduces corpus resources for less studied languages.

15. Appendix: URLs

URLs were accessed on 12 February 2008.

ACQUIS: http://wt.jrc.it/lt/Acquis/
Aix-MARSEC: http://aune.lpl.univ-aix.fr/~EPGA/en_marsec.html
ASBC: http://www.sinica.edu.tw/SinicaCorpus/index.html
AWL: http://language.massey.ac.nz/staff/awl/awlinfo.shtml
Bank of English: http://www.collins.co.uk/books.aspx?group= 153
BASE: http://www2.warwick.ac.uk/fac/soc/celte/research/base/
BAWE: http://www2.warwick.ac.uk/fac/soc/celte/research/bawe
BNC Baby: http://www.natcorp.ox.ac.uk/corpus/baby/index.html
BNC Online: http://www.natcorp.ox.ac.uk/using/index.xml.ID=online
BNC PIE: http://pie.usna.edu/
BNC VIEW: http://corpus.byu.edu/bnc/
BNCWeb: http://escorp.unizh.ch/

BNCWeb CQP Edition: http://es-corp.unizh.ch/
BNC XML Edition: http://www.natcorp.ox.ac.uk/XMLedition/
BYU corpora: http://view.byu.edu/
CECL: http://cecl.fltr.ucl.ac.be/
CEG: http://www.bangor.ac.uk/ar/cb/ceg.php.en
CETEMPublico: http://acdc.linguateca.pt/cetempublico/whatisCETEMP.html
CHILDES: http://childes.psy.cmu.edu/
CHRISTINE: http://www.grsampson.net/ChrisDoc.html
CIC: http://www.cambridge.org/elt/corpus/international_corpus.htm
CLC: http://www.cambridge.org/elt/corpus/learner_corpus.htm
CLEC: http://www.clal.org.cn/corpus/EngSearchEngine.aspx
CLUVI: http://sli.uvigo.es/CLUVI/index_en.html
CME: http://www.hti.umich.edu/c/cme/
COLT: http://www.hf.uib.no/i/Engelsk/COLT/
CORIS: http://corpora.dslo.unibo.it/coris_eng.html
COSMAS: http://corpora.ids-mannheim.de/~cosmas/
Corpus del Espanol: http://www.corpusdelespanol.org/
Corpus do Portugues: http://www.corpusdoportugues.org/
CRATER: http://www.comp.lancs.ac.uk/linguistics/crater/corpus.html
CREA: http://corpus.rae.es/creanet.html
Croatian National Corpus: http://www.hnk.ffzg.hr/default_en.htm
CSLU: http://cslu.cse.ogi.edu/corpora/corpCurrent.html
CSPAE: http://www.athel.com/cspa.html
Czech National Corpus: http://ucnk.ff.cuni.cz/english/
DCPSE: http://www.ucl.ac.uk/english-usage/projects/dcpse/index.htm
DOEC: http://www.doe.utoronto.ca/pub/corpus.html
Early Mandarin: http://www.sinica.edu.tw/Early_Mandarin/
ECCO: http://gale.cengage.com/EighteenthCentury/index.htm
EEBO: http://eebo.chadwyck.com/home
ELRA: http://www.elra.info/
ELSNET: http://www.elsnet.org/
EMILLE: http://www.lancs.ac.uk/fass/projects/corpus/emille
ENABLER: http://www.ilsp.gr/enabler/search_sel.asp
ENPC: http://www.hf.uio.no/iba/prosjekt/
ESPC: http://www.englund.lu.se/corpus/corpus/espc.html
FIDA: http://www.fida.net/eng/index.html
FRANTEXT Database: http://www.lib.uchicago.edu/efts/ARTFL/databases/TLF/
French Development Corpus: http://www.flloc.soton.ac.uk/LDC.html
French Progression Corpus: http://www.flloc.soton.ac.uk/ProgC.html
DWDS corpus: http://www.dwds.de/cgi-bin/rest/loginstart
Global English Monitor Corpus: http://www.corpus.bham.ac.uk/ccl/global.htm
Hellenic National Corpus: http://hnc.ilsp.gr/find.asp
Hungarian National Corpus: http://corpus.nytud.hu/mnsz/index_eng.html
ICAME: http://nora.hd.uib.no/icame.html
ICE: http://www.ucl.ac.uk/english-usage/ice/
ICE-GB: http://www.ucl.ac.uk/english-usage/ice-gb/
ICLE: http://cecl.fltr.ucl.ac.be/Cecl-Projects/Icle/icle.htm
IJS-ELAN: http://nl.ijs.si/elan/
INL: http://www.inl.nl
IPI PAN Corpus: http://korpus.pl/index.php?lang=en&page=welcome
IViE: http://www.phon.ox.ac.uk/~esther/ivyweb/
JPU: http://joeandco.blogspot.com/

KEMPE: http://corp.hum.sdu.dk/cqp.en.html
KNC: http://www.sejong.or.kr/
Korpus: http://corp.hum.sdu.dk/corpustop.en.html
Korpus 2000: http://korpus.dsl.dk/korpus2000/engelsk_summary.php?lang=uk
L-CIE: http://www.ul.ie/~lcie/homepage.htm
Lancaster Babel: http://www.ling.lancs.ac.uk/corplang/babel/babel.htm
LCMC: http://www.elda.org/catalogue/en/text/W0039.html
LDC: http://www.ldc.upenn.edu/
LDC Online: http://www.ldc.upenn.edu/ldc/online/
Lexical Tutor: http://www.lextutor.ca/
LINDSEI: http://cecl.fltr.ucl.ac.be/Cecl-Projects/Lindsei/lindsei.htm
LIVAC: http://www.livac.org/
Longman Corpus Network: http://www.longman.com/dictionaries/corpus/index.html
Longman Learners' Corpus: http://www.longman.com/dictionaries/corpus/learners.html
LUCY: http://www.grsampson.net/LucyDoc.html
MARSEC: http://www.rdg.ac.uk/AcaDepts/ll/speechlab/marsec/
MCLC: http://www.clr.org.en/retrieval
MEMEM: http://www.hti.umich.edu/m/memem/
MICASE: http://lw.lsa.umich.edu/eli/micase/index.htm
MICUSP: http://lw.lsa.umich.edu/eli/eli 1/micusp/index.htm
MidEng: http://etext.virginia.edu/mideng.browse.html
MULTEXT: http://www.lpl.univ-aix.fr/projects/multext/MUL4.html
MUTEXT-East (version 3): http://nl.ijs.si/ME/V3/
National Corpus of Irish: http://www.focloir.ie/corpus/
Nova Beseda: http://bos.zrc-sazu.si/a_beseda.html
OMC: http://www.hf.uio.no/ilos/OMC/English/index_e.html
OTA: http://ota.ahds.ac.uk/
OPUS: http://urd.let.rug.nl/tiedeman/OPUS/
PAROLE: http://www.elda.org/catalogue/en/text/doc/parole.html
Parsed historical corpora: http://www-users.york.ac.uk/~lang18/pcorpus.html
PDT (2.0): http://ufal.mff.cuni.cz/pdt2.0/
PELCRA: http://pelcra.ia.uni.lodz.pl/index_en.php
Penn Treebank: http://www.ldc.upenn.edu/ldc/online/treebank/index.html
PERC: http://www.perc21.org/menu.html
PKU-CCL-Corpus: http://ccl.pku.edu.cn/YuLiao_Contents.Asp
PKU Babel: http://www.icl.pku.edu.cn/icl_groups/parallel/default.htm
PPCME: http://www.ling.upenn.edu/hist-corpora/
PWN Corpus of Polish: http://korpus.pwn.pl/szukaj_en.php
RNC: http://www.ruscorpora.ru
Ruscorpora: http://corpus.leeds.ac.uk/ruscorpora.html
SCCSD: http://ling.cass.cn/dangdai/corpus.htm
SCoSE: http://www.uni-saarland.de/fak4/norrick/scose.html
SCOTS: http://www.scottishcorpus.ac.uk/
Shogakukan Corpus Network: http://www.corpora.jp
Sinica Treebank: http://treebank.sinica.edu.tw/
Sinotefl: http://www.sinotefl.ac.cn/english.asp
Slovak National Corpus: http://korpus.juls.savba.sk/index.en.html
SST: http://leo.meikai.ac.jp/~tono/sst/index.html
SUSANNE: http://www.grsampson.net/SueDoc.html
SWB online: http://www.ldc.upenn.edu/cgi-bin/lol/swb/speechcorpus?&corpus= swb
Talkbank: http://www.talkbank.org/
TalkBank SBCSAE: http://www.talkbank.org/data/Conversation/SBCSAE-zipped.zip

TalkBank SWB: http://www.talkbank.org/media/SWB/
TRACTOR: http://tractor.bham.ac.uk/tractor/catalogue.html
TransSearch: http://www.terminotix.com/eng/index.htm
UCREL: http://ucrel.lancs.ac.uk/
USC Hansard: http://www.isi.edu/natural-language/download/hansard/
USE: http://www.engelska.uu.se/use.html
Xaira: http://www.xaira.org
XGL: http://ariadne.coli.uni-bielefeld.de/indogram/component/option,com_vfm/Itemid,33/dir, Corpora/
ZEN: http://escorp.unizh.ch/

16. Literature

URLs were accessed on 12 February 2008.

Aduriz, I./Aldezabal, I./Alegria, I./Arriola, J./Diaz de Ilarraza, A./Ezeiza, N./Gojenola, K. (2003), Finite State Applications for Basque. In: *Proceedings of'EACL'2003 Workshop on Finite-state Methods in Natural Language Processing*. Budapest, 13–14 April 2003. Available online at: http://citeseer.ist.psu.edu/623753.html.

Altenberg, B./Aijmer, K./Svensson, M. (2001), *The English-Swedish Parallel Corpus (ESPC): Manual of Enlarged Version*. Lund and Göteborg: Universities of Lund and Göteborg.

Armstrong, S./Kempen, M./McKelvie, *D./* Petitpierre, D./Rapp, R./Thompson, H. (1998), Multilingual Corpora for Cooperation. In: Proceedings of the *First International Conference on Language Resources and Evaluation (LREC)*. Granada, Spain, 975–980.

Armstrong-Warwick, S./Thompson, H./McKelvie, D./Petitpierre, D. (1994), Data in your Language: The ECI Multilingual Corpus 1. In: *Proceedings of the International Workshop on Shareable Natural Language Resources*. Nara, Japan. Available at: http://citeseer.ist.psu.edu/205355.html.

Aston, G./Burnard, L. (1998), *The BNC Handbook: Exploring the British National Corpus with SARA*. Edinburgh: Edinburgh University Press.

Auran, C./Bouzon, C./Hirst, D. (2004), The Aix-MARSEC Project: An Evolutive Database of Spoken British English. In: *Proceedings of the Second International Conference on Speech Prosody*. Nara, Japan, 561–564.

Bai, X./Chang, B./Zhan, W. (2002), Building a Large Chinese–English Parallel Corpus. In: Huang, H. (ed.), *Proceedings of the National Symposium on Machine Translation 2002*. Beijing: Electronic Industry Press, 124–131.

Baker, P./Hardie, A./McEnery, T./Xiao, R./Bontcheva, K./Cunningham, H./Gaizauskas, R./Hamza, O./Maynard, D./Tablan, V./Ursu, C./Jayaram, B./Leisher, M. (2004), Corpus Linguistics and South Asian Languages: Corpus Creation and Tool Development. In: *Literary and Linguistic Computing* 19(4), 509–524.

Barlow, M. (1998), *A Corpus of Spoken Professional American English*. Houston, TX: Athelstan.

Beare, J./Scott, B. (1999), The Spoken Corpus of the Survey of English Dialects: Language Variation and Oral History. In: *Proceedings of ALLC/ACH 1999*. Charlottesville, VA. Available at: http://www.iath.virginia.edu/ach-allc.99/proceedings/scott.html.

Biber, D. (1988), *Variation across Speech and Writing*. Cambridge: Cambridge University Press.

Biber, D./Finegan, E./Atkinson, D. (1994), ARCHER and its Challenges: Compiling and Exploring a Representative Corpus of Historical English Registers. In: Fries, U./ Tottie, G./Schneider, P. (eds.), *Creating and Using English Language Corpora*. Amsterdam: Rodopi, 1–14.

Böhmová, A./Hajič, J./Hajičova, E./Hladka, B. (2003), The Prague Dependency Treebank: Three-level Annotation Scenario. In: Abeille, A. (ed.), *Treebanks: Building and Using Syntactically Annotated Corpora*. Dordrecht: Kluwer, 103–127.

Burnard, L. (2002), Where did we Go Wrong? A Retrospective Look at the British National Corpus. In: Ketterman, B./Marko, G. (eds.), *Teaching and Learning by Doing Corpus Analysis: Proceedings of the Fourth International TALC*. Amsterdam: Rodopi, 51–70.

Burnard, L. (2003) Reference Guide for BNC-baby. Available at: http://www.natcorp.ox.ac.uk/corpus/baby/.

Carter, R./McCarthy, M. (2004), Talking, Creating: Interactional Language, Creativity, and Context. In: *Applied Linguistics* 25(1), 62–88.

Cavar, D./Geyken, A./Neumann, G. (2000), Digital Dictionary of the 20th Century German Language. In: Erjavec, T./Gros, J. (eds.), *Proceedings of the Language Technologies Conference*. Ljubljana, Slovenia. Available at: http://nl.ijs.si/isjt00/index-en.html.

Cheng, W./Warren, M. (1999), Facilitating a Description of Intercultural Conversations: The Hong Kong Corpus of Conversational English. In: *ICAME Journal* 23, 5–20.

Cheng, W./Greaves, C./ Warren, M. (2005), The Creation of a Prosodically Transcribed Intercultural Corpus: The Hong Kong Corpus of Spoken English (Prosodic). In: *ICAME Journal* 29, 47–68.

Choukri, K. (2003), Brief Overview of Recent Activities in Europe. In: *Proceedings of COCOSDA Workshop 2003*. Geneva, Switzerland. Available at: http://www.cocosda.org/meet/2003/kc-cocosda.pdf.

Coxhead, A. (2000), A New Academic Word List. In: *TESOL Quarterly* 34(2), 213–238.

Crowdy, S. (1993), Spoken Corpus Design. In: *Literary and Linguistic Computing* 8(4), 259–265.

Culpeper, J./Kytö, M. (1997), Towards a Corpus of Dialogues, 1550–1750. In: Ramisch, H./Wynne, K. (eds.), *Language in Time and Space: Studies in Honour of Wolfgang Viereck on the Occasion of his 60th Birthday*. Stuttgart: Franz Steiner Verlag, 60–73.

Culpeper, J./Kytö, M. (2000), Data in Historical Pragmatics: Spoken Interaction (Re)cast as Writing. In: *Journal of Historical Pragmatics* 1(2), 175–199.

Culpeper, J./Kytö, M. (forthcoming), *Early Modern English Dialogues: Spoken Interaction as Writing*. Cambridge: Cambridge University Press.

Dalli, A. (2001), Interoperable Extensible Linguistic Databases. In: *Proceedings of IRCS Workshop on Linguistic Databases*. Philadelphia, PA, 74–81. Available at: http://www.ldc.upenn.edu/annotation/database/proceedings.html.

Denison, D. (1994), A Corpus of Late Modern English Prose. In: Kytö, M./Rissanen, M./Wright, S. (eds.), *Corpora across the Centuries*. Amsterdam: Rodopi, 7–16.

Du Bois, J./Chafe, W./Meyer, C./Thompson, S. (2000–2005), *Santa Barbara Corpus of Spoken American English* Parts 1–4. Philadelphia, PA: Linguistic Data Consortium.

Ellis, N./O'Dochartaigh, C./Hicks, W./Morgan, M./Laporte, N. (2001), *Cronfa Electroneg o Gymraeg (CEG): A 1 Million Word Lexical Database and Frequency Count for Welsh*. Available at: http://www.bangor.ac.uk/development/canolfanbedwyr/ceg.php.en.

English Language Institute (2003), *MICASE Manual: The Michigan Corpus of Academic Spoken English* (version 1.1). University of Michigan. Available at: http://lw.lsa.umich.edu/eli/micase/MICASE_MANUAL.pdf.

Erjavec, T. (2002), The IJS-ELAN Slovene-English Parallel Corpus. In: *International Journal of Corpus Linguistics* 7(1), 1–20.

Erjavec, T. (2004), MULTEXT-East Version 3: Multilingual Morphosyntactic Specifications, Lexicons and Corpora. In: *LREC 2004 Proceedings*. Paris, France. Available at: http://nl.ijs.si/ME/bib/mte-lrec2004.pdf.

Farr, F./Murphy, B./O'Keeffe, A. (2004), The Limerick Corpus of Irish English: Design, Description and Application. In: *Teanga* 21, 5–29.

Fries, U./Schneider, P. (2000), ZEN: Preparing the Zurich English Newspaper Corpus. In: Ungerer, F. (ed.), *English Media Texts: Past and Present*. Amsterdam: John Benjamins, 1–24.

Garabík, R. (2006), Computer(ized) Linguistic Resources at the Ł. Štúr Institute of Linguistics. In: *Proceedings of the Conference Applied (Computer) Linguistics*. Kiev, Ukraine, 56–59.

Garside, R./Leech, G./Váradi, T. (1992), *Manual of Information for the Lancaster Parsed Corpus.* Lancaster: Lancaster University.

Garside, R./Hutchinson, J./ Leech, G./McEnery, A./Oakes, M. (1994), The Exploitation Of Parallel Corpora in Projects ET10/63 and CRATER. In: *New Methods in Language Processing.* Manchester: UMIST, 108–115.

Garside, R./Leech, G./Sampson, G. (eds.) (1987), *The Computational Analysis of English: A Corpus-based Approach.* Harlow: Longman.

Gautier, G. (1998), Building a Kurdish Language Corpus. Paper presented at ICEMCO 98 6th International Conference and Exhibition on Multilingual Computing. Cambridge, United Kingdom, April 1998. Available at: http://ggautierk.free.fr/e/icem_98.htm.

Gianitsová, L. (2005), Morphological Analysis of the Slovak National Corpus. In: M. Šimková (ed.), *Insight into Slovak and Czech Corpus Linguistics.* Bratislava: Veda, 166–178.

Gillard, P./Gadsby, A. (1998), Using a Learners' Corpus in Compiling ELT Dictionaries. In: Granger, S. (ed.), *Learner English on Computer.* London: Longman, 159–171.

Glover, W. (1998), Toward a Nepali National Corpus. In: Yadava, P./Kansakar, T. (eds.), *Lexicography in Nepal: Proceedings of the Institute on Lexicography, 1995.* Kamaladi, Kathmandu: Royal Nepal Academy, 24–28.

Gómez Guinovart, X./Sacau Fontenla, E. (2004), Parallel Corpora for the Galician Language: Building and Processing of the CLUVI (Linguistic Corpus of the University of Vigo). In: *Proceedings of the Fourth International Conference on Language Resources and Evaluation.* Lisbon, Portugal, 1179–1182.

Grabe, E./Post, B./Nolan, F. (2001), *The IViE Corpus.* Department of Linguistics, University of Cambridge. Available at: http://www.phon.ox.ac.uk/IViE/.

Granger, S. (2003), The International Corpus of Learner English: A New Resource for Foreign Language Learning and Teaching and Second Language Acquisition Research. In: *TESOL Quarterly* 37(3), 538–546.

Granger, S./Tyson, S. (1996), Connector Usage in the English Essay Writing of Native and Non-native EFL Speakers of English. In: *World Englishes* 15(1), 17–27.

Greenbaum, S./Svartvik, J. (1990), The London-Lund Corpus of Spoken English. In: Svartvik, J. (ed.), *The London Lund Corpus of Spoken English: Description and Research.* (Lund Studies in English 82.) Lund: Lund University Press. Available at: http://khnt.hit.uib.no/icame/manuals/LONDLUND/INDEX. HTM.

Gu, Y. (2002), Sampling Situated Discourse for Spoken Chinese Corpus. Manuscript available at: http://ling.cass.cn/dangdai/gu_papers/sampling%20situated%20discourse.pdf.

Guerra, L. (1998), Research in Language and Literature: Old Problems, New Solutions. Paper presented at the conference of *The Future of Humanities in the Digital Age.* Bergen, Norway, 25–26 September 1998. Available at: http://ultibase.rmit.edu.au/Articles/dec98/guerra1.htm.

Gui, S./Yang, H. (2002), *Chinese Learner English Corpus.* Shanghai: Shanghai Foreign Language Education Press.

Hajič, J. (2004), *Complex Corpus Annotation: The Prague Dependency Treebank.* Bratislava, Slovakia: Jazykovedný ústav Ľ. Štúra, SAV.

Haslerud, V./Stenström, A. (1995), The Bergen Corpus of London Teenager Language (COLT). In: Leech, G./Myers, G./Thomas, J. (eds.), *Spoken English on Computer. Transcription, Mark-up and Application.* London: Longman, 235–242.

Hatzigeorgiu, N./Gavrilidou, M./Piperidis, S./Carayannis, G./Papakostopoulou, A./Spiliotopoulou, A./Vacalopoulou, A./Labropoulou, P./Mantzari, E./Papageorgiou, H./Demiros, I. (2000), Design and Implementation of the Online ILSP Greek Corpus. In: *Proceedings of LREC 2000.* Athens, Greece, 1737–1742.

Hoffmann, S./Evert, S. (2006), BNCweb (CQP-Edition) – the Marriage of Two Corpus Tools. In: Braun, S./Kohn, K./Mukherjee, J. (eds.), *Corpus Technology and Language Pedagogy: New Resources, New Tools, New Methods.* Frankfurt am Main: Peter Lang, 177–195.

Holmes, J./Vine, B./Johnson, G. (1998), *Guide to the Wellington Corpus of Spoken New Zealand English*. Wellington, New Zealand: Victoria University of Wellington.

Holmes-Higgin, P./Abidi, S./Ahmad, K. (1994), A Description of Texts in a Corpus: "Virtual" and "Real" Corpora. In: Martin, W./Meijs, W./Moerland, M./ten Pas, E./van Sterkenburg, P./Vossen, P. (eds.), *EURALEX'94 Proceedings*. Amsterdam: Vrije Universiteit, 390–402.

Horváth, J. (1999), Advanced Writing in English as a Foreign Language. A Corpus-based Study of Processes and Products. PhD thesis, Janus Pannonius University.

Huang, C. (2006), Automatic Acquisition of Linguistic Knowledge: From Sinica Corpus to Gigaword Corpus. In: *Language Corpora: Their Compilation and Application. Proceedings of the 13th NIJL International Symposium*. Tokyo, Japan, 41–48.

Huang, C./Chen, K. (1995/1998), *CKIP Technical Report 95-02/98-04*. Taipei: Academia Sinica.

Huang, C./Chen, F./Chen, K./Gao, Z./Chen, K. (2000), Sinica Treebank: Design Criteria, Annotation Guidelines, and Online Interface. In: Bagga, A./Pustejovsky, J./Zadrozny, W. (eds.), *Proceedings of NAACL-ANLP 2000 Workshop: Syntactic and Semantic Complexity in Natural Language Processing Systems*. Seattle, Washington, 29–37.

Hundt, M./Sand, A./Siemund, R. (1998), *Manual of Information to Accompany the Freiburg-LOB Corpus of British English ("FLOB")*. Available at: http://khnt.hit.uib.no/icame/manuals/flob/INDEX.HTM.

Hundt, M./Sand, A./Skandera, P. (1999), *Manual of Information to Accompany the Freiburg-Brown Corpus of American English ("Frown")*. Available at: http://khnt.hit.uib.no/icame/manuals/frown/INDEX.HTM.

Izumi, E./Isahara, H. (2004), Investigation into Language Learners' Acquisition Order Based on the Error Analysis of the Learner Corpus. Paper presented at IWLeL 2004. Tokyo, Japan.

Izumi, E./Uchimoto, K./Isahara, H. (2004), SST Speech Corpus of Japanese Learners' English and Automatic Detection of Learners' Errors. In: *ICAME Journal* 28, 31–48.

Johansson, S./Ebeling, J./Oksefjell, S. (2002), *English-Norwegian Parallel Corpus: Manual*. Oslo: University of Oslo.

Johansson, S./Leech, G./Goodluck, H. (1978), *Manual of Information to Accompany the Lancaster-Oslo/Bergen Corpus of British English, for Use with Digital Computers*. Oslo: University of Oslo.

Kang, B./Kim, H. (2004), Sejong Korean Corpora in the Making. In: *Proceedings of LREC 2004*. Lisbon, Portugal, 1747–1750.

Kim, H. (2006), Korean National Corpus in the 21st Century Sejong Project. In: *Language Corpora: Their Compilation and Application. Proceedings of the 13th NIJL International Symposium*. Tokyo, Japan, 49–54.

Kroch, A./Taylor, A. (2000), *The Penn-Helsinki Parsed Corpus of Middle English. Second Edition*. University of Pennsylvania. Available at: http://www.ling.upenn.edu/hist-corpora/PPCME2-RELEASE-2/.

Kruyt, J. (1995), Nationale tekstcorpora in internationaal perspectief. In: *Forum der Letteren* 36(1), 47–58.

Kruyt, J./Dutilh, M. (1997), A 38 Million Words Dutch Text Corpus and its Users. In: *Lexikos 7* (Afrilex-reeks/series 7), 229–244.

Kruyt, J./Raaijmakers, S./van der Kamp, P./van Strien, R. (1996), Language Resources for Language Technology. In: *Proceedings of the First TELRI European Seminar*. Tihany, Hungary, 173–178.

Kučera, H./Francis, W. (1967), *Computational Analysis of Present-day English*. Providence: Brown University Press.

Kučera, K. (2002), The Czech National Corpus: Principles, Design, and Results. In: *Literary and Linguistic Computing* 17(2), 245–257.

Kytö, M. (1996), *Manual to the Diachronic Part of the Helsinki Corpus of English Texts: Coding Conventions and Lists of Source Texts*. Helsinki: University of Helsinki. Available at: http://khnt.hit.uib.no/icame/manuals/HC/INDEX.HTM.

Kytö, M./Walker, T. (2006), *Guide to* A Corpus of English Dialogues 1560–1760. (Studia Anglistica Upsaliensia 130.) Uppsala: Acta Universitatis Upsaliensis.

Laitinen, M. (2002), Extending the Corpus of Early English Correspondence to the 18th Century. In: *Helsinki English Studies* 2002(2). Available at: http://www.eng.helsinki.fi/hes/Corpora/ extending_the_corpus2.htm.

Lee, D. (2001), Genres, Registers, Text Types, Domains, and Styles: Clarifying the Concepts and Navigating a Path through the BNC Jungle. In: *Language Learning and Technology* 5(3), 37–72.

Leech, G./Smith, N. (2005), Extending the Possibilities of Corpus-based Research on English in the Twentieth Century: A Prequel to LOB and FLOB. In: *ICAME Journal* 29, 83–98.

Lewandowska-Tomaszczyk, B. (2003), The PELCRA Project – State of Art. In: Lewandowska-Tomaszczyk, B. (ed.), *Practical Applications in Language and Computers*. Frankfurt: Peter Lang, 105–121.

Linguistic Data Consortium (1995), SWITCHBOARD: A User's Manual. Philadelphia, PA: LDC, University of Pennsylvania. Available at: http://www.ldc.upenn.edu/Catalog/readme_files/ switchboard.readme.html

MacWhinney, B. (1995), *The CHILDES Project: Tools for Analyzing Talk*. Second Edition. Hillsdale, NJ: Erlbaum.

Malten, T. (1998), Tamil Studies in Germany. Lecture given at Max Mueller Bhavan, Chennai on 17 March 1998. Available at: http://www.tamilnation.org/literature/malten.htm.

Marcus, M. (1999), *Manual of ICAMET (Innsbruck Computer-Archive of Machine-Readable English Texts)*. (Innsbrucker Beiträge zur Kulturwissenschaft, Anglistische Reihe 7.) Innsbruck: Leopold-Franzens-Universität Innsbruck, Institut für Anglistik.

Marcus, M./Santorini, B./Marcinkiewicz, M. (1993), Building a Large Annotated Corpus of English: The Penn Treebank. In: *Computational Linguistics* 19, 313–330.

Marcus, M./Kim, G./Marcinkiewicz, M./MacIntyre, R./Bies, A./Ferguson, M./ Katz, K./Schasberger, B. (1994), The Penn Treebank: Annotating Predicate-argument Structure. In: *Proceedings of the ARPA Human Language Technology Workshop*. Plainsboro, NJ, 114–119.

McEnery, A./Xiao, R./Mo, L. (2003), Aspect Marking in English and Chinese: Using the Lancaster Corpus of Mandarin Chinese for Contrastive Language Study. In: *Literary and Linguistic Computing* 18(4), 361–378.

Milton, J./Chowdhury, N. (1994), Tagging the Interlanguage of Chinese Learners of English. In: Flowerdew, L./Tong, A. (eds.), *Entering Text*. Hong Kong: The Hong Kong University of Science and Technology, 127–143.

Nelson, G. (1996), The Design of the Corpus. In: Greenbaum, S. (ed.), *Comparing English Worldwide: The International Corpus of English*. Oxford: Clarendon Press, 27–35.

Nelson, G./Wallis, S./Aarts, B. (ed.) (2002), *Exploring Natural Language: Working with the British Component of the International Corpus of English*. Amsterdam: John Benjamins.

Nevalainen, T. (2000), Gender Differences in the Evolution of Standard English. In: *Journal of English Linguistics* 28(1), 38–59.

Rayson, P./Tono, Y./Morita, Y./Hoshino, M./Nakamura, T./Aizawa, H./Watanabe, R. (2005), Building a Corpus of Professional English. Poster presented at the *Corpus Linguistics 2005* conference, July 14–17, Birmingham, UK.

Reppen, R./Ide, N. (2004), The American National Corpus: Overall Goals and the First Release. In: *Journal of English Linguistics* 32(2), 105–113.

Rissanen, M. (2000), The World of English Historical Corpora. In: *Journal of English Linguistics* 8(1), 7–20.

Riza, H. (1999), *The Indonesia National Corpus and Information Extraction Project (INC-IX)*. Jakarta: BPP Teknologi.

Rossini Favretti, R./Tamburini, F./de Santis, C. (2004), A Corpus of Written Italian: A Defined and a Dynamic Model. In: Wilson, A./Rayson, P./McEnery, T. (eds.), *A Rainbow of Corpora: Corpus Linguistics and the Languages of the World*. Munich: Lincom-Europa. Available at: http:// corpora.dslo.unibo.it/People/Tamburini/CL2001.pdf.

Sampson, G. (1987), The Grammatical Database and Parsing Scheme. In: Garside, R./Leech, G./Sampson, G. (eds.), *The Computational Analysis of English*. London: Longman, 82–96.

Sampson, G. (1995), *English for the Computer: The SUSANNE Corpus and Analytic Scheme*. Oxford: Clarendon Press.

Sampson, G. (2000), *CHRISTINE Corpus: Documentation*. Sussex: University of Sussex. Available at: http://www.grsampson.net/ChrisDoc.html.

Sampson, G. (2005), *The LUCY Corpus: Documentation*. Sussex: University of Sussex. Available at: http://www.grsampson.net/LucyDoc.html.

Sanchez, M. (2002), CREA: Reference Corpora for Current Spanish. In: *Proceedings of Language Corpora: Present and Future*. Donostia, Spain, 24–25.

Santos, D./Rocha, P. (2001), Evaluating CETEMPúblico, a Free Resource for Portuguese. In: *Proceedings of the 39th Annual Meeting of the Association for Computational Linguistics, ACL'2001*. Toulouse, France, 442–449.

Schmied, J. (1994), The Lampeter Corpus of Early Modern English Tracts. In: Kytö, M./Rissanen, M./Wright, S. (eds.), *Corpora across the Centuries: Proceedings of the First International Colloquium on English Diachronic Corpora. St Catharine's College Cambridge, 25–27 March 1993*. Amsterdam: Rodopi, 81–89.

Schneider, P. (2002), Computer Assisted Spelling Normalization of 18th Century English. In: Peters, P./Collins, P./Smith, A. (eds.), *New Frontiers of Corpus Research*. Amsterdam: Rodopi, 199–214.

Scott, M. (2004), *WordSmith Tools*. Oxford: Oxford University Press.

Sharoff, S. (2006), Methods and Tools for Development of the Russian Reference Corpus. In: Archer, D./Wilson, A./Rayson, P. (eds.), *Corpus Linguistics Around the World*. Amsterdam: Rodopi, 167–180.

Šimková, M. (2005), Slovak National Corpus – History and Current Situation. In: M. Šimková (ed.), *Insight into Slovak and Czech Corpus Linguistics*. Bratislava: Veda, 152–159.

Souter, C. (1993), Towards a Standard Format for Parsed Corpora. In: Aarts, J./Haan, P./Oostdijk, N. (eds.), *English Language Corpora: Design, Analysis and Exploitation*. Amsterdam: Rodopi, 197–214.

Stern, K. (1997), The Longman Spoken American Corpus: Providing an In-depth Analysis of Everyday English. In: *Longman Language Review* 3. Available at: http://www.longman.com/dictionaries/pdfs/Spoken-American.pdf.

Stibbard, R. (2001), Vocal Expression of Emotions in Non-laboratory Speech: An Investigation of the Reading/Leeds Emotion in Speech Project Annotation Data. PhD thesis, University of Reading.

Tan, M. (2005), Authentic Language or Language Errors? Lessons from a Learner Corpus. In: *ELT Journal* 59(2), 126–134.

Taylor, L./Knowles, G. (1988), *Manual of Information to Accompany the SEC Corpus: The Machine Readable Corpus of Spoken English*. University of Lancaster. Available at: http://khnt.hit.uib.no/icame/manuals/sec/INDEX. HTM.

Thompson, P. (2001), A Pedagogically-motivated Corpus-based Examination of PhD theses. PhD thesis, University of Reading, UK.

Tsou, B./Tsoi, W./Lai, T./Hu, J./Chan, S. (2000), LIVAC, a Chinese Synchronous Corpus, and Some Applications. In: *Proceedings of the ICCLC International Conference on Chinese Language Computing*. Chicago, IL, 233–238.

van Bergen, L./Denison, D. (2004), A Corpus of Late Eighteenth Century Prose. In: Beal, J./Corrigan, K./Mosil, H. (eds.), *Models and Methods in the Handling of Unconventional Digital Corpora*, vol. 2. *Diachronic Corpora*. Basingstoke, UK: Palgrave Macmillan, 228–246.

Váradi, T. (2002), The Hungarian National Corpus. In: *Proceedings of the Third International Conference on Language Resources and Evaluation*. Las Palmas, Spain, 385–389.

Wang, J. (2001), Recent Progress in Corpus Linguistics in China. In: *International Journal of Corpus Linguistics* 6(2), 281–304.

Wang, K. (ed.) (2004), *The Development of the Compilation and Application of Parallel Corpora.* Beijing: Foreign Language Education and Research Press.
Wittenburg, P./Brugman, H./Broeder, D. (2000), Summary. In: Broeder, D./Cunningham, H./Ide, N. (eds.), *Proceedings of LREC 2000 Pre-conference Workshop on Meta-descriptions for Multimedia Language Resources.* Athens, Greece. Available at: http://www.mpi.nl/world/ISLE/documents/papers/LREC2000Workshop.pdf.
Xue, N./Xia, F./Chiou, F./Palmer, M. (2005), The Penn Chinese TreeBank: Phrase Structure Annotation of a Large Corpus. In: *Natural Language Engineering* 11(2), 207–238.
Zhan, W./Chang, B./Duan H./Zhang H. (2006), Recent Developments in Chinese Corpus Research. In: *Language Corpora: Their Compilation and Application. Proceedings of the 13th NIJL International Symposium.* Tokyo, Japan, 19–30.

Richard Xiao, Ormskirk (UK)

21. Corpora of less studied languages

1. Why less studied?

1.1. Definitions

This article examines the provision of corpora to represent "less studied languages", sometimes also known as "lesser used languages". This term evidently has vague boundaries. For this volume, the need is to complement the coverage of the world's languages in article 20, "Well-known and influential corpora". That article is devoted predominantly to a variety of corpora for English (often prepared within a foreign context), together with a few corpora for other major national languages (Chinese, Russian, Polish, Korean, German), some major multilingual corpora for Europe and the Indian subcontinent, and (most pertinently to this article) large-scale distributors of language corpora, some of which are in practice global in what they offer.

The vast majority of the world's languages are therefore implicitly the scope of this article, a range that might seem impossible to cover. As it happens, at this point in history – before the full range of corpus description work has been taken up in full earnest – it is still possible to give, if not an exhaustive, then at least a fairly representative survey of this work.

1.2. Value of language corpora for less studied and endangered languages

In Atkins/Clear/Ostler (1992, 13–15), a variety of uses for text corpora were distinguished, which, in principle, can apply to corpora held in any language. In brief, text corpora give evidence in extenso about a **language**, and about the **content** that has been expressed in that language.

As to language, the corpora will be useful to lexicographers, terminologists, translators, technical writers, computational linguists, theoretical linguists and language teachers; as to **content**, they will serve historians, literary critics, sociologists, advertisers and pollsters. It was predicted that these latter content-focused uses would only become significant when large-scale indexed and analysed corpora should start to become available; so they may be less significant in the first flush for the still less developed corpora of less studied languages.

Evidently also, different languages will have different balances of these kinds of experts to be interested in their corpora. Dead languages will not attract advertisers and pollsters; endangered languages are also unlikely to be of great interest to technical writers or translators until the costs of large-scale localization of materials fall massively.

However, since all languages are on a par *qua* languages, a speech corpus will hold significant value for the support of any spoken language, and so will a text corpus for any language that has a literate form. As I remarked in 1998:

> The old quip attributed to [Max] Weinreich, that a language is a dialect with an army and a navy, is being replaced in these progressive days: a language is a dialect with a dictionary, grammar, parser and a multi-million-word corpus of texts – and they'd better all be computer tractable. When you've got all of those, get yourself a speech database, and your language will be poised to compete on terms of equality in the new Information Society.

2. Three main motives for language corpora exemplified

Before undertaking a general review of sources for major corpora, and then a geographically ordered survey of available corpora in various languages, we begin by distinguishing three motives for building corpora of less studied languages.

Corpora developed for less studied languages are predominantly less well backed by investment. The profit motive is largely lacking as a support for the development of corpora for these languages. (Because of the scope of article 20, Japanese corpora must exceptionally also be entered in this article. Japanese is evidently a language of considerable commercial interest, and well-supported by capital investment, cf. section 7.5. below. And evidently, the degree of commercial interest in a language may well change, at least from decade to decade. Arabic, Persian and Turkish, for example, are now probably upwardly mobile in this respect). If investment is to come, it will be justified by patriotic, religious, cultural, or even academic interest. In some cases (e. g. the languages of the western and central Asia), the investment may be triggered by the security concerns of a wealthy foreign power. This means that immediate commercial applications in the development of language technology tend not to be salient for developers. But in practice, three main motives, and hence *grosso modo* three techniques, predominate for the development of large-scale organized collections of texts or sound-files.

Firstly, the focus may be cultural: texts can be gathered into **cultural archives**, to provide convenient and secure access to libraries of important texts that may otherwise be difficult of access. The criteria for exclusion or inclusion will be determined externally, and largely on non-linguistic grounds. These archives may nevertheless provide large-scale resources in particular languages.

Secondly, the focus may be directly linguistic: for a variety of reasons, technical or scientific, there is now often a requirement for a body of material in a given language, which can be profiled for overall properties, used as an input for tests, or mined for quasi-random content. This leads to the construction of what may be called **"artificial corpora"** of documents. They are constructed with whatever data may be accessible at the lowest cost, and essentially regardless of the documents' content, provided they are in the relevant language. They are artificial in the sense that the material has no social or cultural rationale for being collected. Such corpora can be generated by systematic elicitation (a common technique for speech databases, though this tends to require high levels of organization, and hence investment); or they can be generated by what might be called 'systematic opportunism'. In one modern approach, automata can be used to crawl over, and so index, the increasing quantities of documents that happen to appear in some electronic form, thus producing ad-hoc repositories of language materials.

And thirdly, the very threat that some languages face as to their future existence can be turned into a motive for giving them special attention: this leads to work in **language documentation**, a new tradition which, besides producing the traditional 'Holy Trinity' of grammar, dictionary and text-corpus, is increasingly also laying down guidelines for general selection and storage of electronic data on a language, including audio, image and video materials. By its nature this approach is intermediate between the first and second foci: the language documents are valuable because of the cultural tradition that they embody, but nevertheless the danger of loss extends down to the finest points of pronunciation and discourse. As a result, the two imperatives of cultural quality and linguistic quantity are equally felt.

In this context of full-scale documentation, the distinction between "speech database" and "text corpus" increasingly seems artificial. More and more, data is recorded in a multi-tier electronic medium, with synchronized tiers of video, sound and transcriptions, which may analyse gesture and high-level discourse strategies as well as straight text representation. (Multi-modal corpora are discussed specifically in articles 12 and 31. More details of the alternative multi-tier formats currently available can be found at http://www.hrelp.org/documentation/whatisit/).

We now look at one or two significant examples of each motive in action, and the kinds of corpora that they produce.

3. Cultural archives

There are special problems for those who are interested in dead languages, or even modern languages with a significant literate history; these problems are just as real also for those who may be more interested in the cultures which such languages have expressed. A dead language is, by definition, no longer transmitted naturally to new generations; its corpus of memorable writings has become finite, but it is only through familiarity with this corpus that any value can continue to be derived from the language. Likewise, speakers of a language that is still in use, but with past literary riches, may begin to lose touch with them, especially in modern contexts where instant, electronic availability is coming to dominate the modern transmission and storage of texts, even in schools.

An answer to these problems is to endeavour to gather up the cultural riches of the past in electronic collections where they can be easily accessed. This makes them more accessible to teachers and learners, since the necessity of physical proximity to the records is eliminated by electronic communications; but it also makes them available to researchers through new modalities: flexible searching and indexing will allow new visions and insights to be gained. In many cases, there may even be a fear that the language itself will go out of currency; but a cultural archive can be desirable even where the cultural and linguistic traditions are themselves safe. (See article 14 on "Historical corpora").

3.1. For ancient languages

ETCSL Electronic Text Corpus of Sumerian Literature
A recent example of a cultural archive for an ancient (and indeed long extinct) language is the ETCSL, available at http://www-etcsl.orient.ox.ac.uk/edition2/general.php.

This compilation aims to represent the full extent of extant Sumerian literature in romanized transcription. This has largely been transcribed through the Sumerological research activity of the past fifty years, but was not previously available in any single place, or consistent, up-to-date format. Hence, the unitary format of the corpus is an attraction, besides its universal availability, for lay people and specialists in other language traditions. It is encoded in XML following Text Encoding Initiative guidelines (www.tei-c.org, described in article 22, sections 3.1. and 4.2.3.), and the characters used are available in the Unicode repertoire (with a single exception: g with a macron, which represents n). With approximately 550 texts (each assigned an indicative title), its second edition is largely a complete representation of Sumerian literature, with the exception of certain cult songs and prayers, and large numbers of magical incantations.

As a cultural archive it is interesting in that it has chosen to limit itself to romanized transcription (with English translation and bibliographies), without imaging of the underlying tablets, and without any graphic images of accompanying art and architecture attributable to Sumerian civilization. Its focus is evidently to make texts available for reading by interested scholars rather than specifically for electronic collation and comparison.

3.2. For modern languages

AILLA – Archive of Indigenous Languages of Latin America
This is a collection of recordings of naturally occurring discourse, rather than a compilation of accepted works of literature. As such it covers a wide range of genres, including narratives, ceremonies, oratory, conversations and songs. It contains documents (consisting of sound files in MP3 or .wav format, with associated text files in PDF format, as well as associated photographs and line drawings). Its URL is: http://www.ailla.org.

Unlike the ETCSL, it was compiled not merely to enhance accessibility of its constituent documents, but also to ensure their preservation, and not least of all as an act of affirmation of the value of the cultural products of so many American Indigenous communities, many of them apparently nearing assimilation or extinction. Inevitably, it is less consistently formatted than the ETCSL, for instead of supporting one language, it already supports close to a hundred of them. Its elements are all documents which have been deliberately contributed to the corpus by their owners, and many of them have been explicitly created for that purpose.

Nevertheless, the metadata (drawn from OLAC, cf. section 6 below) is consistently applied, and this lends itself to a variety of more powerful electronic searches. It permits search by metadata categories (including identity of speakers, language, geographical region, genre, format of original medium, and file characteristics) and by keywords.

The archive, again unlike ETCSL, is intrinsically open-ended, in that languages can continue to be added. (SIL Ethnologue (Gordon 2005) currently posits about 750 languages in Latin America, so there is major scope for expansion in this way). Furthermore, and more radically, since most of the languages of Latin America are still living, it is also possible for every language's collection to continue to expand, and there is no natural limit to the archive.

4. Artificial corpora

European Speech Database Projects
These projects of the 1990s (http://www.speechdat.org/) have been particularly influential in setting standards for elicited corpora. Their aim has been to establish speech databases for the development of voice operated teleservices and speech interfaces. They were originally undertaken for the major West European languages, but were soon applied more generally, both for minority languages in Europe, and to languages of the wider world.

Notable have been SPEECHDAT (in which 1,000 speakers were recorded over the fixed telephone network, each speaker uttering read and spontaneous items), and SPEECON (recorded items from adult and child speakers (read and spontaneous)). There is also the SPEECHDAT-CAR project, with digits spoken in various noise and driving conditions inside a car.

The corpora remain available from ELRA (cf. section 6 below).

An Crúbadán – corpus by web-crawling
This is a device created by Kevin P. Scannell, and accessible at: http://borel.slu.edu/crubadan/.

Its name means "The Crawler" in Irish, with the base *crúb* – "a paw" – also connoting a somewhat clumsy approach to text handling.

Its purpose is the automatic development of large text corpora for minority languages. It uses web-crawling technology to gather together in one place the quantities of text freely available on the Web, now in a variety of languages. The intent then is that statistical language processing techniques will become applicable to a variety of languages too small to attract the funding directly to build adequate-sized corpora.

It works largely automatically, after a small number of "seed" texts (a few hundred running words) are fed to the crawler. Queries using words from these texts are fed to the Google API, which brings up more candidate texts, which are then in turn statistically evaluated (against the original seed texts) to see if they are in the desired language. The process then runs recursively. The process, begun with Celtic languages, has by now generated text corpora in approximately 130 languages, ranging in size from 95.8 million words (69,502 texts) in Welsh to 7,305 words (20 texts) in Lunda (a Bantu language of the Dem. Rep. Congo). The median languages (such as Konkani or Fijian) have some 290,000 words (though typical Fijian text is three times the length of one in Konkani: there are 98 Fijian texts to 312 in Konkani).

According to Scannell, some of the resulting corpora are being used for lexicography, grammar checking, language recognition, probabilistic text-entry (without a keyboard) and spell-checking.

This kind of technique is discussed further in Ghani/Jones/Mladenić 2004. Although the application of the procedure is language-independent, it should be remembered that the smaller the footprint of a language in the Web, the more unreliable language detection and identification is. Also, Web pages with mixed language content may be mistaken for pages in the target language. The next step, namely direct use of the Web itself as a corpus, is discussed in article 18.

5. Linguistic documentation

5.1. Best Practice in creating a language record: Principles

When languages are endangered, an appropriate response is to record as much as possible of remaining use of the language. In the worst case, these records may survive the last speakers, as evidence of what the language had been. But even where the threat to the continued existence of the language is less extreme, the records may serve as an important resource for speakers in case the language may later be revitalized, or even revived.

This enterprise is complicated by its comprehensive aspirations, namely to provide sets of data which are not restricted to the concerns of a single language discipline, but are instead rich enough to provide a significant basis for many different theoretical and practical uses. Theoretical uses will include at least phonetics, descriptive linguistics, language typology, ethnography, sociolinguistics, lexicography, literary studies, language teaching, language acquisition studies and psycholinguistics; some of these theoretical studies will yield fruits useful to the language-communities under study, but the data themselves must also be available for their own direct use.

Ethically, this poses a number of problems that will need to be addressed and resolved as appropriate for individual languages. Issues of privacy and ownership are particularly concerning in the small language communities whose languages are now highly endangered. The idea of a universal and accessible repository may conflict with imperatives and prohibitions holding among speakers, either because important utterances are sacred, or because speakers have rights to certain linguistic knowledge, and cannot permit it to pass to outsiders within or outside the speaker community. Rights to privacy may also arise, as well as taboos on reference to dead people. In general, the relation of individuals to their language is more specific and personal in small language communities: this general characteristic must always be kept in mind in attempting to build an external, objective repository, not least because it will be crucial in establishing co-operation between witnesses to the language and those creating the documents.

Juridically, copyright issues will arise. The structure of rights and obligations with respect to both memorable and significant texts and more spontaneous utterances in a language will not necessarily conform with the norms of any western legal framework, especially the concept of "fair use". Besides the legitimate interests of direct participants, the political interests of the community as a whole (often going beyond actual speakers of the language) will be a practical constraint on what is possible. As in all politics, manipulation is to be expected.

Logistically, the situation of languages, and their susceptibility to documentation, is highly unequal and highly varied. Communities whose language is endangered will extend along a continuum from those scattered, with relatively low language-esteem, within larger communities, to those separated from such larger communities, but losing the battle to maintain themselves and their language outside it. At any point on this range, a fitting combination of skill and sensitivity will be needed by language researchers in order to build human links, and so create the basis on which a useful repository can be recorded. There are also techniques to elicit material speedily, and counteract the unnatural aspects of the recording situations, knowledge of which has been built up over the past century. Training in this kind of field-work is therefore an essential preparation for any effective work. But far more than in most science, the individual properties, both of the key researchers doing the recording and of the necessarily small number of language-speakers with whom there is interaction, will be crucial to success.

5.2. Best Practice in creating a language record: Examples

Providing a record of a whole language is a vast task, but central to it is the writing of a comprehensive grammar and dictionary, as well as a large and representative corpus of texts. In the modern age, this corpus of written texts can be supplemented – arguably even replaced – by a set of video/audio recordings of the language in use. Standards for the preparation of such multimedia corpora have recently been elaborated, and are available at a number of websites, notably: http://emeld.org/school/index.html (EMELD School of Best Practice), promoting Best Practices in digitizing language data, aiming to guard against physical deterioration of both digital and non-digital storage media; obsolescence of computer hardware and operating systems, which makes the storage media inaccessible; obsolescence of software, which makes file formats unreadable; and undocumented annotation which may make the content uninterpretable.

http://www.hrelp.org/documentation/whatisit/ (Hans Rausing Endangered Languages Programme). This is concerned with archiving and cataloguing, but also looking to the next big challenge, seen as the discovery and widespread use of software interfaces that make the materials easily and flexibly available to a wide range of users.

http://www.mpi.nl/DOBES/INFOpages/applicants/dobes-ling-aspects-lang-doc.html (Max Planck Institute's Project *Dokumentation bedrohter Sprachen* – Documentation of Endangered Languages), with particular attention to the linguistic aspects of what should be in the record.

6. Some general sources for less studied languages

In the remainder of this article, we review the current state of a variety of corpus language resources, before drawing some conclusions on the general problems that beset corpora of this type.

In this section, we look at the gateways and archives which give access to an increasing number of corpora all over the world. In the next, we review, by region, the specific corpora which relate to the languages of particular parts of the world. And finally we consider, more qualitatively, the problems that arise.

OLAC – Open Language Archive Community

This organization, based at http://www.language-archives.org/, has defined a set of metadata categories to classify and give access to significant language resources, and especially corpora. The OLAC website also gives links (via the Linguist List or LDC websites) to all the repositories registered as using its standard.

The standard is summarized in article 22, section 4.2.2. in this volume. The set is based on a subset of the Dublin Core elements, which were conceived as a systematic set of categories for defining the content of any data resource (likewise summarized in article 22 section 4.2.1.). Specialized to define linguistic resources, these elements are extended with codes for Discourse Types, for Language Identification, for Linguistic Field, for Linguistic Data Types and for Participant Roles (http://www.language-archives.org/REC/olac-extensions.html). These make it possible fairly efficiently to browse and research over the Internet any linguistic data resources that are documented according to these standards.

LDC – Linguistic Data Consortium

The Linguistic Data Consortium has been in existence since 1992. (It is covered in article 20 section 13). It offers resources in text and speech from a variety of sources. In fact, its substantial holdings hardly go beyond major languages, but besides English, French, Spanish, German and Russian these do include Japanese, Chinese (Mandarin), Arabic (Egyptian), and Korean. Beyond fairly comprehensive resources on these languages, there are also recordings of telephone speech in Persian (Farsi), Hindi, Tamil and Vietnamese, broadcast news in Czech and newswire text in Portuguese. The full catalogue can be found at http://www.ldc.upenn.edu/Catalog/.

ELRA – European Language Research Association

This contains resources (speech and text) for all the major western European languages. In speech recordings, there are also resources for Swedish, Portuguese, Russian, Greek,

Finnish, Polish, Slovenian, Czech, Slovak, Basque, Welsh, Bulgarian, Hungarian, Romanian, Estonian and a wide range of local varieties of French, German, Dutch and Spanish. The speech resources rely heavily on the products of SPEECHDAT and allied projects (cf. section 4 above).

The text corpora of this association also cover, besides the major western European languages, Danish, Dutch, Swedish, Portuguese, Greek, Catalan and Irish. There are also holdings in Turkish, Persian (Farsi), Arabic, Chinese (Cantonese as well as Mandarin), Hebrew, Korean and Japanese. The full catalogue can be found at http://www.elda.org.

European Corpus Initiative Multilingual Corpus I (ECI/MCI)
The European Corpus Initiative (ECI) supports existing and projected national and international efforts to design, collect and publish large-scale multilingual written and spoken corpora.

ECI has produced the Multilingual Corpus I (ECI/MCI), totaling over 98 million words, which is a highly-unbalanced, ad-hoc compilation of texts in many European languages (including Dutch, Greek, Gaelic, Estonian, Lithuanian, Norwegian, Albanian, Serbian, Czech), as well as Turkish, Japanese, Russian, Uzbek, Chinese and Malay. There are also some parallel corpora between major European languages. The primary focus in this effort is on textual material of all kinds, including transcriptions of spoken material.

The ECI/MCI corpus is available from ELRA, but its full catalogue is available at http://www.elsnet.org/ecilisting.html.

An Crúbadán – corpus by web-crawling
This device is discussed above. Its current products (ad-hoc corpora, for approximately 130 less used languages, led by 96 million words of Welsh) are available at http://borel.slu.edu/crubadan/stadas.html. For access to the corpora, application should be made to the author Kevin Patrick Scannell <scannell@slu.edu>.

DoBeS – Dokumentation der bedrohten Sprachen
This is the repository for the Volkswagen-Stiftung-funded programme of endangered language documentation, held at the Max Planck Institute in Nijmegen. It is accessible at http://corpus1.mpi.nl/ds/imdi_browser/. There are currently resources for:

- Aweti (a Tupian language of Xingú Park in Brazil's Mato Grosso)
- Hocank (a Siouan language of the Mississippi)
- the Chaco languages (Mocoví, Tapieté, Vilela, Wichí, of Argentina)
- Iwaidja (of Croker Island in Australia's NT)
- Kuikúro (a Carib language of Xingú Park in Brazil's Mato Grosso)
- Lacandón (a Mayan language of Yucatán, Mexico)
- Marquesan (a Polynesian language of the Pacific)
- Salar and Monguor (a Turkic and a Mongolian language from the West China)
- Teop (Melanesian, from the North Solomons),
- Tofa (Turkic, of Siberia)
- Trumaí (genetic isolate, spoken in Xingú, Brazil)
- Tsafiki (aka Colorado, a Barbacoan language spoken by the Tsachila in Ecuador)

- Waima'a (Polynesian, of East Timor)
- Wichita (Caddoan, of West Central Oklahoma)

In general, only the descriptive hierarchy is openly available for each language. Further access must be sought from the local contact, usually Corpus.Manager@mpi.nl.

LACITO – Archive of natural speech in "rare" languages
The LACITO Archive provides free access to documents of continuous, spontaneous speech, mostly in 'rare' or endangered languages recorded in their cultural context and transcribed in consultation with native speakers. At present, the archive contains some 127 documents in 26 languages. It contains (mostly narrative) material from eight Austronesian languages of New Caledonia (Drehu, Fagauvea, Iaai, Kwenyii, Nelemwa, Nemi, Xaracuu, Xaragure), four languages of Nepal (Hayu, Limbu, Nepali, Tamang – all but Nepali being Tibeto-Burman), four Caucasian languages (three of them dialects of Circassian)

- Abzakh (Circassian – Adyghe, Caucasus)
- Bjedug (Circassian – Adyghe, Caucasus)
- Shapsug (Circassian – Adyghe, Caucasus)
- Ubykh (North Caucasian)

and ten other languages:

- Araki (Austronesian, Vanuatu)
- Gbaya (Niger-Congo, Central African Republic)
- Lahu (Tibeto-Burman, Thailand)
- Langi (Bantu, Tanzania)
- Ndyuka (English Creole, Guyane)
- Ngazidja (Bantu, Comoros)
- Wuzlam/Ouldeme (Chadic, Cameroon)
- Way ana (Carib, Guyane)
- Yemeni Arabic from Sanaa (Semitic, Yemen)
- Yucuna (Arawak, Colombia)

It can be accessed at http://lacito.vjf.cnrs.fr/archivage/contents_fr.htm.

ELAR – Endangered Language Archive
This will in time become a major repository of corpora derived from the Hans Rausing Endangered Language Documentation Programme. It is accessible at http://www.hrelp.org/archive/.

OGI – Multilingual Corpus
The first publicly available data intended for language ID research is a collection of prompted telephone responses collected at the Oregon Graduate Institute, now available from LDC. It contains speech in eleven languages from about 90 native speakers each. They were recorded at a single site in the US over conventional long distance telephone lines, using a PC, an analog/digital converter, and a telephone interface. The languages are English, Persian (Farsi), French, German, Japanese, Korean, Chinese (Mandarin), Spanish, Tamil, and Vietnamese. The speech is made up of brief responses to questions (e.g., days of the week) and short monologues (up to a minute).

OTA - Oxford Text Archive

The Oxford Text Archive holds several thousand electronic texts and linguistic corpora. Its holdings include electronic editions of works by individual authors, standard reference works such as the Bible and mono-/bilingual dictionaries, and a range of language corpora.

Besides subsections of texts from various periods in English, French, German and Greek, the collection includes 44 languages or families: Afro-Asiatic, Anglo-Saxon, Arabic, Aramaic, Bengali, Chinese, Croatian, Czech, Dutch, Esperanto, Galician, Gujarati, Hanga (Ghana), Hebrew, Hindi, Irish, Italian, Japanese, Kurdish, Latin, Latvian, Malay, Oriya, Pali, Punjabi, Papuan (Amele), Papuan-Australian, Polish, Portuguese, Provençal, Romani, Russian, Sanskrit, Scots, Serbian, Serbo-Croatian, Slovenian, Spanish, Sumerian, Swedish, Tamil, Turkish, Urdu, Welsh.

The OTA is accessible at http://ota.ahds.ac.uk/.

Rosetta-ALL Language Archive

The Rosetta Project is a global collaboration of language specialists and native speakers working to build an online archive of all documented human languages. All documents and data sets are freely available online, as well as archived on a micro-etched nickel disk (intended to be an extremely long-lasting medium).

Rosetta currently serves over 30,000 text pages documenting writing systems, phonology, grammar, vernacular texts, core wordlists, numbering systems, maps, audio files, and demographic/historical descriptions for over 1,000 languages. These are largely stored as text images, rather than coded texts. It includes, for example, the first three chapters of the book of Genesis translated into 1,111 languages, and a further vernacular text, with interlinear glosses in English, for 916 languages.

A major sub-component of the Rosetta archive is the ALL Language Word List Database – a collection of 200-term core vocabulary lists for the languages of the world, currently supporting 1,300 languages. The ALL project supports the growth of this aspect of the Rosetta library with an expectation of increasing the coverage from 1,000 to 2,500 languages.

The Rosetta-ALL Language Archive is accessible at http://www.rosettaproject.org/live.

University of Maryland Parallel Corpus Project

This project has two sets of products, a text of the Bible in Corpus Encoding Standard (CES) format, defined by the European Experts Advisory Council on Language Engineering Standards (http://www.cs.vassar.edu/CES/), and the STRAND bilingual databases, made up of parallel translations automatically mined from the Web.

So far, the version of the Bible available are in only a few languages: Cebuano, Chinese, Danish, English, Finnish, French, Greek, Indonesian, Latin, Spanish, Swahili, Swedish and Vietnamese.

The STRAND bilingual databases are in fact pairs of URLs that identify parallel translations between English and other languages: French, Chinese, Basque, Arabic and Japanese. There is also a large (1.8 GB) opportunistic monolingual database of Russian.

These corpora are available at http://www.umiacs.umd.edu/~resnik/parallel/.

CHILDES database

CHILDES (CHIld Language Data Exchange System) was founded by Brian MacWhinney and Catherine Snow and is located at Carnegie Mellon University (Pittsburgh). The

Max Planck Institute is one of the centers for distribution and support. The CHILDES database has three main components and services:

CHILDES (a public domain data base for corpora on first and second language acquisition); CHAT (transcription guidelines for language acquisition data); CLAN (programs to analyze the data, e. g. search routines, frequency counts).

CHILDES stores acquisition data on a variety of languages and also on bilingual acquisition and acquisition with language disorders, as well as crosslinguistic samples of narrative data. The format of the corpora is non-homogeneous, but over the last years attempts have been made to reformat as many corpora as possible into CHAT-format, so that all CLAN programs can run on them smoothly (CHAT-files are identified by the extension *.cha). CHILDES files are stored in ASCII-format.

The transcripts include data on the learning of 29 different languages: English (American and British), other Germanic languages (Afrikaans, Dutch, German, Swedish), Romance (Catalan, French, Italian, Portuguese, Romanian, Spanish), Slavic (Croatian, Polish, Russian), East Asian (Cantonese, Chinese, Japanese, Thai), Celtic (Irish, Welsh) and others (Basque, Estonian, Persian (Farsi), Greek, Hebrew, Hungarian, Sesotho, Tamil, Turkish).

This database is available at http://childes.psy.cmu.edu/. It has now (2003) been supplemented with a new project TALKBANK (at http://talkbank.org/projects/) which expands the notation to include full multi-tier recording with video, audio and transcriptions.

CHILDES is described further in article 57.

7. A survey of global coverage

Having reviewed some of the major sources of large-scale corpus material on languages round the world, we now take stock of what is actually available at present for languages in different regions, including cultural archives, ad hoc corpora, and language documentation archives in our survey. Our survey cannot be exhaustive, but aims only to take in the major established corpora for less studied languages existing in late 2005, with special emphasis (for convenience) on those accessible over the Web.

7.1. Europe and North Asia

This area is, unsurprisingly, well-provided with cultural archives for ancient languages.

However, some of the general-purpose corpus compilations aimed at modern metropolitan languages (notably the European Union's PAROLE and SPEECHDAT enterprises) have resulted in some auxiliary activity that has produced resources for minority languages.

PERSEUS Digital Library
Perseus is located in the Department of the Classics, Tufts University, USA. In addition to art and archaeology sources, essays, and tools, the classics collection features several hundred works of classical Greek and Roman authors, both in the original language and in translation. Perseus also includes a suite of linguistic tools, linked to lexica, which permit the careful study of Greek and Latin.

It currently contains 489 texts in these two languages, 7,871,366 words in Greek, and 5,269,733 in Latin. It is accessible at http://www.perseus.tufts.edu.

Thesaurus Linguae Graecae
This was founded in 1972 at the University of California at Irvine, USA. TLG has collected and digitized most literary texts written in Greek from Homer to the fall of Byzantium in AD 1453. Its goal is to create a comprehensive digital library of Greek literature from antiquity to the present era.

The Web version currently provides access to 3,700 authors and 12,000 works, approximately 91 million words. It is updated quarterly with new authors and works. It is accessible at http://www.tlg.uci.edu/.

TITUS Thesaurus Indogermanischer Text- und Sprachmaterialien
The University of Frankfurt's TITUS, a "Thesaurus of Indo-European Text- and Language-Materials", was initiated in 1987. It includes searchable files of all the major ancient Indo-European languages; it now runs to over 1 giga-byte of text. It is in fact no longer restricted to purely Indo-European texts, but includes other 'relevant neighbours'. The current list of languages served:

- I. Indic: Vedic, Sanskrit, Buddhist Sanskrit, Pali, Prakrit, Rajasthani, Hindi, Maldivi
- II. Iranian: Avestan, Ancient Persian, Parthian, Middle Persian or Pahlavi, Khotanese-Saka, Sogdian, Modern Persian, Ossetic
- III. Anatolian: Hittite, Luwian, Palaic, Lydian, Lycian, Milyan, Pisidian, Carian
- IV. Tocharian : Lingua A, Lingua B
- V. Armenian: Ancient Armenian
- VI. Baltic: Prussian, Latvian, Lithuanian
- VII. Slavic: Old Church Slavonic, Old Bohemian, Old Polish, Old Slovenian, Old Croatian, Old Russian
- VIII. Germanic: Gothic, Norse, Anglo-Saxon, Old Frisian, Old Saxon, Dutch, Old High German, Middle High German, Modern High German
- IX. Greek: Mycenaean, Homeric, Classical
- X. Italic: Oscan, Umbrian, Latin
- XI. Celtic: Irish, Welsh
- XII. Other Indo-European languages: Albanian, Phrygian, Others
- XIII. Neighbours (Peri-Indo-European):
  - Caucasian: Old Georgian, Middle Georgian, Modern Georgian, Laz, Mingrelian, Svan, Abkhaz, Ude
  - Uralic: Hungarian
  - Semitic: Hebrew, Arabic, Syriac, Ethiopic (Ge'ez and Amharic)
  - Dravidian: Tamil
  - Others: Ancient Cretan, Phaistos disc

It is available at http://titus.uni-frankfurt.de and http://titus.fkidg1.uni-frankfurt.de.

UHLCS University of Helsinki Language Corpus Server
The UHLCS, maintained by the University of Helsinki, was founded late in 1980. From the beginning, the UHLCS contained Finnish, English, and Swedish data. One of the first linguistic corpora in the UHLCS was the HKV-corpus, a syntactically analyzed corpus of Finnish (Hakulinen/Karlsson/Vilkuna 1980).

At present, the UHLCS contains computer corpora of more than 50 languages, including samples of minority languages. There are very large corpora of Finnish, Swedish, English, German, Latin, Russian and Swahili. Already at the beginning of 1990s, the Finnish and Swahili corpora totalled several million words.

The UHLCS contains samples of morphologically-analyzed corpora of most of the Uralic languages and corpora of numerous languages spoken in Europe and North and Central Asia (LENCA-group).

In 2000, the corpora of the Uralic, Turkic, Tungusic, Mongolic, Palaeo-Siberian, Iranian and Caucasian languages were edited for public use. They are predominantly fairly small text corpora (under 100,000 words), drawn from Christian missionary literature, donated to the University of Helsinki by the Institute for Bible Translation (Helsinki and Stockholm). Languages represented include:

- Uralic languages: Livvi, Dvina-Karelian, Ludian, Ingrian, Veps, Liv, Kildin Saami, South Saami, Ume Saami, Erzya, Moksha, East Mari, West Mari, Komi Zyrian, Komi Permyak, Khanty, Mansi, Hungarian, Enets, Nenets, Selkup and Kamas;
- Indo-European languages: Kurdish, Ossete, Tajik, Armenian, Latvian, Lithuanian, Belorussian, Ukrainian, Serbo-Croatian, and Moldavian (Romanian);
- Caucasian languages: Avar, Lak, and Tabasaran;
- Turkic languages: Altai, Azerbaijani, Balkar, Bashkir, Chuvash, Crimean Tatar, Gagauz, Khakas, Kirghiz, Kumyk, Kazakh, Turkmen, Tuvin, Uyghur, Uzbek and Yakut;
- Mongolic languages: Buryat and Kalmyk;
- Tungusic languages: Even, Evenki and Nanai;
- Palaeo-Siberian languages: Chukchi and Koryak.

These corpora are accessible at http://www.ling.helsinki.fi/uhlcs.

CELT Corpus of Electronic Texts (UC Cork, Ireland)

This corpus advertises itself as an Online Resource for Irish history, literature and politics. As of 26 July 2005 it contains 763 texts.

408 source documents are in Irish (from all periods), 260 in English. 17 were written in Latin, and 2 in French. One source text was written in Spanish. There are 70 English, 6 German, and 2 French translations. Some Irish textfiles contain an English translation.

These sources are accessible at http://www.ucc.ie/celt/.

PAROLE Corpas Náisiúnta na Gaeilge

This was the Irish (Gaelic) contribution to the European Union's PAROLE project of 1996–9, which developed text corpora on a given plan for all the EU official languages, together with Irish and Catalan. It consists of approximately 30 million words of text from a variety of contemporary books, newspapers, periodicals and dialogue, approximately 8 million of which are SGML-tagged.

This corpus is available for order at http://www.ite.ie/corpus/.

SPEECHDAT

This project focused on Spoken Language Resources, speech databases for fixed telephone networks including associated annotations and pronunciation lexica.

The databases were for training and testing of typical tele-services. They also provided a phonetically rich set of material usable to train more advanced, vocabulary-independent speech recognition systems. They comprise mostly read speech, but also some spontaneous speech representing common utterance types. The design is based on a 1,000–2,500 speaker collection, which is balanced for sex, age and dialect representation.

The original project developed speech databases for all the official languages of the EU, but also included Welsh. Subsequently, SPEECHDAT-E covered the languages Russian with 2,500 speakers and, with 1,000 speakers, Czech, Slovak, Polish and Hungarian. These databases serve as a resource for the performance of voice driven tele-services.

Lîvõd Tekstõd (Livonian)
This is an example of a single-handed attempt at a cultural archive, with a subordinate aim of language documentation, given that the language retains fewer than ten speakers. Uldis Balodis, a Latvian, has provided electronic access to a set of materials on the endangered Baltic language Livonian, notably the text of the book *Lîvõd Textõd*, a collection of Livonian texts edited by Valda Suvcāne.

It is accessible at http://homepage.mac.com/uldis/livonia/livonia.html.

Sound archives on the World Wide Web with sound recordings from the Saint-Petersburg collections, Voices of Taiga and Tundra
This project has collated a large number of recordings made on phonograph cylinders (1900–1940) and magnetic tapes (1950–1990). Languages so recorded (with the number of archives in each) are:

Khanty and Mansi – (5); Saami – (3); Nenets – (7); Selkup – (1); Ngnanasan – (1); Yakut – (10); Dolgan – (3); Altai – (5); Teleut – (3); Tuvinian – (1); Khakas – (2); Khakas (Khachints) – (2); Khakas (Sagaits) – (1); Khakas (Kyzyls) – (1); Evenki (Tungus) – (14); Even – (5); Orochon – (2); Udehe – (2); Nanai – (6); Chukchi – (6); Koryak – (3); Itelmen – (3); Eskimo – (4); Aleutian – (2); Nivkh – (3); Ket – (4).

Kinds of content in these archives include:

1) texts in languages spoken by the peoples of the North corresponding to the sounds recorded on the cylinders;
2) translations of the texts of the recordings on the cylinders;
3) brief presentations of texts of recordings on the cylinders performed in Russian;
4) notes of the recordings on the cylinders;
5) various descriptions of material from separate collections belonging to different collectors;
6) documents re work done in recording the folklore samples from the peoples of the North onto phonograph cylinders.

Among the folders studied, there is also some material on Mari, Udmurt, Altai, Mongol, and Buryat. Access to the materials can be found through: http://www.mercator-education.org/sjablonen/3/default.asp?objectID=3722 (cf. article 20, section 2 for the Polish National Corpus, Czech National Corpus and Russian Reference Corpus, section 10 for PELCRA and section 11 for TRACTOR).

7.2. North Africa and West Asia

The largest corpora in this area have been Cultural Archives of ancient literatures. More recently, though, the increasing development of language technology for its languages has been supported by the availability of corpora. All of these, though, still originate from external scholars, 'orientalists', rather than local academics and researchers.

ETCSL Electronic Text Corpus of Sumerian Literature
This is discussed above, in section 3.1. It is accessible at http://www-etcsl.orient.ox.ac.uk/edition2/general.php.

There is also a number of other, growing, corpora organized round the cuneiform writing system. These include two being compiled at UCLA:

CDLI Cuneiform Digital Library Initiative
http://cdli.ucla.edu/

stores the form and content of cuneiform tablets dating from the beginning of writing, ca. 3350 B.C., until the end of the pre-Christian era. The number of these documents currently kept in public and private collections is estimated to exceed 500,000 items, of which now more than 125,000 have been catalogued in electronic form by the CDLI.

Digital Corpus of Cuneiform Lexical Texts (DCCLT)
http://cuneiform.ucla.edu/dcclt/

aims to catalog, with photographs and transliterations, the full set of cuneiform lexical lists on clay tablets, not unlike modern dictionaries. The full corpus of cuneiform lexical texts is estimated at 15,000 individual clay tablets and ranges in time from about 3,200 BCE to 100 CE.

West Point Arabic Speech Corpus
available, e. g. at LDC, contains speech data that was collected and processed by members of the Department of Foreign languages at the United States Military Academy at West Point and the Center for Technology Enhanced Language Learning (CTELL). The original purpose of this corpus was to train acoustic models for automatic speech recognition that could be used as an aid in teaching Arabic to West Point cadets. It consists of 8,516 speech files, totaling 1.7 gigabytes or 11.42 hours of speech data. Each speech file represents one person reciting one prompt from one of four prompt scripts.

Arabic Gigaword
This is a comprehensive archive of newswire text data that has been acquired from Arabic news sources by the Linguistic Data Consortium (LDC), at the University of Pennsylvania. The four distinct sources of Arabic newswire are the Agence France Presse, Al Hayat, Al Nahar and Xinhua News Agencies. There are 319 files, totalling approximately 1.1 GB in compressed form (4,348 MB uncompressed, and 391,619,000 words). There is also a Treebank (i. e. a corpus with some level of syntactic analysis) based on the Agence France Presse and Al Hayat data, also available at LDC. The Treebank analyses a fairly small subset of the raw data, but still runs to up to a million words (cf. also section 7.1. UHLCS University of Helsinki Language Corpus Server).

7.3. Southern Africa

University of Pretoria, series of research corpora
The UP research corpora, built by G.-M. de Schryver and D. J. Prinsloo, have been compiled primarily for use in spell-checkers. In 2003, the University of Pretoria *Zulu Corpus* (PZC) stood at 5 million running words (or tokens), and the University of Pretoria *Sepedi Corpus* (PSC) stood at 5.8 million.

University of Stellenbosch, African Speech Technology (AST) Project
This project, completed in 2004, concerned the five languages South-African-variety English, Afrikaans, Xhosa, Zulu and Southern Sesotho, comprising speech databases (of telephone calls, on the SPEECHDAT model) and text corpora.

The text corpora had a target size of one million running words (MRW) for each language (and final figures were English 35.686 MRW; Afrikaans 1.258 MRW, Xhosa 0.697 MRW, Zulu 0.451 MRW, Sesotho 1.226 MRW). Xhosa and Zulu orthographic 'words' tend to be much longer and contain many more morphemes than those in Sesotho (perhaps by a factor of 2.5). The text corpora include a representative selection of genres, including academic articles, journalism, online text and parliamentary proceedings.

7.4. South Asia

EMILLE/CIIL Corpus in 14 Indian languages
The EMILLE Corpus has been constructed as part of a collaborative venture between the EMILLE project (Enabling Minority Language Engineering), Lancaster University, UK, and the Central Institute of Indian Languages (CIIL), Mysore, India. EMILLE is distributed by the European Language Resources Association. It consists of three components: monolingual, parallel and annotated corpora. It is available at http://bowland-files.lancs.ac.uk/corplang/emille/.

(The EMILLE/CIIL Corpus (ELRA-W0037) is distributed free of charge for use in **non-profit-making** research only. The EMILLE Lancaster Corpus (ELRA-W0038) is for **commercial** use only).

There are fourteen monolingual corpora, including both written and (for some languages) spoken data for fourteen South Asian languages: Assamese, Bengali, Gujarati, Hindi, Kannada, Kashmiri, Malayalam, Marathi, Oriya, Punjabi, Sinhala, Tamil, Telegu and Urdu.

The EMILLE monolingual corpora contain approximately 92,799,000 words (including 2,627,000 words of transcribed spoken data for Bengali, Gujarati, Hindi, Punjabi and Urdu). The parallel corpus consists of 200,000 words of text in English and its accompanying translations in Hindi, Bengali, Punjabi, Gujarati and Urdu. The annotated component includes the Urdu monolingual and parallel corpora annotated for parts-of-speech, together with twenty written Hindi corpus files annotated to show the nature of demonstrative use. The corpus is marked up using CES-compliant SGML, and encoded using Unicode.

Clay Sanskrit Library – Corpus materials
http://www.claysanskritlibrary.org/corpus.php

This is to be a searchable version of the content of a new series of Sanskrit texts with parallel translation into English, which is planned to grow to include the whole of the Ramayana, much and then all of the Mahabharata, and all the major and many of the minor works of Sanskrit literature.

In the meantime, a virtual corpus of Sanskrit texts can be located through the Internet, e. g. via http://www.ucl.ac.uk/~ucgadkw/indnet-textarchive.html.

Modern Tamil Prose Tagged Corpus
http://ccat.sas.upenn.edu/plc/tamilweb/tagger.html

This currently contains only text from two short novels, Yuka Santhi written by Jeyakanthan and Kangkaa Snaanam written by Akilan. However, the corpus is tagged, and so may be used to search for specific grammatical categories.

Pongal-2000 Project & Tamil Digital Corpus
The *Pongal-2000* Project is a collaborative undertaking of the Institute of Asian Studies (Chennai), the Institute for Indology and Tamil Studies of the University of Cologne and the University of California-Berkeley, and is directed to creating an electronic compilation of Tamil texts – the Online Tamil Lexicon (OTL) – as well as a Tamil Text Thesaurus (TTT). The project had by 1997 completed conversion of approximately 10 million words from printed text to machine-readable format. The aim is to allow computer access to all major Tamil literary works, classical and modern, via the Internet from anywhere in the world.

Project Madurai & Tamil Ancient Literature
Dr. Kalyanasundaram on Thai Pongal Day 1998 lauched this initiative, open and voluntary, to collect and publish free electronic editions of ancient Tamil literary classics. In June 2003, Tamil Unicode versions of 100 texts from Project Madurai (aproximately 50%) were made available on the Web. They are accessible at http://www.infitt.org/pmadurai/index.html.

ACIP – Thousand Books of Wisdom (Tibetan)
The Asian Classics Input Project (ACIP) was formed for the purpose of preserving the endangered Indo-Tibetan Buddhist literature and making it available to scholars, libraries and researchers. This important body of literature, widespread throughout Central Asia for hundreds of years, was almost completely lost in the last century due to unfavorable political and economic circumstances. Some of these books are now the single last surviving copies that remain in the world. Other books were saved from oblivion through the efforts of libraries such as the U.S. Library of Congress but it is often difficult for scholars to get access to them. Moreover, it has been almost impossible for these books to reach the people who can use them the most: the more than 10,000 Tibetan Buddhist monk-scholars who are living as refugees in India. But now all of this is starting to change. Since 1987, ACIP has been training Tibetan refugees in South Asia to type these endangered books onto computer disks. The Project has established data entry centers in more than a dozen Tibetan refugee communities: monasteries, nunneries, and lay settlements. The ACIP electronic database now contains over 100,000 pages of Buddhist literature from the Kangyur, Tengyur, and Sungbum collections.

The texts are available (each in Roman or Tibetan script) at http://www.worldlibrary.net/ACIP.htm. The collection does not, however, appear to be available as a fully searchable corpus.

Tibetan & Himalayan Digital Library
THDL's Collections constitute its major holdings of texts, videos, images, maps and other data that are at the heart of the library. Users of the library can search across all videos, texts, images and so forth as individual resources, or they can consult specific

organizations of these resources constituting collections based on thematic or geographical criteria. More general approaches to full-text search are under development.

http://iris.lib.virginia.edu/tibet/collections/index.html.

The Language and Linguistics Collections currently contain materials for Tibetan language instruction as well as materials on Tibetan scripts, fonts, and transliteration schemes. The Library expects to expand these resources over time to encompass the entire Himalayan region.

The main foci of the literature section are the cataloging of large collections, such as *The Collected Tantras of the Ancients*, the digitization of texts either in the form of images or marked-up texts, and also as the summary and analysis of texts within the realm of Tibetan and Himalayan Literature. The Literature Collections encompass several projects focused on Tibetan and Himalayan Literature. The Nyingma Project, or the Samantabhadra Collection, was the initial impetus for the Literature Collections. It began as a project to catalog the many editions of *Collected Tantras of the Ancients*. These catalogs are directly connected to scanned images of the folios, kindly provided by the Tibetan Buddhist Resource Center. Ultimately, these catalogs will be connected to digitized versions of the texts that can be searched and downloaded. The Bönpo Project is focused on cataloging and digitizing collections of Bönpo literature. Its initial phase has been to catalog the important *Oral Traditions of Zhang Zhung*. Another project associated with the THDL Literature Collections is the Shechen Monastery Text Input Project. They have entered a number of important Tibetan texts, some of which are available for download in several formats from the Shechen Monastery Text Input page. The THDL Literature Collections provides other resources for the study of Tibetan literature. In the Features box on the left, there are links to a bibliographic guide, which will help the user locate Tibetan texts using the THDL catalogs and other Web resources. The oral commentaries project involves the archiving of audio and video recordings of oral commentaries on a broad variety of Tibetan literary genres, as well as lengthy commentaries on the great classics of Tibetan literature and readings by contemporary poets and novelists. The genres project involves multiple scholars who are compiling a large nested hierarchical guide to Tibetan literary genres, as well as providing on-line resources for the study of this topic.

7.5. East and South-East Asia

BUDSIR – Buddhist Scriptures Information Retrieval in Pali

http://www.budsir.org/

On May 30, 1988, the Digital Tipitaka Development Team under the Mahidol University Computing Center, Thailand, announced the completion of its project to record the 45 volumes of the Pali Tipitaka onto computer, together with the development of an application program, BUDSIR (BUDdhist Scriptures Information Retrieval), for searching it. BUDSIR could search and find every occurrence of every word, sentence, and saying of the Buddha occurring in the Tipitaka promptly, precisely and comprehensively. It was the world's first digital edition of the Tipitaka.

Three years later, 70 volumes of the Atthakatha (Commentary) were added to the database, and three years from then, in August 1994, the Tipitaka and Atthakatha, numbering 115 volumes in all, were recorded on CD-ROM and a more efficient search program, BUDSIR IV, was developed. Then in September, 1996, BUDSIR IV for Windows was developed so that the program can work in a Windows environment. BUDSIR IV for Windows works much the same as previous versions of the program, with fast, accurate and, most importantly, comprehensive search capability.

Malay Concordance Project

The Malay Concordance Project represents a searchable corpus of 3 million words of Malay text, including 8,000 verses, from the 14th century to the 1930s. It is available at http://www.anu.edu.au/asianstudies/ahcen/proudfoot/MCP/.

A second, smaller (1.7 MRW) Malay Concordance Project, which is based purely on classical Malay texts, can be acessed at http://infotree.library.ohiou.edu/single-records/2136.html.

ORCHID corpus

Hitherto, this has been the only Thai text corpus available for research use. ORCHID is a 9-MB Thai part-of-speech tagged corpus initiated by NECTEC, Thailand and Communications Research Laboratory, Japan. ORCHID is available at http://www.links.nectec.or.th/orchid.

University of Virginia (Classical) Japanese Text Initiative

The University of Virginia Library Electronic Text Center and the University of Pittsburgh East Asian Library have sponsored the Japanese Text Initiative, a collaborative effort to make texts of classical Japanese literature available on the World Wide Web. The texts are fully searchable, and cover the full gamut (of out-of-copyright texts) from the earliest days to the present (83 from the period 710 to 1867, and a further 216 for the period 1868 to the present).

http://etext.lib.virginia.edu/japanese/.

Modern Japanese text corpora

In addition to the Cultural Archive provided by the University of Virginia's Classical Japanese text initiative, there are also a number of other essentially literary compilations: Bensei Database (50 texts in classical Japanese), Data Novels (full text Japanese literature published by Computer Shuppan) and Aozora Bunko (out-of-copyright Japanese literature).

The modern Japanese language is also well provided with opportunistic text corpora of considerable size, which can be used for computational linguistic analysis, and the training of various language processors.

The principal annotated corpora are two that were funded through initiatives of the Japanese Government in the 1980s and 1990s. One is the EDR Japanese corpus, a collection of 200,000 sentences with morphological, syntactic and semantic analysis; it forms part of the EDR Japanese Co-occurrence dictionary, available at http://www2.nict.go.jp/r/r312/EDR/index.html. The other is the RWC Text Database, developed by RWCP (Real Word Computing Partnership), issued in 1998, and made up of six sub-corpora: drawn from Japanese MITI white papers, JEIDA Annual reports and surveys, Mainichi-Shimbun articles and Iwanami Dictionary entries, syntactically analysed and manually post-edited. Its source was http://www.rwcp.or.jp/wswg/rwcdb/text/ but has now been suspended.

There is a third corpus made up of 40,000 morphologically and syntactically annotated sentences drawn from newspaper articles (Mainichi-Shimbun), namely the Kyoto Text Corpus, at http://www.kc.t.u-tokyo.ac.jp/nl-resource/corpus-e.html.

The RWC partially, and the Kyoto Text Corpus fully, depend on the 1995 Mainichi-Shimbun CD-ROM, which contains unanalysed newspaper text. This is in fact one of a number of much larger Japanese newspaper text corpora that are available, essentially as annual compilations, from the *Mainichi Shimbun*, the *Yomiuri Shimbun*, the *Asahi Shimbun*, the *Nihon Keizai Shimbun* and the *Nihon Keizai Sangyo Kin'yu Ryutsu Shimbun*.

Modern Japanese speech databases

The main source of spoken corpora for Japanese is ATR. A variety can be found at http://www.red.atr.co.jp/product/02/pro_02.html. There is also the ASJ Continuous Speech Corpus of Japanese newspaper article sentences (306 speakers) at http://www.milab.is.tsukuba.jp/jnas/intstruct.html; the ETL Spoken Dialog Corpus 1998 (with Wizard-of-Oz type dialogues between human and machine) at http://akiba.media-iteraction.jp/ETLSDG/ and the JEIDA Japanese Common Speech Corpus (of monosyllables and digit sequences).

Other specialized speech corpora (together with a vast range of other language technology for Japanese) can be found listed at http://kc.t.u-tokyo.ac.jp/NLP_Portal/lr-cat-e.html.

7.6. Australasia and Pacific

ASEDA – the Aboriginal Studies Electronic Data Archive

http://coombs.anu.edu.au/SpecialProj/ASEDA/fabout.htm

The Australian Institute of Aboriginal and Torres Strait Islander Studies (AIATSIS) holds computer-based (digital) materials about Australian Indigenous languages in the *Aboriginal Studies Electronic Data Archive* (ASEDA). ASEDA offers a free service of secure storage, maintenance, and distribution of electronic texts relating to these languages. Many of these are extended texts, of cultural and/or linguistic interest for particular languages, but there is no text corpus as such. In this, it is like AILLA (cf. above section 3.2.).

PARADISEC – Pacific and Regional Archive for Digital Sources in Endangered Cultures

http://rspas.anu.edu.au/paradisec/

PARADISEC offers a facility for digital conservation and access for endangered materials from the Pacific region, defined broadly to include Oceania, and East and South east Asia. Their research group has developed models to ensure that the archive can provide access to interested communities. Again, many of its archives contain extended texts, of cultural and/or linguistic interest for particular languages, but there is no text corpus as such. In this, it too is like AILLA (cf. above section 3.2.).

7.7. North America

Although various American Indian tribes in this vast area are increasingly establishing their own websites for their languages, there are still relatively few large computer-accessible repositories of texts and recordings. Even a large repository such as the Alaska Native Language Center Archives (http://www.uaf.edu/anlc/), which houses an archive of more than 10,000 items, covering virtually everything written in or about Alaska Native languages, is still constructing its online index, and digitization of the entire archive is still at the proposal stage.

We can quote one example of a digitized resource from this area.

University of Virginia Chiricahua and Mescalero Apache texts
http://etext.lib.virginia.edu/apache/ChiMesc2.html

This is a Web-accessible Apache language linguistic database and text archive, a republication of Hoijer's 1938 monograph originally published by the University of Chicago. It includes

1. 55 Apache language texts (in Chiricahua and Mescalero dialects) representing a variety of genres: stories, songs, prayers and speeches, performed by nine different Apache speakers
2. English translations of the Apache texts, developed by Hoijer in consultation with Apache speakers
3. Ethnological notes to the texts, contributed by Morris Opler, a cultural anthropolo gist
4. Hoijer's linguistic notes, containing morphological analysis of words and phrases as they appear in the texts
5. Hoijer's grammatical outline of Chiricahua and Mescalero Apache language varieties
6. a search-engine for Apache and English language searches
7. a lexicon to the texts developed from Hoijer's linguistic analysis

7.8. Latin America

AILLA – Archive of Indigenous Languages of Latin America
This cultural archive of materials spoken and written in various languages of Latin America is described above: cf. section 3.2.

Maya Hieroglyphic Databases
The Maya Hieroglyphic Database Project http://nas.ucdavis.edu/NALC/mhdhome.html is putting the entire corpus of Maya texts into a graphics database. The hieroglyphic texts on monumental sculpture from the Classic Period (A.D. 250–900) were the first to be included. Now nearly every large site has been partially coded, and images have been scanned and prepared for about 80% of the corpus.

A different approach is taken by the Mayan Epigraphic Database Project http://www3.iath.virginia.edu/med/, which is representing the same corpus not as graphic images, but as sequences of alphanumeric codes.

8. Special problems with corpora of less studied languages

After this review of sites worldwide, we conclude with some general remarks about particular problems besetting work with corpora for less studied languages.

8.1. Corpus motives

The classification of corpus motives and techniques expounded at the outset (section 2) can be applied explicitly to the corpora that we have discovered, distinguishing speech from text corpora, and also separating out the non-text glyph-based databases. The result is Tables 21.1, 21.2 and 21.3.

Tab. 21.1: Corpora including speech, classified by motive

Cultural Archive	Artificial Corpora	Language Documentation
AILLA (Latin America)	CHILDES, TALKBANK	ASEDA (Australian)
	EMILLE (South Asia)	DoBeS
	OGI-Multilingual	ELAR
	SPEECHDAT (Welsh), SPEECHDAT-E (E. Europe)	LACITO
	Stellenbosch AST (African)	PARADISEC (Pacific to SE Asia)
	West Point Arabic	Voices of Tundra & Taiga (Siberian)
	ATR, ASJ, ETL, JEIDA (Japanese)	

Tab. 21.2: Corpora including text, classified by motive

Cultural Archive	Artificial Corpora	Language Documentation
ACIP Thousand Books of Widom (Tibetan)	An Crúbadán	ASEDA (Australian)
AILLA (Latin America)	Arabic Gigaword	DoBeS
Aozora Bunko (Japanese)	CHILDES, TALKBANK	ELAR
Bensei (Japanese)	EDR Japanese Corpus	LACITO
BUDSIR (Pali)	EMILLE (South Asian)	PARADISEC (Pacific to SE Asia)
CELT (Irish)	Malay Concordance	Voices of Tundra & Taiga (Siberian)
Clay Sanskrit	Modern Tamil	

Tab. 2 (cont.)

Cultural Archive	Artificial Corpora	Language Documentation
Data Novels (Japanese)	OGI-Multilingual	
ETCSL (Sumerian)	ORCHID (Thai)	
Livod Textod (Livonian)	PAROLE-Gaeilge (Irish)	
Oxford Text Archive	Rosetta-ALL	
Perseus (Greek, Latin)	RWC Text DB (Japanese)	
Project Madurai (Tamil)	U.Helsinki LCS	
Thesaurus Linguae Graecae	U.Md. Parallel Bible	
Tibetan & Himalayan DL	U.Pretoria Research Corpora (African)	
TITUS (Indo-European etc.)	... Shimbun: Japanese newspaper corpora	
U.Va. Apache		
U.Va. Classical Japanese		

Tab. 21.3: Glyph corpora classified by motive

Cultural Archive	Artificial Corpora	Language Documentation
ETCSL (Sumerian)		CDLI, DCCL (Cuneiform)
		Maya Hieroglyphic
		Maya Epigraphic

There is an evident overlap between the fruits of the Cultural Archive motive for corpus collection, and the fruits of the Language Documentation imperative. In practice, much of what is easiest to find, and hence select and store, in the way of language documentation is what communities naturally offer as 'beautiful or otherwise noticeable utterances' (which is nothing other than Leonard Bloomfield's definition of literature).

There is also a tendency for translations of one culture's Cultural Archive, notably Holy Scriptures, to result in Artificial Corpora for other languages. Hence the Hebrew and Christian Bible underlies the University of Maryland's Parallel Bible, although it is not in itself a Cultural Archive, being rather an artifice to bring together a lot of parallel texts in different languages. Likewise the first three chapters of Genesis were chosen to be the common content among the languages in Rosetta-ALL.

8.2. Difficulties in collection

Less studied languages are as diverse as any other languages, indeed more so, and attempting to find a focus in diversity is one of the hardest things one can attempt. Nevertheless, with the thought in mind that this group includes all the languages which find funding hard to raise, and also all the languages which have fewer than ten million speakers, there are certain generalizations that can be offered.

The low level of funding will be especially problematic where the number of speakers is relatively large: this will tend to mean that the varieties of language to be sampled, and hopefully represented, in a corpus will be more widely spread and differentiated. The corpus will have to be spread thinner in relation to the resources that can be devoted to it. Hence arises the need for the automatic web-crawling approach of An Scrúbadán.

On the other hand, if the speaker-community is very small, say under 100,000 (and 82% of the world's language-communities are in this class), a different kind of problem tends to arise: the speakers usually have a strong sense of ownership of their language, and are intolerant of outsiders who aspire to become involved with it, especially if, as corpus-builders, they seem to be assuming some kind of cultural authority in the community as a whole. Such outsiders will often be resented, and indeed resisted. The problem is compounded, since almost universally there will be different varieties of language even within the smallest communities; and if any selectivity is employed, this may be seen as selecting one variety rather than another as a future standard for the community as a whole. There is thus considerable scope for resentment, both by members of the community towards expert outsiders, but also by different subgroups within the community towards each other. Small-community corpus gathering is therefore by necessity an intensely political activity: and building a political consensus, from within or without, is time-consuming.

Another source of tension in the small community, beyond the purely political, is that – for at least two reasons – it may well be hard to attain an equitable and realistic balance about what goes into the corpus. On the one hand, there may be an artificial bias in the evidence, especially clear if the speaker-community is close to extinction. Language will be concentrated among the old, and usually among the female, biasing any possible record of what the language has been for the community as a whole; furthermore, members of the community may have strong preconceptions about what ought to be in the corpus record, and resist any simple and apparently objective account of the testimony that is offered. A good recent case of this is writing of grammars of Mayan languages by the indigenous OKMA linguists in Guatemala: conscious that the traditional basic word-order in these language is verb-initial, they have resisted use of actual modern examples in their accounts of Kaqchikel and Mam, since these would show a predominant subject-verb-object order, which they attribute to language-contact with Spanish. Instead they appeal to 400-year-old quotations from related languages (e. g. Tz'utujiil) to illustrate their prescriptions (Barrett 2005, 217). Choice of corpus is likely to become increasingly fraught as knowledge of the traditions underlying any given language grows.

8.3. Difficulties in analysis

So much then for particular difficulties in the selection of material that should go into a corpus. What of the problems that will beset analysis of the corpus, including the kind of annotations that will be required, and may become part of the corpus in the wider sense?

Here the corpora of Less Studied Languages are in a different situation from the others, because they will often have a constituency to satisfy beyond the academic and technical personnel who are the main users of large-scale corpora for well-studied (and well-financed) languages. For example, in the bilingual glossing of a language archive, what language should be used as meta-language, and how much of the new archive must be glossed in order to ensure its usefulness? Besides providing for accessibility for searches, and processing to create language technology, there is a need to ensure long-term accessibility of the content of a language archive, to make it legible to those who may not already know the language; and in the case of a highly endangered language, very often these will include members of the very community where the language has been spoken. Evidently, the main consideration in choosing a meta-language is who are the likely users of the archive. When the archive is required as a basis for language maintenance or revitalization, the best meta-language is clearly a local contact language, ideally the language to which the old language community has switched.

A more imponderable question is how much of an archive should be glossed. It is evident that glossing is time-consuming, and 100% is unnecessary: a language makes infinite use of finite means. But how much must be interpreted to secure access to the rest? Related questions, equally hard, are how large (and how varied) a textual corpus must be in order to represent its language, and how big a dictionary needs to be (especially of a small, pre-industrial, community: cf. *How Big is the Lexicon of an Unwritten Language?* (Mallory/Pawley/Trask 2003)). The perpetual obscurity of *hapax legomena* in Homeric Greek and Biblical Hebrew demonstrates that even a well-understood corpus is never totally sufficient to document a language. In Homeric Greek (a corpus of some 175,000 words, assignable to 9,391 distinct lexical entries), there are 3,108 unique occurrences: i. e. 33% of all lemmata. (These data are drawn from the Chicago Homer: http://www.library.northwestern.edu/homer/). If proper names are excluded, there are 2,382 *hapax legomena*, as against 7,780 lexical entries: the proportion is still 31%). In the Hebrew Bible or *TaNaK* (a corpus of just over 300,000 words, from some 8,000 word entries) there are 2,382 of them, i. e. 31% (Ullendorf 1971). And in the British National Corpus, a much more varied corpus, but also over 300 times larger at 100 million words, the rate of *hapax legomena* is even higher, approaching 50%. Even the biggest corpora, it seems, resolutely refuse to repeat themselves; so there is never a clear point at which glossing begins to offer diminishing returns. (See article 37 for more discussion of Zipfian distribution patterns in language).

In a way, the moral of this is profoundly humanistic, since it tends to show that corpora are never totally self-interpreting: rather, they continue to need interpretation by the populations whose languages they represent.

9. Conclusions

This survey has noted the contents of over fifty corpora for less studied languages, i. e. significant collections of documents effectively accessible to computer-search and computer-processing. These corpora come from every continent, though not yet for every literate language or even language family. Corpus linguistics, although it largely derives from Western Europe and North America, is no longer restricted to those areas. Nonetheless, 50 corpora to represent over 6,000 languages (or perhaps the 2,000 languages with some degree of literacy – as estimated by Trond Trosterud. cf. *Ogmios* 11 (15 May 1999), p. 16, http://www.ogmios.org/117.htm) is hardly adequate coverage. This alone gives some idea of the immediate scope for growth in corpus linguistics itself, as well as the other applications for corpora briefly reviewed in section 1.2. above.

It is evident that the motives for compiling these corpora and making them available have been very far from the motives for compilation of the better-known corpora reviewed in article 20. Nevertheless, the widely shared aspirations to create a cultural archive and/or to document an endangered language are highly compatible in their results with the kind of corpus which is required for the quantitative analysis of language, giving rise to a range of studies amply attested in the rest of this volume.

10. Literature

Atkins, Sue/Clear, Jeremy/Ostler, Nicholas (1992), Corpus Design Criteria. In: *Journal of Literary & Linguistic Computing* 7(1), 1–16.

Barrett, Rusty (2005), Review of Five *Oxlajuuj Keej Mayab' Ajtz'iib'* (OKMA) Grammars. In: *International Journal of American Linguistics*, 71(2), 215–220.

Bird, Steven/Simons, Gary (2003), Seven Dimensions of Portability for Language Documentation and Description. In: *Language* 79(3), 557–582.

Ghani, Rayid/Jones, Rosie/Mladenić, Dunja (2004), Building Minority Language Corpora by Learning to Generate Web Search Queries. In: *Knowledge and Information Systems* 7, 56–83.

Gordon, Raymond G., Jr. (ed.) (2005), *Ethnologue: Languages of the World*. Dallas: SIL International.

Hakulinen, Auli/Karlsson, Fred/Vilkuna, Maria (1980), *Suomen tekstilauseiden piirteitä: Kvantitatiivinen tutkimus [Features of Finnish Text Sentences: A Quantitative Study]*. Helsinki: Department of General Linguistics, University of Helsinki.

Mallory, Jim/Pawley, Andrew/Trask, Larry (2003), How Big is the Lexicon of an Unwritten Language? Posted on: *arcling.anu.edu* (11 June 2003), reported in: *Ogmios* 21 (31 July 2003), 17–18, http://www.ogmios.org/217.htm.

Ostler, Nicholas (1998), *Review of Workshop on Language Resources for European Minority Languages*, http://ixa2.si.ehu.es/saltmil/history/review.htm (last visit 15 December 2006).

Ullendorf, Edward (1971), Is Biblical Hebrew a Language? In: *Bulletin of the School of Oriental and African Studies* 31, 241–255.

Nicholas Ostler, Bath (UK)

IV. Preprocessing corpora

22. Annotation standards

This article gives an overview of the state-of-the-art as well as the evolution of annotation and metadata standards to be used for corpus linguistic purposes. It starts with a definition of annotation standards and discusses the necessity of using them. Due to the fact that every annotation standard needs to be implemented using a standardized data or rendering format, section 2 addresses two major formats being used for text encoding purposes: Unicode and XML.

Section 3 introduces the most commonly accepted and widely adopted encoding and annotation standards as well as the goals and aims of the institutions associated with them, and section 4 is dedicated to different metadata standards.

1. What are annotation standards?

By defining "annotation" as the addition of linguistic information to language data (cf. Leech 1997) and "standard" as something that is – at least – widely accepted, the use of the term "annotation standards" implies that there is a well-elaborated set of rules and procedures that is generally accepted, and at the same time frequently used and integrated into common corpus creation and processing tools. Facing the variety of linguistic theories and the heterogeneity of linguistic terms and concepts, one can easily imagine that things appear different in practice. While standards do exist and some of them are used on a large scale, many researchers still do not bother with standards or do not see their importance or the benefits of using them.

There are several aspects relating to the importance of standards:

Whether it is actually possible to systematically find a language resource strongly depends on the existence of metadata referring to the nature of the resource and on its being stored in an accessible repository. Once found, the resource is of much more use to the researcher if the annotation is understandable, either because it is based on standards or documented with standard metadata vocabulary. Long-term storage and retrieval is simplified by means of standardized data formats while automatic language processing also relies strongly on non-ambiguous data to be of any use.

Furthermore, the extent to which established standards are used is determined by the availability of tools that work with this standardized data and vice versa.

Standards in the linguistic context have to comprise a wide range of linguistic theories, languages, research areas and text types. The problems arising from this have been handled in various ways by researchers who have worked on establishing such standards.

Attempts to standardize the encoding of digital text archives and their annotation have been made since the use of computers for text processing became feasible. The formation of the Text Encoding Initiative (TEI, http://www.tei-c.org/) has to be seen as the first major attempt to establish such a standard. At least it was the first attempt that resulted in an outcome that became widely accepted and was actually used. The first draft of the TEI guidelines (called TEI P1) was completed in 1990, the first official version (TEI P3) released in 1994.

Interestingly, the encoding and annotation standards described in this article can often be traced back to the TEI or EAGLES (Expert Advisory Group on Language Engineering Standards, http://www.ilc.cnr.it/EAGLES/home.html) in some manner: The Corpus Encoding Standard (CES) meets the specifications of the TEI guidelines, and MATE (see below) considers itself as an extension of the TEI's line of work. The TEI component used for marking feature structures has been adopted as the basis of the development of the ISO/TC37 standard, which is the first published standard relating to feature structures that has emerged from this committee.

2. Standardized data and rendering formats

A common denominator of the standards that we would like to introduce in this article is their footing on XML and Unicode. Therefore, we will introduce these data formats first.

2.1. XML

Nearly all recent and emerging formats and software programs dealing with textual data either exclusively use XML (eXtensible Markup Language), or implement ways of dealing with XML data. The use of XML can be considered the minimum requirement for encoding texts in a sustainable and computer-processable way.

XML (http://www.w3.org/XML/), is a simplified subset of SGML (Standard Generalized Markup Language, http://www.w3.org/MarkUp/SGML/), and encodes texts by means of a tag structure to identify and classify information. This tag structure consists of tags that define elements which can have attributes. The set of tags, element names, attributes and their permitted values is not defined inside XML itself but in a document grammar, in most cases either a Document Type Definition (DTD) or a Schema. In this way it is possible to use XML for all kinds of documents and applications, hence current linguistic encoding standards are almost exclusively defined using such DTDs or Schemas.

2.2. Unicode

XML uses Unicode (http://www.unicode.org/) as a default for character encoding, an industry standard developed to overcome the problems and incompatibilities resulting from the large amount of character encoding schemes that exist, with the aim of representing every writing system in the world. Unicode is developed in synchronization with ISO 10646, the ISO standard character encoding (cf. http://www.unicode.org/versions/Unicode4.0.0/appC.pdf).

3. Annotation standards

In this section we introduce a number of influential standards for corpus processing and linguistic annotation that are not related to metadata.

3.1. TEI

TEI stands for Text Encoding Initiative (http://www.tei-c.org/) and – though often used as such – is not the name for a standard, but rather a consortium of institutions and projects concerned with the development and maintenance of the TEI standard that is available as a set of guidelines with corresponding document grammars. The formation of the TEI was a result of the Association for Computers and the Humanities' Vassar Conference in 1987. Though the guidelines were created as a kind of standard, the TEI avoided this term as "a commitment to preserving the intellectual autonomy of researchers who encode texts electronically" (Ide/Sperberg-McQueen 1995). The TEI consortium was initiated by the Association for Computers and the Humanities, the Association for Computational Linguistics, and the Association for Literary and Linguistic Computing. Since 2000, it functions as a non-profit organization with the mission of maintaining and developing the TEI standard (http://www.tei-c.org).

The TEI's Guidelines for Electronic Text Encoding and Interchange were first published in April 1994 (under the name "TEI P3") and updated in 1999. The P3 guidelines and DTDs were still based on SGML as their markup language. TEI P4, which was the current edition at the time this article was first submitted, was published in 2002 with the major change that it accommodated XML. It is available online (http://www.tei-c.org/P4X/index.html). The next edition, TEI P5, was released on November 1, 2007.

TEI aims to encode as many possible views (e. g. text components as physical, typographical or linguistic objects) of a text as possible.

The TEI scheme is a modular one, designed to be customized for particular research or production environments. Such a TEI schema for a special purpose consists of a core tag set that is applicable for any TEI document and a base tag set that has to be chosen out of eight different tag sets for different purposes:

- TEI.prose: prose
- TEI.verse: lyrics
- TEI. drama: drama
- TEI. spoken: transcription of spoken language
- TEI. dictionaries: dictionaries
- TEI.terminology: terminological databases
- TEI.mixed and
- TEI.general: text that requires tags from more than one category

The schema can be supplemented with additional tag sets for special purposes such as accuracy markup, graphics etc.

However, this modularity comes at a price: for many researchers, especially the ones working with corpus and computational linguistics, the "raw", uncustomized TEI guidelines are too extensive. The wish to cover a wide range of document types, research areas and almost every conceivable phenomenon not only results in about 400 possible elements but also in various shortcomings that may discourage researchers from using them. Sometimes, different encodings are possible for one and the same phenomenon and some encodings are on such a high level of abstraction that they are not very useful anymore. Moreover, issues concerning ambiguity and hierarchy do not allow for effective validation, which is fundamental for corpus and computational applications.

Furthermore, these problems can lead to a lack of uniformity – having a corpus that complies with TEI guidelines does not necessarily mean that all phenomena in all texts are encoded consistently – something one would expect from a standard.

And even though it is very flexible, TEI does not allow for all possible types of annotation. Especially the fact that the TEI-DTD requires the whole text and annotation to be held in one single XML document that expresses a tree structure leads to problems regarding overlapping hierarchies and to a large overhead.

These objections are, as we have mentioned above, particularly relevant for researchers in corpus and computational linguistics. While famous TEI corpora such as the BNC (cf. article 20) exist, TEI is much more popular and a widely adopted standard in other fields of research, e. g. in literature, in the humanities or in text archives. The TEI website lists over a hundred projects which use the TEI guidelines, and this list is far from complete. The TEI guidelines' compliance to established indexing mechanisms used in libraries also contributes to this success.

The TEI consortium itself has attended to the problems mentioned above: in 1995 it released TEI Lite, a kind of reduced subset of the TEI guidelines, "a useful 'starter set', comprising the elements which almost every user should know about" (Lou Burnard 1995, http://www.tei-c.org/Lite/U5-Intro.html). This subset has become very popular as a starting point for working with the TEI guidelines.

In the same way the TEI created these encoding schemes as TEI-implementations, it is possible to create encoding schemes that conform to the TEI guidelines and narrow them to fit specialized research requirements more adequately. The Medieval Nordic Text Archive (Menota, http://www.menota.org/), for example, developed special guidelines for the encoding and annotation of medieval manuscripts, customized in order to fit their requirements and based on the TEI P4-guidelines. They contain precise instructions on how to encode the phenomena occurring in these manuscripts, meeting an urgent need of researchers that want to start encoding texts right away.

As already mentioned, the next version of the TEI guidelines (TEI P5, http://www.tei-c.org/P5/) is in preparation. The major change compared to previous versions is that TEI schemes, while still expressible in DTDs or W3C Schema Language (http://www.w3.org/XML/Schema), will now use the ISO standard Relax-NG schema language (http://relaxng.org/) as a default for their description.

Further changes include the development of a new XML-based version of the TEI's system supporting the automatic generation of documentation and custom schemas, a revision of TEI's linking system supporting XLink and XPointer (which are important for utilizing stand-off annotation), and a revision of the representation of feature structures, a joint effort with an ISO working group (see "ISO/TC 37/SC4" below).

The development and distribution of TEI P5 are handled via the Open-Source-Software Platform Sourceforge.net (http://sourceforge.net/projects/tei), which reflects a change in focus towards better tools for the creation of derived schemas and the management of TEI conformant resources.

3.2. CES/XCES

As part of their 1996 guidelines, the EAGLES (Expert Advisory Group on Language Engineering Standards, an initiative of the European Commission (EC) within EC DG XIII's Linguistic Research and Engineering program, launched in February 1993) developed the so-called "Corpus Encoding Standard" (CES, now XCES due to the change from SGML to XML). The aim was to determine a minimal encoding level for corpora in order to offer improved ways of data exchange and at the same time to meet the increasing desire of linguists to get an empiricist view on their data.

CES was intended as an exchange format capable of integrating all possible mark-up schemes, meaning that translation between other schemes and CES would be possible in one step and without loss of information.

The principles of the CES (http://www.cs.vassar.edu/CES/CES1-1.html) list nine criteria that were observed in the design of the standard. These criteria and their implementation in CES solve many of the problems of the TEI guidelines mentioned above. The criteria are:

- Coverage: most possible features relevant for language engineering should be encoded in a uniform way disallowing ambiguity and resulting in a very reduced and streamlined tag set.
- Consistency: features should all be encoded in a uniform manner.
- Recoverability: it should be possible to get back/return to the original form of the encoded text by means of a simple algorithm.
- Validatability: tags should not be too abstract and tag hierarchies should be distinct to allow for the automatic validation of structural constraints.
- Capturability: the capturing and the first markup of a text should not be too costly; there should be a minimum requirement that keeps the effort of capturing text low.
- Processability: the conversion of CES-encoded texts into other encodings should be easy and effective.
- Extensibility: schemas should be accessible for later additions and extensions since not every possible case can be considered beforehand.
- Compactness: markup should be as compact as possible without compromising processability.
- Readability: marked up text should still be human readable.

Since a group of people involved with the TEI also contributed to EAGLES, it is not surprising that these criteria read as if they were directly aimed at tackling the problems that kept people from actually using the original TEI guidelines.

The implementation of these criteria, an extension and specialization of the TEI guidelines, "specifies a minimal encoding level that corpora must achieve to be considered standardized in terms of descriptive representation (marking of structural and typographic information) as well as general architecture (so as to be maximally suited for use in a text database). It also provides encoding specifications for linguistic annotation, together with a data architecture for linguistic corpora" (http://www.cs.vassar.edu/CES/).

CES/XCES uses a much reduced subset of TEI tags with more precise semantics and reduced tag content, with a distinct focus placed on morpho-syntactic annotations.

More importantly, XCES allows for the primary text to be separated from its annotations. In this way it is possible to add as many annotation layers to the same primary text as desired. Using this stand-off annotation, in which all annotations are held in separate files from the annotated data, and linked to it by means of pointers, it is possible to annotate overlapping hierarchies, to add multiple annotation layers of the same type and to align parallel texts. Furthermore, the overhead is reduced since not all added annotation layers need to be used when working with the text.

Part of CES/XCES is a documentation providing precise instructions on how to encode texts and which tags to use for which phenomena. This way the problems with the ambiguity given in TEI are eliminated and researchers have a good starting point for work with corpora.

The website lists corpora based on CES/XCES, among others the MULTEXT and PAROLE Corpora (see article 20 for details).

3.3. MATE/NITE

The EU-funded project MATE (Multilevel Annotation, Tools Engineering), managed by the Natural Interactive Systems Group (NIS) (now NISLab, http://www.nis.sdu.dk/) at the University of Southern Denmark, is aimed at developing standards and tools for spoken language dialogue corpora. The project was started in March 1998.

They determined that "the main limitations of the CES are that the CES has mainly focused on written, non-dialogue corpora, such as newspaper texts, and does not go beyond the morphosyntactic level" (http://mate.nis.sdu.dk/information/d12/), and therefore aimed at focusing on requirements for the markup and annotation of spoken corpora, including issues such as overlapping speech, non-hierarchical markup, transcriptions or the annotation of prosody or speech-acts, while enabling cross-level coding, i. e. links between different levels of annotation.

Like CES/XCES, MATE makes use of stand-off annotation. In MATE, all levels of annotation (which are done in coding files) refer to a "transcription" that establishes the anchoring reference to the original data (audio, video, text files); these in turn are collected in one resource file.

One main element of the MATE paradigm is the coding module, which "includes or describes everything that is needed in order to perform a certain kind of markup of a particular spoken language corpus" (http://mate.nis.sdu.dk/information/d12/#-Toc436722285). This module includes precise descriptions on what and how to annotate, the raw data, a declaration of available markup elements, attributes and values with informal descriptions, a guide to the recommended encoding procedure (including examples and other metadata), and the actual coding files mentioned above.

While the MATE encoding schemes are not TEI-compliant, it was intended to provide means for importing and exporting to TEI-compliant XML right from the start.

The general openness of the MATE approach makes it accessible for a wide range of coding schemes; the MATE website lists various compatible coding schemes from different research areas (http://www.dfki.de/mate/d11/annex.html). The encoding scheme was accompanied by the MATE Workbench, a toolset established for displaying and querying the MATE corpora.

The MATE project ended in 2000 and was followed by the NITE (Natural Interactivity Tools Engineering) project, also situated at the NISLab. It focused on the same problems and builds on the work of the MATE project. The MATE encoding scheme was improved and supplemented by the NOM (NITE Object Model), which is based on multi-rooted trees, i. e. multiple element trees can refer to one set of primary data that is optionally augmented by a timeline. The primary data is treated as an annotation layer itself, consisting of an already tokenized text with annotations referring to these tokens. The multiple trees are stored in multiple files and can be viewed as stand-off annotations to that layer, equivalent to MATE's coding files. The MATE Workbench was supplemented with NXT (NITE XML Toolkit), a toolkit that consists, among other things, of a matching query language and API modules for the Java programming language aimed more at developers of specialized applications.

The NITE project ended in 2003, but the NOM and NXT schemes and technology are still maintained and developed as an open-source project on Sourceforge (https://sourceforge.net/projects/nite/).

The list of NITE Corpora (http://www.ltg.ed.ac.uk/NITE/inuse.html) holds well-known corpora like the Switchboard-Corpus (cf. article 20).

3.4. ISO/TC 37/SC4

The International Organization for Standardization (ISO) has a technical committee (TC 37) which deals with "Terminology and other language and content resources". The ISO has a high authority with respect to standards, so the fact that a committee deals with linguistic resources alone is definitely a positive thing. Inside this committee, one of the "special committees" (SC4) deals with "Language resource management", and part of their work is directly related to linguistic annotation. The committee began its work in 2002. At this moment in time, the work of one subordinate working group on the description of feature structures has reached the status of being a published standard.

The Special Committee 4 (SC4) itself is divided into five working groups (WG1-WG5). Together, they deal with matters related to general linguistic annotation, morpho-syntactic and syntactic annotation, and the annotation of feature structures and data categories. The actual projects that are being worked on are:

- Terminology for Language Resource Management (TermLR)
- Linguistic Annotation Framework (LAF)
- Lexical Markup Framework (LMF)
- Feature Structures – Feature Structure Representation (FSR)
- Feature Structures – Feature System Declaration (FSD)
- Morpho-Syntactic Annotation Framework (MAF)
- Word segmentation of written texts for monolingual and multilingual information processing – Part 1: General principles and methods (WordSeg1)
- Word segmentation – Part 2: Chinese, Japanese, Korean (WordSeg2)
- Registry of Standard Data Categories (DCR)
- Computer applications in terminology – Data Categories for electronic lexical resources (DCS)

– A Taxonomy of Temporal Data Categories (TDG)
– Syntactic Annotation Framework (SynAF)
– Multilingual Information Framework (MLIF)
– Semantic Annotation Framework (SemAF)

The special committee is also following the general tendency towards developing more general standards and categories that allow for the description and thus the subsumption of more specialized annotation schemes, creating a kind of meta-structure and data model (meta-standard) for the exchange of linguistic data.

To achieve this goal, it is necessary to distinguish between the user-defined, specialized encoding schemes (here called: document form) and an abstract, general exchange data format (here: data model) and at the same time to ensure the possibility of mapping between them – i. e. the data model behind them has to be compatible. The general format in this context is supposed to be the LAF (Linguistic Annotation Framework, cf. http://www.tc37sc4.org/new_doc/ISO_TC_37_SC4_N31 1_Linguistic%20Annotation %20Framework.pdf), and represents a central pivot point in the committee's work.

LAF allows for any type of user annotation scheme – even if it is not XML-encoded – as long as it is automatically transferable to and from the LAF Dump Format. This dump format is internally represented as a stand-off-annotation on primary (source) data that is considered "read only" and thus protected against alteration.

The representation of linguistic annotation is based on other standards to be developed within the committee. One major problem with respect to this representation is related to the definition of data categories that represent existing and potential future annotations. In this context the committee is planning to establish an open repository of data categories. While this seems to work out fine for existing categories, the modalities required to extend these categories, on the other hand, have not yet been completely elaborated (cf. Trippel/Declerck/Heid 2005).

Formalisms to describe feature structures are an elementary part of linguistic research and often necessary for more complex descriptions. The ISO working group tied in with the TEI's syntax-description for feature structures which had been introduced in TEI-P4 and cooperated with the TEI on a standard for the representation of feature structures. This resulted in the ISO official standard ISO 24610-1:2006, Feature structures – Part 1: Feature structure representation.

Other work items inside the special committee which deal with the actual annotation of linguistic features inside the LAF rely on these standards: the Morphosyntactic Annotation Framework (MAF), which seeks a uniform way of coding morphosyntactic annotation, is for example based on the aforementioned Data Category Register, on the Feature Structure model and on OLAC for metadata. This also applies to other projects.

Since the work of the TC 37/SC4 is still in progress, it is too early to go into detail on the specific work items. However, to get a general idea about the different work areas and their progress it is recommendable to look at the latest papers published by the committee at http://www.tc37sc4.org/document.php.

3.5. Pragmatic annotation

Pragmatic annotation differs from other linguistic annotation more than anything in the way it aims to capture phenomena that cannot be immediately related to the surface of the language data. Categories like illocution, structural relationships between utterances or the context in which an utterance was made often do not link to a well-defined span of textual data – whereas in other annotation contexts, some pragmatic features would fit well into metadata descriptions. Another obstacle on the path to a standardization of pragmatic annotation is the fact that the various branches in pragmatics rarely share the same categories, or that finding these categories is the actual aim of the research.

However, this does not automatically mean that no efforts have been made towards creating pragmatic annotation schemes – a thorough overview can be found in article 29.

4. Metadata standards for language corpora

The term *metadata* is in most cases roughly defined as "data about data" or "information about information". This definition is insufficient, inasmuch as it is applicable to any linguistic annotation referring to single textual units. Metadata, however, provide information on entire texts or even collections of texts.

Depending on context and purpose, several more precise definitions exist. For example Tim Berners-Lee (1997) additionally defines metadata as follows: "Metadata is machine understandable information about web resources or other things".

In this article we define metadata in relation to their use (cf Day 2001) and close to the definition of Schmidt (2004, 146), as "Structured data that represents a resource of information in an information process". Due to the fact that this information process is automated, it is implied that metadata is machine readable.

Using metadata has a long tradition in information and text processing science (e. g. librarianship, see Schmidt 2004, 143), but also in science related to the processing of non-textual data (e. g. geography, physics etc.). Hence metadata are used in every discipline in which large amounts of (textual or non-textual) data have to be managed and described with respect to form and content.

According to the wide range of applications, there have always been approaches to establish metadata standards, most often with the intention of meeting the special needs of a specific branch or field. In the following only those standards intended for the use in corpus linguistic environments or those being used for this purpose due to their high level of interoperability will be introduced.

4.1. Functions and use of metadata standards

The need for standardization of metadata (especially in corpus linguistics) becomes obvious when considering its function in language processing contexts.

First of all, like any kind of annotation, metadata is used to make information (normally a language resource) findable for researchers, and at the same time to grant optimized and systematic access to documents within a corpus. The importance of this role increases in correlation with the growing number of corpora containing large amounts of heterogeneous language data. For this purpose, relevant information on the resource needs to be stored in the form of machine readable data.

The entity representing metadata is the *metadata record*. It is structured into so-called *elements* (or sometimes *attributes*) which describe the resource, such as title, author, language, document-size, etc. The metadata record can either be embedded into the resource it describes, which is common for textual resources, or alternatively stored in a record separate from the resource, which is more practical for non-textual resources. The set of possible entries in a metadata record is the *metadata element set* which is defined by the respective metadata standard being used.

Due to the large variety of linguistic issues and language data being processed, the information given in the metadata may differ. For example, in language transcriptions it may contain information on the speakers' sex, age, dialect etc., whereas in other contexts annotation principles and practice, date of origin, classification of the text etc. may be of higher relevance to researchers. Therefore metadata standards have to establish structures and terminologies (so-called *metadata vocabularies*) to cover as many kinds of information as possible.

Facing the variety of linguistic data, the standardization of metadata is the only way to classify and compare resources across language boundaries. Another aspect referring to relations between documents is the description of coherence relations between resources. Unless the resources are not explicitly connected by means of (hyper-)links within the object data, the linking can be realized by the declaration of metadata (see Trippel/Baumann 2003, 2).

Last but not least, metadata is highly important for the long-term preservation of language resources, as it contains information relevant to the reuse and exchange of the research data, such as legal information, encoding etc.

Taking all the demands mentioned above into consideration, it becomes obvious that it is essential to use metadata standards with a transparent and standardized structure along with a well-defined metadata vocabulary.

4.2. Metadata standards

4.2.1. Dublin Core

One of the most common metadata standards used for digital resources is the Dublin Core metadata element set (DCMES). It has been developed by the DCMI (Dublin Core Metadata Initiative) since 1995. The first part of the name refers to the city of Dublin, Ohio, where the initial work on the development was carried out within a workshop hosted by the OCLC (Online Computer Library Centre). "Core" refers to the fact that the specified element set is an expandable "core" list.

Originally founded in order to develop a standard for the meta-description of online-published texts, the primary aim of the DCMI nowadays is, however, more comprehensive: "the development of simple standards to facilitate the finding, sharing and management of information." (DCMI, http://dublincore.org/about/). This refers not only to textual but to all kinds of data accessible over the Internet.

The DCMI is made up of international researchers belonging to different fields and branches divided into working groups concerned with specific problem domains (see DCMI, http://dublincore.org/groups/). In order to make Dublin Core as applicable as possible to a large variety of resources, it is intended to be kept "as small and simple as possible" using "commonly understood semantics" (Hillmann 2005). "In the diverse world of the Internet, Dublin Core can be seen as a 'metadata pidgin for digital tourists': easily grasped, but not necessarily up to the task of expressing complex relationships or concepts" (ibid.). The scheme exists in two versions different with respect to descriptive depth, namely "simple" and "qualified" Dublin Core.

Simple Dublin Core consists of fifteen facultative elements; each element can appear more than once in arbitrary order within one metadata record. The element set meets the minimum requirements of meta-description.

- **Title:** The name given to the resource.
- **Subject and Keywords:** The topic of the content of the resource.
- **Description:** An account of the content of the resource.
- **Resource Type:** The nature or genre of the content of the resource.
- **Source:** A reference to a resource from which the present resource is derived.
- **Relation:** A reference to a related resource.
- **Coverage:** The extent or scope of the content of the resource.
- **Creator:** An entity primarily responsible for making the content of the resource.
- **Publisher:** The entity responsible for making the resource available.
- **Contributor:** An entity responsible for making contributions to the content of the resource.
- **Rights Management:** Information about rights held in and over the resource.
- **Date:** A date associated with an event in the life cycle of the resource.
- **Format:** The physical or digital manifestation of the resource.
- **Resource Identifier:** An unambiguous reference to the resource within a given context.
- **Language:** A language of the intellectual content of the resource.

Qualified Dublin Core includes the fifteen elements of the Simple Dublin Core plus three additional elements: *Audience, Provenance* and *Rights Holder*. Furthermore, the elements of the Qualified Dublin Core can be specified by sets of "qualifiers" belonging to each element. The qualifiers are seen as a refinement of the element value, not as an extension (for an extensive definition and a complete listing, see Hillmann 2005).

- ***Audience:*** A class of entity for whom the resource is intended or useful.
- ***Provenance:*** A statement of any changes in ownership.
- ***Rights Holder:*** A person or organization owning or managing rights over the resource.

The Dublin Core element set as well as its structure reflect its primary scope, which focuses more on cataloguing and archiving of digital resources than on providing relevant information to linguists. In fact, the major criticism brought up against the use of Dublin Core for corpus linguistic purposes is that most of the categories are underspecified with respect to being used for the annotation of linguistic corpora (see Trippel/Baumann 2003, 5). The DCMI itself admits that Dublin Core may not be sufficient for all purposes and appreciates the development of new standards based on Dublin Core.

4.2.2. OLAC

A prominent metadata standard based on Dublin Core developed especially for archiving linguistic data is the OLAC (Open Language Archives Community) Metadata standard. It originated from the framework of the Open Archives Initiative (OAI), dedicated to the development of "interoperability standards that aim to facilitate the efficient dissemination of content" (OLAC, http://www.openarchives.org/organization/).

The primary intent of the OLAC is the creation of an open worldwide library archive of language resources. Therefore it aims to bring together language processing institutions which constitute a network of data housing and accessing repositories. The metadata scheme developed for this purpose includes all fifteen elements of the Simple Dublin Core (listed in section 4.2.1.). Following the Dublin Core recommendations for qualifying elements, it also includes several qualifiers in addition to the elements of Dublin Core in order to enable the description of language resources with greater precision than the standard Dublin Core refiners. The following listing shows the additional refiners:

Subject:
- ***Subject.language:*** A language which describes or discusses the content of the resource

Resource Type:
- ***Type.functionality:*** Software Functionality
- ***Type.linguistic:*** The nature or genre of the resource from a linguistic standpoint

Format:
- ***Format.cpu:*** The CPU required to use a software resource
- ***Format.encoding:*** An encoded character set used by a digital resource
- ***Format.markup:*** A markup scheme used by a digital resource
- ***Format.os:*** An operating system required to use a software resource
- ***Format.sourcecode:*** A programming language of software distributed in source form

Like in Dublin Core, the elements of the OLAC metadata set can be used repeatedly in arbitrary order. The OLAC metadata set is implemented in XML using the following four additional attributes:

- ***refine:*** used to identify element refinements.
- ***code:*** used to hold metadata values that are taken from a specific encoding scheme.
- ***scheme:*** name for the scheme that constrains how the text in the content of the element is encoded.
- ***lang:*** specifies the language in which the text in the content of the element is written.

Both Dublin Core and OLAC are based on a flat structure, in contrast to the two metadata standards introduced in the following – TEI-Header and IMDI – which use hierarchical structures.

4.2.3. TEI and TEI based metadata

As illustrated in section 3.1. the Text Encoding Initiative (TEI) provides a standard for XML based markup of textual resources. A TEI-compatible text resource consists of a header and a body. While the header contains the document's metadata, the body comprises the encoded text itself.

According to the XML-Structure, the TEI-Header is organized hierarchically into major elements (so-called "principal components") and several sub-elements.

The four major elements are:

```
<teiHeader>
    <fileDesc><!-- ... --></fileDesc>
    <encodingDesc><!-- ... --></encodingDesc>
    <profileDesc><!-- ... --></profileDesc>
    <revisionDesc><!-- ... --></revisionDesc>
</teiHeader>
```

The *File description* (<fileDesc>) contains "a full bibliographical description of the computer file itself" as well as "the source or sources from which the electronic document was derived."

Encoding description (<encodingDesc>) "describes the relationship between an electronic text and its source or sources". Therefore it contains information on encoding conventions, normalizing steps etc. applied during the processing.

Text profile (<profileDesc>) contains "classificatory and contextual information about the text, such as its subject matter, the situation in which it was produced, the individuals described by or participating in producing it, and so forth."

Revision history (<revisionDesc>) provides "a history of changes made during the development of the electronic text." – i.e. information that is necessary for version control of an encoded document.

The <fileDesc> element is the only mandatory element of the TEI-Header, whereas further major and sub-elements are recommended, but not obligatory. A TEI-Header consisting of only this one element is called "minimum header". The structure of the major elements and their respective sub-elements are described in detail in TEIP4 (2002).

The TEI-Header can either be prefixed, as a part of the encoded document (as the name implies, as a "header"), or externally linked to the respective document.

Size and complexity of the TEI-Header strongly depend on its purpose. For corpus linguistic uses in which metadata can be used to describe several levels of a corpus (e.g. the corpus itself or a text-unit within the corpus), the TEI suggests a type-attribute to point to the level the header applies to:

```
<teiCorpus.2>
   <teiHeader type="corpus">
     <!-- header for corpus-level information- -->
   </teiHeader>
 <TEI.2>
   <teiHeader type="text">
     <!-- header for text-level information- -->
   </teiHeader>
   <text><!-- ... --> </text>
 </TEI.2>
 <TEI.2>
   <teiHeader type="text">
   <!-- ... --></teiHeader>
   <text><!-- ... --></text>
 </TEI.2>
 <!-- etc. -->
</teiCorpus.2>
```

The structure and element-set of the TEI-header is defined in the form of a DTD. Like the DCMI, the TEI provides mechanisms for modifying and customizing the TEI-scheme, including the headers (see chapter 29 of the TEI Guidelines). One prominent approach of customizing the TEI-Header has been followed by the EAGLES (see above) that optimized the TEI-Header "to suit the specific needs of corpus-based research." (CES, http://www.cs.vassar.edu/CES/CES1-3.html). The modifications include on the one hand the addition of elements and attributes "for more precision in the specifications" (ibid.), and on the other hand, several attribute values were restricted to presets of values. Since the EAGLES Project at present is continued by ISLE (see below), a complete description of the CES-Metadata is not listed within this article. However, it can be found in chapter 3 of the CES-Documentation (http://www.cs.vassar.edu/CES/CES1-3.html).

4.2.4. EAGLES/ISLE

ISLE (International Standards for Language Engineering) is intended to be the internationally orientated continuation of the EAGLES project mentioned above. The ISLE's programmatic goal, which is crucial for the development of the metadata standard, corresponds to the intention of the OLAC: "The aim of this [...] project is to improve the accessibility/availability of Language Resources on the Internet. We propose to achieve this by creating a browsable and searchable universe of meta-descriptions similar to those devised by other communities on the Internet" (Wittenburg/Broeder/Sloman 2000).

As a result of this aim, the metadata standard IMDI (ISLE Meta Data Initiative) provides – in contrast to OLAC – complex hierarchical structures. Unlike the other metadata standards mentioned above, whose primary focus is placed on cataloguing, IMDI accommodates the special issues of storing information on multi-media and multimodal language resources (such as language transcriptions aligned with audio-visual language records etc.). For this purpose the IMDI distinguishes between two functional categories of metadata: *session-data* and *catalogue-data*. While session-data describes the primary data of a resource ('session'), catalogue-data is used to catalogue the resources.

IMDI catalogue-data:

Name: The name of the corpus.
TitleID: The title of the corpus.
Description: Description of the corpus.
Subject Language: The languages subject to analysis.
Document Language: The languages used for describing/annotating the corpus.
Location: Groups the information about the location of where the corpus content was made.
  Location . Continent: The continent where the corpus content was made.
  Location . Country: The country where the corpus content was made.
  Location . Region: The region or sub-region where the corpus content was made.
Content type: The type of the corpus.
Format: Groups information about the format used in the corpus.
  Format . Text: The format of the text used in the corpus.
  Format . Audio: The format of the audio used in the corpus.
  Format . Video: The format of the video used in the corpus.
Quality: Groups information about the quality of the corpus content.
  Quality . Audio: The quality of the audio data.
  Quality . Video: The quality of the video data.
Smallest Annotation Unit: The smallest annotation unit used in the corpus.
Date: The publishing date of the corpus.
Project: The project for which the corpus was originally created.
Publisher: An entity responsible for making the resource available.
Authors: An entity primarily responsible for making the content of the resource.
Size: Total size of the corpus.

Distribution Form: How the corpora are distributed.
Access: Groups information about access rights.
Pricing: The price of the corpus.

Session-data is used to describe the primary data of a resource including written texts. Therefore it contains "[a]ll information about the circumstances and conditions of the linguistic event, groups the resources belonging to this linguistic event, records the administrative information of the event and describes the content of the event" (IMDI 2003). Due to its complexity, only the major element-groups Session, Project, Content, Actors, Resources and References are listed in the following. For a complete listing and definition of the sub-schemas along with the sub-elements and their definitions, see IMDI (2003).

Session: Bundles all information about the circumstances and conditions of the linguistic event.
Session . Name / Session . Title / Session . Date */ Session . Location / Session . Description / Session . Resource Reference / Session . Key / Session . Project / Session . Content / Session . Resources / Session . Actors / Session . [References]*

Project: Groups the information about the project, for which the session was originally created.
Project. *Name / Project. Title / Project.* Id */ Project. Contact / Project. Description*

Content: Groups the information about the content of the session.
Content . Genre / Content . SubGenre / Content . Communication Context / Content . Task / Content . Modalities / Content . Subject / Content . Languages / Content . Description / Content . Keys

Actors: Groups the information about all the actors in the session.
Actors . Description / Actors . Actor

Resources: Groups information about all the resources associated with the session.
Media File / Written *Resource / Source*

References: Groups documentation associated with the session.
References . Description

4.3. Implementation/mapping between metadata standards

Although various encoding schemes can be used to implement a metadata-standard, most initiatives give precise recommendations for the implementation of the standards they provide. In most cases this is XML or an XML-based schema. An important standard, suitable for cases, in which different metadata standards with different element sets and vocabularies are used within one corpus, is the Resource Description Framework (RDF). It has been developed by the W3C in order to be used for the description and interchange of resources. With the help of RDF it is possible not only to implement metadata standards, but also to map them to different standards that use concurrent vocabularies and structures (for a detailed description, see Tauberer 2006).

5. Outlook

The evolution of standards for linguistic annotation and metadata can be followed from early initiatives such as the TEI or EAGLES through to the efforts of the ISO/TC 37/SC4. The experiences gained by means of the general TEI guidelines showed the way towards more streamlined tag sets and tighter restrictions with respect to tag content in order to enhance the usefulness of automatic processing and eliminate ambiguity.

To facilitate the exchange of data and at the same time allow for the accumulation of larger corpora, we require standardized data models that are able to generalize over specialized tag sets and frameworks, enabling mapping between them. The NITE Object Model tries to accomplish that, and the efforts of the ISO/TC 37/SC4 are heading in the same direction.

A major obstacle on the way to free convertibility between language resources is still represented by the ambiguities between linguistic terms and concepts in different linguistic domains. The efforts to install a public register of data categories in the ISO special committee are aimed at dealing with this problem, as is the General Ontology for Linguistic Description (GOLD, http://www.linguistics-ontology.org/) that originated from the E-MELD (Electronic Metastructure for Endangered Language Data, http://www.emeld.org).

For the linguist who is faced with the decision on how to encode and store data, annotations, and metadata, the situation has only partially improved. The LAF allows any kind of user-defined annotation scheme (as long as the data model is compatible with the LAF dump format), but lacks a recommendation on which encoding scheme actually to use. The EMELD School of Best Practice (focused on the documentation of endangered languages), for example, recommends the use of XML markup, Unicode encoding, OLAC metadata and the linking of terms to an ontology, but does not include any recommendations on how to annotate the data. While these are already useful recommendations since they allow for a simple conversion of the data into another format, the decision on which annotation schema to use will still largely be made on the basis of the tools available for that specific research question.

This leads to the point of why one would want not to use standards. The use of specialized tools for certain research tasks that do not operate on standards is, for example, one good reason. Having old, legacy corpora that are not encoded or annotated in any readily available standard format is another. Also, if one wants to carry out a qualitative analysis on a very small amount of text that one will not ever want to use for any other purpose (and one is sure that nobody else would), it may just be a question of economics when deciding not to bother with standards.

However, modern tools for linguistic annotation and the construction of corpora are mostly standard-aware. The tools available when using the NITE XML Toolkit, for example, enable the annotation of most features a linguist could wish for, including overlapping hierarchics. Furthermore, tools for the conversion a variety of formats, such as different Treebank formats, into the NITE Object Model also exist. Other tools that operate on XML data often allow the importing of files in popular non-XML-encoded schemes (for example, programs for the transcription of spoken language such as ELAN (http://www.mpi.nl/tools/ass.html) or EXMARaLDA (http://www.exmaralda.org) allow the importing of non-XML CHILDES (http://childes.psy.cmu.edu/) data, making further XML based processing possible). It is foreseeable that in the future many tools will pay attention to assuring compatibility with the ISO LAF-standard, guaranteeing the possibility of exchanging and reusing language data on a large scale and making it electronically processable.

The key factor is the possibility of converting between different encoding schemes, and the actual standardization tendencies all seem to be aiming in that direction.

Accompanying this article we set up a WIKI describing tools and formats for creating and managing linguistic annotation. It can be found at http://www.exmaralda.org/annotation/.

6. Literature

Berners-Lee, T. (1997), *Metadata Architecture*. URL: http://www.w3.org/DesignIssues/Metadata.html.

Bray, T./Paoli, J./Sperberg-McQueen, C. M./Maler, E./Yergeau, F. (2004), *Extensible Markup Language (XML) 1.0* (third edition). URL: http://www.w3.org/TR/2004/REC-xml-20040204/.

Calzolari, N./McNaught, J. (1996), *Synopsis and Comparison of Morphosyntactic Phenomena Encoded in Lexicons and Corpora: A Common Proposal and Applications to European Languages*. Technical Report, Expert Advisory Group on Language Engineering Standards (EAGLES). URL: http://dienst.isti.cnr.it/Dienst/UI/2.0/Describe/ercim.cnr.ilc/1996-TR-004.

Carletta, J./Evert, S./Heid, U./Kilgour, J./Robertson, J./Voormann, H. (2003), The NITE XML Toolkit: Flexible Annotation for Multi-modal Language Data. In: *Behavior Research – Methods, Instruments, and Computers* 35(3), 353–363.

Clément, L./de la Clergerie, É. (2005), MAF: A Morphosyntactic Annotation Framework. In: *Proceedings of the 2nd Language and Technology Conference (LT'05)*. Poznan, Poland, 90–94.

Day, M. (2001), Metadata in a Nutshell. URL: http://www.ukoln.ac.uk/metadata/publications/nutshell/.

DCMI (2006) *Dublin Core Metadata Initiative*. URL: http://dublincore.org/.

EAGLES (2000), *Corpus Encoding Standard – Document CES 1*. Title page, Version 1.5. URL: http://www.cs.vassar.edu/CES/.

Farrar, S./Langendoen, D. T. (2003), A Linguistic Ontology for the Semantic Web. In: *GLOT International* 7 (3), 97–100.

Hillmann, D. (2005), *Using Dublin Core*. URL: http://dublincore.org/documents/usageguide/.

Ide, N. (2006), *Linguistic Annotation Framework*. URL: http://www.tc37sc4.org/new_doc/ISO_TC_37_SC4_N31 1_Linguistic%20 Annotation%20 Framework.pdf.

Ide, N./Romary, L. (2004), A Registry of Standard Data Categories for Linguistic Annotation. In: *Proceedings of the Fourth International Conference on Language Resources and Evaluation (LREC 2004)*. Lisbon, Portugal, 135–138. Available at: http://www.cs.vassar.edu/~ide/papers/LREC2004-DCR.pdf.

Ide, N./Sperberg-McQueen, C. M. (1995), The TEI: History, Goals, and Future. In: *Computers and the Humanities* 29(1), 5–15.

IMDI (2003), *IMDI Metadata Elements for Session Descriptions*. Version 3.0.4, MPI Nijmegen. URL: http://www.mpi.nl/IMDI/documents/Proposals/IMDI_MetaData_3.0.4.pdf.

IMDI (2004), *IMDI Metadata Elements for Catalogue Descriptions*. Version 3.0.0, MPI Nijmegen. URL: http://www.mpi.nl/IMDI/documents/Proposals/IMDI_Catalogue_3.0.0.pdf.

IMDI (2006), *ISLE Meta Data Initiative*. URL: http://www.mpi.nl/IMDI/.

ISO 24613:2006 (2006), *Language Resource Management – Lexical Markup Framework (LMF)*. URL: http://www.tc37sc4.org/new_doc/ISO_TC37–4_N1 30_rev9_LMF_15March2006.pdf.

ISO/DIS 24610–1 (2005), *Language Resource Management – Feature Structures – Part 1: Feature Structure Representation*. URL: http://www.tc37sc4.org/new_doc/ISO_TC_37–4_N188_Rev5_24610-1_FSR_20051020.pdf.

Leech, G. (1993), Corpus Annotation Schemes. In: *Literacy and Linguistic Computing* 8(4), 275–281.
Leech, G. (1997), Introducing Corpus Annotation. In: Garside, R./Leech, G. N./McEnery, T. (eds.), *Corpus Annotation: Linguistic Information from Computer Text Corpora.* London: Longman, 1–18.
Leech, G./Wilson, A. (1996), *Recommendations for the Morphosyntactic Annotation of Corpora.* Technical Report, Expert Advisory Group on Language Engineering Standards (EAGLES). URL: http://www.ilc.cnr.it/EAGLES/annotate/annotate.html.
OLAC (2006), *Open Language Archives Community Metadata.* URL: http://www.language-archives.org/OLAC/metadata.html.
Renear, A./Mylonas, E./Durand, D. (1996), Refining our Notion of What Text Really is: The Problem of Overlapping Hierarchies. In: Ide, N./Hockey, S. (eds.), *Research in Humanities Computing.* Oxford: Oxford University Press, 263–280.
Schmidt, I. (2004), Modellierung von Metadaten. In: Henning Lobin, L. L. (ed.), *Texttechnologie.* Tübingen: Stauffenberg, 143–164.
Sperberg-McQueen, C. M./Burnard, L. (2004), *TEI P4 Guidelines for Electronic Text Encoding and Interchange – XML-compatible Edition.* URL: http://www.tei-c.org/P4X/.
Tauberer, J. (2006), *What is RDF.* URL: http://www.xml.com/pub/a/2001/01/24/rdf.html.
Trippel, T./Baumann, T. (2003), *Metadaten für Multimodale Korpora: Verwendung im ModeLex-Projekt.* URL: http://coral.lili.uni-bielefeld.de/modelex/publication/techdoc/modelex_techrep4/.
Trippel, T./Declerck, T./Heid, U. (2005), Standardisierung von Sprachressourcen: Der aktuelle Stand. In: Hess, W./Lenders, W. (eds.), *LDV-Forum* 20(2), 17–29.
Wittenburg, P./Broeder, D./Sloman, B. (2000), *D.B. Meta-description for Language Resources. A Proposal for a Meta Description Standard for Language Resources.* URL: http://www.mpi.nl/ISLE/documents/papers/white_paper_11.pdf.

All URLs were checked on December 15, 2006.

Timm Lehmberg and Kai Wörner, Hamburg (Germany)

23. Development of tag sets for part-of-speech tagging

1. Introduction: Parts-of-speech and pos-tag sets

This article discusses tag sets used when pos-tagging a corpus, that is, enriching a corpus by adding a part-of-speech tag to each word. This requires a tag set, a list of grammatical category labels; a tagging scheme, practical definitions of each tag or label, showing words and contexts where each tag applies; and a tagger, a program for assigning a tag to each word in the corpus, implementing the tag set and tagging-scheme in a tag-assignment algorithm.

We start by reviewing tag sets developed for English corpora in section 1, since English was the first language studied by corpus linguists. Pioneering corpus linguists thought that their English corpora could be more useful research resources if each word was annotated with a part-of-speech label or tag. Traditional English grammars generally provide eight basic parts-of-speech, derived from Latin grammar. However, most tag set developers wanted to capture finer grammatical distinctions, leading to larger tag sets. Pos-tagged English corpora have been used in a wide range of applications.

Section 2 examines criteria used in development of English corpus part-of-speech tag sets: mnemonic tag names; underlying linguistic theory; classification by form or function; analysis of idiosyncratic words; categorization problems; tokenisation issues: defining what counts as a word; multi-word lexical items; target user and/or application; availability and/or adaptability of tagger software; adherence to standards; variations in genre, register, or type of language; and degree of delicacy of the tag set.

To illustrate these issues, section 3 outlines a range of examples of tag set developments for different languages, and discusses how these criteria apply. First we consider tag sets for an online part-of-speech tagging service for **English**; then design of a tag set for another language from the same broad Indo-European language family, **Urdu**; then for a non-Indo-European language with a highly inflexional grammar, **Arabic**; then for a contrasting non-Indo-European language with isolating grammar, **Malay**.

Finally, we present some conclusions in section 4, and references in section 5.

1.1. General-purpose pos-tags for pioneering English corpora

English was the first language of Corpus Linguistics; the first journal of the new research field, the *ICAME Journal* of the International Computer Archive of Modern and Medieval English, reflected this initial focus in its title and contents. Later, Corpus Linguistics extended to other languages. New journals have sprung up to cater for this wider range; for example, the first issue of *Corpora*, the latest Corpus Linguistics journal (founded nearly 30 years after *ICAME Journal*), included papers on Arabic and Spanish (as well as English).

The pioneering Corpus Linguists who collected the Brown corpus, the Lancaster/Oslo-Bergen corpus (LOB), the Spoken English Corpus (SEC), the Polytechnic of Wales corpus (PoW), the University of Pennsylvania corpus (UPenn), the London-Lund Corpus (LLC), the International Corpus of English (ICE), the British National Corpus (BNC), the Spoken Corpus Recordings In British English (SCRIBE), etc. (for references see below; see also article 20) all thought that their corpora could be more useful research resources if the source text samples were enriched with linguistic analyses. In nearly every case (except PoW), the first level of linguistic enrichment was to add a part-of-speech tag to every word in the text, labeling its grammatical category.

The different pos-tag sets used in these English general-purpose corpora are illustrated in Table 23.1, derived from the AMALGAM multi-tagged corpus (Atwell et al. 2000). This corpus is pos-tagged according to a range of rival English corpus tagging schemes, and also parsed according to a range of rival parsing schemes, so each sentence has not just one parse-tree, but "a forest" (Cure 1980). The AMALGAM multi-tagged corpus contains text from three quite different genres of English: informal speech of London teenagers, from COLT, the Corpus of London Teenager English (Andersen/Stenström 1996); prepared speech for radio broadcasts, from SEC, the Spoken English Corpus (Taylor/Knowles 1988); and written text in software manuals, from IPSM, the Industrial Parsing of Software Manuals corpus (Sutcliffe/Koch/McElligott 1996). The example sentence in Table 23.1 is from the software manuals section.

The pos-tagging schemes illustrated in Table 23.1 include: Brown corpus (Greene/Rubin 1981), LOB: Lancaster-Oslo/Bergen corpus (Atwell 1982; Johansson et al. 1986), SEC: Spoken English Corpus (Taylor/Knowles 1988), PoW: Polytechnic of Wales corpus (Souter 1989b), UPenn: University of Pennsylvania corpus (Santorini 1990), LLC: London-Lund Corpus (Eeg-Olofsson 1991), ICE: International Corpus of English (Greenbaum 1993), and BNC: British National Corpus (Garside 1996). For comparison, also included are the simpler "traditional" part-of-speech categories used in the *Collins English Dictionary* (Hanks 1979), and the basic PARTS tag set used to tag the SCRIBE corpus (Atwell 1989).

1.2. Traditional parts-of-speech

School textbooks, in England at least, generally state that there are eight parts-of-speech in English, derived from traditional Latin grammatical categories: *noun*, *verb*, *adjective*, *preposition*, *pronoun*, *adverb*, *conjunction*, and *interjection*. These traditional English parts-of-speech are usually defined in terms of syntactic function (e. g. a noun can function as the head of a noun phrase, the subject or object of a verb), and morphological patterns of grammatical forms (e. g. a noun can have singular and plural forms, but an adjective cannot – in English). These distinctions are explained by showing typical examples. However, this overlooks problematic borderline cases; syntactic and morphological criteria can occasionally conflict. For example, I work in the School of Computing at Leeds University; "computing" after the preposition "of" behaves syntactically as a noun, but morphologically is an inflected form of "compute", a verb. Idiosyncratic words which do not readily fit a category can also be problematic, for example "not". Some grammar descriptions try to cope with problems by extending the categories. For example, the *Collins English Dictionary* extends the traditional eight parts-of-speech by including *determiner* for "this", "that", "my", "his", "a", "some", "any" etc.; and introducing some sub-classifications, for example a distinction between *coordinating conjunctions* "and", "but", "or" etc., and *subordinating conjunctions* "where", "until", "before" etc.

1.3. Why not just use traditional parts-of-speech?

For most linguists developing part-of-speech tag sets and taggers, this is not enough: they may want to capture other grammatical distinctions, including morphological subcategories such as number for nouns and tense and person for verbs, and/or syntactic

Tab. 23.1: Example sentence illustrating rival English pos-taggings (from the AMALGAM multi-tagged corpus)

	Collins English Dictionary	SCRIBE parts	Brown	LOB	Upenn	BNC-C5	BNC-C6	ICE	PoW	LLC
If	s.conjuntion	subcj	CS	CS	IN	CJS	CS	CONJUNC (subord)	B	CC
your	determiner	pos	PP$	PP$	PRP$	DPS	APPGE	PRON(poss)	DD	TB
library	noun	noun	NN	NN	NN	NN1	NN1	N(com,sing)	H	NC
is	verb	be	BEZ	BEZ	VBZ	VBZ	VBZ	V(cop,pres)	OM	VB+3
on	preposition	prep	IN	IN	IN	PRP	II	PREP(ge)	P	PA
a	determiner	art	AT	AT	DT	AT0	AT1	ART(indef)	DQ	TF
network	noun	noun	NN	NN	NN	NN1	NN1	N(com,sing)	H	NC
and	c.conjunction	conj	CC	CC	CC	CJC	CC	CONJUNC(coord)	&	CA
has	verb	verb	HVZ	HVZ	VBZ	VHZ	VHZ	V(montr,pres)	M	VH+3
the	determiner	art	AT	ATI	DT	AT0	AT	ART(def)	DD	TA
Dynix	noun	noun	NP	NP	NNP	NP0	NP1	N(com,sing)	HN	NP
Gateways	noun	noun	NPS	NPS	NNPS	NN2	NN2	N(com,sing)	HN	NP
product	noun	noun	NN	NN	NN	NN1	NN1	N(com,sing)	H	NC
,	(unspecified)	,	,	,	,	PUN	YCOM	PUNC(com)	,	,
patrons	noun	noun	NNS	NNS	NNS	NN2	NN2	N(com,plu)	H	NC+2
and	c.conjunction	conj	CC	CC	CC	CJC	CC	CONJUNC(coord)	&	CA
staff	noun	noun	NN	NN	NNS	NN0	NN	N(com,plu)	H	NC
at	preposition	prep	IN	IN	IN	PRP	II	PREP(ge)	P	PA
your	determiner	pos	PP$	PP$	PRP$	DPS	APPGE	PRON(poss)	DD	TB
library	noun	noun	NN	NN	NN	NN1	NN1	N(com,sing)	H	NC
can	verb	aux	MD	MD	MD	VMO	VM	AUX(modal,pres)	OM	VM+8
use	verb	verb	VB	VB	VB	VVI	VVI	V(montr,infin)	M	VA+0
gateways	noun	noun	NNS	NNS	NNS	NN2	NN2	N(com,plu)	H	NC+2
to	preposition	verb	TO	TO	TO	TOTO	TO	PRTCL(to)	I	PD
access	verb	verb	VB	VB	VB	VVI	VVI	V(montr,infin)	M	VA+0
information	noun	noun	NN	NN	NN	NN1	NN1	N(com,sing)	H	NC
on	preposition	prep	IN	IN	IN	PRP	II	PREP(ge)	P	PA
other	determiner	adj	AP	AP	JJ	AJO	JJ	NUM(ord)	MOC	JS
systems	noun	noun	NNS	NNS	NNS	NN2	NN2	N(com,plu)	H	NC+2
as	(unspecified)	prep	QL	RB	RB	AV021	RR21	ADV(add)	AL	AC
well	(unspecified)	adv	RB	RB”	RB	AV022	RR22	ADV(add)		AC
.	(unspecified)	.	.	.	.	PUN	YSTP	PUNC(per)	.	.

subcategories such as making a distinction between adjectives in attributive and predicative positions. This is why most of the pos-tag sets in Table 23.1 use far more than eight tags.

Before you develop a part-of-speech tag set, or decide to re-use an existing pos-tag set, you should be clear about why you want to pos-tag your corpus. For developers of general-purpose corpus resources, the aim may be to enrich the text with linguistic analyses to maximize the potential for corpus re-use in a wide range of applications. Since these applications are not known in advance, the level of enrichment required is also unknown, so it is tempting to add as much linguistic enrichment as feasible. Corpus linguists have tended to devise pos-tag sets with very fine-grained grammatical distinctions; these pos-tag sets reflect their expert interest in syntax and morphology, rather than specific predicted needs of end-users.

On the other hand, very fine-grained distinctions may cause problems for automatic tagging if some words in English can change grammatical tag depending on function and context. For example, if the tag set tries to distinguish between attributive adjectives and predicative adjectives, then most (but not all) English adjectives have more than one possible tag to choose from according to context, making the task of pos-tagging adjectives non-trivial. This has influenced some pos-tagger developers to favour pos-tag distinctions which avoid computational difficulties. Notwithstanding, other pos-tag designers have chosen to make linguistically-motivated distinctions despite computational problems this may bring; for example, the **Stuttgart-Tübingen Tag Set (STTS)** for German (Schiller/Teufel/Thielen 1995; Thielen et al. 1999; also see http://www.ims.uni-stuttgart.de/projekte/corplex/TagSets/stts-table.html) has exactly this distinction between attributive and predicative adjectives.

1.4. Corpus applications which use pos-tags

As already mentioned, in deciding on the range and number of pos-tags, it makes sense to take into account the potential uses of the pos-tagged corpus. Many English Corpus Linguistics projects reported in *ICAME Journal* and elsewhere have involved grammatical analysis or tagging of English texts (e. g. Leech/Garside/Atwell 1983; Atwell 1983; Booth 1985; Owen 1987; Souter 1989a; O'Donoghue 1991; Belmore 1991; Kytö/Voutilainen 1995; Aarts 1996; Qiao/Huang 1998). Apart from obvious uses in linguistic analysis, some unforeseen applications have been found. As Kilgarriff (2007) put it, "... two external influences need mentioning: (i) lexicography – different agenda but responsible for lots of the actual corpus-building work and innovation, at least in UK; BNC was lexicography-led; (ii) NLP/computational linguistics, which has come into the field like a schoolyard bully, forcing everything that's not computational into submission, collusion or the margins". Further applications include using the tags to aid data compression of English text (Teahan 1998); and as a possible guide in the search for extra-terrestrial intelligence (Elliott/Atwell 2000).

Specific uses and results make use of part-of-speech tag information. For example, searching and concordancing can be made more efficient through use of part-of-speech tags to separate different grammatical forms of a word.

An indelicate annotation is sufficient for many NLP applications, e. g. grammatical error detection in Word Processing (Atwell 1983), training Neural Networks for grammatical analysis of text (Benello/Mackie/Anderson 1989; Atwell 1993), or training statistical language processing models (Manning/Schütze 1999).

2. Criteria for tag set development: Differences between English corpus part-of-speech tag sets

Table 23.1 illustrates a range of alternative English corpus part-of-speech tag sets. The rival tag sets display differences (and similarities) along several dimensions. These dimensions are in effect choices to be made by developers of new pos-tag sets, for English or another language; in developing a new tag set, the designer must decide how to handle each dimension. Once a researcher has decided it would be useful to add part-of-speech tags to their corpus, they must decide on the tag set: decide on the set of grammatical tags or categories, and their definitions and boundaries. It may be attractive to simply adopt an existing tag set, but this still leaves the decision of which of several possible or rival tag sets to adopt, at least for English or other major European languages. If the language being studied is like a virgin, tagged for the very first time (cf. Madonna, 1984), then the researcher does not have the option to adopt an existing tag set; but they may still draw on parallels from other, more experienced languages.

The criteria to consider in deciding or developing the tag set include the underlying differences between the tag sets of Table 23.1. There are also a number of additional design criteria to take account of.

2.1. Mnemonic tag names

Generally the tag names are not arbitrary symbols, but chosen to help linguists remember the categories; for example several tag sets include CC for *Coordinating Conjunction*, and VB for *VerB*. However, sometimes a mnemonic value is not universally agreed. For example, Brown, LOB and UPenn contrast NN for *singular noun* and NNS for *plural noun*, since *-s* is the standard suffix for plurals in English. However, the designers of the BNC tag sets decided that NNS might be mistakenly interpreted as *noun-singular*, so instead use NN1 for *singular noun* and NN2 for *plural noun*. The designers of the ICE tag set decided to use abbreviations rather than acronym-style mnemonics: for example, N(com,sing) for *singular common noun* and N(com,plu) for *plural common noun*.

2.2. Underlying linguistic theory

When a new tag set is developed by a linguist, they will inevitably be swayed by the linguistic theories they espouse. For example, the PoW corpus was collated and annotated by researchers interested in Systemic Functional Grammar, and the pos-tags reflect SFG analysis. Table 23.1 shows that words like "library" and "information" are tagged *noun* in most schemes, but H for *Head* (of a noun phrase) in PoW, showing the function of the noun in the syntactic structure. This makes it easier to parse the pos-tagged corpus with a SFG parser (e. g. O'Donoghue 1993; Souter 1996); but on the other hand a more traditional tagging in terms of nouns etc. would render a corpus more readily parseable by other parsers such as Principar (Lin 1994) or Sextant (Grefenstette 1996).

Another example of theoretical influence is in the ICE tagging scheme, developed later than others, at a time when grammar theories like Generalised Phrase Structure Grammar and Lexical Functional Grammar had promoted the notion that a category is composed of a bundle of features. Whereas earlier tag sets implicitly encoded some grammatical features (e. g. in LOB and Brown, a tag ending S was generally a plural) ICE tags explicitly show the bundle of features. This is more useful for feature-based parsers (e. g. Briscoe/Carroll 1993; Fang 2005).

However, most rival grammar theories like GPSG, LFG, GB etc. differ mainly in how they handle phrase structure, and more complicated structural issues such as the analysis of WH-questions. They generally had little to add to "traditional English grammar" on the issue of word categories, and there are no English corpus pos-tagging schemes which are closely tied to GPSG or LFG, for example.

Some researchers have been more interested in applications beyond linguistics. For example, the UPenn corpus was developed at least partly for researchers in Computer Science, Artificial Intelligence and Machine Learning. Machine Learning researchers using a part-of-speech tagged corpus for their ML experiments may not be concerned whether distinctions conform to a specific linguistic theory; but they will want a tagging which is readily Machine-Learnable.

Some corpus linguists may claim their part-of-speech tag sets are "theory-neutral"; but then why do so many rival part-of-speech tag sets abound? It is really not possible to have a theory-neutral annotation, every tagging scheme makes some theoretical assumptions.

2.3. Classification by form or function?

Traditionally, parts-of-speech are defined in terms of paradigmatic forms (for example, a word is a noun if it can be inflected to singular and plural forms), and syntagmatic functions (for example, a word is a noun if it can appear in specific sentence-slots such as head of a noun phrase). Usually paradigmatic and syntagmatic criteria coincide, but there are some exceptional cases, and different English corpus tag sets may handle these borderline cases differently. For example, in English text, most words with suffix "-ing" are inflected forms of verbs, e. g. "dancing" is derived from the verb "dance", just as "computing" is derived from the verb "compute". So, it is tempting to always tag words with "-ing" suffix as verb-derivatives: VBG in several tag sets. However, "dancing" can also function as an adjective or a noun; and the LOB tag set designers decided to tag "-ing" words according to function rather than form, so "dancing" must be tagged as any one of VBG, NN or JJ depending on syntactic function in context.

2.4. Idiosyncratic words

English has a number of words with special, idiosyncratic behaviour; particles which do not fit into traditional parts-of-speech. Different tag sets may analyse these differently.

For example, "a" is allowed a special *article* tag AT in the Brown and LOB tag sets, but is lumped in with *determiner* DT in the UPenn tag set. The word "to" is always *a preposition* in the *Collins English Dictionary* part-of-speech categories, even when preceding a verb infinitive (e. g. "to go"); whereas most other tag sets have a special tag for infinitival "to", different from the preposition tag for other uses of "to". Another example is the word "one", which has a range of grammatical roles in English. In the LOB tag set, "one" is simply tagged CD1 in all cases, but the ICE tag set has four separate tags for different functions, which a tagger has to try to separately identify.

2.5. Categorization problems

If a corpus linguist wants to design a detailed categorisation scheme, with many more than the eight basic categories, then it is not enough to provide a list of tags: each tag must be defined clearly and unambiguously, giving examples in a "case law" document. The definitions should include how to decide difficult, borderline cases, so that all examples in the corpus can be tagged consistently. For example, the Brown corpus manual specifies a general adverb tag **RB**, and a specialised tag for adverbs used as qualifiers, **QL**. However, it is not clear what limitations there are on the use of **QL**, leading to apparent internal inconsistency in the tagging of adverbs in Brown: a few adverbs appear tagged sometimes **RB** and sometimes **QL**, without any clear rationale. Another example is that most English tag sets have distinct tags for proper nouns and common nouns. It is easy to give prototypical examples of these two categories, but analysis of a corpus tends to throw up problem cases, so the tagging scheme guidelines must specify how to handle these grey areas. For example, product names like "Perrier Water", "International Journal of Corpus Linguistics" could be analysed as including common nouns, or alternatively the name could be tagged as a sequence of proper nouns.

In English, many words can belong to more than one grammatical category; for example, "water" can be used as a noun or a verb. Where a word can have different pos-tags in different contexts, tagging schemes should specify how to choose one tag as appropriate.

However, the UPenn tagging scheme incorporates special 'vertical slash' tags for (very rare) occasions when the part-of-speech is genuinely ambiguous. Consider the sentence: **The duchess was entertaining last night**. (This example is taken from Santorini 1990) Does *entertaining* mean that she was hosting an event, in which case the word would be a present participle verb, *VBG*, or does *entertaining* act adjectively (*JJ*) implying that the Duchess was good company? Either analysis is plausible, and even the surrounding context may not help in reaching a decision; so the Penn Treebank developers allow both tags to apply at the same time in this rare special case. In this case, *entertaining* is legitimately assigned the slash tag *JJ | VBG*. However, in the great majority of other uses of **entertaining**, the context can be used to disambiguate the word, so it should be tagged EITHER **JJ** or **VBG**. (Many cases of genuine ambiguity result in or perhaps reflect syntactic ambiguity, see articles 13 and 28.)

2.6. Tokenisation issues: What counts as a word?

Generally, English text is divided into words by spaces; punctuation and text-formatting can complicate this task of tokenisation, but not much (see article 24). In English, the main exceptions to this generalization are verb-contractions and genitives; and different pos-tag schemes deal with these exceptions differently. In the UPenn scheme, verb contractions and the Anglo-Saxon genitive of nouns are split into their component morphemes, and each morpheme is tagged separately; for example:

children's J children 's parents' → parents'
won't → wo n't
gonna → gon na
I'm → I 'm (from Treebank 1999)

In contrast, the London-Lund tagging scheme uses 'combined tags' for words such as *don't* (VD+0*AN) and *I've* (RA*VH+0). All combined tags have the same form: an asterisk separates the tags for the different tokens that make up the complete combined word. The Brown tagging scheme also uses 'combined tags' for words such as won't (MD*) and I'd (PPSS+HVD). Combined tags come in only these two forms: either negated words have an asterisk appended after their tag or the plus symbol separates the tags for the different tokens that make up the complete combined word.

2.7. Multi-word lexical items

A related problem area is the treatment of multi-word lexical items, also known as idiomatic phrases. For example, "as well" in Table 23.1 is equivalent to "also" or "too". The *Collins English Dictionary* does not specify how to tag this; and the Brown and UPenn tagging schemes insist on one tag per word, treating this as a sequence of adverb/qualifier + adverb. In contrast, the PoW tagging scheme simply supplies one tag (AL) for the phrase. Other tagging schemes include special tags for multi-word lexical items. The LOB tagging scheme introduced Ditto tags, applied to words whose role changes from their normal syntax when applied in certain combinations. The first word of the combination is tagged as normal and all subsequent words are given the first word's tag plus the ditto symbol ("). For example, the combination "so as to" is tagged TO TO" TO". The BNC tag sets C5 and C6 have a more complicated equivalent of ditto-tags: the phrase is given a single tag, AV0 in BNC-C5 or RR in BNC-C6; then each word has a variant of this general tag, with a 2-digit suffix, showing the length of the phrase, and the position within the phrase of this word. So, RR21 means "adverb, 2-word phrase, first word"; and RR22 means "adverb, 2-word phrase, second word".

What counts as a "multi-word lexical item" is also variable. For example, the BNC tag set treats "for example" as a single adverb (RR21 RR22 or AV021 AV022), whereas other tag sets assume this is preposition + noun.

To summarize, there is not always a one-to-one mapping between token and pos-tag. Sometimes a token contains several pos-tags (at least on some level) and sometimes several tokens have a common pos-tag. For more on multi-word lexical patterns, see article 58.

2.8. Target users and/or application

This relates back to section 1. The most important criterion is to satisfy the customer; the final tag set should be evaluated in terms of fit for purpose, and/or customer satisfaction. For example, developers of the LOB corpus thought its main use could be in English language teaching and research, and developed a comparatively complex tag set to reflect fine distinctions of English grammar for learners and teachers. Developers of the UPenn tagged corpus saw more use in language engineering, as a training set for Machine Learning systems which would cope better with a smaller tag set.

Many specific uses of corpora do not need delicate, detailed tag sets. However, the corpus developer should bear in mind the potential for re-use: a small tag set aimed at an immediate customer/application may turn out to be too limited for wider re-use of the corpus in future research. This is one reason why most English corpus pioneers developed sophisticated pos-tag schemes.

2.9. Availability and/or adaptability of tagger software

It is convenient to be able to automate part-of-speech tagging of a corpus, so a part-of-speech tag set which comes with a part-of-speech tagger program has a clear advantage over a purely theoretical tag set. An additional criterion may be the accuracy level of the tagger: it is tempting to adopt a tag set because it can be computed highly accurately, such as the ENGCG tagging system. For a virgin, un-tagged language, it may be possible to adapt a tagger program developed for another language, and this is generally more straightforward if the tag set for the new language parallels the old language tag set.

For example, Brill's tagger (Brill, 1993, 1995) was originally developed for pos-tagging English texts, but has been adapted to several languages including French (Lecomte 1998) and Arabic (Freeman 2001). Similarly, the CLAWS tagger (Leech/Garside/Atwell 1983), originally developed to pos-tag the LOB corpus of British English, has been adapted to other languages including Urdu (Hardie 2003) and Arabic (Khoja/Garside/Knowles 2001, Khoja 2003). In practice, a tagging scheme is inevitably influenced by the tractability of decisions made by the associated tagger program; for example, it is not always easy for a program to decide what function the word "one" has in an English text, so most English tagging schemes (except ICE) just have one tag for "one". It follows that the tag sets assigned to French, Urdu and Arabic texts by taggers originally built for tagging English may have been influenced by the English tag sets assigned by the original programs.

2.10. Adherence to standards

The EAGLES project (see Leech/Barnett/Kahrel 1996) embarked upon the task of setting standards for corpus annotation. The EAGLES guidelines propose a set of grammatical features to recognize in tag sets, including recommended and optional features. A language-neutral "intermediate tag set" is provided, using a numeric (non-mnemonic) coding for each feature; for example, *singular common noun* is N101000, *plural common noun* is N102000, *main verb infinitive* is V0002500100000. Each digit corresponds to a specific EAGLES-recognised grammatical feature; a zero shows this feature is not present (though it may be in other languages, e. g. *gender* in nouns). These intermediate tags are useful in allowing direct computational comparisons of tag sets across two or more languages, but clearly they are hard for humans to digest. Instead, corpus developers are free to use simpler mnemonics, as long as there is a simple mapping between intermediate tags and "human-friendly" tags.

Linguists devising a tag set for a virgin language may try to conform to agreed standards, for example tag sets partly conforming to the EAGLES guidelines have been applied beyond the original EU member-state languages, including to Urdu (Hardie 2003) and Arabic (Khoja/Garside/Knowles 2001). However, this may be an unwarranted imposition: for example, EAGLES guidelines come into conflict with some categories from traditional Arabic linguistics and grammar; and European part-of-speech categories may be quite inappropriate for Malay (Knowles/Don 2003).

Another type of standard is the de-facto widespread adoption of an existing tag set with significant credentials or backers. For example, the Brown Corpus was the first to be part-of-speech tagged, and it was the first major American corpus, which led to its widespread use in American computational linguistics research. Arguably other tag sets evolved from the Brown set, such as LOB and then ICE, have linguistic merit, but they have achieved less exposure in the American-dominated computational linguistics community.

For more on standards in Corpus Linguistics, see article 22.

2.11. Genre, register or type of language

To some linguists, the type of language may have a bearing on the grammatical categories to be employed; for example, they may think that to some extent spoken and written languages have different grammars. Spoken texts may include hesitations, repetitions, false starts, incomplete or partly-inaudible phrases, and other disfluencies not found in written texts; and they may include more informal or non-standard vocabulary and grammar. Some tag sets were developed for specialised corpora, e. g. the PoW corpus of children's conversations, or the Brown and LOB Corpora of written, published English. However the tag sets may still apply to other types of language, for example the LOB tag set was readily applied to the SEC Spoken English Corpus. Other tag sets were developed for corpora which deliberately aimed for a diverse variety of language, e. g. the ICE and BNC corpora contain both written and spoken language, and the respective ICE and BNC tag sets cover both.

2.12. Degree of delicacy of the tag set

It may seem strange to leave this issue to last: arguably the most obvious difference between rival tag sets for English corpora, for instance, is the number of tags, indicating the level of fine-graininess of analysis. However, this decision is heavily influenced by other criteria, which in effect are also decisions about delicacy; and decisions about the target application, available tagger software, standards to be adopted, and genre of the language may leave little room for debate on the appropriate level of delicacy. For example, section 2.8. suggested that the main reason for the difference in number of tags, or degree of delicacy, between the LOB and UPenn tag sets was the target user-group foreseen by the tag set developers.

3. Case studies of tag set development

To illustrate these issues, we outline a range of examples of tag set development and discuss how these criteria apply. First we consider tag sets for an online part-of-speech tagging service for **English**; then design of a tag set for another language from the same broad Indo-European language family, **Urdu**; then for a non-Indo-European language with a highly inflexional grammar, **Arabic**; then for a contrasting non-Indo-European language with isolating grammar, **Malay**.

3.1. Tag sets for an online English corpus part-of-speech tagging service

The AMALGAM project set up a free-to-use part-of-speech tagging service for the English Corpus Linguistics community (Atwell et al. 2000). For this diverse audience, it was decided NOT to develop or adopt a single standard tag set, but to allow users to choose from a range of options from the pioneering English corpus pos-tag sets illustrated in Table 23.1.

The Amalgam project team also tried some experiments with devising a set of mapping rules from one tag set to another (Hughes/Atwell 1994; Atwell/Hughes/Souter 1994; Hughes/Souter/Atwell 1995). The main lesson learnt was that this is non-trivial: the differences between tag sets cover the range of dimensions listed in section 2, and it was not feasible to draw up a simple set of mapping rules coping with all these dimensions of difference.

By offering a choice of the tag sets from Table 23.1, the Amalgam service managed to sit on the fence and leave users to make their own choices with regards to most of the tag set design criteria listed in section 2.

3.1.1. Mnemonic tag names

Users can choose from the mnemonic tag name schemes in Table 23.1, to suit their preferences and needs.

3.1.2. Underlying linguistic theory

Most of the tag sets in Table 23.1 are (claimed to be) "theory-neutral", although the PoW tag set does illustrate one modern "school" or theory of grammar, Systemic Functional grammar. Unfortunately, the Amalgam service could not offer tagging based on other modern theoretical approaches to grammar, such as GPSG or LFG, because no tagged training corpus was available to re-train the tagger.

3.1.3. Classification by form or function?

All of the alternatives illustrated in Table 23.1 were made available. These tag sets generally classify by function: words can have more than one pos-tag, varying according to syntactic context or function.

3.1.4. Idiosyncratic words

The tag sets in Table 23.1 include some variation in treatment of idiosyncratic words; for example, the different treatment of "one" in LOB and ICE mentioned in section 2.4.

3.1.5. Categorization problems

Table 23.1 illustrates one use of the Brown **QL** adverbial qualifier tag, on the word "as" when qualifying the adverb "well". However this is an idiosyncratic qualifier role, in that most other tagging schemes see "as well" as a single multi-word idiom: "as well" is not a typical example to illustrate or define the use of **QL**. Unfortunately, the tagged Brown corpus manual does not define **QL** much more clearly, beyond some more examples of its use.

Table 23.1 also illustrates different attitudes to avoiding inconsistency in distinguishing common and proper nouns, in the software name "the Dynix Gateways product". "Dynix" is clearly a proper name as it does not coincide with any common noun. "Gateways" could also be a proper name; but later in the sentence, "gateways" (without word-initial capital) is unanimously voted as a common noun by every tagging scheme. The BNC, and ICE schemes choose to categorise "Gateways" as a common noun consistently, regardless of word-initial-capital; whereas the Brown, LOB, UPenn, PoW and LLC schemes rule that the word-initial capitals consistently mark out nouns as proper, regardless of possible recurrence in the text in lower-case.

Most tag sets and tagging programs assume a word-type may have more than one pos-tag, but each specific word-token must have one pos-tag, decidable from the context (at least in principle). As explained in section 2.5., the UPenn tag set stands out by allowing "vertical slash" tag-pairs for genuinely ambiguous cases. However, the AMALGAM service was based on an automatic tagging program (the Brill tagger) which was unable to distinguish genuinely ambiguous words from the vast majority of words which can safely be given just one tag; so in practice, "vertical slash" tags are not used in processing texts to be tagged.

3.1.6. Tokenisation: Dividing text into words

The text to be tagged is first passed through a tokeniser which applies various formatting rules to divide the text into words. This can be turned off when mailing data to amalgam-tagger, by specifying 'notoken'. The different English corpus tagging schemes tokenise some special cases differently, as outlined in section 2.6. The AMALGAM tokeniser is in effect a compromise algorithm which tokenizes text the same way for all tag sets, to simplify alignment and direct comparisons of rival taggings of the same text, as illustrated by Table 23.1. Users who require a different tokenization are recommended to tokenise the text themselves, and then turn off tokenization (via 'notoken') when using the Amalgam sevice.

3.1.7. Multi-word lexical items

Table 23.1 illustrates some alternative treatments of the multi-word lexical item "as well". However, this is NOT the direct output of the AMALGAM tagger service: it has been proofread and hand-corrected to reflect the tagging described in the handbooks or other documentation defining each tag set. The Amalgam service (based on the Brill tagger) attempts to supply a pos-tag to every "token" passed from the tokeniser, and it does NOT include a special module for analysis of multi-word lexical items (on the basis that these account for a tiny proportion of the total words in a corpus, not worth the additional processing complexity which would be required to handle these properly). In general, this results in incorrect tagging of most multi-word lexical items.

3.1.8. Target users and/or application

The AMALGAM tagging service was aimed at casual users, who wanted to explore whether and how pos-tags might be useful in their research or teaching, without having to install and set up tagging software on their own computer. As part of such explorative, speculative use, many users tried more than one available pos-tag set, to discover which would be most appropriate to their needs. This implies that an online pos-tagging service should indeed offer a variety of pos-tag sets to choose from, rather than just offering a single scheme.

3.1.9. Availability and/or adaptability of tagger software

The AMALGAM tagging service was powered by the Brill tagger, which could be re-trained to any pos-tag scheme embodied in an existing pos-tagged corpus. The Brill tagger can be freely downloaded from a website, and comes "pre-trained" on the tagged Brown corpus; it was fairly straightforward to re-train with other English pos-tagged corpora.

3.1.10. Adherence to standards

The AMALGAM project did not have access to a corpus tagged with EAGLES guidelines pos-tags, to re-train the Brill tagger; hence EAGLES-tagging is not available. However, the major English tagged corpora, particularly the Brown corpus, have become de-facto standards in Computational Linguistics research, so the Amalgam service does in effect allow users to work with "standard" tag sets. (Atwell et al. 2000, 18) notes: "The most popular schemes are LOB, UPenn, Brown, ICE, and SEC (in that order), with relatively little demand for Parts, LLC, and PoW; this reflects the popularity of the source corpora in the Corpus Linguistics community".

3.1.11. Genre, register or type of language

The tag sets offered by the AMALGAM service aim to cover a wide range of genres, including both spoken and written language. The only constraint noted in the help-file is: "Please note that the tagger is intended for English text – it will not work for languages other than English". This constraint was specified following user feedback that their French texts were not being pos-tagged correctly!

3.1.12 Degree of delicacy of the tag set

User feedback suggests that users select a tag set appropriate to their application on the basis of the above criteria, and NOT simply according to number of tags in the tag set.

3.2. Developing a tag set for another Indo-European language: Urdu

Urdu is outside the original European Union member state languages; however, it is an Indo-European language and hence one might expect that many of the EAGLES standard guidelines could be applied. (Hardie 2003, 2004) demonstrated this by developing a tag set for pos-tagging an Urdu corpus (Baker/Hardie/McEnery/Tayaram 2003).

3.2.1. Mnemonic tag names

The features recognized by the tag set were largely those of the EAGLES guidelines. However, instead of the numerical-code "intermediate tag set", (Hardie 2003, 2004) specifies mnemonic tags reminiscent of the BNC tag set; for example, II for *unmarked postposition* (in BNC-C6, *preposition*); CC for *coordinating conjunction* (as in BNC-C6). In general, the first two letters show the broad word-class, then one character is used to denote each marked grammatical feature. Urdu has more complex inflexional morphology than English, so some tags are quite long; for example, JJF2N for *marked feminine plural nominative adjective*, NNMM1N for *common marked masculine singular nominative noun*.

3.2.2. Underlying linguistic theory

Urdu does not have a long-established tradition of grammatical description, so Hardie based his categories on a modern standard grammar textbook (Schmidt 1999). Other available sources tended to cover only specific aspects of Urdu grammar, for example features which learners need to learn first.

3.2.3. Classification by form or function?

The example tags given in section 3.2.1. are based on morphological form. The tag set also includes some distinct tags for different functions of certain words. However, the focus of Hardie (2003) is on the tag set rather than the tagging program or tagged corpus, and there are no examples which illustrate a form/function conflict.

3.2.4. Idiosyncratic words

Urdu has some idiosyncratic words which do not fit readily into the EAGLES categories; for example, there are special tags PA for the *honorific pronoun "āp"*, AL for *Arabic definite article "al"* found only with Arabic loan-words.

3.2.5. Categorization problems

The tags are defined by examples; Hardie (2003) does not discuss the issue of disambiguation of problem cases, although it does imply that some words may belong to more than one tag-class and hence a tagger will have to select a single tag in context.

3.2.6. Tokenisation: Dividing text into words

This was a challenge: "... many things described in the literature on Urdu grammar as suffixes are actually written as independent words ... For consistency, the (essentially arbitrary) decision was taken to treat every orthographic space as a word break even if it occurs within a lexical word ... Word breaks are also introduced in some places where there is no orthographic space, e. g. where clitics precede/follow another word without a break." (Hardie 2003, 302). This led Hardie to add a tag LL for *non-grammatical lexical element*, to tag the initial token(s) of a multi-token lexical item. For example, Urdu for "telephone" is "teli fon" – the first token "teli" is tagged LL.

3.2.7. Multi-word lexical items

Hardie (2003, 302) notes that the above handling of *non-grammatical lexical elements* is "... only partially analogous to the problem of multi-word idioms in English and similar languages ... In these cases, there is also an analysable internal syntactic structure ... In the Urdu case, it would be very difficult to assign any internal structure to *teli fon* ...". However, Hardie does not discuss or illustrate how "true" equivalents of multi-word idioms would be treated in his tagging system.

3.2.8. Target users and/or application

There was no specific target user group or application, beyond the stated aim of developing a pos-tagger for one of the South Asian languages covered by the EMILLE project (Baker et al. 2003). Hence the tag set was generic and not constrained to a specific application, following the lead of pioneering English tagged corpora.

3.2.9. Availability and/or adaptability of tagger software

Hardie worked within the Lancaster UCREL tradition of Corpus Linguistics, and was undoubtedly influenced by the CLAWS heritage of taggers and tag sets for the LOB and

BNC corpora. However, the tag set for Urdu was designed before a tagger, to ensure it was primarily based on linguistic principles, without compromising to suit computational feasibility or efficiency.

3.2.10. Adherence to standards

As already illustrated, the Urdu tag set fitted EAGLES guidelines, with some minor additions.

3.2.11. Genre, register or type of language

The tag set was developed for the Urdu component of the EMILLE corpus of South Asian languages (Baker et al. 2003), which includes both written texts (e. g. UK government advice leaflets) and spoken texts (e. g. transcripts of UK BBC Asian Network radio broadcasts). Hence, the tag set is not limited to one type of language.

3.2.12. Degree of delicacy of the tag set

Hardie does not explicitly state how many tags there are in his tag set; however, the list of tags in the Appendix shows that the complex morphology of Urdu generates a large number of tags to distinguish many possible combinations of grammatical features. For example, whereas English tag sets generally have a single *preposition* tag, the Urdu tag set has 10 different tags for *postpositions*, to capture possible feature combinations of *unmarked/marked/clitic, masculine/feminine, singular/plural, nominative/oblique*.

3.3. A tag set compatible with Arabic academic traditions

Arabic has been used and studied far longer than English. Classical Arabic was standardized around fourteen hundred years ago, when the Koran became in effect the definitive corpus of the language. Since then Muslim scholars have studied and documented the Arabic language and grammar, keeping it from straying too far from what they believed were the words of God, narrated to Mohammad by an angel, to be passed on verbatim to and by all believers. Modern Standard Arabic has added modern vocabulary, and avoids some of the more complicated grammatical forms, but is essentially the same language.

Western researchers have only recently shown much interest in Arabic, perhaps because of the very different script, morphology, lexis and grammar; and corpus linguists have only recently had open access to Arabic corpora (see Al-Sulaiti/Atwell 2006), and concordancers (Roberts/Al-Sulaiti/Atwell 2006). Corpus linguists have not attempted to apply EAGLES standards to Arabic, a non-Indo-European language. If they did, the tag set arrived at might well seem alien to Arabic linguists and grammarians. The Arabic tag set and part-of-speech Tagger developed by (Khoja/Garside/Knowles 2001; Khoja

2003) came from the Lancaster UCREL tradition of Corpus Linguistics, and like Hardie, Khoja was undoubtedly influenced by the CLAWS heritage of taggers and tag sets for the LOB and BNC corpora. However, Khoja's main influence was traditional Arabic grammatical theory, still used today in Modern Standard Arabic.

3.3.1. Mnemonic tag names

The tags cited in examples in (Khoja 2003) generally use one capital letter (sometimes with an extra lower-case letter) to show each grammatical feature, reminiscent of the LOB and BNC tag sets. For example, VPPl2M is *verb perfect plural second-person masculine;* VISg2FI is *verb imperfect singular second-person feminine indicative*; NPrPDu3 is *noun pronoun personal dual third-person*. This illustrates the complex morphology of Arabic; but there are also some simpler tags, for example NP for *proper noun* (such as a name, by default singular). For the benefit of English-speaking corpus linguists, Khoja has used terminology from English grammar rather than Arabic tradition in naming categories and features; however, the tags do also have equivalents in Arabic script, for the benefit of Arabic linguists.

3.3.2. Underlying linguistic theory

Traditional Arabic grammarians recognize only three main parts-of-speech, which map roughly on to nouns, verbs, and particles. Hence, all pos-tags start with N, V or P. Other EAGLES traditional European categories are subclasses of one of these three, mainly on the basis that they share inflexional patterns; for example, pronouns and adjectives inflect like nouns so they are classed with nouns.

3.3.3. Classification by form or function?

As already stated, traditional Arabic grammar groups words according to their inflexional behaviour, which implies that word-class is dependent on form. A complication peculiar to Arabic is the writing system. Vowels are normally omitted in written Arabic, and left for the reader to infer; unfortunately, vowels can encode grammatical category or feature information. Typically a root or lexical item consists of three consonants, and the vowels between these consonants add grammatical information. For example, the three letters *ktb* can stand for the verb *kataba* meaning 'he wrote', or for the plural noun *kutub* 'books'. The result is that in a written text, many words are rendered ambiguous through lack of vowels, and a tagger has to work out classification of each word taking context or function into account. Human readers of Arabic text manage this disambiguation task, in effect subconsciously tagging the text to understand it.

One major exception to this is the Koran: to ensure it is pronounced (and parsed) correctly, vowels are traditionally included. This makes the Koran a potential "Gold Standard" corpus for Arabic tagging and NLP research.

3.3.4. Idiosyncratic words

Arabic grammatical tradition already recognizes a subclass of *Particle* translated as *Exceptions* by Khoja, to cover some idiosyncratic words which do not fit other patterns: "... These include the Arabic words that are equivalent to the word except and the prefixes non-, un-, and im-." (Khoja 2003, 52).

3.3.5. Categorization problems

Tags are explained by examples, but there is no detailed handbook of "case law" defining how to disambiguate problem cases. As explained above, absence of vowels in most printed text renders many of the words ambiguous. (Khoja 2003) reports results of some initial tagger program experiments, in which 18%–23% of words were unambiguous; but many of the remaining words were not in her lexicon or could not be handled by her stemmer, so these figures are only indicative.

The tagger progam uses the Viterbi algorithm (see article 24) to disambiguate words, and this assumes all words should only have one tag: there is no scope for accepting "truly ambiguous" cases, as in the UPenn tagging scheme.

3.3.6. Tokenisation: Dividing text into words

Particles are sometimes affixes; for example the definite article 'al' is well-known as a prefix in Arabic loan-words in other languages, e. g. algebra, Algarve. These are handled by a compound tag, reminiscent of the Brown tagging scheme. For morphologically complex words a combination of tags is used. For example, the word *walktab* 'and the book' is given the tag PC+NCSgMND, where PC indicates a particle that is a conjunction, and NCSgMND indicates a singular, masculine, nominative, definite noun.

3.3.7. Multi-word lexical items

The prototype tagger reported in (Khoja 2003) was based on a lexicon of under 10,000 word-types, extracted from a corpus of about 50,000 word-tokens. Multi-word lexical items were not considered separately.

3.3.8. Target users and/or application

The Arabic tag set was developed for general Corpus Linguistics research, and so aimed to be generic, analogous to the pioneer English corpus tag sets of Table 23.1.

3.3.9. Availability and/or adaptability of tagger software

The CLAWS system was available to Khoja and her Lancaster colleagues, but her Arabic tag set was not unduly influenced by this: the guiding principle was compatibility with Arabic grammar tradition.

3.3.10. Adherence to standards

The standards adhered to in this case were those of Arabic grammar tradition. However, the English translations of category and feature names were drawn from standard terminology found in the EAGLES guidelines.

3.3.11. Genre, register or type of language

The initial 50,000-word training corpus was extracted from the Saudi Al-Jazirah newspaper (date 03/03/1999); initial tagging experiments were done on other newspaper texts, and a social science paper. However, given that the tag set seems to be as general as analogous tag sets developed at Lancaster such as BNC, we can hope that the tag set will cover other genres, and spoken texts.

3.3.12. Degree of delicacy of the tag set

As with Hardie's tag set for Urdu, the complex inflexional morphology generates many possible combinations of grammatical features, leading to a large number of tags. Khoja states there are 131 tags, but (presumably) this does not include all possible combination-tags for morphologically complex words, such as the example cited above, PC+NCSgMND.

3.4. A tag set for Malay corpus linguistics

Western researchers have also tried to apply Indo-European grammatical concepts to Malay, another non-Indo-European language. In contrast to Arabic, there is no "home-grown" Malay tradition of grammar, other than the ex-colonial tradition of applying concepts from English. Knowles/Don (2003, 2005) are developing a tag set to use in tagging the Dewan Bahasa dan Pustaka (DBP) 80-million-word corpus of Malay texts; their experience suggests that the "English tradition" may be misplaced, and Malay may be better served by a drastically rethought notion of part-of-speech.

3.4.1. Mnemonic tag names

The example tags cited in (Knowles/Don 2003) use Malay tag-names; for example *kata sifat* 'adjective', *kata nama* 'noun', *kata kerja* 'verb'. They do this to distinguish form from function (see below), and also to dissuade users from assuming direct parallels with European or Arabic categories. Unfortunately, they do not present a complete list of tags, but say: "... some of our class labels look like traditional parts-of-speech, but the underlying definitions are entirely different" (ibid., 423).

3.4.2. Underlying linguistic theory

Knowles/Don (2003, 423) note that "... European parts-of-speech are the accepted point of departure for considering grammatical class in Malay (see Asmah, 1993; Sneddon, 1996)". An alternative is to apply the Arabic tradition of three major grammatical categories *noun, verb, particle* (e. g. Abdullah 1974). However, Knowles/Don (2003, 424) argue that a tag set for Malay must take account of 'syntactic drift': "... The class of many words in European languages is made unambiguous by their morphology ... However, in view of the lack of any inflectional morphology, Malay has a large number of simplex forms which belong to no clearly defined class, and appear to 'drift' from one class into another. For example, *masuk* is the normal word for 'enter', which makes it a kind of verb; but it is used in such a way on buildings and in carparks that it could also be taken to be a noun 'entrance'...".

This 'drift' has been recognized by others, for example (Lewis 1947, xvii): "... Malay words change their function according to context. Be prepared for this, and do not attempt to force the language into a set mould. It will escape".

3.4.3. Classification by form or function?

Knowles and Don's radical response to 'syntactic drift' is to separate lexical class or form from syntactic function, and give each word in the lexicon only one class-tag. "... we use the term 'tag' to label a lexical class, and 'slot' to refer to a position in syntactic structure. We maintain the distinction consistently by giving lexical classes Malay labels, and syntactic slots and constructions English labels" (Knowles/Don 2003, 425).

3.4.4. Idiosyncratic words

Knowles and Don's examples include a couple of idiosyncratic words: *relative particle* 'yang' (e. g. 'pintu yang hijau': 'door that is green'); and *negative particle* 'tidak'. In general, Knowles and Don advocate that grammatically idiosyncratic words should NOT be given a special tag, but instead that the idiosyncratic grammatical behaviour should be captured by rules in the parser referring not to tags but to individual word forms: "... for example, the Malay expression corresponding to *o'clock* is a "verb" *pukul* normally meaning 'to hit, strike (e. g. a gong)'. To handle an expression such as *pukul tiga* 'three o'clock', the parser has to test for the specific word *pukul* before a numeral, and so the fact that *pukul* is tagged in the lexicon as a "verb" causes no problem at all" (Knowles/Don 2003, 425).

3.4.5. Categorization problems

As explained above, Knowles and Don's radical approach to categorization problems is to avoid tagging ambiguity by allowing only one tag for each word in the lexicon. They suggest this could even work for English: for example, instead of saying a word like *telephone* is ambiguous between noun and verb, they suggest a single tag or lexical category for words which can function as either nouns or verbs, distinct from lexical categories *noun (only)* and *verb (only)*. Interestingly, this has also been suggested by Machine Learning research on unsupervised learning of word-clusters, (e. g. Atwell 1987; Atwell/Drakos 1987; Hughes/Atwell 1994).

3.4.6. Tokenisation: Dividing text into words

Although Malay lacks inflexional morphology, it does have derivational morphology: for example, *besar* 'big', *membesarkan* 'enlarge', *kebesaran* 'size'; or *baca* 'read', *pembaca* 'reader', *bacaan* 'reading'. Sometimes this leads to problematic tokenisation: for example, "... the "verb" *berbaju* 'wear a shirt' is formed from the "noun" *baju* 'shirt', and this noun can still be followed by an "adjective" such as *merha* 'red' ... the structure is not strictly ((berbaju)(merah)) but (ber(baju merah))" (Knowles/Don 2003, 426).

3.4.7. Multi-word lexical items

The only examples cited by Knowles and Don are multi-word adverbs. There is no separate lexical class of *adverb (only)* in Malay. Instead, a *kata sifat* 'adjective' can also function as a verbal modifier; and Malay also has idiomatic adverbial constructions in which *dengan* 'with' or *secara* 'manner' is followed by a *kata sifat*, e. g. *dengan betul* 'with correct, correctly', *secara betul* 'manner correct, correctly'.

3.4.8. Target users and/or application

The most obvious user of this tag set is Dewan Bahasa dan Pustaka (DBP), the government body responsible for coordinating the use of the Malay language in Malaysia and Brunei. The work should be of wider interest in corpus linguistics, particularly cross-language studies may suggest ways in which the radically different approach to tagging may apply to other languages. As this is a pioneering first attempt to develop a tag set for Malay, analogous to the pioneering English tag sets, Knowles and Don have focused on generic, theoretical issues rather than designing a tag set for a specific application.

3.4.9. Availability and/or adaptability of tagger software

There is no tagger for Malay; furthermore, most existing taggers focus on techniques for choosing the best tag for ambiguous words, which makes them inappropriate for Knowles and Don's model of tagging.

3.4.10. Adherence to standards

Of all the tag sets discussed in this article, this is the furthest from compliance to any standards!

3.4.11. Genre, register or type of language

The sample Knowles and Don have worked on contains only literary texts: four modern novels. However, they make no suggestion that their tag set is limited to literary texts.

3.4.12. Degree of delicacy of the tag set

Knowles/Don (2003, 423) state "... Our tagset currently contains 119 tags in 19 different major classes". However, they only illustrate a few major word-classes, and give no further indication of delicacy of distinctions in the tag set.

4. Conclusions

English corpus linguists have developed a variety of tag sets for part-of-speech tagging, reflecting a range of target applications for pos-tagged corpora, pos-tagging software, linguistic intuitions and theories about categories and degree of delicacy required, adherence to standards, genre or type of language to be analysed, and other factors or constraints. In practice, for many applications of pos-tagged text, a small pos-tag set with few delicate disctinctions is sufficient, and using more complex or delicate tag sets makes little difference. English language researchers may be better off using a pos-tag set for which an accurate tagging software system is readily available; for example, the BNC tag set is widely used by English language researchers, not so much because of its intrinsic superiority over rival tag sets, but because an online pos-tagging service is freely available for tagging of researchers' own texts. This has the knock-on bonus effect of making research results involving part-of-speech information more directly comparable, as the same tag set is used in these results.

Corpus Linguistics has expanded beyond English, and there are now a range of tagging schemes and tagged corpora for at least a few other languages (e. g. German, French, Chinese). However, for corpus linguists studying more exotic languages, particularly non-European languages, there is not the same wealth of existing tag sets to choose from. If a pioneering researcher has developed a pos-tag set for such a language (e. g. Arabic, Urdu, Malay), it is tempting to adopt this as a de-facto "standard" rather than invest time and effort in developing a custom-made tag set. However, the researcher should still evaluate whether an existing tag set is "fit for purpose", as pioneers are not always perfect: the first tag set developed for a language may not suit all applications. If there is no existing tag set for a "virgin" language, the developer can still learn from the range of experiences of Corpus Linguists working with other languages. Hopefully this article can help the researcher in evaluating existing candidates, and if necessary, in developing or revising a tag set suited to the target use or application.

5. Literature

Aarts, Jan (1996), A Tribute to W. Nelson Francis and Henry Kučera: Grammatical Annotation. In: *ICAME Journal* 20, 104–107.

Aarts, Jan/van Halteren, Hans/Oostdijk, Nelleke (1996), The TOSCA Analysis System. In: Koster, C./Oltmans, E. (eds.), *Proceedings of the first AGFL Workshop*. Technical Report CSI-R9604, Computing Science Institute, University of Nijmegen, 181–191.

Abdullah, Hasan (1974), *The Morphology of Malay*. Kuala Lumpur: Dewan Behasa dan Pustaka.

Al-Sulaiti, Latifa/Atwell, Eric (2006), The Design of a Corpus of Contemporary Arabic. In: *International Journal of Corpus Linguistics* 11, 135–171.

Andersen, Gisle/Stenström, Anna-Brita (1996), COLT: A Progress Report. In: *ICAME Journal* 20, 133–136.

Archer, Dawn/Rayson, Paul/Wilson, Andrew/McEnery, Tony (eds.) (2003), *Proceedings of the Corpus Linguistics 2003 Conference*, Lancaster University, UCREL Technical Paper 16.

Asmah, Haji Omar (1993), *Nahu Melayu Mutakhir* (revised edition). Kuala Lumpur: Dewan Bahasa dan Pustaka.

Atwell, Eric (1982), *LOB Corpus Tagging Project: Post-edit Handbook*. Department of Linguistics and Modern English Language, University of Lancaster.

Atwell, Eric (1983), Constituent Likelihood Grammar. In: *ICAME Journal* 7, 34–66.

Atwell, Eric (1987), A Parsing Expert System which Learns from Corpus Analysis. In: Meijs, Willem (ed.), *Corpus Linguistics and Beyond: Proceedings of the Seventh International Conference on English Language Research on Computerised Corpora*. Amsterdam: Rodopi, 227–235.

Atwell, Eric (1989), *Grammatical Analysis of SCRIBE: Spoken Corpus Recordings in British English*. SERC Advanced Research Fellowship Proposal, Science and Engineering Research Council.

Atwell, Eric (1993), Corpus-based Statistical Modelling of English Grammar. In: Souter, Clive/Atwell, Eric (eds.), *Corpus-based Computational Linguistics*. Amsterdam: Rodopi, 195–215.

Atwell, Eric (1996), Comparative Evaluation of Grammatical Annotation Models. In: Sutcliffe/Koch/McElligott 1996, 25–46.

Atwell, Eric (2003), A Word-token-based Machine Learning Algorithm for Neoposy: Coining New Parts of Speech. In: Archer et al. 2003, 43–47.

Atwell, Eric (2004), Clustering of Word Types and Unification of Word Tokens into Grammatical Word-classes. In: Bel, B./Marlien, I. (eds.), *Proceedings of TALN04: XI Conference sur le Traitement Automatique des Langues Naturelles*. ATALA, Volume 1, 27–32.

Atwell, Eric/Al-Sulaiti, Latifa/Al-Osaimi, Saleh/Abu Shawar, Bayan (2004), A Review of Arabic Corpus Analysis Tools. In: Bel, B./Marlien, I. (eds.), *Proceedings of TALN04: XI Conference sur le Traitement Automatique des Langues Naturelles*. ATALA, Volume 2, 229–234.

Atwell, Eric/Demetriou, George/Hughes, John/Schriffin, Amanda/Souter, Clive/Wilcock, Sean (2000), A Comparative Evaluation of Modern English Corpus Grammatical Annotation Schemes. In: *ICAME Journal* 24, 7–23.

Atwell, Eric/Drakos, Nicos (1987), Pattern Recognition Applied to the Acquisition of a Grammatical Classification System from Unrestricted English Text. In: Maegaard, Bente (ed.), *Proceedings of EACL: Third Conference of the European Chapter of the Association for Computational Linguistics*. New Jersey: ACL, 56–62.

Atwell, Eric/Hughes, John/Souter, Clive (1994), AMALGAM: Automatic Mapping among Lexico-grammatical Annotation Models. In: Klavans, Judith/Resnik, Philip (eds.), *The Balancing Act – Combining Symbolic and Statistical Approaches to Language. Proceedings of the Workshop in Conjunction with the 32nd Annual Meeting of the Association for Computational Linguistics*. New Mexico State University, Las Cruces, NM, 11–20.

Baker, Paul/Hardie, Andrew/McEnery, Tony/Jayaram, Sri (2003), Constructing Corpora of South Asian Languages. In: Archer et al. 2003, 71–80.

Belmore, Nancy (1991), Tagging Brown with the LOB Tagging Suite. In: *ICAME Journal* 15, 63–86.

Benello, Julian/Mackie, Andrew/Anderson, James A. (1989), Syntactic Category Disambiguation with Neural Networks. In: *Computer Speech and Language* 3, 203–217.

Black, William/Neal, Philip (1996), Using ALICE to Analyse a Software Manual Corpus. In: Sutcliffe/Koch/McElligott 1996, 47–56.

Booth, Barbara (1985), Revising CLAWS. In: *ICAME Journal* 9, 29–35.

Brill, Eric (1993), *A Corpus-based Approach to Language Learning*. PhD thesis, Department of Computer and Information Science, University of Pennsylvania.

Brill, Eric (1995), Transformation-based Error driven Learning and Natural Language Processing: A Case Study in Part-of-speech Tagging. In: *Computational Linguistics* 21, 543–566.

Briscoe, Edward/Carroll, John (1993), Generalised Probabilistic LR Parsing of Natural Language (Corpora) with Unification-based Grammars. In: *Computational Linguistics* 19, 25–60.

Cure, The (1980), *A Forest*. Fiction Records.

Eeg-Olofsson, Mats (1991), *Word-class Tagging: Some Computational Tools*. PhD thesis. Department of Linguistics and Phonetics, University of Lund, Sweden.

Elliott, John/Atwell, Eric (2000), Is there Anybody out there?: The Detection of Intelligent and Generic Language-like Features. In: *Journal of the British Interplanetary Society* 53(1/2), 13–22.

Fang, Alex (2005), Robust Practical Parsing of English with an Automatically Generated Grammar. PhD thesis, University College London.

Freeman, Andrew (2001), Brill's POS Tagger and a Morphology Parser for Arabic. In: *Proceedings of ACL/EACL 2001 Workshop on Arabic Language Processing: Status and Prospects*. Toulouse, France. Available at: http://www.elsnet.org/acl2001-arabic.html.

Garside, Roger (1996), The Robust Tagging of Unrestricted Text: The BNC Experience. In: Thomas, Jenny/Short, Mick (eds.), *Using Corpora for Language Research: Studies in the Honour of Geoffrey Leech*. London: Longman, 167–180.

Greenbaum, Sidney (1993), The Tagset for the International Corpus of English. In: Clive Souter/Atwell, Eric (eds.), *Corpus-based Computational Linguistics*. Amsterdam: Rodopi, 11–24.

Greene, Barbara/Rubin, Gerald (1981), *Automatic Grammatical Tagging of English*. Providence, RI: Department of Linguistics, Brown University.

Grefenstette, Gregory (1996), Using the SEXTANT Low-level Parser to Analyse a Software Manual Corpus. In: Sutcliffe/Koch/McElligott 1996, 139–158.

Hanks, Patrick (ed.) (1979), *Collins English Dictionary*. London and Glasgow: Collins.

Hardie, Andrew (2003), Developing a Tagset for Automated Part-of-speech Tagging in Urdu. In: Archer et al. 2003, 298–307.

Hardie, Andrew (2004), The Computational Analysis of Morphosyntactic Categories in Urdu. PhD thesis, University of Lancaster.

Hughes, John/Atwell, Eric (1994), The Automated Evaluation of Inferred Word Classifications. In: Cohn, Anthony (ed.), *Proceedings of the European Conference on Artificial Intelligence (ECAI)*. Chichester: John Wiley, 535–539.

Hughes, John/Souter, Clive/Atwell, Eric (1995), Automatic Extraction of Tagset Mappings from Parallel-annotated Corpora. In: *From Texts to Tags: Issues in Multilingual Language Analysis. Proceedings of SIGDAT Workshop in Conjunction with the 7th Conference of the European Chapter of the Association for Computational Linguistics*. University College Dublin, Ireland, 10–17.

Johansson, Stig/Atwell, Eric/Garside, Roger/Leech, Geoffrey (1986), *The Tagged LOB Corpus: Users' Manual*. Bergen University, Norway: ICAME, The Norwegian Computing Centre for the Humanities.

Karlsson, Fred/Voutilainen, Atro/Heikkilä, Juha/Anttila, Arto (1995), *Constraint Grammar: A Language-independent System for Parsing Unrestricted Text*. Berlin: Mouton de Gruyter.

Khoja, Shereen (2003), APT: An Automatic Arabic Part-of-speech Tagger. PhD thesis, Lancaster University.

Khoja, Shereen/Garside, Roger/Knowles, Gerry (2001), A Tagset for the Morphosyntactic Tagging of Arabic. In: Rayson, Paul/Wilson, Andrew/McEnery, Tony/Hardie, Andrew/Khoja, Shereen (eds.), *Proceedings of the Corpus Linguistics 2001 Conference*. UCREL Technical Paper 13, Lancaster University, 341.

Kilgarriff, Adam (2007), Message to *CORPORA@uib.no*, Discussion Forum on the History of Corpus Linguistics.

Knowles, Gerry/Don, Zuraidah Mohd (2003), Tagging a Corpus of Malay Texts, and Coping with "Syntactic Drift". In: Archer et al. 2003, 422–428.

Knowles, Gerry/Don, Zuraidah Mohd (2005), MALEX: Providing Linguistic Information and Tools for Automated Processing of Malay Texts. In: *Proceedings of O-COCOSDA-2005 International Conference on Speech Databases and Assessments*. Jakarta, Indonesia, 138–143.

Kytö, Merja/Voutilainen, Atro (1995), Applying the Constraint Grammar Parser of English to the Helsinki Corpus. In: *ICAME Journal* 19, 23–48.

Lecomte, Josette (1998), *Le categoriseur Brill14-JL5 / WinBrill-0.3*. Technical report, Institut National de la Langue Francaise.

Leech, Geoffrey/Barnett, Ros/Kahrel, Peter (1996), *EAGLES Final Report and Guidelines for the Syntactic Annotation of Corpora*. EAGLES Report EAG-TCWG-SASG/1.5. See also http://www.ilc.pi.cnr.it/EAGLES96/home.html.

Leech, Geoffrey/Garside, Roger/Atwell, Eric (1983), The Automatic Grammatical Tagging of the LOB Corpus. In: *ICAME Journal* 7, 13–33.

Lewis, M. Blanche (1947), *Teach Yourself Malay*. London: English Universities Press.

Lin, Dekang (1994), PRNCIPAR – an Efficient, Broad-coverage, Principle-based Parser. In: *Proceedings of COLING-94*. Kyoto, Japan, 482–488.

Lin, Dekang (1996), Using PRINCIPAR to Analyse a Software Manual Corpus. In: Sutcliffe/Koch/McElligott 1996, 103–118.

Lüdeling, Anke/Evert, Stefan (2003), Linguistic Experience and Productivity: Corpus Evidence for Fine-grained Distinctions. In: Archer et al. 2003, 475–483.

Madonna (1984), *Like a Virgin*. Sire Records.

Manning, Christopher/Schütze, Hinrich (1999), *Foundations of Statistical Natural Language Processing*. Cambridge, MA: MIT Press.

Marcus, Mitchell/Santorini, Beatrice/Marcinkiewicz, Mary Ann (1993), Building a Large Annotated Corpus of English: The Penn Treebank. In: *Computational Linguistics* 19, 313–330.

O'Donoghue, Timothy (1991), Taking a Parsed Corpus to the Cleaners: The EPOW Corpus. In: *ICAME Journal* 15, 55–62.

O'Donoghue, Timothy (1993), Reversing the Process of Generation in Systemic Grammar. PhD thesis, University of Leeds.

Oostdijk, Nelleke (1996), Using the TOSCA Analysis System to Analyse a Software Manual Corpus. In: Sutcliffe/Koch/McElligott 1996, 179–206.

Osborne, Miles (1996), Using the Robust Alvey Natural Language Toolkit to Analyse a Software Manual Corpus. In: Sutcliffe/Koch/McElligott 1996, 119–138.

Owen, Marion 1987. Evaluating Automatic Grammatical Tagging of Text. In: *ICAME Journal* 11, 18–26.

Qiao, Hong Liang/Huang, Renje (1998), Design and Implementation of AGTS Probabilistic Tagger. In: *ICAME Journal* 22, 23–48.

Roberts, Andrew/Al-Sulaiti, Latifa /Atwell, Eric (2006), aConCorde: Towards an Open-source, Extendable Concordancer for Arabic. In: *Corpora Journal* 1, 39–57.

San torini, Beatrice (1990), *Part-of-speech Tagging Guidelines for the Penn Treebank Project*. Technical Report MS-CIS-90-47. University of Pennsylvania: Department of Computer and Information Science. Available at ftp.cis.upenn.edu/pub/treebank/doc/tagguide.ps.gz.

Schiller, Anne/Teufel, Simone/Thielen, C. (1995), *Guidelines für das Tagging Deutscher Textkorpora mit STTS*. Technical Report, Universität Stuttgart and Universität Tübingen. Available at http://www.sfs.nphil.uni-tuebingen.de/Elwis/stts/stts.html.

Schmidt, Ruth (1999), *Urdu: An Essential Grammar*. London: Routledge.

Sleator, Daniel/Temperley, Davy (1991), *Parsing English with a Link Grammar*. Technical Report CMU-CS-91-196, School of Computer Science, Carnegie Mellon University.

Sneddon, James (1996), *Indonesian: A Comprehensive Grammar*. London: Routledge.

Souter, Clive (1989a), The Communal Project: Extracting a Grammar from the Polytechnic of Wales Corpus. In: *ICAME Journal* 13, 20–27.

Souter, Clive (1989b), *A Short Handbook to the Polytechnic of Wales Corpus*. Bergen University, Norway: ICAME, The Norwegian Computing Centre for the Humanities.

Souter, Clive (1996), A Corpus-trained Parser for Systemic-functional Syntax. PhD Thesis, University of Leeds.

Sutcliffe, Richard/Koch, Heinz-Detlev/McElligott, Annette (eds.) (1996), *Industrial Parsing of Software Manuals*. Amsterdam: Rodopi.

Sutcliffe, Richard/McElligott, Annette (1996), Using the Link Parser of Sleator and Temperley to Analyse a Software Manual Corpus. In: Sutcliffe/Koch/McElligott 1996, 89–102.

Taylor, Lolita/Knowles, Gerry (1988), *Manual of Information to Accompany the SEC Corpus: The Machine Readable Corpus of Spoken English*. University of Lancaster: Unit for Computer Research on the English Language. Available at http://khnt.hit.uib.no/icame/manuals/gec/INDEX.HTM.

Teahan, Bill (1998), Modelling English Text PhD Thesis, Department of Computer Science, University of Waikato, New Zealand.

Thielen, Christine/Schiller, Anne/Teufel, Simone/Stöckert, Christine (1999), *Guidelines für das Tagging deutscher Textkorpora mit STTS*. Technical report, Institut für Maschinelle Sprachverarbeitung, University of Stuttgart and Seminar für Sprachwissenschaft, University of Tübingen.

Treebank (1999), *The Penn Treebank Project website*. www.cis.upenn.edu/~treebank/home.html.

Eric Atwell, Leeds (UK)

24. Tokenizing and part-of-speech tagging

This article covers two different topics. Section 1 deals with tokenization and section 2 with part of speech tagging. Both sections are self-contained.

1. Tokenizing

1.1. Introduction

Most natural language processing applications such as part-of-speech taggers, parsers, and stemmers operate on text which is segmented into sentences and *tokens*. Tokens are words, numbers, punctuation marks, parentheses, quotation marks, and similar entities. The segmentation of text is also called *tokenizing*. Here is an example sentence from the Wall Street Journal corpus:

"Most customers don't want to sit in a turboprop for 2 1/2 to three hours," Mr. Lowe said.

Using the tags <S> and </S> as sentence delimiters and newlines as token delimiters, this sentence could be tokenized as follows:

<S>
"
Most
customers
do
n't
want
to
sit
in
a
turboprop
for
2½
to
three
hours
,
"
Mr.
Lowe
said
.
</S>

There is a fundamental difference between the tokenization of alphabetic languages and ideographic languages such as Chinese. Alphabetic languages usually separate words by blanks. A simple tokenizer which replaces whitespace with word boundaries and cuts off punctuation marks, parentheses, and quotation marks at both ends of a word, is already quite accurate. The only major problem is the disambiguation of periods which are either abbreviation periods or full stops. Texts in ideographic languages contain no information about word boundaries. Tokenization is therefore far more difficult. The tokenization of alphabetic and ideographic languages are actually two rather different problems which require different methods.

The rest of this section is organized as follows. Section 1.2. gives an overview of the problems encountered in tokenization. Section 1.3. describes the preprocessing required to transform idiosyncratic text formats into a standard form that the tokenizer can work with. Section 1.4. describes the restoration of words which have been split up during typesetting. Section 1.5. addresses the period disambiguation problem, and section 1.6. presents methods for Chinese tokenization. Finally, section 1.7. suggests further reading.

1.2. Tokenization problems

In alphabetic languages, words are surrounded by whitespace and optionally preceded and followed by punctuation marks, parentheses, or quotes. Sentences usually end with a period (.), a question mark (?) or an exclamation mark (!). A simple tokenization rule can be stated as follows: split the character sequence at whitespace positions and cut off punctuation marks, parentheses, and quotes at both ends of the fragments to obtain the sequence of tokens. Insert a sentence boundary after any occurrence of ".", "?", or "!".

This simple rule is quite accurate because whitespace and punctuation are fairly reliable indicators of word and sentence boundaries. Nevertheless, there are some problems which will be discussed below. Most of them concern the word segmentation problem. Some of them, in particular the period disambiguation problem and the problem of missing whitespace, also affect sentence boundary detection if the word boundaries are not correctly identified. Finally, there is a problem with quoted speech which is only relevant for sentence boundary detection.

Periods

Not all periods are punctuation: periods are also used to mark abbreviations (such as *etc.* or *U.S.A.*) and ordinal numbers (e.g. in the German date expression *1. Oktober 2005*). Only periods acting as sentence markers are separate tokens. The distinction between abbreviation periods and sentence-final punctuation is often difficult. Abbreviation lists help to identify frequent abbreviations, but many abbreviations are rare or created ad hoc and cannot be listed exhaustively. Furthermore, there are potential abbreviations such as *fig.* or *no.* which are truly ambiguous because they might be regular words which are followed by a full stop. Thus the disambiguation of periods requires contextual information. If the next token is a lower-case word, the period is probably part of an abbreviation. If the next token is a capitalized word such as *The*, which is normally written in lower-case, the period is probably a full stop, but it could also belong to an abbreviation in sentence-final position.

Unlike the period, the exclamation mark (!) and the question mark (?) are mostly unambiguous with a few exceptions such as the company name *Yahoo!*.

Ordinal numbers

In German and some other languages, ordinal numbers are followed by a period. Thus *17th* is written *"17."* These ordinal numbers raise the same problem as abbreviations: a number which is followed by a period is either an ordinal number, a cardinal number in sentence-final position, or an ordinal number in sentence-final position. The problem is actually more difficult than the disambiguation of abbreviations because the number itself provides very little information (although numbers between 1 and 12 are more likely to be ordinal numbers than numbers between 1900 and 2010, which often designate years). German ordinal numbers cannot be recognized without contextual information. If a sentence boundary precedes, it is probably indeed an ordinal number. If it is in the range between 1900 and 2010 and the previous word is *April*, it is more likely to be a cardinal number in sentence-final position.

Multiword expressions

So far, it was implicitly assumed that tokens never contain whitespace. The adjective *New York-based* and the number *10 000* show that this assumption is too strict. Neither of them should be split into two tokens.

For applications such as parsing, it might be advantageous to treat certain multiword expressions as a single token. Examples are complex prepositions (*because of*), coordinating conjunctions (*as well as*), subordinating conjunctions (*so that*), adverbial expressions (*at all*), foreign-language phrases (*et cetera, en vogue*), date expressions (*Feb. 1, 2004*), time expressions (*3:30 pm*), and proper names (*Daimler Chrysler AG*). Most of these are difficult to analyze for a parser with standard grammar rules, and it is often unclear which parts of speech to assign to the components.

Recognizers for such multiword tokens are often implemented with regular expression matching using tools such as *Lex* or *Perl* which are available on most Unix systems. The following regular expression, for example, recognizes date expressions.

(May|(Jan|Feb|Mar|Apr|Jun|Jul|Aug|Sep|Oct|Nov|Dec)[.]) [123]?[0−9],(19|20)[0−9][0−9]

The recognition of arbitrary proper names such as *Abdul Aziz bin Abdul Rahman Al Saud* is problematic: they can neither be listed exhaustively nor be described with regular expressions. The recognition and classification of proper names has developed into a separate field, called *Named Entity Recognition*, which is outside of the scope of this article.

Many multiword expressions are ambiguous: *so that* is not a conjunction in the sentence *Ah, so that is the way the wind blows!*, and *at all* is not an adverb in the phrase *at all times*. These ambiguities cannot be resolved without the sentence context. If the next processing step is parsing, the final decision can be left to the parser.

Clitics

Multiword expressions combine several words into a single token. The opposite is often done with clitic expressions (*isn't, ain't, we'll*) which are split into two tokens (is *n't, ai n't*, and *we 'll*). The advantage is that the syntactic analysis of the sentence *He's smart* is analogous to that of *He is smart*. The splitting of clitic expressions produces non-words such as *ai*. In order to distinguish them from regular words, the tokenizer should mark them with a special symbol. For some application, it might be preferable to replace clitic expressions (*we'll*) with regular words (*we will*).

English clitics as well as German clitics (*Stimmt's?* − Is it correct?) and French clitics (*Permettez-vous?* − Would you allow?) are easily identified with suffix matching if exceptions such as *rendez-vous* in French are taken care of. French determiner clitics (*l'Europe* − Europe) can be handled in the same way. The recognition of pronominal clitics in Spanish (*garantizarles* − to guarantee them) and Italian (*applicarlo* − to apply it) is more difficult due to the lack of a separator and requires a morphological analysis. Simple suffix stripping would chop up words such as *Carlo*, as well.

Word-internal punctuation

If the tokenizer just cuts off parentheses and quotation marks at the beginning and the end of a sentence, it will incorrectly split the expressions *relationship(s)* and *"Rambo"-type* and generate the incorrect tokens *relationship(s* and *Rambo"-type*. In order to avoid this, the tokenizer should check − before cutting off a parenthesis or quotation symbol − whether the word internally contains a complementary symbol.

De-hyphenation

Another problem for tokenization arises when words are split during typesetting, leaving a hyphenated word at the end of a line which continues in the next line. The *de-hyphenation* of such forms is not trivial. Three cases have to be distinguished when a line ends, for instance, with the string *pre-*:

- A word such as *preprocessing* was split into *pre-* and *processing*. The hyphen and the newline have to be deleted.
- A word such as *pre-processing* was split into *pre-* and *processing*. Only the newline symbol should be deleted.
- The original text contained a word sequence such as *pre- and post-processing*. Here it is necessary to replace the newline symbol with a word boundary.

Missing whitespace

Sometimes the blank between a punctuation mark and the following word is missing, resulting in strings such as *hours.The* or *however,that* which have to be converted into three separate tokens. Given information about (a) the frequency of word forms $f(w)$, (b) the frequency of word forms in sentence-initial position $f(.w)$, and (c) the size of the corpus from which the counts were extracted N, we can disambiguate using the following rule:

Split the token s.r if f (s)f(.r) > N f (s.r).

Similar rules are applicable to other punctuation marks.

Sentence boundary detection

Tokenization usually includes the identification of sentences. A simple strategy is to put a sentence boundary marker after all occurrences of the tokens ".", "?", and "!". It presupposes that the periods are correctly disambiguated. As mentioned before, this is not trivial because some periods are part of an abbreviation or an ordinal number. Even worse, they are simultaneously sentence and abbreviation markers if an abbreviation happens to occur at the end of a sentence.

Sentence boundary detection is complicated by quoted sentences appearing inside of matrix sentences. The following sentence from the British National Corpus is an example:

"Why not bite the bullet?" said a spokesman.

The insertion of a sentence boundary before the word *said* would create the sentence fragment *said a spokesman*. In this example, the lower-case word after the quotation provides evidence that the sentence is not finished yet. However, such a hint is not always available, as the following sentence from the British National Corpus shows:

"You still don't have an accountant?" Ellis said.

Related problems

A problem which is related to tokenization is *de-capitalization:* when the tokenizer is unsure whether to classify some period as an abbreviation marker or as a punctuation symbol, it helps to know whether the next word is a capitalized word such as *The* which rarely appears in the middle of a sentence (unless it is part of a proper name). Some tokenizers (e. g. Schmid 2000) extract statistical information from corpora in order to guess whether a token is capitalized because the respective word is capitalized, or because it appears in sentence-initial position. Such a tokenizer is also able to de-capitalize words in sentence-initial position.

A more systematic approach to the de-capitalization problem which is also capable of restoring the proper capitalization in headers could be implemented with a Hidden Markov model (HMM, see section 2). Niu et al. (2004) applied HMMs to a very similar problem: the *restoration of case* in an all-upper-case text. And Simard (1998) used HMMs for *accent restoration* in French texts. These topics are beyond the scope of this article, however.

Ideographic languages

In contrast to alphabetic languages, ideographic languages such as Chinese or Japanese do not mark the word boundaries with blanks or any other markers, nor do some phonetic scripts such as Korean or Thai. Most Chinese characters are (single-character) words, but appear in multi-character words as well. Therefore it is difficult to decide where a word ends and where the next word begins.

Chinese word segmentation poses theoretical problems as well: as Wu (1998) pointed out, "the naive notion of a word boundary is essentially alien to Chinese. The notion is borrowed from languages with whitespace-separated characters." Consider the German compound word *Sprachverarbeitung* and its English equivalent *language processing* which is usually split into two words. Should an equivalent Chinese expression be segmented into one or two tokens? Wu advocates a task-oriented approach which places the word boundaries where they are most useful for the application.

Most Chinese tokenizers use a large lexicon. Given a lexicon, a simple tokenizer for Chinese can be implemented with a longest-match strategy: the tokenizer determines the longest character sequence which starts at the current position and is a possible token according to the lexicon. The token is printed and the position pointer is moved behind the token. Then the next token is scanned. This method works quite well because long words are more likely to be correct than short words, but it has two drawbacks. (i) The strategy is too greedy: given a lexicon with the strings AB, ABC, CDED, D, and E (where A, B, C, D, E represent different Chinese characters), it would tokenize the string ABCDED as ABC/D/E/D rather than AB/CDED, although the latter has fewer tokens, (ii) Words which are missing in the lexicon, cannot be recognized. The identification of unknown words is actually the most difficult problem for the tokenization of ideographic languages.

In the following sections, we will have a closer look at some of the tokenization problems encountered in this section and their solutions.

1.3. Pre-processing

Machine-readable texts are stored in a wide variety of idiosyncratic document formats, character sets and typing conventions, which cannot be directly processed by a general-purpose tokenizer. The first processing step is therefore the normalization of the text document to a standard format, namely to a sequence of characters from a standard character set (e. g. Unicode). The formatting information is lost in this step. If it needs to be preserved, because it is relevant for the application, it should be encoded as SGML or XML markup (see article 22 of this volume).

Some formatting information is relevant for tokenization. De-hyphenation, for instance, is trivial if the original file format uses different encodings for hyphens which were inserted during line breaking, and for other hyphens. Formatting information also helps in sentence boundary detection. Headers rarely end with a sentence marker. Once the formatting information has been removed, it is difficult to determine automatically where the header ends and where the first sentence of an article begins. Paragraph markers are useful for sentence boundary detection because paragraph boundaries are also sentence boundaries. Information about headers and paragraph boundaries should be passed to the tokenizer.

1.4. De-hyphenation

Words which were split at line boundaries during typesetting have to be restored to their original form. Given a line ending with some string *x* and a hyphen, and followed by a line starting with some string *y*, the tokenizer needs to disambiguate between three possible output strings, namely (1) the string *xy* (a "regular" word such as preprocessing), (2) the string *x-y* (a hyphenated word such as pre-processing), and (3) the string *x- y* (a truncated word and a regular word such as *pre- and post-processing*).

The first alternative is the most likely one. The third alternative is in most corpora rare enough to be ignored without noticeably degrading the accuracy. Grefenstette/Tapanainen (1994) report on an experiment in which they ran the BNC through the typesetting program *nroff*. 12% of the lines of the formatted text ended in a letter plus hyphen. Simply joining these lines and deleting the hyphen (corresponding to output (1) above) correctly restored 95.1% of the original words.

Grefenstette/Tapanainen (1994) suggested that more informed decisions could be based on lexicon information. Mikheev (2003) implemented a lexicon-based method and reports a reduction of the error rate from 4.9% to 0.9%. He used the following disambiguation rule: if the unhyphenated word form *xy* appears in the lexicon, print *xy*; otherwise if both *x* and *y* are listed in the lexicon as separate words, print the hyphenated form *x-y*; otherwise the unhyphenated form *xy* is printed.

If a lexicon is not available, a word list with frequencies from a tokenized corpus can be used instead. Such a "corpus lexicon" also contains frequent hyphenated word forms (*long-term, full-time*). Furthermore it provides frequency information: the word *makeup* occurs 175 times in the BNC and the word *make-up* 1267 times. *make- up* should thus be de-hyphenated to *make-up* rather than *makeup*. A corpus-derived lexicon can be used in combination with the following disambiguation rule: if the hyphenated word form *x-y* is more frequent than *xy*, print *x-y*. Otherwise if the hyphenated word form *x-y* is less frequent than *xy*, print *xy*. Otherwise if both *x* and *y* are listed in the lexicon as separate words, print *x-y*. Otherwise, print *xy*.

1.5. Period disambiguation

The most difficult problem for the tokenization of alphabetic languages is the disambiguation of periods. Periods either indicate (1) the end of a sentence, or (2) an abbreviation, or (3) an abbreviation at the end of a sentence. In German and a few other languages, the period can also mark (4) an ordinal number, or (5) an ordinal number at the end of a sentence.

If the ambiguity is ignored and all periods are treated as sentence markers, about 93.2% of the sentence boundaries are correctly recognized in the Brown corpus according to Grefenstette/Tapanainen (1994). If all periods which are not followed by whitespace (such as the period in the numeric expression 1,234.56 or the first period of the abbreviation *Ph.D.*) are classified as not sentence-final, the accuracy rises to 93.8%.

Disambiguation heuristics

Many abbreviations consist of a sequence of letter-period pairs (*U.S.A., e.g.*), or of a capitalized letter followed by a sequence of consonants (*Mrs., St., Eds.*). Such character sequences are usually abbreviations, although there are a few exceptions: *Ash.* is more likely to be a name which is followed by a period. If strings of this form are always classified as sentence-internal abbreviations, the accuracy of the sentence boundary detection rises to 97.66%.

Potential abbreviations are often disambiguated by the context. If a period is followed by punctuation such as ",", "?", "!", ":", or ";" or by a lower-case word, it is unlikely to be a sentence marker and the tokenizer should treat the preceding string as an abbreviation. Making use of such unambiguous occurrences of abbreviations, we can automatically extract abbreviation lists from corpora. The results are not perfect, however. Some German newspapers, for instance, write certain organization names (*amnesty international, adidas*) always in lower-case, even at the beginning of a sentence. The last word of the preceding sentence is therefore incorrectly identified as an abbreviation. In order to cope with this and other problems, the abbreviation list needs to be filtered, for example by deleting items which are listed in a lexicon without the period. Unfortunately, the filtering prevents the recognition of abbreviations such as *fig.* and *no.* because *fig* and *no* are words. With automatically extracted abbreviation lists, Grefenstette/Tapanainen (1994) further raised the accuracy of period disambiguation to 98.35%.

Capitalized words which follow a potential abbreviation also provide valuable information. If a period is followed by *Some*, for instance, it is probably not an abbreviation because the capitalized word *Some* typically occurs at the beginning of a sentence. Thus the tokenizer should classify a period as sentence-final if it is followed by a word whose lower-case form is more frequent than its capitalized form. This heuristic fails when an abbreviation is followed by a proper name which is also a regular word as in *Lts. Black and Henley.* In order to tokenize such sentences correctly, *Black* needs to be recognized as a proper name. A detailed discussion of this problem is found in Mikheev (2002).

The heuristic for the extraction of abbreviations from corpora fails to find abbreviations which are typically followed by upper-case words or by numbers. Examples are title abbreviations (*Prof., Mrs.*) which occur in front of names, and certain abbreviations such as *fig.* and *sec.* which are mostly followed by numbers. In order to extract such abbreviations, it is necessary to consider ambiguous occurrences of abbreviations as well. If the string *Mr.* precedes 1000 times an upper-case word and only three times a lower-case word, it is probably an abbreviation unless it is a word which appears mostly at the end of a sentence. To rule out the latter case, it is useful to count how often the potential abbreviation is followed by a capitalized word such as *The* which is normally written in lower-case. If the relative frequency of such words after the potential abbreviation is low, it is probably an abbreviation.

Many abbreviations end with complex consonant clusters (such as *qns* in *eqns.*) which are not found in regular words. Any word ending with such a cluster and followed by a period is probably an abbreviation. Müller/Amerl/Natalis (1980) proposed a sentence boundary detection algorithm which is based on word suffix statistics. Suffix-based recognition of abbreviations is particularly useful in German because of its complex morphology. Abbreviations of English street names such as *Main St.* are easy to recognize by looking up the string *St.* in an abbreviation lexicon. This is more difficult in German where the street names are usually a single word resulting in abbreviations such as *Hauptstr.* or *Koberstädterstr.* Suffix analysis is a way to deal with these complex abbreviations.

The different period disambiguation heuristics discussed so far need to be combined in order to achieve optimal accuracy. This can be done in several ways: one option is to convert the heuristics into rules of the form "If condition C is satisfied then disambiguate the period as y." The rules are ordered according to their reliability and the first matching rule determines the result.

Classification approaches

Another strategy is to treat period disambiguation as a classification problem. The contextual information available for disambiguation is converted into a feature vector, and a classifier is trained on manually disambiguated training data. The classifier learns to assign the correct class (abbreviation, full stop or abbreviation+full stop) to the feature vectors. Riley (1989) implemented a classifier with decision trees (Breiman et al. 1984; Quinlan 1983). He included as features (1) the probability that the word preceding the period occurs in sentence-final position, (2) the probability that the word following the period occurs in sentence-initial position, (3+4) the length of the preceding and the following word, (5+6) whether the preceding/following word is lower-case, upper-case, capitalized or a number, (7) whether the period is followed by punctuation, (8) whether the preceding word with the period is a known abbreviation and the type of the abbreviation. The system was trained on 25 million words from AP news wire and achieved 99.8 % accuracy on the Brown corpus.

Palmer/Hearst (1997) implemented period disambiguators with neural networks as well as decision trees. The feature vector included information about capitalization, punctuation, and the part-of-speech distributions of the six words around the period. The accuracy on *Wall Street Journal* data was 99.0 %. They also evaluated their systems on German and French data with error rates between 1.9 and 0.4 %.

Mikheev (2000) went one step further than Palmer/Hearst (1997) and integrated period disambiguation into part-of-speech (POS) tagging. In the input of the POS tagger, the periods formed separate tokens, and the POS tagger disambiguated the periods by assigning one of three possible tags which indicated whether the period is (1) an abbreviation, (2) a full stop, or (3) an abbreviation and full stop at the same time. He reports an accuracy of 99.8 % on the Brown corpus and 99.69 % on the WSJ corpus for a hybrid system which used unsupervised methods, too.

Reynar/Ratnaparkhi (1997) presented a Maximum-Entropy approach to sentence boundary detection. Their system only uses information which was extracted from the manually tokenized training corpus. They report 98.8 % accuracy on the WSJ corpus and 97.9 % on the Brown corpus. Mikheev (1998) describes a similar system with an accuracy of 99.3 % on WSJ data and 98.7 %o n the Brown corpus.

Unsupervised methods

The drawback of classification-based approaches is the need for manually annotated training data whose creation is expensive and time-consuming. The accuracy of these systems is often impressive on held-out data from the corpus they were trained on, but usually degrades on other corpora. The reason is that abbreviations are much more corpus-specific than other parts of the vocabulary. Abbreviation lists extracted from one corpus are therefore less useful on new corpora. In order to obtain optimal results, classification-based systems need to be retrained for new text types.

Unsupervised methods (Grefenstette/Tapanainen 1994; Mikheev 2002; Schmid 2000) avoid this problem by extracting the required information from raw text. They can even be trained on the corpus which is to be tokenized (unless online processing is required or the corpus is too small). The performance is comparable to the performance of systems which are trained on annotated data. The system described in Schmid (2000), for instance, extracts information about likely abbreviations (*Calif.*), typical abbreviation suffixes (such as *str.* in German), lower-case words appearing in capitalized form after sentence boundaries (*Fortunately*), lower-case words appearing in lower-case after sentence boundaries, proper names, and abbreviations occurring frequently before numbers (*Oct.*, *p.*, *Fig.*, *No.*). The system also extracts statistical information for the disambiguation of potential ordinal numbers in German. It uses a statistically motivated decision rule which combines the different sources of information.

1.6. Tokenization of ideographic languages

The tokenization problem in ideographic languages is rather different from that in alphabetic languages, and so are the methods used to solve it. There are four major strategies: rule-based methods, statistical methods based on word n-grams, tagging approaches, and systems which integrate tokenization with POS tagging or parsing.

Rule-based systems (e. g. Ma/Chen 2003) identify potential words in the character sequence by means of a large lexicon. Overlapping candidate words represent ambiguities which are resolved by rules. The disambiguation rules are developed by hand and use linguistic principles, statistical information, and heuristics. In a second step, the tokenizer detects unknown words with another set of rules.

Statistical systems consider tokenization to be the task of finding the most probable word sequence which yields the character sequence of the sentence to be tokenized. To give an example, assume that the input is ABC (where A, B, and C represent three different Chinese characters) and that A, B, C, AB, and BC are possible words. The set of possible word sequences is then AB C, A BC, and ABC, and the tokenizer needs to compare their probabilities. In mathematical terms, the most probable word sequence for a given character sequence is expressed as follows:

$$\hat{w}_1^n = \operatorname*{arg\,max}_{w_1^n : yield(w_1^n) = c_1^m} p(w_1^n)$$

The formula states that the most probable word sequence $\hat{w}_1^n$ is obtained by (i) computing the set of word sequences w_1^n whose concatenation yields the character sequence c_1^m, (ii) computing the probability $p(w_1^n)$ of each of these word sequences, (iii) determining the maximal probability from all these word sequences (operator **max**), and (iv) returning the word sequence with the maximal probability (operator **arg**).

Probabilities have to be estimated from training data, but it is impossible to directly estimate the probability of sentences of arbitrary length. Hence the sentence probability $p(w_1^n)$ is replaced by a product of simpler bigram probabilities $p(w_1 | <S> p(w_2 | w_1) \ldots p(w_n | w_{n-1})$, where $p(w | w')$ is the probability that word w follows w', and $p(w | <S>)$ is the probability that a sentence starts with the word w. Setting $w_0 := <S>$), the sentence probability can be expressed as follows:

$$(1) \quad p(w_1^n) = \prod_{i=1}^{n} p(w_i | w_{i-1})$$

This *Markov Model* approach (see also Manning/Schütze 1999) assumes that the probability of a word only depends on the preceding word and not on any words appearing earlier. This approximation works quite well for the task at hand because the kind of non-local dependencies which are not represented by the model are seldom relevant for the disambiguation of word boundaries.

The values of the bigram parameters $p(w | w')$ are estimated from counts obtained from a manually tokenized training corpus by dividing the frequency of the word pair $w'w$ by the frequency of the first word w'. This is the so-called *maximum likelihood estimate* (MLE):

$$p(w | w') = \frac{f(w'w)}{f(w)}$$

Due to the Zipfian distribution of the word bigrams (with a few frequent and many rare bigrams), the training corpus is never large enough to contain all possible word bigrams. The probability of a word pair which is not observed in the training data, is 0 according to the ML estimate. The probability of a sentence with such a word pair is 0, too. Thus the tokenizer will never return a word sequence containing an unseen word pair unless there is no other choice. And if there is no alternative because all possible word sequences contain an unseen bigram, then it is impossible to disambiguate between them. In order to avoid this problem, the bigram probabilities have to be *smoothed* by assigning a small probability to unseen word pairs and decreasing the probability of observed word pairs such that the probabilities still sum up to 1. Chen/Goodman (1996) provide an overview of smoothing techniques for word n-gram probabilities.

The Viterbi algorithm (Viterbi 1967; Manning/Schütze 1999) efficiently computes the most likely word sequence for a character sequence. It processes the characters $c_1, \ldots, c_m$ from left to right and computes for each possible word w ending at position i the probability of the most probable word sequence covering $c_1, \ldots, c_i$ and ending with w. This quantity is the *Viterbi*-probability $\delta_w(i)$ of word w at position i. It is obtained by (i) identifying the set of words ending at position $i - |w|$ where $|w|$ is the length of word w, (ii) computing for each word w' in this set the product of its Viterbi probability $\delta_{w'}(i - |w|)$ and the bigram probability $p(w | w')$, (iii) storing the maximal product over all predecessors w' as $\delta_w(i)$ and (iv) storing the best predecessor w' as $\psi_w(i)$.

If W is the set of known words, then the computation of the Viterbi probabilities is mathematically defined as follows:

$$\delta_w(i) = \begin{cases} \max\limits_{w' \in W : w' = c_{i-|w|-|w'|+1}^{i-|w|}} \delta_{w'}(i - |w|)p(w\,|\,w') & \textit{if } w \in W, w = c_{i-|w|+1}^{i} \\ 0 & \text{otherwise} \end{cases}$$

Consider the following abstract example: the character sequence to be tokenized is ABCD. The lexicon comprises the words A, AB, B, BC, D, and BCD. The relevant subset of the bigram probabilities is $p(A\,|<S>) = 0.1$, $p(AB\,|<S>) = 0.02$, $p(B\,|A) = 0.1$, $p(C\,|B) = 0.2$, $p(C\,|AB) = 0.2$, $p(BC\,|A) = 0.01$, $p(D\,|\,C) = 0.01$, $p(D\,|\,BC) = 0.2$, and $p(BCD\,|A) = 0.001$. Figure 24.1 shows the corresponding word lattice. The numbers are the Viterbi probabilities. The length of the surrounding box indicates the start and end position of the respective word. The bold lines (corresponding to the ψ-variables above) connect the words with their best predecessors.

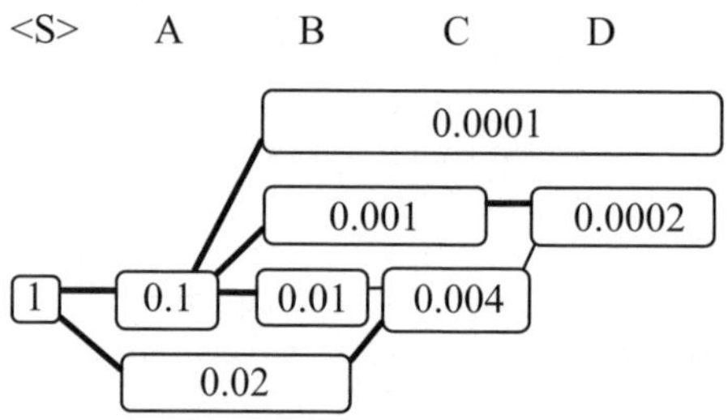

Fig. 24.1: Computation of the Viterbi probabilities

After determining the word with the highest Viterbi probability that ends with the last character (this is the word D in the example), the best word sequence (here A BC D) is obtained by following the bold links backwards from there to the start symbol <S>.

The main problem of statistical tokenizers for Chinese is the recognition of unknown words. The simple bigram approach fails to recognize multi-character words which did not appear in the training corpus. Many unknown words are names. Chinese names consist of a family name with one or two characters and a given name with one or two characters. The number of family names is small and it is possible to list them exhaustively. Names from Western countries are transliterated into a sequence of Chinese characters whose pronunciation is similar to that of the foreign name. Each character corresponds to one syllable and each syllable is usually consistently transliterated in the same way. Therefore there is a small set of characters which tend to be used again and again. The structure of location and organization names is less predictable, but they often end with a character which is typical for the respective class of names.

The simple bigram tokenizer described above usually splits unknown words into smaller units. Many systems recognize unknown words by recombining these fragments in a second step (e. g. Asahara et al. 2003). Others integrate the recognition of unknown words into the statistical model (Sun et al. 2002; Wu/Zhao/Xu 2003).

Tagging-based tokenizers annotate each character c_i with a tag t_i with two possible values which indicate whether character *ci* starts a new word or not. From a statistical point of view, the task of the tagger is to find the most likely tag sequence $\hat{t}_1^n$ for a given character sequence c_1^m:

$$\hat{t}_1^n = \arg\max_{t_1^n} p(t_1^n\,|\,c_1^n)$$

Assuming that the probability of a tag only depends on the current character and the preceding character, we obtain the simple word juncture model proposed by Fu/Luke (2003):

$$\hat{t}_1^n = \arg\max_{t_1^n} \prod_{i=1}^{n} p(t_i \mid c_{i-1}, c_i)$$

Their tagset has two elements indicating the presence or absence of a word boundary between the two characters c_{i-1} and c_i. Xue/Shen (2003) use four different tags, one for characters in word-initial position (LM), one for characters in word-final position (MR), one for inner characters (MM), and one for single character words (LR). They decompose the probability of the tag sequence t_1^n given the character sequence c_1^n into a product of the probabilities of each tag t_i given the k preceding tags t_{i-k}^{i-1} and characters c_{i-k}^{i-1}, the current character c_i and the k following characters c_{i+1}^{i+k}:

$$\hat{t}_{i-k}^{i-1} = \arg\max_{t_1^n} \prod_{i=1}^{n} p(t_i \mid t_{i-k}^{i-1}, c_{i-k}^{i+k})$$

The conditional probabilities are estimated with a maximum-entropy model. The system is very similar to the Maximum-Entropy part-of-speech tagger of Ratnaparkhi (1996) and the reader is referred to that article to obtain more information on Maximum-Entropy models.

Tagging-based tokenizers are not necessarily statistical systems. Goh/Asahara/Matsumoto (2004) use a *support vector machine* classifier (Vapnik 1995) to annotate characters with the tags B (beginning of word), E (end of word), I (word internal), and S (single character word). As features, they use the surrounding characters, the word boundaries assigned to the surrounding characters by a simple forward-matching longest-match segmentation method, the word boundaries assigned by a backward-matching segmentation method, and the tags assigned to the preceding characters by the SVM itself.

All tokenizers for Chinese considered so far, are separate modules. However, it is also possible to integrate segmentation into syntactic analysis with the advantage that higher-level information becomes available for word segmentation. Feng et al. (2004) describe a system which integrates tokenization and part-of-speech (POS) tagging. Using a Hidden Markov model, they compute the best sequence of words and POS tags as follows:

$$\hat{t}_{i-k}^{i-1}, \hat{w}_{i-k}^{i-1} = \arg \max_{t_1^n, w_1^n : yield(w_1^n) = c_1^m} \prod_{i=1}^{n} p(t_i \mid t_{i-2}, t_{i-1}) p(w_i \mid t_i)$$

This POS tagger and tokenizer is very similar to standard HMM POS taggers for tokenized input. The main difference is that the start and end positions of the words are not fixed. (The actual system of Feng et al. (2004) is slightly more complex because it models rhythmic regularities as well.)

Zhang et al. (2003) describe a cascaded Hidden Markov model where the integration of tokenization and POS tagging is less tight. The HMM used for word segmentation resembles the model of Sun et al. (2002). Instead of fully disambiguating the word sequence, they compute the *n* most likely word sequences and leave it to a HMM POS tagger to select the best word sequence.

Wu (2003) integrated tokenization with parsing. Similar to parsers which process the ambiguous output of speech recognizers, their system operates on word lattices which represent all possible word sequences. The word boundary ambiguities are eliminated as a side effect of syntactic disambiguation.

Other languages with ideographic writing systems
The Japanese writing system uses three different types of characters: kanji, hiragana, and katakana. Changes of the character type often indicate word boundaries. This heuristic alone achieves almost 60 % accuracy (Nagata 1997). Most problematic for Japanese word segmentation are sequences of kanji characters which often consist of more than one word. Rule-based (Matsumoto et al. 1999) as well as statistical methods (Ando/Lee 2003) have been applied in Japanese tokenization.

1.7. Further reading

Grefenstette/Tapanainen (1994) give a good overview of the problems encountered in tokenization. German tokenization problems are discussed at length in Klatt (2005). Riley (1989), Palmer/Hearst (1997), and Reynar/Ratnaparkhi (1997) describe period disambiguation methods which are trained on manually annotated text. Unsupervised period disambiguation methods were presented in Grefenstette/Tapanainen (1994), Schmid (2000), and Mikheev (2002). The Proceedings of the SIGHAN Workshops on Chinese Language Processing are a good starting point for learning more about word segmentation methods for Chinese and other ideographic writing systems.

2. Part-of-speech tagging

2.1. Introduction

A part-of-speech (POS) tagger is a program which annotates text with part-of-speech information. Many words are ambiguous with respect to part of speech, as the following sentence shows:

This Trojan virus can exploit programs that store personal data.

In the PENN treebank corpus (Marcus/Santorini/Marcinkiewicz 1993), which serves as a reference corpus for many English POS taggers, the word *This* is either tagged as a determiner (DT) or as a proper name (NP) when it is part of a name such as *This Week.* (See also article 23 of this book on tagsets.) *Trojan* is an adjective (JJ), a singular noun (NN), or a proper name (NP). *can* is a modal verb (MD), or a noun (NN). *exploit* is an infinitive (VB), a non-third person singular present tense finite verb (VBP), or a singular noun (NN). *programs* is a plural noun (NNS) or a third person singular present tense verb (VBZ). *that* is a determiner (DT), a subordinating conjunction (IN), a relative pronoun (WDT), or an adverb (RB) (e. g. in the phrase *not that simple*). *store* is a singular noun (NN), an infinitive (VB) or a finite verb (VBP). Finally, *data* is either a singular noun (NN) or a plural noun (NNS) because it appears with singular (*this data*) as well as plural (*these data*) determiners and verbs. The above sentence should be annotated as follows:

> *This/DT Trojan/JJ virus/NN can/MD exploit/VB programs/NNS that/WDT store/ VBP personal/JJ data/NNS ./SENT*

There are many applications for POS tagging: it is often the first step in syntactic parsing. It is required for the correct lemmatization of words (see article 25). The lemma of the word *building*, for example, is *build* if it is a verb and *building* if it is a noun. And it is used in information extraction, speech synthesis, lexicographic research, term extraction, and other applications.

Early POS taggers (Klein/Simmons 1963; Greene/Rubin 1971) used hand-written rules to assign possible POS tags to words and to disambiguate between them. An important step forward was the application of *Hidden Markov models* (HMM) (Bahl/Mercer 1976; Derouault/Merialdo 1984; Church 1988; Cutting et al. 1992; DeRose 1998) and similar approaches (Garside 1987). Today, there is a wide range of statistical taggers (Schmid 1994b; Armstrong et al. 1995; Ratnaparkhi 1996; Brants 2000), rule-based taggers using manually written rules (Karlsson 1990; Tapanainen/Voutilainen 1994) and automatically induced rules (Brill 1992), and other types of taggers (Benello/Mackie/ Anderson 1989; Nakamura et al. 1990; Schmid 1994a; Màrquez/Padró 1997; Giménez/ Màrquez 2004).

Most POS taggers require a manually annotated training corpus. The creation of such a corpus is time-consuming and forms the main cost factor in the development of part-of-speech taggers for new languages where annotated corpora are not available, yet. For optimal performance, large training corpora of up to a million words are required.

The state-of-the-art accuracy in POS tagging is between 95 % and 98 % depending on the language, the tagset, the size of the training corpus, the coverage of the lexicon, and the similarity between training and test data. These figures are impressive, but an accuracy of 96 % still means that a 20-word sentence is correctly tagged with a probability of just $0.96^{20} \approx 44\,\%$.

2.2. HMM taggers

Hidden Markov model (HMM) taggers are the most widely used approach to part-of-speech tagging due to their accuracy and high processing speed. They are based on a simple statistical model which assumes that the word sequence to be tagged was generated from left to right by a process which randomly selects (i) the part-of-speech of the next word based on the two preceding words (in case of a trigram tagger) and (ii) the next word itself based on the part of speech (which was chosen first).

This model is very simple. When trained on the Wall Street Journal corpus, it generates for example the tag-word sequence "*VVG/intervening TO/to DT/A NN/department IN/by NN/computer POS/'s NN/Stock-market NNS/brokers IN/despite NP/Los SENT/.*" which violates several obvious constraints: it lacks a finite verb; the first word is not capitalized; the capitalized words *A* and *Stock-market* appear in the middle of the sentence, and the word *Los* should be followed by *Angeles*. Nevertheless, Hidden Markov models work surprisingly well.

The probability of a POS tag only depends on the two preceding POS tags in this model, and the probability of the next word only depends on the POS tag. The probability of a tag sequence $t_1, t_2, ..., t_n$ plus word sequence $w_1, w_2, ..., w_n$ is therefore the product of the *contextual* probabilities and the *lexical* probabilities for all word positions ranging from 1 to n:

$$(1) \quad p(t_1, t_2, ..., t_n, w_1, w_2, ..., w_n) = \prod_{i=1}^{n} p(t_i \mid t_{i-1}, t_{i-1}) p(w_i \mid t_i)$$

The lexical probability is the probability of the word (w_i) given the part of speech (t_i). It is zero if the word does not occur with the respective part of speech. The contextual probability is the probability of the tag (t_i) given the preceding tag (t_{i-1}) in case of a bigram tagger and the two preceding tags (t_{i-2} and t_{i-1}) in case of a trigram tagger. The contextual probability is large for a noun following a determiner and an adjective, but small for a verb in the same context.

Consider the sentence *This virus exploits programs* . and the tags DT NN VBZ NNS SENT as an example. In a trigram model, their joint probability is p(DT | <S>) p(*This* | DT) p(NN | <S>,DT) p(*virus* | NN) p(VBZ | DT,NN) p(*exploits* | VBZ) p(NNS | NN,VBZ) *p(programs* | NNS) p(SENT | VBZ,NNS) p(. | SENT). The pseudo-tag <S> represents the context of the first word, namely a sentence boundary.

Parameter estimation

The values of the probability parameters are usually estimated from a manually annotated training corpus. (It is also possible to train HMM taggers on raw text, but the accuracy is lower then. See Elworthy (1994) for a comparison of supervised and unsupervised training.) The contextual probability $p(t \mid t', t'')$ is obtained by dividing the trigram frequency $f_{t',t'',t}$ by the frequency of the context bigram $f_{t',t''}$. The lexical probability $p(w \mid t)$ is the frequency of the joint occurrence of word w and tag t divided by the overall frequency of tag t.

$$p(t \mid t', t'') = \frac{f_{t',t'',t}}{f_{t',t''}}$$

$$p(w \mid t) = \frac{f_{w,t}}{f_t}$$

These are the *Maximum Likelihood* (ML) estimates of the probability parameters. Unfortunately, there are usually many POS trigrams which are perfectly well-formed but do not appear in the training corpus. Examples are the trigram WRB CD NP (*how five U.S.*) and the trigram MD JJ NN (*Will national service*) which do not occur in the first 1.1 million words of the *Wall Street Journal* part of the PENN treebank corpus. The ML probability estimate for unobserved trigrams is zero. Because the probability of a tag sequence is the product of the contextual and the lexical probabilities, it is zero if any of the contextual probabilities is zero, and the tagger will never choose a tag se-

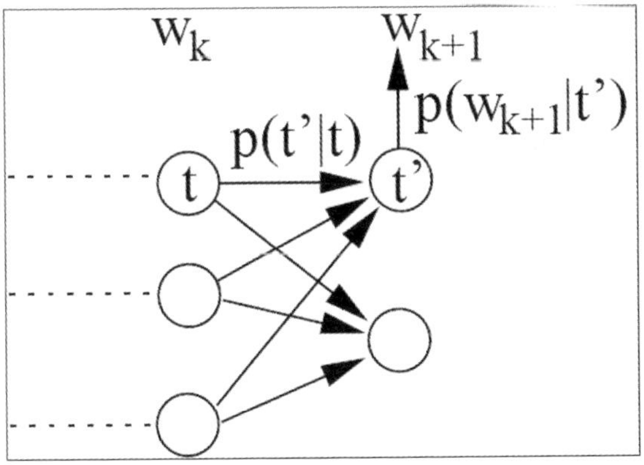

Fig. 24.2: Computation of the Viterbi probabilities

quence with an unknown trigram as long as an alternative without unknown trigrams exists. Furthermore, the tagger is unable to disambiguate if all possible tag sequences contain unknown trigrams and therefore have zero probability.

In order to avoid these problems, the probability estimates have to be *smoothed* by assigning a small probability to unseen trigrams. An overview of smoothing techniques for conditional n-gram probabilities can be found in Chen/Goodman (1996). A special smoothing technique for POS n-grams was presented in Brants (2000).

Viterbi algorithm

The most probable tag sequence for a given word sequence could in theory be computed by (i) enumerating all possible POS sequences, (ii) computing their probability and (iii) returning the most probable sequence. This is not practical, however, since the number of tag sequences grows exponentially with sentence length. HMM taggers instead use the *Viterbi* algorithm (Viterbi 1967; Manning/Schütze 1999) to efficiently determine the best tag sequence.

The Viterbi algorithm (for bigram taggers) is based on the following idea: assume, we have already computed the probability of the most probable (partial) tag sequence ending with tag t at position k. We call it the Viterbi probability $\delta_t(k)$. If t is the only tag of word w_k, then $\delta_t(k)p(t' \mid t)p(w_{k+1} \mid)t')$ is the probability of the best tag sequence ending with tag t' at position $k+1$ (see Figure 24.2). If w_k has more than one possible tag, we have to maximize the expression $\delta_t(k)p(t' \mid t)p(w_{k+1} \mid t')$ over all possible tags t of w_k in order to obtain $\delta_{t'}(k+1)$. The Viterbi probabilities of the other possible tags of word w_{k+1} are computed in the same way.

The formulas for the computation of the Viterbi probabilities of a bigram tagger are as follows:

$$\delta_t(1) = p(t \mid <S>)p(w_1 \mid \mathrm{t})$$

$$\delta_t(k) = \max_{t'} \delta_{t'}(k-1)p(t \mid \mathrm{t}')p(w_k \mid t) \; for \; 1 < k \leq n$$

$$\psi_t(k) = \arg\max_{t'} \delta_{t'}(k-1)p(t \mid \mathrm{t}')p(w_k \mid t) \; for \; 1 < k \leq n$$

The back-pointer $\psi_t(k)$ stores the tag t' for which the product $\delta_{t'}(\text{k}-1)p(t\,|\,t')p(w_k\,|\,t)$ is maximal. The Viterbi probabilities are computed for increasing k ranging from 1 to the sentence length n. Once we know the Viterbi probabilities of the tags of the last word, we can maximize over them to determine the probability $\delta(n)$ of the best tag sequence for the whole sentence and its last element t. Starting with the last tag $t_n = t$, we get the other elements of the best tag sequence via the back-pointers $t_{k-1} = \psi_{t_k}(k)$. The Viterbi probabilities of a trigram tagger are computed according to the following formulas:

$$\delta_{<S>,t}(1) = p(t\,|<S>)p(w_1|\,\text{t})$$

$$\delta_{t',t''}(k) = \max_{t,t'} \delta_{t,t'}(k-1)p(t''\,|\,t,t')p(w_k\,|\,t'')\ for\ 1 < k \leq n$$

Do HMM taggers ignore the right context?

The contextual probabilities of the POS tags depend on the preceding tags, and not on the following tags. Nonetheless, the right context has the same influence on the tagging of a word as the left context because the tagger compares the probabilities of tag sequences and not the contextual probabilities of individual tags.

Consider the two sentences *He knew that fact* and *He knew that they lied.* The tagger annotates the first sentence with PRP VBD DT NN rather than PRP VBD IN NN because a singular noun (NN) is more likely after a determiner (DT) than after a subordinating conjunction (IN). Similarly, the second sentence is annotated with PRP VBD IN PRP VBD rather than PRP VBD DT PRP VBD because $p(\text{PRP}\,|\,\text{IN}) > p(\text{PRP}\,|\,\text{DT})$.

Unknown words

The lexical probability of words which are not observed in the training corpus is zero, causing the same problems as unobserved tag n-grams. If a lexicon with POS information is available, the tagger can smooth the parameters in order to assign a small probability to words which occur in the lexicon but not in the training corpus.

What can be done with words which are not in the lexicon, either? One option is to put unknown and rare words into a class which is treated like a single word. To this end, any word occurring only once in the training data is replaced by the special token <unknown>. Then the parameters are estimated as usual. During tagging, any word which does not occur in the modified training corpus, is also replaced with <unknown> and tagged as usual.

This approach ignores the information from the capitalization, the ending, and other characteristics of the unknown word form. A word such as *pancying*, for example, is either a gerund, an adjective or a noun. The word *Wenying*, on the other hand, is a proper name unless it appears at the beginning of a sentence or in a header.

In order to be able to exploit this information, the tagging formula has to be transformed. It is easy to show that the best tag sequence according to equation 1 is also the best tag sequence according to this formula:

$$(2) \quad \prod_{i=1}^{n} \frac{p(t_i\,|\,t_{i-1},t_{i-1})p(t_i\,|\,w_i)}{p(t_i)}$$

Bayes' theorem which follows from the definition of conditional probabilities, allows us to replace $p(w_i\,|\,t_i)$ with $p(t_i\,|\,w_i)p(w_i)p(t_i)$. The factor $p(w_i)$ is dropped because it is irrelevant for the selection of the best tag sequence.

The prior probability $p(t)$ and the tag probability $p(t|w)$ of known words are directly estimated from the training corpus. The prior probability is estimated by the ratio of the tag frequency and the corpus size. The tag probability estimate is the joint frequency of the tag and the word form divided by the word frequency. Unknown words are divided into disjoint word classes (such as capitalized words, lower-case words ending with *ed*, lower-case words ending with *ing*, etc.) All unknown words in a word class get the same tag probabilities which are estimated on the basis of the known words of that word class. Similar strategies have been presented in (Weischedel et al. 1993; Schmid 1994b; Brants 2000).

Ambiguous output

The decision between two possible POS tags of a word is sometimes so close that the probabilities of the respective tag sequences are almost identical. The Viterbi algorithm will nevertheless return a single analysis. Applications like parsing, however, might prefer to receive both tags in such cases.

By returning all possible tags and their probabilities (given the input sentence), the tagger can leave the decision which tags to consider completely to the following application. The Forward-Backward algorithm (Manning/Schütze 1999) has to be used then instead of the Viterbi algorithm. The Forward-Backward algorithm computes *forward* probabilities $\alpha_t(k)$ according to the following formula, which is identical to the Viterbi formula except for the sum operator 2 which replaces the max operator:

$$\alpha_t(1) = p(t|<S>)p(w_1|t)$$
$$\alpha_t(k) = \sum_{t'} \alpha_{t'}(k-1)p(t|t')p(w_k|t) \; for \; 1 < k \leq n$$

It also computes *backward* probabilities $\beta_t(k)$ for decreasing k (i. e. from right to left):

$$\beta_t(n) = 1$$
$$\beta_t(k) = \sum_{t'} \beta_{t'}(k+1)p(t'|t)p(w_{k+1}|t') \; for \; 1 \leq k < n$$

The forward probability $\alpha_t(i)$ is the sum of the probabilities of all possible partial tag sequences ending with tag t at position i. The backward probability $\beta_t(i)$ is the sum of the probabilities of all partial tag sequences starting with tag t at position i and ending with some tag of the last word. The product $\alpha_t(i)\,\beta_t(i)$ is the probability of all complete tag sequences of the input sentence which assign the tag t to the ith word. Dividing this probability by the overall probability of all tag sequences (which is identical to the sum of the forward probabilities of all tags of the last word), we get the conditional probability of tag t at position i given the input sentence $w_1, w_2, \ldots, w_n$:

$$p(T_i = t|w_1, w_2, \ldots, w_n) = \frac{\alpha_{t_i}\beta_{t_i}}{\sum_{t'}\alpha_{t'}(n)}$$

The Forward-Backward algorithm can also be used to train HMM taggers on unlabeled training data (Cutting et al. 1992). However, the accuracy of such an *unsupervised* training tends to be lower than the accuracy of supervised training with labeled data (Elworthy 1994).

Sen tence-initial capitalization

Sentences always start with a capitalized word. This poses two problems to POS taggers: (i) Words at the beginning of a sentence are not known to the tagger if they only appear in uncapitalized form in the training corpus. (ii) A word such as *Bacon* appearing in the middle of a sentence might be tagged as a regular noun rather than a proper name if the training corpus contains many instances of the regular noun in sentence-initial position.

Problem (i) can be solved by looking up the lower-case form of the first word in addition to the capitalized form. If both forms are found, the tagger should use a frequency-weighted average of the two probability distributions (which only works in combination with the tagging formula of equation 2, however): the probability of the tag t for the sentence-initial word *Bacon* is therefore

$$p(t \mid Bacon)\frac{f_{Bacon}}{f_{Bacon} + f_{bacon}} + p(t \mid bacon)\frac{f_{bacon}}{f_{Bacon} + f_{bacon}}.$$

The second problem could be avoided if sentence-initial words which are normally written in lower-case are de-capitalized in the training corpus.

Ambiguous input

So far, it was assumed that the word segmentation is unambiguous. This is not always the case: in Chinese and other ideographic languages, a sentence is just a sequence of characters without word boundaries, and there are usually several word sequences yielding the same character sequence (see section 1 of this article). The same situation arises when a speech recognizer generates ambiguous output, or when the tokenizer leaves the disambiguation between an abbreviation period and a full stop undecided.

The following modification of the Viterbi algorithm for ambiguous input assumes that s_w holds the start position of the (candidate) word w and e_w its end position. If the end position of w is identical to the start position of w', then w' is a possible successor of w. The Viterbi probabilities are computed by maximizing over all words w ending at position i and over all tags V of the preceding words:

$$\delta_t(1) = p(t \mid <S>)p(w_1 \mid t)$$

$$\delta_t(i) = \max_{t',w:e_w = i} \delta_{t'}(s_w)p(t \mid t')p(w \mid t) \; for \; 1 < i \leq n$$

The back-pointers have to store the length of the current word in addition to the best preceding tag in order to recover the most probable tag sequence.

(Note that the modified tagging formula of equation 2 is not applicable to ambiguously tokenized input, because the prior probability $p(w)$ cannot be dropped in this context.)

2.3. Annotation of training data

HMM taggers and most other part-of-speech taggers require a manually annotated training corpus. The creation of such a corpus begins with the definition of the tagset. All tags in the tagset must be frequent enough to allow the tagger to learn their disambiguation from the training data. Furthermore, it must be possible to disambiguate the tags based on the local syntactic context. Thus purely semantic features should not be represented in the tags. The exact definition of the part-of-speech tags has to be specified in the *tagging guidelines*. The annotators follow these guidelines during the annotation. The guidelines have to be updated permanently as the annotators encounter and solve tagging problems which are not covered by the guidelines, yet. The guidelines ensure the consistency of the corpus and serve as a documentation.

Even if the annotators strictly adhere to the tagging guidelines, we still cannot expect perfect agreement in their decisions because they may make mistakes and sometimes interpret the guidelines differently. In order to detect such problems, the data should be assigned to the annotators in such a way that a part of the data of each annotator is tagged by another annotator. The doubly annotated data can then be used to detect systematic differences between the annotators and to estimate the accuracy of the manual annotation. For optimal quality, all the data is annotated twice and the annotators resolve conflicting annotations in discussion.

Some taggers use a lexicon which contains information about the set of possible parts of speech in addition to the manually annotated training corpus. If a morphological analyzer is available, we can build such a lexicon by (i) extracting a word list from a large corpus, (ii) analyzing the words with the morphology and (iii) extracting the set of possible parts of speech for each word.

2.4. Tagger evaluation

POS taggers are usually evaluated on a manually annotated reference corpus by re-tagging the corpus with the tagger and computing the ratio of correctly annotated words. It is important here to make sure that the evaluation data was not used for the tagger training in any form. Otherwise the accuracy will be over-estimated.

If two POS taggers using the same tagset have to be evaluated on a specific text genre where no manually annotated corpus exists, it can be done by selecting a representative text sample, annotating it with both taggers, and inspecting the words where the annotation of the two taggers differs. Examining 100 or 200 differently tagged words should be sufficient to get a picture of the strengths and weaknesses of the taggers.

2.5. Tagging errors

The error rate of state-of-the-art taggers is between 2 and 5%. If the test data is very different from the training data, the error rate may increase significantly. A major source of errors are unknown words and unknown readings of known words. Even with a sophisticated part-of-speech guesser for unknown words, the error rate is often 4 or 5 times higher on unknown words than on known words (Brants 2000).

Tagging errors also occur when the local context is not sufficient to disambiguate correctly. Consider the following two German sentences:

Er hofft, dass sie keine Fehler machen
(He hopes, that they no mistakes make – He hopes that they make no mistakes)

Sie werden keine Fehler machen
(They will no mistakes make – They will make no mistakes)

In the first sentence, the word *machen* has to be tagged as a finite verb. In the second sentence, it is an infinitive. The local context is exactly the same in both sentences. Thus any bigram or trigram tagger will assign the same tag to *machen* in both sentences and therefore get one of them wrong.

Many training corpora solely consist of newspaper articles because they are readily available in machine-readable form. Questions are not very frequent in these corpora and therefore less accurately tagged than declarative sentences. The same holds for other syntactic constructions which are underrepresented in the training corpus.

Multiword expressions such as *in between*, *all around*, *early on*, *kind of* or *by and large* are problematic as well. Even human annotators have difficulties to assign proper POS tags to the individual words of such expressions.

Last but not least, inconsistencies in the training and test data are an important source of "errors" if errors are determined by comparing the tagger output with a manually annotated gold standard. An example from the PENN treebank is the word *interested* which is sometimes tagged as an adjective (JJ) and sometimes as a past participle (VBN) when it appears in the context *was interested in*.

3. Summary

Tokenization (the segmentation of a text into sentences and words) is one of the easier problems in NLP, at least for alphabetic languages. A simple program which replaces whitespace with word boundaries, cuts off parentheses, quotation, and punctuation marks from the words and inserts sentence boundaries after ".", "!", and "?", is already quite accurate. The main problem remaining is the disambiguation between full stops and abbreviation markers, which can be solved with abbreviation lists and heuristics for the recognition of unknown abbreviations.

In ideographic languages such as Chinese, words are not separated by whitespace. Therefore it is much more difficult to identify word boundaries. Statistical approaches have been successfully applied here. They compute the most likely word sequence according to an n-gram language model. Several extensions of the n-gram model have been proposed in order to deal with unknown words.

Part-of-speech taggers annotate text with part-of-speech information. Although they solely rely on local information for disambiguation and do not attempt to create a global analysis, they perform surprisingly well, achieving a per-word accuracy of more than 95 % if the test data is not too different from the data on which the tagger was developed. A variety of methods have been used to implement POS taggers, including manually written rules, automatically induced rules, Hidden Markov models, and different types of classifiers (decision trees, neural networks, support vector machines). Hidden Markov models are the most widely used approach due to their high processing speed and accuracy. Very important for the performance of HMM taggers are the parameter smoothing method and the POS guessing heuristics for unknown words.

HMM taggers and most other POS taggers have to be trained on manually annotated training data. The creation of such a training corpus is the most expensive part of the development of a POS tagger for a new language.

4. Literature

Ando, R. K./Lee, L. (2003), Mostly-unsupervised Statistical Segmentation of Japanese Kanji Sequences. In: *Journal of Natural Language Engineering* 9, 127–149.

Armstrong, S./Russell, G./Petitpierre, D./Robert, G. (1995), An Open Architecture for Multilingual Text Processing. In: *Proceedings of the EACL-95 SIGDAT Workshop*, Dublin, Ireland, 30–34.

Asahara, M./Goh, C-L./Wang, X./Matsumoto, Y. (2003), Combining Segmenter and Chunker for Chinese Word Segmentation. In: *Proceedings of the Second SIGHAN Workshop on Chinese Language Processing (ACL 2003)*. Sapporo, Japan, 144–147.

Bahl, L. R./Mercer, R. L. (1976), Part-of-speech Assignment by a Statistical Decision Algorithm. In: *IEEE International Symposium on Information Theory*. Ronneby, Sweden, 88–89.

Benello, J./Mackie, A. W./Anderson, J. A. (1989), Syntactic Category Disambiguation with Neural Networks. In: *Computer Speech and Language* 3, 203–217.

Brants, T. (2000), TnT – a Statistical Part-of-speech Tagger. In: *Proceedings of the Sixth Applied Natural Language Processing Conference ANLP-2000*, Seattle, WA. Available at http://www.coli.uni-saarland.de/~thorsten/publications/Brants-ANLP00.pdf.

Breiman, L./Friedman, J. H./Olshen, R. A./Stone, C. J. (1984), *Classification and Regression Trees*. Pacific Grove CA: Wadsworth and Brooks.

Brill, E. (1992), A Simple Rule-based Part of Speech Tagger. In: *Proceedings of the Third Conference on Applied Natural Language Processing*. Trento, Italy, 152–155.

Chen, S. F./Goodman, J. (1996), An Empirical Study of Smoothing Techniques for Language Modeling. In: Joshi, A./Palmer, M. (eds.), *Proceedings of the Thirty-fourth Annual Meeting of the Association for Computational Linguistics (ACL-1996)*. San Francisco: Morgan Kaufmann Publishers, 310–318.

Church, K. W. (1988), A Stochastic Parts Program and Noun Phrase Parser for Unrestricted Text. In: *Proceedings of the Second Conference on Applied Natural Language Processing*, 136–143.

Cutting, D./Kupiec, J./Pedersen, J./Sibun, P. (1992), A Practical Part-of-speech Tagger. In: *Proceedings of the Third Conference on Applied Natural Language Processing*. Trento, Italy, 133–140.

DeRose, S. J. (1988), Grammatical Category Disambiguation by Statistical Optimization. In: *Computational Linguistics* 14(1), 31–39.

Derouault, A.-M./Merialdo, B. (1984), Language Modelling at the Syntactic Level. In: *Proceedings of the 7th International Conference on Pattern Recognition*. Montreal, Canada, 1373–1375.

Elworthy, D. (1994), Does Baum-Welch Re-estimation Help Taggers? In: *Proceedings of the 4th Conference on Applied Natural Language Processing*. Stuttgart, Germany, 53–58.

Feng, J./Liu, H./Chen, Y./Lu, R. (2004). An Enhanced Model for Chinese Word Segmentation and Part-of-speech Tagging. In: *Proceedings of the Third SIGHAN Workshop on Chinese Language Processing (ACL 2004)*. Barcelona, Spain, 28–32.

Fu, G./Luke, K. K. (2003), A Two-stage Statistical Word Segmentation System for Chinese. In: *Proceedings of the Second SIGHAN Workshop on Chinese Language Processing (ACL 2003)*. Sapporo, Japan, 156–159.

Garside, R. (1987), *The Computational Analysis of English: A Corpus-based Approach* (chapter The CLAWS Word-tagging System). London: Longman.

Giménez, J./Màrquez, L. (2004), SVMTool: A General POS Tagger Generator Based on Support Vector Machines. In: *Proceedings of the IV International Conference on Language Resources and Evaluation (LREC'04)*. Lisbon, Portugal, 43–46.

Goh, C.-L./Asahara, M./Matsumoto, Y. (2004), Chinese Word Segmentation by Classification of Characters. In: *Proceedings of the Third SIGHAN Workshop on Chinese Language Processing (ACL 2004)*. Barcelona, Spain, 57–64.

Greene, B./Rubin, G. (1971), *Automatic Grammatical Tagging of English*. Technical report, Department of Linguistics, Brown University, Providence, Rhode Island.

Grefenstette, G./Tapanainen, P. (1994), What is A Word, What is a Sentence? Problems of Tokenization. In: *Proceedings of the 3rd Conference on Computational Lexicography and Text Research (COMPLEX'94)*. Budapest, Hungary, 79–87.

Jiang, F./Liu, H./Chen, Y./Lu, R. (2004), An Enhanced Model for Chinese Word Segmentation and Part-of-speech Tagging. In: *Proceedings of the Third SIGHAN Workshop on Chinese Language Processing (ACL 2004)*. Barcelona, Spain, 28–32.

Karlsson, F. (1990), Constraint Grammar as a Framework for Parsing Running Text. In: *Proceedings of the 13th International Conference on Computational Linguistics (COLING 1990)*. Helsinki, Finland, 168–173.

Klatt, S. (2005), Kombinierbare Textanalyseverfahren für die Korpusannotation und Informationsextraktion. PhD Thesis, Universität Stuttgart.

Klein, S./Simmons, R. (1963), A Computational Approach to Grammatical Coding of English Words. In: *Journal of the Association for Computing Machinery* 10(3), 334–347.

Ma, W-Y./Chen, K-J. (2003), Introduction to CKIP Chinese Word Segmentation System for the First International Chinese Word Segmentation Bakeoff. In: *Proceedings of the Second SIGHAN Workshop on Chinese Language Processing (ACL 2003)*. Sapporo, Japan, 168–171.

Manning, C. D./Schütze, H. (1999), *Foundations of Statistical Natural Language Processing*. Cambridge, MA: MIT Press.

Marcus, M. P./Santorini, B./Marcinkiewicz, M. A. (1993), Building a Large Annotated Corpus of English: The Penn Treebank. In: *Computational Linguistics* 19(2), 313–330.

Màrquez, L./Padró, L. (1997), A Flexible POS Tagger Using an Automatically Acquired Language Model. In: *Proceedings of the 35th Annual Meeting of the ACL (ACL-1997)*. Madrid, Spain, 238–245.

Matsumoto, Y./Kitauchi, A./Yamashita, T./Hirano, Y./Matsuda, H./Asahara, M. (1999), *Japanese Morphological Analysis System ChaSen*. Nara, Japan: Nara Institute of Science and Technology.

Mikheev, A. (1998), Feature Lattices for Maximum Entropy Modelling. In: *Proceedings of ACL-COLING'98*. Montreal, Canada, 845–848.

Mikheev, A. (2000), Tagging Sentence Boundaries. In: *Proceedings of the 1st Meeting of the North American Chapter of the Association for Computational Linguistics (ANLP-NAACL 2000)*. Seattle, WA, 264–271.

Mikheev, A. (2002), Periods, Capitalized Words, etc. In: *Computational Linguistics* 28(3), 289–318.

Mikheev, A. (2003), *The Oxford Handbook of Computational Linguistics* (chapter Text Segmentation). (Oxford Handbooks in Linguistics.) Oxford: Oxford University Press, 201–218.

Müller, H./Amerl, V./Natalis, G. (1980), Worterkennungsverfahren als Grundlage einer Universalmethode zur automatischen Segmentierung von Texten in Sätze. Ein Verfahren zur maschinellen Satzgrenzenbestimmung im Englischen. *Sprache und Datenverarbeitung* 1, 46–63.

Nagata, M. (1997), A Self-organizing Japanese Word Segmenter Using Heuristic Word Identification and Re-estimation. In: *Proceedings of the 5th Workshop on Very Large Corpora*. Beijing, China, 203–215.

Nakamura, M./Maruyama, K./Kawabata, T./Shikano, K. (1990), Neural Network Approach to Word Category Prediction for English Texts. In: Karlgren, H. (ed.), *Proceedings of the 13th International Conference on Computational Linguistics (COLING 1990)*. Helsinki, Finland, 213–218.

Niu, C./Li, W./Ding, J./Srihari, R. K. (2004), Orthographic Case Restoration Using Supervised Learning without Manual Annotation. In: *International Journal on Artificial Intelligence Tools* 13(1), 141–156.

Palmer, D. D./Hearst, M. A. (1997), Adaptive Multilingual Sentence Boundary Disambiguation. In: *Computational Linguistics* 23(2), 241–267.

Quinlan, J. R. (1983), Learning Efficient Classification Procedures and their Application to Chess End Games. In: Michalski, R./Carbonell, J./Mitchell, T. (eds.) *Machine Learning: An Artificial Intelligence Approach*. San Mateo, CA: Morgan Kaufmann, 463–482.

Ratnaparkhi, A. (1996), A Maximum Entropy Model for Part-of-speech Tagging. In: *Proceedings of the Conference on Empirical Methods in Natural Language Processing*. University of Pennsylvania, Philadelphia, PA, 133–142.

Reynar, J. C./Ratnaparkhi, A. (1997), A Maximum Entropy Approach to Identifying Sentence Boundaries. In: *Proceedings of the Fifth Conference on Applied Natural Language Processing*. Washington, D.C., USA, 16–19.

Riley, M. D. (1989), Some Applications of Tree-based Modelling to Speech and Language Indexing. In: *Proceedings of the DARPA Speech and Natural Language Workshop*. San Mateo, CA: Morgan Kaufmann, 339–352.

Schmid, H. (1994a). Part-of-speech Tagging with Neural Networks. In: *Proceedings of the 15th International Conference on Computational Linguistics (COLING 1994)*. Kyoto, Japan, 172–176.

Schmid, H. (1994b). Probabilistic Part-of-speech Tagging Using Decision Trees. In: *Proceedings of the International Conference on New Methods in Language Processing*. Manchester, UK, 44–49.

Schmid, H. (2000), *Unsupervised Learning of Period Disambiguation for Tokenisation*. Technical report, IMS, University of Stuttgart.

Simard, M. (1998), Automatic Insertion of Accents in French Texts. In: *Proceedings of the Third Conference on Empirical Methods in Natural Language Processing (EMNLP)*. Granada, Spain, 27–35.

Sun, J./Gao, J./Zhang, L./Zhou, M./Huang, C. (2002), Chinese Named Entity Identification Using Class-based Language Model. In: *Proceedings of the 19th International Conference on Computational Linguistics (COLING 2002)*. Taipei, Taiwan, 967–973.

Tapanainen, P./Voutilainen, A. (1994), Tagging Accurately – Don't Guess If You Know. In: *Proceedings of the 4th Conference on Applied Natural Language Processing*. Stuttgart, Germany: Association for Computational Linguistics, Morgan Kaufmann, 47–52.

Vapnik, V. N. (1995), *The Nature of Statistical Learning Theory*. New York: Springer-Verlag.

Viterbi, A. J. (1967), Error Bounds for Convolutional Codes and an Asymptotically Optimal Decoding Algorithm. In: *IEEE Transactions on Information Theory* 13, 260–269.

Weischedel, R./Meteer, M./Schwartz, R./Ramshaw, L./Palmucci, J. (1993), Coping with Ambiguity and Unknown Words through Probabilistic Models. In: *Computational Linguistics* 19(2), 359–382.

Wu, A. (2003), Chinese Word Segmentation in MSR-NLP. In: *Proceedings of the Second SIGHAN Workshop on Chinese Language Processing (ACL 2003)*. Sapporo, Japan, 172–175.

Wu, D. (1998), A Position Statement on Chinese Segmentation. Presented at the Chinese Language Processing Workshop, University of Pennsylvania, Philadelphia, 30 June to 2 July 1998. Current draft at http://www.cs.ust.hk/~dekai/papers/segmentation.html.

Wu, Y./Zhao, J./Xu, B. (2003), Chinese Named Entity Recognition Combining a Statistical Model with Human Knowledge. In: *Proceedings of the Workshop on Multilingual and Mixed-language Named Entity Recognition: Combining Statistical and Symbolic Models (ACL 2003)*. Sapporo, Japan, 65–72.

Xue, N./Shen, L. (2003), Chinese Word Segmentation as LMR Tagging. In: *Proceedings of the Second SIGHAN Workshop on Chinese Language Processing (ACL 2003)*. Sapporo, Japan, 176–179.

Zhang, H-P./Liu, Q./Cheng, X-Q./Zhang, H./Yu, H-K. (2003), Chinese Lexical Analysis Using Hierarchical Hidden Markov Model. In: *Proceedings of the Second SIGHAN Workshop on Chinese Language Processing (ACL 2003)*. Sapporo, Japan, 63–70.

Helmut Schmid, Stuttgart (Germany)

25. Lemmatising and morphological tagging

1. Introduction

Lemmatisation is the process of reducing a set of word forms to a smaller number of more generalised representations. In the specific case of inflectional morphology, morphological tagging conserves and makes explicit the information that is discarded by the process of reduction.

Lemmatisation and morphological tagging have a number of concrete applications in natural language processing such as corpus query, document indexing, identification of collocations and determining verb frames. A corpus query system, for example, does not require us to enter all word forms such as 'walk, walks, walking, walked' in a query returning matches relevant to a general search term 'walk' (assuming a lemmatised corpus). An example from the domain of information retrieval is document indexing. Consider the following set of word forms: 'customise, customiser, customisation'. These forms may be reduced to the form 'custom'. Thus a search term which is not an identical string to one of the forms above may nonetheless return documents containing expansions of the reduced form. Applying statistical methods, for example, for identifying collocations in a corpus, benefits from pre-processing in which the individual word forms under consideration are reduced to a more generalised form. A central question, therefore, is how word forms may be meaningfully grouped together and what they are mapped onto.

The consideration of morphological information is essential, for example, for purposes of correctly determining verb frames. For languages with a more flexible constituent order than, say, English, linear ordering alone is insufficient for unambiguously determining grammatical relations such as subject and accusative object – for nouns, for instance, the information we require is frequently indicated by case marking if not on the noun itself then on its determiners. Morphological tagging provides us with precisely this information.

For all such applications, a large number of word forms need to be mapped to an entity representing them. This article describes the theoretical prerequisites for this task and the practical steps required to automatically carry out the mapping from word forms to their respective lemmas and morphological information.

The article is structured as follows: first we discuss the notion of a lemma in a number of application contexts. The concept of a paradigm forms the core of this article and is subsequently dealt with in some detail in section 3. The existence of a paradigm is the prerequisite for the approaches to automated morphological analysis presented in section 4. Since a number of competing analyses are often the product of automated morphological analysis, it is imperative for a disambiguation step to be available. The article concludes with a discussion of potential sources of ambiguity and how such ambiguity may be resolved.

2. Variants of lemmatisation

There are two variants for automatic lemmatisation, one that requires a lexicon and one that does not. The lexicon-based variant can be further sub-divided into two categories: one that consists of an exhaustive list of all potential forms, the so-called full-form approach, and one that implements a paradigm-based approach to generating these forms. CELEX (Baayen/Piepenbrock/Gulikers 1995; see also http://www.kun.nl/celex/) is an example of a widely used full-form listing. Drawbacks are obvious in that such a listing is of necessity inflexible and manual inspection of every form in order to arrive at a mapping to a generalised form is time-consuming and error-prone. The focus in this article will be on paradigm-based approaches.

The approach that does not require a lexicon is known as stemming. Stemming is, as discussed in more detail below, not dependent on any systematic analysis. An approach that does, however, assume the existence of a system relies on knowledge of morphology.

Morphology deals with the smallest meaningful linguistic units, often below word level. The most common sub-division of morphology is into inflection and word formation (compounding, derivation and other processes). Roughly speaking, inflectional morphology accounts for changes in form determined by grammatical function while word formation describes the regular formation of new lexical material as a result of rule application (see Stump 1998 for discussion).

The process of stemming consists of truncating word forms in a relatively arbitrary fashion; on occasion the material that is cut off is identical to inflectional and derivational endings. Since there is no systematic recognition of morphology behind this process, the discarded material is not of further interest and thus stemming has no relevance for morphological tagging. Its purpose is solely the reduction of words to a common representation (for example, as a source of index terms for information retrieval).

The most well-known and widely used stemming algorithm for English to date (which has since been extended to other languages) is the Porter algorithm (Porter 1980).

For each of the approaches to lemmatisation listed above, a more precise formulation can be made of what is meant by lemma. For instance, in a full-form approach it is left to the creator of the listing to decide which form is regarded as the lemma – a lemma has to be explicitly selected and named by the listing's author.

In the paradigm-based approach, a lemma is a name for a class of morphologically related words. As such it is dependent on the underlying theoretical assumptions, the proposed application and convention. As mentioned previously, a set of possible word forms which have some paradigmatic relation are reduced to an entity standing for them all. This abstract entity is the lexeme and the label chosen to designate it is known as lemma. In the example 'walk, walks, walking, walked', the word forms are instantiations of the lexeme known by convention as 'walk'. Note, however, that many researchers use the terms lemma and lexeme differently.

In the case of stemming, the concept of lemma differs from how it is perceived in the paradigm-based approach. Stemming takes individual word forms, and processes the word form strings by rule application, resulting in a reduced form of the original input. This rule application truncates both inflected forms and word forms which are the result of word formation processes – the discarded material may therefore consist of either inflectional or derivational affixes. Since rule application is not based on an existing paradigm, the lemma arrived at may not be linguistically motivated. For example, 'walking' may be reduced to 'walk' by application of a stemming rule that discards the derivational affix '-ing'. This may at first sight appear to be linguistically motivated, whereas the truncated form 'tim' as output of the same process applied to 'timing' shows that this is clearly not the case. A paradigm-based approach would have recognized 'tim' as not being a potential base form that may be combined with '-ing'. Furthermore, the lemma concept within the stemming approach is arbitrary, since the order of application of stemming rules can lead to a number of different outputs. Stemming may be regarded as a special case of lemmatisation in the sense that a variety of word forms are reduced to a generalisation. For our purposes, however, we are only concerned with a linguistically well-founded and sound view of the lemma based on the existence of a paradigm.

Discussion of the notion of a lemma in the context of corpus linguistics can be found in Knowles/Zuraidah (2004). More general treatment of the notions of lemma, lexeme and morpheme is to be found in standard works on morphology (Bauer 2003; Matthews 1974; Booij/Lehmann/Mugdan 2000; Spencer/Zwicky 1998; Aronoff 1994; Luschützky 2000). For an overview of computational morphology, see Ritchie et al. (1992) and Sproat (1992).

3. Paradigm-based approach

In morphology there is not always a one-to-one mapping between form and function. Morphological information is not immediately apparent or even overtly expressed in many word forms. Consider, for example, the plural form *sheep* which is on the surface identical to its singular realisation – the plural morpheme is a zero morph which is not visible but is nonetheless present. On the other hand, however, completely predictable and regular morphological processes exist such as the formation of third person singular in the verb paradigm 'walk' by concatenation of the suffix '-s' to the base form: in such cases a rule may be posited resulting in the correct generation or analysis (in this case) of an inflected form.

3.1. Inflectional paradigms

A prerequisite for paradigm-based processing is an existing inflectional paradigm.

The cloud in Figure 25.1 represents a template for an inflectional paradigm. The lexeme is an abstraction which comprises the base form, a part of speech and a number of pairs made up of word forms and their respective relevant morphological information. The base form is a form to which the word forms can be reduced. Paradigms are language-specific. In a given language, the part of speech assigned to the word form dictates

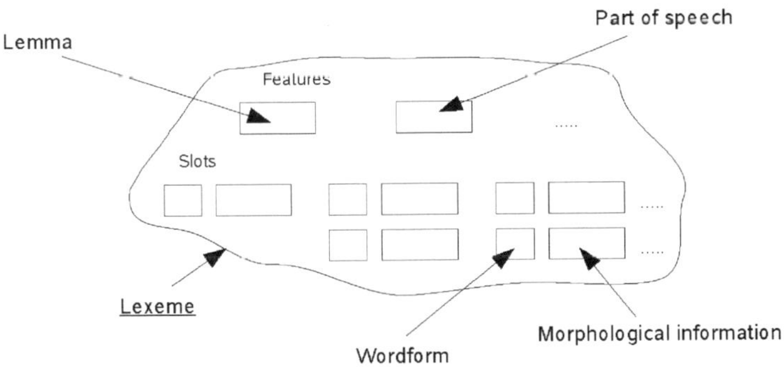

Fig. 25.1: A template for an inflectional paradigm

what information needs to be made explicit. A noun, for instance, may require the features case, number and gender whereas a verb will only share the feature number but differs in that features such as tense and person may be present. Thus, for a given part of speech, the templates will be identical in terms of the distinct types of morphological information present. Note, however, that it is really a matter of long-standing convention that inflectional types are driven by the notion of part of speech. Other means of assigning word forms to some kind of abstraction may be equally valid (see Carstairs-McCarthy 2000 for discussion).

Apart from the generally applicable conditions given above, the level of detail required by an inflectional paradigm is determined by the individual language for which it is realised. It would, for example, be simpler in an isolating language with few bound morphemes such as Chinese or Vietnamese and conversely more complex in an agglutinative language with a rich morphological inventory such as Finnish or Turkish. This means that in agglutinative languages an inflectional paradigm can consist of several hundred potential word forms. It is unsurprising that significant advances have been made in research concerning the computational morphological analysis of such languages, which have also proved relevant to, for example, Indo-European languages. Work on Turkish is reported on in Oflazer (1994), on Finnish in Alkula (2001), on Czech in Hajič (2000) and on Polish in Przepiórkowski/Woliński (2003).

If the paradigm-based approach is to be adopted, criteria for membership in a given part of speech category need to be defined. What these criteria are in detail is not relevant for the process of lemmatisation. Every individual part of speech class has its own predictable and regular characteristics; below the level of part of speech particular phenomena can be identified where word forms and their corresponding morphological information behave in the same way. Subclasses of parts of speech can be posited on the basis of common morphological behaviour. If, for example, the noun 'car' belongs to a subclass which forms plurals by the addition of the inflectional affix '-s' and the noun 'can' is known to belong to the same class, we can infer that its plural will be 'cans'. Given a subclass and a base form, the resulting set of word forms can be generated and thus it is possible to construct the entire lexicon on this basis. This approach does not, however, adequately account for irregular forms and processes like, for example, defective paradigms (verbs such as 'rain') or suppletives ('go, went, gone').

Just as rules may be applied for the generation of possible inflected forms, conversely a base form can be arrived at by means of application of rules to the existing inflected forms. On the basis of knowledge regarding what part of speech certain types of morphological information are assigned to, and since the base form is known, a set of potential lexemes is arrived at. Consider again the word form 'cans'. Facts concerning inflectional affixes of modal verbs rule out a verbal reading, while a plural nominal reading is admissible. If, however, the word form 'can' is present, both nominal and verbal readings are possible. In our model lemmatisation can be understood as the reduction of a word form to a possible set of base forms in order to subsequently arrive at a set of potential lexemes.

Since the string designating the lemma is often identical in surface realisation to the base form, terminological confusion may arise: the abstract notion of lexeme and the concrete instantiation of base form are confused with one another (in fact, both concepts belong to different levels of description).

It follows that a list of base forms and their corresponding subclasses are sufficient to account for the generation of word forms. An exhaustive list of base forms and subclasses is the resource required in order to be able to morphologically analyse word forms.

3.2. Example of the inflectional paradigm for a German noun

From this point onwards, the majority of examples given will be in German. The reason for this is the richer morphology of German compared to English.

Tab. 25.1: Paradigms of the German nouns *Gefährt* 'vehicle' and *Gefährte* 'companion'

	Sg	Pl
Nom	*Gefährt*	*Gefährte*
Gen	*Gefährts*	*Gefährte*
Dat	*Gefährt(e)*	*Gefährten*
Akk	*Gefährt*	*Gefährte*

	Sg	Pl
Nom	*Gefährte*	*Gefährten*
Gen	*Gefährten*	*Gefährten*
Dat	*Gefährten*	*Gefährten*
Akk	*Gefährten*	*Gefährten*

An example is given in Table 25.1, in which the paradigm for two German nouns (*Gefährt* (neuter) 'vehicle' and *Gefährte* (masculine) 'companion') is listed. Along with gender, which (in German) is inherent to nouns, morphological features for possible combinations of number and case also need to be listed. As can be seen, most of the nine possible forms (dative singular can be either *Gefährt* (default) or *Gefährte* (elevated, archaic usage), indicated by the brackets) are not distinct from one another in their surface realisation. This phenomenon is known as syncretism. It is immediately apparent that the morphological analysis of any of these forms leads to highly ambiguous results which then necessitate a further step of disambiguation. This topic is dealt with in section 5.

If the word forms listed in the paradigms above are encountered in running text, there only appear to be four distinct forms (*Gefährt*, *Gefährte*, *Gefährts*, *Gefährten*). Should the morphological information given above also be considered, however, then there are seventeen forms. This differentiation is another potential source of misunderstanding: since, in a given context, each word form mostly only has one correct morphological analysis, it is usually assumed that an analysis can be found for each word form easily and that is exactly what lemmatisation does. In the finer-grained view outlined above, however, it becomes immediately apparent that in most cases there are far more potential results than originally anticipated. The disambiguation of these results, again, is a matter of a subsequent linguistic processing step such as syntactic parsing, or alternatively a disambiguation step which immediately follows lemmatisation.

In the next section, methods for reduction of word forms to a set of corresponding base forms will be presented.

4. Paradigm-based processing

4.1. Prerequisites

As previously shown, an entire paradigm can be generated from the base form, inflectional affixes and the corresponding inflectional rules. These components have to be stored in order to carry out lemmatisation. In addition to inflectional rules, word formation rules also need to be accounted for, since in many languages a considerable number of word forms in a text are the product of word formation processes. Consider the German noun-noun compound *Haustür* 'front door', which is a concatenation of the nouns *Haus* 'house' and *Tür* 'door'; the morphological behaviour of the compound is identical to that of the rightmost component or head. Given the presence of *Haus* and *Tür* as base forms in the lexicon, and word formation rules such as noun + noun = noun, an inflectional rule specific to the compound *Haustür* is not needed, since it inherits the inflectional characteristics of its rightmost element. The same also holds for many derivational processes. This may not be obvious at first sight, since, for example the nominalisation suffix '-ung' in German does not occur on its own but nonetheless all '-ung' derivations display identical morphological behaviour. In conclusion, a combination of lists of base forms, derivational affixes, inflectional rules and word formation rules is the prerequisite for the lemmatisation process.

4.2. Practical application

Given these components, there are basically two ways of performing morphological analysis: reading the word form character by character from left to right or doing the same from right to left.

Consider the example in Table 25.2, which shows how the word form *Freudentränen* is analysed by the freely available German morphological analyser Morphy. The morphological analyser is described in Lezius/Rapp/Wettler (1998) and also featured in the first and only competitive comparison of morphology systems for German (Hausser 1996). In the first two steps, the potential inflectional suffixes '-n' and '-en' are identified. The first potential word form is identified in step 6 – this is the plural nominal word form *Tränen* 'tears', the corresponding base form being *Träne* 'tear'. In step 13, the next complete form *Freuden* 'joys' is identified, made up of the noun *Freude* 'joy' and the linking element '-n', commonly found for phonological reasons in German noun compounding. Note that the word form *Freudentränen* contains many more potential elements than those shown in Table 25.2, for instance the proper name 'Freud', but these

Tab. 25.2: The word form *Freudentränen* 'tears of joy' as analysed by Morphy

#	processing stage	feature(s) recognized
1	Freudenträne - n	inflectional suffix
2	Freudenträn - en	inflectional suffix
3	Freudenträ - nen	-
4	Freudentr - änen	-
5	Freudent - ränen	-
6	Freuden - tränen	plural form of the noun Träne 'tear'
7	Freude - ntränen	-
8	Freud - enträen	-
9	Freu - dentränen	-
10	Fre - udentränen	-
11	Fr - eudentränen	-
12	F - reudentränen	-
13	Freudentränen	noun compound 'tears of joy'

can be ruled out as a result of application of word formation and inflectional rules and the fact that all characters in the string need to be consumed.

The alternative approach is to proceed from left to right, and it uses widely-known finite-state techniques. Finite-state techniques have a long history and are mathematically well-founded and well understood. The most authoritative work to date describing these techniques and their theoretical background is Hopcroft/Ullman (1979). Finite-state methods allow in this case rapid processing of input strings. They are realised by so-called finite-state automata (FSAs), which in their simplest form recognize a sequence of input symbols. Application of such methods in the field of natural language processing is dealt with in Mohri (1997) and Roche/Schabes (1997).

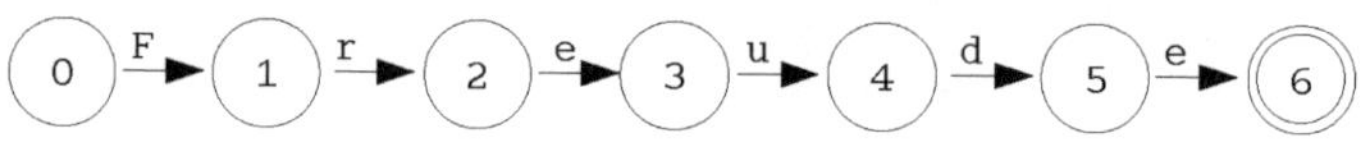

Fig. 25.2: A simple finite-state automaton

An FSA consists of states and transitions; a word in the lexicon can be represented as a sequence of single transitions (see Figure 25.2). The final state shown by convention as two concentric circles is the accepting state, which indicates that the input sequence has been recognized. Inflectional and word form rules based on concatenation can be represented in precisely this manner. In the example given above, *Freude* 'joy' is recognized as a valid entry in the lexicon – this is the most specific level of representation, and strings sharing the same kind of behaviour can be further grouped together in more generalised classes. Word formation rules can thus be expressed by such generalisations.

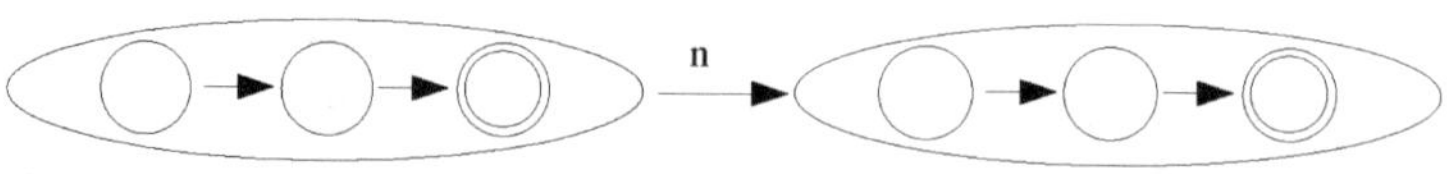

Fig. 25.3: Concatenation of FSAs

In Figure 25.3 a rule is shown that demonstrates that a noun-noun compound is recognized as being the result of a simple concatenation operation which requires an additional linking element '-n'. Such generalisations are referred to as classes; the left-hand component represents FSAs for the class of nouns forming compounds with '-n' and the right-hand component is known in FSA terminology as a continuation class.

Solely recognizing an input string is not sufficient for our purposes, since neither morphological information nor the base form can be acquired in this way. The solution comes in the form of a more specific FSA, this being a finite-state transducer (FST). By FST we understand an automaton that is not only able to recognize input but also to transform it, i. e., an automaton that can read input and write output. When reading the string *Tränen* 'tears', the base form *Träne* 'tear' may be written to the output while the transition that is realised by the plural affix '-n' can be suppressed in the output and instead morphological information stating that it is a plural affix can be written to the output.

Tab. 25.3: Morphological analysis of German noun *Träne* 'tear'

#	wordform	morphological analysis
1	*Tränen*	Träne+NN.Fem.Nom.Pl
2		Träne+NN.Fem.Gen.Pl
3		Träne+NN.Fem.Dat.Pl
4		Träne+NN.Fem.Acc.Pl

How morphological information is presented is subject to notational convention, as shown in Table 25.3. The word form *Tränen* 'tears' is shown with its four possible analyses. The analysis comprises the base form, *Träne* 'tear', the part-of-speech tag (NN denoting common noun), gender (Fem denoting feminine), case (nominative, genitive, dative and accusative) and number (Pl denoting plural). Features are determined by the paradigm. The notation employed is completely arbitrary, here the plus sign separates the base form from the morphological information, and the dot separates morphological features from one another. Other notations are, of course, possible. It should be noted that the FST writes all possible analyses.

4.3. Two-level morphology

Although the FST is the tool of choice for analysing morphological material which is the result of processes of concatenation, it cannot account for others such as deletion or vowel mutation. For this reason the formalism known as two-level morphology was developed and first presented in Kimmo Koskenniemi's PhD thesis (Koskenniemi 1983). In a two-level model, context rules can also be stated for given symbols, and these rules can themselves be compiled into automata and retain the expressive power of FSAs. This is illustrated by the following two examples.

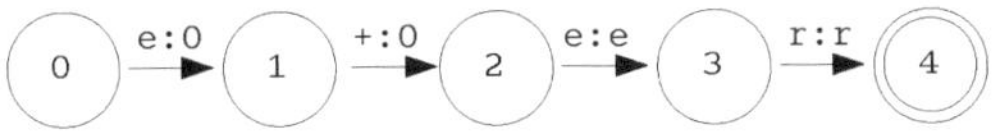

Fig. 25.4: A two-level rule for elision

The adjective *leise* 'quiet' forms its comparative by appending the affix '-er'. The resulting form, however, is *leiser* 'quieter'. For phonological reasons, one 'e' is deleted. Using an FST would require us to postulate an additional lexicon entry 'leis' or else an additional comparative suffix '-r', neither of which is satisfactory, since they do not explain the underlying linguistic principle. Using two-level morphology avoids the two approaches suggested above and offers a more elegant solution, in which a context rule is introduced stating that a superfluous 'e' is deleted in such a context as shown in Figure 25.4. The rule ensures that for all lexicon entries ending in 'e' followed by an inflectional affix also beginning with 'e', the first 'e' is deleted in the output. The advantage is obvious since neither the lexicon nor the inventory of affixes need to be modified or augmented and incorrect forms are not generated.

A morphological process that occurs frequently in German plural formation is vowel mutation (Umlautung), as in *Haus* 'house'/*Häuser* 'houses'. Two-level morphology allows the positing of a rule stating that plural formation with vowel mutation may take place and this rule can be applied to a set of lexicon entries sharing the same morphological behaviour. Again, there is no need for explicit additional lexicon entries containing the mutation (Umlaut). How this functions for analysis can be illustrated by the example of *Freudentränen* 'tears of joy' (see Table 25.2). Here 'Trän' could also conceivably be a plural representation of the noun *Tran* 'oil'. This interpretation is, however, ruled out, since *Tran* is not in the class of nouns where vowel mutation is allowed for plural formation.

Just as for FSTs, two-level morphology generates all possible analyses. This holds for potential permutations of lexicon entries and inflectional rules, and for each of these there may be a set of distinct pieces of morphological information.

A useful overview of the history of finite-state and two-level morphology can be found in Karttunen/Beesley (2005), and more comprehensive accounts are to be found in Beesley/Karttunen (2003) and in chapter 3 of Jurafsky/Martin (2000). An early implementation of two-level morphology is described in Karttunen (1983) and the most well-known freely available implementation is Antworth (1990). Although early work in two-level morphology addressed issues for richly inflected languages, the approach has also been applied to English (cf Karp et al. 1992; Minnen/Carroll/Pearce 2001). A freely available suite of finite-state tools, used extensively for the processing of German, is described in Schmid (2005b) and is available for download at http://www.ims.uni-stuttgart.de/sfst/. An application of these tools for German morphology is presented in Schmid/Fitschen/Heid (2004).

4.4. Discussion and alternative approaches

It is clear that the quality of analysis is heavily dependent on the size and quality of the lexicon. Nonetheless, a larger lexicon does not automatically guarantee better quality analyses, since the larger the lexical resource, the more scope for ambiguity there is. Producing a high quality lexicon is the most labour-intensive part of creating a system for morphological analysis, so as a consequence most freely available systems contain only a small lexicon. Methods for automating lexicon construction have therefore gained increasing importance in the research community as an alternative to purely handcrafting lexicons. Currently the most promising approach consists of a combination of automatic lexicon production with manual post-editing.

The inventory of the lexicon is, however, not confined to lemmas. It may also contain smaller segments such as morphemes. As an example, a recent competition has taken place to evaluate unsupervised learning methods for the segmentation of words into morphemes (Morpho-challenge 2005, http://www.cis.hut.fi/morphochallenge2005/). One of the tasks in the competition was to arrive at morpheme segmentation for three languages on the basis of training data; the segmentation proposed by the machine learning method was compared to a gold standard of manually segmented material. A summary of the task is given and its evaluation is described in Kurimo/Creutz/Varjokallio (2005).

5. Types of ambiguity and disambiguation

It is a common misconception that a lemmatisation process returns a preferred analysis, but we have seen that since all possible forms are returned, there needs to be a subsequent disambiguation step which can either be part of the next component in a pipeline architecture such as syntactic parsing or a free-standing component. It is tempting to create continuation classes in a finite-state transducer which account for ambiguous lexicon entries in order to avoid specific analyses that have a high likelihood of being wrong. An example of such ambiguity is the German noun *Los*, in its nominal reading meaning 'lot' (in the sense of 'fate'), 'ticket' or appearing as an adjectival suffix *-los* '-less'. As a result of the large number of adjectives in German formed with *-los*, there will be many analyses which mistakenly arrive at a noun-noun compound reading – for example, *ahnungslos* 'clueless' may be read as a compound consisting of *Ahnung* 'idea', linking element '-s' and the noun *Los*. Should rules have been previously posited so that a finite-state transducer can exclude such an unwanted analysis, a side effect is that an acceptable noun-noun compound such as *Lotterielos* 'lottery ticket' will then not be correctly identified. For this reason, it is advisable to have a clear distinction between the analysis and disambiguation steps.

A practical solution is to rank the analyses in order of their probability (cf Hakkani-Tür/Oflazer/Tür 2000; Schmid 2005a). In the example above with '-los', an adjectival reading is preferred on grounds of frequency of occurrence; the noun-noun compound readings are not disregarded but are ranked lower. Additionally, part-of-speech information from a tagger (cf. article 24) can be taken into account such that when an adjectival reading is ruled out on these grounds, the rarer cases of acceptable noun-noun compounds will be preferred.

Six possible morphological analyses of *Verbraucher* 'consumer' are given in Table 25.4 (solely with regard to inflectional morphology). If, however, we consider word formation and not just inflection, there are several potential decompositions of the lemma:

(i) *Verbraucher* 'consumer', noun; assuming it is listed in the lexicon. This is the case presented previously,

(ii) *verbrauchen* + *er* 'to consume' + nominalization; assuming a rule exists stating that the derivational suffix '-er' can combine with a verb to form a noun,

(iii) *Verb=Raucher* 'verb + smoker', noun-noun compound; assuming both nouns are stored in the lexicon and there is a noun-noun compounding rule.

(iv) *Verb=rauch+er* 'verb + to smoke' + nominalization; again, assuming the constituents are listed in the lexicon and the respective word-formation rules exist.

The example illustrates the different potential levels of complexity in a morphological analysis system. Depending on whether or not word-formation rules are taken into account, the six purely inflectional analyses in Table 25.4 are augmented by several analyses determined by the presence of word-formation rules. As has already been stated, since lemmatisation is not a process with one canonical outcome, the level of detail is driven by the requirements of its application. Some contexts disregard analyses below the level of inflection, whereas others need to account for productivity in word formation. Should potential nominalisations, for example, be irrelevant to the task at hand, analyses (ii) and (iv) will not exist.

Tab. 25.4: Morphological analyses of the German noun *Verbraucher* 'consumer'

#	wordform	morphological analysis
1	*Verbraucher*	Verbraucher+NN.Masc.Nom.Sg
2		Verbraucher+NN.Masc.Dat.Sg
3		Verbraucher+NN.Masc.Acc.Sg
4		Verbraucher+NN.Masc.Nom.Pl
5		Verbraucher+NN.Masc.Gen.Pl
6		Verbraucher+NN.Masc.Acc.Pl

Note, finally, that although analyses (iii) and (iv) make no sense (verbs cannot be smoked), there is no semantic component to rule them out and thus they are given as potential readings. Semantic disambiguation would require a further processing step.

6. Summary

The problem of lemmatisation consists in the fact that there is no one canonical definition of the process. Natural language processing applications have a variety of requirements, such that in some cases simple stemming suffices and in others knowledge of a paradigm is a prerequisite. Terminological confusion arises as a result. Theoretical and practical levels are therefore often mixed. Given a paradigm, the process of lemmatisation is a simple matter of string transduction, often realised by the use of finite-state techniques. An extension of finite-state approaches is two-level morphology, which remains within the finite-state model but makes a linguistically motivated description possible. Contrary to common belief, the result of lemmatisation is a set of possible analyses rather than a single disambiguated morphological analysis. For this reason, an additional processing step such as syntactic parsing is required in order to arrive at the most plausible analysis.

7. Literature

Alkula, R. (2001), From Plain Character Strings to Meaningful Words: Producing Better Full Text Databases for Inflectional and Compounding Languages with Morphological Analysis Software. In: *Information Retrieval* 4(3/4), 195–208.

Antworth, E. L. (1990), *PC-KIMMO. A Two-level Processor for Morphological Analysis*. Dallas, TX: Summer Institute of Linguistics.
Aronoff, M. (1994), *Morphology by Itself*. Cambridge, MA: MIT Press.
Baayen, R. H./Piepenbrock, R./Gulikers, L. (1995), *The CELEX Lexical Database* (CDROM). Philadelphia, PA: Linguistic Data Consortium, University of Pennsylvania.
Bauer, L. (2003), *Introducing Linguistic Morphology*, 2nd edition. Edinburgh: Edinburgh University Press.
Beesley, K. R./Karttunen, L. (2003), *Finite State Morphology*. Palo Alto, CA: CSLI Publications.
Booij, G./Lehmann, C./Mugdan, J. (eds.) (2000), *Morphologie. Morphology. Ein internationales Handbuch zur Flexion und Wortbildung. An International Handbook on Inflection and Word Formation*, Volume 1 / Halbband 1. Berlin: de Gruyter.
Carstairs-McCarthy, A. (2000), Lexeme, Word-form, Paradigm. In: Booij/Lehmann/Mugdan 2000, 595–607.
Hajič, J. (2000), Morphological Tagging: Data vs. Dictionaries. In: *Proceedings of the First Conference of the North American Chapter of the Association for Computational Linguistics*. Seattle WA, 94–101.
Hakkani-Tür, D. Z./Oflazer, K./Tür, G. (2000), Statistical Morphological Disambiguation for Agglutinative Languages. In: *Proceedings of COLING-2000, the 18th International Conference on Computational Linguistics*. Saarbrücken, Germany, 285–291.
Hausser, R. (ed.) (1996), *Linguistische Verifikation. Dokumentation zur Ersten Morpholympics 1994*. Tübingen: Max Niemeyer Verlag.
Hopcroft, J. E./Ullman, J. D. (1979), *Introduction to Automata Theory, Languages, and Computation*. Reading, MA: Addison Wesley.
Jurafsky, D./Martin, J. H. (2000), *Speech and Language Processing: An Introduction to Natural Language Processing, Computational Linguistics and Speech Recognition*. Upper Saddle River, NJ: Prentice Hall.
Karp, D./Schabes, Y./Zaidel, M./Egedi, D. (1992), A Freely Available Wide Coverage Morphological Analyzer for English. In: *Proceedings of the 14th International Conference on Computational Linguistics*. Nantes, France, 950–955.
Karttunen, L./Beesley, K. R. (2005), Twenty-five Years of Finite-state Morphology. In: Carlson, L./ Ylijyrä, A. (eds.), *A Festschrift for Kimmo Koskenniemi*. Palo Alto, CA: CSLI Publications, 71–83.
Karttunen, L. (1983), KIMMO: A General Morphological Processor. In: *Texas Linguistic Forum* 22, 165–186.
Knowles, G./Zuraidah, M. D. (2004), The Notion of a "Lemma": Headwords, Roots and Lexical Sets. In: *International Journal of Corpus Linguistics* 9(1), 69–81.
Koskenniemi, K. (1983), *Two-level Morphology: A General Computational Model for Word-form Recognition and Production*. PhD thesis, University of Helsinki.
Kurimo, M./Creutz, M./Varjokallio, M. (2005), *Unsupervised Segmentation of Words into Morphemes – Morpho-challenge 2005: An Introduction and Evaluation Report*. Technical report, Helsinki University of Technology.
Lezius, W./Rapp, R./Wettler, M. (1998), A Freely Available Morphological Analyzer, Disambiguator, and Context Sensitive Lemmatizer for German. In: *Proceedings of the COLING-ACL*. Montreal, Canada, 743–747.
Luschützky, H. C. (2000), Morphem, Morph und Allomorph. In: Booij/Lehmann/Mugdan 2000, 451–463.
Matthews, P. H. (1974), *Morphology. An Introduction to the Theory of Word-structure*. Cambridge: Cambridge University Press.
Minnen, G./Carroll, J./Pearce, D. (2001), Applied Morphological Processing of English. In: *Natural Language Engineering* 7(3), 207–223.
Mohri, M. (1997), Finite-state Transducers in Language and Speech Processing. In: *Computational Linguistics* 23(2), 269–311.

Oflazer, K. (1994), Two-level Description of Turkish Morphology. In: *Literary and Linguistic Computing* 9(2), 137–148.
Porter, M. (1980), An Algorithm for Suffix Stripping. In: *Program* 14, 130–137.
Przepiórkowski, A./Woliński, M. (2003), A Flexemic Tagset for Polish. In: *Proceedings of the Workshop on Morphological Processing of Slavic Languages (EACL 2003)*. Budapest, Hungary, 33–40.
Ritchie, G. D./Russell, G. J./Black, A. W./Pulman, S. G. (1992), *Computational Morphology*. Cambridge, MA: Bradford Books, MIT Press.
Roche, E./Schabes, Y. (eds.) (1997), *Finite-state Language Processing*. Cambridge, MA: MIT Press.
Schmid, H. (2005a), Disambiguation of Morphological Structure Using a PCFG. In: *Proceedings of the Human Language Technology Conference and the Conference on Empirical Methods in Natural Language Processing (HLT/EMNLP 2005)*. Vancouver, Canada, 515–522.
Schmid, H. (2005b), A Programming Language for Finite State Transducers. In: *Proceedings of the 5th International Workshop on Finite State Methods in Natural Language Processing*. Helsinki, Finland, 308–309.
Schmid, H./Fitschen, A./Heid, U. (2004), SMOR: A German Computational Morphology Covering Derivation, Composition, and Inflection. In: *Proceedings of the 4th International Conference on Language Resources and Evaluation (LREC 2004)*. Lisbon, Portugal, 1263–1266.
Spencer, A./Zwicky, A. M. (eds.) (1998), *The Handbook of Morphology*. Oxford: Blackwell.
Sproat, R. (1992), *Morphology and Computation*. Cambridge, MA: MIT Press.
Stump, G. T. (1998), Inflection. In: Spencer/Zwicky 1998, 13–43.

Arne Fitschen and Piklu Gupta, Mannheim and Tübingen (Germany)

26. Sense and semantic tagging

1. Introduction

Understanding the meaning of words seems to present little difficulty to human beings. Indeed, children as young as seven years old seem to be able to disambiguate the various meanings of polysemous words in context. Yet, this seemingly trivial task has presented a serious challenge to the natural language processing (NLP) research community amongst others, as witnessed by the crop of recent journal special issues (Ide/Véronis 1998; Kilgarriff/Palmer 2000; Edmonds/Kilgarriff 2002; Preiss/Stevenson 2004).

Researchers in machine translation (MT) have been aware of the difficulty posed by multiple meanings of words since the 1950s and 1960s (Gale/Church/Yarowsky 1993).

However, whilst some researchers have allegedly left the field in frustration (Bar-Hillel, for example, when he could see no way of automatically resolving the meaning of the word "pen" in the sentence "The box was in the pen"; Bar-Hillel 1960), some others have devoted remarkable efforts to word sense disambiguation (WSD).

The WSD algorithms and systems that have been suggested and developed since the 1950s tend to draw on AI-based methods, knowledge-based methods and corpus-based methods (Ide/Véronis 1998). However, more recently, researchers have started to combine various approaches together, as a means of obtaining better results (Stevenson/Wilks 2001).

Several studies have demonstrated that sense identification is a difficult task, even for humans. For example, Fellbaum et al. (1998) showed that humans agree with each other less than 80% of the time when deciding on the appropriate sense for a given corpus example. Véronis (2003) showed that people disagree widely in their judgments on the appropriate dictionary sense for corpus citations and that for some words agreement between the annotators was no greater than chance.

One of the reasons that the WSD task is difficult is that there is no clearly agreed definition of what constitutes a word sense. WSD systems commonly use lexical resources to provide a list of sense definitions but these do not agree on what the senses for each word should be or even how many there are for a particular word. Jorgensen (1990) carried out an experiment to determine whether sense definitions found in dictionaries are realistic models of the human mental lexicon and found that human subjects consistently identify fewer senses than were found in dictionaries. Lexicographers are given detailed instructions on the criteria for sense distinction based on grammatical, etymological and semantic criteria, amongst others, while Jorgensen's subjects were simply asked to sort corpus citations on semantic grounds. However, as Kilgarriff (1997) notes, lexicographers make decisions on whether to 'lump' or 'split' senses that are subjective with a particular target audience in mind. Jorgensen's subjects found concrete nouns easier to define than other classes of words. In addition Fellbaum's subjects found nouns easier to disambiguate. Gentner/France (1988) showed that people are less flexible in their interpretation of nouns than other parts of speech. The clearer delimitation of nominal semantics seems to make the definition and tagging tasks simpler for this part of speech.

A WSD system generally selects a sense from a pool of possible senses of a word that matches a given context. For example, it would tag the word "bank" as a financial institution if it finds that the surrounding words talk about financial issues, and as "river bank" if its context talks about a river. Some WSD systems can even distinguish between "bank" as a financial institution and "bank" as the building containing that institution (or one branch of it), even though such fine-grained sense disambiguation is not always necessary within NLP. Many NLP problems can be solved without access to the full set of dictionary definitions. Let's imagine a scenario in which we only want to know the domain of a journalistic report. In order to understand that the report talks about a crime case, it should be enough to know that many words in the news are about crime, law and the court[s]. For this type of task, what we need is a system that can determine the semantic category (or categories) of each word rather than a system that finds actual word sense definitions.

As we can see, there are a variety of tasks requiring some kind of semantic categorization. A range of terms is used to describe similar techniques from semantic disambiguation, semantic tagging, sense disambiguation down to sense tagging. In this article we shall make distinctions between different categories of the task, based on two factors. Firstly, the type of annotation being applied to words, and secondly on the proportion of words being annotated. The annotations can be semantic tags from a particular taxonomy (e. g. semantic fields of Food, Sport) or componential analysis (e. g. HUMAN, ADULT, FEMALE), or senses from a lexical resource (e. g. LDOCE or WordNet). We distinguish disambiguation from tagging as follows: disambiguation relates to annotation applied to a proportion of the words in a text, whereas tagging relates to the application of annotation to every word in a text. The task of named-entity extraction, for example, which identifies three types of proper names (organization, person and location), two types of temporal expression (date and time) and two types of numbers (money and percentages), can be classified in our scheme as a high-level semantic disambiguation task.

In the remainder of this article, we describe in further detail the motivations for the general task of semantic tagging, present a chronological survey of the methods and taxonomies used, an overview of the evaluation activities and report on research on English and other languages.

2. Motivation for semantic disambiguation

In this section we discuss the motivation for the general task of semantic disambiguation. We can distinguish between semantic disambiguation as an object of study in its own right for linguists or language engineers, and semantic disambiguation as a pre-processing step in a larger language understanding system or application. In this article, we will focus on semantic pre-processing as a constituent of some larger task. We can identify the following applications where semantic disambiguation can assist or is required:

a. Machine Translation (cf article 56): early recognition of the usefulness of semantic analysis came from researchers in Machine Translation (MT), e. g. Weaver (1955); Bar-Hillel (1960). Hutchins/Somers (1992) noted that semantic ambiguity resolution is of use in two stages of MT. First the understanding of sentences in the source language, and second in the generation of sentences in the target language. Transla tion equivalence occurs at the level of word senses rather than words themselves. For example, Ide/Véronis (1998) cite the French word "grille", which, depending on the context, can be translated into English as "railings", "gate", "bar", "grid", "scale", or "schedule".
b. Information retrieval: using ambiguous words as terms in information retrieval systems results in matched documents containing unwanted meanings. For example, in a geographical search for the word "labrador", we would want to exclude senses relating to the labrador retriever breed of dog in order to focus on documents about the large peninsula in north-east Canada. There is an ongoing debate about the usefulness of semantic disambiguation for IR. Krovetz/Croft (1992) carried out experiments comparing query results on a corpus with ambiguous terms with those results obtained after manually disambiguating terms. They concluded that a perfect disambiguation system would improve retrieval performance by only 2%. By contrast, Schütze/Pederson (1995) showed that disambiguation substantially improved infor-

mation retrieval performance by between 7% and 14% on average. Cross-language Information Retrieval is another form of text retrieval in which the user submits the query in one language while the documents being retrieved are written in a different language. This interesting problem combines elements of machine translation with information retrieval. Stevenson/Clough (2004) showed that sense tagging is beneficial for this task.

c. Content analysis: content analysis is concerned with the quantitative analysis of the semantic features of texts. The methodology uses a set of content categories into which the words in the text are classified. The categories may be chosen in advance, or developed based on an initial coding of words or phrases in the text. This pre-coding technique has been used for example in the General Inquirer System developed at Harvard University (Stone et al. 1966). In more recent years, content analysis has had to compete to a greater degree than before with other approaches to textual analysis in the social sciences but there is still considerable interest in the technique, especially in the market research sector (e. g. Kassarjian 1977). Content analysis has been employed for a variety of practical applications including psychological profiling from texts, longitudinal political research, management research and medical sociology (Wilson/Thomas 1997).
d. Semantic Web: since the emergence of the World Wide Web, users of internet search engines have discovered similar problems with search results. The semantic web project (Berners-Lee/Hendler/Lassila 2001) is addressing this as one of its goals. Much research has focused on ontology languages (in addition to the ontologies themselves) for the semantic annotation of Web pages.
e. Corpus linguistics: semantic annotation is helpful for grammatical analysis and corpus annotation. For example, the disambiguation at part-of-speech level between noun and adjective uses of words like “French” and “German” can be resolved by template rules grouping verbs of communication together (which often precede these words) to ensure the following uses “speak French”, “wrote in German”, “read Japanese” are tagged as nouns.
f. Lexicography (cf article 8): semantic annotation, and semantic field analysis in particular, is increasingly being used within lexicography, as a means of distinguishing between the lexicographic senses of the same word. The reason, as Jackson/Zé Amvela (2000, 112) highlight, is that a “semantic field arrangement brings together words that share the same semantic space”, and thus provides “a record of the vocabulary resources available for an area of meaning”. This, in turn, enables “a user of the language, whether a foreign learner or a native speaker, to appreciate often elusive meaning differences between words”. Yet, as Jackson/Zé Amvela also highlight (2000, 113), there is as yet no general-purpose dictionary that uses the semantic field as its organizing principle. Indeed, lexicons using the semantic field principle tend to be based on religious texts and/or be thesaurus-like in nature (e. g. Louw-Nida and Hallig-Wartburg-Wilson). It is worth noting that, many of these semantic category systems agree, to a greater or lesser extent, on the basic major categories that they contain. However, their structure and granularity are very different (Archer et al. 2004). At a finer level of granularity, a sense-annotated corpus would be of particular value to lexicographers, as they would not have to trawl through “money bank” citations when defining “river bank” (Clear 1994).
g. Speech processing: semantic disambiguation is required for determining the correct pronunciation for words in text-to-speech systems (Yarowsky 1997). For example,

German 'Tenor' (tenor, in the sense of 'a male singer with a high voice') and 'Tenor' (tone, in the sense of 'the tone of this article ...'). The first is stressed on the first syllable, the second is stressed on the second syllable. In addition, for speech recognition systems, word segmentation and homophone processing (words which are spelled differently but pronounced the same) will be assisted by semantic disambiguation (Connine 1990).

Having looked at the motivations for semantic and sense annotation, we now turn to a survey of the methods used to carry out this tagging.

3. Survey of methods

3.1. AI-based methods

Initial approaches to automatic sense tagging were firmly rooted in the Artificial Intelligence tradition. Wilks (1975) developed a system for machine translation called "preference semantics". This approach used the selectional constraints on nouns and verbs to select the correct sense. For example, in "John drinks port" we can say that "port" is being used to mean an alcoholic drink (and not a town with a harbor) since it is the direct object of "drink". While this approach was not new, Wilks extended it to allow for novel and metaphorical usages. For example, when presented with the sentence "My car drinks gasoline." Wilks' system would realize that "drinks" was being used metaphorically since none of the existing senses of that verb allow "car" as their subject.

Small (1980) provided an approach which was even more highly lexicalised than that of Wilks, with the lexicon being the source of all information in his system. Through disambiguation a representation for the entire sentence would be built up from the representations of the individual words it contained. Small believes words are idiosyncratic to the extent that an individual word expert, essentially a hand-crafted disambiguator, should be constructed for each. In Small's system word experts contain information which would be stored in the grammar, lexicon, parser or knowledge base in a more conventional system but their size limited this approach.

Hirst (1987) created a system which was less lexicalised and more general than either Small's or Wilks'. His system contained the modules found in a conventional NLP system: a grammar, parser, lexicon, semantic interpreter and knowledge representation language. The disambiguation information and processes were distributed across the different parts of the system. Sentences entered to the system would be translated to the knowledge representation language, and the information in them would be added to the systems knowledge base, so that the whole system constituted a fully working NLP system.

These three systems, reviewed as examples of early approaches, share a lack of extendibility, from their internal lexicon and from the domain in which they were implemented. Each involves, to a greater or lesser extent, a large amount of manual creation of disambiguators.

3.2. Knowledge-based methods

In the 1980's dictionary publishers started to produce electronic versions of their products, dubbed Machine Readable Dictionaries (MRD). Since, as we have seen, the creation of large lexical resources has always been a bottleneck, it was a natural step for researchers to make use of these high coverage resources which had been produced by professional lexicographers. However, a large problem with MRDs was the level of polysemy – they contain a far wider set of potential senses for each word than any of the systems described so far. With the ultimate aim of applying these resources, researchers attempted to disambiguate text relative to the senses in MRDs.

One of the first methods for exploiting the information available in MRDs was produced by Lesk (1986). His strategy was to take the textual definitions from a dictionary and choose the senses which share the most words with other senses. His motivating example was "pine cone". In the dictionary he used "pine" has two senses ('kind of evergreen tree with needle-shaped leaves' and 'waste away through sorrow or illness') while "cone" has three ('solid body which narrows at a point', 'something of this shape whether solid or hollow' and 'fruit of certain evergreen trees'). The correct senses of "pine" and "cone" share the words "evergreen" and "tree" in their definitions. Lesk's implementation compared all potential senses for each ambiguous word within a short, 10-word, context. He estimated that this approach disambiguates 50–70% of words correctly.

A disadvantage of Lesk's approach is that it becomes impractical when attempting to disambiguate all content words for an inventory containing several possible senses for the majority of words; the number of definition overlap computations required is simply too large. Cowie/Guthrie/Guthrie (1992) applied simulated annealing, a numerical minimisation algorithm, as an alternative to calculating all possible combinations. Cowie/Guthrie/Guthrie's implementation of this proposal assigned senses from the machine readable version of the *Longman Dictionary of Contemporary English* (LDOCE) (cf section 4). They reported that 47% of words were correctly disambiguated to a fine-grained level of semantic distinction and 72% to a more rough grained level. MRDs are not the only resources which have been used as knowledge sources for sense tagging; WordNet (cf. section 4) is another commonly used resource, for example (Agirre/Rigau 1996; Banerjee/Pedersen 2002).

3.3. Corpus-based methods

As an alternative to using MRDs, many researchers experimented with automatically acquiring disambiguation information from corpora. An early attempt was carried out by Brown et al. (1991). Their algorithm carried out disambiguation for an English to French machine translation system. Training was carried out on sentence pairs which consisted of an English sentence and its corresponding French translation. Several different disambiguation cues were identified in the sentence pairs, of the type: first noun to the left/right, second word to the left/right etc. A learning algorithm was used to decide which of the cues was most important for each word by maximising mutual information scores between words in the sentence pairs.

Yarowsky (1992) developed a method to identify the most appropriate thesaurus category for each word in text. He used *Roget's Thesaurus* (cf. section 4), with statistical models of the categories in the thesaurus being inferred from unannotated text. An important aspect of this approach was that he used a larger window of words, or context, than had been previously considered in WSD research; Yarowsky used a context of 50 words on either side so that 100 words were considered in the training examples for each ambiguous word. Statistical models for each Roget category were built by extracting contexts around each instance of any word in the category in the corpus. The models themselves were simple Naïve Bayesian models. This approach was tested on 12 polysemous words achieving 92% correct disambiguation.

Sense taggers which automatically induce disambiguation information from text rely on learning algorithms. These can be either supervised or unsupervised. This distinction is often described as a pair of distinct classes but is better viewed as a continuum of techniques. At one end is supervised systems which are provided with a set of pre-defined senses and learn from text in which ambiguous words are annotated with the appropriate sense. Fully unsupervised algorithms lie at the other end of this scale, they do not make use of a pre-defined lexicon but group together corpus examples to automatically cluster word usages into meanings. A good example of this approach can be found in Schütze (1998). The main advantage of unsupervised approaches is that they do not require pre-annotated text which is often costly and time-consuming to produce. However, the sense distinctions they automatically create do not always correspond to those found in lexicons produced by lexicographers and the goal of sense tagging is often to create an explicit link between corpus usages and these resources. The approach described by Yarowsky (1992) creates these links but without the requirement for annotated text, this mixture of supervised and unsupervised methodology combines the advantages of both.

An important claim about the way in which word senses are distributed was made by Gale/Church/Yarowsky (1992b). They concluded that words have "One Sense per Discourse" that is "there is a very strong tendency (98%) for multiple uses of a word to share the same sense in a well-written discourse." (Gale/Church/Yarowsky 1992b, 236). This claim was followed by another, the "One Sense per Collocation" claim: "with high probability an ambiguous word has only one sense in a given collocation" (Yarowsky 1993, 271). This claim was motivated by experiments where several different types of collocations are considered in which it was discovered that a polysemous word was unlikely to occur in the same collocation with a different sense. These are rather striking claims which have important implications for WSD algorithms. If the One Sense per Discourse claim is true then WSD would be best carried out by gathering all occurrences of a word and performing a global disambiguation over the entire text. Local considerations such as selectional restrictions, which have always been regarded as fundamental, would seem to give way to broader considerations.

3.4. Hybrid methods

Stevenson/Wilks (2001) developed an approach which combined the information available in one machine readable dictionary (LDOCE) with information derived from corpora. They noticed that many different sources of linguistic knowledge had been used for WSD but none had appeared more successful than any other and all were limited to some degree. They produced a sense tagger which used several of the information sources in LDOCE (part of speech codes, selectional restrictions, subject codes and textual definitions) using a machine learning algorithm (Daelemans et al. 1998) which combined their output and integrated information from a tagged corpus. When tested it was found that 94% were correctly disambiguated to the broad-grained homograph level and over 90% to the finer-grained level of the LDOCE sense.

Hybrid approaches have also been applied for disambiguation between more coarse-grained semantic field tags (Wilson/Rayson 1993). Here, a combination of part-of-speech tagging, promotion by text domain, approximate sense frequency ranking, auxiliary verb detection and multi-word-expression detection is applied. Precision compared to a manually corrected corpus was reported at 91% (Rayson et al. 2004).

4. Tag sets

An important aspect of any semantic tagging system is the sense inventory it uses. This may vary according to application (a system designed for French-English machine translation may use a very different inventory to one used by lexicographers) and has a profound effect on the difficulty of the task. For example, one inventory may decide not to distinguish between closely related senses while another may choose to do so. An example might be "stake" which has several meanings including "wager" or "share" ("He won £100 on a £5 stake" and "He holds a 10% stake in the company"). Each of these meanings is distinct from the "post" meaning but one lexical resource may choose to list all three possible senses while another may list just two, choosing to combine "wager" and "share" since they are similar. Clearly this leads to different numbers of possibilities for the sense tagger to choose between and, it is reasonable to assume, affects the difficulty of the problem.

Some of the earliest work on WSD used bespoke lexical resources. For example, Wilks (1975), Hirst (1987), Small (1980) and McRoy(1992) all relied on large hand-built lexicons which contained information required to make disambiguation decisions. However, these were extremely expensive to produce, which limited their size.

Machine Readable Dictionaries (MRDs) (Boguraev/Briscoe 1989) started to become available in the language processing community during the 1980's. These resources represented a quantum leap in the quality of lexical resources available to researchers. Produced by trained lexicographers to a professional, publishable standard, these resources were wider in lexical coverage and quality than could be generated by researchers. However, the application of these resources has often been limited by the fact that they are expensive and difficult to obtain. WordNet (Fellbaum 1998) is a lexical resource which is freely-available and large-scale and, as such, has proved very attractive to researchers.

The remainder of this section provides a brief introduction to different types of resources with examples of each.

4.1. WordNet and EuroWordNet

WordNet (Fellbaum 1998) is a semantic database for English originally designed to model the psycholinguistic construction of the human mental lexicon but quickly proved to be an extremely popular resource in language processing since it has been made freely available (http://wordnet.princeton.edu). The basic building block of WordNet is the synset (SYNonym SET): a group of words with closely related meanings. Words with more than one meaning belong to multiple synsets. For example, the noun "car" has 5 different meanings (senses), including a railway car, elevator car, automobile and cable car. One synset for "car" consists of the members: car, motorcar, machine, auto, automobile.

WordNet synsets are connected through a number of relations, the most important of which is hypernymy, the "is a kind of relationship. For example, the hypernym of the synset of "car" previously mentioned consists of the terms "motor vehicle" and "automotive vehicle". This relation organizes the synsets hierarchically, with separate hierarchies for nouns, verbs, adjectives and adverbs.

The vast majority of WSD systems using WordNet have used synsets as semantic tags. However, WordNet is generally acknowledged to contain some extremely fine-grained sense distinctions and it has proved difficult to assign these reliably (Ng/Lee 1996). Consequently some researchers have attempted to assign more general senses from the hierarchy, for example Ciaramita/Johnson (2003) used 26 "supersenses", general semantic classes used by the WordNet lexicographers.

WordNet organises concepts according to their ontological semantics; "tennis player" and "ball boy" are closely related in the hierarchy since they are the same sort of entity (humans) but "tennis player" and "racket" are not closely related. Fellbaum (1998) described this as the "tennis problem". An interesting development bridging this gap is WordNet Domains (Magnini/Cavaglià 2000) in which WordNet synsets have been annotated with domain labels such as medicine, architecture and sport.

EuroWordNet (Vossen 1998) is a multi-lingual lexical resource created by extending the original WordNet to include coverage of Dutch, Italian, Spanish, French, German, Czech and Estonian. Through a number of initiatives it has been extended to cover Basque, Portugese and Swedish (cf http://www.globalwordnet.org). The various language-specific WordNets are linked through a language-independent Inter-Lingual Index (ILI). In practise the ILI is closely based on a version of the original English WordNet. A set of equivalence relations are used to identify concepts which are equivalent across different languages (Vossen 1998). The multilingual aspect of EuroWordNet means that it is possible to semantically tag text in one language and use the resource to identify information about possible translations.

4.2. Machine Readable Dictionaries

LDOCE (Procter 1978) was one of the first and most frequently used dictionaries for language processing. LDOCE uses a three-level embedded structure for sense distinctions. The first, most rough grained, distinction is the homograph level and the second, more fine grained, the sense level with the final, sub-sense, level being optional.

MRDs often draw a distinction between homography and polysemy. Although there is no generally accepted definition of homography, one which is commonly used is to say that two senses of a word are homographic when there is no obvious semantic relation between them. Common examples are "ball" which can be 'a dance' or 'a round object' and "seal" which can mean 'marine mammal' or 'tool for making an impression'.

In LDOCE each homograph is associated with a particular grammatical category. In addition to the textual definitions and example sentences found in most dictionaries, LDOCE also contains additional linguistic information providing further detail about the behavior of each sense. One of the most useful of these are detailed codes describing grammatical behaviour. LDOCE began being used as a sense inventory when the typesetters' tape became available to researchers in the 1980's. In addition to the information in the published dictionary, the tape contained additional information of potential relevance to automatic language processing. Some senses had subject codes, indicating the subject area of text in which that sense is likely to appear, such as "economics" or "banking". Another useful piece of additional information extracted from the typesetters' tape was detail of the selectional preference of each word.

4.3. Thesauruses

Another type of lexical resource which has been used to provide a tag set has been thesauruses (for example, Yarowsky 1992). The thesaurus and dictionary represent very different ways of organising lexical information; in the latter information is accessed through an alphabetically ordered list of headwords, while a thesaurus provides a hierarchy of concepts through which information about words is accessed. WordNet is often described as a thesaurus but this is misleading since each resource organises concepts using very different grounds. As mentioned above, WordNet uses ontological similarity to organise concepts into a hierarchy and, consequently, suffers from the "tennis problem". Conversely, thesauruses are organized around topical semantics, so "tennis player" and "racket" would be closely related as they both refer to the tennis concept.

The most widely known thesaurus is *Roget's International Thesaurus* (Chapman 1977). It is organised in a hierarchical structure with 15 top-level classes, broad subject domains such a *Science and Technology* and *The Body and the Senses*, and also contains some very abstract categories, for example *Behaviour and the Will*. Each class contains a set of large categories which represent sub-domains of the class. There are 1073 of these in the current edition, each numbered according to the order in which they are listed in the book. Large categories underneath the class *Behaviour and the Will* include *Motivation*, *Inducement*, *Pretext* and *Allurement*. The ordering of the large categories can sometimes be used to derive antonyms. For example the first seven large categories under the class *Values and Ideals* are *Ethics*, *Right*, *Wrong*, *Dueness*, *Undueness*, *Duty* and *Prerogative*, although the organisation of ideas into antonyms is less systematic than the ordering into a hierarchy of classes.

5. Evaluation

The approach to evaluation of semantic tagging systems has been a standard one in corpus linguistics: manually annotate a corpus with tags from a predefined set to produce a "gold standard" and then compare the annotation with that produced by a system applied to the same text. While this approach has been generally accepted it is not without its critics. Kilgarriff (1993) argued that the sense distinctions contained in dictionaries do not represent those found in corpora. This far-reaching claim implies that, even with access to vast amounts of world knowledge, humans cannot really carry out word sense disambiguation tasks since the senses in dictionaries do not reflect the senses found in corpora, and therefore the task itself is ill-formed. This claim is echoed by Pustejovsky (1995) and Wilks (1975). Both claimed that words could assume an effectively infinite number of meanings in context and that any effort to enumerate them would necessarily lead to an incomplete lexicon. Despite these objections the "standard" evaluation model is the one most commonly used for sense tagging systems. However, the process of manually annotating text with sense tags is both time-consuming and difficult. Ng (1997) estimated that it would take 16 person-years of effort to manually annotate enough text to train a supervised sense tagger. We have already mentioned studies (section 1) showing that the level of agreement among human annotators may be low.

An innovative solution to this problem was to define sense tags as translations in a parallel corpus. (A parallel corpus contains the same text written in two different languages with the corresponding translation of each sentence identified, cf. article 16). This is an interesting resource since it consists of many examples of sentences and their translations. For example, "bank" can be translated into French as "banque" (when it means financial institution) or "bord" (when it means edge of river). Translations can be automatically extracted from parallel corpora, producing a ready supply of sense annotated text. Brown et al. (1991) and Gale/Church/Yarowsky (1992a) both used the Canadian Hansard, the proceedings of the Canadian Parliament, which is published in both French and English. The meanings of words in English were determined by their translation in the French text, and these roughly corresponded to senses. In this way a level of disambiguation suitable for a machine translation system could be tested and trained without the need for manual annotation. However, these sense inventories may contain different distinctions to those found in MRDs and WordNet.

The use of aligned parallel corpora is essentially a technique which disambiguates text by an indirect means; another approach is to intentionally introduce ambiguity into a text. Yarowsky (1993) did this by creating a corpus containing "pseudo-words", Schütze (1992) calls these "artificially ambiguous words". These are created by choosing two words and replacing all occurrences of either with their concatenation. So all occurrences of, say, "book" or "mug" in a text would be replaced by "book/mug". The goal of the WSD system is to return the original word whenever it finds a pseudo-word.

These techniques for automatically creating annotated corpora are effective ways of generating text annotated with sense-like lexical information and have allowed the creation of extremely large corpora. Yarowsky describes a sense tagged corpus of 460 million words (Yarowsky 1995). They are surely invaluable for WSD systems which require large quantities of tagged data for supervised training algorithms. However, there is the question of how similar these lexical distinctions are to word sense distinctions. The cross-language ambiguities found in parallel corpora do not always reflect the kinds of ambiguities which seem natural in a language and may not correspond to the sense distinctions found in commonly used resources such as LDOCE and WordNet which are produced by professional lexicographers.

Another approach to overcome the sparsity of sense tagged text has been to restrict the evaluation of systems to a small number of lexical items (a "lexical sample"). Under this scheme the performance of systems is judged by how they perform when disambiguating a small number of words (or sometimes just one). For example, Bruce/Wiebe (1994) evaluated their system on a corpus containing 2000 instances of the word "interest" annotated with senses from the LDOCE MRD. Towell/Voorhees (1998) evaluated their system with a lexical sample of three items: the noun "line", verb "serve" and adjective "hard" annotated with synsets from WordNet 1.5. Ng/Lee (1996) produced a larger corpus containing 192,800 occurrences of almost 200 verbs and nouns annotated with senses from the WordNet lexicon. All these evaluation corpora have been made publicly available and have been used to evaluate several systems, allowing direct comparison. But the main disadvantage of these corpora is that they provide annotated examples of only a small set of lexical items. These corpora also tend to provide enough examples for each word to allow the training of a supervised system. But these systems are then limited to the words for which they have training data. In addition, it is possible to evaluate a system which disambiguates all words against one of these corpora (by simply evaluating the performance on the instances where a gold standard exists) but this does not provide a comprehensive evaluation of the system's performance.

The only commonly used corpus in which all (content) words have been manually sense tagged, the SemCor corpus (Landes/Leacock/Tengi 1998) was produced as part of the WordNet project. The corpus is comprised of the Brown corpus (Francis/Kučera 1982) and a novel (Stephen Crane's "The Red Badge of Courage") annotated with their senses from WordNet.

A major recent advance in sense tagger evaluation has been the introduction of the SENSEVAL evaluation exercises (cf. http://www.senseval.org). These provide a uniform framework for comparing the performance of WSD systems. As with any standardised evaluation framework, this approach to evaluation has some disadvantages. Firstly, choices are made for the linguistic assumptions within the framework which may not suit all approaches. A second disadvantage is that there may be the effect that the field is led into an evaluation-led research agenda in which the goal of reporting ever improved results on a particular test set is given undue prominence. However, the overall effect of the SENSEVAL exercises has been highly positive for semantic tagging research. Each SENSEVAL exercise has been accompanied by a meeting which has served as an international focus for WSD research and the evaluation materials created for the exercises provide a valuable resource for researchers where previously there had been a severe shortage of suitable test material.

A wide range of tasks have been included in the SENSEVAL evaluations, the core of which has been all-words and lexical sample disambiguation tasks. Tasks allied to sense tagging, including semantic role labeling and subcategorisation frame acquisition, have also been included. Unlike much of the research into sense tagging, SENSEVAL has also provided evaluation corpora for languages other than English, including Spanish, Italian, Chinese, Basque, Catalan and Romanian. Further details for each of the three SENSEVAL exercises which have been run to date can be found in Kilgarriff/Palmer (2000) and Edmonds/Kilgarriff (2002). In 2007, the nature of the tasks proposed expanded to include semantic analysis and therefore SENSEVAL evolved to become SEMEVAL (semantic evaluations).

Some alternatives to the "standard" evaluation model (using a predefined sense inventory and comparing system output against a manually annotated text) have been suggested. For example, a predefined sense inventory is not necessary for sense discrimination based on sense clustering (Schütze 1998), where word instances are grouped together to represent senses.

Since our focus in this article has been on semantic pre-processing as part of a larger task, another important evaluation methodology presents itself, that of evaluation in an application. In section 1, we discussed how application-driven evaluation for Information Retrieval showed mixed results. Other examples of evaluation by application can be seen from the MT problem. Carpuat/Wu (2005) carried out experiments to determine the WSD accuracy of statistical MT models, and found that statistical MT should benefit from the better predictions made by the WSD models. Vickrey et al. (2005) also show that for the word translation task results were significantly improved.

6. Conclusion

Sense (or semantic) tagging is a useful component of any process which relies on identifying the meaning of a text, and consequently it has a virtually infinite set of applications to corpus linguistics. But, while there has been a long history of research into such tagging, this difficult problem has yet to be fully resolved and, unlike other text processing tasks such as tokenization or part of speech tagging, sense taggers are not commonly available. The choice of sense inventory is critical in the design of sense tagging systems, influencing not just the information it provides but also the possible approaches. It is always useful to bear in mind that sense tagging is not an end in itself (Wilks/Stevenson 1997) and its usefulness will be determined by its contribution to other tasks such as those previously outlined in this article.

7. Literature

Agirre, E./Rigau, G. (1996), Word Sense Disambiguation Using Conceptual Density. In: *Proceedings of 15th International Conference on Computational Linguistics, COLING'96*. Copenhagen, Denmark, 16–22.

Archer, D./Rayson, P./Piao, S./McEnery, T. (2004), Comparing the UCREL Semantic Annotation Scheme with Lexicographical Taxonomies. In: Williams, G./Vessier, S. (eds.), *Proceedings of the 11th EURALEX (European Association for Lexicography) International Congress (Euralex 2004)*. Lorient, France, 6–10 July 2004. Université de Bretagne Sud. Volume III, 817–827.

Banerjee, S./Pedersen, T. (2002), An Adapted Lesk Algorithm for Word Sense Disambiguation Using WordNet. In: *Proceedings of the Third International Conference on Intelligent Text Processing and Computational Linguistics (CICLING-02)*. Mexico City, Mexico, 136–145.

Bar-Hillel, Y. (1960), The Present Status of Automatic Translation of Languages. In: *Advances in Computers* 1, 91–163.

Berners-Lee, T./Hendler, J./Lassila, O. (2001), The Semantic Web. In: *Scientific American* 28(5), 34–43.

Boguraev, B./Briscoe, T. (eds.) (1989), *Computational Lexicography for Natural Language Processing*. London: Longman.

Brown, P./Della Pietra, S./Della Pietra, V./Mercer, R. (1991), Word Sense Disambiguation Using Statistical Methods. In: *Proceedings of the 29th Annual Meeting of the Association for Computational Linguistics (ACL)*. Berkeley, USA, 264–270.

Bruce, R./Wiebe, J. (1994), Word-sense Disambiguation Using Decomposable Models. In: *Proceedings of the 32nd Annual Meeting of the Association for Computational Linguistics (ACL-94)*. Las Cruces, New Mexico, 139–145.

Carpuat, M./Wu, D. (2005), Evaluating the Word Sense Disambiguation Performance of Statistical Machine Translation. In: *Proceedings of Second International Joint Conference on Natural Language Processing (IJCNLP-2005)*. Jeju, Korea, October 2005, 120 125.

Chapman, R. (1977), *Roget's International Thesaurus, Fourth Edition*. New York: Harper and Row.

Ciaramita, M./Johnson, M. (2003), Supersense Tagging of Unknown Nouns in WordNet. In: *Proceedings of the Conference on Empirical Methods in Natural Language Processing (EMNLP 2003)*. Sapporo, Japan, 168–175.

Clear, J. (1994), I Can't See the Sense in a Large Corpus. In: Kiefer, F./Kiss, G./Pajzs, J. (eds.), *Papers in Computational Lexicography: COMPLEX '94*. Budapest, Hungary, 33–48.

Connine, C. (1990), Effects of Sentence Context and Lexical Knowledge in Speech Processing. In: Altmann, G. T. (ed.), *Cognitive Models in Speech Processing*. Cambridge, MA: MIT Press, 281–294.

Cowie, J./Guthrie, L./Guthrie, J. (1992), Lexical Disambiguation Using Simulated Annealing. In: *Proceedings of the 14th International Conference on Computational Linguistics (COLING)*. Nantes, France, 359–365.

Daelemans, W./Zavrel, J./vander Sloot, K./van den Bosch, A. (1998), *TiMBL: Tilburg Memory Based Learner Version 1.0. Technical report, ILK Technical Report 98–03*.

Edmonds, P./Kilgarriff, A. (2002), Introduction to the Special Issue on Evaluating Word Sense Disambiguation Systems. In: *Natural Language Engineering* 8(4), 279–291.

Fellbaum, C. (ed.) (1998), *WordNet: An Electronic Lexical Database and Some of its Applications*. Massachusetts and London: MIT Press.

Fellbaum, C./Garabowski, J./Landes, S./Baumann, A. (1998), Matching Words to Senses in WordNet: Naïve vs. Expert Differentiation. In: Fellbaum 1998, 217–239.

Francis, W./Kučera, H. (1982), *Frequency Analysis of English Usage*. New York: Houghton Mifflin Co.

Gale, W./Church, K./Yarowsky, D. (1992a), Estimating Upper and Lower Bounds on the Performance of Word Sense Disambiguation Programs. In: *Proceedings of the 30th Annual Meeting of the Association for Computational Linguistics (ACL-92)*. Newark, DE, 249–256.

Gale, W./Church, K./Yarowsky, D. (1992b), One Sense Per Discourse. In: *Proceedings of the DARPA Speech and Natural Language Workshop*. Harriman, NY, 233–237.

Gale, W./Church, K./Yarowsky, D. (1993), A Method for Disambiguating Word Senses in a Large Corpus. In: *Computers and the Humanities* 26, 415–439.

Gentner, D./France, I. (1988), The Verb Mutability Effect: Studies of the Combinatorial Semantics of Nouns and Verbs. In: Small, S./Cottrell, G./Tanenhaus, M. (eds.), *Lexical Ambiguity Resolution*. San Mateo, CA: Morgan Kaufman, 343–382.

Hirst, G. (1987), *Semantic Interpretation and the Resolution of Ambiguity*. Cambridge: Cambridge University Press.

Hutchins, J./Somers, H. (1992), *Introduction to Machine Translation*. London: Academic Press.

Ide, N./Véronis, J. (1998), Introduction to the Special Issue on Word Sense Disambiguation: The State of Art. In: *Computational Linguistics* 24(1), 1–40.

Jackson, H./Zé Amvela, E. (2000), *Words, Meaning and Vocabulary: An Introduction to Modern English Lexicology*. London/New York: Cassell.

Jorgensen, J. (1990), The Psychological Reality of Word Senses. In: *Journal of Psycholinguistic Research* 19(3), 167–190.

Kassarjian, H. H. (1977), Content Analysis in Consumer Research. In: *Journal of Consumer Research* 4, 8–18.

Kilgarriff, A. (1993), Dictionary Word Sense Distinctions: An Enquiry into their Nature. In: *Computers and the Humanities* 26, 356–387.

Kilgarriff, A. (1997), I Don't Believe in Word Senses. In: *Computers and the Humanities* 31(2), 91–113.

Kilgarriff, A./Palmer, M. (2000), Introduction to the Special Issue on SENSEVAL. In: *Computers and the Humanities* 34(1), 1–13.

Krovetz, R./Croft, W. B. (1992), Lexical Ambiguity and Information Retrieval. In: *ACM Transactions on Information Systems* 10(2), 115–141.

Landes, S./Leacock, C./Tengi, R. (1998), Building a Semantic Concordance of English. In: Fellbaum 1998, 97–104.

Lesk, M. (1986), Automatic Sense Disambiguation Using Machine Readable Dictionaries: How to Tell a Pine Cone from an Ice Cream Cone. In: *Proceedings of ACM SIGDOC Conference*, Toronto, Canada, 24–26.

Magnini, B./Cavaglià, G. (2000), Integrating Subject Field Codes into WordNet. In: Gavrilidou M./ Crayannis, G./Markantonatu, S./Piperidis, S./Stainhaouer, G. (eds.), *Proceedings of LREC-2000, Second International Conference on Language Resources and Evaluation*. Athens, Greece, 31 May–2 June, 2000, 1413–1418.

McRoy, S. (1992), Using Multiple Knowledge Sources for Word Sense Disambiguation. In: *Computational Linguistics* 18(1), 1–30.

Ng, H. T. (1997), Getting Serious about Word Sense Disambiguation. In: *Proceedings of the SIGLEX Workshop Tagging Text with Lexical Semantics: What, why and how?* Washington, DC, 1–7.

Ng, H. T./Lee, H. B. (1996), Integrating Multiple Knowledge Sources to Disambiguate Word Sense: An Exemplar-based Approach. In: *Proceedings of ACL96*. Santa Cruz, CA, 40–47.

Preiss, J./Stevenson, M. (2004), Introduction to the Special Issue on Word Sense Disambiguation. In: *Computer Speech and Language* 18(3), 201–207.

Procter, P. (1978), *Longman Dictionary of Contemporary English*. London: Longman Group.

Pustejovsky, J. (1995), *The Generative Lexicon*. Cambridge, MA: MIT Press.

Rayson, P./Archer, D./Piao, S. L./McEnery, T. (2004), The UCREL Semantic Analysis System. In: *Proceedings of the Workshop on Beyond Named Entity Recognition Semantic Labelling for NLP Tasks in Association with 4th International Conference on Language Resources and Evaluation (LREC2004)*. 25th May, 2004. Lisbon, Portugal, 7–12.

Schütze, H. (1992), Dimensions of Meaning. In: Werner, R. (ed.), *Proceedings of the 1992 ACM/ IEEE Conference on Super computing* (Minneapolis, Minnesota, United States, November 16–20, 1992). Los Alamitos, CA: IEEE Computer Society Press, 787–796.

Schütze, H./Pedersen, J. (1995), Information Retrieval Based on Word Senses. In: *Proceedings of SDAIR'95*. Las Vegas, Nevada, 161–175.

Schütze, H. (1998), Automatic Word Sense Discrimination. In: *Computational Linguistics* 24(1), 97–124.

Small, S. (1980), Word Expert Parsing: A Theory of Distributed Word-based Natural Language Understanding. PhD Thesis, Department of Computer Science, University of Maryland.

Stevenson, M./Clough, P. (2004), EuroWordNet as a Resource for Cross-language Information Retrieval. In: *Proceedings of the Fourth International Conference on Language Resources and Evaluation*. Lisbon, Portugal, 777–780.

Stevenson, M./Wilks, Y. (2001), The Interaction of Knowledge Sources in Word Sense Disambiguation. In: *Computational Linguistics 27* (3), 321–349.

Stone, P. J./Dunphy, D. C./Smith, M. S./Ogilvie, D. M. (eds.) (1966), *The General Inquirer: A Computer Approach to Content Analysis*. Cambridge, MA: MIT Press.

Towell, G./Voorhees, E. (1998), Disambiguating Highly Ambiguous Words. In: *Computational Linguistics*, 24(1), 125–146.

Véronis, J. (2003), Sense Tagging: Does it Make Sense? In: Wilson, A./Rayson, P./McEnery, T. (eds.), *Corpus Linguistics by the Lune: A Festschrift for Geoffrey Leech*. Frankfurt: Peter Lang, 273–290.

Vickrey, D./Biewald, L./Teyssier, M./Koller, D. (2005), Word-sense Disambiguation for Machine Translation. In: *Conference on Empirical Methods in Natural Language Processing (EMNLP)*. Vancouver, Canada, 771–778.

Vossen, P. (1998), Introduction to EuroWordNet. In: *Computers and the Humanities* 32(2–3), 73–89.

Weaver, W. (1955), Translation. In: Locke, W. N./Booth, A. D., (eds.), *Machine Translation of Languages* (Reprint of mimeographed version, 1949). New York: John Wiley & Sons, 15–23.
Wilks, Y. (1975), A Preferential Pattern-seeking Semantics for Natural language Inference. In: *Artificial Intelligence* 6, 53–74.
Wilks, Y./Stevenson, M. (1997), The Grammar of Sense: Using Part-of-Speech Tags as a First Step in Semantic Disambiguation. In: *Journal of Natural Language Engineering* 4(3), 135–144.
Wilson, A./Rayson, P. (1993), Automatic Content Analysis of Spoken Discourse. In: Souter, C./ Atwell, E. (eds.), *Corpus Based Computational Linguistics*. Amsterdam: Rodopi, 215–226.
Wilson, A./Thomas, J. A. (1997), Semantic Annotation. In: Garside, R./Leech, G./McEnery, A. (eds.), *Corpus Annotation: Linguistic Information from Computer Text Corpora*. London: Longman, 53–65.
Yarowsky, D. (1992), Word-sense Disambiguation Using Statistical Models of Roget's Categories Trained on Large Corpora. In: *Proceedings of the 14th International Conference on Computational Linguistics (COLING)*. Nantes, France, 454–460.
Yarowsky, D. (1993), One Sense per Collocation. In: *Proceedings of the ARPA Human Language Technology Workshop*. Princeton, NJ, 266–271.
Yarowsky, D. (1995), Unsupervised Word-sense Disambiguation Rivaling Supervised Methods. In: *Proceedings of the 33rd Annual Meeting of the Association for Computational Linguistics (ACL-95)*. Cambridge, MA, 189–196.
Yarowsky, D. (1997), Homograph Disambiguation in Text-to-Speech Synthesis. In: van Santen, J. T. H./Sproat, R./Olive, J. P./Hirschberg, J. (eds.), *Progress in Speech Synthesis*. New York: Springer-Verlag, 157–172.

Paul Rayson and Mark Stevenson, Lancaster and Sheffield (UK)

27. Corpora for anaphora and coreference resolution

1. Preliminaries and terminology

This article discusses the importance and availability of corpora annotated with anaphora and coreference information, and other related issues. To start with, it would be important to introduce and define the concepts of anaphora and coreference, and to explain what the differences between them are. Related concepts, such as anaphora resolution and coreference resolution, will be explained as well.

Halliday/Hasan (1976) describe **anaphora** as "cohesion which points back to some previous item". The "pointing back" word or phrase (which is also called a **referring expression** if it has a referential function) is called an **anaphor** and the entity to which it refers or for which it stands is its **antecedent**. The process of determining the antecedent of an anaphor is called **anaphora resolution**. When the anaphor refers to an antecedent and when both have the same referent in the real world, they are termed **coreferential**. Consider the following example

(1) *Sophia Loren* says *she* will always be grateful to Bono. *The actress* revealed that the U2 singer helped *her* calm down when *she* became scared by a thunderstorm while travelling on a plane.

In the first sentence of this example the pronoun *she* is an anaphor, the noun phrase *Sophia Loren* is its antecedent and *she* and *Sophia Loren* are coreferential. This example also demonstrates **coreference**, which is the act of picking out the same referent in the real world. As seen in this example, a specific anaphor and more than one of the preceding (or following) noun phrases may be coreferential thus forming a **coreferential chain** of entities which have the same referent. As a further illustration, *Sophia Loren, she* (from the first sentence), *the actress, her* and *she* (second sentence) are coreferential. Coreferential chains partition discourse entities into equivalence classes and the following coreferential chains can be singled out: {Sophia Loren, she, the actress, her, she}, {Bono, the U2 singer}, {a thunderstorm}, {a plane}.

It is worth mentioning that two items can be anaphoric but not coreferential and vice versa. Bound anaphora exhibits anaphoric, but not coreferential links (***Every man** has **his** own agenda*). The same applies to identity-of-sense anaphora where the anaphor and the antecedent are not coreferential (*The man who gave **his paycheck** to his wife was wiser than the man who gave **it** to his mistress*). On the other hand, there may be cases where two items are coreferential without being anaphoric. **Cross-document coreference** is an obvious example: two mentions of the same person in two different documents will be coreferential, but will not stand in anaphoric relation. For more details see Mitkov (2002).

2. The importance of anaphora and coreference resolution for NLP

The computational treatment of anaphora and coreference has become an increasingly important topic in Natural Language Processing (NLP). The successful identification of anaphoric or coreferential links is vital for a number of applications in the field of natural language understanding including Machine Translation, Automatic Abstracting, Question Answering and Information Extraction.

The interpretation of anaphora is crucial for the successful operation of a **Machine Translation** system. In particular, it is essential to resolve the anaphoric relation when translating into languages that mark the gender of pronouns from languages that do not, or between language pairs that contain gender discrepancies. The importance of coreference resolution in **Information Extraction** led to the inclusion of the coreference resolution task in the Message Understanding Conferences which in turn, stimulated the development of a number of coreference resolution systems. Researchers in **Text Summarisation** are increasingly interested in anaphora resolution since techniques for extracting important sentences are more accurate if anaphoric references of indicative concepts are taken into account as well. More generally, coreference and coreferential chains have been extensively exploited for abstracting purposes (see also article 60). **Cross-Document Summarisation** is a recent area which actively exploits *cross-document coreference resolution*. Coreference resolution has proven to be helpful in **Question Answering** and there are a number of other NLP applications where anaphora or coreference resolution play a major role including an application which focuses on readers with acquired dyslexia, helping them to replace pronouns with their antecedents given their difficulty in processing anaphora. For more information on the importance of anaphora or coreference resolution for NLP, see Mitkov (2002). Finally, a recent application of coreference annotations to the area of text-to-hypertext conversion has been reported in Holler/Maas/Storrer (2006).

3. The importance of corpora for anaphora and coreference resolution

Since the early 1990s research and development in anaphora resolution has benefited from the availability of corpora, both raw and annotated. While raw corpora, successfully exploited for extracting collocation patterns (Dagan/Itai 1990, 1991), are widely available, this is not the case for corpora annotated with coreferential links. The annotation of corpora is an indispensable, albeit time-consuming, preliminary to anaphora resolution (and to most NLP tasks or applications), since the data they provide are critical to the development, optimisation and evaluation of new approaches. The automatic training and evaluation of anaphora resolution algorithms require that the annotation cover not only single anaphor-antecedent pairs, but also anaphoric chains, since the resolution of a specific anaphor would be considered successful if any preceding element of the anaphoric chain associated with that anaphor were identified. Unfortunately, anaphorically or coreferentially **annotated corpora** are not widely available and those that exist are not of a large size.

The act of annotating corpora follows a specific **annotation scheme**, an adopted methodology prescribing how to encode linguistic features in text. Annotation schemes usually comprise a set of ASCII strings such as labelled syntactic brackets to delineate grammatical constituents or word class tags (Botley 1999). Once an annotation scheme has been proposed to encode linguistic information, user-based tools (referred to as **annotation tools**) can be developed to facilitate the application of this scheme, making the annotation process faster and more user-friendly. Furthermore, an **annotation strategy** (often in the form of **annotation guidelines**) is essential for accurate and consistent mark-up. Finally, the quality of the annotated data invariably depends on the level of **inter-annotator agreement**.

The rest of this article will briefly introduce the few existing corpora annotated with anaphoric or coreferential links and will then present the major annotation schemes that have been proposed. Next, several tools that have been developed for the annotation of anaphoric or coreferential relationships will be outlined. Finally, the article will discuss the issues of annotation strategy and inter-annotator agreement.

4. Corpora annotated with anaphoric or coreferential links

One of the few anaphorically annotated resources, the **Lancaster Anaphoric Treebank** is a 100,000 word sample of the Associated Press (AP) corpus (Leech/Garside 1991), marked-up with the UCREL anaphora annotation scheme (see section 5). The original motivation for constructing this corpus was to investigate the potential for developing a probabilistic anaphora resolution program. In late 1989, an agreement was made between the UCREL and IBM Yorktown Heights teams, with funding from the latter, to construct a corpus marked to show a variety of anaphoric or, more generally, cohesive relationships in texts.

Before the anaphoric relationships were analysed and encoded, each text already included the following annotations:

(i) A reference code for each sentence (e. g. A001 69, A001 70, A009 90, A009 91).
(ii) A part-of-speech tag for each word.
(iii) Parsing labels indicating the main constituent structure for each sentence.

The original AP corpus was divided into units of approximately 100 sentences (occasionally a text sample did not include the beginning of the original text), and the syntactic and anaphoric markings were carried out on each of these units, so that the anaphoric reference numbering began afresh with each unit.

The **MUC coreference task** (MUC-6 and MUC-7) gave rise to the production of texts annotated for coreferential links for training and evaluation purposes. The annotated data which complied with the MUC annotation scheme (see section 5), was mostly from the genre of newswire reports on subjects such as corporate buyouts, management takeovers, airline business and plane crashes. (Some of the articles are also about reports on scientific subjects. Management of defence contracts is covered and there are also reports on music concerts, legal matters (lawsuits, etc.) and broadcasting business.) All the annotated texts amounted to approximately 65,000 words.

A **part of the Penn Treebank** (the Penn Treebank is a corpus of manually parsed texts from the Wall Street Journal; see also article 20) was annotated to support a statistical pronoun resolution project at **Brown University** (Ge 1998). The resulting corpus contains 93,931 words and 2,463 pronouns. In addition to providing information on coreference between pronouns and noun phrases, or generally between any two noun phrases, pleonastic pronouns were also marked.

A corpus marked up for coreference was developed from the GENIA dataset as part of the MEDCo annotation project at the Institute for Infocomm Research, Singapore. The annotated resource consists of 228 MEDLINE abstracts with the average length of each document being 244 words (Yang et al. 2004). However, the corpus is not freely available.

A corpus containing around 60,000 words, annotated in a way similar to the MUC annotation scheme with the help of the annotation tool ClinKA (see section 6) has been produced at the **University of Wolverhampton** (Mitkov et al. 2000). The corpus features fully annotated coreferential chains and covers texts from different user manuals (printers, video recorders etc.). **Another 50,000 word annotated corpus** based on documents discussing terrorist attacks from the Reuter newswire corpus was produced at the University of Wolverhampton as part of a project funded by the British Academy (Hasler/

Orasan/Naumann 2006). The mark up covered, among other things, the relations identity, synonymy and generalisation, and specialisation. Both these corpora are available for research purposes.

An ongoing project conducted by members of the **University of Stendahl, Grenoble** and **Xerox Research Centre Europe** (Tutin et al. 2000) is to deliver a 1,000,000 word corpus annotated for anaphoric and cataphoric links. The annotation is limited to anaphor – closest antecedent pairs rather than full anaphoric chains and involves the following types of anaphors: 3rd person personal pronouns, possessive pronouns, demonstrative pronouns, indefinite pronouns, adverbial anaphors and zero noun anaphors. The limitation to annotate anaphor-closest antecedent pairs only makes the corpus more suitable for theoretical linguistic research than for evaluation and testing anaphora resolution systems where full anaphoric or coreferential chains are needed (in evaluating anaphora resolution approaches it is standard to consider any NP preceding the anaphor which is in the same coreferential chain with the anaphor, as the correctly identified antecedent).

Texts annotated for **coreferential links in French** are also reported by Popescu-Belis (1998). The first one, marked up in both MUC's and Bruneseaux and Romary's schemes (see section 5), is part of a short story by Stendhal (*Victoria Accoramboni*). The second one, produced at LORIA, is part of a novel by Balzac (*Le Père Goriot*) and follows Bruneseaux and Romary's scheme. In the first sample all referential expressions (altogether 638) were marked, whereas in the second sample only entities representing the main characters in the novel were annotated (a total of 3,812).

Finally, as a consequence of the increasing number of projects in multilingual anaphora resolution, the need for parallel bilingual and multilingual corpora annotated for coreferential or anaphoric links has become obvious. To the best of this writer's knowledge there are no such corpora yet apart from a small-size **English-Romanian corpus** developed for testing a bilingual coreference resolution system (Harabagiu/Maiorano 2000). Another **parallel English-French** corpus covering texts from technical manuals was annotated for coreferential links at the University of Wolverhampton and exploited by an English and French bilingual anaphora resolution algorithm (Mitkov/Barbu 2002). The English part of the corpus contains 25,499 words and the French part 28,037 words (Mitkov 2002; Mitkov/Barbu 2002).

It should be noted that annotated corpora are an invaluable resource not only to computational linguistics projects but also to different types of linguistic analysis. A corpus of identifiable surface markers of anaphoric items and relationships that can be used to examine current theories, will undoubtedly prove to be very useful in any linguistic studies focusing on anaphora.

5. Annotation schemes

In recent years, a number of corpus annotation schemes for marking up anaphora have come into existence. Notable amongst these are the UCREL anaphora annotation scheme applied to newswire texts (Fligelstone 1992; Garside/Fligelstone/Botley 1997) and the SGML-based (MUC) annotation scheme used in the MUC coreference task (Hirschman/Chinchor 1997a). Other well known schemes include Rocha's (1997) scheme for annotating spoken Portuguese, Botley's (1999) scheme for demonstrative pronouns, Bruneseaux/Romary's scheme (1997), the DRAMA scheme (Passonneau/Litman 1997), the annotation scheme for marking up definite noun phrases proposed by Poesio/Vieira (1998), and the MATE scheme for annotating coreference in dialogues proposed by Davies et al. (1998).

The **UCREL scheme** was initially developed by Geoffrey Leech (Lancaster University) and Ezra Black (IBM). The coding method was then elaborated and tested by its application to corpus texts by the UCREL team, whose feedback triggered further elaboration and testing for the scheme. This development cycle was iterated several times.

The scheme allows the marking of a wide variety of cohesive features ranging from pronominal and lexical NP anaphora through ellipsis to the generic use of pronouns. Special symbols added to anaphors and antecedents can encode the direction of reference (i. e. anaphoric or cataphoric), the type of cohesive relationship involved, the antecedent of an anaphor, as well as various semantic features of anaphors and antecedents. For example, the following text fragment (Tanaka 2000) has been encoded using some of the features of this scheme:

(2) Anything (108 Kurt Thomas 108) does, <REF=108 he does to win. Finishing second, <REF=108 he says, is like finishing last.

As example (2) shows, the UCREL scheme brackets antecedent noun phrases and indicates the direction of pronominal references with arrows ('<' for anaphoric references and '>' for cataphoric references) whilst a string denotes the type of relationship involved (in this case reference rather than substitution). An index number is uniquely assigned to each antecedent and any subsequent references to it. Since elements that are related anaphorically share the same index number, anaphoric chains can be readily identified, either manually or automatically (Botley/McEnery 1991).

The 'indexing mode' may differ depending on whether the antecedent is a single discourse entity, consists of multiple discourse entities, is either one or the other type of discourse entity, or is not quite certain. For instance, in the following example (Tanaka 2000), the antecedents of the anaphoric pronouns *they* and *their* in [A007 18] are felt to be probably *Phil Esposito* (indexed '28') and *Ron Greschner* (indexed '29') but this is not quite certain, hence an uncertainty indicator '?' is marked before each index number:

(3) Right wing (27 Anders Hedberg 27) withdrew because of shoulder problems and was replaced by center (28 Phil Esposito 28), while defenseman (29 Ron Greschner 29) took over for teammate (30 Barry Beck 30) (elbow).
Monday, <REF=?28,?29 they devoted much of <REF=?28,?29 their time to the tenure of Alan Eagleson, executive director ...

Since the process of identifying anaphoric relationships is a complex one and may lead to disagreement between the annotators, it was decided that the UCREL scheme should avoid too detailed a level of analysis. This decision was also prompted by the need to produce a substantial volume of annotated texts for development of an anaphora resolver and, as a consequence, by the need to speed up the annotation. Finally, although the coding scheme was influenced by Halliday/Hasan (1976), the resulting corpus was hoped to be as theoretically neutral as possible, so that it could be used by researchers from a wide range of divergent theoretical positions. This became a further reason for opting for a less detailed type of analysis.

The resulting scheme, therefore, reflects the resolution of the "tension" between the practical requirement to avoid too detailed a level of analysis (caused by the inter-annotator consistency, the speed of marking-up, and the demand for theoretical neutrality) and the requirement to meet potential users' theoretical interests as much as possible (Tanaka 2000). It is worth noting that while the UCREL scheme is probably the most comprehensive one, a drawback is that it did not use SGML or XML for encoding, thus making it difficult for other researchers to use.

In addition to applying the scheme to the data produced for the MUCs, the SGML-based **MUC annotation scheme** (Hirschman/Chinchor 1997a) has been used by a number of researchers to annotate coreferential links (Gaizauskas/Humphreys 1996; Mitkov/Orasan/Evans 1999). Given an antecedent A and an anaphor B, where both A and B are strings in the text, the basic MUC coreference annotation has the form

```
<COREF ID="100"> A </COREF> ...
<COREF ID="101" TYPE="IDENT" REF="100"> B </COREF>
```

So for example in *The Kenya Wildlife Service estimates it loses $1.2 million a year in park entry fees because of fraud*, the anaphor *it* and its antecedent *The Kenya Wildlife Service* would be marked up as

```
<COREF ID="100"> The Kenya Wildlife Service </COREF> estimates
<COREF ID="101" TYPE="IDENT" REF="100"> it </COREF> loses
$1.2 million a year in park entry fees because of fraud.
```

In the MUC scheme, and in the above example, the attribute ID uniquely denotes each string in a coreference relation, REF identifies which string is coreferential with the one which it tags, TYPE indicates the type of relationship between anaphor and antecedent and IDENT indicates the identity relationship between anaphor and antecedent. The MUC scheme only covers the identity (IDENT) relation for noun phrases and does not include other kinds of coreference relations such as set/subset, part/whole etc. In addition to these attributes, the annotator can add two more, the first of which is MIN, which is used in the automatic evaluation of coreference resolution systems. The value of MIN represents the smallest continuous substring of the element that must be identified by a system in order to consider a resolution correct. Secondly, the attribute STATUS can be used and set to the value OPT. This information is used to express the fact that mark-up of the tagged element is optional. Dates, currency expressions and percentages are considered noun phrases.

The MUC scheme stipulates which noun phrases should be marked up as coreferential and when. For example, bound anaphors and their antecedents are regarded as coreferential, and in the example *Most lotions don't give percentages of their ingredients*, a coreference link between *Most lotions* and *their* is recorded. Appositional phrases are considered coreferential to the noun phrase to which they apply, even if they are indefinite (*Reza Khatami, the brother of the President of the Islamic Republic of Iran*, but also *John Smith, a 10-year MUC veteran*). Similarly, all predicate nominals, including indefinite ones, are regarded as coreferential with the subject, allowing a coreference link to be marked not only between *Tony Blair* and *the Prime Minister* in *Tony Blair is the Prime Minister of Britain* but also between *Tony Blair* and *a Prime Minister* in *Tony Blair is a Prime Minister*. Coreference is not recorded if the text only asserts the possibility of identity between two noun phrases such as *Marcelo Rodriguez may be the only person in Los Angeles complaining of too much exposure*; nor can appositives be coreferential if they are negative (*Oliver James, never one for late-night socialising, arrived home at 10.00*...). In particular, two NPs should be recorded as coreferential if the text asserts them to be coreferential at any time (Hirschman/Chinchor 1997b). The MUC annotation scheme also recommends how much of the NP to annotate. The head of a noun phrase is considered as the minimum string to be annotated (such as *task* in the NP *coreference task* or *contract* in the NP *the last contract you will get*). The maximum noun phrase includes all text which may be considered a modifier of the noun phrase (such as *The Love Bug*, or *The Kenya Wildlife Service, which runs the country's national parks* or *A computer virus that may have originated in the Philippines*...).

The view adopted in this article as to the coreferential status of indefinite predicate nominal and indefinite, unspecific appositives is different: they are not considered coreferential with their subjects nor with the NP to which they apply. Van Deemter/Kibble (1999, 90) have criticised the MUC coreference annotation scheme in that "[it] goes well beyond annotation of the relation of coreference as it is commonly understood" since it marks non-referring NPs (which therefore also cannot co-refer) such as quantifying NPs (e. g. *every man, most computational linguists*) as part of the coreferential chain. The authors argue that MUC mixes up coreferential and anaphoric relations (for more on the difference between anaphora and coreference, see section 1 of this article). Van Deemter/Kibble also express their reservation regarding the marking of indefinite NPs and predicate NPs as possibly coreferential arguing that if in the example

(4) Henry Higgins, who was formerly sales director of Sudsy Soaps, became president of Dreamy Detergents.

Henry Higgins, sales director of Sudsy Soaps and *president of Dreamy Detergents* are all marked as standing in the IDENT relation, and if two NPs should be recorded as coreferential if the text asserts them to be coreferential at any time, then one could conclude that Henry Higgins is presently sales director of Sudsy Soaps as well as president of Dreamy Detergents which is not what the text asserts. Van Deemter/Kibble propose alternative solutions in their paper.

However, despite its imperfections, the MUC scheme has the strength of offering a standard format. Also, although it has been designed to mark only a small subset of anaphoric and coreferential relations, the SGML framework does provide a useful starting point for the standardisation of different anaphoric annotation schemes.

The **DRAMA scheme** (Passonneau 1996; Passonneau/Litman 1997) identifies anaphors and antecedents in a text, and marks coreference relationships between them. Although similar to the MUC scheme, the DRAMA scheme classifies and marks different kinds of bridging relationships. DRAMA includes instructions for dealing with some difficult problems of identifying the "markable" entities in dialogues, and allows a wider set of these than does the MUC scheme, such as clauses, verb phrases or adjectival phrases which might be the antecedents of certain anaphors such as *it* and *that*.

Bruneseaux/Romary's scheme (1997) identifies anaphors and antecedents in the text and marks the relationships between them, as is the case with other schemes such as MUC, DRAMA and UCREL. An innovation of this scheme is that it allows references to the visual context to be encoded, due to the fact that the corpora annotated include conversational data in human-computer interaction systems where speakers are using a geological simulation program. This scheme also allows the marking of deixis in the form of pointing and mouse-click gestures.

Poesio/Vieira's (1998) first scheme classified definite noun phrases and their textual relationships with other NPs rather than linking referential expressions as in the MUC and DRAMA schemes. As a result of this, the number of markable entities in this scheme is much more limited. In addition to classifying definite NPs, **Poesio/Vieira's (1998) second scheme** also marked the referential link between referring definite NPs and their antecedents. This latter scheme allowed a wider range of markables than the first scheme.

The **MATE scheme for annotating coreference in dialogues** (Davies et al. 1998) draws on the MUC coreference scheme, adding mechanisms for marking-up further types of information about anaphoric relations as done in the UCREL, DRAMA and Bruneseaux/Romary's schemes. In particular, this scheme allows for the mark up of anaphoric constructs typical in Romance languages such as clitics and of some typical dialogue phenomena. The scheme also provides for the mark up of ambiguities and misunderstandings in dialogue. The MATE scheme consists of a *core scheme* and an *extended scheme*. The core scheme has been developed with a two-fold objective in mind: to (i) produce a scheme which is likely to be reliable in terms of the interannotator agreement and which (ii) offers coverage roughly analogous to that offered by the MUC scheme. The extended scheme enables more detailed annotation of various relationships which can occur between discourse entities such as bound anaphora (*Nobody* likes to lose *his job*), set relationship (see example 6 below), possessive relationship, event relationship etc.; examples of all relationships involved can be found in (Davies et al. 1998). As expected, the inter-annotator agreement for marking-up these more complex relations is considerably lower: once one moves beyond the IDENT relation, it can be difficult to decide how to classify the link between two elements (Poesio/Vieira 1998).

Each discourse entity (de) in the text is given an ID number and <de> tags corresponding to the <coref> tags in the MUC scheme. The <link> pointer specifies the type of link between two discourse entities and lists their IDs as values of the ARGS attribute. For instance, the IDENT relation between the two mentions of *orange juice* in the dialogue

(5) When do we have *orange juice* at Elmira?
We have *orange juice* at Elmira at 6 a.m.

would be tagged as follows

When do we have <de ID="01"> orange juice </de> at Elmira?
We have <de ID="02"> orange juice </de> at Elmira at 6 a.m.
<link type="ident" args="01 02">

Also, the example

(6) *The kids* went to a party last weekend. *Paul* wanted to wear his new suit, but *Jane* insisted on wearing her jeans.

is annotated as follows (as in the previous example, thc ID numbers are chosen as an illustration and may not correspond to the actual enumeration in a real text)

<de ID="85"> The kids </de> went to a party last weekend. <de ID="86"> Paul </de> wanted to wear his new suit, but <de ID="87"> Jane </de> insisted on wearing her jeans
<link type="element" args="86 85">
<link type="element" args="87 85">

where the 'element' link represents a set relation holding when one discourse entity is an element of the set denoted by the other discourse entity.

The strength of the MATE scheme is that while based on the widespread MUC scheme, and adopting the popular SGML standard, similarly to the UCREL scheme it covers a rich variety of anaphoric relations, which makes it a promising general-purpose framework.

Tutin et al.'s (2000) XML-based scheme supports the annotation of a variety of anaphoric relations such as coreference, set membership, substitution, sentential anaphora (exhibited by anaphors whose antecedents are clauses or sentences; sentential anaphora itself may involve coreference or substitution), and indefinite relation which includes all cases not covered by the first four types such as bound anaphora (the scheme does not cover lexical noun phrase anaphora). The annotation scheme encodes the boundaries of each expression, the link between two expressions and the type of relationship between them. The boundaries are marked by means of the <exp> and </exp> tags, with an ID number inserted in <exp>. The link between an anaphor and antecedent is encoded by the <ptr> tag which is added to the anaphor and which is represented as a string containing an *src* antecedent label and a pointer to the ID number of the antecedent. Finally, the type of relation is marked by the 'type' attribute in the <ptr> string. As an illustration, (7)

(7) *Des quatre locomotives de Savoie, l'une* est à redresseurs [...]. Les trois autres montrent une sorte de coexistence ....

Of the four locomotives of Savoie, one is of the erector type [...]. The three others show a kind of coexistence ...

is annotated as follows ('mde' stands for 'membre de' which is the French expression for *set membership*).

<exp id="f50"> Des quatre locomotives de Savoie </exp>, <exp id="f51"> <ptr type="mde" src="f50"/> l'une </exp> est a redresseurs [...]. <exp id="f52"> <ptr type="mde" src="f50"/> Les trois autres</exp> montrent une sorte de coexistence.

Tutin et al.'s scheme can also encode special cases such as identity-of-sense anaphora, ambiguity of anaphors and coordinated (split) antecedents.

Ge's annotation (1998) covers five kinds of relationshsips involving pronouns. The author marks pronouns which have explicit nominal antecedents, pronouns with split antecedents, pronouns pointing to an action or event not represented by a single noun phrase as well as two types of pleonastic pronouns: those that are not specific enough and those that appear in cleft constructions.

Rocha (1997) described a detailed annotation scheme for marking anaphoric references in a corpus of spoken Portuguese dialogues, and extracts from the London-Lund Corpus. Rocha's scheme explores the relationship between anaphora and the topic structure of discourse, by signalling the discourse, segment and subsegment topics. In addition to being able to mark discourse structure features, Rocha's scheme can also mark different aspects of anaphors, such as the type of anaphor (e. g. 'subject pronoun' or 'full noun phrase'), the type of antecedent (implicit, non-surface or explicit, surface antecedent), the topicality status of the antecedent (whether the antecedent is the discourse topic, segment topic or subsegment topic) and the type of knowledge required for the processing of the anaphor (such as syntactic, collocational or discourse knowledge). Rocha's scheme allows for anaphora in spoken (and presumably written) texts to be analysed according to a rich variety of inter-related factors, in a way which extends beyond the descriptive analysis of Halliday/Hasan (which is largely implemented in the UCREL annotation scheme outlined above); however, it is very labour-intensive to apply.

Botley's scheme (1999) describes the different functions of anaphoric demonstratives in written and spoken texts. Essentially, this scheme classifies demonstrative anaphors according to five distinctive features, each of which can have one of a series of values. The features employed are recoverability of the antecedent (e. g. directly recoverable, indirectly recoverable, non-recoverable, not-applicable, e. g. exophoric), direction of reference (anaphoric, cataphoric, not-applicable), phoric type (referential, substitution, not-applicable), syntactic function (non-modifier, non-head, not-applicable) and antecedent type (nominal antecedent, prepositional/factual antecedent, clausal antecedent, adjectival antecedent, no antecedent).

Botley (1999), Davies et al. (1998) and Tutin et al. (2000) provide further discussion on issues relating to the annotation of anaphors and the annotation schemes.

6. Annotation tools

In order to help the human annotator it is necessary to provide him/her with a tool which makes it possible to quickly identify the entities in the discourse and the relations between them. A good graphical interface offers the human annotator trouble-free and efficient interaction with the annotated text. It should also display the resulting annotation in a way that is easy for a user to interpret, hiding unnecessary or hard-to-read aspects of the annotation, such as raw SGML encoding.

The first tool for annotation of anaphoric links, **XANADU**, written by Roger Garside at Lancaster University, is an X-windows interactive editor which offers the user an easy-to-navigate environment for manually marking pairs of anaphors-antecedents within the UCREL scheme (Fligelstone 1992). In particular, XANADU allows the user to move around a block of text, displaying circa 20 lines at a time. The user can use a mouse to mark any segment of text to which s/he wishes to add some labelling. Apart from the text window, there are two primary windows which are always displayed. The first of these contains a set of "command buttons", which for the most part, refer specifically to categories of anaphora that are recognised as being within the scope of the scheme. The second window contains a list of already identified antecedents.

The **DTTool** (Discourse Tagging Tool) enables the annotation of anaphoric relations in Japanese, Spanish and English (Aone/Bennett 1994). This is done in a graphical manner – by the colour-coding of different types of anaphors (e.g. third-person pronoun, definite NP, proper name, zero pronoun, etc.) and antecedents which are displayed on the screen with arrows linking them. For instance, third-person pronouns referring to organisation nouns are highlighted in orange, while definite NPs referring to a person are highlighted in azure blue. The annotated data can be viewed in five different modes: all tags, each anaphor-antecedent pair, all anaphor-antecedent pairs of the same type, all anaphoric chains and the text without any tags.

The **Alembic Workbench** was developed at MITRE, and has been used, among other things, to mark-up coreference relations. The Alembic Workbench is a component of the trainable multilingual information extraction system Alembic (Day/Goldschen/Henderson 1997) and is designed to enable the rapid manual or semi-automatic production of data for training and testing. The data include annotated parts of speech, named entities, coreference chains etc. For the coreference annotation task, the workbench features a right window which produces a sorted list of all tagged elements to facilitate finding the coreferring expressions. The semi-automatic mode applies to simple annotation tasks such as tagging named entities. For instance, if a certain string has been marked as a proper name, the tool proposes that the same string be marked as a proper name if it appears again in the text. The Alembic Workbench offers a choice of tag sets, including all those necessary for the MUC and provides a graphical interface which allows the modification of existing tags and the addition of new ones. In addition, the users of the system are able to construct their own task-specific annotation schemes.

Referee is a discourse annotation and visualisation tool which operates in three modes – reference mode, segment mode and dialogue mode (DeCristofaro/Strube/McCoy 1999). In *reference mode*, the user can mark words or expressions by associating features (e.g. syntactic function, pronominalisation, distance, definiteness etc.) with each of them and assigning coreference. The annotated information can then be easily retrieved. For example, clicking on a specific word will not only display the values of its features (e.g. syntactic function = subject, pronominalisation = no) but will also highlight all other expressions which co-refer with it. At this point the user can update the coreference links or feature values, or store additional information. In *segment mode* the user can partition the text into arbitrarily nested and overlapping segments, whereas the *dialogue mode* enables him/her to code a dialogue by breaking it into turns.

CLinkA is a tool for annotating coreferential links which operates by default on the MUC scheme, but also gives the user the option to define his/her own annotation scheme (Orasan 2000). The program uses two types of tags: one for marking the initial mention of an element in a coreference chain and one for marking the remaining elements of that chain. Similarly to the Alembic Workbench, the following attributes can be added to each tag: (i) counters which uniquely identify every element in the coreference chain and are generated automatically by the program, (ii) index numbers which are uniquely assigned to each antecedent and any subsequent references to it and (iii) values specified by each annotator such as MIN which stands for a "minimal noun phrase" (see the section above on the MUC annotation scheme). CLinkA also displays a right window listing all identified NPs in the text which helps the annotator in linking the coreferential items. The process of annotation is kept as simple as possible. As an illustration, boundaries of entities are identified by mouse clicks and the addition of an entity to an existing chain can be done by clicking on an element already in the chain. To speed up the annotation, the tool offers several features for semi-automatic marking. For instance, identical strings are likely to be in the same coreferential chain and each time the program establishes identity between a new string and an already marked one, the user is asked if she/he would like to add the new string to the chain of the preceding identical string. CLinkA also features a graphical interface for comparing the annotations carried out by different annotators, displaying them in different colours. The tool is language independent and has been used for annotating coreferential links in English, Spanish and Bulgarian. This language independence has been facilitated by the fact that CLinkA is implemented in Java which supports Unicode. In addition, the tool operates on any platform that has a Java Virtual Machine.

CLinkA served as a basis for the development of **PALinkA** – a multipurpose annotation tool which has been successfully used in a variety of annotation tasks such as marking NP coreferential chains (Hasler/Orasan/Naumann 2006), annotation of centering (Mitkov/Orasan 2004), events (Hasler/Orasan/Naumann 2006) and important sentences for summarisation purposes (Hasler/Orasan/Mitkov 2003). The tool offers a user-friendly graphical interface with different colours for the different types of information, which makes it easier to distinguish between them, as well as speeding up the annotation process. PALinkA is easy to use, even for non-computer experts. To mark a unit of text, the annotator uses the mouse to indicate the boundaries of the unit, the tag assigned to the unit, and whatever attributes are required by the tag. To avoid errors, some attributes such as unique IDs and references are determined automatically by the tool.

The set of tags which can be used in the annotation is specified by a preferences file loaded in the tool before annotation starts. The types of tags which can be marked in a text are zero tags which indicate a missing element such as zero pronouns or ellipsis, markables which assign a tag to a span of text, and links between markables. As a result of this, any annotation task which can be broken down into these operation can be completed using PALinkA (Orasan, 2003).

Plug-in support was used in (Hasler/Orasan/Naumann 2006) to facilitate the annotation process by allowing users to run programs which helped them in the annotation process, such as a plug-in to query WordNet about the relationship between two concepts (see Hasler/Orasan/Naumann 2006, section 4.1.). A plugable previewer for the annotation was another change made to PALinkA, due to the fact that the original way of displaying the markables and relations between them (a tree) was appropriate for NP but not event coreference.

Day/Goldschen/Henderson (2000) describe a **cross-document annotation toolset** that supports, among other things, the annotation of cross-document coreference. Individual documents are annotated with pointers to a single entity repository. In turn, the repository maintains references to all the documents (and locations within documents) where information has been individually annotated. Other recent developments relevant to the annotation of coreferential links are the general purpose annotation tool **FAST** (Friendly Annotator for SGML Texts) which operates in three different modes: manual, semi-automatic and fully automatic (Barbu 2000) and the on-going work on **ATLAS**, flexible and extensible architecture for linguistic annotation which will include support for multi-domain, multi-layered and multi-linked annotations (Bird et al. 2000).

In spite of their attractive features, the tools for annotating anaphoric and coreferential relations are still largely based on manual antecedent identification and labelling which is not always easy and straightforward. The manual annotation process imposes a considerable demand on human time and labour. The main reason why annotation of anaphoric or coreferential data has not yet been able to benefit from the level of automation enjoyed by its lexical, syntactic and semantic counterparts (part-of-speech tagging, parsing or word-sense disambiguation, on which see articles 24, 28 and 26 respectively) is the complexity of the linguistic phenomena of anaphora and coreference. However, with a view to accelerating the marking up process, the idea of semi-automatic annotation of anaphoric and coreferential links has already been put forward (Mitkov 1997). It has been suggested that an annotation tool could employ a high precision anaphora resolution system to propose antecedent(s) which are then post-corrected by a human annotator by either choosing from a list of returned antecedents or by manually marking up omitted anaphoric relationships. On a less ambitious but more practical scale CLinkA already provides some level of semi-automatic marking such as the inclusion of two matching NPs in the same coreferential class after consultation with the user.

7. Annotation strategy

The annotation of anaphoric or coreferential relations is a notoriously difficult, time-consuming and labour-intensive task even when focusing on one single variety of the phenomenon (consider the case of demonstrative anaphora – it is well known that when the antecedent is a text segment longer than a sentence, it is often difficult to decide exactly which text portion represents the antecedent). Compared with syntactic analysis, the discourse level analysis of anaphoric relations involves a much more interpretative process, and the possibility of disagreement in interpretation between annotators is much greater than in syntactic analysis (See McEnery 2005 for a detailed general discussion on various issues related to corpus annotation including consistency and accuracy). The complexity of the task imposes a restriction that the annotation process should not follow a detailed level of analysis (as in the case of the UCREL and MUC schemes) but focus instead on identity relation only (MUC scheme). The experience with the MUC annotation scheme shows that even within the narrow domain of NP coreference it is not always easy to decide which NPs should be marked as coreferential. This is indicative of how complex anaphora and coreference are. As a consequence, the annotation process is often considered to be far from reliable in that inter-annotator agreement may be disappointingly low. For related discussion on the complexity of anaphora and coreference see van Deemter/Kibble (1999).

Given the complexity of the anaphora and coreference annotation task, a recent project carried out at the University of Wolverhampton (Mitkov et al. 2000) adopted a less ambitious but clearer approach regarding the variety of anaphora annotated. This move was motivated by the fact that (i) annotating anaphora and coreference is a very difficult task and (ii) the aim was to produce annotated data for the types of anaphora most widely used in NLP: that of identity-of-reference direct nominal anaphora, featuring a relation of coreference between the anaphors (pronouns, definite descriptions or proper names) and any of their antecedents (non-pronominal NPs); since the task of anaphora resolution is considered successful if any element of the anaphoric (coreferential) chain preceding the anaphor is identified, the project addressed the annotation of whole anaphoric (coreferential) chains and not only pairs of anaphors and their closest antecedents. The annotation covered identity-of-reference direct nominal anaphora, which included relationships such as specialisation, generalisation and synonymy, but excluded part-of and set membership relations, which are considered instances of indirect anaphora. Whilst it was obvious that such a corpus would be of less interest in linguistic studies, it was believed that the vast majority of NLP work on anaphora and coreference resolution (and all those tasks which rely on it) would be able to benefit from this corpus by using it for evaluation and training purposes. The view was that the trade-off of a wide coverage, but complicated and potentially error-prone annotation task with low-consistency across annotations, for a simpler, but more reliable annotation task with a NLP-oriented end product, was a worthwhile endeavour.

An annotation strategy in the form of guidelines outlining what to annotate and when to annotate it, and recommending the best annotation practice, can be very helpful to the annotators, and could enhance the annotation consistency and the inter-annotator agreement which are often disappointingly low. The guidelines produced for the objectives of the Wolverhampton project cited above discuss which classes of anaphora should be annotated (identity-of-reference direct nominal anaphora in this particular project), what are the markables (all kinds of NPs including base, complex and coordinated) and advise in which cases two NPs should be marked as coreferential (e. g. definite descriptions in copular relation). These guidelines also explain which types of anaphora or coreference should not be annotated (e. g. identity of sense anaphora, bound anaphora, cross-document coreference), what are non-markables and in which cases NPs should not be marked as coreferential (e. g. copular relation when one of the NPs is indefinite). Useful annotation practices used to improve the inter-annotator agreement included printing out the whole text prior to annotation so that the annotators familiarise themselves with the text, identifying all the noun phrases to be marked as either initial or subsequent mentions, making a note of all troublesome or ambiguous cases and discussing them with other annotators, and ensuring that the annotation is done in one intensive period, as sporadically annotating a file can lead to the annotator having to re-read the document for familiarisation several times. For more details see (Mitkov et al. 2000).

A more recent project at the University of Wolverhampton on the annotation of NP coreference and events (Hasler/Orasan/Naumann 2006) developed even more detailed guidelines as to what should be annotated and what should not be annotated, and explained the way to do that. The annotator had the option to use the **coref** and **ucoref** tags. The **coref** tag was used where there was no doubt that one entity coreferred with another, whilst the **ucoref** tag was used when the annotator was relatively sure of the coreference but there was an element of uncertainty (e. g. *The argument will argue that McVeigh and Nichols were the masterminds of the bombing plot*). The detailed guidelines instructed annotators on the "general strategy" (such as prior to annotation, read the whole text; make a note of troublesome or ambiguous cases and discuss them with other annotators etc.), which elements to consider as markables, what types of coreference to mark, how to annotate coreferential links, how to handle tricky cases etc.

8. Inter-annotator agreement

However difficult the annotation task is, in order to ensure that a specific text or corpus is marked up as correctly and objectively as possible, it is necessary that in addition to adhering to annotation guidelines, each sample be marked by at least two annotators independently. Since there is no guarantee that the annotators will agree on how each instance should be annotated, and with a view to performing quality checks, Mitkov et al. (2000) describe a program which matches all annotations, and flags up instances marked up differently by the annotators. The program works by extracting the full coreference chains from two annotated files and then producing the chains that are present in one file but are not identical to any chains in the file being compared. Similarly, differing elements are output and the number of elements shared between the files is returned. This allows a qualitative assessment of the differences between the annotations as well as subsequent discussion and adjudication.

Orasan (2000) and Mitkov et al. (2000) used the following measure to compute the similarity/closeness of the annotations produced by two different annotators:

$$\mu = \frac{2C}{A + B}$$

where A is the number of items marked by the first annotator, B is the number of items marked by the second and C is the number of items which were marked by both annotators. If both annotators marked the same items then the agreement is equal to 1, otherwise it is a value greater or equal to 0 and less than 1 ($0 \leq \mu \leq 1$). Mitkov et al. (2000) found that the average proportion of shared elements in the corpora annotated varied from 0.66 to 0.72.

Another measure for computing the agreement between annotators used in the literature is the kappa statistic (Carletta 1996). This measure only considers those items marked by both annotators and indicates how many times the annotators used the same tags and the same values for their attributes. The kappa statistic (k) is computed as $k = (P(A) - P(E)) / (1 - P(E))$ where P(A) is the proportion of times the annotators agree and P(E) is the proportion of times that we would expect the annotators to agree by chance. It has been successfully employed for computing the feature-value agreement between annotators in several annotation projects (Davies et al. 1998; Vieira/Poesio

2000). However useful this measure seems, it is not straightforward to compute it with respect to coreference annotation. This is because when the kappa statistic is computed, it is assumed that the possible values of features are known a priori. In the case of the annotation adopted this would mean that the initial mentions of the chains are known. Different models were tried in order to find a solution to this problem, but none were found useful.

Hirschman et al. (1998) conducted a small-scale analysis on the inter-annotator agreement in the coreference task as defined by the Message Understanding Conferences (MUC-6 and MUC-7). The study, which was based on the annotation produced by two annotators, suggested that only 16% of the disagreement cases represented genuine disagreement about coreference since the remainder of the cases were typographical errors or errors of omission. Initially the agreement was in the low 80's but in order to improve it, the authors ran several experiments. In one of the experiments they separated the tagging of the noun phrases from the linking of the actual coreferring expressions, and as a result the inter-annonator agreement climbed to the low 90's. Given the limited scope of the study, the authors suggest that that these results need more extensive evaluation.

Inter-annotator agreement has become an increasingly important and integral part of any report associated with not only providing details about specific annotated resources but also discussing evaluations carried out on specific annotated data.

9. Summary

This article has highlighted the importance of corpora for anaphora and coreference resolution. Corpora annotated with anaphoric or coreferential links are particularly important for research in anaphora resolution. They are invaluable resources for obtaining empirical data and rules in the building of new anaphora resolution approaches and for the training, optimisation and evaluation of existing approaches. The production of annotated corpora is a challenging and time-consuming task, which follows a specific annotation scheme and strategy, and uses task-specific annotation tools. The article has also outlined the existing corpora annotated for coreference, the annotation schemes proposed and the tools developed, and has discussed the related issue of annotation strategy and inter-annotator agreement.

10. Literature

Aone, C./Bennett, S. (1994), Discourse Tagging Tool and Discourse-tagged Multilingual Corpora. In: *Proceedings of the International Workshop on Sharable Natural Language Resources (SNLR)*. Nara, Japan, 71–77.

Barbu, C. (2000), FAST – towards a Semi-automatic Annotation of Corpora. In: *Proceedings of the Second International Conference on Language Resources and Evaluation (LREC)*. Athens, Greece, 501–505.

Bird, S./Day, D./Garofolo, J./Henderson, J./Laprun, C./Liberman, M. (2000), ATLAS: A Flexible and Extensible Architecture for Linguistic Annotation. In: *Proceedings of the Second International Conference on Language Resources and Evaluation (LREC)*. Athens, Greece, 1699–1706.

Botley, S. (1999), Corpora and Discourse Anaphora: Using Corpus Evidence to Test Theoretical Claims. PhD thesis, University of Lancaster, UK.

Botley, S./McEnery, A. (1991), A Graphical Representation Scheme for Anaphoric Links in Natural Language Texts. In: *Proceedings of the 13th Colloquium of the British Computer Society Information Retrieval Specialist Group*. Huddersfield, UK, 127–140.

Bruneseaux, F./Romary, L. (1997), Codage des références et coréférences dans les dialogues homme-machine. In: *Proceedings of the Joint International Conference of the Association for Computers and the Humanities and the Association for Literary and Linguistic Computing (ACH-ALLC '97)*. Ontario, Canada, 15–17.

Carletta, J. (1996), Assessing Agreement on Classification Tasks: The Kappa Statistics. In: *Computational Linguistics* 22(2), 249–254.

Dagan, I./Itai, A. (1990), Automatic Processing of Large Corpora for the Resolution of Anaphora References. In: *Proceedings of the 13th International Conference on Computational Linguistics (COLING'90)*. Helsinki, Finland, vol. III, 1–3.

Dagan, I./Itai, A. (1991), A Statistical Filter for Resolving Pronoun References. In: Feldman, Y. A./Bruckstein, A. (eds.), *Artificial Intelligence and Computer Vision*. Amsterdam: Elsevier Science Publishers B. V. (North-Holland), 125–135.

Davies, S./Poesio, M./Bruneseaux, F./Romary, L. (1998), *Annotating Coreference in Dialogues: Proposal for a Scheme for MATE*. First draft. Available at http://www.hcrc.ed.ac.uk/~poesio/MATE/anno_manual.html.

Day, D./Aberdeen, J./Hirschman, L./Kozierok, R./Robinson, P./Vilain, M. (1997), Mixed-initiative Development of Language Processing Systems. In: *Proceedings of the Fifth Conference on Applied Natural Language Processing, (ANLP97)*. Washington DC, USA, 153–164.

Day, D./Goldschen, A./Henderson, J. (2000), A Framework for Cross-document Annotation. In: *Proceedings of the Second International Conference on Language Resources and Evaluation (LREC)*. Athens, Greece, 199–203.

DeCristofaro, J./Strube, M./McCoy, K. (1999), Building a Tool for Annotating Reference in Discourse. In: *Proceedings of the ACL'99 Workshop on the Relation of Discourse/Dialogue Structure and Reference*. College Park, Maryland, USA, 54–62.

Fligelstone, S. (1992), Developing a Scheme for Annotating Text to Show Anaphoric Relations. In: Leitner, G. (ed.), *New Directions in English Language Corpora: Methodology, Results, Software Developments*. Berlin: Mouton de Gruyter, 153–170.

Gaizauskas, R./Humphreys, K. (1996), Quantitative Evaluation of Coreference Algorithms in an Information Extraction System. Paper presented at the DAARC-1 conference, Lancaster, UK. Reprinted in Botley, S./McEnery, A. (eds.) (2000), *Corpus-based and Computational Approaches to Discourse Anaphora*. Amsterdam: John Benjamins, 143–167.

Garside, R./Fligelstone, S./Botley, S. (1997), Discourse Annotation: Anaphoric Relations in Corpora. In: Garside, R./Leech, G./McEnery, A. (eds.), *Corpus Annotation: Linguistic Information from Computer Text Corpora*. London: Addison-Wesley Longman, 66–84.

Ge, N. (1998), *Annotating the Penn Treebank with Coreference Information*. Internal report, Department of Computer Science, Brown University.

Halliday, M. A. K./Hasan, R. (1976), *Cohesion in English*. London: Longman.

Harabagiu, S./Maiorano, S. (2000), Multilingual Coreference Resolution. In: *Proceedings of ANLP-NAACL2000*. Seattle, WA, 142–149.

Hasler, L./Orasan, C./Mitkov, R. (2003), Building Better Corpora for Summarisation. In: *Proceedings of Corpus Linguistics 2003*. Lancaster, UK, 309–319.

Hasler, L./Orasan, C./Naumann, K. (2006), NPs for Events: Experiments in Coreference Annotation. In: *Proceedings of the International Conference on Language Resources and Evaluation (LREC-2006)*. Genoa, Italy, 1167–1172.

Hirschman, L./Chinchor, N. (1997a), *MUC-7 Coreference Task Definition*. Version 3.0. Available at http://www-nlpir.nist.gov/related_projects/muc/proceedings/co_task.html.

Hirschman, L./Chinchor, N. (eds.) (1997b), *Proceedings of MUC-7*. Fairfax, VA/San Diego, CA: Science Applications International Corporation.

Hirschman, L./Robinson, P./Burger, J./Vilain, M. (1998), The Role of Annotated Training Data. In: *Proceedings of the Workshop on Linguistic Coreference*. Granada, Spain, available at: http://arxiv.org/pdf/cmp-lg/9803001.pdf.

Holler, A./Maas, J. F./Storrer, A. (2006). Exploiting Coreference Annotations for Text-to-hypertext Conversion. In: *Proceedings of the International Conference on Language Resources and Evaluation (LREC-2006)*. Genoa, Italy, 651–654.

Leech, G./Garside, R. (1991), Running a Grammar Factory: The Production of Syntactically Analysed Corpora or Treebanks. In: Johansson, S./Stenström, A-B. (eds.), *English Computer Corpora: Selected Papers and Research Guide*. Berlin: Mouton de Gruyter, 15–32.

McEnery, A. (2005), Corpora. In: Mitkov, R. (ed.), *The Oxford Handbook of Computational Linguistics*. Oxford: Oxford University Press, 448–463.

Mitkov, R. (1997), How Far are we from (Semi-)automatic Annotation of Anaphoric Links in Corpora. In: *Proceedings of the ACL'97/E ACL'97 Workshop on Operational Factors in Practical, Robust Anaphora Resolution*. Madrid, Spain, 82–87.

Mitkov, R. (2002), *Anaphora Resolution*. London: Longman.

Mitkov, R./Barbu, C. (2002), Using Corpora to Improve Pronoun Resolution. In: *Languages in Context* 4(1). Available at: http://clg.wlv.ac.uk/papers/mitkov02.pdf.

Mitkov, R./Orasan, C. (2004), Discourse and Coherence: Revisiting Specific Conventions of the Centering Theory. In: *Proceedings of DAARC2004*. S. Miguel, Azores, Portugal, 109–114.

Mitkov, R./Orasan, C./Evans, R. (1999), The Importance of Annotated Corpora for Natural Language Processing: The Case of Anaphora Resolution and Clause Splitting. In: *Proceedings of the TALN'99 Workshop on Corpora and NLP*. Cargese, France, 60–69.

Mitkov, R./Evans, R./Orasan, C./Barbu, C./Jones, L./Sotirova, V. (2000), Coreference and Anaphora: Developing Annotating Tools, Annotated Resources and Annotation Strategies. In: *Proceedings of the Discourse, Anaphora and Reference Resolution Conference (DAARC2000)*. Lancaster, UK, 49–58.

Orasan, C. (2000), CLinkA – a Coreferential Links Annotator. In: *Proceedings of the Second International Conference on Language Resources and Evaluation (LREC'2000)*. Athens, Greece, 491–496.

Orasan, C. (2003), PALinkA: A Highly Customisable Tool for Discourse Annotation. In: *Proceedings of the 4th SIGdial Workshop on Discourse and Dialogue, ACL-03*. Sapporo, Japan. Available at: http://www.sigdial.org/workshops/workshop4/proceedings/29_SHORT_orasan_palinka-final.pdf.

Passonneau, R. (1996), Instructions for Applying Discourse Reference Annotation for Multiple Applications (DRAMA). Unpublished Internal Document.

Passonneau, R./Litman, D. (1997), Discourse Segmentation by Human and Automated Means. In: *Computational Linguistics* 23(1), 3–139.

Poesio, M./Vieira, R. (1998), A Corpus-based Investigation of Definite Description Use. In: *Computational Linguistics* 24 (2), 183–216.

Popescu-Belis, A. (1998), How Corpora with Annotated Coreference Links Improve Reference Resolution. In: *Proceedings of the First International Conference on Language Resources and Evaluation*, Granada, Spain, 567–572.

Rocha, M. (1997), Supporting Anaphor Resolution with a Corpus-based Probabilistic Model. In: *Proceedings of the ACL'97/EACL'97 Workshop on Operational Factors in Practical, Robust Anaphora Resolution*. Madrid, Spain, 54–61.

Tanaka, I. (2000), The Value of an Annotated Corpus in the Investigation of Anaphoric Pronouns, with Particular Reference to Backwards Anaphora in English. PhD Thesis, University of Lancaster.

Tutin, A./Trouilleux, F./Clouzot, C./Gaussier, E./Zaenen, A./Rayot, S./Antoniadis, G. (2000), Annotating a Large Corpus with Anaphoric Links. In: *Proceedings of the Discourse, Anaphora and Reference Resolution Conference (DAARC2000)*. Lancaster, UK, 28–38.

van Deemter, K./Kibble, R. (1999), What is Coreference and What Should Coreference Annotation be? In: *Proceedings of the ACL99 Workshop on Coreference and its Applications*. College Park, Maryland, USA, 90–96.
Vieira, R./Poesio, M. (1999), Processing Definite Descriptions in Corpora. In: Botley, S./McEnery, T. (eds.), *Corpus-based and Computational Approaches to Discourse Anaphora*. Amsterdam/Philadelphia: John Benjamins.
Vieira, R./Poesio, M. (2000), An Empirically-based System for Processing Definite Descriptions. In: *Computational Linguistics* 26(4), 539–593.
Yang, X./Su, J./Zhou, G./Tan, C. L. (2004), An NP-cluster Based Approach to Coreference Resolution. In: *Proceedings of the 20th International Conference on Computational Linguistics (COLING 2004)*. Geneva. Available at: http://www.comp.nus.edu.sg/~tancl/Papers/COLING04/coling185.pdf.

Ruslan Mitkov, Wolverhampton (UK)

28. Syntactic preprocessing

1. Introduction

Syntactic preprocessing is the next step in text analysis after the annotation on token level. In contrast to lower level annotation it is able to capture structural and in some cases functional aspects of language. There are four general aspects that define approaches to text analysis: (i) type of grammar, i. e. deterministic or probabilistic, (ii) grammar development, i. e. grammar induction or grammar writing, (iii) type of analysis, i. e. phrase-structure or dependency, (iv) depth of analysis, i. e. full parsing or chunking.

Syntactic preprocessing is a means of making the linguistic knowledge inherent in text corpora explicit. The resulting syntactic analysis makes the information accessible to extraction and search tools. Syntactic preprocessing has become an important part of treebank building (cf. article 13 on treebanks) and is used in corpus linguistic research and computational lexicography (cf. articles 5 and 8).

In the following I will give an overview of the different approaches to syntactic preprocessing, while discussing grammar types, grammar development, types of analysis and depths of analysis (section 2). Section 3 gives a brief overview of possible applications. Section 4 discusses the evaluation of syntactic preprocessing.

2. Aspects of syntactic preprocessing

2.1. Grammar type

2.1.1. Symbolic grammars

Symbolic grammars use symbolic elements as triggers to determine the correct syntactic analysis. Lexical knowledge can be included as an additional trigger. An advantage is that a symbolic grammar allows us to formulate precise rules. An analysis can easily be constructed and necessary modifications or corrections can be made. The results of rule application can be predicted and controlled. In some cases, however, symbolic triggers are not sufficient to resolve ambiguities. Long distance context information or world knowledge is necessary for disambiguation. This type of information, however, is difficult to implement, and the necessary relations cannot be established with sufficient reliability. In these cases, heuristics can be used to determine the correct analysis, if we accept that there might be false decisions. Another possibility is to leave the analysis ambiguous, and return all possible parses as a so-called parse forest. Even simple sentences such as *I saw the man with the binoculars* can be subject to ambiguity. In this case, the prepositional phrase *with the binoculars* can either belong to the personal pronoun *I* or to the noun phrase *the man*. The result is two different parse trees. More complex sentences are apt to have more possible analyses. The result is a parse forest.

An example of complex symbolic grammars are unification-based grammars (e. g., in the LFG framework Bresnan 2001, 1982; or in the HPSG framework Pollard/Sag 1987, 1994, Sag/Wasow 1999). These are able to model the hierarchical structure of language, as well as to handle attachment ambiguities, determine relations between constituents, and the function of these constituents.

In order to deal with ambiguities and the various structural possibilities, constraint-based grammars make use of extensive lexical information. Possible structural analyses have to conform to the information present in the lexical database. This can pose a problem, if the information needed is missing. In this case, the grammar cannot provide a valid analysis.

Due to the richness and complexity of the rules and the information used, the grammars usually provide a large number of possible analyses for each sentence. The resulting parse forest cannot be stored and queried efficiently for large corpora. Thus, an additional disambiguation component (statistical or deterministic) has to be applied or the disambiguation has to be performed manually. Disambiguation components may, however, fail to provide the correct analysis and manual disambiguation is labor-intensive and costly.

Context free Grammars (CFG) (Langer 2001) are formal grammars consisting of a set of recursive rewriting rules. The rewriting rules (or productions) replace a terminal and non-terminal symbols by a terminal symbol. A simple CFG for noun phrases (NP) may, e. g., consist of the following rules: NP → PN, NP → ART NN. This CFG is able to analyze NPs such as *John* and *the cake*. In contrast to some other symbolic approaches, CFGs are in general relatively easy and fast to develop. The grammar is modular with only minimal interaction between the rules. The parsing process is usually fast, which makes it feasible to work with large amounts of text.

The grammar, however, can only be kept simple and fast as long as it covers only the basic aspects of a language system. For the automatic analysis of large amounts of text, further so-called robustness rules are required to overcome shortcomings in the grammar. This, however, slows down the parsing process and makes the grammar unwieldy. Charniak (1996), e. g., extracted 10,605 distinct context-free rules from a 300,000 word sample of the Penn Treebank. Only 3,943 of these occurred more than once.

The output of CFG parsers does not include much information. In order to include, e. g., information about agreement or lexical properties, a large number of additional rules is required. The implementation of these rules within the CFG framework is difficult, especially, with respect to disambiguation of agreement features during the parsing process. The more aspects and features are to be considered, the more complicated and complex the rule system, and the more difficult the development of the grammar.

In other words, the CFG framework works well for small grammars which do not have to cover a wide spectrum of phenomena and which do not have to deliver a lot of additional information apart from the structural annotation. If the grammar becomes more complex and/or additional information is required, the CFG framework loses its advantages.

2.1.2. Probabilistic grammars

Probabilistic grammars, in contrast to symbolic grammars, use statistical means to resolve ambiguities. For an overview of probabilistic approaches see chapters 11 and 12 of Manning/Schütze (1999). Probabilistic grammars are trained on text corpora, where training means finding the optimal probability for each grammar rule. The rules are applied to a corpus, and frequency data is collected. The grammar rules are then expanded adding the probabilistic information acquired from the training corpus to the rules. The training can be either supervised or unsupervised. In the case of supervised training, the grammar is trained on a treebank (a syntactically annotated, manually corrected corpus). The advantage of this approach is that the training data is reliable, and the probabilities for each rule can simply be calculated. However, it requires a treebank of a considerable size. Unsupervised training, on the other hand, is performed on corpus data which is not annotated. During the parsing process, all possible analyses are produced, and the probability of each analysis is estimated. If there is more than one analysis, statistical means are used to determine the most probable or the *n* most probable analyses. In this case, the advantage is that we do not need a prerequisite treebank for training. However, probabilities cannot be calculated but have to be estimated.

The use of statistical methods makes the use of comprehensive lexical and linguistic knowledge that symbolic approaches demand unnecessary. Instead of detailed and complex rules, probabilities can be used to determine the correct analysis. Underspecification of rules allows the grammar to deal with phenomena, which are not overtly and actively present in the grammar. This makes probabilistic grammars robust.

However, probabilistic grammars depend on the training corpus they use. Probabilities can only be calculated according to the representation of the different phenomena in the corpus. If the training corpus is not well balanced, the probabilities for the single rules do not reflect normal language use but frequency distributions. But even if the training corpus is well balanced, some phenomena are better represented than others. High-frequency phenomena will in general be preferred over low-frequency phenomena.

The simplest model of a probabilistic grammar is a probabilistic context-free grammar (PCFG). PCFGs were first studied in the late 1960s and early 1970s (Booth/Thompson

1973; Booth 1969). An overview is given in chapter 11 of Manning/Schütze (1999). Jelinek/Lafferty/Mercer (1992) provide a thorough introduction.

PCFGs consist of a set of terminals, a set of non-terminals, a definite start symbol, a set of rules and a corresponding set of probabilities for these rules. Thus, a PCFG is basically a CFG enriched with information about the probability of the rule. The simple NP CFG described above could be put as follows: NP → PN (0.3), NP → ART NN (0.7). In this case, the first rule is assigned a lower probability of 0.3 and the latter rule a higher probability of 0.7. PCFGs have the advantage that they can make use of underspecification. However, they are not as fast as CFGs as they involve more information.

This is even more the case for Head-lexicalized Probabilistic Context Free Grammars (HPCFG). In contrast to PCFGs, HPCFGs capture the lexical dependencies between syntactic units, e. g., between head nouns and a modifying adjective. In order to create a HPCFG the simple PCFG described above is supplemented by the rules PN → *John*, ART → *the* and NN → *cake*. Probabilities are then assigned to head lexicalized rules such as: (NP → PN | NP,*John*), (NP → ART NN | NP,*cake*). An example of a head-lexicalized context free grammar for German is the GRAMOTRON grammar (Schulte im Walde et al. 2001). Within the framework of GRAMOTRON, all grammar rules are indexed by the lemma of the respective syntactic head. The underlying rule system consists of a number of hand-written rules. During training the rules are multiplied by the occurring lexical heads. This leads to a high number of parameters. These parameters need a sizeable amount of working memory which slows down the parsing speed considerably. The GRAMOTRON grammar is unsupervised which makes it less dependent on the training corpus. If necessary, the grammar can be trained anew for each corpus that is to be parsed.

Other approaches based on context free grammars include left corner parsers (Rosenkrantz/Lewis 1970; Demers 1977) that combine bottom-up and top-down processing or bottom-up shift reduce parsers as in the approach of Tomita (1991) and Inui et al. (1997). Probabilistic grammars based on Tree Adjoining Grammars are discussed in Resnik (1992) and Schabes (1992).

2.1.3. Constraint-based grammars

Constraint-based grammars can be either symbolic or probabilistic. An example is the ENGCG (Karlsson et al. 1995) for English. Constraint-based grammars use language constraints to determine the correct analysis. In other words, the grammar does not describe what is grammatical but rather what is ungrammatical in a language. Principally, the constraints are logical formulas which must be satisfied. In reality, however, there are strict and weak constraints. Strict constraints need to be satisfied, weak constraints may be broken under certain circumstances. Foth/Menzel/Schröder (2003) add weights to the constraints in order to give a ranking of strictness.

2.2. Grammar development

2.2.1. Hand-written grammars

Hand-written grammars are grammars for which a grammar writer develops the rules and decides what kind of rules the grammar comprises, and which phenomena the grammar covers. Consequently, the grammar writer has a good control of the rule system, i. e. what the output of the grammar looks like, what kind of language data it can process, and what not.

At the same time, the grammar depends heavily on the expertise of the grammar writer. Only those phenomena are represented in the grammar which the grammar writer has thought of.

Hand-written rules can be used for symbolic grammars, and as a basis for probabilistic grammars. In the latter case, the rules are applied to a corpus after they have been developed by the grammar writer in order to calculate the probabilities for each rule.

2.2.2. Grammar induction

An alternative to writing grammar rules by hand are machine learning techniques. Machine learning algorithms try to infer grammar rules from text corpora. Extensional syntactic descriptions (corpus annotation) are turned into intentional descriptions (rules) (cf. Collins 1999; Charniak 2000). Approaches based on learning can either work on optimal or on suboptimal training data. In the former case, the algorithms try to infer the grammar based on manually annotated language data (usually treebanks, cf. article 13 on treebanks). In the latter case, the grammar rules are built on the basis of annotations which are the result of an automatic process and which can include incorrect analyses.

The big advantage of machine learning is that new resources in the form of text corpora can be exploited to infer a grammar. In the case of optimal learning this means that manual work is invested in corpus annotation rather than in rule writing. The grammar resulting from such machine learning techniques can be either symbolic or probabilistic. The resulting grammar is more or less independent of the grammatical knowledge of the grammar developer as the grammar rules are inferred from existing text corpora rather than being a result of the expertise of the human developer. This, however, makes the grammar depend on the corpus it is derived from, or rather on linguistic phenomena contained in the corpus. Consequently, the grammar covers only those phenomena present in the training data. Charniak (1996) is an example for supervised learning. He induces a maximum likelihood PCFG using the part of speech tags and phrasal categories of the Penn Treebank. Pereira/Schabes (1992) and Schabes/Roth/Osborne (1993) perform a partially unsupervised learning. They trained the grammar on treebank data ignoring non-terminal labels but using the treebank bracketing. They also trained the grammar on unbracketed data, and compared the results. An interesting study comparing different learning methods, their benefits, advantages and disadvantages was conducted by a post-doc research group in the Netherlands (TMR-Network – Learning Computational Grammars, cf. Nerbonne et al. 2001 and http://www.cnts.ua.ac.be/lcg/).

A special case of learning methods is memory based learning algorithms. The most prominent of them is the data oriented parsing approach (DOP) (cf. Bod/Scha 1997 for an overview). The DOP approach extracts tree fragments (called subtrees) from structurally annotated text corpora. The fragments are stored and as such replace the grammar. Language generation and language analysis is performed by combining the memorized fragments to build up a complex hierarchical structure. In the case of parsing, the final structure has to fit the input data.

DOP approaches need a structurally annotated corpus to collect the tree fragments that make up the grammar. Similarly to other learning techniques, the grammar covers only those phenomena present in the training corpus. A similar approach is the memory-based learning approach (Zarvel/Daelemans 1997).

In contrast to other learning approaches, memory based learning techniques are more sensitive to suboptimal data, i.e. they perform much better if the training corpus has correct structural analyses. Besides, memory based approaches make use of large storage (especially the DOP model) to memorize all the collected data. Consequently, memory based approaches are limited by and depend on storage capacity.

2.3. Type of syntactic analysis

Syntactic preprocessing can also be differentiated with respect to the type of syntactic analysis in which it results (cf. article 13 on treebanks).

2.3.1. Phrase-structure based analysis

The most prominent type of analysis in modern linguistics and NLP is a phrase-structure or constituent-based analysis. In the case of a phrase-structure analysis, tokens are grouped together into constituents (e.g. phrases). Each phrase consists of a head and its dependents. The head is a terminal node, a token, the dependents can be either terminal or phrases (i.e. non-terminal nodes) themselves. Relations and dependencies are expressed hierarchically forming tree-like structures. The hierarchical relations can also be labelled to specify the function of the relation.

2.3.2. Dependency structure analysis

Another possibility of structural analysis is to describe linguistic structure in terms of dependencies between words. The idea of dependency grammar is much older than that of the more prominent phrase-structure grammar. The first clear formal statement is made in Tesnière (1959). In a dependency-structure framework, one word is the head of the sentence and all other words depend directly or indirectly on that word. The dependencies are labelled to mark the type of relationship between the words. As dependency relations connect words directly, lexical information is overtly present in dependency grammars. For example in the sentence *John eats the cake*, there would be a pointer from *eat* to *cake* marking the latter as the object of the verb.

An early example of a probabilistic dependency model is the Probabilistic Link Grammar model of Lafferty/Sleator/Temperley (1992). It differs from other dependency grammars in that it assumes bi-directional dependencies. In this framework each word has a left pointing and a right-pointing connector. Rules specify the types of the connections. In order for a sentence to be valid, the rules for each word in the sentence, as well as some global rules, have to be obeyed.

Collins (1996) induces a lexicalized dependency grammar from the phrase-structure of the Penn Treebank. Collins (1997) redevelops a lexicalized dependency-based language model following Collins (1996).

2.4. Depth of analysis

Syntactic preprocessing varies also with respect to the depth of analysis. The syntactic analysis can range from small phrase-structure chunks to a full hierarchical parse including a functional analysis.

2.4.1. Chunking/partial parsing

The output of a chunker can be seen as somewhat in between a corpus with standard preparation (tokenization, lemmatization, PoS-tagging) and a full parse. According to Steven Abney (Abney 1996a, 1) a chunk is "a non-recursive core of an intra-clausal constituent, extending from the beginning of the constituent to its head". Gee/Grosjean (1983) give psychological evidence for chunks, defining them as a structure of word clustering that emerges from a variety of experimental data, such as pause durations in reading and naive sentence diagramming. They speak of "phi-phrases" and define them as an input string broken after each syntactic head that is a content-word.

Thus, the classic notion of a chunk is that of a flat, non-recursive structure. The chunk begins with a function word and ends with the lexical head. This definition excludes all post-head complements and modifiers. Consequently, some chunkers consider a prepositional phrase (PP) to consist only of the preposition itself, as PPs, in general, are head initial structures.

Chunking, chunk parsing or partial parsing is an approach that has become more and more popular. The grammar of chunkers is relatively simple. Rich and complex linguistic and lexicographic information is not required. As the name suggests, chunkers do not aim at annotating the structure of a sentence completely, but try to build "chunks" of words.

Consequently, they are very robust, i. e. they are not apt to fail to parse a sentence because they fail to parse part of the sentence. A chunker analyzes a text as far as possible, and annotates the results.

In general, chunkers do not consider cases resulting in ambiguities such as attachment decisions, or ambiguities involving lexical dependencies. Ambiguous PP attachments are not resolved, the phrase structures are left as separate constituents as the chunk analysis of the following sentence shows: [$_{NP}$ *John*] saw [$_{NP}$ *the woman*] [$_{PP}$*with the binoculars*].

The most prominent chunk parser is the CASS parser, which has been developed within the CASS environment of Steven Abney. The rules are applied in finite-state cascades as described by Abney (1996b). The German CASS grammar developed within the Verbmobil project produces flat, non-recursive structures that are within the chunk definition of Abney (1996a) given above. The grammar includes a small lexicon which is represented using so-called tag-fixes. This means that part-of-speech (PoS) tags can be associated with lexicon classes. In this case, nouns of different lexicon classes would have different PoS-tags indicating their lexical property. Information about the head lemma of chunks is annotated as an attribute of the chunk. A demo version of the German grammar can be accessed via Internet (http://gross.sfs.nphil.uni-tuebingen.de:8080/release/cass.html).

Chunking or partial parsing can be used as an intermediate step towards full parsing. In this case, the output of the chunker or partial parser is used as input for a more elaborate parsing strategy. An example is the partial parser of Brants (Brants 1999). It was used to facilitate the syntactic annotation of the NEGRA corpus (http://www.coli.uni-sb-de/sfb378/negra-corpus/negra-corpus.html, Skut et al. 1997). It is based on cascaded Markov Models, and operates on several layers. The output of each layer serves as the input for the next, higher layer. The system was inspired by other finite-state cascades such as CASS. Brants' partial parser does not follow the longest match strategy but takes the most probable sequence instead. It is even possible to select analyses from lower layers if they fit better with the highest layer. The best path is found using the Viterbi algorithm (Viterbi 1967). For training, the system requires existing treebank data.

Chunking can also more or less be a first step on the way to developing a broad-coverage grammar. The Conexor system, for example, is a symbolic constraint grammar parser (Voutilainen 1994, Voutilainen/Järvinen 1995) primarily built for English. The output of the chunk grammar is simple, non-recursive structures. Lexical information is not available. However, the head lemma of chunks is indicated by a special tag. For some languages, e. g. English (Karlsson et al. 1995), the chunker has been extended to a broad-coverage grammar.

But chunkers or partial parsers do not necessarily have to be a step on the way to a higher level of analysis. Their robustness and efficiency make it desirable to use their output directly in corpus linguistic research and computational lexicography. The YAC chunker for German (Kermes 2003), for instance, was especially designed to meet the needs of extraction processes for linguistic and lexicographic research.

Chunking or partial parsing approaches are as diverse as broad-coverage grammars. Ramshaw/Marcus (1995) use machine learning methods for chunking. Veenstra (1999) and Sang (2002) use memory based techniques. The YAC chunker (Kermes 2003) follows a deterministic approach.

2.4.2. Full parsing

A full parser is based on a complex grammar that can be formulated in various frameworks (e. g. Lexical Functional Grammars (LFG) or Head-Driven Phrase Structure Grammars (HPSG)). These complex grammars are able to model the hierarchical structures of a language. They are powerful enough to handle complex constraints on structures, relations, and attachments. Consequently, they are well suited to handling the problem of attachment ambiguities. In general, they make use of detailed knowledge about the function and usage of words to determine the correct analysis of a sentence. As a result a complete hierarchical annotation is delivered providing rich and complex information about structures, relations and functions.

The rich and complex annotation provides an excellent base for the extraction of linguistic and lexicographic information. All the knowledge inherent in a full syntactic analysis is directly available and accessible to extraction tools. Queries performed on such a basis can be kept simple and nevertheless provide good results with respect to precision and recall. The complexity of the grammars and the use of detailed linguistic and lexicographic knowledge during the parse, however, slow down the parsing speed. Thus, parsing large corpora is time consuming. Besides, if necessary information is lacking, full parsers fail to deliver an analysis. In most cases, even if only part of a sentence cannot be analyzed, the whole sentence is rejected. Full parsers depend heavily on a rich and detailed prerequisite lexicon which provides them with the necessary information. This is a problem for applications meant to extract lexical information, as the information that is to be extracted is already needed for the parsing process.

Besides, the complexity of the rule system and the extensive use of linguistic and lexicographic knowledge not only resolve but also produce ambiguities. In other words, the parser provides a parse forest instead of a single analysis. Some parsers use heuristic or statistical methods to determine the correct parse or to reduce the number of possible parses.

Another possibility to overcome ambiguous or incorrect output is manual correction. However, manual correction is time-consuming and costly. Thus, manual correction is hardly ever used for purposes other than treebank building.

The complex rule system of the underlying grammar can also cause problems. Changes within the grammar can result in unexpected and undesirable interactions between rules. It is usually difficult to determine the cause of the interaction because of the complexity of the rules and the rule system. Consequently, an adaptation to a different text domain can be very complicated and time-consuming

3. Application

Syntactic preprocessing has three major areas of application:

- treebank building
- corpus linguistic research
- computational lexicography

The first application uses syntactic preprocessing to build a syntactically annotated corpus as a resource for further applications. The latter two use the results of syntactic preprocessing as a knowledge source for linguistic and lexicographic research. The syntactic preprocessing differs depending on the respective application, as do the requirements for the syntactic analysis.

3.1. Treebank building

In most cases, treebanks aim for a high percentage of correct syntactic analyses. Thus, even if syntactic preprocessing is involved, the results are manually post-processed. In order to make the post-processing as easy as possible, the analysis of the syntactic preprocessing should come as close to the desired annotation as possible. The parsing tool should thus have the same underlying theoretical assumptions as the annotation of the treebank. A full disambiguation is not necessary as human annotators can choose the correct analysis. Robustness is not as important as the complete analysis of sentences.

If a parse forest is provided, it is however desirable that the correct analysis be amongst the proposed parses. Manual post-processing is feasible for treebank building since, in contrast to the amount of data used in corpus linguistic research and computational lexicography, treebanks are relatively small.

In some cases, the syntactic preprocessing is performed in two steps. In the first step, a chunker or partial parser provides a preliminary analysis. In the second step, a full parser is applied, taking the preliminary analysis as input. Human annotators can correct, disambiguate and modify the analysis after each step. Manual intervention after the first step can facilitate the next step and can improve its performance. This stepwise procedure was used, for example, for building the NEGRA treebank (Skut et al. 1997) using Brants' (1999) partial parser as a first step (cf. article 13 on treebanks).

3.2. Corpus linguistic research and computational lexicography

In recent years, there has been increasing interest in using evidence derived from automatic syntactic analysis in large-scale corpus studies, as well as in exploiting syntactically annotated corpora for computational lexicographic purposes. The goal is a scalable work process for both corpus studies and computational lexicography that is reproducible and can be applied to large amounts of data. Linguistic evidence and lexicographic knowledge is inherent in any text corpus. Syntactic preprocessing makes the inherent information explicit and accessible to linguistic and lexicographic research. Search tools allow us to access the linguistic information.

Let's take for example the sentence *I saw the man with the binoculars*. The sentence contains, for instance, information about the subcategorization frame of the verb *to see*, namely, that it has a subject (here the pronoun *I*) and a direct object (here the NP *the man*). Syntactic preprocessing can make this information explicit by identifying the constituents and their function.

The question is which kind of syntactic preprocessing is best suited for the respective application. In general, the better and more detailed the syntactic preprocessing, the better and faster linguistic knowledge can be extracted. However, the more detailed the syntactic analysis, the more complex the underlying grammar, the more theory dependent, the more time consuming and difficult the grammar development, and the slower the parsing process.

The requirements for syntactic preprocessing as a basis for corpus linguistic and lexicographic research differ from the requirements for treebank building. Large amounts of diverse data have to be processed. Thus, the syntactic preprocessing tool should work on unrestricted text. In other words, there should be no limitation to corpus size. Small as well as large corpora should be processable. The parser should be able to deal with complete sentences as well as with fragmentary text. In order to be reproducible on different text types, the system should not be domain specific. The underlying grammar should be easily adaptable to new text types. No manual checking should be necessary, as manual labor is not feasible for large amounts of text. The system should provide clearly defined and documented interfaces to make the data easily accessible to search tools. There should be a documentation on what is annotated, and how it is annotated. The annotation should be as theory-neutral as possible.

Usually, the linguistic information is extracted from the syntactic annotation in the corpus. If the parser provides a parse, the result of the extraction is a collection of either all possible instances, or the n-best instances, or only the single best instance matching the query.

In some cases, however, the grammar rules themselves contain the linguistic information. In other words, the grammar itself is a kind of lexicon. In this case, the extraction is performed on the grammar itself rather than on corpus material. An example is the GRAMOTRON grammar (Schulte im Walde et al. 2001). If desired, there is however the possibility of performing the extraction on Viterbi parses (Zinsmeister/Heid 2003).

An example of an extraction of lexicographic information from text corpora is the WASPBENCH (cf. Kilgarriff/Tugwell 2001a, http://wasps.itri.bton.ac.uk/), which determines grammatical relations between words using pattern-matching techniques. The most characteristic grammatical patterns of words are presented in so-called word sketches (cf. Kilgarriff/Tugwell 2001b).

Syntactically annotated corpora can also be a source for corpus linguistic studies. Instead of searching through corpora manually, research can rely on the syntactic annotation to find evidence. For more information about the use of syntactically preprocessed corpora see article 8.

4. Evaluation

The evaluation of text analyzing tools is not a trivial question, especially, if the results should be comparable to the results of other tools. There are basically two major problems with respect to evaluation:

(i) What should be evaluated?
(ii) What kind of gold standard should be used?

The PARSEVAL measures of crossing brackets, (labelled) precision, and (labelled) recall (Black 1992, Black et al. 1991) are traditionally used for the quantitative evaluation of parsers. The quality of these measures with respect to giving a good picture of the actual quality of the parser output, however, has been questioned (cf. Manning/Schütze 1999). Besides, the relationship between the PARSEVAL measures and semantic relations has been frequently criticized (Carroll/Briscoe/Sanfilippo 1998; Magerman 1995; Bangalore 1997). The main problem is that text analyzing tools vary significantly with respect to the theory underlying the analysis, as well as with respect to the output they produce.

Thus, a variety of other evaluation measures have arisen, such as, dependency-based, valence-based, exact, or selective category match (sketched in Carroll et al. 2002). The relational evaluation scheme proposed by Briscoe et al. (2002) evaluates parse selection accuracy on named grammatical relations between lemmatized lexical heads, i. e. not the structure itself but the correct assignment of grammatical relations to the lexical heads of structures is evaluated. Kübler/Hinrichs (2002) describe the problems of PARSEVAL measures for partial parsers which prefer partial analyses to uncertain ones. Unattached phrases lead to high losses in precision and recall. Kübler and Hinrichs, thus, prefer a dependency-based evaluation as opposed to a mere phrase structure evaluation.

The second problem is concerned with the gold standard itself. Usually, if there is an existing treebank, it is used for evaluation. However, the parsing tool and the treebank have to be theory-conformant, i. e. the theory underlying the treebank, and the theory underlying the parsing tool have to be the same, or at least similar. Although most treebanks aim at a theory-independent annotation scheme, this is almost impossible. A dependency parser, for example, cannot be evaluated on a phrase structure-based treebank, at least not without comprehensive conversion rules, and vice versa. Even if the underlying theories are similar, problems arise wherever there is a small difference.

The conversion between one or more formats poses problems. The TIGER graph representation used in the TIGER treebank (Brants et al. 2002) (see also the TIGER Project homepage: http://www.ims.uni-stuttgart.de/projekte/TIGER) and the syntactic analysis provided by the LFG grammar, for instance, are very similar at the level of functional/dependency structure, although there are many differences. Thus, a broad coverage LFG grammar was used as one of the tools for building the TIGER treebank. The output of the LFG grammar was manually disambiguated and then automatically transformed into the TIGER export format (cf. Zinsmeister et al. 2001; Zinsmeister/Kuhn/Dipper 2002). The automatic transformation seemed feasible because the relationships between the two formats appeared to be systematic. However, Zinsmeister et al. (2001) report that subtleties had to be handled with care. Forst (2003) then wanted to exploit the existing TIGER treebank as a test suite for the same LFG grammar. However, it was not possible to simply change the direction of the transformation rules. Instead he had to construct new conversion rules. The problem is that although the formats are similar on a functional/dependency level, there are quite a number of differences as well. Cases, where one of the formats is less specific than the other can only be evaluated concerning those aspects present in both formats. Especially problematic are cases, where the analyses are not one to one but *n* to *m*, i. e. where one or more categories in one of the formats can belong to two different categories in the other format, which cannot be subsumed under a single category.

Special problems arise for the evaluation of chunk parsers or partial parsers. Some systems annotate flat structures only, while other systems annotate the internal structure of these chunks as well. In the latter case, should the evaluation be performed on maximal chunks only, or should the whole hierarchy be evaluated? Evaluations based on maximal chunks, however, cannot be compared to evaluations based on the whole constituent structure. The basis of the evaluation is simply not the same. False analyses of parts of a chunk can affect the whole hierarchy, especially if the maximal chunk is false. In this case, embedded structures are usually also false. Besides, it is not necessarily the case that a correct maximal chunk entails correct embedded structures. Usually, it is more difficult to deliver the correct internal structure than to deliver the correct maximal chunk.

Besides, chunkers deviate to a great extent with respect to the structures they annotate. Classic chunkers annotate base chunks only, i. e. flat non-recursive kernels of phrases. Other chunkers extend the chunk definition. They include some embedded structures in pre-head position, which can in some cases include recursive embedding. Some chunkers also include (recursive) embedding in post-head position as long as it does not produce ambiguities, i. e. PP-attachment is usually excluded. The differences are usually caused by the needs of the application the chunker is built for. However, only chunkers with similar output, i. e. similar underlying chunk definitions, and thus, similar structural ranges, can really be compared. Classic chunkers, for example, cannot be compared with partial parsers or recursive chunkers, as the task of the latter is considerably more difficult.

A problem for chunking approaches is also how to evaluate them. For chunking approaches there is no real alternative to a phrase structure based evaluation. Neither relational evaluation nor dependency based evaluation are feasible as grammatical relations and dependencies are not annotated as such.

There are basically three different approaches: (i) manually check the output of the chunker, and extract the numbers necessary for the evaluation, (ii) manually construct a gold standard corpus, which includes the necessary structures, (iii) take an existing treebank as a gold standard. The first and the second approach both have the advantage that they can be adapted to the underlying chunk definition. The first approach, however, is the least desirable as the evaluation in this case cannot be automatized for a new version of the chunker. The second approach has the advantage that once the gold standard is constructed, the evaluation can be repeated as often as desired. However, the construction of such a manually corrected corpus is time consuming and costly. The third approach has the advantage that the manual work has already been performed. The problem in this case is that the analysis of a treebank is deeper than chunk analysis. Thus, the structures of the treebank have to be broken. It is usually easy to extract the base chunks for the reference of a classic chunker. If the chunks correspond directly to explicit parts of the structural annotation of the treebank, the reference is also fairly easy to extract. In most cases, however, the chunks correspond directly to nodes of the treebank. In this case, it is not possible to extract a gold standard directly from a treebank.

5. Conclusion

The goal of syntactic preprocessing is to make linguistic knowledge inherent in text corpora explicit. There are numerous different approaches varying in grammar type, grammar development, type of analysis and depth of analysis. Syntactic preprocessing is used in treebank building. Recently, there is a growing desire to use syntactic preprocessing in large-scale corpus studies and computational lexicography. Statistical studies need large amounts of data. Linguistic research requires detailed information. Thus, corpus linguistics and computational lexicography will continue to make use of syntactic preprocessing.

6. Literature

Abney, S. (1991), Parsing by Chunks. In: Berwick, R./Abney, S./Tenny, C. (eds.), *Principle-based Parsing*. Dordrecht: Kluwer Academic Publishers, 257–278.

Abney, S. (1996a), Chunk Stylebook. Working draft.

Abney, S. (1996b), Partial Parsing Via Finite-state Cascades. In: *Proceedings of the ESSLI '96 Robust Parsing Workshop*. Prague, 8–15.

Bangalore, S. (1997), Complexity of Lexical Descriptions and its Relevance to Partial Parsing. PhD thesis, University of Pennsylvania.

Black, E. (1992), Meeting of Interest Group on Evaluation of Broad-coverage Grammars of English. In: *LINGUIST List 3.587*. Available at: http://www.linguistlist.Org/issues/3/3–587.

Black, E./Abney, D./Flickinger, C./Gdaniec, C./Grishman, R./Harrison, P./Hindle, D./Ingria, R./ Jelinek, F./Klavans, J./Liberman, M./Marcus, M./Roukos, S./Santorini, B./Strzalkowski, T.

(1991), A Procedure for Quantitatively Comparing the Syntactic Coverage of English Grammars. In: *Proceedings of the DARPA Speech and Natural Language Workshop 1991*. Pacific Grove, CA, 306–311.

Bod, R./Scha, R. (1997), Data-oriented Language Processing. In: Bunt, H./Tomita, M. (eds.), *Corpus-based Methods in Language and Speech Processing*. Boston: Kluwer Academic Publishers, 137–173.

Booth, T. L. (1969), Probabilistic Representation of Formal Languages. In: *Tenth Annual IEEE Symposium on Switching and Automata Theory*. Waterloo, Ontario, 74–81.

Booth, T. L./Thompson, R. A. (1973), Applying Probability Measures to Abstract Languages. In: *IEEE Transactions on Computers* C-22, 442–450.

Brants, S./Dipper, S./Hansen, S./Lezius, W./Smith, G. (2002), The TIGER Treebank. In: *Proceedings of the Workshop on Treebanks and Linguistic Theories*. Sozopol, Bulgaria. Available at: http://www.ims.uni-stuttgart.de/projekte/TIGER/paper/treeling2002.pdf.

Brants, T. (1999), Cascaded Markov Models. In: *Proceedings of the 9th Conference of the European Chapter of the Association for Computational Linguistics EACL 1999*. Bergen, Norway, 118–125.

Bresnan, J. (ed.) (1982), *The Mental Representation of Grammatical Relations*. Cambridge, MA: MIT Press.

Bresnan, J. (2001), *Lexical-functional Syntax*. (Blackwell Textbooks in Linguistics 16.) Malden, MA, USA and Oxford, UK: Blackwell.

Briscoe, T./Carroll, J. A./Graham, J./Copestake, A. (2002), Relational Evaluation Scheme. In: *Workshop Proceedings of Beyond PARSEVAL. Towards Improved Evaluation Measures for Parsing Systems*. Las Palmas, Spain, 4–8.

Carroll, J. A./Briscoe, T./Sanfilippo, A. (1998), Parser Evaluation: A Survey and a New Proposal. In: *Proceedings of the First LREC*. Granada, Spain, 447–454.

Carroll, J. A./Frank, A./Lin, D./Prescher, D./Uszkoreit, H. (2002), Proceedings of Beyond PARSEVAL: Towards Improved Evaluation Measures for Parsing Systems. In: *Workshop Proceedings of Beyond PARSEVAL. Towards Improved Evaluation Measures for Parsing Systems*. Las Palmas, 1–3.

Charniak, E. (1996), Treebank Grammars. In: *Proceedings of the Thirteenth National Conference on Artificial Intelligence (AAAI'96)*. Portland, OR, 1031–1036.

Charniak, E. (2000), A Maximum-Entropy-Inspired Parser. In: *Proceedings of the Language Technology Joint Conference ANLP-NA ACL*. Seattle, Canada, 132–139.

Collins, M. J. (1996), A New Statistical Parser Based on Bigram Lexical Dependencies. In: *ACL* 34, 184–191.

Collins, M. J. (1997), Three Generative, Lexicalised Models for Statistical Parsing. In: *ACL* 35/ *EACL* 8, 16–23.

Collins, M. J. (1999), Head-driven Statistical Models for Natural Language Parsing. PhD Thesis, University of Pennsylvania.

Demers, A. J. (1977), Generalized Left Corner Parsing. In: *Proceedings of the Fourth Annual ACM Symposium. IEEE Transactions on Pattern Analysis and Machine Intelligence* 19, 170–182.

Forst, M. (2003), Treebank Conversion – Establishing a Testsuite for a Broad-coverage LFG from the TIGER Treebank. In: *Proceedings of the EACL Workshop on Linguistically Interpreted Corpora (LINC '03)*. Budapest, Hungary. Available at: ftp://www.ims.uni-stuttgart.de/pub/Users/forst/Forst-LINC03.pdf.

Foth, K./Menzel, W./Schröder, I. (2003), Robust Parsing with Weighted Constraints. In: *Natural Language Engineering* 1(1), 1–25.

Gee, J. P./Grosjean, F. (1983), Performance Structure: A Psycholinguistic and Linguistic Appraisal. In: *Cognitive Psychology* 15, 411–458.

Inui, K./Sornlertlamvanich, V./Tanaka, H./Tokunaga, T. (1997), A New Formalization of Probabilistic CLR Parsing. In: *Proceedings of the Fifth International Workshop on Parsing Technologies (IWPT-97)*. MIT, 123–134.

Jelinek, F./Lafferty, J. D./Mercer, R. L. (1992), Basic Methods of Probabilistic Context Free Grammars. In: Laface, P./De Mori, R. (eds.), *Speech Recognition and Understanding: Recent Advances,*

Trends, and Applications. (NATO ASI Series F: Computer and Systems Sciences 75.) Berlin: Springer Verlag, 345–360.

Karlsson, F. A./Voutilainen, A./Heikkilä, J./Anttila, A. (1995), *Constraint Grammar: A Language-independent System for Parsing Unrestricted Text*. Berlin: de Gruyter.

Kermes, H. (2003), Off-line (and On-line) Text Analysis for Computational Lexicography. (Arbeitspapiere des Instituts für Maschinelle Sprachverarbeitung (AIMS) 9(3).) Doctoral Thesis, University of Stuttgart.

Kilgarriff, A./Tugwell, D. (2001a). WASP-bench: An MT Lexicographers' Workstation Supporting State-of-the-art Lexical Disambiguation. In: *Proceedings of MT Summit VII*. Santiago de Compostela, Spain, 187–190.

Kilgarriff, A./Tugwell, D. (2001b). WORD SKETCH: Extraction and Display of Significant Collocations for Lexicography. In: *Proceedings of the Workshop "COLLOCATION: Computational Extraction, Analysis and Exploitation"*, 39th ACL & 10th EACL, July 2001. Toulouse, France, 32–38.

Kübler, S./Hinrichs, E. W. (2002), Towards a Dependency-oriented Evaluation of Partial Parsing. *Workshop Proceedings of Beyond PARSEVAL. Towards Improved Evaluation Measures for Parsing Systems*. Las Palmas, Spain, 9–16.

Lafferty, J. D./Sleator, D./Temperley, D. (1992), Grammatical Trigrams: A Probabilistic Model of Link Grammar. In: *Proceedings of the 1992 AAAI Fall Symposium on Probabilistic Approaches to Natural Language*. Cambridge, MA, 89–97.

Langer, H. (2001), Syntax and Parsing. In: Carstensen, K.-U./Ebert, C./Endriss, C./Jekat, S./Klabunde, R./Langer, H. (eds.), *Computerlinguistik und Sprachtechnologie – eine Einführung*. Heidelberg, Berlin: Spektrum Akademischer Verlag, 377–385.

Magerman, D. (1995), Natural Language Parsing as Statistical Pattern Recognition. PhD Thesis, Stanford University.

Manning, C. D./Schütze, H. (1999), *Foundations of Statistical Natural Language Processing*. Cambridge, M.A.: MIT Press.

Nerbonne, J./Belz, A./Cancedda, N./Déjean, H./Hammerton, J./Koeling, R./Konstantopoulos, S./Osborne, M./Thollard, F./Tjong Kim Sang, E. F. (2001), Learning Computational Grammars. In: Daelemans, W./Zajac, R. (eds.), *Proceedings of CoNLL-2001*. Toulouse, France, 97–104.

Pereira, F./Schabes, Y. (1992), Inside-outside Reestimation from Partially Bracketed Corpora. In: *ACL* 30, 128–135.

Pollard, C./Sag, I. (1987), *Information-based Syntax and Semantics. Volume 1: Fundamentals*. Chicago: University of Chicago Press.

Pollard, C./Sag, I. (1994), *Head-driven Phrase Structure Grammar*. Chicago: University of Chicago Press.

Ramshaw, L. A./Marcus, M. P. (1995), Text Chunking Using Transformation-based Learning. In: *Proceedings of the Third ACL Workshop on Very Large Corpora*. Cambridge, MA, 82–94.

Resnik, P. (1992), Probabilistic Tree-adjoining Grammar as a Framework for Statistical Natural Language Processing. In: *COLING* 14. Nantes, France, 418–425.

Rosenkrantz, D. J./Lewis, P. M. (1970), Deterministic Left Corner Parser. In: *IEEE Conference Record of the 11th Annual Symposium on Switching and Automata*. Santa Monica, CA, 139–152.

Sag, I./Wasow, T. (1999), *Syntactic Theory: A Fundamental Introduction*. Stanford: CSLI Publications.

Sang, E. T. K. (2002), Memory-based Shallow Parsing. In: *Journal of Machine Learning Research* 2 (March), 559–594.

Schabes, Y. (1992), Stochastic Lexicalized Tree-adjoining Grammars. In: *COLING* 14. Nantes, France, 426–432.

Schabes, Y./Roth, M./Osborne, R. (1993), Parsing the Wall Street Journal with the Inside-outside Algorithm. In: *EACL* 6, 341–347.

Schulte im Walde, S./Schmid, H./Rooth, M./Riezler, S./Prescher, D. (2001), Statistical Grammar Models and Lexicon Acquisition. In: Rohrer, C./Rossdeutscher, A./Kamp, H. (eds.), *Linguistic Form and its Computation*. Stanford: CSLI Publications.

Skut, W. T./Brants, T./Krenn, B./Uszkoreit, H. (1997), Annotating Unrestricted German Text. In: *Fachtagung der Sektion Computerlinguistik der Deutschen Gesellschaft für Sprachwissenschaft*. Heidelberg. Available at: http://www.coli.uni-saarland.de/publikationen/softcopies/Skut:1997:AUG.pdf.

Tesnière, L. (1959), *Éléments de Syntaxe Structurale*. Paris: Librairie C. Klincksieck.

Tomita, M. (ed.) (1991), *Generalized LR Parsing*. Boston: Kluwer Academic.

Veenstra, J. (1999), Memory-based Text Chunking. In: *Workshop on Machine Learning in Human Language Technology. ACAI 99*. Chania, Greece. Available at: http://ilk.uvt.nl/~ilk/papers/ACAI.ps.

Viterbi, A. J. (1967), Error Bounds for Convolutional Codes and an Asymptotically Optimum Decoding Algorithm. In: *IEEE Trans. on IT* 13(2), 260–269.

Voutilainen, A. (1994), *Three Studies of Grammar-based Surface Parsing of Unrestricted English Text*. (Technical Report 24.) Helsinki: Department of General Linguistics, University of Helsinki.

Voutilainen, A./Järvinen, T. (1995), Specifying a Shallow Grammatical Representation for Parsing Purpose. In: *Proceedings of the Seventh Conference of the European Chapter of the Association for Computational Linguistics*. Dublin, Ireland, 210–214.

Zarvel, J./Daelemans, W. (1997), Memory-based Learning: Using Similarity for Smoothing. In: *ACL 35/EACL 8*. Madrid, Spain, 436–443.

Zinsmeister, H./Heid, U. (2003), Identifying Predicatively Used Adverbs by Means of a Statistical Grammar Model. In: *Proceedings of Corpus Linguistics 2003*. Lancaster, UK, 932–939.

Zinsmeister, H./Kuhn, J./Dipper, S. (2002), TIGER Transfer – Utilizing LFG Parses for Treebank Annotations. In: *Proceedings of the LFG02 Conference*. Stanford: CSLI Publications, 427–447.

Zinsmeister, H./Kuhn, J./Schrader, B./Dipper, S. (2001), *TIGER Transfer – from LFG Structures to the TIGER Treebank*. (Technical report, IMS.) University of Stuttgart.

Hannah Kermes, Stuttgart (Germany)

29. Pragmatic annotation

1. Introduction: Pragmatics and corpus annotation

Work in the area of pragmatics and corpus annotation is much less advanced than other annotation work (grammatical annotation schemes, for example). In this chapter, we will show the types of advances that have been made over the past decade (see Leech 1997, 12). Until recently, a paper on 'pragmatic annotation' would have largely concentrated on those pragmatic coding schemes that are based on lexical or syntactic units such as anaphors, interjections or modal verbs (see Sampson 1995; Fischer 1996; Fischer/ Brandt-Pook 1998), and would have had very little to say about schemes that capture pragmatic phenomena at or above the level of the conversational act. Over the past decade, however, a number of hand-coded and (semi-)automated schemes capturing information respecting the act, move and/or exchange, as well as various aspects of the context, have been developed. Our particular emphasis will be on such annotation schemes, specifically those which have been applied to *human-human* interaction (for a summary of work relating to *human-machine* interaction, see Baecker/Buxton 1987; Dix et al. 1998; Preece et al. 1994). We will evaluate some of the better-known schemes (e. g., Stiles 1992; Carletta et al. 1997b; Core/Allen 1997), and consider how the nature of a particular scheme is influenced by (i) the research goal, (ii) the medium of data (i. e., spoken versus written), and (iii) the method of tagging (i. e., hand-coding procedures versus (semi-)automated procedures).

The development of pragmatic annotation is not surprising when we consider that corpus linguistics and pragmatics are both concerned with language use and with naturally-occurring data. That said, the prototypical characteristics of corpus linguistics and pragmatics are not always shared ones: the majority of corpus-based studies tend to be large-scale quantitative analyses of written texts – a consequence, perhaps, of there being more corpora of written texts. Yet the reverse is true for pragmatics: that is to say, most pragmatic studies are relatively small-scale qualitative analyses that concentrate on small samples of spoken language data, whether that data be elicited (e. g., through discourse completion tasks) or naturally occurring (e. g., recorded classroom interaction). Another marked difference relates to context. A particular feature of pragmatics research is its concern with language use in context – and, indeed, all the major theories in pragmatics capture some aspect of context. However, the bias of computer searches towards form, that is to say, a letter or string of letters or words (Leech 2000, 679) seems to have resulted in a tendency within corpus linguistics to concentrate on the relationships between those forms (e. g., text and co-text) at the expense of the (situational, sociological and cultural) dynamics of context, particularly at the local, micro level. Thankfully, advances in computer software and the development of pragmatic annotation schemes have allowed researchers to begin to combine qualitative and quantitative accounts and, by so doing, enhance our understanding of pragmatics (see McEnery/ Wilson 2001).

2. Pragmatic information and annotation

In this section, we consider the kind of information that might be viewed as 'pragmatic', and, consequently, the kind of information that might be represented by pragmatic annotation. The field of pragmatics does not have well-defined boundaries. It has a distinctive history, though, beginning with the work of Charles Morris and reaching something of a zenith with the classics associated with John L. Austin, John R. Searle and H. Paul Grice. Notable figures in more recent decades include Geoffrey N. Leech, Stephen C. Levinson, and also Dan Sperber and Deidre Wilson. However, these people are part of a British (and to some extent North American) tradition which views pragmatics as a branch of linguistics. By contrast, the continental European view regards pragmatics as the superordinate field, with disciplines such as linguistics, sociology and psychology as its subordinates. In fact, pragmatics is notoriously difficult to define. Levinson (1983), for example, spends the first thirty or so pages of his influential book on the subject trying to arrive at a definition, but largely fails. A suggestion sometimes made in the literature is that pragmatics involves a triadic relationship:

- Syntax = mono relationship (between linguistic forms)
- Semantics = dyadic relationship (between linguistic forms and world entities)
- Pragmatics = triadic relationship (between linguistic forms, world entities and the user)

This triadic relationship might be expressed by the formula: 'S [= speaker] meant M by utterance U'. Pragmatics researchers have also emphasised that pragmatics focuses on such things as 'meaning in use', 'speaker meaning', 'meaning in context', and 'utterance interpretation'. Note that 'utterance interpretation' means that a definition of pragmatics should include the hearer as well as the speaker. So, the formula should be extended to something like: 'S in context C^1 meant M^1 by utterance U, which was interpreted as M^2 in context C^2 by H [= hearer]'. To use an established example, if somebody said, "It's hot in here", they might intend it to mean, "Please open the window", in the context of a hot room, and the hearer might interpret it in that way by making the same contextual assumptions. On the other hand, the hearer might make different contextual assumptions and assume it to be a comment on, for example, the heated argument that has just taken place in that room. Pragmatic meaning has even less predictability than, say, semantic meaning, and this in turn presents a particular challenge for computational corpus analysis, where (usually) manual- or semi-automated annotation is the only route for comprehensive pragmatic research.

An alternative approach to defining pragmatics is to note that works that regard themselves as pragmatic gravitate towards certain theories and frameworks. It is the concepts and constructs of these theories and frameworks that may provide pragmatic information for annotation. These theories and frameworks emphasise different aspects of a complete pragmatic description. The potential pragmatic meaning of an utterance might be described in terms of five key components: formal, illocutionary, implied/inferred, interactional and contextual. Of course, no component can occur in isolation but is linked in particular ways to the other components (for example, the imperative form "Get out" has the illocutionary force of a command, but it may be a socially impolite way of getting rid of someone, or, in the event of a fire, merely a warning to evacuate a building). These links are a major focus of research interest, not least of all to the researcher employing pragmatic annotation. We will briefly review these five components, highlighting relevant theories and frameworks, as well as their potential for annotation.

2.1. Formal

An utterance involves a certain choice of forms – lexis, grammar, prosody, etc. Some lexical and grammatical forms are conventionally associated with particular pragmatic meanings, and these include speech act verbs (e. g., "I *order* you to be quiet"), hedges (e. g., "*Perhaps* you *might* be quiet"), politeness markers (e. g., "*Please* be quiet") and referring expressions (e. g., "Be quiet please, *darling*"). The corpus linguistic approach here has been to 'search on' particular forms and then to study their functions and contexts of use, as well as to compare the frequencies of particular forms and functions. Examples of researchers who have developed pragmatic coding schemes that are based on lexical or syntactic units (e. g., anaphors, interjections, modal verbs etc.) include Sampson (1995), Fischer (1996) and Fischer/Brandt-Pook (1998). A good example of interactional pragmatic work is Aijmer (1996), who studied the linguistic realisations of various speech acts, such as 'requests', 'thanks' and 'apologies'. In principle, particular forms could be tagged for information regarding their functions and contextual properties. In practice, however, only ad hoc and limited schemes have been devised to date. A particular limitation of this corpus approach relates to the choice of forms. Investigating individual forms is unproblematic, but investigating a collection of forms that represent, for example, a particular speech act leads to the problem of establishing which forms constitute that collection. Researchers have usually resorted to manual readings and qualitative analyses of the data.

2.2. Illocutionary

The philosophers Austin (1962) and Searle (1969, 1975) developed the notion that an utterance can be regarded as an attempt by the speaker to 'do' something. An utterance (or series of utterances) may constitute a particular speech act, such as an assertion, command, promise or curse, in which speakers commit themselves to a particular course of action. The 'illocutionary' meaning or force of a speech act is the speaker's intention in performing the act in a particular context. For a speech act to be successful, certain 'felicity conditions' (Austin 1962, 12−45) should pertain; thus, for example, a promise or a threat both commit the speaker to fulfil the promise or threat in due course. Some quantitative work exists in this area. For example, the *Cross Cultural Speech Act Realization Patterns* (CCSARP) project (see Blum-Kulka/House/Kasper 1989) is a study of data elicited by questionnaire, involving seven different languages or language varieties and 1,088 informants. However, such questionnaire studies elicit small data samples, not long stretches of discourse. Moreover, leafing through the papers in the *Journal of Pragmatics* quickly reveals that the majority of studies contain small-scale qualitative analyses or theoretical descriptions. For this reason, "quantitative accounts [...] would be an important contribution to our understanding of pragmatics" (McEnery/Wilson 1996, 99). In fact, a number of studies (see section 4.1.1. and 4.1.2.) have combined speech act analysis with a corpus and/or computational approach. These studies typically involve the manual- or semi-automated tagging of speech act types, so that they can be placed in more generic groups, and thereby reveal patterns in the discourse. Once a particular form has been assigned to speech act categories, it is possible to investigate, for example, the formal characteristics of those categories. Where do the categories originate? Although Austin's (1962) classification of speech acts was probably the first, most researchers draw on Searle (1976), whose basis for developing the classification was the question 'How many ways of using language are there?' (Searle 1976, 1). His taxonomy consists of five categories (1976, 10−15):

Representatives committing the speaker to the truth of the expressed proposition, e. g., *asserting*, *concluding* [he later renamed this category *Assertives*]

Directives	attempts by the speaker to get the addressee to do something, e. g., *advising, requesting*
Commissives	committing the speaker to a future course of action, e. g., *promising, threatening, offering*
Expressives	expressing a psychological state, e. g., *thanking, apologising, welcoming*
Declaratives	effecting immediate changes in an institutional state of affairs, with extra-linguistic qualities, e. g., *declaring war, christening*

Others have proposed additional categories (for example, Leech 1983, 206, added 'rogatives' to encompass acts like *ask, enquire, query*, and *question*, which previously had been subsumed by 'directives'), or alternative classifications, notably Bach/Harnish (1979). One particular criticism made of these classifications is that they are in fact classifications of the semantics of speech act *verbs*, which cannot be assumed to map straightforwardly onto classifications of illocutionary *acts* (Searle 1976, 8; Leech 1983, 177, 198). Broadly speaking, the earlier the classification – Austin, Searle or Bach/Harnish – the more obviously this is the case. Other researchers have not attempted to devise a classification of illocutionary acts but have opted for a classification of speech act verbs drawn from dictionaries (e. g., Ballmer/Brennenstuhl, 1981, who took 4,800 verbs from German dictionaries and classified them). Studies, including corpus-based or computational studies, have typically adapted such speech act classifications for their particular datasets and annotated acts accordingly (see section 4 onwards). The grand plan of devising a classification that accommodates all kinds of speech act found in all kinds of discourse and at the right level of delicacy seems impossible, but the global classifications that exist do at least present a useful starting point.

2.3. Implied/inferred

Apart from formal or conventionalised aspects of utterances (discussed above), the meanings of an utterance in dialogue cannot be automatically deduced. Understanding an utterance is not merely a matter of decoding a message. Rather, the meanings are induced from the utterance in its context, requiring the analyst to infer a conclusion from all available evidence. We are concerned here both with what the speaker implies and what the hearer infers. The inferential processes involved are usually discussed with reference to Grice's Cooperative Principle (1975) or Sperber/Wilson's Relevance Theory (1986). Relevant corpus-based studies include Archer (2002), who offers an analytical framework that allows for a quantitative investigation of (the various ways in which participants broke) the Gricean maxims within the historical courtroom, and Andersen (2001), whose analytical model for identifying pragmatic markers in a corpus of London adolescent conversation draws on Relevance Theory. Of course, the lack of formal correlates and the sheer complexity of the inferential system place a very heavy burden on corpus-based analysts. McEnery (1995, 24) suggests that the above theories also pose unique problems for the computational analyst; Relevance Theory, for example, is said to be too deterministic in that it seeks out "one intended meaning and one intended meaning alone" for a given utterance. In response, McEnery (1995, 24) advocates that we adopt a probabilistic model that allows analysts to look for "the **optimally** likely meaning rather than the 'correct' or 'successful' interpretation" (original emphasis). We discuss the problems associated with inferential corpus annotation in more detail in section 4.2.

2.4. Interactional

Mention of utterances leads us neatly to interactional considerations. An utterance stands in a certain structural relationship with other utterances in a conversation, and it is this relationship that denotes interactional meaning (thus, for example, an utterance may be regarded as an 'answer' simply because it stands in a certain structural relationship with an utterance regarded as a 'question'). This area has been the focus of study for Conversation Analysis (e. g., Sacks/Schegloff/Jefferson 1974) and Discourse Analysis (e. g., Sinclair/Coulthard 1975). Conversation Analysis (henceforth CA) focuses in particular on (i) turn-taking (e. g., the distribution of talk, turn allocation, turn transition, interruptions, and topic control), (ii) adjacency pairs (e. g., question-answer), and (iii) the overall organisation of conversation (e. g., openings and closings). All of these aspects would be amenable to, and, we would argue, would benefit from, annotation, by which one could study conversational patterns over large datasets. Some researchers have attempted to combine a CA-based approach with annotation. For example, the *Language Interaction in Plurilingual and Plurilectal Speakers* (LIPPS) group have developed a *Linguistic Interaction Database Exchange System* (LIDES), which enables switches in code from one linguistic variety to the other to be tagged (see the *LIDES Coding Manual* 2000 for further details). Such work is extremely rare, however. One reason for this relates to the philosophy behind CA, of course. Engaging in CA is an inductive matter – a matter of revealing the categories that are used. Annotation involves the opposite: the imposition of preformed categories. This being so, annotation can be more naturally equated with the Discourse Analysis model of the Sinclair/Coulthard (1975) type – a speech-act based model, which focuses on structural relationships between utterances, using terms such as 'exchange' or 'move'. Studying discourse taking place in the classroom, Sinclair/Coulthard (1975) described one particular pattern as 'initiation', 'response' and 'feedback' (the IRF model). Thus, the teacher might initiate an exchange with a question (i. e., a particular kind of move), a pupil might then respond with an answer, and finally the teacher might provide feedback with a comment. A Sinclair-Coulthard inspired approach has been used by both computational and corpus-based analysts (see, for example, Carletta et al. 1997a, 1997b; Archer 2005; and sections 4.1.2. and 4.4.). Additional computational work with respect to discourse structure that is not necessarily inspired by the Birmingham School includes Carlson/Marcu/Okurowski (2003), Miltsakaki et al. (2004), Stede (2004) and Baldridge/Lascarides (2005).

2.5. Context

A crucial feature of pragmatics is that it accounts for meanings which are context sensitive. Areas of context for consideration include:

Co-text – the linguistic context. Within pragmatics, this is often taken to involve Conversation Analysis, and not, for example, collocational analysis. There is overlap here with 'interactional meaning', discussed above.

Physical context – the actual setting or environment in which the interaction takes place, (e. g., a church on Sunday morning).

Personal / social context – the social and personal relationships of the interactants to one another, including aspects of power, social distance and role (which are a particular focus of politeness theory, cf. Brown/Levinson 1987; Leech 1983).

Cognitive context – the background knowledge and the shared knowledge of participants in the interaction.

Cultural context – 'institutional' and 'societal' aspects (including the values, beliefs, norms and practices of a culture).

Context in the situational model – the context that is projected by the language itself, or, in other words, the scenario that the interpreter constructs in processing the language (a clear example of this is the fictional world projected by the words of a novel: see, for example, Short/Semino/Culpeper 2000).

Approaches to context within pragmatics often combine several of the above areas, as in Dell Hymes' (e. g., 1972) 'speech events' or Levinson's (1992) 'activity types'. There is also a strong recognition that there are multiple contexts in communication, as seen, for example, by different participants, and that these are always in a state of flux (e. g., somebody might speak to another in their capacity as 'tutor' and then speak to someone else in their capacity as 'friend'). Unfortunately, many researchers working outside pragmatics regularly employ an impoverished notion of context. Often the co-text is taken to be the sum total of all there is to be said about the context. This criticism also applies to corpus-based studies, which, if they consider context at all, confine themselves to the inclusion of a few static values (e. g., the sex of the participants) in the headers of files (see the studies discussed in section 4.3.1.). The major challenge for pragmatic annotation must be to take *full* account of the context.

3. Differentiating between computational pragmatics and corpus pragmatics

As we have used the labels 'computational pragmatics' and 'corpus-based' pragmatics several times in section 2, we believe that it would be useful to define the two approaches (as we see them) and assess their main foci.

With respect to computational pragmatics, we can draw on Jurafsky (2004, 578), who defines the approach as "the computational study of the relation between utterances and action", and also McEnery (1995, 12), whose definition tends to highlight the purpose of computational pragmatics, i. e., "getting natural language processing systems to reason in a way that allows *machines to interpret utterances in context*" (our emphasis). Jurafsky (2004, 579) also stresses this language engineering component, adding that "one futuristic goal of this research is [...] to build artificial agents that can carry on conversations with humans in order to perform tasks like answering questions, keeping schedules, or giving directions". Another related aspect of computational pragmatics mentioned by Jurafsky (2004, 579) is that of " 'computational psycholinguistics' – the use of computational techniques to build processing models of human psycholinguistic performance".

Although, in his seminal article, Jurafsky (2004) acknowledges that computational pragmatics is concerned with a number of areas, (i. e., indexicality, the relation between utterances and action, the relation between utterances and discourse, and the relationship between utterances and the place, time, and environmental context of their being uttered), he nevertheless concurs with Bunt/Black (2000) that the main focus of computational pragmatics is that of inference. Indeed, inference is said to pose "four core inferential problems" for the computational community: abduction (see, e. g., Hobbs 2004), reference resolution (see, e. g., Kehler 2000), the interpretation and generation of speech acts (see, e. g., Jurafsky 2004), and the interpretation and generation of discourse structure and coherence relations (see, e. g., Kehler 2004).

Corpus pragmatics shares this interest in inference (as well as other pragmatic phenomena). However, rather than studying inference as a means of getting computers to understand language, corpus-based analysts study inference so that *they themselves more readily understand language use* (Rayson, personal correspondence). Corpus pragmatics is so named because, like corpus linguistics in general, it involves analysing actual patterns of language use, using a collection of natural texts. Increasingly, these texts tend to be in an electronic form, which means that researchers are able to make use of computers when analysing their data. As this article will reveal, a growing number of corpus-based researchers are also adding annotation to their corpora, and developing software programs to help in their manipulation. Weisser (2003), for example, has developed a tool called SPAACy, which allows human analysts to annotate speech acts semi-automatically. We are, of course, aware that the difference we are painting between the computational analyst and the corpus-based analyst can be a blurry one in practice, not least because "corpora have played a useful role in the development of human language technology to date" and "in return, corpus linguistics has gained access to ever more sophisticated language processing systems" (McEnery 2003, 460).

It is worth noting that the majority of the better-known (corpus-based) pragmatic annotation schemes are devoted to one aspect of inference: the identification of speech/dialogue acts (see McEnery et al. 2006, 40, for a comprehensive list). Unlike the computational studies concerning speech act interpretation, however, corpus-based schemes are, in the main, applied manually, and schemes that are semi-automatic tend to be limited to specific domains. Thus, for example, Weisser's (2003) software tool is limited to the annotation of task-oriented telephone dialogues.

Speech/dialogue act annotation schemes will form a major focus of the rest of this article. Readers interested in other pragmatic annotation schemes, be they manual or (semi-)automatic, are therefore directed to the following (for additional references see Horn/Ward 2004):

- Stede/Heintze (2004), Webber (2004) and Marcu (1999), for articles relating to discourse structure.
- Hahn/Strube/Markert (1996) and Navarro/Martínez-Barco/Muñoz (2002), for articles relating to information structure/information status (especially anaphora resolution methods on definite descriptions).

- Carlson/Marcu/Okurowski (2003) and Kameyama (1998), for articles relating to segmentation issues (note that we also discuss segmentation from a corpus-based perspective in section 5, below).

4. Pragmatic annotation schemes

4.1. Introductory remarks

In this section, we review annotation schemes that capture some of the pragmatic aspects outlined in section 2. The organisation of this section is, broadly speaking, determined by pragmatic area. We begin with schemes that encompass illocutionary force. In practice, those schemes combine, to varying degrees, illocutionary with interactional aspects. We will refer to these schemes as 'dialogue act' schemes, following the existing literature. We then turn briefly to the few schemes dealing with implied/inferred meanings, and then more extensively to contextual schemes. Finally, we give an example of a mixed scheme. We pay particular attention to those schemes that seek to apply annotation systematically, rather than ad hoc or piecemeal.

4.1.1. Dialogue act schemes: A hand-coded scheme

In this section, we will be concentrating on the work of Stiles (1992). Linguists have tended to neglect Stiles' work in the past, perhaps because he is a psychologist, and so tends to publish in that field rather than our own. However, his work is certainly worthy of consideration, as will become apparent.

Stiles designed his taxonomy, which he calls *Verbal Response Mode* or VRM (see Table 29.1), as a means to an end: he wanted to improve psychologists' interactions with their patients, and needed some means of pragmatically analysing their interaction. Using the eight categories of VRM, Stiles assigned each utterance a two-letter interpretative tag. The first letter codifies the *literal form* of the utterance, and the second its *illocutionary function*. So, "Can you pass it?" (where 'it' refers to a very heavy object) would be tagged QQ, while "Can you pass it?" (where 'it' refers to a pen) would probably be tagged QA.

The *form/function* distinction is central to speech act theory, in that words and their force operate by complex means, and the relationship between the two is often tangential or indirect. Moreover, Stiles' categories satisfy the need for discreteness without being cumbersomely detailed, and the easy-to-use (and to remember) tags are ideal for manual tagging. The scheme has the potential to be used qualitatively: "… a useful adjunct in qualitative analyses; it offers clearly defined categories, which investigators can use descriptively" (Stiles 1992, 25). Taking the view that taxonomies may need modification to our specific research needs and data type, the exact criteria for the categories can also be adjusted without much disruption to the others. Indeed, Stiles himself takes the view that categories *should* be adjusted according to the type of discourse being studied. Of course, we might want to refine some of Stiles' labels and definitions. For example, Stiles defines his 'edification' category as 'states objective information'. Since we cannot know

Tab. 29.1: Verbal Response Mode categories (from Stiles 1992, 17)

Type	Code	Description
Disclosure	D	Reveals thoughts, feelings, perceptions or intentions
Edification	E	States objective information
Advisement	A	Attempts to guide behaviour; suggestions, commands, permission, prohibition
Confirmation	C	Compares speaker's experience with others; agreement, disagreement, shared experience or belief
Question	Q	Requests information or guidance
Acknowledgement	K	Conveys receipt of or receptiveness to other's communication; simple acceptance; salutations
Interpretation	I	Explains or labels the other; judgements or evaluations of other's experience/behaviour
Reflection	R	Puts other's experience into words; repetitions, restatements, clarifications

whether a speaker's comments are truly objective, 'states apparently objective information' seems more appropriate. Also, 'edify' usually means 'to instruct and improve', and although Stiles acknowledges that his usage "departs from the dictionary definition" (1992, 75), he does not state *why*. Stiles' scheme also lacks 'unclassifiable' categories, which would allow one to include ambiguous or indeterminate utterances in the analysis. We believe that any classification of pragmatic phenomena should accord proper status to pragmatic indeterminacy, whether this arises because the analyst has insufficient background knowledge or the utterance itself is deliberately ambiguous. Stiles (1992, 100) does include the category 'uncodable' ('U'), which he details briefly, but he does not include it in his main description of the taxonomy, and he restricts it to "utterances that coders cannot understand or hear clearly" (1992, 15).

4.1.2. Dialogue act schemes: (Semi-)automated models

According to Jurafsky (2004), there are two (semi-)automated models of speech act interpretation: the BDI (belief, desire and intention) model and the 'cue-based' or probabilistic model. BDI computational models (e. g., Perrault/Allen 1980) use 'belief logics' inspired by Searle's (1975) explanation of indirect speech acts (of the "Can you pass the salt?" variety). In simple terms, they seek to mimic a hearer's chain of reasoning with respect to satisfactorily met pre-conditions. By contrast, cue-based or probabilistic models (e. g., Jurafsky/Martin 2000) are inspired by Power's (1979) concept of 'conversational games and moves', and Goodwin's (1996) work relating to the 'microgrammar', that is, the specific lexical, collocational, and prosodic features that characterise particular conversational moves. As most well-known studies are in the latter cue-based tradition, cue-based models will be the focus of this section. The reason that cue-based models are more prevalent than BDI models may relate to the fact that computers can search for formal correlates of SA-types more readily than abstract logical aspects.

Cue-based models are not merely interested in identifying illocutionary force, but they also seek to identify interactional meaning. Consequently, practitioners working within the cue-based tradition prefer the term 'dialogue act' to 'speech act'. It is important to note, however, that there is disagreement regarding what constitutes a 'dialogue act'. For example, Bunt (1994) suggests that a dialogue act is a speech act in the context of a dialogue, whilst Core/Allen (1997) suggest that it is an act whose internal structure relates specifically to its dialogue function.

Although a relatively recent development, work on the automatic detection of dialogue acts is quite advanced, and standards for shallow discourse structure annotation now exist. One of the better known, the *Dialogue Act Markup in Several Layers* (DAMSL) tagset, has been designed by the natural language processing community under the *Discourse Resource Initiative* (Core/Allen 1997). Of particular interest is its utilisation of concepts outside the philosophical traditions that first defined speech acts, with the result that we see the inclusion of Schegloff's concept of 'repair' (Schegloff/Jefferson/Sacks 1977), and 'preceding and succeeding discourse' (Schegloff 1968, 1988). Indeed, the DAMSL tagset distinguishes between the *forward-looking* function of an utterance, which differentiates between different SA-based phenomena (cf. STATEMENT = a claim made by the speaker; INFO-REQUEST = a question by the speaker; CHECK = a question by the speaker for confirming information), and the *backward-looking* function, which identifies some sort of pragmatic relationship between utterance U and previous utterances (cf. ACCEPT = accepting the proposal; REJECT = rejecting the proposal; REPEAT-REPHRASE = demonstrated via repetition or reformulation).

The SWBD-DAMSL annotation model (SWBD = Switchboard domain) provides us with an example of work that has utilised – and expanded – the DAMSL tagset (Stolcke et al. 2000). The model consists of approximately 50 basic tags (e. g., QUESTION, STATEMENT, OPINION, BACKCHANNEL, APPRECIATION), which, when combined with diacritics indicating related information, extend to 220, and distinguishes 42 mutually-exclusive utterance types. Here is an example of a conversation taken from the *Switchboard Corpus* of spontaneous human-to-human telephone speech:

Speaker	*Dialogue Act*	*Utterance*
B	STATEMENT	but, uh, we're to the point now where our Financial income is enough that we can consider putting some away –
A	BACKCHANNEL	*Uh-huh/*
B	STATEMENT	– for college,/
B	STATEMENT	so we are going to be starting a regular payroll deduction –
A	BACKCHANNEL	*Um./*
B	STATEMENT	– in the fall/
B	STATEMENT	and then the money that I will be making this summer we'll be putting away for the college fund.
A	APPRECIATION	*Um. Sounds good.*

(Adapted from Stolcke et al. 2000, 7)

This extract shows that each utterance is assigned a unique Discourse Act (DA) label. By 'utterance', Stolcke et al. (2000, 4) mean a 'sentence-level unit', which may or may not correspond to a speaker turn. The tagset is interesting for several reasons. First, it classifies utterances according to a combination of pragmatic, semantic and syntactic criteria. Secondly, it claims not to be 'task-oriented'. Indeed, Stolcke et al. (2000, 4) argue that it is generic in nature, having been applied to a corpus of spontaneous conversational speech – albeit telephone speech. Their claim is important, as similar work has tended to concentrate on specific tasks, which tend to be formulaic and may often be easier to annotate.

Carletta et al.'s (1997a, 1997b) taxonomy is an example of such a task-oriented scheme, having been applied to Map Task dialogues (see Figure 29.1, below). (Note that a Map Task involves participant A's duplication of a route that is present on B's map, but missing from his/her own; for further details see Carletta et al., 1997b, 2.) It is worth noting that Carletta et al. (1997b) purport to have developed a coding scheme that is (potentially) generic. Unlike Stolcke et al. (2000), their scheme is based on conversational moves (i. e., utterance function), game structure, and higher-level transaction structure. Consequently, it shares similarities with the structure adopted by Sinclair/Coulthard (1975), when analysing classroom discourse (see 'interactional meaning' under section 2). Indeed, the 'games' level is roughly equivalent to Sinclair and Coulthard's 'exchange' level, in that it distinguishes between *initiations* and *responses*, etc. A 'game', in turn, is made up of *conversational moves*, beginning with an *initiation* and continuing until the purpose of the 'game' has been achieved. The coding scheme for these 'moves' draws from – and extends – the moves which make up Houghton's (1986) interaction frames, and consists of INSTRUCT, EXPLAIN, CHECK, ALIGN, QUERY-YN, QUERY-W, RESPONSE, ACKNOWLEDGE, REPLY-Y, REPLY-W, CLARIFY, READY. Carletta et al. (1997b, 3) provide a diagram which summarises the procedure followed when assigning these moves. As Figure 29.1 shows, formal and interactional aspects are once again combined (see, in particular, QUERY/REPLY-YN and QUERY/REPLY-W).

Leech/Weisser's (2003) *Speech-Act Annotation Scheme* (SPAAC) is also task-oriented, having been developed primarily for the XML speech act annotation of service dialogues. Two major kinds of telephone dialogue were utilised: telephone operator and service dialogues (provided by British Telecom), and train booking dialogues (provided by the Trainline.com). As its name suggests, the key level of annotation relates to the tagging of speech acts (or dialogue acts), for which SPAAC draws from a tagset of 40 items, including ACCEPT, ACKNOWLEDGE, ANSWER, ANSWER ELABORATE, APPRECIATE, BYE, COMPLETE, CONFIRM, etc. 'Correct' speech act assignment is aided, in turn, by five further dimensions, all of which are tagged:

(a) segmentation (e. g., into utterances, C-units and discourse markers)
(b) syntactic form (e. g., declarative, interrogative, imperative, fragment)
(c) topic or subject matter (e. g., address, arrival, cancel, credit card, date, departure: see train booking dialogues)
(d) mode (e. g., alternative, condition, probability, expletive)
(e) polarity (i. e., positive vs. negative).

The form tagset consists of <decl> (= declarative clause), <q-yn> (yes-no question), <q-wh> (wh-question), <imp> (= imperative), <frag> (=fragment, i. e., a non-clausal unit or incomplete clause lacking a subject), <dm> (=discourse marker), <yes> (= affirmative reply) and <no> (= negative reply). As we might expect, there are some obvious similarities with those schemes already mentioned (cf. QUERY-YN and QUERY-W with <q-yn> and <q-wh>, REPLY-Y and REPLY-N with <yes> and <no>). However, Leech and Weisser also suggest that other (non-questioning/non-answering) form labels

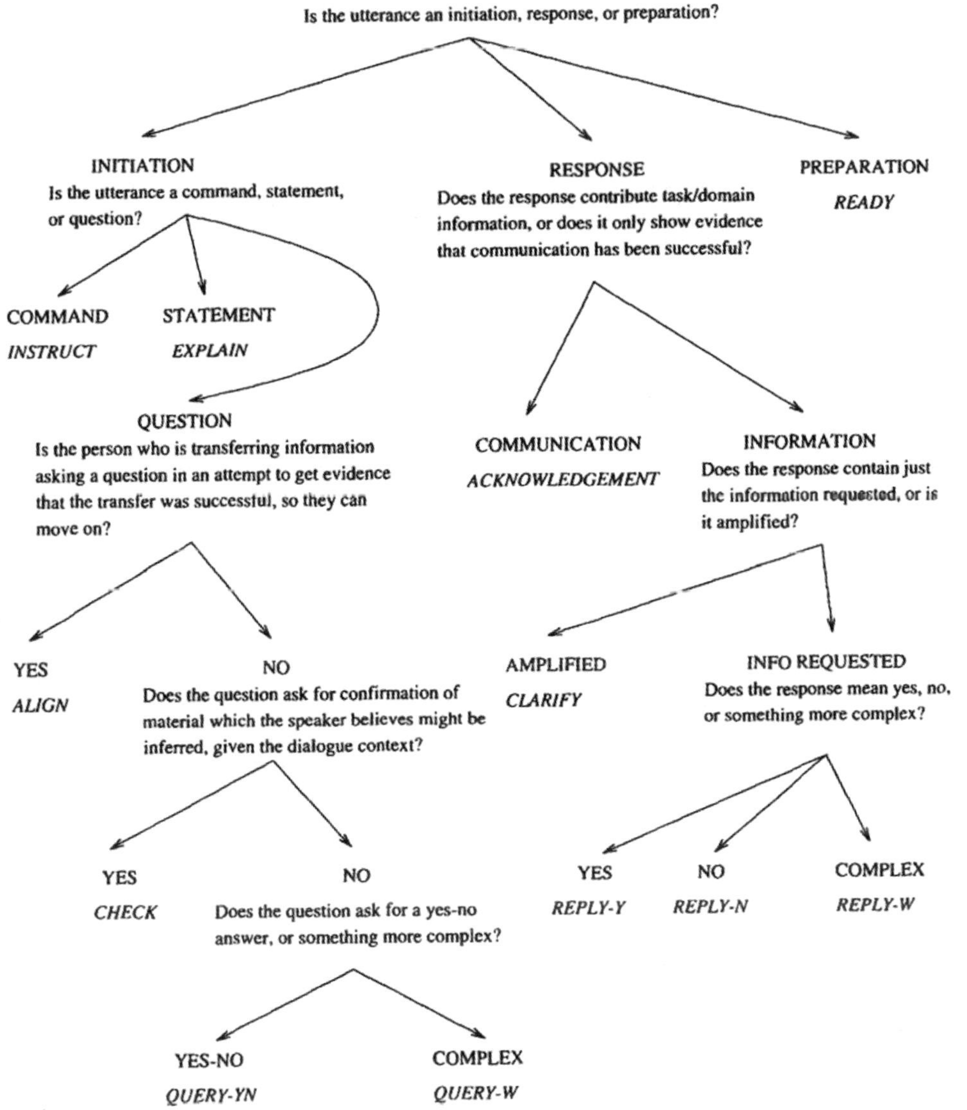

Fig. 29.1: Conversational Move Categories (from Carletta et al. 1997b, 3; original emphasis)

share strong associations with particular speech act labels. For example, an 'inform' is said to be "normally conveyed by a <decl> or (less frequently) a <frag>" (Leech/Weisser 2003, 22). Leech/Weisser (2003, 22) define an INFORM as follows:

> Typically speaker x has the goal of informing speaker y about something speaker x believes that speaker y did not know or was not aware of before, generally without this having been elicited, e. g. *The last train leaves at 1650.*

However, as they go on to explain, informs can be difficult to distinguish in practice, because of their potential overlap with other speech acts, including CONFIRM, EXPRESS-REGRET, EXPRESSWISH, EXPRESSPOSSIBILITY, EXPRESSOPINION, etc. In consequence, Leech/ Weisser (2003, 22)'s INFORM category is 'flexible'. That is:

> [*Inform* is] used where some element of **conveying information** or **making the addressee aware** is present. For example, after a longish period in which the telephone is ringing, the operator may say to the caller: *I'm sorry, **there's no reply**.*

Here, their argument is that, although the information content of the utterance in context is low, the operator is nevertheless making the caller 'explicitly aware of something'.

Leech and Weisser's need to justify the definition and use of their *inform* category illustrates how even apparently straightforward speech act categories like *inform* are problematic to both define and apply to real data.

4.2. Implied/inferred schemes

We have already highlighted two implied/inferred annotation schemes in section 2 that are corpus-based, Archer (2002) and Andersen (2001). As we explained, Archer's (2002) annotation scheme is based on Gricean maxims. Grice (1975) identified four maxims (Quality, Quantity, Relation and Manner) that, taken together, specify what participants have to do in order to converse in a maximally efficient, rational, co-operative way (i. e., speak sincerely, relevantly and clearly, while providing sufficient information). Grice also suggested that, as interactants, we can manipulate these maxims in order to generate an implicature (i. e., cause our interlocutor to look for an additional meaning beyond the surface level meaning). Archer (2002, 10) has used Gricean maxims as annotation categories (and also added two additional categories, 'coop' and 'ambig', which signal surface level cooperation and uncertainty respectively) as a means of distinguishing "those instances when defendants [in the Salem trials of 1692] exhibited a surface level cooperation [with their questioners] (e. g., they did not intend to generate an implicature) from those instances when they flouted the maxims for a particular purpose". Andersen's (2001) scheme for identifying pragmatic markers in a corpus of London adolescent conversation, by contrast, draws on one of the better-known reductionist theories, Relevance Theory. Relevance Theory is based on two principles: a Cognitive Principle, i. e., that human cognition is geared to the maximisation of relevance, and a Communicative Principle, i. e., that utterances create expectations of optimal relevance (Wilson/Sperber 2004).

Although Archer (2002) and Andersen (2001) show that it is possible to draw from both theories to develop a manual-approach to annotation, McEnery (1995) has highlighted potential problems in respect to developing computational pragmatic annotation schemes using Grice (1975) and Sperber/Wilson (1986). As we have already noted, McEnery's (1995) main concern was with using the latter (see section 2), but we will focus here on his main concern in respect of the (computational) use of Grice (1975, 1989), which relates to Grice's (1971) definition of the realisation of the force of an utterance. Put simply, Grice argues that part of the communicative force of an utterance is the intention to communicate itself. That is to say, "U intends to produce in A effect E by A's recognition of that intention" (Grice 1971, 153, cited by McEnery 1995, 16). Using the same example we used in section 2, McEnery (1995, 16) warns that this can lead to 'an infinite regression':

> If speaker A says to hearer B "It is hot in here", part of the force of that utterance is the fact that B knows A wanted to communicate the message C. Yet further to that, A knows that B knows that A wanted to communicate C. Further still, A knows that B knows that A knows that B knows that A wanted to communicate C. This chain of inference could continue forever.

McEnery (1995, 16) goes on to argue that intention has revealed itself to be a major part of the problem of realising the force of an utterance. Indeed, he suggests that "while such communicative intentions are undoubtedly relevant to the formation of the force of an utterance, it is not clear how such factors can be brought into play in determining force within an account of [computational] pragmatics". It should be noted that other theorists offer an alternative to the recursion inherent in Grice's theory, most notably Schiffer (1972), whose mutual knowledge thesis emphasises how a hearer deduces speaker intention through prior assumed mutual knowledge. However, McEnery (1995, 17) insists that this 'answer' merely creates another recursive process:

> At the first order level, there exist the shared assumptions of the speaker and hearer. However, in order to derive this set of assumptions they must both have a set of second order assumptions, i. e. assumptions about what shared assumptions they have. Beyond the second order assumptions are third order assumptions, i. e. assumptions about the assumptions about the shared assumptions, and beyond that fourth, fifth, sixth levels of assumptions and so on, regressing to infinity.

Developing an idea first posited by Leech (1983), McEnery (1995, 25) contends that, first, inferencing should be seen as probabilistic, and, secondly, that Grice's (1982) own *deeming* process appears to confirm this:

> Given that complete understanding is *impossible*, Grice says that the generation of approximations to meaning will lead to the interpretation of an utterance being the *optimum* realisation of the meaning of that utterance. Grice says that these approximations are ones that ought to be deemed to "satisfy a given ideal even though they do not, strictly speaking, exemplify it" – that is utterances may be taken to mean one thing, even though some uncertainty may exist as to whether they definitely do have that meaning. So one may not, strictly speaking, in any model of intention, say that A meant C. But contextually it is legitimate for us to *deem* that A meant C, even though the conditions for determining this to be true are actually unattainable because of the recursions involved.

Put simply, "the modelling of intention is transformed into a probabilistic deeming process rather than an infinite recursion" (McEnery 1995, 25). As such, we can begin to utilise a probabilistic measure of likelihood to gauge the most likely (potential) meaning of a given utterance.

Before we move on to a discussion of contextual schemes, we should point out that corpus-based work which also has a strong computational component has been undertaken with some success, especially in the area of textual coherence. For example, Bean/Riloff (1999) have devised an algorithm for automatically identifying definite noun phrases that are non-anaphoric, using 1600 MUC-4 terrorism news articles as the training corpus. Vieira/Poesio (2000) also draw on a newspaper corpus, but in this case for the purpose of capturing *direct* anaphor (by which they mean those occasions in which both co-specification and identity of the head noun is given). Müller/Strube (2001) build on the work of Vieira/Poesio (2000), but their definition of anaphor is more inclusive (i. e., necessitates co-specification only). Their annotation tool (named MMAX) captures anaphoric and building relations as exhibited in the Heidelberg Text Corpus, a small corpus of written texts describing the city of Heidelberg.

4.3. Contextual schemes

4.3.1. Context as a static construct: The example of the BNC headers

One sort of pragmatic annotation that has attracted interest in recent times involves how contextual information might be encoded in corpora. In fact, most language data must be analysed away from its original source, and linguists of all types must re-create a sense of context so that reasoned interpretations of data become possible. Of course, the issue for corpus annotation is what aspects of the context must be selected for annotation, and the form that that annotation should take. There is, as yet, no universally-adopted scheme for contextual annotation (or, indeed, most types of annotation: but see *Text Encoding Initiative*, TEI). However, the *Expert Advisory Group for Language Engineering Systems* (EAGLES) has surveyed dialogue annotation practices, with the aim of producing a set of guidelines (see http://www.ling.lancs.ac.uk/eagles/ and also Gibbon/Moore/Winski 1998). One of the things highlighted by EAGLES is the issue of where contextual information (e. g., speaker characteristics, channel characteristics, activity types) should be placed. One option is to place such information in the headers of individual files, as in the *British National Corpus* (or BNC), which stores contextual information about the text in a header at the start of each file. These headers, in turn, are structured according to the guidelines produced by the TEI. According to EAGLES, researchers interested in spoken data should provide additional contextual information in external files, linked to the original dataset via pointers (cf Gibbon/Moore/Winski 1998, 732 ff.).

Compared with the rich diversity of potential contextual inputs, as described in the field of pragmatics (see 'context' under section 2), corpora like the BNC have taken a fairly minimalist approach to capturing context. As we have already argued, applying an empirical methodology whereby one can quantify context in some way is a major challenge for a corpus-based approach. This is especially so when one's concern is not with the relatively static characteristics of speakers, but with 'face-to-face' interactions between speakers and hearers. Work in the EAGLES tradition focuses almost exclusively on dyadic interactions (the addressee is normally the other speaker), rather than multi-party talk. One of the main interests of EAGLES is the automated analysis of dialogue. Automatically identifying the addressee in multi-party talk is well beyond the capabilities of current tagging programmes. Even less work has addressed the relevant contextual properties of spoken interaction on a turn-by-turn basis. Putting contextual information in file headers may be reasonable for the general research purposes of corpora such as the BNC, but this practice is inadequate for full pragmatic research.

4.3.2. Context as a dynamic construct: An example of a sociopragmatic annotation scheme

A good example of a sociopragmatic annotation scheme is that developed by Archer/Culpeper (2003), and implemented in the *Sociopragmatic Corpus*. This scheme seeks to identify important contextual factors relating to both speaker *and* addressee at the level of the utterance (as opposed to the text; see Hymes 1972; Levinson 1983, 22), and is designed to interface with three fields – namely, pragmatics, corpus linguistics and (historical) sociolinguistics. These disciplines have their own research goals and methodological preferences. Consequently, when they are combined, they present us with a particular set of difficulties (see Archer/Culpeper 2003, 38–42), and at the heart of these difficulties lies the issue of context. Nevertheless, this scheme demonstrates that it is possible to bridge the gap between text and contexts, and (i) accommodate the investigation of language set in various context(s), for example, speaker/hearer relationships, social roles, and sociological characteristics such as gender, and (ii) treat context(s) as dynamic.

Following TEI guidelines, Archer/Culpeper (2003) transcribe individual utterances using the <u> element, so that <u> signals the beginning of the segment to which the annotation pertains and </u> the end. In the BNC and similar corpora, this <u> element tends to contain a limited amount of information, such as the person id (see the *TEI Guidelines*, http://www.uic.edu/orgs/tei/p3/doc/p3.html). Here is an example:

<u id=1 who=P001>**How are you?**</u>

The approach taken by Archer/Culpeper (2003) is slightly different, since they opt for text-internal coding at the utterance level. This means that participant information is given in the <u> element rather than in the header. The following example is from the Trial of Charles I:

Lord President <u speaker="s" spid="s3tcharl001" spsex="m" sprole1="j" spstatus="1" spage="9" addressee="s" adid="s3tcharl002" adrole1="d" adstatus="O" adage="9">**If this be all you will say,**</u>
<u speaker="s" spid="s3tcharl001" spsex="m" sprole1="j" spstatus="1" spage="9" addressee="m" adid="x" adrole1="n" adstatus="x" adage="x"> **then, Gentlemen, you that brought the Prisoner hither, take charge of him back again.**</u>

The annotation scheme is designed to identify the *specific combination* of sociopragmatic variables affecting each segment. In particular, this means describing who is talking to whom at a given point in time, and in what capacity (cf. the annotation scheme in the BNC, which only describes the static properties of speakers across the whole interaction). The first six tags identify the speaker, and these are followed by corresponding tags to identify the addressee (underlined, to help differentiate them for the reader). The first tag (speaker="s") tells us that the speaker is single, (an individual, and not a group of speakers). The spid="s3tcharl001" tag indicates that the speaker is the Lord President of the courtroom. The spsex="m" tag identifies this speaker as male, and sprole1="j" tells us that he is a judge. He is also of high status (spstatus="1") and over the age of 45 (adage="9"). The addressee tags tell us that the judge is addressing an individual (addressee="s"), who is identified as King Charles I (adid="s3tcharl002"). The adrole1="d" tag tells us that Charles is acting as defendant; adstatus="0" tells us that he is royal; and, again, adage="9" tells us that he is over the age of 45. (See Archer/ Culpeper, 2003, for a complete breakdown of the categories.) Note that if the same speaker addresses a different person, the values for the addressee then change. This may, indeed, occur within the same turn, as shown above, where the second <u> tag marks the point at which the judge addresses other hearers and the utterance continues.

Archer/Culpeper (2003) define segments for tagging in a way that allows them to study multi-party interaction. Multiple roles are a frequently apparent phenomenon, and Archer/Culpeper's (2003) scheme is such that more than one role field may be identified in any given interaction. Clearly, the kinds of information we include here cannot usefully be encoded in a header file. Sceptics may point out that such a scheme is both time-consuming to apply, and, for reason of its complexity, open to error. Our experience of applying it to a corpus of 250,000 words suggests that it is time-consuming but viable for implementation in smaller, more focussed corpora. Moreover, software tools can be developed to speed up the implementation process of a non-automatic annotation scheme quite significantly. For example, once a participant's identity is clarified, the computer can enter static values automatically, leaving the analyst to focus on the beginnings and endings of utterances, as well as dynamic values.

4.4. Mixed schemes: An example

Archer (2005) is an example of a scheme that combines various strands of pragmatic meaning, including the formal, illocutionary, interactional and contextual. Based on an analysis of courtroom interaction from the later Early Modern English period (1640–1760), Archer's work extends the *Sociopragmatic Annotation Scheme* to include an 'interactional intent' field, a 'force' field, and, where applicable, a '(grammatical) form' field. As the 'form' field is relatively self-explanatory, in that it consists of the range of question-types (e. g., *yes-no*, disjunctive, *wh-*, etc.) used in the historical courtroom, we will comment, instead, on the more pragmatically-oriented phenomena, the interactional intent and force fields. The interactional intent field ["stfunc"] relates to the position an utterance occupies in the discourse. In other words, it assesses the interactional/structural purpose of an utterance (that is, what the speaker intends to achieve in interactional/ structural terms at a particular point in the discourse and how he/she does it, see Stenström 1984), so that we have a better understanding of the ways in which (trial) talk is organised. Possible values include:

'initiation'	initiating a new exchange by means of an eliciting device. Prototypical examples include question, request, requirement.

'response'	providing information that has been directly elicited by another participant, usually by responding verbally. Prototypical examples include answer, acceptance, refusal, denial.
'response-initiation'	responding to a direct elicitation of another participant by using and/or following it with an eliciting device. Prototypical examples include an answer immediately followed by a request.
'report'	stating information which has not been directly elicited by another participant. Prototypical examples include statement, explanation.
'follow up'	providing follow-up/feedback to a preceding utterance in some way. Prototypical examples include comment, evaluation.
'follow up-initiation'	providing follow-up/feedback to a preceding utterance by using and/or following it with an eliciting device. Prototypical examples include a comment immediately followed by a question.

The extract below, taken from the Trial of Giles (1680), provides an illustration of the respective values. The recorder was questioning a witness, Elizabeth Crook. When she contradicted evidence given by an earlier witness, William Richmond, he intervened. Shortly after, other participants also became involved. They included the King's Counsel:

Record.	You made the Bed, did not you? [initiation]
Crook,	I did. [response]
Recorder,	Upon your Oath, what time of Night was it? [follow up-initiation]
Crook	I think it was nearer Eleven than Ten. [response]
	[text omitted]
Kings Coun.	What time of Night was it that he was making love to you? [initiation]
Crook,	I think about Ten a Clock. [response]
Kings Coun.	Time passed merrily away with you then. [follow up]
Rich.	It was Twelve a Clock. [report]

Archer's (2005) interactive/structural elements clearly show some resemblance to Sinclair/Coulthard (1975). Carletta et al. (1997b) also show an IRF influence, though their approach is more computational (see section 4.1.2.).

Stenström (1984) and Carletta et al. (1997b) account for many more values at their 'move' level than Archer (2005) does at her 'interactional intent' level (cf. Stenström's (1984, 83–6) 'framing', 'focusing', 'checking' and 'supporting' moves and Carletta et al.'s (1997b) 'instruct', 'explain', 'check', 'align', 'query' and 'acknowledge' moves, etc.) There is a necessary balance in any categorisation between usefulness and ease or consistency of coding. The primary purpose of the 'interactional intent' field is to distinguish between utterances that elicit, respond to, comment on, and terminate an exchange. Archer (2005) argues that further classifications would make the field cumbersome and, thus, potentially more problematic to implement, and that the kind of distinctions that Carletta et al. (1997b) and Stenström (1984) make at this level can be adequately accounted for at a different level (i. e., the force field). For example, we can distinguish the different functions that a question is serving, by identifying that an eliciting move has the force of a question (as opposed to a command or request, for example), and then by clarifying its particular function (e. g., whether it is confirmation-seeking as opposed to information-seeking).

As far as the force field [force=“”] is concerned, Archer (2005), inspired by Searle (1969, 1975) and Wierzbicka (1987), assigns utterances to one (or more) of seven macro categories, e. g., ‘counsel’ (= “w”), ‘question’ (= “q”), ‘request’ (= “r”), ‘require’ (= “c”), ‘sentence’ (= “v”), ‘express’ (= “e”) and ‘inform’ (= “h”). These are viewed as macro categories, and the values they subsume, as “reasonably accurate approximations of the prototypical instances of verbal behaviour describable by means of the English verbs used as labels” (Verschueren 1999, 131−2). By way of illustration, the definitions of four macro-categories are as follows:

Counsel S wants to convey something to A which will help prevent/result in Y [= an event not in A’s best interest], e. g., “My advise to you is, that you would put your self upon your Tryal [sic] … [text omitted] … If you will deal ingenuously with the Court, I think that is best.”

Question S wants A to supply a missing variable by saying/confirming/clarifying something about X [= an action/event/behaviour/person], e. g., “Shall I withdraw?”

Request S wants Z [= an action/event] to happen and hopes to do it/get A to do (or get others to do) it, e. g., “I do humbly move, that I may have time allowed me by this court to send for my Witnesses.”

Require S wants (and expects) A to do something, even though A may be reluctant, or to do something him/herself, in spite of A’s (probable) reluctance, e. g., “My Lord, I demand this, to hear the Commission read”

As the force of some utterances can/may remain indeterminate (due to contextual factors such as status, power and discourse sequencing, for example), Archer’s design also allows for the inclusion of multiple and, indeed, indeterminate forces by using the “m” and “p” values respectively (cf Stiles 1992; see also section 4.1.1.).

5. Segmentation

5.1. Purpose

Segmentation is an essential first stage in preparing data for corpus analysis. Choices of terminology vary (for instance, Stiles (1992) prefers ‘unitizing’), but the practice is the same: it involves dividing a stretch of continuous discourse into its meaningful constituent parts (‘segments’ – a term also used in Phonetics, where it refers to the smallest distinct phonetic unit, typically a vowel or consonant sound) so that interpretative tags relating to those parts may then be applied. Some purists dislike splitting up texts in this way, fearing aesthetic ‘damage’, especially changes to or loss of meaning. However, dividing the whole is very often the best way of making sense of it, and the debate amongst corpus linguists tends to surround not *whether* this should be done, but how it should best be achieved: in other words, on what basis should consistent and accurate divisions be made.

5.2. Some important issues

When we segment something we need to consider our overall aim. This point cannot be overlooked, since the sort of unit we choose will directly determine the results we get. There are many different analytical units, including the word (which computational linguists tend to call *token*), verb, phrase, clause, sentence, turn, utterance, tone group or prosodic unit, idea unit or information unit, discourse unit, etc. The choice of the particular unit will depend on the annotator's research goals. The level of definition required for any particular unit will relate to the abstractness of that unit. Consider the difference between the form of a written question and its illocutionary function; whilst the former can be derived from syntactic/semantic features, the latter is derivable from a mixture of formal and contextual features.

The difficulty of operationalising a particular definition of a unit is related to its tangibility. For instance, although there are debates about what exactly counts as a written English *word* (including whether pause-fillers like 'er' and 'erm' are really words, and whether compounds should be classed as two words or one), words are undoubtedly easier to define because they tend to have distinct orthographic boundaries. By contrast, a *tone group* will require technical definition and analysis, probably with access to original (audio) source material in any given case.

Segmentation requires us not only to state what unit we will be analysing, but also to define it in a way that will enable us to measure one unit against another, and, by so doing, ensure a level of consistency. The utterance is regarded as a key unit of analysis in pragmatics, but it evades easy definition. We should not assume that an utterance is merely a sentence. Indeed, Levinson (1983, 18) argues that the difference between them is 'fundamental'. In the case of the utterance, we might wish to know: how long a typical utterance is; how it relates to other established analytical units (like the conversational turn); whether it must contain a verb (a traditional criterion); whether it is an exact equivalent of any other unit and, if so, why we prefer the term *utterance* to that equivalent; and so on. Stiles (1992, 109) attempts to capture these features by providing the following definition:

> In the VRM taxonomy, an utterance is defined as a simple sentence; an independent clause; a nonrestrictive dependent clause; an element of a compound predicate; or a term of acknowledgement, evaluation, or address.

Notice that his definition attempts to capture a range of formal and functional aspects. It is important that definitions such as this are sufficiently detailed to enable other researchers to replicate the original researcher's work.

The unit of analysis we choose not only determines what a segment looks like (its typical characteristics, length, etc.), but also whether the segmentation must be done by hand, or can be (semi-)automated. In the field of Pragmatics, fully automated segmentation and tagging has not yet been achieved. By contrast, the manual segmentation of speech act phenomena is well-established, notably through the *Cross-Cultural Speech Act Realisation Project*, CCSARP (see Blum-Kulka/House/Kasper 1989). This project devised a way of coding speech acts in a large body of elicited data. The data was elicited by 'discourse completion tasks', a type of questionnaire that requires the informant to produce a speech act appropriate to a particular context. The vast majority of studies applying this methodology have focussed on requests or apologies. The key issue relating to segmentation using the CCSARP framework is making the distinction between 'head act' (HA) and 'support move' (SM). The head act is regarded as the core of the speech act, and usually contains a verb and its grammatically related elements, for example, "Pass me the salt", "I'd like the salt" or "Can you pass me the salt?" Note that the head act can vary, particularly in terms of directness, and that this can be categorised, for example, 'performative', 'want statement' or 'preparatory (ability)'. Support moves are independent elements which pragmatically support the head act in some way (e. g., mitigate the face threat of the act). They include 'alerters' ("excuse me"), 'grounders' ("I really need it"), 'minimizers' ("just a little"), 'disarmers' ("I know you are really busy but ...") and 'politeness markers' ("please"). Although the CCSARP framework has not, as far as we are aware, been applied to corpus data, it is not difficult to envisage its application. The scheme could lead to segmentation and annotation in a corpus as in the following example: [excuse me_SM-ALERTER] [this food tastes bland_SM-GROUNDER] [pass me the salt_HA-PERFORMATIVE] [please_SM-POLITENESS].

5.3. Implementation

Pragmatic interpretations, leading to the implementation of a functional tag (e. g., a speech act), require a complex synthesis/understanding of contextual information that is currently beyond the means of a computer. In other fields, as in part of speech (grammatical) analysis, segmentation and tagging have been computerised for some time (see articles 24 and 26 for more details). A software programme is able to identify words as segments, then assign appropriate grammatical tags from a tagset. In the case of the BNC, this has been achieved using a software programme called CLAWS (Constituent Likelihood Automatic Word-tagging System, see http://www.comp.lancs.ac.uk/computing/research/ucrel/claws/). Here, CLAWS assigns tags from an established tagset (the current version is known as C7), which contains nearly 140 tag categories, like "JJ" for "general adjective", and "NN1" for "singular common noun", etc., and allows for the usual distinctions of grammatical function. There are reports of more than 95% accuracy with this software (rising to 98% using supplementary software), so that computational tagging is typically followed by low-level manual correction. By contrast, Semino/Short (2004) designed a corpus to examine how speech, writing and thought were presented in spoken and written texts, in which all tags were implemented manually. Like speech acts, speech presentation is characterised by both formal *and* functional properties. Consequently, the complexity of software that would allow the automatic segmentation and tagging of speech presentation is such that time and cost constraints presently make it an impossible undertaking – even with direct speech, one of the most formally identifiable modes of speech presentation. Archer/Culpeper (2003; see section 4.3.2.) appear to choose the conversational turn as the unit of analysis in their sociopragmatic tagging of historical texts. However, they digress from this 'turn = segment' procedure when the floor-holder addresses another hearer within the same turn, since the meaning of the interaction could be affected by a contextual change of this type. On the whole, therefore, this tagging has a certain 'neatness', because the 'starts' and 'ends' are normally demarcated by the change of speaker. Here, again, the tagging process is manual, since the segmentation and tagging are dependent on broader discoursal characteristics of the data, rather than specific, and often isolated, phenomena.

By definition, context is an inferred relationship between the linguistic and extra-linguistic. It is not surprising to find, therefore, that tags containing social information have to be implemented manually at present. Archer/Culpeper (2003) suggest that the following issues are also important when implementing sociopragmatic tagging:

> *Choice of categories.* Categories of all types, but particularly social categories, are controversial – there are many different ways in which the social world can be classified.
>
> *Delicacy of categorisation scheme.* The more delicate a categorisation scheme the more accurate the description. On the other hand, the more delicate the scheme, the less likely there will be enough evidence to apply a particular category, and, consequently, the less likely there will be enough evidence to find statistically meaningful results for a particular category.
>
> *Implementation of categories.* There are various types of information that can justify the implementation of a category, including language (e. g., vocatives), secondary sources (e. g., sociological accounts) and inferences (e. g., networks of interaction).

Of course, all of these issues can apply to any type of categorisation scheme, and its implementation.

Another important, but often-overlooked issue, is that the segmentation of speech is quite different from the segmentation of writing (see also article 11). There are considerable structural differences between natural speech (as opposed to, say, speech that is read from a book) and writing. Natural speech contains hesitations (vocalised (filled) and non-vocalised (unfilled) pauses), repetitions, grammatically incomplete phrases, reformulations, anacoluthons, and false starts – treated collectively by some as disfluencies or performance errors – which written language does not (see, for example, Biber et al. 1999, 1052–66). The type and frequency of natural speech features may vary according to the speakers involved, the type of talk (for instance, dialogue compared with monologue), and social setting. These features can make the process of establishing segment boundaries complicated – so complicated that they are sometimes placed in a throw-away category, where the difficulty of making them 'fit' into an otherwise neat scheme (the tagging taxonomy) need not be addressed. This apparent solution is unsatisfactory, since, from a pragmatic point of view, they are meaningful phenomena that can (and probably should) have a direct bearing on our interpretations. For example, a filled pause such as 'erm' could function as a 'softening' preface to a refusal. Consequently, decisions on how to handle these features need to be made at the outset, addressing issues such as what should be excluded, if anything, and why, and how these features can be incorporated in our analysis.

From a practical point of view, and, given the time that pragmatic annotation takes, it is important that we only segment or tag that feature(s) which is relevant to our research goals. For instance, if one were only interested in the clauses that function as questions in a discourse, it would be quite pointless to tag all of the clauses: the questions are likely to make up a smaller proportion of the total, and we would be tagging material we had no intention of using. Thus, in Lampert/Ervin-Tripp's (1993, 170–1) study "to characterize the organization of verbal and gestural moves intended to control the behaviour of others", an initial decision was made to tag only speech acts that had this intent. It is a matter of time and efficiency – and often money – that we know what it is we seek when we approach a corpus, and that only relevant work is undertaken.

Hitherto, we have discussed deductive approaches to segmentation, where the nature of the segment is determined prior to the analysis, and then the corpus is segmented accordingly. Thus, a study of nouns might utilise part-of-speech tagging which requires segmentation at the level of the word, or a study of requests might utilise speech act tagging which requires segmentation at the level of speaker/writer context (speech acts encapsulate speaker intentions). An entirely different approach to segmentation would be an inductive approach, where the nature of the segment is determined by the nature of the data. An obvious data-driven segment is the conversational 'turn'. Turn boundaries are relatively easy to identify, being signalled by grammatical, prosodic and pragmatic features, as well as non-verbal features. Most spoken corpora are segmented according to turns at the point when the spoken data is transcribed for the corpus. However, when our data come from speech situations that are less 'interactive' – a lecture or sermon, for example – the notion of a turn is not very useful, as often there are only a few long turns. Here, a notion such as 'topic' – categorising in some way the content of the discourse – is of much more interest, as are related notions such as 'topic boundary', 'topic-shift' and 'speaking topically'. But definitions of 'topic' are notoriously vague (e. g., it is "what is being talked about"). Brown/Yule (1983, 68) suggest that, "formal attempts to identify topics are doomed to failure". However, recently a group of corpus linguists, notably Eniko Csomay, have been developing an inductive, data-driven approach to identifying discourse segments, specifically in academic discourse (see, for example, Biber et al. 2004; Csomay 2005; Csomay in press). They modified Hearst's (e. g., 1997) discourse segmentation model, called TextTiler, and used it to identify Vocabulary-Based Discourse Units (VBDUs). The modified version of TextTiler works within a 100-words span, comparing the first 50 words of a text with the second and calculating a similarity value (i. e., the extent to which the first 50 words are identical to the second). It then 'slides' one word forward and compares words 2–51 with words 52–101, calculating another similarity value. It continues moving forward one word at a time and each time calculates a similarity value, until the end of the text is reached. A plot of similarity values allows a visual display of vocabulary patterns. Peaks indicate high similarity between two 50-words segments, and valleys low similarity – and thus possible candidates for marking boundaries between VBDUs. Csomay (2005a, 248) concludes:

> In this analysis, shifts in discourse are identified automatically based on the reliable measures of existing vocabulary patterns found in texts. The tracing of vocabulary novelty results in segmenting texts into topically coherent sub-units in full texts [...].

After identifying the units relying on lexical patterns, the linguistic characterizations and corresponding communicative purposes can be explored further.

Clearly, such data-driven segmentation offers exciting potential for the future.

6. The future – towards a 'gold' standard?

Here, we have focussed on recent pragmatic and discoursal annotation work, which seeks to capture information at or above the level of the conversational act (e. g., Stiles 1992; Carletta et al. 1997b; Core/Allen 1997; Stolcke et al. 2000; Archer/Culpeper 2003; Archer 2005). Our main aim has been to highlight the kind of advances that have been made over the past decade in the development and application of such annotation schemes to *human-human* interaction, as well as the types of difficulties that have been encountered. A striking limitation of the current state of the art is the overwhelming dominance of corpus-based approaches to the pragmatics of *English*. There is no principled reason why the schemes and procedures we have discussed in this article could not be applied to other languages. Some adaptation will be necessary, of course, given that different languages have different formal resources for achieving pragmatic meanings; and, vice versa, different pragmatic functions may be encoded (pragmaticalised) in different forms. These differences are in themselves of interest: both devising and exploiting pragmatic annotation schemes for different languages would deepen our understanding of language typologies.

As we have shown, pragmatics research focuses on language and its contexts (e. g., the speaker's intentions, the hearer's understandings, the social contexts, the physical contexts, etc.). Corpus-based approaches to pragmatics tend to involve simple searches on linguistic items and are thus limited to items which have acquired conventional pragmatic meaning (e. g., particular speech act verbs, discourse markers); that is to say, items where the contextual meaning has become part of the conventional word-meaning. Some corpus-based approaches to pragmatics research have engaged in the analysis or annotation of the 'co-text'. However, we would argue that pragmatics is much more than accounting for 'co-text'. Pragmatics is about functional interpretations which are not determined by any particular form alone. Corpus annotation provides a record of those interpretations. Moreover, it is a record that can be accessed by computers to enable systematic, rigorous research into vast collections of data. Whilst this can only serve to strengthen the relationship between corpus linguistics and pragmatics, we believe that annotation should be regarded as an interpretative record only, so as to ensure that we do not over-state the importance of the annotation in relation to the text.

Unlike grammatical annotation, pragmatic annotation cannot be fully automated, though tagging can be computationally-assisted. This has economic implications which affect the nature of the annotation. Researchers tend to devise pragmatic annotation schemes that meet their personal research objectives, unlike grammatical tagging, which is often done to enhance a corpus that is then distributed amongst many researchers pursuing various research agendas. This has the unfortunate consequence that research efforts do not interface with one another. As the EAGLES documentation stated in 1998:

> As yet, there does not seem to exist any complete or systematic typology of dialogues … [However] … there seems to be a definite need for such a classification in order to establish a valid list of criteria that are to be used for annotation: one that is based on actual experience and not on pure introspection. Such a list of criteria can then serve as a basic reference model that would need to be expanded only for special purposes that did not fit any of the existing criteria.

Given that dialogue corpora can be used for many different purposes, and, thus, are open to various types of analyses, segmentation practices, etc., devising a 'basic reference model', acting as a kind of'gold standard', would be a significant challenge. A relatively rigid set of criteria could be designed to capture formatting issues, but criteria that capture 'interpretative' categories or concepts would have to be rather more flexible. For the latter, a set of guidelines and a set of models may be preferable to a set of criteria for a specific model. These guidelines could include aspects we have discussed here, namely, the need to devise an annotation scheme in relation to one's research goals, the need to be systematic enough to ensure replicability (and, by so doing, ensure its usefulness to others), the need to balance delicacy of categorisation with the ability to fill categories with a statistically meaningful quantity of members, and so on. As for a set of models, there clearly needs to be better dissemination of information about models people have devised, so that researchers can build on each others' work rather than, as it were, reinventing the wheel. In writing this article, we hope to have made a small contribution to this endeavour.

7. Literature

Aijmer, K. (1996), *Conversational Routines in English*. Longman: London.

Andersen, G. (2001), *Pragmatic Markers and Sociolinguistic Variation: A Relevance-theoretic Approach to the Language of Adolescents*. (Pragmatics and Beyond Series 84.) Amsterdam/Philadelphia: John Benjamins.

Archer, D. (2002), "Can innocent people be guilty?" A Sociopragmatic Analysis of Examination Transcripts from the Salem Witchcraft Trials. In: *Journal of Historical Pragmatics* 3(1), 1–30.

Archer, D. (2005), *Questions and Answers in the English Courtroom (1640–1760): A Sociopragmatic Analysis*. (Pragmatics and Beyond Series 135.) Amsterdam: John Benjamins.

Archer, D./Culpeper, J. (2003), Sociopragmatic Annotation: New Directions and Possibilities in Historical Corpus Linguistics. In: Wilson, A./Rayson, P./McEnery, A. M. (eds.), *Corpus Linguistics by the Lune: A Festschrift for Geoffrey Leech*. Frankfurt/Main: Peter Lang, 37–58.

Austin, J. (1962), *How to do Things with Words*. Oxford: Oxford University Press.

Bach, K./Harnish, R. M. (1979), *Linguistic Communication and Speech Acts*. Cambridge, MA: M.I.T. Press.

Baecker, R. M./Buxton, W. A. S. (eds.) (1987), *Readings in Human-computer Interaction: A Multidisciplinary Approach*. Los Altos, CA: Morgan-Kaufmann Publishers.

Baldridge, J./Lascarides, A. (2005), Annotating Discourse Structures for Robust Semantic Interpretation. In: *Proceedings of the 6th International Workshop on Computational Semantics. IWCS-6*. Tilburg, The Netherlands. Available at: http://homepages.inf.ed.ac.uk/jbaldrid/baldridge-lascarides-iwcs.pdf.

Ballmer, T. T./Brennenstuhl, W. (1981), *Speech Act Classification: A Study of the Lexical Analysis of English Speech Activity Verbs*. Berlin/New York: Springer-Verlag.

Bean, D./Riloff, E. (1999), Corpus-based Identification of Non-anaphoric Noun Phrases. In: *Proceedings of the 37th Annual Meeting of the Association for Computational Linguistics*. University of Maryland, College Park, Maryland, 373–380.
Biber, D./Johansson, S./Leech, G./Conrad, S./Finegan, E. (1999), *Longman Grammar of Spoken and Written English*. Harlow, England: Pearson.
Biber, D./Csomay, E./Jones, J. K./Keck, C. (2004), A Corpus Linguistic Investigation of Vocabulary-based Discourse Units in University Registers. In: Connor, U./Upton, T. (eds.), *Applied Corpus Linguistics: A Multidimensional Perspective*. Amsterdam: Rodopi, 53–72.
Blum-Kulka, S./House, J./Kasper, G. (1989), *Cross-cultural Pragmatics: Requests and Apologies*. Norwood, NJ: Ablex Publishing Corporation.
Brown, G./Yule, G. (1983), *Discourse Analysis*. Cambridge: Cambridge University Press.
Brown, P./Levinson, S. (1987), *Politeness: Some Universals in Language Usage*. Cambridge: Cambridge University Press.
Bunt, H. (1994), Context and Dialogue Control. In: *Think* 3, 19–31.
Bunt, H./Black, W. (2000), The ABC of Computational Pragmatics. In: Bunt, H./Black, W. (eds.), *Computational Pragmatics: Abduction, Belief and Context*. Amsterdam: John Benjamins, 1–46.
Carletta, J./Dahlbäck, N./Reithinger, N./Walker, M. A. (1997a), *Standards for Dialogue Coding in Natural Language Processing*. Technical Report no. 167, Dagstuhl Seminars. Report from Dagstuhl seminar number 9706.
Carletta, J./Isard, A./Isard, S./Kowtko, J. C./Doherty-Sneddon, G./Anderson, A. H. (1997b), The Reliability of a Dialogue Structure Coding Scheme. In: *Computational Linguistics* 23, 13–32.
Carlson, L./Marcu, D./Okurowski, M. E. (2003), Building a Discourse-tagged Corpus in the Framework of Rhetorical Structure Theory. In: van Kuppevelt, J./Smith, R. W. (eds.), *Current and New Directions in Discourse and Dialogue*. Berlin: Springer, 85–112.
Core, M./Allen, J. (1997), Coding Dialogs with the DAMSL Annotation Scheme. In: *Working Notes of the AAAI Fall Symposium on Communicative Action in Humans and Machines*, November, Cambridge, MA, 28–35.
Csomay, E. (2005a), Linguistic Variation in the Lexical Episodes of University Classroom Talk. In: Tyler, A./Takadam, M./Kim, Y./Marinova, D. (eds.), *Language in Use. Cognitive and Discourse Perspectives on Language and Language Learning*. Georgetown University Round Table on Languages and Linguistics (GURT 2003). Georgetown: Georgetown University Press, 302–324.
Csomay, E. (2005b), Linguistic Variation within University Classroom Talk: A Corpus-based Perspective. In: *Linguistics and Education* 15(3), 243–274.
Dix, A./Finlay, J./Abowd, G./Beale, R. (1998), *Human-computer Interaction*. Hillsdale, NJ: Prentice Hall.
Fischer, K. (1996), Distributed Representation Formalisms for Discourse Particles. In: Gibbon, D. (ed.), *Natural Language Processing and Speech Technology*. Berlin: Mouton de Gruyter, 212–224.
Fischer, K./Brandt-Pook, H. (1998), Automatic Disambiguation of Discourse Particles. In: *Proceedings of the Workshop on Discourse Relations and Discourse Markers*, COLING-ACL, Montreal, Canada, 107–113.
Gibbon, D./Moore, R./Winski, R. (1998), *Handbook of Standards and Resources for Spoken Language Systems*. Berlin: Mouton de Gruyter.
Goodwin, C. (1996), Transparent Vision. In: Ochs, E./Schegloff, E. A./Thompson, S. A. (eds.), *Interaction and Grammar*. Cambridge: Cambridge University Press, 370–404.
Grice, H. P. (1971), Meaning. In: Steinberg, D./Jakobvits, L. (eds.), *Semantics: An Interdisciplinary Reader in Philosophy, Linguistics and Psychology*. Cambridge: Cambridge University Press, 53–59.
Grice, H. P. (1975), Logic and Conversation. In: Cole, P./Morgan, J. L. (eds.), *Syntax and Semantics 3: Speech Acts*. New York: Academic Press, 41–58.
Grice, H. P. (1982), Meaning Revisited. In: Smith, N. (ed.), *Mutual Knowledge*. London: Academic Press, 223–245.
Grice, H. P. (1989), *Studies in the Way of Words*. Cambridge, MA: Harvard University Press.

Hahn, U./Strube, M./Markert, K. (1996), Bridging Textual Ellipses. In: *Proceedings of the 16th Conference on Computational Linguistics, COLING-2006*. Copenhagen, 496–501.

Hearst, M. A. (1997), TextTiling: Segmenting Text into Multi-paragraph Subtopic Passages. In: *Computational Linguistics* 23(1), 33–64.

Hobbs, J. R. (2004), Abduction in Natural Language Understanding. In: Horn/Ward 2004, 724–741.

Horn, L. R./Ward, G. (eds.) (2004), *Handbook of Pragmatics*. (Blackwell Handbooks in Linguistics.) Malden, MA: Blackwell Publishing.

Houghton, G. (1986), The Production of Language in Dialogue: A Computational Model. Unpublished PhD thesis. University of Sussex.

Hymes, D. (1972), Towards Ethnographies of Communication: The Analysis of Communicative Events. In: Giglioli, P. P. (ed.), *Language and Social Context*. Penguin: London, 21–44.

Jurafsky, D. (2004), Pragmatics and Computational Linguistics. In: Horn/Ward 2004, 578–604.

Jurafsky, D./Martin, J. H. (2000), *Speech and Language Processing: An Introduction to Natural Language Processing, Computational Linguistics and Speech Recognition*. Upper Saddle River, NJ: Prentice Hall.

Kameyama, M. (1998), Intra-sentential Centering: A Case Study. In: Walker, M. A./Joshi, A. K./ Prince, E. F. (eds.), *Centering Theory in Discourse*. Oxford: Clarendon Press, 89–112.

Kehler, A. (2000), Discourse. In: Jurafsky, D./Martin, J. H. (eds.), *Speech and Language Processing: An Introduction to Natural Language Processing, Computational Linguistics, and Speech Recognition*. Upper Saddle River, NJ: Prentice Hall, 669–718.

Kehler, A. (2004), Discourse Coherence. In: Horn/Ward 2004, 241–265.

Lampert, M. D./Ervin-Tripp, S. M. (1993), Structured Coding for the Study of Language and Social Interaction. In: Edwards, J. A./Lampert, M. D. (eds.), *Talking Data: Transcription and Coding in Discourse Research*. Hillsdale, NJ, Hove and London: Lawrence Erlbaum Associates, 169–206.

Leech, G. (1983), *Principles of Pragmatics*. Longman: London.

Leech, G. (1997), Introducing Corpus Annotation. In: Garside, R./Leech, G./McEnery, T. (eds.), *Corpus Annotation*. London/New York: Longman, 1–18.

Leech, G. (2000), Grammars of Spoken English: New Outcomes of Corpus-oriented Research. In: *Language Learning* 50(4), 675–724.

Leech, G./Weisser, M./Wilson, A./Grice, M. (1998), *LE-EAGLES-WP4–4. Integrated Resources Working Group. Survey and Guidelines for the Representation and Annotation of Dialogue*. Available at: http://bowland-files.lancs.ac.uk/eagles/delivera/wp4final.htm.

Leech, G./Weisser, M. (2003), Generic Speech Act Annotation for Task-oriented Dialogues. In: Archer, D./Rayson, P./Wilson, A./McEnery, T. (eds.), *Proceedings of the Corpus Linguistics 2003 Conference*. (University Centre for Computer Corpus Research on Language Technical Papers 16(1).) Lancaster, UK, 441–446.

Levinson, S. C. (1983), *Pragmatics*. Cambridge: Cambridge University Press.

Levinson, S. C. (1992), Activity Types and Language. In: Drew, P./Heritage, J. (eds.), *Talk at Work*. Cambridge: Cambridge University Press, 66–100.

Marcu, D. (1999), A Decision-based Approach to Rhetorical Parsing. In: *Proceedings of the 37th Annual Meeting of the Association for Computational Linguistcs* (ACL99). College Park, Maryland, 365–372.

McEnery, T. (1995), Computational Pragmatics: Probability, Deeming and Uncertain References. Unpublished PhD Thesis, Lancaster University.

McEnery, T. (2003), Corpus Linguistics. In: Mitkov, R. (ed.), *The Oxford Handbook of Computational Linguistics*. Oxford: Oxford University Press, 448–463.

McEnery, T./Wilson, A. (1996), *Corpus Linguistics*. Edinburgh: Edinburgh University Press.

McEnery, T./Wilson, A. (2001), *Corpus Linguistics: An Introduction* (2nd edition). Edinburgh: Edinburgh University Press.

McEnery, T./Xiao, R./Tono, Y. (eds.), 2006. *Corpus-based Language Studies: An Advanced Resource Book*. London/New York: Routledge.

Miltsakaki, E./Prasad, A./Joshi, A./Webber, B. (2004), The Penn Discourse TreeBank. In: *Proceedings of the Language Resources and Evaluation Conference*. Lisbon, Portugal. Available at: http://www. seas. upenn. edu/~pdtb/papers/lrec04. pdf.

Müller, C./Strube, M. (2001), Annotating Anaphoric and Bridging Relations with MMAX. In: *Proceedings of the 2nd SIDdial Workshop on Discourse and Dialogue*. Aalborg, Denmark, 90–95.

Navarro, B./Martínez-Barco, P/Muñoz, R. (2002), Solving Definite Descriptions through Dialogue Structure in Spanish. Workshop on Reference Resolution and Natural Language Processing (RRNLP'2002). In: *Proceedings of the Workshop on Reference Resolution and Natural Language Processing*. Alicante, Spain, 77–86.

Perrault, C. R./Allen, J. (1980), A Plan-based Analysis of Indirect Speech Acts. In: *American Journal of Computational Linguistics* 6, 167–182.

Power, R. (1979), The Organization of Purposeful Dialogs. In: *Linguistics* 17, 105–152.

Preece, J./Rogers, Y./Sharp, H./Benyon, D./Holland, S./Carey, T. (1994), *Human-computer Interaction*. Wokingham, UK: Addison Wesley.

Sacks, H./Schegloff, E./Jefferson, G. (1974), A Simplest Systematics for the Organisation of Turn-taking in Conversation. In: *Language* 50(4), 696–735.

Sampson, G. (1995), *English for the Computer*. Oxford: Clarendon Press.

Schegloff, E. A. (1968), Sequencing in Conversational Openings. In: *American Anthropologist* 70, 1075–1095.

Schegloff, E. A. (1988), Presequences and Indirection: Applying Speech Act Theory to Ordinary Conversation. In: *Journal of Pragmatics* 12, 55–62.

Schegloff, E. A./Jefferson, G./Sacks, H. (1977), The Preference for Self-correction in the Organization of Repair in Conversation. In: *Language* 53, 361–382.

Schiffer, S. R. (1972), *Meaning*. Oxford: Clarendon Press.

Searle, J. R. (1969), *Speech Acts: An Essay in the Philosophy of Language*. Cambridge: Cambridge University Press.

Searle, J. R. (1975), Indirect Speech Acts. In: Cole, P./Morgan, J. L. (eds.), *Speech Acts: Syntax and Semantics*. Vol. 3. New York: Academic Press, 59–82.

Searle, J. R. (1976), A Classification of Illocutionary Acts. In: *Language in Society* 5, 1–23.

Searle, J. R. (1979), *Expression and Meaning*. Cambridge: Cambridge University Press.

Semino, E./Short, M. (2004), *Corpus Stylistics: Speech, Writing and Thought Presentation in a Corpus of English Narratives*. London: Routledge.

Short, M./Semino, E./Culpeper, J. (2000), Language and Context(s): Jane Gardam's Bilgewater. In: Bex, T./Burke, M./Stockwell, P. (eds.), *Contextualized Stylistics*. (Studies in Literature 29.) Amsterdam/Atlanta: Rodopi, 131–151.

Sinclair, J./Coulthard, M. (1975), *Towards an Analysis of Discourse: The English Used by Teachers and Pupils*. Oxford: Oxford University Press.

Sperber, D./Wilson, D. (1986), *Relevance: Communication and Cognition*. Oxford: Blackwell.

Stede, M. (2004), The Potsdam Commentary Corpus. In: *Proceedings of the ACL Workshop on Discourse Annotation*. Barcelona, Spain, 96–102.

Stede, M./Heintze, S. (2004), Machine-assisted Rhetorical Structure Annotation. In: *Proceedings of the 20th International Conference on Computational Linguistics, COLING-2004*. Geneva, 425–431

Stenström, A.-B. (1984), *Questions and Responses in English Conversation*. Malmö: Liber Förlag.

Stiles, W. B. (1992), *Describing Talk: A Taxonomy of Verbal Response Modes*. Newbury Park, CA: Sage Publications.

Stolcke, A./Ries, K./Coccaro, N./Shriberg, E./Bates, R./Jurafsky, D./Taylor, P./Martin, R./van Ess-Dykema, C./Meteer, M. (2000), Dialogue Act Modeling for Automatic Tagging and Recognition of Conversational Speech. In: *Computational Linguistics* 26(3), 339–371.

Verschueren, J. (1999), *Understanding Pragmatics*. London: Arnold.

Vieira, R./Poesio, M. (2000), An Empirically-based System for Processing Definite Descriptions. In: *Computational Linguistics* 26(4), 539–593.

Webber, B. (2004), D-LTAG: Extending Lexicalized TAG to Discourse. In: *Cognitive Science* 28(1), 751–779.
Weisser, M. (2003), SPAACy – a Semi-automated Tool for Annotating Dialogue Acts. In: *International Journal of Corpus Linguistics* 8(1), 63–74.
Wierzbicka, A. (1987), *English Speech Act Verbs: A Semantic Dictionary*. Sydney: Academic Press.
Wilson, D./Sperber, D. (2004), Relevance Theory. In: Ward, G./Hord, L. (eds.), *Handbook of Pragmatics*. Oxford: Blackwell, 607–632.

Dawn Archer, Jonathan Culpeper and Matthew Davies,
Preston and Lancaster, Lancashire (UK)

30. Preprocessing speech corpora: Transcription and phonological annotation

1. Introduction

While written language corpora have played a pivotal role in linguistic research for a very long time, large speech corpora for linguistic research (see articles 11 and 47) have only emerged during the last decade of the 20th century. Spurred by the need for ever larger speech corpora for the development of speech technology applications in the late eighties, along with the attendant need for some kind of standardization and interoperability, the speech technology community started making attempts to agree on best practice guidelines for the recording, annotation and evaluation of such corpora. Thanks to annual international conferences like the IEEE Conference on Acoustics, Speech and Signal Processing (ICASSP) and the semi-annual meetings of the Acoustical Society of America, where the speech technology and speech science communities congregate, these efforts have had a strong supra-national and intercontinental nature from the very start. In Europe, the stride towards best practice guidelines and standards for speech corpora was especially supported through the Framework Programmes of the European Commission. The major motivation for this support came from the insight that the development of speech technology enabled services in the inherently multilingual Europe could only be cost-effective if highly similar training corpora were available for all languages. One of the most important results of the involvement of the European Commission was the EAGLES (Expert Advisory Group on Language Engineering Standards) project, dedicated to collecting existent and developing new standards and best practice guidelines and to promoting these in the speech technology and speech science communities, both academic and commercial. The mission of EAGLES was much broader than just speech corpora, but it is fair to say that the success and impact of the EAGLES project has nowhere been as large and as obvious as in this domain. Most probably this is due to the fact that the speech group in EAGLES could build upon the outcome of a successful predecessor project SAM (Speech Assessment Methods; see Fourcin/Gibbon 1994). The EAGLES Handbook, edited by Gibbon/Moore/Winski (1997), and especially the chapter by den Os give an excellent account of the state-of-the-art in the annotation of speech databases in the 1990s. Because speech technology was the single most important driving force for developing speech corpora, it comes as no surprise that virtually all corpora in the eighties and nineties were modeled after the seminal example of the American English Macrophone corpus (Godfrey/Holliman/McDaniel 1992) and the first European follow-up, the Dutch Polyphone corpus (den Os et al. 1995). The Macro-phone/Polyphone paradigm reached its apex in the multilingual collection of SpeechDat databases (Höge et al. 1999), and a sizeable number of corpora that do not go under the SpeechDat name, but that in actual fact adopt all guidelines perfected in the SpeechDat context.

The SpeechDat family of speech corpora is designed with a number of – be it generic – telephone-based speech technology applications in mind: the recordings were meant to train speech recognizers for a number of tasks, such as voice dialing, information services, etc. Because of these objectives, in combination with the technical limitations of the time, the SpeechDat corpora consist of short utterances, most of which were read by known speakers from a prompting sheet. Extemporaneous speech was limited to one-digit numbers, names or yes/no responses to simple questions that were not printed on the prompting sheets. Thus, all relevant metadata (information about the speakers, recording conditions, etc.) were readily available, and it was relatively easy to formulate precise guidelines for the annotation of the speech contents and the validation of the resulting annotations. Also, procedures for reporting and correcting bugs in the annotations could be developed and implemented (van den Heuvel/Höge/Choukri 2002).

At the time when the SpeechDat corpora seemed to have become *the* standard, new alleys were opened in speech technology research, directed at more ambitious applications such as spoken document indexing and retrieval. This line of research goes under the name 'Broadcast News', as do the corpora that were created to support this research. In order to distinguish between speech expressly prompted to be included in some speech corpus on the one hand and recordings of speech produced for normal communicative purposes on the other hand, the term 'found speech' was introduced for the latter category. For these novel applications, corpora comprising large amounts of found speech were needed. As a consequence, new annotation procedures had to be developed, addressing issues such as less readily available and more variable metadata, for example information about the identity of the speakers, the communicative and social setting in which the speech was produced (interview or report), the role of the speakers (anchor or guest), the number of speakers in a fragment, the topic(s) addressed in each item, the acoustic background and channel characteristics, etc., etc. Probably the most authoritative and complete account of the creation and use of the Broadcast News corpora is a special issue of the journal *Speech Communication* (Pallett/Lamel 2002). Unlike what was the case in SpeechDat, recordings can last for more than one hour, without unambiguous separators between utterances of items. In 2001 another special issue of *Speech Communication* was devoted to tools and procedures for annotating large speech corpora (Bird/Harrington 2001).

Inspired by the corpora produced in the speech technology community and the opportunities they were promising for linguistic research, from the mid-nineties onward, linguists and phoneticians started taking advantage of the increasing storage capacity and processing power of modern computer systems by building so called spoken language corpora (Oostdijk/Kristoffersen/Sampson 2004). Spoken language corpora have much in common with speech corpora comprising found speech: most of their content consists of found speech, or else speech elicited in communicative settings that give rise to spontaneous dialogues and multilogues (conversations involving more than two speakers). Therefore, it is not surprising that many of the tools developed for annotating Broadcast News corpora could be re-used for processing spoken language corpora. However, in addition to similarities, there are also differences between speech corpora and spoken language corpora (cf. article 11). Perhaps the most important difference is that the purposes the latter must serve are much more varied, and therefore much less precisely defined. Also, annotations coming with spoken language corpora are expected to be richer, especially at the level of linguistic phenomena and linguistic structure. By necessity, the combination of less precisely specified applications and the need for richer annotations creates uncertainty about what adequate annotations might be, and how these may be provided.

Invariably, the specifications of multi-purpose spoken language corpora comprise an open list of uses to which the corpus might be put. More often than not the applications that are mentioned in the specifications appear to involve different requirements for the annotations, both in terms of the types of annotation and the degree of detail that is necessary. This complicates attempts to define a unique and uniform set of best practice guidelines for the annotation of multi-purpose corpora. For the time being, it is safe to say that there is substantial support in the speech research community for the view that annotations should refrain as much as possible from theory-driven interpretations, as well as from personal interpretations of the semantic contents or the pragmatic function of the speech. Even if the requirement that one should refrain from any kind of theory-driven interpretation seems evident, compliance is sometimes surprisingly difficult, if only because of the lack of theory-neutral terminology. A good example is the annotation of prosodic phenomena, where almost every term seems to be associated with a specific theory (see also article 11). In addition, the default annotation should make it as easy as possible to provide additional, more detailed annotations needed for specific research. Moreover, to keep the expenses of creating large multi-purpose spoken language corpora in terms of time and money within reasonable bounds, basic annotations must be such that they do not require expert knowledge and expertise to provide them in a reliable and dependable manner. Although the latter constraint is admittedly very vague, we suggest that no annotations should be aimed at that would exceed the capabilities of advanced master's students.

It is generally agreed that any spoken language corpus needs at least a precise verbatim transcription, including hesitations, truncated words, and other disfluencies. Moreover, the verbatim transcription must be linked to the speech waveform to enable effective navigation in the corpus. It is not completely clear what level of detail is needed to make the segmentation and time alignment useful for further processing, but alignment at the level of words seems to be sufficient for most – if not all – conceivable applications of multi-purpose spoken language corpora.

There is less agreement on the need for, the usefulness, cost-effectiveness and feasibility of additional linguistic annotations, probably because here specific applications of a corpus lead to diverging requirements. A phonetic transcription using a limited set of symbols corresponding to sounds that can be attributed phonemic status in the language (known as *broad phonetic* (or *phonemic*) transcriptions in the speech technology community; cf. SAMPA (Wells 1997) as an example of a set of phonemic symbols for a large number of languages) might be a welcome asset for speech technology research, while its use for socio-phonetic research may be debatable. Similar arguments appear to hold for other linguistic annotations, such as transcriptions of the prosodic structure, perhaps in conjunction with syntactic annotation. For some applications an annotation, especially of multi-party conversations, in terms of turns and the speech acts implemented by the turns would be of tremendous value, but it is quite likely that such an annotation would require expert capabilities well beyond what can be expected from master's students in Linguistics or Communication. This touches upon the issues of cost-effectiveness and feasibility of several types of annotation that, when asked, many linguists would agree would be extremely useful. However, if annotations can only be created in a reliable (and therefore useful) manner by experts, developers of spoken language corpora are likely to be forced to accept that this is not feasible. Even if there were enough money to pay the experts (which is seldom, if ever, the case) it will probably be impossible to employ them when they are most needed. Cost-effectiveness and feasibility are much less likely to be prohibitive if a well-planned and funded research project needs these annotations. In these cases it is essential that the annotation scheme allow adding additional annotation layers after the completion of the basic corpus. This will probably always be the case if the annotation scheme adheres to the guidelines proposed in article 31 by Wittenburg in the present volume.

In this article the emphasis is on the contents of the basic annotations of multi-purpose spoken language corpora, and on best practice procedures for the completion of the annotation process. Tools that support the corpus creation process will only be dealt with in passing, not least of which because this issue has been covered adequately in recent publications (e. g., Barras et al. 2001). The same holds for the representations of the annotations: we will assume that annotation guidelines will always be sufficiently precise and consistent to allow for their conversion into an XML format that can be imported using a wide range of existing corpus manipulation tools.

2. Orthographic transcription

As previously mentioned, an orthographic transcription is a verbatim account of what was being verbally expressed, including precise indications of hesitations, broken words, laughter, etc. produced by the speaker as part of the message. With recordings of longer stretches of speech and certainly with more spontaneous speech, an orthographic transcription is a prerequisite for being able to access the data. For read speech recorded under laboratory conditions, one might think that having an orthographic transcription is perhaps unnecessary, since one already has access to the original text that the speaker was asked to read out. However, speakers are known to deviate from the text and there are bound to be discrepancies between the original text and what was actually being said. Therefore, as was the default procedure in SpeechDat, it is advisable to derive an initial transcription from the prompting text and direct the subsequent transcription effort specifically to identifying any deviations: the omission or addition of words, hesitations, and false starts. Similar observations can be made with regard to other forms of elicited speech recorded in controlled conditions. It is when one has to deal with other, more spontaneous speech styles, recorded also under less controlled conditions and less favourable circumstances, that producing an orthographic transcription becomes a task demanding a great deal of effort.

Found speech as opposed to elicited speech is characterized by the fact that there is at best limited control over a number of factors. The most important of these are (1) recording conditions, (2) speaker involvement, and (3) content. As regards recording conditions, these may be highly variable. Characteristically, found speech is likely to include background noise, overlapping speech, etc., while the recording quality may be further affected if the recordings are being made by non-professionals. Even if the recordings are made by professionals, using a microphone for each speaker and multichannel recorders, speaker separation becomes extremely difficult if speakers talk simultaneously, and one has to settle for a monaural or – at best – stereophonic broadcast signal. Speech recorded outdoors and in home environments is notoriously difficult to transcribe, if only because professional recording equipment is seldom available in these conditions. The task of transcribing multi-speaker conversations is substantially aggravated if it is not known in advance who the speakers are or what they will speak about. It has been observed that transcriptions of spontaneous conversations contain many stretches of speech that were marked as unintelligible by the transcriber, yet apparently did not invoke requests from the interlocutors to repeat the utterance. Most of the time it is impossible to decide whether the other participant(s) in the conversation did not understand the speaker either, but were able to continue the conversation nevertheless, or whether the familiarity with the speaker and the setting (perhaps combined with better means for separating speaker and acoustic background) helped the other interlocutors in the conversation to understand the present speaker.

2.1. Purpose

As observed above, the orthographic transcription is the most common, and absolutely essential, type of annotation found with speech corpora. It plays an indispensable role in providing access to the data contained in a speech corpus. Provided the transcription is in some way linked to the speech signal, it makes it possible for users to browse and search the corpus. The orthographic transcription is also indispensable for producing further annotations, such as part-of-speech (POS) tagging and syntactic annotation (see articles 24 and 28), which require a written text representation as input. Finally, the orthographic transcription can be useful in speeding up other types of annotation. For example, a first version of a phonetic transcription may be derived automatically from the orthographic transcription (see section 3.1.).

For a multi-purpose corpus, orthographic transcriptions fulfill all conceivable requirements if they are accurate and consistent, and if suitably short segments of the transcriptions are aligned to the original speech signals. In the transcription, it should be possible to obtain a high level of accuracy and consistency. The transcription procedure should be implemented in such a way that the work can be done efficiently, with optimal use of available resources.

2.2. Design considerations for orthographic transcriptions

To make a speech corpus useful for a wide range of research and development purposes, it is essential that the orthographic annotation involve only a minimum level of interpretation. In practice this means, for example, that truncated words and apparent grammatical errors are recorded in the transcript exactly as they occurred. Especially for all speech signal related research, it is extremely important to maintain a close link to the speech signal and have a transcription that captures speaker turns and overlap, and that is sufficiently fine-grained to reflect pauses (between and within words), repeated words or syllables, false starts, etc. One should be aware that there are a number of contexts in which the idea of what transcriptions should include differ from what is commonly understood when talking about speech corpora. Police statements, court proceedings and transcripts of parliamentary debates, as well as commercially provided transcripts of radio and TV broadcasts typically represent what was being said in the form of a 'clean' version. Since in the context in which the transcriptions are being produced there is no immediate use for knowing where or how often hesitations and false starts occurred, such elements do not enter into these transcriptions. However, if transcriptions are available that capture only the contents of the message, it is probably a good idea to use these as the starting point for a conventional orthographic transcription.

Although this may seem counterintuitive at first sight – because potentially relevant information may be lost – it is strongly recommended that standard spelling conventions are adopted and enforced for producing an orthographic transcription. Only then will it be possible to retrieve items regardless of any variation that may have occurred. Of course, even when the language targeted in the corpus is a standard variety, one is bound to come across words that were mispronounced or have a regionally coloured pronunciation. It may be useful to mark these instances so that users can retrieve these separately, or possibly even exclude them from their dataset (cf section 2.3.).

The use of capital letters and punctuation marks deserves special attention. It is commonly argued that capital letters and punctuation find their origin in writing and have no role in the representation of speech. The use of capital letters may be taken into consideration for special items such as acronyms, initials, and proper names in order to single these items out. In a similar fashion, the use of some punctuation marks, e. g. full stop, question mark and ellipsis as sentence delimiter or the full stop with acronyms and initials can facilitate further processing. Experience has shown that the use of other punctuation marks (colon, comma, semicolon, etc.) should be avoided, because more often than not their use requires interpretations of the contents or function of the speech that are open to discussion.

For many research purposes, it is important to be able to distinguish speech produced by different speakers. Therefore, in the orthographic transcription it should be indicated to what speaker particular speech fragments must be attributed and also where the speech of different speakers overlaps. The use of a multi-tiered notation (see article 11 for an example) is an attractive way of representing speaker involvement and interaction. In spontaneous conversations between two or more persons, overlapping speech of several speakers abounds. Often, overlapping speech is difficult or impossible to understand for a transcriber who is not involved as a participant. Intuitively, one might assume that it is straightforward to segment conversations into turns. If this were indeed true, orthographic transcriptions of conversations should always include indicators for the beginning and end of each turn, and each turn should be attributed to a unique speaker. However, in actual practice deciding whether a short utterance of one speaker – even if produced during a pause of the others – constitutes a genuine turn, or whether it was meant solely as a backchannel, requires substantial interpretation. Consequently, segmentation of turns should probably be considered as a 'value added' type of annotation, which cannot be provided independent of some theory of conversation.

While in principle everything said must be accounted for in the orthographic transcription, independently motivated decisions must be made about how to treat speech originating from sources other than the speaker(s) that are immediately involved (e. g. announcements made over a public address system). The same holds for other audible acoustic events, vocal non-speech events such as grunts, laughter, coughing and external noises such as the noise of cars passing or a radio playing. The level of detail with which such non-speech events are described varies a great deal from one resource to the next. For example, in SpeechDat all background speech is indicated as background noise. This is reasonable, because occasional public address announcements on stations or airports cannot be used for training a speech recognition system. However, in other circumstances more detailed transcription of non-speech events is useful. It can be helpful in explaining the apparent sudden disruption of the train of thought. For example, a plane flying by may cause the speaker to pause in the middle of a sentence and possibly briefly comment on the event before continuing with what he or she was saying. A description of the nature and degree of background noise is also useful when selecting training data for a speech recognition experiment.

2.3. Representations

Not all information resulting from an orthographic transcription actually has to go into the verbatim account of what was said in itself: part of the information is probably more appropriately accounted for in the metadata. This certainly holds for characteristics that apply to a complete recording or identified portion of a long recording (such as signal-to-noise ratio, acoustic background, etc.). It also holds for potentially relevant information such as who the speakers were, what their role was in the setting, who was responsible for the transcription, what transcription protocol was used, etc.

Special attention must be paid to the representation of auditory phenomena that are inextricably related to the speech, but that cannot be represented by standardized spelling conventions. Examples are several kinds of hesitations, broken words, false starts and other types of disfluencies. Care should be taken to mark disfluencies as special instances so as to avoid ambiguity with common instances. For example, in the case of a false start, a truncated word may be produced which if left unmarked may be confused with a regular full word, thus yielding noise when the corpus is used. Since hesitations and other types of filled pauses can be represented in a great many different ways, one should consider using a fixed list comprising a limited set of representations. Phenomena such as abnormal lengthening, regionally coloured pronunciation of a word, the fact that a word was pronounced in a foreign language, etc. should preferably be represented as special marks attached to – but separable from – the conventional spelling of the word. This procedure strikes the best possible compromise between the requirements posed by different uses of a corpus.

3. Phonological annotation

If one wants to know not only what was said but also how words were pronounced, an orthographic transcription is not sufficient and additional annotation is required. For many research purposes in areas of phonetics and speech recognition, some kind of phonological annotation or transcription is a prerequisite. However, the nature and the detailedness of such transcription are closely dependent on the specific purpose the transcription is expected to serve. For some purposes (e. g. word segmentation), it may suffice to have a coarse, broad phonetic representation automatically derived from the orthographic transcription, while in other instances only a narrow phonetic transcription will be of use. In this section we will summarize the experience with phonological annotation of large speech corpora that has accumulated over the last decade.

In this article we will distinguish between broad phonetic (or phonemic) transcriptions on the one hand and fine phonetic transcriptions on the other. Phonemic transcriptions represent the speech signal in the form of a sequence of the phonemes of the language. At first sight it may seem trivial to define the phonemes of a language as a closed set (even if text books may disagree on the phonemic status of sounds that occur only in loan words). This was the approach taken in the definition of the SAMPA alphabets for the languages addressed in the SAM project (Wells et al. 1992). In SAM and SpeechDat this approach was adequate because the prompting sheets could be defined so as to elicit only speech that can be transcribed with the symbols from a closed set. However, when found speech must be transcribed the situation becomes much more complicated, if only because found speech almost invariably contains foreign words (if only names). Therefore, one must decide how to represent sounds that are not included in a closed set of native phonemes. In some cases (for some speakers) it may be fully adequate to map foreign sounds onto the nearest native phoneme, but in other cases speakers make it a point to approximate the pronunciation in the language of origin as closely as possible. In the latter cases, one might want to extend the set of transcription symbols so as to cover non-native phonemes (or *xenophones*, cf article 48). Whether or not xenophones are used, phonemic transcriptions should always come with a list of all the symbols that are used and their definition (cf. section 3.4.). Narrow (also called 'fine') phonetic transcriptions use a (much) larger set of symbols (and diacritics) for representing details of the pronunciation that cannot be captured with only phoneme symbols. The level of detail in narrow phonetic transcriptions will also depend on the purpose of the investigation. It is reflected in the list of all symbols and diacritics that may appear in the transcriptions. Therefore, a comprehensive list of all possible symbols and diacritics must be provided.

3.1. Broad phonetic transcriptions: Automatically generated

Once an orthographic transcription is available, it is possible to derive a phonemic transcription from it automatically. In its simplest form, a straightforward translation of the words as they occur in the orthographic transcription into their phonetic representations can suffice. This can either be done by applying a set of grapheme-to-phoneme rules or by substituting the citation (or canonical) forms as listed in a pre-existing pronunciation lexicon. In practice a combination of the two approaches will often be used. There are a number of reasons for this. For some languages a pronunciation lexicon may not exist at all. But even when a pronunciation lexicon is available, it will seldom contain all the words in a corpus that comprises spontaneous conversations or broadcast news. Again, proper names are a guaranteed source of gaps. Also, in languages such as Dutch, German and Swedish that have productive compounding one should be prepared to see a continuous stream of novel words.

To the extent that special items such as acronyms, abbreviations, proper names, and foreign words have been marked in the orthographic transcription, these markers may be exploited to generate specific pronunciation variants where appropriate, either by lexicon look-up or by rule. Special provisions may also be made in order to account for various cross-word phonological processes that affect the pronunciation of words as they co-occur, such as assimilation, degemination (the deletion of one of two identical consonants, often at word boundaries), and the insertion of linking phonemes. Here rules may be implemented that apply only in particular contexts.

If phonemic renderings are generated from the type of orthographic transcriptions defined in section 2, without any further reference to the original speech signals, one should avoid the term 'transcriptions', since this term refers to an account of the sounds that were actually realized. It is more appropriate to use a term like 'phonemic representation'. However, it is quite possible and feasible to obtain automatic phonemic representations that deserve the label 'transcription'. Several automatic procedures can be used to compute the most likely sequence of phonemic symbols, given the speech signal and the orthographic transcription. Invariably, these procedures rely on an automatic speech recognizer that comes with trained acoustic models for all phonemes that must be distinguished. Automatic transcription usually involves an iterative procedure in which additional pronunciation variants of the words in the corpus are generated and then matched against the speech signals (Demuynck/Laureys/Gillis 2002).

State-of-the art automatically generated phonemic transcriptions are certainly good enough for most research in automatic speech recognition (ASR) and synthesis. Most likely, they are also more than adequate for many types of linguistic research. However, it is not possible to give dependable estimates of the accuracy of automatic phonemic transcriptions. Much will depend on the quality of the acoustic models in the speech recognizer, on the details of the iterative transcription procedure, and on peculiarities of the language. For example, in Dutch the distinction between voiced and unvoiced fricatives is rather weak and uncertain. This makes it difficult, if not impossible, to train acoustic models that make the distinction reliably.

Segmentation and alignment
Automatic phonetic transcription is based on an alignment between a hypothetical phonemic representation of the words in the orthographic transcription and the speech signal. Therefore, this procedure yields an automatic segmentation and alignment on phoneme level. It may seem straightforward to convert this into a segmentation and alignment on the word level. However, in actual practice assimilations, degeminations and deletions on word boundaries abound, especially in spontaneous conversational speech. This makes it necessary to specify unambiguous rules for aligning the resulting phonemic transcription with the words in the orthographic transcription. Once this symbolic alignment is in place, the alignment between words in the orthographic transcription and the speech signal comes for free.

3.2. Broad phonetic transcriptions: Generated by human transcribers

It has been noted in the previous subsection that the quality of automatic phonemic transcriptions is very difficult to predict. Therefore, it might be worthwhile to add manual phonemic transcriptions to a corpus. However, it must be realized that this task is very time-consuming and expensive. Moreover, when using (relatively cheap) labour in the form of master's students of Linguistics for the job, one cannot be certain that the quality of the manual transcriptions will exceed that of automatic transcription significantly. Therefore, it is doubtful whether we will ever see large corpora with human phonemic transcriptions.

If one decides to make human phonemic transcriptions, two quite different procedures can be followed. First, one may start with the best possible automatic phonemic transcription, and then ask human transcribers to check and correct the output of the automaton. Alternatively, one can decide to make the transcriptions from scratch, perhaps supporting the transcribers with the result of the orthographic transcriptions. The first method is likely to cause some bias towards the output of the automatic transcriber. This need not be bad, because this bias may result in greater consistency between independently working transcribers. The second method will not be completely bias-free either; experiments in phonetic transcription have shown that phoneticians tend to 'hear' the sounds in the canonical representation of the words if they understand the language, even if the physical presence of the sounds is questionable at best (Cucchiarini 1993).

Segmentation and alignment
Manual phonemic transcriptions do not automatically provide a segmentation and alignment as a byproduct. To obtain a precise link between the transcription and the speech signal, an automatic speech recognition system operating in forced recognition or alignment mode must be used as an additional step. Alternatively, the human transcribers can be requested to make the alignment as part of the transcription procedure. Here too, it is possible to ask human transcribers to check and correct automatic segmentations.

It goes without saying that alignment of manual phonemic transcriptions must solve the same problems due to cross-word assimilations, degeminations and insertions that were mentioned in section 3.1.

3.3. Narrow phonetic transcription

A narrow phonetic transcription aims to represent exactly how a speaker spoke the words he/she said and to record the effects of various articulatory processes involved. This type of transcription can only be made by having an expert transcriber listen carefully to the recording and inspect the audio signal as it is displayed in the form of a waveform and spectrogram. No matter how conscientiously the transcriber goes about the task, transcriptions are inevitably subjective and there is no telling how accurate the transcriptions actually are. This, and the fact that manual transcription is very time-consuming and expensive, has proven to be prohibitive when considering the application of this type of annotation, for example in the case of large (continuous) speech corpora. Especially when many speakers are involved and speech is spontaneous, narrow phonetic transcription of large corpora is considered to be not feasible. Thus, it is not surprising that large corpora contain at best a small subset of samples for which a narrow phonetic transcription is provided. One notable exception is the TIMIT corpus, but this only contains read speech in the form of short and not always meaningful sentences (Garofolo et al. 1986). One of the best known examples of narrow phonetic transcriptions of conversational speech is perhaps the part of the Switchboard corpus that has been transcribed at ICSI (Greenberg 1997).

Phoneticians have different opinions on what is the best procedure for making narrow phonetic transcriptions. Some feel that it is best to create a somewhat rough transcription first and come back later to fill in all the details, while others prefer to cover as many details as possible in a single pass. Those who prefer a multi-pass procedure may or may not want to take a new pass for specific phenomena such as diphthongization, vowel reduction, voicing of stop and fricative consonants, etc. One may or may not want to include the orthographic transcription, or perhaps even a canonical phonemic representation that can be obtained automatically from the orthographic transcription. Little is known about the impact of the details of the transcription procedure on the accuracy of the eventual transcriptions. It is perhaps fair to say that the experience and attention of the transcribers have a bigger impact on the quality of the eventual transcription than the details of the transcription procedure.

Trying to capture all possible details in a narrow phonetic transcription of a large multi-purpose corpus is practically impossible. Even for broad transcriptions starting from a canonical phonemic representation it has been found that one minute of conversational speech takes about 40 minutes to transcribe (Demuynck/Laureys/Gillis 2002). Fine phonetic transcriptions would take a multiple of 40 minutes per minute, and the multiplication factor will depend on the amount of detail one wants to include. In addition, fine phonetic transcriptions can only be created by expert phoneticians. Therefore, one cannot but focus on those details that are considered especially important, and avoid making claims about the accuracy with which other details are captured. For many phonetic and linguistic research projects, information is required about specific details, for example the degree of (de-)voicing, the degree of diphthongization of specific vowels, the exact manner and place of articulation of the [r] phoneme, etc. In the unfortunate (but not unlikely) situation that the details covered in the phonetic transcriptions delivered with the corpus focused on other details, the missing details must be supplemented. Thus, it is likely that researchers will want to add the detailed information that is relevant for their purpose. It has been suggested that the accuracy that can be obtained in transcribing specific phenomena is much higher than what can be expected from a transcription in which phoneticians must pay attention to innumerable details (van Hout/van de Velde 2001). In any case, the likelihood that detail must be added for specific research projects shows that fine phonetic transcriptions must be cast in such a manner that it is easy to make additions. An interesting but as yet unanswered corollary question is whether added detail should eventually replace the less precise original transcriptions.

Narrow phonetic transcriptions can also be obtained automatically, especially if one wants to focus on specific details, like the ones mentioned in the previous paragraph. Starting from a phonemic transcription (produced automatically or manually) and the attendant segmentation of the speech signal, it is possible to apply automatic procedures to classify the sound segments into a number of pre-defined fine grained classes (e. g. Weigelt/Sadoff/Miller 1990). However, once again this cannot be done for every phonetic phenomenon that is conceivably of interest.

3.4. Symbol sets

Once it has been decided what the set of phonemes must be in a phonemic transcription, or what symbols and diacritics may be used in a narrow phonetic transcription, one must select an appropriate representation of these symbols. What 'appropriate' means depends, as usual, very much on the circumstances. The bottom line here is that the representations must be computer readable, but it may also be important that they are easy and transparent to handle for the human transcribers and users.

For phonemic transcriptions, many European corpus creation projects settle for a SAMPA representation (Wells 1997; see also http://www.phon.ucl.ac.uk/home/sampa/), albeit sometimes in a slightly adapted version. In the USA several different computer readable phonetic alphabets are in common use. With very few exceptions, the different representations can be mapped one-to-one onto each other, or onto some underlying XML format. Although an international standard would certainly be preferable, it is unlikely that a widely supported standard will emerge in the foreseeable future. In the meantime, it suffices to provide unambiguous definitions of the symbol representations used in the phonemic and phonetic annotation of a corpus, perhaps accompanied by tools for mapping onto a number of frequently used representations.

4. Prosodic annotation

While it may be possible to derive part of the segmental phonetic information from an orthographic transcription adorned with information about specific articulatory effects, this is not the case with prosodic information. This is the more so if no secondary punctuation marks, such as commas, are used (because these often require a substantial degree of interpretation) (Knowles/Wichmann/Alderson 1996). Because prosody constitutes a very important aspect of speech, one might expect that spoken language corpora come with some kind of prosodic annotation. Unfortunately, linguists do not agree on what a minimal theory-neutral prosodic annotation might or should contain. Virtually all prosodic descriptions rely on a specific theory, if only to define the basic units from which a prosodic transcription can be assembled. To make things even worse, prosody is associated not only with the linguistic level of description, but also with the paralinguistic level, and there is no general agreement on what belongs on one level and what on the other. Given this state of affairs, it does not come as a surprise that prosodic annotations require a great deal of time and effort from extensively trained annotators, and that the level of agreement between annotators can be disappointingly low, especially if annotators are trained by different 'master transcribers'.

It is not surprising either that there are no large (by today's standards) corpora that have been annotated for prosodic information. The London-Lund Corpus (Svartvik 1990) and the Lancaster/IBM Spoken English Corpus (Knowles/Williams/Taylor 1996) are among the better known medium-sized corpora that come with prosodic annotation. The transcriptions fit in the British tradition of prosodic analysis. The basic prosodic features marked in the full transcription are tone unit boundaries, the location of the nucleus (i. e. the peak of greatest prominence in a tone unit), the direction of the nuclear tone, varying lengths of pauses, and varying degrees of stress. Other features comprise varying degrees of loudness and tempo (e. g. allegro, clipped, drawled), modifications in voice quality (pitch range, rhythmicality and tension), and paralinguistic features such as whisper and creak. Indications are given of overlap in the utterances of speakers. There are no data about the reliability of the transcriptions, and because the audio recordings are not publicly accessible, there is no way of assessing the quality of these transcriptions.

Today, the dominant approach in Linguistics to prosodic annotation is no doubt the ToBI framework (Silverman et al. 1992). Of course, ToBI and its language-specific descendants are not theory independent. What is more, it has been shown that the ToBI scheme can only be applied by highly trained labellers, and even then its application is very time-consuming, while there is no guarantee that multiple labellers will reach a high degree of agreement on many of the labels. Syrdal et al. (2001) present a proposal to speed up the labelling procedure. They report the use of a Text-to-Speech (TTS) system to predict the labels from the orthographic transcription; subsequently, labellers were asked to verify the system's predictions. The labelling speed – expressed as the Real Time Factor (RTF) – differed substantially between their labellers; it ranged from 81.77 for the fastest labeller (correcting the predictions of the TTS system) to 215.5 (labelling from scratch). In general, correcting automatic labels was slightly faster than labelling from scratch and the bias due to the suggestions of the TTS system was considered minor. However, all speech processed in this experiment was carefully read by a professional speaker. In the Spoken Dutch Corpus project an attempt to label a small part of the corpus with the Dutch version of ToBI was deemed prohibitive, due to the unavailability of expert labour during the lifetime of the project. Therefore, it was decided to reduce the prosodic labelling to break indices between successive words, the identification of prominent syllables and exceptional lengthening, which can be done with sufficient inter-labeller agreement by students after a relatively short training period (Buhmann et al. 2002). The reduced labels were considered a useful starting point for training prosody modules for TTS systems, as well as for linguistic research.

5. Protocols and guidelines

For a large corpus creation project to be successful, it is absolutely essential to have a complete set of written and tested protocols and guidelines for all individual tasks and stages. The role of these protocols and guidelines is three-fold. First of all, they should provide annotators with clear instructions as to what to transcribe and how to do so. Secondly, they should give insight to future users as to what the annotation comprises. Finally, the guidelines should provide an explicit account of what rules underlie the annotations, so that the results may be evaluated against this set of rules by external evaluators.

The design of good protocols and guidelines is far from trivial. Ideally, they should at the same time be as simple as possible and cover each and every instance that may be encountered. In actual practice, however, it is not easy to strike the right balance between the need for completeness and simplicity. Good guidelines state a small set of basic rules that cover most situations consistently, are non-ambiguous and easy to memorize. In other words, basic guidelines define the spirit of the annotation enterprise. Additional rules may be included to deal with exceptional instances. Where transcribers can be expected to encounter ambiguous situations, the guidelines should provide clear rules that will help them decide on the correct transcription. It is recommended that unnecessary detail be avoided since this will only confuse transcribers and slow them down. The inclusion of typical examples, preferably based on actual cases encountered during the development of the protocols and guidelines, helps annotators more than lengthy theoretical explanations (Hamaker/Zeng/Picone 1998).

It goes without saying that different protocols and guidelines must be developed for the different levels of annotation. It is probably true that the development of protocols for orthographic transcription, at least for Western languages, can profit most from the experiences gained in previous projects. Existing protocols, such as those developed for Switchboard and the Spoken Dutch Corpus, present proven procedures for handling cases that can be considered exceptions to standard spelling rules, such as:

- acronyms
- proper names
- numbers
- spelled letters
- contractions
- foreign words/sounds
- dialect items
- neologisms
- mispronounced words
- truncated words
- unintelligible speech

Where the orthographic transcription also includes a description of non-speech events, it is useful to have a separate transcription layer or tier, preferably one that is synchronized with the other tier(s). Moreover, one may want to consider having a fixed list of items for transcribers to use.

Protocols for the alignment of orthographic transcriptions with the speech signal must specify exactly how deletions, insertions and assimilations across word boundaries must be handled. Other issues that require special attention are stretches of unintelligible speech, and overlapping speech of several speakers.

The protocol for phonetic annotation must specify the set of symbols that may appear in the transcription, as well as their definition in terms of IPA symbols. Also, this protocol should describe the transcription procedure in sufficient detail for external users and evaluators to be able to understand the resulting transcription. For example, it must be clear whether transcribers were instructed to adhere as much as possible to a canonical representation of the words – and only annotate gross deviations – or whether their task was to produce a maximally precise account of the pronunciation, within the constraints of the set of available symbols. The same holds for a prosodic annotation.

6. Procedure

Experience with the creation of multi-purpose corpora has shown that once it has been decided what annotations will be provided, appropriate procedures must be developed that will make it possible to produce high quality annotations, i. e. annotations that are formally correct and relatively error-free, in an efficient and cost-effective manner. Although in principle all annotation layers may be produced in a single pass, the multiple pass approach in which each pass is devoted to a specific subtask is generally preferred. There are various reasons for adopting the latter approach. Dividing up a complex task into a number of distinct, simpler subtasks has the advantage that transcribers can focus on a single task at a time, while being able to benefit from the results obtained in a previous pass. Where appropriate, different parties may be involved for different subtasks, so that different types of expertise can be optimally used. This may even imply that different parts of the annotation task are carried out at different places. For example, phonetic transcription may be contracted to a research group that has dedicated experience in that field. In the Spoken Dutch Corpus project orthographic transcription was performed in several laboratories in the Netherlands and Flanders in parallel, because cross-border transcriptions were deemed too difficult, due to different vocabularies and pronunciation habits. In a multi-pass approach particularly, it is important that the goals of each subtask are specified in detail and that the responsibilities of the different parties involved are absolutely clear.

Where, in the process of arriving at a transcription, a subsequent pass builds on the results obtained in a previous pass, the procedure will automatically involve validation of these results: errors encountered will be spotted and their correction will be required. It is essential to put an effective and at the same time efficient bug reporting and processing procedure in place, to be able to ensure that corrections suggested at one place are finally carried out at all other places where the same speech fragment is being processed. To the extent that results are not used in a subsequent pass, having a separate validation pass is recommended.

Although multi-pass processing in conjunction with explicit protocols and guidelines makes it possible to distribute the work in the creation of a large multi-purpose speech corpus, it is strongly recommended to keep the number of sites as small as possible. This is because protocols and guidelines can only specify the spirit of the rules that must be adhered to. Regular meetings between annotators and supervisors, where recently encountered problem cases can be discussed, add substantially to the quality and consistency of the transcriptions. Very often, transcribers will be confronted with ambiguous cases which they may want to discuss with their supervisors. Even if they finally decide to make a decision themselves, the fact that they can contact the person who is responsible for quality assurance helps them maintain consistency.

In addition to regular meetings to exchange and discuss experiences it is essential that the work of the annotators is checked regularly during the process. This must be done by the supervisor, who is responsible for quality control. The simple fact that the annotators know that their work is being checked helps them to maintain a high quality. Yet, it may happen that individual annotators let their attention and concentration slip, due to fatigue, habituation, or perhaps personal problems. On-line monitoring is especially important when new annotators enter the scene.

It is generally recognized that various types of speech differ a great deal with regard to the degree of difficulty experienced in annotation. Spontaneous speech is on the whole more difficult to process than more formal speech. Here a number of factors are involved. The rate of speech is usually higher in spontaneous speech than it is in more formal and scripted speech styles. The use of substandard forms or dialect, regional pronunciation, as well as the higher number of disfluencies that occur are also known to have a negative effect on the annotation process. A lot of background noise which makes it more difficult to hear what was being said will require greater effort on the part of the transcriber. Other factors that contribute to the degree of difficulty are the extent to which transcribers are familiar with the specific language or language variety. The frequent use of words common to a specific domain but unfamiliar to the transcriber is likely to have a negative effect on the speed of transcription and the correctness of the result. With speech involving multiple speakers, the number of speakers and the amount of overlap that occurs also contribute to making the transcription more difficult. Assigning speech to specific speakers can be problematic, especially when voices sound very similar as is occasionally the case with young females.

For most situations where transcription is perceived as non-trivial, practical arrangements may help facilitate the process. The use of multiple audio channels and visible tiers in the annotation form is quite helpful in this respect. Visualization of the speech signal is generally useful, as is having the possibility of slowing down the recording while listening to it. Technology is available to do this without changing the pitch, but this is not widely used. Online access to a lexicon and a spell checker contribute substantially to keeping the number of errors to a minimum. Obviously, this requires a procedure for rapid updates of the lexicon, each time new words are encountered. In so far as the guidelines specify deviations from standard spelling conventions, the spell checker should be adapted so as to cater for these deviations. In a number of instances, as for example with the transcription of numbers, where a full written form is aimed for, errors may be avoided and transcription speed may be increased by having transcribers simply use numbers and afterwards applying a simple procedure that automatically expands these representations to full, written forms. The same holds true for the annotation of background noises and non-speech sounds generated by the speakers.

7. Tools

As was already mentioned in the introduction to this article, transcription of found speech can be undertaken with relatively simple means, e. g. a replay device that allows the transcriber to listen to (parts of) the recordings repeatedly and a straightforward text editor which permits entering text directly from a keyboard and does not perform any automatic formatting (Barras et al. 2001). If the speech comes in long files, as is likely in the case of broadcast material or recordings of spontaneous conversations, it is important that the audio tools support easy and rapid navigation, in addition to the capability to play short selected intervals of the signal. Signal tools should also offer easy methods for adding time stamps to the signal, e. g. for the segmentation of long recordings into more manageable chunks. An overview of tools that are presently available to support corpus annotation can be found on the LDC's linguistic annotation page (http://www.ldc.upen.edu/Creating/creating-annotated.shtml#Annotation).

Many tools that can be used to support, speed up and possibly improve the quality of the annotations are based on ASR systems. We have already mentioned ASR tools for (semi-)automatic phonetic transcription and segmentation. For fairly formal speech, such as that produced by the anchor persons in news bulletins and similar professionally produced speech, one may consider using an ASR system to produce a raw orthographic transcription, that can subsequently be edited by human transcribers. This is similar to the use of commercial manual transcriptions, which must also be checked and turned into verbatim renderings. In general it holds that well-trained ASR-related tools, when used appropriately, can speed up and improve the manual annotation work. However, the help that can be expected from an ASR system will rapidly diminish as the speech becomes more spontaneous, simply because extant ASR systems still have major problems in dealing with spontaneous speech. Beyond a certain threshold – which is difficult to define – correcting errors made by an automatic device becomes more time-consuming than transcription from scratch.

8. Evaluation

It has already been argued that quality control must be designed into all procedures, protocols and guidelines for the creation of a speech corpus. Having said this, it must be added that quality control standards for the various annotation layers in multi-purpose corpora do not yet exist, and that their development is anything but trivial. This is the more so because protocols and guidelines cannot cover all possible details and ambiguities. In projects like SpeechDat, rather exact evaluation standards have been used for the quality of orthographic transcription, although even there the threshold for the proportion of discrepancies between the actual audio signals and the transcriptions were different for words and non-words (which included background noise). In multi-purpose corpora that comprise conversational speech it is even more difficult to define strict guidelines, if only because it is not always easy to determine whether a stretch of speech is indeed unintelligible. Quality control on other annotation layers is even more difficult. We have already touched upon the problems encountered in prosodic annotation. Similar concerns hold for all forms of phonetic transcription, and there is actually no generally agreed procedure for measuring the quality of phonetic transcriptions (Cucchiarini/Binnenpoorte/Goddijn 2001).

In addition to quality control during corpus creation, some form of formal evaluation is also necessary after the corpus is complete. It has become customary to use the term *validation* for this activity (van den Heuvel/Boves/Sanders 2002). While formal quality monitoring during corpus production is already quite difficult, external validation of the quality of a multi-purpose spoken language corpus is even more difficult. Such validation must involve an assessment of the clarity and completeness of the documentation, which includes the protocols, guidelines and descriptions of the relevant procedures. For the time being, no formal criteria are available for this purpose.

For found speech there is no 'true' reference, not even for the orthographic transcription. This calls into question whether it is at all possible to measure the quality of the annotations of found speech. In the Spoken Dutch Corpus project external validation of the transcription quality was performed by BAS, following the guidelines designed by the sponsors of that project. Essentially, these validation guidelines maintain that transcriptions should be considered correct if they can be motivated against the background of the relevant protocols. Thus, the quality of the orthographic transcription was not measured by making independent transcriptions of a representative sample of the speech and subsequently measuring the proportion of deletions, insertions and substitutions in the transcription that comes with the corpus. Rather, the validators were requested to take the transcriptions as a starting point and check whether these are plausible, given the transcription protocol. Similar procedures must be used for the other annotation layers.

9. Concluding remarks

9.1. Recommendations

Despite the fact that the Spoken Dutch Corpus project was extensively prepared, using all available information and experience from previous comparable enterprises, there were of course some tasks that were underestimated. The single biggest estimation error was the time and effort needed to acquire speech recordings that fitted the design of the corpus, and could be published. There may be almost unlimited amounts of speech to be found, but a multi-purpose corpus needs careful design criteria, which imply for example some balance between communicative settings, speaker characteristics, etc. It is well known that some categories are much more difficult to fill than others. It appears especially difficult to obtain speech of speakers of lower socio-economic status. The selection process is severely aggravated by the need to obtain signed statements from all speakers declaring that they agree to the publishing of their speech. Under European law, radio and TV broadcasts are protected by the same type of copyright as newspapers and magazines; therefore, the fact that speech has been broadcast does not imply that it can be re-published as part of a spoken language corpus.

It is now generally agreed that the London-Lund Corpus and the spoken part of the British National Corpus would have been much more useful if the audio recordings could have been made available. Although one might think that careful annotations can make the original audio recordings redundant, this is not the case, except for a small number of dedicated applications. In actual practice, even verbatim orthographic transcription involves some kind of interpretation of the speech. Transcription protocols just cannot cover all possible ambiguities. Moreover, it has been argued that phonetic and prosodic annotations cannot be completely theory neutral, and that the reliability of such transcriptions leaves room for improvement. Thus, even for the annotation layers that are provided with the basic corpus, many users will require the capability to check and amend the annotations. Moreover, for truly large multi-purpose corpora, default annotations simply cannot contain everything that might be needed for (novel) research. For that reason we have argued that the basic annotation should be considered a starting point for providing the additional annotations needed for specific research endeavours.

Given the importance of the right to publish the original audio recordings, combined with the time and effort it takes to pre-process and annotate speech, it is strongly recommended that all time consuming processing of recordings is postponed until after all signatures have been obtained that are needed for publishing the speech as part of the eventual corpus.

9.2. Standards

It would be of great help if international standards could be developed for speech corpus annotations, as well as for the way in which the quality of such annotations could be assessed. However, 'standards' come in different types and degrees of maturity. It is unlikely that a field like spoken language corpora, which is still in its infancy, will any time soon see the type of formal standards accepted by the International Standards Organization (ISO) or the World Wide Web Consortium (W3C). At the other end of the scale, projects like SAM and EAGLES have provided extremely useful best practice guidelines, which − if adhered to − guarantee a high degree of interoperability between independently created corpora. Thus, one can hope − and expect − that the community will accept and adhere to *de facto standards* for the use of character codes for the representation of orthographic, phonetic and prosodic annotations (cf. Corpus Encoding Standard, http://www.cs.vassar.edu/CES/ and http://www.xml-ces.org/). Note that the use of common character codes does not imply that annotations in different corpora adhere to the same semantics. For example, common character codes may be used to encode different sets of part-of-speech tags or different prosodic phenomena. At this moment it is not clear whether it will ever be possible to define a comprehensive set of POS tags, such that a sub-set would allow accurate tagging for each and every natural language on the globe. The same holds for prosodic phenomena, and probably also for many other language features. Also, one might see emerging standards for the set of metadata that should complete the annotation of specific types of speech, as well as for the representation of these metadata (EAGLES/ISLE Metadata Initiative, http://www.mpi.nl/IMDI/). The reader is encouraged to consult article 31 by Wittenburg for more detailed discussions about formal and *de facto* standards and best practice guidelines.

10. Literature

Barras, C./Geoffrois, E./Wu, Z./Liberman, M. (2001), Transcriber: Development and Use of a Tool for Assisting Speech Corpora Production. In: *Speech Communication* 33(1–2), 5–22.

Binnenpoorte, D./Cucchiarini, C. (2003), Phonetic Transcription of Large Speech Corpora: How to Boost Efficiency without Affecting Quality. In: *Proceedings of the 15th ICPhS*. Barcelona, Spain, 2981–2984.

Bird, S./Harrington, J. (2001), Speech Annotation and Corpus Tools. In: *Speech Communication* 33(1–2), 1–4.

Buhmann, J./Caspers, J./van Heuven, V./Hoekstra, H./Martens, J. P./Swerts, M. (2002), Annotation of Prominent Words, Prosodic Boundaries and Segmental Lengthening by Non-expert Transcribers in the Spoken Dutch Corpus. In: González Rodriguez, M./Paz Suárez Araujo, C. (eds.), *Proceedings of the Third International Conference on Language Resources and Evaluation, Las Palmas de Gran Canaria*. Paris: European Language Resources Association, 779–785.

Burger, S./Weilhammer, K./Schiel, F./Tillmann, H. (2000), Verbmobil Data Collection and Annotation. In: Wahlster, W. (ed.), *Verbmobil: Foundations of Speech-to-speech Translation*. Berlin: Springer, 537–549.

Creer, S./Thompson, P. (2004), Processing Spoken Language Data: The BASE Experience. In: Oostdijk/Kristoffersen/Sampson 2004, 20–27.

Cucchiarini, C. (1993), Phonetic Transcription: A Methodological and Empirical Study. PhD Thesis, Catholic University Nijmegen.

Cucchiarini, C./Binnenpoorte, D./Goddijn, S. (2001), Phonetic Transcriptions in the Spoken Dutch Corpus: How to Combine Efficiency and Good Transcription Quality. In: *Proceedings Eurospeech 2001*. Aalborg, Denmark, 1679–1682.

Demuynck, K./Laureys, T./Gillis, S. (2002), Automatic Generation of Phonetic Transcriptions for Large Speech Corpora. In: *Proceedings of the International Conference on Spoken Language Processing* 1. Denver, USA, 333–336.

Demuynck, K./Laureys, T. (2002), A Comparison of Different Approaches to Automatic Speech Segmentation. In: *Proceedings of the 5th International Conference on Text, Speech and Dialogue*. Brno, Czech Republic, 277–284.

Edwards, J. (2004), The ICSI Meeting Corpus: Close-talking and Far-field, Multi-channel Transcriptions for Speech and Language Researchers. In: Oostdijk/Kristoffersen/Sampson 2004, 8–11.

Fiscus, J. et al. (1998), *Universal Transcription Format Specification*. (http://www.itl.nist.gov/iaui/894.01/tests/bnr/1998).

Fourcin, A./Gibbon, D. (1994), Spoken Language Assessment in the European Context. In: *Literary and Linguistic Computing* 1994 9(1), 79–86.

Garofolo, J./Lamel, L./Fisher, W./Fiscus, J./Pallett, D./Dahlgren, N. (1986), *The DARPA TIMIT Acoustic-phonetic Continuous Speech Corpus CDROM*. Gaithersburg, MD: NIST.

Gauvain, J.-L./Lamel, L./Adda, G. (2002), The LIMSI Broadcast News Transcription System. In: *Speech Communication* 37(1–2), 89–108.

Gibbon, D./Moore, R./Winski, R. (eds.) (1997), *Handbook of Standards and Resources for Spoken Language Systems*. Berlin/New York: Mouton de Gruyter.

Goddijn, S./Binnenpoorte, D. (2003), Assessing Manually Corrected Broad Phonetic Transcriptions in the Spoken Dutch Corpus. In: *Proceedings of the 15th ICPhS*. Barcelona, Spain, 1361–1364.

Godfrey, J./Holliman, E./McDaniel, J. (1992), Switchboard: A Telephone Speech Corpus for Research and Development. In: *Proceedings of the IEEE Conference on Acoustics, Speech and Signal Processing* I. San Francisco, 517–520.

Goedertier, W./Goddijn, S./Martens, J.-P (2000), Orthographic Transcription in the Spoken Dutch Corpus. In: Gravilidou, M./Carayannis, G./Markantonatou, S./Piperidis, S./Stainhaour, G. (eds.), *LREC-2000 (Second International Conference on Language Resources and Evaluation) Proceedings III*. Athens, 1427–1433.

González Ledesma, A./De la Madrid Heizmann, G./Alcántara Plá, M./De la Torre Cuesta, R./ Moreno Sandoval, A. (2004), Orality and Difficulties in the Transcription of Spoken Corpora. In: Oostdijk/Kristoffersen/Sampson 2004, 12–19.

Graff, D. (2002), An Overview of Broadcast News Corpora. In: *Speech Communication* 37, 15–26.

Greenberg, S. (1997), *The Switchboard Transcription Project*. Large Vocabulary Continuous Speech Recognition Summer Research Workshop. Research Report 24. Baltimore, MD: Technical Report Services, Center for Language and Speech Processing, Johns Hopkins University.

Hamaker, J./Zeng, Y./Picone, J. (1998), *Rules and Guidelines for Transcription and Segmentation of the SWITCHBOARD Large Vocabulary Conversational Speech Recognition Corpus*. Version 7.1 October 1, 1998. Mississipi: Mississipi State University.

van den Heuvel, H./Boves, L./Moreno, A./Omologo, M./Richard, G./Sanders, E. (2001), Annotation in the SpeechDat Projects. In: *International Journal of Speech Technology* 4(2), 127–143.

van den Heuvel, H./Boves, L./Sanders, E. (2002), *Validation of Content and Quality of Existing SLR: Overview and Methodology*. (http://www.spex.nl/validationcentre/d11v21.doc).

van den Heuvel, H./Höge, H./Choukri, K. (2002), Give Me a Bug: A Framework for a Bug Report Service. In: González Rodriguez, M./Paz Suárez Araujo, C. (eds.), *Proceedings of the Third International Conference on Language Resources and Evaluation*. Las Palmas de Gran Canaria, 569–572.

Höge, H./Draxler, C./van den Heuvel, H./Johansen, F./Sanders, E./Tropf, H. (1999), SpeechDat Multilingual Speech Databases for Teleservices across the Finish Line. In: *Proceedings Eurospeech'99, Budapest, Hungary 5–9 Sept. 1999*, I. Budapest, 2699–2702.

van Hout, R./van de Velde, H. (2001), Patterns of (r) Variation. In: van de Velde, H./van Hout, R. (eds.), *'r-atics: Sociolinguistic, Phonetic and Phonological Characteristics of/r/. Études & travaux* 4 (a special issue). Bruxelles: ILVP, 1–9.

Keating, P. (1998), Word-level Phonetic Variation in Large Speech Corpora. In: Alexiadou, A. (ed.), *ZAS Working Papers in Linguistics* 11, 35–50.

Knowles, G./Wichmann, A./Alderson, P. (eds.) (1996), *Working with Speech: Perspectives on Research into the Lancaster/IBM Spoken English Corpus*. London: Longman.

Knowles, G./Williams, B./Taylor, L. (eds.) (1996), *A Corpus of Formal British English Speech: The Lancaster/IBM Spoken Corpus*. London: Longman.

Maekawa, K. (2003), Corpus of Spontaneous Japanese: Its Design and Evaluation. In: *Proceedings of the ISCA & IEEE Workshop on Spontaenous Processing and Recognition (SSPR2003)*. Tokyo, 7–12.

Maekawa, K./Korso, H./Furui, S./Isahara, H. (2000), Spontaneous Speech Corpus of Japanese. In: *Proceedings of the Second International Conference on Language Resources and Evaluation (LREC-2000)*. Athens, Greece, 947–952.

Martens, J.-P./Binnenpoorte, D./Demuynck, K./Van Parys, R./Laureys, T./Goedertier, W./Duchateau, J. (2002), Word Segmentation in the Spoken Dutch Corpus. In: González Rodriguez, M./ Paz Suárez Araujo, C. (eds.), *Proceedings of the Third International Conference on Language Resources and Evaluation, Las Palmas de Gran Canaria* VI. Paris: European Language Resources Association, 1432–1437.

Martin, P. (2004), WinPitch Corpus. A Text to Speech Alignment and Analysis Tool for Large Multimodal Corpora. In: Oostdijk/Kristoffersen/Sampson 2004, 48–52.

Oostdijk, N./Goedertier, W./Van Eynde, F./Boves, L./Martens, J.-P./Moortgat, M./Baayen, H. (2002), Experiences from the Spoken Dutch Corpus Project. In: González Rodriguez, M./Paz Suárez Araujo, C. (eds.), *Proceedings of the Third International Conference on Language Resources and Evaluation, Las Palmas de Gran Canaria*. Paris: European Language Resources Association, 340–347.

Oostdijk, N./Kristoffersen, G./Sampson, G. (eds.) (2004), *Compiling and Processing Spoken Language Corpora. LREC-2004 Workshop Proceedings*. Paris, France, ELRA.

den Os, E. (1997), SL Corpus Representation. In: Gibbon/Moore/Winski 1997, 146–173.

den Os, E./Boogaart, T./Boves, L./Klabbers, E. (1995), The Dutch Polyphone Corpus. In: *Proceedings Eurospeech'95*. Madrid, Spain, 829–832.

Pallett, D. (2002), The Role of the National Institute of Standards and Technology in DARPA's Broadcast News Continuous Speech Recognition Program. In: *Speech Communication* 37(1–2), 3–14.

Pallett, D./Lamel, L. (2002), Automatic Transcription of Broadcast News Data. In: *Speech Communication* 37(1–2), 1–2.

Peng, S./Beckman, M. (2003), Annotation Conventions and Corpus Design in the Investigation of Spontaneous Speech Prosody in Taiwanese. In: *Proc. Workshop on Spontaneous Speech Processing and Recognition (SSPR2003)*. Tokyo, 17–22.

Pickering, B./Williams, B./Knowles, G. (1996), Analysis of Transcriber Differences in the SEC. In: Knowles/Wichmann/Alderson 1996, 61–105.

Schiel, F./Berger, S./Geumann, A./Weilhammer, K. (1998), The Partitur Format at BAS. In: *Proceedings of the First International Conference on Language Resources and Evaluation* II. Granada, 1295–1301.

Shriberg, E./Stolcke, A./Hakkani-Tür, D./Tür, G. (2000), Prosody-based Automatic Segmentation of Speech into Sentences and Topics. In: *Speech Communication* 32 (1–2), 127–154.

Silverman, K./Beckman, M./Pierrehumbert, J./Ostendorf, M./Wightman, C./Price, P./Hirschberg, J. (1992), ToBI: A Standard Scheme for Labeling Prosody. In: *Proc. ICSLP-92*. Banff, Alberta, Canada, 867–879.

Svartvik, J. (ed.) (1990), *The London-Lund Corpus of Spoken English. Description and Research.* (Lund Studies in English 82.) Lund: Lund University Press.

Syrdal, A. K./Hirschberg, J./McGory, J./Beckman, M. (2001), Automatic ToBI Prediction and Alignment to Speed Manual Labeling of Prosody. In: *Speech Communication* 33(1–2), 135–151.

Tamburini, F./Caini, C. (2004), Automatic Annotation of Speech Corpora for Prosodic Prominence. In: Oostdijk/Kristoffersen/Sampson 2004, 53–58.

Taylor, L. (1996), The Compilation of the Spoken English Corpus. In: Knowles/Williams/Taylor 1996, 20–37.

Weigelt, L./Sadoff, S./Miller, J. (1990), The Plosive/Fricative Distinction: The Voiceless Case. In: *Journal of the Acoustical Society of America* 87, 2729–2737.

Wells, J. C. (1997), SAMPA Computer Readable Phonetic Alphabet. In: Gibbon, D./Moore, *R.*/ Winski, R. (eds.), *Handbook of Standards and Resources for Spoken Language Systems*. Part IV, section B. Berlin and New York: Mouton de Gruyter. Available at: http://www.phon.ucl.ac.uk/home/sampa/.

Wells, J. C./Barry, W./Grice, M./Fourcin, A./Gibbon, D. (1992), *Standard Computer-compatible Transcription*. SAM Stage Report Sen.3 SAM UCL-037, 28 February 1992. SAM (1992) ESPRIT PROJECT 2589 (SAM) Multilingual Speech Input/Output Assessment, Methodology and Standardisation. Final Report. Year Three: 1. III. 91–28. II. 1992. London: University College London.

Williams, B. (1996a), The Status of Corpora as Linguistic Data. In: Knowles/Wichmann/Alderson 1996, 3–19.

Williams, B. (1996b), The Formulation of an Intonation Transcription System for British English. In: Knowles/Wichmann/Alderson 1996, 38–57.

Nelleke Oostdijk and Lou Boves, Nijmegen (The Netherlands)

31. Preprocessing multimodal corpora

1. General aspects

Multimodality

Multimodal corpora are based on recordings of human communication behavior that include several modalities such as lip, eye and head movements, body postures, gestures, hand shapes, facial expressions, and haptics. For a comprehensive taxonomy, see Bernsen (1994). In general, multimodal recordings include speech information as well, and the prosodic components of the speech signal in particular are considered as types of multimodal information, since they are related to higher levels of linguistic processing. In this article the speech signal is treated as part of a multimodal corpus, but we will not elaborate on its special preprocessing requirements. For details we refer to article 12. A special case of multimodal signals is the Sign Language spoken by deaf people. Sign Languages make use of many modalities such as facial expressions, head, body and in particular arm movements and hand shapes to convey information at all linguistic levels.

Although the nature of the production of multimodal signals is still a subject of ongoing research, and although it is known from various studies (cf. Levelt 1980; Richardson 1984) that we may speak of a tight interaction and therefore synchronization between the modalities during their planning in the human mind, we will assume here for reasons of simplicity that each channel is produced in an independent way. This is a generally accepted view for creating multimodal corpora, since it allows the annotator, for example, to work without a priori constraints when creating annotation structures, i.e., there are no predefined dependencies, for example, between gestures and speech utterances.

Resource types

In multimodal corpora we can distinguish between primary resources, which are the recordings containing the multimodal behavior, and secondary resources, which are the various layers of annotations created by researchers depending on the goals of the project. While the primary resources will not be changed, the secondary resources are in general subject to frequent changes and extensions. Although in general a corpus also contains other linguistic data types such as lexica (lexica can be multimodal if they include, for example, a repository of typical gestures), we will focus in this article on multimedia recordings with annotations of multimodal behavior.

Time axis
The different data streams embedded in the recordings are assumed to share one time axis, i. e. if several cameras and selective recording devices are used, for example, to record facial expressions and gestures in parallel, we assume that the clocks of the recording devices are synchronized. The basic annotations will then refer to the underlying master time. Higher levels of annotations can refer to lower levels either by referring to moments in time or by referring to structural elements in other annotations.

In this article we will therefore first discuss all aspects that are relevant for creating primary resources (section 2). Second, we will describe methods to create annotated sessions as basic units of digital corpora on computers. Third, we will elaborate on creating complex manual annotations for these sessions as the most relevant secondary resource types in multimodal corpora. Fourth, we will briefly describe the state of the art in tools that allow creating annotations. Fifth, we will discuss metadata schemes for multimodal session bundles. Finally, definitions of a number of concepts that are used in this article are given (section 7).

2. Recording phase

2.1. Recording principles

Time axis
Multimodal observations in general are created by using various recording devices, e. g. one or several video cameras to record the movements of body parts from different perspectives, a selective spot recording device to record the exact movements of the pointing finger, etc. All these devices operate on their own time clocks and cannot normally be started at exactly the same moment in time. However, linguistic annotation work has to be based on one underlying time axis. Creating one unified time axis can be achieved in several ways: (1) In modern multimedia labs the start of the recording devices is synchronized electronically where possible, ensuring that all recordings share the same starting point ($t = 0$). (2) Some devices such as high-quality video cameras can be controlled by a master sync. One camera generates the master clock signal for all other cameras assuring that all video frames are taken at exactly the same moment in time. (3) If there are no such possibilities for external timing control the usual practice is to generate an audio/visual signal like clapping one's hands and record it with all devices, or use electronic signals that are recorded in parallel. (4) To do time alignment between the different streams, two moments in time are required – one being the start time. One clock signal can be used as master and for all other clock signals mapping constants can be calculated. Depending on accuracy requirements, the axis transformation can lead to a calculation of new signal values. The simplest case is shown in Figure 31.1, where two samples were taken at time moments t_i and t_{i+1}. The axis transformation may require calculating a new value at t_i^*. Since we do not know the exact signal at that moment the easiest way is to estimate this using linear interpolation. More accurate estimators apply higher order polynomials or are based on underlying mathematical models.

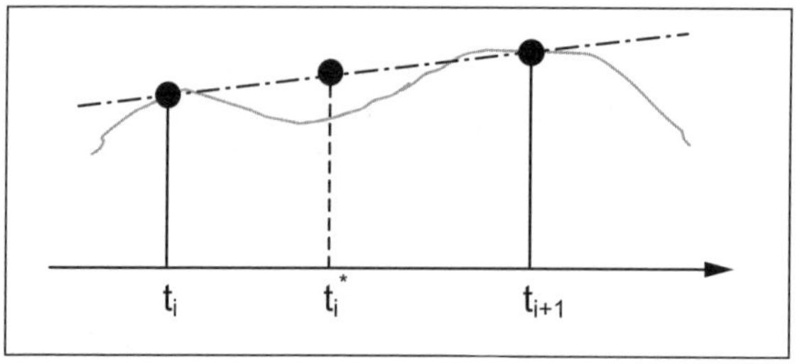

Fig. 31.1.

In contrast to the speech signal, which can be described on the physical level as a one-dimensional signal (sound pressure over time), other multimodal signals are mostly multidimensional. Gestures or Signs, for example, are produced in 3-dimensional space over time. Many recording devices, as for example video cameras, however, only give a 2-dimensional representation of the signal. This limitation can be overcome by using two 2-dimensional devices that are arranged so that their main observation axes form an angle between 0 and 90 degrees ($0 < \alpha < = 90°$). If all geometrical parameters are known, a reconstruction of the 3rd dimension is possible. The general rule is that this reconstruction becomes more accurate the larger the angle is. On the other hand the observation space in the 3rd dimension, the space in which the measurement object can move and will still be recorded with the necessary accuracy, becomes smaller (cf. Woltring 1977).

Sampling principles

In general, measurements of all sorts have to deal with noise and measurement errors. For example, infrared signals are generally known to be noisy due to unexpected reflections, unknown light sources and a high degree of inherent signal noise. Filters can be applied to reduce the noise components. Also, the digitization process itself introduces noise and errors. A smooth eye movement, for example, will be transformed into a step function where we assume that the eye is moved stepwise at equidistant moments in time and where the real positions are associated with a digital number that is close to the real value. It is a well-known principle that we have to be sure that the sample frequency is at least twice as high as the highest frequency component in the signal that we want to register (Nyquist's theorem). Given that we know the highest frequency signal component (f_{max}) we want to register, we should filter out any higher components to not introduce so-called aliasing errors, which are frequency components higher than the sampling frequency mirrored back into the recording $f_{mirror} = f_{comp} \sim f_{sample}$. In those cases where the recording of the position of a body part has to be used to calculate velocity and acceleration, one has to be aware of the fact that the noise component is amplified by the third power (cf. Gustafsson/Lanshammar 1977). In summary, we can say that filtering plays an essential role in preprocessing multimodal corpora. The corpus creators have to be aware of the basic mathematical foundations of digitization and the potential effects on the results. These fundamental digital signal processing principles are described comprehensively in Oppenheim/Schafer (1975) and Rabiner/Gold (1975).

Calibration

For all selective devices that produce quantitative data, a calibration phase has to occur. During the calibration phase a well-known and controlled signal is used to calculate system parameters that allow mapping the recorded values to the application scene. For holistic recordings, such as video, calibration is generally not required, since the recordings show the complete context and human analyzers have to do the analysis in any case. Only for cases where the video signal is going to be used to extract quantitative results (e. g. distance of an arm movement) does a calibration have to be carried out for a given camera position.

2.2. Recording devices

While video cameras record series of frames with qualitative and holistic type of information at a limited sample frequency (50 Hz), selective spot recording devices are used to record the movements of special body parts in a quantitative manner and mostly at a higher frequency. Depending on the modality to be recorded, various techniques can be applied: (1) For the recording of gestures, for example ultrasonic or infrared devices are very popular. Small ultrasonic or infrared emitters are placed on the relevant body parts and appropriate sensors such as ultrasonic microphones (http://www.zebris.de/) or infrared light sensitive cameras (http://www.innovision-systems.com/Products-SelSpot.aspx) are used to detect the location of the emitters. Depending on the technology used, the sample frequencies for such devices can be considerably higher than those of video recordings. (2) To record hand shapes the data glove device (http://www.vrealities.com/glove.html) is very popular. In this device the tensions in resistors placed at the joints of the fingers are used to calculate angles. With the help of an underlying model of the hand, complex hand shapes can be reconstructed from all angle values. (3) To record eye movements, video registration techniques are used most often, although the video frame rate is not fast enough to detect the fastest components of saccadic movements. Here mostly infrared light is emitted to the human eye, and infrared sensitive cameras are used to register reflections such as from the retina (through the iris) and the cornea (http://www.smi.de/). In the case of one reflection, such as that from the retina, head movements cannot be compensated for. With a second reflection, such as that of the cornea, a head movement invariant direction vector can be calculated. Here special reflections, light circles/ellipsoids from the retina and cornea reflections, on a comparatively dark background, can be detected to automatically determine eye gaze. (4) The reflection principle can be applied to many different registrations. Reflectors can be fixed to body parts and lights can be used to yield light spots that can be automatically detected in a video recording. Such a system was offered by the company Hamamatsu Photonics. (5) Pointing gestures can be automatically detected if hand shapes can be clearly identified, using a dark background for the video recordings for example (cf. Nölker/Ritter 1999). (6) Changes in the magnetic field can be recorded if metallic objects change their position. This technique is applied for head movement measurements, for example (http://www.polhemus.com/). (7) Velocity sensors can be used to measure the velocity of a body part; however, the position cannot be reconstructed (http://www.wilcoxon.com/vi_index.cfm/CatS_ID=28). An excellent overview of various sensor systems was created by Daniel Thalmann (http://vrlab.epfl.ch/~thalmann/VR/VRcourse_GestureRecognition_files/frame.htm).

Crucial points in multimodal recordings are the visibility of all relevant parts that have to be recorded and the influence of the measurement technique on the object to be recorded. When observing video recordings of Sign Language, for example, we cannot often see all fingers due to hand rotations. But video cameras can be placed in a way that they observe the scene as human eyes do in a natural scene. We can therefore assume that the movement of the fingers at that moment is not relevant and that we are updating a model of the complete hand in our mind so that we still have a holistic image of the scene. Selective techniques, where emitters are for example positioned on a finger create a problem in so far as hand rotations may lead to erroneous and missing signal values. This can be compensated for by mounting two or even more such emitters on the finger so that at least one will be visible. In such cases an underlying model of the body part will allow to smoothen the discontinuities in the signal.

Techniques also differ in the way they influence the subjects. Mounting emitters on various body parts and fixing the necessary cables will always have an influence on movement patterns. Before generating a multimodal corpus one has to investigate in how far the measurement method will influence the results of the intended studies. The most neutral technique in this respect is to make video recordings. However, if no special light effects are used, almost any analysis will require time consuming manual annotation work. In general, pilot studies have to be carried out to investigate these influences.

As has been indicated, there is a large variety of recording methods and devices for multimodal behavior that can be used, depending on the type of signal to be registered and on the type of analysis planned. It is impossible to give a comprehensive account of all methods and devices. A fundamental difference can be drawn between holistic devices such as video cameras where only qualitative information is available, but where the context is also recorded, and selective devices where highly reduced, but quantitative information is gathered.

Video cameras can be widely used as has been indicated, and therefore some differences between camera types will be described. The principle is that light waves are directed to light sensitive targets (light sensitive semiconductor devices) via lenses and light filters. The photons hitting the lateral target create a sensation that can be measured. To achieve a stable sensation and to improve the signal to noise ratio, the sensations have to be integrated for a small time fragment (Δt). It is assumed that the light emitting objects do not move in this time or that they only move with a limited velocity, since otherwise the image will be noisy and the representation of the object will become blurred. Any technique that increases the amount of light hitting the target chip or that reduces the amount of light necessary to create a stable sensation will allow a reduction of the integration time, and therefore a faster recording of movements. Expensive cameras therefore have excellent optics and very sensitive targets for the chosen frequency range of the light.

The spatial resolution of the camera, i. e. the amount of distinguishable pixels on the sensitive targets, and the size of the mapped object on the target also play an important role. Normal consumer video cameras that are often sufficient to record human behavior are available in two types: (1) with one sensitive target or (2) with three of them. In the first case the target is used to record all three basic colors, i. e. the available pixels on the target are divided. In the latter case there is one target for each basic color which results in a higher resolution. Any of the indicated quality improvements is associated with higher costs.

Of course, it is important to choose geometrical and camera parameters so that the image of the object under investigation has a maximal size on the video target. This guarantees that even details can be analyzed. If for example facial expressions are going to be analyzed, it makes sense to have a video camera setup so that the image of the head covers almost the entire target. Some space has to be left to cope with head movements. If on the other hand Sign Language has to be studied, the recording person has to make sure that all arm and body movements are recorded. This could mean that the resolution for analyzing facial expressions is no longer sufficient. In conflicting cases it is recommended to use multiple synchronized cameras.

2.3. Recording formats and media

Selective recording devices generate highly reduced data and for control and recording purposes they are generally connected directly with computers. Therefore, the generated data can be stored and processed on computers immediately. For video signals the situation is different. The data rate for standard digital video is about 227 Mbit/sec according to ITU-R601 (http://de.wikipedia.org/wiki/CCIR_601) – in general too much to be transferred to and to be stored on computers. Two techniques can be observed: (1) When video is used as the recording technique, but only selective points in the video information are of interest, some real-time processing will be carried out in fast pre-processing units. This method is for example applied in several eye trackers where the pre-processing units detect the reflections in the video signal, calculate their mid points and calculate the final gaze values. Only these values are then sent to the computer to be stored (http://www.sr-research.com/). (2) The complete PAL (Phase Alternating Line Color Coding Standard, http://de.wikipedia.org/wiki/Phase_Alternating_Line) information is highly compressed and first stored on a separate storage medium such as a MiniDV tape or DVD-R. Currently, the most popular format is Digital Video (http://de.wikipedia.org/wiki/Digital_Video), since almost all consumer camcorders support this format. It is optimized for processing on small devices like camcorders and reduces the complete video stream to about 35 Mbit/sec. First cameras are now on the market that directly produce MPEG2 streams at about 6 Mbit/sec which is an open and widely supported standard. Currently, MPEG2 is seen as the backend video format for archiving and digital libraries, and it is supported by a wide range of software products. However, this will change, since video representation technology is still a subject of dynamic developments. Despite the large difference in capacity both compression formats (DV and MPEG2) yield almost the same quality and there is software that allows transforming DV into MPEG2 streams. Both encoding types can be stored on computers, however, MPEG2 is currently being used for long-term preservation or corpus building.

The storage media used for video recordings are currently MiniDV tapes and increasingly often DVD-R. In general, MiniDV tapes allow DV recordings of 90 minutes. A DVD-R can store about 2 hours of MPEG2 streams.

2.4. Elicitation of multimodal behavior

The generation of multimodal corpora requires a clear elicitation strategy that is driven by the goals of the research. For gesture research, for example, one can address the questions (1) how gestures are used to compensate for the weakness of verbal expressions in route directions, (2) how gestures are used to draw the attention of the listener or (3) how gesture planning interacts with speech planning in human interaction. For each of these questions different elicitation strategies have to be applied. For the first question normal passengers can be asked to describe the route to a well-known location and normal observation methods will be sufficient. For the second question one may think of a special laboratory situation where dynamic visual stimuli are offered to create a number of gestures that is statistically sufficient. Still, normal observation methods may be used. The third question addresses the process of speech act planning in the human mind, i. e. exact timing control and interruptions during the planning phase will require special laboratory setups and special techniques such as measuring the gesture, for example, with an ultrasonic device registering the arm movements at a 2 ms interval or even less. Calculating the moment of highest acceleration and changing the stimuli at that moment in time is an adequate elicitation technique. Often laboratories are setup to study special multimodal phenomena such as in the studies of Levelt/Richardson (1984), de Ruiter et al. (2003) or within the SMARTKOM project (http://www.smartkom.org/).

3. Computer-based media handling

3.1. Transmission principles

As has already been indicated, most of the equipment for multimodal recordings that is used today generates digital data, i. e. analog behavior produced by verbal and nonverbal articulators is sampled at discrete moments in time and stored as discrete digital values. Therefore, the recordings can easily be transmitted to computers and further be processed. Because "bytes" are the basic unit of storing and processing in present-day computers, data is often generated in chunks of bytes. The order of bytes, if several are involved in encoding a phenomenon, is defined by the involved software layers (operating system, application).

Multimodal sensors generate sequences of bytes that are transferred via interfaces to the computer. The type of interface is dependent on the transmission bandwidth and the convenience of its development and production. For devices with high speed requirements, such as for example in eye trackers where video information has to be transmitted and processed in real-time, special interface boards will be used that do some form of preprocessing, and these will be directly connected to a high-speed bus of the computer. For most multimodal applications standard computer interfaces such as serial port, parallel port, USB (Universal Serial Bus, http://de.wikipedia.org/wiki/Universal_Serial_Bus), Ethernet, or i-link (http://de.wikipedia.org/wiki/FireWire) are sufficient. In particular the USB link is becoming very popular and its new version (USB 2.0) offers a high speed (up to 480 Mbit/sec), a short latency and off-the-shelf chipsets. Other interface types such as serial and parallel port will be less supported. For fast transmissions such as for video signals from camcorders the i-link was designed, and is supported by almost all DV camcorders. Besides some basic handshaking it is the task of the software (low-level drivers or applications) to determine how reliable the transmission has to be. For the video transmission via the i-link there is often no control whether all information was correctly received, which seems to be a design problem in the i-link protocol. It is known that Adobe Premiere (http://www.adobe.com/de/products/premiere/) at least gives a warning when data was missed. Some freely available capturing programs, however, do not carry out this check, i. e., if the receiving computer is in a moment of heavy workload due to parallel processes one cannot be sure that the stored video stream is complete and therefore without a distortion of the time axis. Depending on the requirements of the study, these aspects have to be investigated carefully.

3.2. Encoding principles

For the encoding of multimodal information many strategies are used on top of the above mentioned byte packaging. There are many variants that are dependent on the nature of the phenomena, the amount of pre-processing and other aspects. For modern eye trackers, for example, we will not only get the gaze position of one (or two) eyes as x and y coordinates for every sample (the sample frequency is dependent on the time resolution of the camera, $f_s <= 50$ Hz), but also the fixations together with time stamps and statistics. Fixations are those eye movement patterns where the eye rests and focuses on an object for some period of time. For such eye trackers we have a regular stream of x and y coordinates, and at irregular moments additional fixation information. Type information or packaging allows differentiating between the two streams.

Since video information is very frequently used and highly standardized, the video encoding principles will be described in more detail. It was already indicated that in general MPEG2 is currently seen as the backend format for multimodal corpora and for long-term preservation. MPEG2 is an encoding standard for video streams with embedded audio created by the Moving Picture Expert Group (MPEG, http://www.chiariglione.org/mpeg/). Its quality is comparable to S-VHS video. It is possible to create MPEG1 and MPEG4 streams from MPEG2. MPEG1 is an older audio/video encoding standard that arose with the emergence of CD-ROMs, has a bit rate of about 1.5 Mbit/sec and has a quality comparable to VHS. MPEG4 is the new standard for Internet streaming of audio/video information and allows the selection of different qualities (> = 500 kbit/sec) for different types of transmission channels. Its video encoding is better than that of MPEG1, i. e. 500 kbit/sec MPEG4 streams have a comparable quality to 1.5 Mbit/sec MPEG1 streams. Actually, MPEG4 is not just a standard for video en/decoding, but also introduced the notion of different media objects that can be combined on the client side based on user wishes. We will not elaborate on these aspects, but refer the reader to the MPEG4 documentation (http://www.chiariglione.org/mpeg/standards/mpeg-4/mpeg-4.htm). It should be noted that MPEG1 just delivers one frame per 40 ms, i. e. no difference is made between half-frames. MPEG2 allows encoding the information per half-frame, i. e. a frame rate of 20 ms is supported.

All MPEG compression algorithms share the same basic principles of video encoding in so far that they apply two compression schemes: (1) Each video frame is subject to a deletion of high frequency components, i. e. sharp transitions are blurred, and (2) across frames compression techniques are used that reduce redundant information such as constant backgrounds. Groups of pictures (GoP) are calculated which consist of one complete key frame (i frame) and a number of predictive frames (p and b frames) that only contain changing information. In general, the user can determine the length of the GoP.

Due to these encoding principles, MPEG streams are not easy to handle when fragments are accessed. If in a streaming application a fragment has to be displayed starting with a frame within a GoP, the media player has to make sure that the previous key frame is taken first, and then all predictive frames have to be used to calculate the actual image. Only when the first frame of the selected fragment has been calculated can the media player start visualizing the stream.

Another point of concern is the compression and packaging of the audio information in the MPEG stream. MPEG2 uses MP3 Level 2 as an audio compression format, which is based on a psychoacoustic analysis of the acoustic information. It is claimed that MP3 reduces all components that are not audible to the human ear, i. e. filtering in the frequency and time domain is applied. Different compression levels can be set. For 192 kbit/sec some studies (cf. van Son 2002) have shown that the normal linguistic type of analysis (spectrogram, pitch, formants) can be carried out without too substantial errors. If compressed audio is not acceptable as in cases where long-term preservation is a must, then a separate linear PCM (Pulse Code Modulation, http://en.wikipedia.org/wiki/Pulse-code_modulation) stream has to be generated during capturing from DV. In multimodal research where time accuracy plays an important role one has to check carefully what exactly the relation between the video and the audio information is. Experience shows that MPEG decoders vary in the way they time align the audio and the video streams. In MPEG1 the misalignment can be greater than 30 msec. The compensation factor to be used can only be estimated when a test tape with an audio/visual transient signal (e. g. a clap of the hand) is processed and analyzed. There are a couple of other video encoding standards such as Cinepak (http://de.wikipedia.org/wiki/Cinepak) and Sorensen (http://www.sorensonmedia.com/) which are not that common and therefore will not be discussed here. The different audio encoding principles are dealt with in article 11.

There is enough software available to transform from DV to MPEG2 streams and from MPEG2 to MPEG1 and MPEG4. For the MPEG algorithms a large number of parameters such as GoP and aspect ratio can be set, i. e. for the transformation step one has to be aware of the most important parameters to create useful output. Since writing correct video codec software is still an art, one has to check the results of a new codec to be sure that the transformation process delivers correct streams.

3.3. Media file formats

Media encoders/decoders (codecs) define how acoustic and visual information is transformed into bit streams and how these are packaged into bytes. File formats determine how these bytes are packaged into files, i. e. which header information is used and how bytes are packaged into words. For video streams, file formats such as AVI (http://de.wikipedia.org/wiki/Audio_Video_Interleave), MOV (http://de.wikipedia.org/wiki/QuickTime) and MPG (http://de.wikipedia.org/wiki/Containerformat) are very popular. Most of the high-quality software products such as Adobe Premiere allow the user to carry out file format conversion. Thus, when specifying the nature of a video object completely one has to specify the file format and the codec used, since an AVI file can include MPEG1, MPEG4, MPEG2 or other streams.

It has to be mentioned that there are more complex media objects. Quicktime and SMIL (http://www.w3.org/TR/SMIL2/) resources can include various tracks of information including pointers that specify the timing relationships between the tracks. With appropriate players these complex resources can be presented. SMIL objects for example can contain layers of annotations as sub-titles. SMIL players such as RealVideo (http://germany.real.com) will show the video, present the audio and at correct moments in time update the sub-title information. The annotation and reference information is contained in XML files. More elaborate web-based exploitation frameworks for annotated media files are currently under development (http://www.mpi.nl/annex).

3.4. Media streaming

The Internet becomes increasingly important for delivering information of all sorts including media. The normal applications make use of the HTTP protocol to select and transmit a resource which can be an HTML-based web-site or a document included as a reference. At the client side the browser will start additional software to visualize the non-HTML resources. In the case of a video stream it will start one of the well known media players such as Windows Media Player, Quicktime or RealVideo. In general this means that a whole resource will first be downloaded and then be played. Some players already support playing while the remaining part of the resource is still being downloaded. The protocol to download the media streams is still HTTP, which is not very efficient due to the protocol overhead.

In many applications it is not useful to play the whole media resource. In particular in multimodal corpora one would like to search for a specific behavioral pattern, get a number of fragments as hits and then play only these fragments. In this case users want to play a media stream from a point t_i to t_{i+1}. Media streaming servers and clients support this feature and they also ensure that media is presented while the rest is downloaded. Further, a more efficient protocol is used, Real Time Streaming Protocol (RTSP, http://www.rtsp.org/), which reduces the overhead, but therefore introduces a time stamp for each package, in order to be able to reconstruct the proper sequence in case of network problems. Protocols such as RTSP also support local caching to handle repetitions more efficiently. Not all media servers and clients support the streaming feature yet. The open source Darwin streaming media server (http://developer.apple.com/opensource/server/str) and the Quicktime client are able to communicate with each other; however, only MPEG4 is supported, i. e. for each media object in the corpus an MPEG4 stream has to be generated beforehand. RealVideo also has a streaming server-client combination; however, the server is not freely available and the codec is proprietary.

4. Multimodal annotation

Annotation models underlie all multimodal annotation representation schemes and determine their expressive power. They are not of primary interest to the end user, since the user will rely on tools that allow creating, manipulating and analyzing annotations. However, the corpus creator has to know in advance whether the tools, and with them their underlying annotation model, are powerful enough to handle all phenomena that are going to be described.

Based on the insights into the complexity of annotation structures for multimodal resources, a few general models have been developed in the last five years. A first workshop on formal annotation schemes was held at LREC 2000 (http://www.lrec-conf.org/lrec2000/www.icp.inpg.fr/ELRA/lrec2000.html). In this section we will discuss three models in more detail: (1) the Annotation Graph Model (AG) by Bird/Liberman (2001), (2) the Abstract Corpus Model (ACM) worked out by Brugman/Wittenburg (2001) and (3) the Language Annotation Framework (cf. Ide/Romary 2003), which is part of the ISO TC37/SC4 standardization work. Other important contributions such as TIPSTER (http://cs.nyu.edu/cs/faculty/grishman/tipster.html), EMU (http://emu.sourceforge.net/) and TIGER (http://www.ims.uni-stuttgart.de/projekte/TIGER/) will not be dealt with in detail, since they were worked out to cover special phenomena as they occur in Treebanks, for example, and corpora generated by NLP (Natural Language Processing) com ponents. XCES (Corpus Encoding Standard, http://www.cs.vassar.edu/XCES/) was worked out as a recommendation mainly for textual corpora. The NITE Object Model (http://www.ltg.ed.ac.uk/NITE/) covers aspects as discussed by AG and ACM.

As has been indicated above, multimodal corpora are based on recording bundles that cover the primary observations created with different devices. We assume that appropriate session bundles were created, i. e. the different streams were prepared in such a way that they share the same starting point and the same time axis (see Figure 31.2).

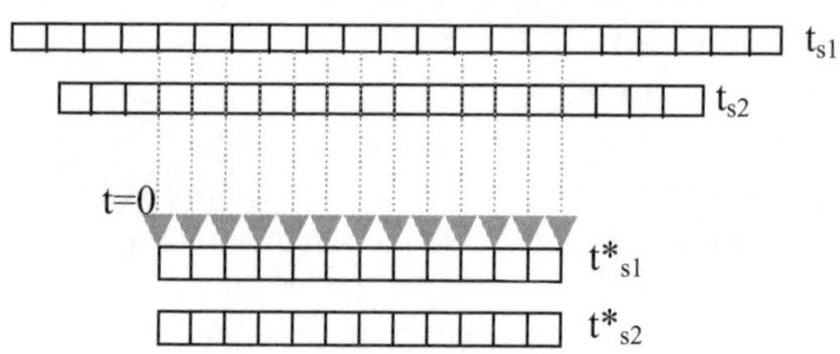

Fig. 31.2: The process of generating a session bundle from the original streams. A fragment is selected that contains the relevant information. The clock t_{s2} is taken as the master clock, i. e. $t_{s2} = t^*_{s2} = t^*_{s1}$, and $t = 0$ is defined. Appropriate samples are generated from stream 1 by interpolation

The session bundle concept is the basis of linguistic analysis that results in linguistic annotations at various levels, i. e. in the following section we assume time-aligned media signals such that all time references are unambiguous.

4.1. Annotation graph model

In their 2001 paper "A Formal Framework for Linguistic Annotation", Bird/Liberman describe the commonalities between the logical structure of the linguistic annotations that they found in many different resources. Based on this broad analysis of existing annotation schemes they developed the Annotation Graph Model (AG) as an abstract formalism. According to AG, annotations can be seen as labeled directed acyclic graphs, where ordered nodes segment the stream of information at some level of linguistic analysis and arc labels can be attributed with type and content information. Some nodes –

anchored nodes – are linked to points in time. Where no time anchoring is given nodes are ordered according to the natural sequence of items. The same is true for cases where the annotations are not continuous as is often the case when for example silences occur which are not explicitly annotated. Seemingly independent parallel streams are indicated by graphs at multiple layers (see Figure 31.3).

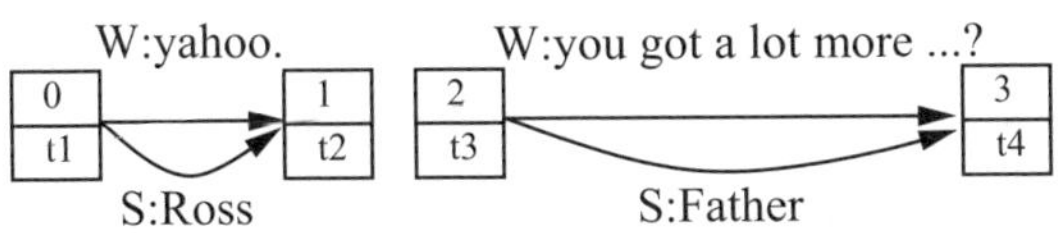

Fig. 31.3: A simple example cited from Bird/Liberman (2001). It includes two utterances that each have a start and end time, i. e. the nodes segmenting the information are time anchored. There is no annotation, however, that connects the two utterances. Further, the two branches each include an indication who the speaker is and what the speaker is saying

Bird/Liberman show how AGs can be represented by XML structures and relational tables. Since the basic AG formalism is based on algebra, queries can be easily formulated using, for example, SQL.

The basic AG formalism does not make statements about hierarchical dependencies and does not include cross-references. Both can lead to annotation structures that are more difficult to maintain and to query.

4.2. Abstract Corpus Model

Brugman/Wittenburg (2001) started their work on the Abstract Corpus Model by analyzing the structural complexity multimodal annotation systems can have, and after several years of experience with multimodal annotations. The goal was to find an abstract framework underlying different annotation systems in use, so that a unifying tool for annotation and exploration could be built. Multimodal recordings contain information from different channels that are assumed to be independent. This means that for example eye, speech articulator and arm movements will occur asynchronously. Any form of overlap can occur as is indicated in Figure 31.4.

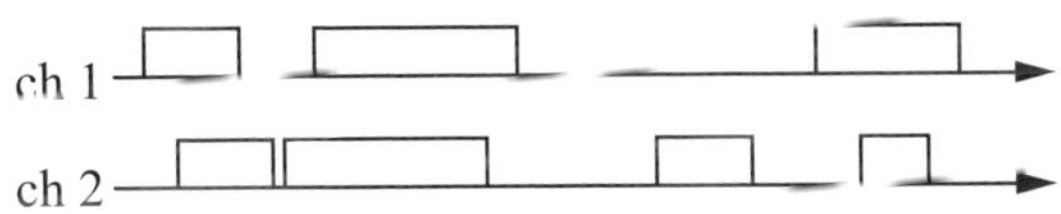

Fig. 31.4: Activities of two multimodal channels that are obviously independent, i. e. a fixation of the eye on an object and arm movements can show any type of overlap

Of course, annotations can include dependencies that will lead to hierarchical annotations as they are well known in speech corpora where the sentence annotation includes the words that are part of the sentence. Words again can be subdivided into morphemes etc., as is shown in Figure 31.5.

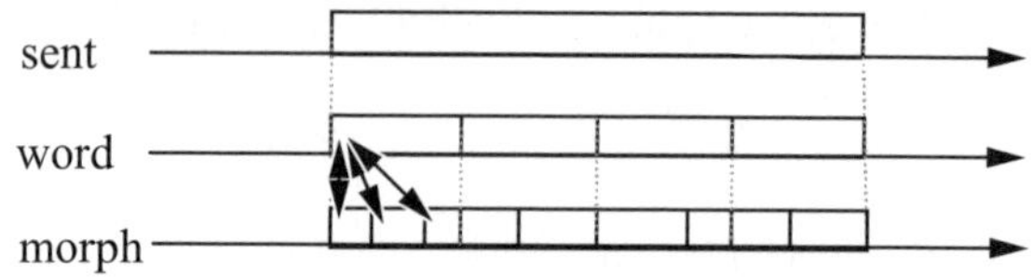

Fig. 31.5: Annotations on dependent tiers that inherit the segment boundaries from the parent tier and in doing so create hierarchical structures as they are common in linguistics

The annotation structures indicated in Figures 31.4 and 31.5 are not yet sufficient to describe all occurring phenomena. Both figures suggest that all segment boundaries refer to moments in time. This, however, is in most cases not true, since precise time alignment is a costly process, i. e. in many cases only larger fragments such as utterances or gestures have time markers. In hierarchical structures the child annotations point to the ID of the corresponding parent segment as is indicated by the arrows in Figure 31.5, i. e. a reference method is required. Hierarchical dependency is an attribute of tier types in ACM, since the information is orthogonal to sequential or temporal order. In addition, it is known that in many cases cross-references are necessary to mark linguistic relationships of all types. The most general case is that we interpret a relation as another annotation type that allows to establish references to several other annotations on one or several different tiers. For these different reference types the same mechanism can be used.

Reference mechanisms are difficult to handle for example in querying, since they could even lead to loops. It is left up to the applications to deal with hierarchies and references in a suitable way. Dependencies, for example, are relevant to consider when shifting an annotation. If the shift operation effects an annotation on a parent tier, it has to be assured that all dependent annotations that inherit timing information are shifted correspondingly, i. e. the tool has to make use of the dependency information in the tier type definition. Searching can include distances of two annotation patterns in terms of time or linguistic units. For dependent tiers it has to be clarified what "distance" in terms of linguistic units actually means.

The discussed structural elements allow the user to create complex annotations as they will occur in multimodal corpora. The ACM was implemented as a set of Java classes that are part of the ELAN annotation tool which was and is applied for various different linguistic projects including hierarchical linguistic encodings and independent multimodal streams. An XML schema is available that allows to make ACM based annotations persistent (http://www.mpi.nl/lat).

4.3. Linguistic Annotation Framework

In 2002 the new ISO TC37/SC4 was set up to work out standards for language resource management. One of the topics to deal with was to define the Linguistic Annotation Framework (LAF) as a generalization of existing annotation schemes. Therefore, its goal is comparable to the work described in sections 4.1. and 4.2. The basic AG model is simple and therefore very convincing; however, it misses a few features that are essential for practical multimodal annotations. This was also stated by Teich/Hansen/Fankhauser (2001). The ACM work was tested on a number of major existing annotation schemes such as those used by CHILDES (http://childes.psy.cmu.edu/), SHOEBOX (http://www.sil.org/computing/shoebox/) and Transcriber (http://trans.sourceforge.net/en/presentation.php), its compliance with AG was shown, and it was tested in many different multimodal studies, but it does not claim completeness. It is the task of the new ISO sub-committee to work on generalization and to include the work of projects such as MATE/NITE, ATLAS (http://sourceforge.net/projects/jatlas/) and MPEG7 (http://www.chiariglione.org/mpeg/standards/mpeg-7/mpeg-7.htm).

4.4. Annotation formats and containers

In section 4.3. the formal principles of annotation schemes were discussed. They can be modeled with modern modeling frameworks such as UML (Universal Modeling Language, http://www.uml-forum.com/) and can be implemented in all their complexity as classes with the help of modern programming languages. Finally, however, after the user has created annotations with the help of some tool supporting a specific annotation model, the complex annotations have to be made persistent in some format and stored in a container. These two aspects cannot be separated for all concrete solutions.

Currently, three solutions are discussed mostly: (1) The complex annotations can be serialized into XML tree structures and stored in the form of separate files or within an XML database. (2) The annotations are stored in the form of relational tables in a relational database management system. (3) The annotations are serialized as Resource Description Framework (RDF, http://www.w3.org/RDF/) assertions which are basically triples and can be stored for example with the help of a relational database management system. All three solutions have their advantages and disadvantages and with the help of transformations they can be converted into each other.

The usage of RDF makes sense where an open relational space is the primary goal such as in ontologies and where relationships defined by structure such as can be found in annotation systems are not so prominent.

XML documents are tree-structured, but together with the Xlink mechanism (http://www.w3.org/TR/xlink/) complex annotations such as those indicated above can be represented. XML-based representations have the advantage that the format is well-described, that they are human readable and therefore acceptable for long-term preservation purposes and that XML is widely agreed upon as an open interchange format. If a DTD (http://de.wikipedia.org/wiki/Dokumenttypdefinition) describing the structure of the XML document is available, or an XML Schema (http://www.w3.org/XML/Schema), which in addition also allows constraining the values, a formal validation can be done. A typical example is given by the EAF schema. XML-files are not suitable for searching directly except if they are stored in an XML database as a special container type. However, then some of the above mentioned advantages are lost, since the database system is a shell encapsulating the content. The type of encapsulation may be proprietary.

Relational databases are special containers based on the entity-relationship data model, i. e. annotations will be stored as a set of related tables. The format these tables are stored in is highly optimized for search and access performance and therefore encapsulated and not human readable. Relational database management systems can be seen as mature transaction machines also offering excellent multi-user access capabilities. Due to the encapsulation, the export possibilities are of extreme importance. It is known that for basically hierarchical documents with deep nesting structures, a proliferation of tables will occur that may lead to non-optimal access patterns.

For the management of corpora or other linguistic data types except for ontologies, both format types are used. In areas where open access and long-term preservation is the primary issue, XML files are the primary choice. Examples are the well-known CHILD ES corpus which was stored as plain text and is now being transformed to XML, the Spoken Dutch Corpus (cf. Oostdijk/Broeder 2003 and article 29), the DOBES archive (http://www.mpi.nl/dobes) and many others.

Relational databases have been used for projects with centralized, highly structured and not sequentially ordered data such as lexica (CELEX, http://www.ru.nl/celex/), typological databases and metadata, but became more popular during the last decade in particular for individually run projects due to the nice user interface building tools. Database solutions are centralized solutions that are in general not so attractive in the world of language resources.

Several projects make use of the advantages of both solutions. For the large and distributed IMDI metadata repository, for example, the individual metadata descriptions are available primarily as XML files to guarantee openness, simplicity and easy integration. For fast searching, however, relational databases are generated by harvesting all metadata records via OAIPMH (http://www.openarchives.org/OAI/openarchivesprotocol.html) type principles. The same principle is applied for the DOBES language resource archive where the long-term preservation requirement and a human readable and open format for all annotations is of primary relevance. The annotations are stored as XML files. For fast searching on the content, however, all annotation data is integrated into fast indexes.

The decision about the primary format and container type is important for every project, since it determines the tools to be used and the type of programming required. It has to be kept in mind that for relational databases the logical structure is kept in tables as well, i. e. when exporting the included data to XML, there is in general no XML schema available and the resulting format is a simple table-like XML representation.

In the future, Web-Services (http://www.w3.org/2002/ws/) will play an important role in accessing corpora independent of their underlying container format. Services such as the access to language resources will be registered with the help of metadata descriptions (UDDI, http://www.uddi.org/) and the offering has to be specified in detail in a kind of programming interface (WSDL, http://www.w3.org/TR/wsdl), i. e. the accessible content and its structure have to be made explicit, so that the underlying container format is not relevant. Any other service can make use of these specifications when accessing the data. It is the web service and the wrappers that will be used to extract the data from the underlying container and to offer it in the way described by the interface specification. This new technology will make the corpora available for Semantic Web like applications.

4.5. Stand-off annotation principle

For many reasons it makes sense to store layers of annotations in different files although they may be closely related. Different annotation layers may be created and maintained by different groups of people as was done for example in the Dutch Spoken Corpus project. The transcription of the spoken utterances was done by specialists, the tokenization and part-of-speech tagging by others with the help of special software. For easy management purposes these groups should then operate as independently as possible and not interfere with the activities of others. Referencing mechanisms as indicated in sections 4.1. and 4.2. can be applied in XML encoded files within and across files.

To avoid getting a proliferation of files, which may also lead to inefficient management, projects normally apply a mixed strategy, i. e. some annotation layers created and maintained by the same group of people may be integrated into one file, while others are kept separate. Increasingly often it will happen that new groups will re-use existing resources and produce improved annotations or add completely new types of annotations. Here too it makes sense not to allow the users to touch the existing files, but to let them create their own ones. For good tools this should not create content access and visualization problems.

In the domain of relational databases this aspect is not relevant, since views and additional tables or fields can be created with differing access attributes. However, since the database approach is centralized, users cannot create these additional layers of information on their own computer and integrate them as easily with other resources.

4.6. Interoperability and presentation

It is obvious that we will be confronted with many different structures in the area of language resources in the future, and that a large variety of linguistic concepts will be used to encode the linguistic phenomena. This raises the question of interoperability at the technical encoding, the structural and the semantic levels, when resources are combined for example for cross-corpus searches.

At the character level there is a trend towards using UNICODE, and there will be improved services for the conversion of legacy character sets to UNICODE. At the structural level we can expect that XML will be used increasingly often and that projects will either make use of some generalized schemas or take the time to define their own schemas. The existence of a schema will allow other people to validate a given resource and to access sub-structures. It will also allow users to convert a given structure into another one by defining and using XSLT styleguides (http://www.w3.org/TR/xslt). Also with respect to structural mapping we can assume that there will be improved services to convert legacy formats into XML structures. However, in some cases the transformation from an XML structured file into another XML structure will be non-trivial, not free from loss of information, and require decisions and procedural treatment.

Transformation templates and style guides will also allow the creation of different presentation formats from XML-structured files. However, to generate printouts in a professional layout, as is required for example for written dictionaries, an appropriate tool has to be made available.

The most problematic aspect for interoperability is the mapping between different linguistic concepts that underlie the annotation tiers, lexical attributes and metadata elements, and that are used as values. Standardizing linguistic encoding seems to be impossible given the differences in languages and in theories, and given the fact that linguists often need flexibility for exploration while coding, in particular in the area of multimodal signals. Nevertheless, first attempts are being made to come at least to a reference framework. The EAGLES (http://www.ilc.cnr.it/EAGLES/home.html), ISLE and TEI (http://www.tei-c.org/) initiatives have begun gathering concepts and defining them. New initiatives such as ISO TC37/SC4 (http://www.tc37sc4.org/) and GOLD (http://linguistlist.org/emeld/tools/ontology.cfm) have started to create formal machine readable ontologies.

The XML-based ISO TC37/SC4 Data Category Registry (cf Ide/Romary 2004) will contain an increasing number of concepts defined according to the ISO 11179 and ISO 12620 standards, i. e. the definitions will include the conceptual space (value range). It will also include relations between concepts insofar as they are part of the definitions, as for example in the following case: "transitive verb" is_a "verb". The GOLD ontology is based on RDF assertions and can therefore contain all types of relations between concepts. When designing a corpus it would of course make sense to reuse as many concepts as possible from the existing ontologies in one's own work or at least to refer to existing categories. Modern tools allow the user to make use of registered linguistic concepts while defining their annotation structure and during annotation. Some examples are LEXUS, which is a new ISO LMF compliant lexicon tool developed at the MPI for Psycholinguistics that can connect to the ISO DCR to make use of existing categories, ELAN, which was extended at the Wayne State University in Detroit to make use of the GOLD ontology, and FIELD, which is a lexicon tool developed at East Michigan University which also makes use of the GOLD ontology. For legacy resources mapping files have to be created to achieve interoperability. We assume that the degree of interoperability at the linguistic encoding level will slowly improve due to tools that connect to existing registries or that allow to establish these mappings.

5. Multimodal annotation tools

After discussing the logical and structural aspects of multimodal annotations, we will devote this section to briefly discussing tools that allow the user to add multimodal annotations to the media streams and therefore to enrich the session bundles. It is obvious that annotation and exploration, i. e. searching, comparing, changing etc., are two highly interacting phases of work. We can expect from a good annotation tool to also be a good exploration tool.

We can distinguish between tools that support manual annotation of multimodal behavior and those that create multimodal annotations automatically based on pattern recognition algorithms. In this section we will focus on manual annotation tools, since automatic annotation is still very limited in its capabilities and it can only be applied to special laboratory situations. Here we will only give a few examples where automatic annotation can be carried out.

(1) Gestures pointing at a map that are displayed on an interactive screen can be detected easily and combined with the speech signal. Automatic annotation of the destination the finger is pointing to is possible. (2) Nölker/Ritter (1999) automatically differentiated between a number of typical hand shapes in a restricted laboratory setup. (3) Ira Cohen et al. (2002) carried out recognition of facial expressions. (4) Eye gaze can be

detected and an automatic annotation can be done of the objects that are in focus during fixations (cf. Pérez et al. 2003).

There are many such special setups, in particular where devices that make quantitative measurements are used. Once calibrated, we can easily calculate meaningful values, map them to the scene and do an automatic annotation. However, when holistic video recordings are made, it is still not possible to do automatic annotation except for very restricted situations. In general multimodal communication is dynamic, with varying backgrounds, i.e. the video frames contain much "noise" that makes it hard to do, for example, robust pattern recognition of moving body parts. In general only time consuming manual annotations help.

Software tools can facilitate this time consuming manual annotation work. They offer the following functionality

- exact media control where one of the streams is made the master (video at a granularity of 20ms, speech at a granularity 50 µs)
- flexible user definable setup of tier structures and types, including support for dependencies and self-defined values
- easy navigation in the media stream, easy segment specification and efficient annotation
- flexible search to detect pattern combinations on different tiers within either a time distance or a distance in terms of units
- support of regular expressions in defining the search patterns
- several views on the selected media and tiers such as a time line view, a subtitle view and a text view
- synchronized viewers where any navigation operation in one view leads to an update in the other viewers
- comparison of two media streams played synchronously
- export defined by a generalized XML schema
- support for various other import and export formats
- printout facility
- platform independence

Currently, we know of a few tools that fulfill these criteria or that come close to it. ELAN (http://www.mpi.nl/lat) meets all of these goals and is widely used for different multimodal annotation projects. A recent study by SPEX (http://www.spex.nl) showed that the timing accuracy of ELAN is exact when working on a PC. Here native media (DirectX) is used. On a MAC, Quicktime is used as a media player and there are no proper codecs yet to guarantee exact timing when playing. ELAN is programmed in Java, freely available under an Open Source license, and a manual is also available.

Signstream (http://www.bu.edu/asllrp/SignStream) is used by some Sign Language researchers. It is MAC based and does not offer the flexibility required above. However it is easy to use. The CLAN tool set (http://childes.psy.cmu.edu/) is used by many researchers world wide. It offers restricted video functionality, and its annotation is utterance based, which may form a limitation for multimodal studies. It has a number of very useful statistical functions.

ANVIL (http://www.dfki.de/~kipp/anvil/) was used by some multimodal projects. Another interesting tool is TASX (http://medien.informatik.fh-fulda.de/tasxforce). Yet, we cannot say in how far the above mentioned criteria are fulfilled in these tools. The

MATE/NITE workbench (http://nite.nis.sdu.dk/publications/NITE-LREC-paper.2.4.2002-F.pdf) does not support multimedia and is therefore not yet a full-blown multimodal tool. The commercially available software Observer (http://www.noldus.com/site/doc200401012)has to be mentioned as a good alternative. An overview about annotation tools is available at the LDC (http://www.ldc.upenn.edu/annotation/) and DFKI (http://registry.dfki.de/) software registries.

The information about tools is aging very quickly. Some of the existing tools are subject to continuous extensions, and new developments are scheduled. However, proper video handling is hard to achieve and requires experts to do the programming.

6. Metadata for resource repositories

Multimodal corpora, and in particular language resource archives, include an increasing number of objects such that the management and discovery tasks cannot be ignored anymore. The Spoken Dutch Corpus includes about 20,000 session bundles with about four different types of resources each (speech, transcription, morphology, syntax). The language archive at the MPI covering multimodal, language development and endangered languages corpora has about 250,000 objects.

Web-based catalogue systems defined by a metadata set and tools are suitable solutions to allow corpus managers to maintain the corpus and users to discover the resources they are looking for.

Currently, there are two mature metadata infrastructures that offer services via the web: (1) OLAC (http://www.language-archives.org/) is inspired by the Dublin Core set that is meant to find web-resources of all sorts. A few additional metadata elements, such as the language a resource is about and the role of the creator, made the OLAC set suitable for language resources. OLAC offers to harvest registered sites according to the OAI PMH and to search on the harvested metadata descriptions.

IMDI (http://www.imdi.eu) is a result of the ISLE (http://www.ilc.cnr.it/EAGLES96/isle/ISLE_Home_Page.htm) and INTERA (http://www.mpi.nl/INTERA/) projects, to which many European researchers including multimodality specialists from different areas contributed for about five years. It offers a more elaborate set compared to OLAC, which allows the user to encode more administrative and in particular linguistic details, and it has the capability to support session bundles. Resources in session bundles share most of the elements except that they have different characteristics such as format, type and creation date. A few elements such as "modalities" and "task" were added to the IMDI core due to the requirements of multimodality experts. However, IMDI can be expanded by individuals or projects at various places by adding their own key-value pairs. If a community requests such extensions so that they are also supported by the editor and the structured search component, special profiles can be added, as was done for example for the European Sign Language community.

IMDI was designed not only to support searching, but also to support browsing as a navigation option and for archive management. The construction of the IMDI domain is very simple in so far as it consists of open XML-based IMDI descriptions linked by URLs, i. e. IMDI files can reside everywhere. It comes with an editor to create session descriptions and IMDI nodes; an XML-based browser; a mechanism to create HTML descriptions on the fly to allow browsing with normal browsers; a structured search component harvesting the registered IMDI sites; a full-text simple search option; a mechanism such that Google can index the IMDI domain; a gateway to OLAC and OAI so that other service providers can harvest all records; and an access rights management system based on metadata and the harvesting of OAI PMH compliant records.

OLAC is used directly by about 35 institutions and IMDI by about 50 institutions world-wide, which already creates an interesting critical mass of open language resource descriptions. However, it is not yet sufficient. We propose that each project should devote some time to create this type of metadata and register it. All resources registered under OLAC and IMDI are searchable and therefore visible to others. Open metadata does not mean that the resources themselves are accessible to everyone, every project can still define access rights to the resources according to their policies.

ISO TC37/SC4 will also take care of metadata descriptions for language resources where the various contributions including the TEI (http://www.tei-c.org/) header recommendations and the IMDI vocabulary will be integrated into a more flexible framework. In doing so all investments in metadata creation will be secured for a longer time.

Summary

In the coming years a rich and more comprehensive metadata landscape will emerge and there will be an increasing pressure to deliver high-quality metadata. These metadata descriptions will allow researchers to easily locate interesting multimodal resources and to gather their own temporary collections for their research purposes. The currently used fixed metadata schemas defined by OLAC and IMDI will not be flexible enough to cope with the different needs. They will be replaced by component-based schemas that are augmented by ontologies such as the ISO Data Category Registry, allowing every project to design its own metadata schema based on the registered vocabularies and therefore guaranteeing semantic interoperability. New types of tools need to be developed to support this flexibility. However, for the next years either OLAC or IMDI should be used depending on the research purpose. These initiatives will ensure that the created metadata descriptions will be transformed into the new framework when it is offered.

7. Definitions

In this article we use a number of concepts that should be clarified to facilitate understanding.

Recording: the resource created by one recording device in a multimodal observation. A video film of one interview taken by a camera can be seen as a recording. A recording bundle comprises the different recordings made during an observation. Two video cameras could have been used to record the same event from different perspectives.

Session: a fragment of a recording that can be seen as an interesting unit of linguistic analysis such as an interview about a certain topic. A session is typically the basic entity of a corpus. A session bundle comprises the appropriate fragments from all recordings. The streams included in a session bundle are assumed to be time aligned.

Stream: the data included in a recording or session and its timing characteristics.

Multimodal channel: the specific modality observed in a recording. Often a video recording, for example, will comprise several modalities such as facial expressions and head movements.

Annotation: a single comment or interpretation associated with a fragment of a stream on an annotation tier.

Annotation tier: the layer of annotations created considering specific linguistic criteria, i. e. orthographic transcription, gesture phases, etc.

Annotation system: the set of annotation tiers used to describe the linguistic content of a session, including its cross-references, hierarchies and other structural aspects.

Multimodal Corpus: consists of a number of session bundles and other secondary linguistic resources such as lexica, notes of all sorts, etc., that were gathered and organized according to a coherent set of criteria with a specific goal in mind.

Language Archive: is a combination of various corpora and other language resources from different contributors and projects that are organized according to a catalogue system.

8. Literature

Bernsen, N. O. (1994), Foundations of Multimodal Representations. A Taxonomy of Representational Modalities. In: *Interacting with Computers* 6(4), 347–371.

Bird, S./Liberman, M. (2001). A Formal Framework for Linguistic Annotation. In: *Speech Communication* 33(1–2), 23–60.

Brugman, H./Wittenburg, P. (2001), The Application of Annotation Models for the Construction of Databases and Tools – an Overview and Analysis of the MPI Work Since 1994. In: Bird, S./Buneman, P./Liberman, M. (eds.), *Proceedings of the IRCS Workshop on Linguistic Databases*. Philadelphia: LDC, 65–75.

Cohen, I./Sebe, N./Garg, A./Lew, M. S./Huang, T. S. (2002), Facial Expression Recognition from Video Sequences. In: *Proceedings of the 2002 International Conference on Multimedia & Expo (ICME-2002)*. Lausanne, Switzerland, 121–124.

de Ruiter, J. P./Rossignol, S./Vuurpijl, L./Cunningham, D./Levelt, W. (2003), SLOT: A Research Platform for Investigating Multimodal Communication. In: *Behavior Research Methods, Instruments, & Computers* 35(3), 408–419.

Gustafsson, L./Lanshammar, H. (1977), *ENOCH – an Integrated System for Measurement and Analysis of Human Gait*. (UPTEC 77:23.) PhD Dissertation, Uppsala University.

Ide, N./Romary, L. (2003), Outline of the International Standard Linguistic Annotation Framework. In: *Proceedings of ACL'03 Workshop on Linguistic Annotation: Getting the Modal Right*. Sapporo, Japan, 1–5. (URL: http://www.cs.vassar.edu/~ide/papers/ACL2003-ws-LAF.pdf).

Ide, N./Romary, L. (2004), A Registry of Standard Data Categories for Linguistic Annotation. In: *Proceedings of the Fourth Language Resources and Evaluation Conference (LREC)*. Lisbon, Portugal, 135–139. (URL: http://www.cs.vassar.edu/~ide/papers/LREC2004-DCR.pdf).

Ide, N./Romary, L./de la Clergie, E. (2003), International Standard for a Linguistic Annotation Framework. In: *Proceedings of HLT-NAACL '03*. Workshop on the Software Engineering and Architecture of Language Technology, Edmunton. (URL: ftp://ftp.inria.fr/INRIA/Projects/Atoll/Eric.Clergerie/ide-romary-clergerie.pdf).

Levelt, W. J. M. (1980), On-line Processing Constraints on the Properties of Signed and Spoken Language. In: Bellugi, U./Studdert-Kennedy, M. (eds.), *Biological Constraints on Linguistic Form*. Weinheim: Verlag Chemie, 141–160.

Nölker, C./Ritter, H. (1999), Grefit: Visual Recognition of Hand Postures. In: Braffort, A./Gherbi, R./Gibet, S./Richardson, J./Teil, D. (eds.), *Gesture-based Communication in Human-computer Interaction*. Berlin: Springer, 61–72.
Oostdijk, N./Broeder, D. (2003), The Spoken Dutch Corpus and its Exploitation Environment. In: *Proceedings of the 4th International Workshop on Linguistically Interpreted Corpora (LINC-03)*. Budapest, Hungary. (URL: http://lands.let.ru.nl/cgn/publs/linc03def.ps).
Oppenheim, A./Schafer, R. (1975), *Digital Signal Processing*. Englewood Cliffs, New Jersey: Prentice-Hall.
Pérez, A./Córdoba, M. L./García, A./Méndez, R./Muñoz, M. L./Pedraza, J. L./Sánchez, F. (2003), A Precise Eye-gaze Detection and Tracking System. In: *Proceedings of the 11th International Conference in Central Europe on Computer Graphics, Visualization and Computer Vision 2003*. University of West Bohemia, Plzen, Czech Republic. (URL: http://wscg.zcu.cz/wscg2003/Papers_2003/A83.pdf).
Rabiner, L. R./Gold, B. (1975), *Theory and Application of Digital Signal Processing*. Englewood Cliffs, New Jersey: Prentice-Hall.
Richardson, G. (1984), Word Recognition under Spatial Transformation in Retarded and Normal Readers. In: *Journal of Experimental Child Psychology* 38, 220–240.
Teich, E./Hansen, S./Fankhauser, P. (2001), Representing and Querying Multi-layer Annotated Corpora. In: Bird, S./Buneman, P./Liberman, M. (eds.), *Proceedings of the IRCS Workshop on Linguistic Databases*. Philadelphia: LDC, 228–237.
van Son, R. J. J. H. (2002), Can Standard Analysis Tools be Used on Decompressed Speech? Paper presented at the COCOSDA2002 meeting, Denver. (URL: http://www.cocosda.org/meet/denver/COCOSDA2002-Rob.pdf).
Woltring, H. (1977), Measurement and Control of Human Movement. PhD Dissertation, University of Nijmegen.

Peter Wittenburg, Nijmegen (The Netherlands)

32. Preprocessing multilingual corpora

1. Introduction

A multilingual parallel corpus is a corpus that contains the same text samples in each of at least two languages, in the sense that the samples are translations of one another. A comparable corpus contains texts in at least two languages which are not translations of each other, but are written in the same genre and on the same topic (see article 16). A sentence alignment is a mapping showing which sentence or sentences of the one text correspond with which sentence or sentences of the other language. Word-level alignment is also possible, and valuable for the production of terminological dictionaries. The focus of this article will be on the preprocessing of parallel corpora, and in particular, on the preprocessing steps of tokenisation (identifying the constituent words, sentences and paragraphs of a corpus, see article 24) and automatic alignment. Figure 32.1, actually a modified segment of the Canadian Hansards adapted from Simard et al. (2000), shows two types of translation analyses – horizontal lines to denote the segmentations of a sentence alignment and numbers in parentheses to denote a word-level mapping. The Canadian Hansards are transcripts of the proceedings of the Canadian Parliament, recorded in both English and French (cf. article 20).

7(1).	7(1).
Le développement(2) est main tenant appréhendé dans la multiplicité de ses dimensions(3).	Development(2) is now understood to involve many dimensions(3);
On n'y voit plus seulement un problème de politique économique(4) et de resources.	it is no longer merely a matter of economic(4) politics and resources.
Les facteurs politiques, sociaux, éducationnels et environmentaux sont concus comme autant de facettes de l'action unifée(5) à développement.	Political, social, educational and environmental factors must be part of an integrated(5) approach to development.
Au moins(6) d'un développement a l'échelle la plus vaste, les jeunes seront agités, frustrés et improductifs.	Without(6) development on the widest scale, the young will be restless, resentful and unproductive.
On se disputera les resources(7) et la creéativité s'égarera.	People will fight for resources(7) and creativity will be misdirected.

Fig. 32.1: A short section of a bilingual corpus, aligned at the sentence and word-level

2. Applications of aligned corpora

Aligned corpora are useful for foreign language learners. They can be used in conjunction with concordancers to show language learners real examples of how a construction in one language has been translated on various occasions into the other (Barlow 2000). They are also useful for bilingual terminology extraction. Multinational organisations such as the European Union continually need to translate product documentation and standardise terminology in technical fields. Human acquisition of technology is an expert task, both slow and expensive, and it is difficult to keep up with the pace of technology development. The production of printed dictionaries involves an inevitable time lag, and commercial dictionaries do not typically contain the subject-specific vocabulary which is often needed. The automatic derivation of bilingual terminology lists offers a solution to both these problems (Gaussier/Langé 1994). Machine Translation, which works best in highly specific technical domains such as weather forecasting (Kittredge 1985), is an important area where such subject-specific electronic dictionaries are particularly useful.

Parallel corpora have a number of other applications in machine translation. With example-based machine translation (EBMT), a large parallel corpus of previously translated phrases is stored (cf. article 56). When a new phrase is entered, the most similar phrase in the corpus is found, and its translation returned (Nagao 1984). Transfer rules, which determine how syntactic structures in one language are translated into the syntactic structures of the other language in traditional machine translation, can also be derived from parallel corpora (Carbonell et al. 2002). Parallel corpora form the basis of statistically-based machine translation (Brown et al. 1990). Parallel corpora can also act as the "gold standard" against which the output of machine translation systems is compared. They also provide data for theoretical linguistic studies (as discussed in article 54).

3. Sentence segmentation and word tokenisation

Most alignment algorithms for parallel corpora require the preprocessing steps of tokenisation (identification of word boundaries) and sentence segmentation (clearly marking where one sentence ends and another begins). Obviously there can be no alignment at the sentence level if we do not know where all the sentence boundaries are, and if we do not identify all the word boundaries correctly, our lexicons derived from word-level alignment will contain a number of non-word sequences (Palmer 2000). In reality, there is no absolute definition for what constitutes a word or a sentence. For example, should *seaside* or *sea side* be one word or two? A lively account of this from a linguist's point of view is given by Aitchison (1999). There are differences between the ways different corpora and applications segment words and sentences. For example, the British National Corpus (BNC) regards *President's* as two word tokens, *President* and *'s*, while the Brown corpus would regard it as a single word token (cf. article 24).

Gale/Church (1991) use manual marking up of sentences (denoted *-d*) and paragraphs (denoted *-D*) before their sentence alignment program can begin. Sentence segmentation involves the recognition of boundaries, typically punctuation (such as a full stop or question mark) at the end of a sentence. Making this assumption, most errors will arise by confusion between full stops denoting abbreviations and those denoting sentence boundaries. There are various heuristics (none absolutely fail-safe) which use the context surrounding the full stop to decide whether it is more likely to denote an abbreviation or end of sentence, such as, does the next word start with an upper case letter? Full stops can also show decimal points (when they are surrounded by numeric characters), and salutations such as *Mr.* Raynar/Ratnaparkhi (1997) suggest that titles such as *Mr.* do not occur at the end of a sentence, and certain suffixes suggest that words are not likely to be abbreviations. Palmer/Hearst (1997) found that the sequences of the parts-of-speech (POS) of the words surrounding the full stop give clues as to its function. Speech quote marks also cloud the issue of sentence segmentation.

Kiss/Strunk (2002) also describe a method for determining whether a full stop denotes an end of sentence or an abbreviation. They regard a word followed by a full stop as a collocation of that word and the full stop. The strength of this collocation, as measured by the log likelihood measure, is greater if the word is an abbreviation, because that abbreviation will always be followed by a full stop. Other words will be weakly collocated with the full stop, since they often occur at other places in a sentence, and thus are not always followed by a full stop. This method will not distinguish between an abbreviation at the end of a sentence and an abbreviation elsewhere in the sentence.

Two successful alignment algorithms circumvent the need for word and sentence segmentation. One is the K-vec algorithm of Fung/Church (1994), where the corpus is simply divided into segments of equal length. The other is Char_align (Church 1993) where alignment is at the level of sequences of four adjacent characters, which may or may not span word boundaries.

4. Sentence alignment

Many algorithms for bilingual sentence alignment exist, and Wu's (2000) excellent chapter on alignment extracts some important general principles. The task of sentence alignment is to discover exactly which sentence or sentences in the first language correspond to which sentence or sentences in the other language. It is often the case that there is no 1:1 alignment between sentences in two languages. For example, Figure 32.2 shows an alignment between two English sentences and one French sentence (i. e. a 2:1 alignment). Strictly speaking, an alignment must be monotonic, meaning that coupled passages (referred to as beads) must occur in the same order on both sides of the corpus. Monotonic sentence aligners will generally propose spurious alignments during non-monotonic passages in translations. Sentence order is generally preserved in translation, but this is not the case for word order. In this article we will use the phrase "word-level alignment", but since word order is generally not preserved in translation, strictly speaking we should say that the words are "set in correspondence".

4.1. Constraints for alignment

The imposition of constraints such as monotonicity helps us a great deal, because myriads of putative alignments are at a stroke declared impossible, cutting down the number of possible alignments from which we must choose the best. Initially there are so many possibilities that even the computer could not look at them all in a reasonable amount of time. For example, to align just 20 sentences of one language with 20 sentences of another, assuming that only 1:1 alignments were allowed (but allowing crossover), would mean having to try about 2,430,000,000,000,000,000 possible configurations before deciding on the best.

Other constraints are anchors, or points in each text which are known to correspond with each other. Some anchors are given by the document structure, and thus tend to be corpus specific, such as labels to identify dates and speakers in the Canadian Hansards, and numbered section headings. It is generally assumed that the very beginning and very end of the two texts are good anchor points. Other anchors are bilingual lexical constraints. In a few cases we can be certain that a word in one language is always translated as the same word in another language, and thus the two sides of the corpus must align wherever this word pair is found. Although less directly useful, we can also make use of word pairs which are mutual translations most, but not all, of the time. Section 5 on word-level alignment describes how such pairs can be discovered and assigned numeric scores according to their translation reliability. Heuristics also exist for the identification of cognates (see section 4.4.) which can also act as partially reliable anchors for related language pairs such as English and French. A related constraint heuristic is referred to as "bands", where it is assumed that "the correct couplings lie not too far from the diagonal between adjacent anchors" (Wu 2000).

One group of alignment methods, described as lexical methods (Kay/Röscheisen 1993; Catizone/Russell/Warwick 1989), make much use of anchor points, especially bilingual word correspondences. They have the advantage that they are more robust to noisy texts (i. e. tolerant of imperfect translations); however, the most easily implemented and fastest corpus alignment techniques are based on relative sentence lengths, which use only paragraph boundaries as anchor points.

4.2. Alignment algorithms based on relative sentence lengths

Alignment methods based on sentence length (Brown/Lai/Mercer 1991; Gale/Church 1991, 1993) operate on a very simple, but surprisingly reliable, premise: short sentences in one language tend to be translated by short sentences in another language, and long sentences in one language tend to be translated by long sentences in the other. Thus the greater the difference between the length of a sentence in language A and the length of a sentence in sentence B, the less likely that they should be aligned. To take this into account, a numerical penalty or cost is imposed whenever the algorithm considers aligning two text segments which differ in length, as given in the following formula:

$$\delta = \frac{l_2 - l_1 c}{\sqrt{l_1 s^2}}$$

l_1 and l_2 are the lengths, in characters, of the two segments. c is a factor which takes into account that equivalent texts might on average be longer in one language than the other. This must be determined empirically for each language pair for which the algorithm is to be used, and can be found simply by dividing the number of characters in the corpus for language A by the number of characters for language B. Gale/Church (1993) found this ratio was 1.06 when language A was French and language B was English. s^2 is the variance in the number of characters in language B per character in language A. If there were always exactly 1.06 characters of French for every character of English, this variance would be 0. However, if we sometimes find other ratios of lengths in characters in individual translation sentence pairs, the variance will be more than 0 (in fact it is 5.6). As we will see in section 8, the variance is high for English and Chinese.

The next stage is to calculate Prob(δ), which is the proportion of sentences which are translations of each other with δ degree of length difference or more. Many statistics textbooks have a table for computing this "integration of a standard normal distribution". Alternatively, Gale and Church give the Abramowitz and Stegun approximation which is in a suitable form for inserting into a computer program. The penalty P is taken to be $P = -100 \ln(\text{Prob}(\delta))$ which is capped at 2500 to prevent having to deal with infinitely large values.

There is also a penalty for bead (or block of mutually aligned sentences) type or cardinality – the more rare the bead type proposed, the higher the penalty. The penalty for a 1:1 pairing (substitution) is 0 (i. e. there is no penalty at all), since this is the most common bead type, 2:1 or 1:2 groupings (contractions and expansions) have a penalty of 250, while 0:1 or 1:0 unpaired sentences (insertions and deletions) have a penalty of 450. Finally, merges, where two sentences of English in total translate two sentences of French, but neither of the English sentences exactly translates either of the French sentences, have a penalty of 440. These penalties were derived empirically, using the formula

$$P = -100 \ln \left(\frac{\textit{probability of alignment type}}{\textit{probability of } 1:1 \textit{ alignment}} \right)$$

The two penalties (for sentence length and cardinality) are added together to give the overall cost of a single bead. The overall cost of aligning the whole bitext is the sum of the costs of the constituent beads, as shown in the example of Figure 32.2. Gale and Church's program could be extended in principle to include any n:m bead type.

Following a two-year transitional period, the new Foodstuffs Ordinance for Mineral Water came into effect on April 1, 1998. Specifically, it contains more stringent requirements regarding quality consistency and purity guarantees.	La nouvelle ordonnance fédérale sur les denrées alimentaires concernant entre autres les eaux minerals, entrée en vigeur le 1er avril 1988 après une période transitoire de deux ans, exige surtout une plus grande constance dans la qualité et une garantie de la pureté.

Fig. 32.2: A short section of the Canadian Hansards

There are three possible alignments of this corpus. Firstly, we might have a 2:1 alignment, where the combination of the two English sentences is translated by the single French sentence. The English sentences are 124 and 106 characters long, while the length of the French sentence is 267 characters respectively. First we consider the scenario where the two English sentences are translated by the single French sentence. The combined length of the English sentences is 230 characters. Using the formula given by Gale/Church (1993), the penalty for this small difference in text lengths is calculated as 57. The penalty for a 2:1 coupling is 250, so the total cost of this alignment is the sum of the two penalties, 57 + 250 = 307.

Secondly, we might have a 1:1 substitution followed by a 0:1 insertion, i. e. the French sentence is completely translated by the first English sentence only, while the second English sentence has no French translation. The overall cost of this alignment is the sum of the costs of the two constituent beads, i. e. 880 + 2404 = 3284. Thirdly we might have a 0:1 insertion followed by a 1:1 substitution, where the first English sentence has no French translation, and the second English sentence alone fully translates the French sentence. The overall cost of this is 3868. These values show that the first scenario, a 1:2 expansion, is the likeliest of the three, since it has the lowest overall cost. For the sake of completeness, we will mention that there is a fourth, albeit unlikely scenario, where none of the text portions are translations of each other. Here the corpus would be divided into three beads, one for the deletion of first English sentence, one for the deletion of the second English sentence, and once for the insertion of the French sentence (various orderings of these are possible, with no difference in cost). The cost of this would be prohibitive, at 8063.

In this small example we have only four possible alignment combinations from which to select the best. In a real corpus, there would be simply too many possible alignment configurations for them all to be examined in turn in a reasonable time, and thus a technique called dynamic programming is used. This means that only certain alignments deemed to be reasonably likely from the outset are examined using the Gale and Church formulas. Theoretically the optimal solution might be overlooked, but a good solution will be found within a reasonable length of time.

4.3. Dynamic programming for sentence alignment

If we wish to align *e* sentences of English with *f* sentences of French by dynamic programming, we should first produce a matrix with $(e + 1)$ rows and $(f + 1)$ columns. The rows are numbered from 0 to *e*, and the columns from 0 to *f*. We start with the trivial assumption that the cost of aligning no sentences of English with no sentences of French is 0, and store this value in row 0, column 0, of the matrix. In every case, the value stored in row *x*, column *y*, is the minimum cost of aligning *x* sentences of English with *y* sentences of French. There is only one way of aligning a sequence of sentences of English with no sentences of French, and that is by a sequence of deletions. Thus the value in row 1, column 0, is the cost of deleting the first English sentence. We add to this value the cost of deleting the second English sentence, and put this result in row 2, column 0. In this way we can easily fill up all the squares in column 0. As well as recording the cost of these partial alignments, we also keep a record that the last step taken in each case was a deletion. Analogous reasoning allows us to fill up all the squares in row 0, by working out the costs of sequences of insertions.

Now we come to fill in the inner cells of the matrix. The value in row 1, column 1, should be the minimum cost of aligning the first sentence of the English text with the first sentence of the French. The word "minimum" now becomes important, because we have a choice of three ways of achieving this alignment: a single substitution, a deletion followed by an insertion, or an insertion followed by a deletion. The cost of a single substitution can be measured directly. To find the cost of a deletion followed by an insertion, remember that we have already found the cost of the deletion, which is stored in row 1, column 0 of the matrix. To this we simply add the cost of inserting the first French sentence. Similarly, to find the cost of an insertion followed by a deletion, find the cost of the insertion at row 0, column 1, then add the cost of the deletion. These three values are compared, and the smallest is retained as the value in row 1, column 1. Once again, as in every case, we record the nature of the most recent bead (substitution, insertion or deletion) to be added to the developing alignment.

Deeper inside the matrix, we have to consider all 6 bead types. In Figure 32.3, the cost of aligning the first three sentences of English with the first two sentences of French is derived from the costs of 6 earlier alignments plus the cost of adding one more bead. The least of these 6 values is the cost of the alignment.

Table 32.1 shows a set of possible values for the situation described in Figure 32.3. These values are calculated using the Gale and Church penalties for the various bead

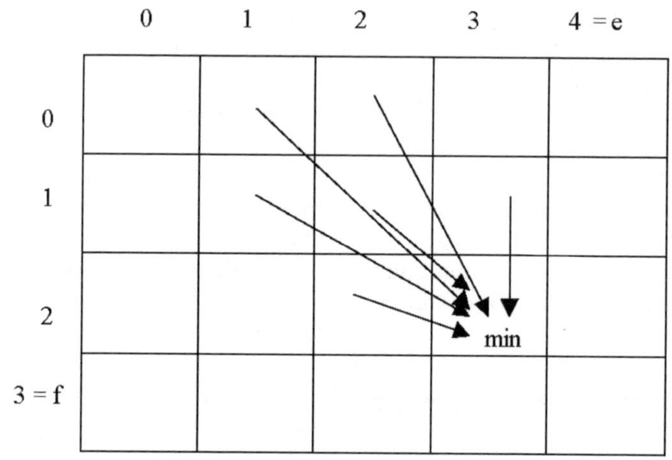

Fig. 32.3: Dynamic programming matrix for sentence alignment

Tab. 32.1: Calculating the cost of a 3 : 2 alignment

Old align	Min cost	Bead to make up 3 : 2	Cost of new bead	Total cost of 3 : 2
1 : 0	450	2 : 2	440	890
2 : 0	900	1 : 2	250	1150
1 : 1	0	2 : 1	250	250
2 : 1	250	1 : 1	0	250
3 : 1	700	0 : 1	450	1150
2 : 2	0	1 : 0	450	450

types, but to simplify the example, penalties based on sentence lengths are ignored. The first column shows the six alignments at the tails of the arrows in Figure 32.3, which can all be transformed into 3 : 2 alignment by the addition of just one more bead. In the second column, the previously found minimum costs of achieving each of these alignments are given. For example, the least cost of producing a 2 : 2 alignment is by proposing two consecutive 1 : 1 alignments, with a total cost of 0. The third column shows the bead type required to transform each alignment in the first column into a 3 : 2 alignment, and the fourth column shows the cost of adding this particular bead type. The final column shows the overall cost of producing a 3 : 2 alignment by each of the six possible routes (rows in the table). In fact we have a tie, with either a 1 : 1 bead followed by a 2 : 1 bead, or a 2 : 1 bead followed by a 1 : 1 bead, with least overall cost (250). Usually such a tie would be resolved by considering the relative sentence lengths, but if not, whichever of the lowest cost alignments is considered first by the program will be chosen.

In general, to find the cost of a partial alignment of x sentences of English with y sentences of French, where the last bead type to be added was of type $a : b$ (coupling a sentences of English with b sentences of French), proceed as follows: Go back to row $(e-a)$, column $(f-b)$, to find the minimum cost of the previous sequence of beads, then add the cost of adding the $a:b$ bead type. It is necessary to work through the matrix systematically, such as from left to right, top to bottom. When all the cells have been filled, the value in row e, column f is the cost of the optimal alignment. We have also kept an implicit record of the sequence of bead types which produced this optimal alignment, and we can retrieve this as follows: See which bead type was the last to be added to the final alignment. If this was an $a:b$ bead type, we trace back to row $(e-a)$, column $(f-b)$, to find the penultimate bead type. This process is repeated until we arrive back at row 0, cell 0.

To overcome the problem of the dynamic programming technique sometimes finding a non-optimal alignment, Chen/Chen (1994) used a technique from artificial intelligence called simulated annealing. The idea of annealing comes from physics, where in order to render some material such as enamel into its most stable configuration, it is first heated, and then slowly cooled again until it falls into this configuration. Heat can be represented in an alignment program by randomness, and the most stable configuration by the optimal alignment, which has least energy (corresponding to least overall cost). Chen/Chen start with any possible alignment, such as one previously found by dynamic programming, which may well not be the best. A number of moves are allowed in the search for a better alignment, e. g. take a sentence from one bead and move it into an adjacent bead. The quality of each alignment is the number of matching part-of-speech (POS) tags on each side. The likelihood of a putative new alignment being adopted is greater if it is better than the old, but it will not always be accepted. Similarly, the randomness in the system means that it is possible for a poorer alignment to be adopted. The reason that seeming improvements are not always made, and even some poorer alignments are chosen, is to prevent the system getting stuck in what is called a local minimum – a sort of dead end, which might be the best among a set of alignments just one step removed from each other, but poorer than the overall best which may be completely different. The search for the optimal alignment continues in this stepwise manner. The degree of randomness in the system gradually gets less until "better" steps are always made, and "worse" steps are never made.

Dynamic programming is also used in bioinformatics for the alignment of protein and DNA sequences (Kruskal 1983), and may even be used by the human body itself for protein folding (Hockenmaier/Joshi/Dill 2006).

4.4. Incorporation of cognates into sentence alignment

Simard/Foster/Isabelle (1992) used the term cognates to describe a pair of words, each from a different language, which are orthographically similar and have similar meaning. This definition would include similar words in languages which are not historically related, such as borrowings and proper nouns, although a linguist's definition of cognates would require historical relatedness. Simard et al. were the first to suggest that the discovery of such word pairs could assist in the process of sentence alignment.

McEnery/Oakes (1996) suggested that such cognates could be discovered in corpora using approximate string matching techniques, such as Dice's similarity coefficient (Dice 1945) and the Damerau-Levenshtein metric (Damerau 1964). Dice's similarity coefficient was adapted by Adamson/Boreham (1974) so it could be used as a measure of orthographic similarity between two words. McEnery/Oakes (1996) used their technique to describe the degree of similarity between a word in one language and its translation in another, such as the Italian *avverbio* and the English *adverb*. First the two words are separated into lists of their adjacent character pairs, or bigrams, as follows: *av-vv-ve-er-rb-bi-io* and *ad-dv-ve-er-rb*.

The number of matching bigrams (*ve*, *er* and *rb*) is 3, while the total number of bigrams in both words is 5 + 7 = 12. Dice's similarity coefficient is twice the number of matches, divided by the total number of bigrams in the two words – which is 6/12 = 0.5. The formula returns a value of 1 if the two words are orthographically identical, and 0 if they have no character pairs at all in common. Empirical results for English-French (McEnery/Oakes 1996) and English-Polish (Lewandowska-Tomaszczyk/Oakes/Wynne 1999) show that the greater the similarity coefficient between a word in one language in a bilingual corpus and a word in the other, the more likely it is that these two words are mutual translations. Hofland (1996) used a combination of bilingual word pairs found by Dice's similarity coefficient with those found in a Norwegian-English dictionary to guide sentence alignment.

Similarly, cognates can be identified using the Damerau-Levenshtein metric, which is the smallest number of operations required to transform one word form into another. This technique is a variant of the Gale and Church sentence alignment algorithm in microcosm. Once again dynamic programming is used, but now we are performing alignment at the character level. Only three operations are allowed: insertions, deletions and substitutions. Thus three operations (a substitution of $v \rightarrow d$ and deletions of *i* and *o*) are required to transform *avverbio* into *adverb*. The number of operations can be transformed to a 0 to 1 scale by dividing by the length in characters of the longer word – in this case two words identical in form will have a score of 0, while two totally dissimilar words will have a score of 1.

Simard et al. (2000) discovered the importance of using only isolated cognates to guide the process of sentence alignment, where a word form is isolated if no similar word form occurs within a certain number of characters. The identification of non-isolated cognates will degrade alignment performance rather than improve it. Cognates which appear in the same aligned region of a corpus (and hence the same context) are unlikely to be 'false friends'. Other linguistic clues can be incorporated into alignment algorithms, such as part-of-speech information and the results of shallow syntactic analysis. Piperidis/Cranias/Papageorgiou (1994) showed that words are more likely to be aligned if they take the same part of speech, and Tiedemann (2003) gives the example that a verb phrase in English is more likely to match a verb cluster in Swedish than a noun phrase.

4.5. Dealing with noisy bitexts

A number of techniques have been designed for the alignment of noisy bitexts (bilingual parallel corpora) or poor quality translations. Wu (2000) lists some reasons why these might occur: non-literal translation, out of order translation, omitted sections, floating passages (such as footnotes, figures and headers), optical character reader (OCR) errors, and sentence segmentation errors. The key to the success of these techniques is that they do not require the original texts to be accurately broken up into paragraphs. The output is a set of anchors rather than a complete mapping of sentences. One such technique is the char_align program of Church (1993), which aligns texts at the character level, using the dot plot technique. Texts should be anchored at character x in English and character y in French if the tetragrams (sequences of four characters) leading up to characters x and y are identical. If so, a dot is placed in cell (x, y) of the dotplot. This only works if there are sufficient cognates in the two languages being aligned. Simard found that about 21 % of the words in a 100 sentence sample of mutual translations in the English-French Canadian Hansards are cognates, which is sufficient for the dotplot technique to work. In contrast, only about 6 % of the words were cognate in a sample of about 100 randomly chosen sentence pairs which were not mutual translations.

Areas which should not be aligned are sparsely populated with dots (due to random correspondences), while a more pronounced diagonal line appears to show where the true correspondences should lie. These diagonal lines can be enhanced by image processing techniques (Chang/Chen 1997). Melamed (1997) describes alignment of noisy bitexts by combining scores for both statistical and linguistic comparisons, such as the presence of cognates, bilingual dictionary matches, and part of speech information.

4.6. Evaluation techniques for sentence alignment

Sentence alignment, like sentence segmentation, can be evaluated using Recall and Precision (Simard et al. 2000). The machine-aligned corpus is compared with a humanly-aligned reference corpus. Precision is the number of sentence pairs aligned by both human and machine, divided by the number of sentence pairs aligned by the machine only. Recall is the number of sentence pairs aligned by both human and machine, divided by the number of sentence pairs aligned by the human only. Here a 2 : 1 alignment of sentences of 10 and 11 in English with sentence 10 in French would mean that the sentence pairs (10, 10) and (11, 10) would be aligned. Both Recall and Precision can also be used with the number of characters aligned by each technique, so the results are not unduly influenced by very short sentences. Gale/Church (1993) stress the importance of the human judge marking the alignments beforehand, so as not to be influenced by seeing the machine output first. This also allows comparison of results for different algorithms with different output formats on a common basis.

5. Word alignment

The two main reasons for performing alignment at the word level are a) to help guide a process of sentence alignment, b) for building bilingual lexicons automatically, and c) to train statistical machine translation systems on the word-aligned corpora.

The earliest work on word alignment was done by Brown et al. (1990), where it was achieved as a by-product of statistical machine translation. Word alignments were produced by the multiplication of three sets of automatically discovered probabilities: a) translation probabilities, e. g. the English "not" aligns with the French "pas" with probability 0.469; b) fertilities, e. g. "not" corresponds with two words in French with probability 0.758; and c) distortion, e. g. what is the probability of the second word in an English sentence aligning with the fifth word of a French sentence?

A number of sentence alignment processes, such as that of Kay/Röscheisen (1993) work in a series of iterated steps. First a rough estimate of which sentences might be aligned is made, which provides enough information to make a first pass at word alignment. Having found a small number of word pairs which are reliable translations, it is possible to make an improved pass at sentence alignment, which in turn enables better word-level alignment. This process continues until no new word pairs can be found.

Daille et al. (1994) built bilingual terminology banks from the International Telecommunications Corpus. The sentence-level alignment of Figure 32.1 was derived first, and this enabled the later word-level alignment. Daille (1995) lists a wide range of statistical measures, all based on the contingency table shown in Figure 32.4. N = a + b + c + d, which is the total number of aligned regions in the corpus (6 in the example of Figure 32.1).

a: number of aligned regions in which both the French and the English words appear	*b:* number of aligned regions in which the French word appears but the English word does not appear.
c: number of aligned regions in which the English word appears but the French word does not appear.appears.	*d:* number of aligned regions in which neither the French nor the English word appears.

Fig. 32.4: A contingency table for word alignment

All these measures are based on the principle that if an English word is the translation of a French word (or vice versa), then in most cases, wherever we have the French word on the left hand side of the corpus, we also have the English word on the right hand side, in the same aligned region. Thus high values of *a* give strong evidence that two words are probably translations of each other, while high values of *d* give weak evidence that they are translations. High values of *b* and *c* (meaning many aligned regions where only one of the two words is found, not both) are evidence that the two words are not translations.

The simplest measure is simple co-occurrence frequency, value *a* in the contingency table. If we want to discover automatically the most likely translation of the English word *development*, it must be one of the words found in a French sentence aligned with at least one English sentence containing *development*. Examples of such words are *le, développement, est, maintenant, apprehendé* and *dans*. Since *développement* and *development* co-occur 3 times (more often than any other French word co-occurs with *development*), the simple co-occurrence frequency suggests that *développement* is the most likely translation of *development*. More sophisticated measures exist, to take into account that the very common words (such as *la*, *de*, and *les* in this example) tend to co-occur frequently with every English word, simply because they are so common and are found throughout the corpus. These more complex measures take not only *a* into account, but also the other values of the contingency table. Daille adapted the simple mutual information measure to produce the cubic association coefficient MI^3, which is given by the formula

$$MI^3 = \log_2 \left(\frac{a^3 N}{(a+b)(a+c)} \right)$$

In the small corpus of Figure 32.2, the MI^3 between *development* and some of its more promising translation candidates in the French part of the corpus is as follows: *développement* 4.17, *la* 2.41, *les* 2.41. Other candidate words, such as *maintenant*, have a MI^3 of 1 or less. Thus the MI^3 measure, like simple co-occurrence frequency, suggests that *développement* is the most likely translation of *development*. Using this method, the most likely translation can be found for each word in the corpus, to build up a complete lexicon. The most effective measures, as determined empirically by Daille, were simple co-occurrence frequency, MI^3, the Fager/McGowan (1963) coeffiecient, and the Log Likelihood measure (Dunning 1993). Fung/Church (1994) suggest a double check: only selected word pairs which have both high MI and t-scores.

Nowadays, researchers wishing to use a "ready-made" word aligner often use the GIZA++ system of Och/Ney (2000).

5.1. Enhancements to statistical word alignment

A number of enhancements have been made to the general procedure described above. Gaussier/Langé/Meunier (1992) were able to eliminate some incorrect high scoring pairs using their best match criterion. For example, they originally created a list of possible candidate translations of the English word *prime* in the Canadian Hansards, consisting of French words found to have a high mutual information score (MI, similar to MI^3, but with the *a* on the top line not cubed) with *prime*. At the top of the list were *sein* (5.63), *bureau* (5.63), *trudeau* (5.34), and *premier* (5.25). Using their best match criterion, they eliminated all candidates which had been found to have a higher MI score with an English word other than *prime*. This left the word *premier* (the correct translation) at the top of the list.

Word-level alignment as described here can be enhanced by stemming rules, for the removal and replacement of common prefixes and suffixes, designed to render alternative grammatical forms of a word equivalent. In the corpus segment shown in Figure 32.2, we have two related pairs of words occurring just once each, *politique* in the same aligned region as *politics*, and *politiques* in the same aligned region as *political*. Since these word pairs occur only once each, we have only weak evidence that they represent translation pairs (MI^3 = 2.58). However, if we recognise that in fact we have two matching pairs of words derived from *polit-*, we now have stronger evidence that these form a translation pair (MI^3 = 3.58). Thus the use of stemming rules can help us better identify translation pairs. French stemming rules have been developed by Savoy (1993), and the most commonly used set of English stemming rules are those of Porter (1980). Similar improvements can be achieved by lemmatisation, where each word is reduced to its dictionary headword. In the calculations presented here, a word has been taken to be any sequence of characters surrounded by white space. Better results would be obtained by preprocessing the corpus to split word pairs forming contractions such as *s'impose* → *se impose*, *l'échelle* → *la échelle*.

When deriving word-level alignments from corpora already aligned at the sentence level, Gaussier/Langé/Meunier (1992) found about 65 % of English words were assigned their correct French translations, 25% had no French word assigned (mainly words with no real French equivalent) and about 10% were aligned with words that were not their correct French translations.

If a bilingual corpus (where the two texts are translations of each other) has not been aligned at the sentence level, it is still possible to use the statistical measures described in this section for word-level alignment. Fung/Church's (1994) K-vec method requires only that the corpus be cut into sections of equal length, and corresponding sections be treated as aligned regions for word length alignment. More complex, and less direct statistical measures can be used for comparable corpora, which contain texts in two languages on the same topic, although they are not translations of each other (Fung/Yee 1988; Peters/Picchi 1998; Gaussier et al. 2004). Here we must start with a small bilingual dictionary, which is augmented with a new word pair from the corpora whenever it can be shown that a sufficient number of collocates of this new word pair are found to correspond in the dictionary.

5.2. Matrix factorisation techniques for word alignment

Goutte/Yamada/Gaussier (2004) achieve word-level alignment from a corpus already aligned at the sentence level, by aligning the words of the two languages through central pivots called cepts, which roughly correspond to individual concepts. More than one word can be aligned with a single cept. The sentences *the licence fee does not increase* and *le droit de permis ne augmente pas* align via four cepts as follows: *the (1) le; licence fee (2) droit de permis; not (3) ne pas; increase (4) augmente*. One matrix is created to store the alignments between the English words and the cepts, and another for the mappings between the cepts and the French words.

These two can be multiplied together to produce the translation matrix, which stores the strength of association between each English word and each French word. An earlier word alignment technique which depended on matrix multiplication was given by Tanaka/Iwasaki (1996).

6. Phrase alignment

Gaussier/Langé (1994) also used statistical measures to work on the problem of finding correspondences between technical terms which were collocations of two content words (such as *station terrienne* and *earth station*) in an aligned International Telecommunications Union (ITU) corpus. The MI between this pair of technical terms was taken to be sum of the following: the MI (as derived above) between *station* and *earth;* the MI between *station* and *station;* the MI between *terrienne* and *earth;* and the MI between *terrienne* and *station*. This was called mutual information with double association.

Lee/Chang/Jang (2006) were interested in aligning named entities such as the names of people and organisations in bilingual documents, as part of machine translation. English named entities were identified either automatically or manually as a preprocessing step, after which the following steps were repeated until all the English named entities were aligned: a) find the set of translation candidates occurring in the target (Chinese) sentence using phrase translation and transliteration (see below); b) evaluate the set of translation candidates, and sort by translation score; and c) align the source and target named entity pair with highest probability.

Following Brown et al. (1990), the phrase translation phase was decomposed into a lexical translation score (the probability of an individual English-Chinese word pair being translations of each other), and a position alignment score such as $P(1 = 2, 2 = 1, 3 = 3)$, the collective probability of the first English word matching the second Chinese word, the second English word matching the first Chinese word, and the third English word matching the third Chinese word. Following Gale/Church (1993), penalties were given for insertions and deletions (such as if a three-word Chinese named entity was proposed as the translation of a two-word English named entity). Names of people and places are typically transliterated into their phonetic equivalents. Thus the system also learns the rules for transliterating English characters into their Pin Yin (Romanised spelling) equivalents. A bilingual dictionary and parallel corpora were used as training data to obtain both the phrase translation and transliteration probabilities.

Other researchers who have used statistical measures to find correspondences between multi-word units are Haruno/Ikehara/Yamazaki (1996), Kitamura/Matsumoto (1996), Smadja/McKeown/Hatzivassiloglou (1996) and McEnery et al. (1997).

7. Structure and tree alignment heuristics

Alignment is not only possible between linear sequences, such as sentences of linear text, but between tree structures. This is important when aligning parse trees from translated texts, to extract phrases for example-based machine translation. The output of tree alignment is a mapping between pairs of coupled nodes. One heuristic for doing this is the crossing constraint (Wu 2000): Suppose two nodes in language-1 (p1 and p2) correspond to two nodes in language-2 (q1 and q2) respectively, and p1 dominates p2. Then q1 must dominate q2. Matsumoto/Ishimoto/Utsuro (1993) give further heuristics for mapping nodes. A cost is associated with any of their heuristics which are not completely fulfilled, and the alignment with least overall cost is the one chosen.

a) Couple leaf nodes (words) that are lexical translations, as found in a bilingual lexicon.
b) Couple leaf nodes that are similar. For example if we have a node for *cat* in English, the correspondence *cat* → *chat* in the English-French dictionary, and a term related to *chat* in the French thesaurus is *tigre*, then the nodes for *cat* and *tigre* will match.
c) Couple internal nodes that share as many coupled leaf nodes as possible.
d) Couple nodes that share as many coupled children or descendents as possible.

Another early method, that of Grishman (1994), assumes that we have a bilingual corpus which has already been aligned at the sentence level, and that both source and target texts have been independently parsed. We also need a bilingual dictionary which lists typical translations for many (but not necessarily all) of the words in the corpus. Node Si in the source parse tree can only be paired with node Ti in the target parse tree if at least one of the following conditions holds true:

1. Ti is a possible translation of Si as found in the bilingual dictionary.
2. There is at least one pair <Sj, Tj> in the alignment such that Si dominates Sj and Ti dominates Tj.

3. There is a pair in the alignment <Sj,Tj> such that Sj immediately dominates Si, Tj immediately dominates Ti, and the syntactic role taken by Ti is a possible translation of the role taken by Si.

Even when these rules are applied, there will be multiple possible alignments. To choose between them, a score for each overall alignment is assigned, which is the sum of the scores of the individual pairings that make up the alignment, which depend on the following four criteria:

1. If Ti is a possible translation of Sj;
2. Whether Si dominates any other nodes in the alignment;
3. If Si immediately dominates other nodes in S which correspond to nodes in T;
4. For each node Tj in the alignment which is immediately dominated by Ti, is the syntactic role a possible translation of the role filled by the node Sj with which it is paired?

All possible alignments between the two trees are considered, and the highest scoring one is chosen as being the most likely.

The various steps for source tree to target tree transformation allowed in Gildea's (2004) model for tree-tree alignment are:

1. Reordering a node's children;
2. Inserting and deleting nodes;
3. Translating individual words at leaf nodes;
4. A single node in the source tree may become two nodes in the target tree and vice versa.

To find the most likely transformation sequence from among a number of possible alternatives, certain probabilities must be learned beforehand from corpora. Related to transformations (1) and (2) above are the reordering probabilities which are in the form *Palign({(1,1)(2,3)(3,2)} | AJXYZ)* meaning "given that the children of node A in the source language appear in the order X, Y, Z, what is the probability of the words corresponding to Y and Z being inverted in the target language?". Such reorderings can include insertions and deletions of individual children. The likelihood of type (3) transformations is given by word to word translation probabilities, and for type (4) we consider the probability of the current node being grouped with one of its child nodes, given the nature of the production rule which decomposes that parent into its child nodes.

In the parse-parse-match scenario, the two sides of the bitext are independently parsed into their constituent structures. Wu (1995), on the other hand, used a biparsing grammar to parse both sides of the bitext simultaneously.

8. Alignment with genetically unrelated language pairs

One of the main challenges when working with languages other than English is character-set dependence. The original set was the ASCII 7-bit set which can encode 128 characters, adequate for English texts, but email systems which still use it require the users of other European languages to circumvent the lack of diacritics by typing, for example, *grüßen* as *gruessen* (German *'to greet'*). There are many larger character sets, such as the 8-bit Latin-1 which covers most Latin-based alphabets with diacritics. Chinese and Japanese require a 2-byte (16 bit) encoding because of their much larger character sets. Examples of character encodings for Chinese are GB and Big5, and TIS 620 for Thai.

The EMILLE project (Baker et al. 2004) has produced monolingual corpora for 14 South Asian languages, and also a parallel corpus of 200,000 words of text in English and its translations in Bengali, Gujurati, Hindi, Punjabi and Urdu. The corpus is marked up in CES-compliant SGML (Baker et al. 1998), which includes sentence and paragraph markers, headings and foreign text (e.g. <s> <p>, <head> and <foreign lang= "eng"> to open sections, and <\s> to close a sentence). Some of the texts were typed in directly using the Unicode word processor Global Writer, and Microsoft Word 2000, running on a Windows 2000 machine, is also Unicode compliant. Other documents were available electronically, such as UK government documents which are available in a wide range of languages, on topics including health, social security and housing. As such, they are rich sources for extracting multilingual term banks in these specific domains. Much material in South Asian languages is encoded in various 8-bit formats. A tool called "Unicodify" was produced by the EMILLE project to convert these various 8-bit encodings into the international standard Unicode, and is available on http://www.ling.lancs.ac.uk/corplang/emille/default.htm.

A number of languages, most notably Chinese and Japanese, consist of unsegmented character sequences without marked word boundaries, and thus automatic word segmentation is generally required before further processing can take place. In particular, sentence alignment algorithms such as that of Brown/Lai/Mercer (1991) rely on estimating sentence length by the number of words in each sentence, which can only be found by segmentation. Problems with word segmentation for Chinese include the low level of agreement between native speakers as to where word boundaries should be, estimated at 70% by Sproat et al. (1996). There was a recent international competition for Chinese word segmentation algorithms, called the First International Chinese Word Segmentation Bakeoff (Sproat/Emerson 2003). One of the entrants (Wu 2003) used the two stage process of word recognition followed by disambiguation. Words were recognised by matching against a lexicon of named entities and derivational morphology rules for the recognition of grammatical variants. Wu also derived heuristics for the identification of new words, not in the lexicon. The next task was to disambiguate between alternative sequences of words which have been proposed in stage one. This may be done by finding which of the possible interpretations allows the most meaningful syntactic parse.

The Gale/Church (1993) sentence alignment algorithm was designed to be language pair independent. A ratio factor *c* is included in one of the formulas to represent the mean ratio of characters in the second language to the number of characters in the first language for a translated text. A second factor, s^2, is included to show the amount of variation in this ratio from sentence to sentence. McEnery/Piao/Xin (2000) found that the lengths of sentences in Chinese are much more poorly correlated with their translation equivalents in English than a closely-related language pair such as English and French, and thus s^2 should be much higher for English Chinese sentence alignment. Another problem is that the Gale and Church program assumes that only 6 types of sentence pairings (1:0, 0:1, 1:1, 2:1, 1:2 and 2:2) occur between translation pairs. However, Chen/Chen (1994) found it was necessary to consider other pairings such as 3:1 and 4:1, since it is common to find several short Chinese sentences matching a single long English one. The Gale and Church algorithm can be extended to incorporate these, but substantial amendments to their computer program are required.

Historically-related languages share cognates, so the correlation between their sentence lengths will be better, and also the cognates themselves can be used to guide the alignment. However, even languages which are not genetically related will contain some similar words due to borrowings and proper nouns. Some of the difficulties inherent in aligning English and Chinese named entities can be overcome if the Chinese is transcribed into its Romanised equivalent, Pin Yin (Lee/Chang/Jang 2006). Successful English-Chinese sentence alignment has been achieved by a number of authors (Fung/McKeown 1997; Wang et al. 2002; Piao 2002).

Prior word segmentation is also required for many sentence alignment procedures involving Japanese. Sentence lengths do not always correspond for Japanese and English, since Japanese function words show little correspondence with their English counterparts, and politeness particles are not always translated. Utiyama/Isahara (2003) align Japanese and English newspaper articles by first performing alignment at the paragraph level (finding the pairs of paragraphs which best match in terms of containing corresponding bilingual dictionary pairs), and then doing sentence alignment using dynamic programming.

9. Conclusion

In this article, we have looked closely at three important preprocessing steps for multilingual parallel corpora, namely segmentation at the sentence level, tokenisation at the word level and alignment. A pair of texts may be aligned at the paragraph, sentence, phrase, word or character level. As well as aligning linear texts, we can also align bilingual parse trees. Alignment techniques are mainly statistical, but may also incorporate linguistic information. We have considered how alignment techniques are evaluated, and the special requirements when aligning texts from non-European languages.

10. Literature

Adamson, G. W./Boreham, J. (1974), The Use of an Association Measure Based on Character Structure to Identify Semantically Related Pairs of Words and Document Titles. In: *Information Storage and Retrieval* 10, 253–260.

Aitchison, J. (1999), *Teach Yourself Linguistics.* London: Hodder Arnold.

Baker, J. P./Burnard, L./McEnery, A. M./Wilson, A. (1998), Techniques for the Evaluation of Language Corpora: A Report from the Front. In: *Proceedings of the First International Conference on Language Resources and Evaluation (LREC)*. Granada, Spain, 135–142.

Baker, P./Hardie, A./McEnery, A./Xiao, R./Bontcheva, K./Cunningham, H./Gaizauskas, R./Hamza, O./Maynard, D./Tablan, V./Ursu, C./Jayaram, B. D./Leisher, M. (2004), Corpus Linguistics and South Asian Languages: Corpus Creation and Tool Development. In: *Literary and Linguistic Computing* 19(4), 509–524.

Barlow, M. (2000), Parallel Texts in Language Teaching. In: Botley, S. P./McEnery, A. M./Wilson, A. (eds.), *Multilingual Corpora in Teaching and Research.* Amsterdam: Rodopi, 106–115.

Brown, P. F./Cocke, J./Della Pietra, J./Della Pietra, V./Jelinek, F./Lafferty, J./Mercer, R./Roosin, P. (1990), A Statistical Approach to Machine Translation. In: *Computational Linguistics* 16(2), 79–85.
Brown, P./Lai, J./Mercer, R. (1991), Aligning Sentences in Parallel Corpora. In: *Proceedings of the 29th Annual meeting of the ACL*, Berkeley, CA, 169–176.
Carbonell, J./Probst, K./Peterson, E./Monson, C./Lavie, A./Brown, R./Levin, L. (2002), Automatic Rule Learning for Resource-limited MT. In: *Proceedings of the Association for Machine Translation in the Americas (AMTA-02)*, Tiburon, CA, 1–10.
Catizone, R./Russell, G./Warwick, S. (1989), Deriving Translation Data from Bilingual Texts. In: *Proceedings of the First International Lexical Acquisition Workshop*, Detroit, MI, 1–6.
Chang, J. S./Chen M. H. (1997), An Alignment Method for Noisy Parallel Corpora Based on Image Processing Techniques. In: *Proceedings of the 35th ACL*, Universidad Nacional de Educacion a Distencia (UNED), Madrid, Spain, 297–304.
Chen, K.-H./Chen, H.-H. (1994), A Part-of-speech-based Alignment Algorithm. In: *Proceedings of COLING'94*, Kyoto, Japan, 166–171.
Church, K. W. (1993), Char_align: A Program for Aligning Parallel Texts at the Character Level. In: *Proceedings of the 31st Annual Meeting of the Association for Computational Linguistics*, Columbus, OH, 40–47.
Daille, B. (1995), *Combined Approach for Terminology Extraction: Lexical Statistics and Linguistic Filtering*. (UCREL Technical Papers 5.) Department of Linguistics, University of Lancaster.
Daille, B./Gaussier, E./Langé, J.-M. (1994), Towards Automatic Extraction of Monolingual and Bilingual Terminology. In: *Proceedings of COLING'94*, Kyoto, Japan, 515–521.
Damerau, F. J. (1964), A Technique for the Computer Detection and Correction of Spelling Errors. In: *Communications of the ACM 7*. New York: ACM Press, 171–176.
Dice, L. R. (1945), Measures of the Amount of Ecologic Association between Species. In: *Geology* 26, 297–302.
Dunning, T. E. (1993), Accurate Methods for the Statistics of Surprise and Coincidence. In: *Computational Linguistics* 19(1), 61–74.
Fager, E. W./McGowan, J. A. (1963), Zooplankton Species Groups in the North Pacific. In: *Science* 140, 453–560.
Fung, P./Church, K. W. (1994), K-vec: A New Approach for Aligning Parallel Texts. In: *Proceedings of COLING'94*, Kyoto, Japan, 1096–1101.
Fung, P./McKeown, K. (1997), A Technical Word and Term Translation Aid Using Noisy Parallel Corpora Across Language Groups. In: *Machine Translation* 12, 53–87.
Fung, P./Yee, L.-Y (1988), An Information Retrieval Approach for Translating New Words from Non-parallel, Comparable Texts. In: *Proceedings of COLING/ACL 98*, Montreal, Canada, 414–420.
Gale, W. A./Church, K. W. (1991), A Program for Aligning Sentences in Bilingual Corpora. In: *Proceedings of the 29th Annual Meeting of the Association for Computational Linguistics*, Berkeley, CA, 177–184.
Gale, W. A./Church, K. W. (1993), A Program for Aligning Sentences in Bilingual Corpora. In: *Computational Linguistics* 19(1), 75–102.
Gaussier, E./Langé, J.-M. (1994), Some Methods for the Extraction of Bilingual Terminology. In: Jones, D. (ed.), *Proceedings of the International Conference on New Methods in Language Processing (NeMLaP)*, 14–16 September 1994, UMIST, Manchester, United Kingdom, 242–247.
Gaussier, E./Langé, J.-M./Meunier, F. (1992), Towards Bilingual Terminology. In: *Proceedings of the Joint ALLC/ACH Conference*. Oxford, United Kingdom, 121–124.
Gaussier, E./Renders, J.-M./Mateeva, I./Goutte, C./Dejean, H. (2004), A Geometric View on Bilingual Lexicon Extraction from Comparable Corpora. In: *Proceedings of the 42nd Meeting of the Association for Computational Linguistics (ACL)*, July 21st–26th, Barcelona, Spain, 526–533.
Gildea, D. (2004), Dependencies vs. Constituents for Tree-based Alignment. In: *Proceedings of the 2004 Conference on Empirical Methods in Natural Language Processing (EMNLP04)*, July 25th–26th, Barcelona, Spain, 214–221.

Goutte, C./Yamada, K./Gaussier, E. (2004), Aligning Words using Matrix Factorisation. In: *Proceedings ofthe 42nd Meeting of the Association for Computational Linguistics (ACL)*, July 21st–26th, Barcelona, Spain, 502–509.

Grishman, R. (1994), Iterative Alignment of Syntactic Structures for a Bilingual Corpus. In: *Proceedings of the 2nd Annual Workshop for Very Large Corpora*, Tokyo, Japan, 57–68.

Haruno, M./Ikehara, S./Yamazaki, T. (1996), Learning Bilingual Collocations by Word-level Sorting. In: *Proceedings of COLING'96*, Copenhagen, Denmark, 525–530.

Hockenmaier, J./Joshi, A. K./Dill, K. A. (2006), Protein Folding and Chart Parsing. In: *Proceedings of the 2006 Conference on Empirical Methods in Natural Language Processing (EMNLP)*, July 22nd, Sydney, Australia, 293–300.

Hofland, K. (1996), A Program for Aligning English and Norwegian Sentences. In: Hockey, S./Ide, N./Perissinotto, G. (eds.), *Research in Humanities Computing*. Oxford: Oxford University Press, 165–178.

Kay, M./Röscheisen, M. (1993), Text-translation Alignment. In: *Computational Linguistics* 19(1), 121–142.

Kiss, T./Strunk, J. (2002), Scaled Log-likelihood Ratios for the Detection of Abbreviations in Text Corpora. In: *Proceedings of the 19th International Conference on Computational Linguistics (COLING'02)*, Aug 24th-Sept 1st, Taipei, Taiwan, 1228–1232.

Kitamura, M./Matsumoto, Y (1996), Automatic Extraction of Word Sequence Correspondences in Parallel Corpora. In: Ejerhed, E./Dagan, I. (eds.), *Proceedings of the 4th Workshop on Very Large Corpora*, Copenhagen, Denmark, 79–87.

Kittredge, R. I. (1985), The Significance of Sublanguage for Automatic Translation. In: Nirenburg, S. (ed.), *Machine Translation: Theoretical and Methodological Issues*. Cambridge: Cambridge University Press, 59–67.

Kruskal, J. B. (1983), An Overview of Sequence Comparison. In: Sankoff, D./Kruskal, J. B. (eds.), *Time Warps, String Edits and Macromolecules: The Theory and Practice of Sequence Comparison*. Reading MA: Addison-Wesley, 1–44.

Lee, C.-J./Chang, J. S./Jang, J.-S. R. (2006), Alignment of Bilingual Named Entities in Parallel Corpora Using Statistical Models and Multiple Knowledge Sources. In: *ACM Transactions on Asian Language and Information Processing*. New York: ACM Press, 121–145.

Lewandowska-Tomaszczyk, B./Oakes, M. P./Wynne, M. (1999), Automatic Alignment of Polish and English Texts. In: Lewandowska-Tomaszczyk, B. and Melia, P. J. (eds.), *PALC'99: Practical Applications in Language Corpora*. Frankfurt a. M.: Peter Lang, 77–86.

Matsumoto, Y./Ishimoto, H./Utsuro, T. (1993), Structural Matching of Parallel Texts. In: *Proceedings of the 31st Annual Meeting of the Association for Computational Linguistics*, Columbus, OH, 23–30.

McEnery, A. M./Langé, J.-M./Oakes, M. P./Véronis, J. (1997), The Exploitation of Multilingual Annotated Corpora for Term Extraction. In: Garside, R./Leech, G./McEnery, A. (eds.), *Corpus Annotation: Linguistic Information from Computer Text Corpora*. London: Longman, 220–230.

McEnery, A. M./Oakes, M. P. (1996), Sentence and Word Alignment in the CRATER Project. In: Thomas, J./Short, M. (eds.), *Using Corpora for Language Research*. London: Longman, 211–231.

McEnery, A. M./Piao, S./Xin, X. (2000), Parallel Alignment in English and Chinese. In: Botley, S. P./McEnery, A. M./Wilson, A. (eds.), *Multilingual Corpora in Teaching and Research*. Amsterdam: Rodopi, 177–189.

Melamed, I. D. (1997), A Portable Algorithm for Mapping Bitext Correspondences. In: *Proceedings of the 35th Annual Meeting of the ACL / 8th Conference of the European Chapter of the Association of Computational Linguistics*, Madrid, Spain, 305–312.

Nagao, M. (1984), A Framework of a Mechanical Translation between Japanese and English by Analogy Principle. In: Elithorn, A./Banerji, R. (eds.), *Artificial and Human Intelligence*. Amsterdam: North Holland Publishing Company, 173–180.

Och, F. J./Ney, H. (2000), Improved Statistical Alignment Models. In: *Proceedings of the Association for Computational Linguistics (ACL)*, Hong Kong, 440–447.

Palmer, D. (2000), Tokenisation and Sentence Segmentation. In: Dale, R./Moisl, H./Somers, H. (eds.), *Handbook of Natural Language Processing*. New York: Marcel Dekker, 11–35.

Palmer, D./Hearst, M. A. (1997), Adaptive Multilingual Sentence Boundary Disambiguation. In: *Computational Linguistics* 23(2), 241–267.

Peters, C./Picchi, E. (1998), CLIR: A System for Comparable Corpus Querying. In: Grefenstette, G. (ed.), *Cross-language Information Retrieval*. Norwell, MA: Kluwer, 81–92.

Piao, S. S. (2002), Word Alignment in English-Chinese Parallel Corpora. In: *Literary and Linguistic Computing* 17(2), 207–230.

Piperidis, H./Cranias, L./Papageorgiou, S. (1994), A New Approach to Automatic Sentence Alignment. Poster presented at Teaching and Language Corpora (TALC94), 10–13 April 1994, Lancaster, United Kingdom. Abstract available at: http://www.comp.lancs.ac.uk/ucrel/talc_handbook.ps.

Porter, M. F. (1980), An Algorithm for Suffix Stripping. In: *Program* 14, 130–137.

Reynar, J. C./Ratnaparkhi, A. (1997), A Maximum Entropy Approach to Identifying Sentence Boundaries. In: *Proceedings of the 5th Conference on Applied Natural Language Processing*, Washington D.C., 16–19.

Savoy, J. (1993), Stemming of French Words Based on Grammatical Categories. In: *JASIS* 44(1), 1–9.

Simard, M./Foster, G./Hannan, M.-L./Macklovitch, E./Plamondon, P. (2000), Bilingual Text Alignment: Where Do we Draw the Line? In: Botley, S./McEnery, A./Wilson, A. (eds.), *Multilingual Corpora in Teaching and Research*. Amsterdam: Rodopi, 38–64.

Simard, M./Foster, G./Isabelle, P. (1992), Using Cognates to Align Sentences in Bilingual Corpora. In: *Proceedings of the 4th International Conference on Theoretical and Methodological Issues in Machine Translation (TMI92)*, Montreal, Canada, 67–81.

Smadja, F./McKeown, K./Hatzivassiloglou, V. (1996), Translating Collocations for Bilingual Lexicons: A Statistical Approach. In: *Computational Linguistics* 22(1), 1–38.

Sproat, R./Emerson, T. (2003), The First International Chinese Word Segmentation Bakeoff. In: *Proceedings of the 2nd SIGH AN Workshop on Chinese Language Processing*, July 2003, Sapporo, Japan. Available at: http://www.sighan.org/bakeoff2003/paper.pdf.

Sproat, R./Shih, C./Gale, W./Chang, N. (1996), A Stochastic Finite-state Word Segmentation Algorithm for Chinese. In: *Computational Linguistics* 22(3), 377–404.

Tanaka, K./Iwasaki, H. (1996), Extraction of Lexical Translations from Non-aligned Corpora. In: *Proceedings of COLING'96*, 580–585.

Tiedemann, J. (2003), Combining Clues for Word Alignment. In: *Proceedings of the 10th Conference of the European Chapter of the ACL (EACL'03)*, April 12th–17th, Budapest, Hungary, 339–346.

Utiyama, M./Isahara, H. (2003), Reliable Measures for Aligning Japanese-English News Articles and Sentences. In: *Proceedings of ACL'03*, July 7th–9th, Sapporo, Japan, 72–79.

Wang, W./Zhao, M./Huang, J. X./Huang, C. N. (2002), Structure Alignment Using Bilingual Chunking. In: *Proceedings of COLING'02*, Aug 24th–Sept 1st, Taipei, Taiwan, 1–7.

Wu, A. (2003), Chinese Word Segmentation in MSR-NLP. In: *Proceedings of the 2nd SIGHAN Workshop on Chinese Language Processing*, Sapporo, Japan, July 2003, 172–175.

Wu, D. (1995), An Algorithm for Simultaneously Bracketing Parallel Texts by Aligning Words. In: *Proceedings of the 33rd ACL*, MIT, Cambridge, Mass., 244–251.

Wu, D. (2000), Alignment. In: Dale, R./Moisl, H./Somers, H. (eds.), *Handbook of Natural Language Processing*. New York: Marcel Dekker, 415–458.

Michael P. Oakes, Sunderland (UK)

33. Searching and concordancing

1. Introduction

This article will deal with the basic techniques of linguistic analysis which involve searching for and finding words and phrases in a corpus, and displaying the results in useful ways. The most common way to display the results of a search in a corpus is in the form of a concordance. In corpus linguistics, a simple concordance is a list of the occurrences of a word, presented one per line along with its immediate context, as in Figure 33.1.

```
rket by setting up more cost effective production facilities based on
ognition that markets are an effective way of generating wealth and
 a national state to exercise effective control of its own affairs has l
s from undertaking the most effective means of monitoring the Sibe
as notes. He always felt that effective musical criticism began by b
it smallpox vaccine remains effective even when stored at relativel
aig Robertson, they have an effective and, at times, elegant midfiel
r his criticisms of the lack of effective policing of what he defends a
 of 1986. The extraordinarily effective popular figure of the masked
ers Situationist film to be an effective oppositional practice. One of
oncept of the spectacle is an effective term which now has a wide cu
les.      This work made an effective bridge to the equally spare a
iunching an inquiry into how effective competition had been in impr
of people already believe an effective education system is the key t
e and get away with it. To be effective this kind of refereeing has to
```

Fig. 33.1: Concordance of 'effective' in a corpus

Concordancing has a long history. One of the first uses of the computer for processing texts was started in 1946 by Father Roberto Busa with the help of IBM to do searches in and generate concordances from the works of Saint Thomas Aquinas. Busa produced the Index Thomisticum, which is available online (Bernot/Alarcón 2005). This work can be seen both as a precursor for work in modern corpus linguistics, but also as the continuation of a long tradition of non-computational work in generating concordances from important texts. In the older tradition, a concordance is an alphabetical list of the principal words used in a book, or body of work, with their immediate text surrounding them.

For many linguists, searching and concordancing is what they mean by doing corpus linguistics. The availability of an electronic corpus allows the linguist to use a computer to search quickly and efficiently through large amounts of language data for examples of words and other linguistic items. When the results of these searches are displayed as a concordance, as in Figure 33.1, the linguist can view the data in a convenient format and start to analyse it in various ways. For other types of analysis and research, searching and concordancing may only be the start of a linguistic investigation. They are ways to verify, identify or classify examples in a corpus, in order to start to develop a hypothesis or a research methodology. Searching and concordancing are important elements in the basic toolkit of techniques which the linguist uses. They are essential for checking results derived by automatic procedures and to examine examples in a text in more detail. These techniques will be examined in more depth in this article.

How do linguists read and analyse concordances? Tognini Bonelli (2001) explores the theoretical basis for reading concordances. She draws attention to the differences between, on the one hand, a linguist reading a text in the usual linear fashion from beginning to end, and on the other hand, a linguist reading the lines of a concordance from a corpus. When reading a concordance, the linguist is looking for patterns of similarity or contrast in the words surrounding the search term. In structuralist terms, when the linguist reads a text, they are reading *parole*, or the way meaning is created in this particular text, and when analysing concordances from a corpus, they can also gain insights into *langue*, or the way that the language system works. In functionalist terms, reading texts allows the reader to concentrate on the poetic, emotive, rhetorical, referential and phatic functions, while concordancing a corpus can foreground the metalingual function of a text (Jakobson 1960).

When the linguist reads concordance lines, the focus of attention is usually on repeated patterns in the vertical direction, or paradigmatic plane. It is also necessary to be able to read each one horizontally, from left to right, to interpret the meaning of the particular example. Reading a set of concordance lines vertically, from top to bottom of the screen, and sorting them in various ways, allows the linguist to see lexical, grammatical and textual paradigms. Simply searching through a corpus and looking at examples one by one is to treat the corpus like a text; it is through concordancing that the patterns of usage and the paradigms are revealed.

Each of the sections below in this article will examine one of the various functions which are available for searching a corpus and for generating and analysing concordances. This article will focus on searching and concordancing in a monolingual text corpus, and the examples given are from English. Some different functions may apply to other types of corpora, and to work on other languages. Some of these differences are referred to briefly in section 17 below. This article is not concerned with search logics, indexing strategies or other techniques from information retrieval – see e.g. Baeza-Yates/Ribeiro-Neto (1999) or Manning/Schütze (1999).

2. Searching for words, phrases and other patterns

2.1. Description

Corpus linguists will typically wish to find certain linguistic items, or sets of linguistic items, in a corpus. The item may be a word, a phrase or some other more complex entity.

The computer can search a corpus quickly for words and phrases. At the simplest level, a search may display one occurrence at a time. More usefully, all the occurrences may be found and displayed for the user.

The process of searching for words in the corpus underpins all of the functions which are described in this article below. They are all either more elaborate ways of searching, or more elaborate ways of displaying the information extracted by a search routine. This section will deal only with the most simple methods of searching in a corpus.

2.2. Example

Figure 33.2 displays the results of opening a corpus file in a word-processing program and searching for the word 'effect'. Note that only one 'effect' is highlighted on screen. References to all corpora and tools mentioned in this article are given in the literature section.

2.3. Analysis with this function

It is possible to search for and find real examples of linguistic items in a corpus. Authentic examples are useful evidence for dictionaries, grammars, textbooks or lecture notes. With the use of a corpus, linguists can find examples which were really used, rather than invented examples. And rather than simply using real examples found when reading a text, using a corpus makes it possible to quickly search across a large collection of texts and find examples which are more typical, and reflect habitual and frequent usage.

Searching for occurrences of a word can also be used to test for its existence in a particular corpus. In this way, a hypothesis that a given feature does not occur can be disproved. However, the non-existence of a linguistic feature in a particular variety of language cannot be proved by its non-existence in a corpus, as the corpus is only a sample and the feature might occur in the much greater population of texts not present in the corpus. Indeed, Chomsky (2002 [1957]) claimed that a corpus (meaning any collection of utterances) can only ever represent a trivial number of the infinite number of possible sentences in a language. Corpus linguists argue, however, that frequencies are interesting and important (for a discussion of these issues see article 3).

While simply searching for and reading examples can be useful, it is preferable to obtain a concordance because then, if results are found, the types of usage which are present can be examined together and compared.

A further use of searching, rather than concordancing, is to search the vast amounts of electronic text available on the web, where the texts cannot all be loaded into a

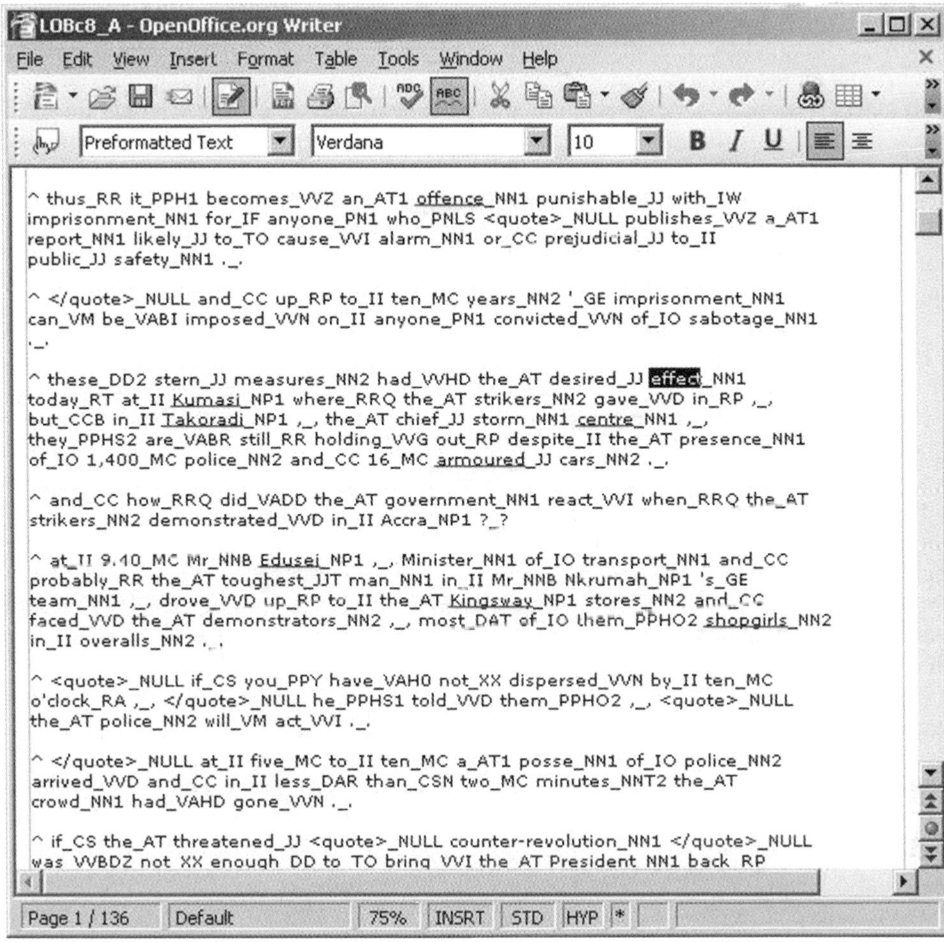

Fig. 33.2: Searching for 'effect' in the Lancaster-Oslo/Bergen (LOB) corpus with a word-processing program

concordance program on the user's computer. Using search engines, the user can search for words or phrases and find many examples. This can be particularly useful for using online text collections, examining new usages in languages which are not yet represented in available corpora, and for investigating emerging modes and styles of electronic communication. Some websites do also offer concordancing online, and systems of returning the results of online searches in the form of concordances are also under development (Renouf/Kehoe/Banerjee 2007). See also article 18

2.4. Technical requirements

Searching in corpora is a task which can be done by a variety of means including the use of scripts, programs, web browsers, word processors, or specialised corpus analysis applications, such as concordancers.

It is possible for users to write their own scripts or programs to search a corpus, if they have the expertise and software tools available to them. In order to obtain a listing of only and all the required examples, in a form that is easy to use, dealing appropriately with markup, along with a suitable amount of co-text, and in a form in which they can easily be read, re-sorted and further analysed, intensive programming and refining of the search program is required. Concordance programs aim to do all of these jobs for the user and present the results of searching a corpus in a useful way. However, a concordance software package might not be able to deal with all types of corpus, and might not be able to carry out all the functions which a user requires, so some programming might be necessary.

A simpler way for linguists to start to search for an example of a string in a corpus is to use a text viewing or editing application, such as a web browser or a word processor. This can be done by loading the corpus text into the application, and then carrying out a simple search (often using the 'Find' command in these programs), where the user types in a word or phrase, and the program displays the section of the text where the next example of the word or phrase occurs. Many applications will allow more complex patterns to be entered as the search term, including wild cards, character ranges, and optional elements. Some applications, such as the IMS Corpus Workbench, will allow regular expressions, which are a powerful way of using a variety of special characters to obtain matches with a set of patterns (using regular expressions one may be able to search, for example, for inflected forms of a word in a non-lemmatized corpus, or for all compounds containing a certain string).

The result of such a search will take the user to the next place in the text where the search term occurs. However, a corpus may be stored in numerous text files and maybe directories, and many applications will not search across more than one file. Opening a corpus in a text editor or word processing program may also be risky, because the user can easily edit the text, perhaps inadvertently, and the program may attempt to correct spelling, silently insert formatting tags, and perhaps alter the file in other ways. The user should also be aware that loading a corpus into a web browser may lead to the browser trying to interpret tags as HTML or as XML; if there are other types of markup in the text it may cause unpredictable and unwanted results in the way the text is displayed. The basic problem is that these programs are designed for reading or editing text documents, but not for searching text corpora.

Concordance programs aim to deal with these potential difficulties and to present the results of searching a corpus in a useful way.

3. Concordances

3.1. Description

A concordance is a listing of each occurrence of a word (or pattern) in a text or corpus, presented with the words surrounding it. A simple concordance of "Key Word In Context" (KWIC) is what is usually referred to when people talk about concordances in corpus linguistics, and an example is shown in Figure 33.1. Concordances are essentially a method of data visualisation. The search term and its co-text are arranged so that the textual environment can be assessed and patterns surrounding the search term can be identified visually. Barlow (2004) defines concordances (and wordlists) as transformations of a text, giving the analyst the opportunity to view different perspectives on a text.

Often a concordance of a particular search term in a corpus will produce too many results for a linguist to read and analyse. In this case a reduced number of examples can be selected. One or two screenfuls is often useful for providing the analyst with at least a preliminary view of the relevant patterns, although the number necessary to examine is heavily dependent on the structure of the corpus, the total number of examples and the type of investigation which is being carried out. If such a sample is chosen, it is important to select them either randomly from the total, or to select every nth example. Otherwise, the software is likely to provide by default the first 40 examples, which may all come from one file, and thus there would be a high risk of a highly biased sample, reflecting only the language usage of one text or variety. Selecting every nth examples is one method of *thinning* a concordance (see section 9).

3.2. Example

Figure 33.1 above shows an example of a concordance.

3.3. Analysis with this function

The primary motivation for the use of concordance data in modern corpus linguistics is the belief that interesting insights into the structure and usage of a language can be obtained by looking at words in real texts and seeing what patterns of lexis and grammar surround them.

The use of concordances is essentially a manual task for human analysts, unlike the use of many computer algorithms to automatically extract information about the occurrence and co-occurrence of words in texts. Automatic extraction of wordlists, collocate lists, etc. can lead the analyst to deal only with words abstracted from the texts where they occur, and taken away from the place where meaning is created. Reading concordances involves looking at words in their context of occurrence in texts, and allows the analyst to see how meaning emerges in the particular case.

Furthermore, reading concordances allows the user to examine what occurs in the corpus, to see how meaning is created in texts, how words co-occur and are combined in meaningful patterns, without any fixed preconceptions about what those units are. It can be a method of approaching the corpus in a theory-neutral way. This is part of what Tognini Bonelli (2001) calls corpus-driven linguistics.

However, interesting results do not spring out as soon as the corpus is loaded into the software. To generate a concordance, the user must select what to search for, and this means approaching the corpus with some pre-conceptions about what words (or other features) will be interesting to look at. One way of avoiding this bias is to make use of a function which some programs have to provide a complete concordance of a text or a corpus, which means making a concordance of every single word. This can be useful for a text, and was the traditional way of making concordances for the study of literary or religious works before the era of the computer. However, a complete concordance of a corpus will usually produce more data than human analysts can cope with.

Even major lexicographic projects are likely to be selective with what words to search for and how many examples to look at in a large corpus. There are other functions, described below, such as making lists of words, collocates and keywords, which can be used as starting points which allow the corpus to suggest things to look for and investigate.

While use of a concordance program may be necessary for corpus-driven work, use of concordances does not necessarily imply that research is corpus-driven. It is perfectly possible to use a concordance program simply to look for data to support a hypothesis which has been arrived at by some means other than analysing the corpus, and most research done using a corpus is probably of this type.

Another important type of work which concordances make possible is data-driven learning. For the language learner, use of a corpus can be a substitute for intuitions which the native speaker acquires through exposure to the mother tongue (e. g. Lamy/ Klarskov Mortensen 1999–2007). See article 7 for more on this topic.

There are many other areas where the qualitative analysis of concordances is essential for identifying and analysing patterns in language. There are some increasingly influential theories which rely on examining collocations and concordances, namely semantic prosody (Louw 1993/2004), semantic preference (Sinclair 2004) and lexical priming (Hoey 2005). See article 45 for more on these topics.

3.4. Technical requirements

Corpus analysis tools will either search through the corpus as a set of text files, or corpora may be pre-indexed, allowing for faster retrieval and more powerful queries. Some tools require corpora to be in particular formats (e. g. plain text, XML, or some other format). Care should be taken to ensure that the particular forms of character and text encoding, file format and markup are being interpreted correctly by the program. This will be more straightforward if the corpus itself is constructed in a fairly standard way and the corpus design and encoding are well documented.

Concordances are usually generated by a program for on-screen display, but it may be essential to save them so that they can be examined again. While a concordance can often easily be generated again by submitting the same query to the same corpus, this may not be possible in some cases. If some complex series of processing steps has been taken, such as sorting, categorising, or thinning the lines (see below), then it may be difficult to reproduce the results. Some of this processing may have to be done by manual selection or annotation, and then this work certainly needs to be saved. There are other reasons why concordances may need to be saved: access to the tools or corpus may be temporary; the corpus may be under development and may change; the tools may be updated and change their functionality in subtle ways. Furthermore, it may be necessary to make the concordance available outside of the program which generates the concordance, so that it can be processed with other tools, or used in teaching, on a website or in a publication. It would therefore be necessary to save the concordance in some portable format, such as HTML. A user should consider whether these functions are available or necessary when selecting (or developing) concordancing software.

The following sections deal with further refinements and enhancements to concordances.

4. Displaying annotations

4.1. Description

A corpus may include various tags, which may encode descriptions of the texts constituting the corpus, elements of the text structure (e. g. paragraphs), or linguistic annotations (e. g. wordclass tags). Concordance software sometimes has the option to hide or display markup.

One possibility is for the concordance software to colour the different parts of speech, so that nouns are red, and verbs blue, for example. This is likely to be easier to read than viewing the concordances with the tags displayed inline with the text. The analyst can see the wordclass categorisation without interruption to the stream of words.

The analyst may wish to be shown tags associated not with the individual words or lines in the concordance, but rather the information associated with the whole text from which the particular concordance line is derived. For example, the name of the file, or title of the text may be useful. Another option would be to indicate, again perhaps by the use of colour contrasts, the category of text from which the example comes. For example, in BNC-Baby, a corpus which is a subset of the British National Corpus, containing 4 million words of written and spoken English, and which is designed to compare and contrast newspapers, fiction, academic writing and spoken conversation, examples from each of these four sub-corpora could be coloured differently.

4.2. Example

Figure 33.3 shows a concordance from the BNC-Baby corpus. This concordance has been produced by Xaira, an XML-aware program, which can recognise and use the metadata and annotations in the corpus in sophisticated ways because it is able to process the XML tags. XML is an international open standard for marking up documents (see article 22). Since the annotations in BNC-Baby are XML tags, XML-aware programs can selectively display or hide the tags.

4.3. Analysis with this function

Viewing the markup associated with concordance lines may sometimes be useful in order to help interpret some of the concordance lines, or to make more patterns visible. It is essential for checking the results of searches using annotations (see section 5 below). When unexpected results are obtained from searching for a particular wordclass tag, for example, it may be necessary to read the tags to find out whether they have been incorrectly assigned, or at least to try to understand the ways in which the wordclass tags have been assigned. There is little consensus in linguistics about how wordclasses should be categorised, and therefore there is a lot of variation in the ways in which different analysts or different programs will assign tags.

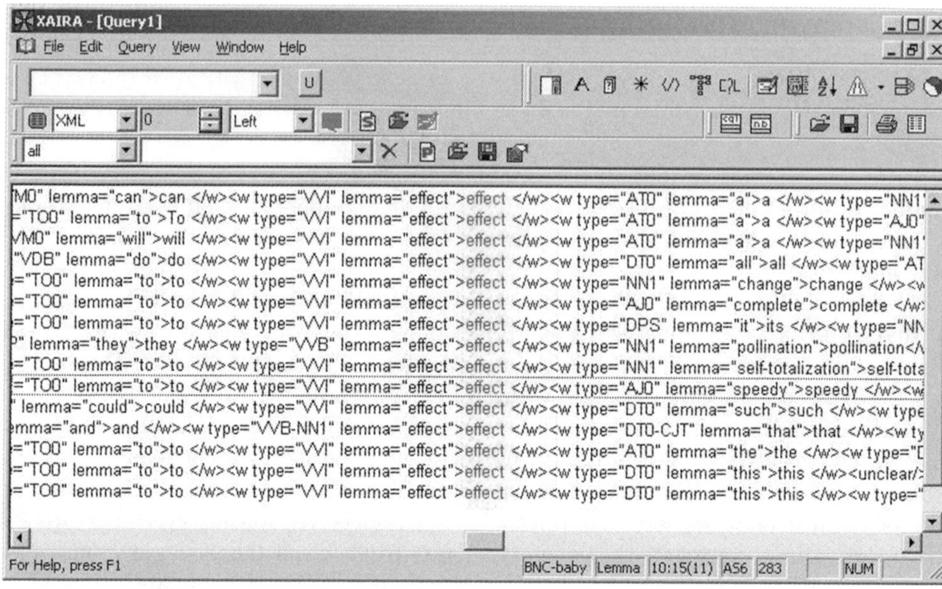

Fig. 33.3: Displaying XML annotations in the BNC-Baby

4.4. Technical requirements

Applying this function usually requires that the corpus text has been annotated. The possibility of implementing this function, and of it being useful to the analyst, depends on the manner in which the markup has been encoded and documented. It is possible in principle that markup could be applied by the software on the fly, but relying on automatic tagging is likely to involve problems of accuracy and consistency as well as additional computational processing.

Displaying information about the source text can help the user to understand the lines of a concordance. Many programs will show the file or text name alongside each concordance line. Others will allow the user to select a line and then view the metadata associated with the text, such as the title, author, date of publication, etc.

The possibilities for selecting elements of the markup and using them to display words or lines differently will become increasingly possible as standards for the encoding of corpora in XML are developed and stylesheet functionality is incorporated into XML corpus analysis tools, to enable the user to adjust and control the display of the output.

5. Using annotation to search

5.1. Description

Corpora often contain various types of tagging. These tags exist in the files in addition to the words which make up the texts, and can include tags which encode descriptions of the corpus and its constituent texts (descriptive metadata), tags which encode information about the text structure, formatting and appearance (structural markup), and tags which encode various levels of linguistic categorisation or analysis of the text (linguistic annotation). It can be useful for the purposes of linguistic analysis to search for examples of words or other units which have been categorised by the use of these tags. In particular, the analyst may wish to exploit the linguistic annotation in a text, such as wordclass tagging (see article 24), or lemmatisation. If a concordancer offers the necessary functionality to interpret the tagging in a sensible way, then it should be possible to search for all examples of a particular word when it is tagged with a particular wordclass categorisation, for example 'effect' as a verb (see Figure 33.4).

Methods for using the descriptive metadata and structural markup are described in the section 'Using metadata' below.

5.2. Example

Figure 33.4 shows a concordance of the word 'effect' where it has been tagged as a verb in the BNC-Baby corpus. The fact that 'cause and effect' is included here is due to a tagging error.

```
months that it's that it's really started to effect this but I know what it is that's because .
:tually interview                       if I do effect all the                       Well you're all g
d with sledgehammers and crowbars 'to effect speedy entry'. Compensation of £8,500 fi
enditure of the 1960s and 70s.          To effect a new social discipline, a new relationshi
 its own alterity and duplicity in order to effect its deconstruction. In this context, we ma
ims that certain forms of literature could effect such a critical, reflective detachment. Thi
e a totality. Although Sartre's inability to effect self-totalization is often presented as a fa
:o the interests of the exploiter. This will effect a displacement or dissolution of self-resp
ıula] as before. The student is invited to effect this reciprocation by means of the fourth
 is a baseline against which attempts to effect change can be measured.
ore ample maintenance and authority to effect the same, We do command the said Chri:
s the chain motion becomes too slow to effect complete untangling of the polymer coils.
time. It is this delay between cause and effect that is fundamental to the observed viscc
:y ny back up to the canopy, where they effect pollination, any slight wind drifting them t
:s in the pattern of home ownership, can effect a change in partisan support.        There
```

Fig. 33.4: 'effect' used as a verb

5.3. Analysis with this function

Exploiting the annotation to specify search terms can help to make more refined, and more grammatically targeted searches. For example, grammar books may say that it is not permissable to say 'less books' or 'less examples', and that it should be 'fewer books' and 'fewer examples'. It is possible to test this prescriptive rule by looking in a corpus at the evidence of what native speakers really say and write. Searching for 'less' immediately followed by a plural noun in the corpus yielded no results, while there were 40 examples of 'fewer' immediately followed by a plural noun.

This does not give conclusive proof that 'less' does not occur before plural nouns, nor that the prescriptive rule is correct. A slightly more sophisticated search pattern (allowing adjectives to occur between 'less' and the plural noun) yielded the following example from this corpus: "even if on the lower rungs with less promotion chances than white men". It is also worth noting that wordclass tags were assigned in this corpus automatically, and it is a possibility that the tagging program would not have been likely to assign a noun tag to a word following 'less', because it might have been programmed with the "rule" which does not permit this sequence.

Searching using the annotation can help to reveal grammatical patterns in the corpus, and it can also be used to find the grammatical patterns which tend to occur with certain words. This tendency for certain grammatical patterns to associate with certain words is known as *colligation* (Firth 1968, see also article 43).

It can also be argued that there is a danger of analysts focussing on the annotations rather than words of the text. Indeed there is a danger of circularity in this methodology, if users simply retrieve the information which has been inserted in the form of annotations by other linguists, or even by themselves, without retrieving any other useful information about the text.

5.4. Technical requirements

Searching with annotation depends on the presence of markup tags in the corpus. The usefulness of the function depends on the quality of the markup, and on the accessibility and quality of the documentation of the markup which is available to the analyst. If the user does not know the tags, or understand the ways in which they have been applied, then it is very difficult to use them and it is easy to misinterpret results. In order to exploit the tagging with software, the software needs to know how to identify and process the tags in the text. (To put this in a more technical way, it is necessary for the corpus analysis application software to be interoperable with the text markup formalism.) For this reason it is useful for the tagging in the corpus to be inserted into the text in a reasonably standardised way, for example as XML tags. XML is a standard way of inserting metadata and markup in a document. If a non-standard form of tagging is used, concordance software is less likely to recognise the markup, and may be unable to differentiate it from the text, or to make use of it in any useful ways. Using non-standard markup can mean that the user is tied to software written specifically to process that markup, which is likely to restrict access to the corpus and reduce its usefulness, especially if the documentation and software specific to the corpus do not survive in the long term.

If the tags are stored separately from the corpus text, in a separate file as "stand-off" markup, then the risk of the tags interfering with the processing of the text is diminished. On the other hand, the computational task of using the tags is made more difficult, and there may be few, if any, standard corpus analysis tools available which can successfully process the tags. However, this type of markup is likely to become more standardised and widely used in the future.

It is not always necessary for a corpus to contain detailed annotation in order to search using wordclass tags and other linguistic categories. An alternative to the use of annotation to carry out analysis of this type is to use lexical and grammatical information which is separate from the text, but which the searching and concordancing programs can make use of. For example, morphological tables may hold lists of inflected forms, which can be used for searches for verb paradigms, as an alternative to annotating all the lemmas in the corpus. One important disadvantage of this approach is that ambiguous occurrences in the corpus are unresolved, or must be resolved "on the fly" by the software each time that the user wishes to make use of them. An important advantage is that the user can conduct searches using annotation on texts which have not been annotated.

6. Expanding the co-text

6.1. Description

Expanding the co-text is a function which can be applied to concordance lines. A concordance line will often be presented to the user as one line on the screen, with perhaps 4 or 5 words visible on either side of the search term. In order for the analyst to be able to read and understand a particular concordance line, it is often necessary to be able to read beyond this limited amount of co-text. It is therefore useful to be able to expand the amount of co-text which is available. Some concordancers only give access to a few extra words or lines; some restrict the scope of the context to some textual unit such as the sentence or paragraph; others allow the analyst to start from the concordance line and read as far as they wish.

6.2. Example

Figure 33.5 shows the concordance of 'effect' in the BNC-Baby corpus (displayed in this case by the MonoConc program), with the expanded co-text for the selected line displayed in the box above the concordance lines.

6.3. Analysis with this function

Being able to read more of the co-text is essential when the analyst wishes to take account of meaning in the text. It may be necessary to read a long way in a text to get enough information to be able to explain the occurrence of a particular linguistic feature in a text.

6.4. Technical requirements

Most concordance programs which make use of a corpus installed locally offer the functionality to expand the co-text. Online concordance programs may restrict the amount

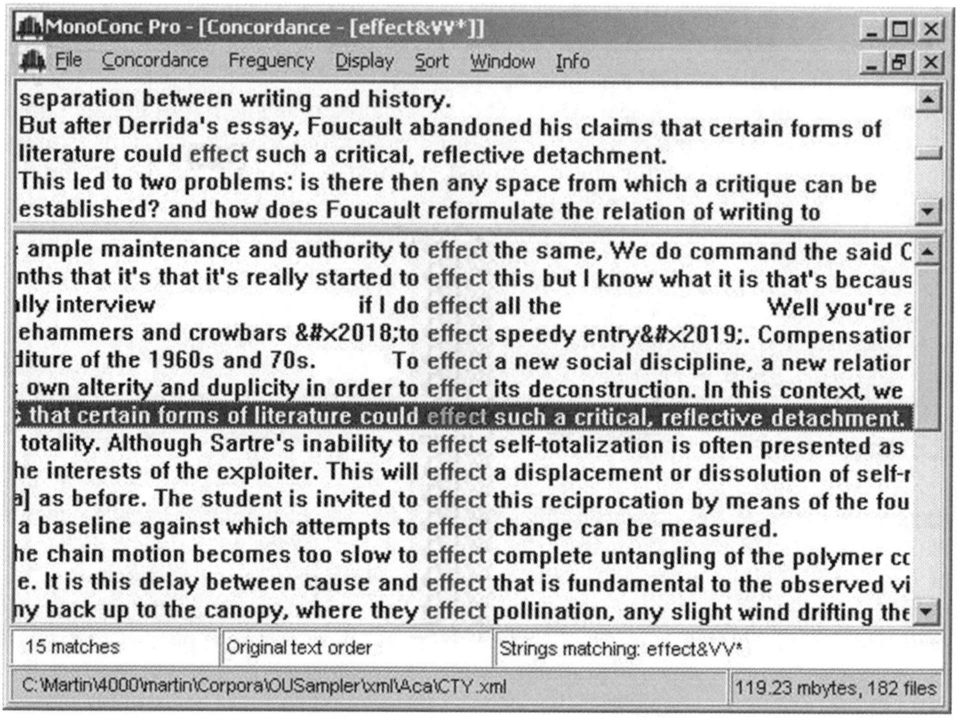

Fig. 33.5: Concordance of 'effect' used as a verb, with expanded context for the selected line

of co-text available in order to prevent the user from downloading an entire text or corpus. This may be necessary because of licensing restrictions on the distribution of the corpus. In this case, it may be necessary to attempt to negotiate access to the full corpus text for more detailed analysis of concordance lines.

7. Sorting

7.1. Description

Sorting is a function which can be applied to concordance lines from a corpus. A concordance program will usually by default present lines in the order in which they occur in the corpus (often called the 'original order'). Sorting the lines on the basis of various criteria may be necessary to reveal patterns in the words surrounding the search term. The criteria according to which lines can be sorted include:

- alphabetically by node (which is only relevant if there is some variation in the node word, such as when wildcards have been used, or when there have been multiple search terms, or search by wordclass or lemma, etc.);
- alphabetically by co-text: words in certain positions around the node word, e. g. one word to the right or left of the node;

– annotations (e. g. grouped together by wordclass tag, or user-defined annotations);
– metadata categories (e. g. text type, sex of speaker);

A further set of options for each of these searches may be made in ascending or descending order (e. g. a-z or z-a in English).

When searching by co-text, it is often useful to try sorting by words in various positions around the search term, for example 1 to 5 places to the left or right. Where the search term is part of a long fixed phrase, it may be necessary to look further away than this, in order to find variation and patterns in the co-text.

It is also possible to sort on the basis of more than one criterion, so that lines which are grouped together according to the first sort criterion are then further ordered, as in Figure 33.6.

```
bility of charging for more services. The effect on the demography of the inner cities cou
ble. How does it change the meaning or effect on the text, as far as you as a reader ...
. this difference is not likely to have any effect on the way in which the individuals will b
The additions to this B-tree have had no effect on the index entries on the left-hand side
ed by some invisible gale which had no effect on the branches of the little trees and eve
vernment and that has inevitably had an effect on the level of the charge.      'This is fi
turn, the Scientific Revolution had some effect on the visual arts. Military engineers, wh
n of personal reference has a noticeable effect on the structure of contributions in conve
y were talking about had had a very bad effect on the Quigleys. Mrs Quigley was hyperv
ent, but is something which also has an effect on the way people behave towards others
s on the prince's function, it also had an effect on the way he fulfilled it. In 1140 the mon
ntanglements begin to have a significant effect on the relaxation times. The undiluted sy
esult, road safety campaigns have little effect on them because they are seen as being
ertions were found to be variable in their effect on timing. IBM files performed better the
n it is introduced, will have a significant effect on transitions. The movement of individu
mpetitive encounter I had an immediate effect on United's performance.      Suddenly '
80pc of its visitors, thus having a major effect on visitor income and support for the est
ts in some of those early films had their effect on Wil he promoted himself to a star on t
 design of the course, conservation and effect on wildlife.      The course boasts a larg
his week as part of a series showing the effect on wildlife of the lowering water table.
nber three so they don't know.'      The effect on women, in a Moslem culture which pe
or female family members can have the effect on women sectioned, of producing less le
.. I felt flattered I I don't usually have an effect on women like that I and thought I loved h
ce in April 1988 have had a devastating effect on young people. At the stroke of a pen th
at his words were starting to have some effect. One or two of the older members were no
```

Fig. 33.6: Concordance sorted by first right then second right

7.2. Example

Figure 33.6 shows a screenful of concordance lines for 'effect' from BNC-Baby, sorted by first word to the right, then second word to the right.

7.3. Analysis with this function

Sorting is often necessary to reveal the patterns of words surrounding the search term. These patterns can more easily be seen by the analyst when repeated occurrences of relevant features are grouped together on the screen. Sorting can help to bring these examples together. In this way, simply sorting on various positions and viewing the lines can reveal patterns which were previously invisible.

7.4. Technical requirements

A concordance program will usually provide the functionality to sort concordance lines. There may be variation in the number of criteria allowed, which criteria may be applied, and the range of co-text over which they may be applied.

8. Searching in concordances

Much of the work of searching and concordancing is about finding out which words tend to occur in the vicinity of other words, and searching in the co-text surrounding the search term in concordance lines may be useful if the analyst is looking for examples of a particular word or pattern. This is a way of searching for the co-occurrence of words and phrases.

The linguist can start to find the words which occur with the search term by sorting the concordance lines and by computing collocations. When some potentially interesting words are suggested by the list of collocates, or by the examination of the concordance lines, the linguist will want to search for the lines in which the word occurs.

Not all concordance programs provide the functionality to search within the concordance lines for a particular word or pattern, or to find co-occurrences of words at all. It may be necessary to use sorting to find the word, although this can be difficult if it is appearing in many different positions around the search term in the KWIC concordance. Words that occur above a certain frequency will appear in a list of collocates, and some programs will allow the user to switch from the collocates list to show a concordance of all the lines in which the collocates appear with the search term.

9. Thinning

9.1. Description

Thinning concordance lines is a function which reduces the number of lines in a concordance, by selecting a subset of the lines based on some criterion. This may be done in order to reduce the number, if there are too many to analyse, or because the analyst is only interested in a particular subset.

Ways of thinning concordance lines include reducing the set to every *n*th occurrence, to *n* per text, or to the first *n* examples (where *n* is any positive integer). A set of concordance lines may also be thinned on the basis of user annotations (see section 10 below).

Searching in results to produce a reduced number of concordance lines (see section 8) can be one way of thinning the concordance lines. Some programs allow the user to search for a string in the concordance lines, and then thin the set of concordances to only those which contain the search string.

9.2. Example

```
tanglements begin to have a significant effect on the relaxation times. The undiluted sy
 even more doses.               Although its effect on the circulation of wild polioviruses ha
their properties would have a beneficial effect on the overall scheme, members heard.
 as rabbits or sheep, has a devastating effect on the fine-leaved bouncy turf rich in spe
ıst, such groups must have had a major effect on the structure of the forest.        The v
ish whether artemether has a beneficial effect on the objective and unambiguous prima
'ernment and that has inevitably had an effect on the level of the charge.       'This is fi
og-meat and biscuits had had a ruinous effect on the housekeeping. Happily Herbert ha
/ were talking about had had a very bad effect on the Quigleys. Mrs Quigley was hyper
 oleoresins of the dipterocarps have an effect on the bacteria of the fore-stomach of col
n but progressive and compensatory in effect. On the circumference of that circle are n
ɔility of charging for more services. The effect on the demography of the inner cities co
ce in April 1988 have had a devastating effect on young people. At the stroke of a pen tl
:ur to her to worry about the devastating effect Paula was having on Edward.        Behln
 and for public health activities. Thus in effect reference centres are indistinguishable f
ı matrix between 'knowledge of a cause/effect relationship between participation progra
nds, detecting a marked distance decay effect.                                   Research p
:rease in blood volume in the lungs I an effect shown by transthoracic impedance techn
time. It is this delay between cause and effect that is fundamental to the observed visc
; so great variety&quot;) give an overall effect that the conclusion is a promotional, or u
e per se , there is some authority to the effect that trespass to goods requires proof of :
Tc interval confirming a largely additive effect; the dose response curves for salbutamc
ıal solution are further examples of this effect.          The fundamentals of light scatteri
v up together than the cross-cousins. In effect, the parallel cousins are as familiar as s
hat if a placebo is to have a therapeutic effect, the patient must believe that it will. Nev
```

Fig. 33.7: The concordance from Figure 33.6 (sorted on right co-text), thinned to display only every 5th occurrence

9.3. Analysis with this function

Thinning lines is often part of the heuristic process of focussing the analysis on a particular area of usage in the corpus. A corpus-driven enquiry will typically start with a search for a particular form, followed by analysis of its meaning and contexts, and then searching for a longer phrase.

Thinning concordance lines is used chiefly for providing an appropriate number of examples for a human analyst to be able to view. This may be done for use in the classroom, so as not to intimidate the student with too many examples. Manually selecting lines is also possible, and may be useful for illustrative or pedagogic purposes, but there is a danger of making a biased selection, and it is important that the person reading the concordance knows that the lines have been manually selected.

If it is intended to generalize from the analysis of the sample, then it is necessary to be aware of the way in which the corpus is structured, and to decide whether the sample is likely to be representative of all the examples. In a similar fashion, if the intention is to generalise about the language on the basis of a corpus, the linguist must also always bear in mind the way in which the texts in the corpus itself have been sampled from the overall population of texts. Analysing only a limited number of the concordance lines may be necessary from a practical point of view, but the analyst must bear in mind that the analysis is based on a sample of a sample.

It is also possible, at least in principle, to apply automatic procedures to thin concordance lines by selecting one or two examples which exemplify typical patterns of usage. This is an attempt to automate the work of finding typical patterns of usage in concordance lines, and may be useful for pedagogical, or for lexicographic applications. Concordance output thinned in this way may be able to show something of the variety of different usages, but will not show patterns of repeated usage in and around the search term. Such a concordance must be read differently. The analyst should not look for repeated occurrences as evidence of typicality, because lines displaying some similarity will have been deleted, and a single typical example allowed to stand for them.

9.4. Technical requirements

A concordance program may be able to thin results, or the same result may be possible by re-running the query with a different search term, or with more filters, for example by searching for a phrase, or by limiting the results to every *n*th occurrence, as described in section 3.

Automatically thinning a concordance to produce typical examples, as discussed above, requires software to implement complex algorithms to interpret the patterns in the co-text and to select typical examples.

10. Categorising

10.1. Description

This is a function which can be applied to concordance lines from a corpus. It is sometimes useful for the analyst to be able to manually categorise the concordance lines, for example to classify different senses of a word which the analyst is able to assign by reading the concordance. Categorising concordance lines can also be used as a way of manually thinning the concordance.

10.2. Example

In the example in Figure 33.8, the analyst has assigned letter codes ('i', 'j', 'r', 'o' and 'n') to each of the 21 concordance lines for 'fast' (every 15th example sampled from BNC-Baby).

easily cultured.
The tubercle bacillus has long been recognised to exist in various guises and seems able to exist interchangeably with and without its cell wall.
When a concerted and invasive effort has been made to find acid fast rods in sarcoid tissue they seem to be present, and acid fast bacteria without cell walls and tuberculostearic acid have also been isolated from lesions of patients with sarcoidosis.

r	Skoda then? No good? if I go too fast! you know, if they put cou
j	ld make that. Oww Think how fast it's gonna be on that. Although game. th
j	tions were reduced to the occasional fast break and the low-percentage shot. Peter S
r	:, for example, was growing twice as fast as the United States' zone, and now emplo
i	auropod could avoid becoming stuck fast in the soft, muddy bottom of a lake. If the ..
j	t's rate of descent was half again as fast as the rest, taking him past the others, and
i	In no time at all Miss Beard was fast asleep. She lay on her back, her usually sa
r	(start to a dull market going nowhere fast. By late afternoon the FT-SE 100 had r
j	1e batsman but the real need is for a fast bowler.' Man in the middle RICHIE Ri
r	.. way I and he couldn't get rid of me fast enough. I felt then as if my whole life I
r	n has caught its radiance. It is rising fast I I swear I can see its motion I above ...
j	:ir engagement. Angus reckoned that fast business expansion was absorbing all her
o	e they seem to be present, and acid fast bacteria without cell walls and tuberculoste
j	3 disgust with the restless owners of fast cars, a temperate man's contempt for drink
r	He knew he would have to work fast. There were already police whistles soundi
n	s of red satin. As I said, he broke his fast and left within the hour.' Corbett rose a
r	being asked. But we've got to move fast.' 'This haste,' said Paul, 'it's ...
j	siness tax. We are also encouraging fast payment by large companies.' He sai
r	in hand to take advantage of another fast growing market. He was optimistic ab

Fig. 33.8: Categorisation codes assigned to concordance lines (using the MonoConc program)

The categorisation has been done as follows: 'r' indicates 'fast' is an adverb, meaning 'quickly'; 'j' indicates that 'fast' is an adjective, meaning 'quick'; 'n' indicates that 'fast' is a noun, meaning 'to go without food', and 'i' indicates that 'fast' is part of an idiomatic expression, partially or fully de-lexicalised. One line has also been tagged 'o', for 'other', and it is often useful to have such a category for problematic examples. Examining more concordances would probably yield more evidence, making it possible to categorise this and other difficult examples, and would involve increasing the number of categories.

10.3. Analysis with this function

Categorising lines manually is necessary where it cannot be done by specifying formal criteria when searching or thinning, either because the functionality is not available, or the necessary level of annotation is not present, or, most likely, because the desired categorisation requires human intervention and analysis. This type of categorisation may therefore be seen as a type of research where the concordance is a tool to help manual, qualitative linguistic analysis.

10.4. Technical requirements

This type of manual annotation of concordance lines is often done on concordance printouts with a pen. Software which allows the annotation to be done on the electronic concordance data makes it possible to sort on the basis of the annotations, and to thin the concordance to leave only those lines with or without a certain manual categorisation.

11. Hiding the node word

11.1. Description

A simple but powerful pedagogic exercise can be created by hiding the search term (or node word) in a KWIC concordance. A human subject can then be shown the concordance lines with the node word invisible, and they must try to guess what the word is. An alternative, or additional, task is to ask the student to identify its wordclass.

11.2. Example

with sledgehammers and crowbars 'to	——	speedy entry'. Compensation of £8,500
nditure of the 1960s and 70s. To	——	a new social discipline, a new relations
ts own alterity and duplicity in order to	——	its deconstruction. In this context, we m
ns that certain forms of literature could	——	such a critical, reflective detachment. Tl
a totality. Although Sartre's inability to	——	self-totalization is often presented as a
the interests of the exploiter. This will	——	a displacement or dissolution of self-re:
ıla] as before. The student is invited to	——	this reciprocation by means of the fourtl
s a baseline against which attempts to	——	change can be measured.
re ample maintenance and authority to	——	the same, We do command the said Ch
the chain motion becomes too slow to	——	complete untangling of the polymer coil
me. It is this delay between cause and	——	that is fundamental to the observed visı
/ ny back up to the canopy, where they	——	pollination, any slight wind drifting then
in the pattern of home ownership, can	——	a change in partisan support. Ther

Fig. 33.9: Concordance with node word concealed

11.3. Analysis with this function

The use of this technique is usually pedagogically motivated. It can be used as a language awareness training exercise for native or non-native speakers.

11.4. Technical requirements

It is useful if the software can do this and print or save the lines with the node word hidden. Otherwise the user can save the concordance and then edit it in another application (such as a text editor or word processor), or even simply print it out and black out the node word with ink.

A related technique that could be useful for teaching purposes would be to conceal the significant collocates where they occur in the concordance lines, and some concordancers can do this automatically.

12. Showing collocates

Collocates are words which tend to occur frequently in the vicinity of the search term. Some concordance software applications can compute the significant collocates of the search term in the corpus, and highlight these words in a particular way in the concordance view, for example by colouring them. In Figure 33.10, the collocates are shown in bold and italic type to differentiate them from other words in the co-text.

ıarket by setting up more ***cost*** **effective** production facilities based on L
ːcognition that markets are ***an*** **effective** ***way of*** generating wealth and
ɔf a national state ***to*** exercise **effective** control ***of*** its own affairs has lc
ɜts from undertaking ***the most*** **effective** means ***of*** monitoring the Siberi
; as notes. He always felt that **effective** musical criticism began by beir
that smallpox vaccine remains **effective** even when stored at relatively
Craig Robertson, they have ***an*** **effective** ***and***, at times, elegant midfielc
For his criticisms of the lack ***of*** **effective** policing ***of*** what he defends as
:y of 1986. ***The*** extraordinarily **effective** popular figure of the masked Sı
ders Situationist film to ***be an*** **effective** oppositional practice. One of tł
concept of the spectacle ***is an*** **effective** term which now has a wide curı
ɔdes. This work made ***an*** **effective** bridge ***to*** the equally spare anc
launching an inquiry into how **effective** competition had been in impro\
t of people already believe ***an*** **effective** education system is the key to

Fig. 33.10: Collocates of the node word

This can help to identify patterns of co-occurrence in the concordance lines, particularly where there are too many examples to see in one screenful, or where the position of the collocate is variable. This is a useful function, because while the linguist may be able see repeated co-occurrences of words and structures, it is not possible to assess the statistical significance of these features simply by looking at them (see article 36).

This method of computing and displaying the collocates does risk obscuring the process of calculation from the user. The linguist should remember that there are various ways to calculate collocates, and choices need to be made regarding, among other things, the collocation window, the basis for establishing what is the expected frequency of co-occurrence, the metric for assessing significance and the thresholds for frequencies and significance. Showing collocates in the concordance window should be seen as only a quick or preliminary indication of potential collocates, which are likely to require more focussed investigation and verification.

Concordance programs will also typically be able to generate lists of significant collocates, sometimes lists of positional collocates, showing which words tend to co-occur in particular positions to the left and right of the node word. Such lists can be invaluable for suggesting further searches to produce concordances and examine patterns of usage. Investigating collocation is a very important part of the corpus linguistics basic toolkit, and is covered in article 58.

13. Using metadata

13.1. Description

With certain corpora and analysis tools, it is possible to restrict the scope of searches to texts (or elements of texts) with particular characteristics. For example, some corpora contain texts which originate in both written and spoken modes. If a corpus is marked-up in such a way that the component texts are clearly marked-up as written and spoken, then searches can be restricted to one section or the other, and frequencies compared.

13.2. Example

Figure 33.11 shows a pie chart from the Xaira program which displays graphically the distribution of the word 'effect' in the BNC-Baby corpus. BNC-Baby is divided into four subsections, each of approximately 1 million words, representing spoken conversation, fictional prose, academic writing and newspapers.

13.3. Analysis with this function

Using metadata to search in particular texts or elements of texts can be particularly useful for research which aims to exploit differences in register, genre, mode and text type among the texts in a corpus.

It should, however, be borne in mind that the design criteria of a corpus may have aimed to sample certain categorisations in a balanced and representative way, while others may simply be indicated and were not carefully sampled and balanced. Sinclair (2005) argues that only elements which are designed to be balanced and representative should be contrasted in research using a corpus.

Careful attention should always be paid to the documentation of the design and implementation of the corpus metadata. For example, Burnard (2000) indicates what the design criteria for the British National Corpus were. He also indicates that, for the spoken, conversational part of the corpus, there is a metadata category which could be used to indicate the sex of the speaker, but which is often only recorded for the main respondent (the person carrying the recording device), and not for the other interlocutors. It is therefore difficult to carry out research to compare the speech of men and women using the BNC, although not impossible (e. g. Rayson/Leech/Hodges 1997).

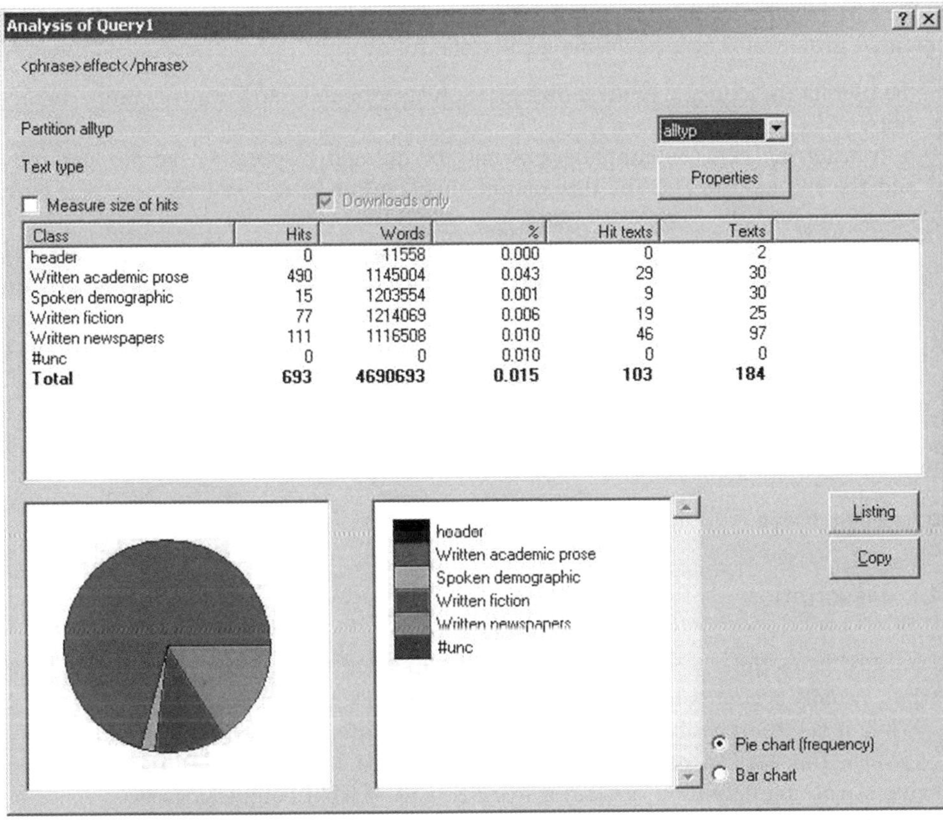

Class	Hits	Words	%	Hit texts	Texts
header	0	11558	0.000	0	2
Written academic prose	490	1145004	0.043	29	30
Spoken demographic	15	1203554	0.001	9	30
Written fiction	77	1214069	0.006	19	25
Written newspapers	111	1116508	0.010	46	97
#unc	0	0	0.010	0	0
Total	**693**	**4690693**	**0.015**	**103**	**184**

Fig. 33.11: Distribution of 'effect'

13.4. Technical requirements

In common with other functions which exploit the markup in a text, application of this function requires access to software which is capable of interoperating with the markup. Successfully doing this is rarer than successful processing of structural markup such as paragraph and page breaks, and annotations associated with individual words, such as wordclass tags. This is because it is necessary for software to recognise and process annotations with a wider, and more complex scope. There may be descriptive metadata which applies to the whole corpus, to sections of it, to subsections, to individual texts, to groupings of texts in different sections, or to certain passages within various texts. For this reason, software which can work with descriptive markup in a sophisticated way will often be tied to a particular corpus, or corpus markup framework.

If the limitations of the corpus markup or the corpus analysis software mean that it is not possible to restrict searches on the basis of metadata categories, then an alternative approach is to put files representing texts from different text types in different folders. Similarly, file naming conventions can be used, so that in effect, codes representing metadata values are encoded in the file name. With these methods, the operating system's method of storing files is exploited to allow the analysis of certain corpus components.

While certain types of analysis can be done this way, there are various limitations and potential problems. These problems include the following:

- the user has to load and analyse different subcorpora and find a way of comparing results;
- in transferring between computers, it may be difficult to preserve the file hierarchy and the file names, and for this reason this solution is not suitable for long term preservation of the corpus metadata;
- it can be difficult, and sometimes impossible to apply multiple metadata categories to define sets of texts – the user may be restricted to one pre-defined categorisation which is fixed in the arrangement of files into folders;
- some operating systems and some concordance programs restrict allowable file names and suffixes, and the number of files in a folder, so a solution may not work in all computing environments.

14. Wordlists

14.1. Description

A wordlist (sometimes written 'word list') is a list of all the different words in a text or corpus, usually accompanied by the number of times each word occurs.

While it is often possible to simply press a button in a software application to make a wordlist, this ease of use may disguise the fact that making a wordlist depends on having a working definition of what a word is, and of what counts as an occurrence of the same word, and that this will vary from language to language.

It is also possible to make lemma lists, where inflected forms of words are counted together as examples of the occurrence of a head word, or lemma. Wordclass tags, or word and tag pairs, may also be counted and listed.

14.2. Example

See Figure 33.12.

14.3. Analysis with this function

Examining the wordlist from a large general reference corpus, as in Figure 33.12, can be useful for finding out about the words which occur most frequently in a language. Examining the wordlist from a text or a specialised corpus can be a starting point for examining the lexis of a particular text or text type. A wordlist from a text or corpus may be compared to the wordlist from a large reference corpus. It may be interesting, for example, to see whether the most frequent words differ from the norm. The lower than usual occurrence of 'of', for example, may be a reflection of a lower amount of post-modifica-

Rank	Frequency	Lemma	Wordclass
1	6187267	the	determiner
2	4239632	be	verb
3	3093444	of	preposition
4	2687863	and	conjunction
5	2186369	a	determiner
6	1924315	in	preposition
7	1620850	to	infinitive-marker
8	1375636	have	verb
9	1090186	it	pronoun
10	1039323	to	preposition
11	887877	for	preposition
12	884599	i	pronoun
13	760399	that	Conjunction
14	695498	you	pronoun
15	681255	he	pronoun
16	680739	on	preposition
17	675027	with	preposition
18	559596	do	verb
19	534162	at	preposition
20	517171	by	preposition

Fig. 33.12: 20 most frequent lemmas in the BNC

tion of noun phrases, which may be a sign of a style which is simpler, or less formal in some way.

Wordlists derived from different components within a corpus may also be compared. Rayson/Leech/Hodges (1997) were able to compare wordlists derived from various sets of speakers in the spoken component of the BNC, and to conduct a quantitative analysis of the utterances of speakers categorized by such factors as sex, age, social group and geographical region.

For a systematic way to find words that occur more or less frequently in a text compared to a reference corpus, a method for determining 'keywords' can be used (see section 15 below).

The most frequent words in a language tend to be grammatical or 'closed class' words. When the user wants to look beyond the most frequent grammatical words in order to see which are the 'content' words which are used most often, a 'stop list' may be used. This is a list of words which the program omits from its searches. Such lists typically contain grammatical, or closed class, words, or simply the most common words in a corpus. If the user is interested in the grammatical words, then it may be necessary to make sure that a stop list is not being used by the program by default. Stop lists are sometimes used by software to prevent users from searching for the most common words, as this would be too big a task for the software, and would produce too many results to analyse manually.

Looking at frequently occurring words may also tell you something about the themes or topics in the texts in a corpus (see more in the section on *Keywords* below).

Obtaining lists of the most frequent words in a corpus can also be used in pedagogic research. Knowing which words occur most frequently can help to indicate which words a learner is most likely to encounter. The top of a wordlist can perhaps be seen as the core vocabulary of a language. The selection of words for learner dictionaries, grammars and other teaching materials is often informed by wordlists obtained from corpora.

14.4. Technical requirements

A utility to make wordlists is usually part of a concordancer or a corpus analysis software package. Although it may not be visible to the user, compiling a wordlist depends on recognising words, or 'tokenising' the text. Being able to count words depends on being able to recognise what a word is, and so some variation in word frequency counts will result from the differing tokenisation algorithms which are employed by different programs.

It is not necessary to use a corpus analysis software package to obtain wordlists from a text or corpus. A simple program can be written in a variety of scripting or programming languages to produce a wordlist. Typically, what such a program will do is send the contents of a file (or a collection of files) through a series of processing steps to (i) remove punctuation characters and other non-word elements, (ii) identify word boundaries, (iii) sort the words into alphabetical order, (iv) identify and count identical words which are adjacent in the sorted list, and (v) sort the wordlist into descending order of frequency.

It is possible to obtain the result by various means, and to make different decisions about what to include or exclude, and how to identify word boundaries, etc. Software usually includes functions to make a wordlist, with varying levels of control of these options.

15. Keywords

15.1. Description

The keywords of a text, in the sense intended here, are words which can be shown to occur in the text with a frequency greater than the expected frequency (using some relevant measure), to an extent which is statistically significant.

Confusingly, the term 'keyword' is used in more than one way in corpus linguistics. It is also used to mean the search term, or node word, as in Keyword in Context (KWIC). The meaning in this section is an important, or 'key', word in a text. This latter usage is inspired by Raymond Williams (1988 [1976], Bennett/Grossberg/Morris 2005), who uses it to signify culturally significant words in the discourse of a society. Mike Scott (2001, Scott/Tribble 2006) introduced the term to corpus linguistics and implemented a method of computing keywords in his WordSmith Tools software.

It is usually most relevant to compute keywords for a text (or a set of related texts) in comparison to a reference corpus, to try to obtain an indication of characteristic lexis in the text (or set of texts).

An interesting development of the notion of keywords is *key key-words*. Scott/Tribble (2006) noted that while words are often computed as *key* in a particular text, they may not be significant across a number of texts of the same type. Those that are *key* across a number of texts in a corpus are called *key key-words*.

15.2. Example

Figure 33.13 shows a list of keywords generated by WordSmith Tools by comparing *A Connecticut Yankee in King Arthur's Court* by Mark Twain with the written component of the British National Corpus, ranked in descending order of their significance, or *keyness*. (The usefulness of such a comparison is discussed in 15.3 below.)

```
I, AND, SIR, KING, YE, IT, MY,
LAUNCELOT, ME, WAS, KNIGHTS, MERLIN,
KNIGHT, ARMOR, CLARENCE, THING,
SANDY, HIM, MARHAUS, THAT, UPON,
TOWARD, MORDRED, GAWAINE, CAMELOT,
SAGRAMOR, SO, DOWLEY, YES, COULDN'T,
MILRAYS, THEN, BUT, THEY, HUNDRED,
PRESENTLY, KING'S, ARTHUR'S, WOULD,
MAN, HAD, WE, ALL, YONDER, THOU,
SLAVE, MIRACLE, OUT, ARTHUR, GOOD,
UNTO, COULD, AH, HATH, MYSELF,
ERRANTRY, LET, SMOTE, ALONG, WELL,
MAGICIAN, NOBLE, HIS, GOT, WHEREFORE,
SWORD, HE, EVERYBODY, THEE, SPEAR,
YOU, ABBOT, PERADVENTURE, OFFENSE,
HERMIT, THEM, PROCESSION,
STRAIGHTWAY, A, YET, MONKS, KAY,
EVER, GUENEVER
```

Fig. 33.13: Keywords in *A Connecticut Yankee*

In the example given in Figure 33.14, the keywords from Shakespeare's *Romeo and Juliet* are given, as calculated in comparison to the rest of Shakespeare's dramatic works. In this way, words which appear relatively more frequently in this play than in the others should appear at the top of the list. The WordSmith Tools program was used for these examples, and the display includes frequency of the words in the text (*Romeo and Juliet*), and in the corpus (the rest of Shakespeare's drama), as well as the frequencies as a percentage of the total number of words in the text or corpus and a calculation of the 'keyness' of the words.

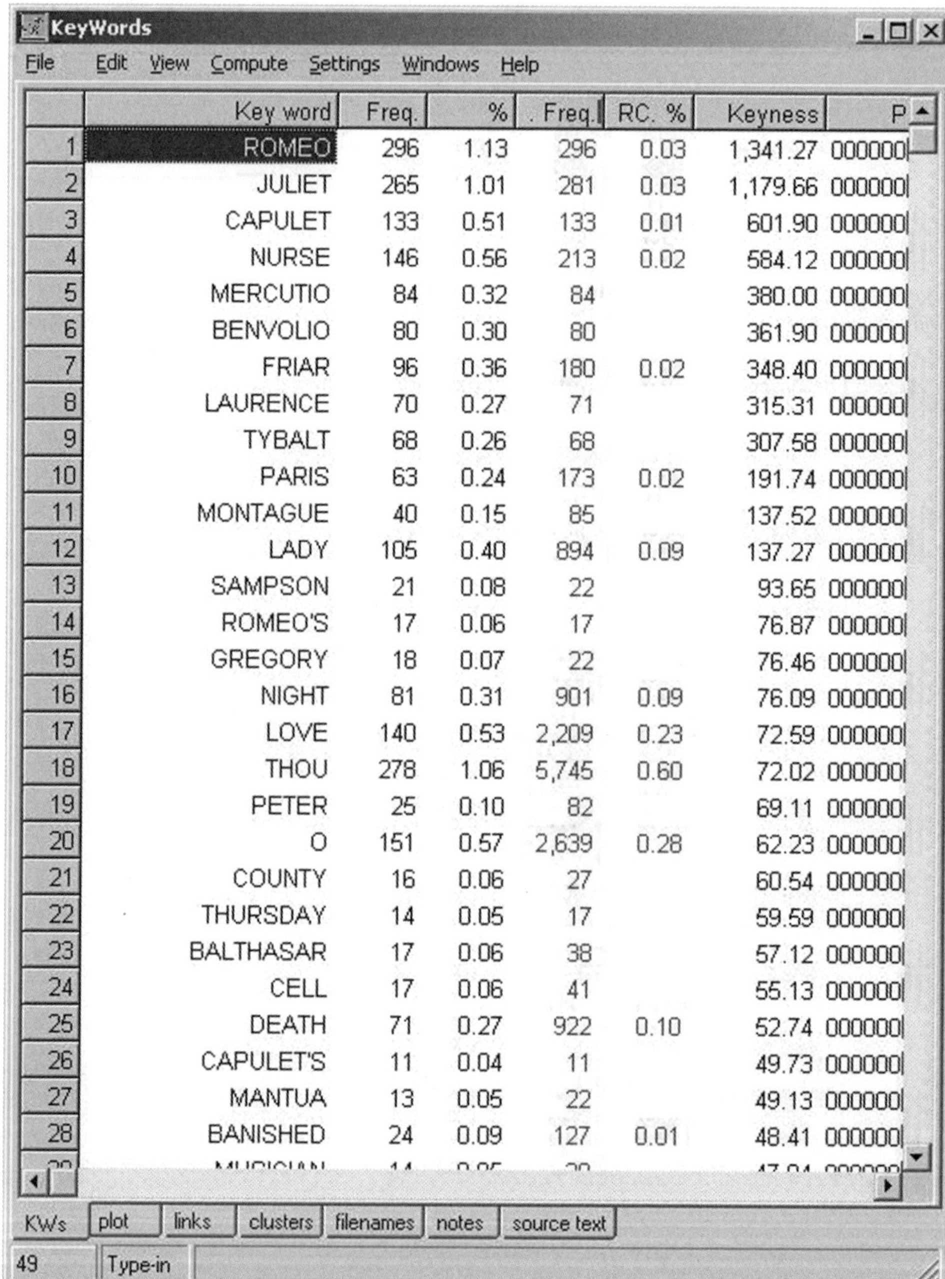

	Key word	Freq.	%	. Freq.	RC. %	Keyness	P
1	ROMEO	296	1.13	296	0.03	1,341.27	000000
2	JULIET	265	1.01	281	0.03	1,179.66	000000
3	CAPULET	133	0.51	133	0.01	601.90	000000
4	NURSE	146	0.56	213	0.02	584.12	000000
5	MERCUTIO	84	0.32	84		380.00	000000
6	BENVOLIO	80	0.30	80		361.90	000000
7	FRIAR	96	0.36	180	0.02	348.40	000000
8	LAURENCE	70	0.27	71		315.31	000000
9	TYBALT	68	0.26	68		307.58	000000
10	PARIS	63	0.24	173	0.02	191.74	000000
11	MONTAGUE	40	0.15	85		137.52	000000
12	LADY	105	0.40	894	0.09	137.27	000000
13	SAMPSON	21	0.08	22		93.65	000000
14	ROMEO'S	17	0.06	17		76.87	000000
15	GREGORY	18	0.07	22		76.46	000000
16	NIGHT	81	0.31	901	0.09	76.09	000000
17	LOVE	140	0.53	2,209	0.23	72.59	000000
18	THOU	278	1.06	5,745	0.60	72.02	000000
19	PETER	25	0.10	82		69.11	000000
20	O	151	0.57	2,639	0.28	62.23	000000
21	COUNTY	16	0.06	27		60.54	000000
22	THURSDAY	14	0.05	17		59.59	000000
23	BALTHASAR	17	0.06	38		57.12	000000
24	CELL	17	0.06	41		55.13	000000
25	DEATH	71	0.27	922	0.10	52.74	000000
26	CAPULET'S	11	0.04	11		49.73	000000
27	MANTUA	13	0.05	22		49.13	000000
28	BANISHED	24	0.09	127	0.01	48.41	000000

Fig. 33.14: Keywords from *Romeo and Juliet*

15.3. Analysis with this function

Keywords are an attempt to characterise the topic, themes or style of a text or corpus. As such, compared to some other forms of analysis using a corpus, keywords analysis tends to focus on the ways in which texts function, rather than on overall characterisations of a corpus, or focussing on isolated linguistic elements in the corpus. For this reason, it is a technique which is popular in various forms of discourse and stylistic analysis (e. g. Culpeper 2002).

It is possible to obtain a lexical characterisation of a text using keywords analysis. The analyst needs to be careful how to interpret results: words can show up as keywords because they are related to the topic, and this is especially likely with proper nouns. Another potential problem is that the value of a keywords analysis depends on the relevance of the reference corpus. Comparing a US nineteenth-century novel with the BNC should produce some keywords typical of the topic and style of the novel, but will also show words which are more typical of US English, words which are more typical of nineteenth-century English, and words which are more typical of prose fiction than the wide range of texts sampled in the BNC. If the aim of the analysis is to identify typical stylistic features of the author, then the novel should more usefully be compared to prose fiction in English of his US contemporaries. If the aim is to identify features typical of only the one novel, it could be compared to the rest of the author's oeuvre.

A final problem relates to frequency and salience. The words which are perceived by the reader as the most significant in a text are not necessarily only those which occur more frequently than the reader would expect. There are other textual devices which can give a particular importance to a word in a text. The fact that a character in a play does not mention his wife's name can be striking and important, for example. Keywords can suggest ways to start to understand the topics or style of a text, and provide statistical evidence for certain textual phenomena, but cannot provide a list of all the interesting words, reveal all stylistic devices, and cannot explain a text.

15.4. Technical requirements

Keywords are calculated by comparing word frequency lists. One interesting aspect of the technique is that it is not necessary to have access to the full texts or corpora used, only to the word frequency list. This has the advantage that researchers who do not have access to the corpus for whatever reason may still be able to access the wordlist and thus calculate keywords. It also means that if the researcher is employing a very large reference corpus, only the wordlist needs to be stored on the computer. So this technique can provide a means of using a large reference corpus where restrictions arise due to size, cost or legal issues. The researchers can conduct their analysis with access to only the wordlists, and keywords can be identified and assessed for their significance purely on the basis of the comparison of lists of out-of-context words. However convenient this may be, it can also be a hindrance to thorough analysis of the actual usage of words in texts. Once a word has appeared in a list of keywords, it is likely to be useful, usually necessary, to look at the concordance lines from the corpus to understand more about whether it is part of a larger unit of words, whether it is occurring only in particular texts, and whether it is playing a particular role in the discourse.

16. Searching for larger units

16.1. Description

Up until now this article has focussed on searching for words which are entered as the search term. Researchers are also interested in using computational methods to find out which sequences of more than one word occur frequently in a corpus. This section deals with using the computer to generate lists of the most frequently occurring sequences of words in a corpus.

16.2. Example

Figure 33.15 contains a list of the 20 most frequently occurring sequences of four words in the BNC, as computed by the online resource Phrases in English (http://pie.usna.edu/explore.html). Note that # represents a number, and that certain sequences count as two words (e. g. "don't") and others as one (e. g. "per cent"), following the ways in which words are defined in the BNC.

```
I don't know
the end of the
at the end of
at the same time
I don't think
for the first time
on the other hand
between # and #
the rest of the
as a result of
in the case of
one of the most
# per cent of the
the Secretary of State
by the end of
from # to #
is one of the
don't want to
to be able to
I don't want
```

Fig. 33.15: 4-grams from the BNC

16.3. Analysis with this function

Various types of multi-word expression may be discovered with these methods. Different sorts of recurring sequences of words are referred to as multi-word expressions, multi-word units, pre-fabricated units (also known as "pre-fabs"), *n*-grams, idioms, phrases and fixed and semi-fixed expressions. Generating lists of such sequences can provide insights into the recurrent phraseology of texts.

The analyst will often find it useful to search for patterns where one of the words is a wildcard, or specified by a part of speech, or a lemma, rather than a literal word form. For example '*preposition* the *noun* of the' proves to be a very common pattern in English. Examining concordances of these variable multi-world expressions will help to show the variety of lexical forms which is produced within and around them, and give some insights into how they are used.

16.4. Technical requirements

Calculating frequencies of multi-word expressions is a computationally complex task. Tools can be optimised for searching for multi-word expressions. All sequences of words of a given length (e. g. all two-, three- and four-word sequences) can be stored in an index, or database. This can give a large improvement to access times and allows computation of the most frequent and significant sequences. It is also possible to make use of lemmatisation and wordclass tagging to find sequences where the forms of some of the words in an expression may vary.

Such work requires considerable pre-processing of the corpus, and then the use of tools designed to access the indexed data.

There is also a complication with identifying the scope and granularity of multi-word expressions. Many patterns appear to be built up of smaller units, with some variable and some fixed elements. For example, some of the entries in the list above overlap, so that for example "I don't want" and "don't want to" appear as separate entries, but many if not most of these will be part of the longer sequence "I don't want to".

17. Searching and concordancing beyond the monolingual text corpus

This article has concentrated on the functions and tools which are commonly used with an English monolingual text corpus. Other types of corpus exist and are widely used. There are corpora of many languages and writing systems (see articles 21 and 20). With some languages it is useful to focus on different forms of analysis from the ones suggested here. There are multilingual corpora, where the focus of research is on comparing languages; similarly there may be corpora which have different versions of a text in one language (e. g. different translations) which the user wishes to compare (see article 16 and 55). And there are corpora which encode and store different modes, in the form of digital audio or video (see articles 11 and 12). Some corpora have streams which need to be aligned, such as audio, a phonetic transcription and an orthographic transcription.

Similar forms of alignment are necessary for various forms of parallel corpus, such as translation corpora (see articles 16 and 55).

Many of the functions described can be used on corpora of other languages; some of the functions reflect basic techniques which have to be implemented in different ways for other types of language; quite different techniques are necessary for other types of corpus.

Parallel corpora require structural markup to indicate the alignment of equivalents units. In the translation corpus, this alignment is typically done at the paragraph or sentence level. Specialist concordance programs exist for displaying both versions to the user, and may have further functionality, such as suggesting potential translation equivalents for the search term.

It is becoming increasingly possible for multimedia corpora to capture in digital form the audio (and sometimes also video) of language events. Current technology for sound or image-based retrieval (e. g. "find me something which sounds like this ...") is rarely successfully implemented in language analysis tools, and corpora still generally require the use of the text transcription or markup for retrieval. A user may search in the orthographic or phonological transcription for occurrences of a particular word (or other unit) and then listen to the linked audio stream as well for each of the concordance lines. The techniques for analysis of spoken data are likely to be subject to significant advances in coming years as more resources and tools become available (see article 31).

While it is hoped that some of the principles outlined above will continue to be of relevance, the corpora of the future are likely to reflect a multilingual and multimedia environment in which distributed online access to resources and to analysis tools is increasingly the norm.

18. Tools and corpora

The following resources and tools were used in producing the examples for this article, or were examined to help with the taxonomy of functions:

- British National Corpus (BNC) and BNC-Baby http://www.natcorp.ox.ac.uk/.
- Bank of English and the 'lookup' tool – this resource is not freely available online. Search for Bank of English and check websites at Collins Dictionaries and at the University of Birmingham for further information.
- Concapp http://www.edict.com.hk/PUB/concapp/.
- Concordance http://www.concordancesoftware.co.uk/.
- IMS Corpus Workbench http://www.ims.uni-stuttgart.de/projekte/CorpusWorkbench/.
- Lancaster-Oslo/Bergen Corpus (LOB), see http://khnt.hit.uib.no/icame/manuals/lob/INDEX.HTM.
- MonoConc http://www.athel.com/mono.html.
- ParaConc http://www.athel.com/para.html.
- Phrases in English (PIE) http://pie.usna.edu/.
- Variation in English Words and Phrases (VIEW) http://view.byu.edu/.
- Sara and Xaira http://www.natcorp.ox.ac.uk/tools/.
- WordSmith Tools http://www.lexically.net/wordsmith/.

There are many other very useful tools available. The fact that they are not included here should not be seen as a reflection on their potential usefulness.

19. Literature

Baeza-Yates, R./Ribeiro-Neto, B. (1999), *Modern Information Retrieval*. Harlow: ACM Press, Addisson Wesley.

Barlow, M. (2004), Software for Corpus Access and Analysis. In: Sinclair, J. (ed.), *How to Use Corpora in Language Teaching*. Amsterdam: John Benjamins, 204–221.

Bennett, T./Grossberg, L./Morris, M. (eds.) (2005), *New Keywords: A Revised Vocabulary of Culture and Society*. Oxford: Blackwell.

Bernot, E./Alarcón, E. (2005), *Index Thomisticus by Roberto Busa SJ and Associates*. Available from: http://www.corpusthomisticum.org/it/index.age [Accessed 2006-10-02].

Burnard, L. (ed.) (2000), *Reference Guide for the British National Corpus (World Edition)*. Available from http://www.natcorp.ox.ac.uk/docs/userManual/ [Accessed 2007-01-11].

Chomsky, N. (2002 [1957]), *Syntactic Structures*. Berlin: Mouton de Gruyter.

Culpeper, J. (2002), Computers, Language and Characterisation: An Analysis of Six Characters in Romeo and Juliet. In: Melander-Marttala, U./Östman, C./Kytö, M. (eds.), *Conversation in Life and in Literature: Papers from the ASLA Symposium 15*. Uppsala: Universitetstryckeriet, 11–30.

Firth, J. R. (1968), *Selected Papers of J. R Firth 1952–59*. Edited by F. R. Palmer. London: Longman.

Hoey, M. (2005), *Lexical Priming: A New Theory of Words and Language*. London: Routledge.

Jakobson, R. (1960), Concluding Statement: Linguistics and Poetics. In: Sebeok, T. (ed.), *Style in Language*. Cambridge, MA: MIT Press, 350–377.

Lamy, M.-N./Klarskov Mortensen, H. J. (1999–2007), Using Concordance Programs in the Modern Foreign Languages Classroom. In: Davies, G. (ed.), *Information and Communications Technology for Language Teachers (ICT4LT), Slough, Thames Valley University*. Available from: http://www.ict4lt.org/en/en_mod2-4.htm [Accessed 2007-04-25].

Louw, W. (1993/2004), Irony in the Text or Insincerity in the Writer? The Diagnostic Potential of Semantic Prosodies. In: Baker, M./Francis, G./Tognini Bonelli, E. (eds.), *Text and Technology*. Amsterdam: John Benjamins, 157–176. [Reprinted in Sampson, G./McCarthy, D. (eds.) (2004), *Corpus Linguistics: Readings in a Widening Discipline*. London: Continuum, 229–241.]

Manning, C./Schütze, H. (1999), *Foundations of Statistical Natural Language Processing*. Cambridge, MA: MIT Press.

Rayson, P./Leech, G./Hodges, M. (1997), Social Differentiation in the Use of English Vocabulary: Some Analyses of the Conversational Component of the British National Corpus. In: *International Journal of Corpus Linguistics* 2(1), 133–152.

Renouf, A./Kehoe, A./Banerjee, J. (2007), WebCorp: An Integrated System for Web Text Search. In: Hundt, M./Nesselhauf, N./Biewer, C. (eds.), *Corpus Linguistics and the Web*. Amsterdam: Rodopi, 47–68.

Scott, M. (2001), Comparing Corpora and Identifying Key Words, Collocations, and Frequency Distributions through the WordSmith Tools Suite of Computer Programs. In: Ghadessy, M./Henry, A./ Roseberry, R. L. (eds.), *Small Corpus Studies and ELT: Theory and Practice*. Amsterdam: Benjamins, 47–67.

Scott, M./Tribble, C. (2006), *Textual Patterns: Keyword and Corpus Analysis in Language Education*. Amsterdam: John Benjamins.

Sinclair, J. (1991), *Corpus, Concordance, Collocation*. Oxford: Oxford University Press.

Sinclair, J. (2004), *Trust the Text: Language, Corpus and Discourse*. London: Routledge.

Sinclair, J. (2005), Corpus and Text: Basic Principles. In: Wynne, M. (ed.), *Developing Linguistic Corpora*. Oxford: Oxbow Books, 1–16. Also online, available from http://www.ahds.ac.uk/linguistic-corpora/ [Accessed 2006-10-02].

Tognini Bonelli, E. (2001), *Corpus Linguistics at Work*. Amsterdam: John Benjamins.

Williams, R. (1988 [1976]), *Keywords*. London: Fontana.

Martin Wynne, Oxford (UK)

34. Searching treebanks and other structured corpora

1. Introduction

A corpus is a collection of written or spoken text compiled for the purposes of linguistic description and analysis. In a parsed corpus, each sentence is given a structured grammatical analysis in the form of a tree. For linguistic purposes it is necessary to augment parsing with manual correction. Automatic parsing of unrestricted text tends to produce incomplete analyses (Briscoe 1996), although these may prove useful in computational applications.

In this book we use the term *treebanks* to refer to parsed corpora whose sentences have been constructed or verified by a linguist. These corpora are (a) much more limited in scale than automatically tagged megacorpora such as the BNC (Aston/Burnard 1998) – a million words is typical, (b) require significant effort to construct and (c) have a wide range of uses from simple exemplification to the evaluation of linguistic theories. As these datasets are collected and annotated, questions arise as to how best to exploit and explore them.

Some applications, such as identifying cases for teaching purposes, simply require the extraction of suitable examples. Others, including general linguistic research and computational generalisation, have rather more complex requirements. These can be considered in two distinct stages:

(i) **Repurposing** the data by focusing on concepts central to a particular research programme or application goal (including designing experiments and extracting a relevant dataset). A query defines a set of results that can then be further evaluated.
(ii) **Evaluating** this data against linguistic hypotheses (Wallis/Nelson 2001) or otherwise generalising from the dataset (articles 42 and 43).

This article is concerned with searching large forests of annotated data. In so doing, we distinguish between an annotation scheme *per se* and the general approach one takes to specifying a query. The critical question is, *by what procedure, and employing which representation, should researchers comb this forest of utterances for linguistic knowledge?*

This paper is organised as follows. Section 2 discusses the *topology* of parsing schemes. By topology we mean the set of structural constraints which define permissible trees and queries. Whereas grammatical schemes differ widely (cf articles 13, 28), structural constraints applied to them vary less. The two most common topologies are *con-*

stituent grammars, including phrase structure grammars (e. g., Marcus et al. 1993; Nelson/Wallis/Aarts 2002), and *dependency grammars*, including constraint grammars (e. g., Karlsson et al. 1995).

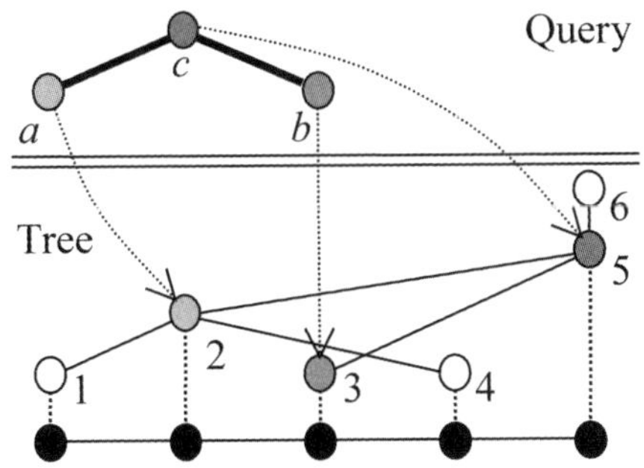

Fig. 34.1: Matching a query to a tree so that <*a*, *b*, *c*> = <2, 3, 5>

Section 3 discusses the relative merits of employing formal logic and diagrammatic models for the purposes of composing a structured query, and the visualisation of resulting cases in a corpus. We distinguish between the process of *matching* a query to a tree in the corpus (Figure 34.1) and any subsequent processes (depending on the application) that may organise and *evaluate* these matching cases. Matching a query against a tree means applying a *proof procedure* to identify configurations of nodes and words (such as <2, 3, 5>) that correspond to a query (<*a*, *b*, *c*>).

Reliably retrieving examples of phenomena from a corpus is not merely a question of applying a single query and yielding a single result. Section 4 considers the problem of retrieving multiple results that may interact with, or even overlap, one another.

Finally, section 5 considers how extending the annotation of corpora impacts on problems of search.

2. Elementary topology

A parsed corpus is segmented into plausible sentences annotated in the form of a tree. In this section we consider corpora with the three distinct topologies summarised in Figure 34.2: (a) part of speech (POS) tagging, (b) dependency or constraint grammar and (c) constituent phrase structure grammar. These three representations broadly cover the gamut of parsed corpora. Section 5 reviews some more complex structural issues.

2.1. A POS-tagged corpus

In Figure 34.2(a), a string of lexical items is connected in sequence. Each word is given a part of speech tag, marked as 'pos' nodes. Typically, this tag will contain a word class category (noun, verb etc.) and further subcategories (plural, past, etc). Different tagsets denote subcategories differently (cf. article 23). CLAWS derivatives such as C5 (McEnery/Wilson 2001) label a common singular noun 'NN1', while ICE (Nelson/Wallis/Aarts

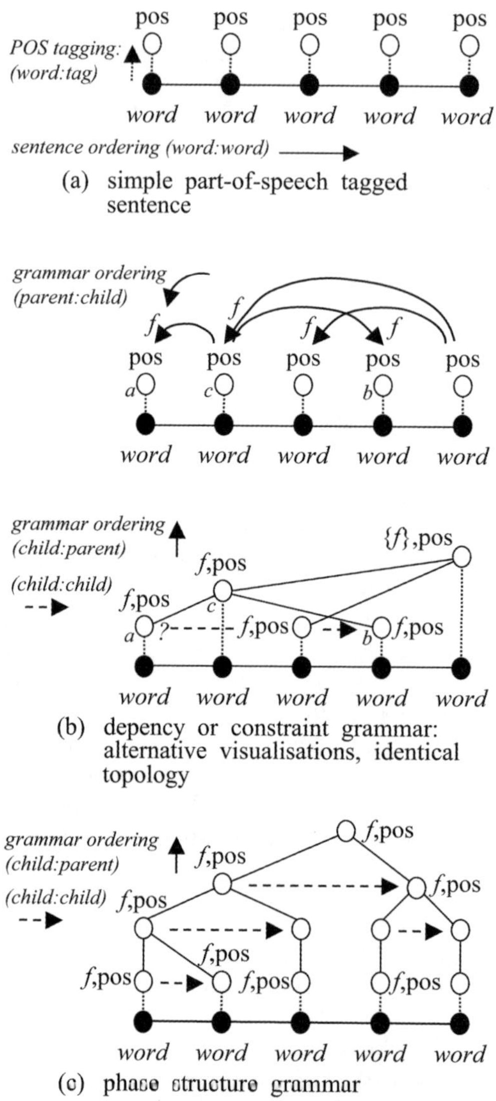

Fig. 34.2: 3 simplified grammatical topologies

2002) spells out each subcategory *feature*, 'N(com, sing)'. ICE notation is more verbose, arguably more transparent, and features are more readily disassociated from each other than C5. As a result one can specify a query for a singular noun as 'N(sing)', rather than the wild card 'NN*1*'.

Table 34.1 lists a range of queries on an ICE POS-tagged corpus. Sentences are sequences of word/tag pairs, so queries might include simple strings; wild cards and logical expressions for words and tags; and sequences of these.

Tab. 34.1: A selection of typical POS-tag queries (ICE notation)

Query	applies to	description
fish	single lexical element	Simple string.
fish*		Wild card.
(expedition or trip)		Logical expression of two simple strings.
{expedition, trip, party}		Set of alternative strings.
<N(sing)>		Word-class tag.
<N or PRON>		Logical expression of two POS tags.
fish* + <N>		Wild card limited by POS tag.
fish* trip	strict lexical sequence	Wild card followed by simple string.
fish* (expedition or trip)		Wild card followed by logical expression.
<N> ? trip		POS tag, any lexical item, simple string.
fishing * trip	lexical sequence	Two simple strings separated by any number of intervening items.

2.2. A dependency grammar corpus

The topology of a typical dependency or constraint grammar is given in Figure 34.2(b). The string of tags in Figure 34.2(a) is extended by the introduction of a named link for each node, marked with an *f*, to another word/tag pair. (In some representations the final ‘head word’ may be linked to a further node.) These links form an acyclic tree where nodes cannot be linked in a loop.

The two visualisations in this figure are isomorphic. The *f* label, which we might call the *function* of the node or link, can be stored with the child node.

Dependency grammars have the following characteristics. A tree contains one node per word and no intermediate constituents. Some, but not all, dependency frameworks permit crossing links.

The most important point, of course, is that these analyses are not merely available to be admired or compared. Queries can exploit the tree.

Queries on a dependency grammar corpus must be able to express relations along the parent-child axis, marked ‘grammar ordering’ in Figure 34.2(b), as well as the sentence axis. In Table 34.1 the space between elements indicates that one word follows another, and ‘+’ connects a word and tag. The presence of additional relational axes means we have to consider how these other relations are distinguished and expressed.

There are two broad traditions for expressing bundles, or *ensembles*, of relations in artificial intelligence. These are *logic-based* and *model-based* representations. In section 3 we discuss the relative benefits of each. But before we discuss how relations are put together in a query, let us first examine how the topology specifies a minimal set of individual relations.

We use the notation ‘**Relation**(*target*, *source*)’ throughout this article, where ‘**Parent**(*c*, *a*)’ means *c* is the parent of *a*. (Mathematical symbols are as follows: ‘$\wedge$’ = and, ‘$\vee$’ = or, ‘$\neg$’ = not, ‘$\forall$’ = for all, ‘$\exists$’ = exists, ‘$\Rightarrow$’ = entails, ‘$\Leftrightarrow$’ = entail each other, ‘$\equiv$’ = is defined as, ‘$\in$’ = member of set, ‘$\{a, b\}$’ = set containing *a* and *b*, ‘$\varnothing$’ = unspecified.)

a) Parent

In our example dependency grammar, the function *f* of a node is equivalent to a label associated with the link from the node to its parent. This has the implication that the function can be treated in a similar way to a feature of the node, and may be optionally included as a constraint in a query on that node.

If a grammatical vector is separable from its function, it is reasonable to elaborate an optimal set of general topological relations between two connected nodes in a query. The pair of diagrams in Figure 34.2(b) have the same topology, so the dependency vector between two word/node pairs (*a* and *c*) is equivalent to the relationship between a 'child' and 'parent' node. A query might express immediate or eventual connection along this axis, which we can denote as '**Parent**(*c*, *a*) ∈ {*Parent*, *Ancestor*}'.

In certain circumstances, parent-child directionality may be unimportant, so this set may include unordered relations, '*Parent/child*' and '*Same branch*'. Stating that '**Parent**(*c*, *a*). = *Parent/child*' would be equivalent to requiring that *a* and *c* were directly connected by a single arrow but that the direction was unspecified. Some small noun groups (or phrases) could be interpreted as having an ambiguous head, so within such a group it is conceivable that a tree may include a bi-directional arrow. Strict dependency is not obligatory in some constraint grammars. However, in the main, unordered **Parent** relations are usually *linguistically meaningless*. In a strict acyclic tree they will match two situations with radically different meanings: either *a* dominates *b* or *b* dominates *a*.

b) NextChild

A second set of relations express the relationship between siblings, indicated by the dashed arrow in Figure 34.2(b). The relevance of this sibling axis depends on whether the order of children has meaning. Dependency grammars may not be restricted by word order. As we saw, some permit crossing links, in which case the actual order may be irrelevant.

If the grammar presumes that function labels specify an ordered set of 'slots' (e. g., subject, verb, direct object), but we do not know that elements *actually* appear in this order, the researcher may relax the ordering requirement. The issue for the linguist is whether an observed sequence is meaningful, i. e., it represents a phenomenon worthy of research.

An optimal set of relations are '**NextChild**(*b*, *a*) ∈ {*Next*, *After*, *Just before/after*, *Before/after*, *Branch after*, *Different branches*}'. The first four relate to sibling order and require that the two nodes share a common parent. '*Next*' and '*After*' state that the second node immediately, or eventually, follows the first in the sequence of children; the '*Before/after*' options are unordered. The last two values of **NextChild**, '*Branch after*' (ordered) and '*Different branches*' (unordered) refer to situations where two nodes might not share the same parent. This can occur if at least one child in the query has an '*Ancestor*' relation (Nelson/Wallis/Aarts 2002, 151–155).

If crossing links are not allowed in the grammar, '*Branch after*' is not required.

c) NextWord

In a lexical or POS-tagged corpus, one may specify a query as a 'wild card' variation of a lexical stream, as in Table 34.1. We define the word-order relation set '**NextWord**(w_2, w_1) ∈ {*Next*, *After*, *Just before/after*, *Before/after*}' by analogy with **NextChild**.

d) HasNode

A final set of relations connects words and nodes. A POS-tagged corpus consists of a sequence of simple pairs of words and nodes, so a 'word plus tag' query (e.g. 'fish* + <N>') will suffice. In a parsed corpus, we may wish to express the concept that a node dominates a word, without requiring that they are directly connected. This distinction can be expressed as '**HasNode**(a, w) $\in$ {*Parent*, *Ancestor*}'.

In summary, to express queries on a corpus analysed with a dependency or constraint grammar, we need to be able to relate words and nodes together with four different types of relation, summarised by the sets **Parent**, **NextChild**, **NextWord** and **HasNode**.

2.3. A phrase structure grammar corpus

A phrase structure grammar adds nodes to those in dependency trees. These nodes represent phrases or clauses and bracket other sets of nodes (including single nodes) below them. A node can either tag a word or bracket a number of nodes (but not both). While a dependency tree has one node per word, a phrase structure tree contains up to twice as many (e.g., in ICE-GB the ratio is approximately 1.8). However, with this in mind, a phrase structure grammar and a dependency grammar have remarkably similar topologies. Compare Figures 34.2(b) and 34.2(c).

A phrase structure grammar is usually applied to a corpus in a descriptive rather than prescriptive manner. This has two possible implications. First, that a *strong ordering* restriction is applied, i.e. that the sentence sequence orders the tree, and prevents crossing links. Second, additional null (notional) words may not be inserted in the sentence, i.e. that the tree is *closed* by the sentence (see section 5.1.). If these topological restrictions are enforced, the query can be similarly constrained using axioms (see below).

For now, let us note that this similar topology means that essentially the same relation sets and axes – **Parent**, **NextChild**, **NextWord** and **HasNode** – are applicable to dependency and phrase structure grammars.

3. Representation, visualisation and matching

Earlier we made a distinction between matching and evaluation. At this point we discuss how relations are composed and visualised to form a query which can be matched against trees. We distinguish between formal *representation* – what a query may be composed of, and how constituents are integrated – and *visualisation*, which is concerned with how the query may be expressed and communicated. Naturally representation impacts on both visualisation and matching, and underpins the design of a search tool.

3.1. Criteria for evaluating query representations

How should we evaluate a query representation? On what basis should we prefer one representation over another? We propose the following set of criteria, in order of decreasing importance.

(i) **Linguistic adequacy.** It should be possible to express any query that has linguistic meaning. This is more important than absolute expressivity – just because one system is more formally expressive than another one does not mean that this expressivity necessarily has a *linguistic* benefit. For example, some query tools can state that two children have the same part of speech, without stating what it is. While expressive, this is of dubious linguistic value. Absolute expressivity may not be required for another reason. In a mature query platform one should be able to combine queries (typically in a logical expression). In summary, *the expressivity of a query system applied to a particular grammar circumscribes the set of linguistic concepts one can retrieve.*

(ii) **Transparency.** A more transparent representation is simply one easier to understand than another, given the same annotation scheme. The main problem that all users of parsed corpora face is sufficiently *learning the grammar* to achieve their goals. An important benefit of a transparent representation is that researchers can learn the grammar and *how it is applied to the corpus* by carrying out queries. Ideally, the user should be able to predict how a query matches examples in the corpus. The *totality* of the expression must be clear. We can see this in Table 34.1. Although lexical queries increase in complexity as one descends, there is a straightforward relationship between each expression and the cases it matches.

(iii) **Expressivity** is a formal property based on the expressivity of individual atoms and relations between them. Two representations are *representationally equivalent* if each can express everything the other can express. Sets ('{*a*, *b*}') and disjoint logical expressions ('$a \vee b$') are equally expressive. One representation is more expressive than another if a distinction can be made in the first that cannot be made in the second. Wild cards are more expressive than simple strings. The option to use unordered **NextChild/Word** relationships increases flexibility. Finally, the ability to relate nodes in a grammatical analysis represents further expressive possibilities.

(iv) **Efficiency** refers to the straightforward computational criterion of the implementation of a search. Although this is relatively unimportant compared to the ability to capture a linguistically meaningful expression, as corpora increase in size and complexity, retrieval efficiency is important in practice. Wallis/Nelson (2000) discuss this question in some detail.

The issues listed here are independent of a particular grammatical analysis. We have noted that different analysis schemes use different formalisms, encode different syntactic, morphological and semantic features, and are based upon different theoretical precepts regarding the meaning of terms. However, linguistic adequacy must ultimately be considered in relation to a particular analysis scheme. The corollary is that if one can identify the same linguistic phenomena in corpora annotated with different frameworks, the actual grammar deployed makes little difference to the results.

3.2. Logic-based queries

So far, we have elaborated four distinct classes of relation which queries must support. At this point we must make a basic decision as to how these relations are combined together. Traditionally there are two approaches: logic and models.

Advocates of a logic-based approach emphasise that logic is supremely expressive, yet despite this expressivity it retains a "clear formal semantics" (Hayes 1977). This means that a logical expression can be evaluated by a series of formal rules. Predicate logic is an extremely general formalism that may be used to express queries by the device of identifying elements and specifying relations between them.

To keep things simple, let us first review the use of logic in a POS-tagged corpus. The examples in Table 34.2 apply to two word sequences, w_1 and w_2, where w_1 immediately precedes w_2, represented by the **NextWord** predicate.

Tab. 34.2: Logical combinations of two-word queries

Query	description
1. $\exists w_1,w_2.(w_1 =$"fishing" $\wedge\ w_2 =$ "trip" $\wedge$ **NextWord**$(w_2, w_1))$	Equivalent to "fishing trip".
2. $\exists w_1,w_2.((w_1 =$ "fishing" $\vee\ w_2 =$ "trip") $\wedge$ **NextWord**$(w_2, w_1))$	Matches "fishing ?" or "? trip".
3. $\exists w_1,w_2.(w_1 =$ "fishing" $\vee\ w_2 =$ "trip" $\vee$ **NextWord**$(w_2, w_1))$	Implausible. Matches "fishing", "trip" *or every word pair where w_1 precedes w_2.*
4. $\exists w_1,w_2.(w_1 =$ "fishing" $\wedge \neg\ (w_2 =$ "trip") $\wedge$ **NextWord**$(w_2, w_1))$	Matches "fishing ?" but not "fishing trip".
5. $\exists w_1,w_2.(w_1 =$ "fishing" $\wedge \neg\ (w_2 =$ "trip" $\wedge$ **NextWord**$(w_2, w_1)))$	Matches "fishing" where fishing is not followed by "trip".

Our first observation is that the expressivity of logic is at the expense of brevity. It is much simpler to write "fishing trip" than the equivalent logical expression. In Query 2, it is easier to list the two alternatives, *fishing* followed by a word ("fishing ?") or a word followed by *trip*, than work out the outcomes from the equivalent logical expression query. Query 3 is highly implausible and likely to be entered in error. It produces three different situations with limited linguistic connection. Permitting a relationship between elements to be optional is not very useful if the elements are left unrelated as a result.

The final pair of queries in Table 34.2 illustrates the importance of the scope of logical negation. The first matches *fishing* followed by any word, provided that this word is not *trip*. The second matches *fishing* except cases where it is followed by *trip*, in other words, it will also match cases where *fishing* is the last word in the sentence.

The problem with logic is twofold. Despite the phrase, 'a clear semantics' does not mean that an expression and its implications are readily understandable. It is easier to comprehend "[fishing ?] or [? trip]" than "$((w_1 =$ "fishing" $\vee\ w_2 =$ "trip") $\wedge$ **Next-Word**$(w_2, w_1))$". Moreover, as this example shows, provided that we allow queries to be *combined* with logic, many of the benefits disappear. We are left with queries like Query 3 in Table 34.2, where the expression specifies a set of alternative constraints on unconnected parts. Much of this expressivity does not seem to be linguistically very useful.

Most examples cited in favour of logic over models contain negation, e. g., 'find all clauses *without* a subject'. Such an expression is easy to understand but difficult to realise in a single conjoint model. However, one can achieve the same result by a process of subtracting the results of one query from those of another – remove the intersection of all clauses containing a subject from the set of all clauses. (In the introduction we distinguished between the evaluation and *organisation* of cases.)

What would a logical language sufficient for queries on a parsed corpus look like? *Tree Query Logic* (TQL, Wallis/Nelson 2000) and *Finite Structure Query* (*fsq*, Kepser 2003) implement queries in first order predicate logic. Below we use a TQL notation for consistency.

TQL employs a number of first order predicates that code for relations between two sorts of element in a tree. In section 2 we discussed a set of plausible topological relations between elements. We now consider how these might be translated into a logical formalism. Figure 34.3 illustrates a simple arrangement of three nodes, x, y and z, and two words, w_1 and w_2, which we will refer to in what follows. Table 34.3 lists a set of predicates sufficient to describe immediate and eventual relationships in a parsed corpus.

Tab. 34.3: Ordered TQL binary predicates

1-step predicate	multi-step predicate	axis	description
Parent(x, y)	**Ancestor**(x, y)	*parent:child*	x dominates y
NextChild(z, y)	**FollowingChild**(z, y)	*child:child*	z is after y in a sequence of children
HasNode(y, w_1)	**HasNodeAbove**(y, w_1)	*node:word*	node y annotates word w_1
NextWord(w_2, w_1)	**FollowingWord**(w_2, w_1)	*word:word*	w_2 is after w_1 in the sentence

Each predicate in the first column takes a single step in one direction along the equivalent axis. These are sufficient to construct a tree structure (or, conversely, a tree can be converted into a logical expression).

One can derive useful unary predicates. These *edges* of the query are indicated by grey 'T' marks in Figure 34.3.

LastWord(w_2) = $\neg\exists w_3$.**NextWord**(w_3, w_2). (there is no w_3 following w_2)

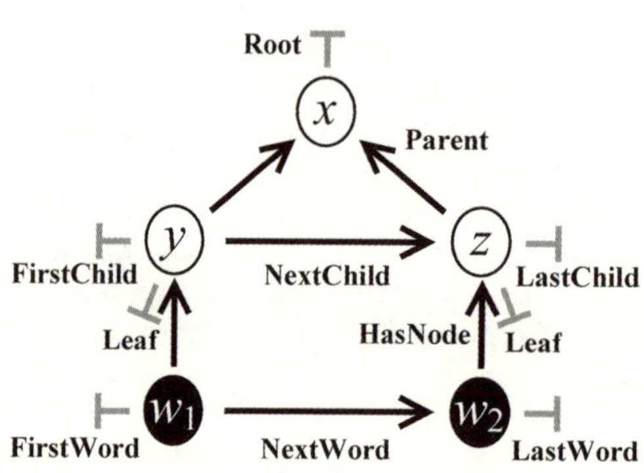

Fig. 34.3: Feasible predicates for a two-sort (word, node) TQL for a phrase structure grammar, after Wallis/Nelson (2000). In a dependency grammar x could also directly annotate a word

A similar process defines **FirstWord, Root, Leaf** etc.

Each single-step predicate can be complemented by another one (in the second column in Table 34.3) which covers an arbitrary number of steps. **FollowingWord** has the same effect as the spatial wild card '*'. If necessary one can derive unordered equivalents from ordered ones, but this is much more useful for model-based representations:

$$\textbf{AdjacentWord}(w_2, w_1) \equiv (\textbf{NextWord}(w_1, w_2) \vee \textbf{NextWord}(w_2, w_1)).$$

It is also necessary to introduce a number of topological axioms. These ensure that unfeasible trees cannot be constructed, including the following.

$$\textbf{Parent}(x, y) \Rightarrow \neg\ \textbf{Parent}(y, x) \quad \text{(circularity)}$$

$$\textbf{FollowingChild}(z, y) \Rightarrow \exists x.(\textbf{Parent}(x, y) \wedge \textbf{Parent}(x, z)). \quad \text{(children share a parent)}$$

Axioms may define the relationship between multiple and single-step predicates, thus:

$$\textbf{Parent}(x, y) \Rightarrow \text{Ancestor}(x, y).$$

Finally, topological properties of the grammar (see section 2) are expressed as axioms:

$$\textbf{FollowingChild}(z, y) \wedge \textbf{HasNodeAbove}(y, w_1) \wedge \textbf{HasNodeAbove}(z, w_2) \Leftrightarrow \textbf{FollowingWord}(w_2, w_1) \quad \text{(tree is ordered by sentence)}$$

$$\neg\exists x.\textbf{Parent}(y, x) \Leftrightarrow \exists w.\textbf{HasNode}(y, w). \quad \text{(tree is closed at words)}$$

We can complete the definition of relations outlined in section 2, and simplify some expressions as a result. However the fundamental problem is that in order to evaluate and comprehend a logical combination of relations one needs to draw a tree in the first place (if you needed to refer to Figure 34.3 to follow the argument above, you have proved my point). If this is the case, perhaps it is preferable to use query representations based on tree diagrams rather than logic.

3.3. Model-based queries

With the exception of *fsq* (Kepser 2003), model-based representations dominate this field. Although less theoretically expressive, models are simply easier to use. At the time of writing, for phrase structure corpora, they have been deployed by *tgrep* and *tgrep2* (Rohde 2001), *CorpusSearch* (Randall 2000), *LDB* (van Halteren/van den Heuvel 1990), *VIQTORYA* (Kallmeyer/Steiner 2003) and *ICECUP III* (Nelson/Wallis/Aarts 2002). Dependency grammar query tools include *TIGERsearch* (Lezius 2002) and *Netgraph* (Ondruška/Mírovský 2005). (See the papers for availability of software.)

The differences between the queries these tools can express are relatively minor, with much of the variation being in the grammar and how results are organised and evaluated.

To evaluate the benefits and costs of employing models to express queries, we will focus our discussion on one of these approaches, ICECUP's *Fuzzy Tree Fragments* (FTFs, Wallis/Nelson 2000) using examples based on the ICE phrase structure grammar, with trees drawn from left to right by default. However, the principles outlined here are common to all of these representations.

A model-based representation is one where elements are considered as part of a coherent whole. In logical terms this means that everything stated should be co-present, i. e., elements and relations are conjoined. Switching from logic to FTFs, therefore, loses negation and disjunction, except within prescribed limits. For example, ICECUP 3.1

(Nelson/Wallis/Aarts 2002) permits logical expressions within nodes and lexical items but only co-occurring combinations of relations. The result of this limitation is a much clearer representation. Let us consider an example.

Consider a query for a clause containing a noun phrase subject and direct object, sketched in Figure 34.4. In logic we would write something like the following:

$\exists x,y,z.$[cat(x)='CL' ∧ (cat(y)='NP' ∧ func(y)='SU') ∧ func(z)='OD' ∧ **Parent**(x, y) ∧ **Parent**(x, z) ∧ (**FollowingChild**(y, z) ∨ **FollowingChild**(z, y))]

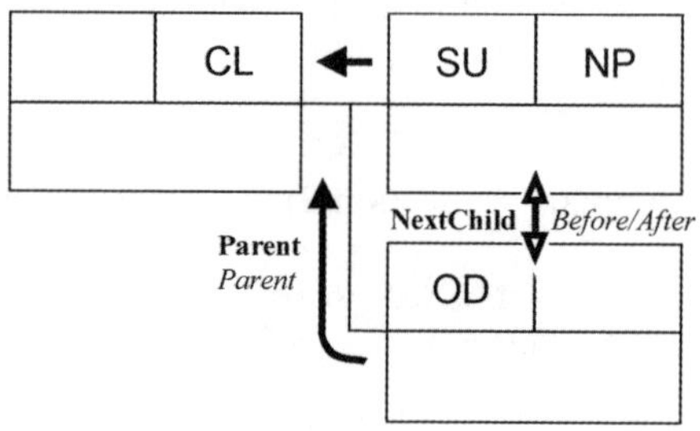

Fig. 34.4: A sketch of a query: a clause (CL) dominating a subject noun phrase (SU,NP) and a direct object (OD), in either order

The model-based representation guarantees a *coherent visualisation*. The total structure in Figure 34.4, representing a specific linguistic event, is immediately apparent and reflects tree structures in the corpus.

A Fuzzy Tree Fragment is a generalised grammatical subtree, containing notional node and word elements, with a series of named relational *links* and *edge* properties at each point. Edges are optionally specified as True or False. Links can take one of a number of values depending on the axis. **Parent** is mandatory and ordered: it must be either *Parent* or *Ancestor*. For the ICE grammar, **NextWord** and **NextChild** may be any of those listed in section 2 except *Branch after* (the grammar is strongly ordered by the sentence ordering).

Figure 34.3 shows how the applicability of particular links and edges depend on the configuration of nodes. Only the top-most node of a query, x, can be a **Root**. If two children are ordered by **NextChild**, the first, y, cannot be a **LastChild** and the second, z, cannot be a **FirstChild**. A similar principle applies to words.

ICE is a closed grammar and all leaf nodes have words attached. As a result the state of the **HasNode** relation may be deduced by the node's **Leaf** status.

Leaf(y) $\Rightarrow \exists w_1$.**HasNode**(y, w_1) (immediate)

Conversely if it is possible that y is not a leaf, **HasNode** is eventual.

3.4. Visualising and matching queries

ICECUP (Nelson/Wallis/Aarts 2002) visualises FTFs by a system of colour-coded arrows, lines and edge markers. Against a grey background, black lines are used to depict the existence of an *immediate* connection (**Parent** in Figure 34.5) and white to indicate an *eventual* or *possible* connection. The absence of a line marks the impossibility of a link. **NextChild** and NextWord relations are depicted by a system of arrows. In Figure 34.5, **NextChild** is *Before/After* (double headed white arrow) and NextWord is unspecified (no arrow). The various edges **(Root, Leaf** etc.) are drawn as white 'possible extensions' to the structure.

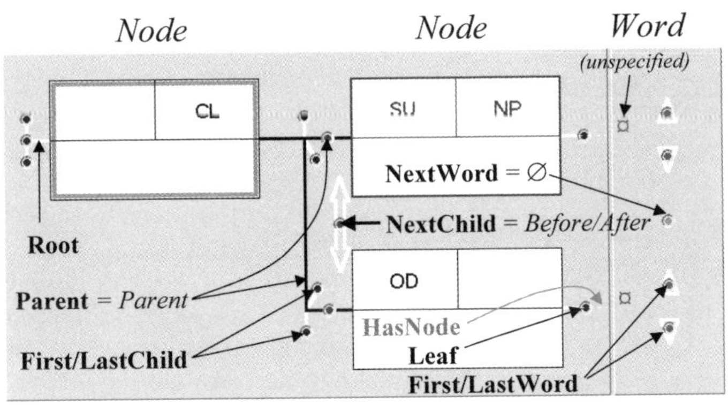

Fig. 34.5: An FTF visualised by ICECUP, (annotated), for the query in Figure 34.4

The benefits of a model-based approach should be immediately apparent. A tree-editing user interface, with extensions to set the status of links, can rapidly construct these fragments. FTFs are *visually coherent* – the total arrangement has meaning to the user – unlike a list of logical relations. A diagram is worth a thousand predicates. They are spatial structures rather than linear lists. This reflects the observation that tree diagrams are easier to follow than bracketed syntax (see, for instance, Quirk et al. 1985, 38). A diagrammatic approach is also readily extensible (see section 5) provided that complexity is carefully managed.

(As an aside, the value of graphical representations has been explored in a number of fields in science. Discussing the history of scientific creativity, for example, Cheng/Simon 1995 argue that selection of the 'right' diagrammatic representation has often proved to be the key to progress.)

The second advantage of employing tree models for queries on parsed corpora is that *it is much easier to visualise matching results*. Our query matches the ICE-GB treein Figure 34.6 twice.

1. [But [it]$_{SU,NP}$ needs [cooking]$_{OD}$ so we can see if it turns out all right]$_{CL}$
2. But it needs cooking [so [we]$_{SU,NP}$ can see [if it turns out all right]$_{OD}$]$_{CL}$ (ICE-GB S1A-012 #107)

We can illustrate these two matching patterns by colouring the nodes of a tree diagram. It is then easy to confirm how our query has matched the tree.

The FTF maps onto every matching tree in this way. Using a simple colour scheme, one can highlight each matching case in turn, and examine how different cases *interact* – for example, identifying that the second case above, *so we can see ...*, is subordinate to the first. This question of interaction is a general issue in corpus research (see below).

Examining matching patterns also reveals overlapping cases, as in the following tree (Figure 34.7).

3. The point is [[you]$_{SU,NP}$ can do [[what]$_{OD}$ [you]$_{SU,NP}$ like]$_{OD,CL}$]$_{CL}$ <laugh>

(ICE-GB S1B-007 #229)

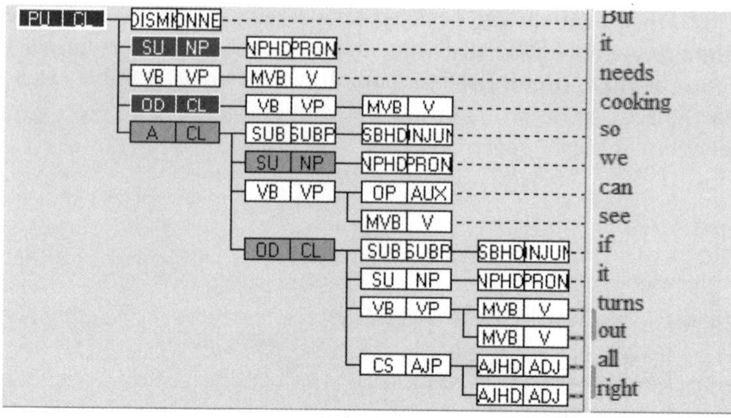

Fig. 34.6: Matching the same tree twice

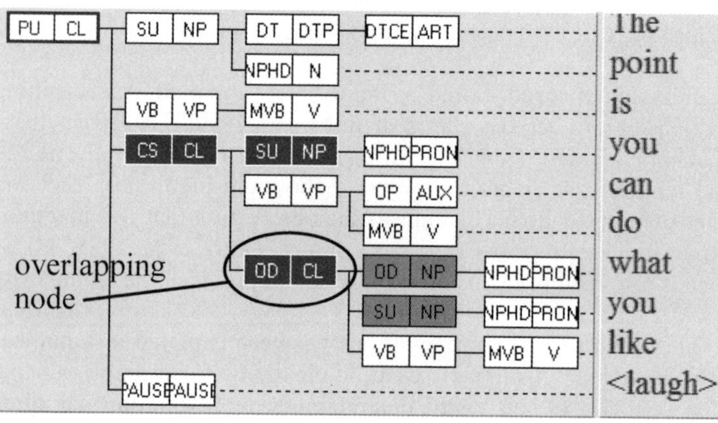

Fig. 34.7: Two cases sharing a node in an ICE-GB phrase structure tree

Here the direct object of the overarching clause *you can do what you like* is also a clause, *what you like*. One matching case is part of another. This example also illustrates the reversibility of constituents.

Although they are drawn as a tree, FTFs can be constructed to search for lexical sequences irrespective of the grammar (Nelson/Wallis/Aarts 2002, 147). The lexical sequence is linked by **NextWord** relations. The tree effectively disappears by attaching **Leaf** nodes, linked, via *Ancestor* relations, to a **Root** node. For every leaf, **NextChild** = ∅. Such an FTF will match once, unambiguously, to any tree annotating the lexical sequence.

ICECUP is an exploratory research platform that provides a 'forgiving' user interface that allows a researcher to construct a query and apply it to a corpus to obtain an exhaustive set of matching cases. The researcher can browse the set of matching cases and combine the results with those of other queries, e. g., by adding another, alternative FTF query, or by applying the results to a subcorpus.

Finally, the tree-model query representation permits one final trick. Tree model queries reflect trees in the corpus. They are *generalised tree structures*. One can *match* a query against a tree in the corpus. A user can also *abstract* a query from a tree or set of trees. Thus ICECUP's 'FTF Creation Wizard' tool constructs a query by taking a portion of a tree and converting it into a query.

4. Case interaction

Case overlap, as defined by a query, reflects a more general problem for researchers: *cases sampled from a corpus are not always independent*. Rather, with a few highly specialised exceptions aside, corpora consist of sequences of running text. Yet any process that *quantifies* results – from counting hits and calculating ratios to forming a dataset and testing hypotheses – effectively assumes that each case is independent from the next.

In fact, two cases in the same passage are less likely to be independent in origin than cases from different texts. Within a passage, two cases that are part of the same utterance are more likely to depend on each other than two more distant cases. Two cases in separate sentences are, on balance, less likely to interact than a pair within the same sentence. And finally cases within the same sentence interact to differing degrees – especially if their extent overlaps.

This problem has always existed in lexical corpora. Topic nouns and certain stylistic patterns obviously predominate in particular texts. In ICE-GB, modal *must* appears 4 times per 1000 words in eleven administrative/regulatory passages, but 0.65 times per 1000 across the corpus. Should each of these cases be treated as independent usages of equal worth, or are their uses due to a particular authorial style or subject matter?

In large lexical corpora such as the 100 million-word *British National Corpus* (Aston/Burnard 1998), a large number of sources and random subsampling can help to minimise the effect. In smaller parsed corpora, the grammatical evidence is both richer and rarer, and cases can appear in clusters for a variety of reasons.

We can consider case interaction as having two sources. The first is *conscious* repetition, including coordination or lexical choice, while the second is *grammatical*, where the use of one construction has consequences for subsequent constructions. Nelson/Wallis/Aarts (2002) offer the following range of possible sources of interaction in query results.

Full overlap. A case fully overlaps another. This is only possible if the query contains unordered relations (and one child can swap position with another).

Partial overlap. Part of one case coincides with part of another. There are two types:

(i) Two overlapping cases match *some of the same nodes* in the tree. This can arise if eventual relationships are employed in an FTF, such as '**NextChild** = *After*'.

(ii) Two cases overlap on different nodes, as in Figure 34.7, where the direct object of one match coincides with the head clause of a second. This is a type of embedding.

Embedding. One match can dominate or subsume another, e. g., a clause in a clause.

Coordination. Coordination normally comprises similar constructions, because one conjoin can usually replace the other or the entire coordinated structure.

Repetition. This occurs naturally for self-correction, reinforcement or stylistic reasons, within an utterance or in conversation.

Finally, it is well known that text genre and sociolinguistic context can lead to certain types of construction being preferred over others, e. g. interrogative clauses in interviews. A corpus sample should be *representative* of the population of utterances one is generalising about.

Strictly, any quantitative assessment of corpus data can only assume sampling independence if each case is sourced from a unique speaker and text. Since this requirement is often too restrictive in practice, an alternative is to try to quantify the *relative independence* of each case against the other cases in the same text. This may be defined as the probability that the case would arise *if the other cases in the text were absent*. To give this account some numbers: an independent case has a probability of 1, two explicitly repeated items within the same text, 0.5, and so on.

Grammatical independence can be estimated by a Bayesian method across the entire sample. If two cases a and b interact, the probability of b given a, $pr(b|a)$, is greater than the probability of b occurring independently, $pr(b)$. This increase in probability, $D(b, a) = pr(b|a) - pr(b)$, represents the dependence of b on a. This calculation must be generalised for all pairs of cases in the same text.

Case interaction is not critical in applications where quantified results are not required, such as obtaining examples for teaching or general exploration. However, this issue is increasingly important when carrying out linguistic research on a corpus. With simple experiments and relatively low-frequency close-interaction, one can 'downplay' the independence of cases, say, by underscoring χ^2 tests. More advanced solutions require the formal abstraction of an experimental model and the evaluation of an experimental sample, as discussed in Wallis/Nelson (2001).

5. Advanced topology

Up to this point we have only considered searching corpora with three types of grammatical topology. We have assumed that each word has a single node annotating it, and vice versa. We have assumed that coordination should be considered as part of the phrase structure. Finally, we have left aside how one might go about extending this basic topology to permit multiple tree analyses or to include other levels of analysis.

5.1. Compounds and missing words

Some parsing schemes do not assume that every word is given a node, but permit the use of compounds or 'ditto tags'. Some grammars, such as Treebank II (Marcus et al. 1994), permit the existence of nodes without words.

ICE treats both *to* and *in order to* as instances of 'particle *to*', adverbial *sort of* as a compound, and many titular proper nouns are analysed as compound nouns. This picture is further complicated by *discontinuous* compounds such as *be (just) going to*. Incidentally, Figure 34.6 shows two compounds, the phrasal verb *turns out* and adjective *all right*.

These situations represent a discontinuity between the grammar and the text. Grammatical relations treat compounds as single elements, while sentence relations assume every word within the compound to be distinct (Figure 34.8).

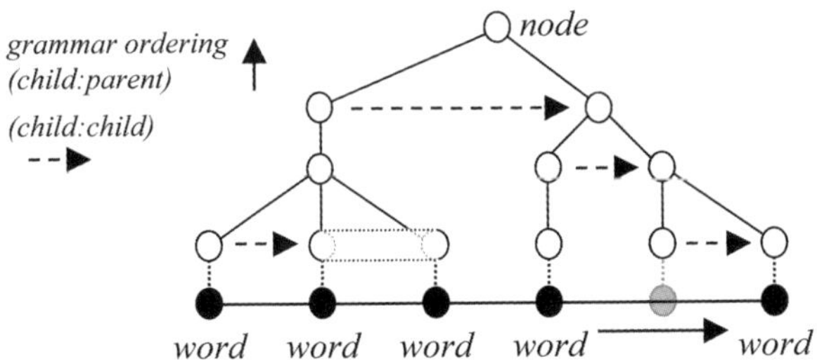

Fig. 34.8: Compounds and missing words

ICECUP solves this problem by employing a *late resolution strategy* (Wallis/Nelson 2000).

(i) Maximally **inflate the proof space** to place elements in every permissible position (including each position within a compound).
(ii) Apply the **proof** method to identify matching combinations of nodes and relations.
(iii) **Collapse the results**, carrying out any necessary simplification (e. g., two matching patterns which differ within the same compound may become one).

Null elements require a different solution. We explicitly increase the ambiguity of the query. Nulls can be accepted into the lexical sequence on the condition that the meaning of '**NextWord** = *Next*' is modified to match two words *separated by zero or more null words*. As a result the **NextWord** restriction may pair one word with several, and only by applying other restrictions is the ambiguity resolved.

ICECUP employs this method for skipping over elements such as pauses, punctuation and discourse markers that can appear at arbitrary locations in the lexical stream.

5.2. Coordination and self-correction

Coordination is not strictly part of phrase structure, but is better understood as being *tangential* to it. Coordinated elements, termed *conjoins*, can appear at many levels in a grammatical tree, from main clauses to verb phrases, e. g., *to swim and to fish*, adjective phrases, e. g., *high and mighty*, to adverbs as in *up and down*. An illustration is given in Figure 34.9.

Different analysis schemes can coordinate structures at slightly differing positions (ICE aims to coordinate phrases, where possible, while Treebank II will coordinate word classes). Coordination also entails a degree of explicit grammatical repetition. Moreover, one phrasal conjoin may contain an element, such as *d* in Figure 34.9, which is absent, but implicitly referred to, in another conjoin, as in the following from ICE-GB (S1A-002 #139).

4. I want to [[perform with a group]$_{CJ}$ and [do some choreography *for my final assessment*]$_{CJ}$]

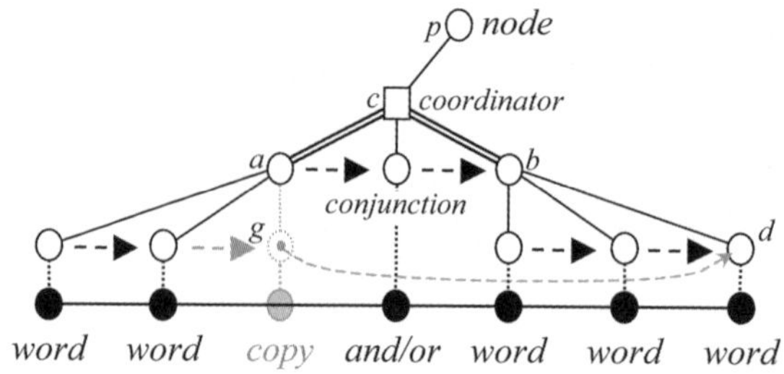

Fig. 34.9: Coordinating *a* and *b*, with gap $g = d$

In this *gapped conjunction* (Marcus et al. 1994), *d* is understood to be part of both phrases, *a* and *b*.

Each instance of coordination involves the insertion of a coordinating node into the tree that brackets conjoins and any intermediate conjunction (*and*, *or*, *but* etc.). The main problem for searching a corpus is that this arbitrary insertion of coordinating nodes into the structure (like the arbitrary insertion of discourse markers, see above) can be a confounding factor that prevents queries matching across the coordinator.

Suppose we have a query which looks for two nodes, *a*, *p*, where **Parent**(*p*, *a*). This will match cases without a coordinator but not those with the additional node. In order to permit the same query to match both coordinated and single phrases the 'immediate' **Parent** relation must be modified to match two nodes separated by zero or more coordinators. Any part of the query at *p* or above will match identical nodes and produce a partial overlap (see section 4 on case interaction).

Marcus et al. (1994) represent gapped conjunctions by introducing a new node (*g* in Figure 34.9) and creating a cross-referencing link $g = d$. Gaps can appear at any position in a conjoin, e. g., *Mary likes Bach and Susan, Beethoven*. Marcus et al. are attempting to recover predicate-argument semantics, '**like**(Mary, Bach) ∧ **like**(Susan, Beethoven)', whereas we are interested in (optionally) matching implied terms against full queries. As with null words and compounds (see 5.1.), the matching method first expands terms and then applies a late resolution strategy.

Every revision of the query system subtly modifies the meaning of the grammar. A query is an abstract tree. If coordination is treated differently from phrase structure in proof, then the meaning of coordinator nodes is distinct.

One of the biggest hurdles facing the parse analysis of spoken material is the identification and analysis of sections of text which are repeated and corrected dynamically by the speaker themselves. So-called *self-correction* is a well-known phenomenon in speech, and a research subject in its own right. However, during the parsing of corpora, self-correction is often only treated as a problem for the parser. ICE notionally 'removes' corrected material by setting an 'ignored' flag and adding surface annotation to show which areas of the text had been replaced by others. However, one interpretation of self-correction is two conjoins coordinated with 'or *rather*', as in:

5. ... the spectacle of seeing his older sister win [a prize]$_{CJ}$ – or, rather, [two prizes]$_{CJ}$

(ICE-GB W2B-006 #83)

The conclusion is that if coordinators can be made to 'disappear' in proof in the way suggested, self-correction could possibly be better represented as a form of *replacement coordination*, with a feature in the earlier material to indicate that it had been replaced.

5.3. Multiple analyses and levels

So far we have assumed that each sentence is given a single tree analysis. What if we permit multiple trees to be stored for the same sentence? We might do this for a number of reasons. Firstly, to represent *fundamental analytical ambiguity*, where additional analyses are (selectively) stored for ambiguous sentences only. Secondly, to represent *different analytical schemes* or *levels of analysis*. Thirdly, to represent *parallel translations*, where each translation is parsed separately. Below we discuss the implications of each of these, very briefly, in turn.

In the case of analytical ambiguity, one might represent an entire 'alternative' tree structure in the corpus, although the ambiguity might be confined to a small part of the tree. Consider a simple situation where a sentence has two interpretations. A query can match either tree independently. If it matches *both* trees, this counts as a single matching case. If it matches one tree, it should count as a single case *given the probability that this tree is the correct analysis*. It follows that each ambiguous tree should be given a prior probability of being correct (i. e. if equally plausible, 0.5 each), and the number of cases in each tree should be multiplied by this prior probability before being taken into account.

One benefit of corpora containing more than one parsing scheme is that they can be used for the contrastive evaluation of grammatical frameworks, *by comparing the effective retrievability of different representations*.

At the time of writing, the cost of multiple parsing has been too high for more than a microcorpus, the AMALGAM MPC (see www.scs.leeds.ac.uk/amalgam/amalgam/multiparsed.html), to be constructed. Consider a corpus parsed with dependency and phrase structure grammars, as in Figure 34.10. We now have three types of element: words, plus two sorts of node (dependency and phrase structure), and two sets of structural relations that are applied to the two types of node.

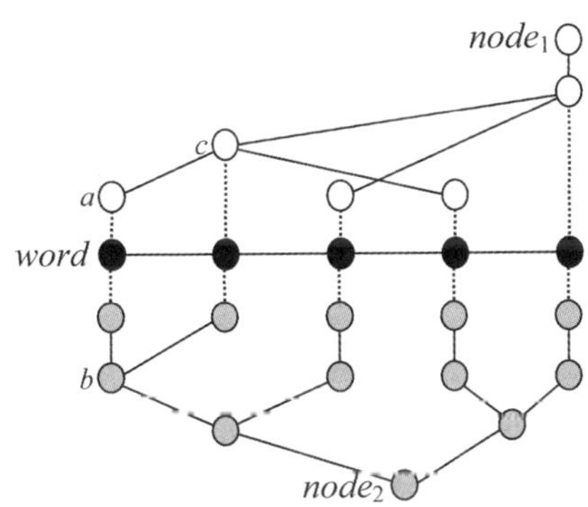

Fig. 34.10: A multi-parsed sentence

Queries on this type of corpus may now *span* the sentence and relate elements on either side together (such as *a* and *b*). In a parallel-parsed corpus, the sentence acts as the reference point for all grammars, allowing a single query to refer to any number of trees. The query representation for any tree necessarily employs the terms and axioms of the relevant grammar. In summary, the possibility of contrasting grammars in this way has two requirements: (a) the definition of a particular evaluative measure (retrievability, i.e., what can be identified or derived from the structure), and (b) the fact that all trees are grounded in the same set of sentences.

A similar principle applies to the integration of a supplementary *morphological* layer of analysis into a parsed corpus. The most integrated representation is where the same topology is carried through below the level of the tree, so a constituent analysis is preferable with a phrase structure grammar, or a dependency analysis with a constraint grammar.

Adding a morphological analysis of each word in a parsed corpus, and extending grammatical queries accordingly, permits new avenues of research. One could investigate the interaction of morphology and syntax, and evaluate morphological dependencies from first principles within grammatical constraints (e.g. within the same phrase or clause.)

Provided that morphological terms can be represented within the same framework as the grammar, we could expect to see networks like Figure 34.11, consisting of an acyclic tree where words are no longer terminals and where morpheme sequences subdivide words. In practice it may be desirable to further extend the annotation to represent morphological compounds, relate morphemes to the lexical string (e.g. indexing a character range in the word) and directly relate morphemes to words.

Corpus queries would then include an explicit **HasNode**(t, w) relation for words and morphemes and relations along the morpheme axis. The interpretation of **NextMorpheme** would be limited, unless otherwise stated, to a sequence of morphemes *within* a word. Thus, to follow the marked arrows in Figure 34.11, one would have to consider two *Ancestors* with attached words, on either side of a **NextWord** relation. (Naturally, it is easier to construct this model than to summarise it.)

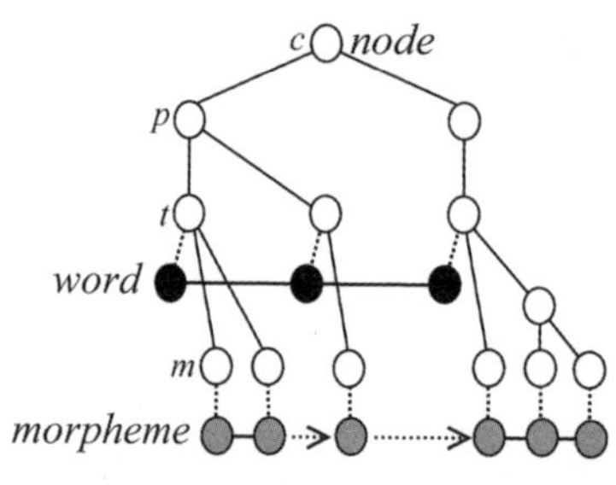

Fig. 34.11: From morpheme to clause: a morpho-syntatic tree

The final corpus typology we will consider is that of parsed translation corpora, where an L1 (first language) sentence is translated into an L2 (second language) sentence and both sentences are parsed. In a phrase structure grammar, one can then map L1 nodes, including phrases and clauses, to L2 nodes (Figure 34.12).

Word-for-word machine translations have well known problems (cf article 32). A solution, in theory at least, is to parse sentences and carry out translation at a phrasal level. An important motivation for carrying out research on this kind of corpus is to identify regular translation patterns and rules.

Although the same grammar may be used for each language, queries are either applied to one or the other language, or form a composite pair linked by the single-place translation arc.

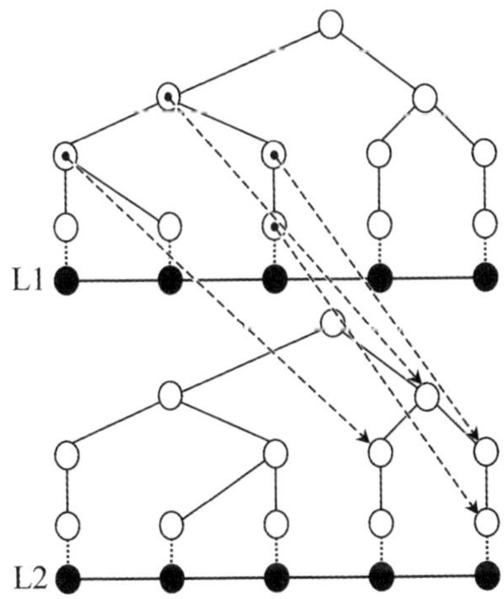

Fig. 34.12: Mapping parsed translations

6. Conclusions

The degree to which a parsed corpus may be exploited depends on the effective use of queries. A clear visual query representation is essential for linguistically educated users and researchers. Model-based queries convey a diagram of the desired total structure, but sacrifice the absolute expressivity of logic. The formal expressivity of logic is often of limited value, however. It may be misleading, and the result is a query platform that is difficult to use by non-specialists. Moreover, a focus on formal expressivity ignores the fact that users must learn the application and meaning of the grammatical annotation in order to carry out research on a parsed corpus.

By contrast, tree models like *Fuzzy Tree Fragments* are cohesive and have an intuitive appeal, the manner in which they have matched against trees in the corpus can be understood, and they may be abstracted from corpus trees. Tools for parsed corpora employ a number of different query systems, with an emerging consensus around the use of treelike models. ICECUP and its brethren have been used for a variety of linguistic tasks, from teaching and research to intensive parse correction (Wallis 2003).

Some of these tools simply concern themselves with retrieving matching cases, although the more mature support an entire exercise of exploring some aspect of the corpus and carrying out simple experiments.

At this point we note that effective experimental research with parsed corpora should take into account the fact that one linguistic event may interact with another. An emerging area of research is in developing experimental methodologies that both incorporate the entire experimental process and automate it as much as possible. An *experimental environment* (Wallis/Nelson 2001) transforms a corpus from being a source of inspiration and statistical distributions to a *locus of theoretical discussion*, where general concepts in linguistics may be evaluated against corpora shared by the entire community, and where interpretations of the results of studies may be widely discussed.

Finally, we discussed some of the implications of more complex corpus topologies, from specific variations on a parsed corpus to the representation of multiple analyses. Notwithstanding our inability to anticipate future developments in corpus linguistics, it seems that model-based 'tree fragment' queries are here to stay.

7. Acknowledgements

Thanks to Dick Hudson, Evelien Keizer, Rolf Kreyer, Anke Lüdeling, Danny Mukherjee, Gerry Nelson, Joakim Nivre, Gabriel Ozon and an anonymous reviewer for their helpful comments on this paper. Initial research was carried out under ESRC grant R000222598. ICECUP III is available from www.ucl.ac.uk/english-usage. Over the years I have been privileged to gain insights from numerous users of ICECUP and to participate in fraternal discussions with authors of other query systems. Every query system is dependent on the quality and reliability of parse analyses, so it is to the unsung galley slaves of corpus annotation that ultimate thanks are due.

8. Literature

Abeillé, A. (ed.) (2003), *Treebanks: Building and Using Parsed Corpora*. Dordrecht: Kluwer.

Aston, G./Burnard, L. (1998), *The BNC Handbook: Exploring the British National Corpus with SARA*. Edinburgh: Edinburgh University Press.

Briscoe, T. (1996), Robust Parsing. In: Cole, R. A./Mariani, J./Uszkoreit, H./Zaenen, A./Zoe, V. (eds.), *Survey of the State of the Art in Human Language Technology*. <http://cslu.cse.ogi.edu/H LTsurvey/ch3n ode9.html>.

Cheng, P. C.-H./Simon, H. A. (1995), Scientific Discovery and Creative Reasoning with Diagrams. In: Smith S./Ward, T./Finke, R. (eds.), *The Creative Cognition Approach*. Cambridge, MA: MIT Press, 205–228.

van Halteren, H./van den Heuvel, T. (1990), *Linguistic Exploitation of Syntactic Databases: The Use of the Nijmegen Linguistic DataBase Program*. Amsterdam: Rodopi.

Hayes, P. J. (1977), In Defence of Logic. In: *Proceedings of the 5th International Joint Conference on AI (IJCAI-5)*, Cambridge, MA, 559–565.

Järvinen, T. (2003), Bank of English and beyond. In: Abeillé 2003, 43–59.

Kallmeyer, L./Steiner, I. (2003), Querying Treebanks of Spontaneous Speech with VIQTORYA. In: *Traitement Automatique des Langues* 43(2), 155–179.

Karlsson, F./Voutilainen, A./Heikkilä, J./Anttila, A. (eds.) (1995), *Constraint Grammar: A Language-independent System for Parsing Unrestricted Text*. (Natural Language Processing 4.) Berlin/New York: Mouton de Gruyter.

Kepser, S. (2003), Finite Structure Query: A Tool for Querying Syntactically Annotated Corpora. In: Copestake, C./Hajič, J. (eds.), *Proceedings of the 10th Conference of the European Chapter of the Association for Computational Linguistics, EACL 2003*. Budapest, Hungary, 179–186.

Lezius, W. (2002), TIGERSearch – Ein Suchwerkzeug für Baumbanken. In: Busemann, S. (ed.), *Proceedings der 6. Konferenz zur Verarbeitung natürlicher Sprache (KONVENS 2002)*. Saarbrücken, Germany, 107–114. See also <http://www.ims.uni-stuttgart.de/projekte/TIGER/TIGERSearch>

Marcus, M./Kim, G./Marcinkiewicz, M. A./MacIntyre, R./Bies, M./Ferguson, M./Katz, K./Schasberger, B. (1994), The Penn Treebank: Annotating Predicate Argument Structure. In: *Proceed-*

ings of the Human Language Technology Workshop. San Francisco: Morgan Kaufmann, 114–119.

Marcus, M./Santorini, B./Marcinkiewicz, M. A. (1993), Building a Large Annotated Corpus of English: The Penn Treebank. In: *Computational Linguistics* 19(2), 313–330.

McEnery, T./Wilson, A. (2001), *Corpus Linguistics*. 2nd ed. Edinburgh: Edinburgh University Press.

Nelson, G./Wallis, S. A./Aarts, B. (2002), *Exploring Natural Language: Working with the British Component of the International Corpus of English*. (Varieties of English around the World.) Amsterdam: John Benjamins.

Ondruška, R./Mírovský, J. (2005), *Netgraph Client Manual*. Institute of Formal and Applied Linguistics, Prague. <http://quest.ms.mff.cuni.cz/netgraph/doc/netgraph_manual.html>.

Quirk, R./Greenbaum, S./Leech, G./Svartvik, J. (1985), *A Comprehensive Grammar of the English Language*. London: Longman.

Randall, B. (2000), *CorpusSearch User's Manual*. Technical report, University of Pennsylvania. <http://corpussearch.sourceforge.net>.

Rohde, D. (2001), *Tgrep2*. Technical report, Carnegie Mellon University. <http://tedlab.mit.edu/dr/Tgrep2>.

Wallis, S. A. (2003), Completing Parsed Corpora: From Correction to Evolution. In: Abeillé 2003, 61–71.

Wallis, S. A./Nelson, G. (2000), Exploiting Fuzzy Tree Fragments in the Investigation of Parsed Corpora. In: *Literary and Linguistic Computing* 15(3), 339–361.

Wallis, S. A./Nelson, G. (2001), Knowledge Discovery in Grammatically Analysed Corpora. In: *Data Mining and Knowledge Discovery* 5(4), 305–336.

Sean Wallis, London (UK)

35. Linguistically annotated corpora: Quality assurance, reusability and sustainability

1. Introduction

The creation and use of linguistically annotated corpora for a wide variety of languages has been one of the most prominent developments in computational linguistics over the last fifteen years. While earlier attempts were largely restricted to morpho-syntactic annotation (part-of-speech tagging, morphological analysis and lemmatization), more recent developments have concentrated on deeper levels of annotation including phrase structure, dependency structure, predicate argument structure, lexical semantics, information structure, and discourse structure. As the complexity of annotation increases and the same data are often annotated with regard to different levels of analysis, questions of quality assurance, reusability and sustainability have become key issues in the creation and maintenance of linguistically annotated corpora. This article surveys the current best practices in each of these three domains, introduces the underlying research issues, and provides pointers to future research directions in these areas.

We will mainly be concerned with textual corpora. Sound recordings of language and other primary data in non-textual modalities are normally transcribed in some way or the other before they are linguistically annotated. We, thus, take the textual representation of language as the starting point of our discussion. For issues of reusability and sustainability of multi-modal corpora, see especially article 31 in this volume.

The remainder of this article is structured as follows: section 2 reviews the different levels of analysis that can be found in current linguistically annotated corpora and gives examples of reuse of data in the sense of multiple use of the same electronic text resource by different researchers or in different research contexts. 'Reuse of text' in the sense of plagiarism is discussed in article 59. Section 3 focuses on the relationship of data reuse and annotation quality as well as transparency of annotation. Section 4 considers corpora with distinct layers (or tiers) of annotation and focuses on issues of alignment and markup. Section 5 is concerned with metadata, documentation and standardization efforts. Section 6, finally, presents an integrated architecture for the sustainable representation of corpus data.

2. Corpus resources and reusability

The first linguistically annotated corpora that went beyond pure morpho-syntactic annotation were concerned with syntactic annotation in the form of phrase structure trees. One of the first efforts of this kind was the Gothenburg Corpus (Ellegård 1978), which was a hand-parsed section of the one million token Brown Corpus of American English (Francis/Kučera 1979). The Gothenburg Corpus comprised approximately 130,000 words and is a small resource by current standards. Its annotation was later reworked according to a very rich and detailed annotation scheme and then published as the SUSANNE Corpus (Sampson 1995) comprising also a small sample of speech from the London-Lund Corpus (Svartvik 1990). An early project involving automatic annotation and manual post-editing was the Lancaster Parsed Corpus (Garside/Leech/Váradi 1992, see also article 13 and article 20). It is based on 144,000 words of the part-of-speech-tagged Lancaster-Oslo/Bergen (LOB) Corpus of British English (Garside/Leech/Sampson 1987). Subsequently, the Penn Treebank project was launched at the University of Pennsylvania, which resulted in the creation of the Penn Treebank for American English. The first preliminary release of the treebank in 1992 presented a corpus of more than 2.8 million tokens of skeleton-parsed text including, among others, a one million token subcorpus of Dow Jones Newswire articles and the one million token Brown Corpus, which was parsed and completely retagged using the Penn Treebank tagset (Marcus/Santorini/Marcinkiewicz 1993). In subsequent releases, minor changes were made with respect to the compilation of material from the Dow Jones News Service and the corpus has since then been referred to as the *Wall Street Journal* corpus. It is fair to say that the Penn Treebank has served as a model of best practice for the creation of treebanks for many other languages. We refer interested readers to article 13 for more detailed information.

This short survey of the first English treebanks shows that the same primary data have found their way into different annotation projects. For example, part of the carefully sampled and balanced Brown Corpus was syntactically annotated in the Gothenburg Corpus as well as in the SUSANNE Corpus. The Brown Corpus as a whole was first part-of-speech-tagged with the Brown tagset (Francis/Kučera 1982); later, it was retagged and parsed as part of the Penn Treebank.

The reuse of resources is not limited to the primary data. The *Wall Street Journal* section of the Penn Treebank is the most prominent example of how an already annotated resource is reused for further annotation. It has not only been used as a reference source for a wide variety of natural language processing applications but has also served as a basis for further linguistic annotation in the areas of semantics and discourse analysis. The annotation of the second release of the Penn Treebank (Penn Treebank II, Marcus et al. 1994), comprises information on phrase structure, basic predicate-argument structure, and some semantic distinctions of adjuncts. Figure 35.1 exemplifies a sentence in the Penn Treebank II bracketing format, which is reminiscent of the programming language LISP. The locative adjunct is marked with the label PP-LOC and the subject with NP-SBJ.

```
( (S
    (PP-LOC (IN In)
      (NP (PDT such) (DT an) (NN environment) ))
    (, ,)
    (NP-SBJ (DT a) (NN market) (NN maker) )
    (VP (MD can)
      (VP (VB absorb)
        (NP (JJ huge) (NNS losses) )))
    (. .) ))
```

Fig. 35.1: Penn Treebank II: *In such an environment, a market maker can absorb huge losses*

The PropBank project created Proposition Bank I (Palmer/Gildea/Kingsbury 2005), which is based on the *Wall Street Journal* section of the Penn Treebank II. PropBank annotates predicate-argument relations in the sense of assigning coarse-grained word senses to the predicates and prototypical semantic roles to the arguments. The annotation process made use of the treebank's phrase structural information: a rule-based argument tagger preprocessed the corpus, which was then manually post-edited. In some cases, the PropBank argument structure disagrees with the Penn Treebank syntactic structure (Palmer/Gildea/Kingsbury 2005, 81 ff.). In Figure 35.2, the subject is marked with the prototypical agent role ARG0, the direct object with the prototypical theme role ARG1, and the locative adjunct-like argument with ARGM-LOC.

The NomBank project (Meyers et al. 2004) again aims at creating a supplementary annotation to the *Wall Street Journal* section of the Penn Treebank. In NomBank 1.0,

```
[ARGM-LOC  In such an environment] , [ARG0  a
market maker] [ARGM-MOD  can]
  [rel  absorb] [ARG1  huge losses] .
```

Fig. 35.2: PropBank; prototypical semantic roles of verbal arguments

nominal predicates are marked, and their arguments are annotated with prototypical semantic roles in accordance with the PropBank annotation.

In the Penn Discourse TreeBank project (Miltsakaki et al. 2004), the *Wall Street Journal* corpus is annotated according to a theory of low-level discourse structure. It treats discourse connectives, sometimes also referred to as *discourse markers*, such as *because*, *when*, *but*, or *as a result* as a kind of predicate between two arguments. In addition to the explicit use of such connectives in corpora, implicit relationships are also annotated by invoking the same connectives. Instead of building on the syntactic annotation of the Penn Treebank, the project decided to use the raw tokenized text for their annotation to avoid errors in the Penn Treebank, and allow for cases where discourse arguments do not align with syntactic structures (Dinesh et al. 2005). The CCGbank (Hockenmaier/Steedman 2005) is the result of an automatic conversion of the whole Penn Treebank into a corpus of Combinatory Categorial Grammar derivations. It pairs syntactic derivations with sets of word-to-word dependencies, which approximate the underlying predicate-argument structure. There are various other projects which have added annotation levels to only parts of the *Wall Street Journal* corpus. For example, the TimeBank Corpus (Pustejovsky et al. 2003) comprises texts from various sources, among them articles from the *Wall Street Journal* corpus, which are annotated with event classes, temporal information, and aspectual information according to the specifications of TimeML (Pustejovsky et al. 2004). The Rhetorical Structure Discourse Treebank (Carlson/Marcu/Okurowski 2003) contains, among other data, a selection of 385 *Wall Street Journal* articles from the Penn Treebank, which were annotated with discourse structure in the framework of Rhetorical Structure Theory (Mann/Thompson 1988). Clauses and larger sequences are hierarchically ordered by a set of discourse relations such as background, elaboration and contrast. For the message understanding competition MUC 6 (1995), a subcorpus of 318 *Wall Street Journal* articles was published, annotated with anaphora and coreference information. The PARC 700 Dependency Bank (King et al. 2003) consists of 700 sentences, which were randomly extracted from one section of the *Wall Street Journal* corpus, syntactically analyzed with a Lexical-Functional Grammar (LFG) parser, and given gold-standard annotations of grammatical dependency relations by manual correction and extension. The FrameNet project (Baker/Fillmore/Lowe 1998), which itself does not aim at creating an annotated corpus resource but a lexical database, provides five texts of the *Wall Street Journal* corpus annotated with FrameNet semantic roles and word senses for evaluation of the relation between its own semantic annotation and the one of PropBank.

There are various examples of multiply annotated data in languages other than English. One of the earliest is the 300,000-token Swedish Talbanken (Teleman 1974) which was manually annotated with morpho-syntactic and syntactic information (see also article 13, section 1). Recently, Talbanken was revived, its format updated and the annotations to some extent automatically re-encoded (see, e. g., Saxena/Borin 2002 and Nilsson/

Hall/Nivre 2006). A major non-English resource is the Prague Dependency Treebank for Czech (Böhmová et al. 2003), which comprises annotation of morpho-syntactic information, surface-oriented dependency structure, and a non-isomorphic tectogrammatical structure including, among others, annotation of semantic roles in the framework of Functional Generative Description (Sgall/Hajičová/Panevová 1986), topic-focus articulation, coreference, and information structure. The German TiGer Treebank (Brants et al. 2004) consists in its second release of 50,000 sentences which are annotated with morpho-syntactic information, part-of-speech tags, phrase structure, and functional dependencies. The SALSA project (Burchardt et al. 2006) enriches the TiGer Treebank with FrameNet relations. The TiGer Dependency Bank (Forst et al. 2004) is a sample of 2,000 sentences from the treebank, which are automatically converted and subsequently extended and corrected in correspondence to the English PARC 700 Dependency Bank. The second major treebank of German, TüBa-D/Z (Hinrichs et al. 2004), consists of about 27,000 sentences in its third release and comprises information on morpho-syntax, phrase structure, topological structure, functional structure, named entities, as well as anaphora and coreference annotation. Another smaller resource is the Potsdam Commentary Corpus (Stede 2004). In addition to morpho-syntax, phrase structure and functional information, it is augmented with discourse relations in the framework of Rhetorical Structure Theory (Mann/Thompson 1988), information structure and anaphoric relations.

These examples show that different aspects of linguistic description come into play in linguistically annotated corpora. In an ideal world, the different annotation levels could be interpreted as distinct analyses of the same data. In the real world, however, they are often maintained as separate resources which are largely disparate. This leads to the question of how to integrate different levels of annotation into a comprehensive corpus resource. It would be desirable to use a combined representation of all levels of information, to be able to search a complex database and to specify restrictions on all levels of annotation. In the context of sustainability an integrated representation is desirable too, since it would allow the specification of general tools and format conversions which reduce the risk of losing one resource or the other due to obsolete formats or software. The representation of different levels of annotation, however, especially if they are created in different projects, places great demands on the data format.

3. Quality and consistency of annotation

Reuse of data is one of the motivations for creating annotated resources in the first place (Leech 1997). The very same corpus data can then be used and interpreted by different researchers potentially from different fields pursuing diverse research questions. Linguistic annotations of corpora can be regarded as useful resources if they are well-formed and consistent. For the annotation, a data format is defined and used, for example, the brackets and the position of the labels in the Penn Bracketing Format. A corpus annotation is *well-formed* if it conforms to this defined format. General markup languages like XML define well-formedness constraints which can be checked by software tools. Therefore, XML-based linguistic annotation may be carried out by means of general or specialized XML tools (see Dipper/Götze/Stede 2004). Moreover, XML provides means of validating annotations formally according to a document grammar that can, for example, be encoded as a Document Type Definition (DTD). If an XML document conforms to such a grammar, the document is said to be *valid* with regard to the document grammar. A document grammar might, for example, require that nouns have to be included in noun phrases. Of course, validity constraints are only formal constructs and do not prevent the annotator from annotating incorrect structure due to wrong analyses. The linguistic adequacy can only be determined through human inspection. Inter-annotator agreement and methods of automatic consistency checking, however, may help to find potential problems.

Consistency in annotation is the most important factor in determining the quality of the annotated resource. *Consistency* here means that the same linguistic phenomena are annotated in the same way, and similar or related phenomena must receive annotations that represent their similarity or relatedness if possible. Consistency is important for all major applications of annotated corpora, regardless of whether they are used as training data in natural language processing (NLP) applications, as gold standard in the evaluation of NLP applications, or as data for qualitative or quantitative linguistic studies. If one phenomenon receives different annotations in the corpus, then a machine learning algorithm cannot learn the regularities concerning the phenomenon, and the evaluation of NLP applications based on inconsistent data is misleading. Even if applications treated this phenomenon consistently, the evaluation would punish the system in cases where the system is consistent, and the annotation is inconsistent. In the case of corpus-based linguistic studies, the linguist is misled by the annotation, either finding only a part of the occurrences of a phenomenon in a quantitative study, or being forced to assume two different phenomena where only a single one exists.

Depending on the techniques used for the creation of the corpora, different strategies for providing consistency can be applied:

(i) Annotation guidelines
(ii) Semi-automatic annotation
(iii) Manual or automatic consistency checking
(iv) Multiple annotation by different annotators

These strategies can be applied independently or in combination, and most of them are independent of the type of annotation. However, some of them necessitate the adaptation of the method to the annotation scheme.

Annotation guidelines are crucial for manual annotation. They describe the general principles in the design of the annotation scheme as well as given examples of different phenomena, and tests for difficult cases. They constitute a set of evolving laws of good annotation practice rather than a comprehensive grammar (the importance of annotation guidelines is also stressed in article 13, section 3.1.). These guidelines provide a list of all symbols used in the annotation such as terminal and non-terminal symbols and their basic definitions. The annotation guidelines provide a resource for the user of the corpus: phenomena can only be searched for in corpora if users know how they are annotated. For example, if linguists search for relative pronouns in the Penn Treebank, they need to know that relative pronouns are annotated as WDT. If they search for subordinating conjunctions, they should be aware that these received the same part-of-speech tag, IN, as prepositions in the Penn Treebank. Additionally, annotation guidelines help in training new annotators and as a reference for annotators when they are unclear on how to annotate certain phenomena. A detailed set of annotation guidelines can help prevent different annotators from making different decisions concerning the same phenomenon. Examples of annotation guidelines are the Penn Treebank part-of-speech tagging guidelines (Santorini 1990), the Penn Treebank II bracketing guidelines (Bies et al. 1995), the PropBank annotation guidelines (Babko-Malaya 2005), and the TimeBank 1.2 documentation (Pustejovsky et al. 2006). Dipper/Götze/Skopeteas (2007) exemplify a joint effort of a number of annotation projects to create common guidelines for phonology, morphology, syntax, semantics, and information structure as realized in the Potsdam Commentary Corpus.

Another possibility of ensuring consistency is the use of software that assists the annotator in the annotation process. *Semi-automatic annotation* is a process in which a program (1) suggests annotations, which then have to be approved or corrected by the annotator, and/or (2) visualizes the annotation so that missing links in the annotation become evident. The first type of program generally uses a machine learning component that is trained on a previously annotated data set. This ensures that suggestions are made for phenomena that are consistent with previous annotations. Thus, to create new annotations, a conscious effort on the part of the annotator is required. Examples for such annotation programs are annotate (Plaehn 1998) and TreeBanker (Carter 1997). The second type of program presents the annotation in such a way that it helps users see gaps in the annotation. Such programs can be useful in the annotation of anaphoric or coreference chains (see article 27). If a link between two coreferent entities is missing, the intended single chain is interrupted, resulting in two different discourse entities. Tools that help with this type of annotation are, for example, MMAX2 (Müller/Strube 2003), PALinkA (Orasan 2003), or WordFreak (cf. https://sourceforge.net/projects/wordfreak/).

Automatic consistency checking is a very general label for annotation-specific strategies to discover inconsistencies. These strategies are dependent on the type of annotation as well as on the annotation scheme. They are based on the assumption that humans will always make mistakes, no matter how careful the annotators are. Thus, it is a good practice to employ global search strategies, which can find questionable annotations (see also *transverse correction* in article 13). In treebank annotation, for example, one can check whether there are clauses in the treebank that have more than one subject. If such examples are found, they need to be checked manually because, in some cases, the double subject may result from coordination rather than from an annotation error. Since these searches are highly dependent on the type of annotation and the annotation scheme, it is difficult to envisage a general tool. Thus, the searches are either implemented as specialized programs or as queries in a tool that is capable of searching the annotated structures. Returning to the example with the two subjects in a clause, tools such as tgrep, which is distributed with the Penn Treebank (see also tgrep2 (Rohde 2001) or tregex (Levy/Andrew 2006)), or TIGERSearch (König/Lezius 2000) query tree structures, can be used to find suspect clauses. A more general approach is to perform a statistical analysis to detect rare constructions, which then need to be checked by humans. Such an approach is based on the assumption that very rare constructions are likely to be errors (cf. Dickinson/Meurers 2005).

The most time-consuming strategy for detecting inconsistencies in the annotation is the multiple annotation of the corpus by different annotators or by the same annotator after a sufficient period of time. This means that every part of the corpus is annotated at least twice. A comparison of these two annotations reveals annotation errors or problematic cases in which the guidelines provide no guidance or are not specific enough to cover the present phenomena. Such multiple annotations allow for the evaluation of *inter-annotator agreement* (also referred to as *inter-coder reliability*, or – if it is a single annotator – as *intra-annotator agreement*), i. e., the degree to which the different annotators agree on a single annotation for a specific sentence or paragraph. If a high inter-annotator agreement is reached, one can conclude that the corpus has been annotated consistently. Brants (2000), for example, reports 92.43 % agreement between two annotators in assigning syntactic annotation to the German NEGRA Corpus and, after a discussion and correction phase, an improved agreement of around 95 %.

High inter-annotator agreement also suggests the conclusion that the annotation scheme is well-balanced between providing enough specialized information and being too specific. If the annotation scheme is too specific, it becomes difficult for the annotators to distinguish the relevant cases, and the annotation becomes inconsistent. One example of such a situation is the annotation of a text with word senses. Most of these annotations are based on the inventory of WordNet (Fellbaum 1998) or related wordnets for other languages. If WordNet provides too few senses for a word, then certain distinctions are lost, and the annotator needs to decide which of the existing categories fits the word or whether to use a superordinate, less specific category. However, if WordNet provides a very fine-grained set of senses, then it is often difficult for the annotator to decide which is the correct sense for the word in question (see also Véronis 2001 and Palmer/Dang/Fellbaum 2007). Thus, finding a good granularity for an annotation is important for ensuring a consistent annotation of the corpus (see also Bayerl et al. 2003b). Additionally, recent studies show that the granularity also influences the quality of NLP applications based on these corpora (cf Kilgarriff/Rosenzweig 2000 for word sense disambiguation, as well as Kübler 2005 and Kübler/Hinrichs/Maier 2006 for parsing). Finally, we would like to point out that inter-annotator agreement is not an absolute measure of quality; there is always the possibility that two annotators just agree by chance. A widely used means for measuring inter-annotator agreement is the *kappa statistic* (Cohen 1960). It compares the observed proportion of agreement with the expected proportion of chance agreement and indicates whether an inter-annotator agreement is at a satisfactory level. As a rule of thumb, a kappa coefficient of less than or equal to 0.67 means that the inter-annotator agreement is too close to chance agreement and that one can therefore not draw any conclusions about it. If it is between 0.67 and 0.80 it allows tentative conclusions; only a value of 0.80 and above allows for definite conclusions about inter-annotator agreement (Krippendorff 1980). For discussions on the interpretation of the kappa coefficient see for example Carletta (1996), Di Eugenio/Glass (2004) and Krenn/Evert/Zinsmeister (2004); article 27 in this volume discusses an alternative measure. New developments concerning the evaluation of linguistically annotated data are presented among others at the biennial Linguistic Resources and Evaluation Conference (LREC) as well as in the Journal on Language Resources and Evaluation.

4. Representation of annotation

This section deals with the question as to how different linguistic levels of annotation are to be technically realized and how they are related to a shared source of primary data. We distinguish conceptual *levels* from technical *layers:* a conceptual level need not correspond to a single technical layer and vice versa (cf. Bayerl et al. 2003a). Different levels, such as the word level (which is a fundamental but still not fully understood level, see the discussion in article 24), the part-of-speech level, and the phrasal level might, for example, be realized by means of one technical layer, as is the case in the Penn Treebank bracketing format (see Figure 35.1).

The type of representation of the annotated corpus is a crucial prerequisite for ensuring its reusability. It is important to use a data format for which there are tools to access and search the corpus. The issue is complicated by the fact that the standards that are developed by international standardization committees are often not widely accepted, an example being the Text Encoding Initiative (TEI) base tagset for the transcription of speech. In most cases, the data format of a specific corpus is chosen to fit the primary application for which it is created. Thus, part-of-speech-tagged corpora, which are mainly used for training statistical part-of-speech taggers, are represented in pure text files, either in a column format, in which each word with its part-of-speech tag is placed on a separate line, or in running text, in which the part-of-speech tag is separated from the word by a special character. Once the annotation becomes more complex, or when there are multiple annotation levels, the issue of representation becomes more difficult. In general, linguistic annotations can belong to one of two conceptually different annotation models: either a sequential model (sometimes also referred to as *graph-based model*) or a hierarchical model (cf. articles 31 and 34).

4.1. Hierarchies and sequences

There are ongoing efforts for defining a representational standard for corpora in which multiple types of annotation are present, for example, morphological, morpho-syntactic, syntactic, lexical-semantic, information structure, or discourse annotation. Bird/Liberman (2001) propose a graph-based representation, in which each type of annotation is treated as an independent layer of graph annotation. The graph approach is very flexible for the representation of text-based corpora as well as speech corpora, each necessitating a different interpretation of the fundamental nodes in the graph. If the underlying data type is text, the position in the sequence of characters serves as the reference point for distinct layers. In contrast, if the underlying data type consists of speech data, the time stamp of each token in the utterance will serve as the basis for the nodes. Additionally, annotation graphs are flexible enough to allow for crossing segment boundaries between layers as well as crossing edges inside a single layer. While this approach is very flexible for the representation of different types of corpora and annotations, it is difficult to imagine a general tool that would allow the user to access the whole range of annotations without having an overly complex and cryptic user interface.

In contrast to flexible annotation schemes designed specifically for multiple layers of annotation, there are annotation schemes that are developed to optimally encode a specific single level of annotation. One example of such an approach is the so-called *Pie-in-the-Sky* initiative (Meyers 2005) which aims at optimizing the representation of semantic information and which should serve as a basis for a general standard in corpus annotation. Hence, semantic information is the main level of organization and the other types of information need to conform to this primary annotation level. Because of the restrictions imposed by the underlying organization of annotations, it would be, e. g., impossible to cross a boundary that is imposed by the semantic annotation. While this restriction may be seen as a disadvantage for representing information other than on the semantic level, one needs to keep in mind that such a representation allows for a very simple and direct access to the semantic data. Thus, it is, for example, much easier to search for a specific type of predicate-argument structure than it would be in a graph-based representation. A similar representation is suggested by (Hinrichs/Kübler/Naumann 2005). Their representation, however, is based primarily on syntactic information. Apart from this level of annotation, the authors include morphological and morphosyntactic as well as anaphoric and coreferential annotations. Again, the decision that the syntactic constituents serve as the basis for the annotation of other levels restricts the annotation especially on the anaphoric and coreference level. However, it also ensures that the two levels are consistent with regard to each other. Thus, a markable, i. e., a potential referring expression, on the referential level will always correspond to a syntactic constituent. This is in contrast to other annotations which have been performed more independently. In PropBank, for example, some of the semantic roles intentionally conflict with the syntactic information in the underlying Penn Treebank (Palmer/Gildea/Kingsbury 2005, 81 ff.). Consequently, if the user needs to align the semantic information from PropBank with the syntactic information from the Penn Treebank, these mismatches must be resolved somehow.

4.2. Embedded and standoff XML markup

Linguistically annotated corpora differ from one another on the conceptual level, for example, as a result of decisions made regarding the development or adoption of a particular tagset, or the choice between a hierarchical or graph-based annotation approach. On the technical level of encoding, annotated corpora differ in the way they combine annotations and textual resources. Since the creation of large linguistically annotated corpora is an extremely time consuming endeavor, many of these corpora are based on technical decisions made in the 1980s. The resulting physical representation is therefore realized as a record-and-field or column-based format and frequently as a bracketing format, often influenced by the syntax of the programming language LISP. Nowadays linguistic (and other) annotations use the syntax of XML, at least as an interchange format. Often, existing linguistic corpora are converted into an XML-annotated resource as well (see, e. g., TiGer Treebank, Prague Dependency Treebank).

The main reason for the use of XML in linguistic annotation is obvious: XML is the lingua franca for text annotation in general (cf. article 31). Hence, XML is supported by most relevant software products, ranging from text editors, databases, and web browsers to libraries for programming languages. Based on experience with the technical development in the last decades, XML was developed as a pure text format without any implicit formatting. This ensures that XML will be accessible in the future, even after it has ceased to play an important role. An additional reason for the widespread use of XML is its flexibility. As a result of this flexibility, the XML annotation in corpora varies tremendously. The most striking difference concerns the connection of markup and annotations. It is possible to embed the markup used to annotate portions of text in the text itself or to refer to this text by means of links. The first technique is called *embedded* or *inline* annotation whereas marking by referencing is usually called *standoff* annotation (Thompson/McKelvie 1997). Both approaches have advantages and drawbacks. Standoff annotation is more flexible and allows for the distribution of different levels of annotation over several independent layers without duplicating the textual resource that is annotated by the different levels. The distribution of annotations of different linguistic levels (e. g., syntactic and discourse structure) over separate annotation layers not only leads to better conceptual modeling but also avoids problems which arise due to the fact that the XML standard forbids overlapping elements. But since XML was designed with the embedded annotation technique in mind, only a few XML software products allow for the processing of standoff annotated corpora in a way acceptable for non-XML experts. This, and the fact that single annotation layers cannot be interpreted or exchanged separately, since they are dependent on the layers they themselves point to, goes against the vision of sustainability of annotated text (see Hilbert/Schonefeld/Witt 2005). To reach more sustainable annotations, standoff annotated documents should also be stored and exchanged as XML documents with embedded XML annotations. Ideally each annotation level is encoded in a single XML file. Several of these XML documents can be merged into a single document if they share their textual primary data (see Witt at al. 2005). Alternatively, a parser which is described by Ide/Suderman (2006) can be used to yield a single XML inline representation. This parser integrates annotations distributed in separate XML standoff layers. Both approaches to merging can deal with overlapping hierarchies (cf. articles 31 and 34), which can be represented by means of milestones (DeRose 2004). Such tools enable users, for example, to merge relevant parts of the Penn Treebank with the annotations of PropBank, NomBank, TimeBank, and the Penn Discourse Treebank.

5. Documentation

It should be clear from the previous sections that the creation of large linguistically annotated corpora is extremely laborious. Of course, this holds also for smaller corpora, but the efforts and the procedures necessary for the creation of corpora do not simply scale linearly with the corpus size.

Typically, the starting point for the creation of a smaller corpus is a single linguistic project that is concerned with a particular research question. To provide empirical evidence, language material is collected, and a corpus is created. This often results in small, special-purpose corpora that are barely reusable in projects concerned with slightly different research tasks. Even though this is a deplorable situation because the numerous small corpora would constitute a valuable resource for linguistics, it is almost impossible to change the situation. Typically individual researchers start collecting language material; afterwards they create a corpus, and later analyze or interpret their data. A single person or even a small group is likely to try to minimize the effort which is invested in the creation of a corpus. However, for the creation of large corpora it is imperative to devote considerable effort to building the prerequisites of corpus reuse and distribution. Ideally, such issues are considered in the early stages of corpus building, otherwise there is a risk of wasting serious amounts of time and money on the creation of annotated data that end up as data graveyards (Schmidt et al. 2006) that are not accessible to the research community.

One of the most important tasks for facilitating reusability is a thorough documentation that goes beyond annotation guidelines described in section 3, which are exclusively directed at the human user. A comprehensive documentation that addresses all corpus-related tasks and that can also be explored by machines comprises different types of information:

– Linguistic tagsets: Linguistic concepts are marked with tags such as NN as a part-of-speech tag for normal nouns or PP-LOC for locative prepositional phrases in the Penn Treebank tagset or ARG0 as a semantic tag in the PropBank tagset.
– Content Models: XML based-annotation schemes often use document grammars to formally define constraints on the use of tags as the content of other tags. To update and to process corpora annotated according to formal document grammars (e. g., DTDs), an extensive documentation of the grammars is extremely important.
– Metadata: as described thoroughly in article 22, the use of metadata, i. e., information describing corpora or sub-corpora, is extremely important for the organization of corpora in general and, especially, for the retrieval of information contained in corpora. The most prominent metadata schemes defined for linguistic data are the ones defined by the Isle Metadata Initiative (IMDI) and by the Open Language Archive Community (OLAC).
– Linguistic Data Categories/Linguistic Ontologies: to ease the interoperability of different linguistic resources some researchers promote the use of linguistic ontologies. Because annotated corpora contain arbitrarily defined tags to refer to linguistic concepts (e. g., number: dual, case: genitive), an ontology, i. e., a formal representation of the concepts, can be used to associate these tags with general linguistic concepts. The Data Category Registry (DCR, ISO 12620-1 (2003)) and the General Ontology for Linguistics (GOLD, Farrar/Langendoen 2003, see also article 22) were developed for this purpose.

Large corpora should be documented on all of these levels. This is not only a prerequisite for the reuse of the corpora. Since large corpora are created and evaluated by several people over a long period of time, extensive documentation is necessary for the creation of a consistent linguistic resource of high quality (cf also section 3).

6. An architecture for the sustainable representation of corpus data

As many linguistic projects collect and annotate corpora, it has become more and more apparent that many of the laboriously acquired resources are not useable and sometimes not even accessible after the research project for which they were created has come to an end.

At the time of writing this article, the issue of sustainability of linguistic data is the subject matter of a joint research project undertaken by the Collaborative Research Centers in Tübingen (SFB 441), in Hamburg (SFB 538), and in Potsdam (SFB 632) (the joint project's homepage is at: http://www.sfb441.uni-tuebingen.de/c2/index-engl.html). Each of these centers has independently developed their own annotated corpora. The joint project has the practical goal of transforming these heterogeneous corpus collec-

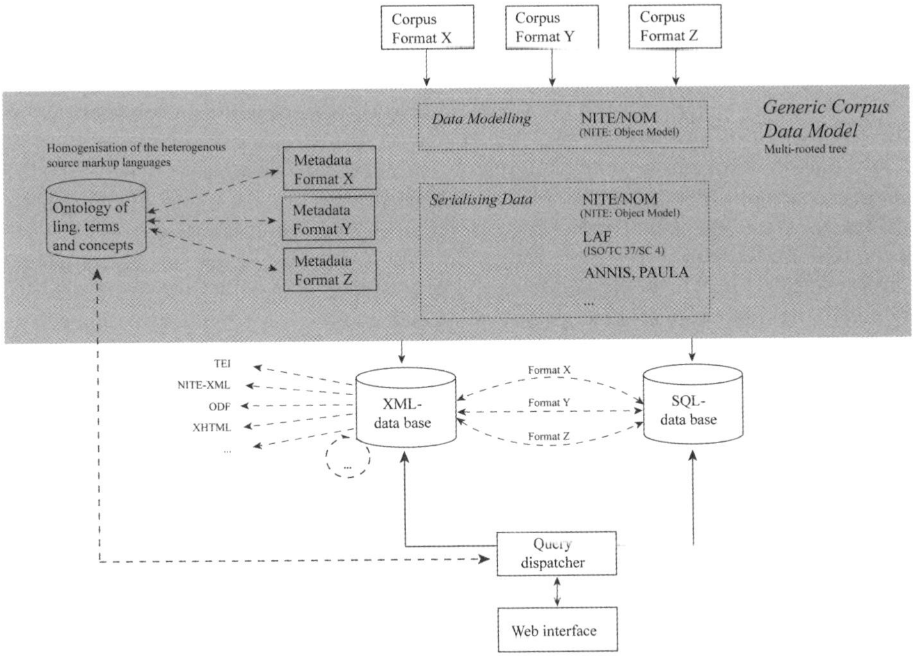

Fig. 35.3: An architecture for sustainable data representation

tions into a uniform data representation. At the same time, the project aims at developing methodologies and rules of best practice for new corpus-oriented projects in general (see also Dipper et al. 2006). Within this project, an architecture for the sustainable representation of corpus data was developed and published in Wörner et al. (2006). A generalized, i. e., less project-specific, version of this architecture is given in Figure 35.3.

The architecture can be subdivided into an input-oriented and an output-oriented part. When dealing with existing corpora, the input-oriented component is necessary for unifying heterogeneous corpus formats. This merging process may result in a document that contains all the information of the source document but its representation belongs to another model, for example, data originally represented in a graph-based model is now represented according to a hierarchical model. In this case, the transformation is an information-preserving (*lossless*) procedure. In other cases, however, the generalized corpus model does not allow for the inclusion of all the information of the source. In such cases, the merging can be regarded as a generalization to the least common denominator. Whether a generalization or unification is used depends heavily on the diversity of the input formats. If they belong to different paradigms, especially if the merging process needs to combine a graph-based format and a hierarchy-oriented format (see section 4), a non-lossless transformation is more likely to be defined and implemented. As a consequence, the result of such a combination is not re-convertible to the input format. To circumvent this drawback, the generalized format needs to allow for the inclusion of information whose sole purpose is to enable back-transformations into the original format.

A corpus represented in a format that conforms to the generic corpus model must contain all the metadata of the original corpus, but potentially represented in another metadata scheme (see article 22).

The output-oriented part of the proposed architecture for the sustainable representation of linguistic data follows the idea that the best way to improve accessibility is to provide the same data in as many different representations as possible. Therefore the data can be partially or completely converted into several linguistic and non-linguistic formats (e. g., TEI, LAF (Ide/Romary/de la Clergerie 2003), or XHTML).

For a general discussion of sustainability we refer the reader to the seminal paper by Bird/Simons (2003) in which they address the problem of portability and sustainability of digitized language data in general with a special emphasis on recorded spoken language. They suggest rules of best practice for the creation, storage and distribution of linguistic resources, which they specify along the following seven dimensions: content, format, discovery, access, citation, preservation, and rights. For example, they recommend the use of Unicode for character encoding and XML for annotation. They strongly recommend using open, non-proprietary standards for storing language data and descriptions. They suggest that creators of corpora document the process for access as part of the metadata, including any licenses and charges. Finally, Bird and Simons recommend making an additional paper print-out of the data, because this is still the most sustainable way of preserving information. An updated version of the rules of best practice is available on the OLAC pages (http://www.language-archives.org). For an exhaustive discussion on aspects of language documentation, interested readers can also consult Gippert/Himmelmann/Mosel (2006).

7. Conclusion

In this article, we discussed linguistically annotated corpora and described an approach for the sustainable representation of such data. The availability of large collections of electronic texts and the need for corpora augmented with linguistic information especially for natural language engineering purposes has led to the creation of larger and larger linguistically annotated corpora. In addition to these large corpora, an immense amount of rather small special-purpose corpora have been annotated as well. Naturally, the creation of all these corpora is a laborious process but the effort involved in the creation of large corpora is not only greater than for the creation of smaller resources, it also requires different strategies: different annotators are involved, heterogeneous software might be used, potentially more levels of information are annotated, the creation of large corpora is more time-consuming (in some cases taking even decades), and so on. For these reasons, every effort should be made that such resources be accessible and reusable after their creation. Therefore, the linguistic community should no longer tolerate corpus-oriented projects ignoring aspects of sustainability and agreement on rules of best practice in corpus creation.

8. Acknowledgements

We would like to thank Stefanie Dipper, Piklu Gupta, and Georg Rehm for their useful comments on earlier versions of this article.

9. Literature

Babko-Malaya, O. (2005), *PropBank Annotation Guidelines*. Available at: http://verbs.colorado.edu/~mpalmer/projects/ace/PBguidelines.pdf.

Baker, C./Fillmore, C./Lowe, J. (1998), The Berkeley FrameNet Project. In: *Proceedings of COLING-ACL*. Montréal, Canada, 86–90.

Bayerl, P./Lüngen, H./Goecke, D./Witt, A./Naber, D. (2003a), Methods for the Semantic Analysis of Document Markup. In: Roisin, C./Munson, E./Vanoirbeek, C. (eds.), *Proceedings of the ACM Symposium on Document Engineering*. Grenoble, France, 161–170.

Bayerl, P./Lüngen, H./Gut, U./Paul, K. I. (2003b), Methodology for Reliable Schema Development and Evaluation of Manual Annotations. In: *Workshop Notes for the Workshop on Knowledge Markup and Semantic Annotation, Second International Conference on Knowledge Capture (K-CAP 2003)*. Sanibel, FL, 17–23.

Bies, A./Ferguson, M./Katz, K./MacIntyre, R. (1995), Bracketing Guidelines for Treebank II Style Penn Treebank Project, University of Pennsylvania. Available at: ftp://ftp.cis.upenn.edu/pub/treebank/doc/manual/.

Bird, S./Liberman, M. (2001), A Formal Framework for Linguistic Annotation. In: *Speech Communication* 33(1–2), 23–60.

Bird, S./Simons, G. (2003), Seven Dimensions of Portability for Language Documentation and Description. In: *Language* 79(3), 557–582.

Böhmová, A./Hajič, J./Hajičova, E./Hladká, B. (2003), The Prague Dependency Treebank: A Three-level Annotation Scenario. In: Abeillé, A. (ed.), *Treebanks: Building and Using Parsed Corpora*. Amsterdam: Kluwer, 103–127.

Brants, S./Dipper, S./Eisenberg, P./Hansen, S./König, E./Lezius, W./Rohrer, C./Smith, G./Uszkoreit, H. (2004), TIGER: Linguistic Interpretation of a German Corpus. In: Hinrichs, E. W./Simov, K. (eds.), *Research on Language and Computation* 2(4), special issue, 597–620.

Brants, T. (2000), Inter-annotator Agreement for a German Newspaper Corpus. In: *Proceedings of the Second International Conference on Language Resources and Evaluation*. Athens, Greece. Available at: http://www.coli.uni-saarland.de/~thorsten/publications/Brants-LREC00.pdf.

Burchardt, A./Erk, K./Frank, A./Kowalski, A./Pado, S./Pinkal, M. (2006), The SALSA Corpus: A German Corpus Resource for Lexical Semantics. In: *Proceedings of the LREC Workshop on Merging and Layering Linguistic Information*. Genoa, Italy, 969–974.

Carletta, J. (1996), Assessing Agreement on Classification Tasks: The Kappa Statistic. In: *Computational Linguistics* 22(2), 249–254.

Carlson, L./Marcu, D./Okurowski, M. E. (2003), Building a Discourse-tagged Corpus in the Framework of Rhetorical Structure Theory. In: van Kuppevelt, J./Smith, R. (eds.), *Current Directions in Discourse and Dialogue*. Dordrecht: Kluwer Academic Publishers, 85–112.

Carter, D. (1997), The TreeBanker: A Tool for Supervised Training of Parsed Corpora. In: *Proceedings of the ACL ENVGRAM Workshop*. Madrid, Spain. Available at: http://xxx.lanl.gov/abs/cmp-lg/9705008v2.

Cohen, J. (1960), A Coefficient of Agreement for Nominal Scales. In: *Educational and Psychological Measurement* 20(1), 37–46.

DeRose, S. (2004), Markup Overlap: A Review and a Horse. In: *Proceedings of Extreme Markup Languages 2004*. Montréal, Canada. Available at: http://www.idealliance.org/papers/extreme/proceedings/html/2004/DeRose01/EML2004DeRose01.html

Di Eugenio, B./Glass, M. (2004), The Kappa Statistic: A Second Look. In: *Computational Linguistics* 30(1), 95–101.

Dickinson, M./Meurers, D. (2005), Detecting Annotation Errors in Spoken Language Corpora. In: *Proceedings of the Special Session on Treebanks for Spoken Language and Discourse at the 15th Nordic Conference of Computational Linguistics (NODALIDA-05)*. Joensuu, Finland, 53–66.

Dinesh, N./Lee, A./Miltsakaki, E./Prasad, R./Joshi, A./Webber, B. (2005), Attribution and the (Non-)alignment of Syntactic and Discourse Arguments of Connectives. In: *Proceedings of the ACL Workshop on Frontiers in Corpus Annotation II: Pie in the Sky*. Ann Arbor, MI, 29–36.

Dipper, S./Götze, M./Skopeteas, S. (eds.) (2007), *Information Structure in Cross-linguistic Corpora: Annotation Guidelines for Phonology, Morphology, Syntax, Semantics, and Information Structure*. (Interdisciplinary Studies on Information Structure (ISIS), Working Papers of the SFB 632, vol. 7.) Potsdam: Universitätsverlag Potsdam.

Dipper, S./Götze, M./Stede, M. (2004), Simple Annotation Tools for Complex Annotation Tasks: An Evaluation. In: *Proceedings of the LREC Workshop on XML-based Richly Annotated Corpora*. Lisbon, Portugal, 54–62.

Dipper, S./Hinrichs, E. W./Schmidt, T./Wagner, A./Witt, A. (2006), Sustainability of Linguistic Resources. In: *Proceedings of the LREC Workshop on Merging and Layering Linguistic Information*. Genoa, Italy, 48–54.

Ellegård, A. (1978), *The Syntactic Structure of English Texts: A Computer-based Study of Four Kinds of Text in the Brown University Corpus*. (Gothenburg Studies in English 43.) Göteborg: Acta Universitatis Gothoburgensis.

Farrar, S./Langendoen, D. T. (2003), A Linguistic Ontology for the Semantic Web. In: *GLOT International* 7(3), 97–100.

Fellbaum, C. (ed.) (1998), *WordNet: An Electronic Lexical Database*. Cambridge, MA: MIT Press.

Forst, M./Bertomeu, N./Crysmann, B./Fouvry, F./Hansen-Schirra, S./Kordoni V. (2004), Towards a Dependency-based Gold Standard for German Parsers – the TiGer Dependency Bank. In: *Proceedings of the COLING Workshop on Linguistically Interpreted Corpora (LINC '04)*. Geneva, Switzerland, 31–38.

Francis, W. N./Kučera, H. (1979), *Manual of Information to Accompany a Standard Corpus of Present-day Edited American English, for Use with Digital Computers*. Technical report, Department of Linguistics, Brown University.

Francis, W. N./Kučera, H. (1982), *Frequency Analysis of English: Lexicon and Grammar*. Boston: Houghton Mifflin.

Garside, R./Leech, G./Sampson, G. (eds.) (1987), *The Computational Analysis of English: A Corpus-based Approach*. London: Longman.

Garside, R./Leech, G./Váradi, T. (compilers) (1992), *Lancaster Parsed Corpus. A Machine-readable Syntactically Analyzed Corpus of 144,000 Words, Available for Distribution through ICAME*. Bergen: The Norwegian Computing Centre for the Humanities.

Gippert, J./Himmelmann, N. P./Mosel, U. (2006), *Essentials of Language Documentation*. Berlin: DeGruyter.

Hilbert, M./Schonefeld, O./Witt, A. (2005), Making CONCUR Work. Paper given at Extreme Markup Languages, sponsored by IDEAlliance. Montréal, Canada.

Hinrichs, E. W./Kübler, S./Naumann, K./Telljohann, H./Trushkina, J. (2004), Recent Developments in Linguistic Annotations of the TüBa-D/Z Treebank. In: *Proceedings of the Third Workshop on Treebanks and Linguistic Theories*. Tübingen, Germany, 51–62.

Hinrichs, E. W./Kübler, S./Naumann, K. (2005), A Unified Representation for Morphological, Syntactic, Semantic, and Referential Annotations. In: *Proceedings of the ACL Workshop on Frontiers in Corpus Annotation II: Pie in the Sky*. Ann Arbor, MI, 13–21.

Hockenmaier, J./Steedman, M. (2005), *CCGbank Manual*. Technical Report MS-CIS-05-09, Department of Computer and Information Science, University of Pennsylvania.

Ide, N./Romary, L./de la Clergerie, E. (2003), International Standard for a Linguistic Annotation Framework. In: *Proceedings of HLT-NAACL'03 Workshop on the Software Engineering and Architecture of Language Technology*. Edmonton, Canada, 25–30.

Ide, N./Suderman, K. (2006), An Open Linguistic Infrastructure for American English. In: *Proceedings of the 5th International Conference on Language Resources and Evaluation*. Genoa, Italy, 621–624.

ISO 12620-1 (2003), *Terminology and Other Language Resources. Data Categories. Part 1: Specification of Data Categories and Management of a Data Category Registry for Language Resources.* (ISO TC37 – Terminology and Other Language Resources.) International Organization for Standardization.

Kilgarriff, A./Rosenzweig, J. (2000), Framework and Results for English SENSEVAL. In: *Computers and the Humanities* 34(1/2), 15–48.

King, T. H./Crouch, R./Riezler, S./Dalrymple, M./Kaplan, R. (2003), The PARC 700 Dependency Bank. In: *Proceedings of the EACL03: 4th International Workshop on Linguistically Interpreted Corpora (LINC-03)*. Budapest, Hungary, 1–8.

König, E./Lezius, W. (2000), A Description Language for Syntactically Annotated Corpora. In: *Proceedings of the COLING Conference*. Saarbrücken, Germany, 1056–1060.

Krenn, B./Evert, S./Zinsmeister, H. (2004), Determining Intercoder Agreement for a Collocation Identification Task. In: *Proceedings of KONVENS 2004*. Vienna, Austria, 89–96.

Krippendorff, K. (1980), *Content Analysis: An Introduction to its Methodology*. Beverly Hills, CA: Sage Publications.

Kübler, S. (2005), How do Treebank Annotation Schemes Influence Parsing Results? Or how not to Compare Apples and Oranges. In: *Proceedings of the International Conference on Recent Advances in Natural Language Processing, RANLP 2005*. Borovets, Bulgaria. Available at: http://jones.ling.indiana.edu/~skuebler/papers/treebanks.pdf.

Kübler, S./Hinrichs, E. W./Maier, W. (2006), Is it Really that Difficult to Parse German? In: *Proceedings of the 2006 Conference on Empirical Methods in Natural Language Processing, EMNLP 2006*. Sydney, Australia, 111–119.

Leech, G. (1997), Introducing Corpus Annotation. In: Garside, R./Leech, G./McEnery, T. (eds.), *Corpus Annotation: Linguistic Information from Computer Text Corpora*. London: Longman, 1–18.

Levy, R./Andrew, G. (2006), Tregex and Tsurgeon: Tools for Querying and Manipulating Tree Data Structures. In: *Proceedings of the 5th International Conference on Language Resources and Evaluation*. Genoa, Italy. Available at: http://idiom.ucsd.edu/~rlevy/papers/levy_andrew_lrec2006.pdf.

Mann, W. C./Thompson, S. A. (1988), Rhetorical Structure Theory: Toward a Functional Theory of Text Organization. In: *Text* 8(3), 243–281.

Marcus, M./Santorini, B./Marcinkiewicz, M. A. (1993), Building a Large Annotated Corpus of English: The Penn Treebank. In: *Computational Linguistics* 19(2), 313–330.

Marcus, M./Kim, G./Marcinkiewicz, M. A., MacIntyre, R./Bies, A./Ferguson, M./Katz, K./Schasberger, B. (1994), The Penn Treebank: Annotating Predicate Argument Structure. In: *ARPA Human Language Technology Workshop*. Plainsbor, NJ, 114–119.

Meyers, A. (2005), *Pie in the Sky Description*. Available at: http://nlp.cs.nyu.edu/meyers/pie-in-the-sky/pie-in-the-sky-descript.html.

Meyers, A./Reeves, R./Macleod, C./Szekely, R./Zielinska, V./Young, B./Grishman, R. (2004), Annotating Noun Argument Structure for NomBank. In: *Proceedings of the 4th International Conference on Language Resources and Evaluation*. Lisbon, Portugal, 803–806.

Miltsakaki, E./Prasad, R./Joshi, A./Webber, B. (2004), The Penn Discourse Treebank. In: *Proceedings of the 4th International Conference on Language Resources and Evaluation*. Lisbon, Portugal. Available at: http://www.ling.upenn.edu/~elenimi/lrec04-lisbon-miltsakaki.pdf.

MUC 6 (1995), *Proceedings of the 6th Message Understanding Conference*. Columbia, MD.

Müller, C./Strube, M. (2003), Multi-level Annotation in MM AX. In: *Proceedings of the 4th SIGdial Workshop on Discourse and Dialogue*. Sapporo, Japan, 198–207.

Nelson, T. H. (1997), Embedded Markup Considered Harmful. In: *WWW Journal* 2(4), 129–134.

Nilsson, J./Hall, J./Nivre, J. (2006), Mamba Meets TIGER: Reconstructing a Treebank from Antiquity. In: Henrichsen, P. J./Skadhauge, P. R. (eds.), *Treebanking for Discourse and Speech*. Copenhagen: Samfundslitteratur Press, 119–132.

Orasan, C. (2003), PALinkA: A Highly Customizable Tool for Discourse Annotation. In: *Proceedings of the 4th SIGdial Workshop on Discourse and Dialog*. Sapporo, Japan. Available at: http://www.sigdial.org/workshops/workshop4/proceedings/29_SHORT_orasan_palinka-final.pdf.

Palmer, M./Dang, H./Fellbaum, C. (2007), Making Fine-grained and Coarse-grained Sense Distinctions. In: *Natural Language Engineering* 13(2), 137–163.

Palmer, M./Gildea, D./Kingsbury, P. (2005), The Proposition Bank: An Annotated Corpus of Semantic Roles. In: *Computational Linguistics* 31(1), 71–106.

Plaehn, O. (1998), *Annotate Bedienungsanleitung*. Technical report, Universität des Saarlandes, Sonderforschungsbereich 378, Projekt C3.

Pustejovsky, J./Hanks, P./Saurí, R./See, A./Gaizauskas, R./Setzer, A./Radev, D./Sundheim, B./Day, D./Ferro, L./Lazo, M. (2003), The TIMEBANK Corpus. *In: Proceedings of Corpus Linguistics 2003*. Lancaster, UK, 647–656.

Pustejovsky, J./Ingria, B./Saurí, R./Castano, J./Littman, J./Gaizauskas, R./Setzer, A./Katz, G./ Mani, I. (2004), The Specification Language TimeML. In: Mani, I./Pustejovsky, J./Gaizauskas, R. (eds.), *The Language of Time: A Reader*. Oxford: Oxford University Press, 545–557.

Pustejovsky, J./Littman, J./Saurí, R./Verhagen, M. (2006), *Timebank 1.2 Documentation*. Available at: http://www.timeml.org/site/timebank/documentation-1.2.html.

Rohde, D. (2001), *Tgrep2*. Technical report, Carnegie Mellon University. Available at: http://tedlab.mit.edu/~dr/Tgrep2.

Sampson, G. (1995), *English for the Computer: The SUSANNE Corpus and Analytic Scheme*. Oxford: Clarendon Press.

Santorini, B. (1990), *Part-of-Speech Tagging Guidelines for the Penn Treebank Project*. 3rd Revision, 2nd Printing. Department of Computer and Information Science, University of Pennsylvania: Technical Report MS-CIS-9047. Available at: ftp.cis.upenn.edu/pub/treebank/doc/tagguide.ps.gz.

Saxena, A./Borin, L. (2002), Locating and Reusing Sundry NLP Flotsam in an E-Learning Application. In: *Proceedings of the LREC Workshop on Customizing Knowledge in NLP Applications: Strategies, Issues, and Evaluation*. Las Palmas, Spain, 45–51.

Schmidt, T./Chiarcos, C./Lehmberg, T./Rehm, G./Witt, A./Hinrichs, E. W. (2006), Avoiding Data Graveyards: From Heterogeneous Data Collected in Multiple Research Projects to Sustainable Linguistic Resources. In: *Proceedings of the E-MELD Workshop 2006*. East Lansing, MI. Available at: http://linguistlist.org/emeld/workshop/2006/papers/schmidt.html.

Sgall, P/Hajičová, E./Panevová, J. (1986), *The Meaning of the Sentence in its Semantic and Pragmatic Aspects*. Dordrecht: Reidel and Prague: Academia.

Stede, M. (2004), The Potsdam Commentary Corpus. In: *Proceedings of the ACL-04 Workshop on Discourse Annotation*. Barcelona, Spain, 96–102.

Svartvik, J. (ed.) (1990), *The London Corpus of Spoken English: Description and Research*. (Lund Studies in English 82.) Lund: Lund University Press.

Teleman, U. (1974), *Manual för grammatisk beskrivning av talad och skriven svenska*. (Lundastudier i nordisk språkvetenskap Serie C, nr 6.) Lund: Studentlitteratur.

Thompson, H. S./McKelvie, D. (1997), Hyperlink Semantics for Standoff Markup of Read-only Documents. In: *Proceedings of SGML Europe'97*. Barcelona, Spain. Available at: http://www.ltg.ed.ac.uk/~ht/sgmleu97.html.

Véronis, J. (2001). Sense Tagging: Does it Make Sense? In: *Proceedings of the Corpus Linguistics 2001 Conference*. Lancaster, UK. Available at: http://www.up.univ-mrs.fr/veronis/pdf/2001-lancaster-sense.pdf.

Witt, A./Goecke, D./Sasaki, F./Lüngen, H. (2005), Unification of XML Documents with Concurrent Markup. In: *Literary and Linguistic Computing* 20(1), 103–116.

Wörner, K./Witt, A./Rehm, G./Dipper, S. (2006), Modelling Linguistic Data Structures. In: *Proceedings of Extreme Markup Languages 2006*. Montréal, Canada. Available at: http://www.idealliance.org/papers/extreme/proceedings/html/2006/Witt01/EML2006Witt01.html.

Heike Zinsmeister, Constance (Germany),
Erhard Hinrichs, Tübingen (Germany),
Sandra Kübler, Bloomington, IN (USA)
and Andreas Witt, Tübingen (Germany)